Abbreviated reference:

I.C.J. Pleadings, Alleged Violations of Sovereign Rights and Maritime Spaces in the Caribbean Sea (Nicaragua v. *Colombia)*, Vol. II

Référence abrégée :

C.I.J. Mémoires, Violations alléguées de droits souverains et d'espaces maritimes dans la mer des Caraïbes (Nicaragua c. Colombie), vol. II

ISSN 0074-4433
ISBN 978-92-1-003215-5
PDF ISBN 978-92-1-106623-4

Sales number
N° de vente : **1296**

PRINTED IN FRANCE/IMPRIMÉ EN FRANCE

ALLEGED VIOLATIONS
OF SOVEREIGN RIGHTS AND MARITIME SPACES
IN THE CARIBBEAN SEA

(NICARAGUA *v.* COLOMBIA)

VIOLATIONS ALLÉGUÉES
DE DROITS SOUVERAINS ET D'ESPACES MARITIMES
DANS LA MER DES CARAÏBES

(NICARAGUA c. COLOMBIE)

INTERNATIONAL COURT OF JUSTICE

PLEADINGS, ORAL ARGUMENTS, DOCUMENTS

ALLEGED VIOLATIONS OF SOVEREIGN RIGHTS AND MARITIME SPACES IN THE CARIBBEAN SEA

(NICARAGUA *v.* COLOMBIA)

VOLUME II

COUR INTERNATIONALE DE JUSTICE

MÉMOIRES, PLAIDOIRIES ET DOCUMENTS

VIOLATIONS ALLÉGUÉES DE DROITS SOUVERAINS ET D'ESPACES MARITIMES DANS LA MER DES CARAÏBES

(NICARAGUA c. COLOMBIE)

VOLUME II

This case, entered on the Court's General List on 26 November 2013 under number 155, was the subject of a Judgment on preliminary objections delivered on 17 March 2016 (*Alleged Violations of Sovereign Rights and Maritime Spaces in the Caribbean Sea (Nicaragua* v. *Colombia), Preliminary Objections, Judgment, I.C.J. Reports 2016*, p. 3) and a Judgment on the merits delivered on 21 April 2022 (*Alleged Violations of Sovereign Rights and Maritime Spaces in the Caribbean Sea (Nicaragua* v. *Colombia), Judgment, I.C.J. Reports 2022*, p. 266).

The documents relating to the case have been published in the following order:

Volume I: Application instituting proceedings; written proceedings.
Volume II: Written proceedings (*continued*); oral proceedings; other documents.

*

For the purposes of this edition, the written pleadings have been reproduced in full in hard copy. Annexes to the written pleadings and other documents are available in electronic format. QR codes for the annexes of these written pleadings and for other documents can be found at the end of each document.

The running heads of the documents reproduced in hard copy contain two sets of page numbers: in addition to the usual continuous pagination, the original pagination of the scanned pleadings appears in brackets; readers should refer to the page numbers in brackets to follow up on any references in the body of the text.

The Hague, 2025.

La présente affaire, inscrite au rôle général de la Cour sous le numéro 155 le 26 novembre 2013, a fait l'objet d'un arrêt sur les exceptions préliminaires rendu le 17 mars 2016 (*Violations alléguées de droits souverains et d'espaces maritimes dans la mer des Caraïbes (Nicaragua c. Colombie), exceptions préliminaires, arrêt, C.I.J. Recueil 2016*, p. 3) et d'un arrêt sur le fond rendu le 21 avril 2022 (*Violations alléguées de droits souverains et d'espaces maritimes dans la mer des Caraïbes (Nicaragua c. Colombie), arrêt, C.I.J. Recueil 2022*, p. 266).

Les documents relatifs à cette affaire ont été publiés dans l'ordre suivant :

Volume I : Requête introductive d'instance ; procédure écrite.
Volume II : Procédure écrite (*suite*) ; procédure orale ; autres documents.

*

Aux fins de la présente édition, les pièces de procédure écrite sont reproduites intégralement en version papier. Les annexes aux pièces de procédure écrite et autres documents sont disponibles au format électronique. Les codes QR qui renvoient à ces annexes et autres documents se trouvent à la fin de chaque document.

Les titres courants des documents reproduits en version papier comportent deux types de folios : outre la pagination continue habituelle, on trouve, entre crochets, la pagination d'origine des pièces scannées, à laquelle il faut se référer en cas de renvoi.

La Haye, 2025.

TABLE OF CONTENTS – TABLE DES MATIÈRES

WRITTEN PROCEEDINGS
(*CONTINUED*)

PROCÉDURE ÉCRITE
(*SUITE*)

INTERNATIONAL COURT OF JUSTICE

ALLEGED VIOLATIONS OF SOVEREIGN RIGHTS AND MARITIME SPACES IN THE CARIBBEAN SEA

(NICARAGUA *v.* COLOMBIA)

REJOINDER OF THE REPUBLIC OF COLOMBIA

VOLUME I

15 November 2018

TABLE OF CONTENTS

PART I

OVERVIEW OF COLOMBIA'S CASE

PART II

COLOMBIA HAS NOT VIOLATED NICARAGUA'S SOVEREIGN RIGHTS OR MARITIME SPACES

PART III

COLOMBIA'S COUNTER-CLAIMS

Chapter 7

PART I

OVERVIEW OF COLOMBIA'S CASE

Chapter 1

INTRODUCTION

1.1 Colombia is filing this Rejoinder pursuant to the Court's Order dated 15 November 2017, which fixed 15 November 2018 as the time-limit for its submission.[1]

1.2 As Colombia will show, Nicaragua's claims rest on a serious mischaracterisation of the facts and a misapplication of the law. When the facts are examined, it will be seen that Colombia's conduct has been entirely in keeping with its customary international law rights in the exclusive economic zone,[2] and has not impeded the exercise of Nicaragua's sovereign rights. Indeed, as shown below and in Annex 71 to this Rejoinder, since the 2012 Judgment,[3] Nicaragua's fishing in the relevant area has increased dramatically, undiminished by any alleged harassment by Colombia.[4]

1.3 With respect to the law, Nicaragua seeks to present its EEZ as if it was its territorial sea, limiting Colombia's freedom of navigation and overflight, as well as other internationally

---

1 *Alleged Violations of Sovereign Rights and Maritime Spaces in the Caribbean Sea (Nicaragua* v. *Colombia), Counter-claims, Order of 15 November 2017, I.C.J. Reports 2017,* p. 315, para. 82 (B).

2 Hereinafter "EEZ".

3 *Territorial and Maritime Dispute (Nicaragua* v. *Colombia), Judgment, I.C.J. Reports 2012*, p. 624 (hereinafter "2012 Judgment").

4 See Annex 71: Ministry of Foreign Affairs of Colombia, *Report on Nicaraguan Fishing Statistics in the Caribbean Sea.*

lawful uses of the sea, to no more than a right of innocent passage. This misguided approach is reflected not only in the way Nicaragua has argued its case,[5] but also in the words of its own President and high-ranking officials.

1.4 For example, on 26 November 2012, just after the Court's Judgment was rendered, President Ortega proclaimed that Nicaragua was "exercising aerial and maritime sovereignty" in the "recovered area" granted by the Court.[6] Similarly, on 13 August 2013, Rear-Admiral Marvin Elías Corrales, stated that President Ortega had instructed the Naval Force to "exercise sovereignty in the sea and jurisdictional airspace restored to Nicaragua by the International Court of Justice".[7] And on 19 August 2015, President Ortega reiterated the point, stating that Nicaragua had "a new territorial sea" of "90,000 square kilometres", in which it would act accordingly under the Court's Judgment.[8] These types of assertions by President Ortega and high-ranking Nicaraguan civil and military authorities claiming

[5] *Alleged Violations of Sovereign Rights and Maritime Spaces in the Caribbean Sea (Nicaragua* v. *Colombia),* Reply of Nicaragua (hereinafter, "NR"), paras. 2.35-2.38.

[6] Annex 1: Message from President Daniel Ortega to the People of Nicaragua, 26 November 2012.

[7] Annex 2: Speeches at the 33rd Anniversary of the Nicaraguan Naval Force, 13 August 2013.

[8] Annex 5: Speeches at the 35th Anniversary of the Nicaraguan Naval Force, 19 August 2015. Similarly, in February 2017, when referring to the 2012 Judgment, President Ortega reiterated that "Nicaragua is already exercising sovereignty in that territorial sea" (Annex 64: La Prensa, *Daniel Ortega did not present results*, 22 February 2017).

Nicaragua's sovereignty over its EEZ are constant and reiterative.[9]

1.5 While such statements are wrong as a matter of law, they show how Nicaragua's case is built on a false legal premise: Nicaragua's EEZ is not territorial sea, and it is not an area over which Nicaragua is entitled to exercise sovereignty.

A. The Unsupported Nature of Nicaragua's Claims Regarding the Alleged Violations of its Sovereign Rights

1.6 Nicaragua's claims rest on two basic contentions. The first is that Colombia has violated Nicaragua's sovereign rights by, as Nicaragua characterizes it, aggregating to itself the right to engage in a "systematic monitoring, surveillance and policing operation" in Nicaragua's EEZ,[10] and installing "a naval

---

[9] For instance, on 1 August 2013, General Spiro José Bassi, Head of the Nicaraguan Air Force, highlighted its participation in the Peace and Sovereignty Mission General Augusto C. Sandino, "exercising sovereignty with our air resources in the air and maritime spaces restored to our People by the International Court of Justice" (Annex 3: Speeches at the 34th Anniversary of the Nicaraguan Air Force, 31 July 2013). Similarly, on 21 February 2015, General Julio César Avilés, Head of the Nicaraguan Army, stated that the "Naval Force, with support from the Air Force, exercises sovereignty" and "particularly (…) since November 2012, it has done so in the waters of the Caribbean that were recognized by the International Court of Justice" (Annex 7: Speeches at the 81st Anniversary of General Augusto C. Sandino's transit to immortality, 21 February 2015). For its part, in March 2017, Congressman Wálmaro Gutiérrez stated that the ICJ had recognized the "sovereignty of Nicaragua up to 200 nautical miles from its coasts in the Caribbean" (Annex 65: El Nuevo Diario, *Congressmen repeal "patriotic tariff"*, 8 March 2017).

[10] NR, para. 2.52.

presence to occupy Nicaragua's waters and treat them as their own".[11] The second is that Colombia has engaged in "an internationally wrongful act" by enacting an Integral Contiguous Zone around the islands of the San Andrés Archipelago.[12] Seemingly as an afterthought, the Reply also adds a new claim never advanced before – namely, that Colombia continues to offer hydrocarbon blocks in areas within Nicaragua's EEZ in violation of Nicaragua's sovereign rights, an allegation that is demonstrably untrue, as Nicaragua is well aware.

(1) THE ALLEGED "INCIDENTS"

1.7 With respect to the first contention, Colombia has in no way acted as if it has "policing powers" within Nicaragua's EEZ; nor has Colombia adopted a policy that treats these waters as its own. When the facts relating to the "incidents" are examined, it will be seen that Colombia's conduct has been responsible and non-threatening. It has been fully in line with the freedoms of navigation and overflight, and other internationally lawful uses of the sea, that it enjoys, to undertake activities aimed, *inter alia*, at observing whether there are any illegal drug trafficking or environmentally harmful practices in the area. Colombia has neither impeded Nicaraguan naval vessels or fishing boats from operating in Nicaragua's EEZ, nor has it violated Nicaragua's sovereign rights, and Nicaragua is

11 NR, para. 2.34.
12 NR, para. 3.8.

unable to show otherwise. In short, there is no policy to usurp Nicaragua's EEZ rights.

1.8 To the contrary, it is Nicaragua that assumes it has full and unfettered sovereignty over its EEZ, not just the limited sovereign rights and jurisdiction that international law allocates to coastal States, such as Nicaragua.[13] For example, while Nicaragua purports to accept that Colombia has freedom of navigation and overflight in Nicaragua's EEZ,[14] it seeks to equate those freedoms with the more limited rights that apply in the territorial sea. Thus, Nicaragua cites UNCLOS – a treaty to which Colombia is not a State party – and refers to Article 18, which is devoted to the right of innocent passage in the territorial sea, not the EEZ, for declaring that "navigation" merely encompasses "the passage of ships or the movement of ships on water".[15] This is tantamount to recognizing no more than a right of innocent passage for Colombia through Nicaragua's EEZ, a proposition that is wholly untenable and finds no support in customary international law or UNCLOS.

---

13 Although Colombia is not a party to the United Nations Convention on the Law of the Sea (hereinafter "UNCLOS"), in any event, Nicaragua is, and as a State party thereto, it is bound by its provisions. Some of the obligations incumbent on a party to UNCLOS are not limited to other States parties to the Convention. Under Article 2(1), "States Parties" is a defined term. Yet, other provisions – e.g. Articles 56 (2) and 58 – establish that the coastal State shall have due regard to the rights and duties "of other States", which is an obligation not limited to States parties.

14 NR, para. 2.13.

15 NR, paras. 2.36 and 2.38.

1.9 The most that can be said is that there is a general principle reflected in Article 58, paragraph 3 of UNCLOS, that, in the EEZ, States shall have due regard to the rights and duties of the coastal State. Colombia has not failed to pay due regard to Nicaragua's sovereign rights. Indeed, Nicaraguan officials recognize that fishing by Nicaraguan boats in the area has significantly increased since the Court's 2012 Judgment,[16] a fact that Colombia documented in its Counter-Memorial and which is supplemented by the information provided in Annex 71 hereto.[17]

1.10 On 28 February 2018, the National Institute of Development Information of Nicaragua (INIDE, from its Spanish acronym) published statistics regarding Nicaraguan fishing in the Caribbean Sea drawn from previous studies carried out by the Nicaraguan Institute for Fishing and Aquaculture (INPESCA, from its Spanish acronym). These show that, since the Court's 2012 Judgment, Nicaragua has enjoyed a 107% increase of total catch from the Caribbean Sea,

16 The Chief of the Nicaraguan Naval Force, Rear-Admiral Marvin Elías Corrales Rodríguez, acknowledged that Nicaraguan fishermen had not been fishing in the area before the Court's Judgment, but that by 18 November 2013, one year after the Judgment, 16 fishing boats were operating in those waters. *Alleged Violations of Sovereign Rights and Maritime Spaces in the Caribbean Sea (Nicaragua* v. *Colombia),* Colombia's Preliminary Objections (hereinafter, "CPO"), Annex 43.

17 *Alleged Violations of Sovereign Rights and Maritime Spaces in the Caribbean Sea (Nicaragua* v. *Colombia),* Colombia's Counter-Memorial (hereinafter "CCM"), para. 3.21 and Graphic No. 2 at p. 107.

with significant increases in the number of Nicaraguan fishing vessels and annual fishing days.[18]

1.11 The table on the following page shows in graphic form this increase. It casts grave doubt on Nicaragua's claim that Colombia's conduct has had an adverse effect on Nicaragua's ability to exercise its sovereign rights over the living resources of its EEZ.

1.12 In the light of the above, the two critical questions are: (i) What are the rights of Nicaragua in its EEZ? and (ii) Is there any evidence that Colombia has violated those rights? As the Applicant in the present case, Nicaragua bears the burden of proving that its sovereign rights have been violated. Although Colombia will show in Chapter 2 that it acts in conformity with its rights and duties pursuant to its legitimate interests in the Southwestern Caribbean Sea, it does not need to prove that its conduct is expressly authorized under international law.

---

18 Annex 71.

Graphic CR 1

Reported Landing of Major Fishery Resources by Nicaragua in the Caribbean Sea 2011-2016 (by Species)

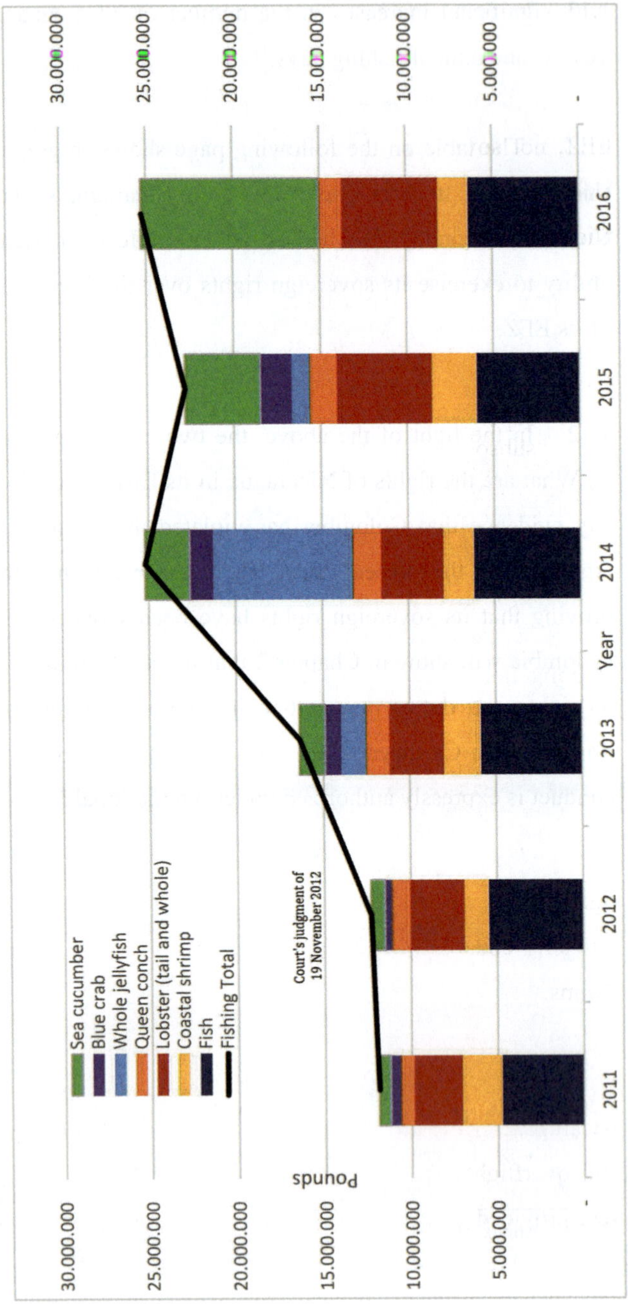

1.13 In considering these issues, it should be recalled that Nicaragua, whether under customary international law or UNCLOS, only possesses sovereign rights and jurisdiction in its EEZ, not sovereignty. Pursuant to Article 56, paragraph 1, of UNCLOS, which reflects customary international law, Nicaragua's sovereign rights exist solely

> "for the purpose of exploring and exploiting, conserving and managing the natural resources, whether living or non-living, of the waters superjacent to the seabed and of the seabed and its subsoil, and with regard to other activities for the economic exploitation and exploration of the zone".

1.14 At the same time, under the customary rule embodied in Article 56, paragraph 2, in exercising these rights, Nicaragua has an obligation to have due regard to the rights and duties of other States, including Colombia.

1.15 None of Colombia's conducts of which Nicaragua complains impeded Nicaragua from exercising its sovereign rights. This is evident from five overriding factors that are mutually consistent and fundamentally undermine Nicaragua's claims.

1.16 *First*, Colombia is fully entitled to be present in Nicaragua's EEZ in the exercise of the freedoms of navigation and overflight, and of other internationally lawful uses of the sea, provided that it has due regard for the sovereign rights of

Nicaragua. Contrary to Nicaragua's assertions,[19] customary international law does not deprive Colombia of the right to observe and collect information about the activities of maritime traffic in the area. In particular, Colombia has compelling interests to be on the look-out for suspicious boats that may be engaged in drug smuggling across the Southwestern Caribbean Sea. Colombia also has a vested interest in the preservation of the environmental integrity of the area, which includes the Seaflower Biosphere Reserve – a unique area of special environmental importance that has been recognized by UNESCO. Furthermore, Colombia has an interest in ensuring the safety and livelihood of the inhabitants of the San Andrés Archipelago, particularly the Raizales – descendant of the enslaved Africans and the original Dutch, British and Spanish settlers – many of whom continue to rely on the sea for their sustenance. Engaging in any of these activities causes no prejudice to Nicaragua. Indeed, it is to the benefit of the international community. Moreover, the activities in question are fully justified as a corollary of Colombia's freedoms of navigation and overflight and other internationally lawful uses of the sea in the region.

1.17 *Second*, Nicaragua has produced no reliable evidence with respect to the "incidents" that are said to underlie its claims. Rather than relying on contemporaneous evidence showing that Colombia engaged in an internationally wrongful

---

19 See NR, paras. 2.26-2.27 and 2.52.

conduct, Nicaragua cites non-contemporaneous and third-party sources, including newspaper articles and indirect reports allegedly furnished from Nicaraguan fishing boats to its Naval Force, well after the events complained of occurred. These are erroneous in fact and insufficient in law. Actually, they are not "incidents" at all. In Chapter 3, therefore, Colombia will demonstrate on a case-by-case basis that Nicaragua has not met its burden of proving that Colombia impeded its vessels from exercising its sovereign rights.

1.18 *Third*, Nicaragua's claims are belied by the contemporaneous statements of its most senior political and military officials. While Nicaragua continues to harp on what it contends is Colombia's "rejection" of the 2012 Judgment,[20] it was Nicaragua's President himself, Daniel Ortega, who referred to the need to downplay what he termed "all this media turbulence" by stating, just three months before Nicaragua filed its Application in this case, that Colombia's Navy "has been respectful and there has not been any kind of confrontation between the Colombian and Nicaraguan Navy".[21] Similarly, it was the Chief of the Nicaraguan Naval Force – someone who would be expected to know if there had been any provocations or "incidents" – who affirmed one year after the Judgment was delivered that "[t]here have not been any conflicts and that is why I want to highlight that in one year of being there we have

---

20 NR, para. 4.44.
21 CPO, Annex 11, p. 118.

not had any problems with the Colombian Navy".[22] And it was General Avilés, the Chief of the Nicaraguan Army, who, on 18 March 2014, four months after the Pact of Bogotá ceased to be in force between Nicaragua and Colombia and the Application was filed, emphasized: "There are no incidents" involving the Colombian Navy.[23]

1.19 *Fourth*, at no time during this period did Nicaragua raise a single complaint to Colombia about any so-called "incidents". The first time Nicaragua sent a note of complaint to Colombia was in September 2014, conveniently just a few weeks before Nicaragua filed its Memorial and well after the Pact of Bogotá had ceased to be in force between Nicaragua and Colombia.

1.20 *Fifth*, while Nicaragua claims that Colombia has engaged in a systematic policy of harassing Nicaraguan fishing vessels, the fact is that statistically, even if those alleged events were true (*quod non*), they are *de minimis* in relation to the combined number of days spent by all Nicaraguan fishing vessels in the area (i.e. fishing trip days). For example, in 2013, the number of events alleged by Nicaragua represents 0.021% of its fishing trip days. As can be seen in Annex 71, similar statistics follow for 2014, 2015 and 2016.[24]

---

22 CPO, Annex 43, p. 355.

23 CPO, Annex 46, p. 367.

24 For 2014, the number of events alleged by Nicaragua represents 0.057% of its fishing trip days; for 2015, it represents 0.018%; and for 2016, it represents 0,005%.

Graphic CR 2
Nicaraguan Annual Fishing Trip Days and Alleged "Incidents" in the Caribbean Sea Involving Nicaraguan Fishing Ships

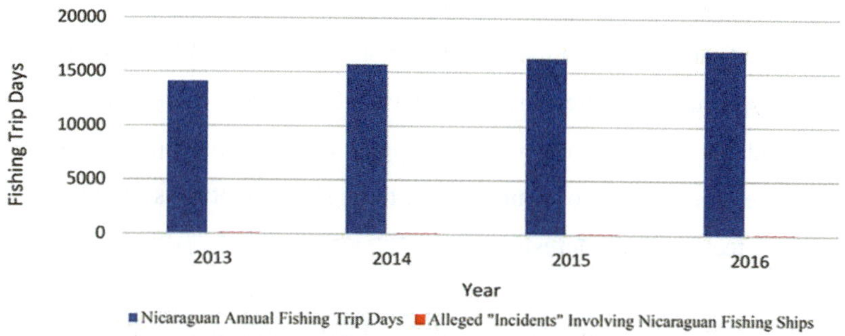

1.21 In short, Nicaragua's claims are not supported by evidence, and they cannot be reconciled with the repeated and consistent affirmations made by its senior officials.

(2) The Contiguous Zone

1.22 Nicaragua has also not demonstrated that Colombia violated Nicaragua's sovereign rights and maritime spaces by its adoption of Decree No. 1946, Article 5 of which provided for the establishment of a contiguous zone around the Colombian islands comprising the San Andrés Archipelago. There is not a single instance that Nicaragua can cite where one of its flagged vessels has been prejudiced or impeded from exercising Nicaragua's EEZ rights within Colombia's contiguous zone.

1.23 Under customary international law, the jurisdictional powers that States can exercise in the contiguous zone, including those enumerated in Decree No. 1946 (as amended), are not incompatible with the sovereign rights a coastal State such as Nicaragua has within its EEZ. Each provides for a distinct set of rights that are not in conflict with each other. In other words, contiguous zone jurisdiction may be exercised by one State in an area that lies within another State's EEZ without displacing the latter's resource-based EEZ rights. Especially in today's world, contiguous zone rights enable a coastal State to exercise a degree of control close to its shores that is essential to protect its vital interests.

1.24 Article 101 of Colombia's 1991 Political Constitution, proclaiming a contiguous zone, states that such a zone "is in accordance with international law". For its part, Article 5 of Decree No. 1946 (as amended) provides that its application "will be carried out in conformity with international law and Article 7 of the present Decree". Article 7, in turn, makes it clear that nothing in the Decree will "affect or limit the rights of other states".[25] Thus, the legislation of which Nicaragua complains expressly provides that it will be applied in conformity with international law and that it will not affect or limit the rights of third States such as Nicaragua.

1.25 Colombia's enactment of the Decree has not affected or limited Nicaragua's sovereign rights or maritime spaces. As noted above, Nicaragua cannot point to any prejudice it has suffered as a result of the adoption of the Decree.

---

25 Decree No. 1946 (as amended) may be found in Annex 7 to the CCM, Vol II at p. 77.

1.26 As Colombia discussed in its Counter-Memorial, and will again demonstrate in this Rejoinder, the jurisdictional powers that the Decree grants to it in the contiguous zone are essential to protect the vital interests of the Archipelago and its inhabitants, and are consistent with customary international law and with State practice. Moreover, the spatial extent of the zone is tailored to the specific geographic characteristics of the islands of the San Andrés Archipelago, and does not prejudice the sovereign rights Nicaragua possesses in the waters of its EEZ.

B. The Real Scope of Colombia's Position and the Constitutional Court's Ruling Regarding the Pact of Bogotá

1.27 Colombia has not denied Nicaragua's sovereign rights and jurisdiction over its maritime spaces, nor has it denied the binding effect of the 2012 Judgment. Yet, Nicaragua clings to an array of political statements devoid of legal content, let alone legal effect. In fact, as demonstrated in Colombia's Preliminary Objections, Counter-Memorial and this Rejoinder, Colombia has not violated Nicaragua's sovereign rights and maritime spaces.

1.28 Moreover, in its Reply Nicaragua asserts that the Constitutional Court's ruling regarding certain provisions of the Pact of Bogotá is a decision that "bar[s] compliance with the 19 November 2012 Judgment".[26] In relation to the scope of the

---

26 NR, p. 191, Submissions, 1 (e).

judgment of Colombia's Constitutional Court, Nicaragua claims that the "Agent of the Respondent merely said that Colombia and its Constitutional Court now recognize the 2012 Judgment as binding"[27] and that "[t]his passage barely clarifies anything."[28]

1.29 Colombia previously referred in both its written and oral pleadings on the preliminary objections to the scope of the 2014 Constitutional Court's ruling regarding the Pact of Bogotá.[29] In the light of Nicaragua's distortion of Colombia's true position, the matter will be briefly revisited to demonstrate the baseless nature of Nicaragua's submission.

1.30 In its Preliminary Objections, Colombia summarized its position as follows:

> "In fact, Colombia has never taken any decision not to comply with the Judgment despite the disappointment of certain constituencies in Colombia with parts of it. On the contrary, both its highest officials and its highest court (the Constitutional Court) have made it clear that the Judgment is binding under international law. However, in order to give effect to the Judgment in its domestic legal order (to make it 'applicable'), it is necessary for Colombia to comply with the requirements of domestic law, in particular with

---

27 NR, para. 1.8.

28 NR, para. 1.8.

29 CPO, paras. 2.41-2.46; *Alleged Violations of Sovereign Rights and Maritime Spaces in the Caribbean Sea (Nicaragua* v. *Colombia)*, Public Sitting, 28 September 2015, CR 2015/22, p. 16, para. 9 and p. 35, para. 18 (Agent).

> Article 101, paragraph 2, of its Constitution. Contrary to what Nicaragua would have the Court believe, there is nothing exceptional in the distinction between the position under international law and domestic law, particularly in States following a dualist approach. Nor is it unusual that time is needed to give effect to an international obligation, whether under a treaty or a judgment."[30]

1.31 Paragraphs 2.38 to 2.46 of the Preliminary Objections further explained the process before the Constitutional Court and its subsequent decision.

1.32 For his part, during the public hearings on the preliminary objections, the Agent of Colombia made it clear that the Constitutional Court "ruled unambiguously that, pursuant to Article 94 of the Charter of the United Nations, judgments rendered by this International Court of Justice are binding and cannot be disregarded".[31] He further asserted that, as a matter of international law, Colombia recognised the binding force of the 2012 Judgment, as confirmed by the Constitutional Court.[32] Counsel for Colombia also explained that, as a matter of domestic law,

> "decisions of the International Court of Justice with respect to boundaries had to be incorporated

30 CPO, para. 2.24.

31 *Alleged Violations of Sovereign Rights and Maritime Spaces in the Caribbean Sea (Nicaragua* v. *Colombia)*, Public Sitting, 28 September 2015, CR 2015/22, p. 16, para. 9 (Agent).

32 *Alleged Violations of Sovereign Rights and Maritime Spaces in the Caribbean Sea (Nicaragua* v. *Colombia)*, Public Sitting, 28 September 2015, CR 2015/22, p. 17, para. 13 (Agent).

> into domestic law in the manner provided for by Article 101 of the Constitution: that is, by means of treaties."[33]

1.33 In its Reply, Nicaragua has chosen to ignore these explanations and to distort Colombia's position. This is so for at least two reasons.

1.34 *First*, the subject-matter of the dispute – as identified by the Court in its 2016 Judgment on Preliminary Objections in the present case – does not cover questions concerning Colombia's compliance with the 2012 Judgment. Rather, the scope of the present proceedings is limited to "the alleged violations by Colombia of Nicaragua's rights in the maritime zones which, according to Nicaragua, the Court declared in its 2012 Judgment appertain to Nicaragua".[34]

1.35 In its Reply, Nicaragua continues to confuse what are in reality two distinct legal questions (compliance with the 2012 Judgment, and "alleged violations of Nicaragua's sovereign rights and maritime spaces") by amalgamating these separate questions into one. Thus, Nicaragua asserts that "[t]he central issue in the present case is precisely that Colombia *not only refused to comply* with the 2012 Judgment but *breached*

---

33 *Alleged Violations of Sovereign Rights and Maritime Spaces in the Caribbean Sea (Nicaragua* v. *Colombia)*, Public Sitting, 28 September 2015, CR 2015/22, p. 37, para. 23 (Bundy).

34 *Alleged Violations of Sovereign Rights and Maritime Spaces in the Caribbean Sea (Nicaragua v. Colombia), Preliminary Objections, I.C.J. Reports 2016* (hereinafter "Judgment on the Preliminary Objections), p. 32, para. 79.

Nicaragua's sovereign rights stemming from it".[35] Yet, even if Nicaragua seeks to portray the former as "the central issue" of its case (i.e. compliance with the 2012 Judgment), in fact the Court has already established that the dispute relates only to one issue: the alleged violations of Nicaragua's sovereign rights and maritime spaces.

1.36 *Second*, Nicaragua misrepresents what Colombia's Constitutional Court actually decided with respect to the 2012 Judgment. As Colombia has already explained, in so far as questions of boundaries are concerned, Colombia's 1991 Political Constitution adopts a dualist approach. Under the Constitution, for a boundary to be established or modified as a matter of Colombian law, a treaty must be signed and ratified. This is the manner in which, according to the Constitutional Court's ruling, the 2012 Judgment will have to be incorporated into domestic law. That in no way means that Colombia has "refused to comply with the 2012 Judgment", as claimed by Nicaragua. To the contrary, the Constitutional Court itself noted that:

> "the decisions rendered by the International Court of Justice, on the basis of the jurisdiction recognized by Colombia through Article XXXI of the Pact [of Bogotá], *cannot be disregarded*, in conformity with what is prescribed in Article 94 of the Charter of the United Nations, that provides that each Member of the United Nations is committed to comply with the decision of the

35 NR, para. 1.9. (Emphasis added).

> International Court of Justice in any case to which it is a party."[36]

1.37 Nicaragua's claim that Colombia has a systematic policy of disregarding the 2012 Judgment is thus unfounded.

C. Colombia's Counter-claims

1.38 In its Order of 15 November 2017, the Court found that Colombia's third and fourth counter-claims are admissible and form part of the current proceedings.[37] Colombia's third counter-claim requests the Court to adjudge and declare that the traditional fishing rights of the inhabitants of the San Andrés Archipelago, including the Raizales, exist and that Nicaragua has infringed those rights to access and exploit their traditional fishing banks. The fourth counter-claim requests the Court to declare that Nicaragua's system of straight baselines, adopted pursuant to Decree No. 33-2013 of 19 August 2013 is contrary to customary international law and violates Colombia's sovereign rights and maritime spaces.

---

[36] CPO, Annex 4, para. 9.10. (Emphasis added).

[37] *Alleged Violations of Sovereign Rights and Maritime Spaces in the Caribbean Sea (Nicaragua* v. *Colombia),* Order of 15 November 2017, paras. 82 (A) and 82 (B).

(1) Nicaragua's Infringement of the Traditional Fishing Rights of the Inhabitants of the San Andrés Archipelago

1.39 Nicaragua's Reply seeks to deny the inhabitants of the San Andrés Archipelago their right to continue exercising their traditional fishing practices in maritime areas of the Southwestern Caribbean Sea, on three main grounds. *First*, Nicaragua asserts that with the adoption of UNCLOS these traditional rights have been extinguished within its EEZ because the coastal State has exclusive sovereign rights to explore and exploit the living resources therein.[38] *Second*, Nicaragua denies that the local inhabitants of the Archipelago even have such rights and contends that Colombia has failed to prove that the rights in question exist.[39] *Third*, even assuming the existence of such rights, Nicaragua denies that it has infringed them.[40] Notwithstanding these denials, Nicaragua nonetheless affirms that

> "it remains open, in the spirit of brotherhood and good neighbourly relations, to work with Colombia to reach a bilateral agreement that takes account of Colombia's and Nicaragua's concerns, including the fishing needs of the Raizales."[41]

1.40 On the first point, Nicaragua's arguments are seriously misguided. Nicaragua does not dispute the fact that traditional

---

[38] NR, paras. 6.7-6.30.
[39] NR, paras. 6.31-6.76.
[40] NR, paras. 6.77-6.95.
[41] NR, para. 6.76.

fishing rights of nationals of one State have been recognized to exist in the territorial sea of another State even though (i) the latter State possesses sovereignty over its territorial sea as opposed to the quite limited sovereign rights that exist in the EEZ, and (ii) UNCLOS does not expressly refer to such rights. Yet, if traditional fishing rights can exist in the territorial sea of another State, it is counterintuitive, to say the least, to maintain that they cannot exist in the EEZ. Indeed, as will be seen, the jurisprudence shows the contrary.[42]

1.41 Nicaragua's second argument – that Colombia has failed to demonstrate that the inhabitants of the Archipelago, including the Raizales, have traditionally fished in what is now part of the waters of Nicaragua's EEZ – is extraordinary in its boldness. For it is no less than Nicaragua's President who has repeatedly referred to and recognized precisely these traditional fishing rights of the Raizales. Indeed, President Ortega has unequivocally stated that "we will respect the historical rights that they have",[43] there will be "open communication channels to ensure the Raizal people their fishing rights",[44] and "the raizal community, living in San Andrés can continue fishing in the Caribbean waters now belonging to Nicaragua and that their rights as native people will not be affected".[45] Quite apart from the witness statements Colombia has filed attesting to historical fishing in the area, unilateral statements such as the above

42 See Chapter 5 *infra*.
43 CCM, Annex 73. See also Annexes 1 and 6 to this Rejoinder.
44 CCM, Annex 74.
45 CCM, Annex 76.

emanating from Nicaragua's highest political authority would had never been made if the traditional fishing rights of the inhabitants of the San Andrés Archipelago did not exist, as Nicaragua now seeks to argue in its Reply.

1.42 As for Nicaragua's third argument – that it has not infringed the traditional fishing rights of the local inhabitants of the San Andrés Archipelago – Nicaragua conveniently adopts a more stringent standard of evidence from the one it applies to its own claims. In this respect, Colombia will show that the Nicaraguan Naval Force harasses and bullies the artisanal fishermen that it intercepts. As a consequence of this conduct, the artisanal fishermen fear getting stopped by the Nicaraguan armed agents, which is why they have been forced to abandon many of their traditional fishing banks.

(2) The Unlawfulness of Nicaragua's Straight Baselines

1.43 In the present case the legality of the straight baselines that Nicaragua enacted pursuant to its Decree No. 33-2013 is squarely in issue, the Court having found that Colombia's counter-claim challenging the legality of Nicaragua's straight baselines is admissible. By enacting its decree, Nicaragua has aggregated to itself, as internal waters, large areas that used to be territorial sea; and has unilaterally extended the breadth of its territorial sea and EEZ in a manner that is contrary to customary international law, as well as the strict conditions for straight baselines set out in Article 7 of UNCLOS, which are binding on Nicaragua.

1.44 As identified by Colombia in its Counter-Memorial and in this Rejoinder, Nicaragua's straight baselines run afoul of several criteria that govern the validity of a system of straight baselines. For example: Nicaragua's coast is not deeply indented and cut into; it does not possess a fringe of islands along the coast in its immediate vicinity that justify straight baselines; its straight baselines fail to respect the requirement that they not depart to any appreciable extent from the general direction of the coast; and the sea areas they purport to appropriate as internal waters lying within the baselines are not sufficiently closely linked to the land domain to be subject to the regime of internal waters. Consequently, they should be ruled to be legally invalid.

D. The Structure of the Rejoinder

1.45 This Rejoinder is organized as follows:

Part I of this pleading introduces Colombia's arguments and explains the legitimate interests that Colombia has. Indeed,

- Chapter 2 will show that Colombia's presence in the Southwestern Caribbean Sea, including in areas within the waters of Nicaragua's EEZ, is fully in line with its rights in this area, including freedoms of navigation and overflight and other internationally lawful uses of the sea.

In Part II Colombia will demonstrate that Nicaragua's allegation that Colombia has violated Nicaragua's sovereign rights and maritime spaces is unfounded in fact and in law, and that Nicaragua has not met its burden of proof for its claims. In particular:

- Chapter 3 will show that, with respect to the "incidents" that Nicaragua relies on for its allegation that Colombia has violated its sovereign rights, the Court's jurisdiction is limited to events that occurred between the date of the Court's 2012 Judgment (i.e. 19 November 2012) and the date when the Pact of Bogotá ceased to be in force between Nicaragua and Colombia (i.e. 27 November 2013, one day after Nicaragua filed its Application). Following that, Colombia will demonstrate, on a case-by-case basis, that none of the "incidents" involved any violation of Nicaragua's sovereign rights. Colombia will also show that it has never authorized industrial fishing in Nicaragua's EEZ and that Nicaragua's claim that Colombia continues to offer petroleum blocks in the waters of Nicaragua's EEZ is false.

- Chapter 4 turns to the second element of Nicaragua's claims – the validity of the contiguous zone established around the islands of the San Andrés Archipelago. Colombia will show that the exercise of its jurisdictional rights in the contiguous zone, and the geographical extent of that zone, are consistent with customary international law, and do not affect Nicaragua's ability to exercise sovereign rights in the waters of its EEZ. Moreover, Colombia will also demonstrate that it is bound by its own legislation to implement the contiguous zone in accordance with international law and in a manner that does not affect the rights of other States, and that Nicaragua has not proved that it has suffered any prejudice as a result of the passage or application of the legislation.

In Part III, Colombia will demonstrate that its two counter-claims found admissible by the Court are well founded. In particular:

- Chapter 5 addresses Colombia's counter-claim that Nicaragua has infringed the traditional fishing rights of the local inhabitants of the Archipelago – rights that Nicaragua, through the declarations of its President, has expressly recognized to exist. Colombia will also show that

Nicaragua's attempt to deny these rights on the basis that they have been extinguished with the adoption of the EEZ regime is misguided.

- Chapter 6 deals with the enactment by Nicaragua, after the 2012 Judgment was delivered, of a system of straight baselines. Colombia will show that these straight baselines do not conform to the conditions imposed under both customary international law and UNCLOS, that they prejudice Colombia, and that they are thus contrary to international law.

- Chapter 7 contains a short summary of Colombia's reasoning. It will be followed by Colombia's Submissions.

Colombia is also filing one volume with the documentary annexes referred to in the Rejoinder, including an Appendix in which Colombia will show that, while the Court lacks jurisdiction to consider the post-critical date events advanced by Nicaragua, none of them evidences any violation of its sovereign rights.

Chapter 2

COLOMBIA'S LEGITIMATE INTERESTS IN THE SOUTHWESTERN CARIBBEAN SEA

A. Introduction

2.1 Nicaragua has portrayed and continues to portray the conduct of Colombia in the Southwestern Caribbean Sea as one of sustained infringement of the EEZ regime,[46] particularly through an allegedly repeated obstruction of Nicaraguan authorities and harassment of Nicaraguan licensed fishing vessels, so as to give the appearance that confrontation and divisiveness prevail over cooperation. This is far from true.[47] Nicaragua speaks at length of "incidents" that would have involved Colombian authorities in the Southwestern Caribbean Sea. As will be seen in Chapter 3, this is not the case. Colombia has never claimed a "general right to engage in policing

[46] NR, para. 2.10.

[47] In fact, there is a friendly and cordial relationship between the Colombian Navy and the Nicaraguan Naval Force. The respective Commanders have met frequently in naval conferences in Buenos Aires (September 2014), Cartagena (August 2015), Mexico (September 2017) and Cartagena (July 2018). Similarly, the two Navies have cooperated in search and rescue operations – for instance, the Colombian A.R.C. "Caldas" assisted when four Nicaraguan marines shipwrecked in *Luna Verde* in December 2013 – and drug interdiction operations – like the recent multilateral Operation "Orion" in April 2018, which led to the seizing of 18.5 tons of cocaine and 1 ton of marihuana, and the capture of 85 people. In addition, in October 2018, two Nicaraguan naval officers attended the VII Naval War Games of Central America and the Caribbean in Cartagena. This type of joint activities would definitely not happen if the Colombian Navy was indeed hostile or had a harassing attitude towards the Nicaraguan Naval Force.

activities in Nicaragua's EEZ."[48] And none of the facts reproached by Nicaragua to Colombia can seriously be qualified as "policing activities."[49]

2.2 The presence of the Colombian Navy in the Southwestern Caribbean Sea is an exercise of its freedom of navigation and overflight, and other internationally lawful uses of the sea, which is wholly consistent with customary international law. As Colombia explained in its Counter-Memorial, it enjoys such rights in waters of the Nicaraguan EEZ. These freedoms allow Colombia to be present in the area and carry out a range of activities, which include observing and informing about practices that prejudice the marine environment or that threaten the habitat and livelihood of the inhabitants of the San Andrés Archipelago who have traditional fishing rights in the area; render assistance to persons and vessels in distress at sea; and cooperate to prevent and interdict drug trafficking and other forms of transnational crime. All of the above is carried out in accordance with customary international law and the relevant treaties applicable to these matters.

2.3 In its Reply, with the intent to challenge Colombia's presence and activities in the Southwestern Caribbean Sea, Nicaragua erroneously reduces freedoms of navigation and overflight, as well as other internationally lawful uses of the sea, to innocent passage. This mistaken conclusion is derived from

---

48 NR, paras. 2.26-2.56.
49 NR, paras. 2.26-2.60.

Nicaragua's apparent belief that the 2012 Judgment granted to it full and unimpeded sovereignty over the waters of its EEZ. However, Colombia will show that Nicaragua's understanding of the freedoms of navigation and overflight, and other internationally lawful uses of the sea, is contrary to international law (Section B), and that its presence in the Southwestern Caribbean Sea, including in the waters of Nicaragua's EEZ, is the legal exercise of these freedoms and an internationally lawful use of the sea, which does not infringe Nicaragua's sovereign rights and jurisdiction (Section C). Further, Colombia will show that it is not acting in a general policing fashion in the waters of the Nicaraguan EEZ, but rather, it is exercising its freedoms and rights to protect legitimate interests and concerns, including the need to prevent transnational crime at sea, drug trafficking, the need to ensure safety for fishermen, the protection of fragile ecosystems and the well-being of vulnerable communities by ensuring a healthy environment for these communities (Section D).

B. Freedoms of Navigation and Overflight, and other Internationally Lawful Uses of the Sea

2.4 Apart from the limited sovereign rights and jurisdiction reserved to the coastal State in the waters of its EEZ, therein other States enjoy freedom of navigation and overflight as well as other internationally lawful uses of the sea – including for their foreign military ships.

2.5 Rather than contesting that Colombia is entitled to freedom of navigation and overflight in Nicaragua's EEZ under customary international law,[50] Nicaragua:

- Tries to limit the scope of these freedoms by asserting that freedom of navigation merely encompasses a right of "passage"[51] (i.e. that a ship can only sail from one point to another).[52]

- Argues that third States do not enjoy the same liberties it does in the waters of its EEZ because

> "the high seas does not have the status of a 'residual regime' in relation to the EEZ so that in the event of doubt as to the existence or scope of coastal State rights in the EEZ the 'high seas presumption' against the existence of coastal State jurisdiction over foreign-flag ships would operate."[53]

- Asserts that "Colombia must establish that the rights that it claims in Nicaragua's EEZ are 'attributed' to it, and not to Nicaragua, by the regime of the EEZ."[54]

2.6 Nicaragua is in error on all three points.

---

[50] NR, para. 2.11.
[51] NR, para. 2.36.
[52] NR, paras. 2.38 and 2.40.
[53] NR, para. 2.8.
[54] NR, para. 2.10.

2.7 *First*, as for the scope of the freedom of navigation, Nicaragua ignores the notion of "freedom", and erroneously reduces it to a mere right to navigate from point A to point B.[55]

2.8 There is no doubt that freedom of navigation entails the freedom of movement of vessels. But freedom of navigation also means the freedom of operations at sea,[56] which encompasses the right to navigate for any lawful purpose.

2.9 *Second*, freedom of navigation in waters of another State's EEZ entails paying due regard to the coastal State's limited sovereign rights, but these are otherwise unaffected.[57] However, some activities that can be freely exercised on the high seas fall under the jurisdiction of the coastal State in its EEZ. Conversely, those activities that do not fall under the

---

55 NR, para. 2.40.

56 R. O'Rourke, *Maritime Territorial and Exclusive Economic Zone (EEZ) Disputes Involving China: Issues for Congress*, Congressional Research Service, 2017, p. 4, available at: http://www.andrewerickson.com/wp-content/uploads/2017/10/CRS_ORourke_China-Maritime-EEZ-Disputes_R42784_20171016.pdf (last visited: 1 November 2018).

57 This has been confirmed by ITLOS in the *M/V 'Virginia G'* case. In this case, the Tribunal addressed the question whether the activity of bunkering while navigating was subject to the exclusive jurisdiction of the coastal State. It held that the coastal State has no competence with regard to bunkering activities not directed to fishermen, thereby implicitly, but necessarily, acknowledging that this activity is encompassed into freedom of navigation, *M/V "Virginia G" (Panama/Guinea-Bissau), Judgment, ITLOS Reports 2014*, p. 4, p. 70, para. 223. Y. Tanaka comments that some countries do no adopt regulation on bunkering activities in the EEZ. This is the case of the U.K. and other States. This is why, except when the coastal State does adopt specific regulation, "fishing vessels remain free to supply and to receive bunkers in the EEZ", Y. Tanaka, "Navigational Rights and Freedoms", in D. R Rothwell, A. G. Oude Elferink, *et al* (eds.), *The Oxford Handbook of the Law of the Sea*, Oxford University Press, 2015, p. 554 (available at the Peace Palace Library).

jurisdiction of the coastal State can be freely exercised by third States while navigating in its EEZ, to the extent, of course, that they do not infringe the rights of the coastal State and of other States. For example, freedom of navigation in the EEZ includes:

> "the right to effectuate operations with regard to the towing and rescue of vessels (...) These actions are connected with the freedom of navigation and, consequently, a coastal State should neither reserve this right to itself, as it may do within its territorial sea, nor demand from other States a prior request about the possibility of conducting such rescue actions."[58]

2.10 Likewise, the freedom of overflight in the EEZ is the same as that enjoyed on the high seas. While contemporary international law transformed large parts of the high seas into EEZ, it has not affected the freedom of overflight over the EEZ.

2.11 The 1944 Chicago Convention, which was concluded before the introduction of the EEZ in international law, distinguished between the territories of the contracting parties and the high seas.[59] When the concept of the EEZ was introduced in UNCLOS III, the Secretariat of the International Civil Aviation Organisation conducted a study on the legal implications of UNCLOS on the Chicago Convention and other air law instruments. That study concluded that:

---

[58] A. A. Kovalev, *Contemporary Issues of the Law of the Sea*, Eleven International Publishing, 2004, p. 56 (available at the Peace Palace Library).

[59] Convention on International Civil Aviation, 7 December 1944, 15 UNTS 296.

> "For all practical and legal purposes, the status of the airspace above the EEZ and the regime over the EEZ is the same as over the high seas and the coastal States are not granted any precedence or priority."[60]

2.12 It follows that the scope of the freedom of overflight over the high seas and in Nicaragua's EEZ is not limited by customary international law, nor by UNCLOS, because the airspace above Nicaragua's EEZ is international. Yet, Nicaragua repeatedly claims to be exercising "sovereignty in the airspace over the waters restored by the International Court of Justice".[61]

2.13 *Third*, Nicaragua is not correct in asserting that, under customary international law as reflected in UNCLOS Article 59, and as far as the EEZ is concerned, if a right is not specifically attributed to third States, then it must be vested on the coastal State.[62] It suffices to read the ordinary meaning of the article to understand that, to the contrary, its sole purpose is to resolve conflicts that could only arise if rights in the EEZ are not automatically attributable to the coastal State.

---

60 International Civil Aviation Organisation, "United Nations Convention on the Law of the Sea – Implications, if any, for the application of the Chicago Convention, its Annexes and other international air law instruments", doc. C-WP/7777 (1984), para. 11.12, in Netherlands Institute for the Law of the Sea (ed.), *International Organizations and the Law of the Sea Documentary Yearbook 3*, 1987, p. 243 (available at the Peace Palace Library).

61 See Annexes 1-5 and 7.

62 NR, para. 2.8.

2.14 In sum, Nicaragua's understanding of the basics of the law applicable in the EEZ is wholly erroneous.

C. Colombia's presence in the Southwestern Caribbean Sea, including in Nicaragua's EEZ, is an exercise of its freedoms of navigation and overflight and an internationally lawful use of the sea, which does not infringe Nicaragua's sovereign rights

2.15 Nicaragua wrongly asserts that the activities carried out by the Colombian Navy in its EEZ are not lawful (Sub-section 1). Moreover, even if these activities were not permitted under the regime of freedoms of navigation and overflight, or were not internationally lawful uses of the sea, *quod non*, it would be for Nicaragua, not Colombia, to prove that they infringe its rights in its EEZ, which it has not done (Sub-section 2).

(1) The Presence of the Colombian Navy falls within the Freedom of Navigation afforded to all States under International Law

2.16 Nicaragua complains that the mere presence of the Colombian Navy in the Southwestern Caribbean Sea, including within the waters of its EEZ, is not an exercise of Colombia's freedom of navigation. However, to the extent that Colombian ships simply observe and inform about unlawful activities, they do not impede the exercise by Nicaragua of its sovereign rights.

2.17 Even with respect to military vessels, while Article 58 of UNCLOS "does not expressly mention military activities or survey activities",[63] it is undisputable that "the naval powers maintain that the language was intended to ensure that traditional freedoms of the seas in article 87 were preserved in the EEZ."[64]

2.18 Moreover, State practice clearly confirms that States are entitled to carry out military operations in a foreign State's EEZ. As has been recalled recently:

> "The United States, like most other countries, believes that coastal states under UNCLOS have the right to regulate economic activities in their EEZs, but do not have the right to regulate foreign military activities in their EEZs.
>
> U.S. military surveillance flights in international airspace above another country's EEZ are lawful under international law, and the United States plans to continue conducting these flights as it has in the past."[65]

2.19 In this sense, that country's Handbook on the Law of Naval Operations clearly states that in the EEZ, as international

---

63 R. Beckham and T. Davenport, "The EEZ Regime, Reflection After 30 Years", *Proceedings from the 2012 LOSI-KIOST Conference on Securing the Ocean for the Next Generation,* 2012, p. 10, available at: https://www.law.berkeley.edu/files/Beckman-Davenport-final.pdf (last visited: 1 November 2018).

64 R. Beckham and T. Davenport, "The EEZ Regime, Reflection After 30 Years", *Proceedings from the 2012 LOSI-KIOST Conference on Securing the Ocean for the Next Generation,* 2012, p. 10, available at: https://www.law.berkeley.edu/files/Beckman-Davenport-final.pdf (last visited: 1 November 2018).

65 R. O'Rourke, *Maritime Territorial and Exclusive Economic Zone (EEZ) Disputes Involving China: Issues for Congress*, Congressional Research Service, 2017, available at: http://www.andrewerickson.com/wp-content/uploads/2017/10/CRS_ORourke_China-Maritime-EEZ-Disputes_R42784_20171016.pdf (last visited: 1 November 2018).

waters,

> "the coastal State cannot unduly restrict or impede the exercise of the freedoms of navigation in and overflight of the EEZ. Since all ships and aircraft, including warships and military aircraft, enjoy the high seas freedoms of navigation and overflight and other internationally lawful uses of the sea related to those freedoms, in and over those waters, the existence of an EEZ in an area of naval operations need not, of itself, be of operational concern to the naval commander."[66]

2.20 Similarly, the Australian Navy considers that "the EEZ regime in UNCLOS *does not* permit the coastal state to limit military activities in its EEZ"[67] because of the high seas freedoms that exist therein, which permit the conduct of military activities, with some limitations, such as to "refrain from unlawful threat, have due regard for the coastal state's rights and duties, due regard for others using the EEZ, and observe obligations under other treaties and rules".[68]

---

[66] United States Navy, "The Commander's Handbook on the Law of Naval Operations", 2017, p. 2-9, available at: http://www.jag.navy.mil/distrib/instructions/CDRs_HB_on_Law_of_Naval_Operations_AUG17.pdf (last visited: 1 November 2018).

[67] Royal Australian Navy, Commander M. H. Miller, "The impact on the Law of the Sea Convention on the roles and activities of the RAN in meeting Australian Government requirements", p. 53, available at: http://www.defence.gov.au/ADC/Publications/Geddes/2005/PublcnsGeddes2005_310310_ImpactoftheLaw.pdf (last visited: 1 November 2018).

[68] Royal Australian Navy, Commander M. H. Miller, "The impact on the Law of the Sea Convention on the roles and activities of the RAN in meeting Australian Government requirements", p. 58, available at: http://www.defence.gov.au/ADC/Publications/Geddes/2005/PublcnsGeddes2005_310310_ImpactoftheLaw.pdf (last visited: 1 November 2018).

2.21 For its part, the United Kingdom's Ministry of Defence asserts that:

> "The long-standing principle of freedom of navigation in international waters allows maritime forces to access areas of national interest and potential threat. This access guarantees freedom of navigation for maritime forces up to 12 nautical miles from a coastline to allow options for intervention at a time and place of national choosing."[69]

2.22 A similar position is adopted by Spain, who also considers that in international waters (including another State's EEZ), "any State may conduct training and exercises with its naval forces, including with real fire", provided that they "respect the purposes for which that exclusive economic zone has been declared."[70]

2.23 Moreover, a warship can even exercise the right of visit in another coastal State's EEZ (a right that the Colombian Navy did not exercise in waters of the Nicaraguan EEZ):

> "[W]arships, military aircrafts, or other ships and aircrafts clearly marked and identifiable as being on government service and duly authorised, may engage in the right of visit (…) the right of visit

---

69 United Kingdom Ministry of Defence, "Joint Doctrine Publication 0 - 10: UK Maritime Power", 5th edition, 2017, p. 37, para. 3.18, available at: https://assets.publishing.service.gov.uk/government/uploads/system/uploads/attachment_data/file/662000/doctrine_uk_maritime_power_jdp_0_10.pdf (last visited: 1 November 2018).

70 Annex 72: Kingdom of Spain, Ministry of Defence, *Law of the Sea Manual*, Volume 1, 27 May 2015.

> applies not only on the high seas, but also in the EEZ, subject to the coastal state rights therein".[71]

2.24 Thus, Colombia may carry out military manoeuvres and surveys in Nicaragua's EEZ so long as they are consistent with international law, in particular Article 2(4) of the UN Charter, and do not trespass on Nicaragua's sovereign rights. More generally, as expressly provided by Article 58 of UNCLOS, which reflects customary international law, in the EEZ, all States "enjoy (...) the freedoms referred to in article 87 of navigation and overflight and of the laying of submarine cables and pipelines, *and other internationally lawful uses of the sea related to these freedoms*".[72]

2.25 In this regard, contrary to what Nicaragua suggests, Colombia is certainly not the only State having its Navy deployed in the area. Many States, both Caribbean and non-Caribbean, have vessels conducting maritime surveillance and other operations in the area. For example, the multinational drug interdiction Operation "Martillo"[73] which involved 15 States from the Americas and Europe,[74] has led to the confiscation of 693 metric tons of cocaine and USD 25 million in bulk cash and the detention of 1,863 suspects and 581 vessels and aircraft,

---

71 E. Papastavridis, *The Interception of Vessels on the High Seas: Contemporary Challenges to the Legal Order of the Oceans*, Hart Publishing, 2013, p. 66 (available at the Peace Palace Library).

72 Emphasis added.

73 See CCM, para. 2.101.

74 Belize, Canada, Chile, Colombia, Costa Rica, El Salvador, France, Guatemala, Honduras, the Netherlands, Nicaragua, Panama, Spain, United Kingdom and United States.

since its launch on January 2012.[75] In this context, Canada has deployed destroyers, frigates, maritime coastal defence vessels, aircrafts and warships in the Caribbean Sea.[76]

2.26 Similarly, the Royal Netherlands Navy has led Operation "Caribbean Venture" and conducted drug interdiction operations in waters of the EEZ of the Dominican Republic and Haiti.[77]

2.27 For its part, the United Kingdom's Royal Navy maintains a "near constant presence in the Caribbean (...) deterring drug traffickers and patrolling the seas".[78]

---

[75] United States Department of Defence, "Operation Martillo Still Hammering Away at Illicit Trafficking", 30 March 2016, available at: https://www.defense.gov/News/Article/Article/708314/operation-martillo-still-hammering-away-at-illicit-trafficking/ (last visited: 1 November 2018); see also United States Southern Command, "Operation Martillo", available at: http://www.southcom.mil/Media/Special-Coverage/Operation-Martillo/ (last visited: 1 November 2018); other maritime interdiction operations before and after the filing of Nicaragua's Application can be found in Annex 70: Ministry of Foreign Affairs of Colombia, *Sample Maritime Drug Interdiction Operations before and after the filing of Nicaragua's Application.*

[76] National Defence and the Canadian Armed Forces, "Operation CARIBBE", available at: http://www.forces.gc.ca/en/operations-canada-north-america-recurring/op-caribbe.page (last visited: 1 November 2018).

[77] Coastguard News, "Royal Netherlands Navy and U.S. Coast Guard seize 13,000 pounds of marijuana and 12 smugglers", 27 May 2015, available at: https://coastguardnews.com/royal-netherlands-navy-and-u-s-coast-guard-seize-13000-pounds-of-marijuana-and-12-smugglers/2015/05/27/ (last visited: 1 November 2018), and "Coast Guard offloads $17 million of cocaine", 20 November 2015, available at: https://coastguardnews.com/coast-guard-offloads-17-million-of-cocaine/2015/11/20/ (last visited: 1 November 2018).

[78] United Kingdom Royal Navy, "Atlantic Patrol Tasking North", available at: https://www.royalnavy.mod.uk/news-and-latest-activity/operations/north-atlantic/atlantic-patrol-tasking-north (last visited: 1 November 2018).

2.28 France has deployed naval vessels to "patrol off the island of Hispaniola to detect and intercept the primary maritime flow of drug trafficking from Colombia and Venezuela".[79]

2.29 The aforesaid is very much in line with Nicaragua's concession that Colombia has a "right to take action in Nicaragua's EEZ if it happens to encounter a ship suspected of the illegal transportation of narcotics, or to search for such a ship if it has a reason to suspect that it is there."[80] Nevertheless, such presence cannot be qualified as an "occupation" of another State's EEZ, as suggested by Nicaragua,[81] since the coastal State's exclusivity in its EEZ does not comprise drug interdiction activities and it is questionable that the figure of occupation applies at all in the EEZ or when there are no hostilities.

(2) The Enjoyment by Colombia of its Freedom of Navigation and Overflight represents an Internationally Lawful Use of the Sea and does not Infringe Nicaragua's EEZ rights

2.30 In accordance with the principle of *onus probandi incumbit actori*, the burden is on Nicaragua to prove that its

---

[79] Ministry of Armed Forces of France, "FAA : coopération franco-américaine en mer des Caraïbes", 17 December 2014, available at : https://www.defense.gouv.fr/espanol/operations/operations/forces-prepositionnees2/forces-de-souverainete/antilles/actualites/faa-cooperation-franco-americaine-en-mer-des-caraibes (last visited: 1 November 2018).

[80] NR, para. 2.34.

[81] NR, para. 2.34.

sovereign rights have been violated.[82] In contrast, the burden is not on Colombia to prove that it did not violate Nicaragua's sovereign rights or to prove that each one of its actions are permitted under international law.

2.31 If the Court finds that Colombia's exercise of its freedoms of navigation and overflight is lawful, as Colombia submits is the case, that disposes of Nicaragua's claims. However, the converse is not true. Thus, even if the Court finds that Colombia's activities are not specifically included within the principle of freedoms of navigation and overflight, or do not constitute an internationally lawful use of the sea, Nicaragua still has to show that they constituted violations of its sovereign rights. In other words, if an activity of Colombia were not specifically recognised as encompassed into its freedoms of navigation and overflight, or another permissible use of the sea, under customary international law, *quod non*, that does not automatically mean that such activity is unlawful *vis-à-vis* Nicaragua. Nicaragua must still prove that Colombia's actions impeded, or materially prejudiced, Nicaragua's ability to exercise its sovereign rights. Since Nicaragua has failed to make

---

[82] *Pulp Mills on the River Uruguay (Argentina* v. *Uruguay), Judgment, I.C.J. Reports 2010*, p. 71, para. 162; *Maritime Delimitation in the Black Sea (Romania* v. *Ukraine), Judgment, I.C.J. Reports 2009*, p. 86, para. 68; *Sovereignty over Pedra Branca/Pulau Batu Puteh, Middle Rocks and South Ledge (Malaysia/Singapore), Judgment, I.C.J. Reports 2008*, p. 31, para. 45; *Application of the Convention on the Prevention and Punishment of the Crime of Genocide (Bosnia and Herzegovina* v. *Serbia and Montenegro), Judgment, I.C.J. Reports 2007*, p. 128, para. 204; *Military and Paramilitary Activities in and against Nicaragua (Nicaragua* v. *United States of America), Jurisdiction and Admissibility, Judgment, I.C.J. Reports 1984*, p. 437, para. 101.

this demonstration, its claims must fail.[83]

2.32 In this regard, it can be recalled that the EEZ is a *sui generis* zone with a distinct legal regime that has been specifically negotiated to balance the interests of coastal States and other maritime States. In its EEZ, "[t]he coastal State's rights relate essentially to the natural resources",[84] and are limited or inexistent with respect to other matters. Concerning the prevention of drug trafficking for example, "the coastal State may assert jurisdiction over foreign vessels suspected of being engaged in drug trafficking only with regard to such activities occurring on artificial islands or other installations pursuant to Article 60 (2), LOSC".[85] Therefore, Nicaragua cannot claim an exclusive jurisdiction for addressing all matters in its EEZ.

2.33 It follows that any suggestion that Colombia violated Nicaragua's sovereign rights merely because it carried out certain observing and informing activities in its EEZ that are not specifically authorized in UNCLOS (to which Colombia is not a party) or under customary international law, is untenable. Nicaragua has to go further to show that its own rights were violated, which it has failed to do.

---

83 See Chapter 3 *infra*.

84 R. R. Churchill and A. V. Lowe, *The Law of the Sea*, 3rd ed., Manchester University Press, 1999, p. 166 (available at the Peace Palace Library).

85 E. Papastavridis, "Crimes at Sea: A Law of the Sea Perspective", in E. Papastavridis, K. N. Trapp (eds.), *La Criminalité en Mer/Crimes at Sea*, The Hague Academy of International Law, Martinus Nijhoff Publishers, 2014, p. 13 (available at the Peace Palace Library).

D. Colombia is exercising its freedoms and rights to protect legitimate interests and concerns

2.34 Nicaragua's Reply completely misses the point that the nature, purpose, and intensity of the exercise by Colombia of its freedoms of navigation and overflight in the area must be assessed in their factual and geographic context, namely in the Southwestern Caribbean Sea, where there are a number of special characteristics that are highly relevant. In an attempt to support its allegations that Colombia has infringed its rights and jurisdiction, Nicaragua distorts Colombia's position by asserting that Colombia claims a "general right to engage in policing activities in Nicaragua's EEZ".[86]

2.35 This is simply not the case. As will be shown, Colombia is not acting in a policing fashion (Sub-section 1). Moreover, contrary to what Nicaragua asserts,[87] the special circumstances of the Southwestern Caribbean Sea further explain and justify the necessity for Colombia to take appropriate measures accepted by international law to prevent transnational organized crime at sea, especially drug trafficking (Sub-section 2). Likewise, since ships flying Colombia's flag also carry out activities in the area, it is Colombia's duty, as the flag State, to provide them safety at sea and other support; this latter obligation is also due to ships of any nationality (Sub-section 3). Lastly, it will be argued that Colombia's observing and

---

86 NR, pp. 19-32.

87 NR, paras. 1.13-1.18.

informing on environmentally-harmful activities does not infringe Nicaragua's rights (Sub-section 4).

(1) COLOMBIA IS NOT ACTING IN A POLICING FASHION

2.36 Nicaragua tries to qualify Colombia's activities in its EEZ as "policing activities".[88] However, none of the facts reproached by Nicaragua to Colombia can be qualified as such, as demonstrated in Chapter 3 below.

2.37 Colombia further notes that, in order to lend support to its case, Nicaragua also complains of what it portrays as wrongful "intent", or "policies" on the part of Colombia. Indeed, Nicaragua's written pleadings show that Nicaragua's focus is not so much on what Colombia's Navy did, but on the significance Nicaragua attributes to Colombia's presence in the Southwestern Caribbean Sea. Nicaragua's case is thus not so much about facts – although Colombia will show in Chapter 3 below that Nicaragua's version of the facts is seriously flawed – but about Colombia's intent or policy that, according to Nicaragua, would qualify as an illegal infringement of its sovereign rights.

2.38 Nicaragua's arguments fail, first, because the law on State responsibility does not attach any consequence to intent;[89]

---

88 NR, paras. 2.26-2.60.

89 International Law Commission, "Commentary to the Draft Articles on Responsibility of States for Internationally Wrongful Acts", *Report of the International Law Commission on the Work of its Fifty-Third Session,*

second, because, in any event, the reasons why Colombia's Navy is present in the area are legitimate; and third, because Colombia has not interfered with Nicaragua's exercise of its sovereign rights since the 2012 Judgment.

2.39 In this regard, the special circumstances of the Southwestern Caribbean Sea, described and explained by Colombia in Chapter 2 of its Counter-Memorial, are relevant, because they form the basis for what is the objective factual and legal context (or "the relevant circumstances", to take the words of UNCLOS Article 59). Needless to say, the mere presence of a navy vessel is not tantamount to occupation – a notion which has a specific legal content in international law. Moreover, as noted above, Nicaragua's unfounded accusations derive from the fact that it wrongly equates EEZ rights to sovereignty over the territorial sea.

2.40 It is striking that Nicaragua does not address or challenge these circumstances as presented in Colombia's Counter-Memorial. Nicaragua only contends that they are irrelevant,[90] an argument that Colombia submits is misguided. For the sake of completeness, some further elements may be added to the relevant context provided in the Counter-Memorial.

A/56/10, Commentary to Article 2, p. 36, para. 10, available at: http://legal.un.org/ilc/documentation/english/reports/a_56_10.pdf (last visited: 1 November 2018).

[90] NR, paras. 1.13-1.18.

(2) Colombia's Navy Presence is Necessary for the Prevention of Transnational Organized Crime at Sea, Especially Drug Trafficking

2.41 Colombia is one of the Caribbean States taking appropriate measures to prevent transnational organized crime committed at sea, including in cooperation with third States. In fact, Colombia's action in this respect is an absolute necessity in the Caribbean Sea, because the area is particularly conducive for drug trafficking.

2.42 In its Reply, Nicaragua asserts that it

> "does not contest Colombia's right to take action in Nicaragua's EEZ if it happens to encounter a ship suspected of the illegal transportation of narcotics, or to search for such a ship if it has reason to suspect that it is there. Nicaragua's complaint is that Colombia has erected and implemented a regime of surveillance and enforcement that treats Nicaragua's EEZ as if it were Colombian national waters".[91]

2.43 This assertion obfuscates completely the reality, visibly misunderstood by Nicaragua. The reality, as illustrated by the map produced in Colombia's Counter-Memorial at Figure 2.6, is that drug trafficking in the area is a widespread phenomenon. Drug trafficking in the Caribbean is not a sporadic event that Colombia's Navy may randomly encounter from time to time. A substantial presence is thus necessary to address drug trafficking in the Caribbean.

---

91 NR, para. 2.34.

2.44 Located between Colombia, Central America, the Caribbean and North America, the San Andrés Archipelago is particularly vulnerable to drug trafficking. As the Commander of the Caribbean Coastguard of Colombia has put it:

> "In both [drug trafficking] routes [to the United States and Europe], the San Andres Archipelago is like a gas station in the middle of the sea, an alternative to find fuel and logistic support".[92]

2.45 An aggravating factor is the poor control exercised by Nicaragua in its maritime areas. This area, and in general the Caribbean coast of Central America, has been described as

> "(...) kind of Wild West that in places has changed little from the days of the pirates. It has hidden ports and forts that are no-go zones for law enforcement, places from which the drug runners operate with complete impunity."[93]

In this respect Nicaragua's assertion that it "shares Colombia's concern regarding law enforcement [and] security" calls for caution.[94] This situation has been particularly well documented by the Foundation *Insight Crime* in 2012,[95] in particular in a

---

92 Annex 60: El Espectador, *Drug traffickers and the Caribbean route,* 31 March 2014.

93 J. G. Stravridis, *Sea Power: The History and Geopolitics of the World's Oceans*, Penguin Press, 2017, p. 294 (available at the Peace Palace Library).

94 NR, para. 1.16.

95 InSight Crime is a foundation dedicated to the study of organized crime, considered by it as the principal threat to national and citizen security

comprehensive report published by Jeremy McDermott[96] on 19 July 2012.[97] Moreover, as evidenced by this report, it is not uncommon for fishing vessels to engage in drug trafficking, and thus try to hide their unlawful conduct behind the appearance of fishing activities. In such circumstances, a strong naval presence is necessary to curb drug trafficking and transnational organized crime more generally, a goal Colombia is committed to.

2.46 Colombia has entered into some 88 bilateral treaties and agreements related to drug trafficking.[98] Most of these agreements have been signed with Caribbean States, including Costa Rica, Cuba, the Dominican Republic, Honduras, Jamaica, Mexico, Panama, Venezuela and the United States. Additionally, the Colombian Navy has concluded agreements on

---

in Latin America and the Caribbean (https://www.insightcrime.org/about-us/#ethical-commitment), with which Colombia has no relation whatsoever.

96 Jeremy McDermott is the Executive Director and co-founder of InSight Crime. He also leads the investigations and coverage of Panama, the Caribbean and South America (except Brazil) and manages the team, which is based primarily in Medellín, Colombia. McDermott has two decades of experience reporting from around Latin America. He is a former British Army officer, who saw active service in Northern Ireland and Bosnia. Upon retiring from the military he became a war correspondent, covering the Balkans, based in Bosnia, then the Middle East from Beirut, before being sent to Colombia to cover the conflict. He has travelled extensively throughout Latin America. Before setting up InSight Crime he worked for many of Britain's most prestigious media outlets, including the BBC, the Daily Telegraph and The Economist. He specializes in drug trafficking, organized crime and the Colombian civil conflict. He has an MA from the University of Edinburgh.

97 J. McDermott, "Bluefields: Nicaragua's Cocaine Hub", InSight Crime, 19 July 2012, available at: https://www.insightcrime.org/investigations/bluefields-nicaraguas-cocaine-hub/ (last visited: 1 November 2018).

98 Ministry of Foreign Affairs of Colombia, Virtual Library of Treaties, available at: http://apw.cancilleria.gov.co/tratados/SitePages/BuscadorExternoForm.aspx (last visited: 1 November 2018).

naval and maritime cooperation with partner authorities from Jamaica, Costa Rica, Mexico, Honduras, the Dominican Republic, Guatemala, Panama and the Netherlands.[99]

2.47 There is no legal requirement that the Colombian Navy, after the Court's 2012 Judgment, cease its operations in waters of Nicaragua's EEZ, so long as the latter's sovereign rights are not impeded.

2.48 As indicated in Colombia's Counter-Memorial, drug interdiction activities carried out by the Colombian Navy between 2009 and 2016 around the San Andrés Archipelago resulted in 59.299 kg of cocaine seized and 163 people arrested for drug trafficking.[100] In addition to aggregate data, in Annex 70, Colombia includes a list of some maritime drug interdiction operations conducted by Colombia individually or jointly with partner States, before and after the filing of Nicaragua's Application.

2.49 In sum, Colombia takes its duty to prevent drug trafficking in the Southwestern Caribbean Sea seriously. Nicaragua, on the other hand, does not.

---

99 CCM, para. 2.107.

100 CCM, footnote 111.

(3) COLOMBIA'S OBLIGATION TO ASSISTS VESSELS IN THE SOUTHWESTERN CARIBBEAN SEA

2.50 As Colombia has previously recalled, the inhabitants of the San Andrés Archipelago, and especially the Raizales, have always depended on what the sea could provide and relied on the trade of its resources with the neighbouring communities across the Southwestern Caribbean Sea.[101] Thus, a fundamental role in this community is played by the many fishermen who have ancestrally fished far away and enjoy traditional fishing rights in areas overlapping with Nicaragua's EEZ.[102] In addition, the inhabitants of the Archipelago rely on a substantial amount of imports from the mainland, many of which are transported by sea.

2.51 As a result, there is a significant marine traffic in and around the San Andrés Archipelago by vessels which navigate both in Colombian and third States' waters, including those of Nicaragua's EEZ. These vessels are of many nationalities and include, of course, Colombian-flagged vessels – over which Colombia has a number of rights, duties and responsibilities, such as to protect and provide relief in cases of security or technical difficulties.

2.52 As a matter of fact, the weather in the Caribbean Sea is unpredictable, creating a high risk for vessels navigating in the

---

101 CCM, Chapter 2, Section C.

102 CCM, Chapter 2, Section C; and Chapter 5 *infra*.

area – especially for the Raizales who have recourse to traditional methods of fishing and sailing.

2.53 It should be stressed that "as individuals, fishers enjoy the rights provided by general human rights treaties"[103] and Article 4(1) of the American Convention on Human Rights provides that Colombia is bound to protect the right to life of fishermen under its jurisdiction as the flag State.[104]

2.54 Moreover, as a State party to the 1979 International Convention on Maritime Search and Rescue,[105] Colombia is under an obligation to establish a marine search and rescue area to assist any vessel or person in distress at sea.[106] Under Article 2.1.10 of the Annex to this Convention,

> "Parties shall ensure that assistance be provided to any person in distress at sea. They shall do so regardless of the nationality or status of such a person or the circumstances in which that person is found."

---

[103] I. Papanicolopulu, "International law and the protection of fishers", in A. del Vecchio (ed.), *International Law of the Sea: Current Trends and Controversial Issues*, Eleven International Publishing, 2014, p. 326 (available at the Peace Palace Library).

[104] M. Rota, "Case-law of the Inter-American Court of Human Rights: Chronicle for the Year 2008", in *Journal for Constitutional Theory and Philosophy of Law,* Vol. 9, 2009, p. 133: "The article 4 of the Convention provides two obligations: the negative obligation to not endanger life (art. 4), and the positive obligation to protect this right, including against the actions of private individuals. Indeed, the Court granted a horizontal effect to the Convention.", available at: https://journals.openedition.org/revus/502 (last visited: 1 November 2018).

[105] Hereinafter "SAR Convention".

[106] SAR areas are based on States' technical capacities and do not necessarily conform to political boundaries.

Colombia's SAR area, as well as that of other Caribbean States (including Nicaragua) is shown in Figures CR 2.1 and CR 2.1a below:[107]

[107] United States Coast Guard, "IMO Maritime SAR Regions", p. 9 (excerpt), available at: https://www.dco.uscg.mil/Portals/9/CG-5R/nsarc/IMO%20Maritime%20SAR%20Regions.pdf (last visited: 1 November 2018).

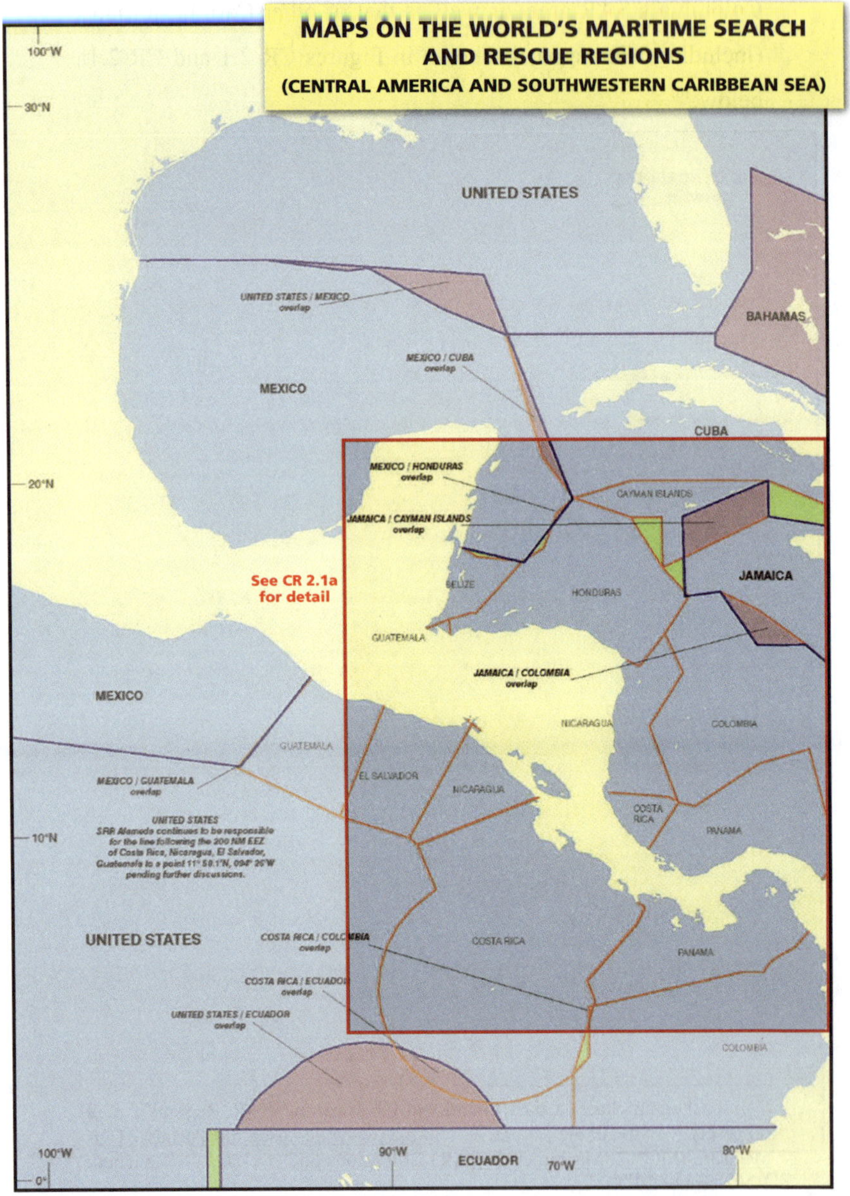

Source: http://docs.imo.org/Shared/Download.aspx?did=75819

Figure CR 2.1

MAPS ON THE WORLD'S MARITIME SEARCH AND RESCUE REGIONS
(EXCERPT OF CENTRAL AMERICA AND SOUTHWESTERN CARIBBEAN SEA)

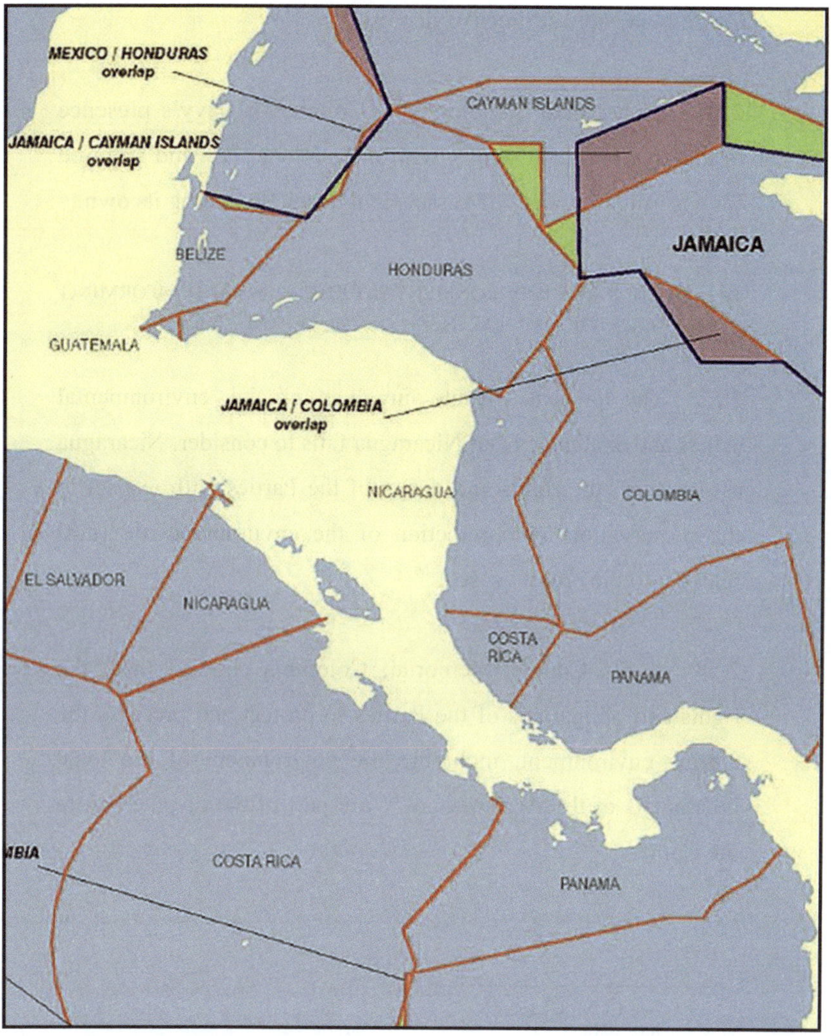

Source: http://docs.imo.org/Shared/Download.aspx?did=75819

Figure CR 2.1a

2.55 Nicaragua, for its part, is not sufficiently equipped to ensure the safety of its vessels in the Southwestern Caribbean Sea. This explains why Nicaraguan fishermen rely on the Colombian Navy at times of distress.[108]

2.56 Rather than 'policing', the Colombian Navy's presence in the area is in conformity with international law and required for ensuring the safety of vessels in the area, including its own.

(4) Colombia's Environmental Observing and Informing Activities do not Infringe Nicaragua's Rights

2.57 The present dispute involves crucial environmental stakes and challenges that Nicaragua fails to consider. Nicaragua asserts that "the rights and duties of the Parties with respect to the preservation and protection of the environment are [not] relevant to the present case".[109]

2.58 In its Counter-Memorial, Colombia showed that "the rights and obligations of the Parties to protect and preserve the marine environment, including the environment of the local inhabitants of the Archipelago"[110] are part of the dispute before the Court.

---

108 See CCM, Chapter 8.
109 NR, para. 1.12.
110 CCM, para. 3.23. See also CCM, paras. 3.24-3.85.

2.59 To portray environmental issues as wholly irrelevant to the case is both incorrect and misleading. It is incorrect because the existence of environmental concerns is central to Colombia's naval presence in the area of the Southwestern Caribbean Sea, as are certain ongoing practices that risk damaging the marine environment. It is misleading because Nicaragua is trying to "distract"[111] or "divert"[112] the Court's attention from one crucial fact, namely that both States, within their different scope of competence, should adopt the appropriate measures to protect the fragile ecosystems of the Southwestern Caribbean Sea and to ensure the right to a healthy environment to the individuals under their jurisdiction, including the Raizales.[113]

2.60 On the other hand, as demonstrated in Colombia's Counter-Memorial, under general international law, the existence of sovereign rights in maritime areas does not exempt a State such as Nicaragua from complying with its international obligations towards other States, including Colombia.[114] Nor does it affect Colombia's rights and duties, such as the duty to cooperate in the protection of the fragile marine environment of the Southwestern Caribbean Sea and the right to ensure the protection, promotion and respect of the right of the population of the Archipelago, including the Raizales, to live in a healthy environment.

---

111 NR, para. 1.11.

112 NR, para. 1.2.

113 For the source of the relevant legal obligations, see CCM, Chapter 3, Section C.

114 CCM, para. 3.3.

2.61 Nicaragua seeks to exclude other States in the Southwestern Caribbean Sea from exercising their rights and complying with their duties, in particular when fragile ecosystems and fragile human communities are at stake, which is at odds with the EEZ regime under general international law. Such an attitude is also detrimental to local communities, which have a right to a healthy environment within the Southwestern Caribbean Sea.

2.62 These issues form part and parcel of the dispute. In accordance with its jurisprudence, it is for the Court itself to determine and delineate the subject-matter of a dispute in an objective manner, taking into account "the Application itself [as well] as subsequent proceedings, the Submissions of the Parties and statements made in the course of the hearings".[115]

2.63 The Court reiterated the same position in the case concerning *Certain Questions of Mutual Assistance in Criminal Matters (Djibouti* v. *France)* when it stated that "it would not confine itself to the formulation by the Applicant when it was called upon to determine the subject of the dispute".[116]

2.64 In its Memorial and Reply, Nicaragua describes the present dispute as one that "originates in Colombia's actions

---

[115] *Case concerning Right of Passage over Indian Territory (Merits), Judgment of 12 April 1960: I.C.J. Reports 1960*, p. 33.
[116] *Certain Questions of Mutual Assistance in Criminal Matters (Djibouti* v. *France), Judgment, I.C.J. Reports 2008*, p. 207, para. 70.

subsequent to the *Judgment*"[117] of 19 November 2012 and, in particular, Colombia's "exercise of purported sovereign rights and jurisdiction in those waters, and its prevention of Nicaragua from exercising its sovereign rights and jurisdiction within its maritime boundaries as fixed by the Court."[118]

2.65 As the Court has noted, in order for it to adjudicate over a State's conduct, such as Colombia's, it must "discharge (…) an assessment of the legality of (…) conduct of States *with regard to the obligations imposed upon them by international law*".[119] The Court cannot undergo this process without considering its wider context, i.e. the exercise of freedom of navigation and overflight plus concerns regarding the protection and preservation of the fragile ecosystems of the Southwestern Caribbean Sea, coupled with the right to a healthy environment of the Raizales and other vulnerable communities of the Archipelago.[120] All of these constitute "other internationally lawful uses of the sea" of the kind that, under customary international law, third States possess in another State's EEZ.

2.66 Nicaragua relies on the Court's Order concerning the admissibility of Colombia's counter-claims to extrapolate that

---

117 *Alleged Violations of Sovereign Rights and Maritime Spaces in the Caribbean Sea (Nicaragua* v. *Colombia),* Memorial of Nicaragua (hereinafter, "NM"), para. 1.35.

118 NM, para. 1.35.

119 *Legal Consequences of the Construction of a Wall in the Occupied Palestinian Territory, Advisory Opinion, I.C.J. Reports 2004,* p. 155, para. 41. (Emphasis added).

120 For the source of the relevant legal obligations see CCM, Chapter 3, Section C.

environmental "rights and obligations are unrelated to Nicaragua's claims".[121] But that is beside the point. That decision cannot prejudge the merits of a case, nor can they prevent a Respondent from formulating its defence on the merits as it deems appropriate.[122]

2.67 Colombia's efforts to cooperate in the preservation and protection of the fragile environment of the Southwestern Caribbean Sea are inextricably linked to the subject-matter of the dispute and are therefore within the scope of the present proceedings.[123] The environmental activities of Colombia in the Southwestern Caribbean Sea, which are limited to observing and informing others of environmental risks and the need to protect the fragile ecosystem, are in accordance with international law.

2.68 The oversimplification of the dispute by Nicaragua is untenable and Colombia respectfully invites the Court to take into account the legitimate environmental concerns in the settlement of the present dispute.

2.69 It is the said legitimate concerns that have prompted Colombia's actions (i.e. observing and informing) in conformity with international law, conducted in accordance with general

---

121 NR, para. 1.20.

122 See e.g. *Certain Phosphate Lands in Nauru (Nauru* v. *Australia), Preliminary Objections, Judgment, I.C.J. Reports 1992*, p. 262, para. 56, and *Oil Platforms (Islamic Republic of Iran* v. *United States of America), Preliminary Objections, I.C.J. Reports 1996*, Separate Opinion of Judge Ranjeva, p. 844.

123 NR, para. 1.22.

international law and have not impaired Nicaragua's sovereign rights and jurisdiction *(a)*; and are consistent with Colombia's responsibilities towards fragile ecosystems and environmentally vulnerable communities *(b)*.

(a) Colombia's environmental concerns are consistent with general international law and the Cartagena Convention, and do not impair Nicaragua's sovereign rights and jurisdiction

2.70 Colombia's conduct has been compatible with the rights of Nicaragua as the coastal State and is in line with the duty that both Nicaragua and Colombia have under general international law and in particular the Cartagena Convention[124] to preserve the fragile environment of the Southwestern Caribbean Sea.

2.71 As noted above, Nicaragua's Memorial attempts to deny the relevance of rights and duties concerning the protection of the environment of the Southwestern Caribbean Sea and the preservation of the right to a healthy environment of the Raizales.

2.72 Nicaragua goes further and vaguely refers to "rights and obligations" that "are not pertinent, insofar as Colombia pretends to exercise them in areas in which Nicaragua has exclusive sovereign rights and jurisdiction".[125]

[124] Convention for the Protection and Development of the Marine Environment of the Wider Caribbean Region. See, in particular: Articles 4, 5 and 10 (in CCM, Annex 17).

[125] NR, para. 1.19.

2.73 In other parts of its Reply, Nicaragua dismisses the "catalogue of measures adopted – and treaties signed – by Colombia since the 1970s in order to protect the environment (…) in the Southwestern Caribbean Sea".[126]

2.74 In yet other parts of its Reply, Nicaragua contests Colombia's understanding of those rights and obligations, asserting that there is a

> "link between them and the harassment and intimidation of Nicaragua's fishing vessels, or the prevention of Nicaragua's authorities from exercising their law enforcement mission and from issuing fishing licenses to Colombia's nationals and foreign boats in zones appertaining to Nicaragua".[127]

2.75 Nicaragua thus purports to avoid discussing the treaties relevant to the Caribbean Sea. Not even a passing mention is made to the Cartagena Convention, which is in fact crucial to understand Colombia's environmental concerns in the Southwestern Caribbean Sea.

2.76 Through its inconsistent approach, Nicaragua confuses the existence of environmental rights and obligations with their implementation.[128]

---

126 NR, para. 1.16.

127 NR, para. 1.20.

128 See, in particular, the duty and right to protect and preserve the biodiversity of the Southwestern Caribbean Sea; the duty to exercise due

2.77 Paragraph 2.73 of Nicaragua's Reply is revealing in this respect. Nicaragua explicitly acknowledges that both Colombia and Nicaragua have a duty to protect the environment of the Southwestern Caribbean Sea and that such duties can be found "in relevant treaties to which both Colombia and Nicaragua are parties". In Nicaragua's own words:

> "No one doubts that Colombia and Nicaragua are under duties to protect the biosphere and to take action against activities such as illegal fishing that threaten it. No one doubts that many of these duties can be found set out in treaties to which both Colombia and Nicaragua are parties, and which require them to take appropriate action '*individually* or jointly'".[129]

2.78 Nicaragua, thus, does not deny that Colombia has duties to protect the marine environment and that compliance with the said duties might entail "individual" actions, such as in the case of Colombia's environmental alerts in the Southwestern Caribbean Sea, which can be conducted as long as they are done in accordance with its obligations under general international law and the Cartagena Convention.

2.79 In that respect, Colombia's environmental activities consisted of informing of the environmental risks at stake and

---

diligence with respect to the environment of the Southwestern Caribbean Sea; and the right and duty to protect the right of the inhabitants of the Archipelago to a healthy, sound and sustainable environment (CCM, Chapter 3, Section C).

129 NR, para. 2.73. (Emphasis added).

the impact of harmful actions taken by fishermen, as shown in several annexes to Colombia's Counter-Memorial.

2.80 A first set of Communications shows that the Colombian Navy vessels informed Nicaraguan vessels about concerns of damage to the marine environment:

- Communication No. 678 of 5 October 2013 mentions that "[a]lso, a QUERY via marine VHF was completed, informing that they were carrying out fishing activities in the 'Seaflower' natural reserve, which is internationally protected by UNES[C]O, reminding it, on numerous occasions, that performing these fishing activities constitutes a breach of international norms…".[130]

- Communication No. 677 of 5 October 2013 also confirms that: "[l]ikewise, a QUERY by marine VHF was performed, informing the fishing boat that it was carrying out a fishing operation in an area of the 'Seaflower' natural reserve, which is internationally protected by UNES[C]O, repeatedly reminding it that it was in violation of international laws while performing such operations in that area".[131]

2.81 In the same vein, a second set of Colombia's Navy Communications alerted on illegal fishing practices by

---

130 CCM, Annex 43.
131 CCM, Annexes 42, 54 and 57.

Nicaraguan fishing vessels:

- Communication No. 375 of 6 August 2013 states: "A.R.C. 801 kept the fishing vessel under surveillance, noticing that it kept artisanal boats carrying out fishing with oxygen tanks".[132]

- Communication No. 059 of 16 October 2013: It is mentioned that "taking into account that lobster fishing with divers is internationally considered as predatory due to its adverse environmental impact, I hereby report this activity to the Command for whatever purposes it sees fit (...)".[133]

2.82 Finally, a third set of Colombia's Navy Communications refer to predatory fishing activities, specifically fishing with divers, which is a practice that undermines the protection and sustainability of the marine environment.[134]

2.83 It is noteworthy that in many of those communications, Colombia did not assert its own jurisdiction, but merely invoked environmental obligations owed by Nicaragua as well. Thus, the nature of Colombia's conduct is simply not of the kind that could create even a potential, let alone an actual, conflict with the enjoyment of Nicaraguan EEZ rights. Under customary

---

132 CCM, Annex 37.
133 CCM, Annex 45.
134 CCM, Annexes 40, 41, 47 and 48.

international law, the regime of the EEZ does not allow a coastal State from denying the rights and duties of other States, including environmental rights and duties.

2.84 Furthermore, such environmental concerns are in line with the very object and purpose of the Cartagena Convention, which was concluded in the light of the contracting parties' recognition of the economic and social value of the marine environment, their responsibility to protect this environment and its ecosystems, and the special hydrographic and ecological characteristics of the region and its vulnerability to pollution and environmental deterioration.[135]

2.85 The Cartagena Convention is based on the customary international law principle obliging States to protect and preserve the marine environment, applied to the specific characteristics of the Wider Caribbean Sea.[136]

2.86 The Convention reflects the same pro-active spirit as customary international law and establishes that its

> "Contracting Parties shall, *individually* or jointly, take all appropriate measures in conformity with international law and in accordance with this Convention and those of its protocols in force to which they are parties to prevent, reduce and control pollution of the Convention area and to ensure sound environmental management, using

---

135 CCM, Annex 17, Preamble.

136 CCM, para. 3.36.

> for this purpose the best practicable means at their disposal and in accordance with their capabilities."[137]

2.87 Colombia rejects Nicaragua's assertions according to which Colombia was engaged "in harassment or any other conduct in Nicaragua's EEZ that falls outside an exercise of its rights in good faith and with due regard for the interests of other States."[138] Colombia also denies that its "obligations in relation to fisheries or the environment or drug trafficking or the repression of other kinds of crime warrant the kind of activities that are in issue in this case."[139]

2.88 It is for Nicaragua to discharge its burden of proof and to demonstrate which of its sovereign rights were infringed. Nicaragua's Reply, as its Memorial, is unhelpful in this regard.

2.89 Nicaragua cannot invoke its own inaction as a pretext to accuse Colombia of "policing" its waters. As Colombia emphasized, the Cartagena Convention invites States parties to ensure sound environmental management through "the best practicable means at their disposal and in accordance with their respective capabilities."[140] This is what Colombia has done through its environmental alerts in the Southwestern Caribbean Sea.

2.90 The environmental concerns of Colombia do not

---

137 CCM, Annex 17, Article 4. (Emphasis added).
138 NR, para. 2.68.
139 NR, para. 2.68.
140 CCM, Annex 17, Article 4.

constitute an internationally wrongful act. On the contrary, they are a fulfilment of its responsibilities with respect to fragile ecosystems and environmentally vulnerable communities.

(b) Colombia is fulfilling its responsibilities towards fragile ecosystems and environmentally vulnerable communities

2.91 The Southwestern Caribbean Sea is host to some very important ecosystems. As the Court has recently stressed, any ecosystem should be protected as a whole.[141] The due diligence that is required from States to protect ecosystems is even greater when the ecosystems at stake are as fragile and interconnected as those in the Southwestern Caribbean Sea (i). In addition, the ecosystems of the Southwestern Caribbean Sea are inextricably linked to the livelihood, survival and basic human needs of vulnerable communities, such as the Raizales (ii).

(i) <u>The ecosystems of the Southwestern Caribbean Sea possess special characteristics which require a greater degree of due diligence</u>

2.92 Because of their fragility and interconnectedness, the ecosystems of the Southwestern Caribbean Sea possess special characteristics. It is only through a greater degree of due diligence that the said special characteristics can be taken into

---

[141] *Certain Activities carried out by Nicaragua in the Border Area (Costa Rica* v. *Nicaragua) – Compensation owed by the Republic of Nicaragua to the Republic of Costa Rica*, Judgment of 2 February 2018, para. 78 (not yet printed).

account and preserved.[142]

2.93 This crucial need to protect the fragile marine and coastal ecosystems of the Southwestern Caribbean Sea found specific expression through the establishment of the Seaflower Marine Protected Area[143] and the Seaflower Biosphere Reserve. The former is part of the latter, which in turn encompasses the total area of the Archipelago. The MPA was designed to protect the biosphere reserve and includes the largest, most productive open-ocean coral reefs in the Caribbean Sea.[144]

2.94 As Colombia explained already in its Counter-Memorial,

> "[The] resources [of the Seaflower Biosphere Reserve area] face a real risk of depletion and even extinction by over-fishing, destructive fishing practices, and pollution from vessels and human activity. Those practices have an adverse knock-on

---

[142] *Certain Activities carried out by Nicaragua in the Border Area (Costa Rica* v. *Nicaragua) – Compensation owed by the Republic of Nicaragua to the Republic of Costa Rica*, Judgment of 2 February 2018, para. 78 (not yet printed).

[143] Hereinafter "MPA".

[144] The Colombian Ocean Commission has explained that: "The Seaflower Biosphere Reserve houses important ecosystems such as tropical dry forests, mangrove forests, seagrass meadows or seagrass beds, soft bottoms and coralline sand beaches, which are very well preserved (Taylor et al, 2011). Likewise, it has more than 77% of the shallow coralline areas of Colombia (Invemar 2005, 2009, Coralina-Invemar 2012), the world's third biggest coral reef, deep ecosystems (including deep corals), key species, great richness and diversity of fish, corals, sponges, gorgonacea, macroalgae, queen conch, lobsters, birds, reptiles, insects, among others, which provide countless ecosystem services such as food, coastal protection, recreation, etc. (Conservation International 2008, Burke et al, 2008)" (*Question of the Delimitation of the Continental Shelf between Nicaragua and Colombia beyond 200 nautical miles from the Nicaraguan Coast (Nicaragua* v. *Colombia),* Counter-Memorial of Colombia, Annex 16).

> effect on other parts of the ecosystem, and endanger the traditional fishing rights of the local population and their very existence, as well as the environment of an internationally recognized biosphere".[145]

2.95 The protection of the ecosystems of the Southwestern Caribbean Sea, which are scattered under various jurisdictions, requires the cooperation of States in the region.

2.96 The conduct of the Colombian Navy, informing and warning of dangers to the ecosystems of the Southwestern Caribbean Sea, in conformity with international law, is aimed at preventing damage to them.

2.97 Nicaragua cannot blow hot and cold. It cannot claim that it cares for the environment, when it is blatantly and without any argumentation asserting in its Reply that the Southwestern Caribbean Sea does not present "special characteristics".[146] Nevertheless, it has not challenged Colombia's lengthy depiction of the special circumstances of the Caribbean Sea.

2.98 It also shows that, far from what it claims in its Reply, Nicaragua is oblivious to, or unaware of, the potential negative impact of the deterioration of fragile ecosystems on the livelihood of vulnerable communities, such as the Raizales.

---

145 CCM, para. 2.10.

146 NR, paras. 1.13-1.18.

(ii) The well-being of the Raizales is intrinsically linked to the sound protection of the environment of the fragile ecosystems of the Southwestern Caribbean Sea

2.99 That the well-being of the Raizales is intrinsically linked to a sound protection of the environment is self-evident. The silence of Nicaragua's Reply with respect to the right of the Raizales to live in a healthy and sustainable environment is even more striking than its denial of the special characteristics of the Southwestern Caribbean Sea.

2.100 Colombia is not arguing in a legal void that the protection of the environment of the Southwestern Caribbean Sea is a prerequisite for ensuring the well-being of indigenous populations and local communities such as the Raizales. International law recognizes the special relationship of indigenous peoples and local communities with the protection of the environment.[147]

2.101 In response to a request made by Colombia, in November 2017 the Inter-American Court of Human Rights[148] rendered a ground-breaking Advisory Opinion where it expounded on State obligations in relation to the environment, in the context of the protection and guarantee of the rights to life and the right to personal integrity, as recognized in Articles 4

---

147 CCM, Chapter 3, Section C (3).

148 Hereinafter "I/A Court H. R.".

and 5 of the American Convention on Human Rights.[149]

2.102 In its Advisory Opinion, the Court confirmed the irrefutable relationship between the protection of the environment and the realisation of human rights, due to the fact that environmental degradation affects the effective enjoyment of other human rights, as follows:

> "47. This Court has recognised the existence of an undeniable relationship between the protection of the environment and the realisation of other human rights, since the environmental degradation and the adverse effects of climate change affect the effective enjoyment of human rights."[150]

2.103 In addition, the I/A Court H. R. emphasised the interdependence and indivisibility between human rights, the environment and sustainable development, since the full enjoyment of all human rights depends on a favourable environment. Having in mind the protection of local communities, the Court stated:

> "54. From this relationship of interdependence and indivisibility between human rights, the environment and sustainable development, multiple connecting points arise with regard to which, as expressed by the Independent expert, 'all human rights are vulnerable to environmental degradation, in the sense that the full enjoyment of

[149] Annex 69: Inter-American Court of Human Rights, Environment and Human Rights, Advisory Opinion OC-23/17 requested by the Republic of Colombia, 15 November 2017 (excerpts).

[150] Annex 69.

> all human rights is contingent upon a favourable environment'".[151]

2.104 The Advisory Opinion lays out a clear legal framework of the shared responsibilities of States to protect the marine environment in the Wider Caribbean region. In order to identify the fundamental principles of international environmental law, the I/A Court H. R. relied extensively on the decisions of the International Court of Justice. It stressed the crucial role of the following duties of States:[152]

- States have the obligation to prevent significant environmental damage, within or outside of their territory;
- States shall regulate, supervise and control the activities under their jurisdiction which may produce significant damage to the environment;
- States must carry out studies on environmental impact when the potential for significant damage to the environment exists;
- States must adopt contingency plans in order to minimize the possibility of serious environmental accidents; and
- States must mitigate the significant environmental damage they may have caused.

151 Annex 69.
152 Annex 69.

2.105 In line with Colombia's submissions, the I/A Court H. R. affirmed that States have the obligation to cooperate in good faith for the protection against significant transboundary environmental damage. It did so in the following terms:

> "7. With the purpose of respecting and guaranteeing the rights of life and integrity of the people under their jurisdiction, States have the obligation to cooperate, in good faith, for the protection against significant transboundary harm caused to the environment."[153]

2.106 This ground-breaking Advisory Opinion also builds on previous decisions of the I/A Court H. R., which had addressed the link between the protection of the environment and the rights of indigenous peoples and local communities.[154]

2.107 The responsibility for Colombia to ensure that the subsistence and traditional fishing activities of the Raizales are not undermined extends to the entire living space of such communities. This responsibility entails, as the Interamerican Commission on Human Rights stated in the *Kuna* case, that:

---

153 Annex 69.

154 I/A Court H. R., *Case of the Kichwa Indigenous People of Sarayaku v. Ecuador (Merits and Reparations), Judgment of June 27, 2012,* paras. 146-147; *Case of the Indigenous People of Mudungandí and the Emberá Indigenous People of Bayano and their Members v. Panama (Merits), 13 November 2012,* paras. 233-234; *Case of Xákmok Kásek Indigenous Community v. Paraguay. Judgment of August 24, 2010 (Merits, Reparations and Costs),* para. 85; *Case of the Sawhoyamaxa Indigenous Community v. Paraguay, Judgment of March 29, 2006 (Merits, Reparations and Costs),* para. 118; *Case of the Yakye Axa Indigenous Community v. Paraguay, Judgment of June 17, 2005 (Merits, Reparation and Costs),* para. 137; *Case of the Saramaka People v. Suriname, Judgment of November 28, 2007 (Preliminary Objections, Merits, Reparations and Costs),* para. 88.

"States are under an obligation to control and prevent illegal extractive activities such as logging, fishing, and illegal mining on indigenous or tribal ancestral territories, and to investigate and punish those responsible."[155]

2.108 The environmental activities that Colombia conducts in the area, consist in informing vessels that they are engaging in activities that are contrary to international law. The discharge of this obligation is especially important in situations where significant harm to fragile ecosystems is in question, or in cases of predatory fishing activities that may "entail catastrophic repercussions for the livelihood and economic well-being of the population"[156] of Colombia.

E. Conclusions

2.109 Colombia has always paid great heed to the protection of the environment, and in particular, to the protection of the fragile ecosystems of the Southwestern Caribbean Sea, shared among several States. In this context, in the spirit of Article 4 of the Cartagena Convention, Colombia has always sought to "jointly, take all appropriate measures" together with other

---

155 Inter-American Commission on Human Rights, *Case of the Kuna Indigenous People of Madungandí and the Emberá Indigenous People of Bayano and their members v. Panama, Report No. 125/12 of November 13, 2012 (Merits)*, para. 234, available at: https://www.oas.org/en/iachr/decisions/court/12.354FondoEng.pdf (last visited: 1 November 2018).

156 *Delimitation of the Maritime Boundary in the Gulf of Maine Area, Judgment, I.C.J. Reports 1984*, p. 342, para. 237.

neighbouring States in order to ensure that the environment of the Southwestern Caribbean Sea is well preserved, and that the right of local communities, including the Raizales, to a healthy environment is fully protected.

2.110 Colombia is also acting in this spirit with respect to the protection of the Seaflower Biosphere Reserve in the context of the UNESCO's Man and Biosphere Program. As to the status of the Seaflower Biosphere Reserve, when UNESCO's International Co-ordinating Council last discussed the issue in June 2014, it called for "the authorities of Colombia and Nicaragua to continue to respect the protected areas of the Seaflower Biosphere Reserve". It also "encouraged Colombia and Nicaragua to work together in the peaceful management of the Seaflower Biosphere Reserve."[157]

2.111 Colombia is indeed open to collaborate with Nicaragua to maintain the level of self-restraint that has allowed the Seaflower Biosphere Reserve to flourish thus far. In this respect, it is worth stressing that the acts of the Colombian Navy in the

---

157 The Council also explicitly invited the parties to: "Evaluate the possibilities to establish a transboundary biosphere reserve. Transboundary biosphere reserves are jointly managed by two or more countries to ensure the conservation of the environment, sustainable development and joint research on issues of relevance of the countries concerned. If the authorities of the two countries so wish, UNESCO can assist in the designation of a transboundary biosphere reserve with all stakeholders concerned." International Co-ordinating Council of the Man and the Biosphere (MAB) Programme, Twenty-sixth session, 10-14 June 2014, Final Report, Document SC-14/CONF.226/15, p. 85, available at: http://www.unesco.org /new/fileadmin/MULTIMEDIA/HQ/SC/pdf/SC-14-CONF-226-14-Information_on_Seaflower-eng-rev.pdf (last visited: 1 November 2018).

Southwestern Caribbean Sea have always sought to maintain the level of environmental protection ensured by the existing international legal regime of the Seaflower Biosphere Reserve as a UNESCO protected reserve.

2.112 In line with the object and purpose of the Cartagena Convention, Colombia is willing "to take all appropriate measures in accordance with international law and in accordance with this Convention to protect the marine environment". Colombia has been doing this in a spirit of cooperation, that it would also like to pursue with Nicaragua, in order to protect the fragile ecosystems of the Southwestern Caribbean Sea and the right to a healthy environment of vulnerable communities.

2.113 To conclude, the presence of Colombia in the Southwestern Caribbean Sea, including in waters of Nicaragua's EEZ, conforms to its freedom of navigation and overflight and thus represents an internationally lawful use of the sea. Therefore, it is wholly consistent with customary international law.

2.114 As previously shown, freedom of navigation consists in the right to navigate for any lawful purpose. In particular, Colombia's presence in the Southwestern Caribbean Sea is motivated by its legitimate concerns in relation to the marine environment, search and rescue, and transnational crimes, in accordance with international law.

2.115 As such, and as it will be shown in the next Chapter of this Rejoinder, the so-called "incidents" alleged by Nicaragua are artificial and over-exaggerated. They simply do not constitute either real incidents or internationally wrongful acts.

PART II

COLOMBIA HAS NOT VIOLATED NICARAGUA'S SOVEREIGN RIGHTS OR MARITIME SPACES

Chapter 3

NICARAGUA'S ALLEGED INCIDENTS IN THE SOUTHWESTERN CARIBBEAN SEA

A. Introduction

3.1 In its Memorial, Nicaragua referred to some 36 "incidents" which it claims represent interference by Colombia with Nicaragua's sovereign rights in its EEZ – of which only 13 are dated before the critical date. These incidents, to which Nicaragua has added a few more in its Reply, are alleged to have involved the threat of the use of force by Colombia's Navy, the harassment of Nicaraguan fishing vessels, the granting of fishing permits to non-Nicaraguan vessels, the offer of hydrocarbon blocks and the prevention of the Nicaraguan Naval Force from being able to exercise its law enforcement mission east of the 82nd West Meridian, in violation of international law.[158] In its Judgment on Colombia's Preliminary Objections, the Court ruled that it had no jurisdiction to consider Nicaragua's claims based on the alleged threat to use force.[159] Colombia will therefore not respond to this aspect of Nicaragua's claims further.

3.2 In Section B, Colombia will demonstrate that, contrary to the arguments advanced by Nicaragua in its Reply, the Court

---

158 NM, paras. 1.9 and 2.22-2.52 and NR, paras. 4.51-4.129.

159 Judgment on the Preliminary Objections, p. 33, para. 78 and p. 42, para. 111(1)(c) (dispositif).

lacks jurisdiction to consider most of these incidents. This is because the vast majority of individual episodes on which Nicaragua relies took place after the "critical date", when the Pact of Bogotá ceased to be in force between Colombia and Nicaragua (27 November 2013).

3.3 With respect to the remainder of the "incidents" which are said to have occurred before the critical date, and thus over which the Court has jurisdiction, Colombia's Counter-Memorial showed that some did not even occur and, in any event, none of them could possibly constitute a violation of Nicaragua's sovereign rights. In other words, they are not incidents at all. On the one hand, Nicaragua's arguments are based on the assumption that Colombia's freedoms of navigation and overflight, and other internationally lawful uses of the sea, merely comprise the right to navigate from Point A to Point B and nothing more. Not only is this proposition untenable as a matter of law, it misses the key point: it is not Colombia that bears the burden of proving that its actions were consistent with its rights; it is for Nicaragua to prove that Colombia's actions violated Nicaragua's sovereign rights – a different question. Not only Nicaragua has presented the flimsiest of evidence to back-up its allegations, but also the material it relies on misrepresents the facts. What is more, Nicaragua also draws unwarranted legal conclusions from them. As Colombia will show in Section C, Nicaragua's Reply offers no new evidence to support any of these so called "incidents", and they remain unproven.

3.4 In its Reply, Nicaragua also contends that Colombia's National Hydrocarbon Agency "continues to act in direct contravention of the 2012 Judgment by offering hydrocarbon blocks in areas within Nicaragua's EEZ."[160] As Colombia will show in Section D, this is a new claim, which is therefore inadmissible. It is also baseless. Colombia has not licensed or awarded any petroleum blocks in areas falling outside its own EEZ.

3.5 The last element of Nicaragua's claim is that Colombia has authorized Colombian licensed vessels to fish in Nicaragua's EEZ. Although Colombia already showed in its Counter-Memorial that this claim is without merit,[161] in Section E, Colombia will again explain how Nicaragua has misrepresented the import of Colombia's licensing regime and has failed to show that Colombia issued any such authorisations. As with the other parts of the claim, this allegation is equally unfounded.

B. The Court Has No Jurisdiction over Events Occurring after 27 November 2013

3.6 Colombia does not contest that the Court has jurisdiction regarding the 13 alleged "incidents" that are said to have occurred before Nicaragua filed its Application and before Colombia ceased to be a party to the Pact of Bogotá. As the

---

160 NR, para. 4.126.

161 CCM, para. 4.46.

Court ruled in its Judgment on Colombia's Preliminary Objections, "[t]he subsequent termination of the Pact as between Nicaragua and Colombia does not affect the jurisdiction which existed on the date that the proceedings were instituted".[162]

3.7 However, the jurisdictional situation regarding the remaining "incidents" that allegedly took place *after* the Pact of Bogotá ceased to be in force between Nicaragua and Colombia is different.[163]

(1) THE LIMITS OF THE COURT'S JURISDICTION *RATIONE TEMPORIS*

3.8 When delineating the extent of its jurisdiction in the present case, the Court in its Judgment on the Preliminary Objections clearly distinguished between pre and post-critical date events. The Court stated that the dispute was circumscribed "to those [events] which allegedly occurred before the critical date".[164] It then reiterated that it would focus on "the alleged incidents that were said to have occurred before Nicaragua filed its Application".[165]

3.9 This conforms to Article XXXI of the Pact of Bogotá, which provides for the compulsory jurisdiction of the Court only "so long as the present Treaty is in force".[166] As a result, the

---

162 Judgment on the Preliminary Objections, p. 26, para. 48.
163 CCM, para. 4.21.
164 Judgment on the Preliminary Objections, p. 33, para. 76.
165 Judgment on the Preliminary Objections, p. 33, para. 77.
166 The full text of Article XXXI reads as follows:

Court has no jurisdiction to rule on the legality of any alleged wrongful acts said to be attributed to Colombia after 27 November 2013 when the Pact was no longer in force for Colombia.

3.10 In considering this issue, it should also be recalled that there are actually two "critical dates", both of which have jurisdictional repercussions. The first – 26 November 2013 – is the date on which Nicaragua filed its Application in these proceedings. As the Court noted in its Judgment on the Preliminary Objections: "The Court recalls that the date at which its jurisdiction has to be established is the date on which the application is filed with the Court."[167] Thus, 26 November 2013 was the critical date for determining whether the Court had jurisdiction over Nicaragua's claims set out in its Application.

> "In conformity with Article 36, paragraph 2, of the Statute of the International Court of Justice, the High Contracting Parties declare that they recognize, in relation to any other American State, the jurisdiction of the Court as compulsory ipso facto, without the necessity of any special agreement so long as the present Treaty is in force, in all disputes of a juridical nature that arise among them concerning:
> a) The interpretation of a treaty;
> b) Any question of international law;
> c) The existence of any fact which, if established, would constitute the breach of an international obligation;
> d) The nature or extent of the reparation to be made for the breach of an international obligation."

167 Judgment on the Preliminary Objections, p. 18, para. 33.

3.11 The second "critical date" relevant here for jurisdictional purposes is the following day, 27 November 2013, which is when the Pact of Bogotá ceased to be in effect for Colombia as a result of its denunciation one year earlier. Once this happened, the compromissory clause appearing in Article XXXI of the Pact providing for the Court's jurisdiction also ceased to be applicable to Colombia *ratione temporis*. While this did not affect the scope of the Court's jurisdiction as established on the date of Nicaragua's Application, it did mean that the Pact no longer provided a basis for jurisdiction for the Court to rule on the legality of any events relied on by Nicaragua after 27 November 2013 for its claim that Colombia violated its sovereign rights.

3.12 The Court has recognised that its jurisdiction can be limited by conditions set out in a compromissory clause in a treaty. As the Court noted in its Judgment in the case concerning *Armed Activities on the Territory of the Congo (New Application: 2002) (Democratic Republic of the Congo* v. *Rwanda)*:

> "The Court recalls in this regard that its jurisdiction is based on the consent of the parties and is confined to the extent accepted by them (...) When that consent is expressed in a compromissory clause in an international agreement, any

> conditions to which such consent is subject must be regarded as constituting the limits thereon."[168]

3.13 In particular, the Court has recognised that temporal limitations in a compromissory clause can have the effect of excluding disputes from the Court's jurisdiction. In the *Certain Property (Liechtenstein* v. *Germany)* case, Liechtenstein relied on Article 1 of the European Convention for the Peaceful Settlement of Disputes of 29 April 1957 as the basis of the Court's jurisdiction for its claim regarding Germany's treatment of certain property of Liechtenstein nationals.[169] Article 27(a) of the European Convention provides that the Convention shall not apply to "disputes relating to facts or situations prior to the entry into force of this Convention as between the parties to the dispute".

3.14 The European Convention came into force as between Lichtenstein and Germany on 18 February 1980. For jurisdictional purposes, therefore, the Court had to determine whether the "facts or situations" in question giving rise to Liechtenstein's claim arose before or after the critical date of 18 February 1980.[170]

---

168 *Armed Activities in the Territory of the Congo (New Application: 2002) (Democratic Republic of the Congo* v. *Rwanda), Jurisdiction and Admissibility, Judgment, I.C.J. Reports 2006*, p. 39, para. 88.

169 *Certain Property (Liechtenstein* v. *Germany), Preliminary Objections, Judgment, I.C.J. Reports 2005*, p. 10, para. 1.

170 *Certain Property (Liechtenstein* v. *Germany), Preliminary Objections, Judgment, I.C.J. Reports 2005*, p. 22, para. 39.

3.15 In the event, the Court found that the "facts or situations" that were the real source of the dispute arose out of a series of confiscation decrees issued in 1945 (the Beneš Decrees) and a 1955 Settlement Convention concluded between the United States, the United Kingdom, France and the Federal Republic of Germany. Since these constituted "facts or situations" prior to the entry into force of the European Convention as between Liechtenstein and Germany, the Court found that it lacked jurisdiction *ratione temporis* to decide the dispute.[171] In other words, the Court has no jurisdiction over "facts or situations" on which a claim is based if those events occurred at a time when there was no jurisdictional bond between the parties.

3.16 Similarly, in the case concerning *Jurisdictional Immunities of the State* (*Germany* v. *Italy)*, the Court held that Italy's counter-claim fell outside the temporal limit of Article 27(a) of the European Convention because the dispute raised by Italy to support its counter-claim related to facts and situations that existed *prior* to the entry into force of the European Convention as between the two parties.[172] Accordingly, the Court held that the dispute fell outside the temporal scope of the Convention and that the counter-claim thus did not come within the Court's jurisdiction and was inadmissible.[173]

---

[171] *Certain Property (Liechtenstein* v. *Germany), Preliminary Objections, Judgment, I.C.J. Reports 2005*, p. 27, paras. 52 and 54 (1)(b).

[172] *Jurisdictional Immunities of the State (Germany* v. *Italy), Counter-claims, Order of 6 July 2010, I.C.J. Reports 2010*, pp. 320-321, para. 30.

[173] *Jurisdictional Immunities of the State (Germany* v. *Italy), Counter-claims, Order of 6 July 2010, I.C.J. Reports 2010*, p. 321, para. 31.

3.17 In short, for the Court to have jurisdiction to consider whether facts alleged by a party in support of its claim constitute a breach of an international obligation by the other party, those facts must have occurred during a period when a jurisdictional basis exists between the parties. In the present case, the "incidents" relied on by Nicaragua that occurred after 27 November 2013 took place at a time when the Pact of Bogotá was no longer in force with respect to Colombia. Just as the Court lacks jurisdiction over claims based on "facts or situations" occurring *before* a basis of jurisdiction exists between the parties to a case, so also does the Court lack jurisdiction to consider "facts or situations" that take place *after* any basis of jurisdiction has lapsed.

3.18 Colombia's consent to the Court's jurisdiction under the Pact of Bogotá was limited *ratione temporis*; it was valid only for "so long as the [Pact of Bogotá] is in force". As the Court in the *Border and Transborder Armed Actions (Nicaragua* v. *Honduras)* case observed, the commitment to submit a dispute to the Court in Article XXXI of the Pact of Bogotá remains "valid *ratione temporis* for as long as that instrument itself remains in force between those States".[174]

3.19 It follows that the Court lacks jurisdiction to consider whether any of the "incidents" that Nicaragua refers to that took place after 27 November 2013 constitute a violation of

---

174 *Border and Transborder Armed Actions (Nicaragua* v. *Honduras), Jurisdiction and Admissibility, Judgment, I.C.J. Reports 1988*, p. 84, para. 34.

Nicaragua's sovereign rights or maritime spaces. It is for this reason that, in its Counter-Memorial, Colombia only addressed the "incidents" referred to by Nicaragua that took place during the period between the date of the Court's Judgment in the original case (19 November 2012) and the date when the Pact of Bogotá ceased to be in force for Colombia (27 November 2013). Colombia will continue to do the same in this pleading, although, *ex abundanti cautela*, Colombia will also show in an Appendix to this Rejoinder how the post-critical date "incidents" cited by Nicaragua are for the most part factually wrong and, in any case, do not amount to a violation of its sovereign rights or maritime spaces.[175]

(2) THE DEFECTS IN NICARAGUA'S JURISDICTIONAL ARGUMENTS

3.20 In its Reply, Nicaragua has advanced a number of arguments in support of the proposition that the Court has jurisdiction to consider whether post-critical date "incidents" constitute a violation of its sovereign rights. Colombia will address the flaws undermining each of Nicaragua's contentions in turn.

3.21 Nicaragua's first argument is that the Court's decision on the admissibility of two of Colombia's counter-claims, which were lodged after the Pact of Bogotá ceased to be in force for Colombia, shows that the Court has jurisdiction over events that

175 See CR, Vol. II.

"represent the continuation of a dispute over which the Court already has jurisdiction" even if the basis of jurisdiction relied on for the principal claims has lapsed in the meantime.[176] However, this is a *non sequitur*: the jurisdictional position *ratione temporis* is not the same for claims and counter-claims.

3.22 Under Article 80, paragraph 2, of the Rules of Court, a counter-claim "shall be made in the Counter-Memorial". That is the earliest a Respondent can file a counter-claim since, by definition, a counter-claim must "counter" the claim detailed in the Applicant's Memorial. It would be unrealistic to oblige a Respondent to file a counter-claim before it had detailed knowledge of the claim itself. Provided that the counter-claim is directly connected with the subject-matter of the claim of the other party and comes within the jurisdiction of the Court, the counter-claim is admissible. Since the date for filing the Counter-Memorial may be after the date on which the basis of jurisdiction for the principal claim has lapsed, as it is in the present case, to rule that a counter-claim, which meets the conditions of Article 80 but could not have been presented earlier, is inadmissible for lack of jurisdiction *ratione temporis* would be unfair to the Respondent State. As the Court noted in its Order on the admissibility of Colombia's counter-claims:

> "the opposite approach would have the disadvantage of allowing the applicant, in some instances, to remove the basis of jurisdiction after

176 NR, paras. 4.10-4.12.

> an application has been filed and thus insulate itself from any counter-claims submitted in the same proceedings and having a direct connection with the principal claim".[177]

3.23 In addition, with respect to its counter-claims that have been ruled admissible, Colombia is not relying on events that took place after the critical date. Rather, the counter-claims are based on facts or situations that transpired between the date of the Court's 2012 Judgment and 27 November 2013; that is, during the period when the Pact of Bogotá still provided a basis of jurisdiction as between the parties. The same holds true for Nicaragua: it is not entitled to rely on acts that took place after the Pact ceased to be in force for Colombia. Contrary to Nicaragua's contention, the Court's Order on the counter-claims does not stand for the proposition that the Court's jurisdiction extends to events after 27 November 2013.

3.24 Equally inapposite is Nicaragua's attempt to rely on what it terms the "*Nottebohm* rule". In so doing, Nicaragua refers to a passage from the Court's Judgment in that case where the Court indicated that, once it has established jurisdiction to entertain a case, "the Court must deal with the claim; it has jurisdiction to deal with all its aspects, whether they relate to jurisdiction, to admissibility or to the merits".[178] But that case did not deal with

---

[177] *Alleged Violations of Sovereign Rights and Maritime Spaces in the Caribbean Sea (Nicaragua* v. *Colombia), Counter-claims, Order of 15 November 2017, I.C.J. Reports 2017*, pp. 310-311, para. 67.

[178] NR, paras. 4.10 and 4.12, citing *Nottebohm case (Preliminary Objections), Judgment of November 18th, 1953: I.C.J. Reports 1953*, p. 123, and *Alleged Violations of Sovereign Rights and Maritime Spaces in the*

the temporal situation that is presented in these proceedings, and it does not support Nicaragua's thesis.

3.25 In *Nottebohm (Liechtenstein* v. *Guatemala)*, the Court ruled that it had jurisdiction with respect to a claim that was introduced by Liechtenstein in an Application that was filed *before* the lapse of Guatemala's optional clause declaration. However, unlike Nicaragua's claims in the present case, Liechtenstein's claim was based solely on events that occurred while Guatemala's declaration was still in effect. Nowhere did the Court indicate in its Judgment that the mere fact that it had been seised meant that it had jurisdiction to consider Guatemala's responsibility for any events that took place *after* its declaration had lapsed. Indeed, the Court noted that "[t]here can be no doubt that an Application filed after the expiry of this period [i.e. after the period during which Guatemala's optional clause declaration was effective] would not have the effect of legally seising the Court."[179]

3.26 Had Nicaragua filed its Application after the 27 November 2013 critical date and based its claim on facts that took place after the Pact lapsed for Colombia, the Court clearly would not have had jurisdiction to entertain the claim. The same result should obtain with respect to Nicaragua's current attempt to rely on post-critical date "facts" for its claim.

Caribbean Sea (Nicaragua v. *Colombia), Counter-claims, Order of 15 November 2017, I.C.J. Reports 2017*, pp. 310-311, para. 67.

[179] *Nottebohm case (Preliminary Objection), Judgment of November 18th, 1953: I.C.J. Reports 1953*, p. 121.

3.27 Nicaragua's next argument is that, because the Court has considered claims "based on facts that occurred after the filing of the Application on multiple occasions"[180], it is therefore entitled to consider facts that occurred after the filing of its Application in this case, including after the Pact of Bogotá ceased to have any effect for Colombia. Relying on the *Certain Questions of Mutual Assistance in Criminal Matters (Djibouti* v. *France), Fisheries Jurisdiction (Federal Republic of Germany* v. *Iceland)* and *LaGrand (Germany* v. *United States of America)* cases, Nicaragua states that the "appropriate test" for considering the existence of jurisdiction over post-Application facts is "whether the facts 'aris[e] directly out of the question which is the subject-matter of [the] Application'".[181] This argument is equally untenable.

3.28 In *Certain Questions of Mutual Assistance in Criminal Matters*, the Court's jurisdiction was based on Article 38(5) of the Rules of Court (*forum prorogatum),* which obviously has no application here. Jurisdiction in the *LaGrand* case was based on a compromissory clause with no resemblance to Article XXXI of the Pact of Bogotá. Similarly, the compromissory clause in *Fisheries Jurisdiction* was far different from that in the Pact.

---

180 NR, para. 4.16.

181 NR, para. 4.18, citing *Fisheries Jurisdiction (Federal Republic of Germany* v. *Iceland), Merits, Judgment, I.CJ. Reports 1972*, p. 203, para. 72 and L*aGrand (Germany* v. *United States of America), Judgment, I.C.J. Reports 2001,* pp. 483-484, para. 45.

These cases cited by Nicaragua are simply inapposite to the situation in these proceedings.

3.29 That being said, Colombia does not contest that, in certain circumstances, the Court can take into account facts that occur after the filing of the Application. But in none of the cases cited by Nicaragua as authority for that proposition, the jurisdictional link between the parties lapsed after the Application was filed; i.e., there was still a continuing jurisdictional basis on which to consider post-Application facts. The present case is fundamentally different. Here, both the consent of Colombia and the jurisdictional link between the parties terminated on the day after Nicaragua's Application was filed. None of the precedents cited by Nicaragua supports the proposition that, in those circumstances, the Court is entitled to take into account facts or situations occurring not only after the Application was filed, but also after the basis of jurisdiction has lapsed.

3.30 Nicaragua tries to counter this point by referring to the Court's provisional measures Order in the *Legality of Use of Force (Yugoslavia* v. *Belgium)* case. But, once again, the effort is unavailing given that the case in question also did not deal with the kind of situation presented here, and the temporal limitation contained in Yugoslavia's Article 36 (2) optional clause declaration was drafted in terms different from the compromissory clause appearing in Article XXXI of the Pact of Bogotá.

3.31 In *Legality of Use of Force (Yugoslavia* v. *Belgium),* Yugoslavia's optional clause declaration provided for the compulsory jurisdiction of the Court in all disputes "arising or which may arise after the signature of the present Declaration".[182] Thus, for jurisdictional purposes, the key question was when the dispute arose. Since the dispute between Yugoslavia and Belgium arose *before* Yugoslavia had deposited its Article 36(2) declaration – i.e. at a time where there was no jurisdictional link between the parties – the Court ruled that there was no *prima facie* basis of jurisdiction such that provisional measures could be prescribed.

3.32 This is very different from Article XXXI of the Pact of Bogotá, which provides for jurisdiction over disputes only "so long as the present Treaty is in force". It is undisputed between the parties that the Pact was not in force when the post-27 November 2013 events on which Nicaragua relies for its claim occurred. Thus, the situation is entirely different from that at issue in *Legality of Use of Force (Yugoslavia* v. *Belgium).* Indeed, citing from the Permanent Court's Judgment in the Preliminary Objections phase of the *Phosphates in Morocco* case, the Court, in its Order on Yugoslavia's request for provisional measures, underscored that "any limitation *ratione temporis* attached by one of the Parties to its declaration of acceptance of the Court's jurisdiction, 'holds good as between

---

182 NR, para. 4.19.

the Parties'".[183] The same holds true for a limitation *ratione temporis* contained in the compromissory clause of a treaty, such as the Pact of Bogotá.

3.33 Notwithstanding this, Nicaragua argues that, as in *Yugoslavia* v. *Belgium*, the focus in the present case should be on when the dispute arose, not when the basis of jurisdiction lapsed, and that Colombia cannot attempt to "slice the dispute in discrete pieces".[184] Accordingly, Nicaragua's thesis is that, because its dispute with Colombia arose before the Pact ceased to have effect for Colombia, the Court's jurisdiction extends to ruling on the legality of Colombia's actions after 27 November 2013 because those acts constitute part of the same dispute.[185]

3.34 This line of argument ignores the temporal limitations of Article XXXI of the Pact for Colombia. It destroys the jurisdictional symmetry of such limitations. Just as the Court has no jurisdiction to rule on facts or situations that arose before the instrument providing for jurisdiction – in this case the Pact – came into effect, so also it lacks jurisdiction to rule on events that transpired after the relevant instrument ceased to be in effect as between the parties to the dispute.

3.35 If taken to their logical conclusion, Nicaragua's contentions would also have the perverse effect of allowing a

---

183 *Legality of the Use of Force (Yugoslavia* v. *Belgium), Provisional Measures, Order of 2 June 1999, I.C.J. Reports 1999*, p. 135, para. 30.

184 NR, para. 4.21.

185 NR, paras. 4.25-4.26.

party to lodge an application against another party after the instrument providing for jurisdiction ceases to be effective by arguing that the underlying dispute arose earlier, while the instrument was still in force. This is clearly not the law; it would run directly contrary to the Court's statement in the *Nottebohm* case that the expiry of the time period when the instrument providing for jurisdiction is effective "would not have the effect of legally seising the Court".[186]

3.36 Based on the foregoing, while the Court has jurisdiction to consider whether the acts of the Colombian Navy between the date of the 2012 Judgment and 27 November 2013 amounted to a violation of Nicaragua's sovereign rights, which they did not, it does not have jurisdiction to consider any events that occurred after 27 November 2013 when the Pact of Bogotá ceased to be in force for Colombia. Nicaragua is simply trying to pad its claim by reference to events falling outside of the Court's temporal jurisdiction.

C. None of the Alleged "Incidents" Constitute a Violation by Colombia of Nicaragua's Sovereign Rights

3.37 There are 13 events that Nicaragua characterizes as "incidents" that occurred before the critical date. Since they form the basis of Nicaragua's claim that Colombia violated its sovereign rights, each event must be examined carefully. Once

---

186 *Nottebohm case (Preliminary Objections), Judgment of November 18th, 1953: I.C.J. Reports 1953*, p. 121.

that is done, it becomes evident that none of them violated Nicaragua's rights.

3.38 This is confirmed by Nicaragua's own conduct during the period in question. As explained below, that conduct is fundamentally inconsistent with the notion that Nicaragua considered Colombia to be engaging in any wrongful conduct at the time.

(1) Nicaragua's Own Conduct Undermines Its Claims

3.39 The first point to note is that Nicaragua never protested any of these "incidents" to Colombia until it was preparing its Memorial for this case, well after the critical date and months after the "incidents" themselves had allegedly occurred. In itself, this strongly suggests that Nicaragua did not consider them to be a violation of its sovereign rights.

3.40 It was not until 13 August 2014, more than eight months *after* Nicaragua filed its Application, that Nicaragua's Foreign Ministry sought information from its Naval Forces as to whether any "incidents" had taken place. And it was only on 13 September 2014, shortly before Nicaragua was due to file its Memorial, that Nicaragua sent a diplomatic note to Colombia alleging that Colombia had infringed its sovereign rights. In these circumstances, it is difficult to avoid the conclusion that Nicaragua was trying to manufacture a case where no basis for one genuinely existed.

3.41 This conclusion is reinforced when it is recalled that, precisely during the period when Nicaragua now asserts that Colombia was engaging in activities that violated its sovereign rights, Nicaragua's senior-most political and military officials were on record as emphasizing the contrary. Those officials are on record as stating that: (i) Colombia's Navy had *not* approached Nicaraguan fishing vessels;[187] (ii) in the one year following the Court's Judgment (i.e. up to the critical date), Nicaragua had *not* had any problems or conflicts with the Colombian Navy and the Navies of both countries had maintained continuous communications;[188] (iii) there were *"no incidents"* even as of March 2014 – that is, some four months *after* Nicaragua had filed its Application;[189] and (iv) the Colombian Navy had been respectful towards Nicaragua and there had not been *any kind of confrontation between the Navies.*[190]

3.42 Recognizing the weakness of its claims, Nicaragua's Reply asserts that "Colombia's 'incident-by-incident' approach tends to obscure the critical context that must inform the Court's evaluation of the facts".[191] Not only is this line of reasoning erroneous – Nicaragua has the burden of showing that specific conduct attributed to Colombia breached its sovereign rights – it

---

187 CCM, para. 4.8 and CPO, Annex 36.
188 CCM, para. 4.8 and CPO, Annex 43.
189 CCM, para. 4.8 and CPO, Annex 46.
190 CCM, para. 4.8 and CPO, Annex 11.
191 NR, para. 4.44.

ignores a crucial element of that conduct and its real context. This is the fact, unrebutted by Nicaragua, that Nicaragua did not raise a single complaint to Colombia at the time, and that its own most senior political and military leaders repeatedly emphasised that there had been no incidents or confrontations involving Colombia.

3.43 Nicaragua tries to pass off the affirmations of its President and senior military officials that there were no incidents, no Colombian approaches to Nicaraguan fishing vessels, no problems or conflicts between the Navies of the two countries, and no confrontations by arguing that all of these statements merely reflected "a deliberate policy of restraint" on Nicaragua's part.[192] This self-serving assertion lacks credibility.

3.44 Had Nicaragua genuinely been following a policy of self-restraint, one would have at least expected reports from the Nicaraguan Naval Force stating that there had been provocations from Colombia, but that the Navy was adopting a low profile and exercising restraint in order to avoid raising tensions.[193] And one would have expected Nicaragua's President to say that there

---

192 NR, para. 4.36.

193 NR, para. 4.37. Nicaragua points to a statement of General Avilés stating that the Nicaraguan Armed Forces were in communication with the Colombian authorities, that "there has been no boarding to fishing vessels" and that business fishermen had declared that the Colombians "have been going around but not boarding, which is serious". Nicaragua tries to spin this statement to suggest that the situation was "serious" (NR, para. 4.38). But it is clear that what the General was referring to was the eventual boarding of fishing boats, which, had it ever occurred, would have been serious, not to the mere presence of Colombian vessels. As admitted by the General, there was never any boarding by Colombia of Nicaraguan fishing boats.

had been incidents, but that Nicaragua had not responded in kind so that the matter would not escalate. Moreover, one would expect Nicaragua to be able to produce contemporary records of such "incidents" and rules of engagement for its Navy instructing Nicaraguan vessels to exercise self-restraint. Yet there is nothing of the kind. Indeed, it is undisputed that the Nicaraguan Naval Force never informed Nicaraguan political officials of any "incidents" until ten months after the Application had been filed, and then only after being prompted by Nicaragua's Foreign Ministry, which was then in the process of preparing Nicaragua's Memorial.

3.45 The statements of Nicaragua's political and military leaders represent positive affirmations that there were no incidents, problems, confrontations or anything else of a provocative nature on the part of Colombia, not evidence of self-restraint. If there were no incidents, there was no reason to exercise self-restraint. In these circumstances, to suggest, as Nicaragua does in its Reply, that these statements were "in no way inconsistent with the fact that Colombia had been engaged in actions against other Nicaraguan vessels that otherwise constituted serious violations of Nicaragua's sovereign rights and jurisdiction" is unconvincing.[194]

3.46 To be clear, Colombia is not relying on these statements to "rehash" the argument that there was no dispute between the

[194] NR, para. 4.40.

parties at the time Nicaragua filed its Application, as Nicaragua mistakenly asserts in its Reply.[195] Rather, the statements from Nicaragua's highest officials contradict Nicaragua's account of the "incidents" and undermine their relevance. As Nicaragua emphasised in its Reply: "[t]he facts are the facts".[196] When coupled with the meagre nature of the "facts" that Nicaragua adduces in support of its claims, the statements of its political and military leaders represent an important element of the context for assessing Nicaragua's claims.

(2) Colombia's Right To Be Present in the Area

3.47 The other side of the equation regarding the context for examining the individual "incidents" relied on by Nicaragua concerns Colombia's right to be present in the area in the exercise of its freedoms of navigation and overflight, and other internationally lawful uses of the sea.

3.48 Contrary to Nicaragua's assertion, Colombia has not adopted a policy of "occupation" of Nicaragua's EEZ – a notion which, as already noted, has a specific legal content in international law and moreover, has nothing to do with rights such as freedoms of navigation and overflight. Rather, as explained in Chapter 2, Colombia has been exercising said freedom of navigation and overflight, as well as other internationally lawful uses of the sea, especially bearing in mind

---

195 NR, para. 4.28.
196 NR, para. 4.29.

that it has a legitimate interest in maintaining a presence in the area in order to assess whether there is maritime shipping that is engaged in illegal activities such as drug trafficking, and to call attention to fishing vessels engaged in destructive environmental activities that they should modify their practices. Colombia also has an interest in ensuring the security and well-being of the inhabitants of the San Andrés Archipelago. None of this amounted to an interference in, let alone violation of, Nicaragua's sovereign rights.

3.49 In accordance with the principle of *onus probandi incumbit actori*, the burden is on Nicaragua to prove that its sovereign rights have been violated.[197] However, as Colombia will demonstrate in the next section, there are serious evidentiary problems with Nicaragua's version of the facts, which render the factual basis for its claims unreliable and incapable of proving any such violation.

3.50 Legally, the EEZ is a *sui generis* zone with a distinct legal regime that was specifically negotiated to balance the interests of coastal States and those of other maritime States.

---

197 *Pulp Mills on the River Uruguay (Argentina* v. *Uruguay), Judgment, I.C.J. Reports 2010*, p. 71, para. 162; *Maritime Delimitation in the Black Sea (Romania* v. *Ukraine), Judgment, I.C.J. Reports 2009*, p. 86, para. 68; *Sovereignty over Pedra Branca/Pulau Batu Puteh, Middle Rocks and South Ledge (Malaysia/Singapore), Judgment, I.C.J. Reports 2008*, p. 31, para. 45; *Application of the Convention on the Prevention and Punishment of the Crime of Genocide (Bosnia and Herzegovina* v. *Serbia and Montenegro), Judgment, I.C.J. Reports 2007*, p. 75, para. 204; *Military and Paramilitary Activities in and against Nicaragua (Nicaragua* v. *United States of America), Jurisdiction and Admissibility, Judgment, I.C.J. Reports 1984*, p. 437, para. 101.

Under customary international law, a coastal State such as Nicaragua, does not have sovereignty in its EEZ; only limited sovereign rights for the purpose of exploring and exploiting, as well as conserving and managing, the natural resources of the waters superjacent to the seabed and of the seabed and its subsoil, and with regard to other activities for the economic exploitation of the zone.[198] The coastal State also has limited jurisdiction in its EEZ. This extends solely to the establishment and use of artificial islands, installations and structures, marine scientific research, and the protection and preservation of the marine environment, none of which are germane since there is no allegation that Colombia interfered with such jurisdictional rights.

3.51 It follows that any suggestion (*quod non*) that Colombia violated Nicaragua's sovereign rights merely because the alleged "incidents" are claimed not to represent the legitimate exercise of the freedoms of navigation and overflight, and other internationally lawful uses of the sea, is untenable. Nicaragua has to go further and to show that its own rights were violated by the failure of Colombia to pay due regard to those rights. As Proelss has observed in his Commentary on UNCLOS:

> "As the *sui generis* nature of the EEZ is inseparably linked to existence of exclusive sovereign rights and jurisdiction of the coastal

---

198 D. Rothwell and T. Stephens, *The International Law of the Sea,* Hart Publishing, 2016, pp. 90-91 (available at the Peace Palace Library). See also UNCLOS Article 56.

> State under Art. 56, this zone ought to be treated as high seas if and to the extent to which these rights and jurisdiction are not affected".[199]

3.52 In *The M/V "SAIGA" (No. 2)* case, for example, the International Tribunal for the Law of the Sea noted that, "while [UNCLOS] attributes certain rights to coastal States and other States in the exclusive economic zone, it does not follow automatically that rights not expressly attributed to the coastal State belong to other States or, alternatively, that rights not specifically attributed to other States belong as of right to the coastal State".[200]

3.53 As will be seen in the next section in which Colombia addresses the specific "incidents", Nicaragua has failed to demonstrate that Colombia's conduct impeded Nicaragua from exercising any of its sovereign rights in its EEZ.

(3) THE INDIVIDUAL "INCIDENTS"

3.54 In this Sub-section, Colombia will address the thirteen individual "incidents" that Nicaragua alleges took place before the Pact of Bogotá ceased to be in force for Colombia. As Colombia will show, the "evidence" produced by Nicaragua

---

[199] A. Proelss, *United Nations Convention on the Law of the Sea: a Commentary*, C.H. Beck / Hart / Nomos, 2017, p. 451 (Proelss Commentary) (available at Peace Palace Library).

[200] *M/V "SAIGA" (No. 2) (Saint Vincent and the Grenadines* v. *Guinea), Judgment, ITLOS Reports 1999*, p. 56, para. 137.

falls well short of demonstrating any violation by Colombia of Nicaragua's sovereign rights.

Incident 1

3.55 Nicaragua asserts that on 19 February 2013, a Colombian naval vessel prevented a Nicaraguan naval vessel from inspecting a Colombian-flagged fishing boat that was operating in the *Luna Verde* area. Colombia has previously explained why the facts show that this alleged "incident" could never have happened because the Colombian vessel was hundreds of miles away at the time.[201]

3.56 In response, Nicaragua's Reply states that the source for the "incident" is not a complaint from the Nicaraguan naval vessel that was allegedly trying to inspect the Colombian boat – indeed, there was no complaint at all raised by the Nicaraguan Naval Force – but rather from a Colombian news article.[202] Nicaragua also admits that the article "does not clarify exactly when the incident took place".[203] That is the sum total of the "evidence" Nicaragua submits for this so-called "incident".

3.57 It is striking that Nicaragua relies solely on a news report from the Colombian news outlet, Caracol, as evidence that the incident occurred, not on any reports from its own naval

201 CCM, para. 4.23.
202 NR, para. 4.51.
203 NR, para. 4.51.

forces.[204] In any event, consistent with its established jurisprudence on this matter, the Court should treat news reports of this kind with considerable caution, particularly since it has been demonstrated that the "facts" in question never took place.

3.58 In the *Armed Activities on the Territory of the Congo (Democratic Republic of Congo* v. *Uganda)* case, for example, the Court observed that "particular caution" should be shown where press information is relied upon as evidence.[205] The Court noted that press articles are secondary evidence which is not capable of proving the existence of facts; at best, such material can only confirm the existence of facts which are established by other evidence. Here, there is no other evidence.

3.59 In *Military and Paramilitary Activities in and against Nicaragua (Nicaragua* v. *United States of America)*, the Court also emphasised the need to treat press reports and secondary sources with caution. As the Court explained:

> "in the present case the Court has before it documentary material of various kinds from various sources. A large number of documents has been supplied in the form of reports in press articles, and some also in the form of extracts from books. Whether these were produced by the applicant State, or by the absent Party before it ceased to appear in these proceedings, the Court has been careful to treat

---

[204] NM, para. 2.39 and Annex 34.

[205] *Armed Activities on the Territory of the Congo (Democratic Republic of the Congo* v. *Uganda), Judgment, I.C.J. Reports 2005*, p. 204, para. 68.

them with great caution; even if they seem to meet high standards of objectivity, the Court regards them not as evidence capable of proving facts, but as material which can nevertheless contribute, in some circumstances, to corroborating the existence of a fact, i.e., as illustrative material additional to other sources of evidence."[206]

3.60 To sum up, with respect to Incident 1, there is no first-hand evidence confirming either the existence, the timing or the specifics of the "incident" Nicaragua is seeking to rely on. There was also no complaint. Nor is there any evidence of prejudice to Nicaragua. That is wholly insufficient for purposes of supporting a claim that Colombia violated Nicaragua's sovereign rights.

Incident 2

3.61 According to Nicaragua, Incident 2 involved the conduct of "military and surveillance manoeuvres" by a Colombian airplane and patrolling by Colombian frigates, which Nicaragua paints as in violation of its sovereign rights.[207] Again, Nicaragua's Reply adds no new evidence relating to this "incident". Instead, Nicaragua once more relies on a few

---

206 *Military and Paramilitary Activities in and against Nicaragua (Nicaragua* v. *United States of America), Merits, Judgment, I.C.J. Reports 1986,* p. 40, para. 62. The Court reiterated this position in a more recent Judgment where it stated: "Evidence of this kind and other documentary material (such as press articles and extracts from books) are merely of a secondary nature and may only be used to confirm the existence of facts established by other evidence". (*Application of the Convention on the Prevention and Punishment of the Crime of Genocide (Croatia* v. *Serbia), Judgment, I.C.J. Reports 2015*, p. 87, para. 239).

207 NM, para. 2.25 and NR, para. 4.54.

Colombian press reports for its claim without producing a shred of evidence of its own that such manoeuvres hindered Nicaragua or Nicaraguan fishing in any way.[208] As is the case for Incident 1, the Court should treat these reports with considerable caution, given that there is no first-hand evidence from either Nicaraguan fishing boats or the Nicaraguan Naval Force to suggest that Nicaragua's account of Incident 2 is accurate or that Nicaragua suffered any prejudice as a result.

3.62 Nicaragua acknowledges that Colombia enjoys freedoms of navigation and overflight in and over Nicaragua's EEZ.[209] Yet, notwithstanding that there was not a single complaint from Nicaragua or its fishermen regarding this event, Nicaragua asserts that it is not credible to view Colombia's actions as benign.[210] The problem with this line of argument is that there is absolutely no evidence to back it up. To the contrary, this was nothing more than the lawful exercise by Colombia of its freedoms of navigation and overflight, as well as other internationally lawful uses of the sea.

3.63 Nicaragua's Reply then goes on to state that, "even if Colombia's conduct on this one occasion viewed in isolation were not considered to have violated international law, the incident must be understood in the larger context as part of a

---

208 NM, para. 2.25 and footnote 69.
209 NR, paras. 2.31 and 2.32.
210 NR, para. 4.56.

pattern of Colombia's persistent and insistent disregard for Nicaragua's sovereign rights and jurisdiction".[211]

3.64. There is no such pattern.[212] Indeed, Nicaragua itself acknowledges that throughout the relevant period fishing by Nicaraguan fishermen increased in its waters;[213] in fact, it increased exponentially, as Colombia demonstrated in its Counter-Memorial[214] and demonstrates as well in this Rejoinder.[215] In other words, any actions said to be attributed to Colombia did not dissuade Nicaraguan fishing vessels from operating in Nicaragua's EEZ. If there is any "pattern" of conduct that is relevant, it is characterized by (i) the paucity of evidence Nicaragua has been able to muster with respect to the "incidents", (ii) Nicaragua's failure to lodge a single protest over any of them, and (iii) the consistent statements emanating from Nicaragua's political and military leaders saying precisely the opposite of what Nicaragua now alleges.

3.65. There is no principle of customary international law or provision in UNCLOS, that prohibits flights by military aircraft over another State's EEZ.[216] As noted by Ambassador Tommy Koh, during the negotiations of UNCLOS concerning military

---

[211] NR, para. 4.58.

[212] See Chapter 1 *supra.*

[213] NR, para. 5.4.

[214] CCM, para. 3.21.

[215] Annex 71.

[216] H. S. Kim, "Military Activities in the Exclusive Economic Zone: Preventing Uncertainty and Defusing Conflict", *International Law Studies*, Vol. 80, 2006, p. 259, available at: https://digital-commons.usnwc.edu/ils/vol80/iss1/9/ (last visited: 1 November 2018).

activities in the EEZ, "[i]t was the general understanding that the text we negotiated and agreed upon would permit such activities to be conducted".[217]

3.66. This is confirmed by the negotiating history of Article 58 of UNCLOS, which does not give coastal States the right to regulate the conduct of foreign military activities in their EEZ. It is significant in this respect that, at the seventh session of the Conference in 1978, Peru proposed a provision requiring foreign warships and military aircraft to "refrain from engaging in manoeuvres or using weapons" in the EEZ without the coastal State's consent.[218] However, this proposal was rejected.

3.67. Moreover, the fact that there was no complaint from Nicaragua is consistent with the repeated affirmations of its President and senior military officials that Colombia had been respectful and that there had been no incidents or confrontations during the period when the "incident" is said to have taken place. In sum, Colombia's actions, which did not involve the use of weapons or the interdiction, let alone boarding, of any Nicaraguan ships, did not constitute a violation of Nicaragua's sovereign rights.

---

[217] T. Koh, cited in J. Van Dyke (ed.), *Consensus and Confrontation: The United States and the Law of the Sea Convention, a Workshop of the Law of the Sea Institute, January 9-13, 1984*, University of Hawaii / Law of the Sea Institute, 1985, pp. 303-304 (available at the Peace Palace Library).

[218] M. H. Nordquist, S. N. Nandan and S. Rosenne (eds.), *United Nations Convention on the Law of the Sea 1982: A Commentary*, University of Virginia / Martinus Nijhoff (Virginia Commentary), Vol. II, 1993, p. 563 (available at the Peace Palace Library).

Incident 3

3.68. Incident 3 involved President Santos delivering a speech on a Colombian frigate, which Nicaragua asserts was engaged in a "sovereignty exercise" involving patrolling by Colombian naval vessels into waters as far west as the 82nd West Meridian.[219] Once again, there is not a shred of evidence from Nicaragua demonstrating where the Colombian vessel was alleged to have navigated. Nor does Nicaragua offer any evidence that Colombia interfered with the exercise by Nicaragua of its sovereign rights in its EEZ. No complaints were made at the time either internally amongst Nicaraguan actors or by Nicaragua to Colombia. In such circumstances, there is no factual or legal basis for finding a violation of Nicaragua's sovereign rights.

3.69. Recognizing that it has no evidence of its own to back up the claim, Nicaragua's Reply refers to a statement made by President Santos during the exercise according to which he said: "We find ourselves patrolling and exercising sovereignty over Colombian waters".[220] But Nicaragua accepts that the exercise was conducted "off the coast of San Andrés", which would have been in Colombian waters. While Nicaragua contends that the

---

219 NM, para. 2.27.
220 NR, para. 4.59.

exercise reached up to the 82nd West Meridian,[221] it produces no evidence to this effect.

3.70. In sum, with respect to Incident 3 as well as the other "incidents", there is no evidence of any violation of Nicaragua's sovereign rights, no demonstration of any prejudice to Nicaragua, which appears not even to have been aware that anything objectionable had occurred, and no complaints from anyone on the Nicaraguan side.

Incident 4

3.71. Incident 4 involved what is said to be a communication by a Colombian naval vessel on 13 October 2013 informing a Nicaraguan vessel (the "Rio Escondido") that, according to Nicaragua's version of events, it was "sailing in Colombian waters".[222] In its Counter-Memorial, Colombia showed that this incident did not happen because on that date the Colombian vessel identified by Nicaragua (the A.R.C. "20 de Julio") was anchored some one hundred miles further south in the territorial sea of San Andrés.[223]

3.72. In its Reply, Nicaragua changed its story. It now argues that, even if Colombia's account is correct, it only suggests that the Nicaraguan vessel may have misidentified the Colombian

---

221 NR, para. 4.59.
222 NM, para. 2.40.
223 CCM, para. 4.26.

ship, not that the "incident" did not happen.[224] Of course, Colombia can only respond to the allegations advanced by Nicaragua. It is Nicaragua that is unable to provide an accurate account of the facts, including identifying the Colombian vessel that was supposed to have been involved, despite bearing the burden of proof for its claims. Nicaragua's only source for its allegations is a letter from the Nicaraguan Naval Force to the Ministry of Foreign Affairs dated 26 August 2014 – some ten months *after* the "incident" is alleged to have occurred – that contains no first-hand or contemporaneous evidence supporting Nicaragua's claim.

3.73. It follows that Nicaragua has not even come close to demonstrating that any such "incident" occurred, let alone that it amounted to a violation of its sovereign rights. Indeed, Nicaragua even goes so far as to distort the 26 August 2014 letter on which it relies. While Nicaragua's Memorial asserted that the Colombian naval commander warned the Nicaraguan vessel that it was sailing "*in* Colombian waters", Nicaragua's own document actually has the Colombian Commander saying simply that the Nicaraguan vessel was sailing "*towards* Colombian waters".[225] Even on Nicaragua's *ex post facto* version of events, therefore, such a statement cannot possibly be construed as an infringement on Nicaragua's sovereign rights.

---

224 NR, para. 4.62.

225 NM, Annex 23 A.

Incident 5

3.74. Incident 5 relates to the alleged harassment at 09:50 hours on 19 October 2013 by Colombian aircraft that are claimed to have flown at a threatening low altitude over a Nicaraguan coast guard vessel and a fishing boat.[226]

3.75. Unlike Nicaragua, which has only relied on indirect reports of the "incident",[227] Colombia filed a contemporaneous Travel Report from one of its naval vessels that was monitoring air traffic in the area on the day in question.[228] That Report indicates that it detected a Colombian aircraft at 11:00 hours that was engaged in "verifying surface and aerial panorama", but no traffic at 09:50 hours as alleged by Nicaragua. Moreover, echo radar indicated that the aircraft was at an altitude of 4,600 feet, which is consistent with Colombian Air Force rules. This cannot be characterized as flying at a "threatening low altitude" as alleged by Nicaragua.

3.76. In the light of the Court's admonishment that: "the Court will treat with caution evidentiary materials specially prepared for this case and also materials emanating from a single source"[229] – which Nicaragua's Annex 23 A gives every indication of being – and that, "[i]t will prefer contemporaneous

---

226 NR, para. 4.64.

227 See for example NM, Annex 20 and Annex 23 A.

228 CCM, Annex 49.

229 *Armed Activities on the Territory of the Congo (Democratic Republic of the Congo* v. *Uganda), Judgment, I.C.J. Reports 2005*, p. 201, para. 61.

evidence from persons with direct knowledge"[230] – as is the case with respect to the Colombian Navy's Travel Report – Nicaragua once again has failed to prove any violation of its sovereign rights.

Incidents 6 and 7

3.77. Nicaragua's allegations regarding these two incidents are similar and can be discussed together. They allegedly involved Colombian aircraft flying at low altitude in a "hostile manner" over Nicaraguan fishing boats and naval vessels. Once again, however, Nicaragua presents no contemporary evidence of these facts and no evidence of any impediment to the exercise of its sovereign rights.

3.78. Colombia demonstrated in its Counter-Memorial that its aircraft were not flying in such a manner, and that it was perfectly legitimate for its aircraft to undertake general observation activities in an area outside of Nicaragua's territorial sea known for maritime drug trafficking.[231] In any event, the Court has already held that the alleged incidents that were said to have occurred before Nicaragua filed its Application relate to the claim on alleged violations of sovereign rights and maritime spaces – rather than that concerning a threat of use of force upon which it stated it did not have

230 *Armed Activities on the Territory of the Congo (Democratic Republic of the Congo* v. *Uganda), Judgment, I.C.J. Reports 2005*, p. 201, para. 61.

231 CCM, paras. 4.31-4.33.

jurisdiction.[232] What remains is the fact that Colombian aircraft were fully entitled to exercise their freedom of overflight. In any case, the naval vessels and fishing boats were never prevented from carrying out their activities and Nicaragua did not protest at the time of their alleged occurrence.

3.79. Once more, Nicaragua is unable to provide any contemporary evidence for these "incidents". It relies on its 26 August 2014 internal letter,[233] almost a year after the events in question, its subsequent diplomatic note to Colombia of 13 September 2014,[234] and a one-page list of "locations". [235] These do not constitute any first-hand evidence of the underlying facts or give their source.

3.80. No new evidence is presented in Nicaragua's Reply. Rather, Nicaragua repeats its mantra that these events must be seen against the context of what is claimed to be a pattern of provocative Colombian actions.[236] However, as Colombia has explained, there was no such "pattern". The true context is that (i) the events in question did not give rise to any contemporary complaint from either the fishing boats or Nicaragua's Naval Force to the Nicaraguan authorities, (ii) Nicaragua itself made no protest to Colombia, and (iii) Nicaragua's military heads confirmed that there were no confrontations or incidents. Those

232 Judgment on the Preliminary Objections, p. 33, para. 77.
233 NM, Annex 23 A.
234 NM, Annex 18.
235 NM, Annex 24.
236 NR, para. 4.66.

facts completely undermine the claims that Nicaragua raises in these proceedings. In short, there was no violation of Nicaragua's sovereign rights with respect to either of these "incidents".

Incident 8

3.81. Incident 8 allegedly involved a Colombian helicopter flying over a Nicaraguan naval vessel on 31 October 2013 at 09:00 hours, and subsequently landing on a Colombian frigate.

3.82. In its Memorial, Nicaragua adduced no evidence to suggest that its vessel was threatened or impeded in any way. It simply relied on second hand reports that were prepared months after the alleged event took place. The Reply adds nothing to Nicaragua's case other than to speculate that, while the helicopter was airborne "it plainly *could* have impermissibly harassed the Nicaraguan vessel".[237] But "could have harassed" is not the same thing as "did harass". The Reply also asserts that Colombia "does not challenge the facts".[238] But this is plainly wrong. In its Counter-Memorial, Colombia introduced contemporary evidence in the form of a Travel Report from its naval vessel, the A.R.C. "Independiente", demonstrating that the helicopter did not take off until 09:42 hours on the day in

237 NR, para. 4.78. (Emphasis added).
238 NR, para. 4.77.

question, well *after* the time when Nicaragua says the "incident" occurred.[239]

3.83. Apart from the fact that there was no complaint issued by Nicaragua at the time, Nicaragua also has not produced any evidence to show that the fishing boat was threatened or impeded in its activities. The mere flying and landing of a Colombian helicopter on a Colombian vessel nearby is entirely consistent with Colombia's freedoms of navigation and overflight, as well as other internationally lawful uses of the sea. It cannot therefore constitute a violation of Nicaragua's sovereign rights.

Incidents 9 and 10

3.84 Incidents 9 and 10 are also based on the same second-hand report – the internal report attached in Annex 23 A to Nicaragua's Memorial – dated some ten months after the "incidents" are said to have occurred. Nicaragua's allegation is that Colombian frigates chased away two Nicaraguan fishing boats, the "Lucky Lady" (Incident 9) and the "Miss Sofia" (Incident 10), stating that they were in Colombian waters. Apart from the lack of any first-hand evidence for these events, to which the Nicaraguan Reply adds nothing, Colombia has explained why these alleged "incidents" could not have happened in the manner recounted by Nicaragua.[240]

---

239 CCM, para. 4.34 and Annex 49.

240 CCM, paras. 4.37 and 4.39.

3.85 In its Counter-Memorial, Colombia presented evidence that the Colombian frigate allegedly involved in Incident 9 was not even in the Caribbean Sea at the time that Nicaragua's Memorial indicated the "incident" occurred.[241]

3.86 In response, Nicaragua tries to explain away its lack of credible evidence by again claiming that the date it gave in its Memorial for Incident 9 was the date the matter was reported to a local naval base, not necessarily the date that the event complained of took place.[242] This rather feeble excuse, which Nicaragua omitted to explain in its Memorial, still leaves Nicaragua unable to provide any specifics about the incident, including when it was said to have transpired or how the fishing boat was prevented from continuing with its activities. In short, the evidence Nicaragua adduces to support its claim is neither reliable nor probative that the incident occurred or that any prejudice to Nicaragua's sovereign rights was caused.

3.87 The same deficiencies undermine Nicaragua's claim based on Incident 10 concerning the "Miss Sofia": no first-hand contemporary evidence; no complaints at the time; no evidence of the fishing boat being prevented from operating in Nicaragua's EEZ. Moreover, the notion that the Colombian vessel – the A.R.C "Almirante Padilla" – contacted the "Miss Sofia" to inform it that it was in Colombian waters, as alleged by Nicaragua, is belied by the fact that, after the "Miss Sofia"

---

241 CCM, para. 4.37, Annex 50.

242 NR, para. 4.80.

abandoned two of its fishermen, it was a Colombian frigate that had to rescue them. The frigate even tried to contact the "Miss Sofia" to return the fishermen, but the latter never bothered to respond.[243] In short, there were no communications between the Colombian vessel and the "Miss Sofia".

3.88 As documented in Annex 53 to Colombia's Counter-Memorial, it was in these circumstances that the A.R.C. "Almirante Padilla" contacted the Nicaraguan coast guard vessel "Rio Escondido". Contrary to Nicaragua's assertion, that contact did not involve any refusal to leave the area or mention of the Court's 2012 Judgment.[244] Rather, having been unable to contact the "Miss Sofia" itself, the Colombian frigate initiated a series of exchanges with the Nicaraguan patrol boat that had been overheard also trying to contact the "Miss Sofia" by radio to arrange for the transfer of the two rescued fishermen. When the "Miss Sofia" could not be reached, arrangements were made to transfer the fishermen to another Nicaraguan fishing boat, the "Caribbean Star", instead. Far from representing a violation of Nicaragua's sovereign rights, Colombia's actions were driven by humane considerations. Significantly, the two fishermen rescued by Colombia never intimated that the Colombian vessel had threatened their fishing boat or crew. Rather, they signed written declarations attesting to their good treatment at the hands of crew onboard the Colombian frigate.[245]

243 CCM, paras. 4.39-4.40 and Annex 53.
244 NR, para. 4.83.
245 CCM, Annex 52.

3.89 Moreover, even if Nicaragua's version of these "incidents" is accepted (*quod non*), which is highly improbable given the Nicaraguan Naval Force's assurances that there were no incidents involving Colombia during this period, Nicaragua has not demonstrated how either the fishing vessels or Nicaragua were prejudiced in a manner that constituted a violation of Nicaragua's sovereign rights.

Incidents 11, 12 and 13

3.90 These last three incidents allegedly involved Colombian airplanes flying over Nicaraguan vessels situated in Nicaragua's EEZ. As Colombia pointed out in its Counter-Memorial, there is no evidence of any hostile actions or prejudice caused to Nicaragua.[246] As before, Nicaragua did not produce any direct source material supporting its allegations, only vague descriptions set out in the later-prepared 26 August 2014 internal document, the sole purpose of which seems to have been a belated attempt to shore up Nicaragua's otherwise undocumented claims at a time when Nicaragua was in the final stages of preparing its Memorial.

3.91 Nicaragua's Reply only contains two brief paragraphs on these "incidents", which largely repeat what it said in its Memorial without providing any new evidence or showing how

[246] CCM, paras. 4.42-4.44.

Nicaragua was prevented from exercising its sovereign rights. In so far as Colombia enjoys freedom of overflight in the EEZ, Colombia's mere overflight over Nicaraguan vessels cannot constitute a violation of Nicaragua's sovereign rights. Notwithstanding the gaps in Nicaragua's case, it is worth noting that, as with all the other "incidents", Nicaragua made no protest at the time – a fact that is consistent with the contemporary statements of Nicaragua's naval officials, political and military leaders stating that there were no incidents.

D. Colombia Has Not Awarded Petroleum Blocks in Nicaragua's EEZ

3.92 Nicaragua alleges in its Reply – and for the first time in the current proceedings – that Colombia is "[o]ffering and awarding hydrocarbon blocks encompassing parts of Nicaragua's EEZ"[247] and that this constitutes a violation of Nicaragua's sovereign rights. No such claim was made in the Application or Memorial. As Colombia will show in Sub-section 1, the claim is inadmissible. Moreover, even if it were admissible (*quod non)*, the claim has no merit (Sub-section 2).

(1) NICARAGUA'S NEW CLAIM IS INADMISSIBLE

3.93 Article 40, paragraph 1, of the Statute provides that the subject of the dispute "shall be indicated" in the Application. This is supplemented by Article 38, paragraph 2, of the Rules of

---

247 NR, para. 4.129.

Court, which stipulates that the Application must specify "the precise nature of the claim". As the Court observed in the *Phosphate Lands in Nauru (Nauru* v. *Australia)* case, these provisions are "essential from the point of view of legal security and the good administration of justice".[248]

3.94 Nicaragua's new claim that Colombia has issued petroleum blocks in violation of Nicaragua's sovereign rights was neither identified as part of the subject of the dispute in Nicaragua's Application; nor was the nature of such a claim ever set out or even mentioned implicitly in that document. Indeed, the claim did not even appear in Nicaragua's Memorial. It has been raised for the first time in the Reply. In such circumstances, the claim is inadmissible.

3.95 In rejecting the admissibility of a late-filed claim in the *Ahmadou Sadio Diallo (Republic of Guinea* v. *Democratic Republic of the Congo)* case, the Court noted that:

> "additional claims formulated in the course of proceedings are inadmissible if they would result, were they to be entertained, in transforming 'the subject of the dispute originally brought before [the Court] under the terms of the Application'".[249]

---

[248] *Certain Phosphate Lands in Nauru (Nauru* v. *Australia), Preliminary Objections, Judgment, I.C.J. Reports 1992*, p. 267, para. 69.

[249] *Ahmadou Sadio Diallo (Republic of Guinea* v. *Democratic Republic of the Congo), Judgment, I.C.J. Reports 2010*, p. 656, para. 39 citing *Territorial and Maritime Dispute between Nicaragua and Honduras in the Caribbean Sea (Nicaragua* v. *Honduras), Judgment, I.C.J. Reports 2007 (II)*, p. 695, para. 108.

As the Court emphasised, "it is the Application which is relevant and the Memorial, 'though it may elucidate the terms of the Application, must not go beyond the limits of the claim as set out therein'."[250]

3.96 In the present case, Nicaragua did not even raise its new claim relating to petroleum blocks in its Memorial. As noted above, the new claim has only appeared in the Reply. It bears no relationship to the original claim, which was based on a series of statements by Colombian authorities, a number of so-called maritime "incidents" (discussed above) and the establishment of the contiguous zone (discussed in the next Chapter). This reinforces the conclusion that the claim should be deemed inadmissible.

3.97 Indeed, the Court has noted that the situation is even more serious when a new claim only appears in the Reply, at a time when the Respondent is no longer able to assert preliminary objections – a right that the Court termed "a fundamental procedural right" in the *Ahmadou Sadio Diallo (Republic of Guinea* v. *Democratic Republic of the Congo)* case. As the Court explained:

---

[250] *Ahmadou Sadio Diallo (Republic of Guinea* v. *Democratic Republic of the Congo), Judgment, I.C.J. Reports 2010*, p. 656, para. 39 citing *Certain Phosphate Lands in Nauru (Nauru* v. *Australia), Preliminary Objections, Judgment, I.C.J. Reports 1992*, p. 267, para. 69 citing the *Case concerning Prince von Pless Administration, Order of 4 February 1933, P.C.I.J., Series A/B, No. 52,* p. 14.

> "This right is infringed if the Applicant asserts a substantively new claim after the Counter-Memorial, which is to say at a time when the Respondent can still raise objections to admissibility and jurisdiction, but not preliminary objections".[251]

3.98 As to the relationship of the new claim to the claim(s) raised in the Application, the Court has stated that "it is not sufficient that there should be links between them of a general nature".[252] Rather, the new claim must either be implicit in the original claim, or it must arise directly out of the question that is the subject-matter of the Application.[253] Nicaragua's new claim relating to alleged petroleum blocks satisfies neither of these tests. It was not implicit in Nicaragua's Application, or even in its Memorial; and it does not arise out of the same questions that were the subject-matter of the Application: the question whether Colombian vessels harassed Nicaraguan vessels in violation of Nicaragua's sovereign rights, and the question concerning Colombia's integral contiguous zone.

---

251 *Ahmadou Sadio Diallo (Republic of Guinea* v. *Democratic Republic of the Congo), Judgment, I.C.J. Reports 2010,* p. 658, para. 44.

252 *Ahmadou Sadio Diallo (Republic of Guinea* v. *Democratic Republic of the Congo), Judgment, I.C.J. Reports 2010*, p. 657, para. 41, citing *Territorial and Maritime Dispute between Nicaragua and Honduras in the Caribbean Sea (Nicaragua* v. *Honduras), Judgment, I.C.J. Reports 2007 (II)*, p. 695, para. 110.

253 *Ahmadou Sadio Diallo (Republic of Guinea* v. *Democratic Republic of the Congo), Judgment, I.C.J. Reports 2010*, p. 657, para. 41, citing the *Case concerning the Temple of Preah Vihear (Cambodia* v. *Thailand), Merits, Judgment of 15 June 1962: I.C.J. Reports 1962*, p. 36 and the *Territorial and Maritime Dispute between Nicaragua and Honduras in the Caribbean Sea (Nicaragua* v. *Honduras), Judgment, I.C.J. Reports 2007*, p. 697, para. 114.

3.99 For these reasons, Nicaragua's new claim is inadmissible.

(2) The Claim Is Without Merit in any Event

3.100 Even if the Court were disposed to consider Nicaragua's new claim, it can readily be shown that the claim has no merit.

3.101 In the first place, it should be recalled that Nicaragua already resorted to the same argument during the hearings on preliminary objections in a different case, and that Colombia had shown that argument to be fallacious. This was the case concerning the *Question of the Delimitation of the Continental Shelf between Nicaragua and Colombia beyond 200 nautical miles from the Nicaraguan Coast (Nicaragua* v. *Colombia).* There, Nicaragua's Agent presented a map by the Colombian National Agency of Hydrocarbons (ANH, from its Spanish acronym) dated 2015 as an example of supposed "unilateral actions of Colombia regarding the exploration or exploitation of the resources, not only over Nicaraguan waters — as established by the Court's Judgment of November 2012 (…)".[254]

3.102 In those hearings, Colombia clarified that there are no existing licenses in the areas concerned; that these areas appear listed in Colombia's ANH maps since well before the 2012

[254] *Question of the Delimitation of the Continental Shelf between Nicaragua and Colombia beyond 200 Nautical Miles from the Nicaraguan Coast (Nicaragua* v. *Colombia)*, Public Sitting, 6 October 2015, CR 2015/27, p. 16, para. 21 (Nicaraguan Agent).

Judgment; and that while two blocks were awarded in 2010 (CAYOS 1 and CAYOS 5) – again, before the 2012 Judgment – they were suspended in 2011, and no contracts were signed afterwards.[255]

3.103 In its Reply, Nicaragua attempts to rehash this argument by stating that "the signature of the relevant contracts remains outstanding"[256] – which is not true. Nicaragua seeks to make a case out of nothing, because as stated, in October 2011 President Santos removed from consideration oil and gas exploration and exploitation in and around the San Andrés Archipelago. Moreover, since 2012 both the Administrative Tribunal of San Andrés and the Council of State (Colombia's highest administrative law tribunal) have confirmed the suspension of activities relating to these two blocks.[257] It follows that there is no possible violation of Nicaragua's sovereign rights in this regard.

3.104 As for the "remaining" nine blocks not awarded in 2010, Nicaragua contends in its Reply that they continue to be offered

---

[255] *Question of the Delimitation of the Continental Shelf between Nicaragua and Colombia beyond 200 Nautical Miles from the Nicaraguan Coast (Nicaragua* v. *Colombia)*, Public Sitting, 7 October 2015, CR 2015/28, p. 40, para. 19 (Wood).

[256] NR, para. 4.128.

[257] Annex 20: Administrative Tribunal of San Andrés, Providencia and Santa Catalina, Judgment on Case No. 88-001-23-31-003-2011-00011-00 filed by the Corporation for the Sustainable Development of San Andrés, Providencia and Santa Catalina (CORALINA) against the National Agency of Hydrocarbons (ANH), 4 June 2012.

by Colombia by reference to a map from the ANH dated 17 February 2017.[258]

3.105 As noted above, Nicaragua's claim and the "evidence" it purports to rely on is inadmissible as it concerns a different subject-matter from the claims it introduced in its Application and has been advanced more than three years after the Court ceased to have jurisdiction between the parties due to the denunciation by Colombia of the Pact of Bogotá.

3.106 Moreover, even if the Court were to consider the map, it does not show any violation of Nicaragua's sovereign rights. Once again, none of these blocks have been the object of any implementation process since 2010. This is because: (i) some of these areas are excluded because they are within a natural park, i.e. the Seaflower Biosphere Reserve and Marine Protected Area, and (ii) as noted by the ANH in its website, "Areas Available" are "those areas that have not been allocated."[259] Thus, there is no existing contract or proposal awarded for the blocks in question (nor there could be), and Nicaragua's sovereign rights remain unaffected.

3.107 What is striking is how Nicaragua's arguments change at its convenience, and how distorted its account of the facts is. Quite simply, Colombia has awarded no petroleum blocks in

---

[258] NR, Figure 4.3.

[259] National Agency of Hydrocarbons, "Lands Map, February 17th 2017", available at: http://www.anh.gov.co/en-us/Asignacion-de-areas/Paginas/Mapa-de-tierras.aspx (last visited: 1 November 2018).

areas falling within Nicaragua's EEZ as delimited by the Court in 2012. It follows that Colombia has not violated Nicaragua's sovereign rights and maritime spaces.

E. The False Accusation that Colombia Has Authorized Fishing in Nicaragua's EEZ

3.108 Nicaragua alleged in its Memorial that Colombia has issued fishing license authorisations to Colombians and nationals of third States to operate in Nicaraguan waters.[260] To support its accusation, Nicaragua submitted as evidence: (i) Resolution No. 5081 issued by the Governorship of the Archipelago Department of San Andrés, Providencia and Santa Catalina on 22 October 2013;[261] (ii) Resolution No. 305 issued by the General Maritime Direction (DIMAR, from its Spanish acronym) on 25 June 2014;[262] and (iii) a Report on the Status of the Natural Resources and the Environment issued by the Office of the Comptroller General of San Andrés, Providencia and Santa Catalina on July 2013.[263]

3.109 In its Reply, Nicaragua reformulated its accusation against Colombia by indicating that: "Colombia has also continued to violate Nicaragua's sovereign rights and jurisdiction by authorizing, encouraging and protecting

260 NM, paras. 2.22, 2.51 and 2.52.
261 NM, Annex 11.
262 NM, Annex 14.
263 NR, Annex 12.

industrial fishing in Nicaragua's EEZ."[264] As "evidence" of the alleged violation, Nicaragua submitted a number of resolutions issued by DIMAR,[265] and the Governorship of the Archipelago Department of San Andrés, Providencia and Santa Catalina – albeit Nicaragua claims these resolutions were issued by DIMAR, it is clear in its own Annexes that they were not.[266]

3.110 Based on the above, Nicaragua asks the Court to declare Colombia's international responsibility for its allegedly "wilful disregard of its international obligations, including the obligation to have due regard for Nicaragua's exclusive sovereign rights to the natural resources of its EEZ"[267] and, therefore that Colombia be ordered to "revoke permits granted to fishing vessels operating in Nicaragua's exclusive economic zone, as delimited in the Court's Judgment of 19 November 2012"[268].

3.111 The first defect in Nicaragua's claim and the "evidence" it submits is that it is based on post-critical date facts. The

---

264 NR, para. 4.101.

265 General Maritime Direction, Resolution No. 0311 of 2013 (26 June 2013) (NR, Annex 7); General Maritime Direction, Resolution No. 305 of 2014 (25 June 2014) (NR, Annex 9, which was already submitted in the Memorial as Annex 14); General Maritime Direction, Resolution No. 0437 of 2015 (27 July 2015) (NR, Annex 12); General Maritime Direction, Resolution No. 0459 of 2016 (27 July 2016)(NR, Annex 16); General Maritime Direction, Resolution No. 550 of 2017 (15 August 2017) (NR, Annex 17).

266 General Maritime Direction, Resolution No. 4997 (NR, Annex 11); General Maritime Direction, Resolution No. 4356 of 2015 (NR, Annex 13); General Maritime Direction, Resolution No. 4780 of 2015 (NR, Annex 14); General Maritime Direction, Resolution No. 2465 of 2016 (NR. Annex 15).

267 NR, para. 4.121.

268 NR, Submissions, para, 1 (d).

resolutions regarding the vessels "Rough Rider" (NR, Annex 11), "Capt. Geovanie" (NR, Annex 13) and "The Saga" (NR, Annex 14) were issued respectively on 10 November 2014, 1 September 2015 and 24 September 2015. The Court lacks jurisdiction to consider whether any of these facts – which took place after 27 November 2013 when the Pact of Bogotá ceased to be in force for Colombia – constitutes a violation of Nicaragua's sovereign rights or maritime spaces.

3.112 Additionally, the special and transitory measures (i.e. exemption from a security tax payment and automatic navigation authorisation) granted for vessels registered in the jurisdiction of the Harbour Masters of San Andrés and Providencia are sovereign acts of the Colombian State materialized in a series of resolutions issued by DIMAR between 2014 and 2017 (NR, Annexes 9, 12, 16 and 17). As these acts also occurred after the Pact of Bogotá ceased to be in effect for Colombia, the Court lacks jurisdiction to consider if they constitute a violation of Nicaragua's sovereign rights or maritime spaces.

3.113 Thus, the only facts with respect to which the Court has jurisdiction are: the resolutions concerning the affiliation of the fishing vessel "Captain KD",[269] and the special and transitory measures granted by DIMAR in Resolution No. 311 of 2013.[270]

---

269 NM, Annex 11.
270 NR, Annex 7.

3.114 However, for the sake of completeness, Colombia will also address Nicaragua's post-critical date facts and evidence to demonstrate that none of these support Nicaragua's complaints either.

3.115 The fact of the matter is that the Colombian fishing industry in the San Andrés Archipelago was devastated by the 2012 Judgment because of its lack of access to areas situated in areas forming part of Nicaragua's EEZ.

3.116 A 2013 Report on the Status of the Natural Resources and the Environment issued by the Office of the Comptroller General of San Andrés, which Nicaragua submits as evidence of its claims, precisely noted that "the great majority of the industrial [fishing] companies have left the islands".[271] That report also indicated that catches of species such as lobster and whitefish had declined to a fraction of their pre-Judgment levels.[272]

3.117 In fact, in 2013, the largest fisheries and export company in San Andrés, Antillana, reported six months after the Judgment that it was ceasing operations "due to the economic unsustainability of the industry after the loss of 75,000 square

---

271 NM, Annex 12.

272 The Report shows that the catch of whitefish fell from 116 tons in 2012 to 27 tons from January to July 2013 and the catch of lobster fell, in that same period, from 133 tons to 36 tons (NM, Annex 12, pp. 190-192).

kilometres of marine spaces in San Andrés".[273] Moreover, the second largest company, King Crab, also stated that it was ceasing operations for the same reason.[274] Rather than granting licenses as before over areas that came to be situated in Nicaragua's EEZ, it was the inability to access these areas that caused a significant collapse of the industry and severe economic hardship to the inhabitants of the Archipelago.

3.118 With regard to the resolutions issued by DIMAR (NM Annex 14; NR Annexes 7, 9, 12, 16 and 17), Nicaragua alleges that through them Colombia has authorised industrial fishing in Nicaragua's EEZ and encouraged such fishing by giving financial incentives.[275] This statement is demonstrably false: they do not grant fishing licenses simply because DIMAR is not the competent authority to grant these permits. Moreover, nowhere in these resolutions are economic incentives granted to promote fishing in Nicaragua's EEZ.

3.119 What these resolutions provide is the following:

(i) They authorize to "stay and operate in the jurisdiction of the San Andrés and Providencia Harbour Master's Office (…) upon authorisation of the Office of the Secretary of Agriculture and

[273] Annex 54: El Universal, *San Andrés' largest fishery is shutting down,* 19 May 2013; and Annex 55: El Isleño, *Chamber of Commerce regrets the closure of Antillana*, 23 May 2013.

[274] Annex 57: Radio Nacional de Colombia, *ICJ ruling jeopardizes industrial fishing in San Andrés*, 13 August 2013.

[275] NR, para. 4.104.

> Fishing of the Government of San Andrés, Providencia and Santa Carolina [sic]".[276]

As can be seen, they do not authorise industrial fishing because fishing permits are issued by the Secretariat of Agriculture and Fishing of San Andrés, not by DIMAR.

(ii) The special and transitory measures, such as the exemption from the payment of the Maritime Security Service, were granted to overcome the "negative economic and social effects" of the 2012 Judgment, but do not refer at all to Nicaragua's EEZ.

3.120 As can be seen, Nicaragua's reading of these DIMAR Resolutions is a mere distortion of the facts. Colombia's issuance of special and transitory measures does not authorise nor encourage industrial fishing in waters of the Nicaraguan EEZ. They only grant certain financial reliefs to the benefit of the fishing fleet registered in San Andrés and Providencia – an act not prohibited by international law, and one that in no way affects or purports to affect Nicaragua's sovereign rights.

3.121 As for the resolutions issued by the Governorship of the Archipelago Department of San Andrés, Providencia and Santa

---

[276] NR, para. 4.104.

Catalina,[277] Nicaragua alleges that through them Colombia issued fishing permits in Nicaragua's EEZ.[278] This statement is incorrect, as the following analysis of each resolution will show:

a. Resolution No. 5081 of 2013:[279] As explained by Colombia in its Counter-Memorial,[280] Nicaragua's assertion is based on the "Whereas" clauses, whilst in the operative part of the permit, Article Three clearly does not include *Luna Verde* bank nor any maritime spaces adjudicated to appertain to Nicaragua by the 2012 Judgment. Indeed, the authorisation is specifically limited to "the Archipelago Department of San Andrés, Providencia and Santa Catalina (Roncador, Serrana and Quitasueño, Serranilla Keys) and Shallows (Alicia and Nuevo)".

b. Resolution No. 4997 of 2014:[281] This resolution merely authorises the disaffiliation of the vessel "Rough Rider" from the permitholder's fishing fleet (see Article One). Thus, it does not grant a fishing permit and in no way evidences that Colombia is granting fishing authorisations in waters of the Nicaraguan EEZ.

---

277 NM, Annex 11 and NR, Annexes 11, 13, 14 and 15.
278 NR, paras. 4.105-4.107.
279 NM, Annex 11.
280 CCM, para. 4.46.
281 NR, Annex 11.

Additionally, the only areas mentioned in the Resolution are "the banks (Roncador, Serrana and Quitasueño, and Serranilla) and Shoals (Alicia and Nuevo), and in the fishing zones that are permitted by the laws, fishing regulations and system of Protected Marine Areas". No mention whatsoever is made of any areas falling within waters of the Nicaraguan EEZ.

c. Resolution No. 4356 of 2015:[282] The same analysis made above with respect to Resolution No. 4997 of 2014 applies to this resolution. *First*, it simply authorizes the disaffiliation of the vessel "Fair Winds" from the permitholder's fishing fleet (see Article One). Thus, it does not grant a fishing permit and in no way evidences that Colombia is granting fishing authorisations in waters of the Nicaraguan EEZ. *Second*, the only areas mentioned in the Resolution are "the banks (Roncador, Serrana and Quitasueño, and Serranilla) and Shoals (Alicia and Nuevo), and the zone where fishing is permitted by the laws". No mention whatsoever is made of any areas falling within waters of the Nicaraguan EEZ.

Simply put, unlike licenses that had been issued before the 2012 Judgment, which listed the *Luna Verde* Bank as

282 NR, Annex 13.

one of the permitted fishing areas,[283] the new Resolutions expressly indicate that the areas where fishing activities are authorised are solely those which the Court has recognised to lie within Colombia's territorial sea and EEZ.

d. Resolution No. 4780 of 2015:[284] Again, this resolution refers to the affiliation of the vessel "The Saga" to the fishing fleet of the permit holder Ms Vianova Forbes James (see Article One). It does not grant a fishing permit, and its purpose is not to indicate the areas in which Colombia is granting fishing authorisations.

As with Resolution No. 5081 of 2013, Nicaragua's claim is based on the "Whereas" clauses. However, operative Article Six only establishes that the "fishing fleet carries out fishing activities in the authorised fishing grounds in the area of the Department of San Andrés, Providencia and Santa Catalina". There is no authorisation to fish at the *Luna Verde* bank or in any maritime spaces recognised to Nicaragua by the 2012 Judgment.

3.122 In sum, the Resolutions issued by the Governorship of the Archipelago Department of San Andrés, Providencia and

---

283 Annex 18: Archipelago Department of San Andrés, Providencia and Santa Catalina, Resolution No. 2479, 13 June 2006; and Annex 19: Archipelago Department of San Andrés, Providencia and Santa Catalina, Resolution No. 20, 13 November 2009.

284 NR, Annex 14.

Santa Catalina submitted by Nicaragua in its Memorial and Reply,[285] do not authorise fishing activities in Nicaragua's EEZ. To the contrary, all of them expressly indicate that the areas where fishing operations can be carried out are areas which the Court recognised fall within Colombia's territorial sea or EEZ (i.e. Roncador, Serrana, Quitasueño, Serranilla, Bajo Alicia and Bajo Nuevo). Nowhere in their operative part is there an authorisation to carry out fishing activities at the *Luna Verde* bank or in other maritime spaces situated within Nicaragua's EEZ.

3.123 Finally, Resolution No. 2465 of 2016,[286] issued by the Governorship of the Archipelago Department of San Andrés, Providencia and Santa Catalina, is completely irrelevant. It refers to the procedure for inscription in the fishermen's book and the identification of artisanal commercial fishermen. Accordingly, it has nothing to do with the granting of fishing permits or any Nicaraguan maritime spaces. To the contrary, Article 8 expressly provides that: "The commercial artisanal fishing activities can only be exercised in the territory that includes the jurisdiction of the Archipelago Department of San Andrés, Providencia and Santa Catalina".

---

285 NM, Annex 11 and NR, Annexes 11, 13 and 14.
286 NR, Annex 15.

F. Conclusions

3.124 Based on the foregoing, it is clear that Nicaragua has not demonstrated any violation of its sovereign rights or maritime spaces by Colombia. This includes the "incidents" that are claimed to have occurred before the critical date when the Pact of Bogotá ceased to be in force between Nicaragua and Colombia, the alleged issuance of fishing permits in Nicaraguan waters and the alleged granting of hydrocarbon exploration and exploitation licences. It follows that Nicaragua's submissions on this aspect of its claims should be rejected.

Chapter 4

THE CONTIGUOUS ZONE OF THE COLOMBIAN ISLAND TERRITORIES IN THE SOUTHWESTERN CARIBBEAN SEA

A. Introduction

4.1 In its Reply, Nicaragua requests the Court to adjudge and declare that "Colombia must revoke, by means of its choice, all laws and regulations which are incompatible with the Court's Judgment of 19 November 2012, including the provisions in Decrees 1946 of 9 September 2013 and 1119 of 17 June 2014 on maritime areas which have been recognized as under the jurisdiction or sovereign rights of Nicaragua".[287]

4.2 It appears from the Reply that, so far as concerns the contiguous zone, Nicaragua claims that Decree No. 1946 (as amended) directly affects its rights under customary international law. Nicaragua claims that the Decree does so because it extends beyond the EEZ delimitation line set out in the 2012 Judgment; because the powers described in the Decree go beyond those permitted under customary international law; and because in certain places the contiguous zone extends to a distance beyond 24 nautical miles from the baselines, also

[287] The wording of the submissions in Nicaragua's Reply is quite different from that in its Application and Memorial, but on each occasion, it would seem that Nicaragua does not seek to challenge Decree 1946 (as amended) in the abstract, but only in so far as Nicaragua's own rights have been directly affected by enactment of the Decree.

allegedly contrary to customary international law. Nicaragua further asserts that the mere adoption of the Decree violates its rights under customary international law, even though it has failed to demonstrate that the Decree has in effect been enforced by Colombia in a manner that has made Nicaragua suffer any harm due to such application.

4.3 As Colombia has shown in its Counter-Memorial, each of these assertions is without merit. In this Chapter, Colombia will address in particular the arguments deployed in Nicaragua's Reply. After describing Decree No. 1946 (as amended) (Section B), the Chapter first shows that, under customary international law, Colombia may lawfully exercise its contiguous zone powers in areas where the contiguous zone overlaps with part of Nicaragua's EEZ (Section C). It next shows that none of the powers provided for in the Decree go beyond those which Colombia is entitled to exercise under customary international law (Section D). The next section explains that the outer limit of the Colombian integral contiguous zone in the Southwestern Caribbean Sea is a lawful simplification of maritime zones and does not encroach upon Nicaragua's rights (Section E). And, finally, it explains that Nicaragua has failed to demonstrate that the enactment and application of the Decree has violated any of its rights under international law (Section F).

B. Decree No. 1946 of 2013 (as amended in 2014)

4.4 Colombia's Political Constitution of 1991 provides for a contiguous zone in accordance with the international law of the sea.[288] This was implemented, so far as concerns the contiguous zone in the Southwestern Caribbean Sea, by Article 5 of Decree No. 1946 concerning the Territorial Sea, Contiguous Zone, and Continental Shelf of the Colombian Island Territories in the Southwestern Caribbean, issued on 9 September 2013 and amended by Decree No. 1119 of 17 June 2014.[289]

4.5 The present section describes these provisions of Colombian law, which are in full conformity with the customary international law of the sea. The section also corrects Nicaragua's distortions and misinterpretations of Colombian domestic law.[290]

4.6 The existence of Colombia's contiguous zone was reflected in Article 101 of the Political Constitution of Colombia

---

288 CCM, para. 5.9.

289 CCM, Annex 7.

290 It is typical of Nicaragua's approach that it even complains about the name given by Colombia under its internal law to the contiguous zone it has declared around the islands and cays of the San Andrés Archipelago. Nicaragua asserts, in footnote 73 of its Reply, that the name 'Integral Contiguous Zone' "is abusive: it corresponds to no accepted notion in international law." Yet States are not required to use UNCLOS terminology when naming zones and features under domestic law. The adjective 'integral' is appropriate in order to reflect the geographical reality that the greater part of the contiguous zone around the Archipelago forms a single zone, not a series of separate contiguous zones.

of 1991,[291] which refers to "the subsoil, the territorial sea, the contiguous zone, the continental shelf, the exclusive economic zone" and which provides that these are "in accordance with international law or the laws of Colombia in the absence of international law."[292] The quoted words confirm, at the level of the Colombian Constitution, that the Colombia's contiguous zone is to be implemented in conformity with international law.

4.7 This principle is further confirmed by the express provisions of the Decrees of 2013 and 2014.[293] Article 1(3) of the 2013 Decree provides that Colombia exercises jurisdiction and sovereign rights over the maritime spaces other than the territorial sea "in the terms prescribed by international law". The commitment to act in conformity with international law is reiterated by the addition in 2014 of a last paragraph to Article 5 (on the contiguous zone), which states that the application of Article 5 "will be carried out in conformity with international law and Article 7" (which itself provides that the rights of other States are not affected or limited by the Decree).

4.8 Decree No. 1946 (as amended) was issued by the President of the Republic of Colombia in exercise of his powers under the 1991 Political Constitution in furtherance of Law 10 of 1978, which provides that the Government shall indicate the

---

291 There had been an earlier reference to the contiguous zone in a law of 1984: see CCM, para. 5.9.
292 CCM, para. 5.9.
293 The background to Decree No. 1946, which was issued by the President of Colombia on 9 September 2013 and amended by Decree No. 1119 of 17 June 2014, was described in CPO, paras. 2.61-2.62.

baselines from which various maritime spaces are measured, and Law 47 of 1993 (concerning the Archipelago Department of San Andrés, Providencia and Santa Catalina). After reciting Article 101 of the 1991 Political Constitution, and relevant provisions of Laws 10 of 1978 and 47 of 1993, the preamble to the Decree proclaims that: "The Republic of Colombia exercises all the rights over its maritime spaces in accordance with International Law".

4.9 Article 1(1) and (2) of the Decree set out a detailed definition of the island territories of Colombia in the Southwestern Caribbean Sea. Article 1(3) provides, *inter alia*, that Colombia "exercises full sovereignty over its insular territories and territorial sea" and "jurisdiction and sovereign rights over the rest of the maritime spaces generated by its insular territories in the terms prescribed by international law". Article 2 provides that "[i]n accordance with (…) customary international law" the maritime spaces generated by the island territories (including the contiguous zone) "are part of Colombia".

4.10 Article 3(1) of the Decree provides that "the Government will indicate the points and baselines for which the width of territorial seas will be measured, along with the contiguous zone". Article 3(2) provides that "[t]hese lines will be drawn in accordance with criteria recognized by customary international law" (which include special criteria related to islands situated on atolls or islands surrounded by reefs). Article 3(3) concerns straight baselines. Article 6 then makes provision for the publication of official thematic maps of the points and baselines, and also of the Integral Contiguous Zone once the points and baselines have been set forth in a Decree.

4.11 Article 4 makes provision for the 12 nautical miles' territorial seas of the island territories.

4.12 Article 5 makes provision for the contiguous zone of the island territories. It comprises three sections. Section 1 provides that the contiguous zone of the island territories extends up to a distance of 24 nautical miles from the baselines. Section 2 provides that "the lines indicated for the outer limits of the contiguous zones will be joined to each other through geodetic lines." Section 3 then describes the faculties of enforcement and control necessary for specified purposes. The final paragraph of Section 3 then includes the following provision, which applies to the whole of Article 5 of the Decree: "The application of this article will be carried out in conformity with international law and Article 7 of the present Decree."

4.13 Article 7 provides that the Decree will not "affect or limit (…) the rights of other states".

4.14 Nicaragua complains that the map of Colombia's contiguous zone included in the Counter-Memorial (Figure 5.1) differs from the map shown at the televised press conference on 9 September 2013, a depiction of which Nicaragua reproduced in its Application and reproduces again at Figure 3.1(a) of its Reply. As stated in Colombia's Preliminary Objections and in its Counter-Memorial,[294] Colombia has not yet issued an official map showing the contiguous zone because technical work is still ongoing to determine the relevant points and baselines according to Article 3 of the Decree, so that they can be proclaimed in accordance with Article 6 of the Decree. Pending such official publication, Figure 5.1 of the Counter-Memorial depicts the integral contiguous zone for illustrative purposes, and – for the purposes of the present case – is nothing more than an accurate illustration of how the Decree should apply in practice.

4.15 As explained in the Counter-Memorial, due to the geography of the region, the contiguous zones of the islands intersect – each island is less than 48 nautical miles from a neighbouring island – and hence the zone which Colombia established is a single, integrated contiguous zone for the Archipelago. Furthermore, for the effective implementation of this contiguous zone, Colombia, in conformity with customary international law, drew geodetic lines to connect the 24-nautical-mile arcs from the islands.

4.16 Nicaragua, in its Reply, accepts "the entitlement of Colombia to a contiguous zone",[295] which necessarily includes the establishment of a contiguous zone for the San Andrés

294 CPO, para. 2.59 and CCM, para. 5.1.
295 NR, para. 3.20.

Archipelago. Nicaragua does, however, dispute the extension of the contiguous zone into its EEZ, the rights exercised within the contiguous zone, and the simplification of the outer limits of the contiguous zone. Colombia will address Nicaragua's objections to the contiguous zone of its island territories in turn.

C. Colombia's Integral Contiguous Zone May Overlap with Nicaragua's EEZ

4.17 Nicaragua attempts to convince the Court that under customary international law, a contiguous zone of one State may not extend into the EEZ of another State. Nicaragua's proposition is that its EEZ rights extinguish any protective rights and powers of Colombia as part of the contiguous zone regime.[296] Nicaragua does not present any convincing evidence or doctrine to that effect. There is none. The Court should thus reject its unfounded *ipse dixit* interpretation of customary international law.

4.18 This Section will show that the right of the coastal State to establish a contiguous zone is independent of, and not incompatible with, any resource-oriented EEZ rights of another State in the same space. Within the contiguous zone, the coastal State only has the right to exercise the degree of control necessary to protect its vital interests within its territory or territorial sea. Colombia will demonstrate that no inherent conflict exists between one State's EEZ rights and another

---

296 NR, para. 3.21.

State's contiguous zone powers, and that, under international law, a coastal State is permitted to exercise its contiguous zone rights, regardless of the existence of another State's EEZ rights in the same maritime space.

4.19 In its Counter-Memorial, Colombia demonstrated that the right of the coastal State to establish a contiguous zone under customary international law is distinct from the right to a contiguous zone in the 1958 Convention on the Territorial Sea and the Contiguous Zone,[297] and later in UNCLOS.[298] The customary right to establish a contiguous zone encompasses the exercise of control necessary to protect the vital interests of the coastal State including, *inter alia*, security interests and environmental protection.[299] Nevertheless, even if the Court were to accept Nicaragua's contention that the customary right to establish a contiguous zone has been codified and is now limited to the precise formulations in Article 24 of the 1958 Convention and Article 33 of UNCLOS, Colombia will demonstrate that both the establishment of its contiguous zone and all the powers specified in Article 5 of Decree No. 1946 (as amended), are in conformity with those provisions.

4.20 For present purposes, the key point is that the jurisdiction and powers vested in the coastal State within the

---

297 Hereinafter "the 1958 Convention".

298 CCM, paras. 5.39-5.54.

299 CCM, para. 5.48.

contiguous zone are different from the sovereign rights a State possesses in its EEZ. As the Virginia Commentary notes:

> "The rights of control exercisable by the coastal State in the contiguous zone, however, differ from its sovereign rights or jurisdiction in the exclusive economic zone, which relate to the natural resources of that zone"[300]

4.21 In the EEZ, UNCLOS Article 56 and customary international law provide that the coastal State has specific, mainly resource-oriented rights, including the exclusive right to exploit the resources of the water column, the sea-bed and its subsoil, and has specific jurisdiction with regard to the establishment and use of artificial islands, installations and structures, marine scientific research and the protection and preservation of the marine environment. These defined rights must be exercised with due regard to the rights and duties of other States in the zone.

4.22 The EEZ regime thus does not bestow sovereignty upon the EEZ coastal State; that State only possesses certain exclusive resource-oriented sovereign rights and jurisdiction in its EEZ, while all other States continue to enjoy their traditional rights and freedoms therein. Hence, the exercise of these specific resource-oriented rights by the coastal State in its EEZ is subject

---

300 Virginia Commentary, p. 275; see also Proelss Commentary, p. 262; J. Carlson, "Presidential Proclamation 7219: Extending the United States' Contiguous Zone – Didn't Someone Say This Had Something to Do with Pollution?", *University of Miami Law Review*, Vol. 55, No. 3, 2001 (available at the Peace Palace Library).

to the obligation to have due regard to the rights and duties of other States, including those in UNCLOS Article 33 and the customary right to establish a contiguous zone.

4.23 Nicaragua contends that Colombia must prove that any rights it claims within Nicaragua's EEZ – in this case, contiguous zone rights – are attributed to Colombia and not to Nicaragua in accordance with UNCLOS Article 59.[301] This argument is misguided; Article 59 has no role to play.

4.24 Article 59 was a new provision negotiated at UNCLOS III with a view to providing a basis for the resolution of any conflict of interests between the coastal State and any other State, in cases where the Convention did not allocate rights or jurisdiction to the coastal State or other States. There is little if any practice concerning Article 59.

4.25 In any event, Nicaragua's reliance on this provision does not assist its case. *First*, Nicaragua simply assumes that Article 59 reflects customary international law but fails to prove its opposability to Colombia. For this reason alone, the Court should disregard any purported relevance of Article 59 to the case. *Second*, even if the Court were minded to consider that Article 59 reflected customary international law, *quod non,* it is clear from its terms, context and negotiating history that Article

---

301 NR, para. 2.10.

59 has no relevance to the question that arises in the present case, that of overlapping contiguous zones and EEZs.

4.26 Article 59 of UNCLOS reads:

> "In cases where this Convention *does not attribute rights or jurisdiction* to the coastal State or to other States within the exclusive economic zone, and a conflict arises between *the interests* of the coastal State and any other State or States, the conflict should be resolved on the basis of equity and in the light of all the relevant circumstances, taking into account *the respective importance of the interests involved* to the parties as well as to the international community as a whole."[302]

UNCLOS Article 59 does not envision, as Nicaragua would have it, the attribution of additional rights to the coastal State in its EEZ. Article 59 only concerns *conflicts of interests* of the coastal State in its EEZ and those of other States: *interests*, not rights or jurisdiction. Furthermore, Article 59 applies only to cases where UNCLOS "does not attribute rights or jurisdiction" to any State. As much of Nicaragua's argument against Colombia's contiguous zone circles around UNCLOS Article 33, it is evident that the Convention does in fact attribute contiguous zone rights and jurisdiction. Hence, Article 59 is inapplicable to the question at hand.

4.27 Nor has Nicaragua shown any *conflict* of interests. As explained below, there is no inherent conflict between the

302 Emphasis added.

resource-related rights and jurisdiction of the coastal State in the EEZ and the control that may be exercised, for specific purposes, by a coastal State in the contiguous zone. Nor has Nicaragua shown any actual such conflict in the present case. Finally, the content of the rule in Article 59 does not assist Nicaragua: even if it applied, Article 59 gives no preference to EEZ rights over the rights of other States, including the latter's contiguous zone rights.

4.28 UNCLOS Article 73 prescribes that any legislation or enforcement by the coastal State within the EEZ must be limited to the specific rights and duties of the State in the EEZ:

> "The coastal State may, in the exercise of its sovereign rights to explore, exploit, conserve and manage the living resources in the exclusive economic zone, take such measures, including boarding, inspection, arrest and judicial proceedings, as may be necessary to ensure compliance with the laws and regulations adopted by it in conformity with this Convention."

Therefore, as part of the EEZ regime, the EEZ coastal State does not possess the right to exercise, beyond its own contiguous zone, control with respect to its customs, fiscal, immigration or sanitary laws and regulations. The absence of such a right as part of the EEZ regime is intentional. During the Conference, it was repeatedly stressed that the EEZ and the contiguous zone regimes conferred separate and distinct types of jurisdictions upon the State.[303] The contiguous zone rights were reserved for the first 24 nautical miles from the coast presumably to protect the freedom of navigation and other rights of all other international users.[304] It is thus clear that not only does the EEZ State lack the right to protect its own interests with respect to customs, fiscal, immigration or sanitary laws and regulations as part of the EEZ regime, but, *a fortiori*, it may not interfere with or purport to safeguard the contiguous zone rights that another State may have in the same area. Under international law, the right and duty to protect such vital interests of the coastal State are vested solely in that State.

4.29 There is no inherent conflict between the rights of the coastal State in the contiguous zone and the rights of another State in its EEZ. At UNCLOS III,

> "the prevailing view (...) was that (...) the envisaged legal regime of the EEZ was intended to

---

303 Virginia Commentary, p. 270; see e.g. Official Records of the Third United Nations Conference on the Law of the Sea: A/CONF.62/C.2/SR.9, *Summary records of meetings of the Second Committee*, 9th meeting, India, para. 3; Indonesia, para. 4; Iraq, para. 11; Algeria, para. 12; A/CONF.62/C.2/SR.22, *Summary records of meetings of the Second Committee*, 22nd meeting, Switzerland, paras. 135-136; A/CONF.62/C.2/SR.26, *Summary records of meetings of the Second Committee*, 26th meeting, Egypt, para. 27; A/CONF.62/C.2/SR.31, *Summary records of meetings of the Second Committee*, 31st meeting, Italy, para. 32; Germany, para. 35; Bahrain, paras. 42-43, available at: http://legal.un.org/diplomaticconferences/1973_los/vol2.shtml (last visited: 1 November 2018).

304 The objection to extending the contiguous zone beyond 12 nautical miles was raised for fear it would "lead to serious disturbance of international communication and the freedom of navigation". J. Symonides, "Origin and legal essence of the contiguous zone", in *Ocean Development & International Law*, Vol. 20, Issue 2, 1989, p. 206 (available at the Peace Palace Library).

> cover entirely different subjects [than the contiguous zone regime], and that there were thus no overlaps in substance between these two maritime zones".[305]

As noted above, the rights of the State in the EEZ mainly concern resources, and its jurisdiction is limited to specified actions in relation to these (UNCLOS Article 56). For example, the EEZ State may regulate the exploitation of resources in the EEZ or regulate traffic to offshore installations. In contrast, contiguous zone jurisdiction is preventive and corrective: therein the coastal State is afforded the necessary powers in order to prevent and punish infringement of its customs, fiscal, immigration or sanitary laws and regulations within its territory or territorial sea. The right to exercise control in the contiguous zone only comes into operation once the event or action develops a potential to adversely affect the essential interests of the coastal State in its territory or territorial sea.

4.30 Thus, if in a given maritime area, State A exercises EEZ rights while State B exercises contiguous zone rights, no conflict should arise, as each State has jurisdiction over events which affect its own rights and interests. In this area of the sea, State A, the EEZ State, would have the right to regulate the enumerated resource exploitations and have jurisdiction over offshore installations, maritime research and an alike; in part of the same maritime area, State B, the contiguous zone State, will exercise the necessary control in the contiguous zone over

---

305 Proelss Commentary, p. 262.

actions and inbound ships which threaten to violate its customs, fiscal, immigration or sanitary laws and regulations and over ships which have transgressed such laws and regulations.[306] As neither State may exercise jurisdiction over events affecting the protective laws and regulations of the other State, there can be no conflict.

4.31 The different jurisdictions in the two maritime regimes were distinguished in UNCLOS III. During the 31st meeting of the Second Committee, which concluded the Committee's discussion on the contiguous zone, the representative of the German Democratic Republic clarified that:

> "[w]ith respect to the rights of the coastal State in the contiguous zone, he said they should include the right to control customs, immigration, fiscal and sanitation regulations. The regulations governing the contiguous zone would not affect the right of the coastal State to utilize the living and mineral resources in the zone adjacent to its territorial sea if the concept of the economic zone was incorporated in the new law of the sea."[307]

---

306 As discussed in the Counter-Memorial, it is Colombia's position that under customary international law, in the contiguous zone the coastal State may exercise necessary control over other actions and events which may adversely affect its vital interests. See CCM, paras. 5.50-5.54.

307 Official Records of the Third United Nations Conference on the Law of the Sea, A/CONF.62/C.2/SR.31, *Summary records of meetings of the Second Committee*, 31st meeting, Germany, para. 35, available at: http://legal.un.org/docs/?path=../diplomaticconferences/1973_los/docs/english/vol_2/a_conf62_c2_sr31.pdf&lang=E (last visited: 1 November 2018).

The representative of Bahrain

> "agreed with the view that the establishment of a contiguous zone for particular purposes beyond the territorial waters of a coastal State was not inconsistent with the concept of an exclusive economic zone since the latter, as its name implied, would be an area in which the utilization of resources and other economic matters were the *sole concern.*
>
> A coastal State's rights in the contiguous zone were of a functional and protective nature."[308]

A contrary proposition would undermine the essential interests of the coastal State in its contiguous zone and the balance struck in the text of UNCLOS.

4.32 The limited jurisdiction of a State in its EEZ was intentional; the Conference rejected the initiative of certain States to transform the EEZ into a 200-nautical-mile territorial sea.[309] While certain voices within the Conference suggested that the contiguous zone should be discarded,[310] the concept was

---

308 Official Records of the Third United Nations Conference on the Law of the Sea, A/CONF.62/C.2/SR.31, *Summary records of meetings of the Second Committee*, 31st meeting, Bahrain, paras. 42-43, available at: http://legal.un.org/docs/?path=../diplomaticconferences/1973_los/docs/english/vol_2/a_conf62_c2_sr31.pdf&lang=E (last visited: 1 November 2018). (Emphasis added).

309 Virginia Commentary, p. 550.

310 Virginia Commentary, p. 269; see e.g. Official Records of the Third United Nations Conference on the Law of the Sea: A/CONF.62/C.2/SR.9, *Summary records of meetings of the Second Committee*, 9th meeting, Mexico, para. 2; Israel, paras. 5-6; Kenya, para. 10, available at: http://legal.un.org/docs/?path=../diplomaticconferences/1973_los/docs/english/vol_2/a_conf62_c2_sr9.pdf&lang=E (last visited: 1 November 2018).

preserved because it differs from the EEZ and confirms the coastal State's customary rights. The jurisdiction and rights bestowed upon the coastal State for each regime are intentionally distinct.[311] During the 31st meeting of the Second Committee, the Italian representative explained that:

> "His position on the contiguous zone was related to his concept of the economic zone. The rights of the coastal State in the economic zone would be purely economic, while its rights in a much more restricted zone would relate to national security, customs, taxation, health and immigration, and the right to guarantee the protection of its territory. If the breadth of the territorial sea was to be reduced and a contiguous zone established beyond it, it should be stated very clearly that the coastal State had different competences over the different parts of the high seas beyond its territorial waters. It would have rights and competences with regard to the protection of its territory in the contiguous zone, while it would have rights and competences with regard to the protection of its clearly defined economic interests in the economic zone measured from the outer limit of the territorial sea. The

---

311 Virginia Commentary, p. 270; see e.g. Official Records of the Third United Nations Conference on the Law of the Sea: A/CONF.62/C.2/SR.9, *Summary records of meetings of the Second Committee*, 9th meeting, Indonesia, para. 4; Iraq, para. 11; Algeria, para. 12; India, para. 3; A/CONF.62/C.2/SR.22, *Summary records of meetings of the Second Committee*, 22nd meeting, Switzerland, paras. 135-136; A/CONF.62/C.2/SR.26, *Summary records of meetings of the Second Committee*, 26th meeting, Egypt, para. 27; A/CONF.62/C.2/SR.31, *Summary records of meetings of the Second Committee*, 31st meeting, Italy, para. 32, available at: http://legal.un.org/diplomaticconferences/1973_los/vol2.shtml (last visited: 1 November 2018). See also J. Carlson, "Presidential Proclamation 7219: Extending the United States' Contiguous Zone – Didn't Someone Say This Had Something to Do with Pollution?", *University of Miami Law Review*, Vol. 55, No. 3, 2001, p. 518 (available at the Peace Palace Library).

> concept, and *the functions of the contiguous zone and the economic zone were thus very different.*"[312]

The Italian position was in line with the position of the representative of Switzerland, who had explained in an earlier meeting on the contiguous zone that:

> "First, the proposed economic zone and the contiguous zone served different purposes: within the economic zone, the coastal State would have exclusive exploitation rights over living and non-living resources; its sole competence in the contiguous zone, however, would be the prevention and punishment of offences against certain rules designed to ensure the maintenance of good order.
>
> Secondly, the type of jurisdiction to be exercised in each zone was completely different: in the exclusive economic zone, the coastal State would have – chiefly legislative – jurisdiction over natural resources and the preservation of the marine environment; in the contiguous zone, it would have the right to punish certain offences committed or to prevent offences likely to be committed by a vessel or its crew on the territory of the coastal State or in its territorial waters. Its competence did not extend to offences that had been or would be committed in the contiguous zone, and there could thus be no application of rules within that zone."[313]

---

[312] Official Records of the Third United Nations Conference on the Law of the Sea, A/CONF.62/C.2/SR.31, *Summary records of meetings of the Second Committee*, 31st meeting, Italy, para. 32, available at: http://legal.un.org/docs/?path=../diplomaticconferences/1973_los/docs/english/vol_2/a_conf62_c2_sr31.pdf&lang=E (last visited: 1 November 2018). (Emphasis added).

[313] Official Records of the Third United Nations Conference on the Law of the Sea, A/CONF.62/C.2/SR.22, *Summary records of meetings of the Second Committee*, 22nd meeting, Switzerland, paras. 136-137, available at:

Similarly, the representative of Iraq explained that:

> "the concept of the contiguous zone differed from that of the economic zone. While he did not oppose the proposals to postpone consideration of the question of the contiguous zone until after the question of the economic zone had been discussed, he pointed out that the concept of the economic zone related only to jurisdiction over resources. The concept of the contiguous zone, on the other hand, involved the jurisdiction of the coastal State in regard to customs, fiscal, sanitation and immigration regulations."[314]

The Indonesian representative pointed out that while:

> "the contiguous zone would lose its importance if the idea of an economic zone were approved, but since the latter would essentially relate to questions of economics and marine resources, his delegation preferred that the concept of the contiguous zone should not be discarded completely, since it involved other powers of the coastal State with regard to customs, fiscal and police control, and sanitation and immigration regulations."[315]

---

http://legal.un.org/docs/?path=../diplomaticconferences/1973_los/docs/english/vol_2/a_conf62_c2_sr22.pdf&lang=E (last visited: 1 November 2018).

314 Official Records of the Third United Nations Conference on the Law of the Sea, A/CONF.62/C.2/SR.9, *Summary records of meetings of the Second Committee*, 9th meeting, Iraq, para. 11, available at: http://legal.un.org/docs/?path=../diplomaticconferences/1973_los/docs/english/vol_2/a_conf62_c2_sr9.pdf&lang=E (last visited: 1 November 2018).

315 Official Records of the Third United Nations Conference on the Law of the Sea, A/CONF.62/C.2/SR.9, *Summary records of meetings of the Second Committee*, 9th meeting, Indonesia, para. 4, available at: http://legal.un.org/docs/?path=../diplomaticconferences/1973_los/docs/english/vol_2/a_conf62_c2_sr9.pdf&lang=E (last visited: 1 November 2018).

4.33 Since State A, the EEZ State, may not exercise its own contiguous zone jurisdiction beyond its contiguous zone, and any contiguous zone jurisdiction it exercises will be limited to preventing the infringement of *its own* vital interests with respect to customs, fiscal, immigration or sanitary laws and regulations, State A does not possess the right to regulate beyond its territorial sea activities which may adversely affect the customs, fiscal, immigration or sanitary laws and regulations of State B. The right and duty to protect itself against such activities and to punish any perpetrators rests solely with State B in that part of State A's EEZ which is State B's contiguous zone.

4.34 Were the coastal State precluded from exercising its contiguous zone rights beyond the territorial sea, its ability to protect its vital interests, as expressed in its relevant laws and regulations, would be severely undermined. The consequences of such a preclusion, would be exacerbated in geographical contexts like that of the San Andrés Archipelago. These effects can be illustrated in several scenarios.

4.35 In the first scenario, if the coasts of the two States are less than 24 nautical miles apart, each State exercises sovereignty within its respective territorial sea. It was for this reason that then President Clinton proclaimed that the contiguous zone of the United States does not extend to the territorial sea of another State.[316]

4.36 In a second scenario, if the coasts of the opposing States are 48 nautical miles apart and the delimitation was the median line, each State would be entitled to a territorial sea of 12 nautical miles and a contiguous zone of up to 12 nautical miles. Whether one or both of the States were to declare an EEZ up to the equidistance line would have no effect on the exercise of contiguous zone rights by either State. In case the States are less than 48 nautical miles apart, the contiguous zones of the States overlap; each State would exercise the necessary degree of control over ships inbound into its respective territorial sea and events that affect its defensive laws and regulations, within their respective overlapping contiguous zones.

4.37 In contrast to Nicaragua's claim that the delimitation of the contiguous zones is part of the delimitation of the EEZ,[317] the possibility of overlapping contiguous zones was recognised in the UNCLOS negotiations, and, according to the Virginia Commentary, was the reason for the removal of the delimitation provision with respect to the contiguous zone.[318] The

---

316 W. Clinton, *Proclamation 7219 – Contiguous Zone of the United States*, 1999, available at: http://www.presidency.ucsb.edu/ws/?pid=56452 (last visited: 1 November 2018).

317 NR, paras. 3.21-3.23.

318 Virginia Commentary, pp. 273-274; other explanations have also been put forward for the removal of the delimitation provision. See H. Caminos, "Contiguous Zone", *Max Planck Encyclopaedia of Public International Law*, para. 16 (available at the Peace Palace Library); Proelss Commentary, pp. 262-263; D. R. Rothwell and T. Stephens, *The*

Commentary quotes the following explanation for the removal of the delimitation provision in the preparatory work of the ISNT/Part II draft:

> "There is no provision in the Convention for the delimitation of contiguous zones. Such a zone cannot, by definition, be extended into the territorial sea of another state. Since the nature of control to be exercised in the contiguous zone does not create any sovereignty over the zone or its resources, *it is possible for two states to exercise control over the same area* if their zones should overlap, for the purpose of prevention of or punishment for infringement of their respective customs, fiscal, immigration or sanitary laws and regulation within their respective territories of territorial sea."[319]

This rationale applies with equal force to delimitations in which the contiguous zone rights of the coastal State are to be exercised within the EEZ of the other State. The contiguous zone does not bestow upon the coastal State any sovereign rights with respect to the resources of the EEZ; nor does it accord it any jurisdiction which could conflict with those assigned to an EEZ State in UNCLOS Article 56(b). It only accords jurisdiction with respect to inbound threats of infringement of the laws and regulations of the coastal State or to outbound

---

International Law of the Sea, Hart Publishing, 2016, p. 90 (available at the Peace Palace Library).

319 Virginia Commentary, pp. 273-274, quoting Commonwealth Group of Experts, *Ocean Management: A Regional Perspective – The Prospects for Commonwealth Maritime Co-operation in Asia and the Pacific*, Commonwealth Secretariat, 1984. (Emphasis added). See also: H. Caminos, "Contiguous Zone", *Max Planck Encyclopaedia of Public International Law*, para. 16 (available at the Peace Palace Library).

perpetrators. Thus, analogous to overlapping contiguous zones, one State's contiguous zone rights may co-exist with another State's EEZ rights.

4.38 Nicaragua refers in its Reply to the United States Proclamation of its contiguous zone in 1999.[320] However, it neglects to mention that in the Proclamation, the United States recognised that the only maritime area where contiguous zone rights may not overlap with rights of other States is the territorial sea. That is why the Proclamation states that the United States contiguous zone cannot extend "within the territorial sea of another nation".[321] In addition, it underlined that it in no way affected the United States' EEZ rights and obligations. This reaffirms the position that exercising contiguous zone rights in no way restricts the sovereign rights of States in other areas, such as the EEZ.

4.39 In the case of delimitations which only accord a coastal State a territorial sea – a scenario in which Colombia finds itself as a result of the 2012 Judgment – the inability to extend the contiguous zone into the EEZ of the opposing State would be devastating to the coastal State's ability to protect its vital interests. The coastal State would thus not be able to prevent infringements of its vital interests in its territorial sea or territorial domain from materializing, and its ability to punish

---

320 NR, para. 3.35.

321 W.J. Clinton, *Proclamation 7219 – Contiguous Zone of the United States*, 1999, available at: http://www.presidency.ucsb.edu/ws/?pid=56452 (last visited: 1 November 2018).

and deter further offenses would also be compromised. The danger to the coastal State would be further exacerbated, since the neighbouring EEZ State would itself not have the jurisdiction to prevent such threats from materializing or to punish offenders that escaped the coastal State's territorial sea. In fact, such a proposition would create the absurd situation in which customary rights, indispensable to the coastal State, would be rendered unenforceable.

4.40 Therefore, Colombia submits that, under customary international law, a coastal State has the right to extend its contiguous zone rights up to 24 nautical miles from the coast. A coastal State has the right to safeguard, at the very least, its vital protective customs, fiscal, immigration, sanitary, environmental, security or cultural heritage laws and regulations regardless of any resource-based rights of other States in the same area. A contrary proposition would deprive the coastal State of the ability to prevent the infringement of its vital protective laws and regulations, as neither it nor its neighbour would be empowered to act.

4.41 Nicaragua, in its Reply, makes several demonstrably fallacious arguments on this issue.

4.42 *First*, Nicaragua claims that the Sketch-map of the contiguous zone presented by Colombia illustrates that Colombia accepts that the maritime boundaries in the north with

Honduras and Jamaica confine its contiguous zone.[322] It is quite puzzling that Nicaragua, after criticizing the same Sketch-map based on the Decree, now purports to take it out of context. The Sketch-map only illustrates the contiguous zone where it is relevant to the case and any depiction of it within Colombia's EEZ serves only to illustrate its simplification. According to the Decree, the integral contiguous zone is not confined by the division of sovereign rights to resources and other jurisdictions with Honduras and Jamaica.

4.43 *Second*, Nicaragua claims that the delimitation of the EEZ and continental shelf between Colombia and Nicaragua in the 2012 Judgment entailed the delimitation of the contiguous zones between the States. Colombia does not consider Nicaragua's argument to have any merit. Nicaragua's argument is not based on what the Court decided in the 2012 Judgment, but rather on the fact that maps presented in that case at some point depicted contiguous zones.[323] Nicaragua never requested a delimitation that included the contiguous zone; it was outside the object of the dispute. Nicaragua's claim directly contradicts the Court's own understanding of what is *res judicata* in its 2012 Judgment.

4.44 Nevertheless, the contiguous zone is not a maritime area subject to be delimited, and even if it was, as Colombia explained above, there was no overlapping of the contiguous

---

[322] NR, para. 3.24.

[323] NR, paras. 3.21-3.23.

zones of the parties to that case and therefore there was no need to delimit them – and the Court obviously did not do that. In any case, even if there had been such an overlap, both the Proelss Commentary, on which Nicaragua heavily relies, and the Virginia Commentary, accept that two contiguous zones may overlap without giving rise to any need for a delimitation.

4.45 *Third*, Nicaragua submits that the contiguous zone rights of Colombia are not included within UNCLOS Article 58,[324] which is part of general international law. The reference in Article 58(1) to Article 87 of UNCLOS (i.e. freedom of the high seas), and the recognition that, except for the listed examples therein, all States have the right to conduct "other internationally lawful uses of the sea related to these freedoms, such as those associated with the operation of ships, aircraft", and the requirement that such uses are "compatible with the other provisions of this Convention", entail a reference to the "*inter alia*" component of Article 87. Thus, under both customary international law and Article 58, all States retain in the EEZ, the traditional high seas freedoms except those assigned to the EEZ State under Article 56 or its customary equivalent. Since contiguous zone rights are traditional high seas rights of the coastal State exercisable in the area adjacent to its territorial sea (and fully compatible with other provisions of the Convention), and such rights were not assigned as part of the EEZ regime to

324 NR, para. 3.21.

the EEZ coastal State, they constitute a lawful exercise of rights of other States within the EEZ of another State.

4.46 For the above reasons, Colombia submits that the Court should reject Nicaragua's objection to the brief overlap of Colombia's contiguous zone into Nicaragua's EEZ. The delimitation performed by the Court in the 2012 Judgment has left the western flank of Colombia's Archipelago with only a territorial sea and two of the islands conforming that Archipelago were granted only a territorial sea.[325] Hence, as a direct consequence of the Court's 2012 Judgment, part of Colombia's contiguous zone perforce lies in waters of Nicaragua's EEZ. In its EEZ, Nicaragua does not possess the right to safeguard Colombia's territory and territorial sea from potential infringement of Colombia's vital interests addressed by its customs, fiscal, immigration or sanitary laws and regulations. Moreover, Nicaragua also lacks the right to detain and punish perpetrators who infringed such vital Colombian interests and have managed to flee seaward from Colombia's territorial sea. Hence, besides the fact that a contiguous zone may lawfully co-exist within the EEZ of another State, if Colombia was precluded from exercising its powers therein the Colombian islands would be exposed to violations of its customs, fiscal, immigration or sanitary laws and regulations, and Colombia

---

[325] *Territorial and Maritime Dispute (Nicaragua* v. *Colombia), Judgment, I.C.J. Reports 2012*, p. 710, para. 235 and p. 714, Sketch-map No. 11.

could not do anything to prevent such threats from materializing. Nor could Nicaragua, for that matter.

D. The Powers Set Out in the Decree Are in Conformity with International Law

4.47 In its Reply, Nicaragua grossly distorts Colombia's position concerning the contiguous zone. Colombia does not claim "that it could potentially extend its contiguous zone over the whole Caribbean Sea (or even further)".[326] And Colombia does not argue that customary international law does not "prescribe[] geographical and material limits to the contiguous zone".[327] What Colombia claims is that no rule of customary international law was violated by the issuance of Decree No. 1946 (as amended).

4.48 *First*, the present section will show that Article 33 of UNCLOS does not reflect present-day customary international law on the contiguous zone. Nicaragua has failed to show otherwise.

4.49 *Second*, the section will show that under existing customary international law, a coastal State is permitted to establish zones contiguous to its territorial sea, of varying breadth and for a range of purposes, going in some respects beyond those expressly envisaged in Article 33 of UNCLOS.

---

326 NR, para. 3.7.
327 NR, para. 3.8.

4.50 *Third*, and in the alternative, even if the Court were to hold that Article 33 of UNCLOS reflects, in whole or in part, rules of customary international law, this treaty provision has been interpreted and applied broadly enough to encompass both the spatial and the substantive content of Article 5 of Decree No. 1946 (as amended).

4.51 *Fourth*, even if the powers set forth in Article 5 of Decree No. 1946 (as amended) were being applied in a manner going beyond what the rules of customary international law on the contiguous zone would permit, that would not in itself mean that such application violated Nicaragua's EEZ rights. Whether that was the case would depend upon the specific powers in question and the circumstances of their application. Colombia will show that based on customary international law all States enjoy extensive freedom of navigation and overflight rights, as well as other internationally lawful uses of the sea within a coastal State's EEZ. The exercise of such rights, even if deemed additional to those that may be exercised in the contiguous zone, *quod non*, is lawful under international law even if, for the purposes of domestic law, they are described as being exercisable as part of a contiguous zone. The question is not whether Colombia's contiguous zone is excessive spatially or in terms of powers, *quod non*, but rather if it has somehow violated the Nicaragua's EEZ rights.

(1) Article 33 does not reflect customary international law

4.52 Any assessment of whether the contiguous zone of the Colombian island territories in the Southwestern Caribbean Sea complies with customary international law must begin by examining whether Colombia's claimed jurisdiction complies with the customary international law concerning the contiguous zone. As elaborated in the Counter-Memorial, under customary international law the interests for the protection of which the coastal State may exercise control in the contiguous zone are not limited to those set out in Article 24 of the 1958 Convention and Article 33 of UNCLOS, but rather have evolved with the threats posed to the coastal State, and include, *inter alia*, the coastal State's security and environmental concerns.[328]

4.53 The customary international law right of the coastal State to establish a contiguous zone to protect its vital interests dates back to the 18th century and was recognised in the 1958 Convention.[329] Article 24 of the Convention provides:

> "1. In a zone of the high seas contiguous to its territorial sea, the coastal State may exercise the control necessary to:

---

[328] CCM, paras. 5.39-5.55.

[329] A. V. Lowe, "The Development of the Concept of the Contiguous Zone", *British Yearbook of International Law*, Vol. 52, 1982 (available at the Peace Palace Library).

(a) Prevent infringement of its customs, fiscal, immigration or sanitary regulations within its territory or territorial sea;

(b) Punish infringement of the above regulations committed within its territory or territorial sea.

2. The contiguous zone may not extend beyond twelve miles from the baseline from which the breadth of the territorial sea is measured.

3. Where the coasts of two States are opposite or adjacent to each other, neither of the two States is entitled, failing agreement between them to the contrary, to extend its contiguous zone beyond the median line every point of which is equidistant from the nearest points on the baselines from which the breadth of the territorial seas of the two States is measured."

UNCLOS Article 33, adopted after only limited discussion by UNCLOS III, provides:

"1. In a zone contiguous to its territorial sea, described as the contiguous zone, the coastal State may exercise the control necessary to:

(a) prevent infringement of its customs, fiscal, immigration or sanitary laws and regulations within its territory or territorial sea;

(b) punish infringement of the above laws and regulations committed within its territory or territorial sea.

2. The contiguous zone may not extend beyond 24 nautical miles from the baselines from which the breadth of the territorial sea is measured."

Article 33 UNCLOS is almost identical to Article 24 of the 1958 Convention, except for the deliberate omission of the latter's paragraph 3 (delimitation).

4.54 In its Reply, referring to the Draft Articles on the Law of the Sea adopted by the International Law Commission (ILC) in 1956, Nicaragua states that: "The matters listed in this draft article reflect State practice contemporary with its adoption".[330] And it adds,

> "none of the elements put forward by Colombia supports its argument, according to which customary international law authorises States to exercise control, in their contiguous zone, over matters other than those listed in Article 33 of UNCLOS".[331]

4.55 This tries to shift the burden of proof. It is Nicaragua that asserts that Colombia's Decree has violated the customary international law on the contiguous zone and the burden is, therefore, on Nicaragua to show that. If Nicaragua's claim is based on the customary status of Article 33, then it is for Nicaragua to establish such status, based on State practice and *opinio juris*. Not only has Nicaragua failed to do so, its own arguments and references undermine its contentions.

---

330 NR, para. 3.30.
331 NR, para. 3.40.

4.56 First, discussions over the various texts negotiated on the contiguous zone show that there were fundamental disagreements as to the texts adopted. At the time of the negotiation of the 1958 Convention and later during UNCLOS III, "customs, fiscal, immigration or sanitary laws and regulations" were considered sufficient, by some, to protect the vital interests of the coastal State. But this was far from a unanimous view. Indeed, during UNCLOS I, Poland proposed an amendment that would add "security" to the list of specified rights in Article 24. While Poland's proposal was adopted by the responsible Committee and gained the support of the majority of the participating States, it did not achieve the necessary two-thirds majority in the Plenary and so was ultimately not adopted.[332]

4.57 Nicaragua itself admits that the final text of Article 24 of the 1958 Convention was a result of compromise. Indeed, the record shows that there was no general agreement among States as to the rights of the State in the contiguous zone. Nicaragua further admits that no real agreement or exchange of views was reached during the UNCLOS negotiations.[333]

4.58 Professor Vaughan Lowe, who has acted as Counsel for Nicaragua, surveys the development of the concept of the contiguous zone, noting that when the 1958 Convention was

---

332 H. Caminos, "Contiguous Zone", *Max Planck Encyclopaedia of Public International Law*, para. 17 (available at the Peace Palace Library).

333 NR, para. 3.33.

concluded, writers such as Fitzmaurice and Lauterpacht still questioned the existence of the concept itself under international law.[334]

4.59 He notes that there was "no uniform practice establishing the agreement of parties to the 1958 Convention upon the interpretation of the contiguous zone article"[335] and that "practice is divergent, and its analysis is complicated by the emergence of claims to pollution, defence and economic zones going beyond the scope of the 1958 contiguous zone article."[336]

4.60 Lowe notes further that Article 24 was "incorporated verbatim, and without significant discussion" by UNCLOS III.[337] He concludes that,

> "*lack of agreement upon its meaning* has not affected its durability. Whatever the shortcomings it might have as a treaty provision, the 1958 formula succeeded in bringing together *a number of different approaches to maritime jurisdiction.*"[338]

[334] A. V. Lowe, "The Development of the Concept of the Contiguous Zone", *British Yearbook of International Law*, Vol. 52, 1982, pp. 158-159 (available at the Peace Palace Library).

[335] A. V. Lowe, "The Development of the Concept of the Contiguous Zone", *British Yearbook of International Law*, Vol. 52, 1982, p. 168 (available at the Peace Palace Library).

[336] A. V. Lowe, "The Development of the Concept of the Contiguous Zone", *British Yearbook of International Law*, Vol. 52, 1982, p. 168 (available at the Peace Palace Library).

[337] A. V. Lowe, "The Development of the Concept of the Contiguous Zone", *British Yearbook of International Law*, Vol. 52, 1982, p. 168 (available at the Peace Palace Library).

[338] A. V. Lowe, "The Development of the Concept of the Contiguous Zone", *British Yearbook of International Law*, Vol. 52, 1982, p. 168 (available at the Peace Palace Library). (Emphasis added).

4.61 Thus, Article 33 of UNCLOS was concluded as a compromise text when no agreement on the scope of the powers to be exercised in the contiguous zone existed. As is usual in such situations, its terms are broad and allow for various interpretations and continuing disagreement between UNCLOS parties. Therefore, those terms did not and do not adequately reflect the status of customary international law on the contiguous zone.

(2) THE CUSTOMARY INTERNATIONAL LAW ON THE CONTIGUOUS ZONE

4.62 Colombia explained in its Counter-Memorial that, under customary international law, based upon State practice and acceptance as law,[339] in an area contiguous to its territorial sea, the coastal State may exercise the control necessary to protect and safeguard its essential interests, including but not limited to those relating to customs, fiscal, immigration or sanitary laws and regulations enacted to protect its interests in its territory and territorial sea. This right enables the coastal State to safeguard its essential interests in such fields as security or drug trafficking, while limiting potential interference with the maritime rights of other States.[340] The rights of the coastal State within the contiguous zone do not extend to the resources of the sea-bed or the water column; nor do they extend to marine

339 CCM, Chapter 5.

340 H. Caminos, "Contiguous Zone", *Max Planck Encyclopaedia of Public International Law*, para. 16 (available at the Peace Palace Library).

scientific research or offshore installations of the contiguous zone.

4.63 This is also what the negotiations over the texts which became both Article 24 of the 1958 Convention and later UNCLOS Article 33 reveal. The broad language aimed at bridging the various views on the contiguous zone was intended to prevent misuse by the coastal State in ways that might undermine the rights and freedoms of other States, in particular their freedom of navigation and other internationally lawful uses of the sea, while still affording the coastal State the control necessary to protect its essential interests. These dual policies must be kept in mind in identifying the extent of contiguous zone rights under customary international law.

4.64 Nicaragua attempts to dismiss the State practice presented by Colombia in its Counter-Memorial by stating that:

> "A careful review of Colombia's Appendix B therefore shows that the State practice from which the Respondent seeks support is, at best, uncertain and does not reflect a general practice. Therefore, it cannot form the content of customary international law"[341]

But it is wholly inconsistent for Nicaragua to claim that Article 33 represents customary international law while at the same time

341 NR, para. 3.39.

asserting that the practice of States presented by Colombia "does not reflect a general practice".

4.65 The Court will encounter here a fundamental flaw recurring throughout Nicaragua's argumentation. Rather than meeting its burden of proof to establish that its rights have been violated by a Decree that is allegedly not in accordance with international law, it attempts to shift that onus to Colombia, as if it were the latter that is supposed to show that it has not violated any of Nicaragua's rights in the EEZ.

4.66 As to State practice itself, Colombia stands by the State practice put forward in its Counter-Memorial demonstrating the general practice and the content and scope of the contiguous zone, in the contemporary world.[342] Following both the 1958 Convention and UNCLOS, States have engaged in a widespread practice of adopting and enforcing legislation that expands the limitations in Articles 24 and 33. States' domestic laws and powers within the contiguous zone have come to encompass varied and legitimate concerns, ranging from security and defence to environmental protection and maritime conservation, and to cultural heritage protection.

4.67 Nicaragua's attempt to set aside this widespread practice fails for several reasons.

---

342 CCM, paras. 5.39-5.55 and Appendix B.

4.68 *First*, Nicaragua seeks to dismiss some of this practice with obscure and unconvincing reasoning. For example:

- That the Court should dismiss the "legislation of Gambia [since it] is old and unclear as it refers to 'any law or right of The Gambia'."[343] i.e. since it is expansive in its application of contiguous zone rights, it should be ignored.

- That the expansive laws of Israel and Cameroon should be ignored since they have yet to declare a contiguous zone, ignoring the substance of the laws.[344]

- That Vietnam only addresses security matters relating to third States' military vessels,[345] when in fact the "Government of the Socialist Republic of Vietnam exercises the control in its contiguous zone necessary *to see to its security* and custom and fiscal interest".[346]

- It dismisses other States' practice with the blanket statement that the practice of certain States is irrelevant because it does not mention "security". However, it is the content of the law, not the specific term used that reflects

343 NR, para. 3.38 and footnote 153.
344 NR, para. 3.38 and footnote 153.
345 NR, para. 3.38 and footnote 153.
346 Vietnam, Statement on the Territorial Sea, the Contiguous Zone, the Exclusive Economic Zone and the Continental Shelf, 1997, available at: https://www.state.gov/documents/organization/58573.pdf (last visited: 1 November 2018). (Emphasis added).

the relevant State practice. For example, Romanian law, while not referring to security, explicitly refers to control in its contiguous zone to prevent "infractions relating to the crossing of the State frontier", clearly a security consideration.[347]

4.69 Nicaragua also attempts to dismiss legislation enacted before UNCLOS as somehow irrelevant.[348] However, when current legislation was enacted is irrelevant; it represents current State practice and evidence of *opinio juris*. Moreover, if considerable legislation pre-dating UNCLOS goes beyond the scope of the latter yet is still in force, it cannot be said that UNCLOS Article 33 reflects customary international law.

4.70 Most critically, Nicaragua is mistaken since the key terms of UNCLOS Article 33 have remained unchanged from the 1958 Convention. Hence, even if the Court were to decide to adopt a cut-off date for relevant legislation and other practice, it should be the adoption of the 1958 Convention and not that of UNCLOS.

4.71 Nicaragua tries to dismiss the State practice presented as insufficient in quantity to establish the predominant State

---

[347] Romania, Act Concerning the Legal Regime of the Internal Waters, the Territorial Sea and the Contiguous Zone, 1990, Article 7, available at: http://www.un.org/depts/los/LEGISLATIONANDTREATIES/PDFFILES/ROM_1990_Act.pdf (last visited: 1 November 2018).

[348] NR, para. 3.38.

practice.[349] However, the practice put forth by Colombia represents the legislation of almost half of the States that have declared a contiguous zone.[350] That is more than sufficient to establish the predominance of practice.

4.72 Additionally, Nicaragua claims that the legislation of the States concerned differs, some claiming rights over security, others over environmental protection and so on.[351] However, Nicaragua misses the point. As explained above, the customary international law on the contiguous zone enables States to protect their interests in their territory and territorial sea with due regard for the rights of other States, such as freedom of navigation rights or EEZ rights. All of the laws and regulations concerned protect their interests in the territory and territorial sea in matters such as security, pollution, cultural heritage and so on. Thus, the State practice identified by Colombia demonstrates a common understanding of the scope and content of customary international law, as a tool to protect the State's essential interests in its territory and territorial sea.

(3) THE CORRECT INTERPRETATION OF ARTICLE 33

4.73 Under Article 33 of UNCLOS the coastal State has the right to exercise up to 24 nautical miles from its coast the control necessary to prevent and punish the infringement of its

---

349 NR, paras. 3.38-3.39.
350 CCM, Appendix B.
351 NR, para. 3.38.

customs, fiscal, immigration or sanitary laws and regulations within its territory or territorial sea.

4.74 Accordingly, even if UNCLOS Article 33 were deemed to enumerate exhaustively the customary international law rights within its contiguous zone, Colombia has the right to exercise the control necessary to prevent any actions or events that may infringe its vital interests within its territory or territorial sea as reflected in "its customs, fiscal, immigration or sanitary laws and regulations". In other words, Colombia has the right to prevent any actions taken by ships within its contiguous zone that may infringe these vital interests of Colombia, including any ships inbound into Colombia's territorial sea, which are suspected of intending to infringe Colombia's customs, fiscal, immigration or sanitary laws and regulations. Moreover, Colombia has the authority under international law to send naval vessels to pursue and apprehend any violators of such interests that fled Colombia's territorial sea and are present in its contiguous zone.

4.75 Treaty terms, including the extent of the terms "customs", "fiscal", "immigration" and "sanitary", are to be "interpreted in good faith in accordance with the ordinary meaning to be given to the terms of the treaty in their context and in the light of its object and purpose."[352]

352 Vienna Convention on the Law of Treaties, Article 31.

4.76 UNCLOS was conceived as an especially long-term treaty, intended by its drafters to put in place a legal order of the seas and oceans.[353] As a "treaty of continuing duration", drafted to endure through improvements in scientific understanding and technological developments, UNCLOS and its terms must be interpreted in an evolutionary manner. In the *Dispute regarding Navigational and Related Rights (Costa Rica* v. *Nicaragua)* case, the Court held that:

> "[W]here the parties have used generic terms in a treaty, the parties necessarily having been aware that the meaning of the terms was likely to evolve over time, and where the treaty has been entered into for a very long period or is 'of continuing duration', the parties must be presumed, as a general rule, to have intended those terms to have an evolving meaning."[354]

4.77 This holding applies to the interpretation of the generic terms "customs", "fiscal", "immigration" and "sanitary" in UNCLOS, which date back over 60 years, at least to the Draft Articles on the Law of the Sea adopted in 1956 by the ILC. The meaning of these terms changes with time and its reference tracks through time both social developments and scientific understanding; for example, the understanding of health and the factors which adversely affect it, has evolved significantly since the 1950s. There is no evidence that the participants in UNCLOS III intended the scope of terms such as these to be

353 UNCLOS, Preamble.

354 *Dispute regarding Navigational and Related Rights (Costa Rica* v. *Nicaragua), Judgment, I.C.J. Reports 2009*, p. 213, para. 66.

frozen in their 1950s understanding. On the contrary, with the recognised objective of protecting the vital interests of the coastal State, the drafters surely intended such terms to be interpreted in an evolutionary manner to assure continuous *effet utile*.

4.78 As explained above, during the drafting of UNCLOS, these generic terms were deemed to cover a coastal State's vital interests in its territory and territorial sea. The purpose of Article 33 was to endow the coastal State with sufficient control to prevent inbound threats to its territory or territorial sea from materialising and to accord adequate control to punish those who violated them, all without compromising the correlative rights of other States. Such a purpose, by its very nature, requires an evolutionary interpretation to the threats of the present, lest the threats to the coastal State evolve with time while the jurisdiction to deal with them does not. The generality of the terms selected enables a coastal State to adapt its control to the evolving threats to its vital interests.

4.79 In its 1956 report to the General Assembly, the ILC explained that:

> "The Commission did not recognize special security rights in the contiguous zone. It considered that the extreme vagueness of the term 'security' would open the way for abuses and that the granting of such rights was not necessary. The enforcement of customs and sanitary regulations will be sufficient in most cases to safeguard the

> security of the State. In so far as measures of self-defence against an imminent and direct threat to the security of the State are concerned, the Commission refers to the general principles of international law and the Charter of the United Nations."[355]

4.80 Two reasons were put forth by the ILC for the omission of an express reference to "security": (1) "security" was considered too wide a term, that could enable the coastal State to extend its jurisdiction and undermine the freedom of navigation; and (2) "customs, fiscal, immigration or sanitary laws and regulations" were considered to be sufficient to cover the security interests of the coastal State.[356]

4.81 Interpretation of a treaty term, including whether the term should be interpreted extensively or restrictively, must be performed in light of the other provisions of the treaty. In this regard, UNCLOS Article 303 is especially enlightening in that it applies a broad and flexible interpretation to the terms in

---

355 International Law Commission, "Commentary to the articles concerning the law of the sea", *Report of the International Law Commission on the Work of its Eighth Session*, A/CN.4/104, Commentary to Article 66, p. 295, para. 4, available at: http://legal.un.org/ilc/documentation/english/reports/a_cn4_104.pdf (last visited: 1 November 2018).

356 International Law Commission, "Commentary to the articles concerning the law of the sea", *Report of the International Law Commission on the Work of its Eighth Session,* A/CN.4/104, Commentary to Article 66, p. 295, para. 4, available at: http://legal.un.org/ilc/documentation/english/reports/a_cn4_104.pdf (last visited: 1 November 2018); See H. Caminos, "Contiguous Zone", *Max Planck Encyclopaedia of Public International Law*, para. 16, (available at the Peace Palace Library); J. Symonides, *The New Law of the Sea*, Polish Institute of International Affairs, 1988, p. 205 (available at the Peace Palace Library).

UNCLOS Article 33. Article 303, entitled "Archaeological and historical objects found at sea" provides that:

> "(1) States have the duty to protect objects of an archaeological and historical nature found at sea and shall cooperate for this purpose.
>
> (2) In order to control traffic in such objects, the coastal State may, in applying article 33, presume that their removal from the seabed in the zone referred to in that article without its approval would result in an infringement within its territory or territorial sea of the laws and regulations referred to in that article."

4.82 UNCLOS Article 303 not only generalises and unifies the terms "customs", "fiscal", "immigration" and "sanitary", but recognises a contiguous zone right which is, *stricto sensu*, far removed from a narrow reading of these generic terms. It interprets the potential removal of "objects of an archaeological and historical nature" to constitute an infringement of the coastal State's "customs", "fiscal", "immigration" and "sanitary" laws and regulations. Not only is this a broad interpretation of the terms in Article 33, but the objective is expanded beyond protecting the vital laws and regulations of the coastal State, to controlling traffic in archaeological and historical objects. UNCLOS Article 303 confirms that "customs", "fiscal", "immigration" and "sanitary" are generic terms providing for the protection of the vital interests of the coastal State, and that such generic terms are to be interpreted accordingly.

4.83 The proposition that the terms of UNCLOS Article 33 should be interpreted in an evolutionary manner has been supported by legal scholarship. The President of UNCLOS III, Ambassador Tommy Koh, deemed the liberal or broad interpretation of the text of UNCLOS Article 33 to represent the majority view of scholars.[357] An evolutionary interpretation of the terms in UNCLOS Article 33 was recently supported in the Proelss Commentary, which warned that

> "[a]n all too narrow interpretation of the purposes enumerated in Art. 33 should therefore not stand in the way of effectively combating new and serious threats, for example those originating in vessel-source pollution."[358]

4.84 In its Reply, Nicaragua has again labelled Colombia's protective control measures in its integral contiguous zone as contrary to the provisions of UNCLOS Article 33, which Nicaragua construes as limiting the authority of the coastal State under customary international law. The latter contention has been rebutted by Colombia in the Counter-Memorial and in this Rejoinder. Colombia will now demonstrate that the former claim

---

357 T. Koh, "The Territorial Sea, Contiguous Zone, Straits and Archipelagos under the 1982 Convention on the Law of the Sea", *Malaya Law Review*, Vol. 29, 1987, pp. 163, 174-175 (available at the Peace Palace Library). Ambassador Koh was referring to the interpretation of the term "territory or territorial sea" with respect to the question whether the coastal State may exercise the same powers with respect to inbound or outbound ships, i.e., whether it may arrest and punish inbound ships. According to Ambassador Koh, the liberal interpretation equating the powers of the coastal State in the contiguous zone and the territorial sea is the majority view. See also: J. Symonides, *The New Law of the Sea*, Polish Institute of International Affairs, 1988, pp. 205-206 (available at the Peace Palace Library).

358 Proelss Commentary, p. 267.

by Nicaragua misrepresents Colombia's contiguous zone. The contiguous zone is in full compliance with customary international law, even if the law were deemed to be limited to a strict reading of the generic terms of UNCLOS Article 33.

4.85 The powers that Colombia may exercise, theoretically, in the contiguous zone are set forth in Article 5(3) of Decree No. 1946 (as amended):

> "3. In developing what has been provided for in the previous numeral, with the purpose of protecting the sovereignty in its territory and territorial sea, in the Integral contiguous zone established in this Article Colombia exercises the faculties of enforcement and control necessary to:
>
> (a) Prevent and control the infractions of the laws and regulations related with the integral security of the State, including piracy and trafficking of drugs and psychotropic substances, as well as conduct contrary to the security in the sea and the national maritime interests, the customs, fiscal, migration and sanitary matters which take place in its insular territories or in their territorial sea. In the same manner, violations against the laws and regulations related with the preservation of the maritime environment and the cultural heritage will be prevented and controlled.
>
> (b) Punish violations of laws and regulations related to the matters indicated in section a) above, committed in its island territories or in their territorial sea."[359]

---

359 CCM, Annex 7. (Emphasis added).

4.86 A careful reading of Article 5(3) shows that Nicaragua's contention that it exceeds the recognised rights of the coastal State in the contiguous zone is meretricious. Decree No. 1946 (as amended) proclaims that Colombia has the right to exercise the control necessary to prevent actions and events that transpire in the contiguous zone, which may adversely affect its vital interests and preventive laws and regulations. The operative part of Article 5(3) extends to the prevention and control of infractions of the laws and regulations with respect to: the security of the State including from piracy and drug trafficking; conduct contrary to security at sea; the national maritime interests; customs, fiscal, migration and sanitary matters; the preservation of the marine environment; and cultural heritage. Under customary international law, all of these competences constitute lawful exercises of control by the coastal State in the contiguous zone, in order to protect vital national interests.[360] Moreover, *none* of these competences displaces or conflicts with Nicaragua's EEZ rights. Thus, even if the whole of customary international law applicable to the contiguous zone were deemed by the Court to be confined to Article 33, *quod non*, Colombia's exercise of control in its contiguous zone would still be in compliance with international law.

4.87 There is no doubt that the exercise of control with respect to "the national maritime interests, the customs, fiscal, migration and sanitary matters" are lawful exercises of control

---

360 CCM, Chapter 5.

by a coastal State in its contiguous zone. Article 5(3) of the Decree is not, however, confined to such generic terms; for the avoidance of doubt, Article 5(3) specifies, in greater detail, several key issues that affect the preventive customs, fiscal, migration and sanitary laws and regulations of Colombia.

4.88 Decree No. 1946 (as amended) provides that Colombia will exercise control to prevent infringement "of the laws and regulations related to the integral security of the State, including piracy and trafficking of drugs and psychotropic substances". Clearly, the exercise of control necessary to prevent and punish piracy and drug trafficking fits neatly in the conventional boundaries of UNCLOS Article 33. Both piracy and drug trafficking contravene the laws and regulations of the coastal State in relation to customs, fiscal and sanitary matters. A coastal State, aware that pirates attack ships inbound and outbound from its territorial sea or that drug trafficking vessels are inbound into its territorial sea or have escaped its territorial sea *en route* to their illicit markets, cannot be left powerless to stop them. A coastal State is clearly allowed to take preventive and corrective measures in its contiguous zone against pirates and drug traffickers, for both affect its vital interests in its territory or territorial sea.[361]

---

361 For example, the United States provides that in its contiguous zone, its Coast Guard may "board and search a foreign vessel suspected of smuggling drugs, carrying illegal immigrants, polluting the ocean, or tampering with sunken ships or other underwater artifacts (…)" See: Office of the Vice President of the United States, *Vice President Al Gore Announces New Action to Help Protect and Preserve U.S. Shores and Oceans*, 1999, available at:

4.89 With respect to other "laws and regulations related to the integral security of the State" and "conduct contrary to the security in the sea", Colombia submits that security has been recognised as part of the customary interpretation of UNCLOS Article 33. As detailed in the Counter-Memorial, the protection of security interests of the coastal State has been adopted by many States as part of their contiguous zone regimes.[362] In 1984, two years after the adoption of UNCLOS and when the 1958 Convention had long been in force, a Commonwealth Group of Experts explained that the coastal State's rights in the contiguous zone include safety laws and regulations: "[i]n a zone contiguous to the territorial sea, the coastal state may exercise the control necessary to prevent infringement of its customs, fiscal, immigration, health and *safety* laws and regulation".[363] In any case, as demonstrated by the examples provided in Article 5(3) of the Decree, i.e. piracy and drug trafficking, the clear intention of the Colombian law is to exercise the necessary control only over events which may adversely affect its laws and regulations in its territory and territorial sea; such actions would fall under the "customs",

---

https://clintonwhitehouse5.archives.gov/textonly/WH/EOP/OSTP/html/999_8.html (last visited: 1 November 2018). It may be recalled that, in contrast to some States in the Southwestern Caribbean Sea, Colombia has invested heavily in its capacity to prevent piracy and drug trafficking in the region. See CCM, paras. 2.98-2.109.

[362] CCM, para. 5.48 and Appendix B.

[363] Commonwealth Group of Experts, *Ocean management: a regional perspective: the prospects for Commonwealth Maritime Co-operation in Asia and the Pacific*, Commonwealth Secretariat, 1984, pp. 33-34 (available at the Peace Palace Library). Emphasis added.

"fiscal", "immigration" and "sanitary" generic categories, insofar as they are embodied in customary international law. If, however, modern security threats are deemed to extend beyond the confines of "customs", "fiscal", "immigration" and "sanitary", a contemporary and evolving interpretation of UNCLOS Article 33 should find such security interests included.

4.90 The prevention and punishment of infringement of its laws and regulations concerning the preservation of cultural heritage is explicitly included in UNCLOS Article 303. Nicaragua submits that Colombia has failed to show that UNCLOS Article 303(2) reflects customary international law.[364] Again, as throughout its Reply, Nicaragua attempts to shift the burden of proof to Colombia. As a party to UNCLOS, Nicaragua has accepted, by ratification, the interpretation of UNCLOS Article 33 as put forth in UNCLOS Article 303(2). If Nicaragua claims that UNCLOS Article 33 reflects customary international law, it must prove it; similarly, if it claims that while UNCLOS Article 33 reflects customary international law, the interpretation in UNCLOS Article 303(2) does not, it must prove it. Nicaragua has failed to do both. Colombia considers it to be irrelevant whether Article 303(2) reflects customary international law since, by ratifying UNCLOS, Nicaragua has accepted the authentic interpretation of the generic terms in Article 33 found in Article 303(2).

---

364 NR, para. 3.51.

4.91 While some controversy exists over as to the scope of the contiguous zone State's right to exercise the necessary degree of control to prevent threats to its "sanitary" laws and regulations,[365] a cogent interpretation, whether originalist or evolving, should accord the coastal State the right to exercise control in its contiguous zone over an environmental threat which threatens to adversely affect its territory or territorial sea. For example, if the coastal State is aware of actions which threaten to pollute and destroy the biosphere within its territory or its territorial sea, threatening both the health of the population and its food security, it would be unthinkable for international law to render the coastal State powerless to stop such actions from materialising.

4.92 Thus, Colombia's intention to exercise a measure of control in its contiguous zone necessary to prevent or punish violations of its laws and regulations with respect to the preservation of the environment is lawful under customary international law as well as consistent with UNCLOS Article 33.

4.93 The English word "sanitary" derives from the Latin word *sanitas*, which means "health".[366] The Oxford English

---

365 Proelss Commentary, p. 267; J. Carlson, "Presidential Proclamation 7219: Extending the United States' Contiguous Zone – Didn't Someone Say This Had Something to Do with Pollution?", *University of Miami Law Review*, Vol. 55, No. 3, 2001 (available at the Peace Palace Library).

366 Oxford Dictionary, *Sanitary,* available at: https://en.oxforddictionaries.com/definition/sanitary (last visited: 1 November 2018).

Dictionary defines the term "sanitary" as: "Relating to the conditions that affect hygiene and health, especially the supply of sewage facilities and clean drinking water." The Merriam-Webster Dictionary similarly defines "sanitary" as "relating to health".[367] In 1984, the Commonwealth Group of Experts, used the term "health" instead of "sanitary" to explain the extent of the rights within the contiguous zone.[368] It is now widely recognised by the scientific community and the general public that environmental damage is a cause of severe health problems. Indeed, the Court has recognised "that the environment is not an abstraction but represents the living space, the quality of life and the very health of human beings, including generations unborn."[369] It would thus be unreasonable to interpret the word "sanitary", which means "health", as not including environmental threats. As one commentator recently wrote "it is the 'sanitary' power that has the greatest potential to be applicable to environmental matters".[370]

[367] Merriam-Webster Dictionary, *Sanitary*, available at: https://www.merriam-webster.com/dictionary/sanitary (last visited: 1 November 2018).

[368] Commonwealth Group of Experts, *Ocean management: a regional perspective: the prospects for Commonwealth Maritime Co-operation in Asia and the Pacific*, Commonwealth Secretariat, 1984, pp. 33-34 (available at the Peace Palace Library).

[369] *Legality of the Threat or Use of Nuclear Weapons, Advisory Opinion, I. C. J. Reports 1996*, p. 226, para. 29.

[370] K. Zou, *Sustainable Development and the Law of the Sea*, Brill Nijhoff, 2017, pp. 51-52.

4.94 While some commentators have argued that "sanitary" was not intended at the Conference to include pollution,[371] several States, including the United States and Canada, have recognised that contiguous zone rights extend to environmental threats, and specifically pollution.[372] On 2 September 1999, President Clinton extended the contiguous zone of the United States to 24 nautical miles, stating in the Proclamation that the "[e]xtension of the contiguous zone of the United States to the limits permitted by international law will advance the law enforcement *and public health interests* of the United States."[373] The same day, Vice-President Gore, referring to President Clinton's Proclamation, announced that

> "[w]ithin the extended contiguous zone, the Coast Guard may now board and search a foreign vessel suspected of smuggling drugs, carrying illegal immigrants, *polluting the ocean*, or tampering with sunken ships or other underwater artifacts, without

---

371 Proelss Commentary, p. 267; see also J. Carlson, "Presidential Proclamation 7219: Extending the United States' Contiguous Zone – Didn't Someone Say This Had Something to Do with Pollution?", *University of Miami Law Review*, Vol. 55, No. 3, 2001 (available at the Peace Palace Library).

372 J. Carlson, "Presidential Proclamation 7219: Extending the United States' Contiguous Zone – Didn't Someone Say This Had Something to Do with Pollution?", *University of Miami Law Review*, Vol. 55, No. 3, 2001 (available at the Peace Palace Library); N. Wulf, "Contiguous Zone for Pollution Control", *Journal of Maritime Law and Commerce*, Vol. 3, 1972, pp. 537-558 (available at the Peace Palace Library); K. Zou, *Sustainable Development and the Law of the Sea*, Brill Nijhoff, 2017, pp. 53-54 (available at the Peace Palace Library).

373 W. Clinton, *Proclamation 7219 – Contiguous Zone of the United States*, 1999, available at: http://www.presidency.ucsb.edu/ws/?pid=56452 (last visited: 1 November 2018). (Emphasis added).

> first obtaining permission from the country where the vessel is registered."[374]

4.95 Such an interpretation is cogent: in the 21st century, it is recognised that a responsibility of the State includes taking actions to protect the health of its population. It would be unthinkable that a coastal State would recognise a potential threat to the marine environment in its contiguous zone and to the health of its population but be prevented from taking action until the threat materialised in its territory or territorial sea. Such a proposition would not only defeat the purpose of the contiguous zone, it would defy common sense.

4.96 The same approach was voiced during UNCLOS III. The representative of Algeria urged the retention of the concept of the contiguous zone, since, *inter alia*, "bearing in mind the level of pollution in the Mediterranean, he felt that his country needed strong regulations to protect the marine environment adjacent to its coasts."[375]

4.97 The Rio+20 Conference concluded that "indigenous peoples and local communities are often the most directly

---

374 Office of the Vice President of the United States, *Vice President Al Gore Announces New Action to Help Protect and Preserve U.S. Shores and Oceans*, 1999, available at: https://clintonwhitehouse5.archives.gov/textonly/WH/EOP/OSTP/html/999_8.html (last visited: 1 November 2018). (Emphasis added).

375 Official Records of the Third United Nations Conference on the Law of the Sea, A/CONF.62/C.2/SR.9, *Summary records of meetings of the Second Committee*, 9th meeting, Algeria, para. 12, available at: http://legal.un.org/docs/?path=../diplomaticconferences/1973_los/docs/english/vol_2/a_conf62_c2_sr9.pdf&lang=E (last visited: 1 November 2018).

dependent on biodiversity and ecosystems and thus are often the most immediately affected by their loss and degradation."[376] In this regard, the situation of the San Andrés Archipelago requires the exercise of control by Colombia over potential environmental damage in the contiguous zone. As Colombia explained in the Counter-Memorial, environmental damage and predatory fishing by Nicaraguan vessels are especially threatening to the Raizales, an indigenous people who depend for their livelihood and their well-being on the environment in this area of the Southwestern Caribbean Sea.[377]

4.98 Thus, under customary international law, Colombia may lawfully exercise control in its contiguous zone to protect the Raizal community from such harm to the ecosystem which threatens their health. Therefore, a hypothetical action which it might take in the contiguous zone, targeted at preventing environmental threats from impacting its territory or territorial sea and not infringing any of the specified EEZ rights of Nicaragua or other lawful international users, would be an internationally lawful use of the sea and the exercise of contiguous zone rights, under customary international law.

---

[376] United Nations General Assembly, "The Future We Want", A/66/L.56, para. 197, available at: http://undocs.org/en/A/66/L.56 (last visited: 1 November 2018).

[377] CCM, Chapter 2, Section C.

(4) The Powers Set Forth in the Decree Are Not Contrary to International Law

4.99 Even if some of the powers set forth in Article 5 of Decree No. 1946 (as amended) were beyond those to which a coastal State is entitled to exercise under the rules of customary international law on the contiguous zone (*quod non*), that would not in itself mean that those powers could not be exercised in Nicaragua's EEZ or necessarily violated Nicaragua's EEZ rights.

4.100 Since the enactment of Decree No. 1946 (as amended) in itself cannot be considered a violation of Nicaragua's rights (see Section F below), the legal issue is not the wording of the Decree, but rather if and how Nicaragua's rights in its EEZ have been violated by Colombia's actions. This is the case whether events took place within the areas covered by the Decree (and Nicaragua has not identified a single such instance) or outside those areas; and whether Colombia considered its actions to be an exercise of its contiguous zone powers or an internationally lawful use of the sea, such as the exercise of its freedoms of navigation and overflight. The answer to this latter question, one that Nicaragua has focused on, is a *non sequitur*. In all cases, the crux of the issue is identifying whether Nicaragua's sovereign rights or maritime spaces were actually violated, not how Colombia characterised its own actions.

4.101 Considering that Nicaragua has failed to point to any violation of its EEZ rights in the Colombian integral contiguous zone, there is no need for the Court to determine the conformity of Decree No. 1946 (as amended) with customary international law. Nevertheless, even if the Court took upon itself that task and found that the Decree were not in conformity with customary international law, that still does not answer the question of whether the rights of Nicaragua in its EEZ have been violated in any way.

4.102 Whether Nicaragua's rights were violated would depend upon the specific powers in question and their application. As Colombia explained above, all States enjoy extensive freedoms of navigation and overflight within the EEZs of other coastal States (including those related to security), as well as other internationally lawful uses of the sea. The exercise of these rights and freedoms additional to those that may be exercised in the contiguous zone may nevertheless be lawful under international law even if, for the purposes of Colombian domestic law, they are categorised and described as being exercisable in the contiguous zone. For international legal purposes, the way domestic law describes itself is not decisive; it is international law's characterisation which is determinative.[378] The exercise of such freedom of navigation would not violate Nicaragua's EEZ rights, which would not have been affected by the terms of the Decree. In other words,

[378] International Law Commission, "Commentary to the Draft Articles on Responsibility of States for Internationally Wrongful Acts", *Report of the International Law Commission on the Work of its Fifty-Third Session*, A/56/10, Commentary to Article 4, p. 42, para. 11, available at: http://legal.un.org/ilc/documentation/english/reports/a_56_10.pdf (last visited: 1 November 2018).

the question is not whether Colombia's contiguous zone legislation is excessive spatially or in terms of powers (*quod non*) but rather if Colombia has actually violated Nicaragua's EEZ rights.

4.103 As explained above, under customary international law, all States retain within the EEZ high seas rights and freedoms not specifically assigned to the EEZ coastal State. All of Colombia's powers under the Decree fit squarely into those residual freedoms. For example, even if control in the contiguous zone related to security were deemed beyond the evolutionary interpretation of Article 33, *quod non*, it would be a lawful exercise of control based on the freedoms of navigation and overflight, and other internationally lawful uses of the seas.

4.104 As Nicaragua, the EEZ coastal State, does not have jurisdiction, as part of the EEZ regime, to exercise control over events that affect Colombia's protective laws and regulations, the exercise of such powers by Colombia does not violate or otherwise interfere with Nicaragua's rights, whether such powers are viewed as within its contiguous zone rights or as an internationally lawful use of the sea.

4.105 At the end of the day, just as Nicaragua has failed to demonstrate more generally a violation of its EEZ rights by Colombia, so it has failed to demonstrate any such violation by the promulgation of the powers contained in Decree No. 1946 (as amended). Colombia thus requests the Court to reject

Nicaragua's argument concerning the extent of the rights in the Decree and to find that all the powers claimed by Colombia in the Decree are lawful exercises of control within a State's contiguous zone or otherwise an internationally lawful use of the sea exercised by Colombia within another State's EEZ.

E. The Outer Limits of Colombia's Contiguous Zone Do Not Contravene Nicaragua's Rights

4.106 This section responds to Nicaragua's contention that the outer limits of Colombia's contiguous zone do not conform with customary international law.

4.107 It is uncontested that all the islands in the San Andrés Archipelago are entitled to a territorial sea and consequently to a contiguous zone. As a result of their naturally unique geographic configuration, the contiguous zones of these islands intersect thus creating an integrated contiguous zone. As Colombia demonstrated in the Counter-Memorial and recalled earlier, the simplification of the contiguous zone through the use of geodetic lines, is essential to enable Colombia to adequately protect its rights within its territorial sea and terrestrial domain.[379] In contrast to Nicaragua's exaggeration, the area beyond 24 nautical miles, but within the contiguous zone that overlaps with Nicaragua's EEZ, is minimal, as can be seen in Figure CR 4.1 below.

---

379 CCM, Chapter 5.

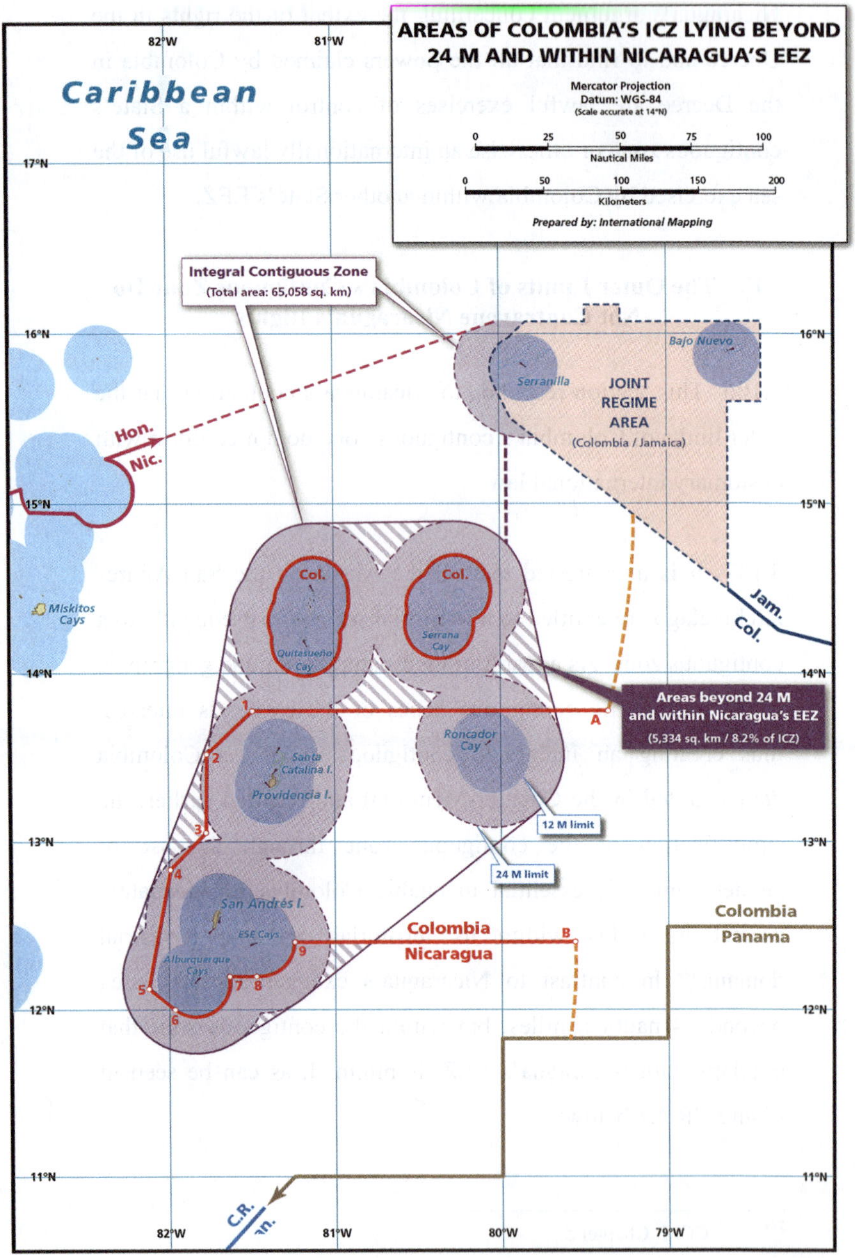
AREAS OF COLOMBIA'S ICZ LYING BEYOND 24 M AND WITHIN NICARAGUA'S EEZ
Mercator Projection
Datum: WGS-84
(Scale accurate at 14°N)
Nautical Miles
Kilometers
Prepared by: International Mapping
Caribbean Sea
Integral Contiguous Zone
(Total area: 65,058 sq. km)
Bajo Nuevo
Serranilla
JOINT REGIME AREA
(Colombia / Jamaica)
Hon.
Nic.
Miskitos Cays
Col.
Col.
Quitasueño Cay
Serrana Cay
Jam.
Col.
Areas beyond 24 M and within Nicaragua's EEZ
(5,334 sq. km / 8.2% of ICZ)
Roncador Cay
Santa Catalina I.
Providencia I.
12 M limit
24 M limit
San Andrés I.
ESE Cays
Alburquerque Cays
Colombia
Nicaragua
Colombia
Panama
C.R.
82°W
81°W
80°W
79°W
17°N
16°N
15°N
14°N
13°N
12°N
11°N

Figure CR 4.1

4.108 In the process of establishing the outer limit of its contiguous zone, Colombia first drew arcs of circle of 24 nautical miles around each of its islands in the Southwestern Caribbean Sea. The result was, however, deemed to be impractical as being unmanageable by the Colombian Navy, or in fact any other naval force under similar circumstances, as is clear when one examines the contours of the contiguous zone without the geodetic lines, as shown in Figure CR 4.2 below.

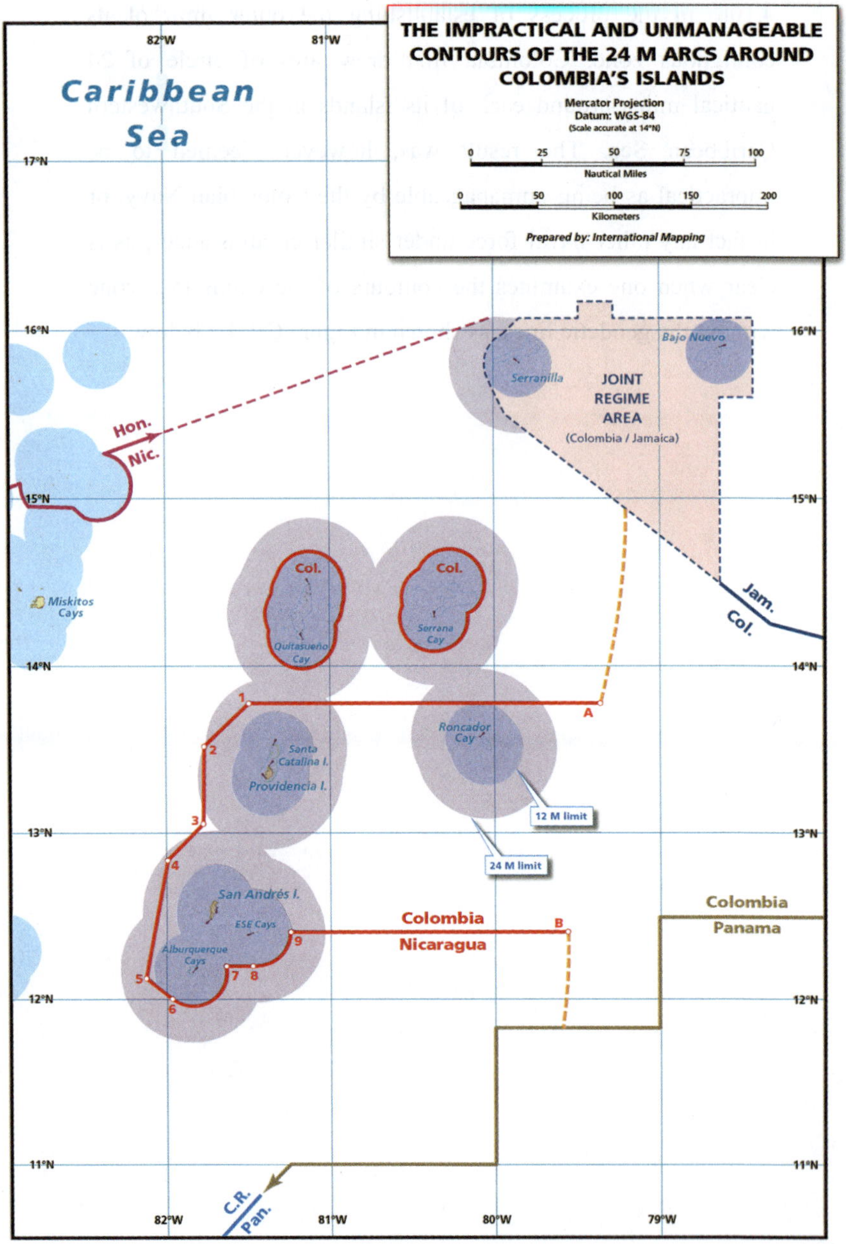
THE IMPRACTICAL AND UNMANAGEABLE CONTOURS OF THE 24 M ARCS AROUND COLOMBIA'S ISLANDS
Mercator Projection
Datum: WGS-84
(Scale accurate at 14°N)
0 25 50 75 100
Nautical Miles
0 50 100 150 200
Kilometers
Prepared by: International Mapping
Caribbean Sea
82°W
81°W
80°W
79°W
17°N
16°N
15°N
14°N
13°N
12°N
11°N
Bajo Nuevo
Serranilla
JOINT REGIME AREA
(Colombia / Jamaica)
Hon.
Nic.
Jam.
Col.
Miskitos Cays
Col.
Quitasueño Cay
Col.
Serrana Cay
Roncador Cay
Santa Catalina I.
Providencia I.
San Andrés I.
ESE Cays
Alburquerque Cays
12 M limit
24 M limit
A
B
1
2
3
4
5
6
7
8
9
Colombia
Nicaragua
Colombia
Panama
C.R.
Pan.

Figure CR 4.2

4.109 The picture says it all. Absent the simplification of the contiguous zone, a tangle of interconnected arcs, imposing significant difficulties in implementation, would be produced. Since Nicaragua has persistently failed to protect the environment and security in this part of the Southwestern Caribbean Sea, it was imperative that Colombia's contiguous zone be manageable and effective. Hence, geodetic lines were used by Colombia to connect the 24-nautical-mile arcs, thus simplifying the outer perimeter of the contiguous zone. As evident from Figure CR 4.3, the use of the geodetic lines created a contiguous zone which enables Colombia to fulfil its obligations toward the residents of the Archipelago, infringes no Nicaraguan right and is clear and understandable for other members of the international community.

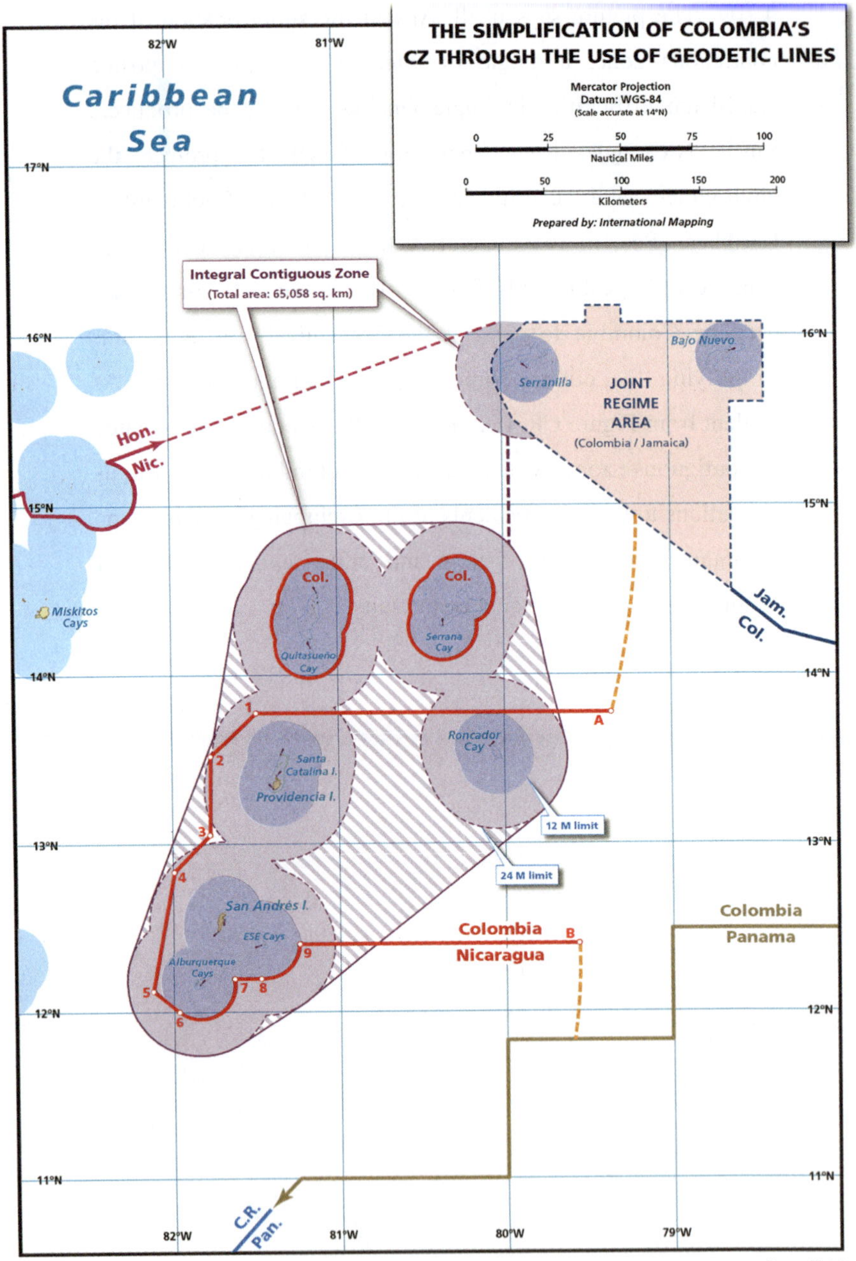
THE SIMPLIFICATION OF COLOMBIA'S CZ THROUGH THE USE OF GEODETIC LINES
Mercator Projection
Datum: WGS-84
(Scale accurate at 14°N)
Nautical Miles
Kilometers
Prepared by: International Mapping
Caribbean Sea
Integral Contiguous Zone
(Total area: 65,058 sq. km)
Hon.
Nic.
Miskitos Cays
Serranilla
Bajo Nuevo
JOINT REGIME AREA
(Colombia / Jamaica)
Jam.
Col.
Col.
Col.
Quitasueño Cay
Serrana Cay
Roncador Cay
Santa Catalina I.
Providencia I.
12 M limit
24 M limit
San Andrés I.
ESE Cays
Alburquerque Cays
Colombia
Nicaragua
Colombia
Panama
C.R.
Pan.
82°W
81°W
80°W
79°W
17°N
16°N
15°N
14°N
13°N
12°N
11°N

Figure CR 4.3

4.110 When reasonable and not excessive, a simplified line has been adapted for maritime zones in analogous circumstances. While the establishment of a contiguous zone does not require, and is not, a delimitation,[380] it is worthwhile to briefly review the judicial practice of delimitation to ascertain whether the use of geodetic lines by Colombia is a lawful practice in determining maritime zones.

4.111 As early as 1951, in *Fisheries,* the Court confirmed that in the particular circumstances of a case, methods of setting maritime boundaries or limits may depart from the general rules.[381] In cases where the geography would otherwise have produced maritime boundaries which are unmanageable or overly complicated, the Court resorted to the use of simplified and manageable lines. For example, in the 2012 Judgment, the Court decided to use a simple and straight delimitation line instead of a complicated line which follows the contours of the coasts:

---

380 As explained by the Commonwealth Group of Experts in 1984, the delimitation provision was removed from the contiguous zone because there is no need to delimit a contiguous zone; two or more contiguous zone jurisdictions may be exercised by different States in the same area. See Commonwealth Group of Experts, *Ocean management: a regional perspective: the prospects for Commonwealth Maritime Co-operation in Asia and the Pacific*, Commonwealth Secretariat, 1984, p. 39 (available at the Peace Palace Library). Hence, as explained above, a contiguous zone of State A and an EEZ of State B, may co-exist and do not require a delimitation, as both regimes bestow distinct, separate and non-conflicting sets of powers upon the States.

381 *Fisheries case, Judgment of December 18th, 1951: I.C.J. Reports 1951,* pp. 128-130.

> "The method used in the construction of the weighted line (…) results in a line which has a curved shape with a large number of turning points. Such a configuration of the line may create difficulties in its practical application. The Court therefore proceeds to a further adjustment by reducing the number of turning points and connecting them by geodetic lines. This produces a simplified weighted line which is depicted on sketch-map No. 10."[382]

Similarly, in its recent Judgment in *Maritime Delimitation in the Caribbean Sea and the Pacific Ocean (Costa Rica* v. *Nicaragua)*, the Court decided on a simplified line for delimitation. The Court said that "[g]iven the complexity of the lines described in the previous paragraph [i.e. the adjusted equidistance line], the Court considers it more appropriate to adopt a simplified line". [383]

4.112 Simplification on a limited scale is an acceptable exercise in maritime delimitation; it fulfils the purpose of arrangements ensuring the orderly management of the oceans. While not a maritime delimitation, the use of a single, simplified line for contiguous zones facilitates the management by the coastal State of its rights and duties and affords foreseeability to the international users as well as other members of the international community.

---

382 *Territorial and Maritime Dispute (Nicaragua* v. *Colombia), Judgment, I.C.J. Reports 2012,* p. 710, para. 235.

383 *Maritime Delimitation in the Caribbean Sea and the Pacific Ocean (Costa Rica* v. *Nicaragua),* Judgment of 2 February 2018, p. 63, para. 158.

4.113 As recognised by the Court in 2012, the San Andrés Archipelago presents an idiosyncratic case for setting maritime boundaries. As Sketch-Map No. 10 in the 2012 Judgment confirms, setting the boundary at the 12-nautical-mile arcs of circle of the Colombian islands would have created difficulties, hence the use of a simplified line was justified.[384] The same should apply to the 24-nautical-mile arcs around *the same* islands. The management of a contiguous zone set to the 24-nautical-mile arcs around the islands would create significant practical, navigational and administrative difficulties, which are exacerbated by the unique challenges facing littoral States of the Southwestern Caribbean Sea.[385] As explained in the Counter-Memorial and in this Rejoinder, the Raizales, whose prosperity and well-being are an urgent national and international priority, depend upon the ability of Colombia to safeguard their vital interests, *inter alia*, through the contiguous zone. Creating an effective and enforceable contiguous zone was thus imperative.

4.114 With these considerations in view, Colombia utilised geodetic lines to connect the arcs to create simplified and manageable lines for the contiguous zone. The use of straight lines to define the limits of the contiguous zone enables the Colombian Navy to efficiently protect vital interests. Moreover, the straight geodetic lines enable the other users of the Southwestern Caribbean Sea to foresee when they enter the

---

384 *Territorial and Maritime Dispute (Nicaragua* v. *Colombia), Judgment, I.C.J. Reports 2012*, p. 710, para. 235 and Sketch-Map No. 10, p. 712.

385 CCM, Chapters 2 and 5.

contiguous zone. Overall, the simplification of the contiguous zone is dictated by the geography in this part of the Southwestern Caribbean Sea.

4.115 Moreover, as Colombia demonstrated above, there is no conflict between the sovereign resource-related rights of the coastal State within its EEZ and the rights of another coastal State within its contiguous zone. The contiguous zone does not bestow upon the coastal State any territorial or sovereign rights. As the ILC stated as early as 1956, "this power of control does not change the legal status of the waters over which it is exercised."[386] In those parts of Nicaragua's EEZ, in which Colombia may exercise contiguous zone rights, whether within 24 nautical miles from the coast or as part of the simplification of the contiguous zone to enable the effective exercise of the contiguous zone rights, Nicaragua would continue to fully enjoy all the sovereign rights and jurisdiction accorded to it under the EEZ regime. Hence, the simplification of the geographical scope of the contiguous zone while providing Colombia with the ability to effectively protect its vital interests, neither undermines nor diminishes Nicaragua's sovereign rights within the EEZ; while the one derives a benefit, the other sustains no loss.

---

[386] International Law Commission, "Commentary to the articles concerning the law of the sea", *Report of the International Law Commission on the Work of its Eighth Session*, A/CN.4/104, Commentary to Article 66, p. 295, para. 1, available at: http://legal.un.org/ilc/documentation/english/reports/a_cn4_104.pdf (last visited: 1 November 2018).

4.116 Without the simplification of the contiguous zone, all maritime shipping would be subject to Colombia's contiguous zone rights within the 24-nautical-mile arcs, while unaffected in the small pockets that form part of the simplification of the contiguous zone. As evident, such areas are limited in size, and it is doubtful if any shipping passing through this area would be able to avoid completely Colombia's contiguous zone rights within the 24-nautical-mile arcs. Moreover, it is questionable if the international community would benefit from a jagged line producing erratic contiguous zone jurisdiction. As explained above, a coherent division of jurisdiction is beneficial to all users of the sea. It is also questionable whether the interests of the international community lie in allowing, unchecked, activities which may threaten the vital interests of a coastal State, for example, drug trafficking, smuggling or pollution.

4.117 Nicaragua contends that the simplification of the contiguous zone is contrary to international law since it extends beyond 24 nautical miles from the coasts of the Colombian islands. Nicaragua submits that States do not establish a contiguous zone that goes beyond 24 nautical miles from the baselines and that the 2012 Judgment is distinguishable since, to quote Nicaragua, the passage

> "concerns the simplification of a common maritime boundary between two States and not the unilateral extension by a State of one of its maritime zones

> beyond the maximum limit authorized by customary international law."[387]

Nicaragua's arguments are misleading.

4.118 In practice, contiguous zones may have been extended by other means. While States have extended their contiguous zones up to 24 nautical miles from baselines, special consideration due to the contours of the coast may have been taken into account in setting those baselines themselves. While not all straight baselines are lawful (like Nicaragua's),[388] maritime zones established on their basis, including contiguous zones, have perforce extended beyond the prescribed 24 nautical miles from normal baselines. Nicaragua's reliance on State practice thus misses the point and fails to undermine Colombia's position that particular cases justify the adjustment of maritime lines. In this case, the Court has confirmed that Colombia's Archipelago is such a special case. The geodetic lines connecting the arcs lead to the same outcome as has the simplified line used by the Court.

4.119 Nicaragua's objection to the use of simplified lines for "the unilateral extension by a State of one of its maritime zones beyond the maximum limit authorized by customary international law"[389] is puzzling. Nicaragua itself purports to use simplified lines – straight baselines – to unilaterally extend its

---

387 NR, para. 3.18.
388 See for example: CR, Chapter 6.
389 NR, para. 3.18.

jurisdiction seaward beyond the distance prescribed by international law. Nicaragua purports to extend its territorial sea and even claim internal waters in areas beyond the distance prescribed by international law! Nicaragua's excessive and unlawful use of simplified lines, and the extent to which such simplified lines is the unilateral extension by a State of one of its maritime zones beyond the maximum limit authorized by customary international law, is shown by figure 7-9 of Nicaragua's Reply:

FIGURE 7.9 OF NICARAGUA'S REPLY: NICARAGUA'S STRAIGHT BASELINES SHOWING AREAS OF INTERNAL WATERS MORE THAN 12 M FROM THE LOW WATER LINE

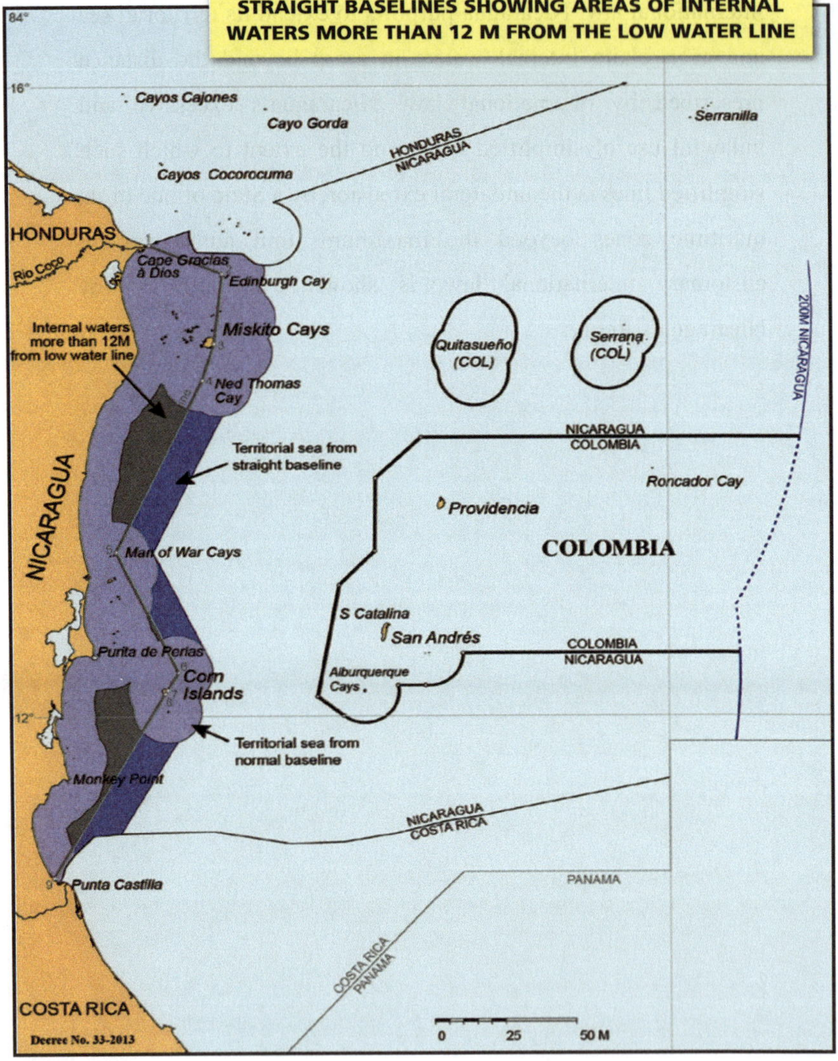

Figure CR 4.4

4.120 As Colombia will explain in Chapter 6 of this Rejoinder, Nicaragua's coast and several remote islands do not constitute an idiosyncratic case that justifies the use of simplified straight baselines for unilaterally projecting seaward all the maritime jurisdictions of the State. Far from it, Nicaragua's baselines are unlawful, exorbitant and in fact reduce the rights of Colombia and the entire international community. The point here is that Nicaragua's use of a simplified line as part of its purported straight baselines demonstrates that Nicaragua's objection to Colombia's simplified line is self-contradictory and hypocritical.

4.121 With no effect upon Nicaragua's rights, *de minimis* effect, if any, on shipping and with significant benefits to Colombia and the rest of the Southwestern Caribbean Sea, Colombia submits that the simplification of the contiguous zone promotes the public order and efficient management of the oceans and is justified based on the law and the facts. Colombia thus requests the Court to reject Nicaragua's argument against the use of a simplified line for its contiguous zone.

F. Neither the Enactment nor the Application of the Decree Violated any Rights of Nicaragua

4.122 It has already been shown that, on its face, Decree No. 1946 (as amended) does not violate Nicaragua's rights under the customary international law of the sea. In its Counter-Memorial, Colombia explained that in any event Nicaragua could not point to any action in the contiguous zone of the Colombian island territories in the Southwestern Caribbean Sea that had prejudiced Nicaragua's rights.[390]

4.123 In its Reply, Nicaragua argues that the mere enactment of Decree No. 1946 (as amended) entails Colombia's international responsibility *vis-à-vis* Nicaragua.[391] In doing so, Nicaragua seeks to make two points: *first*, that the existence of an internationally wrongful act does not depend upon injury; and *second*, that the mere enactment of legislation may constitute an internationally wrongful act.

4.124 Colombia does not contest either of these two points in principle. What it does reject is the distortion of these principles in their putative application by Nicaragua.

4.125 So far as concerns the first point, it is clear from the ILC commentary to Article 2 of the Articles on State Responsibility, quoted by Nicaragua, that whether or not injury is an element of an internationally wrongful act depends entirely on the primary obligation that is alleged to have been breached:

> "there is no exception to the principle stated in article 2 that there are two necessary conditions for an internationally wrongful act –conduct attributable to the State under international law and the breach by that conduct of an international obligation of the State. The question is whether those two necessary conditions are also sufficient.

390 CCM, paras. 5.56-5.57.

391 NR, paras. 3.53-3.60.

> It is sometimes said that international responsibility is not engaged by conduct of a State in disregard of its obligations unless some further element exists, in particular, 'damage' to another State. But whether such elements are required depends on the content of the primary obligation, and there is no general rule in this respect."[392]

4.126 Nicaragua's entire argument on whether, in the present case, the primary obligation requires "damage" consists of the following assertion:

> "In the present case, the primary obligation consists in the preservation of the *exclusive* sovereign rights belonging to Nicaragua in its EEZ in accordance with Articles 56 and 58 of the UNCLOS. By appropriating such rights to itself, Colombia has clearly entailed its international responsibility."[393]

4.127 Colombia rejects this assertion. It is thoroughly misleading to describe the primary rule as "the preservation of the exclusive sovereign rights belonging to Nicaragua in its EEZ in accordance with Articles 56 and 58 of the UNCLOS". Describing a rule in such general terms, such as "preservation" or "appropriation", sheds little, if any, light on the complex interplay between the EEZ State and other States and the obligations owed by other States towards the EEZ State in

---

392 International Law Commission, "Commentary to the Draft Articles on Responsibility of States for Internationally Wrongful Acts", *Report of the International Law Commission on the Work of its Fifty-Third Session*, A/56/10, Commentary to Article 2, p. 36, para. 9, available at: http://legal.un.org/ilc/documentation/english/reports/a_56_10.pdf (last visited: 1 November 2018).

393 NR, para. 3.56. Emphasis in the original

respect of its sovereign rights, jurisdiction and other rights and duties in the EEZ. And even if the obligation is stated in general terms – an obligation not to infringe Nicaragua's EEZ rights – Nicaragua's assertion is circular since it offers no explanation as to how Colombia has "appropriated" Nicaragua's EEZ rights. As explained above, Colombia did not appropriate any EEZ rights to itself, rather Colombia only has the right to exercise, within the contiguous zone, rights which are distinct and different from Nicaragua's EEZ rights.

4.128 Under both UNCLOS and customary international law, the relationship between the sovereign rights, jurisdiction and other rights and duties that the coastal State has and the rights and duties of other States in the EEZ requires a detailed, point-by-point analysis. Nicaragua has not even begun to attempt anything of the sort. Had it done so, it would have become clear that the enactment of Decree No. 1946 in no way violated Nicaragua's EEZ rights nor failed to accord due regard to Nicaragua's rights. As Colombia explained above, all the powers exercisable in accordance with Decree No. 1946 (as amended) are distinct from EEZ rights, are internationally lawful uses of the sea and may lawfully be exercised within another State's EEZ.

4.129 Turning to Nicaragua's second point, while it may be the case that in certain circumstances the mere enactment of legislation may constitute an internationally wrongful act that was not the case with Decree No. 1946 (as amended).

4.130 Nicaragua misstates the law when it says, baldly, that "it is unquestionable that the adoption of a national law or regulation entails the international responsibility of the enacting State."[394] Of course, it is unquestionable that an act of legislation by a State legislator, or a regulation by a government, is an act of the State for the purposes of international responsibility.[395] Thus, the enactment of Decree No. 1946 (as amended) is attributable to Colombia. But whether such enactment entails a breach of an international obligation is quite another matter.

4.131 Whether the mere enactment of Decree No. 1946 (as amended), notwithstanding the lack of any act of implementation or any application whatsoever, can be considered a violation of international law depends upon a close examination of the case-law and the particular facts of the present case, something Nicaragua has failed to perform.

4.132 According to the commentary to the ILC Articles on State Responsibility,

> "The question often arises whether an obligation is breached by the enactment of legislation by a State, in cases where the content of the legislation prima

---

394 NR, para. 3.60.

395 International Law Commission, "Commentary to the Draft Articles on Responsibility of States for Internationally Wrongful Acts", *Report of the International Law Commission on the Work of its Fifty-Third Session*, A/56/10, Commentary to Article 4, p. 40, para. 1, available at: http://legal.un.org/ilc/documentation/english/reports/a_56_10.pdf (last visited: 1 November 2018).

> facie conflicts with what is required by the international obligation, or whether the legislation has to be implemented in the given case before the breach can be said to have occurred. *Again, no general rule can be laid down that is applicable to all cases.*"[396]

4.133 This indicates that the matter is entirely case-specific. Nicaragua cites a number of cases, none of which is comparable to the present one.

4.134 Nicaragua begins with the *Case concerning certain German interests in Polish Upper Silesia*, noting that the Court examined the conformity of a Polish statute with a treaty.[397] Even if this were the case, at best it would show that, in certain circumstances, enactment of legislation can be a violation of international law. But, in fact, the Permanent Court was referring to *the application* of the law rather than its enactment:

> "The Court is certainly not called upon to interpret the Polish law as such; but there is nothing to prevent the Court's giving judgment on the question whether or not, *in applying that law*, Poland is acting in conformity with its obligations towards Germany under the Geneva Convention."[398]

---

396 International Law Commission, "Commentary to the Draft Articles on Responsibility of States for Internationally Wrongful Acts" in *Report of the International Law Commission on the Work of its Fifty-Third Session*, A/56/10, Commentary to Article 12, p. 57, para. 12, available at: http://legal.un.org/ilc/documentation/english/reports/a_56_10.pdf (last visited: 1 November 2018). (Emphasis added).

397 NR, para. 3.58.

398 *Certain German Interests in Polish Upper Silesia (Germany* v. *Poland), P.C.I.J, Series A, No. 7*, pp. 18-19. (Emphasis added).

It is also noteworthy that the matter in question concerned expropriation of property of German nationals through domestic law and its conformity with a treaty, and thus, in such a scenario, the enactment itself altered the property rights of the individuals concerned. This case does not help Nicaragua; the enactment of Decree No. 1946 did not alter or adversely affect any Nicaraguan rights.

4.135 In a footnote, Nicaragua lists a series of human rights cases.[399] It is not surprising that Nicaragua does not make more of these, since they do not assist its contention either. What they do show is that, only when the legislation has a continuing and direct effect on the claimant's human rights, then the legislation itself may amount to a violation of international law. There is indeed considerable jurisprudence from the European Court of Human Rights (ECtHR) supporting the proposition that in certain circumstances the mere enactment of legislation involves a breach of human rights obligations, but this is because of the continuous and direct effect on the individual's human rights.

4.136 In *Dudgeon* v. *The United Kingdom* for example, an Act concerning the criminalization of certain homosexual activities in place in Northern Ireland was contested. One question that arose was if the mere existence of the Act, as opposed to

---

399 NR, footnote 187.

different laws in England and Wales at the time, was of practical consequences. The United Kingdom asserted that,

> "no one was prosecuted in Northern Ireland during the period in question for an act which would clearly not have been an offence if committed in England or Wales. There is, however, no stated policy not to prosecute in respect of such acts."[400]

Thus, officially, prosecution was a matter of discretion.[401]

4.137 The ECtHR opined that:

> "[i]n the personal circumstances of the applicant, *the very existence of this legislation continuously and directly affects his private life* (…) It cannot be said that the law in question is a dead letter in this sphere. It was, and still is, applied so as to prosecute persons with regard to private consensual homosexual acts involving males under 21 years of age (see paragraph 30 above). Although no proceedings seem to have been brought in recent years with regard to such acts involving only males over 21 years of age, apart from mental patients, there is no stated policy on the part of the authorities not to enforce the law in this respect (ibid). Furthermore, apart from prosecution by the Director of Public Prosecution, there always remains the possibility of a private prosecution."[402]

---

[400] European Court of Human Rights, *Case of Dudgeon* v. *The United Kingdom*, 22 October 1981, Series A No. 45, p. 10, para. 30.

[401] European Court of Human Rights, *Case of Dudgeon* v. *The United Kingdom*, 22 October 1981, Series A No. 45, p. 10, para. 31.

[402] European Court of Human Rights, *Case of Dudgeon* v. *The United Kingdom*, 22 October 1981, Series A No. 45, p. 14, para. 41. (Emphasis added).

4.138 The Court placed emphasis on the fact that, as long as there was a possibility that the offensive act, which violated the applicant's right to privacy, may be applied, the legislation was a breach of the United Kingdom's obligations. But it did so because in the circumstances the existence of the law "continuously and directly affected" the individual applicant's personal life.

4.139 In *Modinos* v. *Cyprus*, under similar circumstances, the ECtHR repeated the requirement of continuous and direct effect on the applicant's private life. It stated that:

> "23. It is true that since the Dudgeon judgment the Attorney-General, who is vested with the power to institute or discontinue prosecutions in the public interest, has followed a consistent policy of not bringing criminal proceedings in respect of private homosexual conduct on the basis that the relevant law is a dead letter.
>
> Nevertheless, it is apparent that this policy provides no guarantee that action will not be taken by a future Attorney-General to enforce the law, particularly when regard is had to statements by Government ministers which appear to suggest that the relevant provisions of the Criminal Code are still in force (see paragraph 9 above). Moreover, it cannot be excluded, as matters stand, that the applicant's private behaviour may be the subject of investigation by the police or that an attempt may be made to bring a private prosecution against him.
>
> 24. Against this background, *the Court considers that the existence of the prohibition*

> *continuously and directly affects the applicant's private life.* There is therefore an interference."[403]

4.140 Finally, Nicaragua turns to what it terms "recent law of the sea cases". In fact, it mentions only two: *Virginia 'G'* and *Saiga (No. 2),* claiming that in these cases the International Tribunal for the Law of the Sea (ITLOS) examined the legality of the enactment of legislation.[404] However, what Nicaragua fails to acknowledge is that the Tribunal explained that the issue was pertinent, but for the reason that the *primary obligation* specifically concerned legislation:

> "Under this provision, the rights and obligations of coastal and other States under the convention arise not just from the provisions of the convention but also from national laws and regulations 'adopted by the coastal State in accordance with the provisions of this Convention'. Thus, the Tribunal is competent to determine the compatibility of such laws and regulations with the Convention."[405]

4.141 Other cases could have been mentioned, but presumably were not since they do not help Nicaragua's case. For example, in *Fisheries*, the Court characterised the dispute as follows:

> "The subject of the dispute is clearly indicated under point 8 of the Application instituting proceedings: 'The subject of the dispute is the

---

403 European Court of Human Rights, *Case of Modinos* v. *Cyprus,* 22 April 1993, Series A No. 259, p. 8, para. 24. (Emphasis added).

404 NR, para. 3.59.

405 *M/V "SAIGA" (No. 2) (Saint Vincent and the Grenadines* v. *Guinea), Judgment, ITLOS Reports 1999*, pp. 52-53, para. 121.

> validity or otherwise under international law of the lines of delimitation of the Norwegian fisheries zone laid down by the Royal Decree of 1935 for that part of Norway which is situated northward of 66°28.8' North latitude.' And further on: '.... the question at issue between the two Governments is whether the lines prescribed by the Royal Decree of 1935 as the base-lines for the delimitation of the fisheries zone have or have not been drawn in accordance with the applicable rules of international law'."[406]

4.142 However, what prompted the United Kingdom's application was the implementation of the Royal Decree by Norway against British nationals fishing in the waters covered by it.[407] Thus, it cannot be said that the case stands for the proposition that a law or regulation that contradicts international law on its face necessarily constitutes a breach of international law.

4.143 The same reasoning is found in a decision of a World Trade Organisation (WTO) Panel. On a general note it found that,

> "under traditional public international law, legislation under which an eventual violation could, or even would, subsequently take place,

---

406 *Fisheries case, Judgment of December 18th, 1951: I.C.J. Reports 1951*, p. 125.
407 *Fisheries case, Judgment of December 18th, 1951: I.C.J. Reports 1951*, p. 125.

> does not normally in and of itself engage State responsibility."[408]

This is the case, it added, when obligations "concern only the relations between States, State responsibility is incurred only when an actual violation takes place".[409]

4.144 In the *LaGrand* case,[410] the Court distinguished between the existence of a domestic law and its application in a given case, emphasizing that it is the latter that could constitute a violation of international law. The law in question was not problematic in itself, as it could have been applied in accordance with international law. It was only its application in violation of the Vienna Convention on Consular Relations that may constitute an internationally wrongful act.

4.145 The case law thus indicates that *only* when the domestic law *is applied* in violation of international law an internationally wrongful act may occur.

4.146 Correspondingly, the ILC commentary to the Articles on State Responsibility notes that:

---

[408] World Trade Organisation, *United States – Sections 301-310 of the Trade Act of 1974*, Report of the Panel, WT/DS152/R, 22 December 1999, p. 322, para. 7.80.

[409] World Trade Organisation, *United States – Sections 301-310 of the Trade Act of 1974*, Report of the Panel, WT/DS152/R, 22 December 1999, p. 322, para. 7.81.

[410] *LaGrand (Germany* v. *United States of America), Judgment, I.C.J. Reports 2001*, p. 466, para. 125.

> "In other circumstances, the enactment of legislation may not in and of itself amount to a breach, especially if it is open to the State concerned to give effect to the legislation in a way which would not violate the international obligation in question. In such cases, whether there is a breach will depend on whether and how the legislation is given effect."[411]

4.147 As indicated above, Decree No. 1946 (as amended) provides that it is intended to:

> "Prevent and control the infractions of the laws and regulations related with the integral security of the State, including piracy and trafficking of drugs and psychotropic substances, as well as conduct contrary to the security in the sea and the national maritime interests, the customs, fiscal, migration and sanitary matters which take place in its insular territories or in their territorial sea. In the same manner, violations against the laws and regulations related with the preservation of the maritime environment and the cultural heritage will be prevented and controlled."[412]

4.148 Even if this were not in conformity with the customary international law applicable to the contiguous zone (*quod non*), or the rights of all States within the EEZ (*quod non*), the mere existence of the Decree would not constitute a violation of

---

[411] International Law Commission, "Commentary to the Draft Articles on Responsibility of States for Internationally Wrongful Acts", *Report of the International Law Commission on the Work of its Fifty-Third Session*, A/56/10, Commentary to Article 12, p. 57, para. 12, available at: http://legal.un.org/ilc/documentation/english/reports/a_56_10.pdf (last visited: 1 November 2018).

[412] CCM, Annex 7.

international law. The Decree can and will be implemented in accordance with international law. The Decree itself states that:

> "The application of this article [Article 5 on the contiguous zone] will be carried out in conformity with international law and Article 7 of the present Decree."[413]

And Article 7 reads,

> "Nothing in this Decree will be understood to affect or limit the rights and obligations derived from the 'Treaty on maritime delimitation between the Republic of Colombia and Jamaica' signed between those States on 12 November 1993, *nor will it affect or limit the rights of other states*."[414]

4.149 Decree No. 1946 (as amended), in itself and on its face, is not in conflict with international law and, as in the *LaGrand* case, should only be evaluated based on whether or not its implementation violates Nicaragua's EEZ rights. The Decree itself is in conformity with international law and does not allow for any potential breaches of Nicaragua's EEZ.

4.150 Just as the mere enactment of the Decree is neither contrary to international law nor has violated Nicaragua's rights, the same has to be said about its application. Nicaragua has failed to show a single instance where Colombia has impeded it from exercising its EEZ rights within Colombia's contiguous

---

413 CCM, Annex 7.

414 CCM, Annex 7. (Emphasis added).

zone. The inescapable conclusion is that no Colombian action in the contiguous zone has given rise to any violation of Nicaragua's sovereign rights or maritime spaces.

G. Conclusions

4.151 Decree No. 1946 of 9 September 2013 (as amended by Decree No. 1119 of 17 June 2014) established the contiguous zone of the Colombian island territories in the Southwestern Caribbean Sea, in accordance with international law. It is clear on the face of the Decree that it is to be interpreted and applied in full conformity with the customary international law of the sea.

4.152 There is nothing in customary international law that precludes Colombia's contiguous zone from extending into Nicaragua's EEZ or that precludes Colombia from exercising the corresponding rights and freedoms therein.

4.153 None of the powers provided for in the Decree go beyond those which Colombia is entitled to exercise under customary international law as part of the contiguous zone regime; but even if this were not the case, that would not mean that they were necessarily contrary to international law since a State enjoys residual freedoms of navigation and overflight, as well as other internationally lawful uses of the sea within another State's EEZ.

4.154 The simplification of the outer limit of the Colombian contiguous zone in the Southwestern Caribbean Sea is justified in law and on the facts, and, in any event, does not encroach upon Nicaragua's EEZ rights.

4.155 Finally, Nicaragua cannot argue that the mere enactment of the Decree nor its application has violated any rights of Nicaragua under international law. It has failed to show that it has suffered any injury whatsoever as a result of the enactment or application of the Decree.

PART III

COLOMBIA'S COUNTER-CLAIMS

Chapter 5

NICARAGUA'S INFRINGEMENT OF THE TRADITIONAL FISHING RIGHTS OF THE INHABITANTS OF THE SAN ANDRÉS ARCHIPELAGO

A. Introduction

5.1 Although Nicaragua recognised on numerous occasions, through the statements of its President, the traditional fishing rights of the inhabitants of the San Andrés Archipelago, in particular the Raizales,[415] Colombia must regretfully note that the Applicant is using the current pending proceedings to take the President's words back. Nicaragua's judicial strategy, after the Court ruled Colombia's third counter-claim admissible, is to deny the existence of the vested traditional fishing rights of this vulnerable community,[416] as well as their infringement.[417]

5.2 Nicaragua cannot undo what it has already acknowledged to exist. President Ortega's statements are the Achilles' heel in the Nicaraguan argumentation. Its Reply, which cannot and in fact does not feign ignorance of these declarations,[418] perversely suggests that the President's conciliatory tone merely stands for "the unremarkable proposition that continued fishing in Nicaragua's EEZ by the

---

415 CCM, paras. 3.93-3.94 and Annexes 73-77; CR, Section D *infra*.
416 NR, paras. 6.3-6.76.
417 NR, paras. 6.77-6.95.
418 NR, paras. 6.63-6.76.

Raizales would have the [sic] be the subject of an agreement".[419] In other words, Nicaragua distorts the words of its own President in an attempt to prove that, although it is apparently ready to accommodate the rights of the artisanal fishermen of the Archipelago in a further agreement, it has not recognised the existence of these vested rights as of today.[420] This account reveals the lack of weight of Nicaragua's overall argument, which blurs the distinction between the recognition of the traditional fishing rights regime and the separate matter of the conclusion of technical agreements fleshing out that regime.[421] What is more, Nicaragua's reading of the statements of its Head of State conflicts with the finding, consistently upheld in the jurisprudence, according to which bilateral agreements are not necessary for the perpetuation of acquired rights.

5.3 The express recognition by the President of Nicaragua of the traditional fishing rights of the inhabitants of the San Andrés Archipelago should, in itself, be sufficient to dispose of its belated attempt to repudiate those rights. But Nicaragua has unsurprisingly diverted the focus to other matters. In particular, its Reply relies on convoluted interpretations of UNCLOS, an instrument to which Colombia is not a Party, to assert that all historic rights have somehow evaporated due to the appearance of the EEZ in international law.[422] Nicaragua draws no inference from the fact that the historic rights at stake here are merely

419 NR, para. 6.73.
420 NR, paras. 6.70-6.76 and 6.94.
421 See Section D *infra*.
422 NR, paras. 6.3-6.30.

traditional fishing rights vested on the inhabitants of the Archipelago instead of exclusive sovereign rights of Colombia.[423] To the contrary, Nicaragua erroneously puts all historic rights under the exceptional rights umbrella.[424] Turning the relevant test upside-down, Nicaragua wrongly suggests that, in order not to be extinguished, traditional fishing rights require "express carve-outs" in multilateral or bilateral agreements.[425] What is more, Nicaragua barely hides the fact that its reasoning leads to the disingenuous result according to which traditional rights in general can exist within the land territory, internal waters, territorial sea and archipelagic waters of a State, but not in its EEZ.

5.4 Additionally, Nicaragua criticizes the evidence put forward by Colombia. According to the Applicant, Colombia has neither proven the existence of the traditional fishing rights,[426] nor their infringement by Nicaragua's Naval Force.[427] Partially quoting from the sworn affidavits, Nicaragua's Reply heightens the threshold for establishing the existence of those vested rights in a manner that clearly contradicts the practical

---

423 CPO, Annex 10: Declaration of the President of the Republic of Colombia, 18 February 2013, "Colombian fishermen will be able to exercise – and we have said this clearly – their historical fishing rights in all places where they have been fishing before."; CCM, Annex 1: Press Release from the Ministry of Foreign Affairs with regard to the Seaflower Biosphere Reserve, 30 August 2013, "(…) Colombia is analysing the mechanisms, resources and actions available to it under domestic laws and international law, to promote the defense of national interests, historic fishing rights and the rights of the Colombian population of the Archipelago."

424 NR, para. 6.15.

425 NR, paras. 6.13-6.17.

426 NR, paras. 6.32-6.62.

427 NR, paras. 6.77-6.95.

considerations underpinning the consistent jurisprudence on this matter.[428]

5.5 Nicaragua's stance regarding the law and the evidence attests to the fact that the dispute concerns not only the infringement but also, and in particular, the very existence of the traditional fishing rights, which the Nicaraguan Reply seeks to deny in no less than 25 of the 31 pages devoted to this counter-claim. This is why Colombia respectfully requests the Court to find, on the one hand, that the traditional fishing rights of the inhabitants of the San Andrés Archipelago do exist and, on the other hand, that they have been breached.

5.6 Colombia will first recall the importance of traditional fishing for the inhabitants of the San Andrés Archipelago, the human factor that Nicaragua has ignored in its Reply (Section B). It will then refute Nicaragua's contention according to which the traditional fishing rights have been extinguished either by the emergence of the EEZ or the 2012 Judgment (Section C). After that, Colombia will show that, in any event, Nicaragua has recognised the traditional fishing rights in the aftermath of the appearance of the EEZ and of the 2012 Judgment. Accordingly, even if the Court were to agree with Nicaragua's contention that the vested rights could be superseded solely in the establishment of the regime of the EEZ, *quod non*, nothing precluded the

---

428 *Dispute regarding Navigational and Related Rights (Costa Rica* v. *Nicaragua), Judgment, I.C.J. Reports 2009*, p. 213, para. 141; *The South China Sea Arbitration (Philippines* v. *China), Award of 12 July 2016, PCA Case No. 2013-19*, p. 315, paras. 805-807.

parties to agree otherwise, as they have expressly done (Section D). Afterwards, Colombia will demonstrate that, in light also of the nature of the practices at stake and of the remoteness of the maritime areas in question, it has met the threshold for proving the existence of the traditional fishing rights (Section E). Finally, Colombia will show that the Nicaraguan Naval Force has violated the traditional fishing rights of the inhabitants of the Archipelago (Section F).

B. The Dependence of the Inhabitants of the Archipelago on Their Traditional Fishing in the Southwestern Caribbean Sea

5.7 Colombia already addressed in its Counter-Memorial the historical evolution of the traditional fishing rights at issue, the definition of artisanal as opposed to subsistence and industrial fishing, as well as the social and economic implications of this practice for the inhabitants of the Archipelago, in particular, the Raizal people.[429] Nicaragua, which for the most part does not dispute this "narrative",[430] asserted in its Reply that it is ready to take into account "the fishing needs of the Raizales".[431] While it is true that the Reply has raised challenges to some aspects of the affidavits filed by Colombia that will be addressed in Sections E and F, Nicaragua remained silent with regard to the historical and anthropological developments included in the

---

429 CCM, paras. 2.61-2.86.

430 NR, para. 6.3.

431 NR, para. 6.76.

Counter-Memorial. Rather than reiterating these developments, Colombia will summarize their most fundamental aspects.

5.8 Artisanal fishermen clearly play a crucial role in the San Andrés Archipelago. Aside from its economic and social importance, traditional fishing ensures food security on San Andrés and Providencia.[432] This is why cooperatives, such as "Fish and Farm", and associations, such as the "Association of Fishermen and Farmers of San Andrés and Providencia" (ASOPACFA, from its Spanish acronym), have policies providing that the products must first be sold to the local community.[433] In this respect, there is in fact a degree of overlap between the notions of artisanal and subsistence fishing.[434] While artisanal practices have a commercial component, they also carry an important role for the subsistence of the inhabitants of the Archipelago. Contrary to industrial fishermen, artisanal fishermen do not engage in large-scale fishing activities in boats that trawl with big nets or huge numbers of hooks.[435] However, traditional fishing is not fixed in time in the sense that vessels, gear and techniques are not susceptible of being improved.[436]

---

432 CCM, Annexes 62, 65, 71 and 72.

433 CCM, Annexes 62 and 68.

434 CCM, paras. 2.69-2.70.

435 CCM, para. 2.71.

436 *Award of the Arbitral Tribunal in the Second Stage of the Proceedings between Eritrea and Yemen (Maritime Delimitation)*, Decision of 17 December 1999, R.I.A.A., Vol. XXII, p. 360, para. 106.

5.9 In order to reach the traditional fishing grounds of Cape Bank[437] and the Northern Cays (Serrana, Quitasueño, Roncador, Serranilla and Bajo Nuevo), the artisanal fishermen of the Archipelago initially relied on schooners, sloops and catboats and later, during the second half of the twentieth century, on *lanchas* equipped with outboard or inboard motors.[438] Because of its unique traits, turtling is the activity that mainly attracted the interest of the record keepers, historians and anthropologists who studied the Archipelago.[439] However, fishing was equally important to the men and women of the sea who settled in this remote part of the Southwestern Caribbean Sea. Due to the reduced land available for agriculture, life in the Archipelago always depended on what the sea could offer and the trade of its resources with the other coastal communities.

5.10 The inhabitants of the Archipelago were remarkable seafarers that held close ties with the coastal communities based in the Mosquito Coast, Costa Rica, Panama, Jamaica, the Cayman Islands and continental Colombia. They did not live secluded on their islands, but instead navigated and established settlements in the whole Southwestern Caribbean Sea. The Raizales constitute a distinct ethnic and cultural community and are still present in many of the coastal States of the region. Their intimate connection with the sea is best exemplified by the fact that they navigated, traded and fished in this area of the

---

437 For a description of the geographical area known as Cape Bank, which includes *Luna Verde*, see Section E *infra*.

438 CCM, Annexes 65, 66, 69 and 91.

439 CCM, Annex 93.

Southwestern Caribbean Sea before and after the coming into existence of Nicaragua and Colombia as independent States.

C. The Traditional Fishing Rights Survived the Emergence of the EEZ Regime and the 2012 Judgment

5.11 Nicaragua has made two distinct arguments in its attempt to prove that historic rights *in abstracto*, regardless of their characterisations, can be superseded. First and foremost, Nicaragua relies on the emergence of the EEZ to argue that the vested rights of the inhabitants of the San Andrés Archipelago have been extinguished "as early as 1984" with the crystallisation of the new regime under general international law.[440] Alternatively, Nicaragua indirectly suggests that these rights have been ousted by the 2012 Judgment.

5.12 In relation to the second argument, Colombia's Counter-Memorial[441] has already shown that, according to the consistent jurisprudence, rights vested on the inhabitants of border regions remain unaffected by delimitation processes both on land and in the sea.[442] Colombia's Rejoinder can hence be brief on this point

---

440 NR, para. 6.6.

441 CCM, paras. 3.98-3.111.

442 *Award in the Arbitration regarding the delimitation of the Abyei Area between the Government of Sudan and the Sudan People's Liberation Movement/Army*, Award of 22 July 2009, R.I.A.A., Vol. XXX, p. 408, para. 753; *Award of the Arbitral Tribunal in the First Stage of the Proceedings between Eritrea and Yemen (Territorial Sovereignty and Scope of the Dispute)*, Decision of 9 October 1998, R.I.A.A., Vol. XXII, p. 244, para. 126; *Award of the Arbitral Tribunal in the Second Stage of the Proceedings between Eritrea and Yemen (Maritime Delimitation)*, Decision of 17 December 1999, R.I.A.A., Vol. XXII, p. 361, paras. 110-111; *Arbitration between Barbados and the Republic of Trinidad and Tobago, relating to the*

since Nicaragua does not even attempt to rebut the argument by challenging the jurisprudence. Nicaragua's Reply merely relies on the misleading contention according to which it is apparently "revealing" that Colombia "did not see fit during the previous case to even advert to the existence of the rights it now claims".[443] Regardless of Nicaragua's perceptions as to what is revealing or not, the fact remains that the Court, as well as arbitral tribunals, have consistently denied any role to the conduct of private individuals for the specific purpose of determining the course of boundaries. Accordingly, Nicaragua's conjectures in this regard are wholly irrelevant.

5.13 Colombia will thus focus its attention on Nicaragua's legal argument that the traditional fishing rights "were extinguished with the creation of the EEZ regime".[444] It is worth noting from the outset that Nicaragua's proposition is not premised on the existence of a provision, under conventional or customary law, which would explicitly prohibit traditional fishing rights within the EEZ. With regard to UNCLOS, such an enquiry would indeed be futile since the parties agree that Part V does not proscribe traditional fishing rights. It is therefore not surprising that Nicaragua's Reply, rather than looking for a non-existing prohibition where there is none, self-servingly states

---

Delimitation of the Exclusive Economic Zone and the Continental Shelf between Them, R.I.A.A., Vol. XXVII, p. 227, para. 292*; Land, Island and Maritime Frontier Dispute (El Salvador/Honduras: Nicaragua intervening), Judgment, I.C.J. Reports 1992*, p. 400, para. 66; *German Settlers in Poland, Advisory Opinion, 1923 P.C.I.J. Series B, No. 6*, p. 36.

443 NR, paras. 6.40-6.43.

444 NR, para. 6.5.

that what is required is an "express carve-out", a provision preserving traditional fishing rights.[445] Relying on the maxim *expressio unius est exclusi alterius,*[446] which does not displace the rules of treaty interpretation, Nicaragua swiftly dismisses traditional fishing rights for being allegedly incompatible with the EEZ regime.

5.14 At the heart of Nicaragua's incompatibility plea lies the notion of "exclusivity":[447] the idea that coastal States enjoy sovereign rights *vis-à-vis*, among other things, the exploitation and management of the living resources of the EEZ. While the incompatibility might be true in relation to competing assertions of States aiming at regulating and managing the living resources of the coastal State, Colombia neither claims sovereignty nor sovereign rights within Nicaragua's EEZ.[448] Colombia is not even claiming rights on its own behalf since the traditional fishing rights are in fact private rights vested on the artisanal fishermen of the San Andrés Archipelago.

5.15 Colombia fails to see the reason why traditional fishing rights should be perceived as being contrary to the exclusive

---

445 NR, paras. 6.13-6.17.

446 NR, para. 6.12.

447 NR, para. 6.9.

448 CCM, para. 3.101: "It goes without saying that the customary rights in question, whose content will be developed below, are not tantamount to exclusive sovereign rights; nor do they derogate from the sovereign rights of Nicaragua. These traditional rights are not even to be considered the customary equivalent of a joint regime area (…). Rather the nature of these rights is more limited. They are merely customary rights of access and exploitation that fall well short of a claim of sovereignty or of sovereign rights (…)."

rights of the coastal State within the EEZ. After all, States enjoy full-fledged sovereignty, which is also exclusive, within their territory, but Nicaragua does not dispute that traditional rights have generally been preserved both in the land territory, internal waters and territorial sea of States. Hence, the exclusive nature of the rights involved cannot, by itself, justify Nicaragua's proposition. If traditional rights can subsist within areas where States enjoy sovereignty, *a fortiori* they can also exist within areas in which States merely enjoy sovereign rights.

5.16 In its effort to demonstrate that what is required is a "carve-out" explicitly preserving traditional rights, Nicaragua has sought to depict historic rights as generally being exceptional in nature. Yet, historic is not tantamount to exceptional, and a document of the United Nations Secretariat, which Nicaragua partially quotes,[449] gives a more nuanced account of the debate on the point. Indeed, the 1962 UN study on the *Juridical Regime of Historic Waters Including Historic Bays* does not boil down all instances of historic claims to the assertion of exceptional rights. On the contrary, the authors of the study addressed at length the question whether historic rights necessarily constitute "exceptional regimes",[450] "prescriptive

---

[449] NR, para. 6.15.

[450] United Nations, *Juridical Regime of Historic waters including historic bays – Study prepared by the Secretariat*, Doc. A/CN.4/143, pp. 7-11, paras. 42-61, available at: http://legal.un.org/ilc/documentation/english/a_cn4_143.pdf (last visited: 1 November 2018).

rights"[451] and "exceptions to rules laid down in a general convention".[452] The study sensibly reached the conclusion that it depends on the circumstances. If a certain subject-matter has not been regulated within a convention, such as one of the treaties concluded at UNCLOS I, it is pointless to reserve the historic right in a provision.[453] In others words, it is only when the convention and the historic right clearly conflict that the absence of a carve-out might be of relevance.

5.17 Since historic rights are not necessarily exceptional rights, Nicaragua is mistaken in suggesting that "carve-outs" are always required. The question that arises is whether non-exclusive traditional fishing rights vested in the inhabitants of a border region are incompatible with the coastal State's sovereign rights to such an extent that an express reservation would be required under the relevant applicable law. As stated by Norway in the *Fisheries (United Kingdom* v. *Norway)* case, and quoted in the 1951 Judgment,

> "[t]he Norwegian Government does not rely upon history to justify exceptional rights, to claim areas

[451] United Nations, *Juridical Regime of Historic waters including historic bays – Study prepared by the Secretariat*, Doc. A/CN.4/143, pp. 11-12, paras. 62-68, available at: http://legal.un.org/ilc/documentation/english/a_cn4_143.pdf (last visited: 1 November 2018).

[452] United Nations, *Juridical Regime of Historic waters including historic bays – Study prepared by the Secretariat*, Doc. A/CN.4/143, pp. 12-13, paras. 72-79, available at: http://legal.un.org/ilc/documentation/english/a_cn4_143.pdf (last visited: 1 November 2018).

[453] United Nations, *Juridical Regime of Historic waters including historic bays – Study prepared by the Secretariat*, Doc. A/CN.4/143, pp. 12-13, paras. 75-77, available at: http://legal.un.org/ilc/documentation/english/a_cn4_143.pdf (last visited: 1 November 2018).

> of sea which the general law would deny; it invokes history, together with other factors, to justify the way in which it applies the general law".[454]

In that case, the Court found in favour of Norway because it could not be said that its historic claim conflicted with customary international law, which is the law also applicable to the present case. No carve-out was required and yet, if Nicaragua's approach as to what constitutes conflict were to be followed, Norway's straight baselines decree could have been said to be contrary to the rule according to which the baseline should follow the low-water mark on permanent land. In other words, it is only when the incompatibility is manifest that a carve-out is required.

5.18 Nicaragua in the end mainly relies on one single paragraph of an UNCLOS provision to put forward its thesis that traditional fishing rights have been extinguished in the EEZ.[455] Article 62(3) states that:

> "In giving access to other States to its exclusive economic zone under this article, the coastal State shall take into account all relevant factors, including, *inter alia*, the significance of the living resources of the area to the economy of the coastal State concerned and its other national interests, the provisions of articles 69 and 70, the requirements

---

[454] *Fisheries case, Judgment of December 18th, 1951: I.CJ. Reports 1951*, p. 133; see also M. Bourquin, *Les baies historiques*, Mélanges Georges Sauser-Hall, 1952, pp. 37-51 (available at the Peace Palace Library).

[455] NR, paras. 6.16-6.17.

> of developing States in the subregion or region in harvesting part of the surplus and the need to minimize economic dislocation in States whose nationals have habitually fished in the zone or which have made substantial efforts in research and identification of stocks."

This provision, which has to do with the optimum utilisation of the living resources in the EEZ, mentions the need to minimize economic dislocation in States "whose nationals have habitually fished in the zone". But this reference to "habitual fishing", which could easily encompass industrial fishing from distant fleets and is not equivalent to the notion of "traditional fishing rights", is not concerned with acquired rights vested on individuals and communities. The provision only deals with "giving access to other States" and, far from being incompatible with private rights of artisanal fishermen, can be applied alongside the traditional rights regimes. Because Nicaragua relies on this provision, it is worth mentioning in passing that as of November 2018, that is to say 18 years after it became a Party to UNCLOS, Nicaragua has yet to determine the allowable catch in its EEZ.

5.19 Article 51 of UNCLOS regarding archipelagic waters is the only provision in that instrument that specifically mentions traditional fishing rights in a maritime area. According to Nicaragua, this provision sets the relevant standard: "the fact that there is no analogous provision in Part V can only mean that traditional fishing rights do not exist in the EEZ".[456] But Nicaragua's argument fails to recognise that, notwithstanding the absence of a similar provision within Part II of UNCLOS, traditional fishing rights have not been superseded in the territorial sea either. With regard to this maritime area, it appears that Article 2(3) of UNCLOS, a provision which broadly states that "[t]he sovereignty over the territorial sea is exercised subject to this Convention and to other rules of international law", is equally protective of traditional fishing rights. Thus, when it comes to the EEZ, Nicaragua cannot rely on the absence of an explicit permissive provision to put forward its claim that traditional fishing rights have been extinguished. What is more, Nicaragua cannot ignore the fact that Article 58(2) of UNCLOS on the rights and duties of other States in the EEZ provides, in a manner reminiscent of Article 2(3) that "other pertinent rules of international law apply to the exclusive economic zone in so far as they are not incompatible with this Part".

5.20 Nicaragua's Reply deliberately ignores both the *Award in the Arbitration regarding the Delimitation of the Abyei Area* and the decision in the *Arbitration between Barbados and the Republic of Trinidad and Tobago*, which were already mentioned in the Counter-Memorial.[457] The former concluded that "the transfer of sovereignty should not be construed to extinguish traditional rights to the use of land (or maritime

---

456 NR, para. 6.14.
457 CCM, paras. 3.98 and 3.105.

resources)" without drawing any distinction between different maritime areas.[458] The second specifically mentioned that, notwithstanding the delimitation, Trinidad and Tobago had an obligation to grant "Barbados access to fisheries within [its] EEZ".[459]

5.21 Nicaragua's Reply does, however, clumsily attempt to deny the relevance of the *Award of the Arbitral Tribunal in the Second Stage of the Proceedings between Eritrea and Yemen (Maritime Delimitation)* to the present proceedings. Nicaragua recognises that this award found that traditional fishing rights existed within the EEZ of the coastal States involved.[460] Yet it asserts that, because Article 2(3) of the Arbitration agreement authorized the Tribunal to take into account "any pertinent factor", in addition to UNCLOS, it must follow that the "arbitral tribunal did not rely on UNCLOS in rendering its decision on historic fishing rights".[461]

5.22 Remarkably, Nicaragua's Reply fails to cite a single paragraph from Chapter IV of the Second Stage Award, the

---

458 *Award in the Arbitration regarding the Delimitation of the Abyei Area between the Government of Sudan and the Sudan People's Liberation Movement/Army*, Award of 22 July 2009, R.I.A.A., Vol. XXX, p. 408, para. 753.

459 *Arbitration between Barbados and the Republic of Trinidad and Tobago, relating to the Delimitation of the Exclusive Economic Zone and the Continental Shelf between Them*, R.I.A.A., Vol. XXVII, p. 227, para. 292.

460 NR, para. 6.24.

461 NR, para. 6.29.

section that addressed the "traditional fishing regime".[462] Nicaragua draws no inference from the fact that the Tribunal made no reference to pertinent factors in the relevant paragraphs. But, aside from the fact that the Tribunal explicitly rejected this speculative argument, Nicaragua's explanation is counter-intuitive. Indeed, even if "the tribunal was empowered to look beyond the terms of UNCLOS",[463] no judge or arbitrator would give pre-eminence to a pertinent factor over UNCLOS if the two were truly conflicting and the latter was applicable to the parties. As the Arbitral Tribunal stated:

> "The traditional fishing regime is not limited to the territorial waters of specified islands; nor are its limits drawn by reference to claimed past patterns of fishing. (…) *By its very nature it is not qualified by the maritime zones specified under the United Nations Convention on the Law of the Sea, the law chosen by the Parties to be applicable to this task in this Second Stage of the Arbitration.* The traditional fishing regime operates throughout those waters beyond the territorial waters of each of the Parties, and also in their territorial waters and ports, to the extent and in the manner specified in paragraph 107."[464]

Given the jurisprudence, Nicaragua's applicable law-based explanation is a last-ditch attempt to clutch at straws.

---

462 *Award of the Arbitral Tribunal in the Second Stage of the Proceedings between Eritrea and Yemen (Maritime Delimitation)*, Decision of 17 December 1999, R.I.A.A., Vol. XXII, pp. 356-361, paras. 87-111.

463 NR, para. 6.27.

464 *Award of the Arbitral Tribunal in the Second Stage of the Proceedings between Eritrea and Yemen (Maritime Delimitation)*, Decision of 17 December 1999, R.I.A.A., Vol. XXII, p. 361, para. 109. (Emphasis added).

5.23 Aside from the purported incompatibility theory, Nicaragua stresses that historic rights premised on "[t]he exercise of freedoms permitted under international law cannot give rise to a historic right" because nothing calls for acquiescence if it is done in conformity with international law.[465] This argument, which again assumes that traditional fishing rights are necessarily exceptional rights that must contradict other rules of international law, is not pertinent with regard to non-exclusive traditional rights. The historical controversy over the breadth of the territorial waters demonstrates that traditional fishing rights can crystallise within areas that used to be part of the high seas prior to the extension of the territorial sea from 3 to 6 and 12 nautical miles.

5.24 Similarly, in the *Fisheries Jurisdiction* cases, the Court recognised the United Kingdom's and Germany's historic rights to access and exploit banks located in the Icelandic preferential rights zone.[466] While it is true that the fishing at stake was industrial, this precedent still attests to the fact that historic rights, which do not seek to negate the coastal State's rights, can exist regardless of the fact that the particular maritime area used to be part of the high seas. Nicaragua's own Reply proves the point. By drawing attention to traditional fishing rights in archipelagic waters, Nicaragua implicitly, but inevitably,

---

[465] NR, para. 6.60.

[466] *Fisheries Jurisdiction (United Kingdom* v. *Iceland), Merits, Judgment, I.C.J. Reports 1974*, p. 3; *Fisheries Jurisdiction (Federal Republic of Germany* v. *Iceland), Merits, Judgment, I.C.J. Reports 1974*, p. 175.

recognises that acquired rights can crystallise within areas where the freedom of fishing used to apply, given that archipelagic baselines often enclose maritime areas that used to be high seas.

D. Nicaragua's Express Recognition of the Traditional Fishing Rights

5.25 Colombia reiterates that the debate as to whether traditional fishing rights have been superseded by the appearance of the EEZ becomes purely theoretical when it can be shown that, in any event, both parties have recognised the existence of such vested rights.

5.26 Colombia's main argument is that traditional fishing rights are protected under international law regardless of the maritime area involved and irrespective of any form of recognition from coastal States. Accordingly, for Colombia, President Ortega's statements recognising the rights of the artisanal fishermen of the Archipelago have a purely declaratory effect. They accept already existing rights and customs that can, of course, be subsequently fleshed out in technical agreements. However, Colombia's alternative argument is that if traditional fishing rights were to be considered incompatible with the EEZ, this is without consequence in the present case since the concurrent statements by the Presidents of the two countries can be construed as having a constitutive effect. Nothing precluded Nicaragua and Colombia from reaching the conclusion that the traditional fishing rights of the inhabitants of the San Andrés

Archipelago should be preserved and protected in the aftermath of the 2012 Judgment.

5.27 Rather than neglecting the statements of its own President, Nicaragua in its Reply endeavours to find an explanation for them, which, while upholding the good intentions of its highest representative, also attempts to render his words without troublesome legal consequences. As conveniently put in the Reply, "President Ortega's attempts to strike a conciliatory tone *cannot change the legal situation*".[467]

5.28 Nicaragua does not contest, and neither does Colombia, that President Ortega has shown a measure of goodwill by repeatedly emphasising the need to "respect the ancestral rights of the Raizales".[468] In fact, right after the 2012 Judgment, President Ortega referred to this matter stating that Nicaragua "fully respect[s] the right to fish and navigate in those waters that they have sailed historically and have also survived from the resources of the sea".[469] But for Nicaragua, these references to traditional fishing somehow "fall far short of 'explicit recognitions'".[470] As Nicaragua puts it, the President's statements merely indicate "that artisanal fishing 'rights' do not exist absent an appropriate agreement",[471] and that the declarations stand "only for the unremarkable proposition that

467 NR, Chapter VI, Sub-section (*c*), p. 141. (Emphasis added).
468 NR, para. 6.70.
469 Annex 1: Message from President Daniel Ortega to the People of Nicaragua, 26 November 2012.
470 NR, para. 6.67.
471 NR, para. 6.71.

continued fishing in Nicaragua's EEZ by the Raizales would have the be the [sic] subject of an agreement".[472]

5.29 Aside from the fact that the record shows an altogether different story, Nicaragua's reasoning gives rise to serious difficulties. For example, Nicaragua stresses in relation to the February 2013 statement that, while it is true that President Ortega indicated that Nicaragua will "allow Raizales to continue fishing", that statement constituted "an *exercise* of Nicaragua's sovereign rights and jurisdiction, not the fulfilment of an obligation in *derogation* of Nicaragua's rights".[473] But even if that were to be true, which is doubtful and which nothing in the record supports as can be seen from the transcription of President Ortega's speech,[474] it would not deprive "this public statement of its intended legal effects".[475] For Nicaragua does not, and cannot, dispute the fact that such reading would amount to granting rights to the artisanal fishermen.

5.30 As previously stated, Nicaragua blurs the distinction between recognition of the traditional fishing rights and the separate question of the conclusion of technical agreements to define their exact contours. President Ortega often addresses both matters in conjunction, but the distinction is nevertheless

[472] NR, para. 6.73.
[473] NR, para. 6.72. (Emphasis added).
[474] Annex 6: Speeches at the 79th Anniversary of General Augusto C. Sandino's Transit to Immortality, 21 February 2013.
[475] *Nuclear Tests (Australia* v. *France), Judgment, I.C.J. Reports 1974*, p. 267, para. 43; *Nuclear Tests (New Zealand* v. *France), Judgment, I.C.J. Reports 1974*, p. 472, para. 46.

clear. Thus, on 2 December 2012, the President of Nicaragua stated that:

> "Be sure that we will respect the historical rights that they (the Raizals) have had over those territories. We will find the mechanisms to ensure the right of the Raizal people to fish, in San Andrés, so we can protect those people that live of that territorial sea and also so we can confront drug trafficking in that region."[476]

This statement, on the one hand, expressly recognises pre-existing "historical rights" and, on the other hand, stresses that "mechanisms" should be established to "ensure" the "right of the Raizal people to fish". In other words, the mechanisms are a tool, admittedly an important one, to safeguard the traditional fishing rights, but not a precondition to their existence, which was regarded as an established fact.

5.31 In his 21 February 2013 statement,[477] President Ortega emphasised the importance of establishing a "mechanism", a "commission" or a "consular section", for the sake of fleshing out the content of the traditional fishing rights.[478] This time the emphasis was not on the recognition of the traditional rights, which was taken as a given, but on matters to be clarified such

---

476 CCM, Annexes 73 and 74.

477 CCM, Annex 76. See also: Annex 6: Speeches at the 79th Anniversary of General Augusto C. Sandino's Transit to Immortality, 21 February 2013.

478 CCM, Annex 76. See also: Annex 6: Speeches at the 79th Anniversary of General Augusto C. Sandino's Transit to Immortality, 21 February 2013.

as who and how. The mechanism should "identify the raizal fishermen so that they can keep fishing without problems in the waters that the International Court of Justice reverted to the country [Nicaragua] in the Caribbean Sea".[479] The situation needs to be regulated "because right now there is no way to know how many vessels belong to the raizal community and which are related by [sic] industrial fishing".[480] A consular section in San Andrés would allow to clearly determine, "from there", "how many raizal fishermen are there, which are their boats, so that they can fish freely".[481]

5.32 While it is true that these are all aspects that may require information, Nicaragua's Reply is mistaken in suggesting that "artisanal fishing 'rights' do not exist independently of 'mechanisms to be approved by Nicaragua'".[482] The fact of the matter is that Nicaragua's President has already recognised the existence of the traditional fishing rights as well as their fundamental characteristics. Artisanal fishermen are allowed to

---

479 CCM, Annex 76. See also: Annex 6: Speeches at the 79th Anniversary of General Augusto C. Sandino's Transit to Immortality, 21 February 2013.

480 CCM, Annex 76. See also: Annex 6: Speeches at the 79th Anniversary of General Augusto C. Sandino's Transit to Immortality, 21 February 2013.

481 CCM, Annex 76. See also: Annex 6: Speeches at the 79th Anniversary of General Augusto C. Sandino's Transit to Immortality, 21 February 2013.

482 NR, para. 6.70.

"fish freely"[483] without having to ask for permission from INPESCA in the waters appertaining to Nicaragua.

5.33 Notwithstanding its attempt to diminish the value of its President's statements, Nicaragua concludes that "it remains open, in the spirit of brotherhood and good neighbourly relations, to work with Colombia to reach a bilateral agreement that takes account of Colombia's and Nicaragua's concerns, including the fishing needs of the Raizales".[484] But such bilateral agreement would only serve to put into place the mechanism supplementing the traditional fishing rights regime, whose existence is already established.

E. The Evidence Corroborates the Existence of the Traditional Fishing Rights

5.34 Far from addressing the evidence put forward in Colombia's Counter-Memorial, Nicaragua relies on partial citations so as to dispute the existence of traditional fishing rights in waters of its EEZ. Nicaragua goes further and asserts that Colombia's evidence "disproves its claims".[485] Clearly, Nicaragua believes that anything other than its superficial assessment of the sworn statements must be in vain since, in its contention, the affidavits were made by private persons

---

483 CCM, Annex 76. See also: Annex 6: Speeches at the 79th Anniversary of General Augusto C. Sandino's Transit to Immortality, 21 February 2013.

484 NR, para. 6.76.

485 NR, Chapter VI, Section B, Sub-section (*b*).

interested in the outcome of the proceedings and apparently "prepared in haste for purpose of this litigation".[486]

5.35 This is nothing more than Nicaragua trying to silence the voice of the Raizales. But a full reading of the affidavits discloses an altogether different picture from the one portrayed in Nicaragua's Reply. For the Applicant, the traditional fishing activities did not occur in what are currently waters under its jurisdiction and, if they did (which it begrudgingly admits), they "were too infrequent and of too recent standing to establish either historic rights or a local custom under international law".[487] This dismissive critique is focused on two aspects, spatial and temporal, each of which Colombia will address in turn.

5.36 However, before refuting Nicaragua's fragmented reading of the affidavits, Colombia must draw attention to an aspect that the Applicant purposefully ignored in its Reply. This has to do with the standard of proof for establishing the existence of traditional fishing rights. Colombia is invoking rights vested in a small community of artisanal fishermen that live in an important but, nevertheless, relatively remote region of the Southwestern Caribbean Sea. Under these circumstances, the jurisprudence stresses that the matter of proof must be approached with common sense. For example, in the recent

486 NR, para. 6.50.
487 NR, para. 6.62.

award in the *South China Sea Arbitration*, the Arbitral Tribunal found that:

> "Based on the record before it, the Tribunal is of the view that Scarborough Shoal has been a traditional fishing ground for fishermen of many nationalities, including the Philippines, China (including Taiwan), and Viet Nam. The stories of most of those who have fished at Scarborough Shoal in generations past have not been the subject of written records, and the Tribunal considers that traditional fishing rights constitute an area where matters of evidence should be approached with sensitivity. That certain livelihoods have not been considered of interest to official record keepers or to the writers of history does not make them less important to those who practice them. With respect to Scarborough Shoal, the Tribunal accepts that the claims of both the Philippines and China to have traditionally fished at the shoal are accurate and advanced in good faith."[488]

5.37 Likewise, in the *Dispute regarding Navigational and Related Rights (Costa Rica* v. *Nicaragua)*, the present Court was prepared to recognise the existence of a customary right to fish based on little evidence because it considered, also with sensitivity and common sense, that the practice in question, "especially given the remoteness of the area and the small, thinly spread population, [was] not likely to be documented in any official record".[489]

---

488 *The South China Sea Arbitration (Philippines* v. *China), Award of 12 July 2016, PCA Case No. 2013-19*, p. 315, para. 805.

489 *Dispute regarding Navigational and Related Rights (Costa Rica* v. *Nicaragua), Judgment, I.C.J. Reports 2009*, p. 213, para. 141.

5.38 In other words, Nicaragua's attempt to heighten the burden of proof is misguided considering the nature of the traditional practices and the context in which they took place. Under these circumstances, as previously developed, Colombia considers that the historical documents it gathered are more than adequate to substantiate the proposition that the inhabitants of the Archipelago were men and women of the sea who navigated, traded, turtled and fished throughout the Southwestern Caribbean Sea since time immemorial.[490]

5.39 According to Nicaragua, "historic fishing took place largely in the vicinity of Colombia's islands, not in waters that the Court determined to be part of Nicaragua's EEZ".[491] To support that proposition, Nicaragua merely highlights the fact that the affidavits frequently refer to traditional fishing that occurred in the North Cays (Serrana, Quitasueño, Roncador, Serranilla and Bajo Nuevo).[492] Obviously the artisanal fishermen's sworn statements contain several references to fishing that took place in waters surrounding these islands. Indeed, it would be extraordinary if the traditional banks were to be located only on the Nicaraguan side of the 2012 line. However, it would be equally remarkable if these traditional fishing activities, which Nicaragua takes for granted, were to be located only on the Colombian side of the 2012 line. Nicaragua would have the Court believe that traditional fishing has always

490 CCM, paras. 2.67-2.86.
491 NR, para. 6.51.
492 NR, paras. 6.51-6.54.

for some reasons been restricted to the banks situated within 12 nautical miles of islands such as Quitasueño and Serrana as if the drawing of a line could influence the conduct of the artisanal fishermen retroactively. But, as explained in the Counter-Memorial, bathymetry and of course the affidavits, give the best indication of where traditional fishing took place.

5.40 Indeed, some of the biggest and most important fishing banks, both shallow and deep-sea, are located in the vicinity of the Colombian islands but, nevertheless, in maritime areas adjudicated by the Court to Nicaragua as depicted in Figures 2.4 and 2.5 of Colombia's Counter-Memorial. Yet, despite its so-called "careful examination of Colombia's affidavits",[493] Nicaragua conveniently fails to mention that the artisanal fishermen expressly refer to traditional banks located in waters that had, according to President Ortega himself, "reverted" to Nicaragua.[494]

5.41 Many of the affiants consider that Cape Bank constitutes one of the most important traditional grounds for the artisanal fishermen of the Archipelago. Cape Bank is the vast area of shallow waters that extends from the Mosquito Coast to the 82nd West Meridian and beyond. The fact that some of the affiants refer to the 82nd West Meridian is because such coordinate largely coincides with *Luna Verde* (also known as *La Esquina*) – that is to say, the area where the shallow grounds of Cape Bank

493 NR, para. 6.62.
494 CCM, Annex 76.

give place to its deep sea grounds, which are also crucial for the artisanal fishermen of the Archipelago. *Luna Verde* is simply the part of Cape Bank which is located to the east of the 82nd West Meridian. As stated by Mr George de la Cruz de Alba Barker, an artisanal fisherman based in San Andrés:

> "Cape Bank, what they sometimes call today Luna Verde but I do not know where this name comes from, is the name with which I have known the area since I was a child. Cape Bank goes from Cape Gracias a Dios in Honduras down to Costa Rica. It is not only limited to the area east of the 82nd Meridian and South of the 15th parallel. My parents also fished in this area, and today we generally go there when there is not enough product in the South Cays. Fishing is more abundant in this zone and this is why we go there although it is farther from the South Cays."[495]

5.42 Thus, the affidavits both explicitly and implicitly refer to Cape Bank which is considered by artisanal fishermen as "one of the best places to fish".[496] Indeed, some of the affiants expressly mention "Cape Bank",[497] while others point to locations that are obviously part of its shallow, as well as its deep-sea, grounds such as the "82° West Meridian",[498] "Luna Verde",[499] "Great Corn Island and Little Corn Island",[500]

495 CCM, Annex 71.
496 CCM, Annex 68.
497 CCM, Annexes 62, 65, 68, 70, 71 and 72.
498 CCM, Annexes 63, 64, 65, 69 and 71.
499 CCM, Annex 71
500 CCM, Annex 64.

"Rosalind Bank",[501] "Bobel cay"[502] and "Cape Gracias a Dios".[503] As stated by Mr George de la Cruz de Alba Barker:

> "The fishing banks are mostly located where the sea's depth changes from very shallow to relatively deep. West of Quitasueño these banks are located east of the 82nd Meridian and south of the 15th parallel. But more to the South, to the west of Providencia, they are located on the 82nd Meridian and a little beyond. These are the best areas since Cape Bank is huge and has many resources."[504]

5.43 Likewise, Mr Wallingford Gonzalez Steele Borden declared that he "mostly fish[es] in the 82nd Meridian, west of Providencia, with traps".[505] In its Reply, Nicaragua states that "this vague reference 'to the area of the 82° west of Providencia' does not support Colombia's case" because that meridian "comes very close" to the maritime boundary drawn by the Court.[506] Merely insisting on the proximity between the meridian and the boundary, Nicaragua does not deny that the bathymetry of the region clearly shows that west of Providencia, the shallow and deep-sea grounds of Cape Bank are entirely located within the maritime areas adjudicated to Nicaragua, as shown in Figures 2.4 and 2.5 of Colombia's Counter-Memorial.

---

501 CCM, Annexes 65 and 71.
502 CCM, Annexes 63, 64 and 65.
503 CCM, Annex 63, 69 and 71.
504 CCM, Annex 71.
505 CCM, Annex 63.
506 NR, para 6.54.

5.44 Aside from Cape Bank, the affiants mentioned other important traditional banks that are located on the Nicaraguan side of the 2012 line, such as "Julio Bank",[507] "Far Bank"[508] and "North East Bank".[509] These are mainly deep-sea banks situated in the waters surrounding the North Cays that have at times been named by the artisanal fishermen who discovered them. In these waters, the artisanal fishermen fish "groupers that [they] call 'John Pou', Mandilous, Satten, Red Eyes, Soapfish, Yellow Eyes and Bream" and that are particularly appreciated in the local markets.[510] These deep-sea banks are mainly situated north of Quitasueño, and between, respectively, Providencia and Quitasueño, Quitasueño and Serrana, and Serrana and Roncador. Thus, Mr Landel Hernando Robinson Archbold states that:

> "Unfortunately some of our banks are now in the waters of Nicaragua (…). If I want to fish in North East Bank and in Julio Bank, which are located in Nicaraguan waters between Quitasueño and Providencia, I have to be very careful."[511]

5.45 Likewise, Mr Wallingford Gonzales Steele Borden stressed that:

> "When we fish close to the cay, it is because we are looking for shallow banks. But we also fish farther from the cays in the deep-sea banks located between Providencia and Quitasueño, between

507 CCM, Annexes 62, 63, 64, 65 and 66.
508 CCM, Annexes 63, 64 and 65.
509 CCM, Annexes 62, 64, 65 and 66.
510 CCM, Annex 65.
511 CCM, Annex 62.

> Quitasueño and Serrana, and between Serrana and Roncador. In those areas, there are large fishing banks that are very well known to us, such as 'Far Bank' and 'Julio Bank'. There you find the groupers which are the fish that the cooperative is most interested in. Those fishing banks have names given to them by the people who have discovered them. But no, there is no Wallin[g]ford bank at the moment."[512]

5.46 Mr Ligorio Luis Archbold Howard similarly underlined that:

> "I fish in Nicaragua's waters north and west of Providencia. (…) The fishing grounds of Far bank, North East and Julio Banks are traditional fishing grounds of Providencia and now some of their coordinates are in Nicaraguan waters. They are deep-water banks very important for artisanal fishermen of Providencia because it is where you can find the fish most appreciated by the islanders. We fish from Low Cay off the northern tip of Providencia up to the Southern tip of Quitasueño. I spend 5 or 6 days in Julio Bank, North-East Bank, Far Bank, Low Cay. (…) There are similar deep-sea banks between Quitasueño and Serrana, but I do not know their names. Fishermen try to keep them secret, it is a family tradition. They might have a name but I know that I am not the first one who went there so I did not name them."[513]

5.47 Mr Ornuldo Rodolfo Walters Dawkins, in addition to fishing in the deep-sea banks located in between these islands, also goes farther north where the shallow grounds of *Luna*

---

512 CCM, Annex 63.
513 CCM, Annex 65.

Verde give way to its extended deep-sea banks located to the north and northwest of Quitasueño:

> "I continue to fish in the area between Providencia and Quitasueño. I have fished in Julio Bank, Far Bank, North East Bank and Serrana. But we also fish farther from the cays like for example as far as 35 miles from the North tip of Queena [Quitasueño]."[514]

5.48 In fact, Nicaragua's own written pleadings demonstrate that traditional banks are situated in maritime areas located on the Nicaraguan side of the 2012 delimitation. In paragraph 4.121 of its Reply, Nicaragua based its assertion that "Luna Verde is an area for commercial fishing, not artisanal fishing", on its own Annex 22.[515] Quite apart from the fact that the annexed newspaper article does not state the above, which would make no sense since artisanal and industrial fishing both constitute distinct sub-categories of commercial fishing under Colombian law,[516] that article specifies that the artisanal fishermen lost traditional banks to the "west of Providencia and to the east of Bolivar Key", as well as the area known as *Luna Verde* or *La Esquina*.[517] While the latter was "exploited especially by industrial fishermen", the article clearly indicates that that area is also a traditional ground for artisanal fishermen.[518] Likewise, already in its Memorial, Nicaragua's annexes proved the point.

---

514 CCM, Annex 64.
515 NR, para. 4.121 and Annex 22.
516 Annex 17: Ministry of Agriculture, Decree 2256 of 1991, Article 12.
517 NR, Annex 22.
518 NR, Annex 22.

For example, the 2013 Report of the Office of the Comptroller General of San Andrés on the status of natural resources and the environment, made explicit reference to the 82nd West Meridian, North East Bank and *Luna Verde* or *La Esquina*.[519] With regard to the latter, the Report suggested that this bank was "exploited in greater proportion by industrial fisheries of the Archipelago".[520] Once again, it follows that *Luna Verde* is also a traditional bank exploited by Colombia's artisanal fishermen.

5.49 Unable to maintain that the traditional banks are only located in the Colombian maritime areas as defined in the 2012 Judgment, Nicaragua declares that "at the earliest, artisanal fishermen began venturing into deeper waters closer to Nicaragua only in the 1970s" and that, consequently, "Colombia's assertion that its fishermen have fished in [its] EEZ 'since time immemorial' is [a] profound overstatement".[521] Nicaragua's temporal objection is based on the proposition that traditional fishing rights cannot crystallise over a time frame spanning five decades, which, in itself, is dubious. But what is most problematic is that Nicaragua intentionally distorts the affidavits.

5.50 Technological developments have enabled artisanal fishermen to venture more frequently in the traditional banks located farther from the Archipelago. Nonetheless, the evidence

---

519 NM, Annex 12.
520 NM, Annex 12.
521 NR, para. 6.57.

shows that fishing expeditions to Cape Bank and to the waters surrounding the North Cays were always part and parcel of the culture of the inhabitants of the San Andrés Archipelago. Contrary to what Nicaragua would have the Court believe, Mr Wallingford Gonzalez Steele Borden has not stated that in the 1960s and prior to that decade traditional fishing merely occurred within areas located close to Providencia and San Andrés.[522] On the contrary, he said that:

> "We artisanal fishermen always fished in Roncador, Quitasueño, Serrana and in the area of 82° west of Providencia. We would even go further and reach Bobel Cays close to Cape Gracias a Dios. But at the time the expeditions occurred less frequently because in the sixties we had a lot of fish also around Providencia. We would go in these expeditions to the Northern and Western banks a few times a year and stay there one or two months. With less fish around Providencia we started going more often to these banks. Of course it was easier once engines arrived and we started using *lanchas*. (…) *Lanchas* allow us to reach the grounds with less effort."[523]

5.51 Obviously, the affiants mainly relate to their parents' and their own lifetime experiences because it is the time period that they have witnessed. However, it does not follow, and the artisanal fishermen do not state, that the geographical scope of their fishing activities were previously limited to Providencia and San Andrés. Nor can Nicaragua plausibly argue that those

---

522 NR, para. 6.56.

523 CCM, Annex 63.

activities were "too infrequent".[524] For while it is true that the artisanal fishermen could not go to Cape Bank, *Luna Verde* and the deep-sea banks situated between the North Cays on a daily basis, expeditions that would last weeks or months occurred regularly several times a year. Those expeditions certainly constitute practices that can give rise to traditional fishing rights or local customs.

5.52 In addition to distorting the affidavits, Nicaragua has also misread Colombia's domestic law. Nicaragua's misinterpretation reaches its peak when it asserts that Colombia's legislation prevents artisanal fishermen from fishing beyond 12 nautical miles of San Andrés and Providencia.[525] Partially quoting from DIMAR Resolution No. 121 of 2004, and likewise partially annexing that instrument, Nicaragua wrongly asserts that said instrument "placed tight limits on the areas where artisanal fishermen were permitted to fish".[526]

5.53 But the scope and purpose of that resolution,[527] as can be seen from its title, is to "facilitate", not encumber, artisanal fishing. Also, it establishes a special procedure in relation to coastal (*costera*) and inshore (*de bajura*) artisanal fishing. Contrary to offshore (*de altura*) artisanal fishing, coastal and inshore artisanal fishing occurred, according to Colombian law,

---

524 NR, para. 6.62.
525 NR, para. 6.39.
526 NR, para. 6.39.
527 NR, Annex 6.

within, respectively, 1 nautical mile and 12 nautical miles of the coast.[528]

5.54 Contrary to what Nicaragua asserts,[529] Resolution No. 121 does not, and in fact cannot, prohibit offshore artisanal fishing. In so far as it is not regulated by this resolution, artisanal offshore fishing is perfectly legal to the extent that it is done in conformity with Decree No. 2256 of 1991, which requires the deliverance of a regular, more formal permit.

5.55 Nicaragua has also ignored the fact that both the President and the Foreign Minister of Colombia, as well as other Colombian officials, have repeatedly recognised that many of the traditional fishing grounds of the artisanal fishermen of the San Andrés Archipelago are located on the Nicaraguan side of the 2012 line.[530] However, Nicaragua has pointed to an alleged inconsistency in the Colombian position, which it inferred from two recommendations of a Committee of Experts of the International Labour Organisation (ILO).[531] It appears that the

---

528 Annex 17: Ministry of Agriculture, Decree 2256 of 1991, Article 12.

529 NR, para. 6.39.

530 CCM, Annex 20; CPO, Annexes 10 and 38.

531 NR, paras. 6.32-6.37; ILO, Committee of Experts on the Application of Conventions and Recommendations, "Observations (CEACR) – adopted 2013, published 103rd ILC session (2014), Indigenous and Tribal Peoples Convention, 1989 (No. 169) – Colombia (Ratification: 1991)", available at: https://www.ilo.org/dyn/normlex/en/f?p=1000:13100:0::NO:13100:P13100_COMMENT_ID:3141200 (last visited: 1 November 2018); ILO, Committee of Experts on the Application of Conventions and Recommendations, "Observations (CEACR) – adopted 2014, published 104rd ILC session (2015), Indigenous and Tribal Peoples Convention, 1989 (No. 169) – Colombia (Ratification: 1991)", available at:

Office of Cooperation and International Relations, a section of the Colombian Ministry of Labour, cavalierly concluded, in a letter which Colombia is annexing to this Rejoinder, that the artisanal fishermen of the San Andrés Archipelago could not have been impacted by the 2012 line since the islands and, in particular, the North Cays, as well as their appurtenant territorial sea, remained under Colombian sovereignty.[532]

5.56 This statement was delivered in response to a communication made to an ILO body by the Colombian General Confederation of Labour on behalf of the Raizal Small-Scale Fishers' Associations.[533] Responding to the claim that Colombia had, in particular, breached the Convention concerning Indigenous and Tribal Peoples in Independent Countries (ILO Convention No. 169), the Office of Cooperation and International Relations sought to refute the proposition that the government had not ensured the right of prior consultation of the Raizal people in the context of the *Territorial and Maritime Dispute* case. While that aspect of the communication is comprehensively addressed to in the response of the Office of

---

https://www.ilo.org/dyn/normlex/en/f?p=1000:13100:0::NO::P13100_COMMENT_ID,P13100_LANG_CODE:3182299,en:NO (last visited: 1 November 2018).

[532] Annex 24: Ministry of Labour, Note to the ILO in relation to the application by Colombia of Convention No. 169, 2 September 2013.

[533] Annex 67: General Confederation of Labour, *Submission of complaint on behalf of the General Confederation of Labour and the cooperatives and associations of artisanal fishermen and Raizal groups of the Archipelago of San Andrés, Providencia and Santa Catalina against the Colombian State*, 18 February 2013; and Annex 68: General Confederation of Labour, *Submission of complaint relating to the breach of Convention No. 169 by the Colombian State*, 10 February 2014.

Cooperation and International Relations, that Office significantly failed to provide even a shred of evidence to support its assertion that the traditional fishing sites were precisely located in the vicinity of areas not affected by the decision.

5.57 Moreover, the Office's assertion can hardly be reconciled with the extensive description of "Plan San Andrés" in its response to the ILO. This plan was established by the Colombian Government in the aftermath of the 2012 Judgment to alleviate the adverse effects endured by the artisanal fishermen who had traditionally relied on fishing grounds located in maritime areas that were adjudicated to Nicaragua.

5.58 The Labour Ministry's communication to the ILO indicates that Colombia spent 4.383 million Colombian pesos (some US $ 2.5 million) in marine aquaculture programs intended to provide alternative employment sources for artisanal fishermen; and for six months granted a monthly subsidy of 1.8 million Colombian pesos (more than US $ 1,000) to artisanal fishermen who were certified as such and regularly engaged in this activity before 19 November 2012, the day the 2012 Judgment was rendered.[534]

[534] For the list of requirements to be afforded the monthly subsidy, see Annex 21: Department for Social Prosperity, Resolution No. 02117, 21 December 2012.

5.59 The implementation of the artisanal fishing component of the "Plan San Andrés" was overseen by Monitoring Committees composed by artisanal fishermen, the Ombudsman and the Archipelago's Secretary of Agriculture and Fishing, who in 2013 published the list of subsidies granted (a total of 755 in San Andrés and 275 in Providencia), specifying the beneficiary's name, ID number and cooperative or association to which they belong.[535]

5.60 If Nicaragua's claim that artisanal fishermen were not in fact impaired after the 2012 Judgment from continuing fishing where they had ancestrally done so were true, it would not have been necessary for the Colombian Government to establish a plan and devote a significant amount of money to address what in effect became after November 2012 a pressing social issue.

5.61 In this regard, the communications to the ILO from the General Confederation of Labour on behalf of the Raizal Small-Scale Fishers' Associations actually strengthen the proposition that many traditional fishing banks are located on the Nicaraguan side of the 2012 line. Indeed, the communications received by the ILO clearly indicate that, according to the artisanal fishermen of the Archipelago, traditional fishing used

---

535 Annex 22: Archipelago Department of San Andrés, Providencia and Santa Catalina, List of Beneficiaries of the Artisanal Fishermen Subsidy in San Andrés, 9 April 2013; and Annex 23: Archipelago Department of San Andrés, Providencia and Santa Catalina, List of Beneficiaries of the Artisanal Fishermen Subsidy in Providencia, 9 April 2013.

to take place in areas that were adjudicated to Nicaragua. According to the claimants, Colombia must take:

> "[T]he necessary measures so that the artisanal fishermen workers of San Andrés and Providencia can exercise freely as before their activity of artisanal fishermen in order to seek to improve their social and economic situations, seriously affected by the ruling of the International Court of Justice".[536]

Similarly, the claimants stressed that:

> "Likewise, the Nicaraguan government must adopt measures to allow the Raizal artisanal fishermen to fish in the waters recently adjudicated to that State that were being exploited by this Raizal community".[537]

In other words, it appears that the position of the artisanal fishermen of the Archipelago is coherent regardless of whether their claims are being supported by Colombia in the context of the current proceedings or, on the contrary, brought against the Colombian Government before the ILO. Thus, the communications submitted to the ILO on behalf of the Raizal Small-Scale Fishers' Associations clearly support the existence of traditional fishing rights in the maritime areas adjudicated to Nicaragua.

---

536 Annex 67. See also Annex 68.
537 Annex 67. See also Annex 68.

F. The Evidence Substantiates the Infringement of the Traditional Fishing Rights

5.62 Nicaragua brushed off the evidence attesting to the infringement of the traditional fishing rights by qualifying most of it as amounting to "hearsay".[538] Likewise, Nicaragua also asserted that Colombia did not adduce "contemporaneous evidence" and that "the omission is revealing" considering that Nicaragua is being accused of an "active strategy of intimidation".[539] At the very least, Nicaragua argued, contemporaneous "diplomatic protests" or "complaints made to local authorities" should be expected.[540]

5.63 The Nicaraguan Reply makes no attempt to hide the two different yardsticks that it applies *vis-à-vis*, on the one hand, its own claims and, on the other hand, Colombia's counter-claim. With regard to its own claims, which allegedly also involve the implementation "of a considered policy" demonstrating "Colombia's disregard for Nicaragua's sovereign rights and jurisdiction",[541] Nicaragua appears to be content with the fact that its "evidence" is based on asynchronous second-hand accounts.

5.64 Nicaragua's acute case of selective memory is well portrayed by the fact that its list of so-called "incidents" is based

---

538 NR, paras. 6.79, 6.85, 6.87, 6.89 and 6.91.
539 NR, para. 6.83.
540 NR, para. 6.83.
541 NR, para. 4.45.

on a diplomatic note, which is based on a report from the Nicaraguan Naval Force, which in turn is based on a request from the Nicaraguan Foreign Ministry, that are all far removed temporally from the alleged events to which they refer.[542] While the Colombian affidavits were apparently "prepared in haste for purposes of this litigation",[543] the diplomatic note that was sent three weeks before the filing of the Nicaraguan Memorial is seemingly a perfect piece of evidence despite the fact that it is not backed up with contemporaneous evidence.

5.65 Apart from criticizing the lack of contemporaneous evidence, Nicaragua also stresses that the incidents mentioned in the affidavits are not specific as to the date of occurrence.[544] Yet, Nicaragua again forgets that on many occasions it has provided the date of an indirect report instead of the date of the purported "incident" to support its own claims and that several of the "incidents" it relies on could not have happened as recounted by Nicaragua.[545]

5.66 Aside from highlighting Nicaragua's self-serving double standards, Colombia will go through the evidence once more to demonstrate that Nicaragua has infringed the traditional fishing rights of the inhabitants of the San Andrés Archipelago. Colombia has shown in its Counter-Memorial that by bullying, the Nicaraguan Naval Force has instilled a climate of fear

---

542 See Chapter 3 *supra*.

543 NR, para. 6.50.

544 NR, paras. 6.87, 6.88 and 6.91.

545 See Chapter 3 *supra*, incidents 1, 4 and 9.

amongst the artisanal fishermen, who, as a consequence of this conduct, have been forced to abandon many of their traditional fishing grounds.[546]

5.67 The conduct of the Nicaraguan Naval Force is well portrayed in a number of affidavits annexed to Colombia's Counter-Memorial.[547] While Nicaragua's quick assessment of this part of the counter-claim appears to suggest that, in its opinion, the incidents are trivial in nature, the fact that the Nicaraguan Naval Force requests food, cigarettes or coffee from the fishermen it intercepts, is not only inappropriate, it is serious. When a fisherman is approached, or even worse boarded, by Nicaraguan armed agents, he feels intimidated "since [they] have weapons"[548] and, as understandably put by Mr Antonio Alejandro Sjogreen Pablo, fishermen "cannot say no".[549] There is a sharp contrast with the type of "incidents" alleged by Nicaragua and those suffered by Colombia, in that none of those allegedly involving the Colombian Navy relate to boarding a Nicaraguan vessel or looting the fishermen.

5.68 Let us be clear. These Nicaraguan agents have done worse than stealing lunches and beverages. As stated by Mr George de la Cruz de Alba Barker, "[i]t is common to have our GPS, VHF radio, cigarettes and food supplies taken by them".[550]

546 CCM, paras. 9.11-9.23.
547 CCM, Annexes 67, 69, 70, 71 and 72.
548 CCM, Annex 71.
549 CCM, Annex 72.
550 CCM, Annex 71.

The Nicaraguan Naval Force, he continues, "also strip[s] the boats of all their equipment of any value".[551] As indicated by Mr Alfredo Rafael Howard Newball, "[t]hey stop them, they take away their products, their equipment and they threaten and mistreat them".[552]

5.69 While Nicaragua relies on the ILO's aforementioned recommendations whenever it finds them to be convenient, it surprisingly fails to mention that, according to those recommendations, the complaint on behalf of the artisanal fishermen specified that "Raizal fishers have to cross Nicaraguan maritime territory, which is reported to give rise to difficulties and the payment of fines".[553]

5.70 Nicaragua states that President Santos' statement of 18 February 2013[554] is "pure hearsay".[555] However, it does not deny that President Ortega had to instruct its Naval Force not to detain and not to request permits from the artisanal fishermen prior to and after President Santos' statement.[556] In fact,

---

551 CCM, Annex 71.

552 CCM, Annex. 67.

553 ILO, Committee of Experts on the Application of Conventions and Recommendations, "Observations (CEACR) – adopted 2014, published 104rd ILC session (2015), Indigenous and Tribal Peoples Convention, 1989 (No. 169) – Colombia (Ratification: 1991)", available at: https://www.ilo.org/dyn/normlex/en/f?p=1000:13100:0::NO::P13100_COMMENT_ID,P13100_LANG_CODE:3182299,en:NO (last visited: 1 November 2018).

554 CPO, Annex 10.

555 NR, para. 6.79.

556 Annex 6: Speeches at the 79th Anniversary of General Augusto C. Sandino's Transit to Immortality, 21 February 2013. See also CCM, Annexes 75 and 76.

Nicaragua itself annexes evidence attesting to the occurrence of incidents.[557] Annex 20 of Nicaragua's Reply refers to three incidents that involved the Nicaraguan Naval Force and Raizal fishermen. Annex 12 of Nicaragua's Memorial attests to the fact that the artisanal fishermen are impeded of performing their work because of the conduct of the Nicaraguan Naval Force, which harangues them and, in general, adopts a "very aggressive" behaviour.[558]

5.71 Nicaragua disingenuously suggests that "the most that Colombia's affidavits might be said to establish is that fishermen from San Andrés and Providencia have experienced some uncertainty in the wake of the 2012 Judgment, and that they are reluctant to fish in Nicaragua's waters".[559] Yet, the affiants consistently stress that "there have been incidents with Nicaraguan coastguards"[560] and that, as a consequence, they fear "to get stopped"[561] and being "taken to the Nicaraguan coasts".[562]

5.72 Because of these incidents, many of the artisanal fishermen have stopped going to their traditional banks that are situated in the maritime zones recognised to appertain to Nicaragua or that are located around the Colombian islands. Landel Hernando Robinson Archbold, who is "afraid of the Nicaraguan coast-guard", "do[es] not fish up to la Esquina and

557 NR, Annex 20 and NM, Annex 12.
558 NM, Annex 12.
559 NR, para. 6.92.
560 CCM, Annex 64.
561 CCM, Annex 65.
562 CCM, Annex 71.

Cape Bank" anymore.[563] Ornuldo Rodolfo Walter Dawkins does not fish "beyond the 82nd Meridian" any longer.[564] Ligorio Luis Archbold Howard "do[es] not go all the way to Serrana and Quitasueño because there are more possibilities of getting stopped by Nicaraguan fishermen or coastguard".[565] Orlando Francis Powell states that he is "afraid" of going to traditional banks such as Cape Bank, Quitasueño and Serrana, so "[t]he last time we went in an expedition we went in Roncador because there we do not risk crossing the Nicaraguan coastguards".[566] Eduardo Steel Martinez "currently only fish[es] around San Andrés" because he fears getting stopped by the Nicaragua Naval Force as it sometimes occurs when artisanal fishermen "try to reach Cape Bank or the North Cays".[567] George de la Cruz de Alba Barker says artisanal fishermen "cannot go" anymore to the North Cays or to Cape Bank because "the decision whether they let us pass through, is up to the Nicaraguan coastguard".[568] Antonio Alejandro Sjogreen Pablo explains that because of the conduct of the Nicaraguan Naval Force "plenty of our people stopped going to Cape Bank and the North Cays".[569]

---

563 CCM, Annex 62.
564 CCM, Annex 64.
565 CCM, Annex 65.
566 CCM, Annex 68.
567 CCM, Annex 70.
568 CCM, Annex 71.
569 CCM, Annex 72.

5.73 All of the above clearly substantiates Nicaragua's infringement of the traditional fishing rights of the inhabitants of the San Andrés Archipelago.

G. Conclusions

5.74 Colombia has demonstrated that the inhabitants of the San Andrés Archipelago, in particular the Raizales, have traditionally engaged in artisanal fishing in maritime areas that were adjudicated to appertain to Nicaragua in the 2012 Judgment, as well as in Colombian areas that require navigating through waters of the Nicaraguan EEZ. While Nicaragua has decided in this case, contrary to the position taken by its President, to deny the existence of these recognised fishing rights, it has provided no rational explanation susceptible of justifying why traditional fishing rights should solely be extinguished in the EEZ.

5.75 Quite apart from its irrelevant assessment of the case-law relating to the adjustment of maritime boundaries, Nicaragua has failed to identify even one single precedent, which in either the operative part or the essential reasoning of the decision, stated that non-exclusive fishing rights are extinguished in the EEZ. Regardless of Nicaragua's tortuous reading of UNCLOS, Colombia has also shown that the parties to this case expressly and repeatedly recognised the existence of the traditional fishing rights. This notwithstanding, Colombia has proven that the Nicaraguan Naval Force has repeatedly bullied the artisanal fishermen of the Archipelago, thus discouraging them from reaching their traditional fishing banks.

5.76 By means of this counter-claim, Colombia respectfully requests the Court to find that Nicaragua has infringed the traditional fishing rights of the inhabitants of the San Andrés Archipelago. Colombia also asks the Court to rule that Nicaragua is under an obligation to ensure that the inhabitants of the San Andrés Archipelago, including the Raizales, enjoy unfettered access to: a) the traditional fishing banks located in the maritime areas adjudicated to appertain to Nicaragua; and b) the traditional fishing banks located in the Colombian maritime areas, access to which requires navigating through the maritime areas adjudicated to appertain to Nicaragua. With regard to compensation of the assessable damage, including loss of profit, its form and amount should be determined at a later phase of the proceedings, following established practice.

Chapter 6

NICARAGUA'S VIOLATION OF COLOMBIA'S SOVEREIGN RIGHTS AND MARITIME SPACES THROUGH ITS STRAIGHT BASELINES DECREE

A. Introduction

6.1 In its Counter-Memorial, Colombia submitted a counter-claim challenging the legality, under international law, of Nicaragua's Decree No. 33-2013, enacted in order to establish straight baselines for the measurement of Nicaragua's maritime areas in the Caribbean Sea.[570]

6.2 As Colombia demonstrated in that pleading, Nicaragua's straight baselines are contrary to customary international law, and contrary to Article 7 of UNCLOS, which is binding on Nicaragua. These baselines, which have been enacted following the 2012 Judgment, are drawn from a series of basepoints located on features that the Court used to proceed to the delimitation between Nicaragua and Colombia,[571] with the

---

570 In its Reply, Nicaragua acknowledges that the 2018 Judgment in the case concerning *Maritime Delimitation in the Caribbean Sea and the Pacific Ocean (Costa Rica* v. *Nicaragua)* has an effect on the delimitation of its territorial sea, and indicates that the basepoint set at Harbour Head, is under review. See NR, para. 7.12.

571 The Court declared that "[s]ince [some Nicaraguan] islands are located further east than the Nicaraguan mainland, they will contribute all of the base points for the construction of the provisional median line. For that purpose, the Court will use base points located on Edinburgh Reef, Muerto Cay, Miskitos Cays, Ned Thomas Cay, Roca Tyra, Little Corn Island and Great Corn Island", *Territorial and Maritime Dispute (Nicaragua* v.

addition of two features located on Nicaragua's Caribbean mainland coast not mentioned by the Court.[572] These basepoints are described in the Decree as follows:

Table CR 1
Annex I to Nicaragua's decree No. 33-2013 of 19 August 2013

Item No.	*Latitude (N)* *Deg. Min. Sec.*	*Longitude (W)* *Deg. Min. Sec.*	*Name*
1	15 00 05.9	083 07 43.0	Cabo Gracias a Dios
2	14 49 15.8	082 41 00.0	Edinburgh Cay
3	14 22 31.2	082 44 06.1	Miskito Cays
4	14 08 40.6	082 48 29.0	Ned Thomas Cay
5	13 03 11.6	083 20 38.6	Man of War Cays
6	12 56 10.8	083 17 31.9	East of Great Tyra Cay
7	12 16 55.5	082 57 54.0	Isla del Maiz Pequeña (Little Corn Island)
8	12 10 39.3	083 01 49.9	Isla del Maiz Grande (Great Corn Island)
9	10 55 52.0	083 39 58.1	Harbour Head

6.3 As Colombia explained in its Counter-Memorial, the unlawful consequences of the enactment of this Decree are extreme with respect to the international community as a whole and, in particular, to Colombia and other neighbouring coastal States. Figure CR 6.1 hereunder illustrates its consequences in terms of the artificial and unlawful extension of Nicaragua's maritime claims in the Caribbean Sea.

Colombia), Judgment, I.C.J. Reports 2012, p. 699, para. 201. The basepoint from which Nicaragua departed from the Court's Judgment, without any explanation, is Edinburgh Reef, since the Decree No. 33-2013 refers instead to Edinburgh Cay.

572 CCM, Annex 13 (Decree No. 33-2013, Baselines of the Marine Areas of the Republic of Nicaragua in the Caribbean Sea). Colombia protested against this Decree by letter dated 1 November 2013 to the Secretary-General of the United Nations. Costa Rica and the United States protested as well.

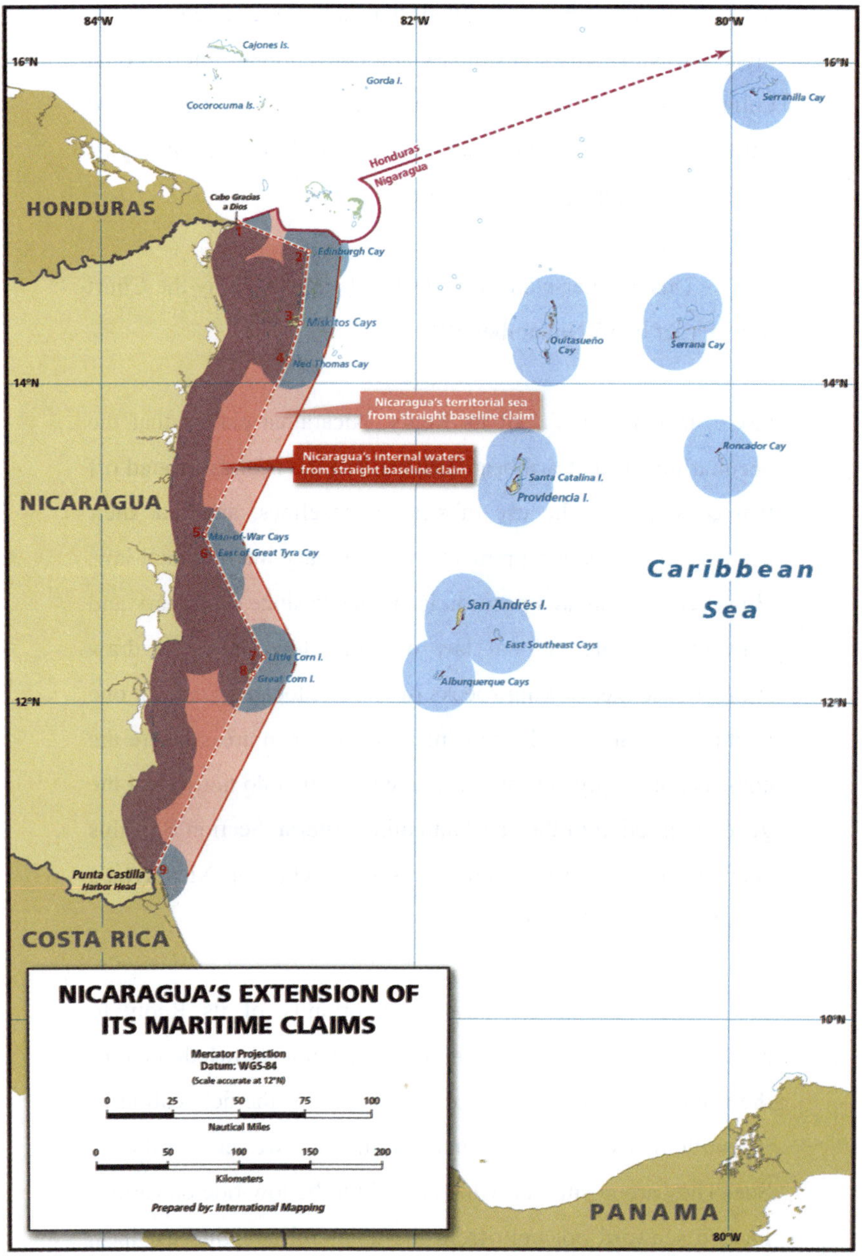
84°W
82°W
80°W
16°N
14°N
12°N
10°N
Cajones Is.
Gorda I.
Cocorocuma Is.
Serranilla Cay
Honduras
Nicaragua
HONDURAS
Cabo Gracias a Dios
Edinburgh Cay
Miskitos Cays
Ned Thomas Cay
Quitasueño Cay
Serrana Cay
Nicaragua's territorial sea from straight baseline claim
Nicaragua's internal waters from straight baseline claim
Roncador Cay
Santa Catalina I.
Providencia I.
NICARAGUA
Man-of-War Cays
East of Great Tyra Cay
Caribbean Sea
San Andrés I.
East Southeast Cays
Little Corn I.
Great Corn I.
Alburquerque Cays
Punta Castilla
Harbor Head
COSTA RICA
NICARAGUA'S EXTENSION OF ITS MARITIME CLAIMS
Mercator Projection
Datum: WGS-84
(Scale accurate at 12°N)
Nautical Miles
Kilometers
Prepared by: International Mapping
PANAMA

Figure CR 6.1

6.4 Colombia has submitted that this Decree entails the breach of Nicaragua's customary and conventional international obligations. It directly violates Colombia's rights and entitlements in the region, including but not limited to, its rights as discussed in the present proceedings.

6.5 This counter-claim was declared admissible by the Court in its Order of 15 November 2017.

6.6 In Chapter VII of its Reply, Nicaragua claims that the peculiarities of its Caribbean coast and of the islands located off that coast justify the use of straight baselines, and that their drawing meets the requirements of customary international law. However, Nicaragua's position is untenable since customary and conventional international law do not allow States to draw straight baselines linking specks of islands, located far from one another and far from their mainland coast, or in areas where the coast is not deeply cut into or indented, or that do not reflect the general direction of the coast and other criteria. Section B of this chapter will set out Colombia's response rebutting Nicaragua's arguments in this regard.

6.7 Nicaragua also took the opportunity of its Reply to pursue a new objective: obtaining a judicial acknowledgment of the use of several new alleged basepoints for the delineation of its entitlements to maritime areas in the Southwestern Caribbean Sea. They are posited on what are said to be low-tide elevations located seaward not only from the unlawful straight baselines, but also from all the nine basepoints previously claimed by Nicaragua. This is the case of the points located on Nee Reef, London Reef and Blowing Rock, none of which had ever been referred to before in the present proceedings.[573]

6.8 Article 16, paragraph 2, of UNCLOS requires State parties, including Nicaragua, to "give due publicity" to the baselines they use for measuring the breadth of their territorial sea, and to "deposit a copy of each such chart or list [of geographical coordinates]" with the Secretary-General of the United Nations.

6.9 But none of the new contended basepoints have been referenced in Nicaragua's own official domestic legal acts. Similarly, the *List of geographical coordinates of points defining the straight baselines from which the breadth of the territorial sea of Nicaragua in the Caribbean Sea is measured* – as contained in Annex I to Decree No. 33-2013 – deposited with the Secretary-General of the United Nations on 26 September

[573] The use by Nicaragua of additional basepoints east of its claimed straight baselines which are in dispute in the current proceedings would have the effect of exacerbating Nicaragua's attempt to encroach into Colombia's maritime zones. The 200-nautical-mile limit from what Nicaragua calls London and Nee Reefs is located at a distance of 3 to 9 nautical miles *east* of the 200-nautical-mile limit measured from the basepoints used by the Court for the purpose of the construction of the provisional median line in its 2012 Judgment. In fact, none of these basepoints were used during the proceedings in the case concerning the *Territorial and Maritime Dispute (Nicaragua* v. *Colombia)*.

2013, contains no reference to these three contended basepoints.[574]

6.10 Since they are not mentioned in the Nicaraguan Decree the legality of which is disputed by Colombia's counter-claim, Colombia will not discuss the existence – undemonstrated by Nicaragua – nor the relevance, if any, of these newly asserted basepoints, which in any event are not opposable to Colombia.

B. Nicaragua's Claimed Baselines Violate the Principles of International Law Governing the Drawing of Straight Baselines

6.11 Colombia's Counter-Memorial demonstrated that the baselines claimed in Nicaragua's Decree No. 33-2013 violate the customary international law principles governing the drawing of straight baselines.[575] Both Nicaragua's recourse to the straight baselines method – which finds no basis in the 2012 Judgment – and the drawing of straight baselines by the Decree, infringe customary international law. In particular:

- Geographical circumstances permitting recourse to straight baselines – i.e. a fringe of islands in the

---

[574] CCM, Annex 13. Article 1 of the Decree No. 33- 2013 provides that: "(t)he straight baselines of the Republic of Nicaragua to be used to measure the breadth of its territorial sea, contiguous zone, exclusive economic zone and continental shelf in the Caribbean Sea shall be established [using the geographical coordinates set forth in Annex I]".

[575] CCM, paras. 10.13-10.65.

immediate vicinity of Nicaragua's Caribbean coast – are not met;[576]

- Nicaragua's drawing of straight baselines contravenes the applicable law since they depart significantly from the general direction of its coast;[577]

- The drawing of the straight baselines is unlawful because it encloses sea areas that are not sufficiently closely linked to the land domain;[578]

- The length of the straight baselines segments claimed by Nicaragua far exceeds any reasonable construction under international law;[579] and

- The effect of Nicaragua's Decree is to illegally expand eastwards its internal waters, territorial sea, EEZ and continental shelf, in detriment to the maritime spaces of Colombia and the rights of the international community as a whole.[580]

6.12 In its Reply, Nicaragua takes issue with each of these points, submitting that its Decree No. 33-2013 meets the conditions of paragraphs 1 and 3 of UNCLOS Article 7. However,

---

576 CCM, paras. 10.33-10.43.
577 CCM, paras. 10.44-.10.45.
578 CCM, paras. 10.46-.10.51.
579 CCM, para. 10.48 and Figure 10.4.
580 CCM, paras. 10.52-10.64.

Nicaragua's arguments are unsupportable in the light of both the relevant geography (Sub-section 1) and the applicable law (Sub-section 2).

(1) THE CONFIGURATION OF NICARAGUA'S ISLANDS DOES NOT JUSTIFY THE USE OF STRAIGHT BASELINES SET BY DECREE NO. 33-2013

6.13 As Colombia will show, contrary to what Nicaragua contends in its Reply, the language and reasoning used by the Court in the 2012 Judgment, whether read alone or in relation with other judgments, cannot be interpreted as recognizing that Edinburgh Cay, Muerto Cay, Miskitos Cays, Ned Thomas Cay, Roca Tyra, Little Corn Island and Great Corn Island form a "fringe of islands" under the rule codified in UNCLOS Article 7. In addition, it will be demonstrated that as a matter of fact the location and features of these features do not satisfy the required criteria for a system of straight baselines.

(a) The Court's case law does not support Nicaragua's claim that its basepoints are posited on a "fringe of islands"

6.14 Nicaragua seems to consider that the existence of a "fringe of islands" cannot be questioned since such qualification would derive from the Court's own words in its 2012 Judgment.[581] But Nicaragua confuses two distinct notions, namely "fringing islands" and a "fringe of islands".

---

581 NR, para. 7.22.

6.15 The Court did use the term "fringing islands" to describe certain Nicaraguan islands on which it selected basepoints for the construction of a provisional median line; the paragraphs referred to by Nicaragua read:

> "[T]he Court (...) considers that Nicaragua's entitlement to a 200-nautical-mile continental shelf and exclusive economic zone has to be measured from the islands fringing ["*les îles côtières*", in the French version] the Nicaraguan coast".[582]

6.16 Of course, in the original case the Court was not called upon to rule on any question involving straight baselines because none existed in the relevant area. Thus, the features considered by the Court in 2012 on which individual basepoints could be situated *fringe* Nicaragua's Caribbean mainland coast in the sense that they *lie off* this coast. They are adjacent to Nicaragua's mainland coast, i.e. they can be said to be *fringing* islands. To the extent that they qualify as islands – which Nicaragua does not prove – they can be designated more accurately as "*des îles côtières*".

6.17 But that does not mean that they form a "fringe of islands" ("*un chapelet d'îles*", in French) within the meaning of the rule embodied in UNCLOS Article 7. "Fringing islands" ("*des îles côtières*") and a "fringe of islands" ("*un chapelet d'îles*") are two different notions, corresponding to distinct geographical situations.

---

[582] *Territorial and Maritime Dispute (Nicaragua* v. *Colombia), Judgment, I.C.J. Reports 2012*, p. 671, para. 135 and p. 678, para. 145 respectively. See also p. 703, para. 214: "the Nicaraguan mainland and fringing islands, and the Colombian islands, are located on the same continental shelf".

A fringe of islands is not just a set of "fringing islands": it is, as interpreted by the Court, a "cluster of islands" or an "island system".[583] Such qualification is nowhere to be found in the 2012 Judgment. The terms "fringing islands" and "fringe of islands" are therefore not interchangeable, and the Court never used the latter in its 2012 Judgment.

6.18 Nicaragua also asserts that Colombia's Counter-Memorial "ignores the fact that the Court gave Nicaragua's fringing islands a different treatment from Serpents' Island in *Black Sea*";[584] Nicaragua explains that:

> "In *Territorial and Maritime Dispute (Nicaragua v. Colombia)*, basepoints on Nicaragua's fringing islands were used in the construction of a provisional equidistance line. To the contrary, Serpents' Island was ignored by the Court in establishing a provisional equidistance line. The Court justified its choice in Black Sea observing that:
>
>> 'Serpents' Island calls for specific attention in the determination of the provisional equidistance line. In connection with the selection of base points, the Court observes that there have been instances when coastal islands have been considered part of a State's coast, in particular when a coast is made up of a cluster of fringe islands. (…) However, Serpents' Island, lying alone and some 20 nautical miles away from the mainland, is not one of a cluster of fringe islands constituting 'the coast' of Ukraine. To count

583 *Maritime Delimitation and Territorial Questions between Qatar and Bahrain, Merits, Judgment, I.C.J. Reports 2001*, p. 103, paras. 213-214. See also CCM, paras. 10.37 and 10.38.

584 NR, para. 7.22.

each of these seven features is part of a cluster of islands lying off Nicaragua's mainland coast.

6.20 This *a contrario* argument is untenable.

6.21 *First*, the only analogy that could be drawn from the two cases is that, in both of them, the Court assessed the relevance of using the maritime features as basepoints in the *construction of a provisional equidistance line*. In none of them did the Court address or decide the issue whether straight baselines could join basepoints posited on specific islands.

6.22 *Second*, in the *Maritime Delimitation in the Black Sea* case, the Court, in connection with the *sole* task of selecting basepoints and of identifying the relevant coast of Ukraine, addressed the question whether coastal islands can be considered as part of a State's coast. As the Court noted, depending on the circumstances, they may. The Court then held, in the paragraph Nicaragua quotes, that: "there have been instances when coastal islands have been considered part of a State's coast, *in particular when* a coast is made up of a cluster of fringe islands".[590] In other words, an island forming part of a cluster of fringe islands is *one of the instances* where it may be regarded as forming part of a State's relevant coast in connection with a maritime delimitation. Contrary to what Nicaragua suggests, this does not imply that any

590 *Maritime Delimitation in the Black Sea (Romania* v. *Ukraine), Judgment, I.C.J. Reports 2009*, pp. 109 and 110, para. 149. (Emphasis added).

maritime feature considered by the Court to be part of a State's coastal configuration necessarily forms part of a cluster of fringing islands for straight baselines purposes.

6.23 The need for an island to be part of a *cluster* of fringing islands is not a criterion for choosing a basepoint for the construction of a provisional equidistance line. It is telling that in its 2012 Judgment, when assessing Quitasueño's capacity to contribute to the construction of the provisional median line, the Court recalled the factors that determined its decision to disregard Serpents' Island as a base point without making any reference to the notion of cluster of islands. The Court explained:

> "In the *Maritime Delimitation in the Black Sea* case, for example, the Court held that it was inappropriate to select any base point on Serpents' Island (which, at 0.17 square km was very much larger than the part of Quitasueño which is above water at high tide), because it lay alone and at a distance of some 20 nautical miles from the mainland coast of Ukraine, and its use as a part of the relevant coast 'would amount to grafting an extraneous element onto Ukraine's coastline; the consequence would be a judicial refashioning of geography, which neither the law nor practice of maritime delimitation authorizes' (*Maritime Delimitation in the Black Sea (Romania* v. *Ukraine), Judgment, I.C.J. Reports 2009*, p. 110, para. 149). These considerations apply with even greater force to Quitasueño. In addition to being a tiny feature, it is 38 nautical miles from Santa Catalina and its use in the construction of the

> Serpents' Island as a relevant part of the coast would amount to grafting an extraneous element onto Ukraine's coastline.'"[585]

Based on this, Nicaragua then alleges that "the Court was well aware of the implications of its findings on Serpents' Island in assessing the treatment of islands in *Territorial and Maritime Dispute*".[586] What such implications are, Nicaragua does not explain. But it contends that the proof of the awareness of the Court results in the "rejection of Colombia's Quitasueño as a base point. The Court found that its considerations concerning Serpents' Island applied 'with even greater force to Quitasueño'".[587]

6.19 From there, Nicaragua does not draw any conclusion regarding the existence of its alleged fringe of islands, and thus the argument is unintelligible. Colombia can only surmise that Nicaragua suggests that, since the Court found in 2009 that Serpents' Island was "not one of a cluster of fringe islands constituting 'the coast' of Ukraine",[588] and then refused to use it as a basepoint in the construction of a provisional equidistance line, the fact that in 2012 the Court used Edinburgh Reef, Muerto Cay, Miskito Cays, Ned Thomas Cay, Roca Tyra, and the Corn Islands as basepoints in the construction of such a line[589] demonstrates that

---

585 NR, para. 7.22.

586 NR, para. 7.23.

587 NR, para. 7.23.

588 *Maritime Delimitation in the Black Sea (Romania* v. *Ukraine), Judgment, I.C.J. Reports 2009*, pp. 109 and 110, para. 149.

589 *Territorial and Maritime Dispute (Nicaragua* v. *Colombia), Judgment, I.C.J. Reports 2012*, p. 699, para. 201.

> provisional median line would push that line significantly closer to Nicaragua."[591]

6.24 The only judicial conclusion that can be drawn from Nicaragua's quotes from the *Maritime Delimitation in the Black Sea* and *Territorial and Maritime Dispute* Judgments is that "[w]hen placing base points on very small maritime features would distort the relevant geography, it is appropriate to disregard them in the construction of a provisional median line".[592] It is this consideration that lead the Court to reject Serpents' Island and Quitasueño as potential basepoints contributing to the construction of the provisional median line, not the fact that they were not part of a cluster of fringing islands.

6.25 *Third*, and more generally, no analogy can be made between the two cases as regards the treatment of islands in the delimitation since their respective geographic contexts are markedly dissimilar. In *Maritime Delimitation in the Black Sea*, the Court proceeded to a delimitation of maritime areas between States with mainly adjacent coasts, Serpents' Island being close to Romania's coast, lying off the Danube's mouth. In contrast, in *Territorial and Maritime Dispute,* the parties' relevant coasts were strictly opposing coasts.

---

591 *Territorial and Maritime Dispute (Nicaragua* v. *Colombia), Judgment, I.C.J. Reports 2012*, p. 699, para. 202.

592 *Territorial and Maritime Dispute (Nicaragua* v. *Colombia), Judgment, I.C.J. Reports 2012*, p. 699, para. 202.

6.26 In sum, whether read alone or in the light of the Court's findings in the *Maritime Delimitation in the Black Sea*, the 2012 Judgment cannot be used as a precedent as regards the nature of Nicaragua's features (Edinburgh Reef, Muerto Cay, Miskitos Cays, Ned Thomas Cay, Roca Tyra, Little Corn Island and Great Corn Island) under the rules reflected in UNCLOS Article 7 or customary international law.[593]

(b) Nicaragua does not demonstrate that its basepoints are posited on islands constituting "a fringe of islands along the coast in its immediate vicinity"

6.27 In its Counter-Memorial, Colombia demonstrated that the islands Nicaragua designated as basepoints in its Decree No. 33-2013 are not a "fringe of islands" in the sense of UNCLOS Article 7.[594] They are neither a group of "islands forming a unity with the mainland", nor "islands which at some distance from the coast form a screen which masks a large proportion of the coast from the sea", as the United Nations Division for Ocean Affairs and the Law of the Sea (DOALOS) described the two main situations "where a fringe of islands is likely to exist".[595]

---

593 It should be added that the Court did not prejudge the baselines drawing method to be used by Nicaragua when observing that the latter "ha[d] yet to notify the baselines from which its territorial sea is measured" (*Territorial and Maritime Dispute (Nicaragua* v. *Colombia), Judgment, I.C.J. Reports 2012*, p. 713, para. 237).

594 CCM, paras. 10.37 and 10.38.

595 DOALOS, *The Law of the Sea – Baselines: An examination of the Relevant Provisions of the United Nations Convention on the Law of the Sea*, p. 21, available at: http://www.un.org/depts/los/doalos_publications/publicationstexts/The%20Law%20of%20the%20Sea_Baselines.pdf (last visited: 1 November 2018). See also CCM, para. 10.36.

6.28 In its Reply, Nicaragua does not dispute that these are the relevant standards to be used to establish the existence of a fringe of islands. However, it argues that its seven islands form, together with numerous unidentified "islands", a group falling into both of these categories[596] and lying in the immediate vicinity of its mainland coast.[597] Nicaragua's both contentions are unsustainable.

(i) Nicaragua fails to demonstrate that the "group" formed by its adjacent islands constitutes a fringe of islands along its coast

6.29 Nicaragua first contends that the islands forming its alleged fringe of islands are not "relatively small in number", in the sense that the Court used in the *Maritime Delimitation and Territorial Questions between Qatar and Bahrain* case, according to which the number of islands is a condition for a "fringe of islands" to exist.[598] There are, Nicaragua alleges, "in total 95

---

596 NR, paras. 7.23-7.35.

597 NR, paras. 7.37-7.42.

598 *Maritime Delimitation and Territorial Questions between Qatar and Bahrain, Merits, Judgment, I.C.J. Reports 2001*, p. 103, para. 214. See also CCM, para. 10.37. Nicaragua contests the relevance of this case as a precedent because this Judgment refers to the situation of an archipelagic State (Bahrain), which Nicaragua is not (NR, para. 7.27). Such reading of the Judgment is biased. It results from the plain language used by the Court that Bahrain being an archipelagic State had no impact on the *general* principle laid down by the Court according to which a group composed of a few islands cannot be a "fringe of islands" under UNCLOS Article 7. The excerpt Nicaragua cited is only an *obiter dictum* following the affirmation of this principle, in which the Court specifies that the only hypothesis in which a fringe of Bahraini islands would exist in the sense of Article 7 is where the alleged fringe includes, besides the islands "relatively small in number", Bahrain's *main* islands; however, in such hypothesis, Bahrain being a multiple-island State, drawing straight baselines between basepoints posited on all its islands including the main ones is allowed by UNCLOS only if

islands that fringe Nicaragua's Caribbean coast".[599] Nicaragua limits itself to setting out a list of these so-called islands in Annex 31 to its Reply, without justifying their insular nature or characteristics or specifying their location. In Figure 7.3 of its Reply entitled "Nicaragua's fringe of islands",[600] the other "islands" allegedly forming a fringe of islands, along with the maritime features on which Decree No. 33-2013 posited basepoints, are not specified. But judging from the blue segments displayed, these supplementary "islands" seem to be located between the Miskitos Cays and the mainland coast, and between the Corn Islands and the mainland coast. Nicaragua does not give any information about these features, including their name and their nature.

6.30 Despite this vagueness, Nicaragua's position can be inferred from Figure 7.3 of its Reply: the "fringe of islands along [its] coast in its immediate vicinity" which supposedly justifies the drawing of straight baselines between the basepoints defined in Decree No. 33-2013 seems to consist of:

- The seven maritime features on which these basepoints are posited; and

---

Bahrain has declared itself to be an archipelagic State under Part IV of the Convention – since Bahrain did not, it is not entitled to draw straight baselines to join its minor islands to each other. The fact that Nicaragua is not an archipelagic State changes nothing to the requirement of a number of islands greater than "relatively small" which is required to qualify a fringe of islands under UNCLOS Article 7.

599 NR, para. 7.26. See also para. 7.20.

600 NR, p. 166.

- Some unidentified features located between the mainland coast and the Miskitos Cays and the Corn Islands.

6.31 This group of features – assuming, *quod non,* that they are islands as defined by customary international law – does not meet, as a whole, the conditions required by UNCLOS Article 7 for the drawing of straight baselines. As the Court has noted, these criteria must be applied "restrictively".[601]

6.32 *First*, this newly defined group of islands *does not form a unity with the mainland.*[602] The only argument made by Nicaragua in its Reply in response is that unity is demonstrated by the fact that, between Nicaragua's mainland coast and, respectively, the Corn Islands and the Miskitos Cays, there are two groups of unidentified maritime features. Since they are unidentified, Nicaragua does not meet its burden of proof.

6.33 Moreover, such a presence, even if it was established and assuming continuity between these features could be demonstrated, would merely illustrate a unity between the mainland and the Miskitos Cays, and between the mainland and the Corn Islands.[603] But the contended fringe of islands at issue is

---

601 *Maritime Delimitation and Territorial Questions between Qatar and Bahrain, Merits, Judgment, I.C.J. Reports 2001*, p. 103, para. 212.

602 CCM, para. 10.39.

603 The point that Nicaragua is thus making, though without the support of any demonstration, is that the "islands" lying between its mainland and Miskitos Cays on the one hand, and those lying between its mainland and Corn Islands on the other hand, form two fringes of islands each arranged on

not the "Miskitos Cays group" or the "Corn islands group", but the *whole group* of islands that Nicaragua has elected to connect, from Edinburgh Reef in the North to Great Corn Island in the south, by straight baselines.

---

an axis perpendicular to the mainland coast. But it bears no consequence – and Nicaragua did not draw any in its Decree No. 33-2013 – as regards the case at hand and generally the ability to draw straight baselines between appropriate basepoints posited on islands pertaining to these "fringes": as DOALOS puts it: "[s]ince the fringe has to be 'along the coast' [Article 7(1)] would not, therefore, apply to islands arranged like stepping stones perpendicular to the coast". See DOALOS, *The Law of the Sea – Baselines: An examination of the Relevant Provisions of the United Nations Convention on the Law of the Sea*, p. 21 available at: http://www.un.org/depts/los/doalos_publications/publicationstexts/The%20Law%20of%20the%20Sea_Baselines.pdf (last visited: 1 November 2018). In any event, Nicaragua's Reply does not demonstrate any continuity/unity between the mainland, middle so-called islands and the Miskitos Cays and between the mainland, middle so-called islands and the Corn Islands.

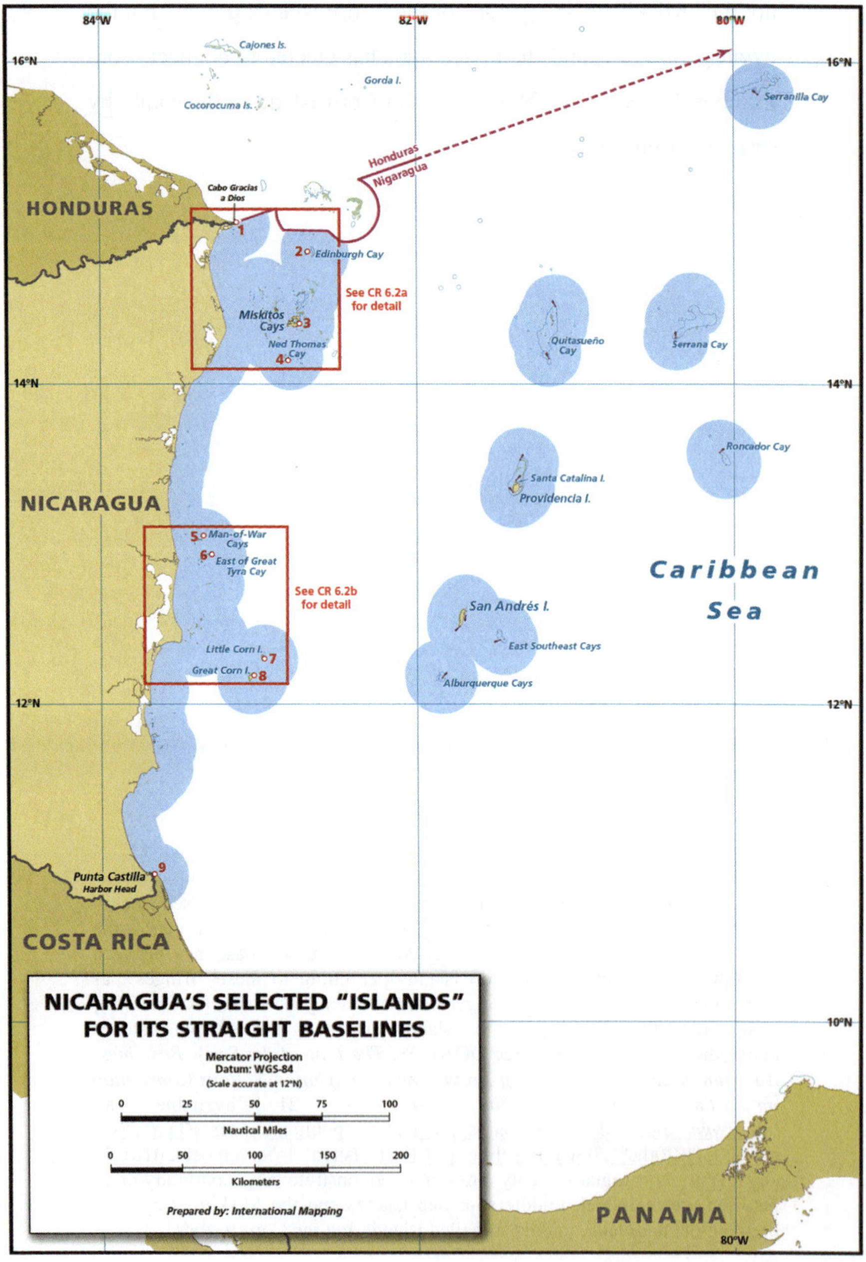

84°W
82°W
80°W
16°N
14°N
12°N
10°N
Cajones Is.
Gorda I.
Cocorocuma Is.
Serranilla Cay
Honduras
Nicaragua
Cabo Gracias a Dios
HONDURAS
1
2
Edinburgh Cay
See CR 6.2a for detail
Miskitos Cays
3
Ned Thomas Cay
4
Quitasueño Cay
Serrana Cay
Roncador Cay
Santa Catalina I.
Providencia I.
NICARAGUA
5
Man-of-War Cays
6
East of Great Tyra Cay
See CR 6.2b for detail
Caribbean Sea
San Andrés I.
East Southeast Cays
Little Corn I.
7
Great Corn I.
8
Alburquerque Cays
Punta Castilla Harbor Head
9
COSTA RICA
NICARAGUA'S SELECTED "ISLANDS" FOR ITS STRAIGHT BASELINES
Mercator Projection
Datum: WGS-84
(Scale accurate at 12°N)
0 25 50 75 100
Nautical Miles
0 50 100 150 200
Kilometers
Prepared by: International Mapping
PANAMA

Figure CR 6.2

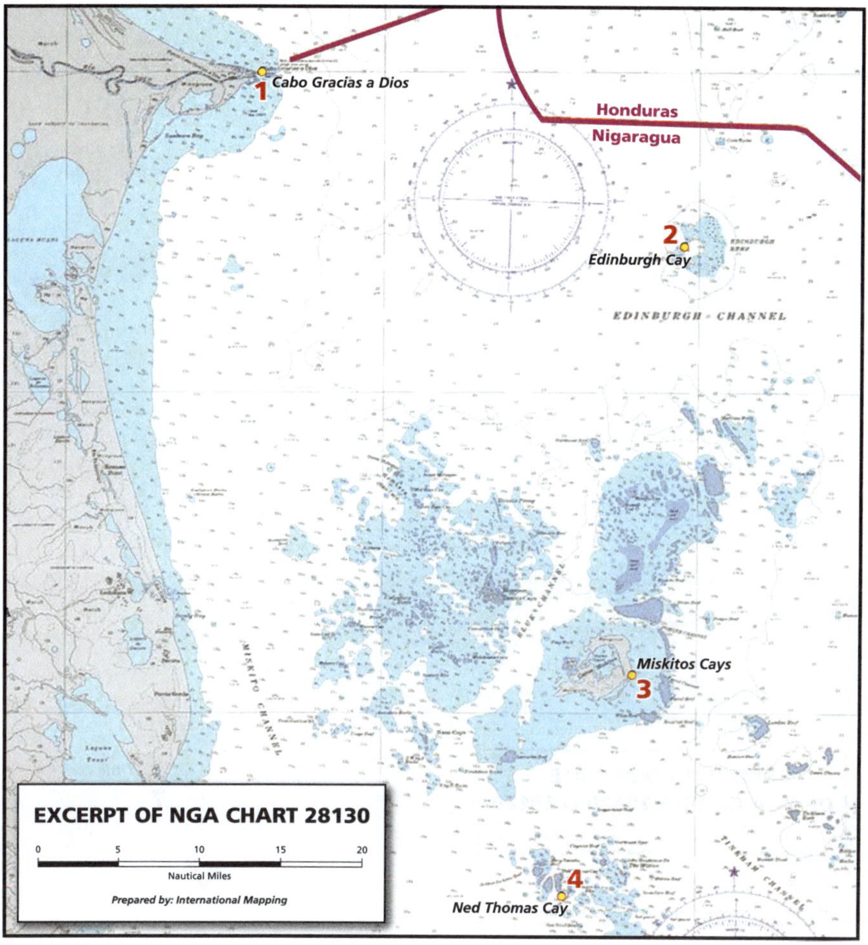

Figure CR 6.2a

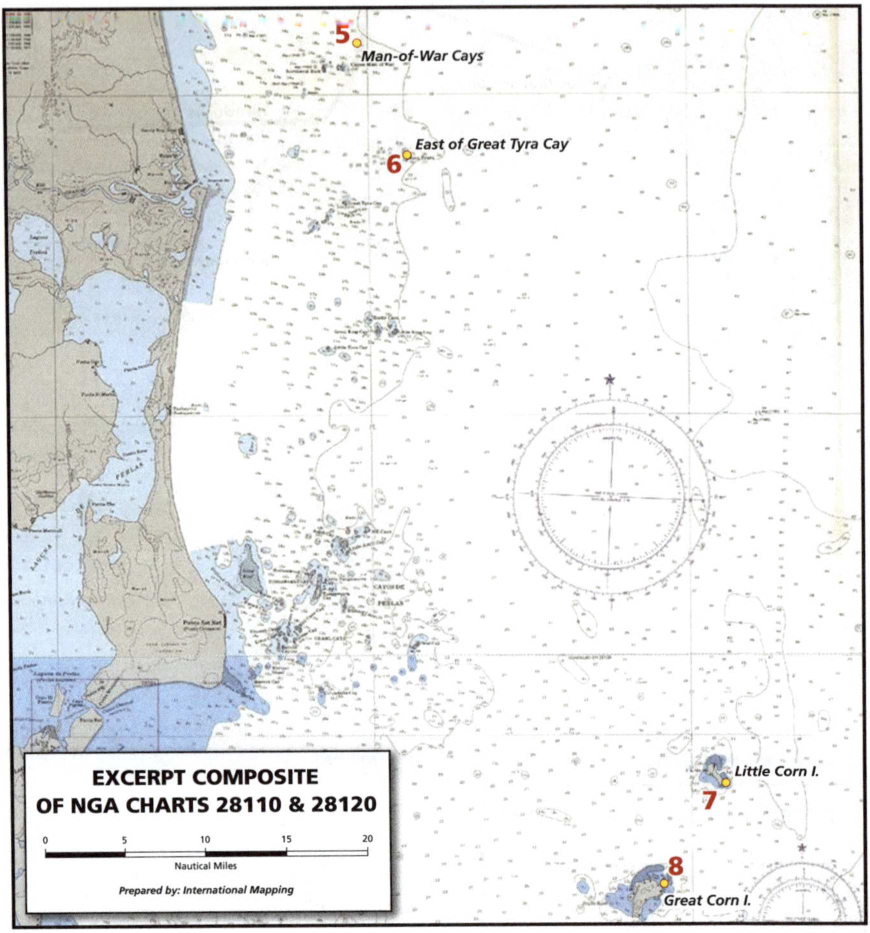

Figure CR 6.2b

6.34 These islands, as a whole, cannot be regarded as forming a unity with the mainland given the large distance between them. Proceeding from north to south, one finds the following features that Nicaragua seeks to join by means of its straight baselines:

- Edinburgh Reef, an isolated and minuscule feature;

- 27 nautical miles from it, the small Miskitos Cays and Ned Thomas Cay to the west of which would be found the unidentified islands relied on by Nicaragua;

- 75 nautical miles to the south, Man-of-War Cays and Great Tyra Cay – also very small features;

- 44 nautical miles further southward, and 85 nautical miles to the north of the next and southernmost basepoint, there are the Corn Islands, a pair of relatively small islands to the west of which the alleged spread unidentified islands would also be found.[604]

As shown on the Figure, the different components of Nicaragua's so-called "fringe of islands" are simply too isolated from each other to be deemed as forming a "unity".

---

604 CCM, Figure 10.4.

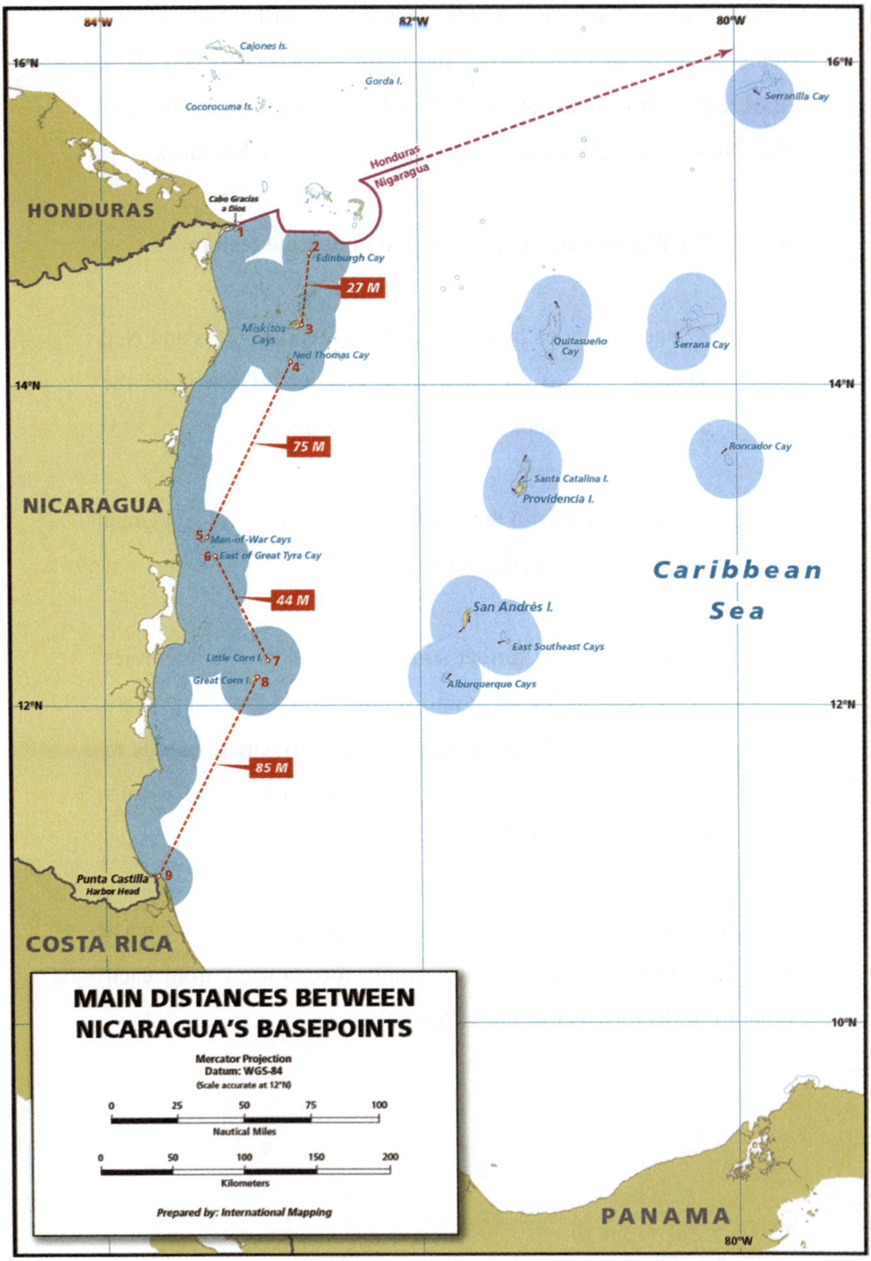

MAIN DISTANCES BETWEEN NICARAGUA'S BASEPOINTS
Mercator Projection
Datum: WGS-84
(Scale accurate at 12°N)
Nautical Miles
Kilometers
Prepared by: International Mapping
84°W
82°W
80°W
16°N
14°N
12°N
10°N
HONDURAS
NICARAGUA
COSTA RICA
PANAMA
Caribbean Sea
Cajones Is.
Gorda I.
Cocorocuma Is.
Cabo Gracias a Dios
Honduras
Nicaragua
Serranilla Cay
Edinburgh Cay
27 M
Miskitos Cays
Ned Thomas Cay
Quitasueño Cay
Serrana Cay
75 M
Roncador Cay
Santa Catalina I.
Providencia I.
Man-of-War Cays
East of Great Tyra Cay
44 M
San Andrés I.
East Southeast Cays
Little Corn I.
Great Corn I.
Alburquerque Cays
85 M
Punta Castilla
Harbor Head

Figure CR 6.3

6.35 *Second*, these maritime features do not form, as required by the rule of customary international law reflected in UNCLOS Article 7, a *continuous* fringe along the coast.[605]

6.36 *Third*, the maritime features of this newly defined "group" *have no or a very limited masking effect* on the mainland coast.

6.37 Nicaragua agrees with Colombia that a controlling precedent in this respect is the *Eritrea/Yemen (second stage)* case, where the arbitral tribunal concluded that what it termed "an intricate system of islands, islets and reefs which guard this part of the coast" was indeed a "fringe system" of the kind contemplated by Article 7 of UNCLOS.[606] Nicaragua contends that its islands do have such a guarding or masking effect.

6.38 According to Nicaragua:

- All its fringing islands and features should be taken into account in the assessment of the masking effect;[607]

---

605 Virginia Commentary, p. 100: the expression fringing islands "covers the case where a number of islands of various size are spread out near the shore so as to form a continuous fringe along the coast". See also CCM, para. 10.36.

606 *Award of the Arbitral Tribunal in the Second Stage of the Proceedings between Eritrea and Yemen (Maritime Delimitation)*, p. 369, para. 151. See NR, paras. 7.31 and 7.32; see also CCM, paras. 10.41-10.42.

607 NR, para. 7.35.

- As regards the appreciation of the masking phenomenon itself,

> "in the light of the Court's case law it would be reasonable to look at the projection of 'all islands and features' between a perpendicular to the general direction of Nicaragua's mainland coast and an angle of 20 degrees to that perpendicular";[608]

- The length of the coast with respect to which the masking effect is to be calculated is the total length of the mainland coast minus the indented part of the coast (see *infra*) from Monkey Point up to the terminus of Nicaragua's land boundary with Costa Rica;[609]

- Basing itself on these self-serving factors, Nicaragua submits that, with respect to the northern part of the coast, "more than 50% of that mainland coast is masked";[610] and that when including the segment from Monkey Point up to the terminus of Nicaragua's land boundary with Costa Rica, 46% of its total mainland coast would be masked, on the basis of a 20-degrees projection. Finally, if a strictly

---

608 NR, para. 7.35.

609 NR, para. 7.36.

610 NR, para. 7.36. Nicaragua purports to illustrate this result by a figure (NR, Figure 7.5) which is notable for lack of any key and incomprehensible: what the pink and green projections are supposed to be representing is not explained, and the names and specifics of the features that are shown as having a masking effect are not identified or documented (the minuscule features just north of Monkey Point, in particular).

frontal projection is used, Nicaragua contends that 25% of the overall coast would be masked.[611]

6.39 These calculations are fanciful. Once again Nicaragua relies on unidentified maritime features, the characteristics of which are simply ignored, thus depriving its calculation of any factual basis.[612] Additionally, Nicaragua relies on a "projection angle" that finds no support in the jurisprudence or international practice. While Nicaragua contends a projection angle of 20% is "reasonable",[613] in reality it is absurd.

6.40 The only element on which Nicaragua relies is a sketch-map (No. 5) used by the Court in the *Maritime Delimitation in the Black Sea (Romania* v. *Ukraine)* case to depict the projection of the parties' relevant coasts along the low-water mark defining the maritime area to be delimited.[614] But this is manifestly irrelevant: the seaward projection of coasts for determining overlapping maritime entitlements says nothing about the masking effect of islands for straight baseline purposes.

6.41 Nicaragua's islands and features do not form an "intricate system of islands"; they do not "guard" the mainland coast (i.e.

---

611 NR, para. 7.34.

612 The list of adjacent maritime features Nicaragua produces in Annex 31 to its Reply provides only the names of the features. It explains nothing about the dimensions or characteristics of each feature.

613 NR, para. 7.35.

614 NR, para. 7.35. The sketch-map is reproduced in *Maritime Delimitation in the Black Sea (Romania* v. *Ukraine), Judgment, I.C.J. Reports 2009*, p. 102.

generate a "masking effect"[615] which covers only 5 or 6% of Nicaragua's entire mainland coast);[616] they do not "cover the coast in such a way as to be considered as its seaward extension";[617] and they do not form a fringe of islands along the mainland coast. Accordingly, they do not justify Nicaragua's system of straight baselines.

(ii) Nicaragua fails to demonstrate that the "group" formed by the maritime features adjacent to its coast lies in its immediate vicinity

6.42 In its Counter-Memorial, Colombia showed that none of the seven islands on which Nicaragua purports to posit its basepoints lies in the "immediate vicinity" of Nicaragua's coast.[618]

6.43 Nicaragua is obviously aware of this deficiency in its claim. In its Reply, therefore, Nicaragua contends that the alleged "fringe of islands" justifying the drawing of straight baselines from Edinburgh Cay up to Great Corn Island not only consists of the seven "main" islands, but also of unidentified maritime

615 As it relates to the measurement of the "masking effect", see for example the method retained by the United States, as illustrated in United States Department of State, Bureau of Oceans and International Environmental and Scientific Affairs, *Limits in the Seas, No. 106, Developing Standard Guidelines for Evaluating Straight Baselines*, pp. 26-27, available at: https://www.state.gov/documents/organization/59584.pdf (last visited: 1 November 2018).

616 CCM, para. 10.41 and Figure 10.2. Even assuming, as Nicaragua claims, that the relevant length of Nicaragua's Caribbean mainland coast was, for the sake of evaluating the masking effect, to be measured from Cabo Gracias a Dios in the north to Monkey Point in the South, this percentage would remain insignificant.

617 S. Kopela, *Dependent Archipelagos in International Law of the Sea*, Brill Nijhoff, 2013, p. 63 (available at the Peace Palace Library).

618 CCM, para. 10.42 and Figure 10.3.

features supposedly lying between the mainland coast and, on the one hand, the Miskitos Cays and, on the other, between the mainland coast and the Corn Islands. Based on this, Nicaragua argues that the "immediate vicinity" requirement applies only to the *inner edge* of the fringe. Since, according to Nicaragua, the westernmost "islands" (not the seven "main" islands) are near the mainland coast, the whole "fringe", including the "main" islands that are not "near" the coast, meets the "immediate vicinity" requirement.

6.44 This argument is wholly unsubstantiated.

6.45 *First*, in both the *Eritrea/Yemen (second stage)* case, and as regards the baselines established by Finland in the area of the Åland islands area and by Norway in the far north of Tromsø, both mentioned by Nicaragua,[619] straight baselines were drawn to enclose an *intricate system of islands,*[620] the inner edge of which is indeed very close to the mainland. This geographical characteristic is absent in the present case, even taking into account all the contended "islands" between the mainland coast and the islands Nicaragua uses as basepoints.

619 NR, paras. 7.38-7.40.

620 This notion was used in the *Award of the Arbitral Tribunal in the Second Stage of the Proceedings between Eritrea and Yemen (Maritime Delimitation)* to designate the fringing islands considered by the Tribunal. The Åland islands form an archipelago, and the Norwegian islands off Tromsø have a configuration similar to the one of the *Skjaergaard* that the Court regarded in the *Fisheries case (United Kingdom* v. *Norway)* as a fringe of islands justifying the drawing of straight baselines.

6.46 *Second*, Nicaragua does not even attempt to identify those "islands" pertaining to the alleged fringe which are said to be located in the "immediate vicinity" of its mainland coast. As noted earlier, it provides no names, no physical description, no coordinates, no distance to the mainland coast except on a sketch which does not display their names,[621] and no demonstration that these features are indeed islands under international law.

6.47 Likewise, Nicaragua fails to demonstrate that there is a "continuity" between the mainland, the unidentified islands allegedly located in the immediate vicinity of the coast, and the "main" islands. As can be seen in Figure 10.3 of Colombia's Counter-Memorial, the majority of the features on which Nicaragua places its basepoints are located beyond 25 nautical miles from the nearest points on the mainland coast.

6.48 Furthermore, Nicaragua is unable to identify State practice that would be widespread enough to establish as a rule of customary law that a distance ranging from 25 to 30 nautical miles[622] between the coast and the islands is generally accepted as not excessive.

6.49 Suffice it to note that the United States (which protested against Nicaragua's Decree No. 33-2013) considers that the "immediate vicinity" criterion is met when the most landward

---

621 NR, Figure 7.3.

622 The exception only being Man-of-War Cays and Great Tyra Cay (11.6 and 12.7 M respectively) and Miskitos Cays (22.4 M). See CCM, para. 10.42 and Figure 10.3.

point of each island lies no more than 24 nautical miles from the mainland coastline,[623] and that the DOALOS, in its 1989 study, observed that:

> "The spirit of article 7, in respect of (…) fringing islands, will be preserved if straight baselines are drawn when the normal baseline and closing lines of bays and rivers would produce a complex pattern of territorial seas and when those complexities can be eliminated by the use of a system of straight baselines. *It is not the purpose of straight baselines to increase the territorial sea unduly*".[624]

6.50 But that is precisely the result that is produced by Nicaragua's attempt to posit a fringe of islands in the immediate vicinity of its coast where such a fringe does not exist.[625]

---

623 International Law Association, *Baselines under the International Law of the Sea, Final Report (2018),* para. 21, available at http://www.ila-hq.org/images/ILA/DraftReports/DraftReport_Baselines.pdf (last visited: 1 November 2018).

624 DOALOS, *The Law of the Sea – Baselines: An examination of the Relevant Provisions of the United Nations Convention on the Law of the Sea*, p. 21, para. 39, available at: http://www.un.org/depts/los/doalos_publications/publicationstexts/The%20Law%20of%20the%20Sea_Baselines.pdf (last visited: 1 November 2018). (Emphasis added).

625 Nicaragua tries to minimize the extent of its claim by stating that "81% of the internal waters that are enclosed by [its] straight baselines already formed part of [its] territorial sea measured from the low-water line" (NR, para. 7.51 and Figure 7.9). But this just highlights the problem. By its newly enacted straight baselines, Nicaragua transforms large areas of what previously formed part of the territorial sea into internal waters, and areas that previously were part of the EEZ into territorial sea.

(iii) The last segment of the claimed straight baselines is inconsistent with Nicaragua's justification for the use of straight baselines in the relevant area

6.51 Nicaragua justifies the southernmost segment of its straight baselines system with the second criterion for drawing straight baselines reflected in UNCLOS, Article 7(1) – namely, the presence of a coastline that is deeply indented and cut into.

6.52 In particular, Nicaragua contends that:

> "the straight baseline between basepoints 8 and 9 defined by Decree No. 33-2013 runs southerly from a basepoint on Great Corn Island to the mainland coast of Nicaragua. That straight baseline does not only enclose the islands that fringe Nicaragua's mainland in that area, but in addition encloses the deeply indented and cut-into coast between Monkey Point and the terminus of the land boundary with Costa Rica."[626]

This is manifestly not the case. A mere glance at the map reveals that the mainland coast lying behind the straight baseline segment between Great Corn Island and Harbour Point is not "deeply indented and cut into".[627] Geography being what it is, Nicaragua cannot demonstrate the contrary.

---

[626] NR, para. 7.18.

[627] Harbour Point is the southernmost of the basepoints posited in Decree No. 33-2013, which Nicaragua announced in its Reply it will amend following the Court's Judgment in the *Maritime Delimitation in the Caribbean Sea and the Pacific Ocean (Costa Rica* v. *Nicaragua)* case that determined the terminus of its land boundary with Costa Rica.

6.53. In sum, Nicaragua's Decree drawing straight baselines is not in conformity with international law. Nicaragua's straight baselines simply do not satisfy the geographical conditions imposed by customary or conventional international law.

(2) THE ABSENCE OF A SUFFICIENTLY CLOSE LINK BETWEEN THE SEA AREAS ENCLOSED AND THE LAND DOMAIN

6.54 Nicaragua's Decree No. 33-2013 draws segments of straight baseline of 44 nautical miles (between basepoints 6 and 7), 75 nautical miles (between basepoints 4 and 5), and as much as 85 nautical miles (between basepoints 8 and 9). The resulting baselines lie at certain points some 30 nautical miles off Nicaragua's mainland coast and enclose 21,500 square kilometres of water now claimed as internal waters – i.e. two-thirds the size of Belgium, larger than Slovenia, twice the size of Lebanon or Jamaica, and almost ten times the size of Luxembourg. These large expanses of waters are obviously not "closely linked to the land domain".[628]

6.55 Nicaragua refers in its Reply to the 1989 baselines study of the DOALOS, and submits that no mathematical test has been developed in State practice to assess straight baselines as regards the link to the land domain required by the rule reflected in UNCLOS Article 7(3).[629]

---

628 CCM, para. 10.48.
629 NR, para. 7.49.

6.56 This misses the point. The question is not whether a mathematical test applies. Rather, it is whether a straight baselines system leads to a reasonable result, by enclosing as internal waters only parts of the sea that can be legitimately seen as closely linked to the land domain. On this question, as rightly said by Fitzmaurice, the dominant consideration is that the waters enclosed really partake of the character of territory, so that it should be reasonable to treat them as internal waters.[630] Thus, the length of the baselines,[631] their distance from the mainland coast, and the surface of water enclosed within such system are obviously relevant, since they objectively reflect whether there is a close connection between the coast and the waters concerned.

6.57 Nicaragua also argues that its newly designated internal waters are in a "fairly close proximity" with its coast, because "a large part of [these internal waters] is studded with the numerous islands and cays that fringe Nicaragua's Caribbean mainland coast".[632] Notwithstanding the fact that Nicaragua does not substantiate this argument in order to demonstrate that these features are linked with the mainland coast through the sea areas enclosed, it concedes that it concerns only limited parts of the sea area, and that "the remaining parts" are not concerned.[633] But it

630 G. Fitzmaurice, "The Law and Procedure of the International Court of Justice", *British Yearbook of International Law*, Vol. 31, 1954, p. 407 (available at the Peace Palace Library).

631 G. Fitzmaurice, "The Law and Procedure of the International Court of Justice", *British Yearbook of International Law*, Vol. 31, 1954, p. 409 (available at the Peace Palace Library).

632 NR, para. 7.52.

633 NR, para. 7.52.

suffices to observe that those "remaining parts" can by no means be considered internal waters to conclude that Nicaragua's system of straight baselines is inconsistent with international law. These baselines exceed "the bounds of what is moderate and reasonable", as the Court characterized the "overarching" standard of compliance in this matter.[634]

C. Conclusions

6.58 In conclusion, for all of the reasons set out above, Nicaragua's newly enacted system of straight baselines does not comport with international law and prejudices Colombia.

6.59 While Nicaragua claims in Decree No. 33-2013 that it has a deeply indented and cut into coastline, and that there is a fringe of islands along its coast and its immediate vicinity, it has not met the burden of proof as to these requirements for the drawing of straight baselines. In fact, the Caribbean coast of Nicaragua is far from being deeply indented and the scarce insular features referred to by Nicaragua do not constitute a fringe of islands to justify the drawing of straight baselines. As a result, Nicaragua is attempting to misappropriate significant maritime areas as its internal waters, artificially expanding its territorial sea belt and limiting the rights of third States in the Caribbean.

---

634 *Fisheries case, Judgment of December 18th, 1951: I.C.J. Reports 1951*, p. 142.

Chapter 7

SUMMARY

A. Nicaragua's Claims

7.1 Nicaragua alleges that Colombia violated its sovereign rights and maritime spaces in four ways:

- By interfering with Nicaraguan fishing boats and naval vessels in its EEZ through a series of so-called "incidents" involving alleged acts of Colombian naval vessels and aircraft;

- By licensing oil exploration blocks in parts of Nicaragua's EEZ;

- By licensing fishing boats to operate in Nicaragua's EEZ; and

- By establishing a contiguous zone which overlaps in places with Nicaragua's EEZ, and which provides for jurisdictional powers and a spatial extent that goes beyond what is permitted under international law.

7.2 Colombia has demonstrated in this Rejoinder that none of these allegations is factually or legally sustainable.

7.3 The parties agree that, under customary international law, Colombia enjoys the freedoms of navigation and overflight, and other internationally lawful uses of the sea related to these freedoms. In an effort to deny Colombia these rights, however, Nicaragua conceives of its EEZ as equivalent to a territorial sea, with Colombia only enjoying right of passage to proceed from one point to another. This is flatly contrary to international law, which places no such limitations on Colombia's, or for that matter, any other State's rights.

7.4 Nicaragua, on the other hand, only enjoys sovereign rights for the purpose of exploring and exploiting, conserving and managing the natural resources within its EEZ, together with other limited jurisdictional powers that are not relevant to this case. None of Colombia's actions have undermined the actual rights of Nicaragua as part of the EEZ regime, as is evidenced by the dramatic increase of Nicaraguan fishing in its EEZ since the 2012 Judgment.

7.5 For its part, Colombia has shown that it has legitimate reasons to be present in the Southwestern Caribbean Sea, including within Nicaragua's EEZ, provided that it has due regard for Nicaragua's sovereign rights.

7.6 Colombia is fully entitled to be on the watch for illegal activities, such as drug trafficking, and environmentally destructive fishing practices that risk damaging the fragile ecosystem of the region and the healthy environment of the inhabitants of the San Andrés Archipelago, including the Raizales. It is also entitled (and bound) to provide assistance to fishing boats in the area when needed.

7.7 With respect to the "incidents" that Nicaragua claims constituted a breach of its sovereign rights, the Court ruled in 2016 that it has no jurisdiction to consider claims based on the alleged threat to use force. Moreover, of the "incidents" which Nicaragua accuses Colombia of having caused in its EEZ, only 13 are purported to have occurred before the critical date when the Pact of Bogotá ceased to be in force between Nicaragua and Colombia. The Court has no jurisdiction to consider post-critical date events. With respect to the alleged incidents which could fall within the Court's jurisdiction, Colombia has demonstrated that some of them simply did not occur and none could possibly constitute a violation of Nicaragua's sovereign rights, as indeed affirmed by contemporaneous acts and statements of Nicaraguan officials who stressed that Colombia's Navy had been respectful and that there had been no incidents following the rendering of the 2012 Judgment.

7.8 With respect to the allegation that Colombia has offered hydrocarbon blocks in areas within Nicaragua's EEZ, the claim is both inadmissible, having not formed part of the subject-matter of the dispute set out in Nicaragua's Application, and baseless as a matter of fact. Colombia has simply not offered any blocks situated within Nicaragua's EEZ for exploration or exploitation. Nor has Colombia issued authorisations to fish in Nicaragua's EEZ. Nicaragua's allegations of the issuance of fishing licenses and authorisations has been demonstrated to be based on a distorted reading of the relevant Colombian regulations and without foundation. The resolutions of the Governorship of the Archipelago Department of San Andrés, Providencia and Santa Catalina simply do not authorize fishing activities in Nicaragua's EEZ.

7.9 There are, in short, no incidents which undermined or violated Nicaragua's EEZ rights and jurisdiction. It follows that Nicaragua's submissions on these claims must be rejected.

7.10 With respect to Colombia's contiguous zone, Decree No. 1946 (as amended) established the integral contiguous zone of the Colombian island territories in the Southwestern Caribbean Sea in accordance with Colombia's rights under customary international law. Indeed, the Decree itself states *expressis verbis* that it is intended to be interpreted and applied in full conformity with customary international law. As Colombia established in the Counter-Memorial and in this Rejoinder, under customary international law, the contiguous zone of one State may lawfully overlap and co-exist with another State's EEZ. There is no inherent conflict between the limited jurisdictional powers of one State within its contiguous zone and the sovereign rights and jurisdiction of another State as part of its EEZ entitlement.

7.11 None of the powers in the Decree exceeds those which Colombia is entitled to exercise under customary international law as part of the contiguous zone regime. Wholly apart from the question of the lawfulness of the Colombia's contiguous zone, a State may exercise the residual freedoms of navigation and overflight, and other internationally lawful uses of the sea related to these freedoms, within another State's EEZ which do not interfere with the specified and limited exclusive economic rights of the other State. Accordingly, all the jurisdictional powers provided for in Decree No. 1946 (as amended) are lawful exercises of the freedoms of navigation and overflight, and other internationally lawful uses of the sea, by a State (Colombia) within another State's EEZ (Nicaragua's). In sum, customary international law does not bar Colombia's contiguous zone from co-existing with Nicaragua's EEZ where they overlap; nor does it preclude Colombia from exercising the freedoms of navigation and overflight, and other internationally lawful uses of the sea, within Nicaragua's EEZ.

7.12 As to the profile of the zone, the simplification of the outer limit of the Colombian contiguous zone in the Southwestern Caribbean Sea is dictated by the geographical facts and is justified in law. The contiguous zones of Colombia's islands meet and overlap; each of the islands is less than 48 nautical miles from the nearest island. The simplification of the contiguous zone around the Colombian island territories through the use of geodetic lines is grounded upon the same rationale which led the Court to simplify the delimitation line in respect of the same islands in the 2012 Judgment. In any event, Colombia's contiguous zone does not, in terms, encroach upon any of Nicaragua's sovereign rights in its EEZ. Under customary international law, the mere enactment of Decree No. 1946 (as amended) does not, in itself, constitute a violation of Nicaragua's rights. Moreover, Nicaragua cannot point to any action taken by Colombia within its contiguous zone that has in any way interfered with the exercise by Nicaragua of its sovereign rights within its EEZ.

B. Colombia's Counter-claims

7.13 Colombia's first counter-claim concerns Nicaragua's violation of the traditional fishing rights of the inhabitants of the San Andrés Archipelago, including the Raizales. Colombia has demonstrated that the inhabitants of the Archipelago, in particular the Raizales, have traditionally engaged in artisanal fishing in maritime areas that have been held to appertain to Nicaragua, as well as in Colombian areas that require navigating through waters of the Nicaraguan EEZ. While Nicaragua, contrary to the public and explicit commitment taken by its President, has denied in these proceedings the existence of these recognized fishing rights, it has failed to identify a single precedent, which in either its operative part or its essential reasoning, stated that non-exclusive traditional fishing rights are extinguished by operation of law in the EEZ. Nicaragua's failure is understandable, since there is no rational explanation as to why traditional fishing rights, which are otherwise recognized as being capable of existing in the territorial sea, should be deemed to be extinguished, by operation of law, in the EEZ.

7.14 Apart from Nicaragua's misreading of UNCLOS and relevant customary international law, Colombia has shown that the parties to this case expressly and repeatedly recognized these traditional fishing rights and are precluded from now denying them. Despite that recognition and the clear law on the matter, the Nicaraguan Naval Force has repeatedly bullied the artisanal fishermen of the Archipelago, impeding them from reaching their traditional banks and lawfully plying their vocation there. This has had a chilling effect in the ability of the local inhabitants to enjoy their traditional fishing rights.

7.15 By means of this counter-claim, Colombia respectfully requests the Court to find that Nicaragua has infringed the traditional fishing rights of the inhabitants of the San Andrés Archipelago, in particular the Raizales. Colombia also asks the Court to rule that Nicaragua is under an obligation to ensure that the inhabitants of the San Andrés Archipelago, including the Raizales, enjoy unfettered access to: a) the traditional fishing banks located in the maritime areas adjudicated to appertain to Nicaragua; and b) the banks located in the Colombian maritime areas, access to which requires navigating through the maritime areas adjudicated to appertain to Nicaragua. With regard to compensation of the assessable damage, including loss of profit, its form and amount should be determined at a later phase of the proceedings, following established practice.

7.16 Colombia's second counter-claim challenges the legality under international law of Nicaragua's Decree No. 33-2013 establishing straight baselines for the measurement of Nicaragua's maritime areas in the Caribbean. Colombia has shown that this Decree breaches Nicaragua's customary and conventional international obligations and directly violates Colombia's rights and entitlements in the Caribbean. In addition to these violations of the principles of international law governing the drawing of straight baselines, Colombia has also shown that the configuration of Nicaragua's islands off its Caribbean coast does not justify the use of straight baselines. Nor can Nicaragua demonstrate that its basepoints are posited on islands constituting the requisite "fringe of islands along the coast in its immediate vicinity". In addition, the islands, as a whole, cannot be regarded as forming a unity with the mainland, another criterion for the drawing of straight baselines that Nicaragua fails to comply with.

SUBMISSIONS

I. For the reasons stated in its Counter-Memorial and Rejoinder, the Republic of Colombia respectfully requests the Court to reject each of the submissions of the Republic of Nicaragua, and to adjudge and declare that

1. Colombia has not in any manner violated Nicaragua's sovereign rights or maritime spaces in the Southwestern Caribbean Sea.

2. Colombia's Decree No. 1946 of 9 September 2013 (as amended by Decree No. 1119 of 17 June 2014) has not given rise to any violation of Nicaragua's sovereign rights or maritime spaces.

   a. There is nothing in international law that precludes the contiguous zone of one State from overlapping with the exclusive economic zone of another State;
   b. The geodetic lines established in the Decree connecting the outermost points of Colombia's contiguous zone do not violate international law;
   c. The specific powers concerning the contiguous zone enumerated in the Decree do not violate international law;

d. No Colombian action in the contiguous zone has given rise to any violation of Nicaragua's sovereign rights or maritime spaces.

II. Further, the Republic of Colombia respectfully requests the Court to adjudge and declare that

3. The inhabitants of the San Andrés Archipelago, in particular the Raizales, enjoy traditional fishing rights in maritime areas adjudicated to appertain to Nicaragua.

4. Nicaragua has violated the traditional fishing rights of the inhabitants of the San Andrés Archipelago.

5. Nicaragua's straight baselines established in Decree No. 33-2013 of 19 August 2013 are contrary to international law and violate Colombia's sovereign rights and maritime spaces.

III. The Court is further requested to order Nicaragua

6. With regard to submissions 3 and 4, to ensure that the inhabitants of the San Andrés Archipelago engaged in traditional fishing enjoy unfettered access to:

a. Their traditional fishing banks located in the maritime areas adjudicated to appertain to Nicaragua;

b. The banks located in Colombian maritime areas, access to which requires navigating through the maritime areas adjudicated to appertain to Nicaragua.

7. To compensate Colombia for all damages caused, including loss of profits, resulting from Nicaragua's violations of its international obligations, with the amount and form of compensation to be determined at a subsequent phase of the proceedings.

8. To give Colombia appropriate guarantees of non-repetition.

CARLOS GUSTAVO ARRIETA PADILLA
Agent of Colombia

The Hague, 15 November 2018

TABLE OF CONTENTS

VOLUME II

Appendix

Annexes

1. Statements by Nicaraguan Authorities

2. Nicaraguan Official Documents

3. Colombian Official Documents

4. Diplomatic Notes

5. Colombian Navy Documents

6. Media Reports

7. Other Documents

8. Photographic Material

Figures, Graphics and Tables

Figures in Chapter 2

Figures in Chapter 4

Figures in Chapter 6

Graphics

Table

QR CODE ACCESS TO APPENDIX AND ANNEXES 1-74

INTERNATIONAL COURT OF JUSTICE

DISPUTE CONCERNING

ALLEGED VIOLATIONS OF SOVEREIGN RIGHTS AND MARITIME SPACES IN THE CARIBBEAN SEA

(NICARAGUA V. COLOMBIA)

ADDITIONAL PLEADING

OF THE REPUBLIC OF NICARAGUA ON COLOMBIA'S

COUNTER-CLAIMS

4 March 2019

TABLE OF CONTENTS

LIST OF ACRONYMS

CR	Colombia's Rejoinder
CCM	Colombia's Counter Memorial
NM	Nicaragua's Memorial
NR	Nicaragua's Reply

LIST OF FIGURES

CHAPTER I. INTRODUCTION

1.1 Nicaragua submits this Additional Pleading on Colombia's counter-Claims in accordance with the Court's Order of 4 December 2018[1]. On 17 November 2016, Colombia filed its Counter-Memorial together with four counter-claims[2]. Colombia counter-claimed that Nicaragua breached:

> (1) "Its duty of due diligence to protect and preserve the marine environment of the Southwestern Caribbean Sea"[3];
> (2) "Its duty of due diligence to protect the right of the inhabitants of the San Andrés Archipelago, in particular the Raizales, to benefit from a healthy, sound and sustainable environment"[4];
> (3) "The artisanal fishing right to access and exploit the traditional banks"[5];
> (4) Colombia's sovereign rights and maritime zones by enacting its straight baselines Decree No. 33-2013 of 19 August 2013[6]

1.2 By Order of 15 November 2017, the Court decided that only the third and fourth counter-claims were admissible[7]. Nicaragua addresses both remaining counter-claims in this Additional Pleading.

1.3 Nicaragua recalls that these proceedings where originally instituted by an Application filed by Nicaragua on 26 November 2013. On 3 October 2014 Nicaragua filed its Memorial stating two claims: (1) that Colombia had violated Nicaragua's maritime zones as delimited in the Court's Judgment of 19 November 2012 and its sovereign rights and jurisdiction in these zones and (2) that Colombia violated the obligation not to use or threaten to use force.[8]

---

[1] I.C.J., Order, 4 December 2018, *Alleged Violations of Sovereign Rights and Maritime Spaces in the Caribbean Sea (Nicaragua v. Colombia), Counter-Claims.*
[2] *See* CCM, Chapters 7-10.
[3] CCM, para. 8.2.
[4] CCM, para. 8.2
[5] CCM, Chapter 9.
[6] CCM, Chapter 10.
[7] I.C.J., Order, 15 November 2017, *Alleged Violations of Sovereign Rights and Maritime Spaces in the Caribbean Sea (Nicaragua* v. *Colombia), Counter-Claims*, paras. 82(A)(3) and (4).
[8] *See* in particular NM, Chapters II and III.

1.4 On 19 December 2014, Colombia raised preliminary objections on which the Court ruled on 17 March 2016 finding that it has jurisdiction over the first of Nicaragua's claims[9], and also that the dispute that existed at the date on which Nicaragua filed its Application did not concern Colombia's violation of the prohibition of the use or threat to use force[10]. Despite the fact that Nicaragua did not engage in further discussion with respect to its second claim in its Reply and will not do so in this Additional Pleading, this does not mean that the facts invoked by Nicaragua in support of this claim have become irrelevant to the dispute between the Parties.[11] On the contrary, Colombia's violations of Nicaragua's sovereign rights and jurisdiction have continued to this day and its conduct has become even more hostile in nature.[12]

1.5 This procedural summary evidences that Colombia has made use of every possible tool in an attempt to distract the Court's attention from the real core issue, which is Colombia's public rejection of the 2012 Judgment and subsequent violations of Nicaragua's sovereign rights and jurisdiction as recognized therein; which, pursuant to Articles 59 and 60 of the Court's Statute is unconditionally binding.

1.6 In Chapter II of this Additional Pleading Nicaragua will demonstrate that Colombia has not established either the existence of the so called "traditional fishing rights" it claims or their alleged infringement by Nicaragua. Furthermore, Nicaragua will show that the current state of the law of the sea does not allow for the survival of any alleged traditional fishing rights within another country's Exclusive Economic Zone.

---

[9] I.C.J., Judgment, 17 March 2016, *Alleged Violations of Sovereign Rights and Maritime Spaces in the Caribbean Sea (Nicaragua* v. *Colombia),Preliminary Objections, Reports 2016*,p. 33, para. 74, and p. 43, para. 111(2).

[10] *Ibid.*, p. 33, para. 78 and p. 42, para. 111(1)(c).

[11] *See* NR, Chapter IV.

[12] Nicaragua will supplement the record of these incidents by presenting evidence of additional events that have occurred since it submitted its Reply.

1.7 Chapter III will prove that Nicaragua has complied with international law in establishing its straight baselines, while Colombia's own practice, which is the standard which Colombia could claim to be held in this case, does not comply with international law.

CHAPTER II. THE TRADITIONAL FISHING RIGHTS THAT COLOMBIA CLAIMS DO NOT EXIST AND NICARAGUA HAS NOT INFRINGED THEM IN ANY EVENT

2.1. Colombia continues to argue that Nicaragua has infringed the "traditional fishing rights" of the inhabitants of the San Andrés Archipelago. This claim fails now, as it did before, for the four reasons Nicaragua explained in its 15 May 2018 Reply. That is:

- "traditional fishing rights" of the sort Colombia claims, even if they may previously have existed, were extinguished by the regime of the EEZ;
- President Ortega's public statements intended to defuse the tense political situation created by Colombia's angry rejection of the Court's 2012 Judgment did not change the legal situation;
- in any event, Colombia has not discharged—and cannot discharge—its burden of proving that the traditional rights it claims ever existed in fact; and
- Colombia has also not discharged its burden of proving that Nicaragua has infringed those putative rights.

2.2. Nothing in Colombia's Rejoinder changes any of these conclusions. Indeed, as Nicaragua will show, Colombia's replies to Nicaragua's arguments only underscore the weakness of its case in all respects. Sections A-D of this Chapter, respectively, demonstrate why Colombia's replies on each of the above four points are unpersuasive.

A. Traditional Fishing Rights Were Extinguished by the EEZ Regime

2.3. Nicaragua showed in its Reply that the adoption of the EEZ regime extinguished traditional fishing rights of the sort that Colombia claims in these proceedings.[13] Colombia disagrees and argues that the traditional fishing rights it claims survived the emergence of the regime of the EEZ.[14] In doing so, however, Colombia is reduced to repeated mischaracterizations of Nicaragua's arguments.

2.4. Colombia claims, for example, that "Nicaragua in the end mainly relies on one single paragraph of an UNCLOS provision [i.e., Article 62(3)[15]] to put forward its thesis that traditional fishing rights have been extinguished in the EEZ."[16] That is not true. In fact, Nicaragua presented a detailed analysis of the text of UNCLOS[17] (which Colombia agrees constitutes customary international law binding on both Parties here), the context,[18] the *travaux préparatoires*[19] and the case law, including the jurisprudence of this Court,[20] all of which confirm the conclusion that the EEZ regime extinguished traditional fishing rights within its waters.

2.5. Indeed, as Nicaragua showed, the entire scheme of the EEZ excludes the possibility of enduring traditional fishing rights for other States and/or their nationals. The very purpose of the regime of the EEZ is to make a coastal State's right over the living resources *exclusive*, exactly as the term "exclusive economic zone" suggests. In the words of the *Virginia Commentary*: "The importance of the concept of exclusivity is that the coastal State, *to the exclusion of other States and entities*, has sole jurisdiction as regards the resources of the zone, and has the right to exercise its discretion in respect of those resources."[21]

---

[13] NR, paras. 6.3-6.30.
[14] CR, Chapter 5, argument heading C.
[15] Article 62(3) provides that "[i]n giving access to other States to its exclusive economic zone under this article, the coastal State shall take into account all relevant factors, including, *inter alia*, … the need to minimize economic dislocation in States whose nationals have habitually fished in the zone or which have made substantial efforts in research and identification of stocks."
[16] CR, para. 5.18.
[17] NR, paras. 6.8-6.12.
[18] *Ibid.*, paras. 6.13-6.17.
[19] *Ibid.*, paras. 6.18-6.21.
[20] *Ibid.*, paras. 6.22-6.29.
[21] Satya N. Nanda & Shabtai Rosenne (eds.), *United Nations Convention on the Law of the Sea 1982: A Commentary*, vol. II (1993), p. 519 (emphasis added).

2.6. Multiple provisions of Part V of UNCLOS make the exclusivity of the coastal States' rights clear. These include, *inter alia*:

- Article 56, which gives coastal States exclusive "sovereign rights for the purpose of exploring and exploiting, conserving and managing the natural resources" of the zone;

- Article 58, which specifies the rights of other States and limits them to the freedom of navigation, overflight, and the laying of submarine cables and pipelines, and other internationally lawful uses of the sea related to these freedoms;

- Article 60, which accords coastal States "the exclusive right to construct and to authorize and regulate the construction and operation" of artificial islands and other installations and structures;

- Article 61, which gives coastal States authority "to determine the allowable catch of the living resources in its exclusive economic zone";

- Article 62(4), which requires nationals of other States fishing in the EEZ to "comply with the conservation measures and with the other terms and conditions established in the laws and regulations of the coastal State"; and

- Article 73(1), which provides that a coastal State "may in the exercise of its sovereign rights to explore, exploit, conserve and manage the living resources in the exclusive economic zone, take such measures, including boarding, inspection, arrest and judicial proceedings, as may be necessary to ensure compliance with the laws and regulations adopted by it in conformity with this Convention".

2.7. All of these provisions make clear that the coastal State has exclusive sovereign rights and jurisdiction over the natural resources of its EEZ. To the extent other States and their nationals may wish to fish in the EEZ of the coastal State, Article 62 makes clear they may only do so with the express authorization of the latter and subject to any conditions it may establish.

2.8. Colombia's Rejoinder tellingly does not engage in an analysis of any of these provisions, much less address their significance as a whole. It confines itself only to the dismissive—and mistaken—assertion that "Nicaragua in the end mainly relies" only on Article 62(3) to show that "traditional fishing rights have been extinguished in the EEZ."[22]

2.9. Article 62(3) is important but, as stated, it is far from the only provision on which Nicaragua relies. The significance of Article 62(3) is that it shows that the drafters of UNCLOS specifically considered what account should be taken of the historical fishing practices of other States and their nationals, and decided that they should constitute only one consideration among others that a coastal State should weigh in exercising its sovereign right to give or deny access to other States to the living resources of its EEZ.

2.10. Indeed, the *travaux* on this point could not be clearer. They underscore the conclusion that flows from the plain text of the Convention. As Nicaragua explained in its Reply, a number of States took the view that the Convention should protect their historic fishing practices in waters that were in the process of being transformed into EEZs.[23] That position was decisively rejected in favour of according coastal States the exclusive sovereign rights provided for in Part V.[24]

2.11. Colombia does not dispute this point. Indeed, it does not say anything at all. Its Rejoinder is entirely silent on the *travaux* and the clear conclusion that

---

[22] CR, para. 5.18.
[23] NR, paras. 6.18-6.21.
[24] *Ibid.*

flows from them. Colombia's silence is a tacit admission that its position now cannot stand in the face of the Convention's negotiating history.

2.12. Another critical point on which Colombia maintains a studied silence is the holding of the Chamber of the Court in the *Gulf of Maine* case, which Nicaragua highlighted in its Reply.[25] As Nicaragua explained, the Chamber ruled that the adoption of the EEZ had the effect of extinguishing any historic fishing rights:

> "Until very recently … these expanses were part of the high seas and as such freely open to the fishermen not only of the United States and Canada but also of other countries, and they were indeed fished by very many nationals of the latter. … But after the coastal States had set up exclusive 200-mile fishery zones, the situation radically altered. *Third States and their nationals found themselves deprived of any right of access to the sea areas within those zones* and of any position of advantage they might have been able to achieve within them. As for the United States, any mere factual predominance which it had been able to secure in the area was transformed into a *situation of legal monopoly to the extent that the localities in question became legally part of its own exclusive fishery zone*. Conversely, to the extent that they had become part of the exclusive fishery zone of the neighbouring State, no reliance could any longer be placed on that predominance."[26]

2.13. The Chamber's holding by itself refutes Colombia's case. By virtue of Nicaragua's 2002 declaration establishing an EEZ, "third States *and their nationals*" were "deprived of any right of access to the sea areas" in that zone. Nicaragua acquired a "legal monopoly" over the natural resources of its EEZ. Colombia's failure even to mention the *Gulf of Maine* case shows that it cannot reconcile its position with the Court's jurisprudence.

---

[25] *Ibid.*, paras. 6.22-6.23.

[26] *Delimitation of the Maritime Boundary in the Gulf of Maine Area (Canada v. United States), Judgment, I.C.J Reports 1984* (hereinafter "*Gulf of Maine*"), p. 246 at pp. 341-342, para. 235 (emphases added).

2.14. Even as it fails to address case law from the Court that is directly on point, Colombia accuses Nicaragua of "deliberately ignor[ing]" the awards in the *Arbitration regarding the Delimitation of the Abyei Area* and the *Arbitration between Barbados and the Republic of Trinidad and Tobago*.[27] According to Colombia, "[t]he former concluded that 'the transfer of sovereignty should not be construed to extinguish traditional rights to the use of land (or maritime resources)'",[28] and the "second specifically mentioned that, notwithstanding the delimitation, Trinidad and Tobago had an obligation to grant 'Barbados access to fisheries within [its] EEZ'".[29] Nicaragua did not previously discuss either decision because neither is relevant to the issues in dispute in this case. Still less can either overcome the weight of the Chamber's ruling in the *Gulf of Maine* case.

2.15. The *Abyie* arbitration is irrelevant for two reasons. It dealt with issues of (a) sovereignty over (b) land territory. This case, in contrast, deals with issues of sovereign rights and jurisdiction over maritime areas in the EEZ. And *Barbados v Trinidad and Tobago* is irrelevant because it does not stand for the proposition Colombia claims. The tribunal did *not* rule that *UNCLOS* obliged Trinidad and Tobago to grant Barbados access to fisheries within its EEZ. It determined only that *in light of specific formal representations that the Agent of Trinidad and Tobago made to the tribunal during the case*, it "ha[d] assumed an obligation … to negotiate in good faith an agreement with Barbados that would give Barbados access to fisheries within the EEZ of Trinidad and Tobago, subject to the limitations and conditions spelled out in that agreement …".[30] Nicaragua, in

[27] CR, para. 5.20.
[28] *Ibid.* (citing *Award in the Arbitration regarding the Delimitation of the Abyei Area between the Government of Sudan and the Sudan People's Liberation Movement/Army*, Award of 22 July 2009, R.I.A.A., Vol. XXX, p. 408, para. 753).
[29] *Ibid.* (citing *Arbitration between Barbados and the Republic of Trinidad and Tobago, relating to the Delimitation of the Exclusive Economic Zone and the Continental Shelf between Them* (hereinafter "*Barbados v. Trinidad and Tobago*"), R.I.A.A., Vol. XXVII, p. 227, para. 292.
[30] *Barbados v. Trinidad and Tobago*, para. 292.

contrast, has never committed itself to, or entered, an agreement with Colombia granting it access to any of the resources in its EEZ.

2.16. Colombia also argues that the *Eritrea/Yemen* case supports it position. As Nicaragua previously showed, however, that case offers no help to Colombia.[31] The tribunal was asked to determine the parties' maritime boundary only at the second stage of the proceedings. Before that, at the first stage, it awarded certain islands to Yemen and, based on its concerns for the livelihoods of Eritrean fishermen who had fished near the islands "since times immemorial", ruled: "Yemen shall ensure that the traditional fishing regime of free access and enjoyment for the fishermen of both Eritrea and Yemen shall be preserved for the benefit of the lives and livelihoods of this poor and industrious order of men."[32]

2.17. At the second stage, the parties specifically asked the tribunal to delimit their maritime boundary, "taking into account the opinion that it will have formed on questions of territorial sovereignty, the United Nations Convention on the Law of the Sea, *and any other pertinent factor"*.[33] In other words, the tribunal was empowered by express agreement of the parties to look beyond the terms of UNCLOS in delimiting the maritime boundary. The *Eritrea/Yemen* decision must therefore be viewed as *sui generis* and its holding limited to the unique circumstances of that case.

2.18. Colombia further suggests that it would be anomalous to find that the EEZ regime extinguished traditional fishing rights. It says

> "Colombia fails to see the reason why traditional fishing rights should be perceived as being contrary to the exclusive rights of the coastal State within the EEZ. After all, States enjoy full-fledged sovereignty, which is also exclusive, within their territory, but Nicaragua does not

[31] *See* NR, paras. 6.24-6.29.
[32] *Eritrea v. Yemen*, First Stage of the Proceedings (Territorial Sovereignty and Scope of the Dispute), Award (9 Oct. 1998), para. 526.
[33] *Ibid.*, para. 7 (emphasis added).

> dispute that traditional rights have generally been preserved both in the land territory, internal waters and territorial sea of States."[34]

2.19. If Colombia "fails to see" the difference between (a) land territory and the territorial sea, and (b) the EEZ, it is the result of willful blindness. The legal regime relating to land sovereignty (including internal waters) is, of course, beyond the scope of UNCLOS and is governed only by general international law. The legal regime relating to the territorial sea is a hybrid; it is governed by both UNCLOS *and* general international law. Article 2(3) of the Convention makes this clear. It provides: "The sovereignty over the territorial sea is exercised subject to this Convention *and to other rules of international law*."

2.20. The legal regime of the EEZ is different from both. It is a novel creation of UNCLOS itself and governed by the provisions of Part V of the Convention. While Article 2(3) makes room for "other rules of international law" to apply broadly in the territorial sea, the same is not true in the EEZ. Under Article 58(2), "other pertinent rules of international law apply to the exclusive economic zone" only "*in so far as they are not incompatible with this Part*."

2.21. Colombia considers Article 58(2) "reminiscent of Article 2(3)"[35] but it is not. Indeed, what is striking about the two provisions is how dissimilar they are. In the territorial sea, other rules of international law apply without qualification. In the EEZ, they apply if and only to the extent that they are not incompatible with the legal regime established in Part V.

2.22. Since Part V of UNCLOS gives the coastal State "exclusive" rights to the fish and other living resources in its EEZ, any derogation from that exclusivity, unless explicitly included in Part V, would be incompatible with that Part of the Convention. The defining characteristic of the EEZ is exactly the exclusivity of

---

[34] CR, para. 5.15.
[35] *Ibid.*, para. 5.19.

coastal States' sovereign rights and jurisdiction. To use the Court's words, the regime of the EEZ gives coastal States a "legal monopoly" over the natural resources in the zone.[36] Other States "*and their nationals* [are] deprived of any right of access to the sea areas within those zones"[37] regardless of their historical fishing practices.[38]

2.23. Precisely for these reasons, Colombia gets no mileage from its citations to the *Fisheries (United Kingdom v. Norway)* case or to the *Fisheries Jurisdiction* cases.[39] With respect to the former, Colombia itself states the reason: "the Court found in favour of Norway because it could not be said that its historic claim conflicted with customary international law."[40] Here, in contrast, it *can* be said that Colombia's historic claim conflicts with the legal regime of the EEZ, which now forms part of customary international law.

2.24. Concerning the *Fisheries Jurisdiction* cases, Colombia says "this precedent … attests to the fact that historic rights, which do not seek to negate the coastal State's rights, can exist regardless of the fact that the particular maritime area used to be part of the high seas."[41] Even if that were true when the case was decided in 1974—eight years before UNCLOS came into existence and ten years before the Court first recognized the EEZ regime "as consonant at present with

---

[36] *Gulf of Maine*, para. 235.
[37] *Ibid.*
[38] Colombia mischaracterizes Nicaragua's argument as being that "what is required is a 'carve-out' explicitly preserving traditional rights." CR, para. 5.16. That is not Nicaragua's position. Carve-outs for historic rights like those contained Articles 15 (concerning the delimitation of the territorial sea), 9(6) (concerning historic bays), or 51(1) (concerning traditional fishing in archipelagic waters) are certainly instructive. But what is required, at very least, is a provision making other rules of international law applicable, like the *renvois* contained in Article 2(3), 19, 21, 31, 34, 87 and 138.
[39] *See* CR, paras. 5.17 & 5.24.
[40] *Ibid.*, para. 5.17.
[41] *Ibid.*, para. 5.24.

general international law"[42]—it is not pertinent today . Historic rights of other States cannot exist in the coastal State's EEZ.

2.25. In the end, Colombia appears to recognize the essential incompatibility between its claim in this case and the EEZ regime. It acknowledges that "the incompatibility may be true in relation to competing assertions of States aiming at regulating and managing the living resources of the coastal State."[43] It tries to get around this problem by repackaging its claims as being about the private rights of its citizens, and taking the position that "Colombia neither claims sovereignty nor sovereign rights within Nicaragua's EEZ. Colombia is not even claiming rights on its own behalf since the traditional fishing rights are in fact private rights vested on the artisanal fishermen of the San Andrés Archipelago."[44]

2.26. This distinction makes no difference. The existence of foreign fishing rights, whether sovereign or private in character, are equally incompatible with the "legal monopoly" the EEZ regime creates for the benefit of coastal States. As the Chamber of the Court clearly stated in *Gulf of Maine*, other States "and their nationals" are equally deprived of access to the resources of the zone without the permission of the coastal State.[45]

2.27. Nicaragua observes by way of conclusion that finding that traditional fishing rights can co-exist with the regime of the EEZ would be inconsistent with the very purpose of UNCLOS. The Convention's first preambular paragraph states that the States Parties were "[p]rompted[] by the desire to settle, in a spirit of mutual understanding and cooperation, *all issues relating to the law of the sea* …". The Conference President, Ambassador T.B. Koh of Singapore, underscored

[42] *Gulf of Maine*, para. 94.
[43] CR, para. 5.14.
[44] *Ibid.* Colombia is, in other words, attempting to exercise diplomatic protection on behalf of its nationals. If this had been alleged when it formulated its Counter-claims, it would have been required to show that its nationals had exhausted local remedies before its claims on their behalf in this case could be considered admissible. *See* International Law Commission ("ILC") *Draft Articles on Diplomatic Protection with commentaries* (2006), Article 14(1).
[45] *Gulf of Maine*, para. 235.

the significance of a comprehensive agreement in his remarks to the Informal Plenary and Group of Legal Experts tasked with preparing the final clauses:

> "Our prime concern is the establishment of a completely integrated legal order for the use of the oceans and its resources and potential. All else must be subordinated to and subserve this purpose. This is the function of the Preamble and the Final Clauses. They must not be allowed to create such contention as would obscure and obstruct the overriding objective, hamper the work of the Conference and imperil our chances of success.
>
> We must seek to preserve intact, and protect, the efficacy and durability of the body of law which we are trying to create in the form of a Convention encompassing *all issues and problems relating to the law of the sea as a package* comprising certain elements that constitute a single and indivisible entity."[46]

2.28. To create space in this "package" agreement "encompassing all issues and problems relating to the law of the sea" for the operation of external legal rules that are incompatible with the "integrated legal order for the use of the oceans and its resources" would introduce exactly the contention and confusion that the drafters of the Convention sought to avoid. Colombia's argument that traditional fishing rights of the sort it claims in this case survived the creation of the EEZ regime must therefore be rejected.

B. President Ortega's Attempts to Diffuse a Tense Political Situation Do Not Change the Legal Situation

2.29. Colombia also claims that President Ortega's statements in which he expressed willingness to take account of Colombia's concerns about the Raizales' fishing practices, provided suitable mechanisms could be put in place, constitute

[46] "Note by the President on the Final Clauses," UN Doc. FC/1 (23 July 1979), *reproduced in* Renate Platzöder (ed.), *Third United Nations Conference on the Law of the Sea: Documents, Vol. XII*, p. 349 (1987) (emphasis added).

an "express recognition" of their traditional fishing rights. It is mistaken. As Nicaragua showed in its Reply,[47] President Ortega's statements were, in fact, exercises in statesmanship intended to diffuse the political tension created by Colombia's rejection of the Court's 2012 Judgment.

2.30. Colombia does not—nor could it—deny the circumstances in which President Ortega's statements were made. Colombia's furious reaction to the 2012 Judgment, which led it to withdraw from the Pact of Bogotá, are well known and indisputable.

2.31. Colombia also does not deny that all of President Ortega's statements "recognizing" the Raizales' traditional fishing rights were expressly conditional:

- in the 26 November 2012 statement in which President Ortega stated that Nicaragua would respect the rights of the inhabitants "to fish and navigate those waters, which they ha[d] historically navigated", he also indicated that "*artisanal fishermen would require an authorization from the relevant Nicaraguan authorities*";[48]

- in the 1 December 2012 statement in which he said that Nicaragua would "respect the ancestral rights of the Raizales", President Ortega noted that "*mechanisms*" *would have to be established in order to* "*ensure the right of the Raizal people to fish*";[49]

- in his February 2013 statement, he expressed openness to working with Colombia, and proposed a bilateral commission to "*work on an agreement between Colombia and Nicaragua to regulate this situation ….*";[50]

[47] NR, paras. 6.63-6.75.
[48] CCM, para. 3.94 (emphasis added).
[49] *Ibid.* (emphasis added).
[50] *Ibid.*, Annex 76 (emphasis added).

- in his November 2014 statement, President Ortega indicated that "while the 2012 delimitation will have to be implemented, guarantees to the Raizal communities of the Archipelago *will also have to be included in the agreement to be negotiated with Colombia*";[51] and

- in his November 2015 statement, he declared that Nicaragua "understand[s] that patience is necessary in order to finally reach the conditions for the Court's Judgment to be ratified by the Colombian Parliament. And there we have engagements, as I said, with the Raizales Brothers regarding their Fishing Rights, *which will have to be arranged later*".[52]

2.32. Colombia tries to take advantage of President Ortega's "recognition" of the Raizales' traditional fishing rights without also accepting the conditions he specified. Even as Colombia acknowledges, as it must, that "President Ortega often addresses both matters in conjunction",[53] it nevertheless argues that Nicaragua "is mistaken in suggesting that artisanal fishing rights do not exist independently of mechanisms to be approved by Nicaragua".[54] But Colombia's argument is defeated by its own words. In its Counter-Memorial, Colombia itself rightly acknowledged that requiring mechanisms to be put in place "would have deprived the recognition of the Raizales' historic fishing rights of any meaning".[55]

2.33. Exactly so. A "right" subject to "authorization", conditioned on the adoption of "mechanisms" or subject to subsequent "agreement", is no right at all. Colombia cannot unilaterally accept Nicaragua's offer to accommodate the Raizales' interests without also accepting the explicit conditions placed on that

---

[51] *Ibid*, para. 3.94 (emphasis added).
[52] *Ibid.*, Annex 78 (emphasis added).
[53] CR, para. 5.30.
[54] *Ibid.*, para. 5.32 (quoting NR, para. 6.70 (internal quotation marks omitted)).
[55] CCM, para. 3.93.

offer. International law is not a buffet from which States are entitled to pick what they want and abjure what they do not.

2.34. Although it does not explicitly say so, Colombia appears to construe President Ortega's statements as giving rise to a binding unilateral undertaking.[56] Viewing the matter through that prism confirms that Nicaragua has not "recognized" the Raizales' traditional fishing rights. The Court stated in the *Nuclear Tests* cases:

> "It is well recognized that declarations made by way of unilateral acts, concerning legal or factual situations, may have the effect of creating legal obligations. …
>
> Of course, not all unilateral acts imply obligation; but a State may choose to take up a certain position in relation to a particular matter with the intention of being bound—the intention is to be ascertained by interpretation of the act. *When States make statements by which their freedom of action is to be limited, a restrictive interpretation is called for.*"[57]

In the case concerning the *Frontier Dispute (Burkina Faso v. Republic of Mali)*, the Court was careful to point out that "it all depends on the intention of the State in question".[58]

2.35. Guiding Principle 3 of the ILC's 2006 "Guiding Principles applicable to unilateral declarations of States capable of creating legal obligations" (the "Guiding Principles") states: "To determine the legal effects of such declarations,

---

[56] *See* CR, para. 5.29, fn 475 (quoting *Nuclear Tests (Australia* v *France), Judgment, I.C.J. Reports 1974*, p. 267, para. 43; *Nuclear Tests (New Zealand* v. *France), Judgment, I.C.J. Reports 1974*, p. 472, para. 46).
[57] *Nuclear Tests (New Zealand* v. *France), Judgment, I.C.J. Reports 1974*, p. 472-473, paras. 46-47; *Nuclear Tests (Australia* v *France), Judgment, I.C.J. Reports 1974*, p. 267, paras. 43-44.
[58] *Case concerning the Frontier Dispute (Burkina Faso v. Republic of Mali)*, Judgment of 22 December 1986, *I.C.J. Reports 1986*, p. 573, para. 39.

it is necessary to take account of their content, of all the factual circumstances in which they were made, and of the reactions to which they gave rise."[59]

2.36. In this case, the circumstances in which President Ortega's statements were made do not reflect an unqualified intent to be bound. As stated, they were made in the context of the highly charged political situation created by Colombia's rejection of the Court's 2012 Judgment. President Ortega was trying to bring Colombia back to the table by offering to take account of the concerns it had expressed.

2.37. Indeed, President Santos' statements following a December 2012 meeting between the two Heads of State make this perfectly clear:

> "We will continue seeking for the rights of Colombians to be restored, that The Hague judgment seriously affected. We met with President Ortega. We explained our position very clearly: we want that the rights of Colombians and the Raizal population, not only in terms of artisanal fishermen rights but other rights, be guaranteed and restored. *He understood.* We told him that we need to handle this situation with cold head, in a diplomatic and friendly fashion, as this kind of issues should be handled to avoid incidents. *He also understood.* We agreed to establish communication channels to address all these points".[60]

2.38. President Ortega *understood,* according to President Santos. He did not *agree.* As President Santos explained, he was urging President Ortega to "handle th[e] situation with [a] cold head, in a diplomatic and friendly fashion [so as] to avoid incidents". That President Ortega did so should not be held against him by finding that he deliberately bound Nicaragua to a legal obligation to respect the traditional fishing rights Colombia claims for the Raizales.

2.39. According to Guiding Principle 7 of the Guiding Principles:

---

[59] ILC, *Guiding Principles applicable to unilateral declarations of States capable of creating legal obligations* (hereinafter "*Guiding Principles*"), Guiding Principle 3 (2006) (emphasis added).
[60] CCM, Annex 74 (emphases added).

> "A unilateral declaration entails obligations for the formulating State *only if it is stated in clear and specific terms. In the case of doubt as to the scope of the obligations resulting from such a declaration, such obligations must be interpreted in a restrictive manner.* In interpreting the content of such obligations, weight shall be given first and foremost to the text of the declaration, together with the context and the circumstances in which it was formulated."[61]

2.40. To the extent that President Ortega statements were made "in clear and specific terms", they were expressly conditioned on working out appropriate "mechanisms", including an agreement, with Colombia. Colombia's case is based on ignoring the conditions President Ortega specified.

2.41. Nicaragua is not "attempt[ing] to render [President Ortega's] words without troublesome legal consequences"[62] or otherwise trying "to diminish the value of its President's statements",[63] as Colombia wrongly contends. To the contrary, Nicaragua stands by those statements in their entirety. As President Ortega indicated, Nicaragua is ready to accommodate Colombia's concerns about the Raizales' artisanal fishing interests, provided that the two sides work out appropriate mechanisms *via* a bilateral agreement that respects Nicaragua's exclusive sovereign rights and jurisdiction as recognized in the Court's 2012 Judgment. As Nicaragua has said before, it remains open in the spirit of brotherhood and good neighbourly relations, to work with Colombia to reach a bilateral agreement that takes account of Colombia's and Nicaragua's concerns, including the fishing needs of the Indigenous population of both nations[64].

---

[61] *Guiding Principles*, Guiding Principle 7 (emphasis added).
[62] CR, para. 5.27.
[63] *Ibid.*, para. 5.33.
[64] NR, para. 6.76.

C. Colombia Has Not Proven the Existence of the Rights It Claims

2.42. In its Reply, Nicaragua showed that Colombia's traditional rights claim should be rejected for the additional reason that it had failed to prove that the Raizales traditionally fished in areas that the Court determined to appertain to Nicaragua in 2012.[65] Colombia's Rejoinder accuses Nicaragua of "trying to silence the voice of the Raizales".[66] Nicaragua is doing no such thing. It is merely taking Colombia's evidence on its own terms for purposes of showing that it does not prove what Colombia says it does.

2.43. Colombia appears to recognize the weakness of its case. It thus begins its response on this point by addressing "the standard of proof for establishing the existence of traditional fishing rights",[67] and arguing for a comparatively lax standard. According to Colombia, "the matter of proof must be approached with common sense" in light of the fact that "Colombia is invoking rights vested in a small community of artisanal fishermen that live in an important but, nevertheless, relatively remote region of the Southwestern Caribbean Sea".[68] It cites to two cases for support, neither of which are apposite.

2.44. First, Colombia cites to the *South China Sea (Philippines v. China)* arbitration, in which the tribunal stated that "traditional fishing rights constitute an area where matters of evidence should be approached with sensitivity".[69] The tribunal never stated, however, that the standard of proof should be lower; it considered only that the absence of "official record[s]"[70] was not necessarily inconsistent with the existence of such rights. More importantly, the issue was not really in dispute in that case. Both parties claimed that their fishermen had

---

[65] NR, paras. 6.47-6.62.
[66] CR, para. 5.35.
[67] *Ibid.*, para. 5.36.
[68] *Ibid.*
[69] *Ibid.* (quoting *South China Sea (Philippines v. China)*, PCA Case No. 2013-19, Award (12 July 2016) (hereinafter "*South China Sea*"), p. 315, para. 805).
[70] *South China Sea*, p. 315, para. 805.

traditionally fished in the vicinity of Scarborough Shoal, the only location at issue.[71] Thus, even assuming that the tribunal adopted a lower standard of proof (*quod non*), it was entirely justified in doing so given the parties' mutual claims.

2.45. The same is true of the second case Colombia cites: *Navigational and Related Rights (Costa Rica v. Nicaragua).*[72] In that case, the Court noted in passing that the subsistence fishing activities in questions were "not likely to be documented in any formal way in any official record",[73] but it did not lower the standard of proof. There too, there was no dispute that there had been subsistence fishing in the area for a very long period of time.[74] Nicaragua did not contest this. The standard of proof issue therefore did not arise.

2.46. In this case, as in any other, "it is the duty of the party which asserts certain facts to establish the existence of such facts".[75] And because Colombia is claiming that the Raizales' alleged traditional fishing rights arose as a matter of local custom,[76] it is required to establish the existence of facts showing a "constant and uniform practice" by the Raizales that was "accepted as law by the Parties".[77] This it cannot do. Indeed, whatever standard of proof may be applied, Colombia's claim still fails. Colombia's evidence simply does not support the

---

[71] *Ibid.* ("With respect to Scarborough Shoal, the Tribunal accepts that the claims of both the Philippines and China to have traditionally fished at the shoal are accurate and advanced in good faith.").

[72] CR, para. 5.36 (quoting *Navigational and Related Rights (Costa Rica v. Nicaragua)*, Judgment, I.C.J. Reports 2009, p. 213, para. 141).

[73] *Navigational and Related Rights (Costa Rica v. Nicaragua)*, Judgment, I.C.J. Reports 2009, p. 213, para. 141.

[74] *Navigational and Related Rights (Costa Rica v. Nicaragua)*, Judgment, I.C.J. Reports 2009, p. 213, para. 141 ("The Court recalls that the Parties are agreed that all that is in dispute is fishing by Costa Rican riparians for subsistence purposes. … Subsistence fishing has without doubt occurred over a very long period. … [T]he Parties agree that the practice of subsistence fishing is long established.").

[75] *Pulp Mills on the River Uruguay (Argentina v. Uruguay)*, Judgment, I.C.J. Reports 2010, p. 71, para. 162.

[76] CCM, p. 140 (Ch. 3, argument heading D(1)).

[77] *Right of Passage over Indian Territory (Portugal v. India), Merits, Judgment, I.C.J Reports 1960*, p. 40; *see also Asylum (Colombia/Peru), Judgment, I.C.J Reports 1950*, p. 276 ("a constant and uniform usage practised by the States in question").

conclusion that the Raizales have fished "since time immemorial"[78] in waters that are now within Nicaragua's EEZ.

2.47. The only evidence Colombia submitted with its Counter-Memorial consisted of 11 affidavits gathered in a period of two weeks in 2016 just before the Counter-Memorial was filed.[79] In its Reply, Nicaragua explained why those affidavits—taken at face value—actually *disprove* Colombia's claims.[80] In particular, they show that any historic fishing took place largely in the vicinity of Colombia's islands, not in Nicaragua's EEZ.[81] Although some of the younger affiants do assert that they have more recently fished in what are now Nicaraguan waters, the clear story that emerges from the affidavits read as a whole is that some Raizales started venturing further from shore only in recent decades as a result of improving technology and the depletion of fish stocks in their traditional, near-shore fishing grounds.[82]

2.48. Colombia's Rejoinder does not respond directly to any of these points. It begins instead with a rhetorical point. Colombia argues that "it would be … remarkable if these traditional fishing activities … were to be located only on the Colombian side of the 2012 line … as if the drawing of a line could influence the conduct of the artisanal fishermen retroactively".[83] Nicaragua, of course, is not arguing that "the drawing of a line could influence the conduct of the artisanal fishermen retroactively". What Nicaragua is arguing is that the evidence shows that Colombia's fishermen historically operated in waters closer to the islands

[78] CCM, para. 3.102 ("The artisanal fishermen of the archipelago have been fishing in their traditional fishing grounds since time immemorial …."); *Ibid.*, para. 2.64 ("Since time immemorial, [the Raizales] have navigated all of the Southwestern Caribbean in search of resources, such as fish and turtles.").
[79] *See* NR, para. 6.50.
[80] *Ibid.*, paras. 6.51-6.57.
[81] *Ibid.*, paras. 6.51-6.55 (citing Annexes 63, 66, 67, 68, 70).
[82] *Ibid.*, paras. 6.55-6.57 (citing Annexes 62, 63, 67).
[83] CR, para. 5.39.

where they reside that now fall on Colombia's side of the boundary, not on Nicaragua's side.

2.49. There is nothing "remarkable" about this. It is true for two simple reasons, both of which are evident from Colombia's affidavits. First, there was no need for the fishermen to venture far from Colombia's islands in the past because there were a lot of fish close to shore.[84] Second, past technological limitations prevented regular distant fishing ventures.[85]

2.50. Colombia attempts to make it appear its affidavits say more than they do by excerpting carefully selected snippets. But a more thorough examination of the statements in their entirety only confirms that none of the Raizales' traditional fishing grounds lie on Nicaragua's side of the maritime boundary.

2.51. Colombia's citations to the affidavits fall into three categories. First, Colombia cites six that expressly refer to Cape Bank,[86] a maritime feature in Nicaragua's EEZ. According to Colombia: "Many of the affiants consider that Cape Bank constitutes one of the most important traditional grounds for the artisanal fishermen of the Archipelago."[87] This is rank mischaracterization of what its affiants said. Colombia tellingly does not cite even a single one of the affidavits (or any other source) for the proposition just stated.[88] Rather, it only cites them for the subsequently stated propositions that "*Luna Verde* is [a] part of Cape Bank",[89] that Cape Bank "is considered by artisanal fishermen as 'one of the best places to fish'",[90] and that "some of the affiants expressly mention 'Cape Bank'".[91] This is a far cry from proving that "Cape Bank constitutes one of the most important traditional grounds". Indeed, a review of the six affidavits

[84] *See, e.g.*, CCM, Annexes 62, 63, 67; *see also* NR, para. 6.56.
[85] *See, e.g.*, CCM, Annexes 63, 65, 69; *see also* NR, para. 6.55.
[86] CR, para. 5.42 (citing CCM, Annexes 62, 65, 68, 70, 71, 72).
[87] *Ibid.*, para. 5.41.
[88] *See ibid.*
[89] *Ibid.* (citing CCM, Annex 71).
[90] *Ibid.*, para. 5.42 (citing CCM, Annex 68).
[91] *Ibid.* (citing CCM, Annexes 62, 65, 68, 70, 71, 72).

Colombia cites about Cape Bank reveals that *none* of them state that it is a traditional fishing ground, much less one of the most important ones.[92]

2.52. Take, for example, one of the affiants that Colombia cites for "expressly mention[ing]" Cape Bank: Mr. Landel Hernando Robinson Archbold.[93] The only time he mentions Cape Bank is to say he does not go there: "I do not fish up to La Esquina and Cape Bank."[94] Another affiant Colombia cites for "expressly mention[ing]" Cape Bank is Mr. George de la Cruz de Alba Barker.[95] But he too does not state that Cape Bank is a traditional fishing ground. To the contrary, when talking about Cape Bank, he admits: "We have been carrying out these activities *since the 1980s and 1990s*."[96] The statements of the other four affiants cited by Colombia similarly do not support Colombia's position.[97]

2.53. The second category of citations (to five affidavits) is to those that "point to locations that are obviously part of [Cape Bank's] shallow, as well as its deep-sea, grounds such as the '82° West Meridian', 'Luna Verde', 'Great Corn Island and Little Corn Island', 'Rosalind Bank', 'Bobel cay' and 'Cape Gracias a Dios'".[98] Although the five affidavits cited do indeed "point to" these locations, none asserts that any of them are traditional fishing grounds. In fact, some of the affidavits prove the opposite.

---

[92] *See* CCM, Annexes 62, 65, 68, 70, 71, 72.
[93] *Ibid.*, Annex 62.
[94] *Ibid.*, Annex 62.
[95] *Ibid.*, Annex 71.
[96] *Ibid.*, Annex 71 (emphasis added). Colombia suggests in passing that traditional fishing rights may crystallise over a timeframe of five decades or less. *See* CR, para. 5.49. Nicaragua does not agree. Although the exact period of time that must elapse for traditional fishing rights to crystallise is not set in stone, a span only of decades is not enough. In the *Eritrea/Yemen* arbitration, the arbitral tribunal recognized a "traditional fishing regime" in an area where fishermen were fishing and navigating "[s]ince times immemorial". *Eritrea/Yemen*, First Stage, Award (9 October 1998), para. 127. Similarly, in the *South China Sea* arbitration, the arbitral tribunal recognized "traditional fishing rights" in an area where fishing had been "carried out for generations". *South China Sea*, p. 315, para. 806. Colombia itself appears to endorse this standard. In its Counter-Memorial, Colombia twice alleged that fishing had taken place "since time immemorial". CCM, paras. 2.64 & 3.102. A timeframe of five decades or less is plainly insufficient.
[97] *See* CCM, Annexes 65, 68, 70, 72.
[98] CR, para. 5.42 (citing CCM, Annexes 63, 64, 65, 69, 71) (footnotes omitted).

2.54. Take, for example, the affidavit of Mr. Domingo Sanchez McNabb.[99] Colombia cites it as one that "point[s] to … Cape Gracias a Dios".[100] And indeed, Mr. McNabb does twice "point to" Cape Gracias a Dios. The first time, he states: "[W]e used to go up to Cabo Gracias a Dios in Honduras *in search of new fishing banks*."[101] The fact that Mr. McNabb would go to Cape Gracias a Dios "in search of new fishing banks" only shows that it is *not* a traditional fishing ground. The second time, Mr. McNabb avers: "Artisanal fishermen began to use some technological elements like, for example, radios, radars and GPS. These technological improvements greatly facilitated the fishing expeditions going farther, to the 82nd meridian and even close to cape Gracias a Dios."[102] Here again, this statement shows that ventures "to the 82nd meridian and even … cape Gracias a Dios" were a recent development, not a historical practice.

2.55. The third category of citations (also to five affidavits) is to those that "mention[] other important traditional banks that are located on the Nicaraguan side of the 2012 line, such as 'Julio Bank', 'Far Bank' and 'North East Bank'".[103] Although the five affiants in question "mention" these fishing banks, that does not prove they are traditional fishing grounds.

2.56. In fact, one affiant states only that he "ha[s] fished" in those banks;[104] another indicates merely that he must be "careful" if he wants to fish in those banks;[105] and another two simply state that the fishermen "know" those banks,[106] or that the banks are "known" to them.[107] None of these statements, even taken at face value, prove that the banks in question are traditional fishing grounds.

---

[99] CCM, Annex 69.
[100] CR, para. 5.42 (citing CCM, Annex 69).
[101] CCM, Annex 69 (emphasis added).
[102] *Ibid.*, Annex 69.
[103] CR, para. 5.44 (citing CCM, Annexes 62, 63, 64, 65, 66).
[104] CCM, Annex 64.
[105] *Ibid.*, Annex 62.
[106] *Ibid.*, Annex 66.
[107] *Ibid.*, Annex 63.

2.57. One—and only one—affiant (Mr Ligorio Luis Archbold Howard) states that the "fishing grounds of Far Bank, North East and Julio Banks are traditional fishing grounds of Providencia".[108] But this lone, bare and conclusory statement does not provide any substantiating information that might enhance its credibility. Indeed, other portions of Mr. Howard's statement tend to undermine it. In particular, he states: "Our parents and grandparents did not know about the maritime limits in those waters; they used to fish in Bobel Cay close to Honduras, Serrana, Quitasueño, Serranilla and Southwest Cay [Alburquerque]".[109]Conspicuously absent from his mention of places his parents and grandparents "used to fish" are Julio Bank, Far Bank and North East Bank.

2.58. By showing that Colombia's affidavits do not support the claim that its artisanal fishermen traditionally fished in waters that are now within Nicaragua's EEZ, Nicaragua is thus not "trying to silence the voice of the Raizales".[110] To the contrary, it is listening carefully to their voices and drawing the conclusions that follow from their own words.

D. Colombia Still Has Not Proven that Nicaragua Infringed the Raizales' Traditional Fishing "Rights"

2.59. Colombia contends that, by its conduct, Nicaragua has infringed the Raizales' traditional fishing rights. This claim fails in the first instance because no such rights exist for the reasons explained above in Sections A-C. It also fails because Colombia has not come forward with any reliable evidence supporting its argument.

2.60. In its Reply, Nicaragua methodically reviewed Colombia's evidence in this respect and showed that none of it is reliable enough to support Colombia's

[108] *Ibid.*, Annex 65.
[109] *Ibid.*
[110] CR, para. 5.35.

claim.[111] Colombia conspicuously did not offer any direct or contemporaneous evidence to support its claims. The evidence cited in its Counter-Memorial consists either of political statements[112] or affidavits from nine of the aforementioned affiants, none of whom claim to have themselves been the object of Nicaragua's conduct.[113] They attest only to actions they understand to have been directed at other people. Their evidence is, in short, hearsay.

2.61. Two years passed between the time of Colombia's November 2016 Counter-Memorial and its November 2018 Rejoinder. And six months passed between Nicaragua's May 2018 Reply and Colombia's Rejoinder. But Colombia submitted no additional evidence in support of this aspect of its claim with its Rejoinder. Nicaragua considers this, by itself, revealing. If Nicaragua were truly conducting the "active strategy of intimidation"[114] and "pillaging"[115] that Colombia claims, it is reasonable to expect the Colombia would have gathered additional evidence during the two years between its Counter-Memorial and Rejoinder.

2.62. Instead of coming forward with new or better evidence, Colombia takes a different tack. In particular, it adopts the *tu quoque* fallacy. As Colombia sees it, Nicaragua cannot complain about the adequacy of Colombia's evidence because its own evidence is equally bad. According to Colombia, Nicaragua's "Reply makes no attempt to hide the two different yardsticks that it applies *vis-à-vis*, on the one hand, its own claims and, on the other hand, Colombia's counter-claim."[116]

2.63. Nicaragua disagrees that the evidence it submitted in support of its claim in chief is comparable to the evidence Colombia presented in support of its

[111] NR, paras. 6.78-6.6.93.
[112] *Ibid.*, para. 6.78-6.79.
[113] *Ibid.*, paras. 6.87-6.93.
[114] CCM, para. 9.4.
[115] *Ibid*, para. 9.5.
[116] CR, para. 5.63.

counter-claim. Among other things, Nicaragua submitted multiple audio warnings the Colombian navy issued to Nicaraguan vessels operating in their own waters.[117] In any event, the quality of the parties' evidence is a matter for the Court to decide. Colombia cannot excuse the inadequacy of its own evidence by hiding behind its criticisms of Nicaragua's.

2.64. In addition to its *tu quoque* defense, Colombia's also returns to the affidavits presented with its Counter-Memorial and cites them again for many of the same, second-hand assertions it previously advanced. It cites, for example, the affidavit of Mr Alfredo Rafael Howard Newball for the proposition that "[t]hey [i.e., the Nicaraguan navy] stop them, they take away their products, their equipment and they threaten and mistreat them".[118] Yet in his affidavit, Mr Newball's assertion is introduced with the statement that "After the 2012 decision, *we do hear that the fishermen have difficulties with the Nicaraguan coastguard.* …"[119] In other words, his statement is based on hearsay about what may have happened to others, not his own personal experience.

2.65. Colombia also cites the affidavit of Mr George de la Cruz de Alba Barker for the assertion that "[i]t is common to have our GPS, VHF radio, cigarettes and food supplies taken by them".[120] But when one examines Mr de la Cruz de Alba Barker's affidavit, he does not appear to be claiming that he himself was the victim of the alleged conduct. His statement is presented in general terms, as if he is referring to conduct experienced by others.[121] Indeed, perhaps more telling is the fact that he claims that "[t]he [fishermen's] associations and co-operatives

[117] *See, e.g.*, NR, Annex 32.
[118] CCM, para. 5.68.
[119] *Ibid.*, Annex 67, p. 6.
[120] CR, para. 5.68.
[121] CCM, Annex 71.

receive complaints of these cases".[122] Yet Colombia has provided no record of any such complaints.

2.66. An analysis of all nine of the affidavits Colombia presented with its Counter-Memorial in support of this aspect of its claim shows that not a single one of its witnesses claims to have himself been the object of any "pillaging" or "intimidation" by Nicaraguan authorities.[123] Colombian cannot build a case on such a weak foundation. As the Court recalled in *Croatia v. Serbia*, "'testimony of matters not within the direct knowledge of the witness, but known to him only from hearsay, [is not] of much weight'."[124]

2.67. The very few other items of evidence that Colombia's Reply refers to are equally unreliable and insufficient to sustain Colombia's case. Colombia points, for example, to the 2014 recommendation of a Committee of Experts of the International Labour Organisation ("ILO") in which it is stated that "Raizal fishers have to cross Nicaraguan maritime territory, *which is reported to* give rise to difficulties and the payment of fines."[125] This too is obvious hearsay, and does not contain any of the specifics the would be required to support a finding of fact.

2.68. More interesting is what the recommendation says about the position of the Government of Colombia:

> "The Government adds that *the waters in which the small-scale fishers of the Raizal community traditionally fished continue to belong to Colombia* and the fishers can

[122] *Ibid.*
[123] *See generally ibid.*, Annexes 63-65, 67-72.
[124] *Application of the Convention on the Prevention and Punishment of the Crime of Genocide (Croatia v. Serbia), Merits, Judgment, I.C.J Reports 2015*, p. 78, para. 197 (quoting *Military and Paramilitary Activities in and against Nicaragua (Nicaragua* v. *United States of America), Merits, Judgment, I.C.J. Reports 1986*, p. 42, para. 68).
[125] CR, para. 5.69 (quoting ILO, Committee of Experts on the Application of Conventions and Recommendations, "Observations (CEACR) – adopted 2014, published 104rd ILC session (2015), Indigenous and Tribal Peoples Convention, 1989 (No. 169) – Colombia (Ratification: 1991)", available at: https://www.ilo.org/dyn/normlex/en/f?p=1000:13100:0::NO::P13100_COMMENT_ID,P13100_LANG_CODE:3182299,en:NO (last visited 21 February 2019).

> continue their work as they did before the ruling of the ICJ of November 2012. With regard to the right of the inhabitants of San Andrés to have access to traditional fishing areas, the Government specifies that *such fishing areas are located precisely around the keys and that these areas were not affected by the ICJ ruling*, as they consisted of territorial waters awarded to Colombia, together with the sovereignty of the islands and the seven keys".[126]

The recommendation thus not only fails to support Colombia's case, it actually defeats it.[127]

2.69. Colombia also mentions Annex 20 to Nicaragua's Reply, which is said to "refer[] to three incidents that involved the Nicaraguan Naval Force and Raizal fishermen",[128] and Annex 12 to Nicaragua's Memorial, which Colombia says "attests to the fact that the artisanal fishermen are impeded of performing their work because of the conduct of the Nicaraguan Naval Force".[129] Neither of those documents constitutes meaningful proof of Colombia's claims.

2.70. Annex 20 to Nicaragua's Reply is a news account from Colombia in which the Commander of the Colombian Navy is quoted for the stated proposition. Few details are provided other than a reference to "an incident in which a Colombian fishing group was inspected and apparently expelled from a border zone between

[126] ILO, Committee of Experts on the Application of Conventions and Recommendations, "Observations (CEACR) – adopted 2014, published 104rd ILC session (2015), Indigenous and Tribal Peoples Convention, 1989 (No. 169) – Colombia (Ratification: 1991)", available at: https://www.ilo.org/dyn/normlex/en/f?p=1000:13100:0::NO::P13100_COMMENT_ID,P13100_LANG_CODE:3182299,en:NO (last visited 8 February 2019).
[127] Colombia is obviously embarrassed about the position it took before the ILO. It expends considerable effort in its Rejoinder trying to explain it away. CR, para. 5.55-5.61. In the end, Colombia is effectively reduced to arguing that the State organ that took the position stated, the Ministry of Labour's Office of Cooperation and International Relations, "failed to provide even a shred of evidence to support its assertion that the traditional fishing sites were precisely located in the vicinity of areas not affected by the decision". CR, para. 5.56. Even if that were true, the point is that Colombia cannot be allowed to speak out of both sides of its mouth. Colombia cannot take one position when it is acting in a defensive posture before the ILO and then expect the Court to accept the opposite proposition when it is acting in an affirmative posture in these proceedings.
[128] CR, para. 5.70.
[129] *Ibid.*

the two countries by the Naval Force of Nicaragua."[130] The reference to a "Colombian fishing group" could just as plausibly be to a commercial fishing group as an artisanal fishing group. More telling in Nicaragua's view is Colombia's response to these alleged incidents. The Commander of the Navy indicated that the Navy would "implement[] all capabilities that the Navy has so that it is ready to enforce respect for all fishermen in the area."[131] In other words, Colombia responded by exercising sovereign rights and jurisdiction in Nicaragua's EEZ.

2.71. Annex 12 to Nicaragua's Memorial is a 2013 "Report on the Status of the Natural Resources and the Environment" prepared by the Comptroller General of the Department of San Andrés, Providencia and Santa Catalina. It is, in other words, a Colombian government document. In any event, all it says is that "Nicaraguan authorities were very aggressive, and now, with this new ruling, they can detain them while transiting through their waters and seize the product, and/or their vessels."[132] In the first place, the context of this statement leaves it unclear whether it is talking about commercial or artisanal fishermen. Moreover, the statement that Nicaraguan authorities were "very aggressive" is entirely unsubstantiated, and so vague and broad as to be effectively meaningless. Still further, the statement that with the 2012 Judgment Nicaragua "can detain" Colombian fishermen is forward-looking; i.e., it is a statement of what *might happen*, not what *has happened*.

2.72. Here again, Nicaragua considers other portions of the report even more revealing. In sections relating to "traditional fishing location[s]" and "industrial fishing location[s]", it states:

[130] NR, Annex 20.
[131] *Ibid.*
[132] NM, Annex 12, p. 11.

> **"Traditional Fishing Location**
>
> San Andres Island artisanal fishermen distribute themselves throughout the entire shelf, using points of reference for fishing grounds such as: Outside Bank (Northern San Andres Island), Under the Lee (Western side of San Andres Island), Southend Bank (Southern San Andres Island), Albuquerque Cays (50 km to the SSW of San Andres Island), and Meridian 82 on the boundary with Nicaragua.
>
> In Providencia and Santa Catalina, fishing takes place in the interior and the exterior of the barrier reef, close to the reef terrace, respecting the park area and the protected marine area. According to Arango and Marquez (1995), the specific work areas are El Faro, Taylor Reef, Morning Star, Northest Bank, South Banks, and North Banks.
>
> **Industrial Fishing Location**
>
> In all of the Banks of the northern area such as Roncador, Serrana and Quitasueño, in the common regime áreas with Honduras and Jamaica, such as Serranilla, Bajos Alicia and Nuevo, and in Luna Verde or La Esquina".[133]

2.73. Consistent with the statements of the Colombian government to the ILO cited above, the report thus suggests that the Raizales' traditional fishing grounds were located principally around the three main islands and that areas located further from shore were the province of industrial fishermen. Colombia has therefore failed to make its case that Nicaragua has infringed the Raizales' traditional fishing right, assuming they even exist (*quod non*).

*

[133] *Ibid.*, p. 9.

2.74. For all the foregoing reasons, Nicaragua respectfully submits that Colombia's counter-claim in respect of the alleged traditional fishing rights of the Raizales should be rejected.

CHAPTER III. NICARAGUA'S BASELINES

3.1. This chapter addresses Colombia's fourth counter-claim to the effect that Nicaragua's legislation on straight baselines is not in accordance with customary international law.[134] This chapter will set out Nicaragua's submission that its legislation on straight baselines is in accordance with both customary law and the relevant provisions of the United Nations Convention on the Law of the Sea (Convention).

3.2. In the Reply, Nicaragua included a discussion of Colombia's straight baseline practice involving both Colombia's Caribbean and Pacific coasts.[135] The Reply concluded that:

> "In seeking to prove that Nicaragua's straight baselines have not been determined in accordance with article 7 of the Convention and the corresponding rules of customary international law, Colombia is relying on an interpretation of those rules that it has not applied to itself in determining its own straight baselines in the Caribbean Sea and the Pacific Ocean. Nicaragua's straight baselines are in accordance with the rules as interpreted and applied by Colombia in establishing its own legislation on straight baselines."[136]

In light of that conclusion one would have expected a forceful rebuttal in the Rejoinder. However, there is only silence. Nicaragua regrets that silence, as it is not particularly helpful in assisting the Court in sorting out the points of agreement and disagreement between the Parties. In view of the significance of Colombia's own practice, section A of the present chapter briefly recapitulates the main points of the Reply in this regard.

---

[134] CCM, para. 7.6.d; CR, para. 6.1.
[135] NR, Chapter 7 *passim*.
[136] NR, para. 7.60.g.

3.3. Nicaragua established its system of straight baselines through Decree No. 33-2013.[137] In addition, Nicaragua has used basepoints on Nee Reef, London Reef and Blowing Rock, which are seaward of the straight baselines, in determining the outer limits of Nicaragua's territorial sea and the 200-nautical-mile limit of its exclusive economic zone. Section B of this chapter addresses the amendment of Decree No. 33-2013 subsequent to the filing of the Reply and the arguments of the Rejoinder in relation to the basepoints on Nee Reef, London Reef and Blowing Rock.

3.4. Section C of this chapter explains that Nicaragua's mainland coast and islands allow the drawing of straight baselines and that these baselines have been established in accordance with international law. The focus of this section is on refuting the Colombian argument to the contrary contained in chapter 6 of the Rejoinder.

3.5. The conclusions of this chapter are contained in Section D.

A. Colombia's Straight Baseline Practice: The Elephant in the Room

3.6. In the Reply, Nicaragua included a discussion of Colombia's straight baseline practice involving both Colombia's Caribbean and Pacific coasts.[138] The Rejoinder does not deign to spend one word on Nicaragua's discussion of Colombia's straight baseline practice. As will be demonstrated in section C of this chapter, that practice remains highly relevant for assessing Colombia's current criticism of Nicaragua's straight baselines. The present section briefly recapitulates the main argument of Nicaragua's Reply on Colombia's straight baseline practice, and the subsequent analysis will cross-refer to the present section.

---

[137] NR, Annex 1.
[138] NR, Chapter 7 *passim*.

3.7. Paragraph 7.8 of the Reply discussed the length of the straight baseline segments of Nicaragua and observed that these straight baselines are unexceptional as regards their length (between 44 and 83 nautical miles) viewed against the practice of other States, and that Colombia's own straight baselines system includes baselines measuring respectively 130.5, 81.6 (two segments), and 76.8 nautical miles in length.

3.8. Paragraph 7.19 of the Reply discussed Colombia's practice in relation of the term "deeply indented and cut into" contained in article 7, paragraph 1, of the Convention. The paragraph showed that the part of the Colombian coast under consideration "is less indented and cut into than the coast of Nicaragua between Monkey Point and the terminus of land boundary with Costa Rica," which is enclosed by Nicaragua's straight baselines. Figure 1 reproduces Figure 7.2 of the Reply, which depicts the relevant Colombian coast and straight baseline.

Figure 1. Colombia's straight baselines

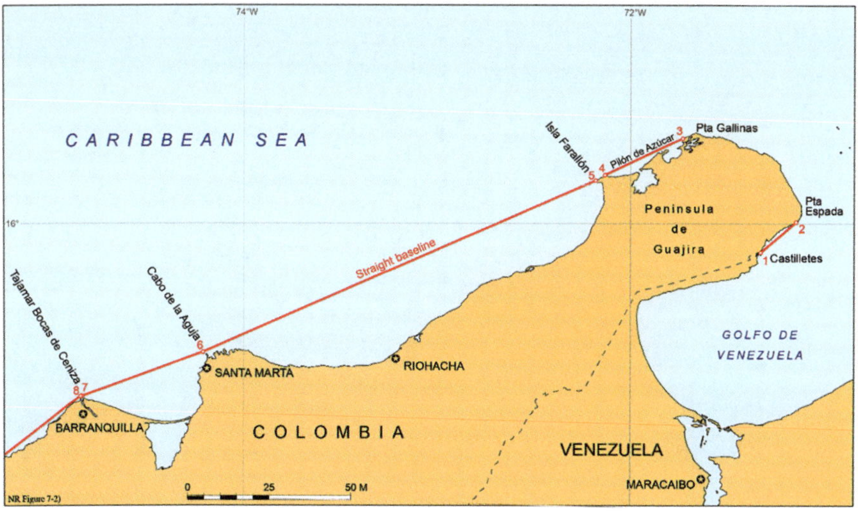

3.9. Paragraph 7.42 of the Reply discussed Colombia's practice in relation to the requirement that a fringe of islands has to lie in the immediate vicinity of the coast to allow the drawing of straight baselines as contained in article 7, paragraph 1, of the Convention. It showed that "Colombia's own baseline practice again indicates that Colombia has not held itself to the standards it now seeks to impose on Nicaragua." One of Colombia's islands discussed in this example is more distant from the coast than one of the islands on which Nicaragua's basepoints are located. It is also more distant from the Colombian coast than many of the islands of Nicaragua that are inside Nicaragua's system of straight baselines. Figure 2 reproduces Figure 7.8 of the Reply, which depicts the relevant Colombian coast, islands and straight baselines.

Figure 2. Colombia's straight baselines (Pacific)

3.10. Paragraph 7.53 of the Reply compared the area of the sea enclosed by Nicaragua's straight baselines to Colombia's enclosure in the area of the Bahia de Bonaventura, in reply to Colombia's argument that Nicaragua was encroaching on the rights of third States. It showed that "Colombia's straight baselines in the Bahia de Bonaventura are thus much more expansive that those of Nicaragua along its Caribbean coast". Figure 3 compares Figures 7.9 and 7.10 of the Reply, which depict the sea areas enclosed by Nicaragua's straight baselines and those enclosed by Colombia's straight baselines in the Bahia de Bonaventura.

Figure 3. Sea areas enclosed by Nicaragua's straight baselines compared with those enclosed by Colombia's straight baselines in the Bahía de Bonaventura

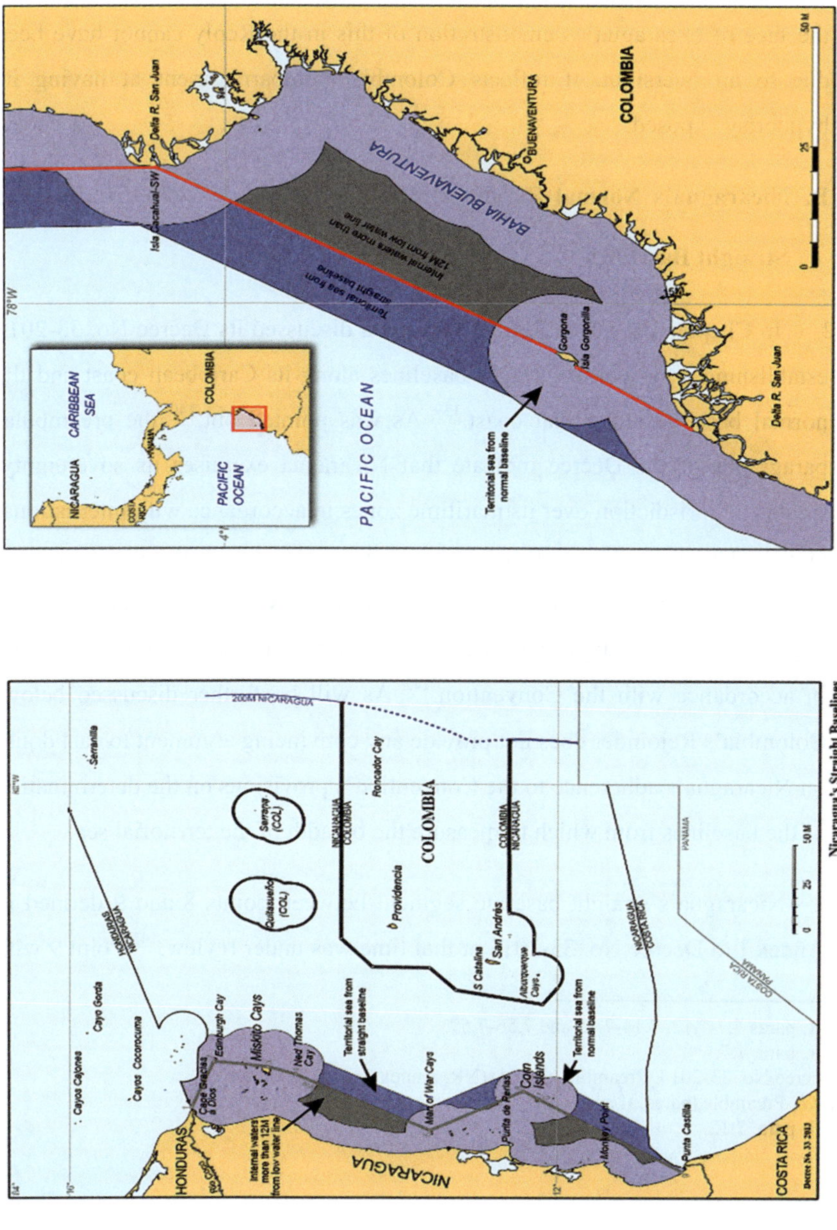

Colombia's Straight Baselines (Pacific) showing areas of internal waters more than 12M from low water line

Figure 7-10

Nicaragua's Straight Baselines showing areas of internal waters more than 12M from low water line

Figure 7-9

Figures 7-9 and 7-10 from NR

3.11 As this review indicates, Colombia's own practice in relation to critical aspects of the regime of straight baselines is comparable to that of Nicaragua and on some points Nicaragua's practice is more moderate. In that light, Colombia's current criticism can only be regarded as insincere. Its silence in the face of Nicaragua's demonstration of this in the Reply cannot have been due to an oversight. It reflects Colombia's embarrassment at having its hypocrisy exposed.

B. Nicaragua's Normal Baselines and Decree No. 33-2013 Establishing Straight Baselines

3.12. In Chapter VII of the Reply, Nicaragua discussed its Decree No. 33-2013 establishing a system of straight baselines along its Caribbean coast and the normal baseline along that coast.[139] As was pointed out,[140] the preambular paragraphs of the Decree indicate that Nicaragua exercises its sovereignty, rights and jurisdiction over its maritime zones in accordance with international law.[141] The preamble further observes that Nicaragua ratified the United Nations Convention on the Law of the Sea on 3 May 2000, and that in the determination of straight baselines in the Caribbean Sea, Nicaragua is acting in accordance with the Convention.[142] As will be further discussed below, Colombia's Rejoinder does not provide any convincing argument to cast doubt on Nicaragua's adherence to the Convention's provisions on the determination of the baselines from which to measure the breadth of the territorial sea.

3.13. Nicaragua's straight baseline segment between points 8 and 9 defined in Annex I to Decree No. 33-2013 at that time was under review.[143] Point 9 with

---

[139] NR, paras 7.7-7.12, 7.14-7.15 and 7.56-7.59.
[140] NR, para. 7.7.
[141] Decree No. 33-2013, Preamble, para. I. (NR, Annex 1).
[142] *Ibid.*, Preamble, paras. II and VI.
[143] NR, para. 7.12.

the geographical coordinates 10° 55' 52.0" N; 083° 39' 58.1" W, was located on the coast of Harbour Head Lagoon. The Court in its Judgment of 2 February 2018 in *Maritime Delimitation in the Caribbean Sea and the Pacific Ocean (Costa Rica v. Nicaragua) and Land Boundary in the Northern Part of Isla Portillos (Costa Rica v. Nicaragua)* confirmed Nicaragua's sovereignty over Harbor Head Lagoon and the sandbar separating it from the Caribbean Sea.[144] However, the Court held that this part of the coast of Nicaragua would not be attributed a territorial sea in the delimitation involving Nicaragua and Costa Rica.[145] As a consequence, point 9 defined in Annex I to Decree No. 33-2013 no longer abutted on Nicaragua's territorial sea.[146] Having completed its review of the implications of the Court's Judgment, Nicaragua has determined the coordinates of the most southern basepoint of its system of straight baselines anew. This new basepoint 9, with geographical coordinates 10° 57'56.6" N; 83° 44' 41.2" W, is located on Barra Indio Maíz (Greytown).[147] This change of Nicaragua's most southern basepoint defining its straight baselines does not make any material difference in relation to Nicaragua's analysis of Decree No. 33-2013 in the context of Colombia's counter claim concerning Nicaragua's straight baselines.[148]

3.14. In the Reply, Nicaragua, explained that the basepoints of its straight baselines have been determined in accordance with articles 5 and 7 of the

[144] *Maritime Delimitation in the Caribbean Sea and the Pacific Ocean (Costa Rica v. Nicaragua) and Land Boundary in the Northern Part of Isla Portillos (Costa Rica v. Nicaragua) Judgment 2 February 2018,* para. 205(2).

[145] *Ibid*, para. 105.

[146] NR, para. 7.12.

[147] Presidential Decree No. 17-2018, Decree of Reform to Decree No. 33 2013, "Baselines of the Maritime Spaces of the Republic of Nicaragua in the Caribbean Sea", Annex I (reproduced in Annex 2 to this pleading) The text of Decree is also available on the website of the Division for Oceans and the Law of the Sea of the UN Secretariat (http://www.un.org/Depts/los/LEGISLATIONANDTREATIES/STATEFILES/NIC.htm) (last visited 21 February 2019).

[148] For the reasons set out at NR, Chapter VII, section F, the change of Nicaragua's most southern basepoint defining its straight baselines does not have any impact on the location of the outer limit of Nicaragua's exclusive economic zone at 200 nautical miles.

Convention, which reflect customary international law. Two of these basepoints are located on the low-water line along Nicaragua's mainland coast, while the remaining seven points are located on the low-water line of Nicaragua's fringing islands.[149] The Rejoinder does not contest that the basepoints that have been used by Nicaragua in this connection are valid basepoints.[150] On the other hand, the Rejoinder does take issue with basepoints of Nicaragua that are located on a number of features off Nicaragua's coast seaward of the straight baselines.

3.15. According to the Rejoinder, the basepoints that Nicaragua has placed along the low-water line of Nee Reef, London Reef off the Miskito Cays and Blowing Rock to the south of Great Corn Island, have never "been referenced in Nicaragua's own official domestic legal acts".[151] The Rejoinder also complains that these points were not included in the list contained in the Annex to Decree 33-2013, and that, in consequence, Nicaragua did not comply with the notification requirements of article 16 of the United Nations Convention on the Law of the Sea.[152] Through these assertions, Colombia demonstrates that it has failed to seriously engage with Nicaragua's domestic legislation and practice and has a poor understanding of article 16 of the Convention.

3.16. As a preliminary point, it may be noted that Nee Reef, London Reef and Blowing Rock are within 12 nautical miles of Cayo Miskito (Nee Reef and London Reef) and Great Corn Island (Blowing Rock). That makes these features, even if they all were low-tide elevations, eligible to be used as part of

---

[149] NR, paras 7.14 and 7.15.
[150] CR, para. 6.2.
[151] CR, para. 6.9.
[152] CR, paras 6.8-6.9.

Nicaragua's baselines in accordance with article 13, paragraph 1, of the United Nations Convention on the Law of the Sea.[153]

3.17. Nicaragua's Law N° 420 on Maritime Spaces of 15 March 2002 provides that the baselines from which the breadth of the territorial sea is measured are straight baselines or the low-water line along the coast.[154] Law N° 420 thus provides for the option of combining the two methods, as Nicaragua as a matter of fact has done along its Caribbean coast.

3.18. In June of 2013, following the Court's 2012 Judgment in *Territorial and Maritime Dispute*, Nicaragua made a submission on the outer limits of its continental shelf to the Commission on the Limits of the Continental Shelf (CLCS) in accordance with article 76 of the Convention. The Executive Summary of Nicaragua's submission has been published on the website of the CLCS.[155] Page 4 of the Executive Summary contains a figure of the 200-nautical-mile-limit of Nicaragua and the basepoints that have been used to determine that limit. This figure is reproduced in Figure 4, while adding Nicaragua's straight baselines. As can be appreciated from Figure 4, the basepoints for determining the 200-nautical-mile limit include basepoints on Nee Reef, London Reef and Blowing Rock, which are located seaward of the straight baselines. In accordance with the Rules of Procedure of the Commission, a communication was circulated to all Member States of the United Nations, including States Parties to the Convention, in order to make

---

[153] Article 13, paragraph 1, provides:

> A low-tide elevation is a naturally formed area of land which is surrounded by and above water at low tide but submerged at high tide. Where a low-tide elevation is situated wholly or partly at a distance not exceeding the breadth of the territorial sea from the mainland or an island, the low-water line on that elevation may be used as the baseline for measuring the breadth of the territorial sea.

[154] Law N° 420 on Maritime Spaces, article 3 (reproduced in Annex 1 to this pleading).

[155] Available at http://www.un.org/Depts/los/clcs_new/submissions_files/nic66_13/Executive%20Summary.pdf. (last visited 21 February 2019)

public the Executive Summary of the submission, including all charts and coordinates contained therein.[156] That is, contrary to what Colombia claims, Nicaragua is not now for the first time using these basepoints, but they were already used and publicized six years ago.

Figure 4. Nicaragua's Submission to CLCS with Straight Baseline added

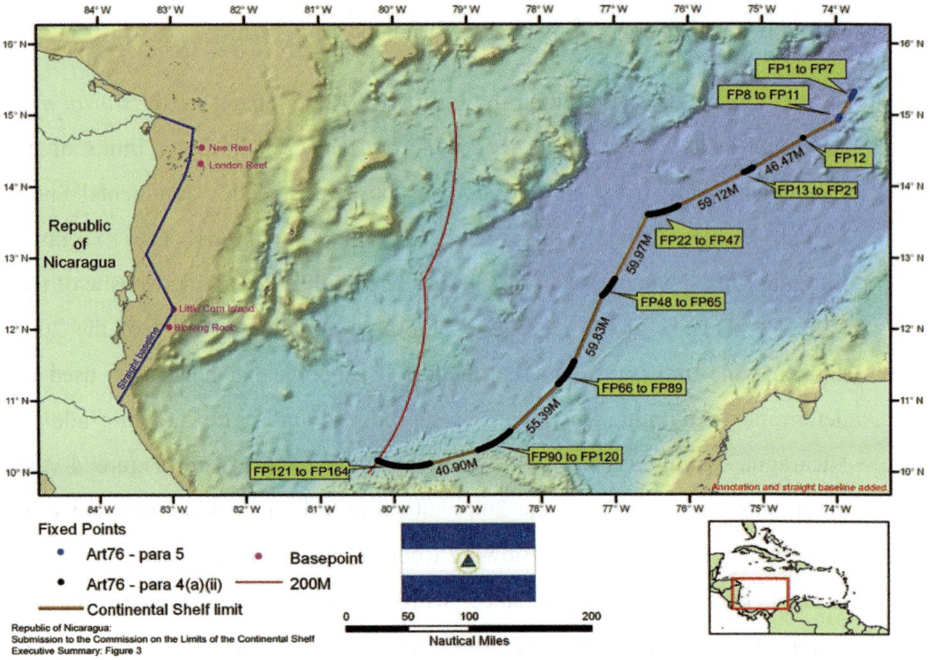

---

[156] Receipt of the Submission made by the Republic of Nicaragua to the Commission on the Limits of the Continental Shelf (CLCS.66.2013.LOS (Continental Shelf Notification) of 1 July 2013; available at http://www.un.org/Depts/los/clcs_new/submissions_files/nic66_13/clcs66_2013.pdf). (last visited 21 February 2019).

3.19. Colombia's claim that the baselines on Nee Reef, London Reef and Blowing Rock are not included in Annex I to Decree 33-2013 is disingenuous, to say the least. As the title of Annex I indicates, it is concerned with providing information on the geographical coordinates of the basepoints of Nicaragua's straight baselines, not the baseline on features beyond those straight baselines.

3.20. The Rejoinder's assertion that Nicaragua did not comply with article 16, paragraph 2, of the Convention, by not including a reference to baselines on Nee Reef, London Reef and Blowing Rock in its 2013 communication to the Secretary-General of the United Nations is equally misguided.[157] Article 16 of the Convention provides:

> "1. The baselines for measuring the breadth of the territorial sea determined in accordance with articles 7, 9 and 10, or the limits derived therefrom, and the lines of delimitation drawn in accordance with articles 12 and 15 shall be shown on charts of a scale or scales adequate for ascertaining their position. Alternatively, a list of geographical coordinates of points, specifying the geodetic datum, may be substituted.
> 2. The coastal State shall give due publicity to such charts or lists of geographical coordinates and shall deposit a copy of each such chart or list with the Secretary-General of the United Nations."

3.21. As article 16, paragraph 1, indicates, the obligation contained in it is concerned with article 7, 9, 10, 12 and 15 of the Convention, and not articles 5 and 13, dealing respectively with the baseline along the coast of the mainland or islands and low-tide elevations. In compliance with article 16, paragraph 2, Nicaragua has submitted information on its straight baselines to the Secretary-General of the United Nations.

3.22. The Rejoinder submits that since the baselines on Nee Reef, London Reef and Blowing Rock are not mentioned in Decree 33-2013, "Colombia will not

[157] CR, para. 6.9.

discuss the existence –undemonstrated by Nicaragua – nor the[ir] relevance, if any".[158] As was set out above, the premise of Colombia's submission is without basis. That Decree 33-2013 did not refer to these baselines is explained by the fact that the Decree was only concerned with straight baselines. As was observed above at paragraph 3.18, the use of the low-water line along Nee Reef, London Reef and Blowing Rock was publicized in 2013 in connection with Nicaragua's continental shelf submission to the CLCS.

3.23. Colombia's submission that Nicaragua has not demonstrated the existence of these basepoints is also wrong as a matter of law. Article 5 of the Convention provides that "Except where otherwise provided in this Convention, the normal baseline for measuring the breadth of the territorial sea is the low-water line along the coast as marked on large-scale charts officially recognized by the coastal State." As the Award of the Annex VII Tribunal in *Guyana v. Suriname* indicates, there is a presumption that the low-water line as marked is the normal baseline. As the Award indicates, that presumption may be challenged by the other party to the proceedings. In *Guyana v. Suriname* the Tribunal concluded in this respect:

> "396. Guyana also objected to Suriname's basepoint S14, which Suriname had identified relying on what Guyana claimed to be an inaccurate chart. The chart in question, NL 2218, was produced by the Netherlands Hydrographic Office (with the assistance of the Maritime Authority Suriname) in June 2005 after the proceedings in this arbitration had commenced. In addition, Guyana claims that another Dutch chart, NL 2014, as well as satellite imagery, "disprov[e] the existence of a low-tide coast at Vissers Bank where Suriname placed its purported basepoint S14."
>
> 396. The Tribunal is not convinced that the depiction of the low-water line on chart NL 2218, a chart recognised as official by Suriname, is inaccurate. As a result, the Tribunal accepts the basepoint on Vissers Bank, Suriname's basepoint S14."

[158] CR, para. 6.10.

3.24. Contrary to Guyana, Colombia has not presented any evidence that the baselines as depicted by Nicaragua in the Executive Summary of its submission to the CLCS might be inaccurate. In that light, there is no reason not to accept the low-water line along Nee Reef London Reef and Blowing Rock as part of the baseline of Nicaragua.

3.25. However, to avoid any doubt that Nicaragua has determined the outer limit of its exclusive economic zone in accordance with the Court's 2012 Judgment in *Territorial and Maritime Dispute* – the Judgment references to a point on that outer limit –[159] the Nicaraguan Navy carried out a survey of Nee Reef and London Reef in January and February of 2019. Basepoints on those reefs control the outer limit of Nicaragua's exclusive economic zone running northwards from Point A established by the Court in 2012. The survey by the Nicaraguan Navy confirms the continued existence of low-tide elevations at both reefs. The report on this survey is included in Annex 5 to this pleading.

3.26. Blowing Rock, to the south of Great Corn Island, is a popular site for scuba diving and regularly visited by tourists. The website of Corn Island Dive Center describes it as:

> "One of Nicaragua's best dive sites, Blowing Rock is a favorite among our divers. Located approximately 7 miles (11 km) from Corn Island, this giant pinnacle of volcanic boulders attracts vast amounts of marine life. The base of the pinnacle rests around 80 feet (24 meters) and towers upwards, breaking the surface to form a small rocky island."[160]

---

[159] The operative part of the Judgment provides that from point 1 on the maritime boundary between Nicaragua and Colombia "the maritime boundary line shall continue due east along the parallel of latitude (co-ordinates 13° 46′ 35.7″ N) until it reaches the 200-nautical-mile limit from the baselines from which the breadth of the territorial sea of Nicaragua is measured" (*Territorial and Maritime Dispute (Nicaragua v. Colombia), Judgment, I.C.J. Reports 2012*, pp. 719-720, para. 251 (4)). The Court refers to the latter point as Point A in paragraph 237 of its judgment.

[160] Dives Sites (available at https://www.cornislanddivecenter.com/dive-sites/) (last visited 31 January 2019)

C. Nicaragua's Mainland Coast and Islands Allow the Drawing of Straight Baselines and These Baselines are in Accordance with International Law

3.27. The current section sets out that the geography of the Nicaraguan coast allows the drawing of straight baselines and that the baselines that have been established are in accordance with customary law as reflected in article 7 of the Convention. Subsection a. explains that the Rejoinder distorts the Reply's discussion of the Court's Judgments in *Black Sea* and *Territorial and Maritime Dispute*. Subsection b. considers the Colombian argument that Nicaragua has provided insufficient data on the islands along its Caribbean coast. That argument misrepresents Nicaragua's presentation of the facts. These islands are a geographic reality that Colombia itself has recognized. Subsection c. explains that the islands adjacent to Nicaragua's coast constitute a fringe of islands in the immediate vicinity of the coast in the sense of article 7, paragraph 1, of the Convention. Subsection d. addresses the point that the southern part of Nicaragua's coast is deeply indented and cut into, another geographical situation that allows the drawing of straight baselines. Finally, subsection e. explains that the waters enclosed by Nicaragua's straight baselines are closely linked to the land domain, as is required by paragraph 3 of article 7.

a. COLOMBIA'S ARGUMENT ON *BLACK SEA* AND *TERRITORIAL AND MARITIME DISPUTE* IS ERRONEOUS

3.28. In the Reply, Nicaragua explained that Colombia's Counter-Memorial had distorted the relationship between Decree 33-2013 and the Court's 2012

Judgment.[161] The Rejoinder does not address the Reply's arguments on the relation between Decree 33-2013 and the Judgment. The Reply also explained that the Counter-Memorial ignored the fact that the 2012 Judgment characterized the islands off Nicaragua's Caribbean coast as fringing islands.[162] The Reply further observed that the Court at the same time referred to the isolated nature of the feature QS32 on the Bank of Quitasueño and in that connection drew a comparison to the Court's treatment of Serpents' Island in *Black Sea*.[163] As the Court observed in relation to Serpents' Island, counting that isolated island "as a relevant part of the coast would amount to grafting an extraneous element onto Ukraine's coastline".[164] Nicaragua submits that these findings indicate that Nicaragua's fringing islands have a close relationship to Nicaragua's mainland coast and that they are in that respect to be distinguished from isolated features that are unconnected to the mainland coast.

3.29. The Rejoinder spins a convoluted argument on the Court's jurisprudence, submitting that the Court made these findings on Nicaragua's islands and Serpents' Island in the context of maritime delimitation disputes.[165] However, one will look in vain in the 2012 Judgment for any support that the Court characterized Nicaragua's islands as fringing islands *because* the case was concerned with maritime delimitation. The islands were characterized as such due to their geographical relationship to the mainland coast of Nicaragua. That geographical relationship did not undergo any changes since 2012.

---

[161] *Territorial and Maritime Dispute (Nicaragua* v *Colombia), Judgment, I.C.J. Reports 2012,* p. 624. NR, para.7.7-7.12.
[162] NR, para. 7.22
[163] NR, paras 7.22-7.23.
[164] *Maritime Delimitation in the Black Sea (Romania v. Ukraine), Judgment, I.C.J. Reports 2009*, pp. 109-110, para. 149.
[165] CR, paras 6.13-6.26

3.30. There is no need to further address the Rejoinder's argument on *Black* Sea and *Territorial and Maritime Dispute*. The whole argument, which takes up a large part of the Rejoinder's Chapter on Colombia's counter claim on Nicaragua's straight baselines, is based on a false premise. The Rejoinder argues that Nicaragua claimed that the Court's 2012 Judgment recognized its coastal islands as a fringe of islands, the term used in article 7, paragraph 1, of the Convention.[166] However, that is not the case. In the Reply, Nicaragua explicitly pointed out that "the 2012 Judgment in two instances refers to respectively the "Nicaraguan fringing islands" and the "islands fringing the Nicaraguan coast"."[167] At no point did the Reply claim that the Court referred to these islands as a fringe of islands in the sense of article 7 of the Convention.

b. Nicaragua's Fringing islands Are a Geographical Reality

3.31. The Parties clearly remain divided on whether Nicaragua's fringing islands constitute a fringe of islands in the sense of article 7, paragraph 1, of the Convention, and its customary law equivalent. However, the focus of Colombia seems to have shifted to some extent. In the Counter-Memorial, Colombia concentrated on the distance of the most seaward islands off Nicaragua's mainland coast, while totally ignoring that between these islands and that mainland coast there are numerous other islands.[168] In the Reply, Nicaragua explained that this was not the proper approach for determining the existence of a fringe of islands, but that instead it is necessary to look at the geographical relationship between all the islands concerned and between those

---

[166] See *e.g.* para. 6.14.
[167] NR, para. 7.22 (footnote omitted). The quotation from the judgment of the Court may be found at *Territorial and Maritime Dispute (Nicaragua v. Colombia), Judgment, I.C.J. Reports 2012*, p. 671, para. 135 and p. 678, para.145.
[168] *See* NR, paras 7.29-7.32.

islands and the mainland coast.[169] The Reply concluded that, looking at the relevant geography from that perspective, there is a fringe of islands along Nicaragua's mainland coast.

3.32. In the Rejoinder, Colombia changes tack and no longer focusses exclusively on the islands on which the basepoints of Nicaragua's straight baselines are located. Nonetheless, Colombia continues to weave this unwarranted focus on the islands on which basepoints are located throughout the Rejoinder.[170] In this additional pleading, Nicaragua to the contrary will focus on the matter that is at the heart of this issue, namely: do the Nicaraguan mainland coast and the entirety of the islands fringing it allow the drawing of straight baselines in accordance with article 7 of the Convention?

3.33. In the Reply, Nicaragua pointed out that there are numerous islands along its Caribbean coast, which are located between that mainland coast and the islands on which the basepoints of its system of straight baselines are positioned. As Nicaragua observed, the total number of the islands along its Caribbean coast is 95, all of which are listed in Annex 31 to the Reply.[171] The Rejoinder complains that Nicaragua does not name all the islands or identify their location and the Rejoinder refers to them as "unidentified features" and "so-called islands".[172]

3.34. Colombia's argument is irrelevant. Article 7 does not contain any requirement that individual features of a fringe of islands have to be identified to qualify for considering them in drawing straight baselines. What counts is the geographical reality and not nomenclature. A fringe of islands is a fringe

---

[169] *See* NR, paras 7.29-7.32.
[170] See *e.g.* CR, paras 6.34 and 6.42.
[171] *See* NR, para. 7.26.
[172] See *e.g.* CR, paras 6.28-6.29, 6.32, 6.34, 6.39, 6.43, 6.47.

of islands because of its location, not the specific identification of each of the islands concerned.

3.35. In any event, Colombia's claims that the islands are unidentified and their location is unspecified are patently incorrect. Annex 31 of Nicaragua's Reply, listing the islands, consists of a table with three columns. The first column is entitled 'Location', providing the location of the group of which individual islands are a part. The second column is entitled 'Cays', providing the names of the specific cays. And the third column provides a count of the numbers of islands in each individual group. On the basis of this information all of these islands can be identified without difficulty on the relevant nautical charts.[173]

3.36. Actually, Colombia never has had any difficulty in identifying the islands that fringe Nicaragua's mainland coast and in recognizing their insular status. The Colombian Rejoinder in *Territorial and Maritime Dispute (Nicaragua v. Colombia)* contains numerous figures that include the islands that are listed in Annex 31 to Nicaragua's Reply in the present proceedings.[174] Figure R-5.4 of the Colombian Rejoinder in that prior case is reproduced as Figure 5 of this pleading. As this Figure shows, Colombia not only had no difficulty in identifying the islands fringing Nicaragua's coast, but also acknowledged that they are entitled to a territorial sea.[175] It may be observed that Colombia's own figure clearly illustrates that all of Nicaragua's islands generate overlapping territorial sea entitlements, conforming their close proximity and interconnectedness.

[173] *See* for example NGA charts 28110, 28120 and 28130 presented by Colombia in CR Figures 6.2a and 6.2b.
[174] See *e.g.* CR, *Territorial and Maritime Dispute (Nicaragua v. Colombia)*, Vol. II, p. 112, Figure R-5.4 and p. 113, Figure R-5.5.
[175] Nicaragua considers that Figure R-5.4 does not necessarily depict the territorial sea of Nicaragua correctly in its entirety. In that connection it may also be noted that this figure was produced prior to Nicaragua enacting its system of straight baselines in 2013.

Figure 5. Nicaragua's Islands and interconnecting Territorial Sea identified by Colombia

CR Figure R 5-4 from *Nicaragua v Colombia* (2012) 112 **Figure R-5.4**

3.37. Even in the current Rejoinder, in which Colombia all of a sudden has difficulty in identifying and locating Nicaragua's islands, the graphics undercut Colombia's story. Figures CR 6.2, CR 6.2a and CR 6.2c, depicted on pages 308 to 310, include the islands the text of the Rejoinder has such difficulty in locating.

3.38. Without going into further detail to refute an argument that is baseless, it suffices to observe that the islands are also identified in academic studies that discuss the importance of the cays and the sea area off Nicaragua's mainland coast for its indigenous population.[176] The sketch map reproduced in Figure 6 is included in Bernard Nietschmann's *Between Land and Water; The Subsistence Ecology of the Miskito Indians, Eastern Nicaragua.*[177] The sketch map identifies the various island groups off Nicaragua's Caribbean coast, most of them by name. Figure 7 contains a sketch map from the study *Indigenes Management mariner Ressourcen in Zentralamerika* and shows the northern part of Nicaragua's coast, including the numerous islands studding the Caribbean Sea off that mainland coast.[178]

[176] For a further discussion of these publications see below at subsection e.

[177] B. Nietschmann *Between Land and Water; The Subsistence Ecology of the Miskito Indians, Eastern Nicaragua* (Seminar Press, New York and London, 1973).

[178] V. Sandner Le Gall *Indigenes Management mariner Ressourcen in Zentralamerika: Der Wandel von Nutzungsmustern und Institutionen in den autonomen Regionen der Kuna (Panama) und Miskito (Nicaragua)* (Geographischen Institut der Universität Kiel; Kieler Geographische Schriften, vol. 116).

Figure 6. Nicaraguan Indigenous Groups

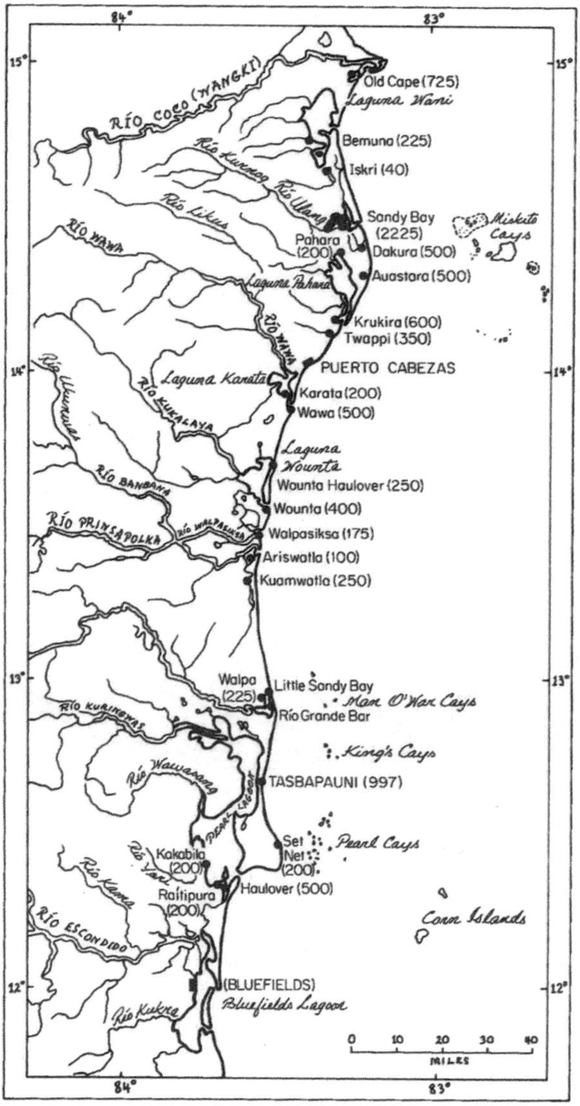

Figure 7. Nicaraguan Indigenous Management of Maritime Areas

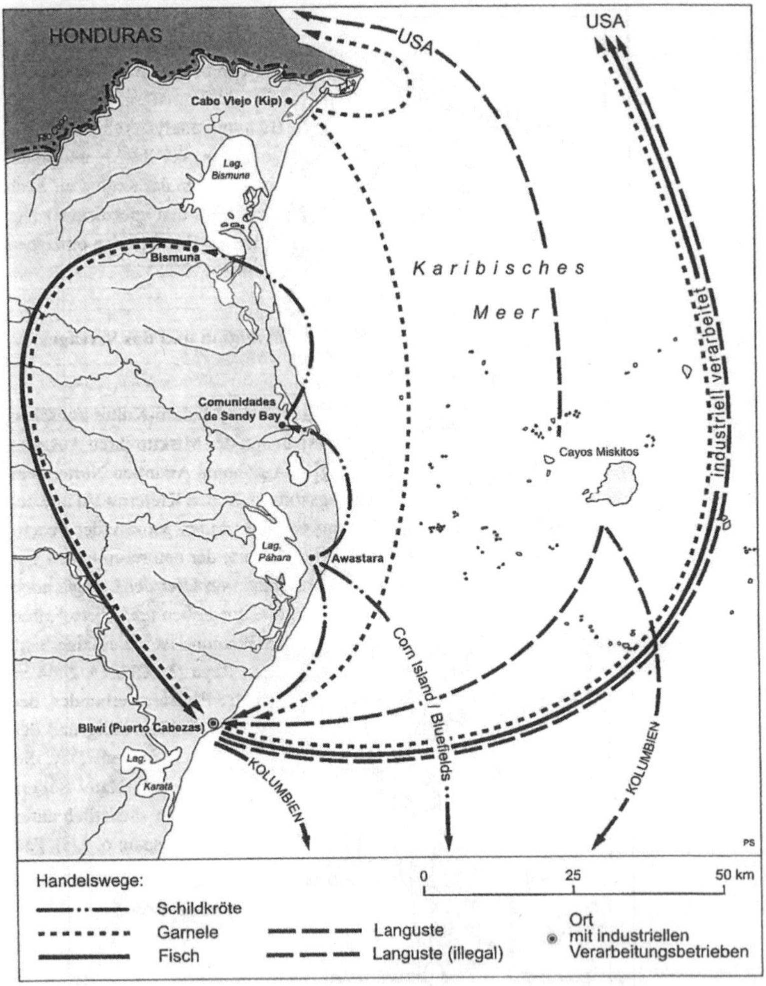

c. Nicaragua's Fringing Islands constitute a fringe of Islands in the Immediate Vicinity of the Coast

3.39. Article 7, paragraph 1, provides that straight baselines may be drawn "if there is a fringe of islands along the coast in its immediate vicinity". Nicaragua submits that this test is met in the case of its Caribbean coast. As was pointed out above, the characterization of these islands as fringing islands in the Court's 2012 judgment in *Territorial and Maritime Dispute* confirms the proximity of the islands to the mainland coast. The number of islands concerned and their location indicates that they constitute a fringe of islands. The different groups of islands, which are listed in Annex 31 of the Reply, inshore are close to the mainland coast and stretch out to sea.

3.40. The Rejoinder contests that the islands along Nicaragua's mainland coast constitute a fringe of islands in the sense of article 7, paragraph 1, and the identical rule of customary international law. In that connection the Rejoinder presents a number of arguments, which will be analyzed in turn.

3.41. First, this is again an instance in which the Rejoinder seeks to rely on the fanciful theory that in looking at the relation of islands and the mainland coast, the focus has to be on the islands on which the basepoints of the system of straight baselines are located. This approach is evident from paragraph 6.34 of the Rejoinder, which, in assessing whether there is a fringe of islands along Nicaragua's coast, exclusively focusses on the islands on which Nicaragua has placed the basepoints of its system of straight baselines. Paragraph 6.34 then concludes: "As shown on the Figure, [which identifies these basepoints] the different components of Nicaragua's so-called "fringe of islands" are simply too isolated from each other to be deemed as forming a "unity"." That conclusion might be warranted if those were the only islands off Nicaragua's mainland coast. However, as should be abundantly clear from the above discussion of the islands off Nicaragua's coast, the geographical reality is completely different from Colombia's imagined reality consisting solely of 7 isolated features.

3.42. The Rejoinder next makes the claim that there is no "*continuous* fringe [of islands] along the coast" and submits that this is required by the rule of customary law as reflected in article 7 of the Convention.[179] Again, the Rejoinder erroneously focusses on the islands on which the basepoints of Nicaragua's straight baselines are anchored, to the exclusion the other islands of the total of 95 listed in Annex 31 to Nicaragua's Reply.[180]

3.43. As indicated above, Colombia's own straight baselines practice belies the restrictive interpretation of what may be considered to be a fringe of islands. As is evident from the example presented in Figures 2 and 3 of this pleading, Colombia has included a group consisting of two islands in its system of straight baselines. What is more, the practice of other States on which Colombia relies contradicts this restrictive interpretation of what constitutes a fringe of islands.[181] For instance, Norway, in the area of the coast off the city of Trondheim, has established a straight baseline between two basepoints identified as NM49 and NM50.[182] These points are located on respectively a rock southwest of Ertenbraken in the Vikna area and Utgrunnskjer in the Frøya area. These two basepoints are almost 85 kilometers apart. This approach indicates that the term fringe of islands does not have the restrictive

---

[179] CR, para. 6.35 (emphasis in the original).

[180] CR, para. 6.35.

[181] In discussing article 7 of the Convention and its customary law equivalent, the Rejoinder among others relies on the practice of Norway, Finland and Yemen (see *e.g.* CR, para. 6.45.)

[182] Regulations relating to the baselines for determining the extent of the territorial sea around mainland Norway; Laid down by Royal Decree of 14 June 2002 pursuant to the Act of 17 May 1814 relating to the Constitution of the Kingdom of Norway and Royal Decree of 22 February 1812 (English text reproduced in *Law of the Sea Bulletin* No. 49, p. 51 (available at http://www.un.org/Depts/los/doalos_publications/LOSBulletins/bulletinpdf/bulletinE49.pdf) (Last visited 21 February 2019).

scope that Colombia seeks to attach to it. A fringe of islands may include separate groups of islands, as is the case for the fringe of islands along the coast of Nicaragua.

3.44. The Rejoinder also submits that the islands along Nicaragua's mainland coast do not form a unity with that coast because the islands have a limited masking effect.[183] Colombia already made this argument in the Counter-Memorial. In the Reply, Nicaragua explained that this argument was defective on a number of counts. First, in determining the masking effect of Nicaragua's islands, the Counter-Memorial failed to take into account a large part of those islands. Second, it was observed that the Counter-Memorial did not offer any explanation as to why it took a strictly frontal projection in determining the extent of the masking effect.[184] The Rejoinder is silent on both counts and also ignores the fact that the Reply pointed out that even under Colombia's restrictive approach, if properly applied, 25 percent of Nicaragua's mainland coast is masked by islands.[185] Instead, the Rejoinder simply continues to rely on the figure of 5 to 6 percent that is based on an erroneous application of Colombia's unjustified method of frontal projections.[186]

3.45. Without providing any explanation as to why Colombia's approach of only using a frontal projection in determining the masking effect of Nicaragua's islands is justified, the Rejoinder criticizes Nicaragua's approach to determining that effect. As Nicaragua explained in the Reply, there is no specific rule for determining the masking effect of islands. However, it was

[183] CR, paras. 6.36 and following.
[184] *See* NR, para. 7.34-7.35.
[185] NR, para. 7.35.
[186] CR, para. 6.41. In a footnote to that paragraph the Rejoinder submits that: "Even assuming, as Nicaragua claims, that the relevant length of Nicaragua's Caribbean mainland coast was, for the sake of evaluating the masking effect, to be measured from Cabo Gracias a Dios in the north to Monkey Point in the South, this percentage would remain insignificant." It is submitted that using the term 'insignificant' for a figure of 25 percent – the percentage under Colombia's methodology to determine the masking effect if properly applied – is inappropriate.

submitted that an analogy might be found in the Court's approach to determining the seaward projection of the relevant coasts in connection with the delimitation of maritime boundaries. As the Reply also pointed out, the Court in those cases has never adopted a strictly frontal projection, a method Colombia proposed without any explanation in the Counter-Memorial.[187]

3.46. In the Rejoinder, Colombia refers to Nicaragua's calculations as 'fanciful' and refers to Nicaragua's reliance of the Court's case law as being 'absurd',[188] relying once again on the incorrect argument that "again Nicaragua relies on unidentified maritime features".[189]

3.47. The Rejoinder argues that Nicaragua's calculation is deprived of any factual basis, because, in making that calculation Nicaragua ignored the characteristics of the islands concerned. This is, using Colombia's own words, a 'fanciful and absurd' argument. In making its calculations, Nicaragua used the western coasts of the islands listed in Annex 31 to the Reply.[190] It is not clear what other characteristics should have been taken into account by Nicaragua in this connection.

3.48. A footnote to the Rejoinder gives a clue about what other characteristics Colombia thinks Nicaragua should have taken into account. That footnote refers to the dimensions of the islands concerned.[191] Indeed, the Rejoinder repeatedly highlights the dimensions of these islands.[192] However, the size of

---

[187] NR, para. 7.35.
[188] CR. para. 6.39.
[189] CR, para. 6.39.
[190] The masking calculations were done using the extent of the western coast of each of the islands – combined into the major groupings identified in NR, Annex 31 – as illustrated by NR Figure 7-5.
[191] CR, para. 6.39, footnote 612.
[192] *See e.g.* CR, para. 6.34 using the words 'miniscule', "small" and "very small" to refer to some of Nicaragua's islands. It should be noted that this characterization is not always completely apt.

islands is irrelevant in determining whether they can qualify as islands that can be taken into consideration in applying article 7 of the Convention. For instance, basepoints NM49 and NM50 of Norway's system of straight baselines, discussed above, are small rocks. Reference may also be had to the case of Yemen. As the Rejoinder observes, Nicaragua and Colombia agree that *Eritrea/Yemen (second stage)* is a relevant precedent in this case.[193] The tribunal there held that islands off the coast of Yemen had a masking effect.[194] The islands concerned are depicted in Figure 7.4 at page 169 of the Reply. As that figure indicates, many of these islands are of very small size. There is no indication in the tribunal's award that the size of islands may disqualify them in considering the masking effect.

3.49. The Rejoinder also criticizes Nicaragua's reliance on the case law on the delimitation of maritime boundaries for determining a methodology to establish the masking effect of islands. Colombia's assertion that the Reply only relies on a sketch map from the Court's judgment in *Black Sea* is misleading.[195] The Reply referred to that sketch map by way of example.[196] That example can be easily supplemented by others examples. It suffices to refer to the Court's discussion of the determination of the relevant coasts of Nicaragua and Colombia in the 2012 Judgment. Those relevant coasts do not project only strictly frontally, i.e. at 90-degree angle.[197]

For instance, the Rejoinder refers to the small Miskito Cays, while the largest of the cays, the homonymous Miskito Cay measures more than 35 square kilometers.

[193] CR, para. 6.37.

[194] *Award of the Arbitral Tribunal in the Second Stage of the Proceedings between Eritrea and Yemen (Maritime Delimitation)*, p. 369, para. 151.

[195] CR, para. 6.40.

[196] NR, para. 7.35, footnote 505, which reads "This [i.e. the rejection of a strictly frontal projection] is for instance illustrated by Sketch-map No.5 included in the Court's judgment in *Black Sea*".

[197] *Territorial and Maritime Dispute (Nicaragua v. Colombia), Judgment, I.C.J. Reports 2012*, pp. 679-680, paras. 151-153 and Sketch map 6.

3.50. The Rejoinder also submits that the analogy that Nicaragua draws between the methods for determining the masking effect of islands and the determination of the relevant coasts in delimitation cases does not hold.[198] However, the Rejoinder does not offer any justification as to why that is so, and as a matter of fact does not offer any guidance at all on how to go about determining the masking effect of islands in the concrete case.

3.51. Nicaragua submits that the analogy with the Court's case law on the determination of the relevant coast in delimitation cases is helpful in determining a methodology for establishing the masking effect of islands. Both situations are concerned with establishing the relationship between different geographical entities: in the case of maritime delimitation law, the relationship between the relevant coast and the relevant area off that relevant coast, and in the case of the masking effect of islands, the relationship between islands and the mainland coast. The rejection of using a strictly frontal projection in the case of determining the relevant area can be seen as a recognition of the fact that geography is too complex to be captured in a dogmatic mathematical approach relying solely on a 90° angle of a frontal projection. Nicaragua submits that this explanation applies with equal force in determining the relationship between islands and the mainland. It would not do justice to the often-complex geographical circumstances to force that relationship into the straitjacket of a 90° angle of a frontal projection as Colombia is doing.

3.52. The example of Yemen further illustrates that Colombia's current pleading concerning the masking effect is far-fetched. Figure 7.4 at p. 169 of the Reply depicts the part of the Yemeni coast that the tribunal considered to be masked

[198] CR, para. 6.40.

by islands.[199] As the Figure illustrates, in particular the central part of the Yemeni coast only has small islands in front of it that, using Colombia's frontal projection method, hardly have any masking effect. The weakness of the Colombian argument is even more clearly illustrated by the practice of Norway. Figure 8 shows a part of the Norwegian coast in the area of the city of Trondheim. In this area, Norway has drawn straight baselines between island groups that are located seaward of the mainland coast. However, those islands only mask the northern and southern extremities of the mainland coast, while most of that mainland coast faces the open sea if one were to apply Colombia's method of frontal projections in determining the masking effect of islands.

Figure 8. Norwegian Straight Baseline in the Trondheim Area

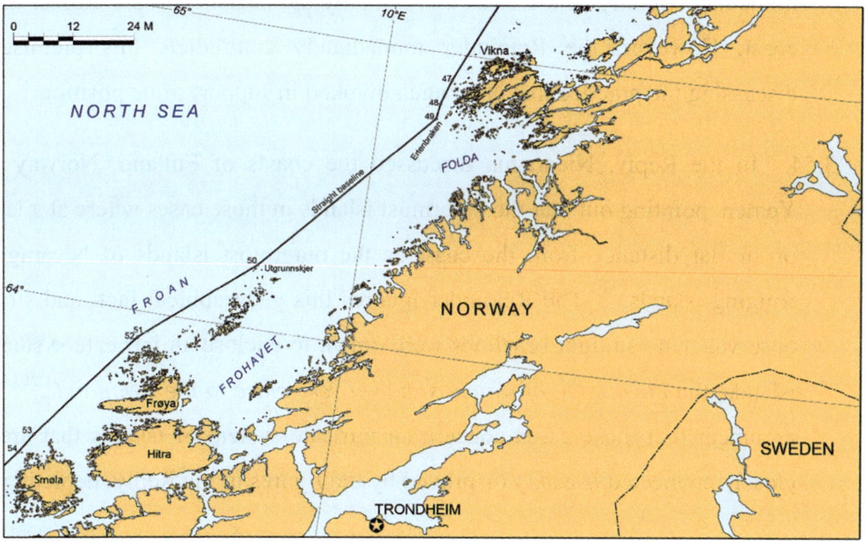

[199] *Award of the Arbitral Tribunal in the second stage of the proceedings (Maritime Delimitation) between Eritrea and Yemen*, p. 369, para. 151.

3.53. The Rejoinder also submits that Nicaragua's Islands do not meet the criterion of being "in the immediate vicinity" of the coast, as is required by article 7 of the Convention and customary international law. In that connection, the Rejoinder again seeks to focus the attention of the Court on the seven islands on which Nicaragua has located basepoints of its straight baselines, and once more harps on its *leitmotif* that the allegedly unidentified islands lying landward of the straight baselines in that connection should not be taken into account.[200] As the Rejoinder observes:

> "Since, according to Nicaragua, the westernmost "islands" (not the seven "main" islands) are near the mainland coast, the whole "fringe", including the "main" islands that are not "near" the coast, meets the "immediate vicinity" requirement. [...] This argument is wholly unsubstantiated."[201]

What Colombia is claiming here is that all islands concerned have to be in the immediate vicinity of the coast and not only the islands that are closest to the coast. However, the Rejoinder immediately contradicts this premise in discussing the practice that Nicaragua invoked in support of its position.

3.54. In the Reply, Nicaragua discussed the coasts of Finland, Norway and Yemen, pointing out that the outermost islands in those cases where at a larger or similar distance from the coast as the outermost islands of Nicaragua's fringing islands.[202] The Rejoinder ignores this geographical fact, and simply observes that "straight baselines were drawn to enclose an intricate system of islands, the *inner edge of which is indeed very close to the mainland*".[203] The argument that these cases concern an intricate system of islands that are all closely connected is easily disproved by the figures in the Reply, depicting the

---

[200] CR, paras 6.42-6.44.
[201] CR, paras 6.43-6.44.
[202] NR, paras 7.38-7.40
[203] CR, para. 6.45 (emphasis of the original deleted; emphasis added).

relevant straight baselines of Norway and Finland.[204] Norway's basepoints 21 and 25 are located on features that are a considerable distance from other islands, and, as was also observed in the Reply, a much larger distance from the mainland.[205] In the case of Finland, reference may in particular be had to basepoint 16 on Flötjan, which, on Colombia's view of things would be an isolated minuscule feature that would not be entitled to a basepoint in the system of straight baselines (see Figure 9 included in this pleading).[206]

Figure 9. Finland's Straight Baselines

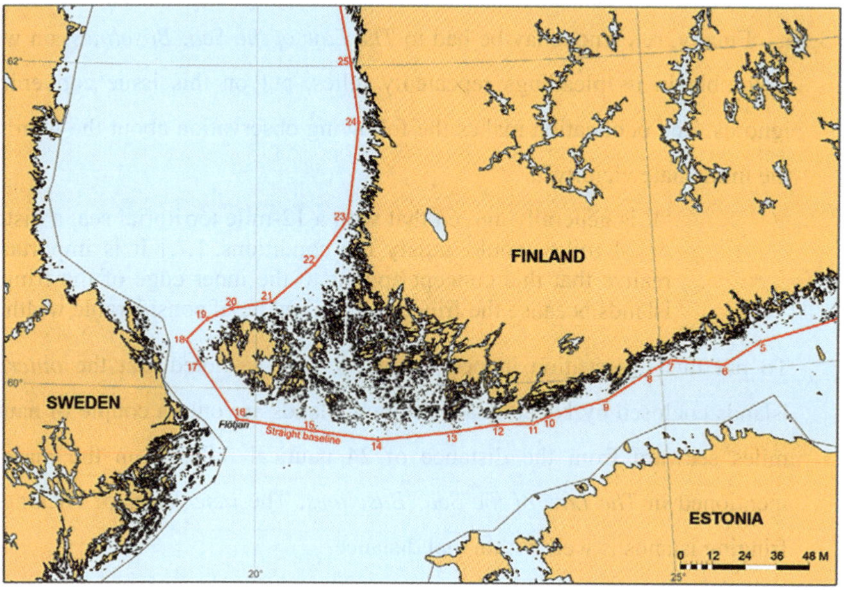

[204] Respectively Figure 7.6 at p. 173 of Nicaragua's Reply and Figure 7.7 at p. 174 of Nicaragua's Reply.
[205] NR, para. 7.39.
[206] Decree No. 993 on the Application of the Act on the Delimitation of the Territorial Waters of Finland of 31 July 1995 (available at http://www.un.org/Depts/los/LEGISLATIONANDTREATIES/PDFFILES/FIN_1995_Decree.pdf, section 1.(Last visited 21 February 2019).

3.55. At this point, it should not come as a surprise that Colombia's argument concerning "an intricate system of islands, the inner edge of which is indeed very close to the mainland" is also disproved by its own straight baselines practice. As is evident from the example presented in Figures 2 and 3, Colombia has included a group consisting of two islands in its system of straight baselines. Colombia's own practice indicates that two islands apparently may qualify as an intricate system of islands. These islands also do not meet the Rejoinder's exacting standard of being very close to the mainland.

3.56. Finally, reference may be had to *The Law of the Sea; Baselines*, on which Colombia in its pleadings repeatedly relies, but on this issue conveniently ignores. The publication makes the following observation about the words "in the immediate vicinity":

> "It is generally agreed that with a 12-mile territorial sea, a distance of 24 miles would satisfy the conditions. [...] It is important to realize that this concept applies to the inner edge of the fringe of islands because the fringe itself might be of considerable width."[207]

To put this observation in perspective, it may be noted that the *outermost* islands enclosed by Nicaragua's fringing islands are only a couple of nautical miles seaward from the distance of 24 nautical miles from the mainland mentioned in *The Law of the Sea; Baselines*. The *inner edge* of Nicaragua's fringing islands is well within that distance.

3.57. The Rejoinder also seeks to conjure up a rule of customary international law to the effect that "a distance ranging from 25 to 30 nautical miles between the coast and the islands is generally accepted as not excessive".[208] There is no

[207] Office for Ocean Affairs and the Law of the Sea, United Nations, *The Law of the Sea; Baselines: An Examination of the Relevant Provisions of the United Nations Convention on the Law of the Sea*, (New York, 1989), para. 46.
[208] CR, para. 6.48 (footnote omitted).

such rule of customary international law. First of all, it may be observed that Colombia agrees that article 7 of the Convention is identical to customary international law on the matter.[209] Article 7 does not contain any reference to Colombia's imaginary rule. Furthermore, in this instance Colombia does rely on *The Law of the Sea; Baselines*. However, instead of quoting that publication's observations on the phrase "in its immediate vicinity", the Rejoinder refers to an argument that is concerned with a different matter.[210] The comment of that publication on the phrase "in its immediate vicinity" as quoted in the preceding paragraph of this pleading, indicates that the inner edge of the fringe of islands may be located at 24 nautical miles from the mainland and the outer edge well beyond that distance as "the fringe itself might be of considerable width".[211] That conclusively disproves Colombia's alleged rule of customary international law.

d. NICARAGUA'S SOUTHERN COAST IS DEEPLY INDENTED AND CUT INTO

3.58. In the Reply, Nicaragua explained that, contrary to what Colombia argued in the Counter-Memorial, Nicaragua relied on the two circumstances that allow the drawing of straight baselines, namely the presence of a fringe of islands or a coast that is deeply indented and cut into.[212] The Rejoinder does not seriously engage with this argument, but simply observes that a "mere glance at the map reveals that the mainland coast lying behind the straight baseline segment between Great Corn Island and Harbour Point (this point is now known as Barra Indio Maíz [Greytown]) is not "deeply indented and cut into". Geography being what it is, Nicaragua cannot demonstrate the

---

[209] See *e.g.* CR, para. 6.35.
[210] CR, para. 6.49.
[211] Office for Ocean Affairs and the Law of the Sea, United Nations, *The Law of the Sea; Baselines: An Examination of the Relevant Provisions of the United Nations Convention on the Law of the Sea*, (New York, 1989), para. 46.
[212] NR, paras 7.17-7.19.

contrary."[213] However, it is not that simple. As the Reply pointed out, Colombia's own practice has been to draw straight baselines along coasts that are less indented and cut into than the coast of Nicaragua between Monkey Point and the terminus of land boundary with Costa Rica.[214] The Rejoinder is silent on this point. Norway's practice in relation to the Trondheim area, discussed above at Figure 8, further illustrates that the Rejoinder's "mere glance at the map" test is deficient. That area can be described as approximately forming a rectangle. The shorter sides are formed by the islands to the north and the south of that sea area. The longer sides by Norway's mainland coast and the straight baselines Norway has established in this area. This indentation is similar to that of the Nicaraguan coast between Monkey Point and the terminus of land boundary with Costa Rica.

e. The Sea Areas within Nicaragua's Straight Baselines Are Closely Linked to its Land Domain

3.59. The Rejoinder takes issue with Nicaragua's explanation as to why the sea areas lying within its straight baselines are "sufficiently closely linked to the land domain to be subject to the regime of internal waters", as is provided by article 7, paragraph 3, of the Convention.[215] The Rejoinder's discussion comes down to the argument that Nicaragua has not proven that there is a sufficiently close link, but does not dispute the calculations that the Reply provides in that connection.[216] And again, the Rejoinder is silent on the Reply's comparison of Nicaragua's and Colombia's practice, which showed that "Colombia's straight

---

[213] CR, para. 6.52.
[214] NR, para. 7.19.
[215] CR, paras 6.54-6.57.
[216] *See*, CR, paras 6.56 and 6.57. For the Nicaraguan argument see NR, paras 7.49-7.53.

baselines in the Bahia de Bonaventura are thus much more expansive than those of Nicaragua along its Caribbean coast".[217]

3.60. Apart from the mathematical test that Nicaragua applied in the Reply to demonstrate that the sea areas lying within its straight baselines are sufficiently closely linked to the land domain to be subject to the regime of internal waters, reference may also be had to the importance of these waters to Nicaragua's indigenous population. In a study published in 2007 focusing on the northern part of Nicaragua's coast, Sandner Le Gall observes that "the area around the Cayos Miskitos on the basis of its natural and spatial characteristics is an important economic area for the Miskito Indians for fisheries, lobster and turtle hunting".[218] The close connection between the Miskito Cays and the mainland coast is also witnessed by the Marine Biological Reserve that Nicaragua has established in this area since 1991, which comprises both a part of the coastal strip and the Cayos Miskitos. The limits of the reserve are identified in Figure 10 of this pleading. This area was designated as a wetland of international importance under the Ramsar Convention on 8 November 2001.[219]

---

[217] NR, para. 7.53. For a depiction of these two cases *see* NR, Figure 7.9 at p. 181 and Figure 7.10 at p. 189.

[218] V. Sandner Le Gall *Indigenes Management mariner Ressourcen in Zentralamerika: Der Wandel von Nutzungsmustern und Institutionen in den autonomen Regionen der Kuna (Panama) und Miskito (Nicaragua)* (Geographischen Institut der Universität Kiel; Kieler Geographische Schriften, vol. 116), p. 223. The original German text reads "*ist das Gebiet um die Cayos Miskitos aufgrund der naturräumlichen Ausstattung zum einen ein wichtiger Wirtschaftsraum für Fischerei, Langusten- und Schildkrötenfang für die Miskito*". *See* Annex 4 to this pleading.

[219] See *Annotated List of Wetlands of International Importance - 48/427*, p. 48 Cayos Miskitos y Franja Costera Immediata (available at https://rsis.ramsar.org/sites/default/files/rsiswp_search/exports/Ramsar-Sites-annotated-summary-Nicaragua.pdf?1549025253). (Last visited 21 February 2019)

Figure 10. Extent of the Cayos Miskitos Marine Biological Reserve

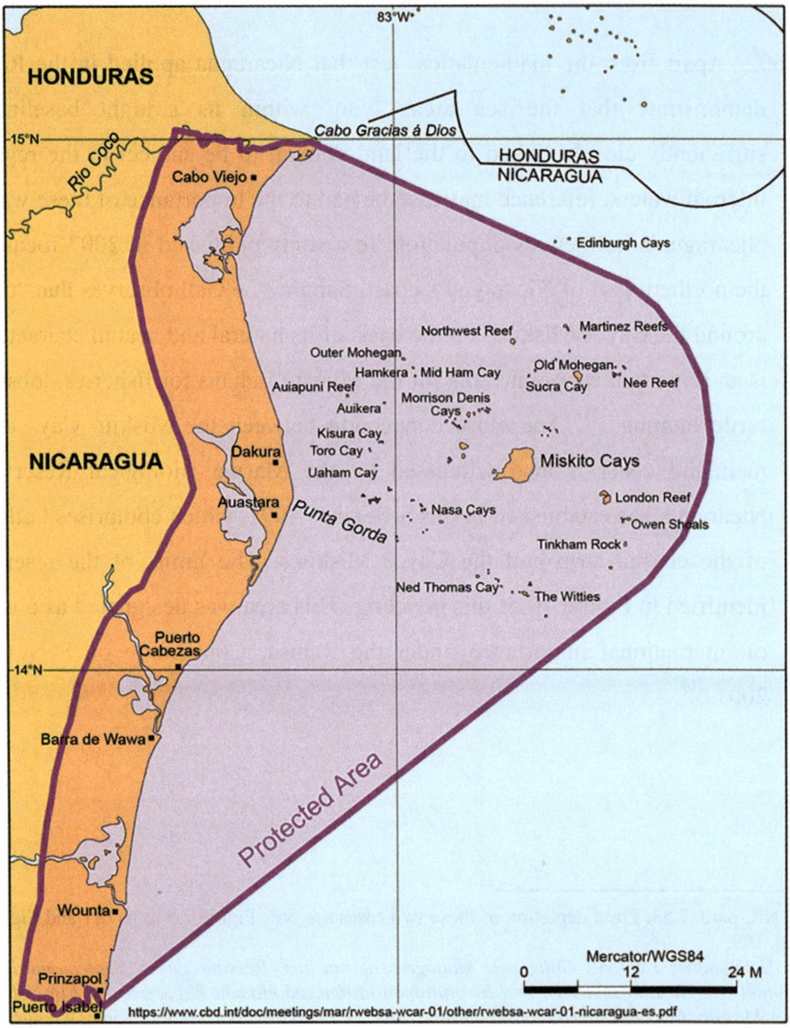

3.61. Niestschmann, in his study *Between Land and Water,* provides a discussion of the shallow waters along Nicaragua's coast from Cape Gracias a Dios in the north to San Juan del Norte in the south:

> "The shelf is widest off Cape Gracias a Dios, going out 75 or more miles and gradually decreasing in width southwards toward San Juan del Norte. It has a very gentle gradient and rarely exceeds 50 fathoms in depth anywhere [...]. This area has the largest sea turtle feeding grounds anywhere in the Western Hemisphere [...], dominated by *Zostera* and *Thalassia* turtle grasses. These marine grasses are efficient producers of energy and make important contributions to the productivity of tropical waters [...]. The underwater marine pastures, or "turtle banks" support remnant populations of the once abundant Atlantic green turtle (*Chelonia mydas mydas*). The turtle banks may occur as isolated patches, 2 to 3 miles in diameter, or in large areas where the banks are close together. [...] Much of the Coastal Miskito food procurement activity, such as patterns and amounts of labor inputs, timing of meat-getting pursuits, and distances travelled, are closely adjusted to the green turtle migratory patterns and habitats."[220]

3.62. Niestschmann provides a more detailed description of the traditional relationship of Nicaragua's indigenous population to the sea areas along the Caribbean coast in the publication *Conservation, Self-determination, and the Miskito Coast Protected Area, Nicaragua.*[221] As he observes:

> "The coastal communities also comprise marine territories. A large part of the Miskito Platform of 900 kilometers in width, is divided en delimited marine territories that often extend for many kilometers from the beach to the sea, depending on the traditional patterns of use of the resources of the biogeography of the continental shelf (Figure 8).[222] Since much of the hunting and

---

[220] B. Nietschmann *Between Land and Water; The Subsistence Ecology of the Miskito Indians, Eastern Nicaragua* (Seminar Press, New York and London, 1973), pp. 92-93. *See* Annex 3 to this pleading.

[221] B. Nietschmann "Conservación, autodeterminación y el Área Protegida Costa Miskita, Nicaragua" *Mesoamérica* 1995 Vol. 29, pp. 1-55. A pdf of the article is available through the website https://dialnet.unirioja.es/descarga/articulo/4011108.pdf (Last visited 21 February 2019)

[222] The reference to Figure 8 likely is a misprint. Figure 7 contained in the publication depicts the tenure areas along the entire Caribbean coast, which are discussed at this point, while Figure 8,

fishing takes place in the open sea where there are reefs and banks of seagrass, the marine territories of the communities extend to the east to include these areas. The marine territories of ten communities of Sandy Bay, and Dakura and Awastara, for instance, extend up to include the coral reef zones and banks of sea food that surround the Cayos Miskitos (see Figure 8), a distance of more than 80 kilometers in its widest part. [...] The Miskito marine and land territory is composed of a continuous extension of lands and waters that traditionally belong to the individual communities."[223]

3.63. Figure 11.A of this pleading reproduces Figure 7 from *Conservation, Self-determination, and the Miskito Coast Protected Area, Nicaragua*, whose caption in English reads *The traditional tenure of the sea of the Miskito communities of the coast*. Figure 11.B shows the same Figure with Nicaragua's straight baselines superimposed. As can easily be appreciated, the two areas overlap to a very large extent. Nicaragua submits that this more than suffices to meet the test that the sea areas lying within its straight baselines are sufficiently closely linked to the land domain to be subject to the regime of internal waters, as is required by article 7, paragraph 3, of the Convention.

---

which is mentioned subsequently in this quotation, focusses on the tenure areas in the area of the Cayos Miskitos.

[223] Nietschmann "Conservación, autodeterminación y el Área Protegida Costa Miskita, Nicaragua" *Mesoamérica* 1995 Vol. 29, p. 17. The Spanish text reads "*Las comunidades costeñas cuentan también con territorios marinos. Gran parte de la Plataforma Miskita de 900 kilómetros de largo está seccionada en territorios marinos delimitados, que se extienden a menudo por muchos kilómetros de la playa al mar dependiendo de patrones tradicionales del uso de recursos y de la biogeografía de la plataforma continental (Figura 8). Como mucha de la caza y pesca en mar abierto se da donde hay arrecifes de coral y bancos de pastos marinos, los territorios marinos de las comunidades se extienden hacia el este para incluir estas áreas. Los territorios marinos de diez comunidades de Sandy Bay y de Dakura y Awastara, por ejemplo, se extienden hasta incluir las zonas de coral y pastos marinos que rodean los Cayos Miskitos (véase la Figura 8), una distancia de 80 kilómetros en su parte más ancha [...] El territorio marino y terrestre miskito está compuesto por una extensión continua de tierras y aguas que por tradición pertenecen a las comunidades individuales.*" Available at https://dialnet.unirioja.es/descarga/articulo/4011108.pdf (Last visited 21 February 2019)

Figure 11. Traditional tenure of the sea of the Miskito communities (A) Original Map (B) Overprinted with Nicaragua's straight baselines

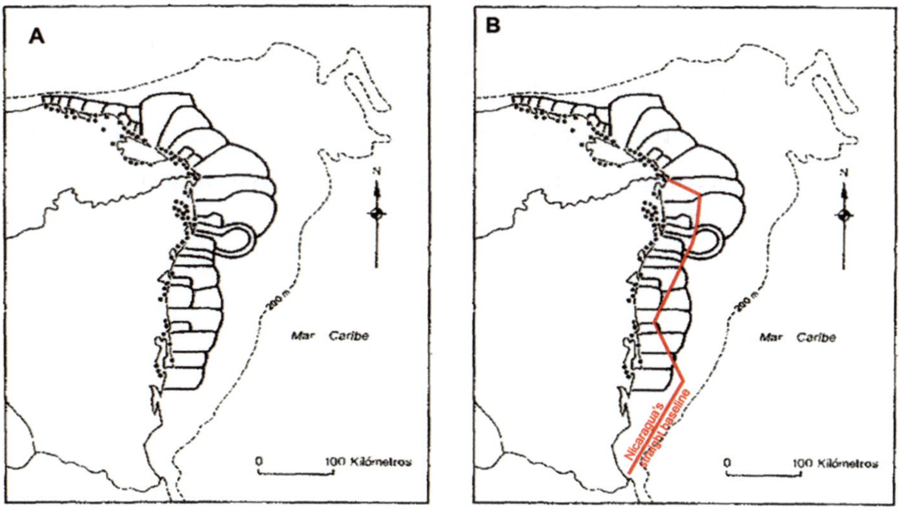

D. Conclusions

3.64. Nicaragua holds that the preceding analysis does not require any adjustment to the Reply's refutation of Colombia's counter-claims on Nicaragua's straight baselines, and the basepoints located seaward of those straight baselines.[224] In summary, Nicaragua's Caribbean coast allows the drawing of straight baselines and these baselines have been established in accordance with article 7 of the Convention and the identical rule of customary international law. The basepoints seaward of those straight

[224] These conclusions are set out in NR, para. 7.60.

baselines on Nee Reef, London Reef and Blowing Rock similarly meet the criteria set out in the relevant provisions of the Convention.

3.65. What is perhaps most striking about the Colombian Rejoinder is its complete silence on Colombia's own practice. Instead of measuring Nicaragua's practice against Colombia's application of the rules of customary international law as reflected in the Convention, Colombia rather prefers to do so against self-serving arguments that have been concocted for the purposes of these proceedings and are in open contradiction to its own practice.

SUBMISSIONS

For the reasons given in its Reply and in this Additional Pleading, the Republic of Nicaragua requests the Court to adjudge and declare that the Counter-Claims of Colombia are rejected.

The Hague, 4 March 2019.

Carlos J. Argüello Gómez

Agent of the Republic of Nicaragua

CERTIFICATION

I have the honour to certify that this Additional Pleading and the documents annexed are true copies and conform to the original documents and that the translations into English made by the Republic of Nicaragua are accurate translations.

The Hague, 4 March 2019.

Carlos J. Argüello Gómez

Agent of the Republic of Nicaragua

LIST OF ANNEXES

QR CODE ACCESS TO ANNEXES 1-6

ORAL PROCEEDINGS

PROCÉDURE ORALE

Corrigé
Corrected

CR 2015/22

International Court
of Justice

THE HAGUE

Cour internationale
de Justice

LA HAYE

YEAR 2015

Public sitting

held on Monday 28 September 2015, at 10 a.m., at the Peace Palace,

President Abraham presiding,

***in the case concerning* Alleged Violations of Sovereign Rights and Maritime Spaces in the Caribbean Sea (Nicaragua *v.* Colombia)**

Preliminary Objections

VERBATIM RECORD

ANNÉE 2015

Audience publique

tenue le lundi 28 septembre 2015, à 10 heures, au Palais de la Paix,

sous la présidence de M. Abraham, président,

***en l'affaire relative à des* Violations alléguées de droits souverains et d'espaces maritimes dans la mer des Caraïbes (Nicaragua c. Colombie)**

Exceptions préliminaires

COMPTE RENDU

Present:	President	Abraham
	Vice-President	Yusuf
	Judges	Owada
		Bennouna
		Cançado Trindade
		Greenwood
		Xue
		Donoghue
		Gaja
		Sebutinde
		Bhandari
		Robinson
		Gevorgian
	Judges *ad hoc*	Daudet
		Caron
	Registrar	Couvreur

Présents :	M.	Abraham, président
	M.	Yusuf, vice-président
	MM.	Owada
		Bennouna
		Cançado Trindade
		Greenwood
	Mmes	Xue
		Donoghue
	M.	Gaja
	Mme	Sebutinde
	MM.	Bhandari
		Robinson
		Gevorgian, juges
	MM.	Daudet
		Caron, juges *ad hoc*
	M.	Couvreur, greffier

The Government of Nicaragua is represented by:

H.E. Mr. Carlos José Argüello Gómez, Ambassador of the Republic of Nicaragua to the Kingdom of the Netherlands,

as Agent and Counsel;

Mr. Vaughan Lowe, Q.C., member of the English Bar, Emeritus Professor of International Law, Oxford University, member of the Institut de droit international,

Mr. Alex Oude Elferink, Director, Netherlands Institute for the Law of the Sea, Professor of International Law of the Sea, Utrecht University,

Mr. Alain Pellet, Emeritus Professor at the University Paris Ouest, Nanterre-La Défense, former member and former Chairman of the International Law Commission, member of the Institut de droit international,

Mr. Antonio Remiro Brotóns, Professor of International Law, Universidad Autónoma de Madrid, member of the Institut de droit international,

as Counsel and Advocates;

Mr. César Vega Masís, Deputy Minister for Foreign Affairs, Director of Juridical Affairs, Sovereignty and Territory, Ministry of Foreign Affairs,

Mr. Walner Molina Pérez, Juridical Adviser, Ministry of Foreign Affairs,

Mr. Julio César Saborio, Juridical Adviser, Ministry of Foreign Affairs,

as Counsel;

Mr. Edgardo Sobenes Obregon, Counsellor, Embassy of Nicaragua in the Kingdom of the Netherlands,

Ms Claudia Loza Obregon, First Secretary, Embassy of Nicaragua in the Kingdom of the Netherlands,

Mr. Benjamin Samson, Ph.D. Candidate, Centre de droit international de Nanterre (CEDIN), University Paris Ouest, Nanterre-La Defense,

Ms Gimena González,

as Assistant Counsel;

Ms Sherly Noguera de Argüello, Consul General of the Republic of Nicaragua,

as Administrator.

Le Gouvernement du Nicaragua est représenté par :

S. Exc. M. Carlos José Argüello Gómez, ambassadeur de la République du Nicaragua auprès du Royaume des Pays-Bas,

comme agent et conseil ;

M. Vaughan Lowe, Q.C., membre du barreau d'Angleterre, professeur émérite de droit international, Oxford University, membre de l'Institut de droit international,

M. Alex Oude Elferink, directeur de l'Institut néerlandais du droit de la mer, professeur de droit international de la mer, Université d'Utrecht,

M. Alain Pellet, professeur émérite à l'Université Paris Ouest, Nanterre-La Défense, ancien membre et ancien président de la Commission du droit international, membre de l'Institut de droit international,

M. Antonio Remiro Brotóns, professeur de droit international à l'Universidad Autónoma de Madrid, membre de l'Institut de droit international,

comme conseils et avocats ;

M. César Vega Masís, vice-ministre des affaires étrangères, directeur des affaires juridiques, de la souveraineté et du territoire au ministère des affaires étrangères,

M. Walner Molina Pérez, conseiller juridique au ministère des affaires étrangères,

M. Julio César Saborio, conseiller juridique au ministère des affaires étrangères,

comme conseils ;

M. Edgardo Sobenes Obregon, conseiller à l'ambassade du Nicaragua au Royaume des Pays-Bas,

Mme Claudia Loza Obregon, première secrétaire de l'ambassade du Nicaragua au Royaume des Pays-Bas,

M. Benjamin Samson, doctorant au Centre de droit international de Nanterre (CEDIN), Université Paris Ouest, Nanterre-La Défense,

Mme Gimena Gonzales,

comme conseils adjoints ;

Mme Sherly Noguera de Argüello, consul général de la République du Nicaragua,

comme administrateur.

The Government of Colombia is represented by:

H.E. Ms María Ángela Holguín Cuéllar, Minister for Foreign Affairs,

H.E. Mr. Francisco Echeverri Lara, Vice Minister of Multilateral Affairs, Ministry of Foreign Affairs,

as National Authorities;

H.E. Mr. Carlos Gustavo Arrieta Padilla, former Judge of the Council of State of Colombia, former Attorney General of Colombia and former Ambassador of Colombia to the Kingdom of the Netherlands,

as Agent;

H.E. Mr. Manuel José Cepeda Espinosa, former President of the Constitutional Court of Colombia, former Permanent Delegate of Colombia to UNESCO and former Ambassador of Colombia to the Helvetic Confederation,

as Co-Agent;

Mr. W. Michael Reisman, McDougal Professor of International Law at Yale University, member of the Institut de droit international,

Mr. Rodman R. Bundy, former *avocat à la Cour d'appel de Paris*, member of the New York Bar, Eversheds LLP, Singapore,

Sir Michael Wood, K.C.M.G., member of the English Bar, member of the International Law Commission,

Mr. Tullio Treves, member of the Institut de droit international, Senior Public International Law Consultant, Curtis, Mallet-Prevost, Colt & Mosle LLP Milan, Professor, University of Milan,

Mr. Eduardo Valencia-Ospina, member and Special Rapporteur of the International Law Commission, President of the Latin American Society of International Law,

Mr. Matthias Herdegen, Dr. h.c., Professor of International Law, Director of the Institute of International Law at the University of Bonn,

as Counsel and Advocates;

H.E. Mr. Juan José Quintana Aranguren, Ambassador of the Republic of Colombia to the Kingdom of the Netherlands, Permanent Representative of Colombia to the OPCW, former Permanent Representative of Colombia to the United Nations in Geneva,

H.E. Mr. Andelfo García González, Ambassador of the Republic of Colombia to the Kingdom of Thailand, Professor of International Law, former Deputy Minister for Foreign Affairs,

Ms Andrea Jiménez Herrera, Counsellor, Embassy of the Republic of Colombia in the Kingdom of the Netherlands,

Le Gouvernement de la Colombie est représenté par :

S. Exc. Mme María Ángela Holguín Cuéllar, ministre des affaires étrangères,

S. Exc. M. Francisco Echeverri Lara, vice-ministre des affaires multilatérales, ministère des affaires étrangères,

comme autorités nationales ;

S. Exc. M. Carlos Gustavo Arrieta Padilla, ancien juge au Conseil d'Etat de la Colombie, ancien *Procurador General de la Nación* et ancien ambassadeur de la Colombie auprès du Royaume des Pays-Bas,

comme agent ;

S. Exc. M. Manuel José Cepeda Espinosa, ancien président de la Cour constitutionnelle de Colombie, ancien délégué permanent de la Colombie auprès de l'UNESCO et ancien ambassadeur de la Colombie auprès de la Confédération helvétique,

comme coagent ;

M. W. Michael Reisman, professeur de droit international à l'Université de Yale, titulaire de la chaire McDougal, membre de l'Institut de droit international,

M. Rodman R. Bundy, ancien avocat à la Cour d'appel de Paris, membre du barreau de New York, cabinet Eversheds LLP, Singapour,

sir Michael Wood, K.C.M.G., membre du barreau d'Angleterre, membre de la Commission du droit international,

M. Tullio Treves, membre de l'Institut de droit international, conseiller principal en droit international public, cabinet Curtis, Mallet-Prevost, Colt et Mosle LLP, Milan, professeur à l'Université de Milan,

M. Eduardo Valencia-Ospina, membre et rapporteur spécial de la Commission du droit international, président de la société latino-américaine de droit international,

M. Matthias Herdegen, docteur *honoris causa*, professeur de droit international, directeur de l'Institut de droit international de l'Université de Bonn,

comme conseils et avocats ;

S. Exc. M. Juan José Quintana Aranguren, ambassadeur de la République de Colombie auprès du Royaume des Pays-Bas, représentant permanent de la Colombie auprès de l'OIAC, ancien représentant permanent de la Colombie auprès des Nations Unies à Genève,

S. Exc. M. Andelfo García González, ambassadeur de la République de Colombie auprès du Royaume de Thaïlande, professeur de droit international, ancien vice-ministre des affaires étrangères,

Mme Andrea Jiménez Herrera, conseiller, ambassade de la République de Colombie au Royaume des Pays-Bas,

Ms Lucía Solano Ramírez, Second Secretary, Embassy of the Republic of Colombia in the Kingdom of the Netherlands,

Mr. Andrés Villegas Jaramillo, Co-ordinator, Group of Affairs before the ICJ, Ministry of Foreign Affairs,

Mr. Giovanny Andrés Vega Barbosa, Group of Affairs before the ICJ, Ministry of Foreign Affairs,

Ms Ana María Durán López, Group of Affairs before the ICJ, Ministry of Foreign Affairs,

Mr. Camilo Alberto Gómez Niño, Group of Affairs before the ICJ, Ministry of Foreign Affairs,

Mr. Juan David Veloza Chará, Third Secretary, Group of Affairs before the ICJ, Ministry of Foreign Affairs,

as Legal Advisers;

Mr. Rear Admiral Luís Hernán Espejo, National Navy of Colombia,

CN William Pedroza, International Affairs Bureau, National Navy of Colombia,

CF Hermann León, National Maritime Authority (DIMAR), National Navy of Colombia,

Mr. Scott Edmonds, Cartographer, International Mapping,

Mr. Thomas Frogh, Cartographer, International Mapping,

as Technical Advisers;

Ms Charis Tan, Advocate and Solicitor, Singapore, member of the New York Bar, Solicitor, England and Wales, Eversheds LLP, Singapore,

Mr. Eran Sthoeger, LL.M., New York University School of Law,

Mr. Renato Raymundo Treves, LL.M., Associate, Curtis, Mallet-Prevost, Colt & Mosle LLP Milan,

Mr. Lorenzo Palestini, Ph.D Candidate, Graduate Institute of International and Development Studies, Geneva,

as Legal Assistants.

Mme Lucía Solano Ramírez, deuxième secrétaire, ambassade de la République de Colombie au Royaume des Pays-Bas,

M. Andrés Villegas Jaramillo, coordinateur, division des affaires portées devant la CIJ, ministère des affaires étrangères,

M. Giovanny Andrés Vega Barbosa, division des affaires portées devant la CIJ, ministère des affaires étrangères,

Mme Ana María Durán López, division des affaires portées devant la CIJ, ministère des affaires étrangères,

M. Camillo Alberto Gómez Niño, division des affaires portées devant la CIJ, ministère des affaires étrangères,

M. Juan David Veloza Chará, troisième secrétaire, division des affaires portées devant la CIJ, ministère des affaires étrangères,

comme conseillers juridiques ;

le contre-amiral Luis Hernán Espejo, marine nationale de Colombie,

le capitaine de vaisseau William Pedroza, bureau des affaires internationales, marine nationale de Colombie,

le capitaine de frégate Hermann León, autorité maritime nationale (DIMAR), marine nationale de Colombie,

M. Scott Edmonds, cartographe, International Mapping,

M. Thomas Frogh, cartographe, International Mapping,

comme conseillers techniques ;

Mme Charis Tan, avocat et *Solicitor* (Singapour), membre du barreau de New York, *Solicitor* (Angleterre et Pays de Galles), cabinet Eversheds LLP, Singapour,

M. Eran Sthoeger, LL.M., faculté de droit de l'Université de New York,

M. Renato Raymundo Treves, LL.M., associé au cabinet Curtis, Mallet-Prevost, Colt et Mosle LLP, Milan,

M. Lorenzo Palestini, doctorant, Institut de hautes études internationales et du développement, Genève,

comme assistants juridiques.

Le PRESIDENT : Veuillez vous asseoir. L'audience est ouverte.

La Cour se réunit aujourd'hui pour entendre les Parties en leurs plaidoiries sur les exceptions préliminaires soulevées par la Colombie en l'affaire relative à des *Violations de droits souverains et d'espaces maritimes dans la mer des Caraïbes (Nicaragua c. Colombie).* Le juge Crawford s'est récusé de l'affaire, conformément au paragraphe 2 de l'article 17 du Statut de la Cour.

J'indique par ailleurs que, pour des raisons dont il m'a dûment fait part, le juge Tomka n'est pas en mesure de siéger aujourd'hui.

Je relève que la Cour ne comptant sur son siège aucun juge de la nationalité des Parties, chacune d'elles s'est prévalue de la faculté que lui confère le paragraphe 2 de l'article 31 du Statut de désigner un juge *ad hoc*. Le Nicaragua avait initialement désigné M. Gilbert Guillaume ; celui-ci ayant démissionné de ses fonctions le 8 septembre 2015, le Nicaragua a désigné M. Yves Daudet. La Colombie a quant à elle désigné M. David Caron.

L'article 20 du Statut dispose que «[t]out membre de la Cour doit, avant d'entrer en fonction, prendre l'engagement solennel d'exercer ses attributions en pleine impartialité et en toute conscience». Et en vertu du paragraphe 6 de l'article 31 du Statut, cette disposition s'applique également aux juges *ad hoc*.

Bien que M. Daudet ait été désigné juge *ad hoc* en d'autres affaires dans lesquelles il a fait des déclarations solennelles, il lui faut, conformément au paragraphe 3 de l'article 8 du Règlement de la Cour, en faire une nouvelle en la présente affaire.

Avant de les inviter à faire leur déclaration solennelle, je dirai quelques mots de la carrière et des qualifications de M. Daudet et de M. Caron.

De nationalité française, M. Daudet est docteur en droit et agrégé de droit public et de science politique. Il a occupé divers postes d'enseignement et de recherche en France métropolitaine, en Martinique, à l'île Maurice, au Maroc et en Côte d'Ivoire. Il a été membre de la délégation française au groupe d'experts, puis à la Conférence des Nations Unies sur le transfert international de technologie. M. Daudet est secrétaire général de l'Académie de droit international de La Haye et professeur émérite de l'Université Paris I (Panthéon-Sorbonne), dont il a été premier vice-président. Il a été désigné pour siéger en qualité de juge *ad hoc* dans l'affaire du *Différend frontalier (Burkina Faso/Niger)* et dans l'affaire relative à l'*Obligation de négocier un accès à l'océan Pacifique (Bolivie c. Chili).* M. Daudet est par ailleurs membre du comité de rédaction de l'*Annuaire français de droit international*, et membre de la Société française pour le droit international et de la branche française de l'Association de droit international/International Law Association. Il a publié de nombreux ouvrages et articles dans différents domaines du droit international.

De nationalité américaine, M. Caron est titulaire d'un doctorat en droit international de l'Université de Leyde et diplômé de l'Académie de droit international de La Haye. M. Caron est doyen et professeur de la *Dickson Poon School of Law du Kings's College London* depuis 2013. Il a également été conférencier, directeur de recherche et directeur d'études auprès de l'Académie de droit international de La Haye. M. Caron, qui a été président de l'*American Society of International Law* de 2010 à 2012, est membre de l'Institut de droit international et, depuis 1991 (avec une interruption de trois années entre 2005 et 2008), membre du comité de rédaction de l'*American Journal of International Law.* Il a également été président de l'Institute for Transnational Arbitration et de la section de droit international de l'*American Association of Law Schools*, membre du conseil exécutif de l'*American Bar Association*, section de droit international, membre élu de l'*American Law Institute*, codirecteur de l'Institut du droit de la mer, et membre de divers comités et groupes d'études de l'*International Law Association.* M. Caron exerce par ailleurs les fonctions d'arbitre, de conseil principal et d'expert dans des arbitrages internationaux. Il est spécialisé dans les questions maritimes et environnementales.

J'invite maintenant MM. Daudet et Caron à prendre l'engagement solennel prescrit par l'article 20 du Statut et je demande à toutes les personnes présentes à l'audience de bien vouloir se lever. Monsieur Daudet.

M. DAUDET :

«Je déclare solennellement que je remplirai mes devoirs et exercerai mes attributions de juge en tout honneur et dévouement, en pleine et parfaite impartialité et en toute conscience.»

Le PRESIDENT : Je vous remercie, Monsieur Daudet. Monsieur Caron.

M. CARON :

"I solemnly declare that I will perform my duties and exercise my powers as judge honourably, faithfully, impartially and conscientiously."

Le PRESIDENT : Je vous remercie, Monsieur Caron. Veuillez vous asseoir. La Cour prend acte des déclarations solennelles faites par MM. Daudet et Caron.

*

Je rappellerai à présent les principales étapes de la procédure en l'espèce.

Le 26 novembre 2013, le Nicaragua a introduit une instance contre la Colombie au sujet d'un différend relatif «aux violations des droits souverains et des espaces maritimes du Nicaragua qui lui ont été reconnus par la Cour dans son arrêt du 19 novembre 2012 en l'affaire du *Différend territorial et maritime (Nicaragua c. Colombie)*, ainsi qu'à la menace de la Colombie de recourir à la force pour commettre ces violations».

Pour fonder la compétence de la Cour, le Nicaragua invoque l'article XXXI du traité américain de règlement pacifique signé le 30 avril 1948, dénommé officiellement «pacte de Bogotá». Il souligne que le 27 novembre 2012, la Colombie a procédé à la dénonciation du pacte, dénonciation qui, en application de l'article LVI de celui-ci, ne devait prendre effet, selon le Nicaragua, qu'au terme d'un an, le pacte cessant ainsi de produire ses effets à l'égard de la Colombie après le 27 novembre 2013. Le Nicaragua soutient que «[d]e surcroît et à titre subsidiaire, la compétence de la Cour réside dans le pouvoir qui est le sien de se prononcer sur les mesures requises par ses arrêts».

Par ordonnance du 3 février 2014, la Cour a fixé au 3 octobre 2014 la date d'expiration du délai pour le dépôt du mémoire du Nicaragua et au 3 juin 2015 la date d'expiration du délai pour le dépôt du contre-mémoire de la Colombie. Le Nicaragua a déposé son mémoire dans le délai prescrit.

Le 19 décembre 2014, la Colombie, se référant à l'article 79 du Règlement, a soulevé certaines exceptions préliminaires d'incompétence de la Cour. En conséquence, par ordonnance du

19 décembre 2014, le président, considérant qu'en vertu des dispositions du paragraphe 5 de l'article 79 du Règlement la procédure sur le fond était suspendue, et tenant dûment compte de l'instruction de procédure V, a fixé au 20 avril 2015 la date d'expiration du délai dans lequel le Nicaragua pourrait présenter un exposé écrit contenant ses observations et conclusions sur les exceptions préliminaires soulevées par la Colombie. Le Nicaragua a déposé un tel exposé dans le délai ainsi fixé, et l'affaire s'est ainsi trouvée en état pour ce qui est des exceptions préliminaires.

*

Conformément au paragraphe 2 de l'article 53 de son Règlement, la Cour, après s'être renseignée auprès des Parties, a décidé de rendre accessibles au public, à l'ouverture de la procédure orale, des exemplaires des exceptions préliminaires et de l'exposé écrit sur ces exceptions. En outre, conformément à la pratique de la Cour, l'ensemble de ces documents sera placé dès aujourd'hui sur le site Internet de la Cour.

*

Je constate la présence à l'audience des agents, conseils et avocats des deux Parties. Conformément aux dispositions relatives à l'organisation de la procédure arrêtées par la Cour, les audiences comprendront un premier et un second tours de plaidoiries. Le premier tour de plaidoiries débute aujourd'hui et se terminera le mardi 29 septembre. Chaque Partie disposera d'une séance de trois heures. Le second tour de plaidoiries s'ouvrira le mercredi 30 septembre et s'achèvera le vendredi 2 octobre. Chaque Partie disposera d'une séance de deux heures.

*

La Colombie, qui sera entendue en premier, pourra aujourd'hui, si besoin, déborder un peu au-delà de 13 heures, compte tenu du temps consacré à ma déclaration liminaire et aux déclarations solennelles des juges *ad hoc*. Je donne à présent la parole à S. Exc. M. Arrieta Padilla, agent de la Colombie. Monsieur l'agent, vous avez la parole.

Mr. ARRIETA:

1. Mr. President, distinguished Members of the Court, it is a great honour for me to address the principal judicial organ of the United Nations, as Agent of the Republic of Colombia. My delegation's task is to demonstrate that there is no jurisdiction in this case. Colombia does this with the utmost respect, convinced that the Court will appreciate that a well-founded objection to jurisdiction is an affirmation of confidence in the Court and in international law; but also convinced that an invocation of the Court in circumstances in which there is manifestly no basis for jurisdiction and no consent to jurisdiction is an abuse of international law and an abuse of the Court itself.

2. I shall not comment on Nicaragua's propensity to resort to the Court, or about its apparent policy to use it as a first instance to solve matters with most of its neighbours that could have been resolved by means of negotiation; but I would like simply to note that, on this particular occasion, it has done so without any valid basis for jurisdiction whatsoever.

3. We agree with the proposition that "[r]ecourse to judicial settlement of legal disputes, particularly referral to the International Court of Justice, should not be considered an unfriendly act between States"[1], but we believe that the law-abiding status of a State is not measured in terms of how many times it goes to court, but in terms of its good neighbourliness and its compliance with international law. Colombia's view, like that of the region, is that, as a matter of principle, judicial settlement should only be resorted to when attempts at negotiation and other forms of direct dialogue have been exhausted. Unfortunately, that has not occurred in this case.

4. Mr. President, I will not conceal my Government's and my countrymen's disappointment with the maritime delimitation effected in the 2012 Judgment. It was, and continues to be, a source of consternation, not only politically, but most painfully, from a human and social perspective. This is particularly so for the inhabitants of the archipelago and especially for the Colombian

---

[1]Manila Declaration on the Peaceful Settlement of International Disputes. Approved by the United Nations General Assembly. Resolution No. 37/10 of 15 November 1982.

Raizal people, whose symbiotic relationship with the sea, in which Nicaragua never had the slightest presence, dates back centuries and who have always seen those areas as their ancestral legacy and their birthright. The sketch-map included in the Court's Judgment depicting the maritime delimitation gave rise to serious concerns that the San Andrés Archipelago, which had always been viewed as a national unit, had somehow been split apart, and that the local inhabitants, who depend on the linkages between their islands for their living, had been deprived of access to their traditional fishing grounds and, so, to a fundamental part of their cultural heritage. In particular, the image of certain of Colombia's islands as enclaves had a powerful psychological effect and was resented by all Colombians.

5. But, notwithstanding, Colombia is absolutely committed to the rule of law, both internally and externally. This is evidenced by our presence here today, to argue these preliminary objections.

6. Mr. President, Members of the Court, the Government of Colombia does not take lightly Nicaragua's grave accusations that our country has threatened to use force, or that Colombia has failed to comply with your 2012 decision. We reject those accusations and, at the same time, we are convinced that the Court lacks jurisdiction to entertain them, for the reasons which will be set out in our preliminary objections, which will be further developed in these hearings. Yet, because once preliminary objections have been raised the only depiction of events before the Court is that presented by the Applicant, a few brief remarks correcting Nicaragua's most serious misrepresentations may be in order.

7. The Court will be relieved to know that the reality in the area could not differ more starkly from Nicaragua's account in its Application and Memorial. To date, there has not been one single episode that could even come close to being construed as a breach of Colombia's international obligations, or as a threat or use of force in contravention of the United Nations Charter. It is striking, really, to see how Nicaragua tries to portray itself as a victim.

8. Mr. President, Nicaragua's Application came as a complete surprise and, quite frankly, was very frustrating for Colombia, given the peaceful situation at sea and the Parties' repeated statements that they were intent on negotiating a treaty to implement the Judgment. Colombia is

convinced that there was not and is not a dispute between the Parties, much, much less one that could possibly form the basis of a case before this honourable institution.

9. Since November 2012, Colombia has been urging the negotiation and conclusion of a treaty with Nicaragua, and has done everything necessary to incorporate the Court's decision into its legal system. In the same spirit, the Government filed a constitutional petition that ended with a decision by our Constitutional Court, in which it ruled unambiguously that, pursuant to Article 94 of the Charter of the United Nations, judgments rendered by this International Court of Justice are binding and cannot be disregarded[2].

10. Colombia's actions in the archipelago since November 2012 have had the purpose of fulfilling its obligations in the area, protecting its archipelago and its people according to international law. Not so Nicaragua. During the past two and a half years it has been unable to control transnational crime in the area, it has failed to provide aid to local and international navigation in the immediate vicinity of the archipelago, and it has tolerated some people's fishing practices, which have been undertaken using inhumane conditions and predatory methods which threaten to break the delicate environmental balance of the San Andrés Archipelago.

11. Colombia has always believed that the post-judgment adjudication situation can be addressed through good faith negotiations between the parties involved. It also believes that those negotiations can lead to a treaty that implements the 2012 Judgment. As will be shown in these proceedings, after the initial shock of the 2012 decision, all the actions of the Colombian authorities have always been oriented toward the application of the decision and we have tried to address those matters in a friendly and constructive manner.

12. Mr. President, as explained, Colombia's denunciation of the Pact of Bogotá on 27 November had immediate effect with respect to the initiation of new procedures against Colombia. Notwithstanding, Nicaragua filed its Application one year later, on 26 November 2013. The timing of its Application was artificial and cynical. Not only was there no dispute at all at that time, but Nicaragua had not even hinted to Colombia that they believed we were violating their maritime spaces or threatening them with the use of force. Rather, Nicaragua files its Application

---

[2]Preliminary Objections of Colombia (POC), Vol. II, Ann. 4, para. 9.10.

on what it thought was the very last day, and, therefore, manufactured a dispute where none really existed.

13. As noted by Colombia in its preliminary objections, Nicaragua's case essentially concerns Colombia's compliance with the Judgment of 19 November 2012. This is clear from the submissions set forth in the Application. Nevertheless, in line with its habit of evading the consequences of weak arguments by changing its submissions throughout the proceedings, Nicaragua has sought in its Memorial to distance itself from its initial formulation. But Nicaragua has failed to change the true nature of the case. Indeed, the substance of its action is belied by two fundamental facts: first, Colombia's recognition that the Judgment is binding, as confirmed by our Constitutional Court; and, second, Colombia's continued availability and openness to dialogue has been constant.

14. Now, Mr. President, distinguished Members of the Court: it is important to explain what was the actual situation as of the date of Nicaragua's Application?

— First, there were no complaints at all, of any kind from Nicaragua regarding Colombia's conduct prior to the lodging of its Application;
— second, President Ortega himself had confirmed as much, and had even credited Colombia's President with the fact that the situation between the two countries at sea was calm and peaceful;
— third, Nicaragua's senior military leaders has said that there had been no incidents at all at sea; on the contrary, they repeatedly insisted that what was happening was a permanent collaboration between the navies; and
— fourth, the Heads of State of both countries were on record as repeatedly saying that the way to deal with the maritime situation in the light of the Court's 2012 decision was by means of bilateral negotiations in order to conclude a treaty on a number of important matters. Those include, among others, the protection of the historical fishing rights of the population, environmental concerns including the all-important Seaflower Reserve, and the fight against transnational crime, boundaries and other matters.

15. Now Mr. President, Members of the Court, pursuant to Article 79, paragraph 7, of the Rules of Court, and Practice Direction VI, the statements and evidence that we will be presenting at

these hearings will be confined to those matters that are relevant to the preliminary objections raised by Colombia. We will not be entering into questions pertaining to the merits of the case and hope that everyone will follow that rule.

16. Mr. President, Members of the Court, allow me now to outline the sequence of Colombia's first round of presentations. You can also find the order of these presentations under tab 1 of the judges' folders.

— To begin with, Sir Michael Wood will explain why the Court lacks jurisdiction under the Pact of Bogotá *ratione temporis*, which is Colombia's first preliminary objection;

— next, Mr. Rodman Bundy will present the facts which Colombia considers relevant for the understanding of my country's second and third preliminary objections;

— following Mr. Bundy, Professor Michael Reisman will elaborate on Colombia's second objection: namely, that on the date of the filing of the Application, there was no dispute between Nicaragua and Colombia with respect to the claims contained in the Application;

— Mr. Eduardo Valencia-Ospina will then explain why, even if Article 31 of the Pact of Bogotá was deemed to constitute a valid basis of jurisdiction, the precondition in its Article II had not been fulfilled on the date of the filing of the Application, which is our third preliminary objection;

— and finally, Professor Tullio Treves will develop Colombia's fourth and fifth preliminary objections, according to which the Court has no inherent power or post-adjudicative jurisdiction upon which Nicaragua can rely.

17. Mr. President, Members of the Court, I thank you for your attention and I would be grateful if you would be so kind as to give the floor to Sir Michael Wood.

Le PRESIDENT: Je vous remercie, Monsieur l'Agent. Je donne maintenant la parole à Sir Michael Wood.

Sir Michael WOOD:

FIRST PRELIMINARY OBJECTION: ARTICLE LVI OF THE PACT OF BOGOTÁ

1. Mr. President, Members of the Court, it is an honour to appear before you, and it is a special honour to do so on behalf of the Republic of Colombia.

2. As the Agent has just explained, I shall deal with Colombia's first preliminary objection: that the Court has no jurisdiction under the Pact of Bogotá because Nicaragua's Application was lodged after the transmission of Colombia's notification of denunciation. This, we say, follows clearly from the second paragraph of Article LVI of the Pact, a provision which Nicaragua largely ignores.

3. Mr. President, Members of the Court, for convenience, the full text of the Pact of Bogotá, in the four authentic languages (English, French, Portuguese and Spanish) is at the back of your folders, at tabs 34 to 37. And Article LVI is also at tab 2, and is now, I hope, appearing on the screen.

4. Article LVI reads:

> "The present Treaty shall remain in force indefinitely, but may be denounced upon one year's notice, at the end of which period it shall cease to be in force with respect to the state denouncing it, but shall continue in force for the remaining signatories. The denunciation shall be addressed to the Pan American Union, which shall transmit it to the other Contracting Parties.
>
> *The denunciation shall have no effect with respect to pending procedures initiated prior to the transmission of the particular notification.*"

5. Mr. President, it is, of course, for the Court to determine whether it has jurisdiction, as is clear from Article XXXIII of the Pact of Bogotá and was highlighted in your recent Judgment in *Bolivia* v. *Chile*[3]. The difference between the Parties turns on the interpretation of Article LVI, and in particular on the interpretation of its second paragraph: "The denunciation shall have no effect with respect to pending procedures initiated *prior to the transmission* of the particular notification."

6. That language could not be clearer — and it is clear in all four authentic languages: "procedures initiated prior to the transmission of the . . . notification", *not* "procedures initiated

[3]*Obligation to Negotiate Access to the Pacific Ocean (Bolivia* v. *Chile), Preliminary Objection,* Judgment of 24 September 2015, para. 38.

prior to the date when the Treaty ceased to be in force for the denouncing State". The application of the general rule of treaty interpretation reflected in Article 31 of the Vienna Convention on the Law of Treaties to Article LVI, taken as a whole, leads to only one conclusion: procedures that a State may seek to initiate after the transmission of the notification are affected by the denunciation.

7. And this result is by no means unusual or surprising. When negotiating States intend that jurisdiction remain for proceedings initiated between notice and the effective date, treaty practice refers to the later date for jurisdictional purposes in clear and unambiguous terms. For example, Article 40 (2) of the European Convention on State Immunity[4] and Article 58 (2) of the European Convention on Human Rights[5] make express reference to the date on which denunciation takes effect.

8. Nicaragua says that it "will demonstrate that Colombia's strained reading of Article LVI of the Pact of Bogotá militates against the object and purpose of the Pact (the settlement of disputes efficiently and definitively), the principle of good faith and does not conform to the rules of treaty interpretation". It is striking, Mr. President, that the rules of treaty interpretation take third place in Nicaragua's thinking; the absence of any consideration of the "ordinary meaning to be given to the terms of the treaty" is remarkable. The rules of treaty interpretation are almost an afterthought, and this is confirmed when one reads Chapter 2 of Nicaragua's Written Statement. The conclusion urged upon you by Nicaragua results from a misapplication of the accepted rules of treaty interpretation. It ignores the actual wording of the second paragraph of Article LVI; it is

---

[4]European Convention on State Immunity, Art. 40:

"(1) Any Contracting State may, in so far as it is concerned, denounce this Convention by means of notification addressed to the Secretary General of the Council of Europe. (2) Such denunciation shall take effect six months after the date of receipt by the Secretary General of such notification. This Convention shall, however, continue to apply to proceedings introduced before the date on which the denunciation takes effect, and to judgments given in such proceedings."

[5]European Convention on Human Right, Art. 58 (1) and (2):

"1. A High Contracting Party may denounce the present Convention only after the expiry of five years from the date on which it became a party to it and after six months' notice contained in a notification addressed to the Secretary General of the Council of Europe, who shall inform the other High Contracting Parties.

2. Such a denunciation shall not have the effect of releasing the High Contracting Party concerned from its obligations under this Convention in respect of any act which, being capable of constituting a violation of such obligations, may have been performed by it before the date at which the denunciation became effective."

dismissive of the *a contrario* argument put forward by Colombia; and it deprives the second paragraph of any *effet utile*.

9. Mr. President, to set the scene, I shall first say a few words about the Pact of Bogotá in general, as well as about the practice of the parties to the Pact in the matter of denunciation. I shall then address the central issue before you, the interpretation of Article LVI of the Pact in accordance with the general rule of interpretation set forth in Article 31 of the Vienna Convention. And finally I shall touch briefly on the *travaux préparatoires* of Article LVI.

The Pact of Bogotá: General

10. Mr. President, first a few words about the Pact of Bogotá. I am, of course, aware that Members of the Court are very familiar with this instrument. I have noted, for example, Judge Cançado Trindade's account of the Pact in his separate opinion last week[6].

11. The Pact was concluded at Bogotá in 1948, during the Ninth International Conference of the American States. It was undoubtedly a pioneering text. It was the culmination of a series of agreements among the countries of the Americas, and the first to be open potentially to all of them. The unique character of the Pact was plain to the negotiators in 1948. So far as concerns dispute settlement, it went much further than the Charter of the Organization of American States (OAS), which itself only contained very general provisions.

12. The Pact contained far-reaching provisions whereby the parties consent to compulsory dispute settlement. At the same time, however, the American States included important limitations on those provisions, including the right to denounce the Pact with immediate effect upon consent to jurisdiction.

13. We described the Pact of Bogotá in our written pleadings[7] and today I shall only refer to some salient features which need to be borne in mind when interpreting Article LVI.

14. The Pact has 60 articles divided into eight chapters. Chapters II through V deal with the specific procedures of dispute settlement, including adjudication before this Court. The remaining chapters contain important substantive obligations and undertakings.

---

[6] *Obligation to Negotiate Access to the Pacific Ocean (Bolivia* v. *Chile), Preliminary Objection,* Judgment of 24 September 2015; separate opinion of Judge Cançado Trindade, paras. 54-58.

[7] POC, Vol. I, Chap. 3 and App. to Chap. 3 (Pact of Bogotá), paras. 3.5-3.7.

15. For example, Article I contains a general yet central undertaking by the parties. It is now on the screen. As you will see, in this Article the parties reaffirm their commitments in the United Nations Charter, and "agree to refrain from the threat or the use of force, or from any other means of coercion for the settlement of their controversies, and to have recourse at all times to pacific procedures.

16. Under Article II of the Pact, the parties are obligated to settle their international disputes by regional procedures before referring them to the United Nations Security Council. Giving priority to regional procedures was a matter of great importance to the American States, which of course is reflected in Chapter VIII of the United Nations Charter.

17. In addition, Article II limits the parties' consent to jurisdiction to disputes that could "not be settled by direct negotiations through the usual diplomatic channels". My colleague, Mr. Valencia-Ospina, will address this point shortly.

18. Article VIII, also in Chapter I, protects the right of individual or collective self-defence in the event of an armed attack as provided for in the Charter of the United Nations.

19. The commitment of American States to the newly formed United Nations, in 1948, to the non-use of force, to the right of self-defence under the Charter, and their commitment to regional settlement before going to the Security Council, are hardly secondary matters under the Pact, particularly when viewed in their historical context in 1948.

20. Article VII contains an important undertaking of the parties to limit their use of the right of diplomatic protection vis-à-vis each other.

21. Article L shows that where it is alleged that a party to the Pact has failed to comply with an ICJ judgment or arbitral award, it is not the role of the Court to monitor compliance, a matter that Professor Treves will deal with later this morning. Rather, the article provides that consultations between the relevant OAS foreign ministers are to be convened before resorting to an outside mechanism, such as the United Nations Security Council.

22. Article LI states that the parties may agree to petition the United Nations General Assembly or the Security Council to request an advisory opinion by this Court on a legal issue, a request they shall submit through the OAS Council.

23. Mr. President, I hope it is clear, from what I have said, that, in addition to the specific procedures for the peaceful settlement of disputes, the Pact also contains substantive rights and obligations of the utmost importance in inter-State relations. While the dispute settlement procedures are important, so too are the substantive rights and obligations set forth in the Pact.

Denunciation practice under the Pact

24. I now turn to the denunciation practice under the Pact of Bogotá. The Pact currently has 14 Contracting Parties, out of the 35 members of the OAS. Two States — El Salvador in 1973 and Colombia in 2012 — have denounced the Pact. You will find the original Spanish text of El Salvador's denunciation, with translations, at tab 4 in the folders. It is similar to Colombia's denunciation, in stating that the denunciation "will begin to take effect as of today"; "*prend effet à compter de ce jour*". No party to the Pact lodged any objection with the OAS to the terms of El Salvador's denunciation, or, indeed, reacted in any way within the OAS or elsewhere. Nor did the OAS Secretariat express any reservations over the terms of the denunciation[8].

25. I now turn to Colombia's denunciation of the Pact. You will find this at tab 5, and it is coming up on the screen. On 27 November 2012, the Minister for Foreign Affairs of Colombia transmitted to the depositary, the General Secretariat of the OAS, a notification of denunciation pursuant to Article LVI of the Pact. The notification stated, and here I quote:

> "that the Republic of Colombia denounces as of today the 'American Treaty on Pacific Settlement'"[9].

The Minister for Foreign Affairs added unequivocally, citing the second paragraph of Article LVI, that Colombia's denunciation of the Pact took effect, and I quote:

---

[8]See also POC, paras. 3.31-3.32.

[9]POC, Vol. II, Ann. 15. The original text in Spanish reads:

> *"Tengo el honor de dirigirme a Su Excelencia, de conformidad con el artículo LVI del Tratado Americano de Soluciones Pacíficas, con ocasión de dar aviso a la Secretaria General de la Organización de Estados Americanos, a su digno cargo, como sucesora de la Unión Panamericana, que la República de Colombia denuncia a partir de la fecha el 'Tratado Americano de Soluciones Pacíficas', suscrito el 30 de abril de 1948 y cuyo instrumento de ratificación fue depositado por Colombia el 6 de noviembre de 1968.*
>
> *La denuncia del Tratado Americano de Soluciones Pacíficas rige a partir del día de hoy respecto de los procedimientos que se inicien después del presente aviso, de conformidad con el párrafo segundo del* artículo *LVI el cual señala que 'La denuncia no tendrá efecto alguno sobre los procedimientos pendientes iniciados antes de transmitido el aviso respectivo'."*

> "as of today with regard to the procedures that are initiated after the present notice, in conformity with Article LVI, second paragraph, providing that '[t]he denunciation shall have no effect with respect to pending procedures initiated prior to the transmission of the particular notification'".

26. The following day, the Secretariat for Legal Affairs of the OAS informed the Contracting Parties to the Pact and the Permanent Missions of the other Member States of the OAS that on 27 November 2012 it had received the Colombian Note by which Colombia "denounced" the Pact of Bogotá[10]. No State party to the Pact — including Nicaragua — reacted in any way.

27. And yet it was one year later, on 26 November 2013, that Nicaragua filed its Application in the current case, seeking to base the Court's jurisdiction on the Pact of Bogotá.

Interpretation of Article LVI: General Rule of Interpretation (Art. 31 VCLT)

28. Mr. President, Members of the Court, these facts are not disputed. What divides the Parties is the legal effect of the transmission of Colombia's notification. I now turn to the text of the Pact, and in particular to Article LVI, second paragraph, to show that the transmission of Colombia's notification of denunciation terminated its consent to the jurisdiction of the Court with immediate effect.

29. I must first recall the precise terms of Article LVI. As I have said, it is at tab 2, and it is on the screen, and I would recall in particular the second paragraph:

> "The denunciation shall have no effect with respect to pending procedures initiated prior to the transmission of the particular notification."

The key words are "transmission" and "notification". The paragraph specifies the date of transmission of the notification as the key date. It distinguishes between procedures initiated before the date of transmission and those that might be sought to be initiated after that date.

30. I think that there is agreement that the applicable rules of interpretation are the customary rules set forth in the Vienna Convention[11].

31. And I need not recall the terms of Article 31 of the Vienna Convention, though our friends opposite seem largely to ignore it. Nicaragua indeed invites you to overlook the ordinary meaning to be given to the actual terms of Article LVI, and instead have regard to its own

---

[10]POC, Vol. II, Ann. 16.

[11]Written Statement of Nicaragua (WSN), para. 2.6.

subjective view of the object and purpose of the Pact and to its own peculiar notion of the application in this case of the principle of good faith.

32. In its Written Statement and in its Memorial[12], Nicaragua claims to apply the rules of treaty interpretation, but in fact, it disregards the ordinary meaning of the words actually used in the second paragraph of Article LVI. Instead, it starts by addressing what it terms "the relationship between Article XXXI and Article LVI"[13] and then it addresses Article LVI, but only its first paragraph[14]. Nicaragua then moves swiftly on to apply its distorted version of the law to the facts, followed by a short discussion of the object and purpose of the Pact to bolster its argument[15].

33. It is only later, when attempting to show the validity of its interpretation of Article LVI, paragraph 1, that Nicaragua sees it fit to mention that Article LVI comprises two paragraphs. In this way, it attempts to make the case that the second paragraph does not sit well with its own interpretation of the first paragraph, which interpretation at this point is treated by Nicaragua as set in stone.

34. But that is not how treaty interpretation works. You cannot interpret a treaty by first discarding one paragraph that you do not like and then feign surprise when that paragraph does not fit your subjective and partial views, views based on ignoring half of the relevant provision. That is the fundamental flaw in Nicaragua's position.

35. Colombia, on the contrary, has provided the Court with a proper interpretation of the Pact, giving due effect to all of its relevant terms, interpreted in good faith and in the light of its object and purpose[16].

36. Mr. President, Members of the Court, I shall now apply the general rule of treaty interpretation to Article LVI[17], but at the same time address Nicaragua's arguments[18]. Let us therefore start with the ordinary meaning to be given to the terms of Article LVI.

---

[12]Memorial of Nicaragua (MN), para. 1.18; WSN, para. 2.6.

[13]WSN, paras. 2.7-2.8.

[14]WSN, paras. 2.9-2.10.

[15]WSN, para. 2.11.

[16]POC, paras. 3.14-3.57.

[17]POC, paras. 3.14-3.32.

[18]WSN, paras. 2.6-2.40.

37. The first paragraph sets out the right of a State party to denounce the Pact, and the steps it must take to exercise that right. A notification of denunciation is to be addressed to the Secretary-General of the OAS (originally the Pan American Union), who then transmits the notification to the other parties to the Pact. That is what happened in the present case, on 27 and 28 November 2012 respectively. Thereafter, the substantive obligations under the Pact continue until the expiry of one year.

38. Then comes the second paragraph of the article. I will not read it again.

39. Mr. President, Nicaragua does everything it can to avoid dealing with the actual text of the second paragraph. But the ordinary meaning of the text leaves no room for doubt. It is clear from the text that procedures initiated after the transmission of the notification are not protected from the effect of denunciation. The drafters, conscious of the need to protect procedures already instituted before the transmission of the notification, stated that such procedures were not affected.

40. The two paragraphs of Article LVI have to be read together. The first paragraph provides that denunciation as regards to the Pact's substantive obligations — such as those that I referred to regarding non-use of force, the obligation to settle disputes peacefully, the obligation to have recourse to the Meeting of Consultation — takes effect after the expiry of the one year's notice. The second paragraph concerns the parts of the Pact dealing with specific procedures for the peaceful settlement of disputes, namely Chapters II to V. It distinguishes between procedures initiated prior to transmission of the notification of denunciation and those that might be initiated after transmission of the notification. By virtue of the second paragraph, denunciation has no effect on the former. But procedures that were not initiated prior to the transmission are not saved by the second paragraph.

41. This interpretation, based upon the ordinary meaning to be given to the terms actually used, allows the whole article, not just part of it, to have an *effet utile*, which is a fundamental principle of treaty interpretation. Nicaragua is simply wrong when it asserts that Colombia's interpretation deprives the first paragraph of any meaning. It is Nicaragua's interpretation that deprives the second paragraph of any or all *effet utile*.

42. Mr. President, I now turn to two arguments made by Nicaragua. First, and I confess I have not fully grasped this argument, Nicaragua makes the bold assertion that what it dismissively

terms "the one-sentence second paragraph of Article LVI" "cannot defeat the Court's jurisdiction under Article XXXI and the first paragraph of Article LVI"; (those were its words). Article XXXI is at tab 8 in the folders, and is now on the screen. Article XXXI — as Members of the Court are well aware — is a treaty provision whereby the parties to the Pact accept the jurisdiction of the Court in terms similar to the optional clause of the Court's Statute.

43. Contrary to Nicaragua's theory, the first paragraph of Article LVI says nothing about consent to jurisdiction. It simply concerns the modalities of denunciation: how, addressed to whom, when.

44. Nicaragua asserts that the second paragraph of Article LVI, and I quote, "does not address 'pending procedures' initiated after a notice of denunciation has been circulated" and that "Colombia's *a contrario* reading of the paragraph . . . cannot stand against the express language of Articles XXXI and LVI, first paragraph, which ensure the effectiveness of Colombia's acceptance of the Court's compulsory jurisdiction for twelve months after notification has been given." That is the end of the quote from Nicaragua.

45. This argument that the general provisions of Articles XXXI and LVI, first paragraph, somehow trump the specific intent of the second paragraph of Article LVI would deprive the second paragraph of its intended purpose and of all *effet utile*. It would lead to the remarkable position that the Parties considered it necessary to state expressly that procedures initiated before transmission of the notification would continue, but remained silent about procedures initiated after transmission of the notification yet somehow intended that they too would continue. How could the drafters have considered it necessary to make express provision in the first case, when one might indeed have expected the procedures to continue, but then remained silent in the second case, when the position would have been much less clear?

46. Nicaragua relies on the words "so as long as the present Treaty is in force" in Article XXXI of the Pact. While ignoring the second paragraph of Article LVI, Nicaragua invokes this short phrase in Article XXXI to bolster its claim that consent to jurisdiction subsists for applications made during the one-year period following the transmission of the notification[19].

---

[19]WSN, paras. 2.16-2.18.

47. Mr President, the general terms of the treaty-based consent to jurisdiction under Article XXXI cannot override the express terms of Article LVI, which specifically addresses the effect of transmitting the notification of denunciation, and its second paragraph in particular, which specifically deals with the question of procedures for the peaceful settlement of disputes following such transmission. Article LVI is the governing provision, not Article XXXI.

48. In order to make its argument based on Article XXXI sound more plausible, Nicaragua, characteristically perhaps, avoids citing the relevant sentence in full. The sentence in question states that the jurisdiction exists "without the necessity of any special agreement so long as the present Treaty is in force". The purpose of this clause is to emphasize that consent to the jurisdiction of the International Court of Justice under the Pact does not require a special agreement, a *compromis*. Its purpose is not to address the extent of the consent *ratione temporis*. Its purpose is not to qualify or override the ordinary meaning of Article LVI, second paragraph. If one reads the two provisions together, it is clear that the words "so long as the present treaty is in force" mean, and can only mean, for so long as the relevant provisions of the Pact are in force in accordance with their terms. Read thus, there is no inconsistency between Article XXXI and Article LVI.

49. Nicaragua makes another argument based on its subjective view of the object and purpose. Dispute settlement by the Court remains subject to the consent of States. However, as Colombia explained in Chapter 3 of its Preliminary Objections[20], the object and purpose of Article LVI is to set out the modalities and effects of denunciation. When progress is made in terms of consent to adjudication in international law, States often insist on safeguards. Article LVI of the Pact of Bogotá is just such a safeguard, and is fundamental to the structure and acceptability of the Pact. Without an effective denunciation clause, the far-reaching provisions on peaceful settlement of disputes, whether through this Court or otherwise, would not have been acceptable to States.

50. There is nothing unusual about the fact that States are willing to consent to the jurisdiction of the Court, but reserve their right to terminate such consent with immediate effect.

---

[20]POC, paras. 3.23-3.32.

We see this with the optional clause and as one author has explained, this is "the price to be paid for adherence by States to the optional clause. And it corresponds to the logic of a jurisdictional system which is still largely based on unfettered sovereignty."[21]

Interpretation of Article LVI: Supplementary Means of Interpretation (Art. 32 VCLT)

51. Mr. President, Members of the Court, I will now turn very briefly to the *travaux préparatoires* of Article LVI of the Pact. Nicaragua in its wisdom has chosen to dismiss summarily our account of the *travaux préparatoires*. At paragraphs 3.33 to 3.52 of our written Preliminary Objections, we set out fully the relevant *travaux préparatoires*. These confirm that the drafters of the Pact consciously chose to word Article LVI so as to limit with immediate effect the initiation of new procedures against the denouncing States, including recourse to this Court, upon the transmission of the notification of denunciation.

52. Nicaragua, in its Written Statement, argues that the meaning of Article LVI is identical to that of Article 9 of the General Treaty of Inter-American Arbitration of 1929[22]. Mr. President, Members of the Court, that is simply not the case. The language, of what later became, almost word for word, the second paragraph of Article LVI, was added to the negotiating text, as we explained in the written Preliminary Objections, in 1938 upon a proposal by the United States of America[23]. It did not exist in the 1929 Treaty. That this was a new issue was highlighted in the text circulated, and was explained orally by Legal Adviser to the United States State Department, Mr. Hackworth[24].

53. Despite this, Nicaragua asserts that the meaning of the text remained identical over the 20 years between 1929 and 1948. Had the text not been changed, Nicaragua would be right! But the text *was* changed, attention was drawn to the change and the meaning of the draft Article was altered accordingly.

---

[21]C. Tomuschat, "Article 36", in A. Zimmermann et al., *The Statute of the International Court of Justice. A Commentary*, 2nd ed., 2012, p. 678; MN 74.

[22]WSN, para. 2.37.

[23]POC, Ann. 25 at p. 5.

[24]*Ibid.*, Ann. 24, Art. XXII at p. 203.

Conclusion

54. Mr. President, Members of the Court, in short, it is Colombia's submission that, in accordance with the terms of Article LVI of the Pact of Bogotá, properly interpreted, the Court does not have jurisdiction in respect of the proceedings commenced by Nicaragua on 26 November 2013. This is because the Application was lodged after the transmission of Colombia's notification of denunciation, which had immediate effect as regards new applications.

55. Mr. President, Members of the Court, that concludes what I have to say and I thank you for your attention. I request that you invite Mr. Rodman Bundy to the podium, to continue our pleadings. Thank you.

Le PRESIDENT : Merci. Je donne maintenant la parole à M. Rodman Bundy.

Mr. BUNDY: Thank you Mr. President, Members of the Court, it is, as always, a great honour to appear before you today and again on behalf of the Republic of Colombia.

THE FACTS RELEVANT TO COLOMBIA'S PRELIMINARY OBJECTIONS

Introduction

1. Now the Court will recall that Colombia's second preliminary objection is that, prior to the filing of Nicaragua's Application on 26 November 2013, there was no dispute between the Parties with respect to the claims advanced in the Application that could trigger the dispute resolution provisions of the Pact, including the Court's jurisdiction[25]. Colombia's third objection is that, even if a dispute could be said to exist, *quod non*, the Parties were not of the opinion that it could not be settled by direct negotiations through the usual diplomatic channels. That is another precondition contained in Article II of the Pact that must be satisfied before the dispute resolution provisions can be resorted to[26].

2. My task this morning is to address the facts that are relevant to these two objections. Professor Reisman and Mr. Valencia-Ospina will come back later to discuss the legal consequences of the facts for jurisdictional purposes.

---

[25]POC, paras. 4.10-4.20.

[26]POC, paras. 4.21-4.73.

3. Both Parties agree that the critical date for assessing whether a dispute existed and, if so, whether the precondition of Article II of the Pact had also been fulfilled, is 26 November 2013, the date of the filing of the Application[27]. And as I will show, prior to that date there was not a whisper of complaint from Nicaragua about Colombia's conduct. In fact, Nicaragua's highest military officials had said precisely the opposite — that there were no incidents or problems. Moreover, senior political leaders on both sides, including the Heads of State of Nicaragua and Colombia, were on record as saying that the implementation of the 2012 Judgment, and any related issues, could be achieved through discussions with a view to reaching a treaty. That scarcely suggests that, when Nicaragua abruptly filed its Application in November 2013, a dispute had arisen, let alone one that could not be settled by direct negotiations through the usual diplomatic channels. In fact, it was not until 13 September 2014 — that is almost ten months *after* the Application was filed — that Nicaragua, for the first time, made any complaint to Colombia about alleged violations of its maritime spaces or threats of the use of force.

The facts placed in their proper perspective

Prior to the Application, there was no dispute and, in any event, the Parties were open to negotiations

4. The Judgment in the *Territorial and Maritime Dispute* case was rendered on 19 November 2012. And Nicaragua refers to the fact that, on that day, Colombia's President Juan Manuel Santos declared that the Judgment was "not applicable"[28] and that, with respect to the enclaving of two of Colombia's islands, Colombia "rejects *this aspect* of the decision issued today" (emphasis added)[29]. Apparently, Nicaragua considers that these words somehow evidence the existence not only of a dispute between the Parties, but one that could not be settled by negotiations.

5. Regrettably, Nicaragua only filed a truncated English translation of the statement made by President Santos, which gives a very misleading picture of what he actually said. I would

---

[27]POC, paras. 4.7-4.8; WSN, para. 4.31.

[28]WSN, paras. 3.6-3.7.

[29]*Ibid.*, paras. 4.34 and 4.35.

respectfully invite the Court to read the complete version that was filed as Annex 6 to Colombia's preliminary objections, which places the President's remarks in their proper context.

6. What actually happened is that, on 19 November 2012, President Santos discussed the Judgment fully and frankly. It is true that the enclaving of Colombia's islands was met with disappointment in Colombia, especially given the historical unity of the San Andrés Archipelago and Colombia's presence in that area. But despite this, President Santos went on to emphasize not once, but *three times*, that Colombia "respects the law", that Colombia "will not discard any recourse or mechanism available to us in international law, to defend our rights", and that "[y]ou may be sure that we shall act with respect for the law — as has been our tradition . . .". The President also drew attention to a point mentioned by Colombia's Agent earlier this morning: namely, that he, as President, had a duty to respect Colombia's Constitution, Article 101 of which provides that boundaries must be established or modified by means of a treaty — a process that necessarily entails the need for negotiations.

7. Those statements of President Santos cannot possibly be read as closing the door to negotiations with Nicaragua, and equally importantly Nicaragua did not view them as such. To the contrary, in the months that followed, the political leaders of both States made it clear that the best manner to deal with the situation arising out of the Judgment was via bilateral negotiations and the conclusion of a treaty.

8. At the beginning of December 2012, Presidents Santos and Ortega met in Mexico City. Two days earlier, Nicaragua's President had declared that: "I want to shake hands with President Santos and say that I and the people of Nicaragua [want] to fix this situation as fraternally as brothers . . ."[30]. For his part, President Santos immediately went on record after the Mexico City meeting as follows:

> "We expressed that we should handle this situation with cold head[s], in an amicable and diplomatic fashion, as this type of matters must be dealt with to avoid incidents. He [President Ortega] also understood."[31]

[30] MN, Ann. 31.

[31] POC, Ann. 9.

President Santos then added: "The way to settle this type of situations is through dialogue"[32], and "[i]f there is a problem, we will call each other"[33].

9. The Parties' mutual intention to resolve matters relating to the Judgment bilaterally was confirmed shortly afterwards. On 13 January 2013, Colombia's Foreign Minister, María Ángela Holguín, referred to the fact that a meeting had been held with President Ortega in order "to open a dialogue and a door to avoid any confrontation and to establish a communication channel"[34]. One month later, President Ortega indicated that he would invite Colombia to establish joint commissions to deal with the implementation of the Judgment. President Ortega also confirmed that, in his discussions with President Santos in Mexico and during the Summit of Latin American States in Chile, the two leaders, and I quote for President Ortega "had always spoken of taking joint measures"[35].

10. In the meantime, the situation at sea was calm. For example, on 5 December 2012, the Chief of Nicaragua's Army, General Avilés, confirmed that Nicaragua was in communication with the Colombian authorities, and that "there has been no boarding to fishing vessels"[36]. In short, there were no complaints emanating from Nicaragua in connection with the events at sea, and channels of communication had been established at both the political and military levels.

11. That situation persisted throughout 2013. On 14 August 2013, President Ortega gave a speech on the occasion of the 33rd Anniversary of Nicaragua's naval forces[37]. Not only did he repeat that Nicaragua sought a dialogue with Colombia, he also stated that, despite what he called the "media turbulence" — and I think we have all seen media turbulence:

> "[W]e must recognize that . . . the Naval Force of Colombia, which is very powerful, that certainly has a very large military power, has been careful, has been respectful and there has not been any kind of confrontation between the Colombian and Nicaraguan Navy".

President Ortega then continued:

---

[32]POC, Ann. 35.

[33]WSN, Ann. 5.

[34]POC, Ann. 37.

[35]MN, Ann. 35 [available only in English]; see also POC, para. 4.50.

[36]POC, Ann. 36, and see also Ann. 37.

[37]POC, para. 4.52.

> "And I [that is, President Ortega] am convinced that, the one who . . . has determined that pacific activity is President Juan Manuel Santos. I am convinced, we hope that this will continue in the same manner until we can reach the dialogue, reach the negotiations so as to conclude the definitive agreements to apply the judgment rendered by the Court in the month of November of last year. We are totally so disposed."[38]

12. On the Colombian side, Foreign Minister Holguín responded positively to President Ortega's proposal for dialogue. On 10 September 2013, she stated that: "We would like to speak with Nicaragua on a path toward a treaty", and that, "[o]ur doors are undoubtedly open"[39]. Two days later, Nicaragua's National Assembly endorsed President Ortega's intention to engage in a dialogue with Colombia to find mechanisms to the conclusion of a treaty with respect to the Judgment[40].

13. Mr. President, Members of the Court, far from evidencing the existence of a dispute, let alone one that could not be resolved by negotiations as Nicaragua alleges, those statements showed a common desire by both Parties, just a few weeks before Nicaragua lodged its Application, to resolve any matters relating to the Judgment by the negotiation of an appropriate treaty.

14. In its Written Statement, Nicaragua acknowledges that the Parties were open to negotiations. However, it tries to explain away the relevance of this by contending that this expressed openness did not concern the subject-matter of this dispute, which Nicaragua says is one involving alleged violations of its maritime rights and the threat of the use of force[41].

15. That is an exercise in semantics that gains no traction. Prior to the deposit of Nicaragua's Application — and even for a significant period afterwards — there was no dispute over any alleged violations of Nicaragua's maritime spaces, or concerning a threat of the use of force, that could have formed the basis of negotiations. That is because there were no claims from Nicaragua at all; only statements from its political and military leaders that the situation was calm, respectful and without incident. So, by the same token, there was no response by Colombia that could have given rise to the level of a dispute.

---

[38]POC, Ann. 11.

[39]WSN, Ann. 8.

[40]MN, Ann. 40.

[41]WSN, para. 4.60.

16. And indeed, even after Colombia proclaimed an Integral Contiguous Zone by Presidential Decree No. 1946 on 9 September 2013 — a decree that Nicaragua harps on in its written pleadings — Nicaragua did not raise any objections. The first time Nicaragua ever referred to this zone was when it filed its Application in the case[42].

17. Nicaragua also claims that the public statements that were made by various officials about matters that could form the basis of a treaty were unrelated to Nicaragua's rights as determined by the Court in its 2012 Judgment[43]. But this too is incorrect. On 10 September 2013, President Ortega himself expressed a willingness to reach a treaty with Colombia. As a published report of President Ortega's remarks indicated and noted at the time: "The 'treaty' proposed by the Nicaraguan president to Colombia must include agreements for fishing, the environment, the fight against drug trafficking 'and all that applies in this area, which has already been decided by the Court,' . . ."[44]. The reference to "all that applies in this area", which has already been decided by the Court, would obviously have included any Nicaraguan concerns it might have had relating to the implementation of the Judgment, to the extent such concerns actually existed.

18. On 12 September 2013, Colombia's President filed an application with the Colombian Constitutional Court requesting the Court — the Constitutional Court — to rule on the constitutionality of the dispute resolution provisions of the Pact of Bogotá in so far as the determination of Colombia's boundaries was concerned[45]. That application focused on whether a treaty was required in order to modify or establish a maritime boundary under Article 101 of Colombia's Constitution[46] — that is, as a matter of internal law.

19. Nicaragua argues that this step indicated that Colombia was of the opinion that no negotiation was possible because Colombia wanted to await the Constitutional Court's decision before taking any further action[47]. That contention is groundless. Not only did the step taken by President Juan Manuel Santos provide a sound constitutional basis for continuing with diplomatic

---

[42]Application, paras. 10 *et seq.*

[43]WSN, para. 4.61.

[44]POC, Ann. 40.

[45]POC, Ann. 2.

[46]POC, paras. 2.40-2.46, and see Anns. 2 and 4 thereto.

[47]WSN, paras. 4.44-4.45.

negotiations, Nicaragua itself, in its written statement, filed a press report referring to the fact that President Santos said, "in the meantime the government [Colombian Government] will try to secure a new treaty with Nicaragua that satisfies both countries"[48]. In the meantime. Indeed, the day after the application to Colombia's Constitutional Court was filed, Nicaragua's President restated his willingness to create a bilateral commission through which the Parties could work together to conclude a treaty on the implementation of the Judgment[49]. Nicaragua clearly had no issue with the Constitutional Court proceedings in Colombia.

20. On 18 November 2013, that is just eight days before Nicaragua filed its Application — eight days — the Chief of Nicaragua's naval forces, Admiral Corrales Rodriguez, in response to a question whether there had been any incidents, any conflicts with Colombia at sea, said the following, and I quote — just eight days before the Application: "There have not been any conflicts and that is why I want to highlight that in one year of being there we have not had any problems with the Colombian Navy."[50]

21. Mr. President, Members of the Court. That was the situation that existed when Nicaragua filed its Application on 26 November 2013. There was no claim by Nicaragua that could have been "positively opposed"[51] by Colombia. And there was no dispute between the Parties regarding either Colombia's compliance with the Judgment or any of the events that Nicaragua now complains of. To the contrary, the Parties had made it crystal clear that they were in favour of negotiating a treaty to deal with the post-Judgment situation.

After the Application, both Governments still did not consider that there was a dispute and, in any event, the Parties were open to negotiations

22. Even after Nicaragua filed its Application, its political leaders continued to declare that negotiation of a treaty with Colombia was a Nicaraguan priority. On 29 January 2014, for

---

[48]WSN, Ann. 7.

[49]POC, Ann. 41.

[50]POC, para. 4.53; Vol. II, Ann. 43 thereto, p. 355.

[51]*South West Africa (Ethiopia* v. *South Africa; Liberia* v. *South Africa), Preliminary Objections, Judgment, I.C.J. Reports 1962*, p. 328.

example, President Ortega stated that, together with President Santos, they had concluded that the two States would sign agreements with respect to boundaries[52].

23. And, as I have said, for its part, Colombia required the conclusion of such a treaty as a matter of domestic law and that was confirmed by the Constitutional Court's ruling handed down in May 2014, in which the Colombian Constitutional Court stated:

> "[T]he decisions rendered by the International Court of Justice, on the basis of the jurisdiction recognized by Colombia through Article XXXI of the Pact, cannot be disregarded, in conformity with what is prescribed in Article 94 of the Charter of the United Nations."[53]

Colombia's Agent mentioned this earlier. The Constitutional Court also held that decisions of the International Court of Justice with respect to boundaries had to be incorporated into domestic law in the manner provided for by Article 101 of the Constitution: that is, by means of treaties.

24. One week later, Nicaragua's President reiterated the need to establish a bilateral commission "so [that] a treaty can come out of it that will allow us to respect, and put in practice the judgment by the ICJ"[54]. Thus, far from indicating that the Parties somehow stood on the brink of a dispute, the record shows both before the filing of the Application and afterwards, that they continued to be ready and willing to negotiate a treaty.

25. In the meantime, Nicaragua's General Avilés, whom I referred to a minute ago, had again confirmed that, according to the permanent communications that had been put in place between the two countries' navies — and I quote from Nicaragua's General — "the area remains without incidents"[55]. This statement, which was made in March 2014, repeated what Nicaragua's military commanders had said before. It underscores the artificiality of the Application that Nicaragua filed in November 2013, alleging that a dispute existed over violations of Nicaragua's maritime spaces and the threat of the use of force. That is completely contradicted by Nicaragua's own senior most military commanders.

26. Mr. President, it was only on 13 September 2014 — that was almost ten months *after* the Application was deposited and on Nicaragua's interpretation of the Pact of Bogatá, ten months

---

[52]POC, Ann. 45.

[53]POC, Ann. 4, para. 9.10.

[54]MN, Ann. 46. [Only available in English]

[55]POC, Ann. 46.

after Colombia's denunciation of the Pact took effect — that Nicaragua sent a Note Verbale to Colombia which, for the first time, referred to any alleged infringements of Nicaragua's sovereign rights[56]. That Note attached a list of so-called "incidents", *none of which* had ever been referred to before, and all of which were directly contradicted by the repeated assurances of the chiefs of Nicaragua's armed forces that there had not been a single incident at sea between the date of the Court's Judgment and the filing of the Application in November 2013 and, indeed, up until at least March 2014, four months after the Application.

27. In these circumstances, Mr. President, distinguished Members, it cannot credibly be said as a matter of fact that, as of 26 November 2013, there was a dispute between the Parties over the events now complained of by Nicaragua. Nor does the record show that the Parties were of the opinion that, to the extent a dispute somehow existed, it could not be settled by direct negotiations through the usual diplomatic channels. Senior leaders of both countries had repeatedly emphasized the desire to negotiate a treaty or treaties relating to the post-Judgment situation.

28. Mr. President, that concludes my presentation. I thank the Court for its courtesy and attention, and I would ask whether, I am not sure after the coffee break or now, the floor could next be given to Professor Reisman. Thank you very much,

Le PRESIDENT : Merci, Monsieur Bundy. La Cour va maintenant marquer une pause de 15 minutes. L'audience est suspendue.

L'audience est suspendue de 11 h 25 à 11 h 40

Le PRESIDENT : Veuillez vous asseoir. L'audience reprend et je donne maintenant la parole au professeur Michael Reisman. Monsieur le professeur.

Mr. REISMAN:

SECOND PRELIMINARY OBJECTION: ABSENCE OF A DISPUTE

1. Thank you Mr. President. Mr. President, Members of the Court, it is an honour to appear before you on behalf of the Republic of Colombia. My assignment is to explain why — even if the

---

[56]POC, Ann. 17.

Court were to find jurisdiction *ratione temporis,* whether under the Pact of Bogotá or under Nicaragua's second basis of jurisdiction — Nicaragua's claims would still fail your jurisdictional requirements because they were not the subject-matter of a dispute at the time of application.

2. The law on this matter may be briefly summarized:

— *first*, even if a putative respondent State is deemed to have consented to jurisdiction, that jurisdiction is effective for a specific case only if there is a dispute;

— *second*, the existence of a dispute is not determined by the subjective assumption of the Applicant but is a matter for "objective determination" by the Court;

— *third*, an objective determination of a dispute requires that the Applicant have indicated to the Respondent, by some modality, the content of its claim, whether legal or factual, and, reciprocally, that the Respondent have indicated, by some modality, its rejection of the claim; and

— *fourth*, the critical date for determining the objective existence of the dispute is that of the filing of the Application.

3. It is hardly necessary to multiply authorities for the law here. From *Peace Treaties* on, the Court has repeatedly confirmed that there must be a dispute and that it is the Court which makes the "objective determination"[57]. As for the critical date for determining the objective existence of a dispute as a condition for jurisdiction — the Court held in *Arrest Warrant*: "The Court recalls that, according to its settled jurisprudence, its jurisdiction must be determined at the time that the act instituting proceedings was filed."[58]

---

[57]*Interpretation of Peace Treaties with Bulgaria, Hungary and Romania, First Phase, Advisory Opinion: I.C.J. Reports 1950,* p. 74; *Nuclear Tests (Australia* v. *France), Judgment, I.C.J. Reports 1974,* pp. 270-271, para. 55; *Nuclear Tests (New Zealand* v. *France), Judgment, I.C.J. Reports 1974*, p. 476, para. 58; *Application of the International Convention on the Elimination of All Forms of Racial Discrimination (Georgia* v. *Russian Federation), Preliminary Objections, Judgment, I.C.J. Reports 2011*, p. 84, para 30.

[58]*Arrest Warrant of 11 April 2000 (Democratic Republic of the Congo* v. *Belgium), Judgment, I.C.J. Reports 2002,* pp. 12-13, para. 26. The Court has emphasized that even for admissibility, the critical date is the date of filing. Thus, the Court held in its 1988 Judgment on *Border and Transborder Armed Actions*: "The critical date for determining the admissibility of an application is the date on which it is filed." *Border and Transborder Armed Actions (Nicaragua* v. *Honduras), Jurisdiction and Admissibility, I.C.J. Reports, 1988*, p. 95, para. 66. The Court maintained this view in the subsequent cases of *Questions of Interpretation and Application of the 1971 Montreal Convention arising from the Aerial Incident at Lockerbie (Libyan Arab Jamahiriya* v. *United Kingdom), Preliminary Objections, Judgment, I. C.J., Reports 1998* pp. 25-26, paras. 42-44; *Application of the International Convention on the Elimination of All Forms of Racial Discrimination (Georgia* v. *Russian Federation), Preliminary Objections, Judgment, I.C.J. Reports 2011*, pp. 84-85, para. 30; and *Questions relating to the Obligation to Prosecute or Extradite (Belgium* v. *Senegal), Judgment, I.C.J., Reports 2012*, pp. 442 and 444-445, paras 46 and 54.

4. Now, making an objective determination is challenging in the contemporary arena, when many States are democratic and have rich communications ecologies. Then their robust internal politics may produce a discordant chorus of many voices from different branches — executive, legislative and judicial — from different departments and from different political factions. Some of the voices may be speaking to domestic audiences while others are vying *to shape* a national political policy rather than authoritatively addressing an external audience, as French authorities did in *Nuclear Tests*[59]. Equally relevant is the moment in time when the voices make themselves heard: some of those voices may reflect initial disappointment with a judgment, to be succeeded by acceptance of it.

5. When there is a chorus of domestic voices, an objective determination naturally looks, in particular, to those of the respective chief executives, as you held in *Georgia* v. *Russia*[60]. Common views of the executives of both States on policy matters are particularly probative. Statements made by military officials as to facts in their domain of expertise are probative as facts, as the Court held in *Congo* v. *Uganda*[61].

6. Mr. President, Nicaragua's Application fails all of these requirements. As I will explain in a moment, the record, when fairly and "objectively" read, shows confirmation of such shared views by the Presidents of Colombia and Nicaragua, a fact which belies the assertion that there was an objective dispute. But first, permit me to correct Nicaragua's misstatement of Colombia's argument as to the modalities of communicating for purposes of objectively establishing that there is a dispute.

7. Colombia's submission was that to fulfil the "objective" requirement, the counter-party has to be informed of the other party's grievance and claim. At several points in its Written

---

[59] *Nuclear Tests (Australia* v. *France), Judgment, I.C.J. Reports 1974*, p. 16, para. 34; *Nuclear Tests (New Zealand* v. *France), Judgment, I.C.J. Reports 1974*, p. 16, para. 35.

[60] *Application of the International Convention on the Elimination of All Forms of Racial Discrimination (Georgia* v. *Russian Federation), Preliminary Objections, Judgment, I.C.J. Reports 2011*, p. 87, para. 37.

[61] As you held in *Armed Activities on the Territory of the Congo (Democratic Republic of the Congo* v. *Uganda)*:

> "The Court will treat with caution evidentiary materials specially prepared for this case and also materials emanating from a single source. It will prefer contemporaneous evidence from persons with direct knowledge. It will give particular attention to reliable evidence acknowledging facts or conduct unfavourable to the State represented by the person making them (*Military and Paramilitary Activities in and against Nicaragua (Nicaragua* v. *United States of America), Merits, Judgment, I.C.J. Reports 1986*, p. 41, para. 64). The Court will also give weight to evidence that has not, even before this litigation, been challenged by impartial persons for the correctness of what it contains." (*Judgment, I.C.J. Reports 2005*, p. 201, para. 61.)

Statement, Nicaragua attributes to Colombia the straw-man argument that I'm quoting Nicaragua, "as a matter of international law no 'dispute' can exist until it has been in some way 'constituted' by the sending of a formal diplomatic Note"[62].

8. Mr. President, what Colombia *actually* argued — and argues — is that while international law does not require a specific modality, "[g]iven Nicaragua's failure to specify the subject-matter of its allegations prior to the submission of its Application, or to raise a complaint, no objective dispute existed between the Parties"[63]. Now, a diplomatic Note can certainly accomplish this, but it is only one of many possible modalities. What counts is that the counter-party be informed *before* the critical date. If an application sufficed *per se* to constitute the objective existence of the dispute, your jurisprudence on this matter would be pointless.

9. Indeed, the Court's constant jurisprudence *(jurisprudence constante)* is particularly clear on the need to demonstrate that the State against whom a complaint is made has had the opportunity to react in some manner so that a "positive opposition of the claim of one party by the other"[64] actually materializes[65]. To paraphrase what the Court held in *Georgia* v. *Russia*, but substituting the names of the Parties in the instant case, what the Court needs to establish in order to determine the existence of a dispute is "whether [Nicaragua] made such a claim [revealing a disagreement on a point of law or fact between the two States] and whether [Colombia] positively opposed it with the result that there is a dispute between them . . ."[66].

10. Mr. President, I turn to Nicaragua's statement of the dispute. In its 2013 Application, Nicaragua defined the "Subject of the dispute" in these words: "The dispute concerns the

---

[62]WSN para. 3.9; see also paras. 3.16-3.20.

[63]POC, para. 4.14.

[64]*Land and Maritime Boundary between Cameroon and Nigeria, Preliminary Objections, Judgment, I.C.J. Reports 1998*, p. 315, para. 89.

[65]See *South West Africa Cases (Ethiopia* v. *South Africa; Liberia* v. *South Africa), Preliminary Objections, Judgment of 21 December 1962: I.C.J. Reports 1962*, p. 328; *East Timor (Portugal* v. *Australia), Judgment, I.C.J. Reports 1995*, pp. 99-100, para. 22; *Questions of Interpretation and Application of the 1971 Montreal Convention arising from the Aerial Incident at Lockerbie (Libyan Arab Jamahiriya* v. *United Kingdom), Preliminary Objections, Judgment, I.C.J., Reports 1998*, p. 17, paras. 21-22; *Arrest Warrant of 11 April 2000 (Democratic Republic of the Congo* v. *Belgium), Judgment, I.C.J. Reports 2002*, p. 13, para. 27; *Certain Property (Liechtenstein* v. *Germany), Preliminary Objections, Judgment, I.C.J. Reports 2005*, p. 18, para. 24; *Armed Activities on the Territory of the Congo (New Application: 2002) (Democratic Republic of the Congo* v. *Rwanda), Jurisdiction and Admissibility, Judgment, I.C.J. Reports 2006*, p. 40, para. 90.

[66]*Application of the International Convention on the Elimination of All Forms of Racial Discrimination (Georgia* v. *Russian Federation), Preliminary Objections, Judgment, I.C.J. Reports 2011*, p. 85, para. 31.

violations of Nicaragua's sovereign rights and maritime zones declared by the Court's Judgment of 19 November 2012 and the threat of the use of force by Colombia in order to implement these violations."[67] Mr. President, Nicaragua never raised any of these claims with nor otherwise manifested them to Colombia prior to the submission of its Application. And it has submitted no evidence to the contrary. Thus Nicaragua fails to show a key element of the requirement as to the objective existence of the dispute.

11. Failing to adduce any evidence that it had raised its claims with Colombia before the date of submission of the Application, Nicaragua cherry-picks statements made by Colombian officials in an effort to show that Colombia was aware of or somehow intuited Nicaragua's "phantom" claims, rejected them, and hence there was a dispute. Nicaragua does this not only by selective quotation, but also by putting a "spin" on the statements, taking them out of context and distorting their meaning. But, logically, if Nicaragua failed to raise its claims against Colombia prior to the submission of its Application, Colombia's communications and statements could not have addressed, let alone opposed non-existent claims. But that impossibility aside, the Colombian statements which Nicaragua selects fail to support its assertion.

12. First, Colombia never stated, in terms that meet the *Peace Treaties* requirement, that "the two sides hold clearly opposite views concerning the question of the performance or non-performance"[68] of the Judgment. Nicaragua — as Mr. Bundy pointed out — reproduces a sentence in which President Santos says that Colombia "emphatically rejects that aspect of the judgment . . ."[69]. I would respectfully invite the Court to review the entire text of President Santos's statement of 19 November 2012, which is in your folders. Mr. President, that the President of Colombia disagreed with and was critical of parts of the Judgment — as was the Foreign Minister — is no cause for surprise, neither are such statements internationally illegal acts, nor do such public expressions of disappointment constitute a declaration of non-compliance with the Judgment. No rule of international law requires a State to rejoice in an adverse judgment. Nicaragua's snippet of the President's speech neglects to cite the President's real message that

---

[67] Application, para. 2.

[68] *Interpretation of Peace Treaties with Bulgaria, Hungary and Romania, First Phase, Advisory Opinion, I.C.J. Reports 1950*, p. 74.

[69] WSN, para. 4.35

"Article 101 of our Constitution says that 'the boundaries fixed in the manner set forth in this Constitution may only be modified by virtue of treaties approved by Congress, and duly ratified by the President'."[70] Nor did Nicaragua quote the President's statement in the speech that "we are committed to find mechanisms and specific strategies, and to produce results — including the negotiation of treaties as may be necessary — so that [the archipelago's inhabitants] rights may at no time be disregarded"[71]. Mr. President, President Santos's entire speech makes clear that, far from a pronouncement of non-compliance with the Judgment, his message specified the modality for implementation of the Judgment, which was to be by treaty, as required by Colombian constitutional law.

13. Nicaragua similarly misrepresents Colombian statements which are alleged to be threats to the use of force. When the Court reads them in full, it will see that they are no more than political affirmations of the commitment to protect Colombian rights in Colombian areas. If such routine political statements are henceforth to be taken as violations of the United Nations Charter, the Security Council's agenda and the Court's docket will quickly become bloated with trivialities.

14. In any event, Mr. President, these are merits questions which the Court need not and should not touch. The decisive point is that at no time up to the critical date of 26 November 2013 did Nicaragua once indicate to Colombia, by *any* modality, that Colombia was violating Nicaraguan sovereign rights and maritime zones declared by the 2012 Judgment or that it was threatening to use force. Not once. It was only almost 10 months *after* filing its Application that Nicaragua, by Note Verbale, accused Colombia of these issues.

15. Nicaragua's contention, Mr. President, that it had refrained from mentioning the alleged threats because it did not want to interfere in Colombia's election process[72] is not worthy of comment. I suggest that the real reason for Nicaragua's failure to raise the issue is that there was none! The Nicaraguan Navy had not reported any incidents and just before Nicaragua filed its Application on 18 November 2013, Nicaraguan Admiral Corrales Rodriguez, eight days before the

---

[70]POC, Vol. II, Ann. 6, p. 89.

[71]*Ibid.*, p. 90.

[72]POC, Vol. II, Ann. 17, p. 151.

Application, reported that there have not been any conflicts[73]. I will not repeat the quotation that had been read by my colleague Mr. Bundy, but he said that there "have not been any conflicts" and that "we have not had any problems with the Colombian Navy".

16. On 14 August 2013, President Ortega announced — this is worth, I think, reviewing:

> "we must recognize that in the middle of all this media turbulence, the Naval Force of Colombia, which is very powerful, that certainly has a very large military power, has been careful, has been respectful and there has not been any kind of confrontation between the Colombian and Nicaraguan Navy, thank God"[74].

17. It was many months *after* the Application that Nicaragua's Ministry of Foreign Affairs requested its own navy to report any alleged incidents that may have taken place. Why and why then? I suggest, Mr. President, in order to fabricate the impression that there was a dispute at the time of its Application.

18. *Peace Treaties* teaches that a dispute exists objectively in "a situation in which the two sides hold clearly opposite views concerning the question of the performance or non-performance of certain treaty obligations"[75]. Nothing in the record shows those required "clearly opposite views" of the subject-matter of the Application at the time of Nicaragua's filing.

19. Mr. Bundy has already referred to President Santos's statement. Comparable views were expressed by Nicaraguan President Ortega. In his speech on 14 August 2013, after referring to drug trafficking, organized crime and the Seaflower Reserve, President Ortega announced:

> "I am convinced, we hope that this will continue in the same manner until we can reach the dialogue, reach the negotiations so as to conclude the definitive agreements to apply the judgment rendered by the Court in the month of November of last year. We are totally so disposed."[76]

Nicaragua's Memorial quotes President Ortega on 9 May 2014 as follows:

> "We propose to the government of Colombia, to President Juan Manuel Santos, to work for a Colombian-Nicaraguan commission so a treaty can come out of it that will allow us to respect and put in practice the judgment by the ICJ."[77]

---

[73]POC, Vol. II, Ann. 43, p. 355.

[74]POC, Vol. II, Ann. 11, p. 118.

[75]*Interpretation of Peace Treaties with Bulgaria, Hungary and Romania, First Phase, Advisory Opinion, I.C.J. Reports 1950*, p. 74.

[76]POC, Vol. II, Ann. 11, p. 119.

[77]MN, p. 54 and Ann. 46, p. 441.

Given the common view of the need for a treaty to implement the Judgment, one can appreciate, all the more, Colombia's surprise at Nicaragua's Application on 26 November 2013[78].

20. Mr. President, Members of the Court, the western Caribbean is a complex arena in which Colombia, for decades, has performed critical international legal roles, including naval interdiction of human trafficking and narco-trafficking, fishing conservation and environmental protection, in addition to discharging its own sovereign responsibility to provide protection for the territory and inhabitants of the Colombian archipelago. Unlike the removal of a border checkpoint in an uninhabited desert, which may be quickly struck, dismantled and hauled away, the delimitation decreed by the Court in 2012 was in a much more complex normative environment, one which requires preparation and adjustments. Both Parties understood this was to be accomplished by treaty. The communications between the two governments and, in Colombia's case, also within it, confirm that the Parties recognize this fact.

21. The Colombian regulations with respect to the contiguous zone must be appreciated in these terms. Up to the time of its Application, the most authoritative statements by high Nicaraguan officials indicated a common view that the implementation of the 2012 Judgment was in the process of being addressed by the counter-party and, thus, was *not* in dispute. President Ortega's statements show that he accepted that the implementation of the Judgment would be by treaty and statements by the Nicaraguan military expressed satisfaction with the comportment of the Colombian Navy. In parallel fashion, none of the statements by Colombian officials, read in their entirety, said more than that the internal procedures necessary for implementing the Judgment in an orderly fashion were in process, pending the completion of which Colombian law would perforce continue to apply. But, Mr. President, for jurisdictional purposes, the two critical points are that, as of the filing of its Application, Nicaragua had not voiced any complaint whatsoever to Colombia with respect to these regulations; and that Colombia only learned about Nicaragua's views on their lawfulness — or lack of it — when it received the Application.

---

[78]See, also, in this regard, the statement of the Foreign Minister: POC, Vol. II, Ann. 44 at p. 359.

22. So for all of these reasons, Colombia respectfully submits that the Court lacks jurisdiction over Nicaragua's Application of 26 November 2013 for, on that date, there was no dispute over the matters raised in the Application.

23. Mr. President, Members of the Court, I thank you for your attention and, Mr. President, may I ask that Mr. Valencia-Ospina be called to address you.

The PRESIDENT: Je donne la parole à M. Valencia-Ospina.

Mr. VALENCIA-OSPINA:

THIRD PRELIMINARY OBJECTION: THE COURT LACKS JURISDICTION BECAUSE THE PRECONDITION OF ARTICLE II OF THE PACT OF BOGOTÁ HAD NOT BEEN FULFILLED AT THE TIME OF THE FILING OF THE APPLICATION

1. Mr. President, Members of the Court, the Government of my country, Colombia, has done me an honour with a deep personal significance by appointing me to plead on its behalf before the highest judicial organ of the United Nations.

2. I have been assigned to address the question of the non-fulfilment of the precondition imposed by Article II of the Pact of Bogotá. I will demonstrate that, at the time Nicaragua filed its Application, the Parties were not of the opinion that the alleged controversy "[could] not be settled by direct negotiations through the usual diplomatic channels", as Article II requires.

3. This third objection is raised as an alternative ground to the two already pleaded. It is nevertheless closely linked to the second objection concerning the absence of a dispute. For while it is true that these grounds are legally distinct, it is equally true that the Court has often relied upon discussions and diplomatic exchanges — such as those that take place during negotiations — in order to disclose the existence of a dispute at the critical date[79].

4. It is in fact undisputed that, prior to the belated Nicaraguan diplomatic Note of 13 September 2014, there were no exchanges between the Parties that addressed the alleged violations of Nicaragua's maritime zones, and much less on the purported threat of or use of force by Colombia. But the Parties have been exchanging views all along on four important

[79] *Mavrommatis Palestine Concessions, Judgment No. 2, 1924, P.C.I.J., Series A, No. 2*, p. 15; *Interpretation of Judgments Nos. 7 and 8 (Factory at Chorzów), Judgment No. 11, 1927, P.C.I.J., Series A, No. 13*, pp. 10-12; *Right of Passage over Indian Territory (Portugal* v. *India), Preliminary Objections, Judgment, I.C.J. Reports 1957*, p. 149.

subject-matters that relate to: *(a)* the implementation of the 2012 Judgment; *(b)* the protection of the historical fishing rights of the population of the archipelago of San Andrés; *(c)* the conservation of the Seaflower Biosphere Reserve; and *(d)* the fight against drug trafficking in the Caribbean Sea.

5. Nicaragua has asserted that the "subject-matters on which the parties kept the door open to eventual negotiations are different from the subject-matter" of its claims[80]. But Nicaragua cannot have it both ways. It cannot, on the one hand, argue that there is an objective dispute by selectively quoting the statements made by the Parties and, on the other hand, put this very same conduct aside because it attests to the fact that negotiations are possible. Nicaragua's move in favour of jurisdiction must fail on either one of those two grounds. Either the conduct discloses the absence of a dispute regarding the claims referred to in the Application, or it reveals that the precondition of Article II of the Pact had not been fulfilled. Should the Court reject the second objection concerning the absence of a dispute, it should still find that the statements made by the highest representatives of both States and the meetings held between them in Mexico and Chile clearly demonstrate that, at the time of the filing of the Application, the Parties did not think that direct negotiations were not the way to proceed.

6. Before going further into the matters in contention, I wish to stress two important points over which the Parties are in agreement:

— first, as already affirmed by the Court in its 1988 Judgment in the *Border and Transborder Armed Actions* case between Nicaragua and Honduras, Article II of the Pact constitutes a precondition to all the procedures of the treaty[81];

— second, the critical date for assessing whether this precondition has been fulfilled is the date of the filing of the Application[82]. The Parties' agreement on this second point can come as no surprise to the Court in view of its conclusions in the 2011 Judgment in the *Georgia* v. *Russian*

---

[80]WSN, paras 4.53-4.65.

[81]*Border and Transborder Armed Actions (Nicaragua* v. *Honduras), Jurisdiction and Admissibility, Judgment, I.C.J. Reports 1988*, p. 69, at p. 94, para. 62; POC, paras. 4.22-4.26; WSN, para. 4.9.

[82]POC, paras. 4.7-4.9; WSN, para. 4.31.

Federation case and the 2012 Judgment in the *Belgium* v. *Senegal* case[83]. However, in view of the opinions held on this issue, I wish to stress that, in the instant case, there is an additional fundamental reason for admitting that the critical date can correspond only to the date of the filing of the Application. The seisin of the Court having occurred at the very last moment before the termination for Colombia of the Pact of Bogotá, the basis of jurisdiction under this instrument has at the very least expired since then. Thus, it would be impossible for Nicaragua to bring fresh proceedings after 26 November 2013. In other words, the situation is markedly different from the one that the Court was confronted with in its 2008 Judgment in the *Croatia* v. *Serbia* case, where it found that all the preconditions to jurisdiction were concurrently fulfilled at a given moment in time after the filing of the Application[84]. This being said, the Parties also agree with the Court's 1988 finding that, "[i]t may however be necessary, in order to determine with certainty what the situation was at the date of filing of the Application, to examine the events, and in particular the relations between the Parties, over a period prior to that date, and indeed during the subsequent period"[85].

7. It is at this stage where agreement ends and disagreement starts. Nicaragua has indeed contested both the meaning of Article II of the Pact and the characterization of the opinion of the Parties put forward by Colombia in its preliminary objections. For Nicaragua, in the opinion of the Parties must be interpreted as signifying in the opinion of one of them — the Applicant — that is to say in Nicaragua's own opinion.

8. In addition, Nicaragua has advanced what it claims to be an "objective" assessment about the opinion of the Parties in order to conclude that both of them were of the good faith belief that the alleged controversy could not be settled by way of direct negotiations. But Nicaragua's own assessment is located at the polar opposite of objectivity. Indeed, I will show that Nicaragua is not only selectively quoting and misconstruing the declarations of Colombia's highest representatives,

---

[83]*Application of the International Convention on the Elimination of All Forms of Racial Discrimination (Georgia* v. *Russian Federation), Preliminary Objections, Judgment, I.C.J. Reports 2011 (I)*, p. 70, at p. 124, para. 130; *Questions relating to the Obligation to Prosecute or Extradite (Belgium* v. *Senegal), Judgment, I.C.J. Reports 2012 (II)*, p. 444, para. 54 and pp. 445-446, paras. 57-59.

[84]*Application of the Convention on the Prevention and Punishment of the Crime of Genocide (Croatia* v. *Serbia), Preliminary Objections, Judgment, I.C.J Reports 2008*, pp. 445-446, para. 96.

[85]*Border and Transborder Armed Actions (Nicaragua* v. *Honduras), Jurisdiction and Admissibility, Judgment, I.C.J. Reports 1988*, p. 95, para. 66.

but also deliberately ignoring the statements made by its own President and military and disregarding the steps taken by the two Presidents. Such omissions speak for themselves. For to quote accurately its President would mean for Nicaragua to explicitly contradict itself, since he has made it abundantly clear that negotiations were possible and indeed the way to proceed.

9. No prospective applicant which is required to fulfil the precondition of Article II of the Pact would publicly declare, only two months prior to the seisin of the Court and the termination for Colombia of the Pact, that diplomatic means are the way to proceed, if it genuinely thought otherwise[86]. Likewise, a State that has recently become an applicant would not publicly assert less than two months after having filed its application that negotiations are still possible, if it thought that that was in fact untrue[87]. While the case law of the Court shows that "negotiations and recourse to judicial settlement have been pursued *pari passu*"[88] and, therefore, that the two means are not mutually exclusive, the situation is of course different when a provision such as Article II of the Pact is applicable. In situations such as the current one, the very fact that Nicaragua has confirmed that negotiations were possible immediately before and after the filing of its Application, demonstrates that the precondition had not been fulfilled at the critical date.

10. I will now proceed to address the meaning of Article II of the Pact before objectively assessing the opinion of the Parties. In so doing, I shall rebut the arguments made by the Applicant in its Written Statement.

The Meaning of Article II of the Pact of Bogotá

The condition presupposes that the Parties must be of the opinion that the controversy "cannot be settled by direct negotiations through the usual diplomatic channels"

11. Article II of the Pact, which now appears on the screen, in its relevant part reads as follows: "in the event that a controversy arises between two or more signatory states which, *in the opinion of the parties*, cannot be settled by direct negotiations through the usual diplomatic channels, the parties bind themselves to use the procedures established in the present Treaty".

---

[86]POC, paras. 4.51-4.52 and Vol. II, Anns. 11, 40 and 41.

[87]*Ibid.*, para. 4.56 and Ann. 45.

[88]*Aegean Sea Continental Shelf (Greece* v. *Turkey), Judgment, I.C.J. Reports 1978*, p. 12, para. 29.

12. Nicaragua has alleged that "Colombia conveniently overlooks" the authentic French text of the same article which refers to "de l'avis de l'une des parties"[89]. But, apart from the English, what about the texts, also appearing on the screen, in Spanish — "en opinión de las Partes" — and Portuguese — "na opinião das Partes" — which clearly refer to the opinion of the Parties? It is rather Nicaragua that is the party that conveniently overlooks these three equally authentic texts, which include Spanish, Nicaragua's and Colombia's own official language, in which the Nicaraguan Senate and Executive incorporated the Pact into its domestic legislation[90]. The Applicant asserts that the phrase "in the opinion of the parties is, on its face, ambiguous", and is "susceptible to either of the interpretations advanced by Colombia and Nicaragua"[91]. On the contrary, what is definitely unambiguous is the fact that the three authentic texts drafted in the Spanish, Portuguese and English languages use the plural "parties" and not the singular form of the term.

13. To buttress its theory that the opinion of only one of the parties is all that is required, Nicaragua resorts to the 1985 Opinion of the Inter-American Juridical Committee on the American Treaty on Pacific Settlement[92]. The Applicant goes even further and dares to criticize Colombia for not having appended that Opinion to its preliminary objections[93]. As a matter of fact Colombia, at paragraph 4.40 of its preliminary objections, did refer to the 1985 Opinion, a document which being in the public domain was identified by its documentary source at footnote 199 of the same pleadings. But let our attention not be distracted by Nicaragua's unfounded criticism, and let us instead look more closely at what Nicaragua does in order to blatantly alter the conclusions of this 1985 Committee's Opinion. Nicaragua contents itself with quoting in its Written Statement and annexing thereto merely two paragraphs of the Opinion[94]. However, such excerpts are simply

---

[89]WSN, para. 4.4.

[90]*La Gaceta*, Diario Oficial, Año LIV, Managua, D.N., Nos. 100, 18 May 1950, p. 966; 118, 9 June 1950, pp. 1138-1139; 121, 18 June 1950, p. 1162; 159, 2 August 1950, pp. 1514-1518; 160, 3 August 1950, pp. 1529-1533.

[91]WSN, para. 4.19.

[92]Opinion of the Inter-American Juridical Committee on the American Treaty on Pacific Settlement (Pact of Bogotá), Organization of the American States Doc. OEA/Ser.G, CP/Doc. 1603/85, 3 Sep. 1985, reproduced in Ann. 23 of Nicaragua's Counter-Memorial in the *Border and Transborder Armed Actions (Nicaragua* v. *Honduras), Jurisdiction and Admissibility, Judgment, I.C.J. Reports 1988*, p. 423.

[93]WSN, paras. 4.24-4.27.

[94]*Ibid.*, para. 4.25 and Ann. 2.

descriptive of the personal views expressed by the Committee's Rapporteur already in his report dated 19 August 1985, and not a reflection of the Committee's conclusions in the Opinion it formally adopted ten days later, on 29 August 1985, which Opinion annexed the Rapporteur's report[95]. Nicaragua does not quote, and does not include in its annexes, the Opinion's clear acknowledgment that the 11-member Committee as a whole rejected the amendment proposed by the Rapporteur. As stated in the paragraph of the Opinion immediately following those quoted by Nicaragua, which now appears on the screen:

> "Although there was a motion by the Rapporteur that an adjustment in the text be recommended to make it consistent with the French version . . ., the amendment voted on for that particular phrase of the second paragraph of Article II was that it [should] read 'in the opinion of one of the parties'. That amendment carried the votes of Drs. Leoro [Rapporteur], Vieira, Callejas-Bonilla, Rabasa and Waaldijk."[96]

In other words, the amendment was supported only by a minority of the full membership of the Committee and, hence, it was rejected. Moreover, the phrase "in the opinion of the parties" in the plural was kept in Article II of the complete text of the Pact adopted by the Committee and reproduced as the concluding part of its Opinion[97]. And yet, Nicaragua unashamedly feels free to assert that "[i]t is thus clear that the conclusion reached by the Juridical Committee is that Article II refers to the opinion of one of the parties to a dispute, not both of them — exactly the opposite of the proposition for which Colombia cites the 1985 Juridical Committee report"[98].

14. However, this is simply not so. What is crystal clear is precisely the contrary. Nicaragua has grossly distorted the Opinion by advancing, as if it were the Committee's interpretation, a reading proposed by the Rapporteur which is precisely the one rejected by the Committee.

15. Moreover, to read Article II of the Pact as meaning that only the opinion of the Applicant matters, as Nicaragua asserts, would lead to a manifestly absurd result. For what purpose would be served by this prerequisite if its fulfilment were to depend solely on the opinion of the party that

---

[95]Opinion of the Inter-American Juridical Committee on the American Treaty on Pacific Settlement (Pact of Bogotá), Organization of the American States Doc. OEA/Ser.G, CP/Doc. 1603/85, 3 Sep. 1985, reproduced in Ann. 23 of Nicaragua's Counter-Memorial in the *Border and Transborder Armed Actions (Nicaragua* v. *Honduras), Jurisdiction and Admissibility, Judgment, I.C.J. Reports 1988*, p. 423.

[96]Opinion of the Inter-American Juridical Committee on the American Treaty on Pacific Settlement (Pact of Bogotá), Organization of the American States Doc. OEA/Ser.G, CP/Doc. 1603/85, 3 Sep. 1985, reproduced in Ann. 23 of Nicaragua's Counter-Memorial in the *Border and Transborder Armed Actions (Nicaragua* v. *Honduras), Jurisdiction and Admissibility, Judgment, I.C.J. Reports 1988*, pp. 431-432.

[97]*Ibid.*, p. 442.

[98]WSN, para. 4.27.

seises the Court? Evidently Nicaragua feels compelled to insist on such reading because it is fully conscious that in the opinion of Colombia direct negotiations were possible.

The condition presupposes an objective assessment of the opinion of the parties

16. The precondition established in Article II of the Pact presupposes an objective assessment of the opinion of the parties. As this Court stated in 1988, "the holding of opinions can be subject to demonstration, and . . . the Court may expect 'the Parties [to provide] substantive evidence that they consider in good faith' a certain possibility of negotiation to exist or not to exist"[99]. The Parties agree with this statement of principle. In practice, however, Nicaragua seeks to demonstrate its bona fide opinion by relying solely on the fact that it is the State that has filed the Application. In the Applicant's own words: "Nicaragua was justified in forming the same view, as the filing of the Application attests."[100]

17. According to the Applicant, Nicaragua had made in the 1988 *Border and Transborder Armed Actions* case "an argument very much like the one Colombia now puts forward"[101]. But what Nicaragua had argued in that case was that the issue "is not whether one of the parties or both of them must think that the dispute cannot be settled by diplomatic means but whether the dispute can in fact be settled by such means"[102]. Nicaragua's contention constitutes yet another deliberate misinterpretation of Colombia's arguments. Colombia has clearly stated in its preliminary objections that the language of Article II of the Pact of Bogotá "points to the importance of the Parties' opinion as to whether the controversy can or cannot be settled by direct negotiations"[103].

18. Moreover, Nicaragua has advanced the untenable proposition that Colombia's analysis of the Court's jurisprudence relating to compromissory clauses, in treaties that provide for recourse to the Court only in the case of a dispute that "is not" or "cannot be" settled by negotiations, is "inapposite"[104]. In its view, the subjective element embodied in Article II implies that it "cannot be

---

[99]*Border and Transborder Armed Actions (Nicaragua* v. *Honduras), Jurisdiction and Admissibility, Judgment, I.C.J. Reports 1988*, p. 95, para. 65.

[100]WSN, para. 4.50.

[101]*Ibid.*, para. 4.12.

[102]*Ibid.*

[103]POC, para. 4.27.

[104]WSN, para. 4.3.

analogized to those other compromissory clauses"[105]. By characterizing Article II of the Pact as "unique", Nicaragua deludes itself by thinking that it can arrive at the conclusion that Colombia simply cannot rely on any such jurisprudential precedent to interpret this provision[106].

19. In this respect, it suffices to emphasize that not even Nicaragua believes what it says. In effect, Nicaragua finds it quite appropriate for itself to refer to the Court's jurisprudence in order to draw purported parallels between the current situation and both the 1988 Advisory Opinion concerning the *UN Headquarters Agreement* and the 1980 Judgment in the *Tehran Hostages* case[107]. It is implausible to attempt such a comparison. In so far as the Advisory Opinion is concerned, there had been extensive negotiations and consultations prior to the filing of the corresponding request. Besides, for the United States its own Anti-Terrorism Act "ha[d] superseded the requirements of the UN Headquarters Agreement to the extent that those requirements [were] inconsistent with th[at] Statute"[108]. Thus, the issue was not one of non-applicability but clearly one of non-compliance with an international obligation. Moreover, in that case the Court was confronted with a provision setting a lower threshold for previous negotiations since the requirement was that the dispute "is not settled" rather than that it "cannot be settled". In relation to the *Tehran Hostages* case, suffice it to recall that, following United States offers to negotiate, the Ayatollah Khomeini "solemnly forb[ade] members of the Revolutionary Council . . . to meet the United States representatives"[109]. Obviously, the very holding of hostages in a diplomatic mission significantly impairs the prospect for further discussions since negotiations with the receiving State are one of the mission's key functions[110].

20. In reasoning on the basis of the jurisprudential distinction between provisions requiring that the dispute "is not settled" and provisions requiring that it "cannot be settled", what Colombia has sought is to describe the appropriate standard against which the opinion of the Parties must be

---

[105]*Ibid.*, para. 4.11 and paras 4.9-4.13.

[106]*Ibid.*, para. 4.3.

[107]WSN, paras 4.47-4.52.

[108]*Applicability of the Obligation to Arbitrate under Section 21 of the United Nations Headquarters Agreement of 26 June 1947, Advisory Opinion, I.C.J. Reports 1988,* p. 23, para. 26.

[109]*United States Diplomatic and Consular Staff in Tehran (United States of America* v. *Tehran), Judgment, I.C.J. Reports 1980*, p. 15, para. 26.

[110]Art. 3, para. 1 (c) of the Vienna Convention on Diplomatic Relations of 18 April 1961.

measured. Article II of the Pact falls squarely in the category of the "cannot be settled" dispute provisions. Hence, the Parties must be of the good faith opinion that negotiations might not just be impractical, but that they would be futile. In any event, even under the Applicant's premise according to which actual negotiations are not necessary to fulfil the precondition of Article II of the Pact, the indisputable fact remains that the statements of the highest representatives of both States and the steps that they have taken attest to their will to settle any alleged controversy by way of negotiations.

The Parties were of the good faith opinion that the alleged controversy could be settled by way of direct negotiations

21. I will now deal with the opinion of the Parties as expressed by their highest representatives and military officials. The evidence, which was also discussed by Mr. Bundy, shows that both Parties were of the opinion that negotiations were possible and indeed the way to proceed. It is abundantly clear from the many declarations made by the President of Nicaragua that the Applicant was never of the opinion that the controversy could not be settled by way of negotiations.

22. The Applicant discusses the conduct of Nicaragua in a single paragraph — 4.37 — of its Written Statement. Out of the numerous declarations made by its President, Nicaragua has chosen to refer to only two: those made on 28 November 2012 and 10 September 2013. But neither of those two declarations attest to the futility of negotiations. In fact, Colombia fails to understand the reason why the November pronouncement by the President of Nicaragua that, "Colombia will recognize the ruling of the International Court of Justice, because there is no other way forward" implies that negotiations are useless[111]. Such characterization of the real meaning of the Presidential statement is obviously in contradiction with the conduct of the Parties at that time, as demonstrated by the constructive meetings between the Presidents of the two countries held soon after in Mexico, in December 2012, and in Chile, in February 2013[112]. In fact, the Applicant has itself admitted that "both Parties had made public statements keeping the door open to eventual

[111]WSN, para. 4.37.

[112]POC, para. 4.50.

negotiations"[113]. According to Nicaragua, it is only at a later time that Colombia shut the door to negotiations[114]. Therefore, the November statement by the Nicaraguan President cannot be read as signifying that in the opinion of the Applicant negotiations were futile.

23. In relation to the declaration of 10 September 2013, Nicaragua does quote its President, but once again it does so selectively[115]. While the President of Nicaragua indeed remarked that there is no question, as Colombia has repeatedly acknowledged, that "[t]he Court decisions are obligatory", the Applicant fails to mention that its President also stated, as shown on the screen, that: "We agree that you can open a dialogue between the Government of Nicaragua and the Government of Colombia, and that these negotiations may produce an agreement that allows us to make the transition in an orderly manner"[116].

24. In an effort to demonstrate that Colombia "ha[d] shut the door to any negotiations", Nicaragua refers to events that occurred in the "two and a half months leading up to the Application"[117]. According to the Applicant, "pending the decision of the Constitutional Court, Colombia was of the opinion that no negotiation was even possible"[118]. However, the statements made by the Colombian President and Minister for Foreign Affairs respectively on 15 and 18 September 2013 indicate that Colombia emphasized the need to conduct negotiations in order to conclude a treaty that would implement the 2012 Judgment. The fact that the adoption of an implementing treaty was one of the key points of Colombia's position is also attested to by the President's speech of 9 September 2013 and the Foreign Minister's declaration of the next day[119]. The need to wait for the ruling of the Constitutional Court cannot therefore be understood as having rendered negotiations futile. In fact, it constituted an important step at the domestic level to give a solid ground to the negotiations on the implementation of the 2012 Judgment.

---

[113]WSN, para. 4.5.

[114]*Ibid.*, para. 4.5.

[115]WSN, para. 4.37.

[116]POC, para. 4.51 and Vol. II, Ann. 40.

[117]WSN, paras 4.38-4.52, Anns. 12 and 39.

[118]*Ibid.*, para. 4.46.

[119]POC, paras 4.68-4.69.

25. To measure the validity of the Applicant's assumption that the complaint to the Constitutional Court made negotiations useless, it suffices to check the declarations made by Nicaragua's Executive and Military before and after the Colombian statements of 15 and 18 September 2013. These declarations, which Nicaragua purposely ignored in its Written Statement, provide concrete evidence of the bona fide opinion of the Applicant's authorities up until the filing of the Application, at the very least.

26. In this respect the official address made by the President of Nicaragua on 14 August 2013 is most enlightening. It shows not only that the relations between the two Parties were good and that the Colombian navy was acting professionally, but also that negotiations concerning the implementation of the 2012 Judgment and related issues were, in the opinion of the Parties, possible[120]. Let us look at the relevant parts of this declaration, now on the screen.

> "Nicaragua respects and is ready to work together with Colombia in protecting the [Seaflower] Reserve zone. We are ready to develop the dialogue, the negotiations between Colombia and Nicaragua that will finally enable us to overcome that situation so that we, Colombians and Nicaraguans, may work further for peace, for stability.
>
> I [President Ortega] am convinced, we hope that this will continue in the same manner until we can reach the dialogue, reach the negotiations so as to conclude the definitive agreements to apply the judgment rendered by the Court in the month of November of last year. We are totally so disposed."

27. Likewise on 13 September 2013 — that is to say after the filing of the complaint before the Constitutional Court that allegedly had rendered negotiations useless — the President of Nicaragua affirmed that he was willing to create a national commission that would meet with a commission from Colombia on the issue of implementation of the 2012 Judgment[121]. In other words, prior to the Colombian statements of 15 and 18 September 2013, Nicaragua was certainly of the bona fide opinion that negotiations were possible.

28. These Colombian statements did not lead Nicaragua to change its opinion. Indeed, on 18 November 2013, the chief of the Nicaraguan navy made a statement concerning the absence of any conflict with the Colombian naval forces stressing that the naval forces of the respective countries maintained continuous communication[122]. The Chief of the Nicaraguan army made a

---

[120]POC, para. 4.52, Ann. 11.

[121]*Ibid.*, para. 4.51, Ann. 41.

[122]*Ibid.*, para. 4.53, Ann. 43.

similar statement on 18 March 2014, that is to say close to four months after the critical date[123]. Even more significantly, as the screen shows, the President of Nicaragua stated on 29 January 2014, in the immediate aftermath of the filing of the Application, that:

> "I had the opportunity to discuss the issue with President Santos in Mexico when Enrique Peña Nieto took office. We concluded that there will be a moment in which we will sign agreements between Colombia and Nicaragua in order to establish, properly, agreements to be ratified by the respective parliaments, these will refer to the boundaries established by the Court . . . Afterwards, we will have to wait until Colombia and Nicaragua discuss to reach an agreement that allows us to establish a way, especially and I so said to President Santos, to guarantee all the rights of the native population."[124]

If this was Nicaragua's opinion merely two months after the filing of the Application, it is evident that that must have been the Applicant's opinion at the critical date. Moreover, on 9 May 2014, the President of Nicaragua reiterated his proposal to create "a Colombian-Nicaraguan commission so [that] a treaty can come out of it that will allow us to respect, and put in practice the judgment by the ICJ"[125].

29. Declarations such as those just mentioned demonstrate that Nicaragua did not interpret the Colombian statements of 15 and 18 September 2013 as having rendered negotiations futile. In other words, Nicaragua's conduct directly contradicts the characterization of the Colombian statements made by the Applicant.

30. Notwithstanding Nicaragua's insistence to the contrary, it is a fact that Colombia has not "repudiated" the 2012 Judgment. The President and the Foreign Minister of Colombia have emphasized that the problem is one of 'applicability' under domestic law and not one of "compliance"[126]. Nicaragua itself has included in its annexes statements of the Executive of Colombia that confirm this distinction[127]. The Executive of Nicaragua was conscious that Colombia was facing "a legal impairment in the application of the ruling" under its domestic system[128]. The issue of incorporation was not unknown to Nicaragua before the filing of the

---

[123]*Ibid.*, para. 4.57, Ann. 46.

[124]POC, para. 4.56, Ann. 45.

[125]MN, para. 2.60, Ann. 46.

[126]POC, Vol. II, Anns. 12, 13, 39 and 42.

[127]WSN, Anns. 4, 6, 7, 8 and 9.

[128]POC, Vol. II, Anns. 41 and 45; WSN, Anns. 4, 6, 7, 8 and 9.

complaint before the Constitutional Court and cannot therefore have led to a change of opinion in its Executive[129].

31. In this context, it is easy to understand the declaration made by the Colombian Foreign Minister — who honours us today with her presence here — as a reaction to the filing of the Application by Nicaragua. As the Minister stated:

> "It is not a big problem. The relations with Nicaragua will not be broken [...] We have [re]called our Ambassador for consultations because sometimes you do not understand how they come to a decision as the last application which that country has submitted in The Hague. I say this, because you go to the Court when all the instances to solve a problem are exhausted."[130]

The Minister's reaction underlines the fact that Colombia was completely taken by surprise by the new additional case brought before the Court. While Nicaragua's and Colombia's highest representatives had made it clear that negotiations were the way to proceed, the Applicant unilaterally seised the Court on the very last moment before the termination of the Pact of Bogotá for the Respondent. In this manner, Nicaragua wished at all costs to preserve the jurisdictional avenue that it hoped was still available to it vis-à-vis Colombia, but in so doing, it failed to fulfil the precondition of Article II of the Pact.

Conclusion

32. Mr. President, Members of the Court, I will now sum up Colombia's third preliminary objection.

33. Nicaragua would have you believe that on the question of whether direct negotiations were possible, the only opinion that matters is its own. To support this self-serving reading of Article II of the Pact, Nicaragua has blatantly altered the content of the 1985 Inter-American Juridical Committee's Opinion. For, in spite of its assertion to the contrary, it is Nicaragua, not Colombia, which has provided a reading of the provision that corresponds exactly to the one rejected by the Juridical Committee.

34. Having supposedly deprived Colombia's conduct of any legal value, Nicaragua would also have you believe that, in its own bona fide opinion, negotiations were useless at the time of the

---

[129]POC, Vol. II, Ann. 12; NWS, Anns. 6 and 7.

[130]POC, paras 4.72-4.73 and Vol. II, Ann. 44.

seisin of the Court. In fact, the Applicant infers such opinion from the very filing of the Application. But what about the numerous statements made by its President that expressly addressed the issue of the implementation of the 2012 Judgment and the viability of direct negotiations through the usual diplomatic channels? Nicaragua either ignores them or selectively cites them. Yet, the President of Nicaragua's statements made on 14 August, 10 and 13 September 2013 and 29 January and 9 May 2014, conclusively demonstrate that the Applicant was of the opinion that direct negotiations were possible before and after and, henceforth, at the critical date[131].

35. Nicaragua has sought to deprive Article II of the Pact of any useful purpose. For if the Applicant's opinion was the only one that mattered, and the filing of an application could alone be sufficient to substantiate such opinion, what would be left of this provision? What would be left of the Court's pronouncement in the 1988 Judgment that it "may expect 'the Parties [to provide] substantive evidence that they consider in good faith' a certain possibility of negotiation to exist or not to exist"[132]?

36. Nicaragua's reading of Article II of the Pact conferring pre-eminence to the French text over the three other authentic texts, coupled with its far from objective assessment of its own opinion, certainly leads to a manifestly absurd result. There is simply nothing left of Article II of the Pact and certainly not a meaningful precondition to be fulfilled prior to the initiation of the Pact's procedures.

37. In conclusion, for the reasons I have explained, the Court lacks jurisdiction over Nicaragua's Application because the precondition imposed by Article II of the Pact has not been fulfilled.

38. Mr. President, Members of the Court, this concludes my presentation. I respectfully ask that you call on my colleague, Mr. Treves.

Le PRESIDENT : Merci, Monsieur Valencia-Ospina. Je donne maintenant la parole au professeur Tullio Treves.

---

[131]POC, Vol. II, Anns. 11, 40, 41 and 45; MN, para. 2.60, Ann. 46.

[132]*Border and Transborder Armed Actions (Nicaragua* v. *Honduras), Jurisdiction and Admissibility, Judgment, I.C.J. Reports 1988*, p. 95, para. 65.

M. TREVES : Merci, Monsieur le président. Monsieur le président, Mesdames et Messieurs les juges, c'est un grand honneur pour moi de plaider devant vous et je suis reconnaissant au Gouvernement de la République de Colombie de m'en avoir donné l'occasion.

QUATRIÈME ET CINQUIÈME EXCEPTIONS PRÉLIMINAIRES : LA COUR N'A PAS UN POUVOIR INHÉRENT POUR JUGER DES DEMANDES DU NICARAGUA

1. La présente plaidoirie porte sur les quatrième et cinquième exceptions préliminaires soulevées par la Colombie. Ces deux exceptions sont distinctes car elles portent respectivement sur l'inexistence d'un pouvoir inhérent de la Cour de juger sur une prétendue inexécution de l'arrêt de 2012 et sur l'inexistence d'un pouvoir inhérent de surveillance sur l'exécution des arrêts. Nous allons néanmoins traiter ces exceptions dans la même plaidoirie puisqu'elles soulèvent, dans la plupart des cas, les mêmes questions. Ces questions ont trait à la base alternative de compétence soulevée par le Nicaragua. Ainsi, elles n'ont pas de lien direct avec les trois premières exceptions qui viennent d'être entendues par la Cour. Ni l'une ni l'autre n'est défensible car elles ne fournissent pas une base de compétence à la Cour.

2. Ma tâche est de démontrer que, contrairement à ce que soutient le Nicaragua, dans la présente affaire la Cour n'est pas compétente au titre d'un «pouvoir inhérent». Cette expression est utilisée, dans les textes en français des arrêts de la Cour, plus fréquemment que «compétence inhérente», terme plus similaire à l'expression «inherent jurisdiction» que l'on trouve dans les textes anglais. Tant il en est ainsi que, dans la présente affaire, les services de la Cour traduisent en français l'expression «inherent jurisdiction» utilisée dans les plaidoiries écrites par «pouvoir inhérent».

3. Cette divergence linguistique couvre une différence de fond, subtile mais importante, ayant trait à la question de savoir à quoi se réfère le terme «inhérent». L'expression «pouvoir inhérent» implique que, au cas où il existe une compétence bien établie basée sur le consentement des parties, celle-ci comprend certains pouvoirs nécessaires à son exercice. L'expression anglaise semblerait, par contre, encourager la mauvaise interprétation que, même en l'absence d'une compétence bien établie basée sur le consentement des parties, la Cour aurait une compétence lui permettant d'agir à l'égard de parties dont le consentement manque. La version française est

cohérente avec le Statut et le principe de la compétence consensuelle. Si on la lit comme le fait le Nicaragua, ce n'est pas le cas de la version anglaise.

4. Le Nicaragua soutient que la compétence de la Cour à juger d'une alléguée violation de l'arrêt du 19 novembre 2012 ou d'une violation des obligations dérivant de l'arrêt découlerait d'un «pouvoir inhérent» *(inherent jurisdiction)* qu'aurait la Cour[133]. Le Nicaragua invite la Cour à exercer ce pouvoir inhérent pour examiner la situation créée par l'allégué comportement de la Colombie qui, à son avis, «remet en cause le fond même» de l'arrêt de 2012. Ce pouvoir inhérent constituerait une «base de compétence à titre subsidiaire en la présente affaire»[134].

5. La Colombie rejette l'allégation du Nicaragua et soutient que la Cour n'a aucun pouvoir inhérent lui permettant de juger d'une affaire distincte, introduite après la conclusion d'une autre affaire entre les mêmes parties et qui a fait l'objet d'un arrêt de la Cour.

6. La compétence à juger sur le fond d'un différend ne s'établit que sur la base des titres de compétence prévus par le Statut. Cela vaut, notamment, pour les différends portant sur l'inexécution d'un autre jugement. C'est ce qu'affirme notamment une étude doctrinale très autorisée

> «tout différend relatif à cette exécution doit être regardé comme un différend distinct de celui réglé par le jugement. La Cour ne saurait dès lors s'en saisir sans un nouvel accord des parties. Aussi a-t-elle jugé à plusieurs reprises qu'elle ne pouvait, ni ne devait envisager l'inexécution de ses arrêts et ne s'est-elle prononcée sur cette exécution que dans les cas où les parties lui avaient donné spécifiquement compétence à cet effet.»[135]

7. L'affaire qui nous occupe correspond exactement à celles envisagées par l'étude que l'on vient de citer : il s'agit d'une affaire portant sur un prétendu nouveau différend, qui requiert un nouveau procès soumis aux règles ordinaires du contentieux, y compris les règles portant sur la compétence. Je dis bien, prétendu nouveau différend puisque, comme l'a souligné mon collègue Michael Reisman, il n'y a pas de différend d'ordre juridique dans cette affaire du fait que le Nicaragua n'a pas rempli les conditions nécessaires à l'existence d'un différend à la date critique.

---

[133] EEN, par. 5.9.

[134] MN, par. 1.32.

[135] G. Guillaume : «De l'exécution des décisions de la Cour internationale de Justice» (1997), dans *La Cour internationale de Justice à l'aube du XXIe siècle, Le regard d'un juge*, Pédone, Paris, 2003, p. 179 (références omises).

8. Dans la présente affaire il n'existe pas un accord des parties conférant à la Cour la compétence pour s'occuper de l'exécution de l'arrêt de 2012 ou d'aspects de celle-ci. Il n'existe pas non plus une disposition de cet arrêt prévoyant la division du procès en plusieurs phases.

9. En outre, l'on ne trouve dans le jugement de 2012 aucune trace d'une réservation de compétence pouvant permettre de ressusciter la compétence de la Cour au cas où certaines conditions devaient se vérifier à l'avenir, comme dans les affaires des *Essais nucléaires*[136]. L'obligation de se conformer aux arrêts de la Cour, consacrée à l'article 94, paragraphe 1, de la Charte des Nations Unies et à l'article 59 du Statut de la Cour, ne saurait se substituer à une clause permettant expressément de «réexaminer la situation» telle qu'on la trouve dans les deux arrêts de 1974 sur les *Essais nucléaires*, respectivement aux paragraphes 60 et 63. Ces clauses des arrêts de 1974 ont un caractère tout à fait exceptionnel, tandis que l'obligation de se conformer aux décisions de la Cour est l'effet normal de tout arrêt de celle-ci. Faire de cette dernière obligation, comme le voudrait le Nicaragua, une base de compétence serait tout à fait erroné car cela permettrait de rouvrir toute affaire où une partie allègue que l'autre ne se conforme pas au jugement qui l'a tranchée.

10. Les arrêts de la Cour que le Nicaragua invoque au soutien de sa position sur l'existence d'un pouvoir inhérent *(inherent jurisdiction)* ne fournissent aucun appui à celle-ci. Ce n'est certainement pas le cas de l'arrêt dans l'affaire de la *Compagnie d'électricité de Sophia*, que le Nicaragua invoque dans son mémoire comme faisant autorité sur l'existence d'un tel pouvoir inhérent[137]. En effet, en acceptant les arguments présentés par la Colombie[138] — le même Nicaragua reconnaît que dans cet arrêt «la question du «pouvoir inhérent» ne s'est pas posée, fût-ce implicitement»[139].

---

[136] *Essais nucléaires (Australie c. France), arrêt, C.I.J. Recueil 1974*, p. 272, par. 60 ; *Essais nucléaires (Nouvelle-Zélande c. France), arrêt, C.I.J. Recueil 1974*, p. 477, par. 63, ainsi que *Demande d'examen de la situation au titre du paragraphe 63 de l'arrêt rendu par la Cour le 20 décembre 1974 dans l'affaire des* Essais nucléaires (Nouvelle-Zélande c. France) *(Nouvelle-Zélande c. France), ordonnance du 22 septembre 1995, C.I.J. Recueil 1995,* p. 297, par. 32.

[137] MN, par. 1.24, note 15.

[138] EPC, par. 5.14.

[139] EEN, par. 5.3.

11. Il ne s'agit non plus des arrêts sur les *Essais nucléaires* de 1974, ni de l'arrêt *LaGrand*[140] de 2001. Ces arrêts, tout en mentionnant des pouvoirs inhérents de la Cour, n'y trouvent pas une base de compétence pour juger d'un différend donné.

12. En effet, dans les arrêts sur les *Essais nucléaires,* la Cour affirme que le «pouvoir inhérent» qu'elle possède «l'autorise à prendre toute mesure voulue ... pour faire en sorte que, *si sa compétence au fond est établie*, l'exercice de cette compétence ne se révèle pas vain»[141]. Ainsi, le «pouvoir inhérent» ne peut s'exercer que dans le cadre d'une affaire à l'égard de laquelle la compétence au fond «est établie» et non vice versa. Ce pouvoir ne saurait pour autant fournir la base de cette compétence.

13. Dans l'affaire *LaGrand,* l'Allemagne soutenait que la Cour avait compétence pour juger de l'inobservance de l'ordonnance du 3 mars 1999 portant mesures conservatoires. Elle faisait valoir comme argument «accessoire et subsidiaire» que cette compétence relevait du pouvoir inhérent de la Cour[142].

14. La Cour ne considéra pas nécessaire d'examiner l'argument accessoire et subsidiaire de l'Allemagne. Elle accepta son argument principal[143], mais elle affirma néanmoins :

> «*Lorsque la Cour a compétence pour trancher un différend*, elle a également compétence pour se prononcer sur des conclusions la priant de constater qu'une ordonnance en indication de mesures rendue aux fins de préserver les droits des Parties à ce différend n'a pas été exécutée.»[144]

15. Ce dernier passage de l'arrêt *LaGrand*, lu hors contexte, donne l'occasion au Nicaragua de faire l'affirmation suivante :

> «Il n'y a aucune raison de ne pas transposer *mutatis mutandis* la position de la Cour concernant son pouvoir inhérent de se prononcer sur le non-respect d'ordonnances en indication de mesures conservatoires aux différends découlant d'un défaut d'exécution de ses arrêts.»[145]

---

[140] *LaGrand (Allemagne c. Etats-Unis d'Amérique), arrêt, C.I.J. Recueil 2001*, p. 466.

[141] *Essais nucléaires (Australie c. France), arrêt, C.I.J. Recueil 1974*, p. 259, par. 23 (les italiques sont de nous) ; *Essais nucléaires (Nouvelle-Zélande* c. *France), arrêt, C.I.J. Recueil 1974,* p. 463, par. 23 (les italiques sont de nous).

[142] *LaGrand (Allemagne* c. *Etats-Unis d'Amérique), arrêt, C.I.J. Recueil 2001*, p. 483, par. 44, où le texte français exceptionnellement utilise «compétence inhérente» comme équivalent de «inherent jurisdiction»), et mémoire de la République fédérale d'Allemagne, par. 3.02.

[143] *LaGrand (Allemagne* c. *Etats-Unis d'Amérique), arrêt, C.I.J. Recueil 2001*, p. 484, par. 45.

[144] *LaGrand (Allemagne* c. *Etats-Unis d'Amérique), arrêt, C.I.J. Recueil 2001*, p. 484, par. 45 (les italiques sont de nous).

[145] EE, par. 5.16.

16. Cette affirmation manque de fondement. Elle ne tient aucunement compte de la différence entre la détermination, dans un jugement sur le fond, adopté dans le cadre d'un différend sur lequel la compétence est établie, du non-respect d'une ordonnance portant mesures conservatoires et un différend ayant pour objet l'allégué non-respect d'un arrêt portant sur une affaire déjà conclue et ayant la force de la chose jugée.

17. Aucun raisonnement par analogie n'est possible. La condition dont la Cour souligne la nécessité en mentionnant ses pouvoirs inhérents dans les affaires des *Essais nucléaires*, à savoir que sa compétence au fond doit être établie[146], n'est pas remplie. Le Nicaragua voudrait faire de cette précondition à leur exercice, la conséquence des pouvoirs inhérents de la Cour. Ce serait mettre la charrue avant les bœufs ! Il s'agit d'une véritable *petitio principii.*

18. Contrairement à ce que dit le Nicaragua, il existe ainsi une raison, une bonne raison en effet, pour ne pas transposer à des différends portant sur le non-respect des jugements l'affirmation de la Cour concernant la compétence en matière d'inexécution d'une ordonnance en indication de mesures provisoires.

19. Les pouvoirs inhérents de la Cour fonctionnent dans le cadre de différends à l'égard desquels sa compétence est établie sur la base d'un titre préexistant. L'on ne saurait les invoquer pour établir une compétence autrement inexistante.

20. Le Nicaragua n'a pas voulu préciser si les pouvoirs inhérents qui, selon lui fondent la compétence de la Cour, concernent un différend portant sur l'exécution de l'arrêt de 2012 ou sur l'inobservance des droits dérivant de celui-ci, en soutenant qu'il s'agirait d'un «intéressant débat juridique» qui appartiendrait au fond et serait sans importance pour ce qui est de la compétence de la Cour[147]. Il n'est pas nécessaire d'entrer ici dans cette discussion. Il n'en reste pas moins que la prétention du Nicaragua de fonder la compétence de la Cour sur un «pouvoir inhérent» de celle-ci est inextricablement liée à l'existence d'une connexion entre l'affaire conclue et la nouvelle affaire. Il s'agit néanmoins de différends distincts pour chacun desquels l'existence d'un titre de compétence est nécessaire.

---

[146] *Essais nucléaires (Australie* c. *France), arrêt, C.I.J. Recueil 1974,* p. 259, par. 23 ; *Essais nucléaires (Nouvelle-Zélande* c. *France), arrêt, C.I.J. Recueil 1974,* p. 463, par. 23.

[147] EEN, par. 5.9.

21. Monsieur le président, Mesdames et Messieurs les juges, je voudrais maintenant partager avec la Cour des réflexions qui renforcent l'argument que, dans la présente affaire en tout cas, la Cour n'a pas un pouvoir inhérent de surveillance sur l'exécution de ses jugements.

22. Il faut remarquer tout d'abord qu'un tel pouvoir n'est pas prévu par le Statut. D'après ce dernier, les seuls cas de compétence de la Cour concernant des arrêts ayant l'effet de la chose jugée ont trait à l'interprétation et à la revision de ces arrêts (art. 60 et 61) et la seule mention dans le Statut de l'exécution d'un arrêt se trouve à l'article 61, paragraphe 3, d'après lequel «la Cour peut subordonner l'ouverture de la procédure en revision à l'exécution préalable de l'arrêt». Nous ne nous trouvons dans aucune des situations envisagées par ces dispositions du Statut.

23. Qui plus est, l'article 94, paragraphe 2, de la Charte des Nations Unies, qui est dans vos dossiers et devrait apparaître sur l'écran, prévoit une procédure à laquelle peut recourir la partie à un litige qui considère que l'autre partie ne satisfait pas aux obligations qui lui incombent en vertu d'un arrêt rendu par la Cour. Cette procédure consiste en un recours au Conseil de sécurité qui, «s'il le juge nécessaire, peut faire des recommandations ou décider des mesures à prendre pour faire exécuter l'arrêt».

24. Compte tenu de cette disposition de la Charte, les Etats américains, afin d'éviter toute divergence entre eux concernant les suites d'un arrêt de la Cour et pouvant impliquer des risques de conflit, adoptèrent une *lex specialis* régionale pour ces divergences. Leur propos était de régler celles-ci «au sein de la famille» sans recourir, si possible, au Conseil de sécurité. Cela s'explique si l'on considère que, au lendemain de la seconde guerre mondiale, les arrangements régionaux se présentaient aux Etats des Amériques comme une protection supplémentaire à celle de la Charte des Nations Unies.

25. La *lex specialis* régionale mentionnée est la procédure prévue à l'article L du pacte de Bogotá. Cet article impose l'obligation de s'adresser à la réunion de consultation des ministres des relations extérieures des Etats parties au pacte à tout Etat partie qui entend recourir au Conseil de sécurité aux fins de l'article 94, paragraphe 2, de la Charte. La réunion des ministres des relations extérieures du pacte de Bogotá est convoquée «afin que celle-ci convienne des mesures à prendre

en vue d'assurer l'exécution de la décision judiciaire[148] ou arbitrale». Le caractère obligatoire de la procédure de l'article L comporte que, pour les Etats liés au pacte, le pouvoir de surveillance sur les suites des arrêts de la Cour appartient au Conseil de sécurité et au conseil des ministres des relations extérieures des Etats parties au pacte, et, partant, non à la Cour internationale de Justice.

26. Il me paraît important de souligner que — quel que soit le point de vue que l'on adopte quant au moment où la dénonciation du pacte par la Colombie déploie ses effets — l'article L et le manque de compétence de la Cour en matière de surveillance sur les suites de ses arrêts qui en découle étaient en vigueur et, partant, obligatoires pour les Parties à la présente affaire au moment de la demande du Nicaragua.

27. Monsieur le président, Mesdames et Messieurs les juges, je ne saurais conclure cette plaidoirie sans souligner que suivre le Nicaragua dans sa revendication d'un pouvoir inhérent pouvant fonder la compétence de la Cour dans la présente affaire serait un précédent dangereux. Le principe selon lequel le consentement des parties est une précondition nécessaire pour établir la compétence de la Cour en serait bouleversé. Et il serait présomptueux de ma part d'insister, devant vous, sur l'importance dirais-je primordiale, dans le cadre d'ensemble du droit international, du principe du consentement tel qu'incorporé dans le Statut de la Cour et d'autres instances juridictionnelles, en tant que base de la compétence des cours et tribunaux internationaux.

28. Au vu de ce qui précède, la Colombie maintient ses quatrième et cinquième exceptions préliminaires.

29. Cette phase des plaidoiries de la Colombie dans la présente affaire est ainsi terminée.

30. Je vous remercie, Monsieur le président, Mesdames et Messieurs les juges, pour votre patience et votre attention.

Le PRESIDENT : Merci, Monsieur le professeur. Voilà qui met un terme au premier tour de plaidoiries de la Colombie. La Cour se réunira de nouveau demain mardi 29 septembre, à 10 heures, pour entendre le Nicaragua en son premier tour de plaidoiries. L'audience est levée.

L'audience est levée à 13 heures.

---

[148] L'article L dit «juridique». Il s'agit d'une faute évidente comme il résulte des autres versions linguistiques : anglais : «judicial» ; espagnol : «judicial» ; portugais: «judicial».

Corrigé
Corrected

CR 2015/23

International Court of Justice
THE HAGUE

Cour internationale de Justice
LA HAYE

YEAR 2015

Public sitting

held on Tuesday 29 September 2015, at 10 a.m., at the Peace Palace,

President Abraham presiding,

***in the case concerning* Alleged Violations of Sovereign Rights and Maritime Spaces in the Caribbean Sea (Nicaragua *v.* Colombia)**

Preliminary Objections

VERBATIM RECORD

ANNÉE 2015

Audience publique

tenue le mardi 29 septembre 2015, à 10 heures, au Palais de la Paix,

sous la présidence de M. Abraham, président,

***en l'affaire relative à des* Violations alléguées de droits souverains et d'espaces maritimes dans la mer des Caraïbes (Nicaragua c. Colombie)**

Exceptions préliminaires

COMPTE RENDU

Present:	President	Abraham
	Vice-President	Yusuf
	Judges	Owada
		Tomka
		Bennouna
		Cançado Trindade
		Greenwood
		Xue
		Donoghue
		Gaja
		Sebutinde
		Bhandari
		Robinson
		Gevorgian
	Judges *ad hoc*	Daudet
		Caron
	Registrar	Couvreur

Présents :	M.	Abraham, président
	M.	Yusuf, vice-président
	MM.	Owada
		Tomka
		Bennouna
		Cançado Trindade
		Greenwood
	Mmes	Xue
		Donoghue
	M.	Gaja
	Mme	Sebutinde
	MM.	Bhandari
		Robinson
		Gevorgian, juges
	MM.	Daudet
		Caron, juges *ad hoc*
	M.	Couvreur, greffier

The Government of Nicaragua is represented by:

H.E. Mr. Carlos José Argüello Gómez, Ambassador of the Republic of Nicaragua to the Kingdom of the Netherlands,

as Agent and Counsel;

Mr. Vaughan Lowe, Q.C., member of the English Bar, Emeritus Professor of International Law, Oxford University, member of the Institut de droit international,

Mr. Alex Oude Elferink, Director, Netherlands Institute for the Law of the Sea, Professor of International Law of the Sea, Utrecht University,

Mr. Alain Pellet, Emeritus Professor at the University Paris Ouest, Nanterre-La Défense, former member and former Chairman of the International Law Commission, member of the Institut de droit international,

Mr. Antonio Remiro Brotóns, Professor of International Law, Universidad Autónoma de Madrid, member of the Institut de droit international,

as Counsel and Advocates;

Mr. César Vega Masís, Deputy Minister for Foreign Affairs, Director of Juridical Affairs, Sovereignty and Territory, Ministry of Foreign Affairs,

Mr. Walner Molina Pérez, Juridical Adviser, Ministry of Foreign Affairs,

Mr. Julio César Saborio, Juridical Adviser, Ministry of Foreign Affairs,

as Counsel;

Mr. Edgardo Sobenes Obregon, Counsellor, Embassy of Nicaragua in the Kingdom of the Netherlands,

Ms Claudia Loza Obregon, First Secretary, Embassy of Nicaragua in the Kingdom of the Netherlands,

Mr. Benjamin Samson, Ph.D. Candidate, Centre de droit international de Nanterre (CEDIN), University Paris Ouest, Nanterre-La Defense,

Ms Gimena González,

as Assistant Counsel;

Ms Sherly Noguera de Argüello, Consul General of the Republic of Nicaragua,

as Administrator.

Le Gouvernement du Nicaragua est représenté par :

S. Exc. M. Carlos José Argüello Gómez, ambassadeur de la République du Nicaragua auprès du Royaume des Pays-Bas,

comme agent et conseil ;

M. Vaughan Lowe, Q.C., membre du barreau d'Angleterre, professeur émérite de droit international, Oxford University, membre de l'Institut de droit international,

M. Alex Oude Elferink, directeur de l'Institut néerlandais du droit de la mer, professeur de droit international de la mer, Université d'Utrecht,

M. Alain Pellet, professeur émérite à l'Université Paris Ouest, Nanterre-La Défense, ancien membre et ancien président de la Commission du droit international, membre de l'Institut de droit international,

M. Antonio Remiro Brotóns, professeur de droit international à l'Universidad Autónoma de Madrid, membre de l'Institut de droit international,

comme conseils et avocats ;

M. César Vega Masís, vice-ministre des affaires étrangères, directeur des affaires juridiques, de la souveraineté et du territoire au ministère des affaires étrangères,

M. Walner Molina Pérez, conseiller juridique au ministère des affaires étrangères,

M. Julio César Saborio, conseiller juridique au ministère des affaires étrangères,

comme conseils ;

M. Edgardo Sobenes Obregon, conseiller à l'ambassade du Nicaragua au Royaume des Pays-Bas,

Mme Claudia Loza Obregon, première secrétaire de l'ambassade du Nicaragua au Royaume des Pays-Bas,

M. Benjamin Samson, doctorant au Centre de droit international de Nanterre (CEDIN), Université Paris Ouest, Nanterre-La Défense,

Mme Gimena Gonzales,

comme conseils adjoints ;

Mme Sherly Noguera de Argüello, consul général de la République du Nicaragua,

comme administrateur.

The Government of Colombia is represented by:

H.E. Ms María Ángela Holguín Cuéllar, Minister for Foreign Affairs,

H.E. Mr. Francisco Echeverri Lara, Vice Minister of Multilateral Affairs, Ministry of Foreign Affairs,

as National Authorities;

H.E. Mr. Carlos Gustavo Arrieta Padilla, former Judge of the Council of State of Colombia, former Attorney General of Colombia and former Ambassador of Colombia to the Kingdom of the Netherlands,

as Agent;

H.E. Mr. Manuel José Cepeda Espinosa, former President of the Constitutional Court of Colombia, former Permanent Delegate of Colombia to UNESCO and former Ambassador of Colombia to the Helvetic Confederation,

as Co-Agent;

Mr. W. Michael Reisman, McDougal Professor of International Law at Yale University, member of the Institut de droit international,

Mr. Rodman R. Bundy, former *avocat à la Cour d'appel de Paris*, member of the New York Bar, Eversheds LLP, Singapore,

Sir Michael Wood, K.C.M.G., member of the English Bar, member of the International Law Commission,

Mr. Tullio Treves, member of the Institut de droit international, Senior Public International Law Consultant, Curtis, Mallet-Prevost, Colt & Mosle LLP Milan, Professor, University of Milan,

Mr. Eduardo Valencia-Ospina, member and Special Rapporteur of the International Law Commission, President of the Latin American Society of International Law,

Mr. Matthias Herdegen, Dr. h.c., Professor of International Law, Director of the Institute of International Law at the University of Bonn,

as Counsel and Advocates;

H.E. Mr. Juan José Quintana Aranguren, Ambassador of the Republic of Colombia to the Kingdom of the Netherlands, Permanent Representative of Colombia to the OPCW, former Permanent Representative of Colombia to the United Nations in Geneva,

H.E. Mr. Andelfo García González, Ambassador of the Republic of Colombia to the Kingdom of Thailand, Professor of International Law, former Deputy Minister for Foreign Affairs,

Ms Andrea Jiménez Herrera, Counsellor, Embassy of the Republic of Colombia in the Kingdom of the Netherlands,

Le Gouvernement de la Colombie est représenté par :

S. Exc. Mme María Ángela Holguín Cuéllar, ministre des affaires étrangères,

S. Exc. M. Francisco Echeverri Lara, vice-ministre des affaires multilatérales, ministère des affaires étrangères,

comme autorités nationales ;

S. Exc. M. Carlos Gustavo Arrieta Padilla, ancien juge au Conseil d'Etat de la Colombie, ancien *Procurador General de la Nación* et ancien ambassadeur de la Colombie auprès du Royaume des Pays-Bas,

comme agent ;

S. Exc. M. Manuel José Cepeda Espinosa, ancien président de la Cour constitutionnelle de Colombie, ancien délégué permanent de la Colombie auprès de l'UNESCO et ancien ambassadeur de la Colombie auprès de la Confédération helvétique,

comme coagent ;

M. W. Michael Reisman, professeur de droit international à l'Université de Yale, titulaire de la chaire McDougal, membre de l'Institut de droit international,

M. Rodman R. Bundy, ancien avocat à la Cour d'appel de Paris, membre du barreau de New York, cabinet Eversheds LLP, Singapour,

sir Michael Wood, K.C.M.G., membre du barreau d'Angleterre, membre de la Commission du droit international,

M. Tullio Treves, membre de l'Institut de droit international, conseiller principal en droit international public, cabinet Curtis, Mallet-Prevost, Colt et Mosle LLP, Milan, professeur à l'Université de Milan,

M. Eduardo Valencia-Ospina, membre et rapporteur spécial de la Commission du droit international, président de la société latino-américaine de droit international,

M. Matthias Herdegen, docteur *honoris causa*, professeur de droit international, directeur de l'Institut de droit international de l'Université de Bonn,

comme conseils et avocats ;

S. Exc. M. Juan José Quintana Aranguren, ambassadeur de la République de Colombie auprès du Royaume des Pays-Bas, représentant permanent de la Colombie auprès de l'OIAC, ancien représentant permanent de la Colombie auprès des Nations Unies à Genève,

S. Exc. M. Andelfo García González, ambassadeur de la République de Colombie auprès du Royaume de Thaïlande, professeur de droit international, ancien vice-ministre des affaires étrangères,

Mme Andrea Jiménez Herrera, conseiller, ambassade de la République de Colombie au Royaume des Pays-Bas,

Ms Lucía Solano Ramírez, Second Secretary, Embassy of the Republic of Colombia in the Kingdom of the Netherlands,

Mr. Andrés Villegas Jaramillo, Co-ordinator, Group of Affairs before the ICJ, Ministry of Foreign Affairs,

Mr. Giovanny Andrés Vega Barbosa, Group of Affairs before the ICJ, Ministry of Foreign Affairs,

Ms Ana María Durán López, Group of Affairs before the ICJ, Ministry of Foreign Affairs,

Mr. Camilo Alberto Gómez Niño, Group of Affairs before the ICJ, Ministry of Foreign Affairs,

Mr. Juan David Veloza Chará, Third Secretary, Group of Affairs before the ICJ, Ministry of Foreign Affairs,

as Legal Advisers;

Mr. Rear Admiral Luís Hernán Espejo, National Navy of Colombia,

CN William Pedroza, International Affairs Bureau, National Navy of Colombia,

CF Hermann León, National Maritime Authority (DIMAR), National Navy of Colombia,

Mr. Scott Edmonds, Cartographer, International Mapping,

Mr. Thomas Frogh, Cartographer, International Mapping,

as Technical Advisers;

Ms Charis Tan, Advocate and Solicitor, Singapore, member of the New York Bar, Solicitor, England and Wales, Eversheds LLP, Singapore,

Mr. Eran Sthoeger, LL.M., New York University School of Law,

Mr. Renato Raymundo Treves, LL.M., Associate, Curtis, Mallet-Prevost, Colt & Mosle LLP Milan,

Mr. Lorenzo Palestini, Ph.D Candidate, Graduate Institute of International and Development Studies, Geneva,

as Legal Assistants.

Mme Lucía Solano Ramírez, deuxième secrétaire, ambassade de la République de Colombie au Royaume des Pays-Bas,

M. Andrés Villegas Jaramillo, coordinateur, division des affaires portées devant la CIJ, ministère des affaires étrangères,

M. Giovanny Andrés Vega Barbosa, division des affaires portées devant la CIJ, ministère des affaires étrangères,

Mme Ana María Durán López, division des affaires portées devant la CIJ, ministère des affaires étrangères,

M. Camillo Alberto Gómez Niño, division des affaires portées devant la CIJ, ministère des affaires étrangères,

M. Juan David Veloza Chará, troisième secrétaire, division des affaires portées devant la CIJ, ministère des affaires étrangères,

comme conseillers juridiques ;

le contre-amiral Luis Hernán Espejo, marine nationale de Colombie,

le capitaine de vaisseau William Pedroza, bureau des affaires internationales, marine nationale de Colombie,

le capitaine de frégate Hermann León, autorité maritime nationale (DIMAR), marine nationale de Colombie,

M. Scott Edmonds, cartographe, International Mapping,

M. Thomas Frogh, cartographe, International Mapping,

comme conseillers techniques ;

Mme Charis Tan, avocat et *Solicitor* (Singapour), membre du barreau de New York, *Solicitor* (Angleterre et Pays de Galles), cabinet Eversheds LLP, Singapour,

M. Eran Sthoeger, LL.M., faculté de droit de l'Université de New York,

M. Renato Raymundo Treves, LL.M., associé au cabinet Curtis, Mallet-Prevost, Colt et Mosle LLP, Milan,

M. Lorenzo Palestini, doctorant, Institut de hautes études internationales et du développement, Genève,

comme assistants juridiques.

Le PRESIDENT : Veuillez vous asseoir. L'audience est ouverte. La Cour se réunit aujourd'hui pour entendre le premier tour de plaidoiries du Nicaragua. Je donne à présent la parole à S. Exc. M. Argüello Gómez, agent du Nicaragua. Monsieur l'Agent, vous avez la parole.

Mr. ARGÜELLO:

1. Mr. President, Members of the Court, good morning, and our greetings to the Colombian delegation. Mr. President it is a renewed honour for me to be pleading once again before you on behalf of my country.

2. The present case was brought before the Court on 26 November 2013 and it concerns the violations of Nicaragua's sovereign rights and maritime spaces by Colombia. These violated rights and maritime spaces were not settled by treaty but were established by the Judgment of this Court of 19 November 2012. So these are also violations of that Judgment.

3. In the presentation of its preliminary objections, Colombia has gone into various topics that pertain to the merits of this case, for which reason Nicaragua generally reserves its rights on all these matters and will only address what is pertinent at this preliminary stage.

The events following the Judgment of 19 November 2012

4. On 19 November 2012 this Court rendered a judgment on the *Territorial and Maritime Dispute (Nicaragua* v. *Colombia)* that involved ten years of litigation. This Judgment attributed sovereignty over all islands and cays in dispute, apart from very substantial maritime spaces for these small features, to Colombia. In many quarters the opinion was that Colombia had won the case. Including the United Nations News, whose headlines read "UN court rules Colombia has sovereignty over islands claimed by Nicaragua"[1].

5. After such lengthy litigation in which preliminary objections were opposed by Colombia and there were two requests for intervention, that resulted in a unanimous decision by the Court. Nicaragua had hoped that it had turned an important page in its relations with Colombia and that that Judgment had brought to an end an ancestral dispute. Unfortunately, we are here today against

---

[1]"UN court rules Colombia has sovereignty over islands claimed by Nicaragua", UN News Centre, 19 Nov. 2012 available at http://www.un.org/apps/news/story.asp?NewsID=43541#.VgmPLXqqpBd (last visited 28 Sept. 2015).

our best wishes because Colombia *not only* refuses to accept the Judgment as binding *ipso facto* but has taken actions that directly violate the rights and maritime areas attributed by the Judgment to Nicaragua. It has breached its obligations under international law arising from that very judgment that should have put an end to Nicaragua's long wait.

6. Following this Court's Judgment, the highest ranking official of Colombia, President Santos, announced that Colombia [tab 1 on] "emphatically reject[ed] that aspect of the judgment rendered by the Court"[2] related to the maritime delimitation that was unanimously decided by its members. President Santos continued to explain that Colombia rejected that part of the judgment due to "omissions, errors, excesses, [and] inconsistencies that [Colombia] cannot accept"[3] and claimed that the Court had "made serious mistakes"[4] [tab 1 off] when deciding on the maritime delimitation. In contrast, Colombia eagerly accepted as "final and unappealable"[5] the section of the judgment adjudicating territorial sovereignty to Colombia over the islands and maritime features.

7. This speech by President Santos was followed by similar statements by the highest civil and military authorities in Colombia and can be seen in Nicaragua's Memorial[6]. Besides they were vastly publicized and covered by international media, thus the international community and this Court is well informed of such statements.

Denunciation of the Pact of Bogotá

8. These statements were followed up on 27 November 2012 by the denunciation of the Pact of Bogotá. [Tab 4 on] President Santos declared that Colombia had done so to make sure that "never again shall we experience what happened through the International Court of Justice's Judgment of 19 November"[7]. [Tab 4 off]

---

[2]Declaration of President Juan Manuel Santos on the judgment of the International Court of Justice, 19 Nov. 2012; Memorial of Nicaragua (MN), Ann. 1.

[3]*Ibid.*

[4]*Ibid.*

[5]*Ibid.*

[6]See Chapter II of Nicaragua's Memorial for the facts.

[7]Declaration of the President of the Republic of Colombia, 28 Nov. 2012; Preliminary Objections of Colombia (POC), Ann. 8.

9. Even after all these unfortunate declarations and the denunciation of the Pact of Bogotá, Nicaragua's President publicly reached out to President Santos and invited him to meet in an effort to forge a constructive dialogue. This first meeting took place on 1 December 2012 in Mexico City on the occasion of the inauguration of the newly elected President of Mexico, Mr. Enrique Pena Nieto. [Tab 5 on] President Santos's position was that that his country would not abide by the Judgment until "we see that Colombians rights, that have been violated, are re-established and guaranteed in the future"[8]. [Tab 5 off]

Purported non-applicability of judgment

10. Colombia claims that the judgment is not applicable without a treaty in accordance with its internal legislation, a special interpretation which is not opposable to Nicaragua nor does it paralyse the application of the judgment. The judgment was given on the basis of an important Treaty signed and ratified by both Colombia and Nicaragua: it is called the Charter of the United Nations and the Statute of the International Court of Justice which forms an integral part of it. There is no further Treaty needed in international law for compliance with a judgment of the International Court of Justice.

11. But if Colombia's need of a treaty were true, then Nicaragua is open to signing today or as soon as possible a treaty that incorporates the text of the Judgment of the Court. If that were done and ratified by the Colombian Congress and Colombian legislation, including Decree 1946 were revised accordingly, Nicaragua would *immediately* request the discontinuance of this case.

12. These are not empty words. President Ortega has repeatedly reiterated Nicaragua's willingness to initiate conversations on different topics related to the implementation of the judgment[9]. He has proposed concrete steps such as the creation of a bilateral commission. Nicaragua was also willing to reach agreements for the autochthonous population of San Andrés (the *raizales*) to practise their artisanal fishing in Nicaraguan waters[10]. All these possibilities were proposed in the context of a treaty that would recognize the rights and jurisdiction attributed to

---

[8]"Government of Colombia will not implement ICJ judgment until the rights of Colombians have been restored"; MN, Ann. 32.

[9]MN, para. 2.53-2.63.

[10]MN, para. 2.54.

Nicaragua by the judgment, despite the fact that no such treaty is necessary for the judgment to be considered effective or binding and that there are no historic fishing rights in those areas.

13. Colombia's reaction to these offers has been negative. Since Colombia deemed that the Court's judgment was "inapplicable" due to conflicts with its internal law that required the signing of a treaty to modify its borders, [tab 6 on] President Santos proceeded to instruct the Colombian navy to deploy and defend the fishing rights of the Colombian vessels "with cloak and sword"[11] [tab 6 off]. President Santos took the repudiation of the Court a step further by taking part in a "sovereignty exercise" on the 82nd Meridian on 18 September 2013, thereby sending a clear message of Colombia's defiance to this Court's decision[12].

14. But apart from the declaration of the non-applicability of the Judgment of the Court, the multiple threats of the use of force in order to cower Nicaraguan fishermen and other possible investors in the exploitation of Nicaragua's natural resources in those maritime spaces continued as is well documented in Nicaragua's Memorial[13].

Statements by military officials

15. Several statements of Nicaraguan military officials have been quoted in which they expressed that there had not been any conflicts with the Colombian navy[14]. Although these are matters that rightfully belong in the merits phase of this case, some observations can be anticipated. These comments by Nicaraguan officers simply reflect the fact that our very small naval forces have been ordered to avoid any engagement with Colombia and, in fact, stay away from the navy as far as possible.

16. The reason for this precaution can be easily understood by reading the declarations of the top military officials of Colombia of even recent date.

17. In an interview with Rear Admiral Luis Hernan Espejo Segura, Commander of the specific Command of San Andrés and Providencia, published in *El Colombiano* on the second

---

[11]MN, para. 1.8.

[12]MN, para. 2.27.

[13]MN, para. 2.22-2.52.

[14]CR 2015/22, p. 34, para. 15 (Bundy).

anniversary of the judgment, that is, in November 2014, his answer to the question as to where the vessels of the Colombian navy were located was: [Tab 2 on]

> "They are exactly in the same waters that they were before the reading of the judgment. The Navy continues to patrol, it continues to be present in each of the maritime spaces since before, during and after the judgment. For us, the jurisdictional scenario has not changed. Among other reasons, because it is a presidential directive derived from our Magna Carta. For that reason, the jurisdiction of the Navy is exactly the same before and after 19 November 2012."[15] [Tab 2 off]

18. For its part, the Ministry of Defence of Colombia announced publicly on 25 June 2015 that the Minister of Defence would make an overflight on the archipelago and the maritime area of the 82 meridian that represents the border with Nicaragua. It was also reported that he would inspect the minor islands in the north, like Serrana and Serranilla and the vessels of the navy that exercise sovereignty over the maritime area[16].

19. [Tab 3 on] The Defence Ministry announced later in its Twitter account that: "Villegas [that is, the Minister] overflew the maritime area around the 82 Meridian, boundary zone with Nicaragua."[17] [Tab 3 off]

20. From the recent declarations of the Colombian officials it is obvious that there has not been confrontation because the Nicaraguan navy has not attempted to interfere with the Colombian navy or try to put a stop to these patrols in Nicaraguan waters. In passing only because this question is for the merits, one might ask: is it conceivable that Nicaraguan fishermen could be blissfully ignorant of the Colombian navy and fish around their destroyers?

1946 Decree creating special zones

21. These threats of use of force and actions taken by the Colombian authorities and its naval forces received a concrete definition of what Colombia considered waters under its jurisdiction. On 9 September 2013 Colombia declared through Presidential Decree 1946 the establishment of

---

[15] "Our Maritime Jurisdiction has not changed: Rear Admiral Espejo", *El Colombiano*, 19 Nov. 2014 available at http://www.elcolombiano.com/nuestra-jurisdiccion-maritima-no-ha-cambiado-contralmirante-espejo-1-DC664410 (last visited 28 Sept. 2015).

[16] "Defence Minister supervises security at 82 Meridian", *El Pais*, 25 June 2015, available at http://www.elpais.com.co/elpais/colombia/noticias/ministro-defensa-revisa-seguridad-meridiano-82 (last visited 28 Sep. 2015).

[17] "Minister Luis Carlos Villegas makes sovereignty visit to San Andres", *Colombia.com*, 26 June 2015, available at http://www.colombia.com/actualidad/nacionales/sdi/117892/ministro-luis-carlos-villegas-realiza-visita-de-soberania-a-san-andres (last visited 28 Sep. 2015).

what was so called Colombia's "Integral Contiguous Zone"[18]. On the screen [tab 7 on], we can appreciate in green colour the extent of this zone[19]. Superimposed to these green zones, is the area of the delimitation as seen in the map that accompanied the Court's Judgment of 19 November 2012. This "integral contiguous zone" is located in areas that were determined by the Court to be Nicaraguan waters. According to this decree this extensive area is under the control of Colombian security, health, fiscal and other authorities. Professor Lowe will expand on the substance and content of this decree. [Tab 7 off.]

22. When it was enacted, Decree 1946, Nicaragua was faced with two fundamental questions in order to decide how to proceed in the defence of its rights. On the one hand, this decree had converted into a legal internal obligation for Colombian authorities, civil and military, the need to act in those zones as provided by the decree. The problem ceased to be capable of solution by a simple order from Colombia's high officials to the military and authorities on the ground that they must respect Nicaragua's rights to its maritime zones. The decree had to be expressly revoked. The other problem looming at that moment was that Colombia had denounced the Pact of Bogotá on 27 November 2012 and this meant that this denunciation would come into effect one year later, that is, on 27 November 2013. After this last date Nicaragua would be left without clear recourse to the instruments of peaceful resolution of conflicts which were at the heart of the Pact of Bogotá. And certainly without any possible unilateral recourse to judicial settlement.

23. At this point Nicaragua reluctantly took the decision to come to the Court before the denunciation of the Pact of Bogotá came into force.

Ancestral fishing rights

24. It is surprising to listen to the emphasis given in Colombia's pleadings, including my colleague, the Agent of Colombia, to purported ancestral fishing rights of the autochthonous population of San Andres, the *raizales*[20]. Surprising not only because these hearings are not appropriate for discussing these rights since they should have been discussed during the merits phase of the case concerning the *Territorial and Maritime Dispute*. But even more so because in

---

[18]Presidential Decree 1946 of 9 Sep. 2013; MN, Ann. 9.

[19]MN, Fig. 2.2. See also Fig. 2.3 showing the location of reported incidents.

[20]CR 2015/22, pp. 14-15, para. 4 (Arrieta).

the extensive arguments in that case, there was no mention of ancestral fishing rights of the *raizales*.

25. If the interest of the autochthonous population of San Andres, the *raizales,* were behind the reluctance of Colombia to apply the Judgment, this problem could be very easily overcome. The *raizal* population is closely tied with the Nicaraguan people living in the Caribbean coast and Nicaragua has their best interests at heart. In President Ortega's speech after the Judgment was delivered, he said that Nicaragua was willing to grant artisanal fishing rights to the *raizales* in waters that the Judgment recognized as Nicaraguan[21].

The Pact of Bogotá

26. After listening to Colombia's interpretation of the Pact of Bogotá, one would wonder why this regional Pact was ever considered a landmark achievement on the pacific settlement of disputes of which the Americas, including the country of the eponymous Pact, were proud. After all, according to Colombia, the procedures it contemplated could only be invoked if both parties to the dispute considered that it could not be settled by direct negotiations[22]. If true, this would imply that any of the procedures it contemplated as binding could only be invoked if both parties were in agreement. On the other hand, if Colombia's interpretation of paragraph 2 of Article 56 of the Pact is correct, then any party to the Pact could denounce it with immediate effects. If these views were accepted the Pact would become such an exercise in futility that the surprising thing is that Colombia thought it necessary to denounce it.

27. Going a bit further into the need to exhaust the possibilities of negotiations before having recourse to the other procedures contemplated in the Pact, it should be recalled that Colombia sent its note of denunciation of the Pact on 27 November 2012 and Nicaragua filed its Application on 26 November 2013, that is, one day before the Pact would cease to be in effect for Colombia. Was it reasonable to suppose that Nicaragua had to continue attempting to negotiate before attempting procedures which would cease to be in effect one day later? This possibility cannot fit in any definition of reasonableness.

---

[21] MN, para. 2.54.

[22] CR 2015/22, pp. 49-51, paras. 11-15 (Valencia-Ospina).

Absence of a dispute

28. The existence of a serious dispute between the Parties has been public knowledge since the day the Judgment was delivered on 19 November 2012. The words of the President of Colombia on that occasion were reproduced by most media and produced a profound consternation in Latin American States and beyond. Among other things, President Santos said, [tab 8 on] "the Court adjusted the line of delimitation, separating the cays of Serrana, Serranilla, Quitasueño and Bajo Nuevo from the rest of the Archipelago"[23]. And then he emphatically stated, "[t]aking into account the above, Colombia — represented by its Head of State — emphatically rejects this aspect of the decision issued today"[24]. [Tab 8 off.]

29. What does this mean? Quite obviously that Colombia does not accept the delimitation carried out by the Court. Did Nicaragua have to expressly inform Colombia: this is a Judgment of the International Court of Justice and its judgments are final and have to be complied with in order that the existence of a dispute be established?

Negotiations

30. The question of the possibility of negotiations is not susceptible of a black or white response. There is no legal impediment for continuing to try to negotiate even after a case has been filed. There are many examples of this. To go no further, in the meeting the President of the Court called to hear the position of the Agents of both Parties on the time-limits for the written pleadings, he reminded both Parties that there was no impediment to reaching agreements outside the Court. If the only way to have recourse to the Court were that there was no possibility of negotiations, then it would be unthinkable that negotiations could go on *pari passu* with litigation.

31. In the circumstances of this case the question of the possibility of successful negotiations became clearly closed when Colombia enacted the 1946 Decree, which in effect, purports to put under Colombian jurisdiction most of the maritime spaces attributed by the Court to Nicaragua. To assume the existence of even a remote possibility of negotiations became totally unfeasible after

[23]Declaration of President Juan Manuel Santos on the Judgment of the International Court of Justice, 19 Nov. 2012; MN, Ann. 1.

[24]*Ibid.*

the denunciation of the Pact came into effect. To insist that negotiations were possible after these events cannot be given serious consideration.

The inherent jurisdiction of this Court

32. Mr. President, Members of the Court, Nicaragua has invoked two sources of jurisdiction. The first one being the Pact of Bogotá, and the second one is the Court's inherent jurisdiction to deal with disputes concerning compliance with its decisions.

33. Nicaragua considers that being the peaceful settlement of disputes the main objective of this tribunal, it is only logical for it to retain its jurisdiction when compliance with the obligations arising from its judgment are the subject-matter of a case. If the Court can order measures to preserve the rights of the parties before a final judgment is given, there cannot be any impediment to take these decisions to guarantee the rights determined in the judgment. It would not serve justice nor be compatible with the character of judicial organ of this Court if it were to bar itself from dealing with such situations.

34. Although Nicaragua considers it certain that the Court's jurisdiction is fully engaged by the Pact of Bogotá, it also considers that the particular circumstances of this case warrant this Court to make use of its inherent jurisdiction to deal with a situation where there is a real threat to peace. A regression in the respect for international law should be avoided at all costs.

35. Although Professor Pellet will elucidate on this topic, allow me to take this opportunity to clarify that whether the rights and obligations that conform the subject-matter of this case stem directly from the Court's Judgment of 19 November 2012 on the *Territorial and Maritime Dispute*, as Colombia argues[25], is very much irrelevant to the case. Therefore Nicaragua is not attempting to hide that fact[26]. Nicaragua is merely stating the obvious, which is that the Judgment produced binding obligations for Colombia, which have been and continue to be violated and this also entails Colombia's responsibility.

36. Mr. President, Members of the Court, the order of the presentations, after closing my own, is as follows:

---

[25]POC, para. 1.5.

[26]Written Statement of Nicaragua (WSN), para. 5.4.

Professor Remiro will elaborate on Colombia's strained and erroneous interpretation of the Pact of Bogotá and demonstrate that it does not conform to the text of the Treaty, the rules of treaty interpretation, nor to the object and purpose of the Pact of Bogotá.

Professor Lowe will then show the existence of an objective dispute prior to the filing of the Application.

Finally, Professor Pellet will address Nicaragua's second basis for jurisdiction, namely, the Court's inherent jurisdiction over obligations arising from its judgments.

Mr. President, this ends my presentation. Thank you and the Members of the Court for your kind attention.

Mr. President, may I ask you now to call Professor Remiro to the podium. Thank you.

Le PRESIDENT: Je remercie M. l'agent du Nicaragua. Je donne à présent la parole au professeur Remiro Brotóns. Monsieur le professeur, vous avez la parole.

M. BROTÓNS : Monsieur le président, Mesdames et Messieurs les juges, c'est un privilège renouvelé de me présenter devant vous et de le faire au nom du Nicaragua.

Compétence de la Cour *ratione temporis* suivant les articles XXXI et LVI du pacte de Bogotá

I. Introduction

1. Le 26 novembre 2013, le Nicaragua a introduit une requête contre la Colombie concernant des violations de ses droits souverains et espaces maritimes reconnus par cette Cour dans son arrêt du 19 novembre 2012, ainsi que la menace de la Colombie de recourir à la force pour commettre ces violations. Le Nicaragua avait fondé la compétence de la Cour, en premier lieu, sur la base de l'article XXXI du pacte de Bogotá [projection] (vous pouvez voir le texte, j'espère, sur l'écran). Etant donné que la Colombie avait procédé à la dénonciation du pacte le 27 novembre 2012 avec, selon notre contradicteur, un effet immédiat sur les procédures entamées par le Nicaragua, ce dernier avait réagi insistant sur le fait que, conformément à l'article LVI, cette dénonciation ne

pourrait entrer en vigueur qu'à expiration du délai d'un an prévu par la clause de dénonciation, c'est-à-dire le 27 novembre 2013[27].

2. Le Nicaragua a argumenté sa position dans son mémoire, déposé le 3 octobre 2014[28]. Or, le 19 décembre, la Colombie a formulé une série d'exceptions préliminaires, la première sur le prétendu manque de compétence *ratione temporis* de la Cour[29]. Le Nicaragua a largement exprimé les raisons qui démentent l'allégation colombienne dans son exposé écrit du 2 avril 2015[30] mais, en vue de la persistance de la Colombie sur ce point[31], il est inévitable d'y revenir aujourd'hui.

3. Monsieur le président, Mesdames et Messieurs les juges, le cœur de la question est l'interprétation de l'article LVI du pacte [projection] (dont le texte se trouve sur l'écran). Les Parties sont en désaccord sur l'interprétation de cette disposition, et les conséquences qui en découlent sont assez lourdes. Si vous suivez l'interprétation faite par la Colombie, la Cour manque de fondement pour s'occuper de cette affaire — même si cette compétence pourrait encore se déduire du pouvoir inhérent de la Cour sur des différends nés de l'inobservance de ses arrêts (un point sur lequel le professeur Pellet reviendra plus tard). Par contre, si vous acceptez la position du Nicaragua, la compétence de la Cour serait établie aussitôt, permettant ainsi de poursuivre la procédure normalement.

4. Ceci est le propos de mon intervention : démontrer à la Cour qu'une application adéquate des règles générales de droit international sur l'interprétation des traités, codifiées aujourd'hui aux articles 31 à 33 de la convention de Vienne de 1969[32], corrobore l'interprétation de l'article LVI du pacte de Bogotá proposée par le Nicaragua en relation avec l'article XXXI, et confirme la compétence de la Cour dans la présente affaire.

---

[27] Requête du Nicaragua, par. 16-17.

[28] Mémoire du Nicaragua (ci-après MN), par. 1.12-1.23 ; voir ordonnance, 3 février 2014, rôle général nº 155.

[29] Exception préliminaire de la Colombie (ci-après EPC), voir en particulier chap. 2, p. 18-21, par. 2.17-2.21 ; chap. 3 et son appendice, p. 41–83, par. 3.1–3.73, et p. 85–89, par. 3A.13A–13, respectivement ; et annexes 14, 15, 16, 19–33.

[30] Exposé écrit du Nicaragua (ci-après EEN), par. 2.1-2.40.

[31] CR 2015/22, p. 19-30.

[32] Nations Unies, *Recueil des traités*, vol. 1155, p. 331.

II. L'article LVI du pacte : paragraphe 1

5. Qu'est-ce que le paragraphe 1 de l'article LVI du pacte nous dit à propos du point que nous discutons ici ? [Projection.] Cette disposition dit, comme vous pouvez le voir, que le pacte «pourra être dénoncé moyennant un préavis d'un an» et que «passé ce délai il cessera de produire ses effets par rapport à la partie qui l'a dénoncé, et demeurera en vigueur en ce qui concerne les autres signataires». Le sens ordinaire, grammatical et logique de la disposition est très clair : le pacte continue à avoir des effets par rapport à l'Etat dénonçant et les autres parties pour un délai d'un an à compter de la date du préavis — j'aimerais bien attirer votre attention sur ce mot : «préavis». C'est le pacte lui-même qui l'utilise.

6. Il est évident que si le pacte continue à avoir des effets pendant un an, il en va de même pour l'article XXXI, selon lequel les Etats parties reconnaissent comme obligatoire de plein droit et sans convention spéciale la juridiction de la Cour sur tous les différends d'ordre juridique «tant que le présent traité restera en vigueur». [Projection.] D'ailleurs, la Cour avait déjà indiqué il y a quelques années que le consentement des Etats à la compétence obligatoire en vertu de l'article XXXI «demeure valide *ratione temporis* tant que cet instrument reste lui-même en vigueur entre ces Etats»[33].

7. La conclusion s'impose sans la moindre ambiguïté. D'une part, selon le premier paragraphe de l'article LVI, le pacte continue à produire des effets et, par conséquent, reste en vigueur et opposable à la Colombie jusqu'au 27 novembre 2013. D'autre part, l'article XXXI du pacte a continué à s'appliquer jusqu'à cette date, en tant que fondement de la compétence de la Cour à l'égard de tout différend d'ordre international entre la Colombie et les autres parties, y compris le Nicaragua. Le Nicaragua avait et a donc le droit d'invoquer pour fonder la compétence de la Cour, cet article, au moment d'introduire sa requête le 26 novembre 2013, alors que la Colombie n'a aucun droit reconnu par le pacte d'autoproclamer l'effet immédiat de son *préavis* de dénonciation le 27 novembre 2012 — ce qui est, d'ailleurs, totalement antinomique.

---

[33] Voir *Actions armées frontalières et transfrontalières (Nicaragua c. Honduras), compétence et recevabilité, arrêt, C.I.J. Recueil 1988*, p. 84, par. 34.

8. D'ailleurs, il s'agit d'un principe bien établi dans la jurisprudence de cette Cour que, une fois dûment saisie à la date de l'introduction de la requête, sa compétence est indépendante à tout changement concernant les bases de ladite compétence[34].

9. Cette interprétation du Nicaragua est cohérente et largement corroborée par l'objet et le but du pacte, ainsi que par le principe de bonne foi, prévus à l'article 31, alinéa 1), de la convention de Vienne de 1969 qui, reflétant la règle générale coutumière dans la matière, prévoit que les traités doivent être interprétés «de bonne foi suivant le sens ordinaire à attribuer aux termes du traité dans leur contexte et à la lumière de son objet et de son but». L'objet et le but du pacte sont, comme indique son titre, le «règlement pacifique» des différends entre les parties. De plus, comme la Cour elle-même l'avait indiqué : «il ressort nettement du pacte que les Etats américains, en élaborant cet instrument, ont entendu renforcer leurs engagements mutuels en matière de règlement judiciaire»[35]. La Cour tiendra compte par la suite des travaux préparatoires pour le confirmer : la sous-commission qui avait préparé le projet estimait que «la principale procédure de règlement pacifique des différends entre les Etats américains devait être la procédure judiciaire devant la Cour internationale de Justice»[36].

III. L'article LVI du pacte : deuxième paragraphe

10. Monsieur le président, Mesdames et Messieurs les juges, la Colombie préfère ignorer l'objet et le but du pacte, la teneur de la règle générale de droit intertemporel convenue par les parties dans le premier paragraphe de l'article LVI et sa relation avec l'article XXXI. La Colombie essaie de fonder un droit de dénonciation du pacte avec des effets immédiats sur la base d'une interprétation *a contrario* du deuxième paragraphe de l'article LVI. Selon la Colombie, si la dénonciation n'a pas d'effet sur les procédures déjà entamées avant la transmission de l'avis en question, il est alors raisonnable d'affirmer, toujours selon nos contradicteurs, que la dénonciation

[34] Voir, par exemple, *Nottebohm (Liechtenstein c. Guatemala), exception préliminaire, arrêt, C.I.J. Recueil 1953,* p. 111, 122–123 ; *Activités militaires et paramilitaires au Nicaragua et contre celui-ci (Nicaragua c. Etats-Unis d'Amérique), fond, arrêt, C.I.J. Recueil 1986,* p. 28–29, par. 36.

[35] Voir *Actions armées frontalières et transfrontalières (Nicaragua c. Honduras), compétence et recevabilité, arrêt, C.I.J. Recueil 1988,* p. 89, par. 46.

[36] *Ibid.*

porte des effets sur toute autre procédure initiée après cette date, à savoir le 27 novembre 2012[37]. Ce raisonnement et la conclusion sont tous les deux erronés et je vais le prouver.

11. Le deuxième paragraphe de l'article LVI du pacte manque de force nécessaire pour ébranler la vigueur de l'article XXXI par rapport à la règle générale intertemporelle du premier paragraphe. Rien dans la phrase du deuxième paragraphe de l'article LVI ne permet à la Colombie de s'évader de son acceptation de la compétence de la Cour conformément à l'article XXXI du pacte «tant que le présent Traité restera en vigueur» — c'est-à-dire, jusqu'au 27 novembre 2013, date d'expiration du délai prévu par l'article LVI. Par ailleurs, il serait contraire au principe de bonne foi de se débarrasser du consentement donné à la compétence de la Cour sur la base de l'article XXXI et le premier paragraphe de l'article LVI par le biais d'une interprétation exorbitante de la portée que pourrait avoir le deuxième paragraphe de la clause. Bien que la Colombie voie dans cette démarche «a powerful argument»[38], elle n'est qu'une coquille vide.

12. On ne peut pas, comme la Colombie prétend, saper la règle générale intertemporelle, adoptée dans des termes positifs et directs, au premier paragraphe de l'article LVI à force de faire dire à une règle particulière — celle du deuxième paragraphe — ce qu'elle ne dit pas. Nous pourrions, certainement, nous abandonner à la spéculation et imaginer pour un instant des scénarios où la règle générale n'existerait pas. Or, la réalité s'impose, la règle générale existe et la règle particulière doit alors s'en tenir à ses propres termes, sans les dépasser : la dénonciation n'aura aucun effet sur les procédures en cours entamées avant la transmission de ladite dénonciation. Point. On ne lit nulle part dans le pacte que : «La dénonciation exclut toute procédure entamée après la transmission de son préavis.»

IV. L'effet utile et inutile de l'interprétation colombienne de l'article LVI

13. Monsieur le président, Mesdames et Messieurs les juges, la Colombie affirme que son interprétation du second paragraphe de l'article LVI est la seule à assurer l'effet utile empêchant ainsi un résultat, elle dit, «manifestement absurde ou déraisonnable»[39]. Et non, non. En fait, bien au contraire. L'effet *utile*, selon la Colombie, de cette disposition aurait comme conséquence

---

[37] EPC, p. 19, par. 2.19 ; p. 41-42, par. 3.1, 3.3 ; p. 52, par. 3.20 ; p. 80-81, par. 3.69 ; p. 83, par. 3.73.

[38] *Ibid.*, p. 81, par. 3.69.

[39] *Ibid.*, p. 50, par. 3.15–3.16 ; p. 75–78, par. 3.60–3.61.

l'ablation de la règle générale du premier paragraphe. A quoi sert de dire, et dire sans conditions, que le pacte «cessera de produire ses effets par rapport à la partie qui l'a dénoncé» une fois passé le délai d'un an d'une dénonciation conçue comme un *préavis* si, à la fin, toute nouvelle requête serait interdite grâce à une interprétation *a contrario* du deuxième paragraphe de l'article LVI ? Voilà cette fois-ci un bel exemple d'un résultat «manifestement absurde ou déraisonnable». La Colombie vous invite, Mesdames et Messieurs les juges, à ignorer, même directement à étrangler, la règle générale du premier paragraphe. Si les requêtes enregistrées une fois notifiée la dénonciation ne bénéficient pas de cette règle, quelle est, alors, sa raison d'être ? ; et son sens ? ; et son utilité ?

14. Il y a cependant des raisons de croire que la Colombie est bien au courant de la faiblesse de la manœuvre interprétative. Notre contradicteur essaie «d'harmoniser» les deux paragraphes de l'article LVI proposant que le premier s'applique aux dispositions qui ne concernent pas les procédures de règlement, alors que le deuxième s'applique aux dispositions relatives à ces procédures[40]. [Projection.] Mais, lorsqu'on observe de plus près, cela n'a ni queue ni tête. Prétendre que la règle principale prévue au premier paragraphe limite ses effets aux dispositions à caractère périphérique à l'objet du pacte et, ensuite, que le deuxième paragraphe gouverne les effets de la dénonciation sur les aspects les plus importants, notamment les procédures de règlement — qui sont la raison d'être du pacte, comme illustre le fait qu'ils occupent 41 des 60 articles[41] — est une absurdité dépourvue de tout sens et fondement.

15. Monsieur le président, Mesdames et Messieurs les juges, seriez-vous prêts à croire que le deuxième paragraphe de l'article LVI a été créé dans le but d'avorter le fonctionnement des procédures de règlement exactement le même jour du *préavis* de la dénonciation ? Seriez-vous prêts à accepter que le deuxième paragraphe de l'article LVI ait été conçu comme une exception dont la portée finirait par annuler même la raison d'être de la règle générale elle-même ? Seriez-vous prêts encore à accepter que le premier paragraphe de l'article LVI n'ait été conçu que pour préserver l'application des articles I à VIII, et L à LX du pacte ?

---

[40] EPC, p. 48–53, par. 3.13–3.22 ; p. 76–78, par. 3.62–3.63.

[41] Articles IX à XLIX du pacte ; voir Nations Unies, *Recueil des traités*, vol. 30, p. 85.

V. Un aperçu de l'ensemble du pacte : le lien indissoluble du chapitre I et les chapitres II à V régissant les procédures de règlement

16. Constatons un fait. La plupart des articles qui, selon la Colombie, font l'objet de cette clause de *survie* ont déjà expiré, une fois leur fonction remplie, lorsque la dénonciation s'est produite, ou bien ils opèrent complètement en marge de cette clause.

17. C'est le cas des dispositions finales du chapitre VIII, le dernier du pacte. C'est le cas de l'article LII, sur la ratification du pacte ; c'est le cas de l'article LIII, sur son entrée en vigueur ; c'est aussi le cas de l'article LIV et de l'article LV, sur la possibilité de l'adhésion et le régime des réserves ; d'ailleurs, c'est le cas de l'article LVI lui-même ; c'est le cas de l'article LVII, sur l'enregistrement du pacte ; c'est le cas de l'article LVIII, avec la relation des traités auxquels le pacte vient à succéder ; c'est le cas de l'article LIX, qui prévoit que ladite succession ne comprend pas les procédures en cours. En ce qui concerne l'article LX [projection] : «Ce Traité aura pour nom : «pacte de Bogotá»... Il est un peu ironique que Bogotá ait renié du pacte qui porte son nom, ainsi que de la compétence obligatoire de la Cour que la délégation de la Colombie avait eu l'honneur de proposer lors de la IXe conférence interaméricaine ; mais, en tout cas, est-ce que le pacte a vraiment cessé de s'appeler «pacte de Bogotá» en Colombie à l'occasion du premier anniversaire de sa dénonciation ?

18. Alors, si le premier paragraphe de l'article LVI ne peut pas s'appliquer aux articles LII à LX du pacte, sa mission est, peut-être, de protéger les articles I à VIII du chapitre I ?

19. Pour commencer, nous sommes confrontés à une difficulté tout au début. Ce chapitre s'intitule «Obligation générale de régler les différends par des moyens pacifiques». Il semble étrange de conserver ce chapitre pendant une année suivant le préavis de dénonciation alors que toutes les voies prévues pour remplir cette obligation deviennent tout d'un coup impraticables. Mais on ne s'arrête pas là.

20. Laissons de côté les articles I et VIII. L'un se réfère à l'obligation des parties de s'abstenir de la menace, de l'emploi de la force ou de n'importe quel autre moyen de coercition pour régler leurs différends ; l'autre laisse à l'abri, en tout cas, l'exercice du droit de légitime défense individuelle ou collective prévu dans la Charte des Nations Unies. Un an après la dénonciation et par la suite, ces règles resteront en vigueur et opposables à la Colombie sur d'autres fondements normatifs.

21. Si nous nous penchons ensuite sur les articles II à VI, d'abord, l'article II établit l'obligation de se servir, avant de recourir au Conseil de sécurité, des procédures du pacte ou d'autres de leur choix si l'une des parties considère que le différend ne peut pas être résolu au moyen de négociations diplomatiques. Puis, l'article III proclame le principe de libre choix et d'égalité entre les procédures du pacte. Pour sa part, l'article IV exige l'épuisement des procédures entamées avant de recourir à une autre procédure. Selon l'article V, lesdites procédures ne peuvent pas s'appliquer aux questions qui, par leur nature, relèvent de la compétence nationale des Etats. Ces procédures, dispose enfin l'article VI, ne pourront pas non plus s'appliquer aux questions déjà réglées au moyen d'une entente entre les parties ou d'une décision arbitrale ou judiciaire, ni à celles régies par des traités en vigueur à la date de la signature du pacte.

22. En d'autres termes, tous ces articles, sans exception, se réfèrent aux procédures de règlement prévues par le pacte de telle manière qu'il est inconcevable que ces dispositions survivent pendant une année après le préavis de la dénonciation sans le cordon ombilical qui les lie à de telles procédures et les nourrit. Les articles II à VI constituent le cadre qui délimite le fonctionnement des procédures prévues dans les chapitres qui suivent — procédures qui sont également l'extension naturelle de l'obligation enracinée dans le premier chapitre. Il est donc naturel qu'on trouve des références et des renvois, et l'article XXXIV est un bel exemple [projection][42]. En fait, c'est sur le deuxième paragraphe de l'article II que la Colombie fonde aujourd'hui l'argumentation de l'irrecevabilité de la requête[43]. Mon collègue, le professeur Lowe abordera cette question plus tard.

23. Il y a donc tout lieu de noter le lien étroit et indissociable qui existe entre les règles du premier chapitre, d'une part, et les règles régissant toute la série de procédures prévues dans les chapitres suivants, d'autre part. La Colombie avait, elle-même, attiré votre attention sur cette relation dans le cadre d'une autre affaire où, en tant que partie défenderesse, elle cherchait à échapper aussi à la compétence de la Cour [projection] :

> «Ce n'est pas l'article XXXI, interprété isolément des autres dispositions pertinentes, qui confère à la Cour sa compétence en l'espèce, mais l'ensemble du

---

[42] L'article XXXIV prévoit que: «Si, pour les motifs indiqués aux articles 5, 6 et 7 de ce Traité, la Cour se déclarait incompétente pour juger le différend, celui-ci sera déclaré terminé.»

[43] EPC, p. 91-129, par. 4.1-4.74 ; CR 2015/22, p. 46-59.

chapitre quatre («Procédure judiciaire»), interprété conjointement avec les dispositions générales du chapitre premier («Obligation générale de régler les différends par des moyens pacifiques»), et, en particulier, l'article VI, auquel les termes de l'article XXXIV renvoient explicitement. L'article XXXI n'est pas un article isolé, mais doit être interprété à la lumière d'autres dispositions pertinentes du pacte[44]».

24. Tout compte fait, il ne nous reste que l'article VII du premier chapitre du pacte en vertu duquel les parties s'engagent à ne pas exercer la protection diplomatique des ressortissants avant l'épuisement des voies de recours internes. Est-ce que le paragraphe 1 de l'article LVI a été adopté pour mieux protéger cette disposition ? Est-ce que le but de cette règle est la seule protection des articles célibataires des chapitres six (portant sur la mise à exécution des décisions de la Cour) et sept (portant sur les avis consultatifs), tous les deux peu pertinents du point de vue du droit intertemporel qui nous occupe ici ?.

25. En fait, et reprenant l'article II invoqué par la Colombie pour contester la recevabilité de la requête, c'est le deuxième paragraphe de cette disposition qui, en vigueur selon la lecture de l'article LVI avancée par la Colombie, joue en faveur de l'interprétation proposée par le Nicaragua. Cette disposition (sur l'écran) prévoit que [projection] :

> «au cas où surgirait un différend qui, de l'avis d'une des parties, ne pourrait être résolu au moyen de négociations directes par voie diplomatique, les parties s'engagent à employer les procédures établies dans ce Traité sous la forme et dans les conditions prévues aux articles suivants».

Ces dispositions ne peuvent être que celles incluses dans les chapitres II à V du pacte consacrés précisément aux procédures de règlement.

26. En somme, et comme on vient de le montrer, l'interprétation que la Colombie prétend faire de l'article LVI du pacte nous amène, si erronément suivie, à laisser la règle énoncée au paragraphe 1 dépourvue de toute signification pratique. On ne peut pas transformer une clause comme le paragraphe 2 de l'article LVI dont la raison d'être est la protection des procédures en cours en une clause excluant des requêtes fondées sur le consentement donné à la compétence de la Cour en vertu de l'article XXXI et le paragraphe 1 de l'article LVI du pacte.

---

[44] Voir *Différend territorial et maritime (Nicaragua c. Colombie)*, exceptions préliminaires, vol. I, juillet 2003, [*traduction du Greffe*], p. 41–42, par . 2.5.

VI. L'effet de *surprise* et le principe de bonne foi

27. En outre, le principe de bonne foi appliqué à un traité dont l'objet est le règlement pacifique des différends entre Etats demande la plus ample protection des attentes en matière de stabilité des procédures y convenues, évitant ainsi que les parties utilisent des actions unilatérales — telle que la faculté de dénonciation — comme un mécanisme de fuite — à moins que l'*élément surprise* se trouve clairement entre les règles du jeu. Mais tel n'est pas le cas ici. Rien dans le pacte ne permet d'affirmer qu'un Etat partie, y compris la Colombie, puisse imposer l'effet immédiat d'une dénonciation. Comment peut-on parler d'un *préavis* de dénonciation si on demande des effets immédiats ? A vrai dire, la Colombie essaie de passer d'un *préavis* de dénonciation à une dénonciation *sans préavis*.

28. La Colombie n'hésite pas à rappeler des déclarations d'acceptation de la compétence obligatoire de la Cour dans le cadre de l'article 36, paragraphe 2, du Statut pour montrer que certaines prévoient des clauses de terminaison d'effet immédiat[45]. Ce recours est clairement inapproprié. Comme on le sait, le fait que le contenu de l'article 36, paragraphe 2, du Statut de la Cour soit incorporé dans l'article XXXI du pacte ne donne pas lieu à son assimilation. L'article XXXI du pacte prévoit une base de compétence de nature conventionnelle soumise à ses propres règles, celles qu'on trouve dans le droit des traités.

29. Comme l'avait fait observer la Cour, même si l'on regarde l'article XXXI comme une déclaration collective d'acceptation de la juridiction obligatoire faite conformément à l'article 36, paragraphe 2, de son Statut, cette déclaration a été incorporée au pacte de Bogotá [projection] :

> «Dès lors elle ne saurait être modifiée que selon les règles fixées par le pacte lui-même. Or l'article XXXI n'envisage à aucun moment que l'engagement pris par les parties au pacte puisse être amendé par voie de déclaration unilatérale faite ultérieurement par application du Statut et la mention du paragraphe 2 de l'article 36 du Statut ne suffit pas par elle-même à produire un tel effet.»[46]

30. La pertinence de la distinction avait été relevée également par l'ancien président de la Cour, Eduardo Jiménez de Aréchaga, affirmant que, grâce à l'article XXXI du pacte, les parties avaient transformé «la relation souple découlant des déclarations unilatérales sous l'article 36, paragraphe 2, en une relation conventionnelle» — ce qui avait permis, écrivait-t-il, d'«établir la

---

[45] EPC, p. 53–55, par. 3.23.

[46] *Actions armées frontalières et transfrontalières (Nicaragua c. Honduras), compétence et recevabilité, arrêt, C.I.J. Recueil 1988*, p. 84, par. 34.

force obligatoire et la stabilité caractéristiques d'un lien conventionnel, et non le régime de la clause facultative». Ainsi les parties au pacte avaient assumé la compétence obligatoire de la Cour dans le cadre de ses relations «à des conditions plus rigoureuses que celles résultant du réseau de déclarations faites en conformité avec l'article 36, paragraphe 2 du Statut». Jiménez de Aréchaga trouvait la confirmation dans deux caractéristiques principales de la clause facultative : «la possibilité de retraits et de nouvelles réserves». Enfin, le maître uruguayen concluait que [projection] :

> «le pacte de Bogotá, une fois accepté par un Etat américain, reste en vigueur indéfiniment, et il peut seulement être dénoncé moyennant un préavis d'un an, demeurant en vigueur pendant toute cette période (art. LVI du pacte de Bogota). Cela signifie que le retrait de l'acceptation de la compétence obligatoire dès que la possibilité d'une requête hostile apparaît à l'horizon a été fortement restreinte.»[47]

31. La Colombie essaie d'attirer l'attention sur le fait qu'aucun Etat n'avait objecté sa démarche au moment de dénoncer le pacte[48]. La seule réponse sur laquelle il convient d'attirer votre attention est l'exercice par le Nicaragua du droit reconnu à l'article XXXI du pacte d'introduire une requête dans le délai d'un an prévu par l'article LVI.

VII. A propos des travaux préparatoires

32. Monsieur le président, Mesdames et messieurs les juges, permettez-moi de dire quelques mots sur les travaux préparatoires du pacte de Bogotá qui, selon la Colombie, confirmeraient son interprétation de l'article LVI[49]. La Colombie s'est efforcée de retrouver l'origine du deuxième paragraphe de cette disposition. Or, la seule conclusion à laquelle on aboutit est qu'il n'y a pas un élément, pas un seul, dans toute cette histoire qui permet de valider l'interprétation de nos contradicteurs. Cela expliquerait la brièveté de la Colombie sur ce point, hier. Personne, absolument personne, fait de commentaires, ni pose de questions sur ce texte ou sa signification. Aucun débat dans la commission en charge, aucune explication des raisons ou des motivations dans les rapports qui accompagnaient les projets. Ce silence est, pour le moins, particulièrement décevant si le but de cette disposition était, comme la Colombie essaie de nous en convaincre ici,

---

[47] Voir E. Jiménez de Aréchaga, «The Compulsory Jurisdiction of the International Court of Justice under the Bogotá and the Optional Clause», Y. Dinstein (ed.), *International Law at a time of perplexity: Essays in honour of Shabtai Rosenne,* Dordrecht [etc.], Martinus Nijhoff, 1989, pp. 356–357.

[48] EPC, p. 21, par. 2.21, p. 59, par. 3.32.

[49] *Ibid.,* p. 60–72, par. 3.33–3.53; p. 78, par. 3.64.

de modifier radicalement la portée des clauses de dénonciation opérant traditionnellement dans le système panaméricain. Mais il y a plus encore.

33. On ne trouve pas non plus de référence au deuxième paragraphe de l'article LVI dans les rapports du comité ni dans les procès-verbaux de la IXe conférence interaméricaine qui avait discuté le projet et a adopté le pacte. La seule référence — assez laconique — à la clause de dénonciation avait été faite par le délégué du Mexique, M. Enríquez, rapporteur de la troisième commission qui s'occupait du règlement de différends et de la sécurité collective, au moment de s'adresser aux membres de la commission de coordination pour expliquer les caractéristiques du projet. Qu'est-ce que M. Enríquez a dit à son audience distinguée ?

34. Le rapporteur a simplement dit que l'article LVI avait été repris du traité général d'arbitrage interaméricain, du 5 janvier 1929[50]. Une fois décidé que le pacte ne serait pas annexé à la charte de l'OEA, «nous avons convenu — explique-t-il — que la meilleure rédaction possible consistait à reproduire l'article 16 du traité de 1929»[51]. [Projection.] Même si le rapporteur encourt un *lapsus linguae* quand il se réfère à l'article 16 [9] d'un traité qui en a seulement neuf, c'est précisément au troisième alinéa de la dernière de ces dispositions que l'on prévoit que [Projection]

> «Le présent traité restera en vigueur indéfiniment, mais il peut être dénoncé par un avis préalable d'un an ; à l'expiration de ce terme il cessera d'être en vigueur en ce qui concerne la Partie qui l'a dénoncé, mais restera en vigueur pour les autres signataires.»

Ni plus, ni moins. Il est fort dommage que cette donnée, non négligeable pour la meilleure compréhension des antécédents et de la portée de l'article LVI, ait été pratiquement ignorée par la Colombie.

35. C'est le pacte de Bogotá lui-même qui, à l'article LVIII, se déclare successeur du traité de 1929[52]. Cela veut dire que toute addition à ce texte doit s'interpréter comme corollaire à cette règle, à moins qu'une autre intention soit manifestée de façon expresse. Cette exigence est plus

---

[50] Société des Nations, *Recueil des traités*, vol. CXXX, nº 2988, p. 135.

[51] IX Conferencia Internacional Americana, Bogotá, Colombia, Marzo 30-Mayo 2 de 1948; voir *Actas y Documentos*, vol. II, MRE de Colombia, Bogotá (1953), p. 541.

[52] Article LVIII: «Les traités, conventions et protocoles ci-après énumérés cesseront de produire leurs effets par rapport aux hautes parties contractantes au fur et à mesure que le présent traité entrera en vigueur en ce qui les concerne au moyen de leurs ratifications successives ... traité général d'arbitrage interaméricain et protocole additionnel d'arbitrage progressif du 5 janvier 1929...»

grande encore lorsque l'intention est régressive par rapport à un traité dont l'objet et le but sont de progresser au lieu de reculer, c'est-à-dire d'élargir le champ des procédures de règlement au lieu de les restreindre.

36. Finalement, il y a tout lieu de remarquer que l'interprétation du deuxième paragraphe de l'article LVI proposée par le Nicaragua selon laquelle cette disposition ne modifie ni comporte une exception à la règle générale prévue au paragraphe 1, non seulement est la seule respectueuse des règles d'interprétation et de l'ensemble du pacte, mais elle est aussi plus cohérente avec, d'une part, les clauses de dénonciation de traités antérieurs portant sur la même matière qui, par ailleurs, conforment l'*acquis* panaméricain[53] ; et, d'autre part, les clauses de dénonciation adoptées dans le cadre de traités multilatéraux à caractère universel ou régional. La relation de traités apportée par la Colombie dans la conviction qu'elle servirait sa cause est devenue une «balle au pied»[54]. Toutes les clauses de dénonciation mentionnées déclarent, sans exception, que les traités concernés restent en vigueur, et ils sont applicables pour un délai de trois, six, ou douze mois après le préavis. En effet, il n'y a pas un seul cas où l'effet immédiat soit la règle. Il est évident que les Etats n'aiment guère les surprises, notamment lorsqu'il s'agit d'assurer la stabilité et d'aider les traités malmenés par le destin à bien mourir.

VIII. Conclusion

37. Monsieur le président, Mesdames et Messieurs les juges, pour conclure, le paragraphe 1 de l'article LVI du pacte de Bogotá proclame, simplement, la vigueur et la continuité des effets et des obligations convenus pour une durée d'un an à partir de la transmission de la dénonciation. Cela implique forcément que l'article XXXI du pacte a continué à avoir toute sa force et est demeuré applicable aux relations entre la Colombie et le Nicaragua jusqu'au 27 novembre 2013. Le deuxième paragraphe de l'article LVI, comme on vient de le montrer, ne peut pas être interprété comme une exception ou une dérogation radicale du principe prévu au paragraphe 1. C'est pourquoi la Cour doit accepter sa compétence sur la requête introduite par le Nicaragua le 26 novembre 2013 sur la base de l'article XXXI du pacte.

---

[53] Voir traité d'arbitrage obligatoire, 29 janvier 1902, art. 22 ; traité général d'arbitrage interaméricain du 5 janvier 1929, art. 9.

[54] EPC, p. 55–58, par. 3.24–3.28.

28. Je vous remercie de votre attention. Monsieur le président, je vous serais très reconnaissant de bien vouloir donner maintenant la parole à mon collège M. Lowe pour la poursuite de la présentation du premier tour de plaidoiries du Nicaragua. Merci.

Le PRESIDENT : Merci, Monsieur le professeur. Je donne maintenant la parole à M. le professeur Vaughan Lowe.

Mr. LOWE:

EXISTENCE OF A DISPUTE

Mr. President, Members of the Court, it is an honour to appear before you again, and to do so on behalf of the Republic of Nicaragua.

1. My task this morning is to address two matters: first, the question whether there really is a dispute between Nicaragua and Colombia (or whether we are all here as a result of some ghastly misunderstanding), and second, the question whether that dispute could be settled by diplomatic means.

2. In its Preliminary Objections dated 19 December 2014, one set of the arguments made by Colombia was made under the heading "There was no dispute with respect to Nicaragua's claims"; and it is those objections that I address now.

3. More specifically Colombia argues that

> "there was no dispute between the two Parties since, prior to filing its Application, Nicaragua failed to make any claims relating to the violation of its 'sovereign rights and maritime zones' or to 'the use of or threat to use force' by Colombia, or to Colombia's Decree 1946 of 2013 that could give rise to a dispute, or any objection to Colombia's conduct relating to the relevant maritime areas"[55].

4. Colombia made it clear yesterday that it does not argue that a formal international claim needs to be made. It is enough that there is "a positive opposition of the claim of one party by the other"[56], and "a dispute exists objectively 'in a situation in which the two sides hold clearly

[55]POC, para. 4.1.

[56]CR 2015/22, p. 41, para. 9 (Reisman).

opposite views concerning the question of the performance or non-performance of certain treaty obligations'"[57].

5. Colombia maintains that "[n]othing in the record shows those required 'clearly opposite views' on the subject-matter of the Application at the time of Nicaragua's filing"[58].

6. It is common ground that there must be a legal dispute in existence on the date when the Application is filed — in this case, 26 November 2013. By that date, as I shall show, Colombia had rejected the Court's Judgment, adopted legislation that contradicted the Court's ruling, and started harassing Nicaraguan fishing vessels in what it said were "Colombian waters" — in fact, waters that had been determined by the Court to belong to Nicaragua.

7. Colombia suggested yesterday that its conduct was all concerned with the "implementation" of the Court's Judgment as required by Colombia's Constitution. But the short answer to that suggestion is that the enactment of contradictory legislation, and the assertion of Colombian title to waters that the Court had decided belong to Nicaragua cannot be described as measures implementing the Court's Judgment; and the suggestion that after 11 years of litigation in the Court over these very waters, Colombia was taken by surprise at Nicaragua's view of its legal rights, recently upheld by the Court, is not at all easy to understand.

The facts

8. I shall not go through all of the facts set out in Nicaragua's Written Statement. That Statement stands as Nicaragua's core submission; and I shall mention only the main points that are important in the context of the arguments put forward in Colombia's opening speech.

9. As the Court will recall, in its 19 November 2012 Judgment[59] it rejected the request for a declaration that Colombia had violated Nicaragua's rights, including violations by way of various maritime activities referred to in Nicaragua's Reply dated 18 September 2009, which had been

---

[57]CR 2015/22, p. 44, para. 18 (Reisman).

[58]*Ibid.*

[59]*Territorial and Maritime Dispute (Nicaragua* v. *Colombia), Judgment, I.C.J. Reports 2012 (II)*, p. 718, paras. 249-250.

submitted in that case[60] The Court said that the boundary had not been settled until the Court gave its Judgment, and that part of the disputed area had been allocated to Colombia.

10. The boundary out to 200 nautical miles was then fixed by the Court. Both Nicaragua and Colombia have known for almost three years the geographical extent of each other's maritime rights, which they must respect. But since November 2012, Colombia's violations of Nicaragua's waters have continued.

11. Chapter II of Nicaragua's Memorial dated 3 October 2014 set out the material facts as they stood prior to that date. Those facts were assembled in four sections. The first dealt with the declarations made immediately after the Court's 2012 Judgment by the President and the Foreign Minister of Colombia. The second dealt with Colombia's notorious Presidential Decree 1946. The third catalogued some of the most significant direct physical violations by Colombia of Nicaragua's maritime rights. All three of those sections refer to facts occurring before Nicaragua's Application was filed with the Court. Some facts occurring after that date were also included, to demonstrate that the problem is continuing. The fourth section of Chapter II of the Memorial provided some context for the account of Colombia's actions, and described Nicaragua's reactions to Colombia's acts. [Tab 22 on]

12. It is not necessary at this stage to go into all of the details of these actions. My present purpose is simply to demonstrate the existence of a dispute between Colombia and Nicaragua.

13. The most striking action was the rejection of the Court's Judgment by Colombia. It began with a clear rejection of the Judgment by the President of Colombia, which you will find at tab 22 of your folder. He said,

> "[i]nexplicably — after recognizing the sovereignty of Colombia over the entire archipelago and holding that it as a unit generated continental shelf and exclusive economic zone rights — the Court adjusted the delimitation line, leaving the Keys of Serrana, Serranilla, Quitasueño and Bajo Nuevo separated from the rest of the archipelago.

---

[60]Reply of Nicaragua (RN), paras. 34-38, and pp. 235-238.

This is inconsistent with what the Court itself acknowledged, and is not compatible with the geographical conception of what is an archipelago.

All of these are really omissions, errors, excesses, inconsistencies that we cannot accept."[61]

14. That is not a paraphrase, inflated by the press to excite the public. It is a statement that was put on to the official website of the Colombian Presidency. [Tab 22 off — tab 23 on]

15. Two days later the Colombian Foreign Minister was reported to have said — you have the text at tab 23 of your folder: "The enemy is the Court which did not base its decision on the law, that Judgment is full of inadequacies and one reads it and cannot believe that the states parties that conform the Court elected those judges to decide such an important Judgment."[62] Colombia then proceeded to denounce the Bogotá Pact.

16. Now, governments must react to developments, and they sometimes express themselves in terms that are calibrated more to the heat of the day's television headlines than to the coolness of long-term diplomacy. It would be a cheap shot if Nicaragua were simply to gather some of the immediate reactions of Colombian politicians to the Court's 2012 Judgment and present them as Colombia's current attitude towards the Court.

17. On the other hand, governments may actually mean what they say publicly, particularly when different ministers make the same point repeatedly. On the face of it, these statements coming out of Colombia had two aspects that could not be ignored by Nicaragua. [Tab 23 off]

18. The first aspect is that two senior officials — the President and the Foreign Minister — rejected the determination of Nicaragua's rights. In common law jurisdictions, there is a concept of "slander of title" — a false claim that a person owns what is in truth someone else's property. In a domestic context, it may seem to be a reflection of the law's ancient preoccupation with property rights; but in international law, it is the first murmuring of the overriding of legal borders. It is a serious matter, that directly challenges the stability of the international system. It is that aspect that brings Nicaragua to the Court.

---

[61] Memorial of Nicaragua (MN), para. 2.3.

[62] MN, para. 2.5.

19. The second aspect is that the repudiation of the Judgment was a direct challenge to the authority of the Court. The Court's Judgment was said to be inexplicable, containing omissions, errors, excesses and inconsistencies that Colombia could not accept, and that aspect of the Judgment was emphatically rejected by Colombia.

20. I do not make this point by way of reporting misbehaviour on the part of Colombia. Nicaragua is a small country on the international stage; like many States, it depends upon international law to safeguard its basic rights; and like many States, it depends upon the Court to speak out when international law is flouted. I say no more about this: but Nicaragua wishes there to be no doubt as to the importance that it attaches to the Court's role in upholding the authority of international law, in the face of undisguised rejections of that authority.

21. Nicaragua sees in Colombia's statements and repudiation of the Court's Judgment, a deliberate, long-term policy of taking from international law what is advantageous to Colombia and rejecting whatever is inconvenient to Colombia. The repudiations were not short-term assertions of national defiance and determination in the face of the Court's Judgment. Indeed, they were preceded, days *before* the Judgment, by military deployments — expressly stated to have the purpose of "exercising and ratifying the Colombian sovereignty" over the waters in dispute. You will see the details in Nicaragua's Memorial, in Annex 50. And as I shall describe shortly, they were followed by a continuing pattern of direct challenges to the boundaries declared by the Court.

22. Let me turn to the second factual development underlying Nicaragua's Application. The repudiations of the Court's authority were not confined to opportunistic statements to the media by politicians. The repudiations continued and were made by a range of high officers of State — the Commander of the Colombian navy, and the Governor of San Andrés, for example. The significance of their repetition by functionaries such as the head of the navy is that it indicates that the remarks have moved well outside the sphere of political comment and have moved into the sphere of settled national policy. And indeed, this was confirmed during the following year. [Tab 24 on]

23. In September 2013 the repudiations of the Court's Judgment were enshrined in national law, in Colombia's Decree 1946, which you will find at tab 24. That decree established a so-called

"Integrated Contiguous Zone"— the ICZ— in which Colombia asserted its "sovereign authority"[63]. Article 5 (3) of the decree provides that

> "the Colombian State shall exercise in the established Integral Contiguous Zone its sovereign authority and the powers for the implementation and necessary control regarding:
>
> *(a)* Prevention and control of violations of the laws and by-laws regarding integral security of the State, including piracy, drug trafficking, as well as behaviours that endanger security at sea and national maritime interests . . ."

And so it goes on. The full text is reproduced as Annex 9 to Nicaragua's Memorial. As is explained in Chapter Three of that Memorial, this decree was amended and the claim embodied in it was strengthened by Decree 1119 of June 2014, mistakenly dated June 2013 in paragraphs 3.23 and 3.24 of the Memorial. [Tab 24 off —tab 25 on]

24. The significance of the claim in Decree 1946 is that the waters over which Colombia asserted its sovereign rights included waters which had been adjudged by the Court to belong to Nicaragua. The overlap is depicted in figure 2.2 of Nicaragua's Memorial, which is now on the screen and set out in tab 25 of your folder[64]. I should also draw your attention the map at Annex 10 to Nicaragua's Memorial, which is the map presented by the Colombian President, in an address to the Colombian people on the day that the decree was issued, setting out again Colombia's ICZ claim[65].

25. Well, you will see on the chart the green area that Colombia established as its Integral Contiguous Zone. It lies across the boundaries determined by the Court. There is a boundary drawn as a bold red line, from Point A in the middle of the chart around to Point B. It proceeds west from Point A on the figure, goes across to Point 1, then south and east through points 1 to 9, and then east to Point B; and that is the line drawn by the Court. The waters outside that "box" are Nicaraguan waters, with the exception of the enclaved waters around Quitasueño and Serrana — a 12-mile territorial sea enclave around each of them, depicted on the chart by a bold red line. The feint dotted lines around Quitasueño and Serrana represent a 24-mile contiguous zone for which the Law of the Sea Convention provides.

---

[63]Quoted in MN, para. 2.12.

[64]MN, para. 2.14.

[65]See MN, paras 2.12 – 2.14.

26. As you can see, Colombia's declared ICZ extends well beyond the boundaries drawn by the Court. Indeed, it extends well beyond any possible claim that Colombia might make to a contiguous zone if it was not constrained by the boundaries with Nicaragua's waters. It is a very plain assertion that parts of Nicaragua's waters belong to Colombia, despite what the Court had said in its 2012 Judgment.

27. Colombia tries to say that the contiguous zone regulations should be seen as an implementation of the Court's Judgment[66]. But how can that be? How can a decree that asserts Colombia's rights over waters that the Court has ruled belong to Nicaragua possibly be an implementation of the Court's Judgment?

28. That decree remains in force today. More than that, Colombia enforces the decree and that takes me to the third category of Colombia's actions: the concrete violations of Nicaragua's legal rights. [Tab 25 off — tab 26 on]

29. In Chapter Two of Nicaragua's Memorial you will find, for example, references to 47 incidents in the Luna Verde fishing grounds, listed and depicted in Annex 24 and in figures 2.3, 2.4 and 2.5.

30. On the screen now is figure 2.3, which is set out at tab 26 in your folder. The bold red lines are the boundaries drawn by the Court in its 2012 Judgment; and the bold blue line is Colombia's claimed Integrated Contiguous Zone — its ICZ. The red dots in and around the area marked as Luna Verde — a rich fishing ground, coloured green on the map — mark the locations of the incidents.

31. You can see that the incidents are not even within Colombia's claimed ICZ. There is no room for any possible belief that these are anything other than Nicaraguan waters. Yet, as Annex 24 of Nicaragua's Memorial records, vessels lawfully within these Nicaraguan waters have been repeatedly harassed and told to leave what were described by Colombian enforcement agencies as Colombian waters.

32. Three things are noteworthy about these incidents. One is that they span the period before and after the initiation of this case. The first dozen or so occurred after the date of the

---

[66]See CR 2015/22, p. 45, para. 21 (Reisman).

Court's Judgment in November 2012 but before Nicaragua's Application was filed in this case on 26 November 2013. There was then a break of about five weeks before they resumed in earnest at the start of 2014. How can Colombia's actions be interpreted, other than as a deliberate — indeed, defiant — repudiation of the Court's Judgment and denial of Nicaragua's rights?

33. The second significant fact is that, as you will see from the excerpts of the conversations between the Colombian naval vessels and the intercepted vessels, set out in Annex 23 (B) to the Memorial, the interceptions were based upon a clear — indeed an explicit and express — opposition of views. The Colombian navy vessels asserted that they were patrolling Colombian waters; the Nicaraguan vessels asserted that they were in Nicaraguan waters. The incidents were all very many miles within the boundaries of the waters that the Court had ruled belong to Nicaragua.

34. The third significant fact is that the incidents involved the armed forces of Colombia and of Nicaragua. These were not only exchanges between fishermen or other private parties. There were exchanges — repeated exchanges, along repeated, consistent lines — between the armed forces of the States. Each side knew that it was acting on behalf of its State, and that the other side was also acting on behalf of its State.

35. Colombia makes much of the fact that there was no naval "confrontation", that no boardings of fishing vessels took place. But the fact that Nicaraguan naval vessels or fishing boats did not square up for a fight with Colombia does not mean that the Colombian harassment was lawful, or that Colombia was entitled to assume that Nicaragua had abandoned the position that it had held throughout the proceedings in this Court and had relinquished its rights over the waters that the Court had just ruled belonged to Nicaragua. [Tab 26 off]

A dispute exists

36. For Colombia now to say that "there was no dispute between the two Parties since, prior to filing its Application, Nicaragua failed to make any claims relating to the violation of its 'sovereign rights and maritime zones' or to 'the use of or threat to use force' by Colombia, or to Colombia's Decree 1946 of 2013 that could give rise to a dispute" is simply disingenuous.

37. The deployments of the Colombian forces were patently intended to demonstrate Colombia's repudiation of the Court's ruling; and so was Decree 1946. It was the entire *purpose* of those steps. And any suggestion that Colombia did not know whether or not Nicaragua disputed Colombia's position is not only absurd: it is flatly contradicted by the recorded exchanges between the naval forces.

38. If Colombia is suggesting that international law requires, as an essential formality, that a specific "claim" must be made before the existence of a "dispute", which can be recognized, Nicaragua would make two points in response.

39. First, Colombia gives no authority for that proposition; and it is incorrect. There is no evidence that international law imposes such a requirement.

40. The most that could be said is that it must be shown that, in the words of the Court, "the two sides held clearly opposite views"[67]. The Court has not required the making of a formal international claim in order to constitute the existence of a "dispute". And as the Court said in the *Headquarters Agreement* case, the lack of any legal argument to justify the conduct of the State does not preclude the existence of a dispute[68].

41. What is important is that each side knows, not simply that there is hostility or discontent between them, but that there is a specific, identified disagreement over a question of law or fact.

42. If that is clear on the facts, there is a dispute, whether or not one the parties chooses to accept that label. As the Court said, in relation to the *Hostages* case, in which Iran had not appeared: "The Court saw no need to enquire into the attitude of Iran in order to establish the existence of a 'dispute' . . ."[69] There comes a point where common sense must bring argument to an end; and as the Court indicated last week in its decision in *Bolivia* v. *Chile*, the Court itself will determine on an objective basis the subject-matter of a dispute between the parties[70].

---

[67] *Interpretation of Peace Treaties with Bulgaria, Hungary and Romania, First Phase, Advisory Opinion, I.C.J. Reports 1950*, p. 74.

[68] *Applicability of the Obligation to Arbitrate under Section 21 of the United Nations Headquarters Agreement of 26 June 1947, Advisory Opinion, I.C.J. Reports 1988,* p. 28, para. 38.

[69] *Ibid.*

[70] *Obligation to Negotiate Access to the Pacific Ocean (Bolivia* v. *Chile), Preliminary Objection,* Judgment of 24 September 2015, para. 26.

43. So, the first point is that there is no legal requirement that a "claim" be presented by one government to another government before a "dispute" can exist between two States.

44. The second point is that it is evident from the record in this case that what international law does require — the clear presentation of positions, so that each side can understand what the disagreement is — is abundantly satisfied.

45. After more than a decade of litigation between Nicaragua and Colombia over this very question of the maritime boundaries between them, and the much publicized rejection of the Court's Judgment by Colombia, and the deployment of the Colombian navy for the explicit purpose of pressing the very claims of which Colombia had failed to persuade the Court, the suggestion that Colombia was in the slightest doubt as to the opposing positions is simply not credible.

Mr. President, I have about 10 or 12 minutes more to go, but you may feel that this is a convenient moment at which to pause for coffee: I am in your hands.

Le PRESIDENT: Oui, Monsieur le professeur. En effet, la Cour va marquer une pause de 15 minutes. L'audience est suspendue.

L'audience est suspendue de 11 h 25 à 11 h 40

Le PRESIDENT : Veuillez vous asseoir. L'audience reprend. Je donne la parole au professeur Vaughan Lowe pour la suite de sa plaidoirie.

Mr. LOWE: Thank you, Mr. President, Members of the Court.

The question of the non-exhaustion of negotiations

[Tab 27 on]

46. I turn to the question whether the dispute could be settled by negotiations between the Parties. The question arises because of the wording of Article II of the Pact of Bogotá. In the English, Spanish and Portuguese texts, the parties to the Pact are bound to use the procedures established in the Pact in relation to a dispute where "the parties" consider that it cannot be settled by direct negotiation through the usual diplomatic channels.

47. In the equally authentic French text, the obligation arises if in the opinion of *one* of the parties it cannot be settled by direct negotiation. As we explain in Chapter IV, of our Written Statement, and as my colleague Professor Antonio Remiro Brotóns has explained, the interpretation of this provision, set out in its various official languages, that best reconciles the texts and accords with the rules on treaty interpretation[71] is, in our submission, that the judgement of the negotiability of a dispute is a matter for the parties to the dispute, and not for a third party, and that, as the French text indicates more clearly, it is enough if one of them holds the view that there is no prospect of a negotiated settlement. After all, if one party believes that a negotiated settlement is not possible, that is a pretty good indication that it is not.

48. More importantly, to make the duty to resort to any of the Bogotá procedures — conciliation, adjudication and so on — dependent upon an *agreement* between the disputing parties that their dispute could not be settled by negotiation would render the entire scheme essentially optional — and that is not at all what the Pact seems to contemplate.

49. And I should add in passing that there is no evidence of any rule of law that requires all possibility of negotiations to be exhausted before any case is referred to the Court or to other international procedures. Indeed, the Court said in *Cameroon* v. *Nigeria* that there is no general rule of international law to this effect[72], and the reference will appear in the transcript.

[Tab 27 off]

50. But in truth, it makes little difference in this case whether one looks for an objective decision or for the opinion of one or of both States. This dispute is clearly one that could not be settled by direct negotiations.

51. In one sense, of course, it can always be said that if the parties to a case sat down and talked they could find a solution to it. But that is not what it means to talk about disputes that cannot be settled by direct negotiation.

52. When a dispute first emerges, as this one did in November 2012, the question whether it can be settled by negotiation is a matter of informed and prudent speculation. A year later

---

[71] See *Mavrommatis Palestine Concessions, Judgment No. 2, 1924, P.C.I.J., Series A, No. 2*, p. 19.

[72] *Land and Maritime Boundary between Cameroon and Nigeria, Preliminary Objections, Judgment, I.C.J Reports 1998*, p. 303, para. 56.

Nicaragua had to make the judgement call, before Colombia's acceptance of the Pact of Bogotá expired, as to whether this dispute could be settled by negotiation or whether it needed to go to the Court. And Nicaragua was convinced that it could not be settled by negotiation.

53. Three years down the road, when Colombia's repudiatory acts that began the dispute are being continued and reaffirmed *after* the initiation of the case, and there has been no sign of any ability to settle even this *case* — let alone settle the broader *dispute* — by negotiation, the position must surely be clear.

54. If this dispute could be settled by negotiation, Nicaragua would have been settling it by negotiation. At the time of the Application, there seemed no hope of a negotiated settlement; and no such settlement has emerged as a possibility since then. If that possibility should emerge in the future, the case could be terminated.

55. The fourth section in Chapter Two of Nicaragua's Memorial sets out details of what is called — perhaps immodestly, but certainly accurately — Nicaragua's restraint. It explains Nicaragua's declarations of its willingness to allow the continuation of traditional artisanal fishing by Colombian fishermen in Nicaraguan waters[73]. It refers to Nicaragua's offer to sit down with Colombia and work out co-operative arrangements for the implementation of the Court's Judgment[74]. And, specifically addressing what appears to be Colombia's main political difficulty in accepting the Court's Judgment, Nicaragua has offered to conclude a bilateral treaty with Colombia to establish the new maritime boundary[75].

56. Have these offers succeeded in resolving the dispute? Obviously not. Have these offers opened up a conversation that might in time produce a solution? No. Did Colombia even *respond* to any of these offers? Well, I leave our friends on the other side to tell you the answer to that question.

57. It is one thing to raise jurisdictional objections to the consideration of an application by the Court. But if an objection is based upon an assertion that a dispute can be settled by direct negotiation, there needs to be some evidence to support it.

---

[73]MN, para. 2.54.

[74]*Ibid.*, para. 2.55.

[75]*Ibid.*, paras. 2.58-2.60.

58. As our Agent has indicated, Nicaragua has been — and still remains — willing to conclude a treaty implementing the Court's Judgment, if that would assist the domestic implementation of the Judgment by Colombia. Nicaragua is also open to make some adaptations to the régime applicable in the areas recognized by the Court to belong to it. But Nicaragua is not willing to change the limits of the area in question; and it is clear that Colombia does not accept those limits and demands a modification of the areas as recognized by the Court. In the *Mavrommatis* case[76] the Court noted that there are disputes where it quickly becomes evident that a deadlock is reached or one of the parties is unable, or refuses, to give way so that there can be no doubt that the dispute cannot be settled by diplomatic negotiation. And this is just such a case.

59. Mr. President, Members of the Court, that concludes my part of the submissions in this round. I thank you for your patience and unless there is any further assistance that I can give you I would ask that you call upon my friend and colleague, Professor Alain Pellet, who will continue Nicaragua's submissions in this round.

Le PRESIDENT : Je vous remercie, Monsieur le professeur, je donne la parole au professeur Alain Pellet.

M. PELLET : Merci beaucoup, Monsieur le président.

COMPÉTENCE INHÉRENTE

1. La pluralité des bases de compétence

1. Monsieur le président, Mesdames et Messieurs les juges, mes collègues ont montré que le refus par la Colombie de respecter votre arrêt du 19 novembre 2012 au mépris du principe de la *res judicata* avait résulté en un différend portant sur le respect des droits souverains du Nicaragua dans certaines zones maritimes de la mer des Caraïbes, que ce différend n'avait pas pu être réglé par la voie de négociations et que la Cour avait compétence pour en connaître en vertu de l'article XXXI du pacte de Bogotá.

2. Comme le dit la sagesse populaire «abondance de biens ne nuit pas» et ce n'est pas parce que la Cour a juridiction sur ce fondement qu'une autre base de compétence ne peut être invoquée

[76] *Mavrommatis Palestine Concessions, Objection to the Jurisdiction of the Court, Judgment, P.C.I.J., Series A, No. 2,* p. 13, and cf. p. 15.

par l'Etat requérant et retenue par elle. Et, depuis la ferme position prise par la Cour permanente dans l'affaire de la *Compagnie d'électricité de Sofia*, la pratique de votre haute juridiction est bien établie et constante : lorsqu'une partie invoque deux bases de juridiction distinctes «[l]e résultat négatif obtenu par l'examen du premier chef de compétence ne dispense cependant pas la Cour de procéder à l'examen de l'autre chef de compétence invoqué à titre distinct et indépendant du premier»[77]. Vous avez procédé de la même façon à maintes reprises :

— dans l'affaire des *Activités militaires et paramilitaires* en 1984[78] ;

— dans celle du *Génocide* entre la Bosnie-Herzégovine et la Serbie[79];

— dans celle des *Activités armées sur le territoire du Congo*[80] ; ou

— dans votre arrêt de 2007 dans *Nicaragua c. Colombie*[81].

3. Bien sûr, si les deux bases de compétence ont la même portée, il est inutile de poursuivre l'examen dès lors que l'une est retenue[82] — sans qu'il y ait de raisons particulières de donner à l'une priorité sur l'autre : cela relève du choix discrétionnaire de la Cour, qui voudra peut-être se fonder sur celle qui recueillerait le plus grand nombre de suffrages. Encore n'est-ce pas complétement évident puisque, dans *Nicaragua c. Etats-Unis* par exemple, la Cour a commencé par affirmer sa compétence, par onze voix contre cinq, sur le fondement des déclarations facultatives faites par les Parties en vertu de l'article 36 du Statut, puis, par 14 voix contre deux, elle a estimé qu'elle avait compétence pour connaître de la requête nicaraguayenne sur la base de l'article XXIV du traité bilatéral d'amitié, de commerce et de navigation conclu en 1956 entre les Parties[83]. Mais cela s'expliquait sans doute par le fait que malgré l'approbation très large que recueillait cette base de compétence conventionnelle, qui ne tombait manifestement pas sous le

---

[77] *Compagnie d'électricité de Sofia et de Bulgarie, arrêt, 1939, C.P.J.I. série A/B nº 77*, p. 80.

[78] *Activités militaires et paramilitaires au Nicaragua et contre celui-ci (Nicaragua c. Etats-Unis d'Amérique), compétence et recevabilité, arrêt, C.I.J. Recueil 1984*, p. 426, par. 77.

[79] *Application de la convention pour la prévention et la répression du crime de génocide (Bosnie-Herzégovine c. Yougoslavie), mesures conservatoires, ordonnance du 13 septembre 1993, C.I.J. Recueil 1993*, p. 338-341, par. 28-32.

[80] *Activités armées sur le territoire du Congo (nouvelle requête : 2002) (République démocratique du Congo c. Rwanda), compétence et recevabilité, arrêt, C.I.J. Recueil 2006*, p. 21, par. 26.

[81] *Différend territorial et maritime (Nicaragua c. Colombie), exceptions préliminaires, arrêt, C.I.J. Recueil 2007 (II)*, p. 873, par. 135.

[82] Cf. *Actions armées frontalières et transfrontalières (Nicaragua c. Honduras), compétence et recevabilité, arrêt, C.I.J. Recueil 1988*, p. 90, par. 48 et *Questions concernant l'obligation de poursuivre ou d'extrader (Belgique c. Sénégal), arrêt, C.I.J. Recueil 2012 (II)*, p. 448, par. 63.

[83] *Activités militaires et paramilitaires au Nicaragua et contre celui-ci (Nicaragua c. Etats-Unis d'Amérique), compétence et recevabilité, arrêt, C.I.J. Recueil 1984*, p. 442, par. 113.

coup de la réserve américaine relative aux traités multilatéraux[84], cette base de compétence n'en était pas moins plus restreinte que celle résultant de la coïncidence des deux déclarations facultatives. D'ailleurs, dans le dispositif de son arrêt de 1984, la Cour précise qu'elle ne retient cette seconde base de compétence «à première vue plus étroite dans sa portée» que «dans la mesure où [la requête] se rapporte à un différend concernant l'interprétation ou l'application» de ce traité[85].

4. Il n'en va pas de même dans notre espèce. Certes, dans l'abstrait, l'article XXXI du pacte de Bogotá confère à la Cour une compétence équivalente à celle résultant de déclarations facultatives concordantes et dépourvues de réserves[86]. Celle reposant sur la nature judiciaire de la Cour -- sur laquelle je vais m'attarder un peu ce matin -- est plus étroite car elle ne peut s'exercer que pour régler le différend entre les Parties résultant de la non-exécution de l'arrêt par celle qui a succombé. Toutefois, aux fins de notre affaire, les deux chefs de compétence se recouvrent complètement puisque le différend entre le Nicaragua et la Colombie a son origine dans le refus de celle-ci d'exécuter votre arrêt de 2012, ce qui prive le Nicaragua de la possibilité d'exercer les droits souverains et la juridiction lui appartenant dans la zone économique exclusive ou sur le plateau continental, délimités par la frontière maritime unique dont vous avez partiellement décidé le tracé.

5. Les deux chefs de compétence invoqués par le Nicaragua vous permettent donc l'un et l'autre de connaître dans son intégralité de l'affaire qu'il vous a soumise. Vous pouvez donc, Mesdames et Messieurs de la Cour, vous fonder indifféremment sur l'un ou sur l'autre ou vous appuyer, pour surplus de droit, sur l'un *et* l'autre, pour rejeter les exceptions préliminaires soulevées par la Colombie. Mon collègue et ami Antonio Remiro Brotóns a montré que votre compétence sur la base du pacte de Bogotá ne faisait pas de doute. Je me propose d'établir qu'il en va de même en ce qui concerne votre compétence inhérente, telle qu'elle découle de la qualité d'organe judiciaire de la Cour.

---

[84] *Activités militaires et paramilitaires au Nicaragua et contre celui-ci (Nicaragua c. Etats-Unis d'Amérique), compétence et recevabilité, arrêt, C.I.J. Recueil 1984*, p. 426, par. 77.

[85] *Ibid.*, p. 442, par. 113.1) *b)*.

[86] *Actions armées frontalières et transfrontalières (Nicaragua c. Honduras), compétence et recevabilité, arrêt, C.I.J. Recueil 1988*, p. 84, par. 33.

2. Ce qui n'est pas l'objet de la requête

6. Avant d'entrer dans le vif du sujet, Monsieur le président, je crois important de préciser à nouveau que, contrairement à ce que la Colombie voudrait faire croire[87], le Nicaragua ne recherche ni la révision, ni l'interprétation de votre arrêt de 2012, ce qu'il aurait pu faire sur la base des compétences — explicites — que les articles 60 et 61 du Statut confèrent à la Cour. Mais tel n'est en aucune manière l'objet de la présente instance :

— il ne s'agit évidemment pas de réviser votre décision : le Nicaragua vous demande au contraire, sinon d'en assurer l'application, du moins de tirer les conséquences de sa *non*-application ;

— il ne s'agit pas davantage d'interprétation : la Colombie ne saurait invoquer une quelconque obscurité de l'arrêt pour ne pas l'appliquer (elle ne le fait d'ailleurs pas) : même s'il ne procède pas à la délimitation complète des espaces maritimes relevant de la juridiction respective des Parties, votre arrêt est parfaitement clair en ce qui concerne ceux qu'elle délimite.

3. L'objet de la requête

7. Le Nicaragua vous prie en revanche, Mesdames et Messieurs les juges, de bien vouloir faire deux choses : d'une part, constater que la Colombie ne s'est pas acquittée de ses obligations claires en vertu de l'arrêt et que, malgré ses dénégations, elle refuse de le faire. Et, *d'autre part*, il vous demande de tirer les conséquences de ce refus, dans la mesure où elles relèvent de votre compétence.

8. Ce «d'autre part» est important, Mesdames et Messieurs de la Cour : s'il ne s'agissait que de constater le manquement (évident et avéré) de la Colombie aux obligations découlant de l'arrêt, celle-ci pourrait soutenir que la requête du Nicaragua est irrecevable car elle reviendrait à demander à la Cour de confirmer le caractère *res judicata* de l'arrêt de 2012. Si l'on en restait là, on peut penser que nous n'en serions guère avancés — encore que la satisfaction soit une forme de réparation qui peut être considérée comme appropriée en l'occurrence[88].

9. Au bénéfice de ces précisions, j'en viens donc à la compétence inhérente de la Cour pour tirer les conséquences — en tout cas, *certaines* conséquences -- d'un refus d'exécution de l'un de ses arrêts.

---

[87] Voir notamment, EPC, par. 5.9-5.11 et 6.14-6.15.

[88] Voir *infra*, par. 38.

4. La notion d'inhérence

10. Je n'ignore évidemment pas, Monsieur le président, que cette compétence inhérente est parfois contestée — et d'abord bien sûr par nos contradicteurs. Mais c'est pour de mauvaises raisons qui, si vous les reteniez, reviendraient à admettre que la Cour, pourtant «organe judiciaire principal des Nations Unies», n'aurait pas tous les attributs inhérents à cette qualité. Après l'avoir montré, je m'attacherai à établir que, contrairement aux assertions de la Colombie[89], cela n'est nullement la conséquence des caractères propres à la juridiction internationale — consensualisme et absence de force exécutoire des décisions. Au contraire, refuser le caractère inhérent des compétences de la Cour dans un cas de ce genre serait totalement incompatible avec ces spécificités.

11. Assurément, Monsieur le président, «*there is nothing in the Statute or the Rules of the Court to authorize 'inherent' jurisdiction*»[90]. Ni le Statut, ni le pacte de Bogotá ne prévoient expressément que la Cour est compétente pour se prononcer sur les suites données (ou non) à ses arrêts. S'il en allait ainsi, il s'agirait d'une compétence non pas inhérente mais explicite. M. de La Palice, qui était toujours vivant lorsqu'il n'était pas encore mort, n'aurait pas dit mieux.

[Projection n° 1 (animation) – Affaires des *Essais nucléaires* (1974), par. 20 et 23]

12. C'est sans doute dans les affaires des *Essais nucléaires* que la Cour a donné la définition la plus générale de cette notion de pouvoir inhérent. «Pouvoir» ou «compétence» ? Mon contradicteur et ami Tullio Treves a dit que la différence était «subtile»[91]. Elle l'est trop pour moi et la vérité me semble être surtout que la Cour utilise assez indifféremment les deux expressions «compétence» ou «pouvoir inhérent» (tout comme «*inherent jurisdiction*» *or* «*inherent power*»[92]). Il «*découle de l'existence même de la Cour, organe judiciaire établi par le consentement des Etats, et lui est conféré afin que sa fonction judiciaire fondamentale puisse être sauvegardée*»[93]. La

---

[89] EPC, par. 6.10-6.11 et 6.14.

[90] EPC, par. 5.6. Voir MN, par. 1.24-1.26 ; EEN, par. 5.10-5.13.

[91] CR 2015/22, p. 60, par. 3 (M. Treves).

[92] Voir d'ailleurs *ibid.* la note de bas de page n° 142 citant l'exemple contraire à sa thèse : «*LaGrand (Allemagne* c. *Etats-Unis d'Amérique), arrêt, C.I.J. Recueil 2001*, p. 483, par. 44 et le mémoire de la République fédérale d'Allemagne dans cette affaire, par. 3.02.

[93] *Essais nucléaires (Australie c. France), arrêt, C.I.J. Recueil 1974*, p. 259, par. 23 ; *Essais nucléaires (Nouvelle-Zélande c. France), arrêt, C.I.J. Recueil 1974*, p. 463, par. 23.

Colombie se plaint que nous ayons cité ceci hors contexte[94] et elle désapprouve la comparaison que nous avons faite entre notre affaire et celles jugées en 1974 avec leur codicille de 1995[95]. Je reviendrai plus tard sur ce dernier aspect. Pour l'instant : intéressons-nous au contexte de la citation.

13. Voici donc le début de celle-ci :

> «A cet égard, il convient de souligner que la Cour possède un pouvoir inhérent qui «l'autorise à prendre toute mesure voulue», d'une part pour faire en sorte que, si sa compétence au fond est établie, l'exercice de cette compétence ne se révèle pas vain, *d'autre part* «pour assurer le règlement régulier de tous les points en litige» ainsi que le respect des «limitations inhérentes à l'exercice de la fonction judiciaire» de la Cour et pour «conserver son caractère judiciaire.» (*Cameroun septentrional, arrêt, C.I.J. Recueil 1963*, p. 29.) Un pouvoir inhérent de ce genre, sur la base duquel la Cour est pleinement habilitée à adopter toute conclusion éventuellement nécessaire aux fins qui viennent d'être indiquées, découle...»[96] -- et puis on a le texte que je vous ai lu tout à l'heure.

N'en déplaise à nos amis de l'autre côté de la barre, qui oublient un peu légèrement le «d'autre part» de la citation projetée en ce moment[97], «l'inhérence» ne se limite nullement à ce qui se passe «en aval», une fois la compétence de la Cour établie ; elle vise, d'une façon générale, à conserver à la Cour son caractère judiciaire. C'est vrai de ses pouvoirs comme de leurs limitations.

[Fin de la projection n° 1.]

14. De plus, comme vous l'avez affirmé, par exemple dans l'affaire de la *Compétence en matière de pêcheries* de 1974 (une grande année pour la compétence inhérente !), vous êtes compétents pour connaître d'une conclusion qui «se fonde sur des faits postérieurs au dépôt de la requête, mais découlant directement de la question qui fait l'objet de cette requête»[98]. Il s'agit là du «prolongement» nécessaire de votre compétence découlant de la qualité d'organe judiciaire de la Cour qui, à ce titre, doit vider complètement les différends qui lui sont soumis afin, pour reprendre votre formule dans cette même affaire, «de considérer le différend sous tous ses aspects»[99]. Encore

---

[94] Voir EPC, par. 5.15.

[95] *Ibid.*, par. 5.16-5.18.

[96] *Essais nucléaires (Australie c. France), arrêt, C.I.J. Recueil 1974*, p. 259, par. 20 ; *Ibid.(Nouvelle-Zélande c. France)*, p. 463, par. 23 -- les italiques sont de nous.

[97] Voir EPC, par. 5.15-5.18 ; CR 2015/22, p. 62-63, par. 12 (M. Treves).

[98] *Compétence en matière de pêcheries (République fédérale d'Allemagne c. Islande), fond, arrêt, C.I.J. Recueil 1974*, p. 203, par. 72 ; voir aussi *LaGrand (Allemagne c. Etats-Unis d'Amérique), arrêt, C.I.J. Recueil 2001*, p. 483-484, par. 45.

[99] *Ibid.*, p. 190, par. 40.

plus frappante est la compétence que vous vous êtes reconnue pour vous prononcer sur la responsabilité d'un Etat qui ne respecterait pas une ordonnance en indication de mesures conservatoires. Le Statut de la Cour ne le prévoit nullement mais, parce qu'elle est un organe judiciaire,

> «[l]orsque la Cour a compétence pour trancher un différend, elle a également compétence pour se prononcer sur les conclusions la priant de constater qu'une ordonnance en indication de mesures conservatoires rendue aux fins de préserver les droits des Parties à ce différend n'a pas été exécutée»[100] (affaire *LaGrand*).

Il s'agit là encore d'un pouvoir inhérent, déduit de la qualité d'organe judiciaire de la Cour et nullement d'une compétence expressément prévue par le Statut ou par un autre texte. Et je continue à ne pas voir pourquoi ce qui vaut pour les mesures conservatoires que vous «indiquez» ne vaudrait point pour les arrêts définitifs et sans recours que vous rendez : dans les deux cas, votre pouvoir inhérent se greffe sur une compétence explicite : d'une part, celle d'indiquer des mesures conservatoires comme le prévoit l'article 41 du Statut ; d'autre part, celle de rendre des arrêts obligatoires, définitifs et sans recours pour les Parties en litige en vertu des articles 59 et 60.

15. Et, pour en finir avec ces généralités sur votre compétence inhérente (et ses limites), Mesdames et Messieurs les juges, j'ajoute qu'elles ne dépendent pas de la volonté des parties, qui ne peuvent les manipuler à leur gré — même si elles le souhaitaient d'un commun accord.

«Il y a», avez-vous dit, dans *Cameroun septentrional*

> «des limitations inhérentes à l'exercice de la fonction judiciaire dont la Cour, en tant que tribunal, doit toujours tenir compte. Il peut ainsi y avoir incompatibilité entre, d'un côté, les désirs d'un demandeur ou même des deux parties à une instance et, de l'autre, le devoir de la Cour de conserver son caractère judiciaire. C'est à la Cour elle-même et non pas aux parties qu'il appartient de veiller à l'intégrité de la fonction judiciaire de la Cour»[101].

Ici encore, on voit mal pourquoi ce qui vaut pour les limitations inhérentes à l'exercice de votre compétence ne vaudrait pas pour votre compétence elle-même : en acceptant de vous saisir — ce qu'ils peuvent faire (ou refuser) librement, les Etats savent que vous êtes un organe judiciaire, que vous exercerez pleinement la compétence qui s'attache à votre qualité d'organe judiciaire. Il n'y a

---

[100] *LaGrand (Allemagne c. Etats-Unis d'Amérique), arrêt, C.I.J. Recueil 2001,* p. 484, par. 45 ; voir aussi : *Activités armées sur le territoire du Congo (République démocratique du Congo c. Ouganda), arrêt, C.I.J. Recueil 2005*, p. 258, par. 263.

[101] *Cameroun septentrional (Cameroun c. Royaume-Uni), exceptions préliminaires, arrêt, C.I.J. Recueil 1963*, p. 29.

rien là de contraire au principe du consentement à la juridiction — c'en est au contraire la conséquence.

5. Ce que la Cour avait refusé d'envisager

16. Monsieur le président, dans ses exceptions préliminaires, la Colombie fait fond[102] sur un article du juge Guillaume dans sa version anglaise. Comme cet article est issu d'une publication française originale, à l'exemple du professeur Treves, je citerai celle-ci pour ne pas faire offense à l'engagement francophone du grand juge. La Cour, écrivait-il, a

> «jugé à plusieurs reprises qu'elle ne pouvait, ni ne devait envisager l'inexécution de ses arrêts et ne s'est prononcée sur cette exécution que dans les cas où les Parties lui avaient donné spécifiquement compétence à cet effet. Ainsi, dans l'affaire opposant le Burkina Faso et le Mali pour la détermination de leur frontière terrestre, les deux Parties avaient demandé à la Chambre de la Cour saisie du dossier de désigner trois experts chargés de les assister dans la démarcation de la frontière ainsi fixée. La Chambre jugea que «rien dans le Statut de la Cour, ni dans la jurisprudence établie» ne s'oppose à ce «qu'elle exerce ce pouvoir» et elle désigna ces experts.
>
> Un tel exemple — c'est toujours le juge Guillaume qui parle — mérite d'être relevé, et l'on pourrait imaginer que dans d'autres cas les Etats parties à un différend confient par voie de compromis à la Cour certaines compétences en ce qui concerne l'exécution des jugements à intervenir. Les exemples conventionnels sont nombreux dans le domaine de l'arbitrage et pourraient aisément être transposés»[103].

17. Monsieur le président, je ne vois pas très bien, ce que la Colombie entend prouver à partir de cette citation. Assurément, ceci montre que les Parties à un différend porté devant la Cour ou tranché par elle, peuvent lui donner mission de contribuer à la mise en œuvre de ses arrêts. Ceci veut dire quoi ? Cela veut dire que le suivi de ses arrêts relève donc bien de la compétence inhérente de la Cour puisque, dans l'affaire *Burkina/Mali* par exemple, la chambre de la Cour accepte d'exercer la mission que lui confèrent les Parties alors même qu'elle constate que celles-ci lui demandent non pas d'appliquer une disposition du Statut de la Cour, «mais d'exercer un pouvoir qui lui est conféré par le compromis». Malgré ce silence du Statut, la Cour estime «que rien dans le Statut de la Cour ni dans la jurisprudence établie ne s'oppose à ce que la chambre exerce ce pouvoir, dont le but est précisément de permettre aux Parties de parvenir à un règlement

---

[102] Voir EPC, par. 6.14. Voir aussi CR 2015/22, p. 61, par. 6 (M. Treves).

[103] G. Guillaume, «De l'exécution des decisions de la Cour internationale de Justice », *Revue suisse de droit international* (1997), p. 438 (notes de bas de page omises) ou *in* G. Guillaume, *La Cour internationale de Justice à l'aube du XXI*[e] *siècle — Le regard d'un juge*, p. 179.

définitif de leur différend en application de l'arrêt qu'elle a rendu»[104]. Il est vrai que, dans le passage que je viens de citer, l'éminent auteur n'envisage son exercice que sur la base d'un accord des parties. Mais ceci parce que, comme l'a souvent répété la Cour elle-même — qu'il cite : elle «ne peut ni ne doit envisager l'éventualité que l'arrêt resterait inexécuté»[105].

6. Quand l'inenvisageable se produit...

18. Or, dans notre espèce, l'éventualité que la Cour se refusait à envisager s'est, incontestablement et très malheureusement, produite.

19. Contrairement aux affaires dans lesquelles votre haute juridiction s'est, très justement, refusée à indiquer, *en amont*, *ce qu'il conviendrait de faire* *si* *la Partie défenderesse* ne s'acquittait pas de ses obligations en vertu de l'arrêt à intervenir, il vous est demandé ici de tirer, *en aval*, les conséquences d'un refus clair et net, je dirais même d'un refus cynique, d'exécution d'un de vos arrêts définitifs. Ce refus a déjà largement été évoqué par notre agent et le professeur Vaughan Lowe, mais quelques exemples tout de même à titre de rappel : «[L]a Colombie, représentée par son chef d'Etat, rejette catégoriquement cet aspect de l'arrêt rendu aujourd'hui par la Cour»[106], «cet aspect» se rapporte à la délimitation maritime entre les deux Etats, ce qui n'est quand même pas un «aspect» secondaire de l'arrêt de 2012 ! Cette déclaration du président colombien lui-même, faite le jour même de la lecture de votre arrêt, a été confirmée on vous l'a dit, à maintes reprises depuis lors :

> «[L]'arrêt de la Cour internationale de Justice n'est pas applicable, et ne le sera pas, tant qu'un traité protégeant les droits des Colombiens n'aura pas été conclu et adopté conformément aux prescriptions de notre Constitution. Et je le redis : sans traité, l'arrêt de la Cour internationale de Justice n'est pas applicable.»[107]

---

[104] *Différend frontalier (Burkina Faso/République du Mali), désignation d'experts, C.I.J. Recueil 1987*, p. 8.

[105] *Activités militaires et paramilitaires au Nicaragua et contre celui-ci (Nicaragua c. Etats-Unis d'Amérique), compétence et recevabilité, arrêt, C.I.J. Recueil 1984*, p. 437, par. 101 (citant *Usine de Chorzów, demande d'indemnité, C.P.J.I.série A n° 17*, p. 63). Voir aussi *Demande en revision et en interprétation de l'arrêt du 24 février 1982 en l'affaire du* Plateau continental (Tunisie/Jamahiriya arabe libyenne) *(Tunisie c. Jamahiriya arabe libyenne), arrêt, C.I.J. Recueil 1985*, p. 229, par. 67 ; et *mutatis mutandis, Essais nucléaires (Australie c. France), arrêt, C.I.J. Recueil 1974*, p. 272, par. 60, et *Essais nucléaires (Nouvelle-Zélande c. France), arrêt, C.I.J. Recueil 1974*, p. 477, par. 63.

[106] Allocution du président Juan Manuel Santos concernant l'arrêt de la Cour internationale de Justice, 19 novembre 2012 (MN, annexe 1).

[107] Déclaration du président Juan Manuel Santos concernant la stratégie globale de la Colombie face à l'arrêt de la Cour internationale de Justice, 9 septembre 2013 (MN, annexe 4) ; voir aussi: présidence de la République de Colombie, communiqué de presse, «Les limites entre la Colombie et Nicaragua continuent d'être celles qui ont été établies dans le traité Esguerra-Barcenas, déclare le président de la Colombie», 2 mai 2014 (MN, annexe 7) ; ou «Santos garantit la continuité de sa politique extérieure à l'égard de l'Amérique latine», *America Economica*, 17 juin 2014 (MN, annexe 48).

Et, tout récemment, la gouverneure de San Andres en oublie même la porte de sortie entrouverte par le président Santos en affirmant : «Nous ne voulons pas appliquer cet arrêt parce que, pour le peuple de San Andres, il est impossible à appliquer.»[108] Et les militaires ne sont pas en reste, qui proclament haut et fort que les limites qu'ils attribuent aux zones sous juridiction colombienne sont restées inchangées après le 19 novembre 2012[109]. Des exemples de ces déclarations figurent sous l'onglet 30 de vos dossiers.

Et, dans ses exceptions préliminaires, la Colombie, tout en affirmant, contre toute raison, n'avoir pas pris la décision de refuser d'appliquer l'arrêt de la Cour, n'en n'explique pas moins : «However, in order to give effect to the Judgment in its domestic legal order (to make it «applicable»), it is necessary for Colombia to comply with the requirements of domestic law.»[110]

20. De l'art de souffler le chaud et le froid ! Du reste, à notre connaissance, la Colombie n'a pas fait quoi que ce soit dans son ordre interne en vue de se conformer à l'arrêt de 2012. Non seulement il n'est pas appliqué, mais encore tout donne à penser qu'il ne le sera délibérément pas et l'adoption du décret 1946 du 9 septembre 2013 rend sa mise en œuvre encore plus improbable. Nous sommes précisément, Monsieur le président, dans l'hypothèse que la Cour s'était, jusqu'à présent, refusée à envisager : celle d'un arrêt restant inexécuté[111].

7. La jurisprudence bien établie des juridictions internationales

21. Dans ce cas de figure — heureusement sans précédent —, la compétence pour tirer les conséquences d'un tel refus est inhérente, en ce sens qu'elle est inéluctablement liée à la notion même d'organe judiciaire dont les décisions, par définition, doivent être exécutées. C'est l'essence même du principe *res judicata* que rappellent les articles 59 et 60 de votre Statut. Et telle est la raison pour laquelle les juridictions internationales — et j'y insiste, Monsieur le président : les

---

[108] Ethel Bent, «Concern for New Defense in The Hague», *El Isleno*, 4 août 2015 (http://xn--elisleo-9za.com/index.php?option=com_content&view=article&id=9965:2015-08-04-15-15-32&catid=60:actualidad&Itemid=96) — ma traduction.

[109] «Our Maritime Jurisdiction has not changed: Rear Admiral Espejo», *El Colombiano*, 19 novembre 2014 (http://www.elcolombiano.com/nuestra-jurisdiccion-maritima-no-ha-cambiado-contralmirante-espejo-1-DC664410). Voir aussi par exemple : «Minister Luis Carlos Villegas makes a sovereignty visit to San Andres», *Colombia.com*, 26 juin 2015 (http://www.colombia.com/actualidad/nacionales/sdi/117892/ministro-luis-carlos-villegas-realiza-visita-de-soberania-a-san-andres).

[110] EPC, par. 2.24 ; voir aussi par. 2.43-2.46.

[111] Voir ci-dessus par. 17.

juridictions internationales, beaucoup plus nettement que les nationales, nous verrons dans quelques instants pourquoi — les juridictions internationales donc, ont considéré avec une belle unanimité, lorsque le problème s'est posé, qu'il leur appartenait de se prononcer sur les cas de non-application des décisions rendues par elles lorsqu'elles étaient saisies d'un tel problème.

22. Je ne vais pas passer en revue de manière complète cette jurisprudence malheureusement assez fournie. Juste quelques exemples :

23. A maintes reprises, en l'absence de toute disposition expresse de son statut, la Cour interaméricaine des droits de l'homme a considéré — comme ses arrêts ne sont pas traduits en français, je vais lire ces extraits assez longs en anglais — «[t]hat one of the inherent attributes of the jurisdictional functions of the Court is to monitor compliance with its decisions»[112]. Similarly, in this same Order, *Blake* v. *Guatemala* of November 27, 2003, the Court of San José de Costa Rica clarified its position as follows :

> «in view of the final and unappealable character of the judgments of the Court, as established in Article 67 of the American Convention, they should be complied with fully and promptly.
>
> Article 68(1) of the American Convention stipulates that «[t]he States Parties to the Convention undertake to comply with the judgment of the Court in any case to which they are parties». The treaty obligations of the States Parties are binding for all the powers and functions of the States.
>
> [T]he obligation to comply with the provisions of the Court's judgments corresponds to a basic principle of the law of the international responsibility of the State, supported by international case law, according to which, a State must comply with its international treaty obligations in good faith *(pacta sunt servanda)* and, as this Court has already indicated and as established in Article 27 of the 1969 Vienna Convention on the Law of Treaties, a party may not invoke the provisions of its internal law as justification for its failure to perform a treaty.»[113]

Ces explications ont été reprises dans des termes très voisins dans plusieurs arrêts de la Cour interaméricaine[114] — vous trouverez, Mesdames et Messieurs les juges, plusieurs extraits pertinents sous l'onglet 31 de votre dossier. Ces explications sont en tous points pertinentes s'agissant de la CIJ dont, tout comme ceux de la Cour interaméricaine, les arrêts sont obligatoires pour les parties

---

[112] *Blake c. Guatemala, ordonnance du 27 novembre 2003*, Cour interaméricaine des droits de l'homme (CIADH), par. 1 ; voir aussi *Garrido et Baigorria c. Argentine, ordonnance du 27 novembre 2007*, CIADH, par. 1, ou *La Prison Miguel Castro Castro c. Peru, ordonnance du 31 mars 2014*, CIADH, par. 2.

[113] *Blake c. Guatemala, ordonnance du 27 novembre 2003*, CIADH, par. 3-5.

[114] Voir notamment *Garrido et Baigorria c. Argentine, ordonnance du 27 novembre 2007*, CIADH, par. 3-5 et *La Prison Miguel Castro Castro c. Peru, ordonnance du 31 mars 2014*, CIADH, par. 2-3.

en litige (ce que précise l'article 59 du Statut), définitifs et sans recours (art. 60), et auxquels chaque membre des Nations Unies s'est engagé à se conformer en vertu de l'article 94, paragraphe 1, de la Charte. Et, bien sûr, la Charte et le Statut relèvent du droit des traités et doivent être appliqués de bonne foi comme l'exige l'article 26 de la convention de Vienne de 1969, sans que les parties puissent «invoquer les dispositions de leur droit interne comme justifiant [leur] non-exécution» (article 27 de la même convention).

24. La Cour européenne des droits de l'homme n'est pas en reste. Selon une formule maintes fois reprises : «L'exécution d'un jugement ou arrêt, *de quelque juridiction que ce soit*, doit ... être considérée comme faisant partie intégrante du «procès» au sens de l'article 6.»[115] L'article 6 de la convention européenne est celui qui porte sur le procès équitable. Les êtres humains y ont droit ; les Etats aussi.

25. Dans un contexte un peu différent — mais toujours international -- les tribunaux administratifs internationaux affirment et justifient également leur compétence inhérente pour se prononcer sur des incidents d'exécution de leurs jugements, et ceci en l'absence de toute clause de juridiction expresse dans leur statut respectif. Ainsi, dans un jugement *Lindsey* de 1965, qui a fait jurisprudence, le Tribunal administratif de l'OIT a considéré :

> «Les trois chefs de demande [du requérant] tendent à obtenir la réparation du préjudice subi par le sieur Lindsey du fait du retard mis par l'UIT à exécuter l'article 7 du dispositif du jugement précité [c'était le jugement n° 61]. Ils portent ainsi sur des droits tirés directement de ce jugement, prononcé dans le cadre de la compétence du Tribunal. Ainsi [c'est le seul fondement] le Tribunal est compétent pour examiner la nouvelle requête du sieur Lindsey, et notamment pour apprécier s'il y a lieu d'accorder une indemnité en réparation du dommage né d'une violation de ces droits.»[116]

Et, comme l'a noté cette même juridiction dans une décision plus récente :

---

[115] Cour européenne des droits de l'homme (CEDH), arrêt du 19 mars 1997, *Hornsby c. Grèce*, requête n° 18357/91, par. 40 — les italiques sont de nous ; voir aussi CEDH, arrêt du 28 juillet 1999, *Immobiliare Saffi c. Italie*, requête n° 22774/93, par. 6 ; arrêt du 27 mai 2004, *Metaxas c. Grèce*, requête n° 8415/02, par. 25 ; arrêt du 11 janvier 2005, *Dubenko c. Ukraine*, requête n° 74221/01, par. 44 et arrêt du 29 mars 2006, *Cocchiarella c. Italie*, requête n° 64886/01, par. 87.

[116] Tribunal administratif de l'Organisation internationale du Travail (TAOIT), jugement n° 82 du 10 avril 1965, *Lindsey c. UIT*, par. 1 ; voir aussi : jugements n° 649 du 18 mars 1985, *Ali Khan c. OIT*, par. 4 ; n° 1620 du 10 juillet 1997, *Moreno de Gomez (n° 2) c. UNESCO*, par. 2 ; ou n° 2327 du 14 juillet 2004, *M. J. M. B. c. OPCW*. *Adde* ; Tribunal d'appel des Nations Unies (TANU), jugement n° 517 du 29 mai 1991, *Van Branteghem*, par. I ; ou TABM, jugement n° 21 du 22 mars 1985, *Martial M.M. van Gent (n° 6) c. BIRD*, par. 3.

> «la jurisprudence du Tribunal est constante sur ce point : toute difficulté sérieuse tenant à l'exécution d'un jugement peut valablement lui être présentée à l'occasion d'un recours en exécution»[117].

Et tout cela encore une fois, sans texte.

26. Dans *Saiga II*, le Tribunal international du droit de la mer n'a pas davantage hésité à reconnaître sa compétence pour se prononcer sur une demande invoquant l'inexécution de son arrêt antérieur concernant la prompte mainlevée du navire[118].

27. Dernier exemple, et pas le moindre, celui de la Cour de justice des Communautés européennes — des Communautés européennes et pas de l'Union — qui, en l'absence *alors* de toute disposition expresse des traités constitutifs, a semblé considérer qu'il allait de soi qu'elle avait compétence pour constater qu'en ne se conformant pas à un arrêt antérieur, un Etat membre avait manqué à ses obligations en vertu du traité de Rome et était responsable de ce fait[119]. Il y avait bien là l'exercice d'une compétence inhérente de la Cour, déduite des articles 169 et 171 du traité imposant aux Etats membres, d'une façon générale — mais seulement d'une façon générale —, de respecter leurs obligations en vertu du traité et les arrêts de la Cour. Le traité de Maastricht de 1992 a «conventionnalisé» cette jurisprudence en consacrant expressément la compétence de la Cour pour se prononcer sur la non-exécution de ses arrêts et en l'autorisant même à prononcer des astreintes contre les Etats concernés[120]. D'inhérente, la compétence de la Cour de justice de l'Union européenne pour se prononcer sur la non-exécution de ses arrêts est ainsi devenue expresse et statutaire.

28. Les mêmes raisons qui ont poussé les autres juridictions internationales à se reconnaître compétentes pour se prononcer sur les difficultés d'exécution de leurs arrêts même en l'absence (habituelle) de dispositions statutaires l'envisageant, valent pour votre haute juridiction, Mesdames et Messieurs de la Cour.

---

[117] TAOIT., jugement n° 2178 du 3 février 2003, *M. M. L. M. c. CICR*, par. 4.

[118] Voir Tribunal international du droit de la mer (TIDM), arrêt du 1er juillet 1999, *Affaire du navire «SAIGA» (No. 2) (Saint-Vincent-et-les Grenadines c. Guinée)*, par. 163-166.

[119] Cour de justice des Communautés européennes (CJCE), arrêt du 13 juillet 1972, *Commission c. Italie* (exécution de l'arrêt 7-68), *Rec.*, p. 533, par. 1 et p. 535, par. 10 ; voir aussi : CJCE., arrêts du 13 juillet 1988, *Commission c. France*, aff. 169/87, *Rec.*, p. 4115, par. 1 et p. 4118, par. 15, ou du 4 février 1988, *Commission c. Belgique*, affaire 391/85, *Rec.*, p. 597, par. 1 et p. 604, par. 29.

[120] Voir l'article 171 2) du traité sur l'Union européenne (7 février 1992) (aujourd'hui article 260 2) du traité sur le fonctionnement de l'Union européenne).

29. Nos contradicteurs opposent cependant à cette conclusion deux autres arguments qu'ils prétendent tirer des caractères propres à la Cour de céans :

— d'une part, la compétence inhérente pour se prononcer sur l'exécution de leurs arrêts ne siérait point aux juridictions internationales — parce qu'elles sont internationales ;

— d'autre part, l'exercice par la Cour de cette compétence serait incompatible avec le rôle que l'article 94, paragraphe 2, de la Charte et l'article L du pacte de Bogotá assignent au Conseil de sécurité et au comité des ministres de l'OEA.

8. Le caractère international de la CIJ rend particulièrement nécessaire l'exercice par la Cour de sa compétence inhérente

30. Je peux être très rapide sur le premier point, Monsieur le président : le fait que la Cour soit une juridiction *internationale*, loin d'exclure qu'elle ait une compétence inhérente aux fins de l'exécution de ses arrêts, en renforce au contraire la nécessité. Ce n'est assurément pas un hasard si ce sont les cours et tribunaux *internationaux* qui ont unanimement ou presque exercé leur compétence inhérente en la matière. S'agissant des juridictions nationales, c'est inutile : leurs décisions sont non seulement obligatoires ; elles sont en outre exécutoires. Il en résulte que l'exécution des décisions des juridictions nationales est le fait de la force publique, ce qui ne laisse guère de place à l'intervention des juridictions ayant adopté ces décisions.

31. Rien de tel dans l'ordre juridique international, dont les auteurs soulignent à l'envi le caractère décentralisé : hors l'hypothèse du chapitre VII de la Charte, c'est à chaque Etat qu'il revient d'assurer l'application du droit international en ce qui le concerne[121]. Lorsqu'un Etat s'y refuse, comme c'est le cas de la Colombie dans notre affaire, le droit international est désarmé. Mais laisser les choses en l'état serait contraire à l'idée même d'un organe *judiciaire*, doté du pouvoir d'adopter des arrêts s'imposant aux Parties. D'où l'inhérence de la compétence des juridictions internationales pour se prononcer sur les difficultés ou les refus d'exécution de leurs décisions.

32. Ceci étant, Mesdames et Messieurs les juges, si le Nicaragua vous demande de bien vouloir reconnaître que vous avez une compétence inhérente à cet égard et de l'exercer, il reconnaît

[121] Voir, par exemple, l'affaire du *Lac Lanoux (Espagne/France)*, sentence du 16 novembre 1957, Nations Unies, *Recueil des sentences arbitrales (RSA)*, vol. XII, p. 310.

évidemment que, en l'exerçant, vous devez aussi respecter les limitations, tout aussi inhérentes, qui résultent de votre qualité d'organe judiciaire. En d'autres termes, il vous appartient de dire le droit, de vous prononcer sur les conséquences de la responsabilité nouvelle qui découle, pour la Colombie, de son refus de mettre en œuvre votre arrêt de 2012 ; mais vous ne sauriez, ce faisant, faire exécuter concrètement votre décision ainsi rejetée par l'Etat défendeur en actionnant une «force publique internationale» — qui n'existe à l'évidence pas.

9. L'article 94 de la Charte ne constitue pas un obstacle à l'exercice par la Cour de sa compétence inhérente

[Projection n° 2 : article 94, paragraphe 2, de la Charte des Nations Unies.]

33. Et c'est aussi en cela que votre intervention ne saurait, d'aucune manière, se confondre avec celle que le paragraphe 2 de l'article 94 de la Charte réserve au Conseil de sécurité. Aux termes de cette disposition :

> «Si une partie à un litige ne satisfait pas aux obligations qui lui incombent en vertu d'un arrêt rendu par la Cour, l'autre partie peut recourir au Conseil de sécurité et celui-ci, s'il le juge nécessaire, peut faire des recommandations ou décider des mesures à prendre pour faire exécuter l'arrêt.»

34. Il s'agit là, Monsieur le président, d'une disposition dont la mise en œuvre est particulièrement aléatoire. Nous sommes fort près du degré zéro de l'obligatoriété :

— «l'autre *peut* recourir au Conseil de sécurité» : rien à redire, ceci est conforme au principe consensuel — et la Cour ne peut davantage se saisir elle-même ;

— «et celui-ci *s'il le juge nécessaire*» : il peut donc ne pas juger nécessaire de faire respecter la qualité d'organe judiciaire de la Cour et accepter la non-exécution de ses arrêts ;

— pour y pallier le Conseil peut se borner à «faire *des recommandations*» — recommander donc de faire ce qui est absolument obligatoire ;

— «ou» — mais seulement *«ou»* — «décider des mesures à prendre *pour faire exécuter l'arrêt*».

[Fin de la projection n° 2.]

35. Au fond, Monsieur le président, tout ce que j'ai dit sur la «mollesse» de cette disposition de la Charte est un peu inutilement professoral et je vous prie de bien vouloir m'en excuser. Car finalement, ce n'est que ce dernier point qui importe : le Conseil de sécurité, *contrairement à la Cour*, a des pouvoirs *d'exécution*. Il ne les a jamais mis en œuvre — et pour une fort bonne

raison : sauf dans un cas que le Nicaragua connaît particulièrement bien ![122], aucun Etat ne le lui a jamais demandé ; c'est qu'en règle générale, Mesdames et Messieurs les juges, vos arrêts sont très remarquablement respectés[123]. Au surplus, la question se pose de savoir si le Conseil pourrait décider de mesures coercitives pour faire exécuter un arrêt de la Cour en l'absence de menace contre la paix[124]. Peu importe en la présente occurrence d'ailleurs puisque, pour l'instant en tout cas, le Nicaragua a choisi de ne pas saisir le Conseil de sécurité.

36. Mais il a saisi la Cour et il l'a fait avec la conviction que son rôle ne se confond pas avec celui du Conseil de sécurité. Comme vous l'avez excellemment dit et répété : «Le Conseil a des attributions politiques ; la Cour exerce des fonctions purement judiciaires. Les deux organes peuvent donc s'acquitter de leurs fonctions distinctes mais complémentaires à propos des mêmes événements.»[125] Au surplus, s'agissant des problèmes liés à l'inexécution des arrêts de la Cour, on peut ajouter que le Conseil a une fonction exécutoire facultative alors que la Cour est appelée à se prononcer sur les conséquences de la non-exécution au plan de la responsabilité de l'Etat concerné, ce qui entre pleinement dans vos compétences.

37. Car, Monsieur le président, c'est de cela — et de cela seulement qu'il s'agit : en ne se conformant pas à un arrêt de la Cour, l'Etat commet un manquement aux obligations qui découlent de cet arrêt. Ce manquement est un fait internationalement illicite qui, comme toute violation du droit, engage la responsabilité de son auteur[126].

38. Dans votre arrêt de 2012, vous aviez refusé — je le reconnais, sans beaucoup de surprise[127] — de considérer que la responsabilité de la Colombie était engagée du fait de ses activités dommageables pour le Nicaragua dans les zones maritimes dont vous aviez reconnu

---

[122] Voir la lettre de la représentante permanente du Nicaragua auprès des Nations Unies en date du 17 octobre 1986 (doc. S/18415).

[123] R. Kolb, *The International Court of Justice*, Hart Publishing, 2013, p. 831-832.

[124] Voir notamment K. Oellers-Frahm, «Article 94 UN Charter », in *The Statute of the International Court of Justice. A Commentary*, OUP, 2012, p. 199-200 et, dans le même ouvrage, C. Brown, «Article 59», p. 1443 et R. Kolb, *The International Court of Justice*, Hart Publishing, 2013, p. 848-854.

[125] *Activités militaires et paramilitaires au Nicaragua et contre celui-ci (Nicaragua c. Etats-Unis d'Amérique), compétence et recevabilité, arrêt, C.I.J. Recueil 1984*, p. 435, par. 95 ; voir aussi *Application de la convention pour la prévention et la répression du crime de génocide (Bosnie-Herzégovine c. Yougoslavie), mesures conservatoires, ordonnance du 8 avril 1993, C.I.J. Recueil 1993*, p. 19, par. 33.

[126] Voir le commentaire de l'article 3 du projet d'articles sur la responsabilité des Etats tel qu'adopté par la Commission du droit international en première lecture, par. 15), *Annuaire de la CDI*, 1973, vol. II, p. 184.

[127] Voir notamment *Frontière terrestre et maritime entre le Cameroun et le Nigéria (Cameroun c. Nigéria; Guinée équatoriale (intervenant)), arrêt, C.I.J. Recueil 2002*, p. 451-452, par. 315 et p. 452, par. 319.

qu'elles relevaient de la juridiction du Nicaragua[128]. Vous aviez considéré que la demande nicaraguayenne de réparation (sous forme d'une déclaration de la Cour) était intervenue «dans le cadre d'une instance concernant une frontière maritime qui n'a jamais été tracée auparavant. Le présent arrêt» -- celui de 2012 donc --, aviez-vous ajouté, «a pour effet de fixer la frontière maritime entre les deux Parties, le Nicaragua et la Colombie, dans l'ensemble de la zone pertinente»[129]. Mais cet arrêt a entraîné une novation juridique : dorénavant — sauf au-delà de la limite des 200 milles marins — les juridictions respectives des Parties sont fixées. En ne respectant pas l'arrêt de la Cour, la Colombie commet un double fait internationalement illicite : elle viole à la fois le principe même de l'autorité de la chose jugée et les droits du Nicaragua dans la zone délimitée. Ces violations engagent la responsabilité de l'Etat défendeur et vous êtes, Mesdames et Messieurs les juges, compétents pour en tirer les conséquences — contrairement au Conseil de sécurité, que l'on imagine mal décider de la forme et des modalités que devraient revêtir les réparations dues pour ces manquements.

[Projection n° 3 : Article L du pacte de Bogotá]

39. Quant à l'argument fondé sur l'article L du pacte de Bogotá, il n'ajoute rien à celui que la Colombie tente de tirer de l'article 94 de la Charte. Comme nous l'avons déjà souligné[130], l'article L instaure une procédure préalable à la saisine du Conseil de sécurité mais ce filtre concerne exclusivement le recours au Conseil ; ce n'est pas ce dont il s'agit en la présente occurrence.

[Fin de la projection n° 3]

10. Premières conclusions

40. Permettez-moi, Monsieur le président, je vous prie, de faire le point :

1) par définition, une compétence inhérente n'est pas expressément prévue ;
2) celle de la Cour pour se prononcer sur l'inexécution (ou la mauvaise exécution) de ses arrêts est la conséquence de sa qualité d'organe judiciaire ;

---

[128] *Différend territorial et maritime (Nicaragua c. Colombie), arrêt, C.I.J. Recueil 2012 (II)*, p. 718, par. 250.

[129] *Ibid.*

[130] Voir EEN, par. 5.28-5.33.

3) celle-ci implique en effet que ses décisions — et ses arrêts au moins autant que ses ordonnances en indication de mesures conservatoires — soient effectivement respectés ;

4) c'est parce qu'il n'existe pas de pouvoir exécutif centralisé dans l'ordre juridique international que les cours et tribunaux internationaux ont estimé, même sans texte, avoir une compétence inhérente pour se prononcer sur les difficultés d'exécution de leurs décisions ;

5) contrairement à ce que soutient la Colombie, le caractère international de la Cour est donc une raison — je dirais même la raison essentielle — qui justifie sa compétence pour tirer les conséquences du mépris dans lequel la Colombie tient votre arrêt du 19 novembre 2012 ;

6) ce faisant, votre haute juridiction, qui est appelée à exercer des compétences purement judiciaires, n'empiéterait nullement sur celle, exécutoire et aléatoire, conférée au Conseil de sécurité par l'article 94, paragraphe 2, de la Charte ; et

7) l'article L du pacte de Bogotá ne joue aucun rôle autonome à cet égard.

Mais il y a plus.

11. La Cour *a* d'ores et déjà exercé la compétence inhérente lui appartenant

41. Monsieur le président, j'ai donné, çà et là, au cours de ma présentation, des exemples montrant que la Cour elle-même s'est, en plusieurs occasions, fondée sur des compétences qu'elle a déduites de son Statut alors même qu'elles n'y sont pas énoncées[131]. Parmi celles-ci la plus notable, qui est aussi la plus proche de notre espèce, est celle que vous avez affirmée en matière de non-respect des mesures conservatoires que vous avez indiquées.

[Projection n° 4 : La jurisprudence *LaGrand*]

42. Dans l'affaire *LaGrand*, vous avez estimé que «[l]orsque la Cour a compétence pour trancher un différend» — compétence expresse découlant dans cette espèce de l'article 36, paragraphe 1, du Statut de la Cour et de l'article premier du protocole de signature facultative à la convention de Vienne sur les relations consulaires, «elle a également compétence pour se prononcer sur des conclusions la priant de constater qu'une ordonnance en indication de mesures rendue aux fins de préserver les droits des Parties à ce différend n'a pas été exécutée»[132]. Et il

---

[131] Voir par. 12-15 ci-dessus et par. 42-46 ci-dessous.

[132] Voir *LaGrand (Allemagne c. Etats-Unis d'Amérique), arrêt, C.I.J. Recueil 2001*, p. 484, par. 45.

s'agit là par contre d'une compétence implicite, inhérente, que la Cour a par ailleurs exercée dans toutes les affaires dans lesquelles le non-respect des ordonnances en indication de mesures conservatoires a été invoqué[133].

[Fin de la projection nº 4]

43. Monsieur le président, je l'ai déjà dit — et c'est une question de bon sens me semble-t-il : ce qui vaut pour de telles ordonnances, dont le caractère décisoire a, au demeurant, longtemps été douteux, vaut évidemment *a fortiori*, quoiqu'en pense le professeur Treves[134], s'agissant du refus d'exécution d'un arrêt «définitif et sans recours». Et d'ailleurs, Mesdames et Messieurs de la Cour, vous l'avez reconnu vous-même d'une manière tout à fait claire.

[Projection nº 5 : Les paragraphes 60 et 63 des arrêts de 1974 dans les affaires des *Essais nucléaires*]

44. Aux paragraphes 60 et 63 rédigés dans les mêmes termes des arrêts de 1974 dans les affaires relatives aux *Essais nucléaires* à la demande respectivement de l'Australie et de la Nouvelle-Zélande, vous avez

> «fait observer que, si le fondement du présent arrêt était remis en cause, le requérant pourrait demander un examen de la situation conformément aux dispositions du Statut ; la dénonciation par la France, dans une lettre du 2 janvier 1974, de l'Acte général pour le règlement pacifique des différends internationaux, qui est invoqué comme l'un des fondements de la compétence de la Cour en l'espèce, ne saurait en soi faire obstacle à la présentation d'une telle demande»[135].

Et il y a sûrement des points communs entre la dénonciation de l'Acte général par la France et la dénonciation du pacte de Bogotá par la Colombie.

En tout cas, c'est en invoquant ce paragraphe que la Nouvelle-Zélande a formé, en 1995, une requête en non-exécution contre la France[136]. Mais ce qui importe pour nous en ce moment ce n'est pas cette demande de la Nouvelle-Zélande, ce sont ces deux paragraphes eux-mêmes 60 et 63 des arrêts de 1974 et de se demander sur quel fondement la Cour a bien pu les adopter.

---

[133] Voir *Activités armées sur le territoire du Congo (République démocratique du Congo c. Ouganda), arrêt, C.I.J. Recueil 2005*, p. 258, par. 263.

[134] CR 2015/22, p. 64, par. 17-19 (M. Treves).

[135] *Essais nucléaires (Australie c. France), requête à fin d'intervention, ordonnance du 20 décembre 1974, C.I.J. Recueil 1974*, p. 272, par. 60 et *Essais nucléaires (Nouvelle-Zélande c. France), arrêt, C.I.J. Recueil 1974*, p. 477, par. 63.

[136] Voir *Demande d'examen de la situation au titre du paragraphe 63 de l'arrêt rendu par la Cour le 20 décembre 1974 dans l'affaire des* Essais nucléaires (Nouvelle-Zélande c. France) *(Nouvelle-Zélande c. France), ordonnance du 22 septembre 1995, C.I.J. Recueil 1995*, p. 288.

45. Dans un curieux passage de ses exceptions préliminaires, la Colombie affirme :

> «Indeed, the Nuclear Test cases confirm the well-established principle that the Court does not retain jurisdiction after a judgment on the subject-matter of the dispute unless the Court has expressly reserved jurisdiction over the case.»[137]

And further :

> «Read in their entirety, the judgments show that unless the Court expressly reserves its jurisdiction over a case, once it delivers its final judgment, the judgment is *res judicata*; there is no 'inherent jurisdiction' over that judgment in anticipation of what might subsequently occur.»[138]

46. Monsieur le président, cela revient à complètement occulter la véritable question ou, pour le dire familièrement, «c'est reculer pour mieux sauter»... Car tout de même, Monsieur le président, quel est le fondement de cette «réserve de compétence» ? Qu'est-ce qui a permis à la Cour d'adopter les deux paragraphes actuellement projetés ? Où cette réserve de compétence trouve-t-elle sa source dans le Statut ? Nulle part — si ce n'est dans la compétence inhérente appartenant à la Cour aux fins de préserver et d'assumer pleinement sa qualité d'organe judiciaire international.

[Fin de la projection nº 5]

47. Monsieur le président, Mesdames et Messieurs les juges, c'est cette compétence inhérente que le Nicaragua vous prie de bien vouloir exercer dans la présente affaire. Elle est la première qui vous en fournit l'occasion puisque, dans celle portée devant la Cour par la Nouvelle-Zélande, les conditions n'en n'étaient pas réunies[139]. Est-il besoin d'ajouter que le fait qu'il s'agit de la première occasion qui vous est donnée de vous prononcer sur ce point montre combien est artificiel l'épouvantail d'un dangereux précédent que brandit la Colombie[140].

48. Pour toutes ces raisons, le Nicaragua vous prie, Mesdames et Messieurs de la Cour, de rejeter les quatrième et cinquième exceptions préliminaires de la Colombie.

---

[137] EPC, par. 5.17.

[138] *Ibid.*

[139] *Demande d'examen de la situation au titre du paragraphe 63 de l'arrêt rendu par la Cour le 20 décembre 1974 dans l'affaire des* Essais nucléaires (Nouvelle-Zélande c. France) *(Nouvelle-Zélande c. France), ordonnance du 22 septembre 1995, C.I.J. Recueil 1995*, p. 306, par. 65.

[140] Voir CR 2015/22, p. 66, par. 27 (M. Treves).

10. Cette présentation clôt le premier tour de plaidoiries du Nicaragua. Je vous remercie très vivement de l'avoir patiemment écoutée.

Le PRESIDENT : Merci, Monsieur le professeur. Ceci met fin à l'audience d'aujourd'hui et clôt le premier tour de plaidoiries. La Cour se réunira de nouveau mercredi 30 septembre 2015, à 16 heures, pour entendre la Colombie en son second tour de plaidoiries. A l'issue de l'audience, la Colombie présentera ses conclusions finales.

Le Nicaragua prendra, pour sa part, la parole le vendredi 2 octobre, à 10 heures, pour son second tour de plaidoiries. A la fin de l'audience, il présentera à son tour ses conclusions finales.

Je rappellerai que, conformément au paragraphe 1 de l'article 60 du Règlement, les exposés oraux devront être aussi succincts que possible. J'ajouterai que le second tour de plaidoiries a pour objet de permettre à chacune des Parties de répondre aux arguments avancés oralement par l'autre ou aux questions posées par les membres de la Cour, le cas échéant. Le second tour ne doit donc pas constituer une répétition des présentations déjà faites par les Parties, qui ne sont, au demeurant, pas tenues d'utiliser l'intégralité du temps de parole qui leur est alloué. Je vous remercie. L'audience est levée.

L'audience est levée à 12 h 50.

____

Corrigé
Corrected

CR 2015/24

International Court of Justice

THE HAGUE

Cour internationale de Justice

LA HAYE

YEAR 2015

Public sitting

held on Wednesday 30 September 2015, at 4 p.m., at the Peace Palace,

President Abraham presiding,

***in the case concerning* Alleged Violations of Sovereign Rights and Maritime Spaces in the Caribbean Sea (Nicaragua *v.* Colombia)**

Preliminary Objections

VERBATIM RECORD

ANNÉE 2015

Audience publique

tenue le mercredi 30 septembre 2015, à 16 heures, au Palais de la Paix,

sous la présidence de M. Abraham, président,

***en l'affaire relative à des* Violations alléguées de droits souverains et d'espaces maritimes dans la mer des Caraïbes (Nicaragua c. Colombie)**

Exceptions préliminaires

COMPTE RENDU

Present:	President	Abraham
	Vice-President	Yusuf
	Judges	Owada
		Tomka
		Bennouna
		Cançado Trindade
		Greenwood
		Xue
		Gaja
		Sebutinde
		Bhandari
		Robinson
		Gevorgian
	Judges *ad hoc*	Daudet
		Caron
	Registrar	Couvreur

Présents :	M.	Abraham, président
	M.	Yusuf, vice-président
	MM.	Owada
		Tomka
		Bennouna
		Cançado Trindade
		Greenwood
	Mme	Xue
	M.	Gaja
	Mme	Sebutinde
	MM.	Bhandari
		Robinson
		Gevorgian, juges
	MM.	Daudet
		Caron, juges *ad hoc*
	M.	Couvreur, greffier

The Government of Nicaragua is represented by:

H.E. Mr. Carlos José Argüello Gómez, Ambassador of the Republic of Nicaragua to the Kingdom of the Netherlands,

as Agent and Counsel;

Mr. Vaughan Lowe, Q.C., member of the English Bar, Emeritus Professor of International Law, Oxford University, member of the Institut de droit international,

Mr. Alex Oude Elferink, Director, Netherlands Institute for the Law of the Sea, Professor of International Law of the Sea, Utrecht University,

Mr. Alain Pellet, Emeritus Professor at the University Paris Ouest, Nanterre-La Défense, former member and former Chairman of the International Law Commission, member of the Institut de droit international,

Mr. Antonio Remiro Brotóns, Professor of International Law, Universidad Autónoma de Madrid, member of the Institut de droit international,

as Counsel and Advocates;

Mr. César Vega Masís, Deputy Minister for Foreign Affairs, Director of Juridical Affairs, Sovereignty and Territory, Ministry of Foreign Affairs,

Mr. Walner Molina Pérez, Juridical Adviser, Ministry of Foreign Affairs,

Mr. Julio César Saborio, Juridical Adviser, Ministry of Foreign Affairs,

as Counsel;

Mr. Edgardo Sobenes Obregon, Counsellor, Embassy of Nicaragua in the Kingdom of the Netherlands,

Ms Claudia Loza Obregon, First Secretary, Embassy of Nicaragua in the Kingdom of the Netherlands,

Mr. Benjamin Samson, Ph.D. Candidate, Centre de droit international de Nanterre (CEDIN), University Paris Ouest, Nanterre-La Defense,

Ms Gimena González,

as Assistant Counsel;

Ms Sherly Noguera de Argüello, Consul General of the Republic of Nicaragua,

as Administrator.

Le Gouvernement du Nicaragua est représenté par :

S. Exc. M. Carlos José Argüello Gómez, ambassadeur de la République du Nicaragua auprès du Royaume des Pays-Bas,

comme agent et conseil ;

M. Vaughan Lowe, Q.C., membre du barreau d'Angleterre, professeur émérite de droit international, Oxford University, membre de l'Institut de droit international,

M. Alex Oude Elferink, directeur de l'Institut néerlandais du droit de la mer, professeur de droit international de la mer, Université d'Utrecht,

M. Alain Pellet, professeur émérite à l'Université Paris Ouest, Nanterre-La Défense, ancien membre et ancien président de la Commission du droit international, membre de l'Institut de droit international,

M. Antonio Remiro Brotóns, professeur de droit international à l'Universidad Autónoma de Madrid, membre de l'Institut de droit international,

comme conseils et avocats ;

M. César Vega Masís, vice-ministre des affaires étrangères, directeur des affaires juridiques, de la souveraineté et du territoire au ministère des affaires étrangères,

M. Walner Molina Pérez, conseiller juridique au ministère des affaires étrangères,

M. Julio César Saborio, conseiller juridique au ministère des affaires étrangères,

comme conseils ;

M. Edgardo Sobenes Obregon, conseiller à l'ambassade du Nicaragua au Royaume des Pays-Bas,

Mme Claudia Loza Obregon, première secrétaire de l'ambassade du Nicaragua au Royaume des Pays-Bas,

M. Benjamin Samson, doctorant au Centre de droit international de Nanterre (CEDIN), Université Paris Ouest, Nanterre-La Défense,

Mme Gimena Gonzales,

comme conseils adjoints ;

Mme Sherly Noguera de Argüello, consul général de la République du Nicaragua,

comme administrateur.

The Government of Colombia is represented by:

H.E. Ms María Ángela Holguín Cuéllar, Minister for Foreign Affairs,

H.E. Mr. Francisco Echeverri Lara, Vice Minister of Multilateral Affairs, Ministry of Foreign Affairs,

as National Authorities;

H.E. Mr. Carlos Gustavo Arrieta Padilla, former Judge of the Council of State of Colombia, former Attorney General of Colombia and former Ambassador of Colombia to the Kingdom of the Netherlands,

as Agent;

H.E. Mr. Manuel José Cepeda Espinosa, former President of the Constitutional Court of Colombia, former Permanent Delegate of Colombia to UNESCO and former Ambassador of Colombia to the Helvetic Confederation,

as Co-Agent;

Mr. W. Michael Reisman, McDougal Professor of International Law at Yale University, member of the Institut de droit international,

Mr. Rodman R. Bundy, former *avocat à la Cour d'appel de Paris*, member of the New York Bar, Eversheds LLP, Singapore,

Sir Michael Wood, K.C.M.G., member of the English Bar, member of the International Law Commission,

Mr. Tullio Treves, member of the Institut de droit international, Senior Public International Law Consultant, Curtis, Mallet-Prevost, Colt & Mosle LLP Milan, Professor, University of Milan,

Mr. Eduardo Valencia-Ospina, member and Special Rapporteur of the International Law Commission, President of the Latin American Society of International Law,

Mr. Matthias Herdegen, Dr. h.c., Professor of International Law, Director of the Institute of International Law at the University of Bonn,

as Counsel and Advocates;

H.E. Mr. Juan José Quintana Aranguren, Ambassador of the Republic of Colombia to the Kingdom of the Netherlands, Permanent Representative of Colombia to the OPCW, former Permanent Representative of Colombia to the United Nations in Geneva,

H.E. Mr. Andelfo García González, Ambassador of the Republic of Colombia to the Kingdom of Thailand, Professor of International Law, former Deputy Minister for Foreign Affairs,

Ms Andrea Jiménez Herrera, Counsellor, Embassy of the Republic of Colombia in the Kingdom of the Netherlands,

Le Gouvernement de la Colombie est représenté par :

S. Exc. Mme María Ángela Holguín Cuéllar, ministre des affaires étrangères,

S. Exc. M. Francisco Echeverri Lara, vice-ministre des affaires multilatérales, ministère des affaires étrangères,

comme autorités nationales ;

S. Exc. M. Carlos Gustavo Arrieta Padilla, ancien juge au Conseil d'Etat de la Colombie, ancien *Procurador General de la Nación* et ancien ambassadeur de la Colombie auprès du Royaume des Pays-Bas,

comme agent ;

S. Exc. M. Manuel José Cepeda Espinosa, ancien président de la Cour constitutionnelle de Colombie, ancien délégué permanent de la Colombie auprès de l'UNESCO et ancien ambassadeur de la Colombie auprès de la Confédération helvétique,

comme coagent ;

M. W. Michael Reisman, professeur de droit international à l'Université de Yale, titulaire de la chaire McDougal, membre de l'Institut de droit international,

M. Rodman R. Bundy, ancien avocat à la Cour d'appel de Paris, membre du barreau de New York, cabinet Eversheds LLP, Singapour,

sir Michael Wood, K.C.M.G., membre du barreau d'Angleterre, membre de la Commission du droit international,

M. Tullio Treves, membre de l'Institut de droit international, conseiller principal en droit international public, cabinet Curtis, Mallet-Prevost, Colt et Mosle LLP, Milan, professeur à l'Université de Milan,

M. Eduardo Valencia-Ospina, membre et rapporteur spécial de la Commission du droit international, président de la société latino-américaine de droit international,

M. Matthias Herdegen, docteur *honoris causa*, professeur de droit international, directeur de l'Institut de droit international de l'Université de Bonn,

comme conseils et avocats ;

S. Exc. M. Juan José Quintana Aranguren, ambassadeur de la République de Colombie auprès du Royaume des Pays-Bas, représentant permanent de la Colombie auprès de l'OIAC, ancien représentant permanent de la Colombie auprès des Nations Unies à Genève,

S. Exc. M. Andelfo García González, ambassadeur de la République de Colombie auprès du Royaume de Thaïlande, professeur de droit international, ancien vice-ministre des affaires étrangères,

Mme Andrea Jiménez Herrera, conseiller, ambassade de la République de Colombie au Royaume des Pays-Bas,

Ms Lucía Solano Ramírez, Second Secretary, Embassy of the Republic of Colombia in the Kingdom of the Netherlands,

Mr. Andrés Villegas Jaramillo, Co-ordinator, Group of Affairs before the ICJ, Ministry of Foreign Affairs,

Mr. Giovanny Andrés Vega Barbosa, Group of Affairs before the ICJ, Ministry of Foreign Affairs,

Ms Ana María Durán López, Group of Affairs before the ICJ, Ministry of Foreign Affairs,

Mr. Camilo Alberto Gómez Niño, Group of Affairs before the ICJ, Ministry of Foreign Affairs,

Mr. Juan David Veloza Chará, Third Secretary, Group of Affairs before the ICJ, Ministry of Foreign Affairs,

as Legal Advisers;

Mr. Rear Admiral Luís Hernán Espejo, National Navy of Colombia,

CN William Pedroza, International Affairs Bureau, National Navy of Colombia,

CF Hermann León, National Maritime Authority (DIMAR), National Navy of Colombia,

Mr. Scott Edmonds, Cartographer, International Mapping,

Mr. Thomas Frogh, Cartographer, International Mapping,

as Technical Advisers;

Ms Charis Tan, Advocate and Solicitor, Singapore, member of the New York Bar, Solicitor, England and Wales, Eversheds LLP, Singapore,

Mr. Eran Sthoeger, LL.M., New York University School of Law,

Mr. Renato Raymundo Treves, LL.M., Associate, Curtis, Mallet-Prevost, Colt & Mosle LLP Milan,

Mr. Lorenzo Palestini, Ph.D Candidate, Graduate Institute of International and Development Studies, Geneva,

as Legal Assistants.

Mme Lucía Solano Ramírez, deuxième secrétaire, ambassade de la République de Colombie au Royaume des Pays-Bas,

M. Andrés Villegas Jaramillo, coordinateur, division des affaires portées devant la CIJ, ministère des affaires étrangères,

M. Giovanny Andrés Vega Barbosa, division des affaires portées devant la CIJ, ministère des affaires étrangères,

Mme Ana María Durán López, division des affaires portées devant la CIJ, ministère des affaires étrangères,

M. Camillo Alberto Gómez Niño, division des affaires portées devant la CIJ, ministère des affaires étrangères,

M. Juan David Veloza Chará, troisième secrétaire, division des affaires portées devant la CIJ, ministère des affaires étrangères,

comme conseillers juridiques ;

le contre-amiral Luis Hernán Espejo, marine nationale de Colombie,

le capitaine de vaisseau William Pedroza, bureau des affaires internationales, marine nationale de Colombie,

le capitaine de frégate Hermann León, autorité maritime nationale (DIMAR), marine nationale de Colombie,

M. Scott Edmonds, cartographe, International Mapping,

M. Thomas Frogh, cartographe, International Mapping,

comme conseillers techniques ;

Mme Charis Tan, avocat et *Solicitor* (Singapour), membre du barreau de New York, *Solicitor* (Angleterre et Pays de Galles), cabinet Eversheds LLP, Singapour,

M. Eran Sthoeger, LL.M., faculté de droit de l'Université de New York,

M. Renato Raymundo Treves, LL.M., associé au cabinet Curtis, Mallet-Prevost, Colt et Mosle LLP, Milan,

M. Lorenzo Palestini, doctorant, Institut de hautes études internationales et du développement, Genève,

comme assistants juridiques.

Le PRESIDENT : L'audience est ouverte. La Cour se réunit aujourd'hui pour entendre le second tour de plaidoiries de la Colombie. J'indique d'abord que, pour des raisons dont elle m'a dûment fait part, la juge Donoghue n'est pas en mesure de siéger aujourd'hui. Je donne à présent la parole à Sir Michael Wood.

Sir Michael WOOD: Thank you, Mr. President.

FIRST PRELIMINARY OBJECTION: ARTICLE LVI OF THE PACT OF BOGOTÁ

1. Mr. President, Members of the Court, the order of speakers in Colombia's second round, responding to what Nicaragua said yesterday, will be as follows.

2. I shall address Colombia's first objection to jurisdiction, based on Article LVI of the Pact of Bogotá.

3. Professor Reisman will follow on the non-existence of a dispute between the Parties.

4. Mr. Valencia-Ospina will address Colombia's alternative argument, that the dispute is not one which, in the opinion of the Parties, could not have been settled by direct negotiations.

5. Professor Treves will then deal with the supposed inherent jurisdiction.

6. Mr. Bundy will then offer some concluding remarks.

7. And he will be followed by the Agent of Colombia, who will read out Colombia's final submissions.

8. Mr. President, in this short intervention, I will respond to what Professor Remiro Brotóns had to say yesterday concerning Colombia's first objection to jurisdiction.

Correct approach to the interpretation of Article LVI

9. The Parties agree on two important points. First, that the core issue is the proper interpretation of Article LVI. Second, that the applicable rules of treaty interpretation are those set forth in the Vienna Convention.

10. Despite the common understanding that the issue of concern is the interpretation of Article LVI, Nicaragua continues to ignore half of its text. That is hardly a good faith interpretation. In an effort to avoid the ordinary meaning of Article LVI, taken as a

whole, Professor Remiro Brotóns yesterday followed the same methodology as that found in Nicaragua's written pleadings. He began with the first paragraph of Article LVI, and only the first paragraph[1]. He then moved straight to Article XXXI, thus concluding Nicaragua's interpretation of the applicable texts[2]. He even said that the consent to the jurisdiction of the Court is based on Article XXXI and the first paragraph of Article LVI[3]. He then supported his conclusion, reached on the basis of Article XXXI and the first paragraph of Article LVI, by referring to his subjective view of the object and purpose of the Pact and of the principle of good faith. And only at this point, he moved on to consider the *travaux préparatoires*, and it was only then that he acknowledged that Article LVI consists of two paragraphs. Rather than interpreting all the elements of Article LVI as a whole, in an effort to reach a harmonious interpretation — as he acknowledged Colombia had done[4] — Nicaragua prefers to contrast the second paragraph of the article with its first paragraph and with Article XXXI in an attempt to deprive the second paragraph of any real meaning. Professor Remiro Brotóns only tells the Court what the second paragraph *cannot* do: for Nicaragua it cannot override Nicaragua's understanding of the first paragraph.

11. Nicaragua has nowhere explained what the purpose of the second paragraph is. The only thing the learned Professor had to say about the second paragraph was that "its *raison d'être* is to protect ongoing proceedings"[5]. Precisely, but the whole question is which procedures are protected by the second paragraph? The answer, we say, is clear — the second paragraph protects procedures initiated prior to the moment of transmission of the notification, not procedures initiated thereafter. This is the only reading of the text that harmonizes its various elements, and ensures that each of the paragraphs has effect.

12. Our colleagues opposite scarcely referred to the actual text of Article LVI, but when they did so they were mistaken. For example, Professor Remiro Brotóns' reliance on the word "*préavis*" in the French version of the article — "notice" in English — seeks to attach a significance to the word that it simply does not bear. Moreover, the thesis advanced by the learned

---

[1]CR 2015/23, pp. 20-21, paras. 4-6 (Remiro Brotóns).

[2]*Ibid.*, p. 21, para. 6 (Remiro Brotóns).

[3]*Ibid.*, pp. 22-23, para. 10 (Remiro Brotóns).

[4]*Ibid.*, pp. 23-24, para. 13 (Remiro Brotóns).

[5]*Ibid.*, p. 27, para. 26 (Remiro Brotóns).

Professor that the specific provision in the second paragraph cannot override what he curiously called the "general rule of intertemporal law" in the first paragraph is contrary to established rules concerning *lex specialis* and *lex generalis*. To accept this thesis would be to deprive more specific rules in treaties of any meaning or purpose.

13. In short, Mr. President, Nicaragua's approach to the interpretation of Article LVI is fundamentally flawed. We set out the correct approach in our written pleadings[6], and I described it again on Monday[7] and I shall not repeat now what I said then.

Object and Purpose

14. Mr. President, Members of the Court, my colleague opposite sought to bolster his interpretation by referring to the object and purpose of the Pact. Yes, the Pact aimed to advance the peaceful settlement of disputes as compared with prior treaties in the Americas. As the Court said in its 1988 Judgment in the *Nicaragua* v. *Honduras* case "the purpose of the American States in drafting [the Pact] was to reinforce their mutual commitments with regard to judicial settlement"[8]. But the Pact advanced that cause within the limits of the consent of the Parties given in the Pact, neither more nor less. You cannot use the general object and purpose of a treaty on pacific settlement to interpret away conditions and safeguards contained therein. Treaties conferring jurisdiction are neither to be interpreted restrictively nor broadly. They are to be interpreted, like any other treaty, in accordance with the Vienna rules. It does not further the cause of judicial settlement to ignore the limits that States place on their consent. Without the assurance that the limits of the consent will be respected, parties will not consent in the first place. It is by no means uncommon for States to denounce a particular treaty setting out procedures for the peaceful settlement of disputes. That in no way diminishes their commitment to the fundamental principle, set out in the United Nations Charter, that disputes must be settled by peaceful means.

15. We see this, for example, with the optional clause. The optional clause undoubtedly serves the object and purpose of the peaceful settlement of disputes. On Monday I drew attention

---

[6]Preliminary Objections of Colombia (POC), Vol. I, Chap. 3.

[7]CR 2015/22, pp. 19-30 (Wood).

[8]*Border and Transborder Armed Actions (Nicaragua* v. *Honduras), Jurisdiction and Admissibility, Judgment, I.C.J. Reports 1988,* p. 89, para. 46.

to the reservations, frequently included in declarations under the optional clause, of the right to withdraw with immediate effect. This may be seen in recent practice. Since 2011, new declarations have been made by Ireland[9], Italy[10], Lithuania[11] and Romania[12], and revised declarations have been made by Greece[13] and the United Kingdom[14]. Each one of these declarations reserves the right to withdraw consent with immediate effect.

16. In the 2014 *Handbook on accepting the jurisdiction of the International Court of Justice: model clauses and templates*[15] — that is, United Nations document A-68/93, which may be found through the Court's website — that Handbook includes the following text as one option for a termination clause in an optional clause declaration:

> "This Declaration will remain in force until notice is given to the Secretary-General of the United Nations withdrawing the declaration, with effect as from the moment of such notification."

17. Professor Remiro Brotóns sought to argue that because, as he claimed, all denunciation clauses in dispute settlement treaties only take effect at the end of the period of notice. Article LVI had to be interpreted in the same way[16]. That, with respect, is a *non sequitur*, but in any event it seems to be based on a false assumption. Thus, Article 72 of the Convention on the Settlement of Investment Disputes Between States and Nationals of Other States (the ICSID Convention) provides that notice of denunciation (which takes effect six months later) pursuant to Article 71 shall not affect rights or obligations of a State arising out of consent to the jurisdiction of the Court

---

[9]Declaration Recognizing as Compulsory the Jurisdiction of the Court by Ireland, http://www.icj-cij.org/jurisdiction/index.php?p1=5&p2=1&p3=1&code=IE (last visited: 29 September 2015).

[10]Declaration Recognizing as Compulsory the Jurisdiction of the Court by Italy, http://www.icj-cij.org/jurisdiction/index.php?p1=5&p2=1&p3=1&code=IT (last visited: 29 September 2015).

[11]Declaration Recognizing as Compulsory the Jurisdiction of the Court by Lithuania, http://www.icj-cij.org/jurisdiction/index.php?p1=5&p2=1&p3=1&code=LT (last visited: 29 September 2015).

[12]Declaration Recognizing as Compulsory the Jurisdiction of the Court by Romania, http://www.icj-cij.org/jurisdiction/index.php?p1=5&p2=1&p3=1&code=RO (last visited: 29 September 2015).

[13]Declaration Recognizing as Compulsory the Jurisdiction of the Court by Greece, http://www.icj-cij.org/jurisdiction/index.php?p1=5&p2=1&p3=1&code=GR (last visited: 29 September 2015).

[14]Declaration Recognizing as Compulsory the Jurisdiction of the Court by United Kingdom, http://www.icj-cij.org/jurisdiction/index.php?p1=5&p2=1&p3=1&code=GB (last visited: 29 September 2015).

[15] Letter dated 24 July 2014 from the Permanent Representative of Switzerland to the United Nations addressed to the Secretary-General, http://www.un.org/ga/search/view_doc.asp?symbol=A/68/963 (last visited: 29 September 2015).

[16]CR 2015/23, pp. 30-31, para. 35 (Remiro Brotóns).

given before such notice was received by the depositary[17]. This means that jurisdiction is preserved only for proceedings that were initiated before the transmission of the notice of denunciation.

Article by Jiménez de Aréchaga and the Court's 1988 Judgment

18. Mr. President. In seeking to justify its position, Nicaragua relied in its written proceedings rather heavily on an article published in 1989 by Eduardo Jiménez de Aréchaga[18]. This was referred to again yesterday by Professor Remiro Brotóns[19]. We have included the full text of this article in your folders at tab 39[20], though I do not think you need turn to it, because the short passage relied upon by our friends opposite has to be read in context. Nicaragua relies on the statement that under the Pact "the withdrawal of the acceptance of compulsory jurisdiction as soon as the possibility of a hostile application looms in the horizon has been severely restricted"[21]. Restricted, perhaps, but not excluded — the distinguished author chose his words carefully. He did not say that jurisdiction persisted throughout the one-year period following transmission of the notification. The context was the distinction between an agreement under Article 36, paragraph 1, of the Statute and the optional clause. The point being made was that when the obligation is "contractualized", to use the author's word, it is not sufficient simply to withdraw a declaration — as under the optional clause. The State has to go much further, it has to denounce an agreement, as in this case, the Pact of Bogotá as a whole. That is politically a much more significant step, a step that States do most certainly not take lightly. In this sense, "contractualization" does indeed place restrictions on States.

---

[17]Article 72 reads:

"Notice by Contracting State pursuant to Articles 70 or 71 shall not affect the rights or obligations under this Convention of that State or of any of its constituent subdivisions or agencies or of any national of that State arising out of consent to the jurisdiction of the Centre given by one of them before such notice was received by the depositary."

[18]Written Statement of Nicaragua (WSN), para. 2.33.

[19]CR 2015/23, p. 28, para. 29 (Remiro Brotóns).

[20]E. Jiménez de Aréchaga, "The Compulsory Jurisdiction of the International Court of Justice under the Pact of Bogotá and the Optional Clause", *International Law at a time of perplexity: Essays in honour of Shabtai Rosenne*, Martinus Nijhoff, 1989, pp. 356-360.

[21]*Ibid.*, p. 357.

19. It was in this context that Professor Remiro Brotóns again cited the Court's statement in the 1988 *Nicaragua* v. *Honduras* case, and he claimed that "the Court itself has recognized that a State's consent to compulsory jurisdiction under Article XXXI of the Pact of Bogotá 'remains valid *ratione temporis* for as long as that instrument itself remains in force between those States'"[22].

20. In its 1988 Judgment this Court was not considering the effect on consent to jurisdiction of the transmission of a notification of denunciation. That question simply did not arise in the case before it. What the Court was actually addressing were arguments put forward by Honduras in an attempt to import the conditions, including the temporal conditions, of its optional clause declaration into its consent to jurisdiction under Article XXXI of the Pact. The Court in 1988 simply did not address Article LVI of the Pact in any way[23].

The various provisions of the Pact of Bogotá

21. Mr. President, Members of the Court, Professor Remiro Brotóns next tries to attack Colombia's interpretation of Article LVI by claiming that the provisions of the Pact of Bogotá are inseparable and that without jurisdiction over procedures initiated under Chapters II through V after the transmission of the notification of denunciation, the Pact would remain an empty shell, as he put it, during the one-year period of notice. He does so by selectively canvassing the articles of the Pact.

22. Mr. President, this argument distorts both the content of the Pact and Colombia's argument. As Colombia demonstrated in its written[24] and oral[25] presentations, a significant number of substantive obligations continue to apply to the denouncing State during the one-year period, even though new procedures cannot be initiated against it.

23. First, Professor Remiro Brotóns conveniently overlooked several important provisions of the Pact. For example, he did not mention Article L on the steps to be taken in the case that a contracting Party fails to carry out a decision of this Court. He did not mention Article LI on

---

[22]WSN, para. 2.11; see also MN, para. 1.23.

[23]*Border and Transborder Armed Actions (Nicaragua* v. *Honduras), Jurisdiction and Admissibility, Judgment, I.C.J. Reports 1988*, p. 84, paras. 33-34.

[24]POC, Vol. I, paras. 3.5-3.7; see also Appendix to Chapter 3 (Pact of Bogotá).

[25]CR 2015/22, pp. 21-23, paras. 10-23 (Wood).

requests for advisory opinions. He summarily dismissed the relevance of Article I on refraining from the threat or use of force and the peaceful settlement of disputes, two very fundamental obligations under the Pact adopted in 1948, just three years after the United Nations Charter. Moreover, Article I in fact contains an obligation to refrain from "any other means of coercion" which is not contained, in terms at least, in the United Nations Charter.

24. Second, the learned professor is wrong to assert that other articles would become redundant. The principles contained in some of them would continue to carry substantive obligations for the denouncing Party and are clearly separable from the procedures in Chapters II to V of the Pact. Article II provides that "[t]he High Contracting Parties recognize the obligation to settle international controversies by regional procedures before referring them to the Security Council of the United Nations" — this is not limited to procedures under Chapters II to V of the Pact. But Article II further provides that,

> "[c]onsequently . . . the parties bind themselves to use the procedures established in the present Treaty, in the manner and under the conditions provided for in the following articles, or, alternatively, such special procedures as, in their opinion, will permit them to arrive at a solution"[26].

This reference to "special procedures" is likewise clearly separable from Chapters II to V.

25. Furthermore, many "procedural" provisions of the Pact will still be in effect after the transmission of the notification of denunciation: they continue to govern any procedures initiated before the transmission and their content and applicability are independent of the ability to initiate new procedures during that period. Moreover, the reservations of Argentina and the United States when signing the Pact, which exclude the applicability of the majority of the procedures under the Pact, demonstrate that the various elements of the Pact can be separated one from another[27].

Travaux préparatoires

26. Mr. President, Members of the Court, Professor Remiro Brotóns finally turned to the *travaux préparatoires* of Article LVI[28]. He asserted that there was "not an element, not a single

---

[26]CR 2015/22, pp. 21-23, paras. 10-23 (Wood).

[27]Reservations of the Pact of Bogotá by United States, http://www.oas.org/juridico/english/sigs/a-42.html#United States (last visited: 29 September 2015); Reservations of the Pact of Bogotá by Argentina, http://www.oas.org/juridico/english/sigs/a-42.html#Argentina (last visited: 29 September 2015).

[28]CR 2015/23, pp. 29-31, paras. 31-35 (Remiro Brotóns).

element" which supported Colombia's interpretation, and that this had explained our brevity on the subject on Monday[29]. To the contrary, we were brief because we had set out the preparatory work fully in our written pleadings[30], and Nicaragua, in its Written Statement in response, had said hardly anything[31]. The learned professor asserts that in 1948 there was no debate in the relevant Commission, no explanation, etc.[32] Well, it may be that the records are limited — not unusual for conferences of that date, or even now, and certainly not unusual in relation to the final clauses of a treaty, or for matters discussed in a drafting committee. But, in fact, as we have shown at length in our written pleadings, the *travaux* do confirm that the drafters of the Pact consciously chose to word Article LVI as they did so as to limit with immediate effect the initiation of new procedures upon the transmission of the notification of denunciation.

27. Nicaragua accepts that the original draft of Article LVI was based on Article 9 of the General Treaty of Inter-American Arbitration of 1929. Yet despite the change, despite the additional sentence, introduced in 1938 to the text which eventually became Article LVI, Nicaragua continues to assert that the meaning of the article remained the same[33]. The change is obvious from tab 9, which is now on the screen, where the two provisions are set out side-by-side.

28. In support of his wholly untenable position, Professor Remiro Brotóns now relies upon one sentence from the records of the 1948 Conference[34]. The Rapporteur of the Third Commission, Mr. Enriquez from Mexico, in his report to the Conciliation Committee said: "We decided that the best drafting would consist on replicating Article 16 [he actually meant Article 9 — it was Article 16, I think, in the Conciliation Treaty — Article 16, *Article 9*] of the 1929 Treaty." Mr. Enriquez then read out both paragraphs of Article LVI (which was then numbered LV). Colombia did not ignore this, as the learned professor claimed[35]. We included what Mr. Enriquez said, in full, and in an English translation, at Annex 31 of our preliminary objections. But it is

---

[29]CR 2015/23, p. 29, para. 31 (Remiro Brotóns).

[30]POC, paras. 3.33-3.52.

[31]WSN, paras. 2.35-2.39.

[32]CR 2015/23, p. 29, para. 31 (Remiro Brotóns).

[33]WSN, para. 2.39.

[34]CR 2015/23, pp. 29-30, paras. 32-34 (Remiro Brotóns).

[35]*Ibid.*, p. 30, para. 33 (Remiro Brotóns).

hardly a sentence of great import — Mr. Enriquez's statement — since it is clear that Mr. Enriquez was referring to the first paragraph of Article LVI, which does indeed follow Article 9 of the 1929 Treaty. He simply could not have been referring to the second paragraph. The second paragraph was clearly new, having been introduced in 1938 — as I said on Monday — upon a proposal by the United States of America[36]. When the new text was introduced, in 1938, the then Legal Adviser to the State Department, Mr. Green Hackworth, emphasized orally that there was a new addition to the draft. And the addition was italicized to draw further attention to the alteration of the text[37].

29. Professor Remiro Brotóns suggested yesterday that the additional paragraph in Article LVI *must be interpreted* so as not to be "regressive" compared with the 1929 General Treaty of Inter-American Arbitration, or indeed other treaties, which the Pact of Bogotá was to replace[38]. That, with great respect, is a false argument. The Pact of Bogotá and the 1929 Treaty, and the other treaties, are wholly different instruments. As its name suggests, the 1929 Treaty was only concerned with a particular form of arbitration. It contained no provisions referring, for example, to the jurisdiction of the then Permanent Court of International Justice.

30. Mr. President, Members of the Court, that concludes my response to what Professor Remiro Brotóns said yesterday.

31. I thank you for your attention and I would ask you to invite Professor Reisman to the podium.

Le PRESIDENT : Merci. Je donne à présent la parole au professeur Michael Reisman.

---

[36]POC, Vol. II, Ann. 25: Delegation of the United States of America, Report of the Meetings of Sub-Committee 1 of Committee I, Consolidation of American Peace Instruments and Agreements, 19 Dec. 1938, p. 5.

[37]*Ibid*, Ann. 24, Art. XXII, p. 203.

[38]CR 2015/23, p. 30, paras. 34-35 (Remiro Brotóns).

Mr. REISMAN:

ABSENCE OF A DISPUTE

1. Mr. President, Members of the Court, I am grateful for the opportunity to return to Colombia's discussion of the "absence of dispute" in order to correct some of Nicaragua's misstatements.

2. This is a proceeding on jurisdiction. Colombia's principal contention is that its consent to jurisdiction ended with immediate effect upon the transmission of its denunciation of the Pact of Bogotá on 27 November 2012. Thus Nicaragua's Application is out of time by one year. But, for the sake of argument, let me assume Nicaragua's contention that Pact Article LVI requires that a year must run for jurisdictional purposes from the date of denunciation; on that assumption, other things being equal, Nicaragua's Application of 26 November 2013, would be admissible because it was lodged one day before Colombia's consent to jurisdiction lapsed.

3. In Nicaragua's view, its Application was admissible but the "critical date" for the Application was one day before the expiration of Colombia's consent to jurisdiction under the Pact. That means that in order to fall within the Court's jurisdiction, events that constituted Nicaragua's grievance must have occurred before that date and, as *Peace Treaties* said, in "a situation in which the two sides hold clearly opposite views concerning the question of the performance or non-performance of certain treaty obligations"[39].

4. How does one determine the objective existence of such a dispute? Yesterday, Professor Lowe cited the *Hostages* case as authority against Colombia's submission that international law requires some modality of communication of a claim to the other party as a means of confirming the objective existence of a dispute. But he only quoted what the Court said about the *Hostages* case in the *Headquarters Agreement* case, namely — and this is the *Headquarters Agreement* summary: "The Court saw no need to enquire into the attitude of Iran in order to establish the existence of a 'dispute'."[40] With respect, Professor Lowe ignored the actual holding

---

[39]*Interpretation of Peace Treaties with Bulgaria, Hungary and Romania, First Phase, Advisory Opinion, I.C.J. Reports 1950,* p. 74.

[40]CR 2015/23, p. 40, para. 42 (Lowe).

and the context of the *Hostages* case in which modalities for establishing the existence of a dispute were fully and amply complied with by the United States. I quote the Court:

> "From the outset of the attack upon its Embassy in Tehran, the United States protested to the Government of Iran both at the attack and at the seizure and detention of the hostages. On 7 November a former Attorney-General of the United States, Mr. Ramsey Clark, was instructed to go with an assistant to Iran to deliver a message from the President of the United States to the Ayatollah Khomeini."[41]

5. The Court went on to note that it was Iran's leader who forbade members of the Revolutionary Council and all the responsible officials to meet the United States representatives[42]. Quoting the Court again:

> "Subsequently, despite the efforts of the United States Government to open negotiations, it became clear that the Iranian authorities would have no direct contact with representatives of the United States Government concerning the holding of the hostages."

6. But there was more. The Court quoted the Security Council "resolution 457 (1979) calling on Iran to release the personnel of the Embassy immediately, to provide them with protection and to allow them to leave the country"[43].

And the Court concluded:

> "In the present instance, neither of the parties to the dispute proposed recourse to either of the two alternatives, [in the 1955 bilateral treaty] before the filing of the Application or at any time afterwards. On the contrary, the Iranian authorities refused to enter into any discussion of the matter with the United States, and this could only be understood by the United States as ruling out, *in limine,* any question of arriving at an agreement to resort to arbitration or conciliation under Article II or Article III of the Protocols, instead of recourse to the Court."[44]

Mr. President, the existence of the dispute was established beyond a shadow of doubt.

7. The Pact of Bogotá, Nicaragua's principal basis of jurisdiction, is particularly relevant in this regard. Under its Article II, not every dispute can be submitted to the Court. As Mr. Valencia-Ospina explained the day before yesterday, Article II preconditions access to Article XXXI's judicial procedure to the demonstration that the parties were of the opinion that the

---

[41] *United States Diplomatic and Consular Staff in Tehran (United States of America* v. *Iran), Judgment, I.C.J. Reports 1980,* p. 15. para. 26.

[42] *Ibid.*

[43] *Ibid.,* p. 16. para. 28.

[44] *Ibid.,* p. 26. para. 49.

relevant dispute or disputes "cannot be settled by direct negotiations through the usual diplomatic channels".

8. Now, Mr. President, the Parties' opinion on the possibility of resolving the dispute through "the usual diplomatic channels" presupposes knowledge of the other Party's legal position. Hence the Pact requires a positive communication of the claim before a dispute can be brought to the Court on its basis.

9. Article II of the Pact refers specifically to negotiations through "the usual diplomatic channels". The Nicaraguan Foreign Ministry is well aware that "the usual diplomatic channels" include such modalities as sending a formal diplomatic Note. The fact that Nicaragua even cared to belatedly send a formal Note on 13 September 2014[45] (almost ten months after the Application was filed) alleging infringement of their sovereign rights as well as the purported use of force by Colombia, means that they were well aware of the meaning of the need for recourse to the "usual diplomatic channels".

10. Now, in the case before you, what events, which are alleged to have occurred before the critical date, can be deemed to constitute "a situation in which the two sides hold clearly opposite views concerning the question of the performance . . ." of a legal obligation and which cannot be settled through "the usual diplomatic channels"? The evidence adduced by Nicaragua to answer this question is selective and contradictory. On 14 August 2013, President Ortega announced that "the Naval Force of Colombia . . . has been respectful and there has not been any kind of confrontation between the Colombian and Nicaraguan Navy . . ."[46]. Eight days before the submission of Nicaragua's Application, Nicaraguan Admiral Corrales Rodriguez declared that "we have not had any problems with the Colombian Naval forces . . ."[47]. Now, nine months later, nine months after having submitted its Application, the Nicaraguan Ministry of Foreign Affairs asked the Admiral for an inventory of "any incidents that may have taken place between the Colombian Navy and the Nicaraguan Navy"[48]. This time, for some reason, the Admiral reported ten low-level

---

[45]POC, Vol. II, Ann. 17.

[46]POC, Vol. II, Ann. 11, p. 118.

[47]POC, Vol. II, Ann. 43, p. 355.

[48]Memorial of Nicaragua (MN), Ann. 23 A, p. 281.

incidents allegedly occurring up to the critical date. Far be it from me to impugn the good faith of Admiral Corrales but it is striking that not one of those events was deemed, at the time of its occurrence, important enough to protest, or otherwise to bring to the attention of the Colombian Government, let alone to Nicaraguan President Ortega.

11. Similarly selective is Nicaragua's presentation of President Santos' speech to the nation on the evening the 2012 Judgment was handed down. The theory that statements by Colombian officials may constitute per se a dispute led Nicaragua to pick out sentences and to read them in ways that create an impression of a defiant non-compliance and repudiation of the Judgment. But the President's statement, for example, that he "emphatically rejects this aspect of the decision" meant absolute disagreement, not an intention of non-compliance. And, incidentally, the disagreement was only with that part of the Judgment dealing with maritime enclaves, not with the whole maritime delimitation. And, indeed, shortly after this sentence in the speech, the President stated: "Therefore, we will not discard any recourse or mechanism available to us in international law"[49] and he went on to inform his countrymen about the method by which Colombia would implement the decision. Mr. President, this is not a declaration of non-compliance.

12. Counsel yesterday said, rightly, that to rely on the first days' reaction of Colombian officials to the Judgment would be "a cheap shot" but he then carefully ignored later statements and the judgment of the Constitutional Court, all of which manifest the intention to comply by means of the conclusion of a treaty. Nor could Nicaragua's Agent resist taking that "cheap shot": the Agent, selecting passages from the President's statement on the day of the Judgment, asserted that it showed "the existence of a serious dispute between the parties" as of the day of the delivery of the Judgment, as purported evidence that "quite obviously . . . Colombia does not accept the delimitation carried out by the Court"[50]. And, Mr. President, I am not sure this goes into the "cheap shot" category, but I note that Nicaragua's propensity is not to quote President Ortega's statement of satisfaction with the comportment of Colombia's President Santos.

13. So, having cited *Hostages* as his authority, we are baffled by Professor Lowe's conclusion that "it is evident from the record in this case that what international law does

[49]POC, Vol. II, Ann. 6, p. 89.

[50]CR 2015/23, p. 17, para. 29 (Argüello).

require — the clear presentation of positions, so that each side can understand what the disagreement is — is abundantly satisfied"[51]. Quite the contrary. By contrast to *Hostages*, not once did Nicaragua protest or otherwise indicate to Colombia that it had grievances or complaints of fact and law that amounted to an objective dispute with Colombia, not once. It simply initiated this case before the Court. Considering that some of Nicaragua's claims involve allegations of threats to use force, its failure to timely protest by any modality renders the existence of that dispute even more doubtful. Nicaragua's efforts to demonstrate the existence of a dispute on these matters at the critical date thus fail.

14. Nicaragua, conscious of the insubstantiality of proving the existence of its claimed dispute before the critical date, argues that the objective existence of the dispute can be proved by reference to events occurring *after* the submission of its Application. In this regard, it sweeps in, again selectively, speeches and events occurring, in some instances almost two years after 26 November 2013, the date of its Application and the crucial date for the purpose of jurisdiction. Now, it may certainly be argued that when consensual jurisdiction continues, there may be a basis in law for sometimes adducing evidence occurring *after* the date of the application. But in this case, such events are inadmissible because the critical date and the end of jurisdiction, even on Nicaragua's reading of the Pact, are only one day apart. Hence no jurisdiction exists after 27 November 2013, the end of the one year period after Colombia's denunciation of the Pact. So, wholly apart from the substantive failure of these various post-Application events to demonstrate an objective dispute, they are also without a basis for jurisdiction.

15. Mr. President, Members of the Court, Nicaragua claims that it is a small State compared to Colombia and, apparently, is entitled to special treatment with respect to the brevity of the period between its Application and the cessation of jurisdiction under the Pact. But it was not a short period: Ambassador Argüello stated that Nicaragua had known of a serious dispute since the delivery of the Judgment[52]. The consequences of Nicaragua's delay and concealment of its action are its own responsibility. Nicaragua has used the Court more than any other Member of the United Nations and it is wise in its ways. It needs and deserves no special treatment, no matter

---

[51]CR 2015/23, p. 41, para. 44 (Lowe).

[52]CR 2015/23, p. 17, para. 28 (Argüello).

how large the respondent State may be. Legally, Mr. President, the Charter teaches that all States are equal.

16. Mr. President, there are compelling reasons for insisting on a demonstration of the objective existence of a dispute as a condition for an otherwise valid basis of jurisdiction. Parties at the international level should know of claims against them and have the opportunity to react to them and to look for ways to resolve them without litigation in order to avert an unnecessarily frictive political — and economic — transaction which can leave in its wake decades if not generations of hostility. The objective existence standard also protects international judicial processes from being exploited with adjudication becoming a tactical device for pressuring a State. And it facilitates the litigation process. In *Certain Property*, where there had been bilateral consultations between Germany and Liechtenstein, you said:

> "The Court thus finds that in the present proceedings complaints of fact and law formulated by Liechtenstein against Germany are denied by the latter. In conformity with well-established jurisprudence . . ., the Court concludes that '[b]y virtue of this denial, there is a legal dispute' between Liechtenstein and Germany."[53]

17. In this case, nothing prevented Nicaragua from communicating its claims and grievances to Colombia through the usual diplomatic channels or by any other modality at any time prior to the termination of jurisdiction under the Pact. Not only did it not protest or otherwise communicate: to the contrary, at the highest levels, it assured Colombia of its satisfaction with its comportment. Recall President Ortega's statement of 14 August 2013 that "there has not been any kind of confrontation between the Colombian and Nicaragua Navy"[54]. Having failed to communicate any "complaints of fact and law", to borrow your language from *Certain Property*, indeed, from expressing at the highest political level, the opposite until the critical date, Nicaragua must bear the responsibility and cannot evade it by claiming to be a "small" country. Now, Mr. President, Members of the Court, that may seem to be a matter of rules, but the rule of law is comprised of rules which are applied to all equally. It is the hallmark of the law.

18. Before concluding, I must comment on Nicaragua's tendency to malign a State that dares to criticize a judgment, or part of a judgment, of the Court while burnishing its own appreciation.

---

[53]*Certain Property (Liechtenstein* v. *Germany), Preliminary Objections, Judgment, I.C.J. Reports 2005,* p. 19, para 25.

[54]POC, Vol. II, Ann. 11.

There is no violation of international law when a State — or a scholar — criticizes a decision of the Security Council, or of the General Assembly or of a judgment of the Court. When, however, a party that has not prevailed undertakes the arduous process of implementing a deeply unpopular judgment, it demonstrates all the more its commitment to international law.

19. Mr. President, yesterday, Professor Lowe mused whether there is really a dispute or "whether we are all here as a result of some ghastly misunderstanding". The Court will surely have realized by now that it is indeed the latter; we are here as the result of a ghastly misunderstanding and none of us should really be here. As a result of Nicaragua's filing of an entirely artificial application, we have been compelled to appear before you to respond to frivolous claims without a jurisdictional base, which are said to constitute a phantom dispute, the subject-matter of which was entirely unknown to Colombia until it was informed by the Registry that, once again, proceedings had been instituted against it. Ghastly, indeed, Mr. President.

20. Mr. President, Members of the Court, I thank you for your attention and ask that Mr. Valencia-Ospina be invited to address you.

Le PRESIDENT : Merci, Monsieur le professeur. Je donne à présent la parole à M. Valencia-Ospina.

Mr. VALENCIA-OSPINA:

THIRD PRELIMINARY OBJECTION: THE COURT LACKS JURISDICTION BECAUSE THE PRECONDITION OF ARTICLE II OF THE PACT OF BOGOTÁ HAD NOT BEEN FULFILLED AT THE TIME OF THE FILING OF THE APPLICATION

Introduction

1. Mr. President, Members of the Court, after having heard Nicaragua's first round of oral pleadings, it becomes necessary to shed more light on the Applicant's misguided interpretation of the applicable law and appreciation of the facts relevant for the third objection.

2. In so doing, I shall concentrate on the objective assessment of the opinion of the Parties. During the first round, Colombia dealt extensively with the interpretation of Article II of the Pact of Bogotá, a question that Nicaragua largely neglected at that round. In this respect I will, therefore, limit myself to highlighting four of the many additional points that could be made.

— First, Nicaragua has now gone as far as to suggest that "the judgment of the negotiability of the dispute is a matter . . . not for a third party"[55]. In other words, the Applicant argues that the Court — contrary to what it stated in the 1988 Judgment[56] — is not entitled to make an objective assessment of the opinion of the Parties but only to take note of what Nicaragua says.

— Second, the fact that the Inter-American Juridical Committee's Rapporteur moved an amendment to Article II of the Pact did not imply that for him the proper interpretation of that provision was the one suggested by the French text. On the contrary, as he explained in his report: "[n]either party is legally in a position to invoke the Pact at the time when, in its individual judgment, a controversy can no longer be settled by diplomatic means"[57]. He thus confirmed the view he had expressed four years earlier that Article II enshrined "a qualified obligation to have recourse to the peaceful means of settlement only when there is a concurrent opinion of the State Parties"[58]; and most significantly, that the terminology in the opinion of the parties "was not a mistake in drafting technique"[59].

— Third, Nicaragua seeks to strengthen its reading of Article II by drawing attention to Article 26 of the OAS Charter which also uses the expression "in the opinion of one" of the Parties[60]. However, the reliance of Article 26 on the term in the singular is virtually effaced by that article's injunction that the "Parties [in the plural] shall agree on some other peaceful procedure that will enable them to reach a solution". In other words, what matters according to Article 26 is in the end the opinion of both Parties since one of them cannot unilaterally determine the procedure to be used.

---

[55]CR 2015/23, p. 42, para. 47 (Lowe).

[56]*Border and Transborder Armed Actions (Nicaragua* v. *Honduras), Jurisdiction and Admissibility, Judgment, I.C.J. Reports 1988,* p. 95, para. 65.

[57]Opinion of the Inter-American Juridical Committee on the American Treaty on Pacific Settlement (Pact of Bogotá), Organization of the American States doc. OEA/SER.G, CP/Doc. 1603/85, 3 Sep. 1985, English Text, Ann. 23 of Nicaragua's Counter-Memorial in the *Border and Transborder Armed Actions* case *(Nicaragua* v. *Honduras), Jurisdiction and Admissibility, Judgment, I.C.J. Reports 1988*, p. 461.

[58]Galo Leoro, F., "La Reforma del Tratado Americano de Soluciones Pacíficas o Pacto de Bogotá", *Anuario Jurídico Inter-Americano*, 1981, p. 48, para. 93.

[59]Galo Leoro, F., "La Reforma del Tratado Americano de Soluciones Pacíficas o Pacto de Bogotá", *Anuario Jurídico Inter-Americano*, 1981, p. 51, para. 106.

[60]WSN, para. 4.28.

— Fourth, counsel for Nicaragua stated that "it is enough if one of [the Parties] holds the view that there is no prospect of a negotiated settlement"[61]. Colombia has rejected this proposition, which, in any event, would be inapplicable in the present case given the repeated statements by the President of Nicaragua emphasizing that negotiations were possible.

The opinion of the Parties

3. Yesterday, the Agent of Nicaragua stated that, "President Ortega has repeatedly reiterated Nicaragua's willingness to initiate conversations on different topics related to the implementation of the judgment"[62]. In fact, he stressed — as if Colombia had reasons to think otherwise — that "[t]hese are not empty words"[63].

4. Colombia certainly appreciates that Nicaragua has recognized on several occasions the many subject-matters over which the Parties are in agreement concerning the possibility to negotiate. Already in its Written Statement, Nicaragua asserted that, "it ha[d] kept the door open to talking about the treaty Colombia wants, including on issues like fishing and environmental protection"[64], that "there were . . . subjects on which negotiations might eventually be had"[65] and that "both Parties had expressed willingness to consider" certain issues[66]. These are correct depictions of the situation at the time of the seisin of the Court.

5. However, in the same Written Statement, Nicaragua proceeded to downplay the value of its assertions. In those pleadings, Nicaragua indeed argued that the subject-matter of the claims it had brought before the Court was different from "the subject matter of the negotiations both Parties had expressed willingness to consider"[67]. In other words, for Nicaragua the alleged violations of its sovereign rights and maritime zones had nothing to do with the implementation of the 2012 Judgment.

---

[61]CR 2015/23, p. 42, para. 47 (Lowe).

[62]*Ibid.*, p. 12, para. 12 (Arguëllo).

[63]*Ibid.*, p. 12, para. 12 (Arguëllo).

[64]WSN, para. 4.7.

[65]WSN, para. 4.56.

[66]WSN, para. 4.59.

[67]WSN, para. 4.59.

6. In fairness, it must be acknowledged that Nicaragua has not repeated this argument in the first round. Nicaragua must have realized that arguing that the Parties are willing to negotiate issues related to the implementation of the 2012 Judgment but not the alleged violations of its maritime zones resulting from that Judgment is artificial and deceptive.

7. Nicaragua has likewise avoided reasserting its argument that, "pending the decision of the Constitutional Court, Colombia was of the opinion that no negotiation was even possible"[68]. In fact, Nicaragua made no mention during the first round of the statements made by the President and Foreign Minister of Colombia on 15 and 18 September 2013[69]. Similarly, Nicaragua has failed to rebut the statements made on 9 and 10 September 2013 by Colombia's Executive that expressed Colombia's willingness to negotiate[70].

8. Instead, for Nicaragua now, what rendered negotiations futile was the enactment of Colombian Decree 1946, a decree that was not protested by Nicaragua prior to the critical date. To quote the Agent of Nicaragua, "the possibility of successful negotiations became clearly closed when Colombia enacted the 1946 Decree"[71]. But this is implausible to say the least. For if the words of the President of Nicaragua "are [to be considered as] not [being] empty"[72], what about his statements made in September 2013, January and May 2014? After all, the Agent of Nicaragua does refer to them in his speech as being instances in which Nicaragua has expressed "willingness to initiate conversations"[73]. Indeed, at the same time he recognizes that the words of his President must be taken seriously, the Agent cites passages from the Memorial that explicitly refer to the September and May statements[74]. The Memorial rightfully emphasizes that the September declaration was made "the day after President Santos introduced Decree 1946 establishing the Colombian 'ICZ'"[75]. How can Nicaragua then demonstrate that the Decree had rendered

---

[68]WSN, para. 4.46 and paras 4.38-4.52, Anns. 12 and 39.

[69]POC, Anns. 13 and 42.

[70]POC, paras 4.68 and 4.69, Anns. 12 and 39; CR 2015/22, p. 55, para. 24 (Valencia-Ospina).

[71]CR 2015/23, p.17, para. 31 (Arguëllo).

[72]*Ibid.*, p. 12, para. 12 (Arguëllo).

[73]*Ibid.*, p. 12, para. 12, fn. 9 (Arguëllo); MN, paras 2.53-2.63.

[74]CR 2015/23, p. 12, para. 12 (Arguëllo); MN, paras 2.58 and 2.60.

[75]MN, para. 2.58.

negotiations futile if on the very next day, and the following months, its President had continued to express such bona fide willingness?

9. The elements of conduct adduced by Colombia "[t]o measure the validity of the Applicant's assumption that the complaint to the Constitutional Court made negotiations useless", are equally relevant to dispose of the new Nicaraguan argument based on the adoption of the Decree[76]. Contrary to what Counsel for Nicaragua stated, these declarations by the Executive of Nicaragua certainly do not support the contention that by the critical date "it quickly bec[a]me evident that a deadlock [had been] reached"[77]. In spite of what Nicaragua would have us believe, it is Colombia and not the Applicant that takes with the utmost seriousness the words of the Nicaraguan President.

10. As it turns out, Nicaragua has itself defeated its own proposition that it had seised the Court because in its opinion direct negotiations were impossible. Rather, its motives were purely opportunistic. For as the Agent of Nicaragua stated, after having recognized that "unilateral recourse" to the Court would be impossible after 27 November 2013[78], Nicaragua "reluctantly took the decision to come to the Court before the denunciation of the Pact of Bogotá came into force"[79]. What the Agent thus emphasizes is Nicaragua's will to preserve the jurisdictional avenue, not the futility of negotiations. Counsel for Nicaragua also stated, in terms that are illuminating, that Nicaragua "had to make [a] judgement (sic) call"[80]. What he meant, of course, is that Nicaragua took this decision not on the basis of whether negotiations were, in the opinion of the Parties, possible, but because it faced the last possible opportunity in which to do so.

11. In this respect, I want to stress that the Agent of Nicaragua's query as to whether it is "reasonable to suppose that Nicaragua had to continue attempting to negotiate before attempting procedures which would cease to be in effect one day later" is simply beside the point[81]. The coming into effect of Colombia's denunciation of the Pact of Bogotá did not relieve an informed

---

[76]CR 2015/22, pp. 55-57, paras 25-29 (Valencia-Ospina).

[77]CR 2015/23, p. 44, para. 58 (Lowe).

[78]*Ibid.*, p. 15, para. 22 (Arguëllo).

[79]*Ibid.*, para. 23 (Arguëllo).

[80]*Ibid.*, pp. 42-43, para. 52 (Lowe).

[81]*Ibid.*, p. 16, para. 27 (Arguëllo).

Applicant from its duty to fulfil the preconditions for the Court's jurisdiction. It cannot trump the positive statements made by the President of Nicaragua immediately before and after the filing of the Application. In light of those explicit statements, the unsubstantiated assertion by Counsel for Nicaragua that "[a]t the time of the Application, there seemed [to be] no hope of a negotiated settlement"[82] could not be further removed from the truth.

12. Also beside the point is Nicaragua's reference to the case law of the Court, according to which negotiations and recourse to judicial settlement can be pursued *pari passu*[83]. For obviously that is only relevant when the Court's jurisdiction is not limited by a clause such as Article II of the Pact. Indeed, in the 1978 Judgment in the *Aegean Sea Continental Shelf* case, the Court did not uphold the argument that in general "the existence of active negotiations in progress constitutes an impediment to the Court's exercise of jurisdiction"[84]. It so acted because under general international law the governing principle is the free choice of means[85]. Had Turkey and Greece been parties to a treaty such as the Pact, the situation would have been very different. In this respect, counsel for Nicaragua's reference to the 1998 Judgment in the *Cameroon* v. *Nigeria* case[86] is also totally irrelevant because the applicable law was likewise general international law and not a treaty in which the parties had agreed to incorporate a precondition of unavailability of negotiations. Nicaragua is well aware that that precedent confirms Colombia's argument since in the very paragraph quoted by the Applicant, the Court also dealt expressly with the question of the special clauses embodied in treaties, which it significantly termed "precondition[s]" and distinguished it from the situation under general international law[87].

13. In fact, as the Court stated in its 2011 Judgment in *Georgia* v. *Russia*, referring to a provision similar to Article II of the Pact, preconditions pertaining to negotiations are "conditions precedent to the seisin of the Court even when the term is not qualified by a temporal element"[88].

---

[82]CR 2015/23, p. 43, para. 54 (Lowe).

[83]*Ibid.*, p. 17, para. 30 (Arguëllo).

[84]*Aegean Sea Continental Shelf, Judgment, I.C.J. Reports 1978*, p. 12, para. 29.

[85]Article 33 of the United Nations Charter.

[86]CR 2015/23, p. 42, para. 49 (Lowe).

[87]*Land and Maritime Boundary between Cameroon and Nigeria (Cameroon* v. *Nigeria), Preliminary Objections, Judgment, I.C.J. Reports 1998,* p. 303, para. 56.

[88]*Application of the International Convention on the Elimination of All Forms of Racial Discrimination (Georgia* v. *Russian Federation), Preliminary Objections, Judgment, I.C.J. Reports 2011 (I)*, p. 124, para. 130.

Moreover, as Colombia has already stressed during the first round, the precondition of Article II of the Pact had to be met at the time of the filing of the Application, also for an additional reason specific to this case. Due to the fact that the jurisdiction under the Pact had, even on Nicaragua's theory, lapsed at the latest on 27 November 2013, it would be impossible for Nicaragua to bring fresh proceedings after that date.

14. For all these reasons, the Applicant must demonstrate that the precondition was met at the latest by the time of the seisin of the Court. Whether the precondition under Article II has been fulfilled later, which in any event it has not been, is irrelevant once jurisdiction under the Pact has expired.

Conclusion

15. Mr. President, Members of the Court, by manufacturing a deadlock which Nicaragua attributes to the authorities of Colombia, the Applicant has made a desperate attempt at diverting the attention of the Court from the analysis of the statements of its own Executive. Yet, as Nicaragua itself admits when quoting the *Georgia* v. *Russia* case, "primary attention" should be "given to statements made or endorsed by the Executives of the two Parties"[89].

16. Consequently, would it not be more appropriate for Nicaragua to objectively assess its own opinion on the basis of all the statements made by its Executive that explicitly recognized that negotiations were the way to proceed? Instead Nicaragua seeks to establish its opinion from an inconclusive element of tacit conduct, namely, the filing of its Application which neither mentioned Article II of the Pact nor referred to the opinion of the Parties concerning the viability of negotiations.

17. Finally, Nicaragua has stated during the first round that it "has been — and still remains — willing to conclude a treaty implementing the Court's judgment" and that it is "open to make some adaptations to the régime applicable in the areas recognized by the Court to belong to it"[90]. For the purpose of this third objection, what really matters is that these assertions confirm what has been stated by the Parties all along, namely, that negotiations are in the opinion of both

---

[89]WSN, para. 4.53.

[90]CR 2015/23, p. 44, para. 58 (Lowe).

Parties still possible. The fact that a treaty has not yet been reached cannot evidence that the precondition under Article II had been met at the relevant time.

18. Mr. President, having arrived at the end of my presentation, may I express my thanks to you and the Members of the Court for your courteous attention and respectfully ask that you call on my colleague, Mr. Treves.

Le PRESIDENT : Merci. Je donne à présent la parole au professeur Tullio Treves.

M. TREVES :

LA COUR N'A PAS UN POUVOIR INHÉRENT POUR JUGER DES DEMANDES DU NICARAGUA (QUATRIÈME ET CINQUIÈME OBJECTIONS PRÉLIMINAIRES)

1. Merci, Monsieur le président. Monsieur le président, Mesdames et Messieurs les juges, ma tâche est aujourd'hui de démontrer que la compétence de la Cour à se prononcer sur la demande du Nicaragua ne saurait trouver sa base sur un pouvoir inhérent qu'aurait la Cour. Pour ce faire, je vais répondre aux arguments, pourtant brillants, soumis par mon collègue et ami Alain Pellet à l'audience d'hier matin.

2. Le leitmotiv de l'argumentation du professeur Pellet est que l'allégué pouvoir (ou compétence) inhérent de la Cour «découle de l'existence même de la Cour»[91] expression utilisée dans les arrêts sur les *Essais nucléaires*, ou, selon une formule que le professeur Pellet utilise aussi, «de la qualité d'organe judiciaire de la Cour»[92]. Ainsi, du simple fait que la Cour est un organe judiciaire (et personne n'en doute), elle serait automatiquement compétente à se prononcer sur toute demande relative à l'inexécution d'un arrêt.

3. Une affaire conclue par un jugement qui l'a tranchée en portant ainsi à exhaustion la compétence de la Cour, donnerait — comme par parthénogénèse — naissance à la compétence à juger sur une autre affaire portant sur la responsabilité internationale découlant des obligations qui incombent à un autre Etat aux termes d'un arrêt de la Cour.

---

[91] CR 2015/23, p. 48, par. 12 (Pellet) citant *Essais nucléaires (Australie c. France), arrêt, C.I.J. Recueil 1974*, p. 259, par. 23 et *Essais nucléaires (Nouvelle-Zélande c. France), arrêt, C.I.J. Recueil 1974*, p. 463, par. 23.

[92] CR 2015/23, p. 46, par. 5 (Pellet).

4. Chacun voit qu'il s'agit d'une idée qui manque de cohérence avec le principe consensuel de la compétence de la Cour. En acceptant cette compétence sur la base de n'importe quel titre prévu par le Statut, les parties acceptent que la Cour se prononce sur l'objet de la demande ou de la question qu'elles soumettent par compromis et non sur une question ayant un objet différent, tel qu'est la prétendue non-exécution de l'arrêt qui a mis fin à l'affaire.

5. Un argument important visant à exclure l'existence d'un pouvoir inhérent qui, à lui seul, fonderait la compétence de la Cour, que la Colombie fait valoir est que les cas d'invocation de pouvoirs inhérents qu'on trouve dans la jurisprudence de la Cour sont tous basés sur la prémisse que la compétence de la Cour soit établie.

6. C'est ce qu'a dit la Cour dans les arrêts sur les *Essais nucléaires* et encore dans l'arrêt *LaGrand* de 2001, dans des passages dûment cités dans ma plaidoirie d'avant-hier[93]. Pour mémoire, dans les affaires des *Essais nucléaires*, la Cour a dit que ses pouvoirs inhérents pouvaient être exercés «si sa compétence au fond est établie»[94] ; dans l'arrêt *LaGrand*, la Cour a dit que son pouvoir de juger sur l'inexécution d'une ordonnance portant mesures conservatoires pouvait s'exercer «lorsque la Cour a compétence pour trancher un différend»[95].

7. Le professeur Pellet semble ne donner aucune importance à ces affirmations de la Cour. Il s'attache à démontrer, toutefois, l'existence de cas envisagés par la Cour où la compétence de celle-ci trouve sa base dans un pouvoir inhérent même en l'absence d'une compétence établie.

8. Ainsi, fait-il valoir que, dans les arrêts sur les *Essais nucléaires,* la Cour, après avoir dit qu'elle possède un pouvoir inhérent l'autorisant à prendre toute mesure voulue «*d'une part* pour faire en sorte que, si la compétence au fond est établie, l'exercice de cette compétence ne se révèle pas vain» dit que cette compétence vaut «*d'autre part* pour assurer le règlement régulier de tous les points en litige ainsi que le respect des «limitations inhérentes à l'exercice de la fonction

---

[93] CR 2015/22, p. 62-63, par. 12 et p. 63, par. 14 (Treves).

[94] *Essais nucléaires (Australie c. France), arrêt, C.I.J. Recueil 1974*, p. 259, par. 23 et *Essais nucléaires (Nouvelle-Zélande c. France), arrêt, C.I.J. Recueil 1974*, p. 463, par. 23.

[95] *LaGrand (Allemagne c. Etats-Unis d'Amérique), arrêt, C.I.J. Recueil 2001*, p. 484, par. 45.

judiciaire»»[96]. Cela indiquerait, d'après M. Pellet, qu'existent des pouvoirs inhérents pour l'exercice desquels la présence d'une compétence établie ne serait pas nécessaire[97].

9. On ne saurait trop lire dans la structure de la phrase que l'on vient de citer. Il n'en reste pas moins que les pouvoirs mentionnés après l'expression «d'autre part» n'ont rien à voir avec une possible compétence sur le fond d'une affaire. En effet, ils ont trait à la régularité procédurale et au fait que la Cour ne saurait se prononcer sur une requête ne correspondant pas à la notion même de la fonction judiciaire. Tel serait un arrêt, comme celui envisagé dans l'affaire du *Cameroun septentrional*, qui n'aurait pas des «conséquences pratiques» ne pouvant pas «affecter les droits ou obligations juridiques existants des parties»[98]. Partant, la Cour est loin d'affirmer un pouvoir inhérent la rendant compétente pour se prononcer sur l'inexécution d'un arrêt.

10. Pour ce qui est de l'arrêt *LaGrand*, invoqué par M. Pellet, il faut souligner d'abord que la décision de la Cour de se prononcer sur l'inexécution d'une ordonnance portant mesures conservatoires adoptée dans le cadre du même procès, ne fut pas prise en accueillant l'argument «accessoire et subsidiaire» de l'Allemagne que la compétence était comprise dans un pouvoir inhérent. La Cour, comme déjà souligné avant-hier[99], n'accepta pas cet argument et affirma que la conclusion de l'Allemagne relative à l'inexécution de l'ordonnance indiquant des mesures conservatoires portait «sur des questions qui découlent directement du différend opposant les Parties devant la Cour, à l'égard desquelles la Cour a déjà conclu qu'elle était compétente»[100].

11. La Cour réaffirme ensuite l'arrêt sur l'affaire de la *Compétence en matière de pêcheries* en soulignant que lorsque la Cour

> «a estimé que, afin de considérer le différend sous tous ses aspects, elle pouvait aussi connaître d'une conclusion qui «se fonde sur des faits postérieurs au dépôt de la requête mais découlant directement de la question qui fait l'objet de cette requête...» (*Compétence en matière de pêcheries (République fédérale d'Allemagne c. Islande), fond, arrêt, C.I.J. Recueil 1974*, p. 203, par. 72)»[101].

---

[96] *Essais nucléaires (Australie c. France), arrêt, C.I.J. Recueil 1974*, p. 259, par. 23 et *Essais nucléaires (Nouvelle-Zélande c. France), arrêt, C.I.J. Recueil 1974*, p. 463, par. 23 — les italiques sont de nous.

[97] CR 2015/23, p. 49, par. 13 (Pellet).

[98] *Cameroun septentrional (Cameroun c. Royaume-Uni, exceptions préliminaires, arrêt, C.I.J. Recueil 1963*, p. 34.

[99] CR 2015/22, p. 63, par. 14 (Treves).

[100] *LaGrand (Allemagne c. Etats-Unis d'Amérique), arrêt, C.I.J. Recueil 2001*, p. 483, par. 45.

[101] *Ibid.*, p. 484, par. 45.

12. C'est sur cette base — et non sur l'idée du pouvoir inhérent — que la Cour affirma que

> «[l]orsque la Cour a compétence pour trancher un différend, elle a également compétence pour se prononcer sur des conclusions la priant de constater qu'une ordonnance en indication de mesures rendue aux fins de préserver les droits des Parties à ce différend n'a pas été exécutée»[102].

M. Pellet affirme que : «Il s'agit là encore d'un pouvoir inhérent, déduit de la qualité d'organe judiciaire de la Cour et nullement d'une compétence prévue expressément par le Statut…»[103]

13. Il semble oublier que c'est un pouvoir inhérent que la Cour n'exerce que quand elle a établi sa compétence et seulement quand elle l'a établie, d'autant plus que les mesures conservatoires sont, par définition, provisoires. C'est pourquoi la transposition de l'affirmation de la Cour relative à sa compétence à se prononcer sur l'inexécution d'une ordonnance portant mesures conservatoires à la compétence pour se prononcer sur l'inexécution d'un arrêt n'est pas soutenable. Ce ne serait pas faire un raisonnement *a fortiori* comme le voudrait M. Pellet[104]. Ce serait suivre un raisonnement possible dans le cadre d'une affaire où la compétence est établie, qui n'est pas admissible pour établir une compétence sur une affaire où une telle compétence n'existe pas.

14. En somme : reste valable l'affirmation faite par le juge Guillaume dans son article «De l'exécution des décisions de la Cour internationale de Justice». En se référant à l'exécution des arrêts de la Cour, l'éminent juge s'exprime ainsi :

> «Par ailleurs, tout différend relatif à cette exécution doit être regardé comme un différend distinct de celui réglé par le jugement. La Cour ne saurait dès lors s'en saisir sans un nouvel accord des parties.»[105]

15. Ces deux phrases, citées dans les plaidoiries orales de la Colombie, sont les seules omises dans la citation faite par M. Pellet de la demi-page de l'article de M. Guillaume qui les suit immédiatement[106]. Elles donnent néanmoins un sens précis à la phrase suivante d'après laquelle la Cour a

---

[102] *LaGrand (Allemagne c. Etats-Unis d'Amérique), arrêt, C.I.J. Recueil 2001*, p. 484, par. 45.

[103] CR 2015/23, p. 50, par. 14 (Pellet).

[104] *Ibid.*, p. 62, par. 43 (Pellet).

[105] Gilbert Guillaume, «De l'exécution des décisions de la Cour internationale de Justice» (1997), dans *La Cour internationale de Justice à l'aube du XXIe siècle, Le regard d'un juge*, Pédone, Paris, 2003, p. 178-179 (références omises).

[106] CR 2015/23, p. 51, par. 16 (Pellet).

«jugé à plusieurs reprises qu'elle ne pouvait, ni ne devait envisager l'inexécution de ses arrêts et ne s'est-elle prononcée sur cette exécution que dans les cas où les Parties lui avaient donné spécifiquement compétence à cet effet»[107].

16. Le sens qu'il faut tirer de cette affirmation est que pour juger d'un différend portant sur l'inexécution d'un arrêt de la Cour, un titre spécifique de compétence est nécessaire, que ce soit un accord *ad hoc* des parties ou une autre forme de consentement.

17. Le professeur Pellet semble confondre la possibilité abstraite de la Cour de se prononcer sur l'inexécution d'un arrêt avec la possibilité concrète de le faire qui requiert un titre spécifique de compétence qui ne saurait être le simple fait que l'objet du différend est une question de responsabilité pour inexécution d'un arrêt déjà adopté. Quand il se demande — et il s'agit évidemment d'une question rhétorique — sur quelle base la Cour a pu adopter les paragraphes 60 et 63 des arrêts de 1974 sur les affaires des *Essais nucléaires*[108], le professeur Pellet donne un exemple de pouvoir inhérent dans l'abstrait — un pouvoir qui ne fonde pas une compétence de la Cour mais qui peut s'exercer à la condition que la Cour soit saisie d'un différend sur lequel sa compétence est établie, ce qui était le cas dans les affaires des *Essais nucléaires*.

18. Monsieur le président, Mesdames et Messieurs les juges, l'invitation que le Nicaragua dirige à la Cour de suivre d'autres juridictions internationales, qui se considèrent investies du pouvoir de juger sur l'inexécution de leurs décisions, peut paraître attrayante dans l'optique d'une hypothétique «fonction judiciaire internationale» dont feraient partie toutes les cours et tous les tribunaux internationaux.

19. L'invitation devient moins attrayante et juridiquement moins persuasive si l'on considère les différences entre votre Cour et les cours et tribunaux internationaux qui se sont déclarés compétents pour juger sur l'exécution de leurs décisions. Il s'agit notamment des cours dont la compétence concerne la protection des droits de l'homme, des tribunaux administratifs internationaux et de la cour très spéciale (quasi domestique) qui était la Cour des communautés européennes. Ni les unes ni les autres ne basent leur compétence sur le consentement des parties.

20. Il faut ajouter que les cours et tribunaux internationaux qui se considèrent investis du pouvoir de juger de l'inexécution de leurs jugements sont moins nombreux que ce qu'il apparaît de

---

[107] Gilbert Guillaume, «De l'exécution des décisions de la Cour internationale de Justice» (1997), dans *La Cour internationale de Justice à l'aube du XXIe siècle, Le regard d'un juge*, Pédone, Paris, 2003, p. 179 (références omises).

[108] CR 2015/23, p. 62, par. 64 (Pellet).

la plaidoirie de M. Pellet. En effet, la position de la Cour européenne des droits de l'homme ne correspond pas à celle de la cour interaméricaine comme on pourrait le croire en écoutant M. Pellet. Dans l'arrêt *Meltex* du 21 mai 2013, la Cour européenne dit en effet :

> «la Cour souligne continuellement qu'il ne relève pas de ses compétences de vérifier si une partie a rempli les obligations que lui impose un des jugements de la Cour. Par conséquent, elle refusa d'examiner des requêtes relatives au manquement des Etats d'exécuter ses jugements, en déclarant de telles requêtes inadmissibles *ratione materiae.*»[109]

21. En outre, contrairement à ce que le Nicaragua a soutenu avant-hier[110], l'arrêt *Saiga II* du Tribunal international du droit de la mer n'a pas utilisé un pouvoir inhérent quand il s'est prononcé sur une demande relative à l'inexécution de son arrêt antérieur portant sur la prompte mainlevée du navire. Le Tribunal était en effet investi d'une demande portant sur la violation d'un ou plusieurs articles de la convention sur le droit de la mer. Et il était compétent pour toute affaire portant sur l'interprétation ou l'application des dispositions de celle-ci[111].

22. Le pas franchi par les cours et tribunaux internationaux dont la compétence est indépendante du consentement des parties aux procès qui se déroulent devant elles est infiniment plus modeste du pas que le Nicaragua invite la Cour à faire en se déclarant pourvue d'un pouvoir inhérent à juger de l'exécution de ses arrêts. Un tel pas, si la Cour devait le faire, pourrait décourager les Etats qui envisagent d'accepter la compétence de la Cour.

23. Non seulement la sagesse d'un tel pas serait ainsi contestable. Sa compatibilité avec le Statut le serait aussi. Comment considérer cohérente avec un Statut qui base la compétence de la Cour sur le consentement des parties à la soumission à la Cour de différends bien définis, la revendication d'un pouvoir «inhérent» de juger de différends portant sur la responsabilité internationale pour violation des obligations contenues dans un arrêt, dont la base serait cet arrêt et que les Etats peuvent considérer avoir définitivement réglé une affaire ?

24. Monsieur le président, Mesdames et Messieurs les juges, nonobstant les arguments portés par le Nicaragua à l'audience d'avant-hier, la Colombie continue à penser que l'article L du pacte

---

[109] Cour européenne des droits de l'homme (CEDH), *Meltex Ltd. c. Arménie*, application nº 45199/09, jugement du 21 mai 2013, par. 28.

[110] CR 2015/23, p. 56, par. 26 (Pellet).

[111] Tribunal international du droit de la mer (TIDM), arrêt du 1er juillet 1999, *Affaire du navire «SAIGA» (No. 2) (Saint-Vincent-et-les Grenadines c. Guinée)*, par. 30.

de Bogotá a une importance dans notre affaire. Lu conjointement à l'article 52, paragraphe 2, de la Charte des Nations Unies (les deux apparaissent sur l'écran), cet article indique que en tout cas d'alléguée inexécution d'un arrêt de la Cour les Etats américains parties au pacte s'obligent à entreprendre tout effort possible pour obtenir une solution pacifique au niveau régional. Pour donner plein effet à ces deux articles, l'obligation de «faire tous leurs efforts» au niveau régional et, notamment, pour les Etats parties au pacte de Bogotá, d'investir la réunion de consultation des ministres des relations extérieures des Etats parties au pacte, doit comprendre non seulement les cas où une partie envisage de recourir à l'article 94, paragraphe 2, de la Charte, mais aussi les cas où elle envisage de recourir à la Cour pour soutenir que l'alléguée inexécution a causé une responsabilité internationale. Or, le Nicaragua n'a entrepris aucun pas au niveau régional avant de recourir à la Cour. La Colombie soumet respectueusement ce fait à la considération de la Cour.

25. Les quatrième et cinquième exceptions préliminaires de la Colombie sont ainsi confirmées.

26. Monsieur le président, Mesdames et Messieurs les juges, je vous remercie pour votre patience. Je vous prie bien, Monsieur le président, de donner la parole à M. Bundy.

Le PRESIDENT : Merci, Monsieur le professeur. Je donne à présent la parole à M. Bundy.

Mr. BUNDY:

CONCLUDING REMARKS

1. Thank you very much, Mr. President, Members of the Court. Having heard my colleagues address Nicaragua's contentions advanced yesterday with respect to each of Colombia's preliminary objections, it falls to me to make some brief concluding remarks.

2. Nicaragua has advanced two bases of jurisdiction for its claims. The first is Article XXXI of the Pact of Bogotá[112]. Now, that was the basis of jurisdiction for the case decided by the Court's Judgment of 19 November 2012. And the second, which Nicaragua put forward as an alternative basis of jurisdiction in its Application, is grounded on a novel theory, which counsel for Nicaragua admitted is nowhere authorized in the Court's Statute, in the Rules of Court or even in the Pact of

---

[112]Application of Nicaragua, paras. 16-17.

Bogotá[113] and that theory is that, even though the case was fully and finally decided in 2012, and was thereafter removed from the List of pending cases before the Court, and I quote from Nicaragua's Application: "the jurisdiction of the Court lies in its inherent power to pronounce on the actions required by its Judgments"[114].

3. Colombia, for its part, has raised five preliminary objections. The first three — the absence of jurisdiction *ratione temporis*, the lack of a dispute, and the failure of Nicaragua to fulfil the [pre]conditions of Article II of the Pact, concern the absence of jurisdiction under the Pact of Bogotá.

4. To be clear, if the Court decides that there is no jurisdiction *ratione temporis* under Article LVI of the Pact, as Colombia believes to be the case, it does not need to reach the question whether, objectively, there was a dispute between the Parties over the subject-matter of Nicaragua's claims as of the critical date — the date of Nicaragua's Application — and similarly, the Court would not need to decide whether Nicaragua had satisfied the requirements of Article II of the Pact prior to instituting these proceedings. However, if the Court were to subscribe to Nicaragua's reading of Article LVI, including the all-important second paragraph, that would still not be the end of the matter, for the Court would still need to decide whether there really was objectively a dispute between the Parties as to the allegations advanced by Nicaragua in its Application, as of the critical date, and whether, if so, the facts show that the Parties were of the opinion, as of 26 November 2013, that such dispute could not be settled by direct negotiations through the usual diplomatic channels. If either of those requirements were not met, there would still be no jurisdiction under the Pact.

5. Colombia's fourth and fifth objections are interrelated and are directed to Nicaragua's alternative theory of jurisdiction. The fourth objection is that the Court has no "inherent jurisdiction" to pronounce on the actions required by one of its previous judgments and the fifth objection is centred on the principle that the Court has no post-adjudication enforcement jurisdiction.

---

[113]CR 2015/23, p. 48, para.11 (Pellet).

[114]Application, para. 18.

6. I think it is pretty evident that Nicaragua has advanced its alternative basis of jurisdiction because it realizes the fragility of its arguments that there is jurisdiction under the Pact of Bogotá. If Nicaragua were as confident as it professes to be that jurisdiction vests under the Pact, there would have been no need for it to conjure up its novel and far-reaching "inherent jurisdiction" theory. As Professor Treves has explained, Nicaragua's alternative basis of jurisdiction does not save Nicaragua because such "inherent jurisdiction" does not exist in the circumstances of this case.

7. I should also add that all of Colombia's preliminary objections have an exclusively preliminary character. In other words, all of them can be decided on the basis of the facts that have been adduced relevant to jurisdiction.

8. That being said, there is one common factor that has a bearing on each of Colombia's objections and that concerns the timing of Nicaragua's Application. I trust that the significance of the fact that Nicaragua lodged its Application on 26 November 2013 — the very last day it could under *its* interpretation of Article LVI of the Pact — will not be lost on the Court.

9. That date had nothing to do with whether a dispute genuinely existed between the Parties at the time. Nor did it have any relation with the question whether, if a dispute actually existed, the Parties — or even Nicaragua alone — considered that the dispute was one that could not be settled by negotiations. No, Mr. President; the date of 26 November 2013 was chosen for pure reasons of expediency. As Nicaragua's Agent acknowledged: "After this last date Nicaragua would be left without clear recourse to the instruments of peaceful resolution of conflicts which was at the heart of the Pact of Bogotá."[115] And it is precisely because there are a host of reasons why there is no jurisdiction under the Pact as of the critical date that Nicaragua had to invent its "inherent jurisdiction" alternative.

10. With respect to the question whether the Court has jurisdiction *ratione temporis*, I would only add one point to what Sir Michael Wood has already said.

11. As Sir Michael explained, the addition of the second paragraph to Article LVI was new in the Pact. The fact that it was a new addition to what had been provided for in previous treaties

---

[115]CR 2015/23, p. 15, para. 22 (Argüello Gómez).

was deliberate, and it was highlighted during the *travaux*. The negotiating States obviously considered the situation where dispute resolution procedures might have been instituted before a party to the Pact denounced it, and they wanted to ensure that such procedures survived the particular notice of denunciation and that is what the second paragraph of Article LVI does. In contrast though, what it does not do and what it does not say is that denunciation shall have no effect with respect to procedures initiated *after* the transmission of the particular notification. The negotiators could perfectly easily have provided for that outcome, but they did not do so.

12. On the screen, you will see the text of the second paragraph of Article LVI, which you are familiar with. "The denunciation shall have no effect with respect to pending procedures initiated *prior to the transmission of the particular notification*." [Emphasis added.]

13. For Nicaragua's interpretation to be valid, what the second paragraph should have said is the following. "The denunciation shall have no effect with *respect* to pending procedures initiated *prior to the date when the Pact ceases to be in force with respect to the State denouncing it*." [Emphasis added.] But that obviously did not happen, and it fundamentally undermines Nicaragua's interpretation of the provision.

14. Then there is the question whether there was a dispute between the Parties concerning the allegations in Nicaragua's Application and, if so, whether it could not be settled by negotiations.

15. According to Nicaragua's Agent and Professor Lowe, the existence of a dispute had been public knowledge since the very day that the Judgment was rendered — 19 November 2012 — as a result of President Santos's remarks that were made really just a few moments after the Judgment was read out[116]. But, as Professor Reisman has shown, that allegation is completely contradicted by what Nicaragua's President and what Nicaragua's highest military commanders said over the next twelve months. The Court will not find a single accusation on the record from these senior State representatives that they considered that a dispute had emerged — you won't find it — whether as a result of President Santos's remarks or otherwise.

---

[116] CR 2015/23, p. 17, para. 28 (Argüello Gómez); p. 42, para. 52 (Lowe).

16. I respectfully invite the Court to look at the record as a whole. There is a consistent pattern of statements emanating from President Ortega that show just the opposite of what our colleagues on the other side contend. I referred to many of these on Monday and counsel for Nicaragua studiously avoided mentioning any of them yesterday. Sometimes, Mr. President, it is instructive to listen to the silences.

17. We also heard yesterday that the Nicaraguan navy did not attempt to interfere with what are alleged to be illegal Colombian patrols in Nicaraguan waters, and that this is the reason there was no confrontation[117]. Apparently, Nicaragua wishes to take credit for the fact that the situation at sea was calm and without incident, as was repeatedly confirmed by Nicaragua's highest military officials. But let us not forget that it was President Ortega himself, on 13 August 2013, who credited *Colombia's* President Santos with the lack of any confrontations in the pacific situation[118].

18. And let us also not forget that, not simply on this occasion, but also on many others right up to the time the Application was filed, both President Ortega and President Santos had confirmed that they welcomed having negotiations, and that Foreign Minister Holguín had expressly stated that Colombia's doors were always open to negotiate a treaty[119]. I hope that responds to my good friend, Mr. Lowe's question whether Colombia ever responded to Nicaragua's offers[120]. It did.

19. Mr. President, Members of the Court: in the light of the factual context, the timing of Nicaragua's Application was artificial. It was lodged when it was because Nicaragua thought it was about to run out of time to institute proceedings under the Pact. But, at that time, there was not a shred of evidence that the Parties had a dispute over the allegations that appeared for the first time in the Application, or that they could not settle any issues relating to the implementation of the Judgment by negotiations. That is, as I said, why we have this far-fetched alternative theory of

---

[117]CR 2015/23, p. 14, para. 20 (Argüello Gómez).

[118]Preliminary Objections of Colombia (POC), Ann. 11; and see CR 2015/22, pp. 33-34, para. 11 (Bundy).

[119]CR 2015/22, p. 34, para. 11 (Bundy), and Written Statement of Nicaragua (WSN), Ann. 8, and Memorial of Nicaragua (MN), Ann. 40.

[120]CR 2015/23, p. 43, para. 56 (Lowe).

inherent jurisdiction expounded by Professor Pellet yesterday. It is supposed to act as some kind of safety net in the event Nicaragua cannot show that it satisfied the conditions for instituting proceedings under the Pact. But, as innovative as Professor Pellet's exposé was, it does not create a basis of jurisdiction where none otherwise exists.

20. Mr. President, Members of the Court, Colombia firmly believes that jurisdiction must be grounded on the fundamental principle of consent, which includes any conditions that are attached to that consent. We have shown that Colombia's consent to jurisdiction in this case does not exist under the Pact of Bogotá, and that there is no basis for implying consent with respect to Nicaragua's theory of "inherent jurisdiction".

Mr. President, that concludes my remarks. I thank the Court for its attention, and I would ask if the floor could now be given to Colombia's Agent. Thank you.

Le PRESIDENT: Merci, Monsieur Bundy. Je donne à présent la parole à S. Exc. M. Carlos Gustavo Arrieta, agent de la Colombie.

Mr. ARRIETA:

1. Mr. President, Members of the Court, as this will be our final presentation in this case and since Nicaragua has made some accusations about Colombia's position purportedly challenging your authority and rejecting your Judgment of 19 November 2012, I wish to stress two very important points before presenting our final submissions:

— *First*, Colombia firmly rejects Nicaragua's tendency to distort Colombian officials' declarations and statements. As Nicaragua recognized yesterday, what they have tried to do is nothing less than a "cheap shot". We believe it is not even that; it has been an outright misrepresentation of those statements. Mr. President, let me say something. It is true that Colombian public opinion does not agree with some aspects of the Judgment; Colombia is, after all, a democracy, and Nicaragua seems to forget that democratic debate about a Court decision is very different from defiance of it. Then, having a dualist system on boundaries is not a sin, we are proud of our constitutional system; but what should be clear, first, is that Colombia is, above all, a law-abiding country, and, second, that we are committed to the

Judgment's implementation. Our Constitutional Court, whose decisions are final, has held that judgments of the International Court of Justice are binding, that they have to be incorporated through treaties in case they affect our boundaries, and that it is our duty to negotiate them. That is the rule of law. And that is the way domestically for us to proceed; it is not, as Nicaragua has misstated, our use of domestic law to justify non-compliance.

— *Second*, as Colombia has made abundantly clear since November 2012, negotiations are the way to proceed for implementation of the Judgment. Now, last, Nicaragua's delegation seems to have fallen in line with President Ortega's declarations. Colombia wishes to confirm to them and to you what we have always said: we are willing to sit at any moment, with Nicaragua, and however many times it should prove necessary, to negotiate a treaty for the implementation of the Court's decision. This has been our position from the very start. I am glad Nicaragua's delegation has accepted it, and hope that they will show the Court that their position regarding negotiations is not purely rhetorical.

2. Mr. President, Members of the Court, I now have the honour formally to read Colombia's final submissions, which are as follows:

> "For the reasons set forth in our written and oral pleadings on preliminary objections, the Republic of Colombia requests the Court to adjudge and declare that it lacks jurisdiction over the proceedings brought by Nicaragua in its Application of 26 November 2013 and that said Application should be dismissed."

3. A copy of the written text of Colombia's final submissions is now being communicated to the Court and transmitted to the Agent of Nicaragua.

4. Mr. President, Members of the Court, before I conclude let me express, on behalf of all the members of the Colombian delegation, our thanks to you, Mr. President, and to the Members of the Court, for your attention and for the efficient manner in which these proceedings have been prepared and conducted. We are very grateful to all concerned: to the Registrar and his staff, to the interpreters, to the translators and to all those who have worked so hard behind the scenes to make this hearing possible.

5. That, Mr. President, concludes Colombia's case. Thank you.

Le PRESIDENT : Excellence, je vous remercie. La Cour prend acte des conclusions finales dont vous venez de donner lecture au nom de la Colombie. Le Nicaragua présentera son second tour de plaidoiries le vendredi 2 octobre, à 10 heures.

L'audience est levée.

L'audience est levée à 17 h 45.

___

Corrigé
Corrected

CR 2015/25

International Court of Justice

THE HAGUE

Cour internationale de Justice

LA HAYE

YEAR 2015

Public sitting

held on Friday 2 October 2015, at 10 a.m., at the Peace Palace,

President Abraham presiding,

in the case concerning **Alleged Violations of Sovereign Rights and Maritime Spaces in the Caribbean Sea (Nicaragua *v.* Colombia)**

Preliminary Objections

VERBATIM RECORD

ANNÉE 2015

Audience publique

tenue le vendredi 2 octobre 2015, à 10 heures, au Palais de la Paix,

sous la présidence de M. Abraham, président,

en l'affaire relative à des **Violations alléguées de droits souverains et d'espaces maritimes dans la mer des Caraïbes (Nicaragua c. Colombie)**

Exceptions préliminaires

COMPTE RENDU

Present:	President	Abraham
	Vice-President	Yusuf
	Judges	Owada
		Tomka
		Bennouna
		Cançado Trindade
		Greenwood
		Xue
		Gaja
		Sebutinde
		Bhandari
		Robinson
		Gevorgian
	Judges *ad hoc*	Daudet
		Caron
	Registrar	Couvreur

Présents :	M.	Abraham, président
	M.	Yusuf, vice-président
	MM.	Owada
		Tomka
		Bennouna
		Cançado Trindade
		Greenwood
	Mme	Xue
	M.	Gaja
	Mme	Sebutinde
	MM.	Bhandari
		Robinson
		Gevorgian, juges
	MM.	Daudet
		Caron, juges *ad hoc*
	M.	Couvreur, greffier

The Government of Nicaragua is represented by:

H.E. Mr. Carlos José Argüello Gómez, Ambassador of the Republic of Nicaragua to the Kingdom of the Netherlands,

as Agent and Counsel;

Mr. Vaughan Lowe, Q.C., member of the English Bar, Emeritus Professor of International Law, Oxford University, member of the Institut de droit international,

Mr. Alex Oude Elferink, Director, Netherlands Institute for the Law of the Sea, Professor of International Law of the Sea, Utrecht University,

Mr. Alain Pellet, Emeritus Professor at the University Paris Ouest, Nanterre-La Défense, former member and former Chairman of the International Law Commission, member of the Institut de droit international,

Mr. Antonio Remiro Brotóns, Professor of International Law, Universidad Autónoma de Madrid, member of the Institut de droit international,

as Counsel and Advocates;

Mr. César Vega Masís, Deputy Minister for Foreign Affairs, Director of Juridical Affairs, Sovereignty and Territory, Ministry of Foreign Affairs,

Mr. Walner Molina Pérez, Juridical Adviser, Ministry of Foreign Affairs,

Mr. Julio César Saborio, Juridical Adviser, Ministry of Foreign Affairs,

as Counsel;

Mr. Edgardo Sobenes Obregon, Counsellor, Embassy of Nicaragua in the Kingdom of the Netherlands,

Ms Claudia Loza Obregon, First Secretary, Embassy of Nicaragua in the Kingdom of the Netherlands,

Mr. Benjamin Samson, Ph.D. Candidate, Centre de droit international de Nanterre (CEDIN), University Paris Ouest, Nanterre-La Defense,

Ms Gimena González,

as Assistant Counsel;

Ms Sherly Noguera de Argüello, Consul General of the Republic of Nicaragua,

as Administrator.

Le Gouvernement du Nicaragua est représenté par :

S. Exc. M. Carlos José Argüello Gómez, ambassadeur de la République du Nicaragua auprès du Royaume des Pays-Bas,

comme agent et conseil ;

M. Vaughan Lowe, Q.C., membre du barreau d'Angleterre, professeur émérite de droit international, Oxford University, membre de l'Institut de droit international,

M. Alex Oude Elferink, directeur de l'Institut néerlandais du droit de la mer, professeur de droit international de la mer, Université d'Utrecht,

M. Alain Pellet, professeur émérite à l'Université Paris Ouest, Nanterre-La Défense, ancien membre et ancien président de la Commission du droit international, membre de l'Institut de droit international,

M. Antonio Remiro Brotóns, professeur de droit international à l'Universidad Autónoma de Madrid, membre de l'Institut de droit international,

comme conseils et avocats ;

M. César Vega Masís, vice-ministre des affaires étrangères, directeur des affaires juridiques, de la souveraineté et du territoire au ministère des affaires étrangères,

M. Walner Molina Pérez, conseiller juridique au ministère des affaires étrangères,

M. Julio César Saborio, conseiller juridique au ministère des affaires étrangères,

comme conseils ;

M. Edgardo Sobenes Obregon, conseiller à l'ambassade du Nicaragua au Royaume des Pays-Bas,

Mme Claudia Loza Obregon, première secrétaire de l'ambassade du Nicaragua au Royaume des Pays-Bas,

M. Benjamin Samson, doctorant au Centre de droit international de Nanterre (CEDIN), Université Paris Ouest, Nanterre-La Défense,

Mme Gimena Gonzales,

comme conseils adjoints ;

Mme Sherly Noguera de Argüello, consul général de la République du Nicaragua,

comme administrateur.

The Government of Colombia is represented by:

H.E. Ms María Ángela Holguín Cuéllar, Minister for Foreign Affairs,

H.E. Mr. Francisco Echeverri Lara, Vice Minister of Multilateral Affairs, Ministry of Foreign Affairs,

as National Authorities;

H.E. Mr. Carlos Gustavo Arrieta Padilla, former Judge of the Council of State of Colombia, former Attorney General of Colombia and former Ambassador of Colombia to the Kingdom of the Netherlands,

as Agent;

H.E. Mr. Manuel José Cepeda Espinosa, former President of the Constitutional Court of Colombia, former Permanent Delegate of Colombia to UNESCO and former Ambassador of Colombia to the Helvetic Confederation,

as Co-Agent;

Mr. W. Michael Reisman, McDougal Professor of International Law at Yale University, member of the Institut de droit international,

Mr. Rodman R. Bundy, former *avocat à la Cour d'appel de Paris*, member of the New York Bar, Eversheds LLP, Singapore,

Sir Michael Wood, K.C.M.G., member of the English Bar, member of the International Law Commission,

Mr. Tullio Treves, member of the Institut de droit international, Senior Public International Law Consultant, Curtis, Mallet-Prevost, Colt & Mosle LLP Milan, Professor, University of Milan,

Mr. Eduardo Valencia-Ospina, member and Special Rapporteur of the International Law Commission, President of the Latin American Society of International Law,

Mr. Matthias Herdegen, Dr. h.c., Professor of International Law, Director of the Institute of International Law at the University of Bonn,

as Counsel and Advocates;

H.E. Mr. Juan José Quintana Aranguren, Ambassador of the Republic of Colombia to the Kingdom of the Netherlands, Permanent Representative of Colombia to the OPCW, former Permanent Representative of Colombia to the United Nations in Geneva,

H.E. Mr. Andelfo García González, Ambassador of the Republic of Colombia to the Kingdom of Thailand, Professor of International Law, former Deputy Minister for Foreign Affairs,

Ms Andrea Jiménez Herrera, Counsellor, Embassy of the Republic of Colombia in the Kingdom of the Netherlands,

Le Gouvernement de la Colombie est représenté par :

S. Exc. Mme María Ángela Holguín Cuéllar, ministre des affaires étrangères,

S. Exc. M. Francisco Echeverri Lara, vice-ministre des affaires multilatérales, ministère des affaires étrangères,

comme autorités nationales ;

S. Exc. M. Carlos Gustavo Arrieta Padilla, ancien juge au Conseil d'Etat de la Colombie, ancien *Attorney General* de la Colombie et ancien ambassadeur de la Colombie auprès du Royaume des Pays-Bas,

comme agent ;

S. Exc. M. Manuel José Cepeda Espinosa, ancien président de la Cour constitutionnelle de Colombie, ancien délégué permanent de la Colombie auprès de l'UNESCO et ancien ambassadeur de la Colombie auprès de la Confédération helvétique,

comme coagent ;

M. W. Michael Reisman, professeur de droit international à l'Université de Yale, titulaire de la chaire McDougal, membre de l'Institut de droit international,

M. Rodman R. Bundy, ancien avocat à la Cour d'appel de Paris, membre du barreau de New York, cabinet Eversheds LLP, Singapour,

sir Michael Wood, K.C.M.G., membre du barreau d'Angleterre, membre de la Commission du droit international,

M. Tullio Treves, membre de l'Institut de droit international, conseiller principal en droit international public, cabinet Curtis, Mallet-Prevost, Colt et Mosle LLP, Milan, professeur à l'Université de Milan,

M. Eduardo Valencia-Ospina, membre et rapporteur spécial de la Commission du droit international, président de la société latino-américaine de droit international,

M. Matthias Herdegen, docteur *honoris causa*, professeur de droit international, directeur de l'Institut de droit international de l'Université de Bonn,

comme conseils et avocats ;

S. Exc. M. Juan José Quintana Aranguren, ambassadeur de la République de Colombie auprès du Royaume des Pays-Bas, représentant permanent de la Colombie auprès de l'OIAC, ancien représentant permanent de la Colombie auprès des Nations Unies à Genève,

S. Exc. M. Andelfo García González, ambassadeur de la République de Colombie auprès du Royaume de Thaïlande, professeur de droit international, ancien vice-ministre des affaires étrangères,

Mme Andrea Jiménez Herrera, conseiller, ambassade de la République de Colombie au Royaume des Pays-Bas,

Ms Lucía Solano Ramírez, Second Secretary, Embassy of the Republic of Colombia in the Kingdom of the Netherlands,

Mr. Andrés Villegas Jaramillo, Co-ordinator, Group of Affairs before the ICJ, Ministry of Foreign Affairs,

Mr. Giovanny Andrés Vega Barbosa, Group of Affairs before the ICJ, Ministry of Foreign Affairs,

Ms Ana María Durán López, Group of Affairs before the ICJ, Ministry of Foreign Affairs,

Mr. Camilo Alberto Gómez Niño, Group of Affairs before the ICJ, Ministry of Foreign Affairs,

Mr. Juan David Veloza Chará, Third Secretary, Group of Affairs before the ICJ, Ministry of Foreign Affairs,

as Legal Advisers;

Mr. Rear Admiral Luís Hernán Espejo, National Navy of Colombia,

CN William Pedroza, International Affairs Bureau, National Navy of Colombia,

CF Hermann León, National Maritime Authority (DIMAR), National Navy of Colombia,

Mr. Scott Edmonds, Cartographer, International Mapping,

Mr. Thomas Frogh, Cartographer, International Mapping,

as Technical Advisers;

Ms Charis Tan, Advocate and Solicitor, Singapore, member of the New York Bar, Solicitor, England and Wales, Eversheds LLP, Singapore,

Mr. Eran Sthoeger, LL.M., New York University School of Law,

Mr. Renato Raymundo Treves, LL.M., Associate, Curtis, Mallet-Prevost, Colt & Mosle LLP Milan,

Mr. Lorenzo Palestini, Ph.D Candidate, Graduate Institute of International and Development Studies, Geneva,

as Legal Assistants.

Mme Lucía Solano Ramírez, deuxième secrétaire, ambassade de la République de Colombie au Royaume des Pays-Bas,

M. Andrés Villegas Jaramillo, coordinateur, division des affaires portées devant la CIJ, ministère des affaires étrangères,

M. Giovanny Andrés Vega Barbosa, division des affaires portées devant la CIJ, ministère des affaires étrangères,

Mme Ana María Durán López, division des affaires portées devant la CIJ, ministère des affaires étrangères,

M. Camillo Alberto Gómez Niño, division des affaires portées devant la CIJ, ministère des affaires étrangères,

M. Juan David Veloza Chará, troisième secrétaire, division des affaires portées devant la CIJ, ministère des affaires étrangères,

comme conseillers juridiques ;

le contre-amiral Luis Hernán Espejo, marine nationale de Colombie,

le capitaine de vaisseau William Pedroza, bureau des affaires internationales, marine nationale de Colombie,

le capitaine de frégate Hermann León, autorité maritime nationale (DIMAR), marine nationale de Colombie,

M. Scott Edmonds, cartographe, International Mapping,

M. Thomas Frogh, cartographe, International Mapping,

comme conseillers techniques ;

Mme Charis Tan, avocat et *Solicitor* (Singapour), membre du barreau de New York, *Solicitor* (Angleterre et Pays de Galles), cabinet Eversheds LLP, Singapour,

M. Eran Sthoeger, LL.M., faculté de droit de l'Université de New York,

M. Renato Raymundo Treves, LL.M., associé au cabinet Curtis, Mallet-Prevost, Colt et Mosle LLP, Milan,

M. Lorenzo Palestini, doctorant, Institut de hautes études internationales et du développement, Genève,

comme assistants juridiques.

Le PRESIDENT : Veuillez vous asseoir. L'audience est ouverte. La Cour se réunit aujourd'hui pour entendre le second tour de plaidoiries du Nicaragua. J'indique d'abord que, pour des raisons dont elle m'a dûment fait part, la juge Donoghue n'est pas en mesure de siéger aujourd'hui. Je donne à présent la parole à M. Argüello Gómez, agent de la République du Nicaragua.

Mr. ARGÜELLO GÓMEZ: Good morning Mr. President, Members of the Court, and good morning to the delegation of Colombia.

1. Mr. President, it was not my intention to submit the Court to a second Agent's speech, even if it will be a fairly short one. But there are some factual statements that have been made that are not entirely accurate or have been placed without indication of the time frame they were made.

Existence of a dispute

2. The first one, which was reiterated by Professor Reisman, Mr. Bundy and Mr. Valencia Ospina, is that it was not credible that there could be a dispute when President Ortega made statements on the occasion of the 33rd anniversary of the Nicaraguan naval forces on 13 August 2013 (published on 14 August) that, in the words of Mr. Bundy, "credit[ing] President Santos with the lack of any confrontations"[1]. And Professor Reisman, for his part, repeated that part of the statement of President Ortega in which he said that "there has not been any kind of confrontation between the Colombian and Nicaraguan Navy"[2].

3. This statement is used to attempt to prove that there was no dispute that merited filing an application on 26 November 2013. The point is that this argument forgets to mention that after those words of President Ortega were delivered in August, President Santos decreed on 9 September 2013 the creation of the special zone of jurisdiction called the Integrated Contiguous Zone and located in the maritime spaces that the 2012 Judgment attributed to Nicaragua — Decree

[1]CR 2015/24, p. 42, para. 17 (Bundy).

[2]*Ibid.*, p. 21, para. 10 (Reisman).

No. 1946. In fact, Professor Reisman's speech which addressed the general question that Colombia has titled as "Absence of a Dispute"[3] does not mention Decree 1946 at all.

4. After the Decree on 9 September 2013, it was followed up on 18 September by an order of President Santos to the high command of the Armed Forces to defend with "cloak and sword"[4] the continental shelf that Colombia has in the Caribbean.

5. These orders were soon put into effect. The first incidents with the Colombian navy that we have documented in the Nicaraguan Memorial began on 13 October 2013[5]. The Memorial documents ten incidents provoked by the Colombian Armed Forces between that date and 25 November 2013, one day before the Application was filed. In one of these incidents on 17 November 2013 the Commander of the Colombian frigate *Almirante Padilla* ordered the Captain of the Nicaraguan flag lobster boat *Miss Sofia* out of the area located clearly in Nicaraguan waters attributed by the Judgment. When the Nicaraguan boat established communication with the Colombian Officer explaining that he was in Nicaraguan waters he was told that they did not recognize the Judgment of the International Court of Justice.

6. It is remarkable that faced with these facts Professor Reisman can say that

> "we [that is, Colombia] have been compelled to appear before you to respond to frivolous claims without a jurisdictional base, which are said to constitute a phantom dispute, the subject-matter of which was entirely unknown to Colombia until it was informed by the Registry that, once again, proceedings had been instituted against it"[6].

Negotiations

7. The other important fact that has not been reported faithfully by Colombia is that President Ortega has never stated that Nicaragua is willing to negotiate the content and decisions of the 2012 Judgment. President Ortega is perfectly aware that the application of a judgment of the International Court of Justice does not depend on negotiations, nor has he ever stated that he would

---

[3]*Ibid.*, p. 19 (Reisman).

[4]"Santos orders defense of the continental shelf with cloak and sword", *El Espectador,* 19 Nov. 2013; Memorial of Nicaragua (MN), Ann. 41.

[5]Letter from the Nicaraguan Naval Force to the Ministry of Foreign Affairs reporting on incidents with the Colombian Navy in Nicaragua's Exclusive Economic Zone, 26 Aug. 2014; MN, Ann. 23A. See also Diplomatic Note from the Minister for Foreign Affairs of Nicaragua, to the Minister for Foreign Affairs of Colombia, 13 Sep. 2013; MN, Ann. 18.

[6]CR 2015/24, p. 25, para. 19 (Reisman).

accept to do so. In the clear wording of Article 60 of the Statute of the Court a judgment is final and without appeal.

8. In all President Ortega's statements this understanding emerges clearly that the Judgments of the Court must be complied with. What he has indicated is that Nicaragua is willing to sign a Treaty containing — that is, transcribing the pertinent wording of the Judgment — if that facilitates the implementation by Colombia. But he has never implied that Nicaragua agrees that the implementation of the Judgment is subservient to the signing of a treaty. The fact that Nicaragua agreed to discuss questions of fisheries, security and environmental issues or even commercial matters is not because they are relevant or necessary for implementing the Judgment. These are matters of good neighbourly relations which Nicaragua is anxious to establish and maintain for the benefit of both countries.

9. In Nicaragua's Written Statement, Chapter 4, paras. 4.5 to 4.7 and Section III B, it explains its position on the question of the possibility of negotiations. The very clear fact is that the subject-matter of this dispute as stated in the Application is not the same subject-matter on which the Parties have expressed willingness to negotiate. Nicaragua is not willing and has never agreed to negotiate the terms of the Judgment, that is, the delimitation it establishes. And Colombia is only willing to negotiate if it also involves negotiating the terms of the Judgment.

Nicaragua's statements on negotiations

10. The statements of President Ortega speak for themselves. The following are statements published in the media — including the official government media — and readily available as indicated in the footnotes.

11. On 10 September 2013 in a message to the nation he stated, [tab 36 on] "that the only objective of an eventual treaty with Colombia is to enforce the ruling by the International Court of Justice of The Hague (ICJ), which restituted rights to Nicaragua in the Caribbean Sea"[7]. He added,

---

[7] "Treaty with Colombia must serve to enforce ICJ judgment", *Radio La Primerisima*, 10 Sep. 2013, available at http://www.radiolaprimerisima.com/noticias/148607/tratado-con-colombia-debe-servir-para-cumplir-fallo-cij; see also "Daniel Ortega says that a treaty would only be to comply with judgment", *El Tiempo*, 10 Sep. 2013, available at http://www.eltiempo.com/archivo/documento/CMS-13056908.

"Now, Colombia and Nicaragua have to sit together so that the ruling by the Court is implemented."[8] [Tab 36 off]

12. During the Reception of the Central American Torch in the Plaza of the Revolution on 12 September 2013 President Ortega reiterated: [tab 37 on]

> "We are ready; we are willing to create the corresponding commission so that it meets with a commission from the brotherly Colombian people, of the Government of Colombia, so that we work together in order to enable *the implementation of the Court's ruling* so that it rests underpinned, ratified; because the ruling was delivered *and it is a simple matter of incorporating it so that it is recorded in a treaty between Colombia and Nicaragua.*"[9] (Emphasis added.)
>
> "In such treaty, Colombia and Nicaragua would proceed to comply with the ruling, to the ruling by the ICJ of The Hague. Such is the path to Peace, the path of Unity, the path of Fraternity."[10] [Tab 37 off]

13. The two previous declarations of President Ortega were made two months before the Application was filed. But the same position was recently reiterated by President Ortega. During the Ceremony of the 36th Anniversary of the Nicaraguan Army on 3 September 2015 he stated: [tab 38 on]

> "And now, it is time for Colombia to respect international law . . . How? By moving toward a dialogue with Nicaragua; for what? So that the *Ruling is fully implemented*, which must lead to the approval and acknowledgement by the National Assembly and the Colombian Congress of the new maritime boundaries set forth by the ruling pursuant to international law, by the highest Court that exists in our Planet, which is the International Court of Justice that ruled in favor of Nicaragua."[11] (Emphasis added.) [Tab 38 off]

Colombian statements

14. Colombia for its part has maintained the position expressed by its President on the day the Judgment was delivered in the remarkable statement that has been quoted by Nicaraguan counsel and its Agent — in passing, one must wonder why our distinguished Colombian colleagues

---

[8] "Treaty with Colombia must serve to enforce ICJ judgment", *Radio La Primerisima*, 10 Sep. 2013, available at http://www.radiolaprimerisima.com/noticias/148607/tratado-con-colombia-debe-servir-para-cumplir-fallo-cij.

[9] "President Daniel urges Colombia to honor commitments to peace and international law", *El 19 Digital*, 12 Sept. 2013 available at http://www.el19digital.com/articulos/ver/titulo:13092-presidente-daniel-insta-a-colombia-a-honrar-compromisos-con-la-paz-y-el-derecho-internacional; emphasis added.

[10] "President Daniel urges Colombia to honor commitments to peace and international law", *El 19 Digital*, 12 Sept. 2013, available at http://www.el19digital.com/articulos/ver/titulo:13092-presidente-daniel-insta-a-colombia-a-honrar-compromisos-con-la-paz-y-el-derecho-internacional.

[11] "President Daniel and Comrade Rosario participate in the ceremony of the 36th Anniversary of the Army of Nicaragua", 3 Sept. 2015, available http://www.el19digital.com/articulos/ver/titulo:33155-presidente-daniel-y-companera-rosario-participan-en-acto-del-36-aniversario-del-ejercito-de-nicaragua; emphasis added.

believe that quoting the words of the President of Colombia are cheap shots on Nicaragua's part President Santos' words were: [Tab 39 on]

> "The Court adjusted the line of delimitation, separating the cays of Serrana, Serranilla, Quitasueño and Bajo Nuevo from the rest of the Archipelago."[12]
>
> "Taking into account the above, Colombia — represented by its Head of State — emphatically rejects that aspect of the Judgment rendered by the Court today."[13] [Tab 39 off]

15. That is, Colombia rejects the limits fixed by the Court that in its views separate the cays of the archipelago. If we couple these words with the enactment of Decree 1946 — which in effect unites the waters of the main islands with all the cays — it is clear that the intention is to disregard the rights of Nicaragua recognized in the 2012 Judgment. It is indeed not a sign of willingness to implement the Judgment; it is a clear statement to the contrary.

16. The declarations of the President of Colombia and the enactment of Decree 1946 are not an offer to implement the Judgment with or without a treaty. As President Santos explained in his declaration on the so-called "integral strategy of Colombia on the Judgment of the International Court of Justice" given on 9 September 2013, he said: [tab 40 on] "1. We decided that without a treaty, the Judgment is not applicable. 2. We consolidated our archipelago by declaring an Integral Contiguous Zone."[14] [Tab 40 off]

17. President Santos makes it perfectly clear that the object of Decree 1946 establishing the Integral Contiguous Zone was to consolidate the maritime areas between the archipelago since, as he stated in his very first speech on 19 November 2012, Colombia could not accept that it should be separated. [Tab 41 on] On the screen we can appreciate what Decree 1946 does with the delimitation established by the Court[15].

18. From the statements and actions by Colombia, it is clear that it is not willing to negotiate the full implementation of the Judgment which is a condition *sine qua non* for Nicaragua to accept

---

[12]Declaration of President Juan Manuel Santos on the Judgment of the International Court of Justice, 19 Nov. 2012; MN, Ann. 1.

[13]Declaration of President Juan Manuel Santos on the Judgment of the International Court of Justice, 19 Nov. 2012; MN, Ann. 1.

[14]Declaration of President Juan Manuel Santos on the integral strategy of Colombia on the Judgment of the International Court of Justice", 9 Sep. 2013; MN, Ann. 4.

[15]See MN, fig. 2.2.

negotiations. There was then absolutely no meeting of minds on the question of negotiations when the Application was filed and this situation persists today.

19. The statement made by the distinguished Agent of Colombia in his closing words that Colombia was willing "to negotiate a treaty for the implementation of the Court's decision"[16] in effect carefully conditions the implementation to negotiations. This only brings us back to square one. It is not a question of negotiating the implementation but as President Ortega stated very simply what had to be done was "a simple matter of incorporating it (that is the text of the Judgment) so that it is recorded in a treaty between Colombia and Nicaragua"[17]. For Nicaragua it is clear that the implementation of a Judgment of the Court is final and not subject to negotiations. [Tab 41 off]

Comments by counsel for Colombia

20. Now I will address some comments by counsel for Colombia. Mr. Valencia-Ospina stated that it was manifest that Nicaragua filed its Application not because there was a dispute that could not be solved by negotiations but only because of what he calls the "purely opportunistic"[18] reason that Nicaragua wished to preserve the basis of jurisdiction and not because of the futility of negotiations. While it is true that Nicaragua waited until the last day to file its Application, this only shows forbearance on Nicaragua's part in the hope that the Colombian democracy would come to its legal senses and comply with international law. It is also evident and perfectly justified that Nicaragua did not wish to let the Pact of Bogotá be out of force for Colombia and thus let scape the possibility of having recourse to the procedures of the Pact due to the opportunistic denunciation made by Colombia. Furthermore, it is incontestable that Nicaragua had the right to file the Application at any moment before the denunciation came into force on 27 November 2013.

21. Mr. Bundy commented that "it is [clear] that Nicaragua has advanced its alternative basis of jurisdiction [the inherent jurisdiction] because it [recognizes] the fragility of its arguments that

---

[16]CR 2015/24, p. 44, para. 1.2 (Arrieta).

[17]"President Daniel urges Colombia to honor commitments to peace and international law", *El 19 Digital*, 12 Sep. 2013, available at http://www.el19digital.com/articulos/ver/titulo:13092-presidente-daniel-insta-a-colombia-a-honrar-compromisos-con-la-paz-y-el-derecho-internacional.

[18]CR 2015/24, p. 29, para. 10. (Valencia-Ospina).

there is jurisdiction under the Pact of Bogotá"[19]. It is surprising that such a distinguished jurist can put in doubt that it is only sensible for parties to invoke all existing bases of jurisdiction. Besides, when this additional basis of jurisdiction was suggested by Nicaraguan counsel, it was accepted by Nicaragua readily because it considered that this position reflects the best interests of international law and of this Court.

22. Professor Reisman states that "Nicaragua claims that it is a small State compared to Colombia and . . . is entitled to special treatment with respect to the brevity . . . between its Application and the cessation of jurisdiction under the Pact"[20]. Mr. President, in the 31 years I have been representing Nicaragua in different cases before this Court, Nicaragua has never asked for special treatment or ever received it. Whenever Nicaragua has called attention to the fact that it is a small State, it has been only to emphasize its great dependence on international law. Professor Reisman is well documented and has written on the *Nicaragua* v. *United States of America* case so presumably is aware that Nicaragua never asked for special treatment in that case . . . much less would it do so with Colombia. In any event, it is surprising that the exercise of a right by Nicaragua when it considered opportune to do so, that is to file its Application, should be treated as a request for special treatment.

23. Finally, Mr. President, we are not here — and I quote again Professor Reisman — to "malign a State that dares to criticize a judgment . . . of the Court"[21]. We are criticizing a country that is not willing to comply with a judgment of the Court and that openly takes actions that violate the terms of that judgment. Apparently the people of Chile — a great democracy — were not very happy with the judgment in its case with Peru, but they implemented the judgment. To go no further, I have to confess that I was not happy when the Court decided that a rock 1 metre in diameter in the area of Quitasueño allowed Colombia rights to several thousand square kilometres of maritime areas, a rock whose existence was only established by Colombian employees and has never been seen by Nicaraguans. But, like Chile, we accept the judgment as final and binding and are not here to change the Judgment but to implement it.

---

[19] *Ibid.*, p. 40, para. 6 (Bundy).

[20] CR 2015/24, pp. 23-24, para. 15 (Reisman).

[21] *Ibid.*, p. 24, para. 18 (Reisman).

24. Professor Virally commented on what to do if a superpower does not comply with its international obligations and, for Nicaragua, Colombia is a superpower. He said that what was left was the mobilization of shame. So one must not confuse the mobilization of shame with maligning.

Mr. President, Members of the Court, this ends my presentation. Thank you for your kind attention. Now Mr. President, may I ask you to call Professor Remiro to the podium.

Le PRESIDENT : Merci, Monsieur l'agent. Je donne à présent la parole au professeur Antonio Remiro.

M. REMIRO BROTÓNS :

COMPÉTENCE DE LA COUR *RATIONE TEMPORIS* SUIVANT LES ARTICLES XXXI ET LVI DU PACTE DE BOGOTÁ

I. Introduction

1. Monsieur le président, Mesdames et Messieurs les juges, je reprends la parole aujourd'hui afin de clarifier certains points concernant l'article XXXI et l'article LVI du pacte sur lesquels la Colombie essaie, à notre avis, de semer la confusion. Toutefois, et rappelant les indications de M. le président nous invitant à la concision en conformité avec le Règlement de la Cour, mes mots seront brefs. Avant d'entrer dans le détail, je voudrais tout d'abord assurer à nos amis de l'autre côté que nous sommes complètement convaincus de la compétence de cette Cour pour entendre l'affaire que le Nicaragua lui a soumise sur la base de l'article XXXI et de l'article LVI du pacte — même si, en tant que professeur, le regret sera de ne pas bénéficier des réflexions de la Cour au sujet de sa compétence inhérente en tant qu'organe judiciaire — encore que, après tout, elle puisse retenir les deux fondements à sa compétence qui se renforcent sans s'exclure. Par ailleurs, si la Colombie est complètement sûre que le pacte ne donne pas à la Cour la base de compétence nécessaire, la question qui vient à l'esprit est celle de savoir pourquoi elle perd son temps avec d'autres objections préliminaires, y compris celles qui postulent que le pacte est en effet en vigueur ?

2. Le Nicaragua soutient que sa propre interprétation de l'article LVI en relation avec l'article XXXI du pacte reste intacte après deux tours de plaidoiries de la Colombie, et il réaffirme

la position systématiquement adoptée tant dans son exposé écrit du 2 avril 2015 qu'au premier tour de ses plaidoiries, le 29 septembre[22]. Le Nicaragua est convaincu d'avoir prouvé que la Cour est compétente pour connaître de l'affaire qui lui est soumise, dès lors que l'on applique la règle générale d'interprétation au second paragraphe de l'article LVI. En ce qui concerne ce paragraphe, le Nicaragua a mis en évidence l'artificialité de la manœuvre tentée par la Colombie afin de faire obstacle à l'application de l'article XXXI et du premier paragraphe de l'article LVI, dispositions auxquelles la Colombie essaie d'échapper.

3. Nous sommes pourtant convaincus que, sous les apparences, la Colombie cherchait à confondre la Cour et c'est pour cela que nous avons procédé à les démanteler par une revision de chacune des 19 dispositions sur 60 qui, selon la Colombie, pourraient bénéficier de la clause de *survie* pendant le délai d'un an après la transmission du préavis de la dénonciation prévu au premier paragraphe. Cette démarche portait également sur l'article L, si important pour l'exécution des arrêts, mais pas tellement pour établir la compétence de la Cour, article que, selon la Colombie, nous avons ignoré[23]. La Colombie n'écoute pas, ou bien elle lit mal[24]. Cet aperçu de l'ensemble du pacte nous a permis d'établir le lien indissoluble des articles II à VI du premier chapitre, qui proclame l'obligation générale de régler les différends par des moyens pacifiques, avec les chapitres II à V, qui régissent les procédures de règlement prévues pour remplir cette obligation.

II. L'article LVI du pacte confirme la compétence de la Cour

4. La Colombie essaie de vous convaincre que seul doit être considéré le deuxième paragraphe de l'article LVI à condition de vous engager dans un raisonnement *a contrario* et d'accepter que ledit paragraphe dit ce qu'il ne dit pas. En d'autres termes, selon la Colombie, cette disposition est utile uniquement si on accepte que, grâce à elle, le préavis produit un effet immédiat. La Colombie va jusqu'à affirmer que, autrement, le résultat serait «absurde et déraisonnable». Mais si tel était le cas, alors la question que nous devions nous poser est celle de comprendre les motifs des auteurs du pacte pour «tricoter» une rédaction si machiavélique. Est-ce

---

[22] CR 2015/23, p. 19-32, par. 1-38 (Remiro Brotóns).

[23] CR 2015/24, p. 15, par. 23 (Wood).

[24] CR 2015/23, p. 27 (Remiro Brotóns).

qu'il ne serait pas plus logique et raisonnable d'avoir prévu de manière expresse que l'introduction de nouvelles requêtes et procédures étaient exclues dès la transmission du préavis ?

5. Mercredi, la Colombie a montré sur l'écran ce que le deuxième paragraphe de l'article LVI dit et, d'autre part, ce que le Nicaragua, selon la Colombie, souhaite[25]. [Projection.] Vous l'avez maintenant sur l'écran. Mais la Colombie se trompe car le Nicaragua n'a aucun problème avec cette disposition. Le Nicaragua considère que le deuxième paragraphe de l'article LVI a un sens utile si on le prend tout simplement au pied de la lettre. On pourrait certes parler de son caractère accessoire, mais il ne faut pas confondre ce qui n'est pas nécessaire avec ce qui est inutile.

6. Certes, les auteurs du pacte pourraient avoir omis la règle du deuxième paragraphe de l'article LVI vu que la règle du premier paragraphe suffisait pour protéger les procédures en cours déjà entamées à la date du préavis. Mais cela ne rend pas le paragraphe 2 forcément inutile ; être *superflu* ne signifie pas être dépourvu d'effet *utile* : le deuxième paragraphe continue à remplir sa fonction plus spécifique. Il est là pour assurer à nouveau que personne ne puisse mettre en doute que le pacte s'applique aux procédures déjà entamées à la date du préavis de la dénonciation.

7. Ce contre quoi le Nicaragua se bat n'est donc pas le second paragraphe de l'article LVI, mais la manœuvre que la Colombie tente afin de nous faire lire ce que le texte ne dit pas et d'en faire la seule vérité absolue. Finalement, je voudrais attirer encore une fois l'attention sur les dangers de dérive de la démarche qu'elle nous propose. Si la Colombie avait raison, nous serions en présence d'une clause à effets assez corrosifs sur la compétence de la Cour cachée derrière un texte pourtant apparemment clair, totalement incompatible avec le premier paragraphe de l'article LVI ainsi que, par ricochet, avec l'article XXXI, dispositions que la Colombie s'accorde le privilège d'ignorer dans son aventure interprétative. La position colombienne est totalement incompatible avec une interprétation de bonne foi, conforme à l'objet et au but du pacte.

8. En outre, il serait très fâcheux d'admettre que l'esprit de l'article LVI consiste à établir l'effet immédiat de la dénonciation sur les chapitres II à V du pacte tout en maintenant les circonstances — articles II à VI du premier chapitre — qui pourraient empêcher la survie des

[25] CR 2015/24, p. 41 (Bundy).

procédures déjà entamées le jour de la dénonciation. Il serait particulièrement pervers de prétendre, d'une part, que la Cour manque de compétence pour examiner les requêtes introduites à compter de la date du préavis de la dénonciation, et d'autre part, d'assurer la continuité des dispositions permettant à l'Etat auteur de la dénonciation de faire échouer les procédures en cours à cette date. On ne peut pas accepter sans nuire à la réputation des auteurs du pacte que le premier paragraphe a été conçu comme une sorte de pelle dans les mains de l'Etat dénonçant qui souhaite tout d'un coup enterrer les rares procédures ouvertes.

9. C'est pourtant ce que la Colombie est en train de pratiquer au cours des présentes plaidoiries. D'abord, notre contradicteur nie la compétence de la Cour, puis il essaie de se retrancher derrière l'article II pour mettre fin à la procédure.

10. Si on accepte la thèse avancée par la Colombie concernant l'article LVI, son interprétation reposerait sur un principe résultant d'une lecture *a contrario* d'une règle particulière qui prévaudrait sur la règle générale écrite, claire et précise, dont elle découle. En somme, la Colombie prétend pulvériser le premier paragraphe de l'article LVI. Ce paragraphe, Mesdames et Messieurs les juges, prend son sens en relation à la compétence obligatoire de la Cour uniquement s'il protège cette compétence vis-à-vis des requêtes qui pourraient être formulées pendant le délai prévu au premier paragraphe. Sinon, on comprend mal sa pertinence.

11. Certes, un raisonnement *a contrario* peut être un moyen auxiliaire, parmi tant d'autres, pour déterminer la portée d'une règle, ou comme moyen de confirmation d'une interprétation à laquelle on est arrivé par d'autres voies. Toutefois, il serait très imprudent d'utiliser l'interprétation *a contrario* comme seule méthode et d'en déduire la neutralisation totale d'une disposition au mépris de la règle générale d'interprétation codifiée à l'article 31, paragraphe 1, de la convention de Vienne sur le droit des traités de 1969. Si l'on applique la règle générale d'interprétation aux deux paragraphes de l'article LVI, on arrive aux conclusions proposées par le Nicaragua. Tous deux répondent aux mêmes principes de stabilité, certitude et sécurité ; tous deux gardent entre eux l'harmonie souhaitée ainsi que la cohérence logique et axiologique. L'interprétation donnée par la Colombie du paragraphe deux ne peut pas vider de toute substance les valeurs et les intérêts protégés au premier paragraphe. Le premier paragraphe conserve ainsi toute son utilité. Le deuxième paragraphe aussi. Le pacte aussi. Et cela répond à l'objet et au but du pacte en

conformité avec le principe de bonne foi. Tout cela est absent lorsqu'on retient l'interprétation *a contrario* du deuxième paragraphe avancée par la Colombie où l'harmonie fait totalement défaut.

12. Jusqu'ici je me suis occupé du point fondamental de la position du Nicaragua sur la compétence de la Cour qui découle de l'article XXXI et de l'article LVI du pacte de Bogotá. Néanmoins, comme la Colombie a consacré une partie non négligeable de sa plaidoirie de mercredi dernier à se pencher sur des éléments secondaires, je suis obligé d'attirer votre attention sur eux. Je commencerai par les travaux préparatoires.

III. Les travaux préparatoires

13. Rien d'écrit ni de publié concernant les travaux préparatoires ne permet à la Colombie de conforter l'interprétation du second paragraphe de l'article LVI qu'elle tente péniblement de vous faire avaliser. Les représentants de la Colombie peuvent spéculer autant qu'ils veulent sur ce qui aurait pu se passer dans le comité de rédaction ou — pourquoi pas — au cours des petits déjeuners de ses membres à l'hôtel. Mais la vérité est que la seule mention des origines de l'article LVI se lit dans la déclaration du rapporteur de la commission chargée du projet, enregistrée dans les comptes rendus.

14. Le rapporteur informait que la commission considérait que le plus convenable serait, une fois que le pacte ne serait pas annexé à la charte de l'Organisation des Etats américains, de *reproduire* («replicate», «reproducir») l'article 16 (l'article 9 en réalité), du traité de 1929. Et après une lecture intégrale du texte de l'article LVI, tout le monde semblait être d'accord. Certes, la phrase du deuxième paragraphe ne figurait pas dans le traité de 1929, mais l'absence de réaction aux propositions des fonctionnaires du département d'Etat qui l'avaient proposée en 1938 doit s'interpréter, inévitablement, dans le sens que celle-ci allait dans la même direction. On ne peut pas absolument déduire de cela que le second paragraphe cherchait à entraver l'application de la règle contenue dans le premier paragraphe.

15. L'autre jour la Colombie a affirmé sans aucune base que le commentaire du rapporteur se circonscrivait au premier paragraphe de l'article LVI[26]. Mais, en tout cas, la question qu'on devrait se poser est pourquoi le rapporteur ne dit rien sur un paragraphe, le second, qui est, selon la

[26] CR 2015/24, p. 17, par. 28 (Wood).

Colombie, appelé à révolutionner la pratique du système interaméricain. La vérité est que la précision qu'il a apportée n'était pas celle que la Colombie a essayé de vous faire croire il y a deux jours. Le rapporteur croyait fermement, tout comme ses collègues, que l'article LVI reproduisait l'article 16, en fait l'article 9 du traité de 1929. Cela m'amène de manière raisonnable à conclure qu'aucun d'entre eux ne pensait véritablement que le second paragraphe, dont personne n'a parlé, était une sorte de bombe à retardement insérée au cœur du pacte et donnant à chaque partie une clef permettant d'activer une destruction instantanée. La structure et la portée de l'article LVI dans son intégralité nous fait penser que tel n'était absolument pas le cas. L'intention des auteurs du pacte était celle de consolider et d'aller au-delà des obligations assumées auparavant, et non pas de régresser.

IV. Les clauses de dénonciation d'effets immédiats dans la pratique conventionnelle

16. Une clause, celle du deuxième paragraphe de l'article LVI qui, telle que la Colombie l'interprète, reste sans équivalent dans le droit des traités. Une clause exceptionnelle, unique dans l'espèce. La clause de «mort subite». Comme le Nicaragua l'a fait remarquer, il n'y a pas, dans la pratique des traités, de clauses portant des tels effets immédiats[27]. Les représentants de la Colombie ont cherché encore et encore très péniblement, dans les collections et recueils des clauses à alléger le fardeau de sa solitude interprétative. Mais, il semble évident qu'ils ont échoué. La Colombie a été obligée de tourner les yeux à nouveau vers les déclarations d'acceptation de la compétence de la Cour en vertu du paragraphe 2 de l'article 36 de son Statut pour venir nous dire qu'on trouve, là encore, fréquemment des expressions prévoyant des effets immédiats[28]. Le Nicaragua doit rappeler à nos amis que l'article LVI est une clause conventionnelle réglée et régie par le droit des traités — et non une déclaration unilatérale qui, comme on le sait, n'est régie que par la volonté de son auteur.

17. L'ancien président de la Cour, Jiménez de Aréchaga, avait remarqué cette distinction, et le Nicaragua a considéré opportun de le mentionner du fait de sa double condition d'autorité académique et judiciaire. Mercredi, la Colombie a eu la courtoisie de nous offrir le texte complet

[27] CR 2015/23, p. 31, par. 36 (Remiro Brotóns).

[28] CR 2015/24, p. 12-13 (Wood).

du maître uruguayen publié dans les essais en hommage à Shabtai Rosenne, seulement pour remarquer que, selon le maître, l'article LVI du pacte avait restreint, mais non exclu, les effets de la dénonciation sur l'acceptation de la compétence obligatoire de la Cour. «Restricted, but not excluded», on a souligné[29]. La Colombie n'aime pas les adverbes. Jiménez de Aréchaga a écrit : «severely restricted» (fortement restreinte) ; donc les effets sont «severely restricted», not «restricted», *tout court*. Et cette conclusion est établie après que l'éminent auteur a mentionné que le pacte peut seulement être dénoncé moyennant un préavis d'un an, et demeure en vigueur pendant toute cette période en conformité avec l'article LVI. Mesdames et Messieurs les juges, à vous d'en tirer les conclusions.

18. Tout d'un coup, prêt à tout pour échapper au dédale que la Colombie elle-même s'est fabriqué, eureka ! Notre contradicteur croit avoir identifié dans le champ des traités un gilet de sauvetage : l'article 72 de la convention de Washington de 1965[30]. Avant de me tourner vers cette disposition, il vaut peut-être la peine de reprendre, d'abord, l'article 71, qui dit que :

> «Tout Etat contractant peut dénoncer la présente Convention par notification adressée au dépositaire de la présente Convention. La dénonciation prend effet six mois après réception de ladite notification.»

En ce qui concerne l'article 72 [projection à l'écran], il prévoit que la notification de la dénonciation en vertu de l'article 71 :

> «ne peut porter atteinte aux droits et obligations dudit Etat ... aux termes de la présente Convention qui découlent d'un consentement à la compétence du Centre donné par l'un d'eux antérieurement à la réception de ladite notification par le dépositaire».

19. Selon la Colombie, «This means that jurisdiction is preserved only for those arbitration proceedings which were initiated before the transmission of denunciation.»[31]

20. Mais le gilet n'était qu'un mirage. La Colombie lit mal à nouveau. L'article 72 de la convention de Washington, loin de supporter la cause de la Colombie, au contraire, devient une autre balle qu'elle se tire dans le pied, et pour les raisons suivantes, parmi d'autres. D'abord, cette disposition se réfère au consentement, et non aux procédures entamées sur la base dudit

[29] CR 2015/24, p. 14, par. 18 (Wood).

[30] *Ibid.*, p. 13-14 (Wood).

[31] *Ibid.*, p. 13, par. 17 (Wood).

consentement, une distinction que la pratique arbitrale s'est efforcée de bien tirer[32] ; deuxièmement, s'il s'agit de consentements donnés avant la notification de la dénonciation, il n'y a pas de doute qu'en ce qui concerne le pacte de Bogotá, ce consentement avait été donné au moment de la ratification. Troisièmement, et plus fondamentalement, ce que l'article 72 prétend empêcher est que l'expiration du délai prévu de six mois à compter de la notification puisse mettre un terme ou perturber la compétence déjà établie sur la base du consentement découlant des traités, des lois, ou des contrats, où ce dernier ne peut pas être retiré de façon unilatérale.

21. En ce qui concerne l'article 72, la dénonciation, même une fois devenue effective, ne fait pas obstacle pour qu'un tribunal puisse entendre des requêtes enregistrées après cette date. C'est pourquoi on trouve des cas comme celui du Venezuela, dont la dénonciation de la convention CIRDI n'a pas empêché l'enregistrement de requêtes ultérieures à la date de la notification, le 24 janvier 2012[33], mais aussi après la date où la dénonciation est devenue effective, six mois après, le 25 juillet[34]. L'article 72 de la convention CIRDI donc a été adopté pour protéger la compétence du centre non seulement dans les cas initiés après la notification de la dénonciation et avant la date de son effectivité, mais aussi pour les cas enregistrés après l'expiration des six mois requis pour que la dénonciation devienne effective[35].

22. Par ailleurs, faire appel aux travaux préparatoires ou faire des recherches de la pratique conventionnelle sont des exercices accessoires, c'est-à-dire qu'ils ne constituent pas une nécessité là où les textes sont clairs et précis.

---

[32] *Venoklim Holding BV c. República Bolivariana de Venezuela* (ICSID Case nº ARB/12/22), 3 avril 2015, p. 21, par. 74.

[33] Voir *Saint-Gobain Performance Plastics Europe* v. *Bolivarian Republic of Venezuela*, ICSID Case nº ARB/12/13) ; *Venoklim Holding BV c. República Bolivariana de Venezuela* (ICSID Case nº ARB/12/22 ; *Valle Verde S.Financiera S.L.* v. *Bolivarian Republic of Venezuela*, (ICSID Case nº ARB/12/18 ; en ce qui concerne la Bolivie, *ETI Eurotelecom International NV* v. *Plurinational State of Bolivia* (ICSID Case nº ARB/07/28).

[34] Depuis le 25 juillet 2012, une dizaine d'affaires ont été enregistrées concernant le Venezuela, voir le site du centre du règlement des différends relatif aux investissements («cases»): icsidworldbank.org (dernière consultation : 30 septembre 2015).

[35] Voir Christoph Schreuer, «Denunciation of the ICSID Convention and Consent to Arbitration», M. Waibel, A. Kaushal, K-H Liz Chung, and C. Balchin (eds.), «The Backlash against Investment Arbitration: Perceptions and Reality», Alphen aan den Rijn: Kluwer Law International, 2010, p. 353–368, notamment p. 355-366.

V. Conclusion

23. Le premier paragraphe de l'article LVI prévoit clairement et sans conditions la survie de tous les effets, des droits et des engagements du pacte pendant un délai d'un an à compter de la transmission du préavis. Le second paragraphe s'occupe d'aborder la question de savoir quoi faire avec les procédures en cours à cette date. Ce paragraphe donne la réponse à cette situation : la dénonciation ne portera pas atteinte aux procédures entamées et permet que la saisine de la Cour pourrait produire ses effets au-delà du délai prévu. Le silence n'implique pas que la Cour manque de compétence pour entendre les affaires initiées entre la transmission du préavis et la date où deviendra effective la dénonciation parce que le fondement de cette compétence a été déjà établi sur la base de l'article XXXI du pacte, qui continue à être en vigueur en vertu du premier paragraphe de l'article LVI.

Monsieur le président, Mesdames et Messieurs les juges, je vous remercie de votre attention et je vous prie, Monsieur le président, de bien vouloir donner la parole à mon collègue le professeur Lowe pour la poursuite de la présentation du Nicaragua.

Le PRESIDENT : Merci, Monsieur le professeur. Je donne maintenant la parole au professeur Vaughan Lowe.

Mr. LOWE:

The existence of a dispute

1. Mr. President, Members of the Court, the first point that Colombia made in its second round speeches in respect of the argument that there was, at the critical date, no dispute between the two States is that there was no prior notification of the dispute to Colombia, comparable to the notifications to Iran by the United States in the *Hostages* crisis.

2. Of course, no one expects that every case that yields a passage worthy of quotation should have facts that are materially identical to the case in which they are quoted. We referred to the *Hostages* case to show that the Court has taken the view that sometimes the position of States is so obvious that demands for proof in a particular form are unnecessary and unrealistic, separating the Court from its footing in the real world and limiting its capacity to help settle current disputes between actual States in real time.

3. That said, it is common ground that the two States must understand that their disagreement is over a particular point of law or fact. Professor Reisman alluded to the forms of communication that Nicaragua might have used to give Colombia explicit notice of the dispute. But he did not say what it was that Colombia did not understand, and when that state of ignorance subsisted.

4. Recall the facts: from 2001 to 2012 — 11 years — Nicaragua and Colombia exchanged pleadings concerning the maritime boundaries. In November 2012 the Court announces its decision in a fully reasoned Judgment. There is an immediate reaction. Colombia — *Colombia* — rejects the Judgment, repeatedly, and specifically in respect of the maritime boundaries.

5. My good friend Mr. Bundy referred to the significance of silences. Among them, you will note that there has been no denial or explanation of the facts concerning the attempts to exclude Nicaraguan vessels from Nicaraguan waters that Colombia declared were its own; no denial or explanation of the enactment into Colombian law of that unilateral appropriation of Nicaraguan territory, in Decree 1946; no suggestion that Colombia is prepared to reverse its expropriation of the Nicaraguan waters.

6. Why does Colombia think that the onus was on Nicaragua to deliver a formal protest? It was Colombia that was violating the Court's Judgment, clearly and openly. It was Colombia whose conduct called for an explanation. If I go and steal someone's wallet, does he have to notify me that he considers it to be his property and that my actions violate his rights? If he sues me, is it any answer to say that he never gave me any notice that he objected to me taking it? Does international law say that the Court cannot move in relation to a dispute brought before it, unless that dispute has previously been spelled out for the wrongdoer in diplomatic correspondence? In our submission, there is no such requirement in international law; and if the Court is to remain capable of dealing with disputes in the messy reality of the real world, there can be none.

7. But consider what Colombia *did* know. After 11 years of pleading the case in The Hague — and, of course, numerous political exchanges and statements between the Parties in Central America, as well — Colombia knew that Nicaragua did not accept Colombia's claim to sovereign rights out to the 82nd meridian, or to the waters of the extended archipelago. That question was argued fully, in both technical and legal detail, before the Court; and the Court delivered its Judgment. It is idle to pretend that Colombia did not know that Nicaragua still

maintained its claims after the Court had ruled. What possible basis was there for supposing that Nicaragua would say, "well, the Court has awarded us this area in response to our pleadings, but we are not sure whether we still assert any claim to it"? As we said: the idea is not only absurd, it is flatly contradicted by the exchanges between the naval vessels of the two sides, the evidence on which is not challenged by Colombia.

8. There you have it. A clear statement of Nicaraguan rights in November 2012, equally clearly opposed by Colombia's assertion of rights over Nicaraguan waters. A clear opposition of views on a question of fact or law. [Tab 45 on] It is interesting to see how Colombia presents the position. Tab 26 of its judges' folders sets out extracts from statements dated 1 December 2012. It is headed "Ortega and Santos talk in Mexico about *dispute*": "nobody wants a warlike confrontation. This is the last recourse. The way to settle this type of situation is through dialogue. A reasonable dialogue where the positions are clearly established and expressed, just as we expressed to President Ortega as the Colombian position." It seems that Colombia had recognized the existence of a dispute and had a clearly established position by December 2012. [Tab 45 off]

9. Professor Reisman refers to the irrelevance of incidents after the filing of the Application. But, with respect, that conflates, on the one hand, the complaint with, on the other hand, the evidence of the complaint. Nicaragua's complaint, which existed and was demonstrated by the facts at the time of Nicaragua's Application, is in short that Colombia is in breach of its obligations not to violate what are recognized, as a consequence of the Court's Judgment, to be Nicaragua's maritime zones — the full text is in the Application.

10. The Application is made out on the basis of the facts as they stood on 26 November 2013 — on that we agree. But for our part, we submit that later facts can be adduced in order to cast light on earlier facts, in order to determine the extent of the breach and its consequences, and so on. But these are matters for the merits stage, and for now I shall focus on events prior to 26 November 2013.

No negotiated solution was foreseeable

11. Professor Reisman and Mr. Valencia Ospina and Mr. Bundy all ask how President Ortega can say that Nicaragua is open to negotiations, and how the Nicaraguan navy can

say that it has no problems with the Colombian navy, if there was no possibility of a negotiated solution. They also labour the point that Nicaragua filed its Application the day before the expiry of the one-year notice period for the termination of the Pact of Bogotá by Colombia.

12. To take that last point first: that is how time-limits work. Something done within the time-limit is effective; something done outside the time-limit is not. Nicaragua acted within the time-limit.

13. Colombia says that the timing was opportunistic, and had everything to do with the expiry of the notice period and nothing to do with the existence of a real dispute.

14. But, consider the position. [Tab 46 on] From 2001 to 2012, Nicaragua and Colombia are litigating in the Court. The Court delivers its Judgment in November 2012. Colombia has made its position in relation to the Judgment clear, already in November 2012, and has denounced the Pact of Bogotá at the same time. If Nicaragua had initiated the case in December 2012, or the following March or May, Colombia would no doubt have said that Nicaragua had not allowed any real chance to find a negotiated solution.

15. Perhaps, despite the harassment of Nicaraguan vessels in Nicaraguan waters, which had had been duly noted in the regular daily logs, and were later consolidated in reports at the request of the government, negotiations might have been possible. Perhaps the harassment was a temporary display for the benefit of the Colombian population, from which Colombia would consider that it could decently withdraw in the context of some wider adjustment of relations between the two States in order to conclude a negotiated settlement.

16. What might have led Nicaragua to believe that there was a real possibility of such a negotiated solution? Colombia refers to statements made on 13 August 2013 by President Ortega noting the lack of any confrontation between the Colombian and Nicaraguan navies. Do those statements show that Nicaragua had cause to think that negotiations were possible?

17. Well, it is true that in August 2013 the two sides were both exploring the possibility of a negotiated solution, and one presumes were doing so in good faith. They were, no doubt, keen to create an atmosphere in which amicable talks might proceed. But what legal weight should we attach to that? When the President or Foreign Minister of Colombia makes a statement, such as their reactions to the Judgment, it is rightly said that this must be taken in context, and not read as a

considered formulation of the State's position on a question of international law. The same is true here.

18. Yes: complimentary remarks made by President Ortega on 13 August 2013, and later by Nicaraguan navy officers, can be taken as sincere and true. But a statement that there has been no confrontation cannot be treated as a general confirmation of the possibility of a negotiated solution — there is some considerable distance between saying that no one fired a gun at the people on the other side, and saying that the two sides have an agreement in sight. And the statements cannot be taken as permanently valid positions that determine Nicaragua's rights and duties for an indefinite time in the future. For consider what happens next.

19. After the bonhomie of mid-August 2013, on 23 August the Vice President of Colombia is reported as saying that "[t]he judgement of the Court of The Hague is unenforceable in our country. It cannot apply now, in five years or ten years time."[36] It is true, too, that the Vice President goes on to say that Colombia is preparing an appeal against the judgment, pending which it must be respected: but that scarcely clarifies the position.

20. Just over two weeks later, on 9 September, Colombia adopts Decree 1946 — Nicaragua's Memorial, Annex 9 — claiming sovereign authority over Nicaraguan waters. I took you through that on Tuesday.

21. Let me take you also to the declaration of President Santos on the "integral strategy of Colombia on the Judgment of the International Court of Justice", which he announced to the Colombian people on that same day, 9 September. As with all these statements, you will of course read the full text, which is in Nicaragua's Memorial, Annex 4; but this one is rather long, so let me just give you the first paragraph, which sums it up.

"1. We decided that without a treaty, the Judgment is not applicable.
2. We consolidated our archipelago by declaring an Integral Contiguous Zone.
3. We advanced in environmental and social protection in the Seaflower Reserve.
4. We stopped Nicaragua's expansionist plans by declaring the unification of two continental seabeds which jointly extend from San Andrés to Cartagena."

That is Colombia's publicly declared strategy.

---

[36]Memorial of Nicaragua (MN), Ann. 38.

22. The next day, 10 September, Colombia's Foreign Minister is reported as saying that "[o]ur doors are undoubtedly open to speak with Nicaragua" but the same news item says that President Santos assured that the new maritime delimitation is inapplicable as long as there is no treaty between the two States; it was what *La Prensa* called "a new gesture that rejects the verdict"[37].

23. Two days later, on 11 September, President Ortega holds out an olive branch: "We understand the position taken by President Santos, but we cannot say that we agree with the position of President Santos . . . We do agree that it is necessary to dialogue."[38]

24. The following day, 12 September, the Nicaraguan Assembly endorses that position[39].

25. What is Colombia's response? On 12 September, President Santos files a suit in the Constitutional Court. The full request appears as Nicaragua's Memorial, Annex 15, and it is worth reading.

26. This is not the Colombian Government clearing the way to adopt a treaty implementing the Court's Judgment. The request is for a ruling that Articles XXXI and L of the Pact of Bogotá are unconstitutional and inapplicable (and you will note the word "inapplicable"). Article XXXI, you will recall, gives jurisdiction to the International Court of Justice; Article L says that if a Bogotá Pact Party fails to carry out obligations imposed upon it by a decision of the International Court of Justice, other Parties shall, before resorting to the Security Council of the United Nations, propose a meeting of consultation of Ministers for Foreign Affairs to agree upon appropriate measures to ensure the fulfilment of the judicial decision.

27. How was Nicaragua supposed to view that move? The Application — at page 233 in Nicaragua's Memorial — says:

> "This request is based on the fact that the challenged norms are unconstitutional in the abstract. The references to the judgments of the International Court of Justice only seek to illustrate that what the text of the challenged norms says and permits has had an interpretation with clear, precise and very serious legal effects for Colombia."

---

[37]Written Statement of Nicaragua (WSN), Ann. 8.

[38]MN, Ann. 39.

[39]MN, Ann. 40.

Is this an interesting inquiry into the constitutional status of what Colombia calls the *lex specialis*?[40] Or is it a move to resist the implementation of the Judgment?

28. Then, on 19 September:

> "The President of the Republic, Juan Manuel Santos, ordered the high command of the Armed Forces to defend with 'cloak and sword' the continental shelf that Colombia has in the Caribbean Sea. During the speech by the Navy Commander, Vice Admiral Hernando Wills, he reiterated that his forces comply with the order of the Head of State to exercise sovereignty throughout the Colombian [territorial] sea. The high command even said that the Colombian frigates operate in the 82 meridian, and added that the judgment of The Hague is inapplicable and that his duty is to defend all the Colombian maritime space."[41]

Then there are the episodes of harassment of vessels in Nicaraguan waters to which the Agent referred.

29. This is the background against which Nicaragua had to decide whether the dispute was going to find a negotiated solution, or whether it needed to prepare, print and file an application to the Court before Colombia left the Bogotá Pact in November 2013. None of these details, all of them set out in Nicaragua's pleadings, has been contested by Colombia.

30. It was a political judgment, made in Managua by government officials, supported by the full range of government information and advice. The signs were that Colombia's position was hardening, with the "Integrated Strategy", the adoption of Decree 1946, and the instructions to the Colombian navy. You have heard our Agent say that Nicaragua considered that there was no prospect of a settlement of this escalating dispute by negotiation; and in our submission, there is no evidence on the basis of which that view could be contradicted. [Tab 46 off]

31. Apart from the submissions on Article II of the Bogotá Pact and the significance of the — or insignificance — of the French text, you have not heard any submissions on the standard of proof applicable to this question — whether Nicaragua's view must stand unless it is shown to be unreasonable, or the Court should take its own view *de novo*. But in our submission, whatever view is taken, the facts speak for themselves. There was a dispute; Colombia knew that there was a dispute; it knew exactly what that dispute was; and there was no reason to suppose that it could be settled by negotiation.

---

[40]CR 2015/22, p. 65, para. 25 (Treves).

[41]MN, Ann. 41.

32. Colombia points out, correctly, that there have been indications since November 2013 of the willingness of Nicaragua and of Colombia to look for a negotiated solution. They ask how that is to be reconciled with the view that the dispute cannot be settled by negotiation.

33. As our Agent has said, the answer is that Nicaragua is — and always has been — open to discussions on the arrangements for fishing and so on that will be applied within the maritime zones of each State; but Nicaragua is absolutely not prepared to give up the maritime boundaries that the Court has drawn. Colombia is open to discussions on what it calls "implementation", but it has shown no sign of a willingness to withdraw its assertion of sovereign rights over Nicaraguan waters, based on Decree 1946, contrary to the Court's Judgment. And, until Colombia is willing to yield on that point, there can be neither a negotiated settlement, nor compliance with the Court's Judgment.

34. For these reasons, we submit that Colombia's arguments that there is no dispute, and that if there were a dispute it would be capable of settlement by negotiation, are not supported by the facts and should be dismissed.

35. Mr. President, Members of the Court: that concludes my part in this second round of Nicaragua's submissions; and unless I can assist you further I would ask you to call upon my friend and colleague Professor Alain Pellet to continue Nicaragua's submissions.

Le PRESIDENT: Merci, Monsieur le professeur. Je donne à présent la parole au professeur Alain Pellet.

M. PELLET :

COMPÉTENCE INHÉRENTE ET CONCLUSIONS

1. Merci beaucoup, Monsieur le président. Monsieur le président, Mesdames et Messieurs de la Cour, non ! L'invocation d'une seconde base à la compétence de la Cour n'est pas le signe du moindre doute du Nicaragua quant à la validité de celle fondée sur le pacte de Bogotá[42] ! Mais puisqu'il y en a deux, qui se renforcent l'une l'autre, pourquoi ne pas les invoquer l'une et l'autre ? D'autant plus que, si elles vous permettent, toutes deux, d'examiner complètement la requête du

---

[42] Voir CR 2015/24, p. 40, par. 6 (Bundy).

Nicaragua, les conditions de leur mise en œuvre sont différentes. Et je relève à cet égard que nos amis de l'autre côté de la barre, qui font si grand cas de leur argument fondé sur le non-épuisement des possibilités de négociations, reconnaissent eux-mêmes que cette prétendue condition n'est en tout cas pas applicable à la compétence inhérente de la Cour du fait de sa nature d'organe judiciaire[43]. Dont acte.

2. Au bénéfice de cette remarque, je répondrai dans un premier temps aux objections que m'ont opposées mes excellents collègues et amis, principalement le professeur Tullio Treves et, dans une mesure moindre, M. Bundy ; puis, dans un second temps, je résumerai, très brièvement, les raisons clefs qui doivent, croyons-nous, conduire la Cour à rejeter les exceptions préliminaires de la Colombie.

I. La compétence inhérente de la Cour
(Les quatrième et cinquième exceptions préliminaires de la Colombie)

3. Monsieur le président, bien entendu, il n'entre pas dans mes intentions de reprendre, dans son entier, toute ma démonstration du premier tour relative à la compétence inhérente de la Cour. Je note cependant le silence total de nos contradicteurs sur un certain nombre de points importants — notamment sur la compétence exécutoire, mineure et aléatoire, conférée au Conseil de sécurité par l'article 94, paragraphe 2, de la Charte ; de ce fait, ils reconnaissent implicitement que cette disposition ne constitue pas un obstacle à l'exercice par la Cour de ses fonctions purement judiciaires[44]. Je relève du même coup que la Colombie semble avoir abandonné sa cinquième exception préliminaire, puisque le professeur Treves a admis avant-hier que la Cour pouvait «juger d'un différend portant sur l'inexécution d'un [de ses] arrêt[s]»[45]. Les Parties demeurent cependant divisées sur la question de savoir si la Cour peut connaître d'un tel différend sur le fondement de sa compétence inhérente. A cet égard, il me semble que nos amis de l'autre côté de la barre ont principalement opposé sept arguments à ceux que j'avais fait valoir mardi :

1) dans son principe, le pouvoir inhérent que nous invoquons serait incompatible avec le fondement consensuel de la compétence de la Cour ;

---

[43] CR 2015/24, p. 42-43, par. 19-20 (Bundy) ; voir aussi *ibid.*, p. 30, par. 12 (Valencia-Ospina).

[44] Voir CR 2015/23, p. 58-60, par 33-39 (Pellet).

[45] CR 2015/24, p. 36, par. 16 (Treves).

2) plus précisément, ce pouvoir ne pourrait être exercé qu'une fois la compétence de la Cour établie ; ni
3) l'analogie que j'ai faite avec votre compétence pour vous prononcer sur des mesures conservatoires ; ni
4) les nombreux précédents que j'ai cités de juridictions internationales qui exercent une telle compétence inhérente ne seraient pertinents ;
5) la question du fondement de la possibilité d'un réexamen de la situation envisagée dans les affaires des *Essais nucléaires* serait purement rhétorique ;
6) la conjonction de l'article 52 de la Charte des Nations Unies et de l'article L du pacte de Bogotá imposerait la recherche d'une solution régionale du différend préalablement à la saisine de votre Cour ; et
7) la reconnaissance par la Cour de sa compétence inhérente dans notre affaire serait lourde de dangers pour son avenir même.

Je crois n'avoir rien oublié et ce plan figure dans les dossiers des juges.

4. Sans avoir ni le temps ni le besoin de m'y attarder, je répondrai successivement à chacune de ces objections.

1. Dans son principe, le pouvoir inhérent de la Cour serait incompatible avec le fondement consensuel de sa compétence

5. Monsieur le président, l'insistance mise par nos contradicteurs à invoquer l'incompatibilité de la compétence inhérente de la Cour avec le principe consensuel qui préside à l'établissement de sa juridiction me semble témoigner d'une incompréhension (certainement voulue !) de la notion même d'inhérence. D'abord, par définition même, une compétence inhérente n'est pas une compétence expresse et il n'y a pas lieu de s'indigner, comme l'a fait M. Bundy (pas le professeur Treves — il faut lui rendre cette justice), de ce qu'elle ne soit «*nowhere authorized in the Court's Statute, in the Rules of Court or even in the Pact of Bogotá*»[46] : le fût-elle, elle ne serait plus inhérente. En revanche elle est impliquée tant par la Charte que par le Statut, qui ont institué la Cour en tant qu'organe judiciaire ; c'est-à-dire, par définition aussi, en tant qu'organe dont les parties à ce traité se sont engagées à exécuter les décisions.

---

[46] CR 2015/24, p. 38-39, par. 2 (Bundy).

6. Cet engagement conventionnel, qui découle *ipso facto* de la participation au Statut de la Cour, constitue la conséquence nécessaire, on pourrait même dire l'essence même, de la reconnaissance de la nature d'organe judiciaire à votre haute juridiction. En ratifiant la Charte (et, du même coup, le Statut), la Colombie a accepté — c'est bien de consentement qu'il s'agit — le caractère exécutoire (et *self-executing*, inconditionnel) des arrêts de la Cour. C'est d'ailleurs bien pour cela qu'elle s'est, à maintes reprises, refusée à envisager la possibilité que l'un de ses arrêts pût ne pas être exécuté.

2. Le pouvoir inhérent de la Cour ne pourrait être exercé qu'une fois sa compétence établie

7. Mon contradicteur ne nie pas qu'une telle compétence — inhérente — existe ; mais en un raisonnement curieusement circulaire, il affirme qu'elle n'existe que si ... la compétence de la Cour est préalablement établie. C'est fort étrange, Monsieur le président :

— la Cour a une compétence inhérente ;

— mais celle-ci n'est établie que…

— lorsque la compétence de la Cour est établie !

C'est à peu près exactement ce qu'a dit le professeur Treves au paragraphe 13 de sa plaidoirie : on peut, a-t-il dit, accepter l'idée que la Cour a une compétence inhérente «dans le cadre d'une affaire où la compétence est établie», mais ceci «n'est pas admissible pour établir une compétence sur une affaire où une telle compétence n'existe pas»[47]. C'est à en perdre toute boussole cartésienne !

8. Au demeurant, si ce que veut dire le professeur Treves est que la compétence inhérente ne peut surgir de nulle part et doit trouver un ancrage dans une compétence expresse appartenant à la Cour en vertu d'un texte constitutif — la Charte ou le Statut — nous ne le contestons pas. Et nous admettons tout à fait que, lorsqu'elle est inhérente, la compétence de la Cour est forcément dérivée. Mais c'est bien le cas dans notre affaire : la Cour a rendu son arrêt en 2012 dans l'exercice de sa juridiction en tant qu'organe judiciaire ; et c'est cet arrêt — ou plutôt le refus de la Colombie de l'appliquer — qui établit son pouvoir inhérent de tirer les conséquences de son rejet par la Colombie.

---

[47] CR 2015/24, p. 35, par. 13 (Treves).

3. Il n'y aurait aucune analogie entre la compétence de la Cour pour se prononcer sur le non-respect de mesures conservatoires et sur l'inexécution d'un arrêt

9. En troisième lieu, mon savant ami s'agace par ailleurs que je suggère une analogie entre la compétence inhérente que nous vous demandons de vous reconnaître en matière de non ou de mauvaise exécution de vos arrêts, et celle qu'indiscutablement vous exercez s'agissant des demandes portant sur l'inexécution de mesures conservatoires indiquées sur le fondement de l'article 41 du Statut. Et pourtant, malgré le déplaisir de mon contradicteur, j'ai du mal à comprendre en quoi l'analogie serait irrecevable : la compétence de la Cour pour indiquer des mesures conservatoires est expressément prévue à l'article 41 du Statut ; celle, inhérente, pour se prononcer sur leur non-exécution découle de celle-ci ou même, plus largement, de votre compétence pour trancher les différends qui vous sont soumis ; la compétence de la Cour pour rendre des arrêts obligatoires pour les parties et sans recours fait expressément l'objet des articles 59 et 60 du Statut ; pourquoi celle, inhérente, pour se prononcer sur leur non-exécution n'en découlerait-elle pas ?

[Projection n° 1 : La jurisprudence *LaGrand*]

10. A l'appui de ses dires, M. Treves s'appuie sur l'arrêt de 2001 dans l'affaire *LaGrand* qui a, le premier, reconnu la compétence de la Cour pour se prononcer sur le non-respect des mesures conservatoires indiquées en vertu de l'article 41 et qui est le seul à s'en être expliqué. Il y est dit — et ce passage est celui-là même cité par mon contradicteur à l'appui de ses dires[48] :

> «Lorsque la Cour a compétence pour trancher un différend, elle a également compétence pour se prononcer sur des conclusions la priant de constater qu'une ordonnance en indication de mesures rendue aux fins de préserver les droits des Parties à ce différend n'a pas été exécutée.»[49]

Qu'est-ce que cela, Monsieur le président, sinon l'affirmation d'une compétence inhérente en l'absence même de toute disposition statutaire la prévoyant expressément ?

[Fin de la projection n° 1]

11. J'ajoute que le choix de la Cour d'extrapoler sa compétence pour se prononcer sur la non-exécution de mesures conservatoires à partir de celle lui appartenant pour trancher un différend alors qu'elle eût pu se contenter de se référer à l'article 41 de son Statut, conforte notre argument :

---

[48] CR 2015/24, par. 12.

[49] *LaGrand (Allemagne c. Etats-Unis d'Amérique), arrêt, C.I.J. Recueil 2001*, p. 484, par. 45.

cette très large compétence justifie aussi bien la compétence inhérente de la Cour concernant l'inexécution de ses ordonnances en mesures conservatoires que celle de ses arrêts.

4. Les positions prises par les autres juridictions internationales en faveur de leur compétence inhérente en cas d'inexécution ne seraient pas pertinentes

12. Monsieur le président, l'analogie que j'ai faite entre la compétence inhérente, qui nous paraît appartenir à la Cour en cas de difficulté d'exécution de ses arrêts, et la position prise par les autres juridictions internationales qui ont eu à se prononcer sur la question ne trouve pas davantage grâce aux yeux de l'éminent avocat de la Colombie qui, adroitement, s'efforce de flatter votre haute juridiction en écartant, de manière un peu méprisante la jurisprudence fortement argumentée de ces cours et tribunaux. Il y a longtemps pourtant que vous êtes descendus de la tour d'ivoire où vos prédécesseurs avaient longtemps cru bon de s'enfermer et que vous prêtez attention à la jurisprudence des autres juridictions internationales[50].

13. Au demeurant, il est fort discutable que la base de la compétence de celles-ci puisse être définie comme n'étant pas consensuelle[51] : toutes ces juridictions (sauf peut-être les tribunaux administratifs internationaux — et encore on pourrait le discuter) tiennent leurs compétences d'un traité auquel les Etats soumis à la juridiction en question sont volontairement devenus parties — et d'ailleurs en vertu de l'article 36, paragraphe 1, du Statut, «[l]a compétence de la Cour s'étend à ... tous les cas spécialement prévus dans la Charte des Nations Unies ou dans les traités et conventions en vigueur». Au demeurant, cet aspect ne joue aucun rôle dans le raisonnement des cours et tribunaux dont j'ai cité la jurisprudence mardi dernier[52]. Et je me permets de vous renvoyer en particulier, Mesdames et Messieurs les juges, à la motivation très serrée des arrêts de la Cour interaméricaine des droits de l'homme et des jugements du Tribunal administratif de l'OIT. Pour reconnaître leur compétence en cas de difficulté d'exécution de leurs décisions, ces juridictions s'appuient essentiellement sur le caractère obligatoire et sans appel de leurs décisions et sur l'engagement conventionnel des Etats ou des organisations internationales ayant accepté leur juridiction de les mettre en œuvre.

---

[50] A. Pellet, «Article 38», *in* A. Zimmermann, Ch. Tomuschat and K. Oellers-Frahm, *The Statute of the International Court of Justice : a Commentary*, 2e ed., OUP, Oxford, 2012, p. 858-862.

[51] CR 2015/24, p. 36-37, par. 18-22 (Treves).

[52] CR 2015/23, p. 54-56, par. 23-27 (Pellet).

14. Et ceci est vrai aussi pour le Tribunal international du droit de la mer (TIDM) et pour la Cour européenne des droits de l'homme.

15. En ce qui concerne le premier, il est exact que, dans l'affaire *Saïga II*, le TIDM avait été appelé à se prononcer sur la violation par la Guinée d'un certain nombre de dispositions de la convention des Nations Unies sur le droit de la mer, en conséquence justement du non-respect de l'arrêt antérieur (il datait de 1997) du Tribunal — exactement comme il vous est demandé, Mesdames et Messieurs les juges, de vous prononcer sur la violation des droits, coutumiers cette fois, du Nicaragua dans les zones maritimes lui revenant, en vertu de votre arrêt de 2012. Je me réfère au document figurant à l'onglet 49 de vos dossiers. Le Tribunal y relève expressément que «[l]es droits dont se prévaut Saint-Vincent-et-les Grenadines comportent celui «d'obtenir *une prompte exécution de l'arrêt rendu par le Tribunal* le 4 décembre 1997»»[53]. Puis, il se prononce sans hésitation (et sans base statutaire) sur «la demande de Saint-Vincent-et-les Grenadines selon laquelle la Guinée aurait violé ses droits, aux termes de la convention, en ne procédant pas à la prompte mainlevée de l'immobilisation du Saïga et à la prompte libération des membres de son équipage, *conformément à l'arrêt rendu par le Tribunal le 4 décembre 1997*»[54] pour, d'ailleurs, rejeter cette demande.

16. Quant à la Cour européenne des droits de l'homme, il est vrai que sa jurisprudence est moins significative en la matière que celle de son homologue interaméricaine — mais pour une raison simple et qui se retourne contre l'argumentation du professeur Treves — ou plutôt, peut-être, qui explique son silence gêné sur un point fort important : contrairement à ceux de la Cour de San José, les arrêts de celle de Strasbourg peuvent faire l'objet d'une procédure exécutoire de la part du comité des ministres du Conseil de l'Europe. Dès lors, il n'y a plus de raison pour que la Cour européenne, dans les cas où une telle procédure peut intervenir, exerce une compétence inhérente qui ferait double emploi avec celle, explicite et sans doute plus efficace, conférée au comité. C'est, du reste, très exactement ce que dit la Cour de Strasbourg dans l'arrêt *Meltex* qu'a

---

[53] Tribunal international du droit de la mer (TIDM), *Affaire du navire «SAIGA» (No. 2) (Saint-Vincent-et-les Grenadines c. Guinée)*, arrêt du 1er juillet 1999, par. 97 - les italiques sont de nous ; voir aussi par. 163-177 («Exécution de l'arrêt du 4 décembre 1997» et «Réparation»).

[54] *Ibid.*, par. 183 11) - les italiques sont de nous ; voir par. 183 12).

cité M. Treves[55] et dont vous trouverez également les extraits pertinents dans vos dossiers — sous l'onglet 50 : assurément, dans le paragraphe 28 (auquel M. Treves s'était référé), la Cour fait application de sa jurisprudence par laquelle elle se refuse à «examiner des requêtes relatives au manquement des Etats d'exécuter ses jugements»[56]. Mais mon contradicteur omet de citer les deux paragraphes, fort éclairants, qui, respectivement, précèdent et suivent ce paragraphe 28. Sous le nº 27, la Cour rappelle que — je le cite en anglais, il n'y a pas l'air d'y avoir de traduction française — «[a]lthough the Court can in certain situations indicate the specific remedy or other measure to be taken by the respondent state, it still falls to the Committee of Ministers to evaluate the implementation of such measures under Article 46, paragraph 2, of the Convention»[57] ; et la Cour de Strasbourg précise au paragraphe 28 que son abstention d'exercer une compétence dans ce domaine est la *conséquence* de celle qui est reconnue au comité des ministres — le passage cité par M. Treves commence par l'adverbe «consequently» («en conséquence»), il a été remplacé par des points de suspension dans sa citation[58]. Enfin, dans les paragraphes suivants, la Cour rappelle — je cite l'arrêt à nouveau — que «the Committee of Ministers' role in this sphere does not mean that measures taken by a respondent State to remedy a violation found by the Court cannot raise a new issue undecided by the judgment and, as such, form the subject of a new application that may be dealt with by the Court»[59].

17. Si je me suis un peu attardé sur cet exemple, Monsieur le président, c'est que je le crois très significatif. Il confirme ce sur quoi j'avais fortement insisté mardi[60] et que le professeur Treves a passé pudiquement sous silence : la raison de l'exercice de leur compétence inhérente en matière d'exécution de leurs décisions par les juridictions internationales s'explique par l'absence de procédure exécutoire ; lorsqu'une telle procédure existe — comme c'est le cas en partie pour la Cour de Strasbourg —, il n'y a plus lieu de recourir à la notion de compétence inhérente. L'exemple de la position de la Cour de justice des communautés puis de

---

[55] CR 2015/24, p. 37, par. 20 (Treves).

[56] *Ibid.* — traduction de M. Treves.

[57] *Ibid.*, par. 28 — références à la jurisprudence omises.

[58] CR 2015/24, p. 37, par. 20.

[59] *Ibid.*, par. 29 — référence à la jurisprudence omise ; voir aussi par. 30-33 ; MN, par. 1.27 et EEN, par. 5.34-5.35.

[60] Voir CR 2015/23, p. 57-58, par. 30-32 (Pellet).

l'Union européenne le confirme également — ici encore le silence gardé par M. Treves est éloquent. Mr. Bundy said «Sometimes, Mr. President, it is instructive to listen to the silences»*. As Simon and Garfunkel rightly sang, the truth can be whispered in the *Sounds of silence*[61]. J'avais prévu de vous faire entendre quelques notes de cette magnifique chanson, mais il semble que quelques notes de musique ne sied pas à la dignité de ces lieux. Dommage, c'est vraiment une très belle chanson.

5. La question du fondement de la possibilité d'un réexamen de la situation envisagée dans les affaires des *Essais nucléaires* serait purement rhétorique

18. Mon estimé contradicteur n'est guère plus disert sur la question de savoir sur quel fondement la Cour a pu réserver la possibilité d'un réexamen de la situation dans ses arrêts de 1974 relatifs aux *Essais nucléaires*. Il se borne à la qualifier de «rhétorique»[62] — pourquoi rhétorique ? Monsieur le président, je ne suis pas très savant, et j'ai horreur des mots compliqués ; même «rhétorique» est de ceux sur lesquels j'hésite ; j'ai donc cherché dans le dictionnaire pour essayer de comprendre en quoi ma question l'était. Et j'ai constaté avec intérêt que cela veut dire qu'elle n'appelle pas de réponse (apparemment parce que celle-ci va de soi)[63]. Et, c'est — en effet — sans doute la bonne explication : compte tenu de la nature d'organe judiciaire international de la Cour, sa compétence pour se prononcer sur l'exécution de ses arrêts relève assurément de l'évidence. En tout cas, le professeur Treves n'a pas donné d'autre explication quant à ce qui a permis à la Cour de réserver, dans ses arrêts de 1974, la possibilité d'un réexamen de la situation en cas de non-exécution.

19. Notre contradicteur s'est expliqué un peu davantage sur le paragraphe 23 de ces mêmes arrêts sur les *Essais nucléaires* — il s'agit du fameux passage dans lequel la Cour affirme qu'elle «possède un pouvoir inhérent qui l'autorise à prendre toute mesure voulue, d'une part pour faire en sorte que, si sa compétence au fond est établie, l'exercice de cette compétence ne se révèle pas

---

[61] Simon and Garfunkel, «The Sound of Silence», 1964 (album: Wednesday Morning, 3 A.M.) (https://www.google.nl/url?sa=t&rct=j&q=&esrc=s&source=video&cd=1&cad=rja&uact=8&ved=0CCIQtwIwAGoVChMI95nTqpWgyAIVx-kUCh1QtQYu&url=http%3A%2F%2Fwww.youtube.com%2Fwatch%3Fv%3D4zLfCnGVeL4&usg=AFQjCNFkZyKeWjHKgxa2KMScjtH-zYTAMw&bvm=bv.104226188,d.d24).

[62] CR 2015/24, p. 36, par. 17 (Treves).

[63] Http://www.linternaute.com/dictionnaire/fr/definition/question-rhetorique/ et http://examples.yourdictionary.com/rhetorical-question-examples.html.

* CR 2015/24, p. 42, par. 16 (Bundy).

vain...»[64] Jusqu'ici, M. Treves est content : il ne s'agit pas de compétence inhérente puisque, la Cour postule, dans cette hypothèse, que «sa compétence au fond est établie». Mais les choses se gâtent ensuite pour M. Treves car ce pouvoir inhérent peut aussi être utilisé «*d'autre part* pour assurer le règlement régulier *de tous les points en litige* ainsi que le respect des «limitations inhérentes à l'exercice de la fonction judiciaire» de la Cour et pour «conserver son caractère judiciaire»». Clairement, ceci veut dire, par contraste, que ce pouvoir inhérent peut être utilisé non pas lorsque la compétence de la Cour au fond est établie mais pour l'établir (ou au contraire pour refuser de l'exercer — et ce sont les limitations) ; étant entendu cependant, je l'ai dit, que ce pouvoir inhérent dérive toujours d'une compétence préexistante[65].

> «Un pouvoir inhérent de ce genre, sur la base duquel la Cour est pleinement habilitée à adopter toute conclusion éventuellement nécessaire aux fins qui viennent d'être indiquées, *découle* — et je cite toujours les arrêts de 1974 — *de l'existence même de la Cour, organe judiciaire établi par le consentement des Etats*, et lui est conféré afin que sa fonction judiciaire fondamentale puisse être sauvegardée.»[66]

Je ne pense pas, Monsieur le président, qu'il soit nécessaire de commenter à nouveau ce passage : il parle pour lui-même : la Cour a des pouvoirs inhérents, découlant de sa nature d'organe judiciaire pour exercer une compétence qui lui est expressément reconnue ou pour en établir une, dérivée, si cela est nécessaire pour qu'elle puisse pleinement s'acquitter de sa mission. Pour paraphraser la célèbre formule de la Cour dans son avis de 1949 relatif aux pouvoirs implicites de l'ONU dans l'affaire du *Comte Bernadotte*, «[s]elon le droit international, [la Cour] doit être considérée comme possédant ces pouvoirs qui, s'ils ne sont pas expressément énoncés dans [le Statut], sont, par une conséquence nécessaire, conférés à [la Cour] en tant qu'essentiels à l'exercice des fonctions de celle-ci»[67].

---

[64] *Essais nucléaires (Australie c. France), arrêt, C.I.J. Recueil 1974*, p. 259, par. 23 ; *Essais nucléaires (Nouvelle-Zélande c. France), ibid.*, p. 463, par. 23.

[65] Voir par. 8 ci-dessus.

[66] *Essais nucléaires (Australie c. France), arrêt, C.I.J. Recueil 1974*, p. 259, par. 23 ; *Essais nucléaires (Nouvelle-Zélande c. France), ibid.*, p. 463, par. 23 — les italiques sont de nous.

[67] *Réparation des dommages subis au service des Nations Unies, avis consultatif, C.I.J. Recueil 1949*, p. 182.

6. La conjonction de l'article 52 de la Charte des Nations Unies et de l'article L du pacte de Bogotá imposerait la recherche d'une solution régionale du différend préalablement à la saisine de votre Cour

[Projection n° 2 : Article 52, paragraphe 2), de la Charte des Nations Unies et article L du pacte de Bogotá]

20. Avant de conclure sur la compétence inhérente, une brève observation sur un point nouveau, Monsieur le président, si vous le voulez bien. Revenant sur l'article L du pacte de Bogotá, le professeur Treves a affirmé :

> «Lu conjointement à l'article 52 de la Charte des Nations Unies, *qui apparaît sur l'écran,* cet article indique [qu'en] cas d'alléguée inexécution d'un arrêt de la Cour les Etats américains parties au Pacte s'obligent à entreprendre tout effort possible pour obtenir une solution pacifique au niveau régional.»[68]

21. Un coup d'œil sur les extraits de ces dispositions, qui sont projetées en ce moment, suffit : elles concernent exclusivement la saisine *du Conseil de sécurité* ; ce n'est pas lui mais votre haute juridiction que le Nicaragua a choisi de saisir.

[Fin de la projection n° 2]

7. La reconnaissance par la Cour de sa compétence inhérente pour se prononcer sur la non-exécution de ses arrêts serait lourde de dangers pour son avenir même

22. Je termine cette première partie de ma présentation de ce matin (la seconde sera nettement moins longue !) par quelques mots sur l'apocalypse promis à la Cour par la Colombie si elle en venait à reconnaître sa compétence inhérente comme l'y invite le Nicaragua[69]. Selon le professeur Treves, «[u]n tel pas, si la Cour devait le faire, pourrait décourager les Etats ... [d']accepter la compétence de la Cour»[70]. On se demande vraiment pourquoi les Etats seraient découragés d'accepter la compétence de la Cour s'ils ont la certitude que celle-ci ferait ce qui est en son pouvoir pour aider à la bonne exécution de ses arrêts (comme elle le fait d'ailleurs lorsqu'ils le lui demandent conjointement) en tirant les conséquences de leur non-exécution, ceci, bien sûr, dans les limites inhérentes à sa compétence purement judiciaire — c'est-à-dire en se plaçant sur le terrain de la responsabilité ; un terrain qui relève par excellence — «inhéremment» si

---

[68] CR 2015/24, p. 37-38, par. 24 (Treves).

[69] *Ibid.*, p. 37, par. 22-23 (Treves). Voir aussi les exceptions préliminaires de la Colombie (EPC), par. 5.3, et CR 2015/22, p. 66, par. 27 (Treves).

[70] CR 2015/24, p. 37, par. 22 (Treves).

l'adverbe existait en français, «inherently» indeed — de la compétence de la Cour[71]. Cette assurance que la haute juridiction s'acquitterait pleinement de sa mission de régler effectivement, complètement, durablement, les différends qui lui sont soumis devrait au contraire inciter les Etats à la saisir, par contraste avec l'«à quoi bon ?» que l'indifférence que vous manifesteriez à l'égard de l'exécution de vos arrêts risquerait de susciter.

II. Quelques remarques conclusives

23. Monsieur le président, Mesdames et Messieurs les juges, j'en viens à quelques dernières remarques récapitulatives — pas un résumé de ce que nous avons dit, une tentative pour mettre en exergue quelques traits saillants.

24. Le premier de ces aspects, crucial, est, bien sûr, qu'il y a un différend entre les Parties et qu'il n'est pas raisonnable de prétendre le contraire. Je ne suis pas certain que de longs raisonnements soient nécessaires pour l'établir : en 2001, le Nicaragua a saisi la Cour d'une requête complexe ; vous avez rejeté certaines de ses demandes (les plus nombreuses, à vrai dire...) et vous en avez accueilli d'autres dans votre arrêt de 2012 ; la Colombie se refuse à exécuter celles qui donnent raison au Nicaragua. Voilà qui suffit, me semble-t-il, à établir qu'il existe un différend entre les Parties — et ce différend est né le jour même où vous avez rendu votre arrêt puisque c'est ce jour-là que le président colombien a rejeté catégoriquement l'«aspect» («ese aspecto») de l'arrêt concernant rien moins que la délimitation maritime[72].

25. Certes, depuis lors, la Colombie s'est efforcée d'atténuer le caractère outrancier de cette position et l'effet désastreux qu'elle a eu au plan international. Dorénavant, malgré quelques «ratés»[73], la thèse officielle est que la Colombie dans sa grande mansuétude pourrait appliquer l'arrêt, à condition qu'un traité soit conclu à cette fin avec le Nicaragua ; faute de quoi il demeurerait «inapplicable». Première remarque — et essentielle : les arrêts de la Cour sont obligatoires de plein droit et *rien* n'autorise un Etat à en subordonner l'application à quelque

---

[71] Cf. l'article 36, par. 2 *c)* et *d)* du Statut.

[72] Allocution du président Juan Manuel Santos concernant l'arrêt de la Cour internationale de Justice, 19 novembre 2012 (mémoire du Nicaragua, annexe 1).

[73] Ethel Bent, «Concern for New Defense in The Hague», *El Isleno*, 4 août 2015 (http ://xn--elisleo-9za.com/index.php?option=com_content&view=article&id=9965 :2015-08-04-15-15-32&catid=60 :actualidad&Itemid=96).

condition que ce soit, non plus évidemment qu'à s'abriter derrière les exigences prétendues de son droit interne pour ne pas l'exécuter ou à ne prévoir de le faire que conditionnellement. Cela suffit pour rejeter le principal argument de la Colombie à l'appui de sa prétention assez extravagante selon laquelle il n'y aurait pas de différend entre les deux Etats.

26. Moyennant quoi, le Nicaragua, bon prince, a fait savoir que, si ce n'était que cela, il serait disposé à conclure un traité avec la Colombie en vue d'appliquer — mais d'appliquer pleinement — l'arrêt dans son entièreté, notre agent l'a rappelé solennellement mardi dernier[74], ainsi qu'à envisager des aménagements au régime juridique des zones marines reconnues par l'arrêt comme relevant de la juridiction du Nicaragua, sans qu'il soit question toutefois de remettre en cause les limites de ces zones[75]. Las ! La Colombie se dit prête à négocier — mais sans accepter le préalable de l'application intégrale de l'arrêt de 2012 en matière de délimitation. Bien au contraire, l'adoption du décret n° 1946 déclarant une «zone contiguë intégrale», la saisine de la Cour constitutionnelle (et la décision de celle-ci), le renforcement du contrôle militaire des zones reconnues par la Cour comme nicaraguayennes — et j'en passe ! — portent témoignage de l'intention délibérée de la Colombie de ne pas appliquer l'arrêt et de rendre les négociations parfaitement vaines. Chacun des deux Etats campant sur ses positions, inébranlables dès l'origine, l'impasse était totale et si le principe de ce qu'on pourrait appeler «l'épuisement préalable des possibilités de négociations» devait s'appliquer, il est clair que les conditions en seraient remplies.

27. Un tel principe n'existe assurément pas en droit international général et la Colombie ne le prétend d'ailleurs pas — la seconde base de compétence invoquée par le Nicaragua n'est donc pas concernée. En revanche, nos contradicteurs soutiennent *mordicus* que ce prétendu principe s'imposerait en vertu des versions anglaise, espagnole et portugaise de l'article II du pacte de Bogotá ; s'il fallait l'interpréter ainsi, cela signifierait qu'une partie pourrait bloquer indéfiniment toute possibilité de règlement pacifique en prétendant que des négociations sont possibles. Ceci n'est ni raisonnable, ni conforme à la vocation même du «Traité américain de Règlement pacifique». Dès lors, la version française semble infiniment plus apte à atteindre le résultat recherché et, dans un cas de ce genre, comme l'a d'ailleurs rappelé la Cour dans l'affaire

---

[74] CR 2015/23, p. 12, par. 11 (agent).

[75] *Ibid.*, par. 12 (agent).

LaGrand[76], il convient d'appliquer le principe (ayant valeur coutumière) énoncé dans l'article 33, paragraphe 4, de la convention de Vienne sur le droit des traités et d'adopter «le sens qui, compte tenu de l'objet et du but du traité, concilie le mieux ces textes». Je ne crois pas faire preuve d'un chauvinisme linguistique excessif en pensant qu'en l'occurrence le texte français doit s'appliquer : la conviction raisonnable d'une des Parties selon laquelle les négociations sont dans l'impasse doit suffire pour qu'il soit possible de recourir aux autres procédures établies par le pacte de Bogotá. Cette interprétation s'impose d'autant plus en l'espèce que la Cour peut contrôler l'appréciation unilatérale du Nicaragua.

28. Parmi les modes de règlement envisagés par le pacte, le règlement judiciaire tient une place de choix puisque l'article XXXI constitue une manière de déclaration facultative collective, ce qui ouvre largement la compétence de la Cour de céans. Et c'est ce moyen que le Nicaragua a choisi d'actionner tant en 2001 lorsqu'il a saisi la Cour de son *Différend terrestre et maritime* avec la Colombie, qu'en 2013 lorsqu'il lui a demandé de faire respecter les droits souverains et les espaces maritimes que l'arrêt de 2012 lui a reconnus.

29. Vous ne le savez que trop, Mesdames et Messieurs les juges, la Colombie a cru pouvoir faire échapper ce différend à la compétence de la Cour en dénonçant le pacte de Bogotá avec effet immédiat — au mépris du texte tout à fait clair de l'article LVI, paragraphe 1, de celui-ci qui en autorise la dénonciation «moyennant un préavis d'un an», étant entendu que «passé ce délai il cessera de produire ses effets par rapport à la partie qui l'a dénoncé». C'est clair et net et il n'y a pas là matière à interprétation : intervenue le 27 novembre 2012, la dénonciation du pacte par la Colombie a fait que celui-ci ne produit plus d'effets à son égard depuis le 27 novembre 2013. Le paragraphe 2 de l'article LVI tire les conséquences de ce principe en ce qui concerne les procédures entamées avant cette dénonciation en précisant qu'elle n'aura aucun effet sur ces procédures. Et si je veux bien concéder que la formule utilisée pour le dire est ambiguë (puisqu'elle vise les «procédures en cours entamées avant la transmission de l'avis de dénonciation»), l'ambiguïté est facile à lever à la lumière du contexte — et d'abord du paragraphe 1 qui doit, lui aussi, avoir un effet utile — à la lumière aussi des travaux préparatoires et de l'objet et du but du pacte de Bogotá.

---

[76] *LaGrand (Allemagne c. Etats-Unis d'Amérique), arrêt, C.I.J. Recueil 2001*, p. 502, par. 101.

30. Au demeurant, Monsieur le président, ces problèmes d'interprétation ne présentent aucune pertinence en ce qui concerne le second chef de compétence de la Cour (alternatif et cumulatif) invoqué par le Nicaragua : sa compétence inhérente pour tirer les conséquences de la non-exécution de l'arrêt de 2012 par la partie colombienne. Je viens d'en parler aussi longuement que le temps qui m'est alloué le permettait et je ne pense pas qu'il soit utile que je m'y attarde à nouveau — sauf à relever une nouvelle fois que la compétence inhérente que vous possédez en la matière ne se confond nullement avec celle que l'article 94, paragraphe 2, de la Charte des Nations Unies prévoit en faveur du Conseil de sécurité : la sienne est éminemment politique, la vôtre est judiciaire ; la sienne est de nature exécutoire, la vôtre se situe sur le terrain de la responsabilité ; la sienne est terriblement aléatoire et incertaine ; les Etats doivent trouver dans l'exercice de la vôtre un élément rassurant et fiable contribuant à la mise en œuvre effective des arrêts que vous rendez conformément à la mission qui est la vôtre : trancher les différends qui vous sont soumis de manière complète et effective.

31. Mesdames et Messieurs de la Cour, c'est toujours un honneur insigne et, j'ose ajouter, un plaisir, de plaider devant vous ; je vous suis reconnaissant de me l'accorder et au Nicaragua de m'en donner l'occasion.

32. Monsieur le président, je vous prie de bien vouloir appeler l'ambassadeur Argüello à la barre pour la lecture des conclusions finales de la République du Nicaragua.

Le PRESIDENT : Merci, Monsieur le professeur. Je redonne à présent la parole à l'agent du Nicaragua, S. Exc. M. Argüello Gómez.

Mr. ARGÜELLO GÓMEZ:

FINAL SUBMISSIONS

Thank you, Mr. President, Members of the Court. At this time enough has been said about the preliminary objections of Colombia and I will limit the next few moments to simply expressing orally the final submissions that Nicaragua is filing with the Court.

> "In view of the reasons Nicaragua has presented in its Written Observations and during the hearings, the Republic of Nicaragua requests the Court:
>
> — to reject the preliminary objections of the Republic of Colombia; and
>
> — to proceed with the examination of the merits of the case."

Mr. President, Members of the Court, with this reading of its submissions Nicaragua puts an end to its oral pleadings and expresses its gratitude to the Court for their patience and kind attention to these pleadings.

Mr. President, the Nicaraguan team also wishes to thank the Registrar and all those officials of the Registry that have collaborated in organizing these very efficient hearings, including the excellent team of interpreters and translators who have arduously worked to keep up with our different accents. The Nicaraguan team also wishes to extend its thanks and congratulations to the Colombian team.

Thank you, Mr. President, Members of the Court.

Le PRESIDENT : Merci, Monsieur l'agent. Un juge a des questions à poser aux Parties. Je vais lui donner à présent la parole. Monsieur le juge Cançado Trindade.

Judge CANÇADO TRINDADE: Merci, Monsieur le président.

In the course of the proceedings along this week, both contending Parties referred to the relevant case law of contemporary international tribunals, in particular in respect of the question of their inherent powers or *facultés*. Having listened attentively to their oral arguments, I have three questions to address to both Parties, so as to obtain further precisions, at conceptual level, from both of them, in the context of the *cas d'espèce*.

> "First: Do the inherent powers or *facultés* of contemporary international tribunals ensue from the exercise itself, by each of them, of their international judicial function?
>
> Second: Do the distinct bases of jurisdiction of contemporary international tribunals have an incidence on the extent of their *compétence de la compétence*?
>
> Third: Do the distinct bases of jurisdiction of contemporary international tribunals condition the operation of the corresponding mechanisms of supervision of compliance with their respective judgments and decisions?"

Thank you, Mr. President.

Le PRESIDENT : Je vous remercie, Monsieur le juge. Le texte de ces questions sera communiqué aux Parties, sous forme écrite, dès que possible. Les Parties sont invitées à soumettre leurs réponses écrites à ces questions le 9 octobre à 18 heures au plus tard. Toutes observations qu'une Partie pourrait souhaiter présenter, conformément à l'article 72 du Règlement de la Cour, sur les réponses de l'autre Partie devront être communiquées le 16 octobre à 18 heures au plus tard.

Ceci nous amène au terme des audiences consacrées aux exceptions préliminaires présentées par la Colombie en la présente affaire. Je tiens à remercier les agents, conseils et avocats des deux Parties pour leurs interventions. Conformément à la pratique, je prierai les agents de rester à la disposition de la Cour pour tous renseignements complémentaires dont elle pourrait avoir besoin.

Sous cette réserve, je déclare close la procédure orale sur les exceptions préliminaires en l'affaire relative à des *Violations de droits souverains et d'espaces maritimes dans la mer des Caraïbes (Nicaragua c. Colombie)*. La Cour va maintenant se retirer pour délibérer. Les agents des Parties seront avisés en temps utile de la date à laquelle la Cour rendra son arrêt. La Cour n'étant saisie d'aucune autre question aujourd'hui, l'audience est levée.

L'audience est levée à 12 heures.

___

Corrigé
Corrected

CR 2021/13

International Court
of Justice

THE HAGUE

Cour internationale
de Justice

LA HAYE

YEAR 2021

Public sitting

held on Monday 20 September 2021, at 3 p.m., at the Peace Palace,

President Donoghue presiding,

***in the case concerning* Alleged Violations of Sovereign Rights and Maritime Spaces in the Caribbean Sea (Nicaragua *v.* Colombia)**

VERBATIM RECORD

ANNÉE 2021

Audience publique

tenue le lundi 20 septembre 2021, à 15 heures, au Palais de la Paix,

sous la présidence de Mme Donoghue, présidente,

***en l'affaire relative à des* Violations alléguées de droits souverains et d'espaces maritimes dans la mer des Caraïbes (Nicaragua c. Colombie)**

COMPTE RENDU

Present:	President	Donoghue
	Vice-President	Gevorgian
	Judges	Tomka
		Abraham
		Bennouna
		Yusuf
		Xue
		Sebutinde
		Bhandari
		Robinson
		Salam
		Iwasawa
		Nolte
	Judges *ad hoc*	Daudet
		McRae
	Registrar	Gautier

Présents :	Mme	Donoghue, présidente
	M.	Gevorgian, vice-président
	MM.	Tomka
		Abraham
		Bennouna
		Yusuf
	Mmes	Xue
		Sebutinde
	MM.	Bhandari
		Robinson
		Salam
		Iwasawa
		Nolte, juges
	MM.	Daudet
		McRae, juges *ad hoc*
	M.	Gautier, greffier

The Government of Nicaragua is represented by:

H.E. Mr. Carlos José Argüello Gómez, Ambassador of the Republic of Nicaragua to the Kingdom of the Netherlands,

as Agent and Counsel;

Mr. Alex Oude Elferink, Director, Netherlands Institute for the Law of the Sea, Professor of International Law of the Sea at Utrecht University,

Mr. Vaughan Lowe, QC, Emeritus Chichele Professor of Public International Law, University of Oxford, member of the Institut de droit international, member of the Bar of England and Wales,

Mr. Lawrence H. Martin, Attorney at Law, Foley Hoag LLP, member of the Bars of the United States Supreme Court, the District of Columbia and the Commonwealth of Massachusetts,

Mr. Alain Pellet, Emeritus Professor of the University Paris Nanterre, former Chairman of the International Law Commission, President of the Institut de droit international,

Mr. Paul Reichler, Attorney at Law, Foley Hoag LLP, member of the Bars of the United States Supreme Court and the District of Columbia,

as Counsel and Advocates;

Ms Claudia Loza Obregon, Legal Adviser, Ministry of Foreign Affairs of Nicaragua,

Ms Tessa Barsac, Consultant in International Law, Master (University Paris Nanterre), LLM (Leiden University),

as Assistant Counsel;

Mr. Robin Cleverly, MA, DPhil, CGeol, FGS, Law of the Sea Consultant, Marbdy Consulting Ltd,

as Scientific and Technical Adviser;

Ms Sherly Noguera de Argüello, MBA,

as Administrator.

The Government of Colombia is represented by:

H.E. Mr. Carlos Gustavo Arrieta Padilla, former Judge of the Council of State of Colombia, former Attorney General of Colombia and former Ambassador of Colombia to the Netherlands,

as Agent;

H.E. Mr. Manuel José Cepeda Espinosa, former President of the Constitutional Court of Colombia, former Permanent Delegate of Colombia to UNESCO and former Ambassador of Colombia to the Swiss Confederation,

as Co-Agent;

Le Gouvernement du Nicaragua est représenté par :

S. Exc. M. Carlos José Argüello Gómez, ambassadeur de la République du Nicaragua auprès du Royaume des Pays-Bas,

comme agent et conseil ;

M. Alex Oude Elferink, directeur de l'Institut néerlandais du droit de la mer, professeur de droit international de la mer à l'Université d'Utrecht,

M. Vaughan Lowe, QC, professeur émérite de droit international public à l'Université d'Oxford, titulaire de la chaire Chichele, membre de l'Institut de droit international, membre du barreau d'Angleterre et du pays de Galles,

M. Lawrence H. Martin, avocat au cabinet Foley Hoag LLP, membre des barreaux de la Cour suprême des Etats-Unis d'Amérique, du district de Colombia et du Commonwealth du Massachusetts,

M. Alain Pellet, professeur émérite de l'Université Paris Nanterre, ancien président de la Commission du droit international, président de l'Institut de droit international,

M. Paul Reichler, avocat au cabinet Foley Hoag LLP, membre des barreaux de la Cour suprême des Etats-Unis d'Amérique et du district de Colombia,

comme conseils et avocats ;

Mme Claudia Loza Obregon, conseillère juridique auprès du ministère des affaires étrangères du Nicaragua,

Mme Tessa Barsac, consultante en droit international, master (Université Paris Nanterre), LLM (Université de Leyde),

comme conseils adjoints ;

M. Robin Cleverly, MA, DPhil, CGeol, FGS, consultant en droit de la mer, Marbdy Consulting Ltd,

comme conseiller scientifique et technique ;

Mme Sherly Noguera de Argüello, MBA,

comme administrateur.

Le Gouvernement de la Colombie est représenté par :

S. Exc. M. Carlos Gustavo Arrieta Padilla, ancien juge au conseil d'Etat colombien, ancien *Procurador General de la Nación* et ancien ambassadeur de Colombie aux Pays-Bas,

comme agent ;

S. Exc. M. Manuel José Cepeda Espinosa, ancien président de la Cour constitutionnelle de Colombie, ancien représentant permanent de la Colombie auprès de l'UNESCO et ancien ambassadeur de Colombie auprès de la Confédération suisse,

comme coagent ;

H.E. Ms Marta Lucía Ramírez Blanco, Vice-President and Minister for Foreign Affairs of the Republic of Colombia,

H.E. Mr. Everth Hawkins Sjogreen, Governor of San Andrés, Providencia and Santa Catalina, Colombia,

as National Authorities;

Mr. W. Michael Reisman, McDougal Professor of International Law at Yale University, member of the Institut de droit international,

Mr. Rodman R. Bundy, former *avocat à la Cour d'appel de Paris*, member of the Bar of the State of New York, partner at Squire Patton Boggs LLP, Singapore,

Sir Michael Wood, KCMG, member of the International Law Commission, member of the Bar of England and Wales,

Mr. Eduardo Valencia-Ospina, former Registrar and Deputy-Registrar of the International Court of Justice, member and former Special Rapporteur and Chair of the International Law Commission, former Chair of the Latin American Society of International Law,

Mr. Jean-Marc Thouvenin, Professor at the University Paris Nanterre, Secretary-General of the Hague Academy of International Law, associate member of the Institut de droit international, member of the Paris Bar, Sygna Partners,

Ms Laurence Boisson de Chazournes, Professor of International Law and International Organization at the University of Geneva, member of the Institut de droit international,

H.E. Mr. Kent Francis James, former Ambassador of Colombia to Belize, former Ambassador of Colombia to Jamaica,

as Counsel and Advocates;

Mr. Andrés Villegas Jaramillo, LLM, Co-ordinator, Group of Affairs before the International Court of Justice at the Ministry of Foreign Affairs of Colombia, member of the Legal Sub-Commission of the Caribbean Sea Commission, Association of Caribbean States,

Mr. Makane Moïse Mbengue, Professor at the University of Geneva, Director of the Department of Public International Law and International Organization, associate member of the Institut de droit international,

Mr. Luke Vidal, member of the Paris Bar, Sygna Partners,

Mr. Eran Sthoeger, Esq., member of the Bar of the State of New York, Adjunct Professor of International Law at Brooklyn Law School and Seton Hall Law School,

Mr. Alvin Yap, Advocate and Solicitor of the Supreme Court of Singapore, Squire Patton Boggs LLP, Singapore,

Mr. Lorenzo Palestini, PhD, Lecturer at the Graduate Institute of International and Development Studies and at the University of Geneva,

as Counsel;

S. Exc. Mme Marta Lucía Ramírez Blanco, vice-présidente et ministre des affaires étrangères de la République de Colombie,

S. Exc. M. Everth Hawkins Sjogreen, gouverneur de San Andrés, Providencia et Santa Catalina, Colombie,

comme représentants de l'Etat ;

M. W. Michael Reisman, professeur de droit international à l'Université de Yale, titulaire de la chaire McDougal, membre de l'Institut de droit international,

M. Rodman R. Bundy, ancien avocat à la Cour d'appel de Paris, membre du barreau de l'Etat de New York, associé au cabinet Squire Patton Boggs LLP (Singapour),

Sir Michael Wood, KCMG, membre de la Commission du droit international, membre du barreau d'Angleterre et du pays de Galles,

M. Eduardo Valencia-Ospina, ancien greffier et greffier adjoint de la Cour internationale de Justice, membre et ancien rapporteur spécial et président de la Commission du droit international, ancien président de l'association latino-américaine de droit international,

M. Jean-Marc Thouvenin, professeur à l'Université Paris Nanterre, secrétaire général de l'Académie de droit international de La Haye, membre associé de l'Institut de droit international, membre du barreau de Paris, cabinet Sygna Partners,

Mme Laurence Boisson de Chazournes, professeure de droit international public et organisation internationale à l'Université de Genève, membre de l'Institut de droit international,

S. Exc. M. Kent Francis James, ancien ambassadeur de Colombie au Belize et ancien ambassadeur de Colombie en Jamaïque,

comme conseils et avocats ;

M. Andrés Villegas Jaramillo, LLM, coordonnateur du groupe chargé des affaires portées devant la Cour internationale de Justice au sein du ministère des affaires étrangères de la Colombie, membre de la sous-commission juridique relevant de la Commission de la mer des Caraïbes de l'Association des Etats de la Caraïbe,

M. Makane Moïse Mbengue, professeur à l'Université de Genève, directeur du département de droit international public et organisation internationale, membre associé de l'Institut de droit international,

M. Luke Vidal, membre du barreau de Paris, cabinet Sygna Partners,

M. Eran Sthoeger, membre du barreau de l'Etat de New York, professeur adjoint de droit international à la Brooklyn Law School et à la faculté de droit de l'université de Seton Hall

M. Alvin Yap, avocat et *solicitor* à la Cour suprême de Singapour, cabinet Squire Patton Boggs LLP (Singapour),

M. Lorenzo Palestini, PhD, chargé d'enseignement à l'Institut de hautes études internationales et du développement et à l'Université de Genève,

comme conseils ;

H.E. Mr. Juan José Quintana Aranguren, Head of Multilateral Affairs, former Ambassador of Colombia to the Netherlands,

H.E. Mr. Fernando Antonio Grillo Rubiano, Ambassador of the Republic of Colombia to the Kingdom of the Netherlands and Permanent Representative of Colombia to the Organisation for the Prohibition of Chemical Weapons,

Ms Jenny Sharyne Bowie Wilches, Second Secretary, Embassy of Colombia in the Netherlands,

Ms Viviana Andrea Medina Cruz, Second Secretary, Embassy of Colombia in the Netherlands,

Mr. Sebastián Correa Cruz, Third Secretary,

Mr. Raúl Alfonso Simancas Gómez, Third Secretary, Group of Affairs before the International Court of Justice,

Ministry of Foreign Affairs of Colombia;

Rear Admiral Ernesto Segovia Forero, Chief of Naval Operations,

CN Hermann León, Delegate of Colombia to the International Maritime Organization,

CN William Pedroza, National Navy of Colombia, Director of Maritime and Fluvial Interests Office,

Navy of the Republic of Colombia;

Mr. Scott Edmonds, Cartographer, Director of International Mapping,

Ms Victoria Taylor, Cartographer, International Mapping,

as Technical Advisers;

Mr. Gershon Hasin, LLM, JSD, Yale Law School,

as Legal Assistant;

Mr. Mark Taylor Archbold, Consultant for the National Unit of Disaster Risk Management,

Mr. Joseph Richard Jessie Martinez, Consultant for the National Unit of Disaster Risk Management,

as Advisers.

S. Exc. M. Juan José Quintana Aranguren, chef des affaires multilatérales, ancien ambassadeur de Colombie aux Pays-Bas,

S. Exc. M. Fernando Antonio Grillo Rubiano, ambassadeur de la République de Colombie auprès du Royaume des Pays-Bas et représentant permanent de la Colombie auprès de l'Organisation pour l'interdiction des armes chimiques,

Mme Jenny Sharyne Bowie Wilches, deuxième secrétaire, ambassade de Colombie aux Pays-Bas,

Mme Viviana Andrea Medina Cruz, deuxième secrétaire, ambassade de Colombie aux Pays-Bas,

M. Sebastián Correa Cruz, troisième secrétaire,

M. Raúl Alfonso Simancas Gómez, troisième secrétaire, groupe chargé des affaires portées devant la Cour internationale de Justice,

ministère des affaires étrangères de la République de Colombie ;

Le contre-amiral Ernesto Segovia Forero, chef des opérations navales,

Le capitaine de vaisseau Hermann León, représentant de la Colombie auprès de l'Organisation maritime internationale,

Le capitaine de vaisseau William Pedroza, marine nationale de Colombie, chef de la direction chargée des intérêts maritimes et fluviaux,

marine de la République de Colombie ;

M. Scott Edmonds, cartographe, directeur de International Mapping,

Mme Victoria Taylor, cartographe, International Mapping,

comme conseillers techniques ;

M. Gershon Hasin, LLM, JSD, faculté de droit de l'Université de Yale,

comme assistant juridique ;

M. Mark Taylor Archbold, consultant auprès de l'unité nationale de gestion des risques de catastrophe,

M. Joseph Richard Jessie Martinez, consultant auprès de l'unité nationale de gestion des risques de catastrophe,

comme conseillers.

The PRESIDENT: Please be seated. The sitting is open.

Before we start our judicial proceedings today, I would like to pay tribute, on behalf of the Court, to Judge James Crawford, our esteemed colleague and friend, who passed away on 31 May of this year.

Judge Crawford, an active and highly regarded Member of the Court since 2015, was a towering figure in international law and a role model for generations of lawyers. Born in 1948 in Adelaide, Australia, Judge James Crawford studied law and humanities at the University of Adelaide and obtained a doctorate in jurisprudence at Oxford University. In his extraordinary career, Judge Crawford distinguished himself both as an academic and as a practitioner. He was Professor of Law at the University of Adelaide, Challis Professor of International Law at the University of Sydney and, until his election to the Court, Whewell Professor of International Law at the University of Cambridge, where he also directed the Lauterpacht Centre for International Law. As an academic, he created an astonishing body of scholarship, including seminal works on key topics such as State responsibility and the creation of States in international law. As a practitioner, he was a well-renowned and a seasoned barrister, having been called to the Bar of the Supreme Court of New South Wales in 1987 and appointed senior Counsel in 1997. He also became a member of the Bar of England and Wales and co-founded a highly successful set of chambers in London in 2000.

Within his home country, Judge Crawford held a number of key positions, including being a member of the Australian Law Reform Commission, where he spearheaded the effort to recognize Aboriginal customary laws. At the international level, he had considerable experience as an arbitrator in the settlement of investor-state disputes and left his mark as a member of the International Law Commission from 1992 to 2001, where he served as Special Rapporteur on State responsibility for internationally wrongful acts, playing a crucial role in the adoption by the Commission of the final text of these draft Articles. As a member of the Institut de droit international, Judge Crawford made a significant contribution to the study and development of many other areas of international law.

Prior to his election to the International Court of Justice, Judge Crawford had already gained a wealth of experience pleading before this Bench. He first appeared as counsel before the Court in the case concerning *Certain Phosphate Lands in Nauru* in 1991. He was thereafter to become a regular fixture in the Great Hall of Justice, addressing the Court in close to 30 contentious and advisory proceedings.

When Judge Crawford became a Member of this Court in February 2015, the qualities that had earned him his reputation as a giant in international law were immediately apparent. With his singularly agile mind, brilliant analytical skills and fine drafting, he was a true asset to this institution. He cared deeply about the Court and was firmly committed to the accomplishment of its mandate through constructive dialogue and reasoned debate.

Beyond Judge Crawford's remarkable professional achievements, he will also be remembered in equal measure for his warm, unassuming personality and his sharp sense of humour. The countless tributes that poured in following his untimely death are a testament to the deep respect and affection he inspired as a teacher, mentor and colleague.

Judge Crawford's passing is an enormous loss to international law and international justice, and to this Court, where he is sorely missed.

I would like now to invite you to stand and observe a minute's silence in memory of Judge James Crawford.

[The Court observed a minute's silence]

The PRESIDENT: Please be seated.

The Court meets today and will meet in the coming days to hear the Parties' oral arguments on the merits of the case concerning *Alleged Violations of Sovereign Rights and Maritime Spaces in the Caribbean Sea (Nicaragua* v. *Colombia)*. Today, the Court will hear the first round of oral argument of Nicaragua.

Owing to the ongoing concerns and restrictions related to the COVID-19 pandemic, the Court has decided to hold these oral proceedings in a hybrid format, under Article 59, paragraph 2, of its Rules. The Court will continue to fulfil its mission through all means at its disposal, pending the normalization of the health situation.

The Court has taken great care to ensure the smooth conduct of this hybrid hearing. The Parties participated in technical tests over the course of the past week. Those tests were comprehensive and included, for example, tests of the interpretation system and the process for displaying demonstrative exhibits such as PowerPoint slides and maps. However, while these tests can reduce the risk of technical difficulties, they cannot eliminate them. In the event that we experience any such difficulty, such as a loss of any audio input from a remote participant, I may have to interrupt the hearing briefly to allow the technical team to solve the problem.

In a hybrid hearing such as this one, all judges are able to view the speaker and any demonstrative exhibits, regardless of whether they are in the Great Hall or joining via video link. I would note that the following judges are present with me in the Great Hall of Justice: Vice-President Gevorgian and Judges Tomka, Abraham, Bennouna, Yusuf, Sebutinde and Nolte; while Judges Xue, Bhandari, Robinson, Salam and Iwasawa and Judges *ad hoc* Daudet and McRae are participating by video link. For reasons duly made known to me, Judge Cançado Trindade is unable to sit with us in these oral proceedings, either in person or by video link.

For this hybrid hearing, the Registrar informed both Parties that each of them could have up to four representatives present in the Great Hall of Justice at any one time and that the Court could make available, should a Party so desire, an additional room in the Peace Palace from which other members of the delegation could follow the proceedings via video link. The Registrar also informed the Parties that participation via video link would be available to the members of each delegation who would not be present in the Peace Palace.

*

Since the Court included upon the Bench no judge of the nationality of either Party, each Party proceeded to exercise the right conferred upon it by Article 31, paragraph 3, of the Statute to choose a judge *ad hoc* to sit in the case. Nicaragua first chose Judge Gilbert Guillaume, who resigned on 8 September 2015, and subsequently Professor Yves Daudet. Colombia first chose Professor David Caron and subsequently, following the death of Professor Caron in February 2018, chose Professor Donald McRae.

Article 20 of the Statute provides that "[e]very Member of the Court shall, before taking up his duties, make a solemn declaration in open court that he will exercise his powers impartially and conscientiously". Pursuant to Article 31, paragraph 6, of the Statute, that same provision applies to judges *ad hoc*.

Professor Daudet has already made his solemn declaration at the sitting held on 28 September 2015, on the occasion of the proceedings on the preliminary objections raised by Colombia.

Since this is the first time that Professor McRae is participating in this case, he is required, in accordance with Article 8, paragraph 3, of the Rules of Court, to make a solemn declaration in relation to the present case.

Before inviting Professor McRae to make his solemn declaration, I shall first, in accordance with custom, say a few words about his career and qualifications.

Professor McRae, of Canadian and New Zealand nationalities, is Professor Emeritus and former Dean of Common Law at the Faculty of Law, at the University of Ottawa. He has extensive experience as counsel in the context of international fisheries and boundary arbitrations, and he has also appeared before this Court as counsel in *Request for Interpretation of the Judgment of 15 June 1962 in the Case concerning the* Temple of Preah Vihear *(Cambodia* v. *Thailand)*. In the framework of the World Trade Organization, he has appeared as counsel before that organization's dispute settlement panels and Appellate Body and has also served as a member of several WTO panels. In addition, he has been a member and chair of various investment tribunals, including cases brought under the Convention on the Settlement of Investment Disputes between States and Nationals of Other States and Chapter 11 of the North American Free Trade Agreement. He currently chairs an Arbitral Tribunal convened pursuant to Annex VII of the United Nations Convention on the Law of the Sea. Professor McRae is the former Editor-in-Chief of the Canadian Yearbook of International Law and has published widely on international law, including on law of the sea and international trade law. He is a member of the Institut de droit international, a member of the Royal Society of Canada, a Companion of the Order of Canada, and an Officer of the New Zealand Order of Merit. He was a member of the International Law Commission from 2007 to 2016. Professor McRae also served as judge *ad hoc* in the case concerning the *Obligation to Negotiate Access to the Pacific Ocean (Bolivia* v. *Chile)*.

I shall now invite Professor McRae to make the solemn declaration prescribed by the Statute, and I request all those present to rise. Professor McRae, please proceed.

Mr. McRAE:

> "I solemnly declare that I will perform my duties and exercise my powers as judge honourably, faithfully, impartially and conscientiously."

The PRESIDENT: Thank you, Professor McRae. Please be seated. I take note of the solemn declaration made by Professor McRae and declare him duly installed as a judge *ad hoc* in the case concerning *Alleged Violations of Sovereign Rights and Maritime Spaces in the Caribbean Sea (Nicaragua* v. *Colombia)*.

*

I shall now briefly recall the principal procedural steps in this case.

On 26 November 2013, the Government of the Republic of Nicaragua filed in the Registry of the Court an Application instituting proceedings against the Republic of Colombia concerning a dispute in relation to, first, alleged violations by Colombia of Nicaragua's rights in maritime zones which, according to the Applicant, the Court declared to appertain to Nicaragua in its 2012 Judgment in the case concerning *Territorial and Maritime Dispute (Nicaragua* v. *Colombia)* and, secondly, the threat of use of force by Colombia in the course of these violations.

As a basis for the Court's jurisdiction, Nicaragua invoked Article XXXI of the American Treaty on Pacific Settlement signed on 30 April 1948, and officially designated, according to Article LX thereof, as the "Pact of Bogotá".

By an Order of 3 February 2014, the Court fixed 3 October 2014 and 3 June 2015 as the respective time-limits for the filing of a Memorial by Nicaragua and a Counter-Memorial by Colombia. Nicaragua filed its Memorial within the time-limit thus fixed.

On 19 December 2014, within the time-limit prescribed by Article 79, paragraph 1, of the Rules of Court of 14 April 1978 as amended on 1 February 2001, Colombia raised preliminary objections to the jurisdiction of the Court.

By a Judgment of 17 March 2016, the Court found that it had jurisdiction, on the basis of Article XXXI of the Pact of Bogotá, to entertain the dispute between Nicaragua and Colombia regarding the alleged violations by Colombia of Nicaragua's rights in the maritime zones which, according to Nicaragua, the Court declared in its 2012 Judgment appertain to Nicaragua.

By an Order of 17 March 2016, the Court fixed 17 November 2016 as the new time-limit for the filing of the Counter-Memorial of Colombia. Colombia filed that pleading within the time-limit thus prescribed. In Part III of its Counter-Memorial, Colombia, making reference to Article 80 of the Rules of Court, submitted four counter-claims.

At a meeting held by the President of the Court with the representatives of the Parties on 19 January 2017, Nicaragua indicated that it considered the counter-claims contained in the Counter-Memorial of Colombia to be inadmissible. By letters dated 20 January 2017, the Registrar informed the Parties that the Court had decided that the Government of Nicaragua should specify in writing, by 20 April 2017 at the latest, the legal grounds on which it relied in maintaining that the Respondent's counter-claims were inadmissible, and that the Government of Colombia should present its own views on the question in writing, by 20 July 2017 at the latest. Nicaragua and Colombia submitted their written observations on the admissibility of Colombia's counter-claims within the time-limits thus fixed.

By an Order of 15 November 2017, the Court found that two of the four counter-claims were admissible — namely, the third and the fourth. The third counter-claim concerns the alleged violation by Nicaragua of the customary artisanal fishing rights of the local inhabitants of the San Andrés Archipelago to access and exploit their traditional fishing grounds; the fourth counter-claim relates to the adoption by Nicaragua of Decree No. 33-2013 of 19 August 2013, which is alleged to have established straight baselines and to have had the effect of extending Nicaragua's internal waters and maritime zones beyond what international law permits, thereby violating Colombia's sovereign rights and maritime spaces. By the same Order, the Court directed Nicaragua to submit a Reply and Colombia to submit a Rejoinder relating to the claims of both Parties in the current proceedings, and fixed 15 May and 15 November 2018 as the respective time-limits for the filing of those pleadings. The Reply of Nicaragua and the Rejoinder of Colombia were filed within the time-limits thus fixed.

By an Order dated 4 December 2018, the Court authorized the submission by Nicaragua of an additional pleading relating solely to the counter-claims submitted by Colombia and fixed 4 March

2019 as the time-limit for the filing of that pleading. The additional pleading was filed by Nicaragua within the prescribed time-limit.

Following the closure of the written proceedings, by letter of 23 September 2019, the Nicaraguan Government, referring to Article 56 of the Rules of Court, requested the authorization of the Court to produce 19 new documents. By letter dated 3 October 2019, the Government of Colombia informed the Court that it was opposed to the granting of that request. By letters dated 16 October 2019, the Parties were informed that the Court had authorized the production of the above-mentioned documents by Nicaragua, and that the opportunity was available to Colombia to comment thereon and to submit documents in support of its comments. Within the time-limit of 16 December 2019, as fixed by the Court for that purpose, Colombia transmitted to the Court its comments on the new documents, as well as supporting exhibits and audio-visual material.

By letter of 30 July 2021, Nicaragua, referring to Article 56 of the Rules of Court, further requested the authorization of the Court to produce four additional new documents. By letter dated 16 August 2021, the Government of Colombia informed the Court that it objected to the production of these documents. By letters dated 1 September 2021, the Parties were informed that the Court had authorized the production of two of these new documents, and that the opportunity was available to Colombia to comment thereon and to submit documents in support of its comments. Within the time-limit of 9 September 2021, as fixed by the Court for that purpose, Colombia transmitted to the Court its comments on the two new documents, as well as supporting exhibits.

*

Pursuant to Article 53, paragraph 2, of its Rules, the Court decided, after consulting the Parties, that copies of the written pleadings and documents annexed would be made accessible to the public, with the exception of certain annexes to and figures included in Colombia's written pleadings. In particular, the Court acceded to Colombia's request that these materials not be made accessible to the public on the basis that, under Colombian legislation, they are classified as secret or reserved for reasons of national security. While the Parties may, during this hearing, refer to the titles of these confidential documents as they appear in the list of annexes, they may not read out quotations from them nor display slides showing all or part of them. With the exception of the above-mentioned materials, and in accordance with the Court's practice, all pleadings and documents annexed will be placed on the Court's website in due course.

*

I would now like to welcome the delegations of the Parties. I note here the presence in the Great Hall of Justice of the Agent of Nicaragua and the Agent of Colombia, each accompanied by members of their respective State's delegation. I further note that other members of the delegations of the Applicant and the Respondent will be participating in the hearings by video link.

In accordance with the arrangements on the organization of the proceedings that have been decided by the Court, the hearings will comprise a first and second round of oral argument. The first round will begin with Nicaragua's presentation today of its arguments on its own claims, from 3 p.m. to 6 p.m. On Wednesday 22 September, Colombia will present its first round of argument, both on the claims of Nicaragua and on its own counter-claims, from 11 a.m. to 1 p.m. and then from 3 p.m. to 6 p.m. On Friday 24 September, Nicaragua will present its observations on the counter-claims of Colombia, from 3 p.m. to 5 p.m.

The second round of oral argument will open on the afternoon of Monday 27 September, with Nicaragua addressing the Court on its own claims from 3 p.m. to 5 p.m. On Wednesday 29 September, Colombia will present its second round of argument on the claims of Nicaragua and its own counter-claims, from 3 p.m. to 6 p.m. On Friday 1 October, Nicaragua will present its reply on the counter-claims of Colombia, from 3 p.m. to 4 p.m.

In this first sitting, Nicaragua may, if so required, avail itself of a short extension of time beyond 6 p.m., in view of the time taken up by these introductory remarks.

I shall now give the floor to the Agent of Nicaragua, H.E. Mr. Carlos José Argüello Gómez. You have the floor, Your Excellency.

Mr. ARGÜELLO GÓMEZ:

1. Good afternoon. Thank you, Madam President, distinguished Members of the Court. It is always an honour to be before you, representing my country.

2. Before beginning my presentation, I would like to add my tribute to the memory of Judge James Crawford. As a member of the Bar that has had the honour of pleading before this Court, I was able to appreciate first-hand the eloquence and high academic standards of Judge Crawford, not only as a judge but also in his role as counsel in some of the many cases in which he pleaded before the Court, several in which Nicaragua was a party, including the case of the *Territorial and Maritime Dispute (Nicaragua* v. *Colombia)* which is the background of the present case before the Court.

3. Madam President, nine years ago, in April 2012, during the oral pleadings in the *Territorial and Maritime Dispute*, after an exhausting and exhaustive procedure that began with Nicaragua filing its Application on 6 December 2001 and went through preliminary objections filed by Colombia, and later the request to intervene by two States that had a special relation with the maritime interests of Colombia, I stated in my presentation:

> "So finally, more than ten years after Nicaragua filed its Application, we find ourselves in what is hopefully the final run in a case that has outrun, in length of time, the classic example of a long drawn out case: the *Barcelona traction* or the more recent case of *Cameroon* v. *Nigeria*."[1]

4. Unfortunately that hope turned out to be wishful thinking. Twenty years after we filed our Application in December of 2001 and nine years after the Judgment of the Court in this case on 19 November 2012, we are back to where we started.

5. When the *Territorial and Maritime Dispute* was filed, the situation was that Colombia claimed the 82nd meridian as a line of delimitation. On screen, we can appreciate a map of the area at the time the Application was filed. The position of Colombia was clear. All areas east of the meridian including the land (islands and cays), water and continental shelf were claimed by Colombia.

6. The Court decided at the preliminary objections phase of the case in its Judgment of 13 December 2007 that the 82nd meridian was *not* a line of delimitation but recognized Colombian sovereignty over the three main islands.

7. In its Judgment of 19 November 2012, the Court attributed sovereignty over all the islands and cays in dispute to Colombia as well as very substantial maritime areas to these small features.

---

[1] *Territorial and Maritime Dispute (Nicaragua* v. *Colombia)*, CR 2012/8, p. 16, para. 13 (Argüello).

8. This maritime delimitation was unanimously decided by the Court, including the judges *ad hoc* appointed by the Parties, and was considered in many quarters to be especially beneficial to Colombian interests. The UN News headline read "UN court rules Colombia has sovereignty over islands claimed by Nicaragua"[2].

Reaction of Colombian authorities to the 2012 Judgment

9. The day the Judgment was delivered, the President of Colombia was very happy with the attribution of sovereignty to Colombia over the islands, but he stated that the other aspects of the Judgment on maritime delimitation were unacceptable and that Colombia "emphatically rejects that aspect of the judgment rendered by the Court today"[3].

10. The Foreign Minister of Colombia went even further, questioning the professional credentials of the Members of the Court. She stated that

> "[t]he enemy is the Court which did not based its decision on the law, that Judgment is full of inadequacies and one reads it and cannot believe that the states parties that conform the Court elected those judges to decide such an important Judgment"[4].

11. Other officials even questioned the moral capacity of Members and staff of the Court. For example, Ambassador Noemí Sanín, former Foreign Minister of Colombia, made some very offensive comments that I will not repeat here. She and a former deputy Minister of Justice wrote a book on the Judgment reiterating and amplifying these comments[5]. They were rewarded last year by the President of Colombia by appointing them as delegates of the presidency to the Colombian Foreign Affairs Commission. This Commission is charged, among other things, with reviewing and approving Colombia's position before this Court.

12. The object of recalling this event is not to cause embarrassment to the other Party for a diplomatic gaffe that is best forgotten. Because it was not a gaffe provoked by a passing emotion. *It is* the position that Colombia has consistently maintained since the Judgment was read. Colombia

---

[2] "UN court rules Colombia has sovereignty over islands claimed by Nicaragua", UN News, 19 Nov. 2012, available at https://news.un.org/en/story/2012/11/426062-un-court-rules-colombia-has-sovereignty-over-islands-claimed-nicaragua#.VgmPLXqqpBd (accessed 14 Sept. 2021).

[3] Memorial of Nicaragua (MN), p. 23, para. 2.4.

[4] MN, p. 23, para. 2.5.

[5] "La llegada del Dragón. ¿Falló la Haya?", Noemí Sanín, Miguel Ceballos, 2013, available at https://www.amazon.com/llegada-del-Drag%C3%B3n-%C2%BFFall%C3%B3-Haya/dp/9583043451 (accessed 14 Sept. 2021).

today still will not accept that Nicaragua has maritime areas east of the 82nd meridian. It is this position that according to President Santos's statement they will defend with "cloak and sword"[6].

13. This initial reaction when the Judgment was delivered on 19 November was followed by the denunciation of the Pact of Bogotá on 27 November 2012, on which occasion President Santos stated that "[t]he borders between nations cannot be in the hands of a court of law. They must be drawn by agreement between the countries involved."[7]

14. On 18 September 2013, President Santos reiterated that the Judgment of the Court was not applicable. That the only way to affect Colombian territorial rights was by means of a treaty that had to be approved in accordance with the internal laws of Colombia[8].

15. On 2 May 2014, the Constitutional Court of Colombia determined that the Judgment could only be implemented by means of a treaty approved by Congress and ratified by the President[9].

16. Madam President, this is a disingenuous decision of the Constitutional Court. It should have been evident to *that* court that the Judgment of *this* Court was given on the basis of at least two treaties ratified by Colombia: the Charter of the United Nations and the Pact of Bogotá. Any supposed need for another treaty to implement the Judgment is simply an excuse for not complying.

17. During the lengthy process that led to the 2012 Judgment, Colombia had many opportunities for claiming that its Constitution did not allow that territorial questions be decided by the International Court of Justice. In fact, Colombia presented preliminary objections to the jurisdiction of the Court[10], but there is not one sentence in all the pleadings and arguments of Colombia in those 11 years of judicial process in which there is any hint that Colombia could not comply with the Judgment of the Court.

18. This is all the more telling if it is recalled that one of the arguments of Nicaragua for the invalidity of the 1928 Treaty — that is the treaty which was the basis for Colombia's claim of rights in that area — was precisely that it was a treaty that violated the mandates of the Nicaraguan

[6] MN, p. 5, para. 1.8.

[7] MN, p. 372, Ann. 29.

[8] MN, pp. 30-31, para. 2.17.

[9] MN, Ann. 16.

[10] *Territorial and Maritime Dispute (Nicaragua* v. *Colombia), Preliminary Objections, Judgment, I.C.J. Reports 2007 (II)*, p. 832.

Constitution[11]. What would be the situation if after the Court's Judgment attributing sovereignty to Colombia over the main islands of San Andrés and Providencia, Nicaragua had said that it could not accept the Judgment because it went against its Constitution? What would have been the situation of Nicaragua before world opinion and before this Court even though the constitutional question had been placed before the Court by Nicaragua?

Colombia continues to violate Nicaragua's rights

19. Madam President, the refusal of Colombia to comply with the Judgment and respect Nicaragua's rights in the Caribbean Sea has been consistently maintained to this day; it is one of open challenge to the authority of the Court. Mr. Reichler will go into more detail on all the activities by Colombian authorities that violate Nicaragua's rights. At this point, I will only briefly mention some very recent examples of Colombia's determination to continue ignoring and violating Nicaragua's rights.

20. Former President Uribe of Colombia, also a member of the Colombian Foreign Affairs Commission, recently reiterated a call for a referendum on the limits of Colombia with Nicaragua in the Caribbean Sea[12]; that is, on whether the Colombian people accept the Judgment of the Court. Mr. Uribe was president when the first Judgment of the Court on the preliminary objections was delivered on 13 December 2007, in which the Court determined that the 82nd meridian was not a boundary. Present-day President Duque himself had first proposed a referendum several years before being elected during his campaign for the presidency on 14 February 2018 calling for "a great popular consultation so that Colombians may reaffirm the position of the country of not being willing of ceding one millimetre beyond the 82nd meridian in the conflict of limits with Nicaragua"[13].

---

[11] *Territorial and Maritime Dispute (Nicaragua* v. *Colombia)*, Memorial of Nicaragua, pp. 108-115, available at https://www.icj-cij.org/public/files/case-related/124/13870.pdf (accessed 16 Sept. 2021).

[12] "President Duque welcomes Uribe's proposal on 'popular consultation' to confirm border with Nicaragua. The initiative seeks to recognize the 82nd meridian as the limit with the Central American country", Semana, 1 Sept. 2021, available at https://www.semana.com/nacion/articulo/presidente-duque-ve-con-buenos-ojos-propuesta-de-uribe-sobre-consulta-popular-para-confirmar-limite-con-nicaragua/202112/ (accessed 14 Sept. 2021).

[13] "This Ivan Duque's proposal to govern Colombia", Radio Nacional de Colombia, 14 Feb. 2018, available at https://www.radionacional.co/cultura/esta-es-la-propuesta-de-ivan-duque-para-gobernar-colombia (accessed 16 Sept. 2021).

21. A few weeks ago, on 1 September, President Duque reiterated his proposal for a referendum and again stated that the 82nd meridian was still the border with Nicaragua[14]. The fact that this proposal for a referendum and this reiteration of Colombian claims of sovereignty up to the 82nd meridian was made practically on the eve of these hearings can only be construed as a direct challenge to the authority of the Court. *What more can one say?*

22. If there were any possible misunderstanding that these proposals for a referendum made by President Duque are simply political rhetoric, the following document will dispel this notion. The Colombian Ocean Commission — presided by the Vice-President and Foreign Minister of Colombia, Mrs. Marta Ramírez de Rincón — published a document in July of this year titled "Colombian Maritime Interests". The document states:

> "Colombia has a territory of approximately 2,070,408 km^2, of which . . . 44.85% [corresponds] to maritime territory (approximately 589,560 km^2 in the Caribbean . . .)"[15].

23. The document contains a graphic which is before you now. Out of 100 per cent of the territory of Colombia, 55 per cent is the mainland and 28.46 per cent is the Caribbean[16]. You will note several points that result from this document released under the authority of the Vice-President of Colombia:

— *First*, that the boundary with Nicaragua not only continues to be drawn down the 82nd meridian, a question that had already been decided by the Court in its Judgment of 2007 in the preliminary objections of the case.

— *Second*, that the northern boundary of the Colombian maritime "territory" is not the boundary fixed by the Court in the Judgment in the case of *Nicaragua* v. *Honduras*, but according to Colombia still is the boundary in a Treaty between Colombia and Honduras of 1986.

— *Third*, that the southern boundary of the Colombian maritime "territory" with Costa Rica is drawn in accordance with the Treaty of 1977 between Colombia and Costa Rica, and completely

---

[14] "President Duque welcomes Uribe's proposal on 'popular consultation' to confirm border with Nicaragua. The initiative seeks to recognize the 82nd meridian as the limit with the Central American country", Semana, 1 Sept. 2021, available at https://www.semana.com/nacion/articulo/presidente-duque-ve-con-buenos-ojos-propuesta-de-uribe-sobre-consulta-popular-para-confirmar-limite-con-nicaragua/202112/, (accessed 14 Sept. 2021).

[15] "Colombian Maritime Interests", Colombian Ocean Commission, July 2021, p. 11, available at https://cco.gov.co/83-publicaciones/881-intereses-maritimos-de-colombia.html (accessed 14 Sept. 2021).

[16] "Colombian Maritime Interests", Colombian Ocean Commission, July 2021, p. 12, available at https://cco.gov.co/83-publicaciones/881-intereses-maritimos-de-colombia.html (accessed 14 Sept. 2021).

ignores the Judgment of the Court in which it determined the boundary between Nicaragua and Costa Rica in the Caribbean.

24. Madam President, shortly after assuming military command of the area of San Andrés and Providencia, Rear Admiral Hernando Mattos Dager gave an interview to the local media published on 3 January of this year, in which he reaffirmed that the Navy would watch over the Seaflower Biosphere Reserve. He stated: "For us, the Biosphere Reserve continues to be indivisible no matter if there is a Judgment that fixes its limits."[17] He further indicated: "We maintain our presence in the area and punish those actions that threaten the protection of this natural reserve, as for example the case of the substantial seizure of parrot fish that was recently undertaken"[18].

25. This Biosphere Reserve was created by Colombia in the year 2000[19] when Nicaragua had announced it would be bringing the case to the Court. The Biosphere Reserve encompasses all the area that was in dispute with Nicaragua and that was settled by the Judgment of the Court in 2012. The assertion by the military commander of the area, that Colombia will continue patrolling the area and controlling the environment including fisheries is simply stating that the Judgment of the Court will not be recognized, nor the maritime areas of Nicaragua be respected.

26. Just last week, as you Madam President recalled, Colombia, in a last-minute manoeuvre, invoked the confidentiality of more than 80 documents annexed to its pleadings in order to conceal to the public the extent of the violations of Nicaragua's rights of which it was the author.

27. In conclusion, we have the President of Colombia calling for a referendum tabling the rejection of the 2012 Judgment of the Court, a publication of the Vice-President including the maritime areas of Nicaragua as Colombian, and the military commander of the area reaffirming that the Colombian Navy will ignore the Judgment. All of this just during the past few weeks and months.

28. Madam President, what can we hear from the distinguished representatives of Colombia now before the Court that will contradict what the highest civil and military authorities have said?

---

[17] "We must prepare for possible similar events", El Isleño.com, 3 Jan. 2021, available at http://xn--elisleo-9za.com/index.php?option=com_content&view=article&id=21112%3Adebemos-prepararnos-ante-posibles-eventos-similares-en-las-islas&catid=60%3Aactualidad&Itemid=96 (accessed 14 Sept. 2021).

[18] "We must prepare for possible similar events", El Isleño.com, 3 Jan. 2021, available at http://xn--elisleo-9za.com/index.php?option=com_content&view=article&id=21112%3Adebemos-prepararnos-ante-posibles-eventos-similares-en-las-islas&catid=60%3Aactualidad&Itemid=96 (accessed 14 Sept. 2021).

[19] Https://coralina.gov.co/en/areas-protegidas-m/reserva-de-biosfera-seaflower.

Unless there is a declaration from the highest authority that Colombia will respect Nicaragua's rights resulting from the Judgment, what else can we listen to? What are we doing here?

29. The reality is that this is a singular situation. There have been several instances in which States decided not to appear before the Court, but none of those non-appearing States has made the incredibly disparaging statements that the Colombian authorities have made against the Court. Even in those situations — some very tense, like that during the *Hostages* case or the *Nicaragua* case against the United States — the non-appearing States have shown respect to the Court and somehow tried to resolve the issue *sub judice*.

30. Madam President, in the submissions of Nicaragua in its Memorial and Reply, the Court is requested to adjudge that Colombia must give "appropriate guarantees of non-repetition of its internationally wrongful acts"[20]. In the past the Court has noted on these types of requests that, "there is no reason to suppose that a State whose act or conduct has been declared wrongful by the Court will repeat that act or conduct in the future, since its good faith must be presumed" and therefore assurances and guarantees of non-repetition will be ordered only "in special circumstances"[21].

31. Madam President, the present circumstances are certainly "special" since the highest authorities of Colombia have repeatedly stated, even on the eve of these hearings, that they will not comply with the Judgment of the Court. The question then would be to determine what an appropriate guarantee would be. We wait to hear how Colombia thinks it can be relied upon to comply with the Court's Judgment.

32. Nicaragua for its part has reached the conclusion that any guarantee must also involve the continued cognizance of the Court on the question of compliance. For this reason, Nicaragua will include in its final submissions a request that the Court should remain available until it is evident that Colombia has complied with the Judgment of the Court and is respecting the rights of Nicaragua.

33. Madam President, Members of the Court, to conclude my pleading — the list of speakers who will follow me today is in this order: Professor Pellet will give a general presentation of the case before you; Mr. Reichler will discuss the facts regarding Colombia's violations of Nicaragua's rights

---

[20] See MN, p. 108; Reply of Nicaragua (RN), p. 192.

[21] *Dispute regarding Navigational and Related Rights (Costa Rica* v. *Nicaragua), Judgment, I.C.J. Reports 2009*, p. 267, para. 150.

and Professor Lowe will explain why Colombia's Integral Contiguous Zone is inconsistent with international law and will end his presentation with our request for remedies.

34. Thank you for your kind attention. May I please ask you to call Professor Pellet, Madam President.

The PRESIDENT: I thank the Agent of Nicaragua for his statement and I now invite Professor Alain Pellet to take the floor. You have the floor, Sir.

M. PELLET : Thank you very much, Madam President.

PRÉSENTATION GÉNÉRALE

1. Madame la présidente, Mesdames et Messieurs de la Cour, permettez-moi de dédier cette plaidoirie à la mémoire de mon ami de trente ans, James Crawford. Bien que je rende hommage à la manière dont, Webex mis à part, la Cour et son Greffe ont parfaitement su pallier les problèmes posés par le mauvais virus, j'espère que, une fois celui-ci terrassé, nous pourrons nous retrouver dans la solennité du Grand Hall de Justice sans appréhension et sans limitation du nombre de plaideurs et du public.

2. Madame la présidente, il me revient de faire une présentation générale de l'affaire telle que le Nicaragua la perçoit. J'insisterai sur les principaux points qui divisent encore les Parties, ainsi que sur les déficiences flagrantes de l'argumentation de la Colombie. Dans un premier temps, je montrerai que, quoi qu'en dise l'Etat défendeur, l'affaire n'est évidemment pas dépourvue de tout lien avec son refus obstiné de mettre en œuvre l'arrêt rendu par la Cour le 19 novembre 2012. J'examinerai ensuite la manière très particulière qu'a la Colombie de se targuer de droits qu'elle n'a pas et de dénier au Nicaragua ceux qui lui appartiennent. Enfin, je dirai quelques mots de la façon, tout aussi singulière, dont la Colombie s'efforce de limiter la portée de votre examen.

I. La portée de la requête et le refus de la Colombie d'appliquer l'arrêt de 2012

3. Madame la présidente, selon le fameux aphorisme de Louis Henkin et malgré l'opinion contraire de quelques universitaires chagrins[22], «[a]lmost all nations observe almost all principles of international law and almost all of their obligations almost all the time»[23]. Ce qui est vrai pour le droit international en général l'est tout autant — réserves académiques incluses[24] — s'agissant des arrêts de la Cour[25]. C'est ce qui confère un aspect exceptionnel à la présente affaire, qui résulte du refus continu de la Colombie de respecter la délimitation maritime que vous avez unanimement fixée dans votre arrêt de 2012[26].

1. Le refus persistant de la Colombie d'appliquer l'arrêt de 2012

4. Comme l'a signalé l'ambassadeur Argüello il y a un instant, tandis que la Colombie a accueilli avec entrain la décision relative à sa souveraineté sur l'archipel de San Andrés — qu'elle considère comme «définitive et sans appel», elle a, pour l'essentiel, rejeté le reste de l'arrêt en raison, selon les mots du président Santos, «d'omissions, d'erreurs, d'excès, d'incohérences que nous ne

---

[22] Voir notamment K. Davis et B. Kingsbury, «Obligation Overload: Adjusting the Obligations of Fragile or Failed States», Hauser Globalization Colloquium, 2010 (https://www.iilj.org/wp-content/uploads/2016/11/Davis-et-al-Obligation-Overload-2010.pdf).

[23] L. Henkin, *How Nations Behave: Law and Foreign Policy,* Columbia UP, New York, 2e éd., 1979, p. 47.

[24] E.A. Posner, «The Decline of the International Court of Justice», *John M Olin Program in Law and Economics Working Paper* No. 233, 2004, p. 26-31 https://chicagounbound.uchicago.edu/cgi/viewcontent.cgi?article=1499&context=law_and_economics ; M. Reisman, «Metamorphoses: Judge Shigeru Oda and the International Court of Justice», *The Canadian Yearbook of International Law*, 1995, p. 185-222.

[25] Voir notamment le recensement opéré par E.A. Posner, *ibid.*, p. 26-31, faisant en particulier référence à *Essais nucléaires (Nouvelle-Zélande c. France)*, *Personnel diplomatique et consulaire des Etats-Unis à Téhéran (Etats-Unis d'Amérique c. Iran)*, *Activités militaires et paramilitaires au Nicaragua et contre celui-ci (Nicaragua c. Etats-Unis d'Amérique)*, *Frontière terrestre et maritime entre le Cameroun et le Nigéria (Cameroun c. Nigéria ; Guinée équatoriale (intervenant))*, *LaGrand (Allemagne c. Etats-Unis d'Amérique)*, *Avena et autres ressortissants mexicains (Mexique c. Etats-Unis d'Amérique)*. Voir aussi : A. Azar, *L'Exécution des décisions de la Cour internationale de justice*, Bruxelles, Bruylant, 2003 ; L. Nemer Caldeira Brant, *L'autorité de la chose jugée en droit international public*, LGDJ, 2003, p. 244-245 ; A. Ben Mansour, *La mise en œuvre des arrêts et des sentences des juridictions internationales*, Larcier, 2011 ; A. Llamzon, «Jurisdiction and Compliance», *EJIL* 2008, p. 815-852 ; M. Kamto, «Considérations actuelles sur l'inexécution des décisions de la Cour internationale de Justice», *Liber Amicorum Judge Thomas Mensah*, 2007, p. 215-233 ; E. Edynak, «L'exécution des décisions de la Cour internationale de justice en matière de délimitation maritime», *Les annales de droit*, 2013, p. 61-92 ; M. Shaw, *Rosenne's Law and Practice of the International Court: 1920-2015*, Brill, 5e éd., 2016, vol. I, chap. 4, par. 39-58.

[26] *Différend territorial et maritime (Nicaragua c. Colombie), arrêt, C.I.J. Recueil 2012 (II)*, p. 624.

pouvons accepter»[27]. Dans la foulée, la Colombie a dénoncé le pacte de Bogotá[28] en protestation contre l'arrêt de la Cour[29].

5. Le refus s'est fait, en apparence, moins catégorique après que le Nicaragua vous a saisi de l'affaire qui nous occupe, le 26 novembre 2013. Peut-être aiguillonnée par ses conseils, conscients du caractère intenable de cette fin de non-recevoir, la Colombie a cherché une manière moins injurieuse de faire obstacle à l'application de votre arrêt. Une sentence, en date du 2 mai 2014, de la Cour constitutionnelle (saisie par le président de la République) lui en a donné l'occasion :

> «[L]es décisions de la Cour internationale de Justice ayant trait à des différends frontaliers devront être incorporées dans l'ordre juridique interne au moyen d'un traité dûment ratifié et approuvé conformément aux dispositions de l'article 101 de la Constitution»[30].

6. Cette exigence vise, de manière assez navrante, à tenter de justifier *ex post*, deux ans après l'arrêt de la Cour, le refus abrupt du président Santos. Le résultat est que la Colombie s'est trouvée encouragée à considérer, de fait, votre arrêt de 2012 comme nul et non avenu. Cette attitude ne pose pas seulement de graves problèmes de principe ; elle a aussi des répercussions négatives très concrètes sur l'exercice par le Nicaragua des droits qui lui appartiennent dans les zones maritimes dans lesquelles votre arrêt lui a reconnu des droits souverains. La Colombie *continue* de violer ceux-ci ; elle *continue* de considérer ces zones comme lui appartenant ; elle *continue* à envoyer sa marine intimider les pêcheurs nicaraguayens...

7. Tout cela est fait sous le couvert de la sentence opportunément adoptée par la Cour constitutionnelle qui a été, par la suite, largement mise en avant par les autorités colombiennes pour

---

[27] Allocution du président Juan Manuel Santos concernant l'arrêt de la Cour internationale de Justice, 19 novembre 2012 (MN, annexe 1). Voir aussi «Santos Guarantees Continuity in his Foreign Policy with Latin America», *America Economica*, 17 juin 2014 (http://www.americaeconomia.com/politica-sociedad/politica/santos-garantiza-continuidad-en-su-politica-exterior-con-latinoamerica?utm_source=feedburner&utm_medium=feed&utm_campaign=Feed%3A+america-economia+(Am%C3%A9rica+Econom%C3%ADa en espagnol, et Mémoire du Nicaragua (MN), annexe 48 pour la traduction anglaise.)

[28] Lettre de la ministre colombienne des affaires étrangères au secrétaire général de l'Organisation des Etats américains, 27 novembre 2012 (GACIJ No.79357) (MN, annexe 19).

[29] Voir notamment Déclaration du président Juan Manuel Santos concernant la dénonciation du pacte de Bogotá, 28 novembre 2012 (MN, annexe 2).

[30] Arrêt C-269/14 du 2 mai 2014, *Actio popularis* d'inconstitutionnalité contre les articles II (en partie), V (en partie), XXXI et L de la loi n° 37 de 1961 portant approbation du traité américain de règlement pacifique (pacte de Bogotá) (Exceptions préliminaires de la Colombie (EPC), vol. II, annexe 4, p. 40) — traduction du Greffe.

ne pas s'acquitter des obligations résultant de l'arrêt de 2012[31] au prétexte que «tant qu'un nouveau traité n'aura pas été signé, les limites entre la Colombie et le Nicaragua demeureront celles qui ont été établies dans le traité Esguerra-Bárcenas, autrement dit, celles qui existaient avant que la Cour internationale de Justice rende son arrêt»[32]. Et ceci, Madame la présidente, est, en traduction, une citation extraite du discours du président Santos prononcé juste après que la sentence de la Cour constitutionnelle a été rendue ; cette citation figure sous l'onglet nº 4 du dossier des juges. Et, notre agent y a insisté, cela a continué — je saute moult épisodes...

8. Le 10 octobre 2019, la vice-présidente colombienne, Mme Marta Lucía Ramírez, critiquée après la publication d'une vidéo dans laquelle elle déclarait que «la mer de San Andrés était déjà perdue» en raison de l'arrêt de 2012, a assuré, sans même se référer à la possibilité de conclure un traité, qu'«à aucun moment je n'ai dit que le gouvernement se conformait [à l'arrêt,] ni qu'il devait s'y conformer»[33].

9. Bien que le Nicaragua eût fait savoir, par la voix de son président, qu'il n'était pas opposé à la conclusion d'un traité donnant effet à l'arrêt de 2012[34], aucune initiative ne semble avoir été prise pour procéder conformément aux prescriptions de la Cour constitutionnelle. Et les atteintes aux droits exclusifs du Nicaragua dans sa ZEE se poursuivent. Ainsi, il a été confirmé, récemment, que la marine nationale colombienne continue d'effectuer des patrouilles permanentes le long du 82e méridien[35]. Et, cette année encore, plusieurs cartes marines officielles ont été publiées

---

[31] Voir notamment : ««It is possible to negotiate with Nicaragua in The Hague»: Carlos Gustavo Arrieta Colombia's agent to The Hague says there is bilateral disposition», *El Tiempo*, 22 novembre 2014 (Réplique du Nicaragua (RN), annexe 23 — non traduite) ; «Colombian Ambassador Reasoned Refusal to Abide by ICJ Ruling», *El Nuevo Diario,* 4 septembre 2015 (RN, annexe 25 — non traduite) ; «The Burden Falls on Nicaragua», *El Espectador*, 19 mars 2016 (RN, annexe 30 — non traduite).

[32] Discours du président Santos, 2 mai 2014 (MN, annexe 7).

[33] Trinchera, «¿Se rindió Colombia ante el fallo de La Haya de 2012?», 10 octobre 2019, https://www.trincheraonline.com/2019/10/10/se-rindio-colombia-ante-el-fallo-de-la-haya-de-2012/ — espagnol original : «En ningún momento he dicho ni que el Gobierno lo esté acatando (el fallo de La Haya), ni que se debe acatar, ni que hemos renunciado (al mar)».

[34] «Daniel : 40 ans après le martyre d'Allende, la paix doit prévaloir», *El 19 Digital*, 11 septembre 2013 (MN, annexe 39). Voir aussi «L'Assemblée nicaraguayenne favorable au dialogue avec la Colombie», *El Universal*, 12 septembre 2013 (MN, annexe 40) ; «Le Nicaragua propose à la Colombie de collaborer en vue de la mise en œuvre de l'arrêt de La Haye», *AFP*, 9 mai 2014 (MN, annexe 46) (http://www.noticiasrcn.com/internacional-america/nicaragua-propone-coordinar-fallo-haya-colombia).

[35] El Nuevo Siglo, «La Armada continúa patrullando el meridiano 82», 7 décembre 2019 https://www.elnuevosiglo.com.co/articulos/12-2019-la-armada-continua-patrullando-el-meridiano-82.

reproduisant les limites revendiquées par la Colombie avant que la Cour rende son arrêt[36], notamment celle projetée il y a un instant par l'agent ou une autre émanant de l'agence nationale des hydrocarbures. Plus remarquable encore : dans un discours prononcé tout dernièrement, le 1er septembre dernier, que notre agent a aussi évoqué, le président Duque a répété que la frontière maritime entre la Colombie et le Nicaragua était constituée par le 82e méridien et qu'il n'excluait pas de la faire confirmer par référendum[37].

10. Madame la présidente, il n'est peut-être pas inutile de rappeler une évidence : en vertu des articles 59 et 60 du Statut de la Cour, l'arrêt de 2012 est inconditionnellement obligatoire et définitif (dans son ensemble). De même, conformément à l'article 94 de la Charte des Nations Unies, les parties doivent se conformer à la décision de la Cour et ne peuvent pas se retrancher derrière leurs règles constitutionnelles pour s'y soustraire[38]. Comme la Colombie l'écrit, très justement, dans sa duplique : «For international legal purposes, the way domestic law describes itself is not decisive; it is international law's characterisation which is determinative.»[39]

2. L'objet de la requête — ses liens avec l'arrêt de 2012

11. En ce qui me concerne, je persiste à considérer que la Cour est dotée d'un pouvoir inhérent pour tirer les conséquences de la non-application de ses arrêts. Cela dit, comme vous l'avez relevé à juste titre dans votre arrêt de 2016 sur la compétence, «[l]e Nicaragua ne cherche pas à faire exécuter l'arrêt de 2012 en tant que tel»[40] ; et c'est la raison pour laquelle vous ne vous êtes pas prononcés sur cette question de principe, que le Nicaragua avait soulevée à titre subsidiaire[41]. L'objet de la présente affaire, tel que vous l'avez précisé, est de déterminer les conséquences des «violations par la

---

[36] Agencia Nacional de Hidrocarburos de Colombia, Mapa de Tierras, 2m_tierras_010621, https://www.anh.gov.co/hidrocarburos/oportunidades-disponibles/mapa-de-tierras. Voir aussi : Presentation of Ministerio de Defensa Nacional, Dirección General Marítima, Autoridad Marítima Colombiana, p. 22 (Contract No. 245 DIMAR — ANH Year 2018).

[37] Https://www.semana.com/nacion/articulo/presidente-duque-ve-con-buenos-ojos-propuesta-de-uribe-sobre-consulta-popular-para-confirmar-limite-con-nicaragua/202112/.

[38] Voir Commission du droit international (CDI), Projet d'articles sur la responsabilité de l'Etat pour fait internationalement illicite et commentaires y relatifs, 2001, art. 3 et 12 (https://legal.un.org/ilc/texts/instruments/french/commentaries/9_6_2001.pdf).

[39] Duplique de la Colombie (DC), par. 4.102.

[40] *Violations alléguées de droits souverains et d'espaces maritimes dans la mer des Caraïbes (Nicaragua c. Colombie), exceptions préliminaires, arrêt, C.I.J. Recueil 2016 (I)*, p. 42, par. 109.

[41] *Ibid.*, p. 39, par. 104 ; voir aussi p. 41, par. 107.

Colombie des droits du Nicaragua dans les zones maritimes dont celui-ci affirme qu'elles lui ont été reconnues par l'arrêt de 2012»[42].

12. Contrairement à ce qu'affirme la Colombie dans sa duplique, le Nicaragua does not «confuse what are in reality two distinct legal questions (compliance with the 2012 Judgment, and "alleged violations of Nicaragua's sovereign rights and maritime spaces") by amalgamating these separate questions into one»[43]. Comme la Cour l'a noté à juste titre, le Nicaragua constate que la Colombie ne respecte pas les droits souverains qui lui appartiennent dans la zone économique exclusive que l'arrêt de 2012 lui a reconnue. Or, comme vous l'avez fermement rappelé, «[p]river une partie du bénéfice d'un arrêt rendu en sa faveur doit, de manière générale, être considéré comme contraire aux principes auxquels obéit le règlement judiciaire des différends»[44].

13. L'affirmation de la Colombie appelle en outre trois observations :

— En premier lieu, elle revient à contester la position que vous avez prise dans votre arrêt sur les exceptions préliminaires : comme je l'ai rappelé, vous vous êtes abstenus de vous prononcer sur votre compétence concernant les questions relatives aux suites données (ou pas) à vos arrêts précisément *parce que* vous considérez que la requête du Nicaragua porte sur la question, distincte, du respect des droits lui appartenant — ce que vous avez constaté dans votre arrêt[45].

— D'ailleurs, et c'est ma deuxième observation, ce faisant vous avez confirmé un état de droit existant et n'avez pas accordé au Nicaragua de nouveaux droits : selon la jurisprudence dominante, ces droits préexistaient à votre arrêt[46].

— Troisièmement : de toute manière, la responsabilité de la Colombie ne pourrait être recherchée pour son comportement antérieur à l'arrêt de 2012 ; le Nicaragua ne vous le demande d'ailleurs pas. Toutefois, pour paraphraser votre arrêt de 2002 cette fois, dans *Cameroun c. Nigéria*, celui de 2012 «précise de manière définitive et obligatoire la frontière ... maritime entre les deux Etats.

---

[42] *Violations alléguées de droits souverains et d'espaces maritimes dans la mer des Caraïbes (Nicaragua c. Colombie), exceptions préliminaires, arrêt, C.I.J. Recueil 2016 (I)*,, p. 34, par. 79.

[43] DC, par. 1.35

[44] *Application de la convention pour la prévention et la répression du crime de génocide (Bosnie-Herzégovine c. Serbie-et-Monténégro), arrêt, C.I.J. Recueil 2007 (I)*, p. 91, par. 116.

[45] *Violations alléguées de droits souverains et d'espaces maritimes dans la mer des Caraïbes (Nicaragua c. Colombie), exceptions préliminaires, arrêt, C.I.J. Recueil 2016 (I)*, p. 42, par. 109, cité *supra*, par. 10.

[46] *Plateau continental de la mer du Nord (République fédérale d'Allemagne/Danemark) (République fédérale d'Allemagne/Pays-Bas), arrêt, C.I.J. Recueil 1969*, p. 22, par. 18. Voir aussi *Délimitation maritime dans la région située entre le Groenland et Jan Mayen (Danemark c. Norvège), arrêt, C.I.J. Recueil 1993*, p. 66-67, par. 64.

Tout doute étant levé à cet égard, la Cour [n'aurait pas dû être appelée à] envisager l'hypothèse dans laquelle [la Colombie] ... ne respecterait pas» les droits souverains du Nicaragua tels qu'ils sont reconnus par l'arrêt[47]. Et tel est pourtant le cas en l'espèce.

14. C'est dire — et je vous cite à nouveau — que :

> «L'arrêt rendu en 2012 est incontestablement pertinent en la présente affaire, en ce qu'il détermine la frontière maritime entre les Parties et établit donc laquelle d'entre elles a des droits souverains en vertu du droit international coutumier dans les espaces maritimes qui font l'objet de la présente affaire.»[48]

II. Les droits respectifs des Parties en cause dans la présente affaire

15. Mesdames et Messieurs les juges, les droits appartenant au Nicaragua, quels sont-ils ? Ce sont ceux — seulement ceux, mais tous ceux — qui sont reconnus à un Etat riverain sur la ZEE par le droit international coutumier.

16. A cet égard également une précision s'impose.

17. Contrairement au Nicaragua, la Colombie n'est pas partie à la convention des Nations Unies sur le droit de la mer. Et elle se prévaut abondamment — surabondamment même — de cette situation pour écarter l'application des dispositions conventionnelles qui ne lui conviennent pas[49]. Mais cela ne l'empêche pas de tenter de tirer avantage de la convention lorsque celle-ci impose des obligations spécifiques aux Parties, quand bien même ces obligations ne sauraient être rattachées à une règle coutumière. Ainsi au paragraphe 4.90 de sa duplique, la Colombie rappelle avec insistance que

> «[a]s a party to UNCLOS, Nicaragua has accepted, by ratification, the interpretation of UNCLOS Article 33 as put forth in UNCLOS Article 303(2). ... [Therefore] Colombia considers it to be irrelevant whether Article 303(2) reflects customary international law since, by ratifying UNCLOS, Nicaragua has accepted the authentic interpretation of the generic terms in Article 33 found in Article 303(2).»[50]

---

[47] Voir *Frontière terrestre et maritime entre le Cameroun et le Nigéria (Cameroun c. Nigéria ; Guinée équatoriale (intervenant)), arrêt, C.I.J. Recueil 2002*, p. 452, par. 318.

[48] *Violations alléguées de droits souverains et d'espaces maritimes dans la mer des Caraïbes (Nicaragua c. Colombie), exceptions préliminaires, arrêt, C.I.J. Recueil 2016 (I)*, p. 41-42, par. 109.

[49] Voir, par exemple, DC, par. 1.8, 2.33, 4.25, 4.48, 5.3 ; voir aussi contre-mémoire de la Colombie (CMC), par. 5.39.

[50] DC, par. 4.90. Voir aussi DC, p. 7, note 13.

Certes, Madame la présidente, *pacta tertiis non nocent* — mais *nec prosunt* ! [illegible], les traités ne nuisent pas aux tiers mais ceux-ci ne peuvent pas non plus en profiter...

18. De notre côté, nous acceptons pleinement que seul le droit coutumier, raisonnablement interprété, fait droit entre les Parties. Nous admettons aussi que les dispositions de la convention puissent être complétées sur certains points par une pratique générale acceptée comme étant le droit — mais il en faudrait beaucoup pour qu'elle soit *modifiée* de cette manière alors qu'elle est expressément reconnue comme faisant droit entre la très grande majorité des Etats du monde ; à l'inverse, on peut légitimement considérer que cette acceptation particulièrement générale crée, après quarante ans, une présomption — non irréfragable, certes, mais solide — en faveur de la coutumiérisation de ces dispositions, sauf objections persistantes, spécifiques et publiques.

19. Mes collègues élaboreront davantage sur ce point à propos de certaines règles dont la Colombie donne une interprétation exorbitante — ou trop extensive, ou trop restrictive, selon les besoins de sa démonstration. Je m'en tiendrai pour ma part à une remarque générale sur un point récurrent dans la duplique et qui me paraît présenter une certaine importance : la question des droits des Etats non riverains («tiers», pour faire court) dans la ZEE.

20. Dans toute sa duplique, la Colombie tient un double langage qui peut être résumé en deux formules antagonistes :

— pour l'Etat tiers, tout ce qui n'est pas interdit est permis ;

— pour l'Etat côtier, tout ce qui est expressément permis doit être interprété restrictivement.

21. Ce diptyque est directement contraire à la position très sage du TIDM qui, dans l'affaire *Saïga II*, a déclaré — dans un passage d'ailleurs bizarrement cité par la Colombie elle-même[51] :

> «si la Convention attribue certains droits aux Etats côtiers et aux autres Etats dans la zone économique exclusive, il ne s'ensuit pas automatiquement que les droits qui n'ont pas été expressément attribués à l'Etat côtier reviennent aux autres Etats ou que, à l'inverse, les droits qui n'ont pas été attribués de manière spécifique aux autres Etats reviennent à l'Etat côtier»[52].

---

[51] DC, par. 3.52.

[52] *Navire «SAIGA» (No. 2) (Saint-Vincent-et-les Grenadines c. Guinée), arrêt, TIDM Recueil 1999*, p. 56, par. 137.

1. Tout ce qui n'est pas interdit n'est pas permis

22. Pour des exemples de la première proposition (tout ce qui n'est pas interdit est permis) — que je tiens de toute manière pour inexacte dans sa généralité :

1) dès le paragraphe 1.12 de sa duplique, la Colombie affirme que «it does not need to prove that its conduct is expressly authorized under international law» — et, en effet, elle ne se soucie pas de le prouver ;

2) au paragraphe 2.33, la Colombie invoque un droit de contrôle sur un certain nombre d'activités menées dans la ZEE du Nicaragua «that are not specifically authorized in UNCLOS (to which Colombia is not a party) or under customary international law» ;

3) au paragraphe 5.13, la défenderesse affirme qu'il n'existe pas de «provision, under conventional or customary law, which would explicitly prohibit traditional fishing rights within the EEZ» in order to prevail itself of such rights.

23. Fort de cette conviction l'Etat défendeur prétend, plus généralement, à quantité de droits qu'il pourrait exercer dans la ZEE du Nicaragua alors que certains ne peuvent même pas l'être en haute mer.

24. D'une manière très générale, la volonté de la Colombie de tirer profit du droit international sans en respecter les obligations caractérise toute son argumentation. Pour ne prendre que trois exemples topiques :

— la Colombie fait le plus grand cas de l'obligation de tenir «dûment compte des droits et obligations des autres Etats» lorsque cette obligation incombe au Nicaragua[53] ; mais, alors que cette directive irrigue la convention de Montego Bay aussi bien que le droit coutumier de la mer dans son ensemble, l'Etat défendeur ne se montre guère soucieux de la mettre en œuvre dans sa «zone contiguë intégrale» ; l'expression est d'ailleurs parlante : l'ajout de l'adjectif «intégrale» entend clairement signifier qu'il s'agit de balayer toute prétention contraire ;

— autre exemple, également lié à l'instauration de cette zone d'un genre nouveau : la Colombie prétend relier, de façon assez incongrue, les îlots éloignés et inhabités de Quintasueño, Roncador, Serrana, Serranilla et Bajo Nuevo ; ceci ne correspond assurément pas à la vocation des zones

---

[53] DC, par. 4.22.

contiguës «tout court», qu'elles soient définies par la convention de 1982 ou par le droit coutumier ;

— troisième exemple, très remarquable : il concerne la manière dont la Colombie présente son argumentation à l'appui de la mesure reconventionnelle qu'elle a introduite au sujet des lignes de base droites du Nicaragua ; ces lignes seraient illicites car contraires aux dispositions de l'article 7 de la CNUDM (dont elle admet *pro causa* qu'il reflète des règles coutumières[54]) notamment du fait que la distance entre les points de base retenus serait excessive ; or celle qui sépare certains des points de base que la Colombie elle-même a adoptés est nettement supérieure. La Colombie s'est appliqué les critères mêmes qu'elle reproche au Nicaragua d'avoir choisis ; et,

— dans le même esprit, dans la loi n° 10 du 4 août 1978 proclamant sa ZEE, la Colombie revendique des droits souverains et une juridiction *exclusifs* dans cette zone[55], tout en empêchant le Nicaragua d'exercer *ces mêmes droits* dans la ZEE que la Cour lui a reconnue.

25. La prétention de la Colombie à exercer contrôles et contrainte en vue de la protection de l'environnement dans la ZEE nicaraguayenne illustre particulièrement bien mon propos. L'article 56 de la convention sur le droit de la mer précise que «l'Etat côtier a ... juridiction, conformément aux dispositions pertinentes de la Convention, en ce qui concerne ... la protection et la préservation du milieu marin»[56] ; la Colombie ne semble pas le contester dans son principe[57]. Quant à l'article 33, paragraphe 1 a), sur la zone contiguë, il énumère les domaines dans lesquels «l'Etat côtier peut exercer le contrôle nécessaire en vue de prévenir les infractions à ses lois et règlements douaniers, fiscaux, sanitaires ou d'immigration sur son territoire ou dans sa mer territoriale». «Juridiction» en matière de protection de l'environnement d'un côté (pour la ZEE), absence de toute mention de l'autre (pour la zone contiguë). La Colombie n'en affirme pas moins «that [it] has duties to protect the marine environment and that compliance with the said duties might entail "individual" actions»[58]

[54] Voir DC, par. 6.2, 6.13 ou 6.26.

[55] Articles 7 et 8 de la loi n° 10 du 4 août 1978 fixant les règles en matière de mer territoriale, de zone économique exclusive et de plateau continental et régissant d'autres matières.

[56] Art. 56, par. 1 *b)* iii).

[57] Voir DC, par. 3.50 ou 4.21.

[58] DC, par. 2.78.

— actions individuelles que l'Etat défendeur, sans les nier, tente de minimiser afin d'en édulcorer le caractère illicite.

2. Tout ce qui est permis ne doit pas être interprété restrictivement

26. Le ton change lorsqu'il s'agit d'interpréter les droits du Nicaragua dans sa ZEE. C'est que (selon la Colombie) — et l'on en arrive à la seconde proposition — tout ce qui est expressément permis doit être interprété de manière restrictive.

27. Faute de trouver, dans le droit conventionnel ou coutumier, le moindre argument qui lui permettrait de justifier des limites à la juridiction du Nicaragua en matière de protection de l'environnement dans sa ZEE, la Colombie invoque la convention de Carthagène de 1983 en faisant totalement fi de son texte et de sa portée. En particulier, de deux de ses traits essentiels : d'une part, il s'agit d'un traité-cadre, essentiellement *non self-executing*, qui invite les Etats parties à approfondir leur coopération, notamment par la conclusion d'accords spécifiques ; d'autre part, la mise en œuvre de ses dispositions est subordonnée au respect du droit international[59]. A en croire la Colombie, les dispositions expresses de la CNUDM, ou leur équivalent coutumier, conférant des droits exclusifs à l'Etat côtier dans certains domaines n'en feraient pas partie.

28. Cette désinvolture colombienne à l'égard des droits du Nicaragua dans sa zone économique exclusive ne se borne pas à la protection de l'environnement, elle s'étend aussi à la pêche. A cet égard, la Colombie sort ce qui paraît lui tenir lieu d'atout-maître à maints égards dans cette affaire : les droits des Raizals.

29. Ici encore, l'article 56 est catégorique :

> «1. Dans la zone économique exclusive, l'Etat côtier a des droits souverains aux fins d'exploration et d'exploitation, de conservation et de gestion des ressources naturelles, biologiques ou non biologiques, des eaux surjacentes aux fonds marins, des fonds marins et de leur sous-sol» ;

mais cela ne dissuade pas la Colombie de se faire, avec ardeur, la championne des droits de pêche des Raizals car «the ecosystems of the Southwestern Caribbean Sea are inextricably linked to the livelihood, survival and basic human needs of vulnerable communities, such as the Raizales»[60]. Et d'invoquer, dans une bien-pensance admirable, «the right of the Raizales to live in a healthy and

---

[59] Voir notamment les articles 3 1), 6 1) et 4) ou 16.

[60] DC, par. 2.91 ; voir aussi, presque dans les mêmes termes, par. 2.98 ou 2.100.

sustainable environment»[61] together with its responsability «to ensure that the subsistence and traditional fishing activities of the Raizales are not undermined extends to the entire living space of such communities»[62]. A cette fin, la Colombie prétend être en droit d'exercer son contrôle sur tout dommage environnemental potentiel et s'opposer à ce qu'elle qualifie de pêches prédatrices des bateaux du Nicaragua menaçant les Raizals dans sa zone contiguë intégrale[63] et, plus largement encore, dans la ZEE du Nicaragua. Tout ceci alors même qu'elle semble reconnaître «la nature exclusive» des droits souverains du Nicaragua dans sa zone économique[64] tout aussi exclusive — et l'exclusivité est d'ailleurs la marque de ce qui est «souverain» ; et l'adjectif «exclusive» pour caractériser la zone économique ne laisse aucun doute à cet égard.

30. La question de la réalité de ces droits historiques sera abordée durant les audiences consacrées aux demandes reconventionnelles de la Colombie.

31. Je relève en outre que, si le Nicaragua a indiqué qu'il était disposé à discuter les droits de pêche éventuels des Raizals, il ne s'agissait que d'une offre de négociation, qui, elle non plus, n'est pas «self-executing» : le président Ortega «announced that it was agreed to "*open communication channels* to ensure the Raizal people their fishing rights"»[65]. Il n'a pas *reconnu* les droits de pêche traditionnels des Raizals, il a *proposé* de négocier pour leur assurer des droits. Et c'est bien ainsi que le président Santos l'avait compris : «These communication channels are a significant complement.»[66] Il faut noter au surplus que la Colombie n'a jamais invoqué les prétendus droits historiques des Raizals dans ses plaidoiries dans l'affaire du *Différend territorial et maritime*.

32. Mais il y a plus : la protection des droits allégués des Raizals, dont elle se dit tellement soucieuse, sert à la Colombie non seulement de prétexte pour s'adjuger, sans aucune base juridique, des «obligations» de protection de l'environnement ou de droits en matière de pêcheries dans la ZEE nicaraguayenne, mais aussi de justification pour revendiquer une zone contiguë «intégrale» aux

---

[61] DC, par. 2.99 ; voir aussi par. 2.107, 2.109.

[62] DC, par. 2.107.

[63] *Ibid.* ; voir aussi par. 4.99.

[64] DC, par. 5.15.

[65] CMC, annexe 77, «Radio La Primerísima, Daniel ratified to Colombia his vocation for peace», 2 décembre 2012 — les italiques sont de moi (annexe non traduite). Voir aussi CMC, annexe 78, El 19 Digital, *President Daniel receives letters of credence from the ambassadors of Colombia, El Salvador, Germany and Italy*, 6 November 2015.

[66] *Ibid.*

contours très excessifs pour, en réalité, étendre les pêcheries industrielles colombiennes, comme le professeur Lowe le montrera tout à l'heure.

III. La portée des conclusions des Parties et de leur examen par la Cour

33. Mesdames et Messieurs les juges, la Colombie utilise une autre tactique pour s'exonérer de ses responsabilités : elle s'efforce de limiter la portée de votre examen, d'une part en interprétant de manière erronée et très excessive les conséquences de sa dénonciation du pacte de Bogotá ; d'autre part en analysant de manière tout aussi fallacieuse, mais cette fois abusivement restrictive, les conditions auxquelles l'exercice de votre compétence serait soumis.

1. Les conséquences de la dénonciation du pacte de Bogotá

34. Après avoir traité la Cour d'«ennemie de la Colombie»[67] — rien que ça ! —, la ministre colombienne des affaires étrangères a dénoncé le pacte de Bogotá dans une lettre adressée au secrétaire général de l'OEA le 27 novembre 2012[68]. Les conséquences de cette dénonciation doivent bien sûr être appréciées au regard du texte du pacte.

35. Conformément aux dispositions de l'article LVI, reproduit à l'onglet n° 5 du dossier des juges, la dénonciation colombienne a pris effet le 27 novembre 2013. La Colombie entend interdire à la Cour de connaître de tout fait postérieur à cette date. Sa position repose sur une confusion.

36. Il résulte de cet article LVI que la Cour ne pourrait se prononcer sur des faits postérieurs à la terminaison du pacte, qui ferait l'objet d'un nouveau différend, distinct de celui actuellement soumis à la Cour pour lequel celle-ci a reconnu avoir compétence. Mais l'article LVI n'empêche en aucun cas la Cour de décider de la licéité — ou de l'illicéité — de faits postérieurs qui ne font que confirmer que la Colombie n'a nullement l'intention de reconnaître les droits souverains de la juridiction du Nicaragua dans la ZEE que l'arrêt de 2012 lui a reconnus.

37. Il en va d'autant plus certainement ainsi qu'il s'agit de faits illicites à la fois composites et continus[69]. Du fait de son refus de reconnaître les limites des conséquences résultant de sa

---

[67] «The Colombian Foreign Minister Calls The Hague an Enemy», *El Nuevo Herald*, 28 novembre 2012 (MN, annexe 30).

[68] Voir ci-dessus note 28.

[69] Voir les articles 14 et 15 des Articles de la CDI sur la responsabilité de l'Etat pour fait internationalement illicite.

dénonciation du pacte, la Colombie a passé entièrement sous silence dans son contre-mémoire les événements qui ont pris place après cette date fatidique et qu'elle a relégués dans une annexe à sa duplique.

38. Les deux affaires citées par la Colombie à l'appui de ses efforts pour écarter ces développements du débat — celle relative à *Certains biens* et celle sur les *Immunités juridictionnelles de l'Etat*[70] — sont sans aucun intérêt dans notre espèce : il s'agissait de savoir si des faits *antérieurs* à l'acceptation de la compétence de la Cour pouvaient relever de sa juridiction. Dans notre affaire, la question est de savoir quelle est la pertinence de faits *postérieurs* pour apprécier la validité de comportements à l'égard desquels la Cour a, d'ores et déjà, reconnu qu'elle avait compétence.

39. D'ailleurs, la Colombie elle-même recourt abondamment à des événements postérieurs à votre saisine pour établir le bien-fondé de ses prétentions. Pour n'en donner que deux exemples parmi beaucoup d'autres :

— tous les développements de sa duplique selon lesquels la conduite du Nicaragua minerait ses prétentions (ce sont les paragraphes 3.39 à 3.46) reposent *entièrement* sur des faits *postérieurs* à la dénonciation du pacte ; et,

— pour se défendre contre les griefs du Nicaragua relatifs à l'octroi du permis de pêche dans sa ZEE, la Colombie invoque une série de résolutions de la direction générale maritime (la DIMAR) adoptées entre 2014 et 2017[71].

Du reste, très couramment, la Cour n'hésite pas à se fonder sur des faits postérieurs à l'introduction de la requête (ou du compromis) pour motiver ses décisions[72].

40. Dans le même esprit, la Colombie fait une mauvaise querelle au Nicaragua lorsqu'elle prétend que celui-ci a introduit dans sa réplique une nouvelle réclamation («a «new claim»») portant sur les permis pétroliers qu'elle aurait proposés en violation des droits souverains du Nicaragua[73].

41. C'est confondre une conclusion et un moyen. En l'espèce, il s'agit d'un simple argument — un moyen — à l'appui de la conclusion par laquelle le Nicaragua prie la Cour de déclarer que la

---

[70] Voir DC, par. 3.13-3.16.

[71] Voir DC, par. 3.112.

[72] Voir RN, par. 4.15-4.26.

[73] DC, par. 3.94.

Colombie agit en violation des droits souverains et de la juridiction lui appartenant dans les zones maritimes que la Cour lui a reconnues par son arrêt de 2012. Conformément à votre jurisprudence constante : «Il ne découle pas ... du paragraphe 2 de l'article 38 du Règlement de la Cour que la latitude dont dispose l'Etat demandeur pour développer ce qu'il a exposé dans sa requête soit strictement limitée.»[74] La Cour a souligné en particulier qu'une telle conclusion ne saurait être tirée de ses décisions selon lesquelles la date pertinente pour apprécier la recevabilité d'une requête est la date de son dépôt car «ces prononcés ne se réfèrent pas au contenu des requêtes»[75] ; dès lors, «des incidents supplémentaires constituent des faits supplémentaires» pouvant être invoqués durant la procédure[76].

42. Autant une conclusion supplémentaire (*a submission*) modifiant substantiellement des demandes énoncées dans la requête ou s'y ajoutant — comme dans l'affaire *Diallo*, dont la Colombie fait grand cas[77] — ne serait pas recevable à ce stade, autant un moyen à l'appui d'une demande existante ne se heurte à aucune objection — du moment que l'autre partie est en mesure d'y répondre. C'est le cas ; la Colombie s'est en effet essayée à répliquer — à tort, comme Me Reichler le montrera dans un instant. Pour surplus de droit, j'ajoute que, en tout état de cause, si la Cour considérait qu'il s'agit d'une conclusion (au sens de *submission*), elle ne fait que préciser les demandes initiales du Nicaragua, et serait sans conteste recevable[78].

---

[74] *Frontière terrestre et maritime entre le Cameroun et le Nigéria (Cameroun c. Nigéria), exceptions préliminaires, arrêt, C.I.J. Recueil 1998*, p. 318, par. 99. Voir aussi *Demande en interprétation de l'arrêt du 11 juin 1998 en l'affaire de la* Frontière terrestre et maritime entre le Cameroun et le Nigéria (Cameroun c. Nigéria), exceptions préliminaires *(Nigéria c. Cameroun), arrêt, C.I.J. Recueil 1999 (I)*, p. 38, par. 15.

[75] *Ibid.*, se référant à *Questions d'interprétation et d'application de la convention de Montréal de 1971 résultant de l'incident aérien de Lockerbie (Jamahiriya arabe libyenne c. Royaume-Uni), exceptions préliminaires, arrêt, C.I.J. Recueil 1998*, p. 26, par. 44, et *Questions d'interprétation et d'application de la convention de Montréal de 1971 résultant de l'incident aérien de Lockerbie (Jamahiriya arabe libyenne c. Etats-Unis d'Amérique), exceptions préliminaires, arrêt, C.I.J. Recueil 1998*, p. 130, par. 43) ; voir aussi *Demande en interprétation de l'arrêt du 11 juin 1998 en l'affaire de la* Frontière terrestre et maritime entre le Cameroun et le Nigéria (Cameroun c. Nigéria), exceptions préliminaires *(Nigéria c. Cameroun), arrêt, C.I.J. Recueil 1999 (I)*, p. 38, par. 15.

[76] *Demande en interprétation de l'arrêt du 11 juin 1998 en l'affaire de la* Frontière terrestre et maritime entre le Cameroun et le Nigéria (Cameroun c. Nigéria), exceptions préliminaires *(Nigéria c. Cameroun), arrêt, C.I.J. Recueil 1999 (I)*, p. 38, par. 15.

[77] DC, par. 3.95. Voir *Ahmadou Sadio Diallo (République de Guinée c. République démocratique du Congo), fond, arrêt, C.I.J. Recueil 2010 (II)*, p. 651, par. 21.

[78] Voir notamment *ibid.*, p. 656-657, par. 40 ; *Différend territorial et maritime (Nicaragua c. Colombie), arrêt, C.I.J. Recueil 2012 (II)*, p. 665, par. 111-112 ; *Différend territorial et maritime entre le Nicaragua et le Honduras dans la mer des Caraïbes (Nicaragua c. Honduras), arrêt, C.I.J. Recueil 2007 (II)*, p. 695, par. 110, citant partiellement *Certaines terres à phosphates à Nauru (Nauru c. Australie), exceptions préliminaires, arrêt, C.I.J. Recueil 1992*, p. 265-266, par. 65.

2. La question de l'intérêt pour agir

43. Madame la présidente, revenant insidieusement sur des questions de recevabilité de la requête, la Colombie prétend que la Cour ne peut se prononcer sur la conformité au droit international coutumier du décret de 1946 établissant une zone contiguë «intégrale» autour de l'archipel de San Andrés et de nombreux îlots inhabités qui en sont très éloignés, ceci car le Nicaragua n'aurait pas démontré que ses droits propres dans la ZEE auraient été violés[79].

44. Ils l'ont été, comme mes collègues le démontreront incessamment. Mais la question qui m'intéresse dans l'immédiat est un peu différente. Elle est de savoir si le Nicaragua serait recevable à se plaindre de l'établissement de cette zone, dans l'hypothèse où, contre toute attente, la Cour considérerait que l'extension et le régime de la «zone contiguë intégrale» que la Colombie s'est attribuée ne portent aucune atteinte aux droits du Nicaragua dans la zone maritime lui revenant conformément à l'arrêt de 2012.

45. Outre que l'on peut s'interroger sur la tardiveté de cette exception, la réponse ne peut faire aucun doute : que ce soit en vertu de la convention de Montego Bay ou du droit international coutumier, la délimitation — ou peut-être faudrait-il dire la «délinéation» puisqu'il s'agit de l'extension vers le large des espaces marins relevant d'un Etat particulier — intéresse la communauté internationale des Etats dans son ensemble et les obligations des Etats côtiers dans ces espaces sont l'exemple même d'obligations *erga omnes*[80].

46. Madame la présidente, Mesdames et Messieurs les juges, la Colombie n'a pas respecté les droits souverains et la juridiction du Nicaragua dans la zone économique exclusive que vous lui avez reconnue par votre arrêt de 2012. Elle y effectue des contrôles et des actes de contrainte à l'égard de navires — y compris nicaraguayens — en vue de faire respecter des droits imaginaires qu'elle aurait (ou qu'auraient ses ressortissants) en matière de protection de l'environnement et de pêcheries. Ce faisant l'Etat défendeur remet en cause non seulement l'autorité de vos arrêts mais aussi les principes fondamentaux du droit de la mer et «l'ordre juridique» des océans. Il cause en outre des préjudices

---

[79] Voir, par exemple, DC, par. 4.51.

[80] Voir, par exemple, *Pêcheries (Royaume-Uni c. Norvège), arrêt, C.I.J. Recueil 1951*, p. 132. Voir aussi sentence du tribunal arbitral rendue au terme de la première étape de la procédure entre l'Érythrée et la République du Yémen (souveraineté territoriale et portée du différend), décision du 9 octobre 1998, Nations Unies, *Recueil des sentences arbitrales*, vol. XXII, p. 250, par. 153.

matériels et moraux au Nicaragua, dont celui-ci est fondé à demander réparation, comme le montrera le professeur Lowe.

Madame la présidente, je vous remercie et je vous prie de bien vouloir donner la parole à Me Reichler.

The PRESIDENT: I thank Professor Pellet and I now give the floor to Mr. Paul Reichler. You have the floor, Sir.

Mr. REICHLER:

THE FACTS REGARDING COLOMBIA'S VIOLATIONS OF NICARAGUA'S RIGHTS

1. Madam President, Members of the Court, it is always an honour for me to appear before you, and it is a privilege to do so on behalf of Nicaragua in these proceedings. I am deeply grateful to the Court for allowing counsel to plead virtually from their home countries, and thus avoid the risks of international travel during this period of heightened public health concern.

2. Madam President, I want to applaud you for your very moving tribute to Judge Crawford today. He was indeed one of a kind. His passing is most definitely a great loss to the Court and the world, as it is for his many friends who loved and admired him, myself included.

3. My task today is to address the facts pertaining to the present dispute, concerning Colombia's violations of Nicaragua's sovereign rights and jurisdiction in Nicaragua's exclusive economic zone and continental shelf, as delimited by the Court in the Judgment of 19 November 2012.

4. I will discuss these facts under three headings in the following order: *first*, facts concerning Colombia's rejection of the Court's 2012 Judgment, including its refusal to accept the boundary established by the Court, and its ongoing insistence — to the present day — on its own sovereign rights and jurisdiction in areas located on Nicaragua's side of the delimitation line; *second*, facts concerning Colombia's establishment of a so-called Integral Contiguous Zone, encompassing parts of Nicaragua's EEZ and continental shelf, in furtherance of Colombia's assertion of sovereign rights and jurisdiction beyond the limits of the maritime areas attributed to it by the Court, and the revival, and maintenance to this day, of its pre-Judgment claim to all of the maritime space east of the

82nd meridian; and *third*, facts concerning the Colombian Navy's physical interference with Nicaragua's exercise of sovereign rights and jurisdiction in its EEZ, based on the assertion that the 2012 Judgment is inapplicable, and that Colombia is therefore entitled to exercise its own sovereign rights and jurisdiction in these waters.

5. Although, for clarity, I will discuss these three sets of facts under separate headings, they are all very closely linked, and constitute inseparable parts of the same dispute. All of Colombia's wrongful actions, including those of its navy, since Nicaragua's Application was filed, relate back to Colombia's rejection of the 2012 Judgment, its refusal to accept the boundary with Nicaragua established by the Court, and its reassertion of a claim to the entire area east of the 82nd meridian, the same claim that Colombia advanced before the Court, and the Court rejected.

6. In fact, pursuant to this revived claim, the Colombian Navy, upon confronting Nicaraguan coast guard vessels in this area, warned them, in recorded audio messages, some of which you will hear today, that the Court's Judgment was inapplicable, exactly as the President of Colombia first declared in November 2012; that all of the waters east of the 82nd meridian were Colombian, and that Nicaragua had no jurisdiction in these waters.

I. Colombia's rejection of the 2012 Judgment and the boundary fixed by the Court

7. The statements by Colombia's President denouncing the 2012 Judgment, disavowing it and rejecting the boundary fixed by the Court are set out in Nicaragua's Memorial. My purpose in reading some of them aloud today is not to rub salt in Colombia's self-inflicted wounds; nor is it to inflame passions by recalling remarks that are truly disturbing, not only for their impact on Nicaragua's own hard-won rights, but for their disregard of the rule of law, and for the sanctity of the judgments issued by the world's supreme judicial authority. Rather, Nicaragua invokes these statements here for the sole reason that they constitute the origin of the dispute that is presently before the Court, as well as the basis and the alleged justification for the actions subsequently carried out by Colombia, including by its navy, in flagrant violation of Nicaragua's rights, as determined by the 2012 Judgment. As such, these statements explain, and cannot be separated from, the unlawful conduct to which they gave rise, and thus, like those actions, constitute part of a single, indivisible dispute.

8. To be precise, Colombia did not reject or disavow the entire 2012 Judgment. It was perfectly content to accept and applaud the Court's ruling on sovereignty over disputed islands, which its President, Juan Manuel Santos, described as "a final and unappealable judgment on this issue"[81]. Colombia's rejection of the Judgment was selectively limited to the maritime boundary in the Caribbean Sea, which President Santos described as riddled with what he called "omissions, errors, excesses and inconsistencies that we cannot accept"[82]. The conclusion, in the President's own words, was: "Colombia — represented by its Head of State — emphatically rejects that aspect of the judgment rendered by the Court today"[83].

9. Within 10 days of the Judgment, Colombia formally denounced the Pact of Bogotá, withdrawing its acceptance of the Court's compulsory jurisdiction[84]. President Santos left no doubt that this was in further rejection of the Court's Judgment: "I have decided that the highest national interests demand that the territorial and maritime boundaries be fixed through treaties, as has been the legal tradition of Colombia, and not through judgments rendered by the International Court of Justice."[85]

10. It might have been hoped that Colombia, disappointed with this aspect of the Judgment, would eventually reconcile itself to it, and that its extreme reaction would ultimately give way to conduct more befitting a responsible State, like the one that gave the name of its capital to a historic agreement — the Pact of Bogotá — under which the States Parties agreed to submit their disputes with one another to the Court. Unfortunately, this was not the case. Ten months after the Judgment, in September 2013, President Santos again declared:

> "The Judgment of the International Court of Justice is not applicable — it is not and will not be applicable — until a treaty that protects the rights of Colombians has been celebrated, a treaty that will have to be approved in accordance with our

---

[81] "Declaration of President Juan Manuel Santos on the Judgment of the International Court of Justice", 19 Nov. 2012, Spanish original available at https://www.cancilleria.gov.co/newsroom/news/alocucion-presidente-juan-manuel-santos-fallo-corte-internacional-justicia.

[82] *Ibid.*

[83] *Ibid.*

[84] Letter from Colombia to Secretary General of the Organization of American States dated 27 Nov. 2012 (GACIJ No. 79357).

[85] "Colombia denounces the Pact of Bogotá after Judgment of the ICJ", Deutsche Welle, 28 Nov. 2012, Spanish original available at https://www.dw.com/es/colombia-denuncia-pacto-de-bogot%C3%A1-tras-fallo-de-la-cij/a-16414772.

Constitution. I repeat the decision I have made: the judgment of the International Court IS NOT APPLICABLE”[86].

11. Of even greater concern, upon making this statement, President Santos ordered the Armed Forces High Command to “defend with ‘cloak and sword’ the continental shelf Colombia has in the Caribbean Sea”[87]. The High Command understood this as a call to defend the entire maritime area historically claimed by Colombia east of the 82nd meridian, notwithstanding the delimitation effected by the Court’s 2012 Judgment. Vice Admiral Hernando Wills Velez, the Commander of the Colombian Navy, responded to the President’s call by declaring that his forces would “comply with the order of the Head of State to exercise sovereignty throughout the Colombian Caribbean Sea”, since “the judgment of The Hague is inapplicable” and the Colombian Navy would fulfil its duty “to defend all the Colombian maritime space”[88].

12. And that is exactly what the Colombian Navy proceeded to do, including by interfering with, and preventing, Nicaragua’s exercise of its sovereign rights and jurisdiction in its own EEZ, in areas that unmistakably fall on the Nicaraguan side of the boundary fixed by the Court, as I will describe in the third part of my presentation.

13. To conclude this first part, it is indisputable, and Colombia does not seriously attempt to dispute, that it denounced, rejected and refused to accept the maritime boundary fixed by the Court in its 2012 Judgment, and that, as of September 2013, by order of its President, its armed forces had pledged to disregard that Judgment and enforce Colombia’s claims against Nicaragua, including its purported sovereign rights and jurisdiction, in areas east of the 82nd meridian that the Court had determined to fall within Nicaragua’s EEZ. Nor can it now be disputed that this has remained Colombia’s official position until today. This is what its current President, Ivan Duque, said as recently as 1 September 2021: “The 82nd Meridian is the boundary we have today with Nicaragua and that is why we are very clear that our Constitution says that Colombia’s limits can only be

---

[86] “Declaration of President Juan Manuel Santos on the integral strategy of Colombia on the Judgment of the International Court of Justice”, 9 Sept. 2013, Spanish original available at https://www.cancilleria.gov.co/newsroom/news/colombia-presenta-su-estrategia-integral-frente-fallo-haya (emphasis in original).

[87] “Santos orders defense of the continental shelf with cloak and sword”, *El Espectador*, 19 Sept. 2013, Spanish original available at https://www.elespectador.com/politica/santos-ordena-defender-plataforma-continental-a-capa-y-espada-article-447445/.

[88] *Ibid.*

modified through treaties; we are defenders of its integrality."[89] All of these statements by Colombia's Presidents can be found at tab 6 of your judges' folders.

II. Colombia's establishment of an Integral Contiguous Zone and renewed claim to all of the maritime space east of the 82nd meridian

14. This brings me to the second part of my presentation, Colombia's establishment of an Integral Contiguous Zone, and the renewal of its claim to all maritime space east of the 82nd meridian, despite the Court's rejection of that claim. The Integral Contiguous Zone was established by Presidential Decree No. 1946, on 9 September 2013[90]. Article 5 describes the "Contiguous Zone of the Western Caribbean Sea Insular Territories". Paragraph 1 of that Article declares a contiguous zone of 24 miles around the Western Caribbean Insular Territories, but this is expressly without prejudice to the provisions of paragraph 2, which extend it beyond 24 miles in order to "connect" the contiguous zones of the various islands of the San Andrés Archipelago, so that they form "a continuous zone and uninterrupted zone of the whole of the San Andrés, Providencia and Catalina Department"[91].

15. Upon introducing this Decree, President Santos displayed a map illustrating the extent of the newly created Integral Contiguous Zone[92]. This slide shows President Santos displaying his map. Next is the same Integral Contiguous Zone displayed by President Santos superimposed on the maritime boundary established by the Court, as reflected in sketch-map No. 11 from the Judgment. Here, we have highlighted in pink the areas where the Integral Contiguous Zone overlaps waters attributed by the Court to Nicaragua as its EEZ. As can easily be seen, the Integral Contiguous Zone depicted by President Santos in 2013 substantially transgresses areas subject to Nicaragua's exclusive sovereign rights and jurisdiction. All three of these maps of Colombia's Integral Contiguous Zone are at tab 7 of your judges' folders.

---

[89] "Presidente Duque ve con buenos ojos propuesta de Uribe sobre 'consulta popular' para. confirmar límite con Nicaragua", *Semana*, 1 Sept. 2021, Spanish original available at https://www.semana.com/nacion/articulo/presidente-duque-ve-con-buenos-ojos-propuesta-de-uribe-sobre-consulta-popular-para-confirmar-limite-con-nicaragua/202112.

[90] Presidential Decree 1946 of 9 Sept. 2013, Spanish original available at https://www.cancilleria.gov.co/sites/default/files/Normograma/docs/decreto_1946_2013.htm.

[91] *Ibid.*

[92] Map presented by President Juan Manuel Santos, 9 Sept. 2013, Spanish original available at https://www.cancilleria.gov.co/print/7196 (mins. 7:43-8:16).

16. Here is another map of the Integral Contiguous Zone, provided by Colombia in its Rejoinder. This map, which is also at tab 8 of your folders, is helpfully entitled, by Colombia itself: "Areas of Colombia's ICZ lying beyond 24 M and within Nicaragua's EEZ"[93]. I am tempted to say: "QED". But there is much more to say, and it gets much worse for Colombia.

17. First, Colombia's transgression of Nicaragua's EEZ was exacerbated by the powers Colombia attributed to itself in its Integral Contiguous Zone. According to President Santos: "In this Integral Contiguous Zone we will exercise jurisdiction and control over all areas related to security and the struggle against delinquency, and over fiscal, customs, environmental, immigration and health matters and other areas as well."[94] This Presidential Decree is at tab 9 of your folders.

18. At tab 10, you will find that Decree 1946 itself specifies that

> "the Colombian State shall exercise in the established Integral Contiguous Zone *its sovereign authority* and the powers for the implementation and the necessary control regarding: *[inter alia]* environmental protection, cultural patrimony and the exercise of historic rights to fishing held by the State of Colombia"[95].

Colombia later modified the Decree by deleting the reference to fishing rights[96]. But, in practice, Colombia has continued to assert and enforce them, as you will soon see. In its Rejoinder, Colombia acknowledges that, under international law, "[t]he contiguous zone does not bestow upon the coastal State any territorial or sovereign rights"[97]. But those are exactly the rights that Decree 1946 expressly attributes to Colombia in its Integral Contiguous Zone, and that Colombia itself has continuously exercised.

19. As Professor Lowe will show, the rights a coastal State may exercise in a properly established contiguous zone, that is, one that does not extend across an international boundary, do not include control of fishing or environmental protection[98]. And, as Mr. Martin will show on Friday,

---

[93] Rejoinder of the Republic of Colombia (RC), Volume II, 15 Nov. 2018, Figure CR 4.1.

[94] "Declaration of President Juan Manuel Santos on the integral strategy of Colombia on the Judgment of the International Court of Justice", 9 Sept. 2013, Spanish original available at https://www.cancilleria.gov.co/newsroom/news/colombia-presenta-su-estrategia-integral-frente-fallo-haya.

[95] Presidential Decree 1946 of 9 Sept. 2013, Art. 5.3. *(a)*. Spanish original available at https://www.cancilleria.gov.co/sites/default/files/Normograma/docs/decreto_1946_2013.htm.

[96] Presidential Decree 1119 of 2014 (modifying and adding to Presidential Decree of 9 Sept. 2013), Spanish original available at https://www.dimar.mil.co/sites/default/files/normatividad/dec11192014_0.pdf.

[97] RC, Vol. I, para. 4.115.

[98] See United Nations Convention on the Law of the Sea, Articles 33 (on contiguous zone) and 55-75 (on exclusive economic zone).

Colombia has no fishing rights, historic or otherwise, in any of the areas the Court determined to be within Nicaragua's EEZ. Yet, in practice, as I will come to in the final part of my presentation, Colombia has invoked its Integral Contiguous Zone, and the powers declared thereunder, as well as its resurrected claim to all of the maritime area east of the 82nd meridian, to justify its exercise of sovereign rights and jurisdiction in Nicaragua's EEZ, including its authorization of Colombian and foreign-flagged vessels to fish in Nicaragua's waters; and its prevention of Nicaraguan-authorized vessels from fishing or conducting marine scientific research in those same waters.

20. By 2014, it became clear that Colombia's pretentions to sovereign rights and jurisdiction in the areas determined by the Court to belong to Nicaragua went well beyond the limits of the Integral Contiguous Zone. President Santos declared at that time that Colombia's exclusive rights and jurisdiction extended over the entire area that Colombia had claimed prior to the Court's Judgment, as if the Judgment were never issued, that is, all the waters east of the 82nd meridian: "In consequence, for our country as long as a new treaty is not signed — the limits of Colombia with Nicaragua continue to be those established in the [1928] Esguerra-Bárcenas Treaty. That is to say, the limits previous to the International Court of Justice's Judgment."[99] This statement is at tab 11 of the folders.

21. This was not a mere rhetorical exercise. It was the position and policy of the Colombian State, as pronounced by the Head of State himself. And it has remained Colombia's official position. To this day, Colombia claims that its maritime rights and jurisdiction are limited not by the boundary fixed by the Court, but by the 82nd meridian, and that everything to the east is theirs, in complete abnegation of Nicaragua's judicially determined rights in this area. This map, which is at tab 12 of the folders, is from a PowerPoint presentation given by the Commander of the Colombian Navy, Admiral Hernando Wills Vélez, on 3 March 2015. It remains available today on a navy-connected website[100]. It is captioned "Areas of Responsibility of the National Navy". The map depicts Colombia's maritime boundaries in the Caribbean Sea and the Pacific Ocean. In the Caribbean, boundaries are shown with all of Colombia's neighbours, including Nicaragua, where the

---

[99] "Nicaragua Fears Losing the Sea", Taringa!, 3 May 2014, Spanish original available at http://www.taringa.net/posts/info/17784410/Nicaragua-teme-perder-el-mar.html.

[100] Admiral Hernando Wills Vélez, *Proyectando el Futuro, Poder Marítimo Colombiano*, pp. 5-6 (Areas of Responsibility of the National Army), Spanish original available at https://cidin.co/index.php/cidin/article/view/58/167.

boundary is depicted as the 82nd meridian. This is where, according to Colombia, Nicaragua's maritime jurisdiction ends.

22. The same PowerPoint presentation by the Commander of the Colombian Navy also includes this map, captioned "National Navy Areas of Operation"[101]. It, too, is at tab 13. I call your attention to the blue dot, in the upper left part of the map. As you can see, this dot is just to the east of the 82nd meridian, which depicts the outer limit of the Navy's area of operation in this zone. The map identifies the CESYP as the naval component responsible for enforcing Colombia's jurisdiction here. The initials stand for *Comando Específico de San Andrés y Providencia*, or, in English, "Specific Command for San Andrés and Providencia"[102].

23. And this is from a map published by the Colombian National Hydrocarbon Agency showing oil blocks that are described as available for concession, in relation to the boundary fixed by the Court in 2012[103]. The entire map is at tab 15. What you see here is the northwesternmost portion of the map, which shows that, in 2017, Colombia held out as available for concession oil blocks bounded in the west by the 82nd meridian, as if the Court's 2012 Judgment had never been issued. This map is still accessible on the National Hydrocarbon Agency's website[104]. After these oral hearings were scheduled, and soon before they were to commence, Colombia cleverly updated its website with a more sanitized version of the map[105], but the 2017 version has remained accessible along with it. The oil blocks along the 82nd meridian indisputably infringe on Nicaragua's EEZ and continental shelf. Colombia asserts that it has not awarded any concessions in these areas[106]. We have no reason to challenge that assertion. Experienced international oil companies would not be so foolish as to bid for exploration or drilling rights in a maritime area disputed by two States, especially when

---

[101] Admiral Hernando Wills Vélez, *Proyectando el Futuro, Poder Marítimo Colombiano*, pp. 5-6 (Areas of Responsibility of the National Army), Spanish original available at https://cidin.co/index.php/cidin/article/view/58/167, p. 7.

[102] See for example "Comandante Fuerza Aérea visits the San Andrés Archipelago", Spanish original available at https://www.fac.mil.co/es/noticias/comandante-fuerza-aerea-visita-el-archipielago-de-san-andres.

[103] Agencia Nacional de Hidrocarburos de Colombia, Mapa de Tierras (2m_tierras_172017.pdf), 17 Feb. 2017, available at https://www.anh.gov.co/Asignacion-de-areas/Documents/2m_tierras_170217.pdf; see also RN, p. 113, para. 4.129, Figure 4.3.

[104] *Ibid.*

[105] Agencia Nacional de Hidrocarburos de Colombia, Mapa de Tierras (2m_tierras_010621), available at https://www.anh.gov.co/hidrocarburos/oportunidades-disponibles/mapa-de-tierras.

[106] RC, Vol. I, paras. 7.8; 3.92-3.99.

the International Court of Justice has already ruled against Colombia's claim. But the fact remains: various Colombian State organs, most conspicuously the Colombian Navy, continue to depict and regard these areas, up to the 82nd meridian, as subject to Colombia's exclusive sovereign rights and jurisdiction.

24. The Commander of Colombia's Navy has expressly confirmed this. In a 2019 interview, Admiral Evelio Ramírez Gáfaro was asked: "Does the Navy patrol the 82nd Meridian and help the Colombian fishermen in that jurisdiction?" The Admiral responded, as shown on your screens and at tab 16 of the folders:

> "The Navy has a permanent presence in that area. The operations carried out in the Archipelago of San Andrés, Providencia and Santa Catalina have resulted in . . . the capture of 29 persons for the crime of illegal fishing and the seizure of 15,460 kilograms of queen conch. In addition, our presence in the area of operations of the Archipelago Department creates conditions of security and tranquillity for the Colombian fishermen and artisanal fishermen of the region."[107]

25. In February 2021, Colombia protested the adoption of legislation by the Nicaraguan National Assembly protecting the Nicaraguan Caribbean Biosphere Reserve, which lies entirely within Nicaragua's EEZ and continental shelf, as determined by the Court[108]. Colombia's Note claimed that it alone may exercise jurisdiction over this area, which it still considers part of what it denominated as its own Biosphere Reserve before the 2012 Judgment. This was precisely the position expressed by Rear Admiral Hernando Mattos Dager, the Chief of Colombia's Naval Command for San Andrés and Providencia, the naval unit charged by Colombia with protection of the Reserve, just prior to the dispatch of Colombia's 2021 diplomatic Note: "For us, the Biosphere Reserve continues to be indivisible no matter if there is a court judgment that fixes its limits"[109]. None of these facts is, or can credibly be, disputed.

26. And these are not separate, isolated events. They are manifestations and integral parts of the same dispute, which arose from Colombia's denial of and refusal to recognize Nicaragua's rights in the maritime areas found to be Nicaraguan by the Court in its 2012 Judgment, and Colombia's

---

[107] "La Armada continúa patrullando el meridiano 82", *El Nuevo Siglo*, 7 Dec. 2019, Spanish original available at https://www.elnuevosiglo.com.co/articulos/12-2019-la-armada-continua-patrullando-el-meridiano-82.

[108] Letter to the Court of 30 July 2021 from Nicaragua's Agent submitting Carta del Ministerio de Relaciones de la República de Colombia a la Embajada de la República de Nicaragua, 15 Feb. 2021, S-DVRE-21-003007.

[109] "Debemos prepararnos ante posibles eventos similares", El Isleño.com, 3 Jan. 2021, Spanish original available at http://www.xn--elisleo-9za.com/index.php?option=com_content&view=article&id=21112:debemos-prepararnos-ante-posibles-eventos-similares-en-las-islas&catid=60:actualidad&Itemid=96.

insistence that it alone enjoys sovereign rights and jurisdiction in all such areas lying east of the 82nd meridian, just as if the Court's Judgment were never issued. This is the dispute that Nicaragua presented to the Court in its Application, over which the Court accepted jurisdiction when it rejected Colombia's preliminary objection in this regard in its Judgment of 17 March 2016.

27. These are the facts pertaining to the Integral Contiguous Zone, and the reassertion of Colombia's claim to the entire area east of the 82nd meridian, and they are all well established by the evidence.

III. Colombia's physical acts of interference with Nicaragua's exercise of its sovereign rights and jurisdiction within its EEZ

28. Madam President, I turn now to the third and final part of my presentation, which addresses Colombia's physical acts of interference with Nicaragua's sovereign rights and jurisdiction —

The PRESIDENT: Excuse me, Mr. Reichler. May I kindly interrupt you before you begin the next section of your presentation.

Mr. REICHLER: Absolutely, Madam President.

The PRESIDENT: It seems like this would be a good time to adjourn for a coffee break of ten minutes.

Mr. REICHLER: Very well. I agree. Thank you, very much, Madam President.

The Court adjourned from 4.45 p.m. to 5 p.m.

The PRESIDENT: Please be seated. The sitting is resumed. I now give the floor back to Mr. Reichler to continue his presentation.

Mr. REICHLER:

28. Thank you, Madam President. I turn now to the third and final part of my presentation, which addresses Colombia's physical acts of interference with Nicaragua's sovereign rights and jurisdiction in its own EEZ, as defined by the Court in its 2012 Judgment. In its written pleadings, Nicaragua identified and offered proof of 51 such acts by Colombia's armed forces, particularly its

navy, from the beginning of 2013 to the end of 2018. These, too, are not separate, isolated events, but manifestations of the same dispute that began with Colombia's rejection of the Court's 2012 Judgment, its denial of Nicaragua's rights thereunder, its reversion to its pre-Judgment position that the boundary is the 82nd meridian, and its attribution to itself of sovereign rights and jurisdiction that exclusively belong to Nicaragua under the 2012 Judgment.

29. I will focus today on some of the more egregious of these actions by the Colombian Navy, which are sufficient in themselves to prove that Colombia has repeatedly, and deliberately, violated Nicaragua's rights in areas the Court adjudged to belong to Nicaragua, but which Colombia, in defiance of the Court's Judgment, continues to claim as its own.

30. As set out in Nicaragua's written pleadings, the Colombian Navy began to interfere with Nicaragua's sovereign rights and jurisdiction in its EEZ as early as February 2013, less than three months after the Court's Judgment and Colombia's rejection of it[110]. These violations continued and grew bolder thereafter. In the face of Colombia's denials of wrongdoing in its Counter-Memorial, Nicaragua's coast guard vessels began to record their radio communications with the offending Colombian naval ships. All of these recordings, including the ones I will play for you today, have been submitted as evidence annexed to Nicaragua's Reply.

31. On 18 March 2015, Nicaraguan coast guard vessel *CG-401* encountered the Colombian naval frigate *ARC Independiente* in the location now shown on your screens, and at tab 17 of your folders, well within Nicaragua's EEZ[111]. *CG-401* asked the *ARC Independiente* to state its objective in navigating in Nicaragua's waters[112]. The Colombian frigate responded, as you will now hear in the original Spanish, and see on your screens in English translation: "I inform you that you are in Colombian jurisdictional waters. The Colombian State has established that the ruling of The Hague is not applicable; therefore, the units of the navy of the Republic of Colombia will continue to exercise sovereignty of these waters."[113] A transcription of the original Spanish, and a translation

---

[110] See MN, 3 Oct. 2014, paras. 2.39 *et seq*.

[111] RN, Ann. 2, Daily Navy Reports 2015-2017, p. 210 (map); para. 4.92; see also RN, Ann. 32, Audio Transcription of 18 Mar. 2015.

[112] RN, Ann. 32, Audio Transcription of 18 Mar. 2015.

[113] *Ibid.*

into French as well as English, are provided in your judges' folders. The same is true for the other incidents I will describe today.

32. The next one occurred five days later. On 23 March 2015, Nicaragua's *CG-401* again encountered Colombia's *ARC Independiente* within Nicaragua's EEZ, as shown here, and at tab 18[114]. This time, the Colombian ship was positioned approximately 300 metres from a Honduran-flagged industrial fishing vessel, the *Lucky Lady*, which had not been licensed by Nicaragua to conduct fishing activities. As *CG-401* approached the *Lucky Lady*, the *ARC Independiente* intervened, and issued the following warning to the Nicaraguan coast guard vessel, which I will not play aloud to save time, but you can see in transcription:

> "I inform you that the Colombian government has not abided by the ruling in The Hague; until that happens, the boats that are in the area, are under the protection of the government of Colombia. I invite you to maintain caution in these cases, keep the caution, captain, to avoid situations that you might regret later. Please refrain yourself from any intentions you have on that motorboat."[115]

33. These were not isolated incidents. Far from it. On 26 March 2015, three days later, Nicaragua's *CG-401* encountered the Colombian naval frigate *ARC 11 de Noviembre* in Nicaragua's EEZ, as depicted on the chart now on display, which is at tab 19 of your folders[116]. You can hear, and see in transcription, the message delivered by the Colombian ship: "I inform you that I am in the Colombian Archipelago of San Andrés and Providencia, protecting the historic fishing rights of the Colombian State, guaranteeing the security of all vessels present in the area and implementing operations against transnational crimes." After the captain of the Nicaraguan vessel protested that they were in Nicaraguan waters as determined by the International Court of Justice, the Colombian frigate responded:

> "Coast Guard of Nicaragua, this is the *ARC 11 de Noviembre*. According to the Colombian government, the ruling of The Hague is inapplicable, which is why I am in the Colombian Archipelago of San Andrés and Providencia, carrying out the work that I already informed you, and I invite you to maintain the caution required in these cases."[117]

---

[114] RN, Ann. 2, Daily Navy Reports 2015-2017, p. 211 (map); see also RN, para. 4.108.

[115] RN, Ann. 32, Audio Transcription of 23 Mar. 2015.

[116] RN, Ann. 2, Daily Navy Reports 2015-2017, p. 212; RN, Ann. 32, Audio Transcription of 26 Mar. 2015; RN, para. 4.122.

[117] RN, Ann. 32, Audio Transcription of 26 Mar. 2015.

34. On the same date, while it was still in Nicaragua's EEZ, the *ARC 11 de Noviembre* ordered a Nicaraguan-flagged and Nicaraguan-licensed fishing vessel, the *Doña Emilia*, to stop fishing in what it called Colombian waters[118]. The incident occurred here, as depicted on the screen now and at tab 20 of your folders. The Colombian naval vessel's message was also recorded, and it was submitted as part of Annex 32 to Nicaragua's Reply[119].

35. On 5 April 2015, Nicaraguan coast guard vessel *BL-405* encountered another Colombian naval frigate, the *ARC San Andrés*, in the location depicted in the chart now on display, and at tab 21, and initiated communication with it[120]. Again, you can hear Colombia's response, and see the now-familiar words on your screens: "I inform you that I am in the Colombian Archipelago of San Andrés and Providencia, protecting the historic fishing rights of the Colombian State and guaranteeing the security of all vessels present and implementing operations against transnational crime."[121]

36. The same two vessels had another encounter two days later, on 7 April 2015[122], as now depicted on your screens and at tab 22 of your folders[123]. This time the *ARC San Andrés* broadcast this message to the Nicaraguan coast guard vessel, shown on your screens now:

> "I inform you that at this time your unit is 1.2 away from the *ARC San Andrés*, [Coast Guard] unit of the Republic of Colombia, it is located in [the] jurisdictional waters of the Archipelago of San Andrés and Providencia, enforcing the historic [fishing] rights of fishermen from the Republic of Colombia."[124]

37. On 12 September 2015, Nicaragua's *BL-405* encountered the industrial fishing vessel *Miss Dolores*, flying the Tanzanian flag, in this location, also shown at tab 23 of your folders[125]. It attempted to hail this unlicensed vessel, but received instead the following response from a nearby Colombian frigate:

---

[118] RN, Ann. 2, Daily Navy Reports 2015-2017, p. 213 (map); RN, para. 4.93; see also RN, Ann. 32, Audio Transcription of 28 Mar. 2015; see also RN.

[119] RN, Ann. 32, Audio Transcription of 28 Mar. 2015.

[120] RN, Ann. 2, Daily Navy Reports 2015-2017, p. 215 (map); see also RN, para. 4.95.

[121] RN, Ann. 32, Audio Transcription of 5 Apr. 2015.

[122] RN, Ann. 32, Audio Transcription of 7 Apr. 2015; see also RN, para. 4.97.

[123] RN, Ann. 2, Daily Navy Reports 2015-2017, p. 216 (map).

[124] RN, Ann. 32, Audio Transcription of 7 Apr. 2015.

[125] RN, Ann. 2, Daily Navy Reports 2015-2017, p. 220 (map); see also RN, para. 4.109.

> “[T]his is the Coast Guard of the Navy of the Republic of Colombia, good afternoon. I inform you that I am in the Colombian Archipelago of San Andrés and Providencia, protecting the historical fishing rights of the Colombian State, guaranteeing the security of all vessels present in the area. You have not been authorized by the Colombian government to exercise visitation rights on the *Miss Dolores* flagship of Tanzania, which is fishing for the Colombian government. I ask you to stay away from the boat. We will remain in the area to guarantee its protection. I invite you to maintain the caution required in these cases.”[126]

Here again, the audio recording is part of the record, and you are invited to verify the accuracy of our transcriptions, in English, French and Spanish. I am not playing the tape today in order to stay within my allotted time.

38. The frequency of Colombia’s interventions, to assert and exercise its purported sovereign rights within Nicaragua’s EEZ, to deny Nicaragua the exercise of its lawful rights, to protect Colombian-licensed industrial fishing vessels in Nicaragua’s waters, and repeatedly deliver the same message that the Court’s Judgment was not applicable, make clear that these incidents were part of a larger, government policy to assert Colombian jurisdiction over all of Nicaragua’s waters east of the 82nd meridian. As declared by the Commander of Colombia’s naval forces in San Andrés and Providencia, Rear Admiral Andrés Vásquez Villegas, on 3 December 2015: “There are no vetoed areas for our fishermen. We will continue to exercise national sovereignty and defend our sovereignty in the jurisdictional waters of Colombia.”[127] This is at tab 24 of the folders.

39. Shortly after this statement, on 12 January 2016, the Honduran-flagged *Observer* was seen fishing in Nicaragua’s EEZ by coast guard vessel *CG-403*, at this location, and as depicted at tab 25 of your folders[128]. The *Observer* was informed that it was in Nicaragua’s waters and required a licence from Nicaragua to fish there[129]. The *Observer* responded, as recorded by the *CG-403*: “I did not know because the Colombian authorities allowed us to come and fish. They ordered us to come and work here.”[130] A few hours later, the *CG-403* spotted the *Observer* fishing in the same area and attempted to hail it again[131]. This time, the recorded response came from a nearby Colombian naval

---

[126] RN, Ann. 32, Audio Transcription of 12 Sept. 2015.

[127] “There are no vetoed zones for the fishermen in San Andrés: National Navy”, *El País*, 3 Dec. 2015 (RN, Ann. 26).

[128] RN, Ann. 2, Daily Navy Reports 2015-2017, p. 223 (map); RN, para. 4.113.

[129] RN, Ann. 32, Audio Transcription of 12 Jan. 2016.

[130] RN, Ann. 32, Audio Transcription of 12 Jan. 2016.

[131] RN, Ann. 2, Daily Navy Reports 2015-2017, p. 224 (map); RN, para. 4.114.

frigate: "This is the vessel of the Navy of the Republic of Colombia. I inform you that the motorboat *Observer* is authorized to fish in this area by the Colombian maritime authority, according to the historic fishing rights of the State of Colombia."[132] When the *CG-403* objected, the Colombian naval vessel responded: "I inform you that the *Observer* and all Colombian vessels that are in the area are authorized by the Colombian General Maritime Directorate to carry out fishing activities in the area."[133]

40. A similar incident occurred on 6 January 2017. On that date, the Nicaraguan coast guard vessel *CG-405* encountered the Honduran-flagged *Capitán Geovanie* fishing without a licence in Nicaragua's EEZ, as depicted here, and at tab 26 of the folders[134]. *CG-405* ordered the *Capitán Geovanie* to leave the area, but a Colombian frigate soon arrived and instructed the *Capitán Geovanie*: *[original recording in Spanish]* "This the Coast Guard of Colombia. Upon receipt, proceed and continue your fishing task. You are in historically Colombian waters and our duty is to protect your task."[135] The Colombian frigate then turned its attention to Nicaragua's *CG-405*: *[original recording in Spanish]* "This is the Coast Guard of Colombia. Upon receipt, proceed to abort any attempt to board and any attempt to abort the fishing of the *Capitán Geovanie* motorboat." In response to the Nicaraguan coast guard vessel's protest, the Colombian vessel insisted: *[original recording in Spanish]* "The *Capitán Geovanie* is authorized by the Colombian maritime authority, fishing in historically Colombian waters."[136]

41. On 10 December 2018, Nicaragua's coast guard vessel *BL-405* encountered once again, the Honduran fishing vessel *Observer* conducting illegal fishing in Nicaragua's EEZ, as depicted here, and at tab 27 of your folders[137]. This time, the Nicaraguan authorities were able to board the *Observer*, where they discovered over 5,000 pounds of lobster and 150 lobster traps, as well as a

---

[132] RN, Ann. 32, Audio Transcription of 12 Jan. 2016.

[133] *Ibid.*

[134] RN, Ann. 2, Daily Navy Reports 2015-2017, p. 229 (map); RN, para. 4.118.

[135] RN, Ann. 32, Audio Transcription of 6 Jan. 2017.

[136] *Ibid.*

[137] Letter of the Agent of Nicaragua to the International Court of Justice, Ref.: HOL-EMB-098-2019, 23 Sept. 2019, p. 2.

Colombian fishing licence[138] and a departure certificate issued in San Andrés in November 2018[139], Nicaragua has submitted both of these official documents to the Court. The *BL-405* took the *Observer* into custody and began to escort it to a port in Nicaragua. Due to mechanical problems, the *Observer* stalled, and had to be towed by *BL-405*[140].

42. The following day, 11 December 2018, the Colombian Navy intervened. The frigate *ARC-53 Antioquia* ordered the *BL-405* to release the *Observer*[141]. The *BL-405* refused[142]. The Colombian frigate followed closely the *BL-405*, with the *Observer* in tow, and then, as the vessels manoeuvred for position, the tow line connecting *BL-405* with the *Observer* severed[143]. Notwithstanding Colombia's interference with Nicaragua's law enforcement efforts in its own EEZ, the *BL-405* managed to retake control of the *Observer* and to bring it to the Nicaraguan mainland at Bluefields[144].

43. In its written response, Colombia makes two assertions. First, it claims the *Observer* was merely transiting Nicaragua's waters, with lobster caught elsewhere. But the captain of the *Observer* has admitted that the boat was caught fishing in Nicaragua's waters without a Nicaraguan licence[145]. Second, Colombia claims that its naval frigate was threatened by the manoeuvres made by the much smaller Nicaraguan coast guard vessel. That is like an elephant claiming to be threatened by a mouse. But, even if Nicaragua's mouse were somehow endowed with supernatural powers, the real question — for which Colombia has no answer — is: why was a Colombian naval frigate challenging and interfering with Nicaragua's enforcement of its sovereign right to prevent illegal fishing activities in its own EEZ by a Honduran-flagged fishing boat?

---

138 Colombian Certificate of Fishing Patent (*ibid.*, Ann. 18 *(i)*).

139 Colombian Set Sail (*ibid.*, Ann. 18 *(g)*).

140 Letter of the Agent of Nicaragua to the International Court of Justice, Ref.: HOL-EMB-098-2019, 23 Sept. 2019, p. 3; Affidavit by Officer Bismarck Isidro Valle Castro (Ann. 17 *(b)*).

141 Letter of the Agent of Nicaragua to the International Court of Justice, Ref.: HOL-EMB-098-2019, 23 Sept. 2019, p. 2.

142 *Ibid.*

143 *Ibid.* and Anns. 17 *(b)*, 17 *(f)*, 17 *(g)*, 17 *(h)* and 17 *(i)*.

144 See Letter of Vice-Minister of the Interior of Nicaragua, Luis Cañas Novoa, to Minister for Foreign Affairs of Nicaragua, Denis Moncada Colindres, Mar. 2019 (*ibid.*, Ann. 11).

145 Judgment of Nicaragua's Supreme Court of Justice No. 086, 26 Oct. 2020, p. 14. Spanish original available at https://www.poderjudicial.gob.ni/pjupload/sconten2012/pdf/certificacion_caso_observer.pdf; see also diplomatic Note MRE/DM-DM/DGAJST/00585/12/18 dated 22 Dec. 2018 (Ann. 6 to Letter of the Agent of Nicaragua to the International Court of Justice, Ref.: HOL-EMB-098-2019, 23 Sept. 2019, p. 2)

44. These incidents, all of them except for the last one, have occurred in or near the rich fishing area known as Luna Verde, depicted here in green, and at tab 28 of your folders. As you can see, it is plainly within Nicaragua's EEZ. Nevertheless, Colombia has made no secret of its encouragement of Colombian and foreign-flagged vessels to fish at Luna Verde. For example, resolution No. 4780, issued by the General Maritime Directorate of the Department of the Archipelago of San Andrés and Providencia on 24 September 2015, grants an "Industrial Commercial Fishing Permit" to the owner of the company Pesquera Serranilla to fish in "the area known as 'la esquina' or 'luna verde', which includes our insular territory and fishing zones"[146]. As this permit makes clear, it licenses "Industrial Commercial" fishing. That is what Colombia has regularly licensed at Luna Verde, in Nicaragua's EEZ. The evidence thus belies Colombia's claim that it only licenses small-scale, artisanal fishing by local island inhabitants in these waters. As Mr. Martin will show on Friday, even if Colombia's issuance of fishing licences were limited to artisanal fishing, which is not the case, this would still violate Nicaragua's exclusive fishing rights in its EEZ under well-established principles of customary international law.

45. These Colombian resolutions expressly authorize fishing by industrial commercial vessels "within the maritime jurisdiction of the Department of the Archipelago of San Andrés and Providencia", the contours of which are depicted on this official map[147]. The Court will observe that this purported maritime jurisdiction includes all the waters east of the 82nd meridian, as well as the notation, at the bottom left of the map: "Cortesía Armada República de Colombia", which means, "Courtesy of the Navy of the Republic of Colombia". These official Colombian documents are at tab 29 of your folders.

46. Colombia has also usurped Nicaragua's exclusive authority to license marine scientific research in its EEZ. On 8 October 2018, the Colombian naval frigate *ARC-51 Almirante Padilla* stopped the Mexican-flagged research ship, the *Dr. Jorge Carranza Fraser*, which had been licensed by Nicaragua under a research project funded by the United Nations Food and Agricultural

---

[146] General Maritime Directorate, Resolution No. 4780 of 2015 (24 Sept. 2015), Preamble, Recital 1 (RN, Ann. 14); see also RN, para. 4.106.

[147] General Maritime Directorate, Resolution No. 2465 of 2016 (30 June 2016), Art. 4; see also *ibid.*, Art. 8. (RN, Ann. 15); see Government of the Department of the Archipelago of San Andrés, Providencia and Santa Catalina, *Territorio*, https://www.sanandres.gov.co/index.php/archipielago/mapas/territorio, *y mapa geográfico* https://www.sanandres.gov.co/index.php/archipielago/mapas/mapa-geografico.

Organization[148]. The incident occurred along this route, depicted in red on this map, which was submitted to the Court by Colombia, and is included in the judges' folders at tab 30. Although the entire route followed by the Mexican research vessel, as shown by Colombia, was within Nicaragua's EEZ, the Colombian frigate forced it to leave the area, and prevented it from completing its mission. These facts are confirmed by correspondence from the Director General of Mexico's National Institute of Fishing and Aquaculture, which is part of the Mexican Department of Agriculture, to his Nicaraguan counterpart[149]. The Mexican Director General's letter, dated 16 April 2019, which is at tab 31 of your folders, and shown here in relevant part, explained that his institute's research vessel had been unable to complete its mission due to:

> "an interception by a marine military patrol from the government of a third country to the Jorge Carranza Fraser vessel during the cruise in the areas near the missing transects, indicating that it was sailing without permits in the waters of its marine jurisdiction, escorting the vessel Jorge Carranza Fraser until it departed the area".

47. There is no doubt about the identity of the "third country" referred to here by the Mexican official. Colombia itself acknowledges this. Nor is there any doubt that the Mexican vessel was navigating within Nicaragua's waters when it was "intercepted" by a "marine military patrol" from a third country. Colombia's own map, which I just showed you, demonstrates this.

48. All of this evidence — as well as the evidence of the dozens of other, similar incidents described in Nicaragua's pleadings — demonstrates the hypocrisy of Colombia's insistence, in its Rejoinder, that its actions in these waters have allowed Nicaragua to "continue to . . enjoy [its] sovereign rights . . [in its EEZ]"[150]. The evidence also belies Colombia's assertion that its actions reflect nothing more than its exercise of the right of freedom of navigation[151]. Earlier this month, Colombia's own President let the cat out of the bag, again, and dispensed entirely with these pretexts, as I displayed on your screens earlier: "The 82nd Meridian is the boundary we have today with Nicaragua". Freedom of navigation? That is not what the President of Colombia said. Nor is it what the Colombian Navy itself repeatedly told Nicaragua it was protecting. Rather, in the recorded words

---

148 Scientific Fishing Permit extended to Mexican vessel *Dr. Jorge Carranza Fraser*. Letter of the Agent of Nicaragua to the International Court of Justice, Ref.: HOL-EMB-098-2019, 23 Sept. 2019, p. 2, and Ann. 16.

149 Letter from the National Institute of Fisheries and Aquaculture of Mexico to the Nicaraguan Institute of Fisheries and Aquaculture, 16 Apr. 2019, OFICIO-RJL-INAPESCA-DG-058-2019; Letter of the Agent of Nicaragua to the International Court of Justice, Ref.: HOL-EMB-098-2019, 23 Sept. 2019, Ann. 12.

150 RC, Vol. I, para. 4.115.

151 See RC, Vol. I, pp. 33-78.

of its naval commanders, it was engaging, repeatedly, in the exercise of Colombia's sovereign authority over these waters, and especially to protect Colombia's "historic fishing rights" in areas the Court declared to constitute Nicaragua's EEZ[152].

49. Colombia seeks to minimize the incidents by arguing that Nicaragua itself played them down in its public statements, avoiding mention of conflicts with Colombia at sea up to early 2014[153]. Nicaragua has already explained that its statements were intended to minimize tensions with a vastly more powerful neighbour, and to give Colombia time and space to accommodate itself to the Court's Judgment and an eventual settlement with Nicaragua on terms consistent with that Judgment[154]. However, as Colombia's violations of Nicaragua's rights continued, and grew more intrusive and threatening, Nicaragua began to protest them more vigorously, and to make recordings of them to provide irrefutable proof of those violations. Colombia has yet to offer a credible explanation of its actions.

50. Faced with its inability to defend the indefensible, Colombia seeks refuge in a casuistic jurisdictional argument that would erase all these incidents from the case, as if they never took place, on grounds that they are beyond the scope of the present dispute, hence outside the Court's jurisdiction. In its Counter-Memorial, Colombia simply refused to address any of the incidents that post-dated 27 November 2013, the date of its withdrawal from the Pact of Bogotá, arguing that these incidents were each separate disputes, each of which arose after the jurisdictional title for Nicaragua's Application had lapsed[155]. In its Rejoinder, Colombia likewise refused to discuss any of these incidents in the main body of its text, relegating its response to an appendix[156].

51. Madam President, Colombia can run from these incidents, but it cannot hide from them. Certainly not behind a half-baked jurisdictional argument. In its Judgment of 17 March 2016, the Court rejected Colombia's second preliminary objection, and affirmed its jurisdiction over: the

[152] See, *inter alia*, Audio Transcription of 18 Mar. 2015, Audio Transcription of 23 Mar. 2015, Audio Transcription of 5 Apr. 2015, Audio Transcription of 7 Apr. 2015, Audio Transcription of 12 Sept. 2015 and Audio Transcription of 12 Sept. 2015 (RN, Ann. 32).

[153] RC, Vol. I, paras. 1.18; 3.41-3.45 *et seq*, citing *Alleged Violations of Sovereign Rights and Maritime Spaces in the Caribbean Sea (Nicaragua* v. *Colombia)*, Preliminary Objections of Colombia, Ann. 46, p. 367.

[154] RN, para. 4.33, paras. 4.27-4.42; RC, Vol. I, Appendix, p. 14, para. 4.

[155] Counter-Memorial of the Republic of Colombia (CMC), Vol. I, 17 Nov. 2016, pp. 165-168.

[156] RC, Vol. I.

"dispute concerning the alleged violations by Colombia of Nicaragua's rights in the maritime zones which, according to Nicaragua, the Court declared in its 2012 Judgment appertain to Nicaragua"[157]. The Court found that this dispute existed as of the time that Nicaragua filed its Application on 26 November 2013, which it regarded as the critical date for jurisdictional purposes[158].

52. Colombia would interpret the Court's Judgment as limiting its jurisdiction only to acts by Colombia which occurred before that date. But the Judgment of 17 March 2016 does not say that. It does not limit the Court's jurisdiction to acts occurring before 26 November 2013; it affirms jurisdiction over the dispute that arose prior to that date. Thus, as Professor Pellet has explained, acts by Colombia afterwards that are part of the same dispute inevitably fall within the jurisdictional scope of this case.

53. The Court was called upon to decide what was fundamentally the same question, that is, whether subsequent and ongoing violations of the applicant State's rights relate back to the date the dispute arose, or whether they constitute new and separate disputes, in the case concerning *Legality of Use of Force (Yugoslavia* v. *Belgium).* In that case, NATO's bombing of targets in Yugoslavia, which was the subject of the dispute between the parties, began on 24 March 1999. This was before Yugoslavia made its Article 36 (2) declaration on 25 April 1999 and filed its Application four days later. Yugoslavia, like Colombia here, attempted to slice the dispute into discrete pieces. It argued that each bombing incident gave rise to a new and separate dispute distinct from the original one, such that bombings after 25 April 1999 fell within the jurisdiction of the Court even though the NATO bombing campaign began before that date.

54. The Court upheld Belgium's preliminary objection on the ground that the individual bombing incidents after Yugoslavia's Article 36 (2) declaration were part of the same dispute that arose prior to it, and thus, like the dispute itself, fell outside the scope of its jurisdiction. The Court explained that "each individual air attack could not have given rise to a separate subsequent dispute", because "Yugoslavia has not established that new disputes, distinct from the initial one, have arisen

---

[157] *Alleged Violations of Sovereign Rights and Maritime Spaces in the Caribbean Sea (Nicaragua* v. *Colombia), Preliminary Objections, Judgment, I.C.J. Reports 2016*, p. 35, para. 79.

[158] *Ibid.*, p. 9, para. 1, p. 39, para 101.

between the Parties since 25 April 1999 in respect of subsequent situations or facts attributable to Belgium"[159].

55. This was not the first time the Court ruled as such. In the *Fisheries Jurisdiction* case (*Germany* v. *Iceland*), Germany alleged violations of its rights by Iceland that post-dated its Application. The Court had no difficulty holding that it had jurisdiction over these actions, on the ground that they constituted part of the same dispute that was submitted in the Application:

> "The Court cannot accept the view that it would lack jurisdiction to deal with this submission. The matter raised therein is part of the controversy between the Parties, and constitutes a dispute relating to Iceland's extension of its fisheries jurisdiction. The submission is one based on facts subsequent to the filing of the Application, but arising directly out of the question which is the subject-matter of that Application [over which the Court had jurisdiction]."[160]

56. The same is true here. Colombia's violations of Nicaragua's EEZ rights after November 2013 were unquestionably part of the same dispute raised by Nicaragua in its Application over which the Court affirmed its jurisdiction. In the Court's language, the "dispute concerning the alleged violations by Colombia of Nicaragua's rights in the maritime zones which, according to Nicaragua, the Court declared in its 2012 Judgment appertain to Nicaragua"[161]. Because the Court ruled that it has jurisdiction over *this* dispute, all of the individual incidents that form part of it, or relate back to it, necessarily fall within the same jurisdictional competence. Just as each post-Application bombing of Yugoslavia did not give rise to a new dispute, separate from the one that arose when the bombings first commenced, neither did the Colombian Navy's recurring and repeated violations of Nicaragua's sovereign rights and jurisdiction in Nicaragua's EEZ constitute new disputes separate from the one raised by Nicaragua in its Application. And, just as Iceland's post-Application actions arose directly out of the subject-matter of Germany's Application, Colombia's actions after 2013 arose directly out of the subject-matter of Nicaragua's Application.

---

[159] *Legality of Use of Force (Yugoslavia* v. *Belgium), Provisional Measures, Order of 2 June 1999, I.C.J. Reports 1999 (I)*, pp. 134-135, paras. 29-30.

[160] *Fisheries Jurisdiction (Federal Republic of Germany* v. *Iceland), Merits, Judgment, I.C.J. Reports 1974*, p. 203, para. 72.

[161] *Alleged Violations of Sovereign Rights and Maritime Spaces in the Caribbean Sea (Nicaragua* v. *Colombia), Preliminary Objections, Judgment, I.C.J. Reports 2016*, p. 34, para. 79.

57. As a consequence, Colombia cannot escape its international responsibility for violating Nicaragua's rights on jurisdictional grounds, any more than it can avoid its responsibility on the merits.

58. Madam President, Mr. Vice-President, Members of the Court, this concludes my presentation today. I thank you for your kind courtesy and patient attention, and I ask that you give the floor to my esteemed colleague, Professor Lowe.

The PRESIDENT: I thank Mr. Reichler and I now give the floor to Professor Vaughan Lowe.

Mr. LOWE: Thank you, Madam President. It is a privilege to appear before you and an honour to have been entrusted with this part of Nicaragua's submissions. May I begin by joining in the tribute to the late Judge Crawford. A colleague, a friend and an inspiration.

COLOMBIA'S INTEGRAL CONTIGUOUS ZONE IS INCONSISTENT WITH INTERNATIONAL LAW AND REMEDIES

1. Madam President, Members of the Court, nine years after your 2012 Judgment, Colombia is persisting in its attempts to establish Colombian maritime zones in areas that the Court has ruled are part of Nicaragua's EEZ. Colombia has no right to create special zones or an integral contiguous zone in Nicaragua's EEZ, period.

2. I shall focus on Colombia's Integral Contiguous Zone — its ICZ — which violates international law in various ways that I shall address shortly. But the main point is that Colombia must not continue to deny Nicaragua's rights under international law.

3. In 2012 the Court said that "the maritime boundary between Nicaragua and Colombia throughout the relevant area has now been delimited as between the Parties"[162]. That maritime boundary is shown on Sketch-map No. 11 in the Judgment, which is tab 32 in your folder[163].

---

[162] *Territorial and Maritime Dispute (Nicaragua* v. *Colombia), Judgment, I.C.J. Reports 2012 (II)*, p. 718, para. 250.

[163] *Territorial and Maritime Dispute (Nicaragua* v. *Colombia), Judgment, I.C.J. Reports 2012 (II)*, p. 714, para. 238.

4. Colombia did not accept the Court's Judgment. In 2013 it declared what it called "an Integral Contiguous Zone through which we have unified the contiguous zones of all our islands and keys in the Western Caribbean Sea. We will continue to exercise full jurisdiction and control in this zone."[164]

5. The area of the ICZ is depicted in Figure 2.2 in Nicaragua's Memorial as an overlay on the Court's Sketch-map No. 11. It is on the screen, shaded in green, and it is tab 33 in your folder. As you can see, it extends, in the words of the Colombian President, "from the south, where the Albuquerque and East-Southeast keys are situated, and to the north, where Serranilla Key is located. Of course, it includes San Andrés, Providencia and Santa Catalina, Quitasueño, Serrana and Roncador islands, and the other formations in the area"[165]. Around half of the green ICZ lies in areas that the Court has determined are Nicaragua's maritime zones, as defined by the 2012 maritime boundary, which is drawn in red.

6. The details of the ICZ are set out in Colombia's Presidential Decree 1946 of 9 September 2013, which is tab 10 in your folder[166].

7. Nicaragua objected to the ICZ for three reasons: (i) it infringed the EEZ that the Court had decided in 2012 belonged to Nicaragua[167]; (ii) it asserted jurisdiction over matters not properly encompassed within a contiguous zone under customary international law (Colombia not being a party to UNCLOS)[168]; and (iii) it exceeded the maximum breadth of the contiguous zone — 24 nautical miles from the territorial sea baseline — as permitted under international law[169].

8. Nicaragua and Colombia have exchanged substantial written pleadings on this question; and Nicaragua maintains in full the arguments that it has set out there. Here, I shall address the key points that remain in dispute after Colombia's Rejoinder.

9. Colombia's essential argument is that "[u]nder customary international law, the jurisdictional powers that States can exercise in the contiguous zone, including those enumerated in

---

164 "Declaration of President Juan Manuel Santos on the integral strategy of Colombia on the Judgment of the International Court of Justice, 9 September 2013", MN, Ann. 4, p. 135.

165 MN, Ann. 4, p. 135.

166 MN, Ann. 9.

167 MN, paras. 3.18, 3.20, 3.27.

168 MN, paras. 3.21-3.26.

169 MN, paras. 3.18-3.20.

Decree No. 1946 . . . are not incompatible with the sovereign rights a coastal State such as Nicaragua has within its EEZ"[170].

10. The main elements of Colombia's argument are:

(a) first, that the contiguous zone is not a maritime zone that needs to be delimited, but rather a "functional area" within which a coastal State has certain rights to protect its vital interests[171];

(b) second, the interests that it can protect are not confined to the four — customs, fiscal, immigration and sanitary regulations — set out in UNCLOS, Article 33, which Nicaragua says reflects customary international law;

(c) third, the provision in Article 33 (2) that "[t]he contiguous zone may not extend beyond 24 nautical miles from the baselines from which the breadth of the territorial sea is measured" does not apply as a matter of customary international law to Colombia's western islands within the ICZ;

(d) fourth, there is no incompatibility or conflict between Colombia's contiguous zone rights and Nicaragua's EEZ rights, which can coexist and overlap; and

(e) fifth, in any event, it is not the *declaration* of the ICZ but only its actual *implementation* that could amount to a violation of international law.

(a) *The contiguous zone is a maritime zone to be delimited*

11. I begin with the argument that the contiguous zone is not a maritime zone that needs to be delimited but a vague "functional area" of legal competence. International law has acknowledged what are in effect such areas. Under the doctrine of "constructive presence"[172] a coastal State could act against a foreign ship that stayed on the high seas while it used small boats to communicate with the shore, for example in order to smuggle narcotics into or out of the State.

12. There was no fixed distance from shore within which the ship on the high seas had to be located; nor was there a fixed list of coastal laws or interests whose violation justified reliance on the

---

[170] RC, para. 1.23.

[171] CMC, para. 5.34.

[172] See e.g. UNCLOS, Art. 111 (4); *The Arctic Sunrise Arbitration (Netherlands* v. *Russia)*, PCA Case No. 2014-02, Award on the Merits, 14 August 2015, para. 253; US Navy, *The Commander's Handbook on the Law of Naval Operations*, (Aug. 2017 ed.), para. 3.11.2.2.5, available at https://www.hsdl.org/?view&did=806860; C. J. Colombos, *International Law of the Sea* (6th ed., 1967), pp. 173-175; (former ITLOS Judge) H. Caminos, "Contiguous Zone", in *Max Planck Encyclopedia of Public International Law* (2012), para. 4.

constructive presence doctrine. One could say that, within a reasonable distance beyond its territorial sea, a coastal State could enforce its laws protecting its important interests. But this was a matter of its rights on what remained the high seas. It was not the assertion of control over a defined area of the sea.

13. Similarly, in the case of hot pursuit, a coastal State may pursue a foreign ship that has violated its laws out of its territorial sea (or, in the case of violations of customs, fiscal, sanitary and immigration laws, out of its contiguous zone) and arrest it on the high seas or in the EEZ of third States[173]. There is no fixed geographical limit, as long as the ship pursued has not entered the territorial sea of its own or a third State[174].

14. Constructive presence and hot pursuit are examples of limited functional rights of a coastal State beyond its territorial sea for the protection of its vital interests. Within reason, and subject to the duty to have due regard to the interests of other users of the sea and to respect the sovereignty of other States in their territorial seas and their rights in other maritime zones, States could exercise these rights anywhere. There is no defined zone in which they exercise those rights. But that is *not* what we are dealing with here.

15. Colombia's ICZ is quite different. It is a defined zone in which Colombia says, these are *our* waters, subject to *our* control, within which you must look to *our* laws, because as long as you are in this defined zone, we have the right to prevent and punish infringements of our laws. Whatever Colombia may say here, according to the Constitution[175] and the laws[176] of Colombia, the ICZ is fully a part of Colombia.

16. Colombia says that the fact that its domestic law describes the ICZ as a Colombian "zone" is not decisive[177]. A State might indeed claim a contiguous zone that is consistent with UNCLOS Article 33 but call it, say, a "security zone". Using a name that is inappropriate is, in itself, no offence. But that is not the point.

---

173 See e.g. UNCLOS, Art. 111.

174 UNCLOS, Art. 111 (3).

175 Art. 101, available at https://www.constituteproject.org/constitution/Colombia_2015.pdf?lang=en.

176 See MN, paras. 3.23-3.25; Presidential Decree No. 1119 of 17 June 2013, MN, Ann. 13; Presidential Decree No. 1946 of 9 September 2013, (Art. 2), MN, Ann. 9.

177 RC, para. 4.102.

17. Colombia has indicated that it intends to delimit the zone — to define its boundary — when technical work on the relevant baselines is complete[178]. It asserts that the boundary "enables the Colombian Navy to efficiently protect vital interests" and will "enable the other users of the Southwestern Caribbean Sea to foresee when they enter the contiguous zone"[179]. Like the old signs at the checkpoints in occupied Berlin, the ICZ boundary will in effect announce "[y]ou are now entering the Colombian sector".

18. The designation of the area as the Colombian Integral Contiguous *Zone* matters precisely because Colombia says that foreign ships need to know when they are entering the Colombian ICZ. It is a defined Colombian maritime zone, in which Colombia asserts its "full jurisdiction and control"[180].

19. Article 24 of the 1958 Territorial Sea Convention provided for the delimitation of the contiguous zone, with the median line as the default rule. The suggestion that the absence of any such provision in UNCLOS Article 33 shows that there is no need to delimit contiguous zones and that they may overlap[181] is misconceived and, as one of the authorities cited by Colombia puts it, "a very academic approach"[182].

20. One obvious explanation for the omission of a delimitation provision from Article 33, as those authorities note[183], is that such a provision is superfluous because the contiguous zone is part of the EEZ, for whose delimitation provision *is* made, in UNCLOS Article 74.

21. And the very nature of the contiguous zone points to its status as a distinct, defined maritime zone. UNCLOS Article 303 makes provision in relation to archaeological and historical objects in the contiguous zone. It says that a coastal State may "presume that their removal from the sea-bed in the [contiguous] zone . . . without its approval" is an offence under its laws.

---

178 RC, para. 4.14.

179 RC, para. 4.114.

180 "Declaration of President Juan Manuel Santos on the integral strategy of Colombia on the Judgment of the International Court of Justice", 9 September 2013, MN, Ann. 4, p. 135.

181 RC, paras. 4.37 and 4.34.

182 *The United Nations Convention on the Law of the Sea: A Commentary*, Alexander Proelβ, editor (hereinafter *"Proelss Commentary"*), p. 263.

183 See H. Caminos, "Contiguous Zone", in *Max Planck Encyclopedia of Public International Law* (2012), para. 16; *Proelss Commentary*, pp. 262–263; D. R. Rothwell and T. Stephens, *The International Law of the Sea* (2nd ed., 2016), pp. 81-82.

22. That provision makes no practical sense if the area of sea-bed in question falls within the overlapping contiguous zones of two States. Which of them is to give approval? As the *Virginia Commentary* recognized[184], delimitation is necessary in order to define the area within which each State is competent. That is why Article 8 of the 2001 Convention for the Protection of the Underwater Cultural Heritage asserts that "States Parties may regulate and authorize activities directed at underwater cultural heritage *within their contiguous zone*"[185].

23. Colombia, of course, itself asserts the right to safeguard its cultural heritage laws in its Integral Contiguous Zone; and that would plainly interfere with the rights of Nicaragua[186].

24. My final point on this first issue is that Colombia cannot point to a single State that has asserted contiguous zone rights without declaring a contiguous zone within defined limits. When States claim a contiguous zone, they claim a defined *zone*. Colombia, of course, has defined its Integral Contiguous Zone precisely, in Decree 1946.

25. Similarly, there is no evidence of States carving out or reserving their position in relation to contiguous zone rights when they delimit maritime boundaries — for example by establishing a contiguous zone straddling the delimited boundary. There is, for example, no such provision in Colombia's 1977 maritime boundary treaty with Costa Rica[187].

(b) *A contiguous zone is confined to the protection of customs, fiscal, immigration and sanitary laws*

26. On the second issue, concerning the list of laws and regulations that may be protected in the contiguous zone, it is again what Colombia cannot show you that is more pertinent than what it can.

27. In its Rejoinder, Colombia argued that the terms "'customs', 'fiscal', 'immigration' and 'sanitary'" laws are "generic terms providing for the protection of the vital interests of the coastal

---

[184] *Virginia Commentary*, Vol. V (1989), para. 303.6

[185] Http://www.unesco.org/new/en/culture/themes/underwater-cultural-heritage/2001-convention/official-text/; emphasis added.

[186] Decree 1946 of 2013, Art. 5 (3) *(a)*.

[187] Https://www.un.org/depts/los/LEGISLATIONANDTREATIES/PDFFILES/TREATIES/COL-CRI1977MC.PDF, Arts. 1 and 2.

State" in general in the contiguous zone[188], and that "all States retain within the EEZ high seas rights and freedoms not specifically assigned to the EEZ coastal State"[189].

28. To take the latter point, the EEZ does *not* have the "residual high seas character" that Colombia claims[190]: as UNCLOS, Article 55, makes clear, it is a zone "subject to the specific legal régime established in this Part" of the Convention.

29. The same is true in customary international law: the basic UNCLOS EEZ principles are a prime example of treaty provisions "reflecting, or . . . crystallizing, received or at least emergent rules of customary international law"[191], to borrow the Court's words from the *North Sea Continental Shelf* cases.

30. The United States' State Department geographer showed in his 1986 study of the exclusive economic zone that State practice developed alongside the successive drafts of UNCLOS, with national legislation based on those drafts. The graphic — your tab 34 — shows the number of claims made each year during the United Nations Conference, and the great leap in claims in the late 1970s. It was the concept of the EEZ *as developed by the United Nations Conference on the Law of the Sea* that was adopted in State practice[192].

31. As for the interests protected by the contiguous zone, exactly the same formula — "customs, fiscal, immigration or sanitary laws and regulations" — was adopted in Article 24 of the 1958 Territorial Sea Convention and then in Article 33 of UNCLOS.

32. There was no suggestion during the drafting that the contiguous zone should allow open-ended controls in relation to any matter that the coastal State considered to engage its "vital interests"[193].

33. That remains the case. As Captain Roach's 2020 study shows, "there are relatively few instances of claims to a contiguous zone that exceed the rights permitted coastal States under

---

[188] RC, para. 4.82 and cf. paras. 4.19 and 4.72.

[189] RC, para. 4.103.

[190] CMC, para. 5.23.

[191] *North Sea Continental Shelf (Federal Republic of Germany/Denmark), Judgment, I.C.J. Reports 1969*, p. 34. para. 50.

[192] See Table 7 in R. W. Smith, *Exclusive Economic Zone Claims: An Analysis and Primary Documents* (1986), pp. 35–37, and cf. pp. 29–40.

[193] RC, para. 4.82.

international law. Excessive contiguous zone claims relate to security and to underwater cultural heritage."[194]

34. Roach identifies 103 States claiming contiguous zones as of 2019[195], and only 16 of them as claimants to control security as a contiguous zone interest[196]. That is hardly a "general practice". He also lists the equally numerous protests made against those claims[197], which undermines any suggestion that the practice of these 16 States is "a general practice *accepted as law*".

35. All 168 Parties to UNCLOS may, of course, assert jurisdiction over archaeological and historical objects found at sea, in accordance with the terms of UNCLOS Article 303, paragraph 2 of which treats them as falling within Article 33.

36. But there is no evidence whatsoever to support Colombia's argument that "UNCLOS Article 303 confirms that 'customs', 'fiscal', 'immigration' and 'sanitary' are generic terms providing for the protection of the vital interests of the coastal State, and that such generic terms are to be interpreted accordingly"[198]. How does that work? States may exercise controls for purposes x, y, and z; x, y and z are important interests; therefore, States may protect all important interests? I do not think so.

37. Customs, fiscal, immigration and sanitary laws and regulations: State practice provides no basis for the assertion of any wider rights of control, let alone for a general, "generic" right to protect whatever Colombia may consider to be its "vital interests".

(c) *The contiguous zone may not extend beyond 24 nautical miles from the baseline*

38. On the third issue, the breadth of the contiguous zone, UNCLOS Article 33 (2) says "[t]he contiguous zone may not extend beyond 24 nautical miles from the baselines from which the breadth of the territorial sea is measured".

39. As can be seen from the chart now on your screen (your tab 35), Colombia's ICZ extends beyond 24 nautical miles. Its south-eastern margin is, at its furthest, over 50 nautical miles from the

---

[194] J. A. Roach, *Excessive Maritime Claims* (4th ed., 2020), p. 146.

[195] J. A. Roach, *Excessive Maritime Claims* (4th ed., 2020), p. 145, Table 6.

[196] J. A. Roach, *Excessive Maritime Claims* (4th ed., 2020), p. 149, Table 8.

[197] J. A. Roach, *Excessive Maritime Claims* (4th ed., 2020), pp. 146–149.

[198] RC, para. 482.

nearest baselines, on Roncador and East Southeast Cays. In the north, the "pan-handle" corridor inserted to connect the ICZ around Serranilla with that around Quitasueño and Serrana is in places 45 nautical miles from the nearest baselines.

40. This chart — your tab 36 — shows the ICZ, and all the parts of it that are shaded red lie more than 24 nautical miles from the nearest Colombian baselines. That is about one third of the ICZ. But Colombia has no right to establish a contiguous zone extending so far. It interferes not only with Nicaragua's rights, but with the rights of *all* foreign vessels in those waters.

41. The position is the same under customary international law. As of July 2021, the United Nations Division for Ocean Affairs and the Law of the Sea ("DOALOS") identifies only one State, the Democratic People's Republic of Korea, that claims a greater breadth for its contiguous zone — a 50-nautical mile zone established by an army command in 1977[199]. Another State in the DOALOS table, Lithuania, specifies co-ordinates containing its contiguous zone[200]: but the line so drawn lies entirely within 24 nautical miles of the baselines and conforms to Article 33[201].

42. There is no basis in State practice for a right to extend a contiguous zone beyond 24 nautical miles from the baseline. On the rare occasions when wider claims have been made, they have been actively opposed by States and subsequently withdrawn, as Roach's 2020 study shows[202].

43. Colombia has no right to establish a maritime zone — whether the ICZ or a special zone such as the Seaflower Marine Biosphere Reserve[203], in what the Court has determined to be Nicaragua's EEZ, including the waters around the enclaves around Quitasueño and Serrana[204]. And Colombia has no right to establish a contiguous zone of more than 24 nautical miles in any waters.

44. Columbia's suggestion that the ICZ is no more than a "simplification" of the complicated zone that would result from using the territorial sea baseline, analogous to the straight baseline in the *Anglo-Norwegian Fisheries* case, is not credible.

---

[199] Available at https://www.un.org/Depts/los/LEGISLATIONANDTREATIES/PDFFILES/table_summary_of_claims.pdf (accessed 15 July 2021).

[200] Available at https://www.un.org/Depts/los/LEGISLATIONANDTREATIES/STATEFILES/LTU.htm

[201] Cf. J. A. Roach, *Excessive Maritime Claims* (4th ed., 2020), p. 145, table 6.

[202] J. A. Roach, *Excessive Maritime Claims* (4th ed., 2020), pp. 151–153.

[203] See MN, paras. 2.16, 2.57; Anns 5, 11, 12, 23B, 33 and 46.

[204] *Territorial and Maritime Dispute (Nicaragua* v. *Colombia), Judgment, I.C.J. Reports 2012 (II)*, p. 713, para. 238.

45. There is no legal basis for claiming that such circumstances are ever relevant to the outer limit of the contiguous zone. The contiguous zone is always drawn from the territorial sea baseline. But in any event, the configuration of Colombia's islands is *not* an "exceptional geographical or socio-economic circumstance"[205]. The 24-nautical-mile contiguous zone contours are depicted in this figure — your tabs 37 and 38 — by purple shading — the inner blue shading represents the 12-nautical-mile territorial sea. Colombia calls this "a tangle of interconnected arcs, imposing significant difficulties in implementation"[206].

46. There are roughly half a dozen roughly circular areas, five of which overlap with one another. That is nothing like the complexities resulting from the 120,000 or so islands in the "skærgaard" that justified the use of simplifying straight baselines in the *Anglo-Norwegian Fisheries* case[207], which Colombia cites in support of its position[208]. Nor is it remotely comparable with the many States that do have complex coastlines and offshore islands.

(d) *Colombia's contiguous zone rights and Nicaragua's EEZ rights conflict and cannot overlap*

47. I turn to Colombia's fourth point: the argument that its contiguous zone rights and Nicaragua's EEZ rights can coexist, overlapping in the same space.

48. The first response to this is that the premise underlying it is incorrect. To take one example, Decree 1946 asserts Colombia's "*sovereign authority* and the powers for the implementation and the necessary control regarding . . . violations of laws and by-laws regarding environmental protection . . . and the exercise of historic rights to fishing held by the State of Colombia"[209].

49. Colombia asserts that authority and those powers in areas in which, under UNCLOS and customary international law, *Nicaragua* has "sovereign rights for the purpose of exploring and exploiting, conserving and managing the natural resources, whether living or non-living, of the waters", and in addition "jurisdiction . . . with regard to . . . the protection and preservation of the marine environment"[210]. Colombia asserts those very same rights in its own EEZ under its 1978 EEZ

[205] CMC, para. 5.29

[206] RC, para. 4.109.

[207] *Fisheries (United Kingdom* v. *Norway), Judgment, I.C.J. Reports 1951*, p. 127.

[208] CMC, para. 5.29.

[209] Decree 1946 of 2013, Art. 5 (3) *(a)*.

[210] UNCLOS, Art. 56 (1) *(a)* and *(b)*.

law, including what it calls "*exclusive* jurisdiction for . . . the preservation of the marine environment"[211]. The jurisdictional clash is obvious. As was apparent to the ITLOS in the *Saiga* and the *Virginia G* cases[212].

50. Whose law does a vessel look to? If, for example, a United States vessel in the Nicaraguan EEZ is authorized by Nicaragua to fish there, and is approached by a Colombian law enforcement vessel and told that those waters are part of Colombia's ICZ, must it submit to Colombia's control? EEZ rights and Colombia's ICZ rights do not address entirely different matters as Colombia claims, especially given the breadth of the rights asserted by Colombia.

51. The second response is that regardless of the jurisdictional conflict, Colombia has no right to arrogate to itself such rights in such locations. It has the right to establish a contiguous zone around its islands, out to a maximum distance of 24 miles but in no case beyond the maritime boundary delimited by the Court, and to do so for the purposes listed in Articles 33 and 303 of UNCLOS. And that is all.

52. Colombia says that the inability to establish the ICZ would be "devastating to the coastal State's ability to protect its vital interests"[213]. But why? Despite establishing an EEZ in 1978[214], Colombia managed without establishing a contiguous zone until 2013, when it says that "as a result of the 2012 Judgment" it found itself in a position where it was accorded only a territorial sea[215].

53. That, of course, is inaccurate. As can be seen from Figure 3.2 of Nicaragua's Reply, tab 39 in your folder, only the uninhabited banks of Quitasueño, which has only one minute feature above water at high tide[216], and Serrana, which is so small that neither the Court nor Colombia placed a

---

[211] Act No. 10 of 1978, Art. 8, available at https://www.un.org/Depts/los/LEGISLATIONANDTREATIES/PDFFILES/COL_1978_Act.pdf.

[212] *The M/V "SAIGA" Case (Saint Vincent and the Grenadines* v. *Guinea), Prompt Release, Judgment, ITLOS Reports 1997*, paras. 63–65; *The M/V "SAIGA" Case (Saint Vincent and the Grenadines* v. *Guinea), Prompt Release, ITLOS Reports 1997*, paras. 70–72; *The M/V "SAIGA" (No. 2) Case (Saint Vincent and the Grenadines* v. *Guinea), ITLOS Reports 1999*, paras. 131, 136; *The M/V "Virginia G" Case (Panama/Guinea-Bissau), Judgment, ITLOS Reports 2014*, paras. 208–217.

[213] RC, para. 4.39.

[214] Act No. 10 of 4 August 1978 establishing rules concerning the territorial sea, the exclusive economic zone and the continental shelf and regulating other matters, available at https://www.un.org/depts/los/LEGISLATIONANDTREATIES/PDFFILES/COL_1978_Act.pdf.

[215] RC, para. 4.39.

[216] *Territorial and Maritime Dispute (Nicaragua* v. *Colombia), Judgment, I.C.J. Reports 2012 (II)*, p. 644, para. 36, and cf. p. 692, para. 181.

base point on it[217], were accorded no maritime zone beyond 12 nautical miles in 2012. What "vital interests" of Colombia are jeopardized by having only a 12-mile territorial sea around each of them?

54. It is true that the 24-mile contiguous zone around Providencia, Roncador, San Andrés and the Albuquerque Cays is curtailed — but it has to be. That is the direct result of the Court's 2012 delimitation. And Colombia has no right to establish a Colombian maritime zone within Nicaragua's EEZ.

55. Despite all that it says in its written pleadings in this case, the website of the *Cancilleria* of Colombia sets out a definition of the contiguous zone that is much more faithful to the UNCLOS definition:

> "The contiguous zone is a maritime area recognized by international law, immediately following the territorial sea and extending 12 nautical miles for a total of 24 miles. It applies to both the mainland and the islands and cays. In the Contiguous Zone, monitoring is mainly carried out to prevent violations of customs, fiscal, immigration or health regulations; States may also punish in this space those infractions on these matters committed in the territory or in the Territorial Sea."[218]

Colombia knows full well what the law is; and it should comply with it.

(e) *Nicaragua's claim does not require material harm; but Nicaragua is suffering material harm*

56. Finally, I turn to the suggestion that no breach of international law arises from the establishment of the ICZ unless and until it causes Nicaragua material injury.

57. To be clear, Nicaragua maintains that there *has* been material injury, and has asked the Court to declare Colombia liable to compensate Nicaragua for such injury. The amount of compensation due for that material injury is a question reserved for a subsequent phase of this case. Here, the Court is asked to address the basic principles of Colombia's legal rights and duties.

58. Nicaragua explained in its Reply that the mere enactment of legislation may constitute an internationally wrongful act[219]. Colombia says that its ICZ Decree "can and will be implemented in accordance with international law"[220] — presumably, those parts of international law that Colombia

---

[217] *Territorial and Maritime Dispute (Nicaragua* v. *Colombia), Judgment, I.C.J. Reports (II)*, p. 699, para. 202.

[218] ¿Qué es la zona contigua?, available at https://www.cancilleria.gov.co/que-la-zona-contigua (accessed 31 Aug. 2021).

[219] RN, para. 3.57.

[220] RC, para. 4.148.

chooses to accept. It says that the ICZ Decree "should only be evaluated based on whether or not its implementation violates Nicaragua's EEZ rights"[221].

59. That is not so. Your 2012 Judgment was not concerned with instances of the implementation of States' powers: it was concerned with the delimitation of maritime zones. The ICZ is a plain and direct repudiation of that Judgment, and of Nicaragua's rights. Colombia cannot say to the world: "Foresee when you enter our ICZ that we control shipping there", and then say to the Court: "Don't worry, despite what we have declared and enacted, we will only act within our rights under international law."

60. The ICZ is a declaration by Colombia of what it considers to be its rights to control foreign shipping. The rights it claims are plainly in excess of those to which it is entitled under customary international law and under the Court's 2012 Judgment; and Nicaragua asks the Court to say so.

61. But again I emphasize that, as Nicaragua has demonstrated in its written pleadings — and as Mr. Reichler has shown you today — Colombia has gone far beyond making declarations that violate Nicaragua's rights under customary international law. It has repeatedly sent its Navy to prevent Nicaragua from exercising its exclusive sovereign rights and jurisdiction in its own EEZ, as delimited by the Court in 2012. And Colombia has attempted to exercise for itself those same rights — over fishing, marine scientific research and environmental protection — in waters that the Court has determined fall within Nicaragua's EEZ.

Relief requested

62. The remedies that Nicaragua requests from the Court are set out in the submissions on page 191 of its Reply. In summary, Nicaragua seeks an order, first, that Colombia must respect the maritime boundary delimited by the Court in 2012, and Nicaragua's sovereign rights and jurisdiction therein, and must revoke Colombian laws and instruments to the contrary; second, that Colombia must compensate Nicaragua for all damages caused by its violations of its international legal obligations, in an amount to be determined subsequently; and third, that Colombia must give appropriate guarantees of non-repetition. Our Agent will read out the request for relief in full at the end of these proceedings.

[221] RC, para. 4.149.

63. That brings my submissions, Madam President, Members of the Court, to a close. I thank you for your kind attention and unless I can be of any further assistance to you, this is the conclusion of Nicaragua's submissions on its claims, in this first round of oral proceedings. Thank you.

The PRESIDENT: I thank Professor Lowe, whose statement brings this sitting to a close. The oral proceedings in the case will resume at 11 a.m. on Wednesday 22 September, when Colombia will present its first round of argument, both on the claims of Nicaragua and on its own counter-claims.

The sitting is adjourned.

The Court rose at 6.10 p.m.

____

Corrigé
Corrected

CR 2021/14

International Court of Justice

THE HAGUE

Cour internationale de Justice

LA HAYE

YEAR 2021

Public sitting

held on Wednesday 22 September 2021, at 11 a.m., at the Peace Palace,

President Donoghue presiding,

***in the case concerning* Alleged Violations of Sovereign Rights and Maritime Spaces in the Caribbean Sea (Nicaragua *v.* Colombia)**

VERBATIM RECORD

ANNÉE 2021

Audience publique

tenue le mercredi 22 septembre 2021, à 11 heures, au Palais de la Paix,

sous la présidence de Mme Donoghue, présidente,

***en l'affaire relative à des* Violations alléguées de droits souverains et d'espaces maritimes dans la mer des Caraïbes (Nicaragua c. Colombie)**

COMPTE RENDU

Present:	President	Donoghue
	Vice-President	Gevorgian
	Judges	Tomka
		Abraham
		Bennouna
		Yusuf
		Sebutinde
		Bhandari
		Salam
		Iwasawa
		Nolte
	Judges *ad hoc*	Daudet
		McRae
	Registrar	Gautier

Présents :	Mme	Donoghue, présidente
	M.	Gevorgian, vice-président
	MM.	Tomka
		Abraham
		Bennouna
		Yusuf
	Mme	Sebutinde
	MM.	Bhandari
		Salam
		Iwasawa
		Nolte, juges
	MM.	Daudet
		McRae, juges *ad hoc*
	M.	Gautier, greffier

The Government of Nicaragua is represented by:

H.E. Mr. Carlos José Argüello Gómez, Ambassador of the Republic of Nicaragua to the Kingdom of the Netherlands,

as Agent and Counsel;

Mr. Alex Oude Elferink, Director, Netherlands Institute for the Law of the Sea, Professor of International Law of the Sea at Utrecht University,

Mr. Vaughan Lowe, QC, Emeritus Chichele Professor of Public International Law, University of Oxford, member of the Institut de droit international, member of the Bar of England and Wales,

Mr. Lawrence H. Martin, Attorney at Law, Foley Hoag LLP, member of the Bars of the United States Supreme Court, the District of Columbia and the Commonwealth of Massachusetts,

Mr. Alain Pellet, Emeritus Professor of the University Paris Nanterre, former Chairman of the International Law Commission, President of the Institut de droit international,

Mr. Paul Reichler, Attorney at Law, Foley Hoag LLP, member of the Bars of the United States Supreme Court and the District of Columbia,

as Counsel and Advocates;

Ms Claudia Loza Obregon, Legal Adviser, Ministry of Foreign Affairs of Nicaragua,

Ms Tessa Barsac, Consultant in International Law, Master (University Paris Nanterre), LLM (Leiden University),

as Assistant Counsel;

Mr. Robin Cleverly, MA, DPhil, CGeol, FGS, Law of the Sea Consultant, Marbdy Consulting Ltd,

as Scientific and Technical Adviser;

Ms Sherly Noguera de Argüello, MBA,

as Administrator.

The Government of Colombia is represented by:

H.E. Mr. Carlos Gustavo Arrieta Padilla, former Judge of the Council of State of Colombia, former Attorney General of Colombia and former Ambassador of Colombia to the Netherlands,

as Agent;

H.E. Mr. Manuel José Cepeda Espinosa, former President of the Constitutional Court of Colombia, former Permanent Delegate of Colombia to UNESCO and former Ambassador of Colombia to the Swiss Confederation,

as Co-Agent;

Le Gouvernement du Nicaragua est représenté par :

S. Exc. M. Carlos José Argüello Gómez, ambassadeur de la République du Nicaragua auprès du Royaume des Pays-Bas,

comme agent et conseil ;

M. Alex Oude Elferink, directeur de l'Institut néerlandais du droit de la mer, professeur de droit international de la mer à l'Université d'Utrecht,

M. Vaughan Lowe, QC, professeur émérite de droit international public à l'Université d'Oxford, titulaire de la chaire Chichele, membre de l'Institut de droit international, membre du barreau d'Angleterre et du pays de Galles,

M. Lawrence H. Martin, avocat au cabinet Foley Hoag LLP, membre des barreaux de la Cour suprême des Etats-Unis d'Amérique, du district de Colombia et du Commonwealth du Massachusetts,

M. Alain Pellet, professeur émérite de l'Université Paris Nanterre, ancien président de la Commission du droit international, président de l'Institut de droit international,

M. Paul Reichler, avocat au cabinet Foley Hoag LLP, membre des barreaux de la Cour suprême des Etats-Unis d'Amérique et du district de Colombia,

comme conseils et avocats ;

Mme Claudia Loza Obregon, conseillère juridique auprès du ministère des affaires étrangères du Nicaragua,

Mme Tessa Barsac, consultante en droit international, master (Université Paris Nanterre), LLM (Université de Leyde),

comme conseils adjoints ;

M. Robin Cleverly, MA, DPhil, CGeol, FGS, consultant en droit de la mer, Marbdy Consulting Ltd,

comme conseiller scientifique et technique ;

Mme Sherly Noguera de Argüello, MBA,

comme administrateur.

Le Gouvernement de la Colombie est représenté par :

S. Exc. M. Carlos Gustavo Arrieta Padilla, ancien juge au conseil d'Etat colombien, ancien *Procurador General de la Nación* et ancien ambassadeur de Colombie aux Pays-Bas,

comme agent ;

S. Exc. M. Manuel José Cepeda Espinosa, ancien président de la Cour constitutionnelle de Colombie, ancien représentant permanent de la Colombie auprès de l'UNESCO et ancien ambassadeur de Colombie auprès de la Confédération suisse,

comme coagent ;

H.E. Ms Marta Lucía Ramírez Blanco, Vice-President and Minister for Foreign Affairs of the Republic of Colombia,

H.E. Mr. Everth Hawkins Sjogreen, Governor of San Andrés, Providencia and Santa Catalina, Colombia,

as National Authorities;

Mr. W. Michael Reisman, McDougal Professor of International Law at Yale University, member of the Institut de droit international,

Mr. Rodman R. Bundy, former *avocat à la Cour d'appel de Paris*, member of the Bar of the State of New York, partner at Squire Patton Boggs LLP, Singapore,

Sir Michael Wood, KCMG, member of the International Law Commission, member of the Bar of England and Wales,

Mr. Eduardo Valencia-Ospina, former Registrar and Deputy-Registrar of the International Court of Justice, member and former Special Rapporteur and Chair of the International Law Commission, former Chair of the Latin American Society of International Law,

Mr. Jean-Marc Thouvenin, Professor at the University Paris Nanterre, Secretary-General of the Hague Academy of International Law, associate member of the Institut de droit international, member of the Paris Bar, Sygna Partners,

Ms Laurence Boisson de Chazournes, Professor of International Law and International Organization at the University of Geneva, member of the Institut de droit international,

H.E. Mr. Kent Francis James, former Ambassador of Colombia to Belize, former Ambassador of Colombia to Jamaica,

as Counsel and Advocates;

Mr. Andrés Villegas Jaramillo, LLM, Co-ordinator, Group of Affairs before the International Court of Justice at the Ministry of Foreign Affairs of Colombia, member of the Legal Sub Commission of the Caribbean Sea Commission, Association of Caribbean States,

Mr. Makane Moïse Mbengue, Professor at the University of Geneva, Director of the Department of Public International Law and International Organization, associate member of the Institut de droit international,

Mr. Luke Vidal, member of the Paris Bar, Sygna Partners,

Mr. Eran Sthoeger, Esq., member of the Bar of the State of New York, Adjunct Professor of International Law at Brooklyn Law School and Seton Hall Law School,

Mr. Alvin Yap, Advocate and Solicitor of the Supreme Court of Singapore, Squire Patton Boggs LLP, Singapore,

Mr. Lorenzo Palestini, PhD, Lecturer at the Graduate Institute of International and Development Studies and at the University of Geneva,

as Counsel;

S. Exc. Mme Marta Lucía Ramírez Blanco, vice-présidente et ministre des affaires étrangères de la République de Colombie,

S. Exc. M. Everth Hawkins Sjogreen, gouverneur de San Andrés, Providencia et Santa Catalina, Colombie,

comme représentants de l'Etat ;

M. W. Michael Reisman, professeur de droit international à l'Université de Yale, titulaire de la chaire McDougal, membre de l'Institut de droit international,

M. Rodman R. Bundy, ancien avocat à la Cour d'appel de Paris, membre du barreau de l'Etat de New York, associé au cabinet Squire Patton Boggs LLP (Singapour),

Sir Michael Wood, KCMG, membre de la Commission du droit international, membre du barreau d'Angleterre et du pays de Galles,

M. Eduardo Valencia-Ospina, ancien greffier et greffier adjoint de la Cour internationale de Justice, membre et ancien rapporteur spécial et président de la Commission du droit international, ancien président de l'association latino-américaine de droit international,

M. Jean-Marc Thouvenin, professeur à l'Université Paris Nanterre, secrétaire général de l'Académie de droit international de La Haye, membre associé de l'Institut de droit international, membre du barreau de Paris, cabinet Sygna Partners,

Mme Laurence Boisson de Chazournes, professeure de droit international public et organisation internationale à l'Université de Genève, membre de l'Institut de droit international,

S. Exc. M. Kent Francis James, ancien ambassadeur de Colombie au Belize et ancien ambassadeur de Colombie en Jamaïque,

comme conseils et avocats ;

M. Andrés Villegas Jaramillo, LLM, coordonnateur du groupe chargé des affaires portées devant la Cour internationale de Justice au sein du ministère des affaires étrangères de la Colombie, membre de la sous-commission juridique relevant de la Commission de la mer des Caraïbes de l'Association des Etats de la Caraïbe,

M. Makane Moïse Mbengue, professeur à l'Université de Genève, directeur du département de droit international public et organisation internationale, membre associé de l'Institut de droit international,

M. Luke Vidal, membre du barreau de Paris, cabinet Sygna Partners,

M. Eran Sthoeger, membre du barreau de l'Etat de New York, professeur adjoint de droit international à la Brooklyn Law School et à la faculté de droit de l'université de Seton Hall,

M. Alvin Yap, avocat et *solicitor* à la Cour suprême de Singapour, cabinet Squire Patton Boggs LLP (Singapour),

M. Lorenzo Palestini, PhD, chargé d'enseignement à l'Institut de hautes études internationales et du développement et à l'Université de Genève,

comme conseils ;

H.E. Mr. Juan José Quintana Aranguren, Head of Multilateral Affairs, former Ambassador of Colombia to the Netherlands,

H.E. Mr. Fernando Antonio Grillo Rubiano, Ambassador of the Republic of Colombia to the Kingdom of the Netherlands and Permanent Representative of Colombia to the Organisation for the Prohibition of Chemical Weapons,

Ms Jenny Sharyne Bowie Wilches, Second Secretary, Embassy of Colombia in the Netherlands,

Ms Viviana Andrea Medina Cruz, Second Secretary, Embassy of Colombia in the Netherlands,

Mr. Sebastián Correa Cruz, Third Secretary,

Mr. Raúl Alfonso Simancas Gómez, Third Secretary, Group of Affairs before the International Court of Justice,

Ministry of Foreign Affairs of Colombia;

Rear Admiral Ernesto Segovia Forero, Chief of Naval Operations,

CN Hermann León, Delegate of Colombia to the International Maritime Organization,

CN William Pedroza, National Navy of Colombia, Director of Maritime and Fluvial Interests Office,

Navy of the Republic of Colombia;

Mr. Scott Edmonds, Cartographer, Director of International Mapping,

Ms Victoria Taylor, Cartographer, International Mapping,

as Technical Advisers;

Mr. Gershon Hasin, LLM, JSD, Yale Law School,

as Legal Assistant;

Mr. Mark Taylor Archbold, Consultant for the National Unit of Disaster Risk Management,

Mr. Joseph Richard Jessie Martinez, Consultant for the National Unit of Disaster Risk Management,

as Advisers.

S. Exc. M. Juan José Quintana Aranguren, chef des affaires multilatérales, ancien ambassadeur de Colombie aux Pays-Bas,

S. Exc. M. Fernando Antonio Grillo Rubiano, ambassadeur de la République de Colombie auprès du Royaume des Pays-Bas et représentant permanent de la Colombie auprès de l'Organisation pour l'interdiction des armes chimiques,

Mme Jenny Sharyne Bowie Wilches, deuxième secrétaire, ambassade de Colombie aux Pays-Bas,

Mme Viviana Andrea Medina Cruz, deuxième secrétaire, ambassade de Colombie aux Pays-Bas,

M. Sebastián Correa Cruz, troisième secrétaire,

M. Raúl Alfonso Simancas Gómez, troisième secrétaire, groupe chargé des affaires portées devant la Cour internationale de Justice,

ministère des affaires étrangères de la République de Colombie ;

Le contre-amiral Ernesto Segovia Forero, chef des opérations navales,

Le capitaine de vaisseau Hermann León, représentant de la Colombie auprès de l'Organisation maritime internationale,

Le capitaine de vaisseau William Pedroza, marine nationale de Colombie, chef de la direction chargée des intérêts maritimes et fluviaux,

marine de la République de Colombie ;

M. Scott Edmonds, cartographe, directeur de International Mapping,

Mme Victoria Taylor, cartographe, International Mapping,

comme conseillers techniques ;

M. Gershon Hasin, LLM, JSD, faculté de droit de l'Université de Yale,

comme assistant juridique ;

M. Mark Taylor Archbold, consultant auprès de l'unité nationale de gestion des risques de catastrophe,

M. Joseph Richard Jessie Martinez, consultant auprès de l'unité nationale de gestion des risques de catastrophe,

comme conseillers.

The PRESIDENT: Please be seated. The sitting is open. For reasons duly made known to me, Judges Xue and Robinson are unable to join us for this morning's sitting. The Court meets today to hear the first round of oral argument of Colombia, both on the claims of Nicaragua and on its own counter-claims. Colombia has two sittings in which to present its arguments, this morning, from 11 a.m. to 1 p.m., and this afternoon, from 3 p.m. to 6 p.m. I shall now give the floor to the Co-Agent of Colombia, H.E. Mr. Manuel José Cepeda Espinosa. You have the floor, Your Excellency.

Mr. CEPEDA ESPINOSA:

1. Madam President, distinguished judges, it is a great honour to represent the Republic of Colombia before the International Court of Justice in this Great Hall of Justice.

2. Madam President, allow me to convey to you my deepest gratitude for having rendered homage to the late James Crawford, a renowned professor and admired judge of this Court. He was well known to Colombia; as you noted, prior to acceding to the Bench, he was lead counsel for Colombia in a case involving our territorial and maritime interests before this same tribunal. My country joins in the tribute to his memory, regrets his loss and honours his legacy.

3. Let me start by addressing upfront what we heard on Monday from the Agent of Nicaragua, Mr. Carlos Argüello. He attempted to present an image of Colombia as a rogue country that does not care about the law or this high court. If this were the case, why would Colombia be here pleading before you? The presence of Colombia before this Court is an indication of my country's old tradition of respect for international law and the procedures for the peaceful settlement of disputes.

4. On Monday, Nicaragua drew a picture of Colombia that completely distorts our legal tradition, our constitutional law and Colombia's position and policy.

5. Nicaragua's Agent is of course not obliged to know Colombian constitutional law. Obviously, he is not aware that Article 101 of the Colombian Constitution expressly states since 1991, that is, ten years before Nicaragua filed its first application against Colombia, that Colombia's limits "can only be modified by virtue of a treaty".

6. On the other hand, his assertion that Colombia has invoked its domestic law as "simply an excuse for not complying"[1] is clearly extravagant. This is not the position of Colombia.

[1] CR 2021/13, p. 20, para. 16.

7. This wild accusation compels me to dwell on the attempts that Colombia has made to resolve the differences with Nicaragua through diplomatic channels.

8. Allow me to remind you that in 1977, 1995 and 2001 Colombia proposed to Nicaragua to resolve their differences through a treaty. Nicaragua refused. It preferred to litigate before this Court. It was Nicaragua's right to do so. But what Nicaragua cannot do is hide extremely relevant facts and later declare itself surprised because Colombia had not invoked before the need for a treaty. In its Judgment on preliminary objections of 13 December 2007, the Court referred to those negotiations. The Court highlighted that "Nicaragua emphasizes, in this connection, that the negotiations concerned, *inter alia*, the delimitation of the respective maritime area of the Parties"[2].

9. Nicaragua knows this. Nicaragua alleged this before this Court. And now Nicaragua declares itself surprised. How convenient for Nicaragua!

10. Colombia's willingness to initiate conversations was also publicly expressed after the 2012 ruling of this Court.

11. Colombia took the initiative to start conversations with Nicaragua with a view to signing a treaty on various issues, including some of which are now the subject of these judicial proceedings, such as fishing rights and the environment. Colombia expressed its willingness to Nicaragua early and publicly, in a meeting held between the two Heads of State while in Mexico during the inauguration of President Enrique Peña Nieto on 1 December 2012. Afterwards, in furtherance of this announcement, a list of topics to be discussed and a *modus operandi* were preliminarily agreed upon. Nicaragua decided to abruptly end the conversations in 2015. Colombia left the door open. Nicaragua slammed it shut.

12. Nicaragua refused to continue the talks in 2015 and, in this way, it self-servingly created the circumstances to accuse Colombia of rejecting the 2012 Judgment because a treaty has not been concluded. And then it invokes the absence of such a treaty as proof of Colombia's violation of Nicaragua's economic rights. The Court very well knows that the absence of a treaty proves nothing regarding the alleged incidents at sea.

---

[2] *Territorial and Maritime Dispute (Nicaragua* v. *Colombia), Preliminary Objections, Judgment, I.C.J. Reports 2007 (II)*, p. 867, para. 113.

13. I should underline that these talks were unilaterally interrupted by Nicaragua before its domestic political situation deteriorated so dramatically that the Organization of American States has condemned the actions of the Nicaraguan Government and the European Union has imposed sanctions on Nicaragua's highest officials.

14. On Monday, Nicaragua also omitted something that, this time, Nicaragua should have known, because it is in the case file. When the Constitutional Court, in its decision of May 2014, referred to the need for a treaty to "incorporate" the 2012 Judgment, it also said that the rulings of the International Court of Justice had binding international effects and that Colombia had a "duty to comply [with it] in good faith"[3], until a treaty was concluded. The Constitutional Court went on to say that Colombia "recognizes the binding character of the decisions adopted by an international court in the performance of treaties previously entered into, approved and ratified by Colombia"[4].

15. In sum, Colombia is a dualist country in matters of territorial and maritime boundaries. This does not mean that Colombia does not or cannot abide by international judicial decisions. What it means, as in any other dualist system, is that certain steps must be fulfilled for the judgment to have domestic legal effects. This does not undermine the judgment's binding force in the *international* legal order.

16. Nicaragua has stated that the Constitutional Court's decision was opportunistic, and that Colombia acted in bad faith. That, simply, is not true. This decision followed a precedent that had existed for many years. Actually, in 1999, two years before Nicaragua's first Application against Colombia, the Constitutional Court had stated that "the modification of boundaries, which entails a transfer of territory with respect to the existing consolidated boundaries at the time the Constitution of 1991 was approved, requires . . . an international treaty"[5].

17. This is a separate question to that of whether Colombia requires a treaty to respect the 2012 Judgment. In fact, Colombia does not need a treaty to refrain itself from violating Nicaragua's sovereign rights.

---

[3] Preliminary Objections of the Republic of Colombia (POC), Vol. II, Ann. 4, para. 9.9.

[4] *Ibid.*, para. 9.11.

[5] Constitutional Court of Colombia, Decision C-1022 of 1999, available at https://www.corteconstitucional.gov.co/relatoria/1999/C-1022-99.htm (accessed 21 Sept. 2021).

18. Colombia's position has been open and clear from the outset. It is well recorded in the Court's Judgment on preliminary objections in 2016, in which it is stated:

> "Colombia accepts that the Judgment [of 2012] is binding upon it in international law. The Colombian Constitutional Court took the same position in its decision of 2 May 2014. The question that has arisen in Colombia is how to implement the 2012 Judgment domestically, having regard to the relevant constitutional provisions and the nature of Colombia's legal system with respect to boundaries."[6]

19. In conclusion, two things must be distinguished. In the light of Colombia's domestic law, a treaty is necessary to modify boundaries, but this does not mean that the judgments of this Court have no effects at the international level, even in the absence of a treaty. Most of these effects have actually to do with the international rights and freedoms of the Parties to the present case.

20. We return, then, to the subject-matter of this case and the real questions at issue here: has Colombia infringed the sovereign rights of Nicaragua? Can Nicaragua ignore the sovereignty of Colombia over the islands of the Archipelago by denying them the right to a zone contiguous to its territorial sea? Has Nicaragua violated the traditional fishing rights of artisanal fishermen from the San Andrés Archipelago? Can Nicaragua by decree convert into internal waters 21,500 sq km of sea far away from its continental coast?

21. Nicaragua seeks not only to distort Colombia's domestic law, but to deny Colombia's basic rights and freedoms recognized by international law.

22. If Nicaragua had continued the discussions started in 2012, we would not be in these judicial proceedings that deal with Nicaragua's claims and Colombia's counter-claims.

23. The Court would recall that Nicaragua came before it to contend that Colombia was threatening or using force against Nicaragua in violation of the Charter of the United Nations and customary law. That was pure invention. In its Judgment on preliminary objections, the Court unanimously decided there was simply no dispute on this matter[7]. Since then, and putting aside for the time being the counter-claims of Colombia, only the claims related to the alleged violations of the rights invoked by Nicaragua fall under the jurisdiction of the Court. I recall that these claims are essentially grounded on alleged "incidents" that no one heard about at the time of Nicaragua's

---

[6] *Alleged Violations of Sovereign Rights and Maritime Spaces in the Caribbean Sea (Nicaragua* v. *Colombia), Preliminary Objections, Judgment, I.C.J. Reports 2016 (I)*, p. 28, para. 57.

[7] *Ibid.*, p. 42, para. 111 (1) *(c)*.

Application. All information pertaining to these events magically emerged after the filing of the Application and shortly before Nicaragua's Memorial in the present case was due.

24. Aware of its poor arguments and evidence, Nicaragua has tried to make up for the defects in its claims with rhetorical and political arguments. Madam President, permit me to remind the Court that Colombia is a country committed to peace, respect for the rule of law, international co-operation, and the defence of democratic principles. Nicaragua, in contrast, uses the language we have heard, a language which would not be used by the representative of a democratic country where the separation of powers is an effective principle.

25. In its pleadings, Nicaragua insists on quoting, and misquoting, out of context statements attributed to Colombian officials or former officials, including some found in recent Colombian press, in an effort to discredit Colombia. With regard to some of them, Nicaragua did not even provide a translation, as required by Practice Direction IX*bis*. If anything, the statements resulting from internal political debates in Colombia are evidence of the vigour of a democratic and pluralistic society. Nothing more.

26. Obsessed with atmospherics, Nicaragua tries to make a storm in a teacup full of words. Nicaragua is alarmed by the words "cloak and sword", a pure rhetorical figure used by a former president. Then, Nicaragua quotes more words from the current President, taken imprecisely from a weekly magazine but has failed to point to any presidential order to violate Nicaragua's rights. In Colombia, presidents, as well as other officials and politicians, are accustomed to being in the eye of the political storms. Yes, we debate a lot. We debate all the time. We debate about everything. A democratic reality that apparently escapes Nicaragua's comprehension. Words, particularly in a political argument quoted out of context, are not illicit acts under international law. Peaceful navigation and overflight are not either.

27. Colombia, like any other State, enjoys freedom of navigation and overflight, and other internationally lawful uses of the sea related to these freedoms, throughout the Caribbean Sea. Nicaragua, at odds with international law, purports to deny Colombia these essential freedoms.

28. Nicaragua unsuccessfully tries to build a case to support its Application — an Application, I would remind the Court, filed just one day before Colombia's denunciation of the Pact of Bogotá took effect. In fact, Nicaragua attaches negative connotations to the exercise of the right of Colombia

to withdraw from this treaty. Nicaragua does not accept that Colombia has even this basic prerogative.

29. Of the 13 so-called incidents which occurred before the critical date, Nicaragua has not proven any violation of its rights by Colombia. Nicaragua did not even protest them before filing the Application. Nicaragua did not protest these alleged "incidents" earlier because, in fact, they were neither incidents, nor did Colombia's actions constitute any violation of Nicaragua's sovereign rights. Nicaragua did not even mention one of them, on Monday, even though they were the origin of its Application and are the only ones that fall under the jurisdiction of this Court. To compensate for the precariousness of its case, Nicaragua has attempted four times to add post-critical date events, all inconsequential.

30. Moreover, the official fishing statistics released by Nicaragua itself confirm that Colombia's alleged systematic policy of violating Nicaragua's sovereign rights has never existed. If anything, these statistics show that Nicaragua's fishing activity has increased exponentially[8]. Nicaragua can only point to a few fishing-related alleged "incidents" during each year. As Colombia will explain, these were actually "non-events". And these "incidents", if we take the year 2013, would have represented a mere 0.021 per cent of the total fishing days carried out by Nicaragua's fishing fleet. This means that 99.98 per cent of Nicaraguan fishing activities in the Caribbean during that year were not affected by Colombia, according to Nicaragua. The statistics for the following years lead to similar conclusions. Moreover, from 2017 until now they amount to zero. That, certainly, demonstrates the absence of any Colombian policy to impede their activities; on the contrary, they show a policy of respect for international law.

31. Furthermore, throughout the course of these proceedings Nicaragua has failed to prove that its flagged or licenced vessels could not continue fishing or that the catch was confiscated. It has failed to prove, case by case, that Colombia violated Nicaragua's sovereign rights. That is why it has tried to bundle those events together and has sought to portray them as a pattern of conduct by Colombian authorities. However, adding nothing to nothing results in nothing. That, Madam President, distinguished judges, it is scarcely a "pattern" of illegal conduct.

---

[8] CMC, Vol. II, Ann. 71.

32. Madam President, judges of the Court, such precarious evidence, so many late attempts to amend it, so many distortions of what happened, make one thing clear: neither in 2013 nor now does Nicaragua have a serious case.

33. Colombia has exercised its freedoms of navigation and overflight, and other internationally lawful uses of the sea related to these freedoms, which are guaranteed by international law. All States can benefit from these freedoms, including Colombia. However, Nicaragua seeks to curtail the scope of these freedoms, which is equivalent to subverting a cardinal principle of international law. The profound and disruptive implications of equating these freedoms to mere passage are self-evident.

34. Throughout the course of these proceedings, Nicaragua has denied that "the rights and duties of the Parties with respect to the preservation and protection of the environment . . . are relevant to the present case"[9]. In fact, this statement has been backed by its actions, particularly by systematically engaging in predatory fishing practices under inhumane conditions[10].

35. This is a shocking position when the international community awaits, urgently, international action to avoid ecological disasters. The preservation of the marine environment is a duty of all States, especially when the habitat of the communities of the Archipelago and the region is at stake. The Seaflower Biosphere Reserve constitutes the habitat within which thousands of Colombian inhabitants of the Archipelago live.

36. In addition to the preservation of the marine environment, the presence of Colombia in the Caribbean Sea, especially in the south-western sector, is due to other imperatives, such as the interdiction of drug trafficking and other illegal activities. Colombia is present in the area in compliance with its international duties. Colombia plays a leading role in joint operations against drug trafficking in which France, the Netherlands, the United States, Costa Rica, and other Caribbean and Central American countries participate, including Nicaragua. Thirty-eight States take part in Operation Orion, a multilateral effort against drug trafficking. It is unclear, to say the least, why Nicaragua maintains that all these countries can be present in the area, but Colombia cannot.

---

[9] RN, para. 1.12.

[10] *The New York Times*, "For Nicaragua's Lobstermen, Deadly Dives Are All Too Common", 24 Jan. 2021, available at https://www.nytimes.com/2021/01/24/world/nicaragua-lobsters-fishing.html (accessed 21 Sept. 2021).

37. Madam President, distinguished judges, it is worth recalling that Colombia has sovereignty over all the islands that make up the Colombian Archipelago. International law extends the exercise of sovereignty to the territorial sea of the islands and allows for the exercise of certain protective functions in a zone contiguous to the territorial sea. By claiming that Colombia cannot exercise contiguous zone functions around the islands of our Archipelago, Nicaragua is contradicting international law.

38. All the above leads to a simple conclusion: all of Nicaragua's claims are unsubstantiated and artificial. They are founded on words, not conduct.

39. Consequently, what remains of this case initiated by Nicaragua are Colombia's legitimate rights at sea and our two counter-claims.

40. Colombia considers that Nicaragua is infringing the traditional fishing rights of the Raizal people who inhabit the Archipelago of San Andrés, Providencia and Santa Catalina. It is doing so first and foremost by seeking to deny the existence of these rights, a denial which is the underlying main point of contention between the Parties.

41. Not only has Nicaragua prevented the Raizales from fishing, but it has also intimidated them by intercepting their modest boats. This abuse is one more injustice that the Raizal people have had to suffer. This is a community whose members are descendants of slaves brought from Africa to be exploited during the colonial period and who, more than two centuries ago, found in these islands a space of freedom in which to live in harmony with the sea. Two centuries after they found their freedom, Nicaragua seeks to curtail the Raizales' access to their traditional fishing grounds on which their culture and subsistence as a fishing community depends.

42. Finally, Colombia also considers that Nicaragua has acted in manifest violation of international law by drawing a system of straight baselines far away from its continental coast without fulfilling the international law requirements for doing so. Colombia and other States have sent corresponding notes of protest.

43. Madam President, Members of the Court, the order in which Colombia's counsel will address you in the first round will be as follows:

— First, Mr. Kent Francis James will recall the traditional rights of the Raizal people, to which Colombia attaches paramount importance.

— He will be followed by Sir Michael Wood, who will address the content of the applicable international law in the context of this case and highlight the serious legal flaws upon which Nicaragua builds its arguments.

— Professor Laurence Boisson de Chazournes will speak about the importance of Colombia's activities of observation and information for environmental purposes and their legality.

— Mr. Rodman Bundy will come next. He will explain that Colombia has not violated any of Nicaragua's sovereign rights. We expect Mr. Bundy to begin his statement shortly before the lunch break and to continue in the afternoon.

— Professor Michael Reisman will then show why the contiguous zone of the Colombian islands in the Archipelago and its extent, far from illegal, are in harmony with customary international law.

— Turning to our first counter-claim, Mr. Eduardo Valencia Ospina will describe Nicaragua's infringement of the traditional fishing rights of the inhabitants of the San Andrés Archipelago.

— And to conclude our first round, Professor Jean-Marc Thouvenin will demonstrate the blatant illegality of Nicaragua's straight baselines.

44. Madam President, distinguished judges, I thank you for your attention. May I ask Madam President to now give the floor to Mr. Kent Francis James, who will deliver the first pleading on behalf of Colombia. Thank you.

The PRESIDENT: I thank the Co-Agent of Colombia for his statement. I now invite H.E. Mr. Kent Francis James to take the floor. You have the floor, Sir.

Mr. JAMES:

THE TRADITIONAL RIGHTS OF THE RAIZAL PEOPLE

Introduction

1. Madam President, distinguished judges, it is an honour to appear before the principal judicial organ of the United Nations, and to do so as a member of Colombia's legal team in this important case.

2. Colombia's Co-Agent has just outlined Colombia's response to the arguments that Nicaragua has advanced during these proceedings and the basic elements of Colombia's counter-claims. In my brief presentation, I will make references to the human, historical, social and environmental context which informs the various elements of this case, and which need to be taken into account when assessing the claims and counter-claims of the Parties.

3. Both claims and counter-claims involve matters relating to the south-western Caribbean Sea. The Court's decision in this case will have an important impact on the people that inhabit this area.

Who are the Raizales?

4. The name Raizales comes from the word "roots" in Creole[11]. For almost 400 years, the Raizales have inhabited and derived economic sustenance from the Archipelago of San Andrés and the associated maritime areas.

5. The Raizales from the Archipelago of San Andrés, Providencia and Santa Catalina are Colombian. And within Colombia's diversity they are also Caribbean people, whose lives are intimately connected with the sea.

6. The Raizales depend on traditional fishing rights extending over large maritime areas at issue in this case. This is clear from Colombia's first counter-claim. Because of that dependence on the sea, the Raizales' livelihood can only be preserved if the maritime areas are protected and conserved without being subject to harmful and destructive fishing practices.

7. Over the centuries, the Raizales have established a stable community with footprints in the Archipelago of San Andrés, Providencia and Santa Catalina. But not only there. The Raizales' movements throughout the region have never been constrained.

8. When the Dutch arrived in the Archipelago, they established commercial relations with the inhabitants of the Mosquito coast. Also, in the first decades of the seventeenth century, the English arrived. Then there was a mixture of indigenous people from the Caribbean, together with enslaved Africans, and British, Dutch, French, German, Spanish and Chinese, among others. Currently, the Raizales are mostly Creole — Black Kriols to be precise.

---

[11] CMC, para. 2.64.

9. African men and women were brought in large numbers to the Archipelago through enslavement — owing to the customs of human trafficking of the time. But in many aspects (language, religion, customs) the British markedly influenced the Raizales. Hence the Puritan heritage.

10. Almost 200 years ago, when the United Kingdom ended the trade of slaves, a son from the island of Providencia, Philip Beekman Livingston Jr., of British parents, in his early twenties, also began in 1834 a campaign for the emancipation of Blacks in the area[12], which included the Mosquito coast and the Corn Islands. He freed the slaves from his family, giving them property and land, instructing them to read, write and in mathematics, as well as organizing entrepreneurial activities for their own benefit. His acts of humanity influenced others to also emancipate all those enslaved on the islands.

11. The Raizales then began planting coconut for export to the United States of America. Other products, such as bird eggs and guano, were also of economic interest. But the main livelihood for the Raizales has always come from the sea[13].

The Raizales' relationship with the sea

12. For the Raizales the sea is home, shelter, livelihood and support. The Raizales have worked the sea as artisanal fishermen and sailors. While based in the islands of the Archipelago, they have always maintained contact with the continent and with other islands in the Caribbean.

13. The Raizales generally navigate without having sight of land, with minimal instruments for this purpose; this is part of the ancestral knowledge of the Raizal people. The Raizales have always sailed and enjoyed the products of the sea without any restrictions from the political limits established by man.

14. The sea is a vital space for the Raizales, a trade route for Creole peoples in the south-western Caribbean. It is their economic heritage.

---

[12] M. Aguilera, *Geografía económica del archipiélago de San Andrés, Providencia y Santa Catalina*, Banco de la República, Centro de Estudios Económicos Regionales, Documentos de trabajo sobre economía regional, No. 133, 2010, p. 5.

[13] J. Bond and R. Meyer de Schauensee, "The Birds", *The Academy of Natural Sciences of Philadelphia*, Monographs, No. 6, Results of the Fifth George Vanderbilt Expedition (1941), Wickersham Printing Company, 1947, p. 10.

15. The sea is also their cultural heritage. In fact, followers of the Raizales' faith are baptized in the sea. It is a cemetery for those who left and have not returned. It is the source of true and fictional stories, of tales, of fables, of adventures, of amusement and sadness. As the Raizales say: it is a gift of God.

16. The habitat of the Raizales is formed by islands, islets, cays, atolls and banks. These range from San Andrés and the islands in its proximity, which include South South-West Cays and East South-East Cays to the islands of Serranilla and Bajo Nuevo; passing through Roncador, Serrana and Quitasueño; and the islands of Old Providence and Kathleena. This habitat is an essential part of the Raizales' history, their livelihood, their culture.

The importance of fishing and the environment

17. Madam President, distinguished judges, the sea provides the Raizal people and the people of the Archipelago with food security. The banks and areas that are traditionally fished are reference points that are essential to the Raizales' livelihood and habitat. They include banks close to the Colombian islands. They also include, but are not limited to banks farther out, such as Luna Verde, Cape Bank, Julio Bank, North-East Bank and Far Bank. These are much more than 12 nautical miles from the coast, and since 2012, problems have arisen for the Raizales when they sail to fish in these areas. Eduardo Valencia-Ospina will address these matters in detail.

18. The Raizales are artisanal fishermen who use environmentally friendly techniques such as "handlining" and "breath-hold diving". These are sustainable methods and practices geared to the special characteristics of the western Caribbean maritime area. By contrast, other methods, such as fishing with divers who use scuba tanks, oxygen compressors or explosives, cause serious harm.

19. Unsustainable extraction of marine resources is a threat to all communities' survival and specially the Raizal people. International developments such as Sustainable Development Goal 14, which calls on States to conserve the oceans, seas and marine resources, are very much in line with the Raizales' ethos and traditions.

20. Also, because of its importance, the protection and preservation of the sea with its fisheries is engrained in the Raizales' fishing practices. The Raizales participated in promoting the designation by UNESCO of a world biosphere reserve — the Seaflower Reserve[14].

21. The maritime spaces covered by the reserve also contain one of the most extensive coral reef ecosystems on the planet[15]. The reserve took its name in honour of the *Seaflower*, a ship that carried some of the first Britons to settle on the island of Providencia. The *Seaflower* had a sister ship — the *Mayflower* — whose history is well known. Professor Boisson will address in detail the importance of the environment for this case.

22. Your Excellencies, as we have said, the Raizal people of San Andrés, Providencia and Santa Catalina have a natural bond with the sea: they live off it and consider it part of their natural habitat. Any restrictions of their historical and cultural traditions would have a significant and negative impact on their way of life and identity.

23. Madam President, distinguished judges, I thank you for your attention and I would be grateful if the floor could now be given to Sir Michael Wood. Thank you.

The PRESIDENT: I thank Mr. James. I now invite Sir Michael Wood to take the floor.

Sir Michael WOOD:

THE APPLICABLE LEGAL RÉGIME AND THE RIGHTS OF THE PARTIES

1. Madam President, Members of the Court, it is an honour to appear before you on behalf of Colombia. On a personal level, may I say that it is a pleasure to be in The Hague and to be once again in the Peace Palace. May I first join in the tributes that have been paid to Judge Crawford. His passing is a great loss to the Court and to all of us.

2. My statement will be in two parts. First, I shall recall the basic elements of the specific legal régime at issue in this case. It is necessary to do so because Nicaragua presents the Court with a false picture in its pleadings. Second, I will explain that Colombia's activities fall squarely within the

---

[14] UNESCO, Man and the Biosphere (MAB) Programme, Sixteenth session, 6-10 Nov. 2000, Final Report, doc. SC.2000/CONF.208/CLD.16, p. 21, para. 122, available at https://unesdoc.unesco.org/ark:/48223/pf0000122703_fre (in French) and https://unesdoc.unesco.org/ark:/48223/pf0000122703 (in English) (accessed 21 Sept. 2021).

[15] Colombia's National Natural Parks, Old Providence McBean Lagoon National Natural Park, available at https://www.parquesnacionales.gov.co/portal/en/ecotourism/caribbean-region/old-providence-mcbean-lagoon-national-natural-park/ (in English) (accessed 21 Sept. 2021).

freedoms and rights enjoyed by all States in the areas in question. Colombia has at all times had due regard to Nicaragua's rights and duties and has not violated any of Nicaragua's rights.

3. Madam President, it is important to bear in mind the complex nature of the maritime area at issue in this case — the south-western Caribbean. As perhaps you can see on the screen, but anyway it is at tab 2 in your folders, the south-western Caribbean is a semi-enclosed sea bordered by seven coastal States: to the south and west, Colombia, Panama, Costa Rica and Nicaragua, with Jamaica, Haiti and the Dominican Republic to the north.

4. Colombia is not some distant maritime power; it is a coastal State in the south-western Caribbean, with an extensive mainland coast and numerous islands, including those of the San Andrés Archipelago. Colombia's activities and presence in the south-western Caribbean are a natural consequence of these geographical realities. In this context, Nicaragua's references on Monday to maps depicting the "area of operation" of the Colombian Navy or to statements about having a presence in various maritime areas are of no significance[16]. States' navies regularly operate in areas beyond their maritime jurisdiction, even globally, to protect their interests[17]. There is nothing unique or remarkable about Colombia having maritime interests and presence outside its jurisdictional waters. The peace and environmental sustainability of the south-western Caribbean are essential components of Colombia's well-being and form part of its national identity.

5. Madam President, the applicable law in this case is closely related to this geographical situation. Account needs to be taken not only of the customary international law of the sea but also of a range of conventional and customary rules applicable to the Caribbean Sea, not least the Cartagena Convention[18], to which both Colombia and Nicaragua are parties. These particular rules, in turn, assist a correct understanding of the customary international law of the sea, which applies between the Parties (since of course Colombia is not a party to UNCLOS).

---

[16] CR 2021/13, p. 48 (Reichler); p. 29 (Pellet).

[17] E.g. French Navy 2021, Information file, available at https://www.google.com/url?sa=t&rct=j&q=&esrc=s&source=web&cd=&ved=2ahUKEwjr_4-e-o3zAhVl_rsIHVm2BF8QFnoECAIQAQ&url=https%3A%2F%2Fwww.defense.gouv.fr%2Fcontent%2Fdownload%2F612927%2F10259719%2FDIM_2021_ANGLAIS.pdf&usg=AOvVaw0JyrdXDKRtNx75E7CSvtR1.

[18] Convention for the Protection and Development of the Marine Environment in the Wider Caribbean Region, CMC, Ann. 17.

I. The specific legal régime applicable to the areas at issue in this case

6. Madam President, Members of the Court, the present case raises a number of important issues. A central question, and the one on which I shall focus today, concerns the nature, scope and content of the specific legal régime applicable under customary international law. This régime governs the rights, duties and jurisdiction of coastal States, and the freedoms, rights and duties of other States[19]. In the end, the question before the Court is whether any of Colombia's specific actions that are within the scope of this case have in fact violated Nicaragua's sovereign rights and jurisdiction. The case is not about determining the international responsibility of the State for political statements made by its officials. It is about actions taken, not determining abstract legal questions.

7. On Monday, Professor Pellet devoted a large part of his intervention to abstract and generalized criticisms of Colombia's approach to the law. He himself nowhere described the specific legal régime applicable to the maritime area in question. Professor Pellet accused Colombia of being opportunistic in identifying the rules of customary international law and "taking advantage" of UNCLOS to impose obligations on Nicaragua, even though Colombia is not a party to UNCLOS[20]. In fact, Madam President, unlike Nicaragua, Colombia has been consistent in applying the correct methodology for identifying rules of customary international law, as it derives from your case law and as was recognized in the recent work of the International Law Commission. Colombia has been consistent in its approach, identifying rules of customary international law on the basis of State practice and *opinio juris*. Unlike Nicaragua, Colombia does not just "presume" that a treaty rule necessarily reflects customary international law. Moreover, notwithstanding the fact that Colombia is not a party to UNCLOS, it is obvious that Nicaragua must comply with its obligations thereunder, as this Court itself recognized[21].

8. In its pleadings, Nicaragua adopts a wholly mistaken approach to the specific legal régime applicable within an EEZ, and seeks to deny Colombia the rights and freedoms recognized by international law. Professor Pellet did nothing to correct that on Monday. The essence of the applicable régime is that the coastal State has "sovereign rights *for the purpose of exploring and exploiting, conserving and managing the natural resources*, whether living or non-living, of the

---

[19] Cf. UNCLOS, Art. 56.

[20] CR 2021/13, p. 31 (Pellet).

[21] *Territorial and Maritime Dispute (Nicaragua* v. *Colombia), Judgment, I.C.J. Reports 2012 (II)*, p. 669, para. 126.

waters superjacent to the sea-bed and of the sea-bed and its subsoil"[22]. All other States enjoy the high seas freedoms of navigation and overflight, and other internationally lawful uses of the sea related to those freedoms[23]. In addition, the rules of international law concerning the high seas and other pertinent rules of international law apply[24].

9. Thus, the specific legal régime gives the coastal State certain rights and duties but they are limited in scope and nature, and relate mainly to the exploration, exploitation, conservation and management of natural resources. As for the coastal State's jurisdiction with regard to the protection and preservation of the marine environment, it too is specific and limited; it is not exclusive[25]. Under customary international law, all States have environmental rights and duties in the area in question. This basic legal framework has to be read with more specific rules, including those set out in the Cartegena Convention.

10. Nicaragua challenges all this. It does not accept the EEZ for what it is, a specific legal régime essentially concerned with natural resources. Nicaragua apparently takes the wholly mistaken view that the area in question is to be equated to sovereignty and to the territorial sea. This can be seen from the statements of its high officials.

11. As you will see on the screen and at tab 3 in your folders, already in late 2012, President Ortega spoke of "exercising this aerial and maritime *sovereignty*"[26]. And in 2015, he spoke of "a New Territorial Sea"[27] awarded by the Court to Nicaragua. The Head of the Nicaraguan Naval Force also spoke about "exercising *sovereignty* in the Sea and Jurisdictional Airspace"[28]. The Head of Nicaragua's Army spoke of "Sovereign Seas, particularly of our waters in the Caribbean restored by the Judgment of the International Court of Justice of November 2012"[29]. And in its Note Verbale of 16 February 2021, which Nicaragua has just introduced into these proceedings, Nicaragua described "the waters on which the Nicaraguan Caribbean Biosphere Reserve is found" as being

---

[22] Cf. UNCLOS, Art. 56.1 *(a)* (emphasis added).

[23] Cf. UNLCOS, Art. 58.1.

[24] Cf. UNCLOS, Art. 58.2.

[25] Cf. UNCLOS, Art. 56.1 *(b)* (i); see also Arts. 193-194, 205-208.

[26] RC, Ann. 1 (emphasis added).

[27] RC, Ann. 5.

[28] *Ibid.* (emphasis added).

[29] *Ibid.*

"indisputably part of our Caribbean *territory*". These are just a few examples[30]. Earlier this year, even the Agent of Nicaragua made statements to the media confirming that Nicaragua views the waters in question as *territory under its sovereignty*[31].

12. Madam President, these are not just loose words. They reflect a deep-seated Nicaraguan attitude, a Nicaraguan position with practical implications, as we shall see.

13. Nicaragua continues to assert that "Colombia must establish that the rights that it claims in Nicaragua's EEZ are 'attributed' to it, and not to Nicaragua, by the regime of the EEZ"[32]. In other words, it seeks to argue that other States do not enjoy the same liberties as it does in and over the waters off its coast, because the area is not a "residual regime"[33].This wilful misunderstanding seeks to reverse the burden of showing that an activity is not permitted. Also, according to Nicaragua, freedom of navigation merely encompasses a right of "passage" — sailing from one point to another and nothing more[34]. According to Nicaragua, it is for Colombia to show that it has other rights. But that is not how the specific legal régime works. All States enjoy the freedoms of navigation and overflight and of the laying of submarine cables and pipelines, and other internationally lawful uses of the sea related to those freedoms. And they also benefit from the rules of international law concerning the high seas and other pertinent rules of international law.

14. Madam President, Nicaragua's vision of the specific legal régime recalls 200-nautical-mile territorial sea claims from the 1940s and 1950s. But the law developed in a different direction. State practice evolved in the 1970s, in parallel with the negotiations at the Third United Nations Conference on the Law of the Sea. A specific legal régime extending 200 nautical miles from baselines emerged. This régime did not grant sovereignty to the coastal State. Rather, the coastal State enjoyed certain exclusive rights with respect to natural resources[35]. By the late 1970s, this régime had gained general acceptance[36]. A coastal State's zone is *not* sovereign territory, it is *not*

[30] See RC, Anns. 1-5, 7 (emphasis added).

[31] Dr. Carlos Argüello, Representative of Nicaragua before the International Court of Justice in The Hague, interview with Alberto Mora, Live Magazine, Channel 4, 2 Feb. 2021, available at http://nicaraguasandino.com/ley-que-declara-y-define-reserva-de-biosfera-del-caribe/.

[32] RN, para. 2.10.

[33] RN, paras. 2.08, 2.16.

[34] RN, paras. 2.38 and 2.40.

[35] *Continental Shelf (Libyan Arab Jamahiriya/Malta), Judgment, I.C.J. Reports 1985*, p. 33, para. 34.

[36] See Virginia Commentary, Vol. II, pp. 548-550.

territorial sea. The zone is subject to a régime that was painstakingly negotiated in the 1970s, to balance the interests of coastal States and the interests of all other States. "The coastal State's rights relate essentially to the natural resources"[37] — that is a quote, and a correct quote in my view, from the book by Professors Churchill and Lowe on the Law of the Sea. The other side of that coin is that the coastal State enjoys no special rights with respect to other matters. And, at the same time, it has a positive obligation to have due regard to the rights of other States[38].

15. Due regard must be given also to the coastal State's particular rights. Subject to that, the rights of all other States are no different from their rights on the high seas. High seas freedoms and the rules of international law applicable to the high seas apply within the zone. In other words, those activities relating to freedom of navigation and overflight that do not fall within the exclusive rights of the coastal State can be freely exercised by other States while navigating in or flying over its zone, subject to having due regard to the coastal State's rights and to the high seas rights exercised by other States. The rights of all States there include the right to conduct activities that do not involve any sailing at all. For example, "bunkering on the high seas is part of the freedom of navigation to be exercised under the conditions laid down by the Convention and other rules of international law"[39]. That is a quote from the Law of the Sea Tribunal.

16. In short, Madam President, Members of the Court, the freedoms of navigation and overflight, and other internationally lawful uses of the sea, in and over the coastal State's zone, are the same as those freedoms anywhere on the high seas. They apply to all ships and aircraft. They go beyond "passage". They include the right to navigate and overfly for any purpose.

17. As with freedom of navigation, freedom of overflight is the same as that enjoyed over the high seas[40]. As has been stated by the International Civil Aviation Organization (ICAO) — and is now on your screens, and at tab 4: "For all practical and legal purposes, the status of the airspace

---

[37] R. R. Churchill and A. V. Lowe, *The Law of the Sea*, 3rd ed., Manchester University Press, 1999, p. 166: see also RC, para. 2.32; D. P. O'Connell, *The International Law of the Sea*, Vol. 1, p. 552(1982).

[39] *M/V "Norstar" (Panama* v. *Italy), Judgment, ITLOS Reports 2018-2019*, p. 10, para. 2.19; See also *M/V "Virginia G" (Panama/Guinea-Bissau), Judgment, ITLOS Reports 2014*, p. 70, para. 223.

[40] Cf. UNCLOS, Art. 58.

above the EEZ and the regime over the EEZ is the same as over the high seas and the coastal States are not granted any precedence or priority"[41].

18. Nicaragua has tried to make much of alleged incidents involving overflight by Colombian aircraft. Mr. Bundy will demonstrate later today that these allegations are factually groundless, as has already been shown in Colombia's written pleadings[42]. But in any event, Madam President, the basis of these allegations is Nicaragua's misconceived understanding of the law relating to overflight over the zone. Nicaragua repeatedly purports to exercise what it calls "sovereignty" in the airspace over waters beyond its territorial sea[43]. But the freedom of overflight is not limited under international law; as ICAO explained, the airspace above the zone has essentially the same status as the airspace over any other area where high seas rights and freedoms apply. A coastal State's sovereignty over its airspace extends only to the airspace above its territorial sea.

19. To make a broader point, Madam President, Nicaragua's written pleadings focus less on what it claims Colombia actually did, but more on what it says was Colombia's "intent" and whatever general significance Nicaragua reads into Colombia's presence in the south-western Caribbean[44]. Forgive me for stating the obvious, but this is a court that adjudicates between States based on law and facts, not on speculation.

II. The presence of the Colombian Navy is an exercise of the freedoms of navigation and overflight and other internationally lawful uses of the sea

20. Madam President, Members of the Court, I now turn to the second part of my statement and will say a few words about the factual background to this case. Those who follow me will go into these matters in more detail. As we have seen, under international law, in a coastal State's zone all ships and aircraft enjoy the high seas freedoms of navigation and overflight and other internationally lawful uses of the sea related to these freedoms[45].

---

[41] International Civil Aviation Organization, "United Nations Convention on the Law of the Sea — Implications, if any, for the application of the Chicago Convention, its Annexes and other international air law instruments", doc. C-WP/7777 (1984), para. 11.12, Netherlands Institute for the Law of the Sea (ed.), *International Organizations and the Law of the Sea Documentary Yearbook 3*, 1987, p. 243.

[42] CMC, Chap. IV.A (2); RC, Chap. 3.C.

[43] RC, Ann. 3, Reading of Order No. 0061-2013 by the Commander-in-Chief of the Nicaraguan Army. See RC, Anns. 1-5 and 7 for similar statements on Nicaraguan sovereignty over the maritime areas in question; See also RC, para. 2.12.

[44] See, for example, MN, paras. 2.02-2.21; RN, paras. 2.1, 2.35, 4.36, 4.45, 4.112 and 4.130.

[45] Cf. UNCLOS, Art. 58.

21. To find State practice to this effect we need look no further than the Caribbean Sea, where Caribbean and non-Caribbean States alike routinely conduct maritime surveillance and other operations. As the Co-Agent has already mentioned this morning, Colombia's Navy and coast guard are by no means the only ones operating in the area. As has been shown in detail in our written pleadings, Belize, Canada, Chile, Colombia, Costa Rica, El Salvador, France, Guatemala, Honduras, the Netherlands, Panama, Spain, the United Kingdom and the United States, among others, all conduct activities in this area, unilaterally, bilaterally and jointly[46].

22. This established practice in the south-western Caribbean confirms that Nicaragua cannot claim "exclusive jurisdiction" so as to deny Colombia and all other States the rights and freedoms recognized by international law. The suggestion that Colombia and other States violate Nicaragua's sovereign rights simply because they carry out certain observing and informing activities in the area, that is, observing what is happening there and informing those involved of the consequences of their actions[47], that suggestion is untenable. Such activities fall squarely within all States' rights to exercise the freedoms of navigation and overflight and other internationally lawful uses of the sea. How this presence, how these activities, have violated Nicaragua's rights is left unanswered by Nicaragua.

23. Nicaragua repeatedly refers to this as "policing", or as Professor Pellet put it on Monday, "contrôles et contrainte"[48]. This is an attempt to convey a false image of the activities concerned, to create the impression that Colombia is omnipresent and a threatening force in the Caribbean. The reality is completely different. The Colombian "presence", in fact, normally consists of a single coast guard vessel. Occasionally a second Colombian coast guard vessel may also navigate in the area at the same time. This is the "presence" Nicaragua goes on and on about: one, or occasionally two, vessels in a vast maritime area.

24. In any event, the presence of naval vessels from many nations in the south-western Caribbean is unsurprising, given the challenging circumstances in the area, circumstances which Nicaragua has so far not seen fit to address in these proceedings.

---

[46] CMC, paras. 2.101-2.109; RC, paras. 2.23-2.29.

[47] RN, para. 2.10.

[48] CR 2021/13, p. 34 (Pellet).

25. It should be noted that Nicaragua itself was largely absent from the south-western Caribbean at the time when that maritime area was, as it still is, experiencing significant challenges. The nature and extent of these challenges have been thoroughly explained in our written pleadings[49]. I will highlight just a few points concerning transnational organized crime and drug trafficking, assistance to vessels at sea, and the protection of the environment.

Transnational organized crime and drug trafficking

26. Madam President, Members of the Court, Colombia is one of the Caribbean States taking appropriate measures to prevent transnational organized crime at sea, including in co-operation with other States. In fact, Colombia's actions are an absolute necessity in the Caribbean Sea; the area was and continues to be particularly afflicted by drug trafficking[50], arms trafficking and other serious criminal activities. Nicaragua itself concedes, in its Reply, that Colombia has a right to take action in the area "if it happens to encounter a ship suspected of the illegal transportation of narcotics, or to search for such a ship if it has a reason to suspect that it is there"[51].

27. As we explained in our Counter-Memorial, Colombia's Navy has a base on San Andrés, which performs a vital role in the efforts against illicit drug trafficking. In addition, on Serrana, Serranilla, Roncador and Cayo Bolívar, Colombia has built accommodation for naval detachments, including solar panels and water collection facilities for the use of the navy infantry corps and the fishermen who inhabit or visit the islands and cays. It has also built radio stations and lighthouses[52]. These efforts place Colombia at the forefront of the fight against drug trafficking in the Caribbean, a fact that is well recognized internationally[53].

28. Colombia has entered into some 88 bilateral arrangements to fight drug trafficking[54]. It is also a party to international coalitions established to that end. These have included, for example, Operation Martillo. Launched in 2012 and only recently terminated, that operation was a coalition of

---

[49] CMC, Chap. 2; RC, paras. 2.34-2.108.

[50] CMC, para. 2.97 and the accompanying Figure 2.6; RC, paras. 2.41-2.49.

[51] RN, para. 2.34.

[52] CMC, paras. 2.98-2.100.

[53] CMC, paras. 2.104-2.108.

[54] CR, para. 2.46, referring to Ministry of Foreign Affairs of Colombia, Virtual Library of Treaties, available at http://apw.cancilleria.gov.co/tratados/SitePages/BuscadorExternoForm.aspx (accessed 12 May 2019).

14 countries, including, I note, Nicaragua[55]. This successful operation depended on the presence of vessels from some 14 countries in the relevant maritime areas. As was stated by the United States Department of Defense: "In support of the operation [Operation Martillo], U.S., partner nation and allied forces' ships and aircraft provide *persistent presence* in select maritime zones"[56].

29. The presence of Colombia's vessels in the south-western Caribbean is no different from the presence of vessels from other States, including non-Caribbean States, and is part of vital anti-narcotics co-operation. In fact, it is the presence of naval vessels from a range of States that is the cornerstone of these indispensable efforts. For Nicaragua to come before this Court, and single out Colombia in order to paint this presence as some evil plot, is incomprehensible.

30. Madam President, Colombia takes the threat of drug trafficking seriously. This was true in 2013 when Nicaragua initiated these proceedings, as Operation Martillo demonstrates, and it remains true today. That is why Colombia invited the Nicaraguan Navy to participate in the new multilateral Operation Orion, launched in April 2018. Phase VII of that operation was carried out earlier this year and was co-ordinated by the Colombian Navy. Thirty-eight States (including Nicaragua) participated[57]. The Chief of the Nicaraguan Army applauded the "high level of cooperation" with the Colombian Navy against drug trafficking, through participation in Operation Orion[58].

31. Under customary international law, beyond its territorial sea a coastal State has no sovereign rights or jurisdiction that are specifically relevant to action against drug trafficking. But like all States, Nicaragua is obliged under specific conventions to co-operate with other States in the suppression of drug trafficking at sea[59].

---

[55] CMC, paras. 2.101-2.102.

[56] US Southern Command, "Operation Martillo Still Hammering Away at Illicit Trafficking", available at https://www.southcom.mil/MEDIA/NEWS-ARTICLES/Article/985770/operation-martillo-still-hammering-away-at-illicit-trafficking/ (emphasis added).

[57] Naval Campaign press release of 3 Aug. 2021, available at https://www.cgfm.mil.co/en/blog/naval-campaign-orion-vii-largest-multilateral-operation-against-drug-trafficking-history-has; Presidency of the Republic press release of 3 Aug. 2021, available at https://www.cgfm.mil.co/en/blog/results-operation-orion-vii-show-together-we-are-more-effective-against-international-drug.

[58] Speech of General Julio César Avilés, Chief of the Nicaraguan Army, of 21 Feb. 2020, available at https://www.lavozdelsandinismo.com/nicaragua/2020-02-21/acto-en-conmemoracion-del-86-aniversario-del-transito-a-la-inmortalidad-del-general-de-hombres-y-mujeres-libres-augusto-c-sandino-21-2-2020-texto-integro/.

[59] See UNCLOS, Art. 108 and Art. 58 (2).

Assistance to vessels at sea

32. Madam President, Members of the Court, I now turn to assistance to vessels at sea. As explained in our written pleadings, there is significant maritime traffic in and around the San Andrés Archipelago and beyond. These vessels include, of course, Colombian flagged and licenced vessels.

33. The weather in this part of the Caribbean Sea is increasingly unpredictable, creating a high risk for vessels navigating in the area — and not only for the Raizales. Colombia has rights and obligations towards all vessels, Colombian and others alike, including to protect and provide relief in cases of security or technical difficulty.

34. As was pointed out in our Rejoinder[60], Colombia is a State party to the International Convention on Maritime Search and Rescue, the primary international agreement on search and rescue at sea. Under the Annex to the Convention, excerpts of which are in your folders at tab 5, States are required to "provide the most appropriate assistance available" within their designated search and rescue region[61]. Moreover, all parties to the Convention are under an obligation to provide assistance to any person in distress at sea, regardless of nationality or circumstances[62].

35. On your screen now — and at tab 6 — you can see Colombia's designated search and rescue region. It covers parts of many States' EEZs. Colombia is acting in accordance with its obligations under the Convention when it provides technical and humanitarian assistance to vessels in distress in the south-western Caribbean. Several examples of such assistance provided by the Colombian Navy to Nicaraguan vessels in distress may be found in Appendix A of our Counter-Memorial.

36. Let me recall in this context that coastal States have both rights and *duties* under international law. But Nicaragua, for its part, is not sufficiently equipped at present to ensure the safety of vessels in the southern Caribbean. This explains why Nicaraguan fishermen rely on the Colombian Navy at times of distress[63].

37. Most importantly, Colombia — like Nicaragua and all coastal States — has an obligation to promote the establishment, operation and maintenance of "an adequate and effective search and

---

[60] RC, paras. 2.50-2.56.

[61] International Convention on Maritime Search and Rescue 1979, Annex, Art. 2.1.9.

[62] *Ibid.*, Annex, Art. 2.1.10.

[63] CMC, Chap. 8, see also Appendix A; RC, para. 2.55.

rescue service regarding safety on and over the sea"[64]. It is hard to see how Colombia's humanitarian actions in helping others have harmed Nicaragua's rights in any way. If anything, they should be welcomed by Nicaragua as they were by its distressed fishermen.

Protection of the environment

38. Madam President, and lastly, I turn briefly to the protection of the environment. The relevant rights and obligations of Colombia and Nicaragua for protecting the environment, particularly in the context of the fragile south-western Caribbean, have been explained in our written pleadings[65]. International law imposes upon States *obligations* as well as granting them rights with respect to the environment. Under customary international law, States are obliged to "protect and preserve the marine environment".

39. This obligation of conduct, a "due diligence" obligation[66], requires a State to proactively ensure that the relevant rules are enforced. The Court explained this in *Pulp Mills*; the text is on the screens (tab 7), but given the time, I will not read it out aloud.

40. In addition to this due diligence obligation, under international law, States must exercise their sovereign rights "in accordance with their duty to protect and preserve the marine environment"[67]. Measures are to "include those necessary to protect and preserve rare or fragile ecosystems as well as the habitat of depleted, threatened or endangered species and other forms of marine life"[68]. Moreover, States are under a positive obligation to "endeavour . . . to observe, measure, evaluate and analyse . . . the risks or effects of pollution of the marine environment"[69].

41. Colombia's environmental activities in the south-western Caribbean are limited to observing, evaluating and informing others of environmental risks, and the need to protect the fragile ecosystem and natural habitat of vulnerable communities, such as the Raizales. They are in no way contrary to international law and are fully compatible with the rights and obligations of the coastal

---

[64] As reflected in UNCLOS, Art. 98 (2).

[65] RC, paras. 2.57-2.108.

[66] *Request for Advisory Opinion submitted by the Sub-Regional Fisheries Commission, Advisory Opinion, 2 April 2015, ITLOS Reports 2015*, p. 40. para. 129.

[67] Cf. UNCLOS, Art. 193.

[68] Cf. UNCLOS, Art. 194 (5).

[69] Cf. UNCLOS, Art. 204 (1).

State. Professor Boisson de Chazournes will explain this in more detail shortly. Nicaragua, for its part, seems indifferent to the potential negative impact of the deterioration of fragile ecosystems on the livelihood of vulnerable communities, such as the Raizales.

42. Madam President, Members of the Court, the international community cannot ignore the scourge of drugs, the well-being of those in peril at sea, or irreversible damage to the environment, including to significant and unique ecosystems, especially when these ecosystems are the habitat of a vulnerable community. Instead of addressing the fact that it is failing to meet its own obligations, Nicaragua points the finger at Colombia's proportionate and limited actions to safeguard the essential interests of the international community from grave and imminent damage to the environment, as well as from other harm. Nicaragua's passiveness has contributed to unimpeded drug trafficking and to the danger posed to the environment in the south-western Caribbean — and to the well-being of those dependent on it, including the Raizales. By contrast, Colombia's actions in no way impair Nicaragua's essential interests.

43. Madam President, that concludes my intervention and I request that you invite Professor Boisson de Chazournes to the podium. I thank you.

The PRESIDENT: I thank Sir Michael and I now invite Professor Laurence Boisson de Chazournes to take the floor.

Mme BOISSON DE CHAZOURNES :

L'IMPORTANCE DES ACTIVITÉS D'OBSERVATION ET D'INFORMATION DE LA COLOMBIE À DES FINS ENVIRONNEMENTALES ET LEUR LICÉITÉ

1. Madame la présidente, Mesdames et Messieurs les juges, c'est un honneur pour moi de me présenter devant vous aujourd'hui au nom de la République de Colombie. Permettez-moi tout d'abord de rendre un hommage appuyé au professeur, juge et ami James Crawford.

2. Le moins que l'on puisse dire c'est que, durant son premier tour de plaidoiries, le Nicaragua a confirmé les craintes maintes fois exprimées par la Colombie devant la Cour de céans quant à son mépris flagrant des considérations environnementales. Dans la fable concoctée par les conseils du

Nicaragua, l'environnement ne serait qu'un instrument de «contrôles»[70], de «contrainte»[71], ou encore de «désinvolture»[72] visant à nier les droits reconnus aux Etats côtiers par le droit international. En plus d'être inquiétantes, de telles élucubrations juridiques sont anachroniques et en total déphasage avec ce qui est requis des Etats membres de la communauté internationale en vertu du droit international contemporain. Mais pis, ces élucubrations ont pour effet de réduire à néant l'importance des considérations environnementales dans l'appréciation par la Cour de la licéité des actions menées par la Colombie.

3. Et pourtant, la Colombie n'aura cesse de le répéter : l'environnement est bel et bien au cœur du présent différend. Et si la Cour venait à faire abstraction des considérations environnementales, comme l'y invite le Nicaragua et cela sans aucune base juridique, elle ignorerait un élément intégral du différend dont elle est saisie.

4. Mesdames et Messieurs les juges, c'est dans un espace maritime *particulier* que le différend porté devant vous s'inscrit : celui de la mer des Caraïbes. Cette mer semi-fermée se caractérise par la fragilité de ses écosystèmes, lesquels écosystèmes servent d'habitat naturel, social, économique et culturel à une communauté non moins vulnérable, à savoir les Raizals, ainsi que M. Kent Francis James vient de l'expliquer. Ces deux dimensions — environnementale et humaine — font de l'espace en cause dans le présent différend un espace particulier à protéger et à préserver.

5. C'est ce souci à la fois de protection et de préservation qui a conduit des membres de la communauté internationale, notamment les Etats qui «sont particulièrement intéressés»[73], à élaborer un *corps de règles spéciales* pour garantir la durabilité de la mer des Caraïbes. Le corpus en question trouve assise dans la convention de Carthagène. Le Nicaragua et la Colombie, tous deux parties à cet instrument conventionnel, sont tenus d'agir conformément à ce régime juridique spécifique mis en place dans le contexte de l'espace environnemental et humain particulier que constitue la mer des Caraïbes. Ce régime doit prendre toute sa place au cœur de l'écheveau des droits et obligations en cause dans la présente affaire.

---

[70] CR 2021/13, p. 34, par. 25 (Pellet).

[71] *Ibid.*

[72] *Ibid.*, p. 35, par. 28 (Pellet).

[73] *Plateau continental de la mer du Nord (République fédérale d'Allemagne/Danemark) (République fédérale d'Allemagne/Pays-Bas), arrêt, C.I.J. Recueil 1969*, p. 43, par. 74.

6. La convention de Carthagène fait partie des sept conventions administrées par le Programme des Nations Unies pour l'environnement (PNUE). L'organisation onusienne a interpellé, à maintes reprises, la communauté internationale sur les menaces qui pèsent sur les habitats sensibles de la mer des Caraïbes[74].

7. Partant, il ne fait point de sens, comme le fait le Nicaragua, de reprocher à la Colombie d'agir avec toute la diligence requise en menant des activités d'observation et d'information afin de sauvegarder les écosystèmes de la mer des Caraïbes, des écosystèmes connus tant pour leur fragilité que pour leur importance dans la réalisation des besoins vitaux des Raizals et de la préservation de leur habitat. Le régime spécial mis en place à travers la convention de Carthagène, de pair avec les obligations qui pèsent tant sur le Nicaragua que la Colombie en vertu du droit international coutumier de la mer comme l'a souligné Sir Michael Wood, requièrent la protection et la conservation de ces écosystèmes, et notamment des ressources halieutiques qui les peuplent.

8. Je démontrerai, tout d'abord, que la protection des écosystèmes de la mer des Caraïbes et, par ricochet, la préservation de l'habitat des Raizals, font bel et bien partie du différend qui oppose le Nicaragua à la Colombie (**I**). Pour prendre la mesure des accusations infondées du Nicaragua, la Cour se doit d'accorder une attention singulière à la particularité de l'espace maritime que constitue la mer des Caraïbes, et plus précisément les écosystèmes fragiles et les habitats sensibles du sud-ouest de la mer des Caraïbes (**II**). L'appréhension de ces aspects permettra ainsi à la Cour de constater que la Colombie a conduit des activités d'observation et d'information à des fins environnementales dans la mer des Caraïbes en plein respect du droit international, et notamment de la convention de Carthagène. Ce faisant, la Colombie ne saurait avoir enfreint les droits souverains du Nicaragua (**III**).

I. Les aspects environnementaux font partie intégrante du présent différend

9. Contrairement à ce que le Nicaragua a prétendu dans ses écritures[75] et lors du premier tour des plaidoiries orales, les aspects environnementaux du présent différend sont loin d'être artificiels

---

[74] Voir, par exemple, PNUE, *Une stratégie de survie pour nos océans et nos côtes*, Genève, 2000, p. 11, disponible à l'adresse suivante : https://unep.ch/iuc/info/seas/RSbooklet-F.pdf.

[75] RN, par. 1.19-1.20.

ou marginaux. Les hésitations et volte-face du Nicaragua témoignent par elles-mêmes du manque total d'assurance du Nicaragua sur la question.

10. Dans sa réplique, le Nicaragua se réfugiait principalement derrière le fait que la Cour a déclaré inadmissibles les demandes reconventionnelles de la Colombie en relation avec l'environnement, afin de nier toute pertinence aux aspects environnementaux[76]. Le Nicaragua semble s'être rendu enfin à l'évidence puisqu'aucun de ses conseils n'a réitéré ces arguments fort douteux à l'oral.

11. Il va de soi que la Cour n'a jamais indiqué que la protection de l'environnement et de l'habitat naturel des Raizals est exclue du présent différend. Ce n'est qu'à présent que la Cour *peut* et *doit* apprécier «la licéité de la conduite éventuelle [de la Colombie] au regard des obligations que le droit international [lui] impose»[77] ; ce n'est qu'à présent que la Cour *peut* et *doit* s'exprimer sur le fait de savoir si la Colombie est en mesure, en vertu du droit international, d'observer si les écosystèmes fragiles de la mer des Caraïbes sont menacés par les navires, y inclus tout navire nicaraguayen, et le cas échéant informer lesdits navires du caractère illicite et dommageable de leurs activités ou opérations.

12. Afin d'esquiver les aspects environnementaux, le Nicaragua est demeuré silencieux sur les écosystèmes de la mer des Caraïbes durant son premier tour de plaidoiries. Nulle mention n'a été faite de la mer des Caraïbes ; et nulle référence n'a été faite aux écosystèmes. Quel silence assourdissant !

13. En plus d'être assourdissant, c'est un silence qui en dit long sur l'absence de perspective environnementale du Nicaragua. Et, en agissant de la sorte, le Nicaragua a fait fi des questions environnementales et n'a pas répondu aux arguments factuels et juridiques précis que la Colombie a soulevés tout au long de ses écritures. La Cour doit en tirer toutes les conséquences juridiques dans la mesure où le Nicaragua, pour paraphraser votre juridiction, refuse d'assister la Cour dans le règlement du différend, *dans toute sa dimension*[78].

---

[76] RN, par. 1.21 et par. 2.15.

[77] *Conséquences juridiques de l'édification d'un mur dans le territoire palestinien occupé, avis consultatif du 9 juillet 2004, C.I.J. Recueil 2004 (I)*, p. 155, par. 41.

[78] *Usines de pâte à papier sur le fleuve Uruguay (Argentine c. Uruguay), arrêt, C.I.J. Recueil 2010 (I)*, p. 71, par. 163.

14. Les préoccupations légitimes de la Colombie sur la protection des environnements concernés ne constituent pas un «prétexte pour s'adjuger … des «obligations» de protection de l'environnement»[79] comme le soutient à tort le professeur Pellet. Ces préoccupations découlent de la sensibilité et de la vulnérabilité des écosystèmes et des habitats qui composent ces environnements, et en particulier celui des Raizals.

II. La particularité des écosystèmes et des habitats de l'environnement marin du sud-ouest de la mer des Caraïbes et de l'habitat des Raizals

15. L'espace en cause dans le présent différend est celui de l'environnement marin du sud-ouest de la mer des Caraïbes. Il n'est point réduit au territoire du Nicaragua et encore moins à sa mer territoriale ou à sa zone économique exclusive (ZEE) ; les écosystèmes qui en dépendent ne sont pas la propriété du Nicaragua. L'environnement marin en cause repose sur des écosystèmes qui sont interdépendants, interreliés et formant un tout naturel. C'est l'interdépendance et la fragilité de ces écosystèmes qui requièrent que tout Etat riverain de la mer des Caraïbes y prête une attention particulière (**A**). A cette vulnérabilité écosystémique est liée une vulnérabilité humaine. En effet, les écosystèmes en question sont également particuliers et sensibles du fait de la fonction qu'ils remplissent : ils servent d'habitat, de cadre de vie et de subsistance pour les communautés autochtones vivant dans l'espace marin du sud-ouest de la mer des Caraïbes, et notamment pour les Raizals (**B**).

A. La fragilité des écosystèmes de l'environnement marin du sud-ouest de la mer des Caraïbes

16. Le Nicaragua est sans doute frappé d'amnésie juridique lorsqu'il affirme, comme il l'a fait dans ses écritures, de manière péremptoire, que l'environnement marin du sud-ouest de la mer des Caraïbes ne présente pas de caractéristiques spéciales[80]. En effet, il s'inscrit en porte-à-faux avec la convention de Carthagène, à laquelle il est partie. Le préambule de cette convention, que vous trouvez à l'onglet n° 9 du dossier des juges, évoque avec force «les caractéristiques hydrographiques et écologiques *spéciales* de la région»[81]. L'une des caractéristiques spéciales a trait aux écosystèmes.

---

[79] CR 2021/13, p. 36, par. 32 (Pellet).

[80] RN, par. 1.13.

[81] Dossier des juges, onglets n°s 8 et 9, convention de Carthagène (les italiques sont de moi).

En particulier, une réserve de biosphère dont l'importance est reconnue par l'UNESCO[82] se trouve naturellement interconnectée à cette portion de la mer des Caraïbes[83]. Il s'agit du Seaflower Biosphere Reserve, inscrit par les instances de l'UNESCO dans son réseau mondial des réserves de biosphère à la demande de la Colombie en septembre 2000[84].

17. Les préoccupations environnementales de la Colombie sont donc loin d'être inédites et n'ont aucun lien avec les questions de délimitation maritime comme l'a sous-entendu l'agent du Nicaragua. Ces préoccupations ne sont d'ailleurs pas propres à la Colombie.

18. L'Assemblée générale des Nations Unies a, par exemple, depuis 1999, pleinement reconnu la fragilité des écosystèmes de cette région, en incluant l'environnement marin du sud-ouest de la mer des Caraïbes à son agenda. Dès la première de ces résolutions sur la question, ainsi que vous le verrez à l'onglet n° 10 du dossier des juges, l'Assemblée générale a mis en relief le caractère semi-fermé de la mer des Caraïbes et la vulnérabilité qui en résulte pour les écosystèmes[85].

19. Les résolutions subséquemment adoptées soulignent toutes la fragilité des écosystèmes en réitérant que la mer des Caraïbes «renferme une diversité biologique exceptionnelle et des écosystèmes extrêmement fragiles»[86]. Comme cela apparaît à l'onglet n° 11 du dossier des juges, les résolutions de l'Assemblée générale prennent également note du fait que les chefs d'Etat et de gouvernement de l'Association des Etats de la Caraïbe — dont le Nicaragua et la Colombie sont

---

[82] DC, par. 2.110-2.111. Voir aussi, International Co-ordinating Council of the Man and the Biosphere (MAB) Programme, Twenty-sixth session, 10-14 June 2014, Final Report, Document SC-14/CONF.226/15, p. 85, disponible à l'adresse suivante : http://www.unesco.org /new/fileadmin/MULTIMEDIA/HQ/SC/pdf/SC-14-CONF-226-14- Information_on_Seaflower-eng-rev.pdf.

[83] CMC, vol. II, fig. 2.2, p. 676.

[84] International Co-ordinating Council of the Man and the Biosphere (MAB) Programme, Sixteenth session, 6-10 November 2000, Final Report, Document SC.2000/CONF.208/CLD.16, p. 21, disponible à l'adresse suivante : (français) https://unesdoc.unesco.org/ark:/48223/pf0000122703_fre ; (anglais) https://unesdoc.unesco.org/ark:/48223/pf0000122703 (dernière consultation le 20 septembre 2021).

[85] Dossier des juges, onglet n° 10, résolution 54/225 du 22 décembre 1999 :

> «la zone de la mer des Caraïbes, qui est presque totalement séparée de la haute mer par des masses continentales ou insulaires, est caractérisée par une diversité biologique exceptionnelle et des écosystèmes très fragiles, tels que le deuxième système corallien du monde, le fait que la plupart des Etats, pays et territoires sont fortement tributaires de leurs zones côtières et du milieu marin en général pour répondre à leurs besoins et réaliser leurs objectifs en matière de développement durable».

[86] Voir la résolution 73/229 du 20 décembre 2018. Voir également résolutions 55/203 du 20 décembre 2000, 57/261 du 20 décembre 2002, 59/230 du 22 décembre 2004, 61/197 du 20 décembre 2006, 63/214 du 19 décembre 2008, 65/155 du 20 décembre 2010, 67/205 du 21 décembre 2012, 69/216 du 19 décembre 2014 et 71/224 du 21 décembre 2016.

membres — se sont fermement engagés à prendre les mesures requises pour garantir que la mer des Caraïbes soit désignée «zone spéciale dans le contexte du développement durable»[87].

20. La Cour, en tant qu'organe judiciaire principal des Nations Unies, et conformément à sa pratique jurisprudentielle, se doit d'accorder une attention particulière à ces nombreuses résolutions de l'Assemblée générale des Nations Unies. Ces résolutions ont pour dénominateur commun d'encourager *tous* les Etats côtiers de la mer des Caraïbes et de la communauté internationale dans son ensemble à protéger les écosystèmes fragiles de cette mer semi-fermée.

21. Les positions du Nicaragua s'inscrivent ainsi à contre-courant des positions de la communauté internationale telles que reflétées dans ces résolutions mais aussi dans les rapports du Secrétaire général de l'ONU. Et vous trouverez dans l'onglet n° 12 du dossier des juges, un extrait du Rapport du Secrétaire général dans lequel il est fait état du fait que cette mer semi-fermée représente «le plus complexe, sur le plan géopolitique, des grands écosystèmes marins dans le monde» et «le patrimoine commun des peuples de la région des Caraïbes»[88].

22. Afin de minimiser, dans le contexte du présent différend, l'importance des caractéristiques spéciales de l'environnement marin du sud-ouest de la mer des Caraïbes, le Nicaragua a soutenu dans ses écritures que les caractéristiques en cause ne sont pertinentes qu'à des fins de délimitation et ont déjà été prises en compte par la Cour dans l'affaire du *Différend territorial et maritime*[89].

23. Toutefois, le Nicaragua se trompe. Les caractéristiques spéciales de la mer des Caraïbes existent en dehors des questions de délimitation. Les écosystèmes demeurent des écosystèmes indépendamment des frontières tracées ci et là et des questions de souveraineté. En d'autres termes, et pour paraphraser la Cour, il convient «d'appréhender l'écosystème *dans son ensemble*»[90].

---

[87] Dossier des juges, onglet n° 11, résolution 71/224 du 21 décembre 2016, par. 2. Voir aussi le paragraphe 11 de la même résolution, dans laquelle l'Assemblée générale «*[s]e félicite*, à cet égard, de la désignation de la région des Caraïbes comme zone spéciale, laquelle a pris effet en mai 2011».

[88] Dossier des juges, onglet n° 12, «Vers le développement durable de la mer des Caraïbes pour les générations présentes et à venir» et son annexe «Progrès réalisés dans l'application de la résolution 71/224 de l'Assemblée générale, rapport de la Commission de la mer des Caraïbes de l'Association des Etats de la Caraïbe», doc. A/73/225, 24 juillet 2018, par. 1 de l'annexe.

[89] RN, par. 1.13.

[90] *Certaines activités menées par le Nicaragua dans la région frontalière (Costa Rica c. Nicaragua), indemnisation, arrêt, C.I.J. Recueil 2018 (I)*, p. 37, par. 78 (les italiques sont de moi).

24. La convention de Carthagène s'inscrit dans cette logique écosystémique. Son objet et son but sont d'encourager les Etats parties à adopter une approche d'ensemble en matière de protection de l'environnement de la mer des Caraïbes, notamment pour préserver son «équilibre écologique»[91].

25. C'est du fait de l'objectif de préservation de l'équilibre écologique que la Colombie mène des activités d'observation et d'information à des fins environnementales dans la mer des Caraïbes en conformité avec l'objet et le but de la convention de Carthagène, ainsi qu'avec le droit international coutumier. La Colombie n'enfreint d'aucune manière les droits du Nicaragua. Je reviendrai sur ce point.

B. La vulnérabilité de l'habitat des Raizals

26. Les écosystèmes de l'environnement marin du sud-ouest de la mer des Caraïbes constituent un habitat dans lequel évoluent les Raizals, et dont la qualité de leur vie ainsi que de leur santé dépend. Dans plusieurs de ses résolutions sur la mer des Caraïbes, l'Assemblée générale des Nations Unies a mis en exergue le lien intrinsèque entre la protection des écosystèmes et la préservation des habitats des communautés[92]. Pour les Raizals, leur habitat n'est pas qu'une «source régulière» de subsistance… Il remplit une fonction *vitale*. Ainsi que l'a souligné avec autorité la Cour interaméricaine des droits de l'homme dans un avis consultatif pionnier,

> «[there is] an undeniable relationship between the protection of the environment and the realization of other human rights, in that environmental degradation … affect[s] the real enjoyment of human rights»[93].

27. Mesdames et Messieurs de la Cour, là encore que peut reprocher le Nicaragua à la Colombie ? Tout simplement, rien. La Colombie a le devoir, cela notamment en vertu de ses obligations découlant de la convention interaméricaine des droits de l'homme, de respecter, de

---

[91] Voir dossier des juges, onglet nº 8, préambule de la convention de Carthagène, qui met l'accent sur «la menace que la pollution et le fait que l'environnement ne soit pas suffisamment pris en compte dans le processus de développement font peser sur le milieu marin, son équilibre écologique, ses ressources et ses utilisations légitimes».

[92] Voir résolution 73/229 du 20 décembre 2018.

[93] Dossier des juges, onglet nº 13, Cour interaméricaine des droits de l'homme, avis consultatif OC-23/17, 15 novembre 2017, demandé par la République de Colombie, *The Environment and Human Rights (State obligations in relation to the environment in the context of the protection and guarantee of the rights to life and to personal integrity: interpretation and scope of Articles 4(1) and 5(1) in relation to Articles 1(1) and 2 of the American Convention on Human Rights)*, par. 47.

protéger et promouvoir le droit à un environnement écologiquement sain des Raizals, et ce au-delà de sa juridiction nationale[94].

28. Le droit des Raizals à vivre dans un habitat écologiquement sain est étroitement lié à la préservation des écosystèmes de l'environnement marin du sud-ouest de la mer des Caraïbes et à la lutte contre les pratiques de pêche déprédatrices. Cela est d'autant plus vrai dans le contexte latino-américain que la Cour interaméricaine des droits de l'homme dans l'avis consultatif que je viens de mentionner, s'appuyant à maintes reprises sur la jurisprudence de la Cour de céans, a reconnu le lien inextricable et intrinsèque entre les droits de l'homme, la protection de l'environnement et le développement durable[95].

29. Il apparaît clairement que, dans le contexte latino-américain, le facteur humain joue un rôle considérable dans la protection de l'environnement, et surtout lorsque les communautés en cause dépendent pour leur existence et leur mode de vie d'un environnement particulier, comme c'est le cas des Raizals. La Cour est donc invitée, comme elle l'a fait dans l'affaire *Diallo*, à interpréter les droits et obligations en question à la lumière de la jurisprudence constante de la Cour interaméricaine des droits de l'homme relative au droit à un environnement sain des communautés autochtones[96]. Plus spécifiquement, il est important que la Cour garde à l'esprit que, dans le contexte du système interaméricain des droits de l'homme, la notion de «compétence» («jurisdiction» en anglais), interprétée de bonne foi en tenant compte du contexte ainsi que de l'objet et du but de la convention interaméricaine, signifie «that it is not limited to the concept of national territory, but covers a broader concept that includes certain ways of exercising jurisdiction beyond the territory of the State in question»[97].

---

[94] Dossier des juges, onglet n° 13, Cour interaméricaine des droits de l'homme, avis consultatif OC-23/17, 15 novembre 2017, demandé par la République de Colombie, *The Environment and Human Rights (State obligations in relation to the environment in the context of the protection and guarantee of the rights to life and to personal integrity: interpretation and scope of Articles 4(1) and 5(1) in relation to Articles 1(1) and 2 of the American Convention on Human Rights)*, par. 104 *a)* et *c)*.

[95] *Ibid.*, par. 59.

[96] Voir, par exemple, CMC, par. 3.80-3.82.

[97] Dossier des juges, onglet n° 14, Cour interaméricaine des droits de l'homme, avis consultatif OC-23/17, 15 novembre 2017, demandé par la République de Colombie, *The Environment and Human Rights (State obligations in relation to the environment in the context of the protection and guarantee of the rights to life and to personal integrity: interpretation and scope of Articles 4(1) and 5(1) in relation to Articles 1(1) and 2 of the American Convention on Human Rights)*, par. 74.

30. Cela permettra à la Cour de se rendre à l'évidence : aucun droit souverain du Nicaragua n'a été violé par les activités d'observation et d'information à des fins environnementales ; ces dernières relèvent de la «compétence» de la Colombie à l'aune de la jurisprudence établie de la Cour interaméricaine des droits de l'homme.

31. En accordant «une grande considération à l'interprétation adoptée par cet organe indépendant, spécialement établi en vue de superviser l'application de ce traité»[98], la Cour contribuera au renforcement de la protection des communautés locales dans l'archipel des Caraïbes ainsi qu'à «la nécessaire clarté et ... l'indispensable cohérence du droit international»[99].

32. Il va donc de soi que les considérations expansionnistes de souveraineté invoquées par le Nicaragua ne peuvent pas éclipser les «considérations élémentaires d'humanité»[100]. Les zones économiques exclusives (ZEE) de chacun des Etats côtiers de la région font partie d'un environnement écosystémique et humain particulier et sensible. Elles n'existent pas en isolation clinique du reste de l'environnement marin de cette mer.

III. Les activités d'observation et d'information de la Colombie à des fins environnementales s'inscrivent dans le cadre de la convention de Carthagène

33. Madame la présidente, Mesdames et Messieurs les Membres de la Cour, en présence d'un environnement marin caractérisé par une vulnérabilité écologique et humaine, le problème qui se pose à la Cour est celui de l'étendue des droits et obligations des Etats riverains de la mer des Caraïbes en matière de protection de l'environnement marin.

34. Lesdits droits et obligations concourent tous vers un seul et même objectif : la protection des écosystèmes et des habitats fragiles du milieu marin de la mer des Caraïbes.

35. Cette exigence de protection découle, de prime abord, de l'obligation coutumière de diligence qui est «requise» de tous les Etats en matière environnementale et dont la jurisprudence de la Cour de céans s'est faite l'écho à plusieurs occasions[101]. Elle découle également, comme je l'ai

---

[98] *Ahmadou Sadio Diallo (République de Guinée c. République démocratique du Congo), fond, arrêt, C.I.J. Recueil 2010 (II)*, p. 663-664, par. 66.

[99] *Ibid.*

[100] *Détroit de Corfou (Royaume-Uni c. Albanie), fond, arrêt, C.I.J. Recueil 1949*, p. 22.

[101] Voir, par exemple, *Projet Gabčíkovo-Nagymaros (Hongrie/Slovaquie), arrêt, C.I.J. Recueil 1997*, p. 41, par. 53, et p. 78, par. 140 ; *Usines de pâte à papier sur le fleuve Uruguay (Argentine c. Uruguay), arrêt, C.I.J. Recueil 2010 (I)*, p. 55-56, par. 101.

évoqué, de l'obligation de protection de l'environnement marin reflétée dans la partie XII de la convention du droit de la mer, à laquelle, je le rappelle, le Nicaragua est partie.

36. Mais ce n'est pas que le droit international coutumier qui est en jeu. L'obligation de protection des écosystèmes de la mer des Caraïbes *dans son ensemble* repose en outre sur le régime spécial qui découle de la convention de Carthagène. Cette dernière sert de pilier majeur au régime juridique régissant la protection de l'environnement marin dans la région des Caraïbes. La Cour se doit d'apprécier les obligations de fond de la Colombie et du Nicaragua à l'aune de la convention de Carthagène comme elle l'a fait récemment entre le Costa Rica et le Nicaragua en tenant compte des conventions régionales applicables dans les relations entre les parties au différend[102]. La convention de Carthagène est un «accord détaillé et complet englobant la protection et le développement de l'environnement marin»[103]. Cet accord est *self-executing* et loin d'être un traité-cadre au sens où veut l'entendre le professeur Pellet ! En le qualifiant de la sorte, c'est le Nicaragua et non la Colombie qui fait «totalement fi de son texte et de sa portée»[104].

37. Le préambule de la convention de Carthagène indique clairement que les Etats qui l'ont négociée et ratifiée étaient tout à fait conscients «du *devoir* qui leur incombe de protéger le milieu marin de la mer des Caraïbes dans l'intérêt et pour l'agrément des générations présentes et futures»[105]. Et c'est à cette fin que les mêmes Etats se sont fixé comme «l'un de leurs principaux objectifs»[106] la «protection des écosystèmes du milieu marin» de la mer des Caraïbes[107].

38. Mesdames et Messieurs les juges, la convention de Carthagène a bel et bien été conclue dans l'idée que chaque Etat partie a un devoir de protection et de préservation de l'environnement marin dans sa globalité et son ensemble, y compris pour l'habitat des communautés vulnérables.

---

[102] *Certaines activités menées par le Nicaragua dans la région frontalière (Costa Rica c. Nicaragua)* et *Construction d'une route au Costa Rica le long du fleuve San Juan (Nicaragua c. Costa Rica), arrêt, C.I.J. Recueil 2015 (II)*, p. 726, par. 174 : «La Cour examinera à présent les allégations concernant la violation, par le Costa Rica, des obligations de fond lui incombant au titre du droit international coutumier et des conventions internationales applicables.»

[103] Convention pour la protection et la mise en valeur du milieu marin dans la région des Caraïbes, 2012, p. 12, disponible à l'adresse suivante : https://wedocs.unep.org/bitstream/handle/20.500.11822/27875/SPAWSTAC5_2012-fr.pdf?sequence=2&isAllowed=y.

[104] CR 2021/13, p. 35, par. 27 (Pellet).

[105] Dossier des juges, onglet nº 8, préambule de la convention de Carthagène (les italiques sont de moi).

[106] Dossier des juges, onglet nº 8, préambule de la convention de Carthagène.

[107] *Ibid.*

39. Cette interprétation est corroborée par le contexte de la convention qui permet de donner aussi un effet utile aux termes minutieusement choisis par les rédacteurs de la convention.

40. Comme cela apparaît à l'écran, l'article 10 de la convention de Carthagène prévoit la possibilité pour les parties d'adopter des mesures «individuelles» en vue de la protection des écosystèmes. Les mesures «individuelles» prises par la Colombie dans le cadre de ses activités d'observation et d'information à des fins environnementales ne constituent pas des mesures «unilatérales» comme l'entend le Nicaragua. Ce sont des mesures autorisées par ledit régime conventionnel mais aussi par le droit international coutumier contemporain.

41. Par conséquent, il ne fait pas de doute que la Colombie a le devoir, mais aussi est en droit — en vertu de la convention de Carthagène ainsi que du droit international général —, de mener des activités d'observation et d'information à des fins environnementales en vue de la préservation des écosystèmes fragiles du sud-ouest de la mer des Caraïbes et de l'habitat des Raizals, y compris dans la zone économique exclusive du Nicaragua, laquelle est indissociable de ces écosystèmes.

42. Madame la présidente, Mesdames et Messieurs de la Cour, qu'y a-t-il de mal à ce que la Colombie observe et informe lorsque des bateaux battant différents pavillons, y compris nicaraguayen, s'engagent dans des pratiques déprédatrices des ressources halieutiques, composantes essentielles de la biodiversité ? Qu'y a-t-il de mal à ce que la Colombie observe et informe en cas d'activités de pêche illégale, non reportée et non régulée susceptibles d'affecter de manière significative les écosystèmes fragiles de la mer des Caraïbes et le droit des Raizals de vivre dans un habitat écologiquement sain et durable ?

43. L'argument du Nicaragua qui consiste à dire qu'il a des droits exclusifs dans sa zone économique exclusive et que ces droits exclusifs empêcheraient tout autre Etat, et en particulier la Colombie, de procéder à des activités licites en relation avec l'environnement dans ladite zone n'est pas fondé. Le régime de la zone économique exclusive n'a jamais eu pour objectif d'exclure la possibilité pour des Etats tiers de mener des activités licites dans le cadre de la liberté de navigation et des autres usages pacifiques qui leur sont reconnus par le droit international coutumier.

44. Dans sa zone économique exclusive, un Etat doit s'assurer que ladite zone ne soit pas utilisée «aux fins d'actes contraires aux droits d'autres Etats»[108]. Le droit de protéger l'environnement marin du sud-ouest de la mer des Caraïbes et le droit des populations raizales à vivre dans un habitat sain font sans aucun doute partie de ces droits que le Nicaragua doit respecter et veiller à préserver.

Conclusion

45. Pour conclure, Madame la présidente, je crois pouvoir dire sans me tromper que rarement un Etat a été accusé gratuitement de la sorte devant la Cour. Le Nicaragua n'y est pas allé de main morte. Il a parlé sans cesse dans ses écritures et de façon quasi obsessionnelle de harcèlement et de «policing». Faute de pouvoir prouver ses dires, il décrit désormais la Colombie comme ayant le pouvoir de créer des «droits imaginaires»[109] dans les espaces maritimes du Nicaragua.

46. Mais, si imagination il y a, c'est du côté du Nicaragua qu'il faut aller la chercher. Comme je l'ai souligné, les activités d'observation et d'information à des fins environnementales de la Colombie s'inscrivent dans le cadre de ce que le droit international applicable au présent différend permet, notamment lorsque des écosystèmes fragiles et des habitats vulnérables comme celui des Raizals sont en cause. De telles activités ne violent en aucun cas les droits souverains du Nicaragua.

47. Mesdames et Messieurs les juges, en considérant les faits invoqués par le Nicaragua, la Colombie vous demande respectueusement de prendre dûment compte des instruments et principes juridiques qui vous ont été présentés, et en particulier le régime spécial de la convention de Carthagène et les principes de droit international coutumier applicables.

48. La Colombie aurait souhaité qu'un climat de coopération entre le Nicaragua et la Colombie s'instaure afin de protéger au mieux les écosystèmes de l'environnement du sud-ouest de la mer des Caraïbes et l'habitat des Raizals. Le régime spécial mis en place à travers la convention de Carthagène invite en effet les Etats parties à cette convention à identifier de manière proactive des solutions et stratégies en vue de la préservation de ces écosystèmes fragiles et essentiels pour l'environnement global. L'arrêt de pratiques déprédatrices de pêche qui ont sans aucun doute un effet

---

[108] *Détroit de Corfou (Royaume-Uni c. Albanie), fond, arrêt, C.I.J. Recueil 1949*, p. 22.

[109] CR 2021/13, p. 40, par. 46 (Pellet).

nocif sur l'environnement compte parmi ces solutions et stratégies. Malheureusement, l'attitude du Nicaragua durant le premier tour de plaidoiries orales traduit son manque de volonté à s'engager de bonne foi dans cette voie. Espérons que la Cour pourra jouer un rôle décisif dans l'instauration d'un tel climat de coopération.

49. Je vous remercie de votre attention. Madame la présidente, puis-je vous demander de donner la parole à M. Rodman Bundy ?

The PRESIDENT: I thank Professor Boisson de Chazournes for her remarks, and I invite Mr. Bundy to take the floor now. Mr. Bundy, we started a few minutes late this morning, so if you wish to continue until approximately five minutes after the hour, that would be fine.

Mr. BUNDY:

COLOMBIA DID NOT VIOLATE NICARAGUA'S SOVEREIGN RIGHTS

1. Thank you very much. Madam President, Members of the Court. As always, I am aware of the honour of appearing before the Court — I am glad to be in the Great Hall — and the opportunity to represent the Republic of Colombia. I would also like to associate myself with the remarks of others regarding the untimely passing of Judge Crawford. He was a good friend and colleague, and even a good opponent, and he will be sorely missed.

Introduction

2. My colleagues having dealt with the legal framework within which Nicaragua's claims fall to be assessed, my task this morning and continuing into the afternoon is to address the first part of Nicaragua's claim. This principally involves the assertion that the conduct of Colombia's naval vessels and aircraft have violated Nicaragua's sovereign rights and maritime spaces under customary international law.

3. This aspect of the case relates to a number of events — or, to put it another way — a number of alleged wrongful acts that Nicaragua has referred to in its written pleadings. *Thirteen* of these events are said to have taken place *before* 27 November 2013, the day that Colombia's denunciation of the Pact of Bogotá took effect. That was one day after Nicaragua lodged its Application on 26 November 2013. In other words, these 13 events formed the main basis on which Nicaragua filed

its Application alleging a violation of its sovereign rights. They inevitably constituted the subject-matter of the Application because there was nothing else. That being the case, it was astonishing, to say the least, that none of Nicaragua's counsel made the slightest reference to any of these events in their first-round presentations on Monday. While Colombia was accused of trying to "erase" events that took place after the Pact of Bogotá ceased to be in force for Colombia[110], it is Nicaragua that seeks to erase the very elements that formed the basis of its Application.

4. The rest of the events adduced by Nicaragua relate to matters that allegedly transpired *after* the critical dates of 26 and 27 November 2013. As I will explain, quite apart from the fact that these events did not form part of the subject-matter of the Application, the Court lacks jurisdiction *ratione temporis* under the Pact of Bogotá to consider any events claimed to have occurred after 27 November 2013.

5. In order to demonstrate the ill-founded nature of Nicaragua's claims, my presentation will be in three parts.

6. In the first part, I will address the 13 elements of Nicaragua's claim over which the Court has jurisdiction because they relate to events that are said to have occurred at a time when Colombia was still bound by the Pact of Bogotá. But I will show that these are not really "incidents" — as Nicaragua calls them — at all. They are "non-events" unsupported by any contemporary evidence, which at the time were not viewed by Nicaragua as having the slightest impact on its sovereign rights, and which did not in any manner violate those rights. As I said, it was striking that none of Nicaragua's counsel made any reference to these events on Monday, although there was nothing else on which Nicaragua's Application could be based.

7. In the second part of my presentation, I will turn to matters referred to by Nicaragua that took place *after* the critical date when Colombia was no longer a party to the Pact of Bogotá. Contrary to what was asserted on Monday, Colombia has shown in Appendix 1 to its Rejoinder that none of these events can be deemed to rise to the level of a violation of Nicaragua's sovereign rights.

8. Notwithstanding that, the key threshold point is that the Court lacks jurisdiction to consider whether any of these so-called "post-critical-date incidents" violated Nicaragua's sovereign rights,

---

[110] CR 2021/13, p. 59, para. 50 (Reichler).

because as of 27 November 2013, Colombia was no longer bound by the Pact of Bogotá. Under Articles XXXI and LVI of the Pact — Nicaragua only mentioned Article LVI on Monday, but XXXI, as I will show, is crucial — under Articles XXXI and LVI of the Pact, Colombia did not consent to the Court's jurisdiction to rule on any dispute concerning the existence of facts, if established, that are claimed to have taken place *after* the Pact was no longer in force.

9. In the third part of my pleading, I will briefly address two new Nicaraguan claims that were not mentioned in the Application, and not even mentioned in the Memorial, which Nicaragua now advances as violations of its sovereign rights. These concern the allegation and the assertion that Colombia has entered into petroleum contracts for the exploration and exploitation of hydrocarbons in maritime areas where Nicaragua has sovereign rights, and its claim that Colombia has licensed fishing boats to fish in violation also of Nicaragua's sovereign rights. And as I shall show, neither of these allegations is true[111].

I. Alleged events prior to the critical date

10. With that introduction, Madam President, I think if I could start for a couple of minutes more, I could give a flavour of the pre-critical-date events: the events on which the Application must have been based, that are said to have occurred before 26 November 2013 when Nicaragua filed its Application. So I am dealing with the events that allegedly occurred before the critical date, between the Court's 2012 Judgment and 26-27 November when the Pact of Bogotá ceased to be in force for Colombia. These are the events which I have said that Nicaragua is clearly embarrassed to discuss even though they must have formed the basis of the Application. Now, to assist, I have had placed in tab 20 of your folders a chronological list of these events together with the dates of certain key statements made by Nicaraguan officials, which provide very important context for Nicaragua's claims and represent clear admissions against interest. Given that Colombia has addressed the details of each event in its written pleadings, I will limit myself to summarizing the main points[112].

11. My first point is that Nicaragua has not filed a single piece of first-hand evidence for any of these so-called "incidents". There are no contemporary reports of any such events; no documented

---

[111] CMC, para. 4.46; RC, paras. 3.111-3.123.

[112] See CMC, pp. 168-186, and RC, pp. 111-128.

facts; no complaints by Nicaraguan fishermen or the Nicaraguan Naval Force at the time; and no protests to Colombia. In itself, this is a strong indication that Nicaragua did not consider that Colombia was violating its sovereign rights. And it undoubtedly explains Nicaragua's silence on these matters on Monday.

12. For example, the first two events (Nos. 1 and 2 on the list in tab 20) are based on no more than vague media reports emanating from *Colombian* sources that do not evidence any violation of Nicaragua's sovereign rights. Given that there is no first-hand evidence or complaints from Nicaragua, it is not surprising that Nicaragua has not, despite several rounds of written pleadings, been able to specify where the matters of which it complains took place or how its sovereign rights were supposedly violated.

13. The third item on the list is based on a statement referred to on a Colombian website in September 2013, reportedly made by former President Santos when he visited the island of San Andrés to the effect that Colombia was carrying out a "sovereignty exercise" "off the coast of San Andrés"[113], a Colombian island, *in Colombian waters*. However, Nicaragua has again not submitted any evidence showing how Nicaragua's sovereign rights were violated.

14. Apart from these deficiencies, it is appropriate to recall the Court's observation in the *Croatia* v. *Serbia* case that evidence such as press articles are merely of a secondary nature and may only be used to confirm the existence of facts established by other evidence[114]. With respect to Nicaragua's assertions, there is no other evidence.

15. As for the next ten items on the list — Nos. 4 through 13 — the only so-called "evidence" Nicaragua has submitted is an account attached to a letter dated 26 August 2014 —, almost a year after the Application — sent by Rear Admiral Marvin Corrales, who was the Head of Nicaragua's Naval Force, to the Nicaraguan Ministry of Foreign Affairs in response to a query from the Ministry asking whether there had been any "incidents". This single source, prepared almost a year *after* Nicaragua filed its Application and to which no contemporaneous supporting documentation was attached, was filed as Annex 23-A to Nicaragua's Memorial. Given that Admiral Corrales' letter was

[113] MN, para. 2.27.

[114] *Application of the Convention on the Prevention and Punishment of the Crime of Genocide (Croatia* v. *Serbia), Judgment, I.C.J. Reports 2015 (I)*, p. 87, para. 239. See also *Military and Paramilitary Activities in and against Nicaragua (Nicaragua* v. *United States of America), Merits, Judgment, I.C.J. Reports 1986,* p. 40, para. 62.

sent just a few weeks before Nicaragua filed its Memorial, and long after the events complained of allegedly occurred, it is pretty clear that it was prepared for purposes of this litigation.

16. But that is scarcely sufficient to prove any violations on Colombia's part. As the Court observed in its Judgment in the *Armed Activities* case between the Democratic Republic of the Congo and Uganda: "The Court will treat with caution evidentiary materials specially prepared for this case and also materials emanating from a single source. It will prefer contemporaneous evidence from persons with direct knowledge."[115] In the present case, there is no such evidence.

Thank you, Madam President, distinguished judges, I think that may be an appropriate point to pause.

The PRESIDENT: I thank Mr. Bundy, whose statement — the beginning of his statement — brings to an end this morning's sitting. Oral argument in the case will resume this afternoon at 3 p.m.

The sitting is adjourned.

The Court rose at 1.05 p.m.

---

[115] *Armed Activities on the Territory of the Congo (Democratic Republic of the Congo* v. *Uganda), Judgment, I.C.J. Reports 2005*, p. 201, para. 61.

Corrigé
Corrected

CR 2021/15

International Court of Justice

THE HAGUE

Cour internationale de Justice

LA HAYE

YEAR 2021

Public sitting

held on Wednesday 22 September 2021, at 3 p.m., at the Peace Palace,

President Donoghue presiding,

***in the case concerning* Alleged Violations of Sovereign Rights and Maritime Spaces in the Caribbean Sea (Nicaragua *v.* Colombia)**

VERBATIM RECORD

ANNÉE 2021

Audience publique

tenue le mercredi 22 septembre 2021, à 15 heures, au Palais de la Paix,

sous la présidence de Mme Donoghue, présidente,

***en l'affaire relative à des* Violations alléguées de droits souverains et d'espaces maritimes dans la mer des Caraïbes (Nicaragua c. Colombie)**

COMPTE RENDU

Present:	President	Donoghue
	Vice-President	Gevorgian
	Judges	Tomka
		Abraham
		Bennouna
		Yusuf
		Xue
		Sebutinde
		Bhandari
		Salam
		Iwasawa
		Nolte
	Judges *ad hoc*	Daudet
		McRae
	Registrar	Gautier

Présents :	Mme	Donoghue, présidente
	M.	Gevorgian, vice-président
	MM.	Tomka
		Abraham
		Bennouna
		Yusuf
	Mmes	Xue
		Sebutinde
	MM.	Bhandari
		Salam
		Iwasawa
		Nolte, juges
	MM.	Daudet
		McRae, juges *ad hoc*
	M.	Gautier, greffier

The Government of Nicaragua is represented by:

H.E. Mr. Carlos José Argüello Gómez, Ambassador of the Republic of Nicaragua to the Kingdom of the Netherlands,

as Agent and Counsel;

Mr. Alex Oude Elferink, Director, Netherlands Institute for the Law of the Sea, Professor of International Law of the Sea at Utrecht University,

Mr. Vaughan Lowe, QC, Emeritus Chichele Professor of Public International Law, University of Oxford, member of the Institut de droit international, member of the Bar of England and Wales,

Mr. Lawrence H. Martin, Attorney at Law, Foley Hoag LLP, member of the Bars of the United States Supreme Court, the District of Columbia and the Commonwealth of Massachusetts,

Mr. Alain Pellet, Emeritus Professor of the University Paris Nanterre, former Chairman of the International Law Commission, President of the Institut de droit international,

Mr. Paul Reichler, Attorney at Law, Foley Hoag LLP, member of the Bars of the United States Supreme Court and the District of Columbia,

as Counsel and Advocates;

Ms Claudia Loza Obregon, Legal Adviser, Ministry of Foreign Affairs of Nicaragua,

Ms Tessa Barsac, Consultant in International Law, Master (University Paris Nanterre), LLM (Leiden University),

as Assistant Counsel;

Mr. Robin Cleverly, MA, DPhil, CGeol, FGS, Law of the Sea Consultant, Marbdy Consulting Ltd,

as Scientific and Technical Adviser;

Ms Sherly Noguera de Argüello, MBA,

as Administrator.

The Government of Colombia is represented by:

H.E. Mr. Carlos Gustavo Arrieta Padilla, former Judge of the Council of State of Colombia, former Attorney General of Colombia and former Ambassador of Colombia to the Netherlands,

as Agent;

H.E. Mr. Manuel José Cepeda Espinosa, former President of the Constitutional Court of Colombia, former Permanent Delegate of Colombia to UNESCO and former Ambassador of Colombia to the Swiss Confederation,

as Co-Agent;

Le Gouvernement du Nicaragua est représenté par :

S. Exc. M. Carlos José Argüello Gómez, ambassadeur de la République du Nicaragua auprès du Royaume des Pays-Bas,

comme agent et conseil ;

M. Alex Oude Elferink, directeur de l'Institut néerlandais du droit de la mer, professeur de droit international de la mer à l'Université d'Utrecht,

M. Vaughan Lowe, QC, professeur émérite de droit international public à l'Université d'Oxford, titulaire de la chaire Chichele, membre de l'Institut de droit international, membre du barreau d'Angleterre et du pays de Galles,

M. Lawrence H. Martin, avocat au cabinet Foley Hoag LLP, membre des barreaux de la Cour suprême des Etats-Unis d'Amérique, du district de Colombia et du Commonwealth du Massachusetts,

M. Alain Pellet, professeur émérite de l'Université Paris Nanterre, ancien président de la Commission du droit international, président de l'Institut de droit international,

M. Paul Reichler, avocat au cabinet Foley Hoag LLP, membre des barreaux de la Cour suprême des Etats-Unis d'Amérique et du district de Colombia,

comme conseils et avocats ;

Mme Claudia Loza Obregon, conseillère juridique auprès du ministère des affaires étrangères du Nicaragua,

Mme Tessa Barsac, consultante en droit international, master (Université Paris Nanterre), LLM (Université de Leyde),

comme conseils adjoints ;

M. Robin Cleverly, MA, DPhil, CGeol, FGS, consultant en droit de la mer, Marbdy Consulting Ltd,

comme conseiller scientifique et technique ;

Mme Sherly Noguera de Argüello, MBA,

comme administrateur.

Le Gouvernement de la Colombie est représenté par :

S. Exc. M. Carlos Gustavo Arrieta Padilla, ancien juge au conseil d'Etat colombien, ancien *Procurador General de la Nación* et ancien ambassadeur de Colombie aux Pays-Bas,

comme agent ;

S. Exc. M. Manuel José Cepeda Espinosa, ancien président de la Cour constitutionnelle de Colombie, ancien représentant permanent de la Colombie auprès de l'UNESCO et ancien ambassadeur de Colombie auprès de la Confédération suisse,

comme coagent ;

H.E. Ms Marta Lucía Ramírez Blanco, Vice-President and Minister for Foreign Affairs of the Republic of Colombia,

H.E. Mr. Everth Hawkins Sjogreen, Governor of San Andrés, Providencia and Santa Catalina, Colombia,

as National Authorities;

Mr. W. Michael Reisman, McDougal Professor of International Law at Yale University, member of the Institut de droit international,

Mr. Rodman R. Bundy, former *avocat à la Cour d'appel de Paris*, member of the Bar of the State of New York, partner at Squire Patton Boggs LLP, Singapore,

Sir Michael Wood, KCMG, member of the International Law Commission, member of the Bar of England and Wales,

Mr. Eduardo Valencia-Ospina, former Registrar and Deputy-Registrar of the International Court of Justice, member and former Special Rapporteur and Chair of the International Law Commission, former Chair of the Latin American Society of International Law,

Mr. Jean-Marc Thouvenin, Professor at the University Paris Nanterre, Secretary-General of the Hague Academy of International Law, associate member of the Institut de droit international, member of the Paris Bar, Sygna Partners,

Ms Laurence Boisson de Chazournes, Professor of International Law and International Organization at the University of Geneva, member of the Institut de droit international,

H.E. Mr. Kent Francis James, former Ambassador of Colombia to Belize, former Ambassador of Colombia to Jamaica,

as Counsel and Advocates;

Mr. Andrés Villegas Jaramillo, LLM, Co-ordinator, Group of Affairs before the International Court of Justice at the Ministry of Foreign Affairs of Colombia, member of the Legal Sub-Commission of the Caribbean Sea Commission, Association of Caribbean States,

Mr. Makane Moïse Mbengue, Professor at the University of Geneva, Director of the Department of Public International Law and International Organization, associate member of the Institut de droit international,

Mr. Luke Vidal, member of the Paris Bar, Sygna Partners,

Mr. Eran Sthoeger, Esq., member of the Bar of the State of New York, Adjunct Professor of International Law at Brooklyn Law School and Seton Hall Law School,

Mr. Alvin Yap, Advocate and Solicitor of the Supreme Court of Singapore, Squire Patton Boggs LLP, Singapore,

Mr. Lorenzo Palestini, PhD, Lecturer at the Graduate Institute of International and Development Studies and at the University of Geneva,

as Counsel;

S. Exc. Mme Marta Lucía Ramírez Blanco, vice-présidente et ministre des affaires étrangères de la République de Colombie,

S. Exc. M. Everth Hawkins Sjogreen, gouverneur de San Andrés, Providencia et Santa Catalina, Colombie,

comme représentants de l'Etat ;

M. W. Michael Reisman, professeur de droit international à l'Université de Yale, titulaire de la chaire McDougal, membre de l'Institut de droit international,

M. Rodman R. Bundy, ancien avocat à la Cour d'appel de Paris, membre du barreau de l'Etat de New York, associé au cabinet Squire Patton Boggs LLP (Singapour),

Sir Michael Wood, KCMG, membre de la Commission du droit international, membre du barreau d'Angleterre et du pays de Galles,

M. Eduardo Valencia-Ospina, ancien greffier et greffier adjoint de la Cour internationale de Justice, membre et ancien rapporteur spécial et président de la Commission du droit international, ancien président de l'association latino-américaine de droit international,

M. Jean-Marc Thouvenin, professeur à l'Université Paris Nanterre, secrétaire général de l'Académie de droit international de La Haye, membre associé de l'Institut de droit international, membre du barreau de Paris, cabinet Sygna Partners,

Mme Laurence Boisson de Chazournes, professeure de droit international public et organisation internationale à l'Université de Genève, membre de l'Institut de droit international,

S. Exc. M. Kent Francis James, ancien ambassadeur de Colombie au Belize et ancien ambassadeur de Colombie en Jamaïque,

comme conseils et avocats ;

M. Andrés Villegas Jaramillo, LLM, coordonnateur du groupe chargé des affaires portées devant la Cour internationale de Justice au sein du ministère des affaires étrangères de la Colombie, membre de la sous-commission juridique relevant de la Commission de la mer des Caraïbes de l'Association des Etats de la Caraïbe,

M. Makane Moïse Mbengue, professeur à l'Université de Genève, directeur du département de droit international public et organisation internationale, membre associé de l'Institut de droit international,

M. Luke Vidal, membre du barreau de Paris, cabinet Sygna Partners,

M. Eran Sthoeger, membre du barreau de l'Etat de New York, professeur adjoint de droit international à la Brooklyn Law School et à la faculté de droit de l'université de Seton Hall,

M. Alvin Yap, avocat et *solicitor* à la Cour suprême de Singapour, cabinet Squire Patton Boggs LLP (Singapour),

M. Lorenzo Palestini, PhD, chargé d'enseignement à l'Institut de hautes études internationales et du développement et à l'Université de Genève,

comme conseils ;

H.E. Mr. Juan José Quintana Aranguren, Head of Multilateral Affairs, former Ambassador of Colombia to the Netherlands,

H.E. Mr. Fernando Antonio Grillo Rubiano, Ambassador of the Republic of Colombia to the Kingdom of the Netherlands and Permanent Representative of Colombia to the Organisation for the Prohibition of Chemical Weapons,

Ms Jenny Sharyne Bowie Wilches, Second Secretary, Embassy of Colombia in the Netherlands,

Ms Viviana Andrea Medina Cruz, Second Secretary, Embassy of Colombia in the Netherlands,

Mr. Sebastián Correa Cruz, Third Secretary,

Mr. Raúl Alfonso Simancas Gómez, Third Secretary, Group of Affairs before the International Court of Justice,

Ministry of Foreign Affairs of Colombia;

Rear Admiral Ernesto Segovia Forero, Chief of Naval Operations,

CN Hermann León, Delegate of Colombia to the International Maritime Organization,

CN William Pedroza, National Navy of Colombia, Director of Maritime and Fluvial Interests Office,

Navy of the Republic of Colombia;

Mr. Scott Edmonds, Cartographer, Director of International Mapping,

Ms Victoria Taylor, Cartographer, International Mapping,

as Technical Advisers;

Mr. Gershon Hasin, LLM, JSD, Yale Law School,

as Legal Assistant;

Mr. Mark Taylor Archbold, Consultant for the National Unit of Disaster Risk Management,

Mr. Joseph Richard Jessie Martinez, Consultant for the National Unit of Disaster Risk Management,

as Advisers.

S. Exc. M. Juan José Quintana Aranguren, chef des affaires multilatérales, ancien ambassadeur de Colombie aux Pays-Bas,

S. Exc. M. Fernando Antonio Grillo Rubiano, ambassadeur de la République de Colombie auprès du Royaume des Pays-Bas et représentant permanent de la Colombie auprès de l'Organisation pour l'interdiction des armes chimiques,

Mme Jenny Sharyne Bowie Wilches, deuxième secrétaire, ambassade de Colombie aux Pays-Bas,

Mme Viviana Andrea Medina Cruz, deuxième secrétaire, ambassade de Colombie aux Pays-Bas,

M. Sebastián Correa Cruz, troisième secrétaire,

M. Raúl Alfonso Simancas Gómez, troisième secrétaire, groupe chargé des affaires portées devant la Cour internationale de Justice,

ministère des affaires étrangères de la République de Colombie ;

Le contre-amiral Ernesto Segovia Forero, chef des opérations navales,

Le capitaine de vaisseau Hermann León, représentant de la Colombie auprès de l'Organisation maritime internationale,

Le capitaine de vaisseau William Pedroza, marine nationale de Colombie, chef de la direction chargée des intérêts maritimes et fluviaux,

marine de la République de Colombie ;

M. Scott Edmonds, cartographe, directeur de International Mapping,

Mme Victoria Taylor, cartographe, International Mapping,

comme conseillers techniques ;

M. Gershon Hasin, LLM, JSD, faculté de droit de l'Université de Yale,

comme assistant juridique ;

M. Mark Taylor Archbold, consultant auprès de l'unité nationale de gestion des risques de catastrophe,

M. Joseph Richard Jessie Martinez, consultant auprès de l'unité nationale de gestion des risques de catastrophe,

comme conseillers.

The PRESIDENT: Please be seated. The sitting is open. For reasons duly made known to me, Judge Robinson is unable to join us for this afternoon's sitting. The Court meets this afternoon to hear the continuation of Colombia's first round of oral argument, including on its own counter-claims.

I shall now give the floor to Mr. Bundy to continue the statement that he began this morning. Go ahead, Mr. Bundy.

Mr. BUNDY:

COLOMBIA DID NOT VIOLATE NICARAGUA'S SOVEREIGN RIGHTS (CONTINUED)

17. Thank you very much, Madam President. Before the break I discussed the fact that the first three of Nicaragua's 13 pre-critical-date allegations are supported by no more than vague media accounts — actually published in Colombia, not Nicaragua — with no supporting evidence to corroborate them or to prove any violation on Colombia's part. I also mentioned that the rest of the 13 pre-critical-date allegations are also unsupported by any contemporary evidence, only a 26 August 2014 internal letter prepared shortly before Nicaragua filed its Memorial, which also had no supporting documentation. But aside from these deficiencies in Nicaragua's claims, during precisely the time when these events were claimed to have occurred in 2013, Nicaragua's senior-most military and political officials were on record as repeatedly affirming that there had been *no incidents* with Colombia.

18. For example, on 14 August 2013, a couple of months before the Application was filed, President Ortega publicly stated that Colombia's Navy "has been respectful and there has not been any kind of confrontation between the Colombia and [the] Nicaraguan Navy"[1]. Three months later, on 18 November 2013 — this was just eight days before the Application was filed and *after* the first ten of Nicaragua's alleged "incidents" — Admiral Corrales, the Head of the Navy, said the following, and you can also find this in tab 21: "There have not been any conflicts and that is why I want to highlight that in one year of being there we have not had any problems with the Colombian

[1] POC, Ann. 11.

Navy"[2]. And he went on to say: "Yes, we have not had any conflicts in those waters. I even think our presence has strengthened the security stability for the fishing vessels, which if at the beginning were few, now are 16 fishing boats"[3].

19. And on 18 March 2014, well after *all* of the pre-critical-date events that Nicaragua relies on and *after* the filing of its Application, Nicaragua's Chief of the Army, General Avilés, said the same thing. You will see this at tab 22 and on the screen: "There are no incidents."[4]

20. On Monday, Mr. Reichler struggled with these admissions against interest. He claimed that the statements of Nicaragua's senior-most officials were simply trying to minimize tensions with Colombia[5]. With respect, however, this post-facto attempt to explain away the obvious is specious. None of the statements that I just referred to even intimate that Nicaragua considered that Colombia was violating its sovereign rights, or that Nicaragua did not react out of self-restraint in order not to raise tensions. To the contrary, all of the statements clearly affirmed in straightforward terms: there were no incidents.

21. Coupled with the absence of evidence, these statements fundamentally undermine Nicaragua's entire claim. They also contradict any notion of a Colombian "policy" to interfere with Nicaraguan vessels or Nicaragua's sovereign rights. If anything, as Admiral Corrales himself noted, Nicaragua's fishing in the area increased significantly after the Court's 2012 Judgment, which certainly does not suggest that Nicaraguan fishermen considered themselves impeded by Colombia's presence in the area.

22. In this connection, it is worth recalling the Court's Judgment in the *Military and Paramilitary Activities* case between Nicaragua and the United States where the Court stated the following — and you will find this in tab 23 and on the screen:

> "The Court takes the view that statements of this kind, emanating from high-ranking official political figures, sometimes indeed of the highest rank, are of particular probative value when they acknowledge facts or conduct unfavourable to the

---

[2] POC, Ann. 43, p. 355; judges' folder, tab 21.

[3] POC, Ann. 43, p. 356; judges' folder, tab 21.

[4] POC, Ann. 46, p. 367; judges' folder, tab 22.

[5] CR 2021/13, p. 59, para. 49 (Reichler).

State represented by the person who made them. They may be then construed as a form of admission."[6]

The same point was repeated by the Court in its 2005 Judgment in the *Democratic Republic of the Congo* v. *Uganda* case[7].

23. Now if we turn to the allegations Nos. 4-13: in these cases, too, there is no evidence to back up the claims. Let me go through them briefly.

No. 4

24. Item No. 4 supposedly concerned a Colombian vessel claimed by Nicaragua to have interfered with its own vessels on 13 October 2013. But Colombia showed in its written pleadings that its naval ship was not even in the area on the day in question[8]. And while Nicaragua alleges in its pleadings that some Colombian vessel warned a Nicaraguan ship that it was sailing "in Colombian waters"[9], this is a distortion of Admiral Corrales' own 23 August 2014 letter, because that document stated that the Colombian vessel warned that the Nicaraguan boat was sailing "towards Colombian waters" — not that it was in Colombian waters, in other words, towards Colombia's territorial sea around Quitasueño only a few miles away[10]. That scarcely constitutes a violation of Nicaragua's sovereign rights.

Nos. 5, 6, 7 and 8

25. Items 5, 6 and 7 on the list are claimed to have involved low flying Colombian aircraft that are said to have intimidated Nicaraguan fishing and naval vessels in October 2013. But once again, Nicaragua has no contemporary evidence to support its assertions. Moreover, the statements of its military leaders, coupled with the lack of any protest whatsoever from Nicaragua, belie the claim.

26. Event No. 8 involved a Colombian helicopter that is said to have landed on a nearby Colombian vessel on 31 October 2013. Nicaragua argues in its Reply that the helicopter "could

[6] *Military and Paramilitary Activities in and against Nicaragua (Nicaragua* v. *United States of America), Merits, Judgment, I.C.J. Reports 1986*, p. 41, para. 64.

[7] *Armed Activities on the Territory of the Congo (Democratic Republic of the Congo* v. *Uganda), Judgment, I.C.J. Reports 2005*, p. 210, para. 61.

[8] CMC, para. 4.26; RC, para. 3.71.

[9] MN, para. 2.40 and Ann. 18.

[10] MN, Ann. 23-A; see also RC, para. 3.73.

have" — those were Nicaragua's words, "could have" — harassed a Nicaraguan naval vessel[11]. But that is pure speculation with no evidence to back it up, quite apart from the fact that the Nicaraguan vessel again made no complaint.

Nos. 9 and 10

27. With respect to the next item on the list, Item 9, Nicaragua asserts that Colombia harassed a Nicaraguan fishing boat. But once again, Madam President and distinguished judges, Nicaragua simply falls back on its 26 August 2014 letter — the Admiral Corrales letter — a single source, without supporting documentation, prepared for the case well after the event was alleged to have occurred, but shortly before Nicaragua filed its Memorial.

28. The same lack of evidence characterizes item No. 10 on the list, which is another allegation that Colombia interfered with a Nicaraguan fishing boat. The allegation is also unsupported by the facts. In fact, it was a Colombian vessel — a Colombian naval vessel — that had to rescue two Nicaraguan fishermen, who had been abandoned by the crew of a Nicaraguan fishing boat, and then deliver them safely to a different Nicaraguan vessel[12]. Far from constituting a violation of Nicaragua's sovereign rights, this was an example of co-operation by the Colombian Navy.

Nos. 11, 12 and 13

29. And as for the last three pre-critical-date events said to have taken place in November 2013 — these were Nos. 11, 12 and 13 — Nicaragua's treatment is, to say the least, economical, even in its written pleadings. It asserts that, in each instance, Colombian aircraft flew low over Nicaraguan vessels in an act of intimidation. But, again there is no contemporary evidence to support the claims. And as for the other events I have discussed, there were no Nicaraguan complaints that its sovereign rights were violated, only statements from the Head of Nicaragua's Naval Force affirming that there were no problems with the Colombian Navy.

30. Madam President, distinguished judges, I scarcely need to belabour the point. Nicaragua has simply not come close to sustaining its burden of proving that any of these alleged events amounted to a violation of its sovereign rights. Hence, I would suggest, Nicaragua's total silence on

---

[11] RN, para. 4.78.

[12] CMC, para. 4.40; RC, para. 3.87.

this on Monday. The only truly probative evidence that exists is found in the contemporary statements from Nicaragua's senior-most military and political figures affirming that there were no "incidents" or problems to complain about. Those statements are consistent with the absence of any contemporary complaints from Nicaragua to Colombia or evidence to back the claims up. But they fundamentally undermine the claim that Colombia violated Nicaragua's sovereign rights or maritime spaces.

II. The lack of jurisdiction to consider the post-critical date event

31. Given the weakness of its case, Nicaragua has also introduced a number of post-critical-date events in an attempt to save its case. And this brings me to the second part of my presentation, in which I will explain why the Court lacks jurisdiction to consider any events that are alleged by Nicaragua to have taken place in violation of its sovereign rights *after* the critical date of 27 November 2013.

32. There is no doubt that the bedrock of the Court's jurisdiction lies in the principle of consent. As the Court underscored in its Judgment on jurisdiction and admissibility in the *Congo* v. *Rwanda* case: "When that consent is expressed in a compromissory clause in an international agreement, any conditions to which such consent is subject must be regarded as constituting the limits thereon"[13]. Now the Pact of Bogotá contains such limits, and they are critical in this case, but they have been ignored by Nicaragua, including in its pleadings on Monday.

A. No jurisdiction under the Pact of Bogotá

33. It is undisputed that the Pact of Bogotá ceased to be in force for Colombia on 27 November 2013 — one year after Colombia denounced it. Because Nicaragua's Application was filed the day before the Pact lapsed for Colombia, the Court ruled in its Judgment on Colombia's preliminary objections that it had jurisdiction under the Pact over the dispute that was the subject-matter of the Application, which involved by necessity pre-critical-date events. As the Court noted in its 2016 Judgment:

---

[13] *Armed Activities in the Territory of the Congo (New Application: 2002 (Democratic Republic of the Congo* v. *Rwanda), Jurisdiction and Admissibility, Judgment, I.C.J. Reports 2006*, p. 39, para. 88. See also the *Order of 10 July 2002* in the same case, *I.C.J. Reports 2002*, p. 241, para. 57.

> "it is not the denunciation *per se* that is capable of having an effect upon the jurisdiction of the Court under Article XXXI of the Pact, but the termination of the treaty (as between the denouncing State and the other parties) which results from the denunciation"[14].

34. Given the termination of the Pact for Colombia, the situation is different for Nicaragua's post-critical-date alleged wrongful acts. Colombia's consent to jurisdiction no longer existed after the Pact of Bogotá terminated for it. As the Court will recall, Article LVI of the Pact provided that it could be "may be denounced upon one year's notice, at the end of which it shall cease to be in force with respect to the state denouncing it" (tab 24 of the judges' folder). As I shall now explain, no jurisdictional basis exists for the Court to rule on any of the facts alleged to have occurred *after* the Pact ceased to be in effect for Colombia.

35. But it is not simply Article LVI that is relevant here. The question of jurisdiction over post-critical-date alleged wrongful acts also falls to be considered under Article XXXI of the Pact. This is the key compromissory clause, but it was conspicuously ignored by both Professor Pellet and Mr. Reichler on Monday. They never very mentioned that clause. They only focused on Article LVI. Yet it is Article XXXI that not only contains the Contracting Parties' consent to the Court's jurisdiction, but equally importantly, the *limits* of that consent, including consent to the Court's jurisdiction *ratione temporis* to decide disputes referred to in that Article. To demonstrate the point, it may assist if I place the text of Article XXXI on the screen and you will also find it in tab 25.

36. Now, as can be seen, Colombia declared that it recognized the compulsory jurisdiction of the Court in relation to any other Contracting Party without the need for special agreement "*so long as the present Treaty is in force*, in all disputes of a juridical nature that arise among them concerning" — and here I refer to subparagraphs *(b)* and *(c)* — "*(b)* [a]ny question of international law" and "*(c)* [t]he existence of any fact which, if established, would constitute the breach of an international obligation" (emphasis added).

37. Under Articles XXXI and LVI of the Pact, therefore, there was a clear temporal limitation to Colombia's consent to the Court's jurisdiction over a dispute concerning the existence of any fact which, if established, could constitute the breach of an international obligation. That consent only existed "as long as the present Treaty is in force". As the Court stated in its Judgment on jurisdiction

---

[14] *Alleged Violations of Sovereign Rights and Maritime Spaces in the Caribbean Sea (Nicaragua* v. *Colombia, Preliminary Objections, Judgment, I.C.J. Reports 2016 (I)*, p. 20, para. 38.

in the *Armed Actions* case between Nicaragua and Honduras, the Pact "defines with precision the obligations of the parties", and "it remains valid *ratione temporis* for as long as that instrument itself remains in force between those States" [15].

38. In the present case, after the critical date of 27 November 2013, the Pact was no longer in force for Colombia and there was thus no longer any such consent. And that is why Colombia maintains that the Court does not have jurisdiction *ratione temporis* to rule on events that are alleged to have occurred after that date.

39. In the *Certain Property* case between Liechtenstein and Germany referred to by Professor Pellet on Monday[16], Liechtenstein relied on a compromissory clause that bears similarity to Article XXXI, subparagraph *(c)* of the Pact of Bogotá. In the *Certain Property* case, Article 1 of the European Convention for the Peaceful Settlement of Disputes provided that the Contracting Parties submitted to the Court's jurisdiction all international legal disputes which may arise between them concerning, *inter alia*, "the existence of any fact which, if established, would constitute a breach of an international obligation": the same as Article XXXI *(c)* of the Pact of Bogotá. Now the Court in that case found that the "facts or situations" that were the real source of the dispute *predated* the entry into force of the European Convention and that it therefore lacked jurisdiction *ratione temporis*[17]. Here, the facts that Nicaragua relies on for all of the alleged "incidents", except for the first 13, relate to a period *after* the Pact was no longer in force for Colombia. Just as the Court had no jurisdiction to rule on whether pre-treaty facts constituted a breach of an international obligation in the *Certain Property* case, so also it lacks jurisdiction to rule on whether *post-treaty facts* constitute a breach of an international obligation in this case. Contrary to Professor Pellet's contention on Monday, there are no reasons for treating the two situations differently with respect to jurisdiction *ratione temporis*.

40. For his part, Mr. Reichler referred to the *Legality of Use of Force* case between Yugoslavia and Belgium, and he argued that it makes no difference that the title of jurisdiction in this case lapsed

---

[15] *Border and Transborder Armed Actions (Nicaragua* v. *Honduras), Jurisdiction and Admissibility, Judgment, I.C.J. Reports 1988*, p. 84, para. 34.

[16] CR 2021/13, p. 38, para. 38 (Pellet).

[17] *Certain Property (Liechtenstein* v. *Germany), Preliminary Objections, Judgment, I.C.J. Reports 2005*, pp. 26-27, para. 52.

after Nicaragua submitted its Application because, to use the words from Nicaragua's Reply, "the only relevant question is whether the 'dispute' arose within the temporal limitations of the jurisdictional title"[18].

41. But once again, this argument is misplaced. For counsel ignores the fact that Yugoslavia's Article 36 (2) optional clause declaration was drafted in a very different manner than Article XXXI of the Pact of Bogotá. In its optional clause declaration, Yugoslavia recognized the Court's jurisdiction over all disputes "*arising or which may arise* after the signature of the present Declaration". The question before the Court was therefore whether the *dispute* arose before or after Yugoslavia's optional clause declaration. And since the Court concluded that the dispute arose before that declaration was made, it ruled that there was no prima facie jurisdiction allowing for the indication of provisional measures.

42. In contrast however, Article XXXI of the Pact contains no language conditioning jurisdiction on when the dispute arose. Rather, it provides for jurisdiction over disputes concerning facts that, if established, could constitute a breach of an international obligation only "so long as the present Treaty is in force". In these circumstances, the ruling in *Yugoslavia-Belgium* that Nicaragua tries to rely on is simply not apposite. The compromissory clauses are different.

43. Mr. Reichler also referred to the *Fisheries Jurisdiction* case *(Germany* v. *Iceland)* to support his argument that the Court has jurisdiction over alleged violations that post-date the Application[19]. Once again, this case is of no assistance to Nicaragua.

44. In the *Fisheries Jurisdiction* case, the Court had jurisdiction under Article 36, paragraph 1, of the Statute pursuant to an Exchange of Notes between the parties dated 19 July 1961. That Exchange provided that, in the event Iceland extended its fisheries jurisdiction, and upon giving six months' notice of such extension, the matter shall be referred to the Court at the request of either party.

45. Counsel relies on a passage from the Court's Judgment in that case[20], holding that it had jurisdiction over one of Germany's submissions that was based on facts subsequent to the filing of

---

[18] CR 2021/13, pp. 60-61, paras. 53-54, and see RN, para. 4.26.

[19] CR 2021/13, p. 61, para. 55 (Reichler).

[20] *Fisheries Jurisdiction (Federal Republic of Germany* v. *Iceland), Merits, Judgment, I.C.J. Reports 1974*, p. 203, para. 72.

the Application but arising directly out of the question which was the subject-matter of the Application[21]. But that's not our situation here. The question is not whether facts subsequent to the Application can be added. The fact is that Nicaragua fails to take into account that, unlike the Pact of Bogotá, the Exchange of Notes between Germany and Iceland conferring jurisdiction on the Court did not contain any conditions other than the prior giving of six months' notice of any extension of Iceland's fisheries limits. In particular, there was no temporal limit to matters that the Court could rule on as there is in Article XXXI of the Pact.

46. Madam President, distinguished judges, the bottom line is that neither Professor Pellet nor Mr. Reichler pointed to a single case where the Court or its predecessor has ever ruled on the legality of a State's conduct when that conduct occurred at a time when there was no applicable jurisdictional title between the parties to the case. No example. Given the terms in which Article XXXI of the Pact of Bogotá is drafted, there is no jurisdictional basis for the Court to consider whether facts that occurred after the Pact ceased to be in force for Colombia, even if established, constituted a breach by Colombia of international law or an international obligation.

B. Nicaragua's claims are unsupported in any event

47. Yet, even if the Court had jurisdiction over post-critical-date events *(quod non)*, Nicaragua has failed to prove that these events amount to a violation of its rights. Since Colombia addressed each of these post-critical-date events in detail in Appendix 1 to its Rejoinder, I will simply draw your attention to some of the basic problems undermining Nicaragua's claims.

48. First, if we go back to the slides that Mr. Reichler presented on Monday and included in the folders, there is not a single reference to Nicaraguan fishing vessels being prevented from exercising their activities by Colombia's Navy. You may recall that in most of the exchanges, the Colombian vessels indicated that they were protecting Colombia's historical fishing rights, providing security for all vessels, and implementing measures against transnational crimes.

49. With respect to historical fishing, the Colombian Navy's statements are in no way inconsistent with the position of Nicaragua's own Head of State, President Ortega, who had clearly stated that Nicaragua "will authorize their fishing in that area, where [the Colombian fishermen] have

---

[21] CR 2021/13, p. 61, para. 55 (Reichler), and see RN, para. 4.16.

historically practiced fisheries, both artisanal and industrial fisheries"[22], and President Ortega also said: "I have told President Santos, and I have said publicly, that the Raizales can continue fishing. That Nicaragua will not affect them in their rights."[23] Regrettably, it was Nicaragua's Naval Force that did not respect what their own President had affirmed, but Colombia's allegations in the light of those affirmations by the Head of State of Nicaragua would not constitute a violation of any rights. Mr. Valencia-Ospina will come back to this later this afternoon. As for providing security for all vessels, this did not constitute any violation of Nicaragua's sovereign rights. And with respect to implementing measures against transnational crimes, Nicaragua itself conceded in its Reply that it "does not contest Colombia's right to take action in Nicaragua's EEZ if it happens to encounter a ship suspected of the illegal transportation of narcotics, or to search a ship if it has reason to suspect it is there"[24].

50. The key point is that at no time did Colombia interfere with the navigation of Nicaraguan vessels, board any vessels or carry out enforcement actions. If anything, the contemporaneous evidence shows that, even when Nicaraguan fishing vessels were observed to be carrying out predatory fishing practices in environmentally sensitive areas, Colombia simply informed them of that fact and invited them to change their practices, which, unfortunately, they did not do. Mere advisory statements of this kind without any physical interference, particularly when they are made in the face of blatantly illegal fishing practices, do not remotely rise to the level of a violation of Nicaragua's rights.

51. In other words, any such alleged incidents — even if one assumes for purposes of argument that they took place, and fall within the jurisdiction of the Court — did not affect the ability of Nicaraguan fishing boats to operate or constitute a violation of Nicaragua's sovereign rights.

52. Counsel for Nicaragua also harped on the *Observer* incident in their first round. But Colombia has shown in its written pleadings that our opponents' version of events is demonstrably misleading and incorrect.

---

[22] MN, Ann. 27.

[23] RC, Ann. 6.

[24] RN, para. 2.34.

53. First, Colombia submitted video evidence — you have it on the record — video evidence of the incident that shows that it was Nicaragua that engaged in blatantly illegal activities contrary to international rules of navigation, including the COLREGS, when it attempted to approach the *Observer* vessel.

Second, the vessel was not caught fishing in violation of Nicaragua's sovereign rights. It was apprehended in the middle of the night, in a location where the depths of the water precluded fishing and when no fishing activities were taking place. As Colombia showed in its written pleadings, the *Observer* was merely transiting on route between Colombia's islands.

Third, contrary to what Mr. Reichler said on Monday[25], there was no fishing licence on the *Observer* to fish in Nicaraguan waters. There was only a permit to leave port and another authorization to operate in the waters of the San Andrés Archipelago with no mention of any other areas.

Fourth, and again contrary to counsel's assertion[26], the captain of the *Observer* never admitted that he was caught fishing in Nicaraguan waters without a Nicaraguan license. The captain, who was actually on the ship, never admitted that.

54. While time does not permit me to engage in a point-by-point rebuttal of counsel's intervention on Monday, let me just briefly mention two other matters raised in Nicaragua's first round. If necessary, I will come back in the second round on these.

55. With respect to the assertion that Colombia licensed an "industrial commercial" fishing vessel to fish in contravention of Nicaragua's sovereign rights, counsel also unfortunately misstates the facts. Under tab 29 of Monday's folders, Nicaragua only produced extracts from a resolution of Colombia's General Maritime Directorate in order to assert that a Ms Vianova Forbes James received a commercial fishing permit to fish in the Luna Verde bank. This is incorrect. The document in question is not a fishing permit; it is a permit for a different Honduran-flagged vessel, the *Saga*, to be affiliated with Ms James' fleet. The reference to Luna Verde is in the preamble in this document and does not purport to license Ms James to fish there.

---

[25] CR 2021/13, p. 54.

[26] CR 2021/13, p. 56, para. 43 (Reichler).

56. And as for Nicaragua's remarks about a Mexican research vessel, the *Dr. Jorge Carranza Fraser*, being escorted away by Colombia[27], this is another "non-event". Suffice it to note that the Mexican Government never raised the slightest complaint to Colombia.

III. Nicaragua's allegations regarding petroleum concessions and fishing permits

57. Madam President, this brings me to the final part of my presentation in which I shall respond to Nicaragua's contention that Colombia has violated its sovereign rights by issuing licenses to companies to explore for and exploit petroleum, and boats to fish, in violation of Nicaragua's rights. I can be relatively brief because, once again, the so-called evidence adduced by Nicaragua does not support the claim.

58. With respect to petroleum activities, I have two principal points to make. First, the claim is a new one, not raised in the Memorial let alone the Application. As the Court has often emphasized, it is the Application that defines the subject-matter of the dispute. And the Memorial, "though it may elucidate the terms of the Application, must not go beyond the limits of the claim as set out therein"[28]. This new claim regarding petroleum contracts goes well beyond the subject-matter of the dispute as circumscribed by the Application. It does not deal with any alleged interference with Nicaraguan vessels by Colombia's Navy. And it does not deal with Colombia's contiguous zone; those were the subject-matter of the Application. It deals with an entirely different matter — the alleged licensing of commercial petroleum contracts. As such, Colombia submits the claim is not admissible.

59. But be that as it may, my second point is that the factual assertion by Nicaragua that Colombia continues to license petroleum blocks in areas where Nicaragua possesses sovereign rights is wrong. Now we have explained this in the Rejoinder[29], but let me just reiterate that any offshore blocks that were designated before the Court's 2012 Judgment were suspended in 2011, and contracts were never signed by Colombia and have not been pursued. Moreover, Colombia's courts have prohibited any petroleum activities within the Seaflower Reserve. Other blocks that Nicaragua refers

---

[27] CR 2021/13, pp. 57-58, paras. 46-47 (Reichler).

[28] *Ahmadou Sadio Diallo (Republic of Guinea* v. *Democratic Republic of the Congo), Judgment, I.C.J. Reports 2010 (II), p.* 656, para. 39; *Certain Phosphate Lands in Nauru (Nauru* v. *Australia), Preliminary Objections, Judgment, I.C.J. Reports 1992*, p. 267, para. 69; *Prince von Pless Administration, Order of 4 February 1933, P.C.I.J., Series A/B*, No. 52, p. 14.

[29] RC, paras. 3.101-3.107.

to are based on a map produced by the Colombian National Agency of Hydrocarbons. But these too have not been implemented and will not be pursued, and will not be offered. In short, there are no existing contracts covering petroleum activities in any areas where Nicaragua has sovereign rights, and no proposals for any of the blocks shown on the map to be awarded. Indeed, on Monday, Nicaragua's counsel accepted that Colombia has not awarded any concessions in those areas[30]. There is no possible violation of Nicaragua's rights in these circumstances.

60. And as for the allegation that Colombia has authorized fishing in violation of Nicaragua's sovereign rights, this also has no merit. Nicaragua's claim was based on a number of resolutions issued by the Colombian General Maritime Direction, which is known as DIMAR, and the Governorship of the Archipelago Department of San Andrés, Providencia and Santa Catalina. However, contrary to Nicaragua's contentions, none of those documents purports to authorize fishing beyond Colombia's EEZ.

61. In Colombia's Rejoinder, Colombia explained very carefully how, notwithstanding that these resolutions on which Nicaragua purports to rely post-date the critical date of 27 November 2013, Nicaragua has misread what they say[31]. First, DIMAR has no competence to issue fishing licences and does not do so. Competence for issuing fishing permits rests with the Secretariat of Agriculture and Fishing of San Andrés. Second, none of the resolutions relied on by Nicaragua stipulate that fishing is permitted in Nicaraguan waters. They mention banks around the Colombian islands of Roncador, Serrana, Serranilla and Quitasueño as places where fishing is authorized, but they do not purport to authorize fishing anywhere else. And third, the resolutions only authorize fishing vessels to operate "in the jurisdiction of the San Andrés and Providencia Harbor Master's Office" and they grant certain financial relief to the fishing fleet registered in San Andrés and Providencia. In sum, they provide no support for the claim that Colombia violated Nicaragua's sovereign rights.

62. Madam President, distinguished judges, I believe I have shown that there is not a scintilla of evidence to support any of the pre-critical-date claims of Nicaragua despite the fact that these alleged wrongful acts must have formed the basis of the Application. Similarly, the evidence does

---

[30] CR 2021/13, pp. 57-58, para. 23 (Reichler).

[31] RC, paras. 3.108-3.123.

not support the assertion that Colombia engaged in wrongful acts that violated Nicaragua's rights *after* the Pact ceased to be in force for Colombia, notwithstanding the *ratione temporis* jurisdictional problem. In these circumstances, there are no grounds for the contention advanced by Nicaragua's Agent, and again by Professor Pellet, that Colombia has engaged in a continuing violation of Nicaragua's rights[32]. It has not.

63. What Nicaragua has done is to introduce claims against Colombia by means of an Application dated 26 November 2013 for which there is absolutely no supporting evidence and with respect to alleged events that Nicaragua did not even deem fit to address on Monday. Nicaragua then tried after the Application in subsequent pleadings, and again on Monday, to manufacture a case based on alleged wrongful acts that were said to have occurred *after* the Pact of Bogotá was no longer in force for Colombia — in other words, at a time when there was no jurisdictional title between the Parties. And it did this based on its "continuous wrongful acts" theory. But there can be no continuity between what is nothing, i.e. the events leading up to the Application before the critical date, and post-critical date allegations that are equally unfounded and over which the Court lacks jurisdiction.

Conclusions

64. Madam President, distinguished judges: let me conclude with a summary of Colombia's position with respect to the first strand of Nicaragua's claim. I have five brief points.

(i) First, all of the so-called "incidents" on which Nicaragua relies that are said to have taken place before the critical date of 27 November 2013, and which must have formed the basis of the Application, are in reality non-events that involved no violation of Nicaragua's sovereign rights. They are unsupported with any direct or contemporary evidence. And they are flatly contradicted by the statements of Nicaragua's political and military leaders at the time and the failure of Nicaragua to raise the slightest protest. No wonder they were not discussed on Monday.

(ii) Second, with respect to the elements of Nicaragua's claim that took place after Colombia ceased to be bound by the Pact, the Court lacks jurisdiction *ratione temporis* under Articles XXXI and LVI of the Pact to consider whether, even if such facts were to be

[32] CR 2021/13, p. 21, para. 19 (Argüello); CR 2021/13, p. 27, para. 6 (Pellet).

established, they amounted to a violation of Nicaragua's sovereign rights. Nicaragua has simply ignored the temporal limits of the compromissory clause contained in Article XXXI of the Pact.

(iii) Third, even if jurisdiction existed over post-critical date events — *quod non* — Nicaragua has not sustained its burden of proving that Colombia's conduct violated its rights.

(iv) Fourth, Nicaragua's contentions that Colombia licensed petroleum and fishing activities in violation of Nicaragua's sovereign rights are incorrect.

(v) And fifth, and finally, Nicaragua's "continuing wrongful acts" theory is jurisdictionally flawed in law, and unsupported in fact.

Madam President, that concludes my presentation. I thank the Court for its attention, and I would be grateful if the floor could now be given to Professor Reisman, who will be presenting virtually. Thank you very much.

The PRESIDENT: I thank Mr. Bundy. I now invite the next speaker, Professor Michael Reisman, to take the floor. You have the floor, Sir.

Mr. REISMAN:

THE CONTIGUOUS ZONE

1. Thank you, Madam President. Madam President, Members of the Court, it is an honour to appear before you on behalf of the Republic of Colombia. I too would like to take a moment to express my respect and admiration for Judge James Crawford and to recognize the profound loss that his death means to our profession.

2. Madam President, in my presentation, I will explain why Colombia's contiguous zone Decree No. 1946, as amended, is lawful and does not infringe any Nicaraguan right[33]. For brevity, I will refer to the Colombian Decree as "Decree 1946" or "the Decree".

3. As a preliminary point, it was quite puzzling to see Nicaragua manoeuvring around the fact that the Decree of which it complains has been amended. Especially since Nicaragua recognized this

---

[33] The Decree's disputed Article 5 is entitled "The Contiguous Zone of the Island Territories in the Western Caribbean Sea".

fact in the written pleadings[34], and even limited its claims in the Reply to the powers in the amended Decree[35]. Therefore, as far as Nicaragua's claims against Decree 1946 rest on its quotes from the obsolete version, they have become theoretical. And the Court does not deal with theoretical questions[36].

4. As Colombia's submissions clarify, the map it produced in the record is the most accurate illustration of the contiguous zone[37]. Colombia will publish official charts depicting its contiguous zone when ready. In its pleadings, Nicaragua repeatedly emphasized the word "integral", as if its use under Colombian domestic law conveys some ominous spatial conveyance. But it is simply "integral" because the geography of the area dictates so. It is not a new type of zone.

5. It is also important to underline that Colombia has sovereignty over all the islands composing the Archipelago of San Andrés, Providencia and Santa Catalina. Each island, great or small, is entitled, under customary international law, as a matter of right, to a territorial sea and a contiguous zone. It is not for Nicaragua to decide which of Colombia's archipelagic islands and their territorial seas are entitled to be protected by contiguous zone powers.

6. And contrary to Nicaragua's rhetoric, this case is not about a purported "repudiation" of the 2012 Judgment — which, we should say, is not in issue — but about whether Colombia violates Nicaragua's enumerated rights or jurisdictions. And the Decree is a lawful exercise of Colombia's sovereignty.

A. The controlling legal issues

7. Madam President, Nicaragua raises four objections to the Decree. First, it contends that, as a general rule, customary international law denies a State a protective contiguous zone if its territorial sea abuts another State's EEZ. Second, it contends that a State may not resort to *any* reasonable geodetic lines to simplify the jagged and indented contours of its contiguous zone. Third, it contends that customary international law confines contiguous zone powers to those enumerated in UNCLOS

---

[34] RN, para. 2.59, submission 1 *(c)*.

[35] RN, para. 3.41.

[36] *Northern Cameroons (Cameroon* v. *United Kingdom), Preliminary Objections, Judgment, I.C.J. Reports 1963*, p. 37.

[37] RC, p. 212, Figure CR 4.3.

Article 33 and that, unlike the rest of customary international law, or indeed the terms of treaties, the substance of these powers cannot evolve to adjust to new circumstances. Finally, Nicaragua contends that Colombia's mere enactment of the Decree *ipso facto* violated its rights.

8. Each of Nicaragua's contentions is wrong. The powers in the Decree are lawful under customary international law, and do not conflict with any right Nicaragua might have. The modest use of geodetic lines to smooth out and simplify the otherwise impractical outer limits of the contiguous zone is dictated by geography. The rights and the simplification cause no injury to Nicaragua.

9. Inasmuch as Colombia is not party to UNCLOS, customary international law is the applicable law. But instead of adducing State practice and *opinio juris* to evidence its restrictive interpretation, Nicaragua simply assumes that UNCLOS provisions on the contiguous zone mirror a static, and restrictive, rule of customary international law, as of 1956, 1982 and the present.

B. The relationship between the exclusive economic zone and the contiguous zone

10. Within the EEZ, high seas freedoms of other States continue in effect, as do customary contiguous zone rights of an adjacent State, for an EEZ is not a State's "waters", even less is it its territorial sea. As Sir Michael Wood has shown, the exclusive economic zone is not a territorial sea. All the EEZ State has are the enumerated economic rights and accompanying jurisdictions for "exploring and exploiting, conserving and managing the natural resources" of the zone. An EEZ does not displace pre-existing customary contiguous zone rights.

11. UNCLOS Article 56 (1) *(b)*, which is in your folders, does not itself bestow any general jurisdiction upon the EEZ State. Rather, it provides the EEZ State with such jurisdiction "as provided for in the relevant provisions of this Convention". Such jurisdiction is not residual or general but is only what is specified in the text of the Convention.

12. To argue that Decree 1946, as amended, somehow violated or "appropriated" rights or jurisdictions which Nicaragua might claim, Nicaragua must show precisely which resource rights or which jurisdictions the Decree violates. Instead, Nicaragua claims a violation of unspecified "sovereign rights". I will demonstrate that Decree 1946, as amended, does not violate or displace any of Nicaragua's rights or jurisdictions.

13. A copy of UNCLOS Article 33, entitled "Contiguous zone", is in tab 27 of your folders. You will note that Article 33 is located in Part II of UNCLOS, entitled "Territorial sea and contiguous zone", and not in Part V, entitled "Exclusive economic zone".

14. Conceptually, the protective powers which may be exercised in the contiguous zone form part of the territorial sea régime which itself originated in customary international law as a protective zone. Contiguous zone rights remain protective rights which a coastal State may lawfully call into operation in the waters adjacent to its territorial sea. None of these protective powers displaces any of a neighbouring EEZ State's rights. As the ILC recognized in 1956, "this power of control does not change the legal status of the waters over which it is exercised"[38]. This power existed in customary international law when that area was high seas and it remains so, as Article 58 makes clear, after the EEZ régime assigned a coastal State specific resource rights there.

15. A State's contiguous zone powers are all for the protection of the State's territory and territorial sea. They are distinct from the rights and jurisdictions of a coastal State in its EEZ and do not contradict them, as was recognized at the Conference. The Proelss Commentary explains that

> "the prevailing view at the Conference, however, was that, first, an enlarged territorial sea would in no way compromise the rationale of creating an adjacent 'prevent and punishment zone', and second, the envisaged legal régime of the EEZ was intended to cover entirely different subjects, and that there were thus no overlaps in substance between these two maritime zones."[39]

16. An EEZ State may not prevent and punish infringements of its *own* customs, fiscal, immigration or sanitary laws and regulations in its territory or territorial sea, beyond its own contiguous zone. *A fortiori*, Nicaragua, in the name of asserted EEZ rights, may not prevent or punish violations of *Colombia's* customs, fiscal, immigration or sanitary laws and regulations. Only Colombia may exercise such powers in a zone contiguous to its territorial sea.

17. Madam President, in certain geographical circumstances, the contiguous zones of two States or a contiguous zone and an EEZ of another State overlap. If the coasts of the two States are less than 24 nautical miles apart, each State will have only a territorial sea and neither State may exercise contiguous zone powers in the territorial sea of its neighbour, for this would, indeed, infringe a coastal State's sovereignty. That is the only impermissible overlap. As the United States explained

---

[38] *Yearbook of the International Law Commission (YILC)*, 1956, commentary to Article 66, para. 1.

[39] Alexander Proelss, *The United Nations Convention on the Law of the Sea: A Commentary* (2017), p. 262.

when it proclaimed its contiguous zone: "The contiguous zone of the United States extends to 24 nautical miles from the baselines of the United States determined in accordance with international law, but in no case within the territorial sea of another nation."[40]

18. As much as Nicaragua would wish it, the western Caribbean is not its territorial sea.

19. When the coasts of two States lie 48 or more nautical miles apart, and they apply equidistance to delimit their respective maritime entitlements, each State will have a 12-nautical-mile contiguous zone which entirely overlaps with its own EEZ. The overlap is not duplicative or legally redundant, as its EEZ rights and contiguous zone rights are different.

20. But if the two States' coasts are between 48 and 24 nautical miles apart — let's say, 40 nautical miles apart — the two States' contiguous zones overlap, as you can see on the screen. If equidistance is applied to delimit their EEZs, the contiguous zone of each State will also overlap with the contiguous zone and the EEZ of the other. The nature of contiguous zone powers allows for such overlaps.

21. As the Virginia Commentary explains:

> "Since the nature of control to be exercised in the contiguous zone does not create any sovereignty over the zone or its resources, it is possible for two states to exercise control over the same area if their zones should overlap, for the purpose of prevention or punishment for infringement of their respective customs, fiscal, immigration or sanitary laws and regulations within their respective territories or territorial sea."[41]

This is why the provision on the delimitation of contiguous zones was removed, not because it was "superfluous" as Nicaragua suggests.

22. Nicaragua's proposition that an overlap is inconsistent with potential conflicts over the regulation of archaeological objects, is misconceived, as is Nicaragua's own reliance on the Virginia Commentary[42]. The Commentary did not suggest that the delimitation of contiguous zones was necessary. Rather it recognized that contiguous zones may overlap and referred any theoretical disputes to the dispute settlement mechanism. The Virginia Commentary says: "Since the Convention did not adopt any provision regarding the delimitation of the contiguous zone, the

---

[40] Proclamation 7219 of 2 September 1999, https://www.govinfo.gov/content/pkg/CFR-2000-title3-vol1/pdf/CFR-2000-title3-vol1-proc7219.pdf.

[41] Virginia Commentary, pp. 273-274, quoting Commonwealth Group of Experts, *Ocean Management: A Regional Perspective — The Prospects for Commonwealth Maritime Co-operation in Asia and the Pacific*, Commonwealth Secretariat, 1984; emphasis added.

[42] CR 2021/13, p. 67, para. 22 (Lowe).

possibility of disputes arising out of conflicting claims by states whose coasts are opposite or adjacent to each other cannot be ruled out, and Part XV, therefore, will be applicable."[43]

23. It is difficult to see why Nicaragua believes this passage supports its proposition that contiguous zones may not overlap, for it clearly supports the contrary position. But even if such theoretical conflicts occur, and the objects are not related to the cultural heritage of one of the States, UNCLOS Article 303 (1) imposes a duty of co-operation between the States, which may simply resolve any disagreement.

24. An overlap of a contiguous zone and an EEZ may occur when the territorial sea of an island of one State borders the EEZ of the other State. Then the island's contiguous zone, ordinarily 12 nautical miles in breadth, extends perforce into the other State's EEZ.

25. Madam President, this is the situation before you. Because Colombia's archipelagic islands have a territorial sea, their contiguous zone adjacent to this territorial sea extends into the adjoining waters, regardless of whether Nicaragua claims resource rights in the overlapping area.

26. Bear in mind that the term "zone", whether used for the exclusive economic zone or the contiguous zone, does not designate comprehensive or residual rights *to* a body of water, but rather specific rights *in* a body of water which otherwise retains its character of high seas. For these powers, the term "zone" is descriptive of specific powers within a space rather than constitutive of a comprehensive spatial conveyance. Thus, it is wrong to say that a contiguous zone right "violates" the EEZ of another State. Because a contiguous zone right does not displace any of the rights of the EEZ State, the only possible claim could be that it has been applied in a particular instance without "due regard" to a specific EEZ right of the other State. Yet even then that would not undermine the overall legality of the contiguous zone powers.

27. The fact that contiguous zone powers were not "delimited" by the Court in 2012 does not mean, as Nicaragua would have it, that they were implicitly denied. Rather, the Court's decision is consistent with the fact that a contiguous zone does not require a delimitation as these powers are non-exclusive and do not conflict with any resource-related rights and jurisdictions of another State.

---

[43] Virginia Commentary, para. 303.6.

The primary audience for indicating the contiguous zone is the coast guard or navy of the State concerned.

28. Madam President, for these reasons Colombia submits that under customary international law, when circumstances so require, it may lawfully exercise contiguous zone powers within the space in which its contiguous zone extends into an area where Nicaragua claims to exercise certain resource rights.

C. The simplification of the seaward limit of the contiguous zone

29. Nicaragua's second contention concerns Colombia's simplification of the contours of the seaward limit of its contiguous zone.

30. Because of the proximity of the islands comprising the Archipelago, their contiguous zones overlap. As can be seen, the overlap is dictated by geography, not legislative initiative.

31. The adoption of lines to simplify maritime jurisdiction is recognized in international law as a pragmatic and lawful technique.

32. Madam President, Members of the Court, when you recognized the complexity created by the modified arcs, you replaced them with a simplified line. The management difficulties which concerned you apply to the 24-nautical-mile intersecting arcs around the islands. The practical, navigational and administrative difficulties led Colombia to employ a similar simplification for the extent of its contiguous zone powers.

33. Colombia submits that the simplification of a maritime jurisdiction, when employed on a reasonable, contextually appropriate and not excessive scale, may be a lawful method, akin, *mutatis mutandis*, to the power under international law to draw straight baselines in appropriate circumstances[44]. Simplification then ensures the orderly management of the oceans[45].

34. As is evident from the map, without simplification, the contiguous zone of Colombia would be a tangle of interconnected arcs, representing difficulties in its practical application.

35. Not only can a simplification be lawful under international law but, in contrast to straight baselines which have *exclusionary* effects on international users, smoothing the contours of

[44] See e.g. *Fisheries (United Kingdom* v. *Norway), Judgment, I.C.J. Reports 1951.*

[45] *Territorial and Maritime Dispute (Nicaragua* v. *Colombia), Judgment, I.C.J. Reports 2012 (II)*, p. 710, para. 235.

contiguous zone powers has no adverse effects on the rights or interests of other States and no effects whatsoever on Nicaragua's rights. Should circumstances require it, it enables Colombia to effectively protect these legitimate interests in a fragile area such as the San Andrés Archipelago.

36. Colombia submits that the simplification of the contours of its contiguous zone promotes the public order and efficient management of a legitimate use of the oceans and, on the law and facts, is justified. Colombia thus requests the Court to reject Nicaragua's argument against the use of a simplified geodetic line for its contiguous zone.

D. Contiguous zone powers

37. Madam President, Nicaragua distorts the powers claimed in Decree 1946, as amended, by repeatedly quoting from a version it knows to be obsolete[46]. I will proceed assuming that what Nicaragua meant to argue is that the powers in Decree 1946, *as amended*, exceed what UNCLOS Article 33 allows. Nicaragua misses the point. It is customary international law that determines the rights of Colombia in its contiguous zone in accordance with *current* State practice and *opinio juris*. Colombia's study of State practice, found in Appendix B to the Counter-Memorial, shows that States have claimed powers in their contiguous zones for security and defence matters, environmental concerns and effects on cultural heritage.

38. Even assuming, for the sake of argument, that the contiguous zone powers of a coastal State under customary international law are confined *stricto sensu* to those in Article 33, the question becomes the current meaning of the treaty's generic terms: "customs", "fiscal", "immigration" and "sanitary". You have instructed that when interpreting generic terms in long-term treaties, it should, as a general rule, be presumed that the Parties "have intended those terms to have an evolving meaning"[47].

39. That instruction applies to the generic terms in Article 33 which date back, over 60 years, to the ILC's 1956 Draft Articles on the Law of the Sea. Such terms should be interpreted in an evolutionary manner to enable a coastal State to protect its territorial sea and land domain from changing inbound threats without compromising the correlative rights of other States.

---

[46] E.g. CR 2021/13, pp. 46 and 71.

[47] *Dispute regarding Navigational and Related Rights (Costa Rica* v. *Nicaragua), Judgment, I.C.J. Reports 2009*, p. 243, para. 66.

40. Scholars have voiced support for an evolutionary interpretation of Article 33 to ensure their relevance to evolving threats. The Proelss Commentary admonished that: "[a]n all too narrow interpretation of the purposes enumerated in Article 33 should therefore not stand in the way of effectively combating new and serious threats, for example those originating in vessel source pollution"[48].

41. The powers set out in Decree 1946 are:

1. to safeguard the security of the islands including from piracy and drug trafficking;
2. to protect against conduct contrary to security at sea;
3. to defend its national maritime interests, customs, fiscal, migration and sanitary matters;
4. to preserve the islands' marine environment; and
5. to guard the Archipelago's cultural heritage.

42. As Colombia's survey of State practice shows, for many of these powers there is evidence of an emerging custom. Moreover, the contingent exercise of these powers, should the necessity arise, would deprive Nicaragua of nothing as the powers are neither incompatible with nor displace any of Nicaragua's rights and jurisdictions. As Nicaragua lacks the powers to protect and preserve *Colombia's* islands' environment, security or cultural heritage, and, of course, no rights to act in a manner which violates Colombia's protective laws and regulations, the Decree neither conflicts with nor displaces a corresponding Nicaraguan power. The powers in Decree 1946 are, it is submitted, consistent with customary international law on the contiguous zone and the EEZ.

43. Decree 1946 provides, that the application of these powers "will be carried out in conformity with international law". On Monday, Nicaragua attempted to downplay Colombia's commitment in this regard. That may reflect the attitude of others, but not Colombia's for whom this solemn commitment is not undertaken lightly.

44. In 1956, the ILC deemed it unnecessary to include "security" because "[t]he enforcement of customs and sanitary regulations will be sufficient in most cases to safeguard the security of the State"[49]. Other security related threats would concern circumstances that would be covered under self-defence. At the first UNCLOS conference, the motion to include "security" did not attain the

---

[48] Alexander Proelss, *The United Nations Convention on the Law of the Sea: A Commentary* (2017), p. 267.

[49] *YILC*, 1956, Commentary to Article 66, para. 4.

necessary two-thirds support, but Colombia submits that under modern conditions an evolving interpretation of Article 33 may now include Decree 1946's types of security concerns: specifically, "piracy and trafficking of drugs and psychotropic substances".

45. These concerns would, in any event, come under the protection of the coastal State's "customs", "fiscal" and "sanitary" laws and regulations. Nicaragua seems to forget that these activities fall under the rights of third States through the operation of the principle set forth in UNCLOS Article 58, paragraph 2.

46. Nicaragua's objection to the Decree's inclusion of cultural heritage is ironic, as its own law on its contiguous zone claims such a power. As Colombia's survey of State practice demonstrated, multiple States have claimed powers to protect cultural heritage in their contiguous zone, reflecting the presumption in UNCLOS Article 303.

47. Nicaragua objects to Colombia's power to protect the Archipelago's marine environment from threats or acts emanating from the contiguous zone. Nicaragua has failed to show which of its enumerated environmental jurisdictions in Part XII the Colombian Decree violates. For instance, UNCLOS Article 220, paragraph 6, empowers a State within its EEZ, to address marine pollution to its coastline, but not to the coastline of another State. It is UNCLOS Article 221 which provides an example of the allocation of jurisdiction in one such scenario. Both provisions are in your folders at tab 35.

48. Article 221 provides that, consistent with customary and conventional law, a State may "take and enforce measures beyond the territorial sea proportional to the actual or threatened damage to protect their coastline or related interests, including fishing, from pollution or threat of pollution following upon a maritime casualty or acts relating to such a casualty". Article 221, paragraph 2, sets no spatial limit for this power and the events activating this right are cast in broad terms. In any event, none of the provisions in Part XII or anywhere else in the UNCLOS grant an EEZ State the jurisdiction to protect the environment of another State's territorial sea and land territory. That right and responsibility rests with Colombia, as part of its contiguous zone powers, none of which violates Nicaragua's specific environmental jurisdictions.

49. The control necessary to protect the marine environment and to respond to environmental threats in general is included within UNCLOS Article 33's "sanitary" power. The etymology of the

word "sanitary", the Latin "sanitas", means "health". Recently, the Inter-American Court of Human Rights confirmed that a healthy environment is a human right which States have a duty to protect. Indeed, Nicaragua's own contiguous zone law employs the term "health".

50. At this moment, Madam President, one hardly need marshal authority for the right and obligation of States to take appropriate actions to protect the health of their populations. If a threat to a State's territory and territorial sea is emanating from events in the contiguous zone and portends adverse effects on the health of its population, must the State wait for the threat to materialize in its territory or its territorial sea, before acting to abate it? Many States exercise environmental protection measures as part of their contiguous zone powers, as set out in Colombia's survey of State practice.

51. For example, in 1999, the United States, a non-State party subject only to customary international law, proclaimed, in its contiguous zone, powers to control drug smuggling, pollution, and underwater artifacts[50].

52. Both the customary law on the contiguous zone and the interpretation of Article 33 have evolved in response to the changing perils to the members of the international community. Nicaragua urges an obsolete construction of the customary international law on the contiguous zone. Obsolete and even hypocritical, as the scope of its own contiguous zone law shows.

53. Earlier this week, Nicaragua criticized Colombia for describing its contiguous zone powers as protecting "vital interests". Yet Colombia's Decree 1946, as amended, provides for a closed list of these vital interests, each subject to evolutionary interpretation. By contrast, consider the breadth and scope of Nicaragua's Law No. 420, which defines the extent of *its* contiguous zone powers[51].

54. As you can see, in its contiguous zone, Nicaragua claims the unqualified right to prevent and punish violations of its "criminal" laws and regulations in its territory or territorial sea. Apparently, domestic criminal laws may extend, at the State's will, to include prohibitions far beyond the generic terms of UNCLOS Article 33. The sincerity of its objection to mere evolutionary interpretation of generic terms is cast into doubt by its own, unlimited, version of contiguous zone powers. Nicaragua complains that "only" 16 States claimed security powers in their respective

---

[50] The White House, Office of the Vice President, "Extension of Federal Enforcement Zone in U.S. Coastal Waters Will Help Prevent Violations of Environmental, Customs, or Immigration Laws", 2 Sept. 1999, available at https://clintonwhitehouse4.archives.gov/CEQ/990902a.html.

[51] Nicaragua Law No. 420, Art. 6.

contiguous zone. Nicaragua is the *only* State claiming the unlimited power to control infringements of its criminal law.

55. For these reasons, Nicaragua's objection to Decree 1946's specific powers should be rejected.

E. Decree 1946 is not *ipso facto* an internationally wrongful act

56. Madam President, Nicaragua claims that Colombia's mere enactment of Decree 1946 constitutes an internationally wrongful act. But as the ILC explains, the applicable standard depends on the primary obligation, which, in this case, is one of conduct. Therefore "whether there is a breach will depend on whether and how the legislation is given effect"[52].

57. Nicaragua argues that the obligation which the Decree violated is "the preservation of the exclusive sovereign rights belonging to Nicaragua in its EEZ in accordance with Articles 56 and 58 of the UNCLOS"[53]. Its argument is misconceived. Should an occasion require Colombia to *exercise* its rights or *perform* its duties in any overlapping area, the applicable standard of conduct is to have "due regard" to Nicaragua's rights, in accordance with UNCLOS Articles 56 and 58 (3).

58. The "due regard" obligation, as the arbitral tribunal in *Chagos Marine Protected Are*a recently explained, would not be an obligation to "avoid any impairment" of a State's right within the EEZ but to balance the competing rights[54]. And, indeed, Decree 1946, which provides expressly that its application "will be carried out in conformity with international law", represents such a commitment.

59. Colombia's obligation with regard to Nicaragua's rights may only be violated, if at all, through the *mis-application* of the Decree, not its *enactment*.

60. The lawfulness of the Decree cannot be evaluated based solely on whether its application, in a specific incident, has failed the "due regard" obligation. The powers enumerated in Decree 1946 are, as has been shown, consistent with international law. Moreover, Nicaragua has failed to prove that it suffered any injury by the enactment of Decree 1946 or by any purported failure by Colombia

---

[52] *YILC*, Draft Articles on Responsibility of States for Internationally Wrongful Acts, with Commentaries, 2001, Vol. II, Part Two, Art. 12, para. 12.

[53] RN, para. 3.56 (emphasis omitted).

[54] *Chagos Marine Protected Area Arbitration (Mauritius* v. *United Kingdom), Award of 18 March 2015*, para. 519.

to accord "due regard" to any of its rights. As to the question of whether the Decree, in itself, is inconsistent with or impedes Nicaragua's claimed rights, the answer is simple. It does not.

F. Conclusion

61. Madam President, all of Nicaragua's arguments against Decree 1946 have been shown to fail. Colombia's contiguous zone and its spatial extent are lawful under customary international law. So are the powers which may be exercised therein. Nicaragua cannot extinguish the legal effects of Colombia's sovereignty over each one of the Archipelagic islands, great or small.

62. Madam President, Members of the Court, thank you for your attention. Madam President, unless this is an appropriate moment for a break, may I ask you to call on my colleague Eduardo Valencia-Ospina, to commence Colombia's counter-claims.

The PRESIDENT: I thank Professor Reisman. It is indeed a suitable time for a coffee break, so the Court will observe a coffee break of 10 minutes before giving the floor to the next speaker. The sitting is adjourned.

The Court adjourned from 4.20 p.m. to 4.35 p.m.

The PRESIDENT: Please be seated. The sitting is resumed and I shall now give the floor to Mr. Eduardo Valencia-Ospina. You have the floor.

Mr. VALENCIA-OSPINA: Madam President, distinguished judges, may I be permitted to join the Court and others who have paid tribute to the late Judge James Crawford, whose memory I had the occasion to publicly exalt at the recent session of the International Law Commission.

COUNTER-CLAIM: NICARAGUA'S INFRINGEMENT OF THE TRADITIONAL FISHING RIGHTS OF THE INHABITANTS OF THE SAN ANDRÉS ARCHIPELAGO

I. Introduction

1. It is an honour for me to appear before you on behalf of my country, the Republic of Colombia. It is also a privilege to do so in the interest of the inhabitants of the San Andrés Archipelago and, in particular, the Raizales, who are listening very closely in their native Caribbean

islands. This morning Mr. Kent Francis James set the background against which to properly appreciate the importance of fishing for their survival.

2. This afternoon, Colombia takes the floor to reassert their rights in the context of two counter-claims, one of which is of *immediate relevance* and *paramount importance* to the artisanal fishermen and communities of the San Andrés Archipelago, hereinafter referred to as "the artisanal fishermen", who rely on fishing for their sustenance and livelihood. Colombia firmly believes that the two counter-claims, declared admissible in 2017[55], are well founded in law and in fact. They are not, as Nicaragua dismissively puts it, "an attempt to distract the Court's attention from the real core issue"[56]. The counter-claims touch upon crucial questions such as the basic needs of the inhabitants of the San Andrés Archipelago, as well as Nicaragua's straight baselines decree, which caused the unlawful extension of the Nicaraguan internal waters, territorial sea and EEZ. Their assessment by the Court, rather than impeding it, will greatly contribute to the sound administration of justice.

3. Although Colombia raised the question of Nicaragua's infringement of the traditional fishing rights, what is the underlying main point of contention is *the very existence* of these traditional rights[57]. Nicaragua does not simply ask to be cleared of all responsibility for the bullying of the artisanal fishermen. It asks for more. Nicaragua wants this Court to find that there are *no* traditional fishing rights whatsoever or, in other words, that the fishermen *cannot* fish where they have been doing so customarily, even before the coming into existence of Colombia and Nicaragua as independent States more than 200 years ago.

4. Nicaragua's two-tiered strategy is both unexpected and unfortunate. Unexpected because the highest representatives of both Parties have *explicitly* recognized the existence of these traditional fishing rights. Unfortunate, because we are dealing with an extremely delicate issue pertaining to social necessity, which Nicaragua "is ready to accommodate", as it has remarkably written, although of course not today before this Court[58].

---

[55] *Alleged Violations of Sovereign Rights and Maritime Spaces in the Caribbean Sea (Nicaragua* v. *Colombia), Counter-Claims, Order of 15 November 2017, I.C.J. Reports 2017*, p. 289.

[56] Additional Pleading of Nicaragua on Colombia's Counter-Claims (APN), para. 1.5.

[57] APN, pp. 5-27, paras. 2.3-2.58; RN, pp. 121-145, paras. 6.3-6.76.

[58] RN, para. 6.76; APN, para. 2.41.

5. Nicaragua "denies that the inhabitants of the San Andrés Archipelago have a vested 'right' to conduct artisanal fishing". Yet at the same time it not only recognizes the "fishing needs of the Raizales", but declares that "it remains open, in the spirit of brotherhood and good neighbourly relations" to reach a bilateral agreement on this matter[59]. With due respect, Nicaragua's judicial strategy reveals the weakness of its argument. The traditional fishing régime obviously needs to be fleshed out. However, the conclusion of technical arrangements should not be confused with *the existence* and *recognition of the existence* of the traditional fishing rights. Nicaragua struggled to diminish the relevance and value of its President's statements[60]. Likewise, Nicaragua struggled to distort and play down the affidavits of the artisanal fishermen annexed to Colombia's written pleadings[61]. Nicaragua's repeated assertion that it "remains open" to find a solution that includes "the fishing needs of the Raizales" does not strengthen its case based on the alleged non-existence of the traditional fishing rights. It does the exact opposite.

6. My presentation will be divided in two parts. The *first* is devoted to the existence and scope of the traditional fishing rights of the inhabitants of the San Andrés Archipelago. The *second* addresses the infringement of those rights by the Nicaraguan Naval Force.

II. The existence and scope of the traditional fishing rights of the artisanal fishermen

7. Colombia must embark anew in the examination of the affidavits annexed to its Counter-Memorial[62]. Unfortunately, Nicaragua has deemed it appropriate to rely on selective quotations from those affidavits in order to put forward two unsustainable propositions, which convey the wrong picture about the geographic and temporal scopes of the traditional fishing rights at stake. However, before going into the affidavits, it is important to stress once more that Nicaragua's assertions are disproved by the words of its *own* President, who indeed has recognized the existence of the traditional fishing rights. Three statements he made after the delivery of the 2012 Judgment must be considered in succession.

---

[59] RN, para. 6.76.

[60] RN, paras. 6.63-6.76; APN, paras. 2.29-2.41.

[61] RN, paras. 6.47-6.62; APN, paras. 2.47-2.58.

[62] CMC, Anns. 62-72.

8. On 26 November 2012, in the immediate aftermath of the Judgment, President Ortega stated with reference to the fishermen of the San Andrés Archipelago that

> "Nicaragua will authorize their fisheries in that area, where they have historically practiced fisheries, both artisanal and industrial fisheries, in that maritime area, in that maritime space, where even before the ruling by the Court, the permit was granted by Colombia and now, the permit is granted by Nicaragua"[63].

This first statement constitutes an *explicit* recognition that the fishermen of the San Andrés Archipelago have *historically* fished in an artisanal manner in maritime areas located off the coast of Nicaragua. This brings us to the second statement, the very next month.

9. On 2 December 2012, when President Ortega met with Colombian President Santos during the inauguration of Mexican President Peña Nieto, the Nicaraguan President adopted a *more concrete* stance, recognizing *not only* the artisanal and historical fishing practices at stake, *but also* the traditional *rights* vested in the Raizales. He stated:

> "Be sure that we will respect the historical rights that they (the Raizals) have had over those territories. We will find the mechanisms to ensure the right of the Raizal people to fish, in San Andrés, so we can protect those people that live of the territorial sea"[64].

10. Remarkably, President Ortega spoke of "historical *rights*" of the Raizales. He stated that mechanisms will have to be established *"to ensure"*, that is, to make certain or guarantee that those rights *already existing* are effective instead of purely theoretical. His reference to the "territorial sea" is inaccurate. It again reflects Nicaragua's tendency to equate the EEZ with the territorial sea[65]. What matters, however, is that Nicaragua's President had clearly in mind traditional rights to navigate and exploit banks in maritime areas located off the coast of Nicaragua. Let me stress again that, if the first statement of November 2012 amounts to an *explicit* recognition of the long-standing artisanal fishing *practices*, the ensuing statement in December of that same year *elevates* those practices to the *higher level of rights* protected by law. The third relevant statement confirms this.

11. On 21 February 2013, during the commemoration of the death anniversary of General Sandino, President Ortega was even more precise by declaring before the whole Nicaraguan nation:

---

[63] MN, Ann. 27.

[64] CMC, Anns. 73 and 74.

[65] Cf. CR 2021/14, pp. 22-34 (Wood).

> "I told President Santos, and I have said publicly, that the [Raizales] can continue fishing. That Nicaragua will not affect them in their Rights as Original people, that they can continue fishing. And that we work an Agreement, an Agreement between the Government of Colombia and Nicaragua, so that we can regulate this well. Because how do we know that all the boats that are fishing there are from the Raizal Community, and which ones are fisheries not related to the Raizal Community, or even has to do with industrial fishing?"[66]

12. As stressed by President Ortega, the bottom line is that the Raizales have the right to "fish freely"[67]. As the Nicaraguan President puts it, while "[i]ndustrial fishing . . . has to request permission from INPESCA [the Nicaraguan Institute for Fishing and Aquaculture]", the Raizales, as well as their companies, "can fish freely" because, he says, these waters "are their original areas as Original People, the same as of our Brothers on the Caribbean Coast"[68]. He then asks: why can the artisanal fishermen fish "once and for all"? "Because", says President Ortega, "they already have a permanent permit there". "Because they are in their lands, they are in their waters, they are in their natural habitat"[69]. This statement constitutes an *explicit* and *indisputable* recognition of the traditional fishing rights of the artisanal fishermen.

13. Nicaragua has put forward two propositions in its written pleadings, which directly contradict its President's recognition of the traditional fishing rights.

— According to the first, the artisanal fishermen only fish in the waters surrounding the islands of San Andrés, Providencia and Santa Catalina, and when they engage in longer fishing expeditions, they merely do so in the waters immediately adjacent to the other Colombian islands, such as Quitasueño, Serrana and Roncador[70]. In other words, Nicaragua alleges that they do not sail to Cape Bank and Luna Verde, despite the fact that these banks, which are *largely* more significant in terms of size and resources, are located at a similar, if not shorter, distance from San Andrés and Providencia than the distance between these two islands and Quitasueño, Serrana and Roncador.

---

[66] RC, Ann. 6.

[67] *Ibid.*

[68] *Ibid.*

[69] *Ibid.*

[70] RN, paras. 6.51-6.54.

— According to the second, the artisanal fishermen *do fish* in Cape Bank and Luna Verde, but they started doing so only in the 1970s, that is to say fifty years ago[71]. There is apparently nothing traditional in what constitutes, according to Nicaragua's misguided perception, a contemporary phenomenon, the logical outcome of technological developments[72].

14. Nicaragua's partial reading of the affidavits shows that there can be *no effective substitute* for the careful examination of the annexes at pages 373 to 427 of the Counter-Memorial. Obviously, those affidavits are replete with references to traditional fishing in the surroundings of what the artisanal fishermen sometimes call the "Northern Islands", that is to say, Quitasueño, Serrana and Roncador. It is, therefore, *extremely* convenient for Nicaragua to "cherry-pick" those excerpts from the affidavits which allow it to convey the erroneous impression that artisanal fishing mainly took place in Colombian maritime areas.

15. Likewise, it can be easily understood why the artisanal fishermen's affidavits often focus on the time period they have directly witnessed, that is, up to the last six decades. But at the same time those fishermen vividly recall that, prior to the 1960s, artisanal fishing by their forebears did take place in waters situated off the coast of Nicaragua. Before outboard and inboard engines became increasingly common in the San Andrés Archipelago, artisanal fishermen relied on catboats, schooners and sloops to reach Cape Bank, Luna Verde *and* the other traditional banks. Such expeditions certainly required more preparation, time and effort, but they nevertheless occurred regularly during the appropriate seasons. This is not surprising, considering that the Raizales are a seafarer coastal community that has held close connections with its sister communities based in the Mosquito Coast, Panama, Costa Rica, Jamaica and the Colombian mainland. In other words, Colombia does not deny that improvements in technology *facilitate* the fishing expeditions of the artisanal fishermen. Colombia, however, *does refute* Nicaragua's assertion that, prior to these developments, traditional fishing did not take place in Cape Bank and Luna Verde in a manner sufficient to give rise to a customary practice.

16. To further elucidate the thrust of my presentation, I must turn to the bathymetric Figure 4 included for illustration purposes in the judges' folders at tabs 41 to 43, which depicts the shallow

---

[71] RN, paras. 6.55-6.58; APN, para. 2.47.

[72] RN, para. 6.55.

banks in blue as well as the deep-sea banks in purple. It provides an accurate visual representation of the banks mentioned by the artisanal fishermen.

17. When I speak of shallow banks, I refer to areas where the sea-bed is located at *less* than 200 metres of depth. In this zone, there is enough light for photosynthesis to take place. It is in these nutrient-rich inshore waters that fishermen find the highest concentration of biodiversity, in particular the fish that thrive and form an essential resource of these sunlit waters.

18. On the other hand, when I speak of deep-sea banks, as the artisanal fishermen call them, I am not referring to the open-ocean offshore waters but to banks located at sea-bed depths greater than those that characterize the shallow banks. They are nevertheless at depths usually well under the 500-metre isobath. They are adjacent to the shallower nutrient-rich waters and, overall, present more commonalities with inshore rather than offshore waters. There are, of course, small shallow banks in the maritime areas located on the Colombian side, but *nothing* compares, even remotely, to the shallow and deep-sea banks located off the coast of Nicaragua.

19. Turning to the Colombian maritime areas, there exists, west of San Andrés, Providencia and Santa Catalina, two contiguous troughs each of which reaches depths *greater* than 2,000 metres, resulting in only narrow shelf areas. The situation does not improve towards the east. On the contrary, east of San Andrés, Providencia and Santa Catalina, we mainly find open-ocean offshore waters, that is, depths much greater than 500 metres. The sole limited exceptions are the banks surrounding Roncador and the East South-East Cays, but the size of these banks, like the size of the banks surrounding San Andrés, Providencia and Santa Catalina, again *pales* in comparison to the shallow and deep-sea banks located near the Archipelago and midway between Colombia and Nicaragua.

20. Admittedly, there are larger shallow and deep-sea banks located around Quitasueño and Serrana, two of the Northern Islands. Yet, they are not by themselves capable of meeting the food security needs of the inhabitants of the San Andrés Archipelago, which brings me to address the other side of the equation, that is, the Nicaraguan side.

21. Cape Bank is *by far* one of the most quoted banks in the affidavits[73]. Cape Bank is in fact *massive*. It is an area around 30 nautical miles in width, that extends for more than 100 nautical miles

[73] CMC, Anns. 62, 65, 68, 70, 71 and 72.

offshore from the entire Mosquito Coast. To the north, it reaches areas located well beyond 100 nautical miles from Cabo Gracias a Dios. East of Puerto Cabezas, Cape Bank extends beyond the 82nd west meridian in the area known as Luna Verde. Luna Verde extends significantly farther east of that meridian, at a distance of approximately 100 nautical miles from Nicaragua's mainland. From Luna Verde, the eastern edge of Cape Bank then follows a south-south-west direction. This limit, the green line on the figure, is commonly referred to as La Esquina by the artisanal fishermen. This is where the shallow grounds of Cape Bank give place to its deep-sea grounds.

22. La Esquina constitutes one of the *most* important points of reference for the artisanal fishermen. West-north-west of Providencia, La Esquina largely follows the 82nd west meridian in the south, but curves eastwards towards the north, in a north-north-east azimuth. This explains why that Meridian is also mentioned by the artisanal fishermen in their affidavits. To the north, in the area known as Luna Verde, La Esquina is located significantly east of that meridian. To the south, on the other hand, La Esquina follows a north-east to south-west direction that brings it west of the 82nd west meridian.

23. The artisanal fishermen have navigated and exploited *every ground* of Cape Bank. There are in the affidavits common references to fishing in the waters surrounding Bobel Cay, Cabo Gracias a Dios and Rosalind Bank, as well as the Corn Islands[74]. But when the artisanal fishermen speak of La Esquina, Luna Verde or the 82nd west meridian, when they broadly mention Cape Bank, they are *generally* referring to fishing grounds that are located around the eastern edge of Cape Bank. The artisanal fishermen thus fish in the shallow and deep-sea banks located, respectively, to the west and to the east of the green line shown in the figure.

24. Aside from the eastern edge of Cape Bank, the artisanal fishermen commonly refer to traditional banks north of Providencia, again in maritime areas located off the coast of Nicaragua. These banks include, but are not limited to, those discovered and named by the Raizales as Julio Bank, North East Bank and Far Bank[75]. They are located between the Northern Islands and, in particular, between Quitasueño and Providencia, as well as north of Quitasueño, not far from Luna Verde. The artisanal fishermen living in Providencia are those who most often refer to them. It

[74] CMC, Anns. 63, 64, 65, 69 and 71.

[75] CMC, Anns. 62, 63, 64, 65 and 66.

is there, instead of closer to the shallow banks of the Northern Islands, that the artisanal fishermen find the fish of particular interest to the communities living in the San Andrés Archipelago[76].

25. Instead of going now through each of the affidavits individually, I will focus on key findings that can be gathered by reading the sworn statements as a whole.

26. Let me start by recalling that the Raizales who were interviewed in San Andrés, Providencia and Santa Catalina were artisanal fishermen long before they became adults. Their parents, grandparents, uncles and aunts taught them the arts of their trade before they could reach adulthood and the same is true with regard to these ancestors. Artisanal fishermen are part of something bigger than their individual selves because, each time they set sail, they carry the traditions of their forebears with them. The south-western Caribbean Sea thus represents much more than a source of subsistence to the artisanal fishermen. To the inhabitants of the Archipelago and, in particular, the Raizales, the sea constitutes an ancestral vital maritime space *as important as* the islands that it surrounds. The relationship that the artisanal fishermen entertain with the sea could be described in part as semi-mystical and it involves a great deal of emotions[77].

27. Nicaragua stated in its Reply that it is "revealing that Colombia did not see fit during the previous *[Territorial and Maritime Dispute]* case to even advert to the existence of the rights it now claims"[78]. This is not true. In his very opening speech at the merits hearing of 2012, the Agent of Colombia stressed, "[s]ince the nineteenth century, the population of the San Andrés Archipelago had been conducting fishing activities up to the Mosquito Coast", which "have always been so essential for the archipelago's inhabitants that depriving them of these resources would entail serious consequences for their livelihood"[79]. In any event, what matters is what Colombia has explicitly stated in the present case. While the practice of private individuals *does not* affect the course of maritime and land boundaries, maritime and land boundaries, in turn, *do not* affect traditional rights vested on the inhabitants of border regions[80]. The jurisprudence in this regard, an excerpt of which

---

[76] CMC, Ann. 65.

[77] Cf. in particular CMC, Ann. 69.

[78] RN, para. 6.41.

[79] *Territorial and Maritime Dispute (Nicaragua* v. *Colombia)*, CR 2012/11, p. 14, para. 24 (Londoño).

[80] CMC, paras. 3.98-3.111.

you can see on the screen, *decisively* favours Colombia[81], an inconvenient reality that Nicaragua seeks to circumvent by relying exclusively on another argument, the alleged specificity of the EEZ, the *one and only* maritime area where, *according to Nicaragua*, traditional rights have been superseded. This issue has been amply dealt with in the written pleadings[82].

28. What the Court will also find in the affidavits is an explanation of what constitutes artisanal fishing, as distinguished from subsistence and industrial fishing, as well as a description of its evolution in terms notably of means and methods. Artisanal fishing is a form of commercial fishing[83], which also entails, in addition to direct consumption, selling part of the catch. In this regard, artisanal fishing is different from subsistence fishing, which only aims to provide food on the fisherman's family table. However, *despite* its commercial connotations, artisanal fishing has *much* in common with subsistence fishing. As stated in most affidavits, artisanal fishing ensures food security in the San Andrés Archipelago[84]. As the artisanal fishermen so often stress, artisanal fishing plays a crucial role for the subsistence of the inhabitants of San Andrés, Providencia and Santa Catalina. The line separating artisanal from subsistence fishing is overall a thin and blurry one. What differentiates artisanal from industrial fishing are the methods involved and the two activities' production scales[85].

29. One can usually tell whether a fisherman is engaged in artisanal fishing simply by looking at his boat and fishing gear. Artisanal fishermen use lines with up to approximately ten hooks, harpoons and sometimes traps. Artisanal fishing is *not*, however, an activity frozen in time. It has *inevitably* evolved and, no doubt, will continue to do so with technological developments. The affidavits give ample account of the evolution of the artisanal fishermen's boats[86], who first adapted

---

[81] *Award in the Arbitration regarding the delimitation of the Abyei Area between the Government of Sudan and the Sudan People's Liberation Movement/Army, Award of 22 July 2009, Reports of International Arbitral Awards (RIAA)*, Vol. XXX, p. 408, para. 753; *Award of the Arbitral Tribunal in the First Stage of the Proceedings between Eritrea and Yemen (Territorial Sovereignty and Scope of the Dispute), Decision of 9 October 1998, RIAA*, Vol. XXII, p. 244, para. 126; *Award of the Arbitral Tribunal in the Second Stage of the Proceedings between Eritrea and Yemen (Maritime Delimitation), Decision of 17 December 1999, RIAA*, Vol. XXII, p. 361, paras. 110-111; *Arbitration between Barbados and the Republic of Trinidad and Tobago, relating to the Delimitation of the Exclusive Economic Zone and the Continental Shelf between Them, RIAA*, Vol. XXVII, p. 227, para. 292; *Land, Island and Maritime Frontier Dispute (El Salvador/Honduras: Nicaragua intervening), Judgment, I.C.J. Reports 1992*, p. 400, para. 66; *German Settlers in Poland, Advisory Opinion, 1923, P.C.I.J., Series B, No. 6*, p. 36.

[82] RC, pp. 246-257, paras. 5.11-5.24.

[83] CMC, Anns. 62 and 65.

[84] Cf. in particular CMC, Anns. 65 and 71.

[85] CMC, Anns. 62, 65 and 68.

[86] CMC, Anns. 62, 63, 64, 65 and 67.

their wooden sailing boats to leave space for outboard engines and, later, replaced many of these vessels with fiberglass *lanchas*[87]. Some of the artisanal fishermen's boats nowadays have inboard engines, as well as small refrigeration systems instead of boxes filled with ice and salt. The navigation equipment also evolved: sextants and other instruments have been replaced by GPS and other electronics.

30. Despite the evolution of the means and methods involved, artisanal fishermen have kept to their artisanal practices and remained faithful to the main aim of their activity, which is to sell products to *their* community living in the Archipelago. There is clearly a social component to artisanal fishing, which is highlighted, among other things, by the policies adopted by the fishing co-operatives and associations based in the San Andrés Archipelago[88]. Artisanal fishermen often share their boats and fishing gear with other artisanal fishermen. They likewise borrow the boats and gear of the co-operatives to which they are often affiliated. Theirs is *first of all* a community-driven activity, one which aims at filling the needs of the inhabitants of the San Andrés Archipelago and, in particular, the Raizales, who, as you know by now, are the descendants of the enslaved Africans and the original European settlers, who have acquired their own specific culture in the last four centuries.

31. Contrary to the statements of its President, Nicaragua disputes that the artisanal fishermen of the San Andrés Archipelago have traditionally fished in waters situated off its coast. It asserts that artisanal fishing occurs within close distance of the Colombian islands and that fishing that takes place in Cape Bank and Luna Verde is a recent phenomenon. Counsel for Nicaragua of course know that it is impossible to pinpoint the precise moment when artisanal fishermen started venturing in and exploiting the grounds of Cape Bank, Luna Verde or the banks located between the Northern Islands. One point with ancestral traditions is that it is difficult to determine with precision when they originated. But for the artisanal fishermen interviewed, it is absolutely clear that, as much as themselves, their forebears navigated and exploited those banks.

32. There is nothing exceptional for artisanal fishermen based in San Andrés, Providencia and Santa Catalina to sail to Cape Bank, be it La Esquina or some of its internal banks located closer to the Miskito Cays or the Corn Islands. In fact, the route to Cape Bank, which *time and time again*

---

[87] Cf. in particular CMC, Ann. 91.

[88] CMC, Anns. 62 and 65.

must have been used by the sister communities living both in the Archipelago and on the Mosquito Coast, is *shorter* than the route to the Northern Islands. The artisanal fishermen have fished in all the waters surrounding these features, be it statically or while navigating from an island to another, trolling with one or a few lines. Likewise, they have fished in the waters of Luna Verde which, when compared to the waters of Roncador and Serrana, are in fact located *significantly* closer to Providencia.

III. The infringement of the traditional fishing rights by the Nicaraguan Naval Force

33. Regarding the affidavits, Nicaragua asserts that all the accounts relating to the bullying of the artisanal fishermen by its Naval Force amount to hearsay[89]. In its written pleadings, Nicaragua stressed that Colombia has adopted a *tu quoque* fallacy to justify its own claims, implying that Colombia's evidence appears to Nicaragua as equally inadequate as Colombia asserts that the evidence put forward by Nicaragua is[90]. Yet, the truth of the matter is that, under the conditions provided for by the Court's jurisprudence, affidavits and second-hand accounts *do constitute* admissible evidence before the Court[91]. Those conditions are amply met in relation to the affidavits and accounts from the Raizales.

34. The affidavits are consistent. Besides, the International Labour Organization's (ILO) recommendations, which Nicaragua cites only when it deems them convenient to its cause, are also consistent[92]. As the ILO has put it, "Raizal fishers have to cross Nicaraguan maritime territory, which is reported to give rise to difficulties and the payment of fines"[93]. Moreover, Nicaragua's own annexes, No. 12 of its Memorial and No. 20 of its Reply, are likewise consistent. They do refer to certain occurrences that have taken place[94]. And it will be recalled that President Ortega *himself* had

---

[89] APN, para. 2.60.

[90] APN, para. 2.62.

[91] Cf. for example *Territorial and Maritime Dispute between Nicaragua and Honduras in the Caribbean Sea (Nicaragua* v. *Honduras), Judgment, I.C.J. Reports 2007 (II)*, p. 731, para. 244.

[92] RC, para. 5.69.

[93] ILO, Committee of Experts on the Application of Conventions and Recommendations, "Observations (CEACR) — adopted 2014, published 104rd ILC session (2015)", Indigenous and Tribal Peoples Convention, 1989 (No. 169), Colombia (Ratification: 1991).

[94] RC, para. 5.70.

to instruct General Avilés *not* to detain or otherwise interfere with the artisanal fishing activities of the inhabitants of the San Andrés Archipelago[95].

35. Yet, Nicaragua asserts that "the most that Colombia's affidavits might be said to establish is that fishermen from San Andrés and Providencia have experienced some uncertainty in the wake of the 2012 Judgment, and that they are reluctant to fish in Nicaragua's waters"[96]. This is an egregious understatement. What the affidavits, the ILO recommendations and Nicaragua's own annexes all indicate is that there have been occurrences between the artisanal fishermen and the Nicaraguan Naval Force. It is the latter that has instilled a climate of fear among the artisanal fishermen. This is confirmed in recent press articles that attest *not only* to the difficult situation of the artisanal fishermen[97], *but also* to the aforementioned occurrences, which include the arrest and detention of the fishermen by the Nicaraguan Naval Force[98].

36. As portrayed in the affidavits, artisanal fishermen are approached and *boarded* by the Nicaraguan Naval Force. In the best-case scenario, the Nicaraguan agents take food, cigarettes and coffee from the fishermen who, of course, cannot refuse. But in the worst-case scenario, the Nicaraguan Naval Force takes the GPS, VHF radios, the products and all the fishing and navigation gear of value, leaving them adrift without the proper equipment[99].

37. The artisanal fishermen have stopped going to many of their traditional banks due to these occurrences with the Nicaraguan Naval Force. The encounters take place on the way to Cape Bank, when the artisanal fishermen are navigating along La Esquina, or when the Raizales are navigating and fishing between the Northern Islands.

---

[95] CMC, Ann. 76.

[96] RN, para. 6.92.

[97] "Siete años del fallo de La Haya: la crisis de los pescadores de San Andrés", press report by Radio Nacional de Colombia, 19 Nov. 2019, available at https://www.radionacional.co/cultura/siete-anos-del-fallo-de-la-haya-la-crisis-de-los-pescadores-de-san-andres (accessed 22 Sept. 2021); "La voz de las mujeres isleñas sobre el fallo de La Haya", press report by Radio Nacional de Colombia, 23 Nov. 2018, available at https://www.radionacional.co/cultura/la-voz-de-las-mujeres-islenas-sobre-fallo-de-la-haya (accessed 22 Sept. 2021); "La penosa situación de los pescadores de San Andrés", press report by Semana, 8 Feb. 2014, available at https://www.semana.com/nacion/articulo/pescadores-de-san-andres/376713-3/ (accessed 22 Sept. 2021).

[98] "San Andrés: entre la corrupción y el riesgo sanitario", press report by RCN, 16 Nov. 2019, available at https://www.noticiasrcn.com/nacional/san-andres-entre-la-corrupcion-y-el-riesgo-sanitario-349613 (accessed 22 Sept. 2021); "El fallo de la Haya se acató y se aplicó", press report by Caracol, 9 Oct. 2019, available at https://caracol.com.co/programa/2019/10/09/6am_hoy_por_hoy/1570633564_762159.html (accessed 22 Sept. 2021).

[99] Cf. in particular CMC, Anns. 67 and 71.

38. Quite apart from Nicaragua's *irrelevant* assessment of the jurisprudence relating to the drawing of maritime delimitations, such as the *Gulf of Maine* case, Colombia has demonstrated that traditional rights vested on indigenous people run with the land, as well as with the sea. In other words, while the practice of private individuals *does not* affect the course of maritime and land boundaries, maritime and land boundaries, in turn, *do not* affect traditional rights vested on indigenous people[100].

39. No doubt this Court will hear from Nicaragua a plea in favour of exclusivity, the idea that there can be no limitations whatsoever to its sovereign rights as a coastal State. The notion of exclusivity, however, is in no way specific to the EEZ. States enjoy full-fledged sovereignty, which is also exclusive, within their territory and territorial sea. Yet, nobody, *not even* Nicaragua, suggests that traditional rights are incompatible with the exclusive rights that a State enjoys within its territory. As shown in the screen, the Eritrea-Yemen Tribunal rightly found that traditional fishing régimes are not limited by the maritime zones specified under UNCLOS[101]. On the contrary, this Tribunal, which was composed of *no less* than three former Presidents of the International Court of Justice, rightly found that the traditional fishing régime operated *beyond* the territorial waters of the parties to the proceedings[102].

40. In its written pleadings Colombia has already addressed in depth this argument. I can, therefore, limit myself to pointing out that this whole debate — as to whether traditional fishing rights have been superseded by the appearance of the EEZ — becomes *purely theoretical* when it can be shown, as my pleading has done, that in any event both Parties have recognized the existence of such traditional rights.

41. For the reasons stated in this pleading, Colombia has demonstrated that the artisanal fishermen of the San Andrés Archipelago enjoy traditional fishing rights in the maritime areas off the coast of Nicaragua. It has also shown that, notwithstanding the Nicaraguan President's

---

[100] Cf. *supra* fn. 83 and 84.

[101] *Award of the Arbitral Tribunal in the Second Stage of the Proceedings between Eritrea and Yemen (Maritime Delimitation), Decision of 17 December 1999, RIAA,* Vol. XXII, p. 361, para. 109.

[102] *Ibid.*

recognition of these rights, the Nicaraguan Naval Force has bullied the artisanal fishermen of the San Andrés Archipelago, thus breaching the rights of this vulnerable community.

Madam President, distinguished judges, this concludes my presentation. I thank you for your attention and request that you invite Professor Thouvenin to the podium.

The PRESIDENT: I thank Mr. Valencia-Ospina, and I now invite the next speaker, Professor Jean-Marc Thouvenin, to take the floor.

M. THOUVENIN : Merci beaucoup, Madame la présidente.

Demande reconventionnelle : illégalité du décret nº 33-2013

1. Madame la présidente, Mesdames et Messieurs les juges, c'est un honneur de paraître devant vous aujourd'hui, pensant avec émotion au temps où le juge Crawford siégeait parmi vous. Et ce, pour présenter les arguments de la Colombie au soutien de sa demande reconventionnelle relative au décret nicaraguayen nº 33-2013 fixant ses lignes de base attachées à sa côte caribéenne. Ce décret est reproduit à l'onglet nº 46 du dossier des juges.

2. Droites, et fort éloignées de la côte, ces lignes de base ont pour effet mécanique de repousser les limites des espaces maritimes du Nicaragua vers l'est, et d'empiéter sur les droits de la Colombie. Comme on l'a vu depuis le début de ces plaidoiries, ce qui est en jeu dans cette affaire, c'est la liberté de navigation, en particulier celle des navires colombiens dont le Nicaragua s'évertue à contester la simple présence en mer. Or, les lignes de base droites nicaraguayennes procèdent de la même démarche en portant un coup supplémentaire à la liberté de navigation. Elles transforment en mer territoriale, sous le régime du passage inoffensif, de vastes espaces de zone économique exclusive où la liberté de navigation devrait prévaloir. Elles apparaissent en orange sur la carte projetée. Ces lignes de base transforment aussi en eaux intérieures des espaces de mer territoriale ou même de zone économique exclusive. On les voit en rouge vif sur la carte. Ces lignes projettent tout aussi mécaniquement la zone économique exclusive et le plateau continental du Nicaragua plus à l'est. C'est cela que le Nicaragua conteste.

3. Madame la présidente, après un débat assez tendu entre les Parties à propos de la recevabilité de cette demande reconventionnelle, la Cour s'est dite compétente pour en connaître à raison du lien

de connexité entre, d'une part, les demandes au principal du Nicaragua concernant le décret colombien établissant une zone contiguë, et, d'autre part, le décret nicaraguayen établissant des lignes de base. La Cour a souligné à cet égard : «à travers leurs demandes respectives, les Parties poursuivent le même but juridique puisque chacune espère voir la Cour déclarer le décret de l'autre contraire au droit international»[103].

4. La question posée à la Cour par la demande reconventionnelle de la Colombie est donc circonscrite. Elle est de savoir, et elle est uniquement de savoir, si le décret nicaraguayen n° 33-2013, par lequel cet Etat a fixé ses lignes de base droites en mer des Caraïbes, est contraire au droit international. Selon la Colombie, c'est le cas, et c'est ce que je vais démontrer.

5. Ce faisant, je ne discuterai pas de ce dont le Nicaragua voudrait faire le cœur du débat, et sur quoi j'imagine, hélas, que la Cour va devoir consacrer un temps d'écoute inutile, à savoir des actes de droit interne colombiens fixant ses propres lignes de base[104]. Il est évident que la demande reconventionnelle est limitée à la seule question de savoir si le décret nicaraguayen d'août 2013 est conforme ou non aux exigences du droit international.

6. Je ne discuterai pas davantage des prétentions nouvelles que le Nicaragua fait valoir quant à des points de base qu'il entendrait poser sur de prétendus hauts-fonds découvrants qui se situeraient à l'est des lignes de base droites établies par le décret contesté[105]. Cette question est hors sujet et hors de la juridiction de la Cour puisqu'elle est sans aucun lien avec le décret dont la contestation par la Colombie a été acceptée par la Cour comme recevable au titre de la demande reconventionnelle[106]. Au demeurant, rien ne soutient la thèse exposée dans la plaidoirie additionnelle du Nicaragua, selon laquelle cet Etat pourrait proclamer, comme point de départ de la mesure de l'étendue de ses zones maritimes en rapport avec une portion spécifique de sa côte, *à la fois* une ligne de base droite reliant deux points de base posés sur des îles, *et, en même temps,* des points de base prétendument posés sur des hauts-fonds découvrants se situant au large de cette ligne de base droite[107]. Le Nicaragua ne peut

---

[103] *Violations alléguées de droits souverains et d'espaces maritimes dans la mer des Caraïbes (Nicaragua c. Colombie), demandes reconventionnelles, ordonnance du 15 novembre 2017, C.I.J. Recueil 2017*, p. 307, par. 53.

[104] RN, par. 7.19 et 7.53 ; pièce additionnelle du Nicaragua relative aux demandes reconventionnelles de la Colombie (ci-après «PAN»), par. 3.6 à 3.11.

[105] RN, par. 7.8 et 7.57 ; PAN, par. 3.15 à 3.26.

[106] DC, par. 6.10.

[107] PAN, notamment, par. 3.19 à 3.22.

pas avoir deux lignes de base *au même endroit* de sa côte, tout comme il ne peut pas avoir deux lignes de délinéation de sa mer territoriale, ou encore deux lignes de délinéation de sa zone économique exclusive.

7. En tout état de cause, la Colombie a présenté une demande reconventionnelle à propos du seul décret proclamant des lignes de base droites. J'en resterai donc, comme je le dois, à la question dont la Cour est saisie. Pour l'aborder il est opportun de commencer par rappeler le droit applicable, avant de constater que les lignes de base consignées dans le décret nicaraguayen n'y sont nullement conformes.

I. Droit applicable

8. Madame la présidente, c'est suffisamment rare pour être souligné : les Parties semblent en accord sur les règles de droit international coutumier qui président à la détermination des lignes de base[108]. La règle de principe pose que c'est la laisse de basse mer le long de la côte qui doit servir de fondement au tracé de la ligne de base. Mais le Nicaragua a préféré faire valoir l'exception à cette règle, bien qu'elle ne soit invocable qu'à propos des côtes dont les abords sont les plus tourmentés. Cette exception coutumière, dont l'existence a été relevée par la Cour internationale de Justice dans l'affaire des *Pêcheries anglo-norvégiennes* jugée en 1951[109], se reflète dans l'article 4 de la convention de Genève de 1958 sur la mer territoriale et la zone contiguë, dont le texte est reproduit presque mot à mot à l'article 7 de la convention des Nations Unies sur le droit de la mer. Selon ces textes :

> «[Dans les régions où la ligne côtière présente de profondes échancrures et indentations] (texte de 1958), [Là où la côte est profondément échancrée et découpée] (texte de 1982), ou s'il existe un chapelet d'îles le long de la côte, à proximité immédiate de celle-ci, la méthode des lignes de base droites reliant des points appropriés peut être employée pour tracer la ligne de base à partir de laquelle est mesurée la largeur de la mer territoriale (textes de 1958 et 1982).»

9. Il est donc constant que la possibilité de recourir à des lignes de base droites, évidemment plus avantageuses que des lignes de base normales pour l'Etat côtier, et plus désavantageuses pour tous les autres Etats, n'est reconnue par le droit international coutumier que dans des cas véritablement exceptionnels. Dans l'affaire *Qatar c. Bahreïn*, la Cour a constaté

---

[108] CMC, par. 10.24 à 10.29 ; RN, par. 7.13.

[109] *Pêcheries (Royaume-Uni c. Norvège), arrêt, C.I.J. Recueil 1951*, p. 116.

«que la méthode des lignes de base droites, qui déroge aux règles normales de détermination des lignes de base, ne peut être appliquée que si plusieurs conditions sont remplies. Cette méthode doit être appliquée de façon restrictive.»[110]

10. Il faut, je crois, conserver cette précision bien claire à l'esprit : la «méthode doit être appliquée de façon restrictive», seulement lorsque les conditions requises sont objectivement réunies. Mais même lorsque tel est le cas, les lignes de base droites que l'Etat côtier peut alors tirer doivent être conformes à certaines exigences. La règle coutumière à cet égard est codifiée par le texte du paragraphe 2 de la convention de 1958, repris à l'identique au paragraphe 3 de l'article 7 de la convention de 1982 :

«Le tracé des lignes de base droites ne doit pas s'écarter sensiblement de la direction générale de la côte et les étendues de mer situées en deçà doivent être suffisamment liées au domaine terrestre pour être soumises au régime des eaux intérieures.»

II. Le décret du Nicaragua ne respecte pas les règles relatives au recours et au tracé des lignes de base droites

11. Madame la présidente, Mesdames et Messieurs les juges, la Colombie soutient que le décret nicaraguayen n'est pas conforme à ces règles. D'autres Etats partagent ce constat : le Costa Rica a élevé une protestation[111] ; et il en va de même des Etats-Unis qui contestent avec force arguments les «excessive straight baselines» du Nicaragua[112]. Vous trouverez le texte de ces protestations au dossier des juges, à l'onglet n° 49.

12. Comme je vais maintenant le montrer, ces protestations sont justifiées car, non seulement les conditions ne sont pas réunies pour que le Nicaragua soit autorisé à tracer des lignes de base droites, mais, au surplus, à supposer même que les conditions soient réunies — *quod non* —, les lignes droites revendiquées par le Nicaragua ne sont pas conformes aux règles se rapportant à leur tracé.

---

[110] *Délimitation maritime et questions territoriales entre Qatar et Bahreïn (Qatar c. Bahreïn), fond, arrêt, C.I.J. Recueil 2001*, p. 103, par. 212.

[111] Nations Unies, lettre datée du 23 octobre 2013, adressée au Secrétaire général par le représentant permanent du Costa Rica auprès de l'Organisation des Nations Unies, Assemblée générale des Nations Unies, 25 octobre 2013, doc. A/68/548 (disponible à l'adresse suivante : documents-dds-ny.un.org/doc/UNDOC/GEN/N13/531/15/pdf/N1353115.pdf).

[112] U.S. diplomatic note No. 070 of 6 March 2014, 2014 Digest chapter 12, pp. 542-543 (disponible à l'adresse suivante : 2009-2017.state.gov/documents/organization/244504.pdf) ; U.S. Department of Defense, *Freedom of Navigation Report for Fiscal Year 2014*, p. 2 (disponible à l'adresse suivante : policy.defense.gov/Portals/11/Documents/gsa/cwmd/20150323%202015%20DoD%20Annual%20FON%20Report.pdf) ; voir aussi le *Freedom of Navigation Report for Fiscal Year 2015*, p. 1 (disponible à l'adresse suivante : policy.defense.gov/Portals/11/Documents/gsa/cwmd/FON_Report_FY15.pdf).

A. Les conditions ne sont pas réunies pour que le Nicaragua puisse recourir à des lignes de base droites

1. La côte nicaraguayenne n'est pas «profondément échancrée et découpée»

13. Madame la présidente, Mesdames et Messieurs les juges, il vous suffira sans doute de jeter un regard à la configuration de la côte caraïbe du Nicaragua pour percevoir que les conditions ne sont manifestement pas réunies pour que des lignes de base droites soient tirées par le Nicaragua tout au long de sa côte. Permettez-moi tout de même, au risque d'enfoncer des portes ouvertes, d'en administrer la démonstration.

14. La première des deux situations géographiques dans lesquelles un Etat peut prétendre tracer des lignes de base droites est celle dans laquelle sa façade maritime présente une ligne de côte particulièrement tourmentée. La côte doit, selon l'exception coutumière codifiée aux articles 4 et 7 des conventions de 1958 et 1982, présenter de profondes échancrures et indentations, c'est-à-dire être profondément échancrée et découpée.

15. Le type de côte visé ici ressort de manière particulièrement frappante de la description faite de la côte norvégienne par la Cour dans l'affaire des *Pêcheries anglo-norvégiennes*. Cette côte est, selon la Cour :

> «[p]rofondément découpée sur tout son parcours, [et] ouvre à tout instant des échancrures qui pénètrent dans les terres, sur une distance souvent très considérable : le Porsangerfjord, par exemple, pénètre à l'intérieur du continent sur une longueur de 75 milles marins»[113].

Elle est encore, ajoute la Cour : «découpée en fjords larges et profonds»[114].

16. La formule des textes codificateurs que l'on trouve tant dans la convention de 1958 que dans celle de 1982 n'est donc pas une figure de style. Elle reflète correctement la règle coutumière selon laquelle, exception faite de la seconde hypothèse sur laquelle je reviendrai dans un instant, seule une côte profondément échancrée et découpée de tout aussi profondes indentations est susceptible de donner droit au tracé de lignes de base droites. Des échancrures, des concavités, des failles, ne sauraient suffire : les tourments de la côte doivent être *profonds*.

17. Il suffit de regarder la ligne de la côte caraïbe du Nicaragua — qui est maintenant projetée — pour percevoir qu'elle ne répond en rien à cette exigence. Elle n'est ni tourmentée, ni

---

[113] *Pêcheries (Royaume-Uni c. Norvège), arrêt, C.I.J. Recueil 1951*, p. 127.

[114] *Ibid.*

profondément échancrée et découpée, et personne n'y verra de profondes indentations. Elle est tout au contraire remarquablement stable.

18. On voit, bien sûr, qu'elle change légèrement de parcours vers le sud, de Punta Perlas à Monkey Point puis jusqu'à la frontière avec le Costa Rica. Mais cette portion de côte n'est pas pour autant profondément échancrée et découpée. Ses légères concavités sont des figures géographiques dont la règle ne dit nullement qu'elles autorisent à recourir à la ligne de base droite sans lien avec la côte proclamée par le Nicaragua à cet endroit.

2. L'introuvable chapelet d'îles le long et à proximité immédiate de la côte

19. Passant à la seconde hypothèse, vous constaterez, Madame la présidente, Mesdames et Messieurs les juges, qu'il n'y a pas davantage de chapelets d'îles le long et à proximité immédiate de cette côte que de profonds tourments.

***a)* Le critère**

20. Les termes «chapelet d'îles le long de la côte, à proximité immédiate de celle-ci»[115] retranscrivent fidèlement la jurisprudence de la Cour dans l'affaire des *Pêcheries anglo-norvégiennes*[116]. A l'époque, selon la Cour, le critère à remplir pour pouvoir tirer des lignes de base droites entre des îles situées en face d'une côte était que cette côte soit «bordée par un archipel tel que le «skjærgaard»»[117]. En français, «skjærgaard» signifie «barrière», et, en anglais, «rock rampart». L'image est particulièrement juste puisque cette formation est constituée d'environ 120 000 éléments insulaires[118]. Ceci suggère que pour qu'il soit permis de déroger aux lignes de base normales, la configuration côtière et insulaire doit présenter un aspect exceptionnel[119], laissant apparaître une sorte de barrière d'îles difficilement franchissable entre la côte et le large.

21. La règle coutumière codifiée depuis lors se formule très légèrement différemment, sans plus de référence à la notion d'archipel, laquelle pourrait peut-être donner lieu à controverses, mais

[115] Convention des Nations Unies sur le droit de la mer, art. 7, par. 1.

[116] *Pêcheries (Royaume-Uni c. Norvège), arrêt, C.I.J. Recueil 1951*, p. 116.

[117] *Ibid.*, p. 129.

[118] C. Lathrop, «Baselines», *in* Donald R. Rothwell, Alex G. Oude Elferink, Karen N. Scott, Tim Stephens, *The Oxford Handbook of the Law of the Sea,* Oxford, 2015, p. 85.

[119] *Ibid.*, p. 86.

l'esprit reste le même. De par le nombre, la forme et la disposition des îles en question, la formation insulaire qui en résulte doit en effet ressembler, ou à tout le moins, inspirer la comparaison avec un *chapelet*, c'est-à-dire, pour prendre une image comparable, avec un «collier» d'îles tenant fermement ces dernières dans un alignement relativement cohérent.

22. Ce chapelet d'îles doit, selon l'exception coutumière, être disposé «le long de la côte, à proximité immédiate de celle-ci»[120]. *A contrario*, les chapelets d'îles qui ne sont pas «le long de la côte», c'est-à-dire ceux qui lui sont plutôt perpendiculaires ou, autrement dit, qui s'éloignent de la côte, sont sans pertinence et ne sauraient justifier d'exception.

23. Sont également dénués d'effet les chapelets d'îles qui ne sont pas «à proximité immédiate» de la côte. Du reste, les dernières îles d'un chapelet d'îles perpendiculaire à la côte perdent progressivement tout rapport de proximité immédiate avec cette dernière, ce qui confirme qu'elles ne sauraient satisfaire le critère permettant de tirer des lignes de base droites.

24. Le Bureau du droit de la mer et des affaires maritimes de l'Organisation des Nations Unies a fort utilement décliné cette règle à des cas concrets dans son étude de 1989 sur les lignes de base, et son travail sur ce point précis est tout à fait remarquable. Il avait conclu à l'existence de deux types pertinents de chapelets d'îles permettant de déroger à la règle relative à la ligne de base «normale».

25. Le premier cas se présente :

> «lorsque les îles semblent constituer un tout avec la terre ferme. Ces îles paraissent imbriquées dans la côte et, sur les cartes à petite échelle, sont représentées comme un prolongement de la terre ferme.»[121]

26. Alternativement, le second cas est observé lorsqu'existe :

> «une formation d'îles-barrières située à quelque distance de la côte et masquant une grande partie du littoral depuis la mer. ... La côte peut aussi être masquée par une multitude d'îlots qui, du seul fait de leur nombre, pourraient être comparées à un chapelet.»[122]

---

120 Convention des Nations Unies sur le droit de la mer, art. 7, par. 1.

121 Bureau des affaires maritimes et du droit de la mer, *Lignes de base : examen des dispositions relatives aux lignes de base dans la Convention des Nations Unies sur le droit de la mer*, New York, 1989, p. 41, par. 44 (disponible à l'adresse suivante : www.un.org/Depts/los/doalos_publications/publicationstexts/f_88v5_baselines_highres.pdf) ; voir aussi Virginia Commentary, p. 100, cité in CMC, par. 10.36.

122 *Ibid.*, p. 23, par. 45.

***b)* Les prétendues îles nicaraguayennes**

27. Madame la présidente, Mesdames et Messieurs les juges, ceci posé, j'en viens au cas d'espèce.

28. Le Nicaragua prétend que le nombre d'îles se trouvant au large de ses côtes est très élevé puisqu'il s'établirait à pas moins de 95[123]. Ces dernières îles se trouveraient entre la côte et les îles principales à partir desquelles ses lignes de base droites sont tracées[124]. C'est cet ensemble d'îles qui, selon le Nicaragua, formerait un chapelet d'îles le long et à proximité immédiate de sa côte.

29. Cette thèse est sans fondement, pour trois raisons déterminantes.

30. *En premier lieu*, le Nicaragua n'apporte aucunement la preuve des faits qu'il allègue. Il se borne à donner une liste de ses prétendues îles en annexe 31 à sa réplique. Or, l'existence de ces prétendues îles doit se prouver, une liste de noms n'étant manifestement pas une preuve[125].

31. D'autant moins que la simple lecture de cette liste soulève des doutes. Ainsi, «Pigeon Cay», «White Rock», «Guano Cay», «Frenchman's Cay» et «Sister Cays» y apparaissent chacune deux fois, et sont donc comptabilisées deux fois.

32. Le doute s'épaissit davantage, pour dire le moins, lorsque l'on regarde d'un peu plus près ce qu'il en est de la première des îles revendiquées par le Nicaragua pour poser ses points de base, à savoir Edinburgh Cay. Cette prétendue île est d'une particulière importance puisque, comme on le sait, le décret contesté trace 8 segments de lignes de base droite à partir d'une série de 9 points de base, Edinburgh Cay étant le deuxième d'entre eux. Ceci est représenté sur la carte en haut à gauche de votre écran, qui est un extrait de l'annexe 2 au décret contesté.

33. L'ennui est qu'Edinburgh Cay n'est pas une île, selon les cartes marines à grande échelle qu'utilise le Nicaragua, comme la carte «NGA Nautical Chart 28130, Cabo Gracias a dios to Puerto Isabel», produite en annexe 5 à sa plaidoirie additionnelle. En effet, comme vous pouvez le constater en regardant l'extrait présenté en bas à gauche de l'écran, que l'on ne peut comprendre qu'à la lumière de la légende de la carte que nous avons reproduite à droite de l'écran[126], Edinburgh Cay n'a

[123] RN, par. 7.20.

[124] PAN, par. 3.33.

[125] DC, par. 6.29.

[126] «U.S. Chart No. 1 – Symbols, Abbreviations and Terms used on Paper and Electronic Navigational Charts», NGA, 13th ed., 15 avril 2019 (accessible à l'adresse suivante : msi.nga.mil/Publications/Chart1).

rien que l'on puisse légalement qualifier d'île. Pourtant, le Nicaragua prétend y poser un point de base.

34. Le Nicaragua n'a donc aucunement prouvé la géographie marine dont il se prévaut.

35. *En deuxième lieu*, il est manifestement inexact que les 95 prétendues îles forment *un* chapelet d'îles «le long de la côte, à proximité immédiate» de cette dernière, de la frontière avec le Honduras jusqu'à hauteur de Monkey Point.

36. En effet, même en admettant, pour les besoins de la discussion, que les 95 prétendues îles existent, elles seraient localisées dans *trois* zones géographiques distinctes[127], indépendantes et éloignées les unes des autres ; la disposition des îles et îlots au sein de ces zones serait en outre largement orientée perpendiculairement à la côte, en direction du large. Au demeurant, il suffit de regarder la carte pour voir que ces îles ne produisent aucun effet masquant. A supposer même que leur existence soit prouvée, elles ne donneraient donc pas à voir un chapelet d'îles situées le long et à proximité immédiate de la côte du Nicaragua en mer des Caraïbes[128].

37. C'est dire que là où le critère pour tracer des lignes de base droites requiert que la côte concernée soit «masquée par une multitude d'îlots qui, du seul fait de leur nombre, pourraient être comparées à un chapelet»[129] d'îles, le Nicaragua ne présente que quelques îles, rochers et hauts-fonds découvrants concentrés dans trois zones géographiques distinctes et éloignées les unes des autres.

38. Le Nicaragua défend sa thèse en faisant valoir la pratique norvégienne qui montrerait que relier des groupes d'îles séparées de dizaines de milles marins ne serait pas incompatible avec l'existence d'*un* chapelet d'îles le long de la côte[130].

39. Mais, outre que la pratique norvégienne à laquelle le Nicaragua se réfère n'est pas constitutive de la règle de droit, il est clair que la côte norvégienne en cause est radicalement différente de celle qui nous occupe. Là encore, il suffit de la regarder pour voir qu'elle illustre parfaitement la première hypothèse dans laquelle un chapelet d'îles est susceptible d'autoriser le recours à des lignes de base droites, celle dans laquelle les îles :

---

[127] RN, fig. 7.5.

[128] CMC, par. 10.39 à 10.43 ; DC, par. 6.32 à 6.41.

[129] Bureau des affaires maritimes et du droit de la mer, Lignes de base : examen des dispositions relatives aux lignes de base dans la Convention des Nations Unies sur le droit de la mer, New York, 1989, p. 23, par. 45 (disponible à l'adresse suivante : www.un.org/Depts/los/doalos_publications/publicationstexts/f_88v5_baselines_highres.pdf).

[130] PAN, fig. 8.

«semblent constituer un tout avec la terre ferme. Ces îles paraissent imbriquées dans la côte et, sur les cartes à petite échelle, sont représentées comme un prolongement de la terre ferme.»[131]

40. Comme on le voit sur cette carte à petite échelle, la configuration de la côte norvégienne donne l'impression que les îles sont tellement imbriquées avec la côte qu'elles forment une baie que la ligne de base droite viendrait fermer. Ici, les eaux intérieures se situant entre la côte et la ligne apparaissent nettement comme *«inter fauces terrarum»*, selon le critère posé par la Cour dans son arrêt de 1951 dans l'affaire des *Pêcheries*[132], c'est-à-dire «entre les mâchoires de la côte», ou, en anglais, «in the jaws of the land»[133].

41. On ne peut certainement pas en dire autant des îles nicaraguayennes, lesquelles ne semblent nullement former un tout avec la terre, et ne sont d'ailleurs jamais représentées comme un prolongement de la terre ferme. Il n'y a ici rien qui ressemble, même de loin, à des «mâchoires» de la côte, entre lesquelles les eaux revendiquées par le Nicaragua comme intérieures seraient enferrées.

42. *En troisième et dernier lieu*, si les îles nicaraguayennes ne forment pas *un* chapelet d'îles, puisqu'elles forment à l'évidence trois groupes distincts, elles ne forment pas davantage *trois* chapelets d'îles, qui, chacun, s'étendrait le long des portions de la côte au large desquelles elles sont situées, justifiant des lignes de base droites à ces endroits.

43. En effet, leur orientation générale n'est pas parallèle à la côte, mais lui est perpendiculaire[134]. Elles sont positionnées non pas comme le serait un chapelet étendu parallèlement à la côte, mais, pour prendre là encore une image, comme le seraient des osselets jetés au large par un enfant positionné sur la côte[135]. C'est pourquoi leur effet masquant est pratiquement insignifiant puisque, par hypothèse même, l'effet masquant de dix petites îles perpendiculaires à la côte n'a aucun effet cumulatif de ce point de vue.

44. C'est d'ailleurs l'un des éléments, l'un des éléments *seulement* car il y en a bien d'autres, qui distingue la configuration en discussion ici de celle qui était examinée dans l'affaire

---

[131] Bureau des affaires maritimes et du droit de la mer, Lignes de base : examen des dispositions relatives aux lignes de base dans la Convention des Nations Unies sur le droit de la mer, New York, 1989, p. 22, par. 44.

[132] *Pêcheries (Royaume-Uni c. Norvège), arrêt, C.I.J. Recueil 1951*, p. 130.

[133] Coalter G. Lathrop, «Baselines», *in* Donald R. Rothwell, Alex G. Oude Elferink, Karen N. Scott, Tim Stephens, *The Oxford Handbook of the Law of the Sea,* Oxford, 2015, p. 80.

[134] CMC, par. 10.42.

[135] Allant apparemment dans le même sens, voir PAN, par. 3.39.

Erithrée/Yemen. Dans cette affaire, les îles discutées par le tribunal, notamment Tiqfash, Kutama et Uqban, se situent dans le prolongement de la presqu'île de Ras Isa, selon une projection presque parallèle à la côte. Le tribunal y a spontanément vu un «intricate system of islands, islets and reefs which guard this part of the coast»[136], c'est-à-dire une formation correspondant non pas à une, mais aux deux hypothèses formulées par le Bureau du droit de la mer que j'ai évoquées tout à l'heure. Et pour cause : non seulement ces îles yéménites paraissent en effet «imbriquées dans la côte», parce qu'avec la grande île de Kamaran, elles se situent dans le prolongement exact de la presqu'île de Ras Isa, le long de la côte, et donnent l'impression de prolonger cette presqu'île, mais encore, parce qu'elles ont un effet très masquant à raison de leur nombre et de leur disposition le long de la côte et non pas vers le large.

45. La côte nicaraguayenne et ses îles ne présentent *aucune* ressemblance avec ce cas.

46. Il faut ajouter que la disposition des îles vers le large interdit au Nicaragua de prétendre que ses îles les plus éloignées, jusqu'à 24 milles marins de la côte, sont à «proximité immédiate» de la côte[137].

47. La Cour notera, bien sûr, que les Parties ont déjà fait valoir leurs vues sur la question de savoir si plus de 20 milles marins des côtes est, ou non, une distance incompatible avec l'idée d'une «proximité immédiate». La Colombie admet que la règle de la proximité immédiate n'est pas mathématique. Elle a cependant un sens. Elle traduit l'exigence que le chapelet d'îles le long de la côte forme une certaine unité avec cette dernière, même si ce chapelet ne s'y imbrique pas mais au contraire s'en détache. Or, plus une île est éloignée de la côte, moins il est possible de prétendre qu'elle forme une unité avec cette dernière. En l'espèce, on ne perçoit *aucune* unité géographique entre la côte et les îles nicaraguayennes par lesquelles passent les lignes de base contestées.

---

[136] *Sovereignty and Maritime Delimitation in the Red Sea (Eritrea/Yemen)*, PCA Case No. 1996-04, Award of the Arbitral Tribunal in the Second Stage - Maritime Delimitation, 17 décembre 1999, par. 151, p. 45.

[137] CMC, par. 10.42.

B. Les lignes de base droites tirées par le Nicaragua ne sont pas conformes aux exigences du droit international

48. Madame la présidente, Mesdames et Messieurs de la Cour, à supposer, contrairement à ce que je viens de démontrer, que les conditions géographiques soient réunies pour que le tracé de lignes de base droites soit possible, ces dernières doivent assurer deux résultats :

— d'une part, le tracé des lignes de base droites ne doit pas s'écarter sensiblement de la direction générale de la côte[138] ;

— d'autre part, les étendues de mer situées en deçà doivent être suffisamment liées au domaine terrestre pour être soumises au régime des eaux intérieures[139].

49. Le système de lignes de base du Nicaragua échoue sur ces deux aspects, que j'aborderai tour à tour.

1. Les ruptures avec la direction générale de la côte

50. L'exigence que les lignes de base droites suivent la direction générale de la côte correspond au principe selon lequel le recours à de telles lignes doit demeurer exceptionnel et ne viser qu'à simplifier le tracé des lignes de base[140]. Il n'autorise pas l'Etat côtier à tracer n'importe quelle ligne, qui serait trop éloignée de ce qu'est la ligne de base «normale», laquelle suit les méandres de la côte.

51. En l'espèce, les lignes tracées par le Nicaragua ne sauraient être considérées comme suivant la direction de la côte, laquelle est simplement ignorée à au moins trois endroits.

52. Entre Cape Gracias a Dios et Edinburgh Cay — Edinburgh Cay dont j'ai indiqué tout à l'heure qu'elle n'est pas une île selon les cartes utilisées par le Nicaragua —, la prétendue ligne de base du Nicaragua, qui prend une direction est-sud-est sur environ 30 milles marins, fait un angle presque droit avec la ligne de la côte qui se dirige au sud-ouest. Non seulement cette ligne n'a-t-elle rien en partage avec la direction de la côte, mais elle démontre à elle seule que le système de lignes de base droites nicaraguayen est artificiel et non conforme aux prescriptions du droit international.

53. Entre Man of War Cay et Little Corn Island — c'est l'image au centre —, la ligne prend une direction sud-est alors que la côte suit une direction sud. Ceci conduit la prétendue ligne de base nicaraguayenne à s'éloigner de 17 milles marins supplémentaires de la côte, puisque Man of War

---

138 CMC, par. 10.44.

139 CMC, par. 10.46 et 10.47.

140 CMC, par. 10.44.

Cay est à environ 12 milles marins de la côte, tandis que Little Corn Island se trouve à 30 milles marins de la côte.

54. Enfin, entre Great Corn Island et le point terminal du système de lignes de base droites du Nicaragua — il s'agit du point 9 tout au sud, l'image est celle de droite à l'écran —, la ligne n'a strictement rien à voir avec la direction de la côte.

55. C'est d'ailleurs ce que le Nicaragua semblait faire valoir dans le cadre de son différend avec le Costa Rica. A gauche, vous voyez la direction générale de la côte dans la partie sud, telle que montrée par le Nicaragua à la page 95 de son contre-mémoire du 8 décembre 2015 dans l'affaire de sa délimitation maritime avec le Costa Rica. A droite, vous voyez la ligne de base, qui *en principe* devrait être fidèle à la direction générale de la côte, mais qui ne l'est pas du tout. Le décalage est patent.

2. L'absence de lien avec le domaine terrestre pour justifier d'une soumission au régime des eaux intérieures

56. J'en viens au dernier test, celui du lien avec le domaine terrestre des eaux que le Nicaragua entend réclamer comme étant ses eaux intérieures.

57. Ce lien devrait en l'espèce être fermement établi, j'allais dire «sauter aux yeux», vu les étendues d'eau concernées. La Cour notera d'ailleurs que la surface de mer revendiquée par le Nicaragua au large de ses côtes continentales comme relevant de ses eaux intérieures, c'est-à-dire soumises à sa souveraineté au même titre que son territoire terrestre, représente environ 21 500 kilomètres carrés[141]. C'est l'équivalent de plus de deux fois le territoire de la Jamaïque, de la totalité du territoire terrestre d'El Salvador ou de Bélize, des deux-tiers de la surface du territoire de la Belgique, et de la moitié de la surface du pays où nous nous trouvons[142]. Dans un cas aussi extrême, les éléments attestant que les eaux revendiquées sont suffisamment liées au domaine terrestre pour être soumises au régime des eaux intérieures doivent être patents. Ils sont, en l'espèce, inexistants.

58. Sur le plan purement géographique, aucun lien particulier n'existe entre les eaux revendiquées comme intérieures et la configuration de la côte et des prétendues îles côtières. La surface insulaire présente dans ces eaux est quantité négligeable par rapport à la très grande surface

---

[141] CMC, par. 10.48.

[142] DC, par. 6.54.

desdites eaux. Ces prétendues îles n'enclavent nullement les eaux en cause de manière à en faire des eaux susceptibles d'être soumises au régime des eaux intérieures[143]. Elles ne forment aucune des «mâchoires» insulaires qui, ensemble avec la côte, enclaveraient ces eaux. Le très faible effet masquant des prétendues îles nicaraguayennes ne fait d'ailleurs que souligner que ces eaux sont bien davantage liées à la mer qu'à la terre. Quant aux lignes de base droites artificiellement tirées entre Mistikos Cay et Man of War Cay, et entre Corn Islands et le point 9, elles ne sauraient justifier, à elles seules, d'un lien entre les eaux qu'elles englobent et la côte.

59. Au demeurant, le Nicaragua n'avance aucun argument sérieux justifiant d'un quelconque lien entre les eaux revendiquées comme intérieures et son territoire. Il se borne à prétendre que 81 % de ces eaux relèverait de ce qui serait sa mer territoriale s'il traçait des lignes de base normales le long de sa côte[144]. La belle affaire ! Que l'on sache, cela ne justifie en rien de les réclamer comme *eaux intérieures*.

60. Le Nicaragua allègue que ces eaux ont été exploitées par les Nicaraguayens, qui les utilisent comme lieux de pêche et d'autres activités[145], ou encore qu'une zone biologique protégée a été établie au nord de la zone[146]. Mais il n'explique nullement en quoi ces pratiques pourraient justifier qu'il exerce une souveraineté pleine, entière et exclusive sur les vastes espaces maritimes qui s'étendent entre les lignes de base normales et les lignes de base droites qu'il revendique comme étant ses eaux intérieures.

61. Accessoirement, un regard sur la carte représentant la zone de la réserve biologique couvrant Miskitos Cay, d'une part, et la bande côtière adjacente, d'autre part, telle qu'elle figure sur le site Internet recensant les sites couverts par la convention Ramsar sur les zones humides, montre l'absence de lien entre les deux sites[147]. On le voit sur cette carte du site couvert par la convention Ramsar au niveau de Miskitos Cay : ledit site ne rencontre pas la côte. Il en reste détaché et ne forme nullement une unité avec elle.

---

[143] CMC, par. 10.50.

[144] RN, par. 7.51.

[145] PAN, par. 3.60 à 3.63.

[146] PAN, par. 3.60.

[147] Disponible à l'adresse suivante : rsis.ramsar.org/RISapp/files/666/pictures/NI1135map2001.pdf.

62. Madame la présidente, Mesdames et Messieurs les juges, j'en viens à la conclusion, à vrai dire fort simple, de ma plaidoirie. Elle est que rien ne justifie que le Nicaragua soit autorisé à recourir à un système de lignes de base droites pour établir sa ligne de base dans la mer des Caraïbes, et qu'en tout état de cause les lignes qu'il établit sont dénuées de tout fondement en droit international. Le décret contesté est donc bien contraire au droit international.

Madame la présidente, Mesdames et Messieurs les juges, je vous remercie de votre patiente attention. J'ai le plaisir de vous rendre trois minutes sur l'horaire puisque ces mots concluent, du côté de la Partie colombienne, son premier tour de plaidoiries orales.

The PRESIDENT: I thank Professor Thouvenin, whose statement brings to an end this afternoon's sitting. Oral argument in the case will resume on Friday 24 September at 3 p.m., when Nicaragua will present its observations on the counter-claims of Colombia.

The sitting is adjourned.

The Court rose at 6 p.m.

Corrigé
Corrected

CR 2021/16

International Court of Justice

THE HAGUE

Cour internationale de Justice

LA HAYE

YEAR 2021

Public sitting

held on Friday 24 September 2021, at 3 p.m., at the Peace Palace,

President Donoghue presiding,

***in the case concerning* Alleged Violations of Sovereign Rights and Maritime Spaces in the Caribbean Sea (Nicaragua *v.* Colombia)**

VERBATIM RECORD

ANNÉE 2021

Audience publique

tenue le vendredi 24 septembre 2021, à 15 heures, au Palais de la Paix,

sous la présidence de Mme Donoghue, présidente,

***en l'affaire relative à des* Violations alléguées de droits souverains et d'espaces maritimes dans la mer des Caraïbes (Nicaragua c. Colombie)**

COMPTE RENDU

Present:	President	Donoghue
	Vice-President	Gevorgian
	Judges	Tomka
		Abraham
		Bennouna
		Yusuf
		Xue
		Sebutinde
		Bhandari
		Robinson
		Salam
		Iwasawa
		Nolte
	Judges *ad hoc*	Daudet
		McRae
	Registrar	Gautier

Présents :	Mme	Donoghue, présidente
	M.	Gevorgian, vice-président
	MM.	Tomka
		Abraham
		Bennouna
		Yusuf
	Mmes	Xue
		Sebutinde
	MM.	Bhandari
		Robinson
		Salam
		Iwasawa
		Nolte, juges
	MM.	Daudet
		McRae, juges *ad hoc*
	M.	Gautier, greffier

The Government of Nicaragua is represented by:

H.E. Mr. Carlos José Argüello Gómez, Ambassador of the Republic of Nicaragua to the Kingdom of the Netherlands,

as Agent and Counsel;

Mr. Alex Oude Elferink, Director, Netherlands Institute for the Law of the Sea, Professor of International Law of the Sea at Utrecht University,

Mr. Vaughan Lowe, QC, Emeritus Chichele Professor of Public International Law, University of Oxford, member of the Institut de droit international, member of the Bar of England and Wales,

Mr. Lawrence H. Martin, Attorney at Law, Foley Hoag LLP, member of the Bars of the United States Supreme Court, the District of Columbia and the Commonwealth of Massachusetts,

Mr. Alain Pellet, Emeritus Professor of the University Paris Nanterre, former Chairman of the International Law Commission, President of the Institut de droit international,

Mr. Paul Reichler, Attorney at Law, Foley Hoag LLP, member of the Bars of the United States Supreme Court and the District of Columbia,

as Counsel and Advocates;

Ms Claudia Loza Obregon, Legal Adviser, Ministry of Foreign Affairs of Nicaragua,

Ms Tessa Barsac, Consultant in International Law, Master (University Paris Nanterre), LLM (Leiden University),

as Assistant Counsel;

Mr. Robin Cleverly, MA, DPhil, CGeol, FGS, Law of the Sea Consultant, Marbdy Consulting Ltd,

as Scientific and Technical Adviser;

Ms Sherly Noguera de Argüello, MBA,

as Administrator.

The Government of Colombia is represented by:

H.E. Mr. Carlos Gustavo Arrieta Padilla, former Judge of the Council of State of Colombia, former Attorney General of Colombia and former Ambassador of Colombia to the Netherlands,

as Agent;

H.E. Mr. Manuel José Cepeda Espinosa, former President of the Constitutional Court of Colombia, former Permanent Delegate of Colombia to UNESCO and former Ambassador of Colombia to the Swiss Confederation,

as Co-Agent;

Le Gouvernement du Nicaragua est représenté par :

S. Exc. M. Carlos José Argüello Gómez, ambassadeur de la République du Nicaragua auprès du Royaume des Pays-Bas,

comme agent et conseil ;

M. Alex Oude Elferink, directeur de l'Institut néerlandais du droit de la mer, professeur de droit international de la mer à l'Université d'Utrecht,

M. Vaughan Lowe, QC, professeur émérite de droit international public à l'Université d'Oxford, titulaire de la chaire Chichele, membre de l'Institut de droit international, membre du barreau d'Angleterre et du pays de Galles,

M. Lawrence H. Martin, avocat au cabinet Foley Hoag LLP, membre des barreaux de la Cour suprême des Etats-Unis d'Amérique, du district de Colombia et du Commonwealth du Massachusetts,

M. Alain Pellet, professeur émérite de l'Université Paris Nanterre, ancien président de la Commission du droit international, président de l'Institut de droit international,

M. Paul Reichler, avocat au cabinet Foley Hoag LLP, membre des barreaux de la Cour suprême des Etats-Unis d'Amérique et du district de Colombia,

comme conseils et avocats ;

Mme Claudia Loza Obregon, conseillère juridique auprès du ministère des affaires étrangères du Nicaragua,

Mme Tessa Barsac, consultante en droit international, master (Université Paris Nanterre), LLM (Université de Leyde),

comme conseils adjoints ;

M. Robin Cleverly, MA, DPhil, CGeol, FGS, consultant en droit de la mer, Marbdy Consulting Ltd,

comme conseiller scientifique et technique ;

Mme Sherly Noguera de Argüello, MBA,

comme administrateur.

Le Gouvernement de la Colombie est représenté par :

S. Exc. M. Carlos Gustavo Arrieta Padilla, ancien juge au conseil d'Etat colombien, ancien *Procurador General de la Nación* et ancien ambassadeur de Colombie aux Pays-Bas,

comme agent ;

S. Exc. M. Manuel José Cepeda Espinosa, ancien président de la Cour constitutionnelle de Colombie, ancien représentant permanent de la Colombie auprès de l'UNESCO et ancien ambassadeur de Colombie auprès de la Confédération suisse,

comme coagent ;

H.E. Ms Marta Lucía Ramírez Blanco, Vice-President and Minister for Foreign Affairs of the Republic of Colombia,

H.E. Mr. Everth Hawkins Sjogreen, Governor of San Andrés, Providencia and Santa Catalina, Colombia,

as National Authorities;

Mr. W. Michael Reisman, McDougal Professor of International Law at Yale University, member of the Institut de droit international,

Mr. Rodman R. Bundy, former *avocat à la Cour d'appel de Paris*, member of the Bar of the State of New York, partner at Squire Patton Boggs LLP, Singapore,

Sir Michael Wood, KCMG, member of the International Law Commission, member of the Bar of England and Wales,

Mr. Eduardo Valencia-Ospina, former Registrar and Deputy-Registrar of the International Court of Justice, member and former Special Rapporteur and Chair of the International Law Commission, former Chair of the Latin American Society of International Law,

Mr. Jean-Marc Thouvenin, Professor at the University Paris Nanterre, Secretary-General of the Hague Academy of International Law, associate member of the Institut de droit international, member of the Paris Bar, Sygna Partners,

Ms Laurence Boisson de Chazournes, Professor of International Law and International Organization at the University of Geneva, member of the Institut de droit international,

H.E. Mr. Kent Francis James, former Ambassador of Colombia to Belize, former Ambassador of Colombia to Jamaica,

as Counsel and Advocates;

Mr. Andrés Villegas Jaramillo, LLM, Co-ordinator, Group of Affairs before the International Court of Justice at the Ministry of Foreign Affairs of Colombia, member of the Legal Sub-Commission of the Caribbean Sea Commission, Association of Caribbean States,

Mr. Makane Moïse Mbengue, Professor at the University of Geneva, Director of the Department of Public International Law and International Organization, associate member of the Institut de droit international,

Mr. Luke Vidal, member of the Paris Bar, Sygna Partners,

Mr. Eran Sthoeger, Esq., member of the Bar of the State of New York, Adjunct Professor of International Law at Brooklyn Law School and Seton Hall Law School,

Mr. Alvin Yap, Advocate and Solicitor of the Supreme Court of Singapore, Squire Patton Boggs LLP, Singapore,

Mr. Lorenzo Palestini, PhD, Lecturer at the Graduate Institute of International and Development Studies and at the University of Geneva,

as Counsel;

S. Exc. Mme Marta Lucía Ramírez Blanco, vice-présidente et ministre des affaires étrangères de la République de Colombie,

S. Exc. M. Everth Hawkins Sjogreen, gouverneur de San Andrés, Providencia et Santa Catalina, Colombie,

comme représentants de l'Etat ;

M. W. Michael Reisman, professeur de droit international à l'Université de Yale, titulaire de la chaire McDougal, membre de l'Institut de droit international,

M. Rodman R. Bundy, ancien avocat à la Cour d'appel de Paris, membre du barreau de l'Etat de New York, associé au cabinet Squire Patton Boggs LLP (Singapour),

Sir Michael Wood, KCMG, membre de la Commission du droit international, membre du barreau d'Angleterre et du pays de Galles,

M. Eduardo Valencia-Ospina, ancien greffier et greffier adjoint de la Cour internationale de Justice, membre et ancien rapporteur spécial et président de la Commission du droit international, ancien président de l'association latino-américaine de droit international,

M. Jean-Marc Thouvenin, professeur à l'Université Paris Nanterre, secrétaire général de l'Académie de droit international de La Haye, membre associé de l'Institut de droit international, membre du barreau de Paris, cabinet Sygna Partners,

Mme Laurence Boisson de Chazournes, professeure de droit international public et organisation internationale à l'Université de Genève, membre de l'Institut de droit international,

S. Exc. M. Kent Francis James, ancien ambassadeur de Colombie au Belize et ancien ambassadeur de Colombie en Jamaïque,

comme conseils et avocats ;

M. Andrés Villegas Jaramillo, LLM, coordonnateur du groupe chargé des affaires portées devant la Cour internationale de Justice au sein du ministère des affaires étrangères de la Colombie, membre de la sous-commission juridique relevant de la Commission de la mer des Caraïbes de l'Association des Etats de la Caraïbe,

M. Makane Moïse Mbengue, professeur à l'Université de Genève, directeur du département de droit international public et organisation internationale, membre associé de l'Institut de droit international,

M. Luke Vidal, membre du barreau de Paris, cabinet Sygna Partners,

M. Eran Sthoeger, membre du barreau de l'Etat de New York, professeur adjoint de droit international à la Brooklyn Law School et à la faculté de droit de l'université de Seton Hall,

M. Alvin Yap, avocat et *solicitor* à la Cour suprême de Singapour, cabinet Squire Patton Boggs LLP (Singapour),

M. Lorenzo Palestini, PhD, chargé d'enseignement à l'Institut de hautes études internationales et du développement et à l'Université de Genève,

comme conseils ;

H.E. Mr. Juan José Quintana Aranguren, Head of Multilateral Affairs, former Ambassador of Colombia to the Netherlands,

H.E. Mr. Fernando Antonio Grillo Rubiano, Ambassador of the Republic of Colombia to the Kingdom of the Netherlands and Permanent Representative of Colombia to the Organisation for the Prohibition of Chemical Weapons,

Ms Jenny Sharyne Bowie Wilches, Second Secretary, Embassy of Colombia in the Netherlands,

Ms Viviana Andrea Medina Cruz, Second Secretary, Embassy of Colombia in the Netherlands,

Mr. Sebastián Correa Cruz, Third Secretary,

Mr. Raúl Alfonso Simancas Gómez, Third Secretary, Group of Affairs before the International Court of Justice,

Ministry of Foreign Affairs of Colombia;

Rear Admiral Ernesto Segovia Forero, Chief of Naval Operations,

CN Hermann León, Delegate of Colombia to the International Maritime Organization,

CN William Pedroza, National Navy of Colombia, Director of Maritime and Fluvial Interests Office,

Navy of the Republic of Colombia;

Mr. Scott Edmonds, Cartographer, Director of International Mapping,

Ms Victoria Taylor, Cartographer, International Mapping,

as Technical Advisers;

Mr. Gershon Hasin, LLM, JSD, Yale Law School,

as Legal Assistant;

Mr. Mark Taylor Archbold, Consultant for the National Unit of Disaster Risk Management,

Mr. Joseph Richard Jessie Martinez, Consultant for the National Unit of Disaster Risk Management,

as Advisers.

S. Exc. M. Juan José Quintana Aranguren, chef des affaires multilatérales, ancien ambassadeur de Colombie aux Pays-Bas,

S. Exc. M. Fernando Antonio Grillo Rubiano, ambassadeur de la République de Colombie auprès du Royaume des Pays-Bas et représentant permanent de la Colombie auprès de l'Organisation pour l'interdiction des armes chimiques,

Mme Jenny Sharyne Bowie Wilches, deuxième secrétaire, ambassade de Colombie aux Pays-Bas,

Mme Viviana Andrea Medina Cruz, deuxième secrétaire, ambassade de Colombie aux Pays-Bas,

M. Sebastián Correa Cruz, troisième secrétaire,

M. Raúl Alfonso Simancas Gómez, troisième secrétaire, groupe chargé des affaires portées devant la Cour internationale de Justice,

ministère des affaires étrangères de la République de Colombie ;

Le contre-amiral Ernesto Segovia Forero, chef des opérations navales,

Le capitaine de vaisseau Hermann León, représentant de la Colombie auprès de l'Organisation maritime internationale,

Le capitaine de vaisseau William Pedroza, marine nationale de Colombie, chef de la direction chargée des intérêts maritimes et fluviaux,

marine de la République de Colombie ;

M. Scott Edmonds, cartographe, directeur de International Mapping,

Mme Victoria Taylor, cartographe, International Mapping,

comme conseillers techniques ;

M. Gershon Hasin, LLM, JSD, faculté de droit de l'Université de Yale,

comme assistant juridique ;

M. Mark Taylor Archbold, consultant auprès de l'unité nationale de gestion des risques de catastrophe,

M. Joseph Richard Jessie Martinez, consultant auprès de l'unité nationale de gestion des risques de catastrophe,

comme conseillers.

The PRESIDENT: Please be seated. The sitting is open. The Court meets this afternoon to hear the observations of Nicaragua on the counter-claims of Colombia.

I shall now give the floor to the Agent of Nicaragua, His Excellency Mr. Carlos José Argüello Gómez. You have the floor, Your Excellency.

Mr. ARGÜELLO GÓMEZ:

1. Madam President, Members of the Court, good afternoon. Today we will address the two counter-claims filed by Colombia that were admitted by the Court.

2. The first counter-claim requests the Court to declare that Nicaragua has infringed the customary artisanal fishing rights of the local inhabitants of the San Andrés Archipelago, including the indigenous Raizal people, to access and exploit their traditional fishing grounds[1].

3. Colombia has presented to the Court the three classic types of argument identified by Aristotle: the logical appeal *(logos)*, the ethical appeal *(ethos)* and the emotional appeal *(pathos)*.

4. As a starting-point, it must be clear that the only valid argument before this Court is the logical appeal, that is the legal argument, and on that count there are absolutely no legal rights, residual or otherwise, of the Raizal population of the small islands of San Andrés, Providencia and Santa Catalina to any purported fishing in the Nicaraguan EEZ. With respect to the purported infringement of these rights of the local inhabitants, it must be said at the outset that Colombia has failed to offer any credible evidence that Nicaragua has interfered with any fishing by these people, whether or not they have any rights in Nicaragua's EEZ, which Nicaragua denies. This argument or pleading by Colombia will be addressed by Mr. Lawrence Martin. I will say a few words on the other two arguments, or rather appeals.

5. Mr. Valencia explained that his pleading was also addressed to "the inhabitants of the San Andrés Archipelago and, in particular, the Raizales, who are listening very closely in their native Caribbean islands"[2]. So in a certain sense, my words must take that into consideration.

6. Hence, to begin, let me make it clear that I am not underestimating the arguments basically developed by Mr. James and Mr. Valencia but as I will briefly indicate below, if the Raizal

[1] See CMC, Chap. 9, and RC, Chap. 5.

[2] CR 2021/15, pp. 36-37, para. 1 (Valencia-Ospina).

population is suffering any problems, it is *not* due to Nicaragua or to the Court's Judgment of 2012, but to the Colombian governments.

The Court's 2012 Judgment

7. I will begin with the 2012 Judgment.

8. In this Judgment, the Court attributed sovereignty over all the islands and keys in dispute to Colombia as well as very substantial maritime areas around these small features[3]. The total land area of the islands and keys is approximately 45 sq km with a population today of approximately 80,000, including a minority of Raizales[4]. The land area of the Caribbean coast of Nicaragua, which is about one third of the total land area of the country, is around 45,000 sq km and has a population of approximately 1 million[5].

9. Thus the relevant Nicaraguan continental land area was more than a thousand times larger than all the islands put together, and the population was more than twenty times more extensive. As you can appreciate in the image on the screen. Notwithstanding this, Colombia (that is the islands) was awarded approximately 24 per cent of the maritime area that was to be divided. When Nicaragua was presenting its pleadings on delimitation in the 2012 case, it could not present arguments based on this disparity because the jurisprudence of the Court is constant that the land mass or the population is not taken into consideration in a delimitation[6].

10. So, on the basis of the Judgment, the islands and their population came out extremely well. Much better than the Caribbean people of Nicaragua. If the decision had been based on strict equity, *lato sensu*, the Colombian islands would have been attributed at most a territorial sea, and the small rocks or keys a very small token area.

11. Madam President, Mr. James made a very emotional plea based on the situation of his people, the Raizales, that according to a census is presently less than half of the population of the

---

[3] *Territorial and Maritime Dispute (Nicaragua* v. *Colombia), Judgment, I.C.J. Reports 2012 (II)*, pp. 718-720.

[4] Secretaría de Planeación Departamental, Gobernación del Archipiélago, "Ficha Técnica de Indicadores Económicos y de Desarrollo", Aug. 2020, p. 9, available at https://www.sanandres.gov.co/index.php/gestion/planeacion/publicaciones/13057-ficha-tecnica-de-indicadores-san-andres-providencia-y-santa-catalina/file (accessed 24 Sept. 2021).

[5] Demographic Data, Pro Nicaragua, available at https://pronicaragua.gob.ni/es/descubre-caribe/ (accessed 24 Sept. 2021).

[6] See for example *Continental Shelf (Libyan Arab Jamahiriya/Malta), Judgment, I.C.J. Reports 1985*, p. 41, para. 50; *Maritime Delimitation in the Area between Greenland and Jan Mayen (Denmark* v. *Norway), Judgment, I.C.J. Reports 1993*, p. 74, para. 80.

islands. The Government of the Archipelago itself published a census in August 2020 and the Raizal population is a total of 26,076 with 23,396 living in the islands[7].

12. But, as indicated before, it must be pointed out that the problems of the Raizales did not begin with the Court or with Nicaragua. These problems began in the 1950s when the Government of Colombia declared San Andrés a free port and started promoting tourism. There was a massive influx of people from the mainland that sidelined the Raizales. The Raizales have a name for what happened, they call it the "colombianization" of the islands. The newcomers took over the most lucrative businesses and the Raizales were marginalized[8].

13. The Judgment of the Court did not make matters worse. It simply served as an excuse to point the finger away from the Colombian Government for the problems of the Raizal population. The main detrimental impact of the Judgment is supposedly the loss of fishing areas. Let us look briefly on this issue.

Alleged artisanal fishing rights

14. Firstly, the claim is that these fishing areas that have been presumably curtailed by the Judgment are identified as ancestral fishing grounds. Let us go back a bit in history.

15. According to the historical data the population of San Andres in 1843 was 1,285 inhabitants, out of which 56.8 per cent were farmers, 31.8 per cent did domestic work, and the rest were fishermen or other related activities[9]

16. This means that circa 1850, about 11 per cent of the population of 1,285 persons were fishermen; that is, about 130 persons if we include women, children and the elderly. Is it conceivable that these people needed to fish outside the territorial waters of the islands? And by territorial waters I refer to the 3-nautical-mile limit usually accepted in the 19th century. Is it conceivable that this

---

[7] Secretaría de Planeación Departamental, Gobernación del Archipiélago, "Ficha Técnica de Indicadores Económicos y de Desarrollo", Aug. 2020, p. 9, available at https://www.sanandres.gov.co/index.php/gestion/planeacion/publicaciones/13057-ficha-tecnica-de-indicadores-san-andres-providencia-y-santa-catalina/file (accessed 24 Sept. 2021).

[8] See for example Natalia Guevara, "San Andrés Isla, Memorias de la colombianización y Reparaciones", available at https://repositorio.unal.edu.co/bitstream/handle/unal/2862/09CAPI08.pdf?sequence=23&isAllowed=y#:~:text=En%20los%20a%C3%B1os%20veinte%20se,hablo%20espa%C3%B1ol%2C%20yo%20soy%20colombiano%E2%80%A6 (accessed 24 Sept. 2021).

[9] Adolfo Meisel, *La estructura económica de San Andrés y Providencia en 1846* (2009), p. 5, available at https://repositorio.banrep.gov.co/bitstream/handle/20.500.12134/454/?sequence=1 (accessed 24 Sept. 2021).

small group of people had needed and established fishing rights in an area the size of the Adriatic Sea?

17. In 1925, the population had increased to approximately 5,000 inhabitants[10]. Even with this increase in population, most of them were farmers dedicated to the copra industry and not fishermen. But even if they had all been fishermen, did they need and use the equivalent — and again, I repeat: did they need and use the equivalent extent of the Adriatic Sea to fish?

Present day fishing

18. Madam President, the artisanal fishermen of the islands even today do not go much beyond the area of the main islands. According to a publication of the Colombian Institute of Marine and Coastal Investigations in 2011, most of the artisanal fisheries

> "were concentrated in the areas contiguous to the islands of Providencia and San Andrés and the Cays of Albuquerque and Bolívar. The Cays of Roncador, the Serrana Banks and Quitasueño presented a low frequency of fishing by unit of area, which indicates that artisanal fishing is not frequent in those areas due to their distance from Providencia and San Andres."[11]

19. In Colombia, a government program was set up to support the artisanal fishermen of the islands supposedly to help them out after the Judgment of the Court. According to the published report of 8 April 2013, a total of 275 people were registered and paid[12].

20. In the Caribbean coast of Nicaragua there are hundreds of thousands of people, Afro-descendants like the Raizales, quite a few of them Creoles and even with close family ties with the Creoles or Raizales, living in the islands; there are also the numerous descendants of the different Aborigines in the Mosquito Coast that lived there centuries before the Afro-descendants arrived in

---

[10] See for example "Los Raizales del Archipiélago de San Andrés, Providencia y Santa Catalina", available at https://thearchipielagopress.co/los-raizales-del-archipielago-de-san-andres-providencia-y-santa-catalina/ (accessed 24 Sept. 2021)

[11] INVEMAR-ANH, 2011, "Estudio Línea base ambiental y pesquera en la Reserva de Biosfera Seaflower (Archipiélago de San Andrés, Providencia y Santa Catalina) como aporte al conocimiento y aprovechamiento sostenible de los recursos para la región — Fase I", Informe técnico final, Santa Marta, p. 4, available at http://cinto.invemar.org.co/alfresco/d/d/workspace/SpacesStore/06068ed3-6a62-4939-8119-86364328efa6/Estudio%20linea%20base%20ambiental%20y%20pesquera%20en%20la%20reserva%20de%20biosfera%20seaflower%20(Archipielago%20de%20San%20Andres,%20Providencia%20y%20Santa%20Catalina)%20como%20aporte%20al%20conocimiento%20y%20aprovechamiento%20sostenible%20de%20los%20recursos%20para%20la%20region%20-%20FASE%20I?ticket=TICKET_00ba8ac51399410cd995d2e5731889fb33f6721c (accessed 24 Sept. 2021).

[12] See Comité de apoyo, acompañamiento y seguimiento al componente pesquero artesanal del plan archipiélago de San Andrés, Providencia y Santa Catalina, Beneficiarios Aprobados-Listado Definitivo para avalar el segundo pago del subsidio, 8 Apr. 2013, available at https://www.sanandres.gov.co/index.php/170-agricultura/pescadores-artesanales/1183-listado-pescadores-artesanales-subsidio-tercer-pago (accessed 15 Sept. 2021).

the area. All of these Nicaraguan people have depended on fishing for their subsistence: the Afro-descendants including the Creoles or Afro-Europeans, the Miskitos (which is the largest component of the population), the Sumu (Amerindian), Garifuna (Afro-Indians), the Rama (Amerindian), and some Chinese.

Nicaraguan artisanal fishing

21. The Nicaraguan Government is very aware of the ancestral rights of its indigenous and ethnic communities. There is a Nicaraguan law on the Communal Property of the Indigenous People and Ethnical Communities of the Atlantic Coast dating from 2003, that mandates, in Article 33, the following:

> "The indigenous and ethnic communities of the coast, islands and cays of the Atlantic, have exclusive rights to use the maritime resources for communal and artisanal fishing, within the 3 miles adjacent to the coast and 25 miles around the adjacent cays and islands."[13]

22. In parenthesis, Madam President, it could be pointed out that one of the reasons Nicaragua declared straight baselines — the legality of which is also the basis of a counter-claim of Colombia — is because it considered it appropriate in view of the rights of the population to fish and exploit those areas within 25 nautical miles of the adjacent islands and keys. End of parenthesis.

23. In order to regulate the exercise of these rights of artisanal fishing, the Institute of Fisheries of Nicaragua keeps a registry of the artisanal fishermen in the country. On the Caribbean side of Nicaragua, according to the publication of 2018, there are 8,907 artisanal fishermen registered[14]. It is well to recall that the number of registered Colombian artisanal fishermen in the islands was 275 in the year 2013.

President Ortega's statements

24. President Ortega made several statements shortly after the 2012 Judgment about the possibility and even desirability of negotiating a fishing agreement for the benefit of the Raizal

[13] Communal Property Regime Law of Indigenous Peoples and Ethnic Communities of the Autonomous Regions of the Atlantic Coast of Nicaragua and the Rivers Bocay, Coco, Indio and Maiz, Law 445, 2003, available at https://www.poderjudicial.gob.ni/pjupload/costacaribe/pdf/Ley_445.pdf (accessed 24 Sept. 2021).

[14] *Fishery and Aquaculture Yearbook of Nicaragua*, Nicaraguan Institute of Fisheries, 2018, p. 83, available at http://www.inpesca.gob.ni/images/Anuarios%20Pesqueros/Anuario%20Pesquero%20y%20Acuicola%202018.pdf (accessed 24 Sept. 2021).

community. This offer to negotiate was never accepted by Colombia. From the quote of President Ortega, cited by Mr. Valencia, it should be clear that his emphasis is on an agreement.

> "I told President Santos, and I have said publicly, that the [Raizales] can continue fishing. That Nicaragua will not affect them in their Rights as Original People, that they can continue fishing. And that we work an Agreement, an Agreement between the Government of Colombia and Nicaragua, so that we can regulate this well. Because how do we know that all the boats that are fishing there are from the Raizal Community, and which ones are fisheries not related to the Raizal Community, or even has to do with industrial fishing?"[15]

25. Finally, it should be noted that if there are any people that could point to ancestral fishing rights in all this area, including the islands and the mainland coast, it is the Miskitos, whose presence in the area goes back much further in time than that of the Raizales in the islands.

Colombia's second counter-claim: straight baselines

26. Madam President, the second counter-claim requests the Court to declare that Nicaragua, by adopting Decree No. 33-2013 of 19 August 2013, which established straight baselines and, according to Colombia, had the effect of extending its internal waters and maritime zones beyond what international law permits, has violated Colombia's sovereign rights and jurisdiction[16]. Professor Alex Oude Elferink will address this issue fully. At this point, some short comments.

27. To begin, there is some apparent misconception that the question of Nicaragua's straight baselines is in some way related to the issue of Colombia's creation of a so-called Integral Contiguous Zone (ICZ). There is no connection. Nicaragua's straight baselines are located inside indisputable Nicaraguan waters. Colombia's ICZ is located in Nicaragua's EEZ. The only comparison of Nicaragua's straight baselines could be with the straight baseline system that Colombia has along its coasts and which will be discussed later, in spite of Professor Thouvenin's averment that we should not do so[17].

28. Colombia's rights of innocent passage through the waters enclosed by the straight baselines has not been and cannot be affected. The right of innocent passage is guaranteed in Article 8 of UNCLOS, that states:

---

[15] CR 2021/15, p. 40, para. 11 (Valencia-Ospina).

[16] See CMC, Chap. 10; RC, Chap. 6.

[17] CR 2021/15, p. 51, para. 5 (Thouvenin).

> "Where the establishment of a straight baseline in accordance with the method set forth in article 7 has the effect of enclosing as internal waters areas which had not previously been considered as such, a right of innocent passage as provided in this Convention shall exist in those waters."

29. Indeed customary law cannot be less accommodating for third countries' rights. This right is accorded to vessels of all states, including non-parties to the Convention.

30. There have been no incidents in that area with Colombia or any other State. It has in no way affected Colombia's rights or is the issue really connected in any way with the present case. If there was a connection, we would also be discussing Colombia's straight baselines and the impact that has had or could have for Nicaragua.

31. Professor Thouvenin has pointed out that the area enclosed by these straight lines is comparable to the size of Belgium and of some other countries[18]. As a legal argument, that is not relevant per se because that depends on the size and configuration of the coastline. UNCLOS, as well as customary law, permits the drawing of straight baselines in the same way it permits archipelagic lines that frequently enclose enormous spaces around a group of small islands.

32. The figure on the screen, helps us to discuss what could be of interest in the allusion made by Professor Thouvenin: the straight baselines used by Colombia — and we refer just to those on its Caribbean coast — enclose areas as large as 21,670 sq km, bigger than El Salvador and more than half the size of The Netherlands[19], as you can appreciate on the screen.

33. Perhaps the most insidious claim of Colombia is that the straight baseline system extended the Nicaraguan EEZ. Any expert on the law of the sea would immediately see through this. It is not a theoretical question but a physical geometrical issue. Straight baselines, almost invariably, do not affect the extent of the EEZ. This could only be affected by the base points used to draw those lines. The base points used by Nicaragua are unimpeachable.

34. Professor Thouvenin attempted to dispute one of the base points, Edinburgh Cay. Professor Oude Elferink will address this but let me point out that a base point on this key was used in the *Nicaragua* v. *Honduras* delimitation and for the drawing of the provisional equidistance line

---

[18] CR 2021/15, p. 62, para. 57 (Thouvenin).

[19] Areas taken from worldometers.info (accessed 24 Sept. 2021).

in *Nicaragua* v. *Colombia* by the Court. Even more to the point, it was used by Colombia itself as a base point in its Counter-Memorial in the maritime dispute with Nicaragua[20].

35. Professor Thouvenin also stated that these lines project Nicaragua's exclusive economic zone and continental shelf further east, and that this is what Colombia disputes[21]. But he volunteered no argument on this question besides that simple statement.

36. On the screen are some graphics that show the effect of the baselines on the outer limit of the EEZ.

37. On the slide in the image right now, it shows that 200-nautical-mile limit drawn from the Nicaraguan straight baselines. The next image now on the screen compares the limits measured from the straight and from the normal baselines, and we can see that the normal baseline limit actually extends further east than the limit drawn from the straight baselines.

38. Now, the graphic on screen is taken from the Colombian Counter-Memorial in the *Territorial and Maritime Dispute* and shows the base points used by Colombia to draw its median line between the San Andrés Archipelago and Nicaragua.

39. Now, in this last map, Colombia's base points have been used to draw the 200-nautical-mile limit which is the red line on the screen. The blue line now on screen is the 200-nautical-mile limit drawn from the straight baselines. The two lines are very close; if anything, the line resulting from Colombia's base points lies further to the east.

40. In conclusion, Madam President, the straight baselines of Nicaragua have no practical effect on the outer limit of its EEZ as Colombia claims.

41. Madam President, Members of the Court, thank you for your attention. May I ask you to call Mr. Lawrence Martin, please.

The PRESIDENT: I thank the Agent of Nicaragua. I now invite the next speaker, Mr. Lawrence Martin, to take the floor.

---

[20] *Territorial and Maritime Dispute (Nicaragua* v. *Colombia)*, Counter-Memorial of the Republic of Colombia (11 Nov. 2008), p. 393, Figure 9.2.

[21] CR 2021/15, p. 50, para. 2 (Thouvenin).

Mr. MARTIN:

THE RAIZALES DO NOT HAVE TRADITIONAL FISHING RIGHTS IN NICARAGUA'S EEZ AND EVEN IF THEY DID, THEY HAVE NOT BEEN VIOLATED

1. Madam President, distinguished Members of the Court, good afternoon. Like friends before me, let me first note my deep sadness at Judge Crawford's passing. He was a kind teacher, a wise judge, and sometimes an intimidating adversary. Like all of us, I will miss that mischievous twinkle in his eye very much.

2. It falls to me today to respond to Colombia's counter-claim relating to the alleged traditional fishing rights of the Raizales. This counter-claim fails on the facts and the law. The rights Colombia alleges do not exist and even if they did, Nicaragua has not violated them.

3. I will address four points this afternoon. *First*, the traditional fishing rights Colombia claims are fundamentally incompatible with the régime of the exclusive economic zone. Even if, decades ago, the Raizales "traditionally" fished in what is now Nicaragua's EEZ — which has not been shown — the advent of the EEZ gave Nicaragua exclusive rights to the exploitation of the living resources in that zone.

4. *Second*, contrary to what you heard from Colombia on Wednesday, President Ortega never recognized the existence of any such rights. What he did was indicate a willingness to accommodate Colombia's concerns, and the Raizales themselves provided appropriate mechanisms could be worked out between the Parties.

5. *Third*, the evidence Colombia has presented to support this counter-claim, even taken at face value, does not support the existence of the rights it claims.

6. *Fourth*, and finally, even if the Raizales had the rights Colombia asserts — but they do not — the evidence does not support the allegation that Nicaragua violated them.

I. Traditional fishing rights are incompatible with the régime of the EEZ

7. I turn to my first point: traditional fishing rights are inconsistent with the institution of the EEZ. On Wednesday, you heard Mr. Valencia-Ospina say "[n]o doubt this Court will hear from

Nicaragua a plea in favour of exclusivity"[22]. Well, yes. And that really should not be controversial. A coastal State's rights to fish in its EEZ are "exclusive", exactly as the name of the zone indicates. Nobody else has any such rights. Before the EEZ became law, everyone and anyone could fish in the areas that were then high seas. After it became law, only the coastal State could fish in its own EEZ (unless it authorized others to do so).

8. A Chamber of this Court made exactly this point nearly 40 years ago in the *Gulf of Maine* case. I apologize for the length of this quotation, but it is all very much relevant. The Chamber held:

> "Until very recently . . . these expanses were part of the high seas and as such freely open to the fishermen not only of the United States and Canada but also of other countries, and they were indeed fished by very many nationals of the latter. . . . But after the coastal States had set up exclusive 200-mile fishery zones, the situation radically altered. *Third States* ***and their nationals*** *found themselves deprived of any right of access to the sea areas within those zones* and of any position of advantage they might have been able to achieve within them. As for the United States, any mere factual predominance which it had been able to secure in the area was transformed into a *situation* ***of legal monopoly*** to the extent that the localities in question became legally part of its own exclusive fishery zone."[23]

9. We first noted this aspect of the Chamber's Judgment in our May 2018 Reply[24]. Colombia conspicuously had nothing to say about it in its November 2018 Rejoinder. There is only a single citation to the *Gulf of Maine* case in the entire Rejoinder, and that is on an entirely different point[25]. Nor did we hear anything about it on Wednesday. We consider this silence telling. By itself, the Chamber's ruling is fatal to Colombia's case. In its EEZ, Nicaragua is in a "situation of legal monopoly" that deprives "[t]hird States *and their nationals* . . . of any right of access to the sea areas" within that zone.

10. Rather than come to terms with the clear consequences of the *Gulf of Maine* decision, Colombia, at least in its written pleadings, tried a couple of other tactics to avoid it. It argued first that, in effect, that which is not prohibited is permitted[26]. It also argued that there is nothing

[22] CR 2021/15, p. 49, para. 39 (Valencia-Ospina).

[23] *Delimitation of the Maritime Boundary in the Gulf of Maine Area (Canada/United States of America), Judgment, I.C.J. Reports 1984* (hereinafter "*Gulf of Maine*"), pp. 341-342, para. 235; emphases added.

[24] RN, para. 6.23.

[25] RC, para. 2.108, fn. 156.

[26] RC, para. 5.13.

incompatible between Nicaragua's exclusive *sovereign* rights and a finding that the Raizales *as individuals* have a traditional right to fish in Nicaragua's EEZ[27].

11. Both arguments are, in the first instance, defeated by the Chamber's plain holding in *Gulf of Maine*. Whereas Colombia said that which is not prohibited is permitted, the Chamber said that coastal States enjoy a "legal monopoly" over fishing in their EEZs. Whereas Colombia said there is nothing inconsistent between sovereign and individual fishing rights, the Chamber said that the institution of the EEZ deprives "third States *and their nationals*" of any right of access.

12. The result, moreover, is plainly the one dictated by the text of UNCLOS, as well as by its context and the *travaux*, all of which equally inform the content of customary international law. We made these points at length in our written pleadings[28] and I will only highlight the essential elements here, all the more because Mr. Valencia-Ospina did not bother to touch on *any of them* on Wednesday.

13. With respect to the text and context, Colombia said in its Rejoinder that "Nicaragua in the end mainly relies on one single paragraph of an UNCLOS provision [i.e. Article 62 (3)] to put forward its thesis that traditional fishing rights have been extinguished in the EEZ"[29]. That, of course, is incorrect. Article 56, which gives coastal States the exclusive "sovereign rights for the purpose of exploring and exploiting, conserving and managing the natural resources" of the zone[30], is the foundation of our case.

14. Article 62 (3) is important, but it is far from the only other provision on which we rely. The Court well knows that Article 62 (3) provides that when the coastal State does not have the capacity to harvest the resources up to the allowable limit (which *the coastal State* sets), one of the factors it should consider in giving access to other States is "the need to minimize economic dislocation in States whose nationals have habitually fished in the zone"[31]. This is the only provision in Part V dealing with the issue of other States' nationals who have traditionally fished in the zone. And it does not give or recognize any rights in respect of other States' nationals.

---

[27] RC, para. 5.14.

[28] RN, paras. 6.7-6.21; APN, paras. 2.4-2.11.

[29] RC, para. 5.18.

[30] UNCLOS, Art. 56; see RN, paras. 6.8-6.9.

[31] UNCLOS, Art. 62 (3).

15. The provisions of Part IV dealing with archipelagic States provide a telling contrast. Article 51 (1) states that "an archipelagic State . . . shall recognize traditional fishing rights . . . in certain areas falling within archipelagic waters"[32]. This shows that when the drafters of the Convention wanted to protect traditional fishing rights, they knew how to do so. The absence of an analogous provision in Part V can only mean that traditional fishing rights do not exist in the EEZ.

16. Other provisions on which we rely include Article 58, Article 60, Article 61, Article 62 (4) and Article 73 (1), as made clear in our written pleadings[33].

17. All of these provisions and the rest of Part V make it indisputable that the very purpose of the régime of the EEZ, both conventional and customary, is to make a coastal State's rights over the living resources *exclusive*. According to the Virginia Commentary: "The importance of the concept of exclusivity is that the coastal State, *to the exclusion of other States and entities*, has sole jurisdiction as regards the resources of the zone, and has the right to exercise its discretion in respect of those resources."[34]

18. The *travaux* are to precisely the same effect 17. The *travaux* are to precisely the same effect. This too is another point on which Colombia maintains a very studied silence. Nicaragua showed in its written pleadings that during the UNCLOS negotiations, some States took the view that the Convention should protect their historic fishing practices in waters that were in the process of being transformed into EEZs. To cite just two examples:

— Japan and the Soviet Union took the view that coastal States should not have *exclusive* rights in the EEZ. They proposed instead that they should have only *preferential* rights, which would entitle them to an allocation of resources subject to "duly [taking] into account . . . the interests of traditionally established fisheries of other States"[35]; and

— Malta and Zaire proposed that historic fishing rights should be preserved in the EEZ[36].

---

[32] UNCLOS, Art. 51 (1).

[33] RN, paras. 6.10-6.12; APN, para. 2.6.

[34] Myron H. Nordquist, Satya N. Nandan & Shabtai Rosenne (eds.), *United Nations Convention on the Law of the Sea, 1982: A Commentary*, Vol. II (1993), p. 519; emphasis added.

[35] Japan, Proposals for a régime of fisheries on the high seas, UN doc. A/AC.138/SC.II/L.12 (1972); USSR, Draft article on fishing (basic provisions and explanatory note), UN doc. A/AC.138/SC.II/L.6 (1972).

[36] Leonardo Bernard, "The Effect of Historic Fishing Rights In Maritime Boundaries Delimitation", Law of the Sea Institute Conference Papers, Securing the Ocean for the Next Generation (Harry N. Scheiber, ed., May 2012).

19. In contrast, a larger number of States, particularly developing States, strenuously objected to the protection of other States' alleged historic fishing practices in the waters adjacent to their coasts[37]. The latter position received widespread support at the 1974 Caracas Session[38] and ultimately prevailed. The "Main Trends" working paper produced that year recognized that the coastal State would have exclusive sovereign rights and jurisdiction over the natural resources in the EEZ[39]. That principle was subsequently embodied in Article 56 of the Convention.

20. Colombia does not deny any of this. They said nothing about the *travaux* on this point in their written pleadings. We also heard nothing about it on Wednesday. Colombia, it seems, is well aware that this point too is fatal to its case.

21. Instead of grounding its analysis in the text, context and *travaux* of UNCLOS, Colombia points to irrelevancies. In its Rejoinder, it says: "If traditional rights can subsist within areas where States enjoy sovereignty, *a fortiori* they can also exist within areas in which States merely enjoy sovereign rights."[40] In Colombia's view, a contrary result would somehow be "disingenuous"[41]. Mr. Valencia-Ospina tried to raise a similar point when he put a quotation from the *Abyei* arbitration on the screen on Wednesday[42].

22. We do not agree. In the first place, the question of whether or not traditional fishing rights can exist in the territorial sea is not before the Court and need not be addressed. In the second place, and in any event, there would be nothing "disingenuous" about finding that such rights could exist in the territorial sea but not the EEZ.

23. To state the obvious, the territorial sea and the EEZ are different legal animals. The former has an ancient history and the applicable legal régime is a hybrid; it is governed by both UNCLOS

---

[37] See e.g. Declaration of Latin American States on the Law of the Sea (8 Aug. 1970); Montevideo Declaration on the Law of the Sea (8 May 1970), in *American Journal of International Law (AJIL)*, Vol. 64, No. 5 (1970); Declaration of Santo Domingo, UN doc. A/AC.138/80 (7 June 1972).

[38] J. Stevenson and B. Oxman, "The Third United Nations Convention on the Law of the Sea: The 1974 Caracas Session", *AJIL*, Vol. 69, No. 1 (1975), p. 2.

[39] Third United Nations Conference on the Law of the Sea (UNCLOS III), "Working Paper of the Second Committee: Main Trends", UN doc. A/CONF.62/L.8/Rev. 1, Ann. II, App. I (1974), p. 120.

[40] RC, para. 5.15.

[41] RC, para. 5.3.

[42] CR 2021/15, pp. 44-45, para. 27 (Valencia-Ospina).

and general international law. Article 2 (3) of the Convention provides: "The sovereignty over the territorial sea is exercised subject to this Convention *and to other rules of international law*."

24. The legal régime of the EEZ is very different. It is a creation of UNCLOS and governed by the provisions of Part V of the Convention. There is no reason to think the customary régime is any different and Colombia has made no effort to demonstrate that it is. While Article 2 (3) makes room for "other rules of international law" to apply broadly in the territorial sea, the same is not true in the EEZ. Under Article 58 (2), "other pertinent rules of international law apply to the exclusive economic zone" only *"in so far as they are not incompatible with this Part"*. And since Part V of UNCLOS gives the coastal State *exclusive* rights to the fish and other living resources in its EEZ, any derogation from that exclusivity, unless explicitly included in Part V, would plainly be incompatible with that Part of the Convention.

25. At the end of the day, the only authority that Colombia can even try to point to, to support its position, is the *Eritrea-Yemen* arbitration[43]. As we made clear in our written pleadings, that case was very different from this one. It was unique in that the applicable law included more than just UNCLOS[44]. More important still, in that case, there was actually an express agreement between the parties to respect traditional fishing rights in the EEZ. Specifically, Eritrea and Yemen had concluded a Memorandum of Understanding (MOU) prior to the arbitration that stated in relevant part that they "shall permit fishermen who are citizens of the two States . . . to fish in the territorial waters of the two States, *the contiguous zone and the Exclusive Economic Zone* of the two countries in the Red Sea . . . provided that the fishermen of the two countries . . . be granted official licenses" upon application[45]. That case therefore cannot serve as any kind of precedent in this one.

II. President Ortega never recognized such rights

26. I turn now to the second of my four points. Colombia also argues that whatever the status of traditional fishing rights under customary international law, Nicaragua's President Ortega has

---

[43] CR 2021/15, p. 49, para. 39 (Valencia-Ospina).

[44] RN, paras. 6.25-6.29; *Eritrea/Yemen*, Award of the Arbitral Tribunal in the First Stage —Territorial Sovereignty and Scope of the Dispute, 9 Oct. 1998, para. 7.

[45] Memorandum of Understanding between the State of Eritrea and the Republic of Yemen for Cooperation in the Areas of Maritime Fishing, Trade, Investment, and Transportation (15 Nov. 1994), para. 1; emphasis added, reproduced in *Eritrea/Yemen*, PCA Case No. 1996-04, Award of the Arbitral Tribunal in the Second Stage—Maritime Delimitation, 17 Dec. 1999, Ann. 3.

expressly recognized the existence of these alleged rights in five public statements made between 2012 and 2015.

27. Colombia is plainly conscious of the weakness of its case on this score. According to the Rejoinder: "Colombia's main argument is that traditional fishing rights are protected under international law regardless of the maritime area involved and irrespective of any form of recognition from coastal States."[46] Its argument about President Ortega's statements is, in other words, offered only by way of back-up, although Mr. Valencia-Ospina did seem to try and make it the centre of Colombia's case on Wednesday.

28. In any event, President Ortega's statements very obviously do not themselves constitute a concession of the rights Colombia alleges. To the contrary, read both on their face and in light of the context in which they were made, they are very obviously not the words of an international lawyer, but those of a Head of State trying to grapple, as diplomatically as possible, with the fallout from Colombia's furious rejection of the Court's 2012 Judgment.

29. Nicaragua's Agent, Mr. Reichler, both recalled on Monday that when the Court issued its unanimous decision on delimitation in November 2012, the response from Bogotá was less than welcoming. Rather than inflame this delicate situation, President Ortega sought to de-escalate it and nudge Colombia in the direction of respecting the Court's Judgment by indicating that there was room to accommodate Colombia's stated concerns.

30. Indeed, then President Santos expressly recognized this reality. Following a meeting with President Ortega in Mexico City in December 2012, he stated:

> "We will continue seeking for the rights of Colombians to be restored, that The Hague judgment seriously affected. We met with President Ortega. We explained our position very clearly: we want that the rights of Colombians and the Raizal population, not only in terms of artisanal fishermen rights but other rights, be guaranteed and restored. *He understood.* We told him that we need to handle this situation with [a] cold head, in a diplomatic and friendly fashion, as this kind of issues should be handled to avoid incidents. *He also understood. We agreed to establish communication channels to address all these points.*"[47]

31. President Ortega "understood" Colombia's concerns. That does not mean he "agreed" with them. According to President Santos himself, the only point on which the two Presidents "agreed"

---

[46] RC, para. 5.26.

[47] CMC, Ann. 74; emphases added.

was that they would "establish communication channels to address all these points". This is an express acknowledgment that, rather than being agreed, Colombia's concerns about the Raizal fishermen remained to be addressed.

32. It should therefore not be surprising that President Ortega's public statements fall far short of the "explicit recognitions"[48] of the Raizales' alleged fishing rights in Nicaragua's EEZ that Colombia says they are. All of his statements expressly condition Nicaragua's willingness to accommodate Colombia's concerns on appropriate "authorization", or on "agreements" or "mechanisms" being worked out.

33. Specifically:

— In the 26 November 2012 statement in which President Ortega stated that Nicaragua would respect the rights of the inhabitants "to fish and navigate those waters, which they ha[d] historically navigated", he also indicated that "*artisanal fishermen would require an authorization from the relevant Nicaraguan authorities*"[49].

— In the 1 December 2012 statement in which he said that Nicaragua would "respect the ancestral rights of the Raizales", President Ortega noted that *"mechanisms"* would have to be established in order to "ensure the right of the Raizal people to fish"[50]. (I note that both of these statements were made before the meeting between the two Presidents, at which President Santos characterized President Ortega's position as "understanding" Colombia's concerns, not "agreeing" to them.)

— In his February 2013 statement, the first one after the bilateral meeting, President Ortega expressed openness to working with Colombia, and proposed a bilateral commission to "work on an agreement between Colombia and Nicaragua to regulate this situation"[51].

— In his November 2014 statement, President Ortega indicated that "while the 2012 delimitation will have to be implemented, guarantees to the Raizal communities of the Archipelago *will also have to be included in the agreement to be negotiated with Colombia*"[52]; and, finally,

[48] CMC, para. 3.93.

[49] MN, Ann. 27, emphasis added; see CMC, paras. 3.93-3.94.

[50] CMC, Anns. 73, 74, emphasis added; see CMC, para. 3.94.

[51] CMC, Ann. 76, emphasis added; see CMC, para. 3.94.

[52] CMC, Ann. 77, emphasis added; see CMC, para. 3.94.

— in his November 2015 statement, President Ortega declared that Nicaragua "understand[s] that patience is necessary in order to finally reach the conditions for the Court's Judgment to be ratified by the Colombian Parliament. And there we have engagements, as I said, with the Raizales Brothers regarding their fishing rights, *which will have to be arranged later.*"[53]

34. Now, here before the Court, Colombia seeks to avail itself of President Ortega's ostensible "recognition" of the Raizales' traditional fishing rights, but without also accepting the conditions he specified.

35. As Colombia sees it, by insisting that there are no rights without also appropriate mechanisms, we are "blur[ring] the distinction between recognition of the traditional fishing rights and the separate question of the conclusion of technical agreements to define their exact contours"[54]. We disagree. We are not blurring any distinction. Our point is that Nicaragua has been consistent in stating that it would be willing to formally recognize the Raizales' alleged historic fishing practices, but only as part of an agreement in which Colombia recognizes and accepts the boundary delimited by the Court in 2012. Indeed, the two issues cannot be separated. Any negotiation concerning Raizal fishing rights is necessarily dependent on Colombia's recognition of the boundary established by the Court.

III. Colombia has not proven the existence of the rights it claims

36. That brings me to the third part of my presentation, concerning the evidence Colombia offers to prove the existence of the alleged traditional fishing rights it claims. We say that evidence not only fails to demonstrate that the rights claimed ever existed: it actually proves they do not.

37. In its written pleadings, and again on Wednesday, Colombia claimed that the Raizales' alleged traditional fishing rights arose as a matter of local custom[55]. Colombia is therefore required to establish the existence of facts showing a "constant and uniform practice" by the Raizales that was "accepted as law by the Parties"[56]. Colombia has come nowhere close to meeting this burden.

---

[53] CMC, Ann. 78, emphasis added; see CMC, para. 3.94.

[54] RC, para. 5.30.

[55] See CMC, p. 140 (Chap. 3, argument heading D(1)); CR 2021/15, p. 41, para. 15 (Valencia-Ospina).

[56] *Right of Passage over Indian Territory (Portugal* v. *India), Merits, Judgment, I.C.J Reports 1960*, p. 40; see also *Asylum (Colombia/Peru), Judgment, I.C.J Reports 1950*, p. 276.

38. One might ask in the first instance whether, even if it were shown that the Raizales has historically fished up to the 82nd meridian *(quod non)*, how it could possibly have been accepted as law by Nicaragua? At all times before, and still now after, the 2012 Judgment, Colombia has claimed that it alone has sovereign rights and jurisdiction up to that line. Nicaragua, for its part, has at all times disagreed. Indeed, the very purpose of the first case, as well as this one, is to challenge Colombia's right to exercise such rights. Nicaragua has therefore never accepted Colombian fishing up to the 82nd meridian as law.

39. In any event, Colombia relies exclusively on affidavits from 11 fishermen collected over a 13-day period, less than a month before it submitted its Counter-Memorial in November 2016. We first challenged the sufficiency of that evidence in our May 2018 Reply. Colombia thus had ample opportunity to supplement the record if it had anything else to offer. It did not. By itself, that conspicuous omission underscores the poverty of Colombia's case.

40. Before addressing the content of Colombia's affidavits, however, it may be more useful to start with Colombia's own words. In February 2013, a Colombian labour syndicate complained to the ILO Committee of Experts on the Application of Conventions and Recommendations — or CEACR — that the 2012 Judgment had negative implications for the Raizales' traditional fishing rights[57]. Colombia defended itself against the complaint by stating, in part, that the "traditional fishing sites are precisely located in the vicinity of areas *not affected by the ICJ judgment* since it is a question of territorial sea"[58].

41. This was not a mere slip of the tongue. After the labour syndicate restated its complaint to the Committee in 2014, Colombia reiterated the same point, stating:

> "With regard to the right of the inhabitants of San Andrés to have access to traditional fishing areas, . . . *such fishing areas are located precisely around the keys and that these areas were not affected by the ICJ ruling*, as they consisted of territorial

[57] International Labour Organization (ILO), Committee of Experts on the Application of Conventions and Recommendations (CEACR), "Observation (CEACR), adopted 2013, published 103rd ILC session (2014)", Indigenous and Tribal Peoples Convention, 1989 (No. 169), Colombia (Ratification: 1991), available at http://www.ilo.org/dyn/normlex/en/f?p=NORMLEXPUB:13100:0::NO::P13100_COMMENT_ID:3141200.

[58] ILO, CEARC, "Observation (CEACR), adopted 2013, published 103rd ILC session (2014)", Indigenous and Tribal Peoples Convention, 1989 (No. 169), Colombia (Ratification: 1991), available at http://www.ilo.org/dyn/normlex/en/f?p=NORMLEXPUB:13100:0::NO::P13100_COMMENT_ID:3141200.

waters awarded to Colombia, together with the sovereignty of the islands and the seven keys."[59]

42. The Court does not need me to remind it of the evidentiary weight it has historically placed on statements against interests like these[60]. Nicaragua finds it particularly disingenuous for Colombia to take one position before the ILO but then take precisely the opposite position in these proceedings.

43. Colombia is very obviously embarrassed about this. In its Rejoinder, it tries to explain away its own admissions as "cavalier[] conclu[sions]"[61]. It says the office that made these statements, the Ministry of Labour's Office of Co-operation and International Relations, "failed to provide even a shred of evidence to support its assertion that the traditional fishing sites were precisely located in the vicinity of areas not affected by the decision"[62].

44. These statements are not so easily dismissed. They were made by an organ of the State, and thus attributable to Colombia itself. Moreover, these were not the only times that Colombia took this same position. It did so also before this Court in the earlier case between the Parties. Specifically, the portion of Colombia's 2008 Counter-Memorial in the *Territorial and Maritime Dispute* case discussing the issue of "access to resources" states that

> "it is important to point out that since mid-nineteen [sic] century the population of San Andrés and Providencia have relied for their subsistence on the fisheries, turtle hunting, guano exploitation and other food resources in *Roncador, Quitasueño, Serrana, Serranilla and Bajo Nuevo*"[63].

45. But, of course, none of Roncador, Quitasueño, Serrana, Serranilla or Bajo Nuevo is located in Nicaragua's EEZ.

46. In light of these multiple admissions, it is perhaps not surprising that Colombia's hurriedly gathered affidavits, even if they are credited, actually tend to disprove its case. Consistent with the position that Colombia took before the ILO Committee and before this Court in the previous case,

---

[59] ILO, CEARC, "Observation (CEACR), adopted 2013, published 103rd ILC session (2014)", Indigenous and Tribal Peoples Convention, 1989 (No. 169), Colombia (Ratification: 1991), available at http://www.ilo.org/dyn/normlex/en/f?p=NORMLEXPUB:13100:0::NO::P13100_COMMENT_ID:3141200.

[60] *Military and Paramilitary Activities in and against Nicaragua (Nicaragua* v. *United States of America), Merits, Judgment, I.C.J. Reports 1986*, p. 41, para. 64; *Armed Activities on the Territory of the Congo (Democratic Republic of the Congo* v. *Uganda), Judgment, I.C.J. Reports 2005*, p. 201, para. 61.

[61] RC, para. 5.55.

[62] RC, para. 5.56.

[63] *Territorial and Maritime Dispute (Nicaragua* v. *Colombia)*, Counter-Memorial of the Republic of Colombia (11 Nov. 2008), para. 9.78.

the affidavits show that the Raizales' principal fishing activities were near shore around the features over which Colombia has sovereignty.

47. On Wednesday, Mr. Valencia-Ospina said that "there can be no effective substitute for the careful examination of the" affidavits[64]. We cannot agree more. Nicaragua therefore invites the Court to read them carefully. Although some of the younger affiants do assert that they have more recently fished in what are now Nicaraguan waters, the clear story that emerges from their affidavits is that some Raizales started venturing further from shore only in recent years as a result of improving technology and the depletion of fish stocks in their traditional, near-shore fishing grounds[65]. That is, the areas *historically* fished are those close to shore, in the territorial seas of Colombia's insular features. There was no "constant and uniform practice" of the Raizales fishing in areas falling within Nicaragua's EEZ.

48. Given Colombia's assertion that the Raizales have been fishing in waters that the Court determined appertain to Nicaragua in 2012 since "time immemorial"[66], it is instructive to look at the affidavits of the two oldest fishermen: Mr. Jonathan Archibald Robinson, born in or around 1928[67], and Mr. Alfredo Rafael Howard Newball, born in or around 1930[68].

49. Mr. Robinson states:

> "I began to fish when I was 18 years old [that is, circa 1946] . . . My father was a fisherman. *I fished most of my life in Serrana, Roncador and Quitasueño*. I used to go in long fishing expeditions of even one month in these cays to lay traps for turtles, fishing and collecting seabirds' eggs. . . . In 1950 I arrived in Providencia again and I started to fish, *I raised eight children selling salted fish from Serrana, Roncador and Quitasueño*, up to this day."[69]

He also speaks of "fish[ing] around the island" of Providencia[70].

50. To be sure, Mr. Robinson does say: "I have fished in Nicaraguan waters; we fished in Quenna [that is, Quitasueño] and all that zone because in those days there were no limits."[71] But

[64] CR 2021/15, p. 41, para. 14 (Valencia-Ospina).

[65] RN, paras. 6.55-6.57 (citing CMC, Anns. 62, 63, 67).

[66] CMC, para. 3.102.

[67] CMC, Ann. 66.

[68] CMC, Ann. 67.

[69] CMC, Ann. 66.

[70] *Ibid.*

[71] *Ibid.*

Quitasueño, of course, is a Colombian feature and the reference to "all that zone" is far too vague to be given any legal significance.

51. He also says: "I have fished between Serrana and Quitasueño, and between Quitasueño and Roncador, fishing in deep waters."[72] In the first instance, this is purely an individual statement: *he* has fished. He does not speak of these areas as being a common fishing area for others. Moreover, in contrast to the way he describes fishing around Serrana, Roncador and Quitasueño, he conspicuously does not say that he habitually fished in these areas, merely that he "has" done so.

52. Mr. Newball's affidavit is to similar effect. He states: "My grandfather taught me to be a sailor since I was 8 years old [that is, circa 1938] . . . In those old days, we would go to the North Cays [i.e. Quitasueño, Roncador, Serranilla and Serrana] to do artisanal fishing . . . The fishing more often took place in the banks where there were cays in order to be able to sleep [there] at night."[73] In other words, the fishing typically took place around the features over which Colombia has sovereignty, exactly as Colombia itself represented to the ILO Committee.

53. Interestingly, a bit further down in his affidavit, Mr. Newball states: "Fish are more scarce nowadays. Artisanal fishermen have to go farther more often to survive."[74]

54. The same themes emerge in the affidavit of Mr. Domingo Sánchez McNabb, who was born much later, in or around 1960[75]. He states: "I have personally had experiences fishing in the North Cays for up to 42 days without seeing dry land; we used to go up to Cabo Gracias a Dios in Honduras or to Bajo Nuevo *in search of new fishing banks*."[76] What is interesting is that when speaking about locations other than the "North Cays", it is for the purpose of finding "new" — not traditional — fishing banks.

55. Mr. McNabb then goes on to describe the changes that he has seen over time, first in the 1970s when outboard engines were introduced and then when they started using new kinds of boats called "Kingfivers". Even then, however, the focus was still very much on Colombia's cays. He describes the new Kingfivers as being

[72] CMC, Ann. 66.

[73] CMC, Ann. 67.

[74] *Ibid.*

[75] CMC, Ann. 69.

[76] *Ibid.*

"very fast and adapted for outboard engines. Besides, they had an autonomy of 4 to 5 days for travelling to the *South Cays (Bolívar and Alburquerque)* and the *North Cays (Quitasueño, Roncador, Serranilla and Serrana). Fishing in the North Cays* began by the artisanal fishermen living on the islands of Providencia. First, they used to go in search of sea turtles and eggs, and later they began to fish for conch, lobster and deep-sea fish of higher value in the islands markets."[77]

56. Things began to change, he says, when "[t]he demand for fishing products due to the increase in tourism, commerce and population growth led to fishing in the farther zones of the North of the Archipelago more often"[78]. These more recent, distant expeditions were greatly facilitated he said by the advent of radios, radars and GPS. According to Mr. McNabb: "These technological improvements greatly facilitated the fishing expeditions going farther, to the 82nd meridian and even close to cape Gracias a Dios."[79]

57. On Wednesday, Mr. Valencia-Ospina spent a great deal of time talking about Cape Bank and arguing that "[t]he artisanal fishermen have navigated and exploited every ground of Cape Bank". In its Rejoinder, Colombia pointed to six affidavits that expressly mention Cape Bank to support that proposition[80]. But a review of those six affidavits shows that, while they may "mention" Cape Bank, *none of them* actually state that Cape Bank is a traditional fishing ground, much less one of the most important ones[81]. We made this point at some length in our Additional Pleading on Colombia's Counter-Claims and rather than further burdening the Court now, I respectfully refer to the relevant paragraphs in footnote[82].

58. Colombia's contention that its fishermen have fished in Nicaragua's EEZ "since time immemorial" is thus unsupported by Colombia's own evidence, even taking it at face value. Even accepting that these facts have been established, *quod non*, such scant practice beyond the 12-nautical-mile limits of Colombia's insular possessions over just a few decades at most is not nearly enough to give rise to the traditional fishing rights that Colombia claims.

---

[77] CMC, Ann. 69.

[78] *Ibid.*

[79] *Ibid.*

[80] RC, para. 5.42.

[81] See CMC, Anns. 62, 65, 68, 70, 71, 72.

[82] APN, paras. 2.51-2.57.

IV. Colombia has also not proven that Nicaragua violated those rights

59. Madam President, that brings me to the final part of my intervention this afternoon. Even if the Raizales had the rights that Colombia claims — which they do not — Colombia has not met its burden of proving that Nicaragua has done anything to violate them.

60. The evidence Colombia submits to prove its case consists of the same affidavits of the fishermen it used to try to prove the existence of the rights in the first place. Before discussing the content of those affidavits, it is useful to pause a moment to consider what Colombia has *not* submitted. There is not a single piece of contemporaneous evidence proving that Nicaragua ever interfered with the Raizales' alleged rights. No incident reports, no transcripts of any radio calls, nothing. Nor are there even any diplomatic Notes from Colombia to Nicaragua protesting the latter's supposed actions. Surely, if Nicaragua had conducted the campaign of "harassment"[83], "pillaging"[84] and "intimidation"[85] that Colombia alleges, someone in Bogotá would have spoken up. No one did.

61. Perhaps Colombia will say that we are being formalistic, that it is unreasonable to expect contemporaneous incident reports from or about artisanal fishermen operating in the middle of the Caribbean. To that potential objection, I would point out that, according to a publicly available book — published by the Central Bank of Colombia in 2016, the same year Colombia's affidavits were produced — artisanal fishermen are required to submit detailed paperwork to the Fish & Farm Coop:

> "The fishermen plan their fishing activity like this: they send a request to the cooperative with the budget . . . Once they return, they report to the port captaincy and the cooperative, where they take the product, value it, deduct expenses and collect surpluses."[86]

62. Inasmuch as fishermen are specifically required to report on their fishing trips when they return, including to the port captaincy, it is not at all unreasonable to expect contemporaneous reports of incidents if they actually occurred.

---

[83] CMC, para. 9.7.

[84] CMC, para. 9.5.

[85] *Ibid.*

[86] María Aguilera Díaz, "Geografía económica del archipiélago de San Andrés, Providencia y Santa Catalina", in Adolfo Meisel Roca & María Aguilera Díaz (eds.), *Economía y medio ambiente del archipiélago de San Andrés, Providencia y Santa Catalina* (2016), pp. 101-102, available at https://repositorio.banrep.gov.co/bitstream/handle/20.500.12134/456/?sequence=1 (accessed 23 Sept. 2021; free translation).

63. Indeed, one of Colombia's affiants, Mr. Orlando Francis Powell, specifically states that incident reports, albeit of a different sort, exist. Specifically, he states: "There have been incidents with illegal fishermen from other countries, they have been reported to the local authorities (the Department's [provincial] Fishing Secretariat, Port Captaincy, Coast Guard), through the action of the co-operatives or associations."[87] The absence of similar reports relating to Nicaragua's alleged conduct is revealing.

64. In any event, turning to the content of the affidavits themselves, there is nothing that might genuinely be considered proof of the very serious allegations that Colombia makes. Of the 11 affidavits Colombia presented, nine refer in some way to the alleged bad behaviour on the part of Nicaragua[88]. And, of these, three mention only that they are "afraid" of potential interference from Nicaragua, without mentioning any specific conduct that is alleged to have taken place[89].

65. The specific references, with page numbers, are included in footnotes to this speech. Again, we invite the Court to examine each of these nine affidavits carefully. *Not a single one* describes incidents of harassment or pillaging that are alleged to have occurred to the affiant himself. They address things that are said to have happened to other people, sometimes in exceedingly general terms. They are, in other words, pure hearsay. Mr. Valencia-Ospina tried to dismiss this concern by stating that "second-hand accounts do constitute admissible evidence before the Court"[90]. That may technically be true, but the Court has previously made clear that such statements are not to be given "much weight"[91].

66. Take the allegation of Mr. Newball for example. He says only: "After the 2012 decision, we do hear — *we do hear* — that the fishermen have difficulties with the Nicaraguan coastguard. They stop them, they take away their products, their equipment and they threaten them and mistreat

---

[87] CMC, Ann. 68.

[88] CMC, Ann. 62, pp. 374-375; Ann. 64, p. 386; Ann. 65, pp. 391-392; Ann. 67, p. 404; Ann. 68, p. 408; Ann. 69, p. 413; Ann. 70, p. 416; Ann. 71, pp. 420-421; Ann. 72, p. 426.

[89] CMC, Ann. 68, p. 408, Ann. 70, p. 416, Ann. 71, pp. 420-421.

[90] CR 2021/15, p. 47, para. 33 (Valencia-Ospina).

[91] *Application of the Convention on the Prevention and Punishment of the Crime of Genocide (Croatia* v. *Serbia), Judgment, I.C.J. Reports 2015 (I)*, p. 78, para. 197.

them."[92] The affiant himself did not experience any such difficulties. No specific incidents involving others are identified, and no evidence of them is provided.

67. Or take the statement of Mr. Eduardo Steele Martínez, who says: "I do not go to the North Cays because I fear to fish in these areas. The fear relates to the fact that artisanal fishermen sometimes get stopped by the Nicaraguan coastguards that take their food when they try to reach Cape Bank or the North Cays."[93] Again, no personal experience, no specific incidents are identified, and no evidence about any of them is provided.

68. Tellingly, when there are references to incidents that are alleged to have happened to specific people, they are always in the third person[94]. For instance, Mr. Robinson states: "I know that Minival Ward, a member of the co-operative, was attacked by Nicaraguan fishermen when going to the North Cays."[95] Not only is this hearsay, it refers to alleged conduct by private Nicaraguan citizens, not Nicaraguan authorities. And there is no direct evidence from Mr. Ward himself.

69. Another example is Mr. Ornuldo Rodolfo Walters Dawkins, who says: "I know that apart from what we hear in the media, there is the one with [the] *Condorito*, who[se] [crew] were taken to Nicaragua and mistreated 5 years ago."[96] This one is not only hearsay, it concerns an event said to have happened in 2011, before the Court even issued its 2012 Judgment. No statement from any of those allegedly mistreated has been provided.

70. There is one affiant who alleges that he had direct interaction with what he believed to be the Nicaraguan coastguard. It is Mr. Ligorio Luis Archbold Howard, who describes the following "incident": "A few years ago, while I was navigating on a sailboat northwest of Quitasueño, towards Honduras, I was stopped by a fast *lancha* with people that were armed. They identified themselves as the coastguard of Nicaragua."[97] That is it. He was "stopped". He was not harassed, nothing was stolen; he does not say he was even prevented from fishing. This is not the stuff of which serious international cases are made.

---

[92] CMC, Ann. 67.

[93] CMC, Ann. 70.

[94] CMC, Ann. 62, p. 374; Ann. 64, p. 386; Ann. 65, p. 391; Ann. 69, p. 413.

[95] CMC, Ann. 62.

[96] CMC, Ann. 64.

[97] CMC, Ann. 65.

71. For all these reasons, Madam President, Colombia's counter-claim relating to the alleged traditional fishing rights of the Raizales must be rejected. The rights not only do not exist; they have also not been violated.

72. Madam President, thank you for your customary courtesy and kind attention. May I ask that you invite Professor Oude Elferink to the podium?

The PRESIDENT: I thank Mr. Martin, and I shall now give the floor to Professor Alex Oude Elferink. You have the floor, Sir.

Mr. OUDE ELFERINK:

NICARAGUA'S BASELINES

A. Introduction

1. Madam President, Members of the Court, it is an honour to appear before you today, and a privilege to speak on behalf of the Republic of Nicaragua. I would like to associate myself with the remarks that have been made regarding the untimely passing of Judge Crawford. He will be sorely missed.

2. Madam President, today I will be addressing Colombia's counter-claim concerning Nicaragua's straight baselines, which issue was pleaded by Professor Thouvenin this Wednesday.

B. Colombia's graphics

3. Madam President, at the outset I would like to briefly discuss Professor Thouvenin's use of graphics. On screen, we have his Figure 1, which he showed at the very outset of his presentation, on the left[98]. We have replicated that figure on the right-hand side of the slide, which is at tab 13 of the judges' folder. As a preliminary point, it may be noted that Colombia's figure uses an incorrect location of Nicaragua's base point 9. Nicaragua adjusted that base point in 2018 to bring it in line with the Judgment of 2 February 2018 in the case between Nicaragua and Costa Rica concerning their land and maritime boundary[99]. The bright red colouring on Figure 1 no doubt was chosen to

---

[98] See CR 2021/15, p. 50, para. 2.

[99] Presidential Decree No. 17-2018, Decree of Reform to Decree No. 33 2013, "Baselines of the Maritime Spaces of the Republic of Nicaragua in the Caribbean Sea", Ann. I (reproduced in Ann. 2 to this pleading). The text of the decree is also available on the website of the Division for Oceans and the Law of the Sea of the United Nations' Secretariat (http://www.un.org/Depts/los/LEGISLATIONANDTREATIES/STATEFILES/NIC.htm) (accessed 21 Feb. 2019).

heighten its dramatic effects. Later in his presentation, Professor Thouvenin compared the extent of the waters enclosed by Nicaragua's straight baselines to the territory of Jamaica, El Salvador, Belgium and the Netherlands[100]. Now, what his figure did not show, and what his comparison ignored, is that most of the waters that are inside Nicaragua's straight baselines previously formed part of Nicaragua's territorial sea. You now see this illustrated in the figure on the right-hand side of the screen; it is the area that is now in white. This actually concerns 81 per cent of the maritime area inside Nicaragua's straight baselines. The remaining area is just over 3,800 sq km.

4. The extent of Nicaragua's territorial sea prior to the establishment of its straight baselines also puts the claim that Nicaragua is limiting the navigational rights of other States in a different perspective[101]. There are two points to be made in that respect. First, straight baselines may indeed change the navigational régime of sea areas. That is inherent to the régime of straight baselines. Second, the change is not near as dramatic as has been suggested. As the applicable law indicates, the right of innocent passage is maintained in the internal waters inside the straight baselines, to the extent they previously did not have that status[102]. That concerns all of the area that was coloured in red on Professor Thouvenin's Figure 1.

5. Let me point you to one other misleading figure that Professor Thouvenin used to build his argument. This is Figure 14 at tab 58 of Colombia's judges' folder. It shows Nicaragua's mainland and Miskito Cay. Professor Thouvenin used this figure to argue that there was no connection between the two[103]. Well, that first of all completely ignores that Miskito Cay is in the immediate vicinity of the mainland coast. They are less than 24 nautical miles apart. Even more importantly, this figure does not include any of the other cays and drying reefs that are situated in the Cayos Miskitos. We have added these to the figure. This figure is at tab 13 of today's judges' folder. As may be appreciated, this provides a completely different picture of the situation. There is an intricate system of islands and reefs in close proximity to the mainland.

---

[100] CR 2021/15, p. 62, para. 57.

[101] See CR 2021/15, p. 50, para. 2.

[102] See UNCLOS, Art. 8.

[103] CR 2021/15, p. 63, para. 61.

6. Madam President, allow me to also mention a figure that Professor Thouvenin did not show you. He submitted that Nicaragua's straight baselines have pushed the outer limit of Nicaragua's exclusive economic zone to the east[104]. I am sure the Court would be interested in seeing that explained in a figure. Well, he did not do so. The reason is simple. It is not possible to produce such a figure. The establishment of Nicaragua's straight baselines, as was also pointed out by the Agent earlier today, has had no effect whatsoever on the 200-nautical-mile limit. For further details, I respectfully refer the Court to Nicaragua's written pleadings on this matter[105]. The absence of an effect of Nicaragua's straight baselines on its 200-nautical-mile line can be illustrated by a figure. The figure on screen, which is at tab 13 of your judges' folder, shows the 200-nautical-mile limit that would result from using the straight baselines as a blue dotted line and the 200-nautical-mile limit measured from the low-water line as a magenta line. At no point is the 200-nautical-mile limit that would be generated by the straight baselines seaward of the actual 200-nautical-mile limit that is generated by Nicaragua's normal baseline along the low-water line.

7. To conclude this argument on graphics, Colombia's graphics and related argument should be treated with much caution. I will be reverting to some of these graphics subsequently.

C. Nicaragua's combined use of the normal baseline and straight baselines is permitted

8. I do need to elaborate a little further on Professor Thouvenin's argument in relation to Nicaragua's 200-nautical-mile limit. He made two points. First, he submitted that the base points on Nicaragua's low-water line had nothing to do with Colombia's counter-claim on straight baselines and that as such they are beyond the jurisdiction of the Court. Columbia's counter-claim indeed did not impugn the validity of Nicaragua's baseline along its low-water line. But that is not the point. Colombia claims that Nicaragua's straight baselines pushed Nicaragua's 200-nautical-mile limit east[106]. To be able to assess that point, the Court has to take cognizance of all of Nicaragua's baselines, not only its straight baselines.

[104] See CR 2021/15, p. 50, para. 2.

[105] See APN, paras. 3.15-3.26.

[106] See CR 2021/15, p. 50, para. 2.

9. Professor Thouvenin's second point to reject the use of the normal baseline in combination with straight baselines was that a State cannot use two types of baseline at the same time[107]. Although, Colombia's Co-Agent this Wednesday was adamant that "Colombia has been consistent in its approach, identifying rules of customary international law on the basis of State practice and *opinio juris*"[108]. Professor Thouvenin offered nothing to demonstrate the existence of an alleged rule of customary international law prohibiting the use of different baselines at the same time. To be frank, it is an absurd proposition. The normal baseline is the default rule, and nothing in Article 7 of the Convention indicates that a normal baseline cannot be located seaward of a straight baseline that is drawn landward of the feature on which that normal baseline is located.

D. Nicaragua's straight baselines

10. I now turn to the discussion of Nicaragua's straight baselines. I will first discuss the applicable law. Although Colombia and Nicaragua are in agreement that Article 7 of the United Nations Convention on the Law of the Sea reflects customary international law[109], they do not agree about the specific implications of its provisions. Next, I will be discussing the different elements of the law that are relevant for assessing the validity of Nicaragua's straight baselines. These elements in particular concern the following. First, the length of Nicaragua's straight baselines. Second, the complementary requirements of the presence of either a fringe of islands or a coast that is deeply indented or cut into[110]. Third, the requirement that the fringe of islands has to be in the immediate vicinity of the coast[111]. Fourth, the requirement that straight baselines must not depart to any appreciable extent from the general direction of the coast[112]. And, finally, the requirement that the sea areas lying within the lines must be sufficiently closely linked to the land domain to be subject to the régime of internal waters[113].

---

[107] CR 2021/15, p. 51, para. 6.

[108] CR 2021/14, p. 24, para. 7.

[109] See e.g. RC, para. 6.45; APN, para. 3.64.

[110] United Nations Convention on the Law of the Sea, Art. 7 (1).

[111] *Ibid.*

[112] *Ibid.*, Art. 7 (3).

[113] *Ibid.*

***(a)* The applicable law and its interpretation**

11. I now turn to a brief discussion of the applicable law. Since the Parties are in agreement that the applicable law is provided by customary international law, which is identical to Article 7 of the Convention, it might seem that I could be very brief indeed. There is, however, one point that needs to be brought to the attention of the Court. Colombia during these pleadings at times suggests that Nicaragua is required to prove the existence of quite specific rules of international law, which go beyond the language of Article 7 of the Convention[114]. This raises a point of principle that merits emphasizing. The determination of a rule of customary international law that is more specific than Article 7 of the Convention requires the presence of *opinio juris* and a settled practice. It is upon Colombia to prove the existence of such a rule of customary law. As a Chamber of the Court observed in the *Gulf of Maine* case, the presence of customary rules "in the *opinio juris* of States can be tested by induction based on the analysis of a sufficiently extensive and convincing practice, and not by deduction from preconceived ideas"[115]. Colombia has not engaged in this kind of analysis of State practice. Its claims concerning rules of customary law that go beyond the language of Article 7 of the Convention are deduced from Colombia's idea of what the law should be, not what the law is.

12. In this connection, it is also pertinent to briefly refer to Colombia's own straight baseline practice. Nicaragua in its written pleadings has provided a detailed comparison of its straight baselines and those of Colombia[116]. In summary, from this comparison it may be concluded that Colombia's own practice on all counts reflects a more expansive interpretation of the law than Nicaragua's practice. This Wednesday, Colombia finally engaged with Nicaragua's argument. Or, I should rather say, desperately sought to avoid doing so. Professor Thouvenin submitted that an internal act of Colombia — he was referring to Colombia's straight baselines legislation — had nothing to do with Colombia's counter-claim concerning Nicaragua's straight baselines[117]. However, it has everything to do with this matter. One has to assume, Colombia being the law-abiding nation it claims to be, that Colombia's straight baselines have been established in accordance with the

---

[114] See e.g. RC, para. 6.48.

[115] *Delimitation of the Maritime Boundary in the Gulf of Maine Area, Judgment, I.C.J. Reports 1984*, p. 299, para. 111.

[116] Reply of Nicaragua (RN), Chap. 7 *passim*, and APN, para. 3.9.

[117] CR 2021/15, p. 51, para. 5.

applicable rules of customary international law. Colombia's straight baselines thus illustrate how Colombia considers the law has to be interpreted and applied. Colombia cannot now adopt a different and self-serving standard to assess the legality of Nicaragua's straight baselines.

(b) The length of Nicaragua's straight baselines

13. I will now turn to a discussion of the different elements of Article 7 as they relate to Nicaragua's straight baselines along its Caribbean coast. Let me first briefly address the length of these straight baselines. The individual segments of Nicaragua's straight baseline system measure between 44 and 83 nautical miles. This makes these straight baselines unexceptional as regards their length in the light of State practice in the application of the straight baseline provisions of Article 7 of the Convention and customary international law. Colombia itself has established straight baselines along its mainland coast in the Caribbean Sea and the Pacific Ocean, which include baselines measuring respectively 130.5, 81.6 and 76.8 nautical miles in length[118].

(c) The presence of a fringe of islands

14. I now turn to the question of whether there is a fringe of islands along Nicaragua's coast that allows the drawing of straight baselines.

15. During these proceedings, Colombia has had difficulty in identifying the islands that are located along Nicaragua's coast[119]. This Wednesday, Professor Thouvenin again raised this point[120].

16. Let me start by showing you a figure. The figure that is now on screen is included in Nicaragua's Additional Pleading on Colombia's Counter-Claims[121]. It is taken from the Colombian Rejoinder in the *Territorial and Maritime Dispute*. As this figure from that prior case indicates, Colombia had no difficulty then in identifying the islands fringing Nicaragua's coast. It may, moreover, be observed that this figure clearly illustrates that all of Nicaragua's islands generate overlapping territorial sea entitlements, confirming their close proximity and interconnectedness with Nicaragua's mainland coast. That the islands are in the immediate vicinity of the mainland, as

---

118 Figures included in "Straight Baselines: Colombia", *Limits in the Seas*, No. 103, United States Department of State, Office of the Geographer, 30 Apr. 1985 (available at https://www.state.gov/documents/organization/58565.pdf), pp. 4-5 and 7.

119 APN, paras. 3.31 *et seq*.

120 CR 2021/15, para. 28 *et seq*.

121 APN, Figure 5.

is required by Article 7, is confirmed by the baselines study of the United Nations Office for Ocean Affairs and the Law of the Sea, which observes that with a 12-nautical-mile territorial sea, a distance of 24 nautical miles would satisfy the conditions of "in the immediate vicinity". The study adds that "[i]t is important to realize that this concept applies to the inner edge of the fringe of islands because the fringe itself might be of considerable width"[122]. It may be noted that the outermost islands enclosed by Nicaragua's straight baselines are just over 24 nautical miles from Nicaragua's mainland.

17. Professor Thouvenin in his discussion on islands also questioned the status of Edinburgh Cay, which is one of the islands that has been used by Nicaragua as a base point for its system of straight baselines. He pointed to a nautical chart that indicated that Edinburgh Cay was not charted as an island[123]. However, charts of the United Kingdom Hydrographic Office (UKHO) that were part of Nicaragua's case files in *Territorial and Maritime Dispute between Nicaragua and Honduras* show that there are several islands on Edinburgh Reef[124]. You will find this figure at tab 14 of the judges' folder. In its Judgment in that case, the Court placed a base point for delimiting the territorial sea between Nicaragua and Honduras on Edinburgh Cay[125].

18. Professor Thouvenin also submitted that there were three separate groups of fringing islands along Nicaragua's mainland coast, implying that straight baselines may not be used to connect such allegedly separate groups. Before looking into that argument in more detail, let me remind you of Colombia's own practice on this point. As you may appreciate from the figure that is now on screen and at tab 14 of the judges' folder, in the Pacific, Colombia has drawn straight baselines to a fringe of islands consisting of just two islands. These islands are also more distant from the Colombian coast than many of the islands of Nicaragua that are inside Nicaragua's system of straight baselines.

---

[122] United Nations, Office for Ocean Affairs and the Law of the Sea, *The Law of the Sea. Baselines: An Examination of the Relevant Provisions of the United Nations Convention on the Law of the Sea* ,1989, New York, para. 46.

[123] CR 2021/15, pp. 57-58, paras. 32-34.

[124] See *Territorial and Maritime Dispute between Nicaragua and Honduras in the Caribbean Sea (Nicaragua* v. *Honduras)*, Vol. III.

[125] See *Territorial and Maritime Dispute between Nicaragua and Honduras in the Caribbean Sea (Nicaragua* v. *Honduras), Judgment, I.C.J. Reports 2007*, pp. 760-763, para. 321 (3).

19. Returning to Professor Thouvenin's argument on fringing islands, he relied on the study on baselines of the United Nations Office for Ocean Affairs and the Law of the Sea. The study refers to two types of fringing islands. First, he discussed the "skjærgaard" of the Norwegian coast, emphasizing that the "skjærgaard" forms a barrier. As he said, the "skjærgaard" forms "une sorte de barrière d'îles difficilement franchissable entre la côte et le large"[126].

20. In discussing the "skjærgaard" along Norway's coast, Professor Thouvenin used a figure of the Norwegian straight baselines in the Trondheim area. Now, if the "skjærgaard" is such a defining feature that acts as a barrier between the coast and the sea, one would expect that the straight baselines would conform to that barrier. Well, they do not. Please have a look at base point 50. If the Norwegian system of straight baselines had been intended to delineate the barrier that the "skjærgaard" constitutes, the straight baselines would have turned east to link to the islands forming the "skjærgaard" in that area, as identified by Colombia itself, and would have followed that barrier. This is illustrated by the red lines that have been added to the figure which is at tab 14 of the judges' folder. Well, the straight baseline does not turn east. It continues approximately in the same direction to link to base point 49. To give you some further perspective, which Professor Thouvenin did not, these two base points are around 46 nautical miles apart. And a large part of the straight baseline connecting these two points is located beyond the outer limit of the territorial sea, measured from the low-water line along the coast. This makes it completely untenable, especially if one were to adopt the restrictive view that Colombia has adopted for the purposes of these proceedings, to argue that base points 49 and 50 are located in the same group of fringing islands. The Norwegian approach indicates that the term fringe of islands does not have the restrictive scope that Colombia now seeks to attach to it. A fringe of islands may include separate groups of islands, as is the case for the islands along the coast of Norway and of Nicaragua.

21. Professor Thouvenin also referred to another type of fringing islands that are also discussed in the study on baselines of the United Nations Office for Ocean Affairs and the Law of the Sea[127]. The study observes that a fringe of islands may be constituted "by a swarm of small islands which

---

[126] CR 2021/15, p. 55, para. 20.

[127] CR 2021/15, p. 56, para. 56.

by their number justify consideration as a fringe"[128]. As an example, the study refers to the myriad islands of the Archipelago of the Recherche, off the western coast of Australia[129]. This example was not discussed this Wednesday, and it is instructive to have a closer look at it.

22. According to a number of sources, the myriad islands in the Archipelago of the Recherche number around one hundred[130]. As Nicaragua's Reply detailed, there are 95 islands off Nicaragua's Caribbean coast[131].

23. The baselines study of the United Nations Office for Ocean Affairs and the Law of the Sea observes that the mainland coast of Western Australia is "screened" by the islands of the Archipelago of the Recherche. The figure on screen, which is at tab 15 of the judges' folder, shows the straight baselines along the Archipelago of the Recherche. In particular to the west of the town of Esperance, there is only a limited number of small islands, but they are all included in the Australian system of straight baselines. This example again belies the high threshold Colombia is now seeking to impose on Nicaragua in relation to the criterion of fringing islands.

***(d)* A deeply indented and cut-into coast**

24. Madam President, I now turn to the discussion of the second condition that allows the drawing of straight baselines, namely a coast that is deeply indented and cut into. This condition is in particular relevant for the southern part of Nicaragua's mainland coast, between the Corn Islands and Nicaragua's land boundary with Costa Rica. Colombia, in its written pleadings and again this Wednesday, had no difficulty in submitting that this condition was not met by Nicaragua's coast[132].

25. While running the risk of seeming to be repetitive, it is pertinent to again draw the Court's attention to Colombia's own practice. A number of Colombia's straight baselines are drawn between points on the mainland coast of Colombia where there are no fringing islands. Colombia in those

---

[128] United Nations, Office for Ocean Affairs and the Law of the Sea, *The Law of the Sea. Baselines: An Examination of the Relevant Provisions of the United Nations Convention on the Law of the Sea*, 1989, New York, para.45.

[129] *Ibid.*

[130] Rebecca Brewin, "A look around the Recherche Archipelago", ABC Local, available at (https://www.abc.net.au/local/photos/2015/01/23/4167422.htm (accessed 20 Aug. 2021); "Attraction Archipelago of the Recherche", available at https://www.westernaustralia.com/en/Attraction/Archipelago_of_the_Recherche/56b2669daeeeaaf773cf9316 (accessed 20 Aug. 2021).

[131] RN, Ann. 31.

[132] See also APN, para. 3.58.

instances must have relied on the assumption that its coast is deeply indented and cut into. One of these areas is now on screen. This concerns Colombia's Caribbean coast between base points 5 and 6. This part of the coast of Colombia actually is less indented and cut into than the coast of Nicaragua between Monkey Point and the terminus of the land boundary with Costa Rica, which you now have on screen, alongside Colombia's Caribbean coast. This figure is at tab 16 of the judges' folder.

(e) The general direction of the coast

26. Article 7 (3) of the Convention requires that "[t]he drawing of straight baselines must not depart to any appreciable extent from the general direction of the coast". As the Judgment of the Court in the Anglo-Norwegian *Fisheries* indicates, the focus in this connection should be on the overall direction of the coast under consideration, not that of specific localities[133]. That leaves the question how to determine whether this requirement has been met.

27. The baselines study of the United Nations Office for Ocean Affairs and the Law of the Sea observes in this connection that a maximum departure of no more than 20 degrees has been suggested as a general rule[134]. The study qualifies this figure by observing that the geographical situation of a fringe of islands may be such that "the lines joining it to the coast must form an angle greater than 20 degrees"[135].

28. Nicaragua has prepared an assessment of its straight baselines in light of the criterion proposed by the baselines study of the United Nations Office for Ocean Affairs and the Law of the Sea. An illustration of this assessment is now on screen. As is also recognized by the study, determining the general direction of the coast is not without difficulty[136]. However, it is considered that a straight line between the termini of Nicaragua's land boundaries with Costa Rica and Honduras provides a reasonable representation of the general direction of that coast. That general direction results in an angle of between 1 and 22 degrees with the individual baseline segments of Nicaragua, which is in the range of the 20 degrees figure. The only exceptions are, first, the straight baseline

---

[133] For a further discussion see RN, paras. 7.44-7.48.

[134] United Nations, Office for Ocean Affairs and the Law of the Sea, *The Law of the Sea. Baselines: An Examination of the Relevant Provisions of the United Nations Convention on the Law of the Sea* (1989), New York, para. 54.

[135] *Ibid.*

[136] *Ibid.*, para. 55.

running from the southern bank of the boundary river with Honduras to the Miskito Cays and, second, the straight baseline between Man of War Cays and the Corn Islands. However, the Miskito Cays themselves constitute the relevant coast and the baseline closely follows the general direction of that coast. A relevant analogy is provided by Finland's Åland Islands. Finland's straight baselines are aligned with the general configuration of the Åland Islands, and not Finland's mainland coast[137]. In the case of the straight baseline between Man of War Cays and the Corn Islands, that line is drawn in such a way as to allow the inclusion of all islands fringing Nicaragua's mainland coast in its system of straight baselines.

29. In conclusion, none of Nicaragua's straight baselines depart to any appreciable extent from the general direction of the coast, meeting the requirement contained in this respect in Article 7 (3) of the Convention and customary international law.

30. This is also yet another instance in which Colombia's current parsimonious interpretation of the law is in stark contrast with its own straight baseline practice. This concerns the straight baseline between base points 6 and 7 on Colombia's Caribbean coast. The coast behind the straight baseline consists of two segments that are almost at a straight angle. The angles of these two segments with the straight baseline between point 6 and 7 are respectively 64 and 40 degrees. This figure is at tab 16 of the judges' folder.

31. Professor Thouvenin, this Wednesday, tried to graphically illustrate the divergence of Nicaragua's straight baselines from the general direction of the coast. Yet another example of the opportunistic use of graphics. He discussed three sections of Nicaragua's system of straight baselines[138]. As regards the first section he discussed, in the area of the Miskito Cays, I already explained some moments ago that one should not only look at the general direction of the mainland coast, but also the islands themselves, which Professor Thouvenin did not do. He also did not mention the angle that the third sector he discussed makes with the general direction of the coast. As I just mentioned it is 22 degrees, within the range of 20 degrees mentioned in the study on baselines of the United Nations Office for Ocean Affairs and the Law of the Sea.

---

[137] See further RN, para. 7.40, and Figure 7.7.

[138] See CR 2021/15, pp. 61-62, paras. 51-55, and Colombia's judges' folder, 22 Sept. 2021, tab 56, Figure 9, and tab 57, Figure 10.

32. Furthermore, one may question whether the 20-degrees range provides a general criterion that is applicable in all cases. Let me again revert to the Archipelago of the Recherche. The two westernmost straight baselines make angles of respectively 17 and 36 degrees to the general direction of the Australian mainland coast. This figure is at tab 17 of the judges' folder.

***(f)* Close linkage of the enclosed waters with the land domain**

33. A further requirement contained in Article 7 of the Convention and customary law is that "the sea areas lying within the lines must be sufficiently closely linked to the land domain to be subject to the régime of internal waters". In its written pleadings, Colombia applied a mathematical test of its own design to test this requirement. As regards the deficiencies of Colombia's mathematical test, I respectfully refer you to Nicaragua's written pleadings, cited in the footnote[139]. Let me just remind the Court of Figure 3 of Nicaragua's Additional Pleading on Colombia's counter-claims that is at tab 17 of the judges' folder. Applying Colombia's mathematical test to Colombia's own straight baselines reveals a much more expansive approach than is the case for Nicaragua. Thirty-two per cent of the internal waters enclosed by Colombia's straight baselines in the area on screen would not be part of Colombia's territorial sea measured from the low-water line. On the other hand, only 19 per cent of the internal waters enclosed by Nicaragua's straight baselines would not be part of Nicaragua's territorial sea measured from the low-water line. This again confirms that Colombia seeks to impose a standard on Nicaragua that it did not apply to itself.

34. This Wednesday, Professor Thouvenin also observed that Nicaragua has relied on the fact that the waters enclosed by Nicaragua's straight baselines had been used by its indigenous peoples[140]. Well, that was not exactly the main thrust of Nicaragua's argument. Nicaragua, in its written pleadings, relied on anthropological research that evidenced that most of the waters concerned had been divided in traditional tenure areas. A figure illustrating these areas is now on screen and at tab 18 of the judges' folder. Their location is compared to Nicaragua's straight baselines on the right-hand side. The division in tenure areas is comparable to similar management approaches on

---

[139] RN, paras. 7.43-7.53; APN, para. 3.59.

[140] CR 2021/15, p. 63, para. 60.

land. It has nothing to do with an open-access régime that would have been applicable under a State-centred law of the sea approach.

E. Colombia's rights are not infringed by Nicaragua's baselines

35. Colombia, in its written pleadings, and this Wednesday, has contended that Nicaragua, by establishing its system of straight baselines, has infringed Colombia's rights in two ways[141]. First, the régime of internal waters enclosed by straight baselines is different from the régime of the territorial sea and the exclusive economic zone. Second, following the establishment of Nicaragua's straight baselines, the territorial sea in part extends into areas that were formerly part of Nicaragua's exclusive economic zone. As a consequence, Colombia alleges, other States have more limited rights in Nicaragua's maritime domain.

36. As I have argued during my presentation, Nicaragua's straight baselines are in conformity with Article 7 of the Convention and customary international law. Moreover, Colombia's current interpretation of the law is contradicted by its own practice on straight baselines. That Colombian practice instead supports Nicaragua's application of the law.

37. Nicaragua is entitled to determine the status of the waters landward and seaward of its straight baselines in accordance with international law: internal waters landward of the straight baselines, and territorial sea, contiguous zone, exclusive economic zone and continental shelf seaward of the straight baselines. During these proceedings, Colombia has not provided any evidence that Colombia's rights in the waters enclosed by Nicaragua's straight baselines have been infringed. In particular, Colombia has not reported any single incident concerning the alleged violation of Colombia's rights in these waters.

38. Colombia also claims that Nicaragua's straight baselines have moved the outer limit of Nicaragua's exclusive economic zone seaward[142]. It is clear from my presentation that no such thing has happened. The outer limit of Nicaragua's exclusive economic zone in the Caribbean Sea has remained unaltered because Nicaragua has base points seaward of the straight baselines. These base

---

[141] CMC, para. 10.52; RC, para. 1.43.

[142] CMC, para. 10.52.

points on Nicaragua's low-water line have been determined in accordance with the Convention's Articles 5 and 13, which reflect customary international law.

39. Unless I can be of further assistance, Madam President, Members of the Court, that brings me to the end of my submissions, and of Nicaragua's submissions on Colombia's counter-claims in the first round of oral pleadings. I thank you for your attention.

The PRESIDENT: I thank Professor Oude Elferink, whose statement brings to an end the first round of oral argument. The Court will reconvene on Monday 27 September at 3 p.m. to hear Nicaragua's second round of pleadings.

Nicaragua will present its final submissions on its own claims on the afternoon of Monday 27 September. For its part, Colombia, on the afternoon of Wednesday 29 September, following its second round, will present its final submissions on the claims of Nicaragua and on its own counter-claims. On the afternoon of Friday 1 October, Nicaragua will present its final submissions on the counter-claims of Colombia.

As the Parties and their counsel turn to their preparation for the second round of these oral proceedings, I take this opportunity to remind them of Article 60, paragraph 1, of the Rules of Court, pursuant to which the oral statements are to be as succinct as possible. The Court has emphasized this requirement in Practice Direction VI. The Parties should not use the second round to repeat statements that they have previously made. The second round is an opportunity to respond to points that were made earlier in these oral proceedings. Moreover, the Parties are not obliged to use all the time allotted to them.

The sitting is adjourned.

The Court rose at 4.45 p.m.

____

Corrigé
Corrected

CR 2021/17

International Court of Justice

THE HAGUE

Cour internationale de Justice

LA HAYE

YEAR 2021

Public sitting

held on Monday 27 September 2021, at 3 p.m., at the Peace Palace,

President Donoghue presiding,

***in the case concerning* Alleged Violations of Sovereign Rights and Maritime Spaces in the Caribbean Sea (Nicaragua *v.* Colombia)**

VERBATIM RECORD

ANNÉE 2021

Audience publique

tenue le lundi 27 septembre 2021, à 15 heures, au Palais de la Paix,

sous la présidence de Mme Donoghue, présidente,

***en l'affaire relative à des* Violations alléguées de droits souverains et d'espaces maritimes dans la mer des Caraïbes (Nicaragua c. Colombie)**

COMPTE RENDU

Present:	President	Donoghue
	Vice-President	Gevorgian
	Judges	Tomka
		Abraham
		Bennouna
		Yusuf
		Xue
		Sebutinde
		Bhandari
		Robinson
		Salam
		Iwasawa
		Nolte
	Judges *ad hoc*	Daudet
		McRae
	Registrar	Gautier

Présents :	Mme	Donoghue, présidente
	M.	Gevorgian, vice-président
	MM.	Tomka
		Abraham
		Bennouna
		Yusuf
	Mmes	Xue
		Sebutinde
	MM.	Bhandari
		Robinson
		Salam
		Iwasawa
		Nolte, juges
	MM.	Daudet
		McRae, juges *ad hoc*
	M.	Gautier, greffier

The Government of Nicaragua is represented by:

H.E. Mr. Carlos José Argüello Gómez, Ambassador of the Republic of Nicaragua to the Kingdom of the Netherlands,

as Agent and Counsel;

Mr. Alex Oude Elferink, Director, Netherlands Institute for the Law of the Sea, Professor of International Law of the Sea at Utrecht University,

Mr. Vaughan Lowe, QC, Emeritus Chichele Professor of Public International Law, University of Oxford, member of the Institut de droit international, member of the Bar of England and Wales,

Mr. Lawrence H. Martin, Attorney at Law, Foley Hoag LLP, member of the Bars of the United States Supreme Court, the District of Columbia and the Commonwealth of Massachusetts,

Mr. Alain Pellet, Emeritus Professor of the University Paris Nanterre, former Chairman of the International Law Commission, President of the Institut de droit international,

Mr. Paul Reichler, Attorney at Law, Foley Hoag LLP, member of the Bars of the United States Supreme Court and the District of Columbia,

as Counsel and Advocates;

Ms Claudia Loza Obregon, Legal Adviser, Ministry of Foreign Affairs of Nicaragua,

Ms Tessa Barsac, Consultant in International Law, Master (University Paris Nanterre), LLM (Leiden University),

as Assistant Counsel;

Mr. Robin Cleverly, MA, DPhil, CGeol, FGS, Law of the Sea Consultant, Marbdy Consulting Ltd,

as Scientific and Technical Adviser;

Ms Sherly Noguera de Argüello, MBA,

as Administrator.

The Government of Colombia is represented by:

H.E. Mr. Carlos Gustavo Arrieta Padilla, former Judge of the Council of State of Colombia, former Attorney General of Colombia and former Ambassador of Colombia to the Netherlands,

as Agent;

H.E. Mr. Manuel José Cepeda Espinosa, former President of the Constitutional Court of Colombia, former Permanent Delegate of Colombia to UNESCO and former Ambassador of Colombia to the Swiss Confederation,

as Co-Agent;

Le Gouvernement du Nicaragua est représenté par :

S. Exc. M. Carlos José Argüello Gómez, ambassadeur de la République du Nicaragua auprès du Royaume des Pays-Bas,

comme agent et conseil ;

M. Alex Oude Elferink, directeur de l'Institut néerlandais du droit de la mer, professeur de droit international de la mer à l'Université d'Utrecht,

M. Vaughan Lowe, QC, professeur émérite de droit international public à l'Université d'Oxford, titulaire de la chaire Chichele, membre de l'Institut de droit international, membre du barreau d'Angleterre et du pays de Galles,

M. Lawrence H. Martin, avocat au cabinet Foley Hoag LLP, membre des barreaux de la Cour suprême des Etats-Unis d'Amérique, du district de Colombia et du Commonwealth du Massachusetts,

M. Alain Pellet, professeur émérite de l'Université Paris Nanterre, ancien président de la Commission du droit international, président de l'Institut de droit international,

M. Paul Reichler, avocat au cabinet Foley Hoag LLP, membre des barreaux de la Cour suprême des Etats-Unis d'Amérique et du district de Colombia,

comme conseils et avocats ;

Mme Claudia Loza Obregon, conseillère juridique auprès du ministère des affaires étrangères du Nicaragua,

Mme Tessa Barsac, consultante en droit international, master (Université Paris Nanterre), LLM (Université de Leyde),

comme conseils adjoints ;

M. Robin Cleverly, MA, DPhil, CGeol, FGS, consultant en droit de la mer, Marbdy Consulting Ltd,

comme conseiller scientifique et technique ;

Mme Sherly Noguera de Argüello, MBA,

comme administrateur.

Le Gouvernement de la Colombie est représenté par :

S. Exc. M. Carlos Gustavo Arrieta Padilla, ancien juge au conseil d'Etat colombien, ancien *Procurador General de la Nación* et ancien ambassadeur de Colombie aux Pays-Bas,

comme agent ;

S. Exc. M. Manuel José Cepeda Espinosa, ancien président de la Cour constitutionnelle de Colombie, ancien représentant permanent de la Colombie auprès de l'UNESCO et ancien ambassadeur de Colombie auprès de la Confédération suisse,

comme coagent ;

H.E. Ms Marta Lucía Ramírez Blanco, Vice-President and Minister for Foreign Affairs of the Republic of Colombia,

H.E. Mr. Everth Hawkins Sjogreen, Governor of San Andrés, Providencia and Santa Catalina, Colombia,

as National Authorities;

Mr. W. Michael Reisman, McDougal Professor of International Law at Yale University, member of the Institut de droit international,

Mr. Rodman R. Bundy, former *avocat à la Cour d'appel de Paris*, member of the Bar of the State of New York, partner at Squire Patton Boggs LLP, Singapore,

Sir Michael Wood, KCMG, member of the International Law Commission, member of the Bar of England and Wales,

Mr. Eduardo Valencia-Ospina, former Registrar and Deputy-Registrar of the International Court of Justice, member and former Special Rapporteur and Chair of the International Law Commission, former Chair of the Latin American Society of International Law,

Mr. Jean-Marc Thouvenin, Professor at the University Paris Nanterre, Secretary-General of the Hague Academy of International Law, associate member of the Institut de droit international, member of the Paris Bar, Sygna Partners,

Ms Laurence Boisson de Chazournes, Professor of International Law and International Organization at the University of Geneva, member of the Institut de droit international,

H.E. Mr. Kent Francis James, former Ambassador of Colombia to Belize, former Ambassador of Colombia to Jamaica,

as Counsel and Advocates;

Mr. Andrés Villegas Jaramillo, LLM, Co-ordinator, Group of Affairs before the International Court of Justice at the Ministry of Foreign Affairs of Colombia, member of the Legal Sub-Commission of the Caribbean Sea Commission, Association of Caribbean States,

Mr. Makane Moïse Mbengue, Professor at the University of Geneva, Director of the Department of Public International Law and International Organization, associate member of the Institut de droit international,

Mr. Luke Vidal, member of the Paris Bar, Sygna Partners,

Mr. Eran Sthoeger, Esq., member of the Bar of the State of New York, Adjunct Professor of International Law at Brooklyn Law School and Seton Hall Law School,

Mr. Alvin Yap, Advocate and Solicitor of the Supreme Court of Singapore, Squire Patton Boggs LLP, Singapore,

Mr. Lorenzo Palestini, PhD, Lecturer at the Graduate Institute of International and Development Studies and at the University of Geneva,

as Counsel;

S. Exc. Mme Marta Lucía Ramírez Blanco, vice-présidente et ministre des affaires étrangères de la République de Colombie,

S. Exc. M. Everth Hawkins Sjogreen, gouverneur de San Andrés, Providencia et Santa Catalina, Colombie,

comme représentants de l'Etat ;

M. W. Michael Reisman, professeur de droit international à l'Université de Yale, titulaire de la chaire McDougal, membre de l'Institut de droit international,

M. Rodman R. Bundy, ancien avocat à la Cour d'appel de Paris, membre du barreau de l'Etat de New York, associé au cabinet Squire Patton Boggs LLP (Singapour),

Sir Michael Wood, KCMG, membre de la Commission du droit international, membre du barreau d'Angleterre et du pays de Galles,

M. Eduardo Valencia-Ospina, ancien greffier et greffier adjoint de la Cour internationale de Justice, membre et ancien rapporteur spécial et président de la Commission du droit international, ancien président de l'association latino-américaine de droit international,

M. Jean-Marc Thouvenin, professeur à l'Université Paris Nanterre, secrétaire général de l'Académie de droit international de La Haye, membre associé de l'Institut de droit international, membre du barreau de Paris, cabinet Sygna Partners,

Mme Laurence Boisson de Chazournes, professeure de droit international public et organisation internationale à l'Université de Genève, membre de l'Institut de droit international,

S. Exc. M. Kent Francis James, ancien ambassadeur de Colombie au Belize et ancien ambassadeur de Colombie en Jamaïque,

comme conseils et avocats ;

M. Andrés Villegas Jaramillo, LLM, coordonnateur du groupe chargé des affaires portées devant la Cour internationale de Justice au sein du ministère des affaires étrangères de la Colombie, membre de la sous-commission juridique relevant de la Commission de la mer des Caraïbes de l'Association des Etats de la Caraïbe,

M. Makane Moïse Mbengue, professeur à l'Université de Genève, directeur du département de droit international public et organisation internationale, membre associé de l'Institut de droit international,

M. Luke Vidal, membre du barreau de Paris, cabinet Sygna Partners,

M. Eran Sthoeger, membre du barreau de l'Etat de New York, professeur adjoint de droit international à la Brooklyn Law School et à la faculté de droit de l'université de Seton Hall,

M. Alvin Yap, avocat et *solicitor* à la Cour suprême de Singapour, cabinet Squire Patton Boggs LLP (Singapour),

M. Lorenzo Palestini, PhD, chargé d'enseignement à l'Institut de hautes études internationales et du développement et à l'Université de Genève,

comme conseils ;

H.E. Mr. Juan José Quintana Aranguren, Head of Multilateral Affairs, former Ambassador of Colombia to the Netherlands,

H.E. Mr. Fernando Antonio Grillo Rubiano, Ambassador of the Republic of Colombia to the Kingdom of the Netherlands and Permanent Representative of Colombia to the Organisation for the Prohibition of Chemical Weapons,

Ms Jenny Sharyne Bowie Wilches, Second Secretary, Embassy of Colombia in the Netherlands,

Ms Viviana Andrea Medina Cruz, Second Secretary, Embassy of Colombia in the Netherlands,

Mr. Sebastián Correa Cruz, Third Secretary,

Mr. Raúl Alfonso Simancas Gómez, Third Secretary, Group of Affairs before the International Court of Justice,

Ministry of Foreign Affairs of Colombia;

Rear Admiral Ernesto Segovia Forero, Chief of Naval Operations,

CN Hermann León, Delegate of Colombia to the International Maritime Organization,

CN William Pedroza, National Navy of Colombia, Director of Maritime and Fluvial Interests Office,

Navy of the Republic of Colombia;

Mr. Scott Edmonds, Cartographer, Director of International Mapping,

Ms Victoria Taylor, Cartographer, International Mapping,

as Technical Advisers;

Mr. Gershon Hasin, LLM, JSD, Yale Law School,

as Legal Assistant;

Mr. Mark Taylor Archbold, Consultant for the National Unit of Disaster Risk Management,

Mr. Joseph Richard Jessie Martinez, Consultant for the National Unit of Disaster Risk Management,

as Advisers.

S. Exc. M. Juan José Quintana Aranguren, chef des affaires multilatérales, ancien ambassadeur de Colombie aux Pays-Bas,

S. Exc. M. Fernando Antonio Grillo Rubiano, ambassadeur de la République de Colombie auprès du Royaume des Pays-Bas et représentant permanent de la Colombie auprès de l'Organisation pour l'interdiction des armes chimiques,

Mme Jenny Sharyne Bowie Wilches, deuxième secrétaire, ambassade de Colombie aux Pays-Bas,

Mme Viviana Andrea Medina Cruz, deuxième secrétaire, ambassade de Colombie aux Pays-Bas,

M. Sebastián Correa Cruz, troisième secrétaire,

M. Raúl Alfonso Simancas Gómez, troisième secrétaire, groupe chargé des affaires portées devant la Cour internationale de Justice,

ministère des affaires étrangères de la République de Colombie ;

Le contre-amiral Ernesto Segovia Forero, chef des opérations navales,

Le capitaine de vaisseau Hermann León, représentant de la Colombie auprès de l'Organisation maritime internationale,

Le capitaine de vaisseau William Pedroza, marine nationale de Colombie, chef de la direction chargée des intérêts maritimes et fluviaux,

marine de la République de Colombie ;

M. Scott Edmonds, cartographe, directeur de International Mapping,

Mme Victoria Taylor, cartographe, International Mapping,

comme conseillers techniques ;

M. Gershon Hasin, LLM, JSD, faculté de droit de l'Université de Yale,

comme assistant juridique ;

M. Mark Taylor Archbold, consultant auprès de l'unité nationale de gestion des risques de catastrophe,

M. Joseph Richard Jessie Martinez, consultant auprès de l'unité nationale de gestion des risques de catastrophe,

comme conseillers.

The PRESIDENT: Please be seated. The sitting is open. I would like to note that, today, the following judges are present with me in the Great Hall of Justice: Vice-President Gevorgian and Judges Tomka, Bennouna, Sebutinde and Nolte; while Judges Abraham, Yusuf, Xue, Bhandari, Robinson, Salam and Iwasawa, and Judges *ad hoc* Daudet and McRae are participating by video link.

The Court meets this afternoon to hear Nicaragua's second round of oral argument on its own claims.

I shall now give the floor to Professor Alain Pellet. You have the floor, Sir.

M. PELLET :

LES BIZARRERIES JURIDIQUES DES THÈSES COLOMBIENNES

1. Madame la présidente, Mesdames et Messieurs les juges, la semaine dernière, la Colombie a plaidé une affaire dans laquelle nous avons du mal à reconnaître celle que le Nicaragua vous a soumise par sa requête du 26 novembre 2013. Comme l'ambassadeur James s'agissant des Raizals, Laurence Boisson de Chazournes a beaucoup fait vibrer la corde sensible en mettant en accusation la politique environnementale nicaraguayenne qui serait «au cœur du présent différend»[1] — tandis que, pour Jean-Marc Thouvenin, «ce qui est en jeu dans cette affaire, c'est la liberté de navigation»[2].

2. Dans un premier temps, je m'emploierai donc à nouveau à remettre l'affaire sur ses rails en rappelant de quoi il s'agit et… de quoi il ne s'agit pas. Cela me conduira à revenir sur l'étendue de la compétence de la Cour et la prétendue irrecevabilité de l'invocation par le Nicaragua de certains faits survenus postérieurement à l'introduction de la requête. Je dirai ensuite quelques mots, plus largement, des vains efforts de la Colombie pour manipuler le droit applicable.

I. L'objet de l'affaire

3. Madame la présidente, l'objet de l'affaire qui nous réunit est décrit, de manière claire et suffisante, par le premier membre de phrase du paragraphe 2 de la requête : «Le différend porte sur des violations des droits souverains et des espaces maritimes du Nicaragua qui lui ont été reconnus par la Cour dans son arrêt du 19 novembre 2012...» Le même paragraphe ajoutait : «ainsi que sur la

---

[1] CR 2021/14, p. 35, par. 3 (Boisson de Chazournes).

[2] CR 2021/15, p. 50, par. 2 (Thouvenin) ; voir aussi, par exemple, CR 2021/14, p. 14, par. 27 (Cepeda Espinosa).

menace de la Colombie de recourir à la force pour commettre ces violations». Mais, dans votre sagesse, vous avez retenu, par votre arrêt du 17 mars 2016, l'exception préliminaire soulevée à l'encontre de cette seconde demande — elle ne fait donc pas l'objet du présent différend : contrairement à l'Etat défendeur, le Nicaragua se plie, lui, aux décisions de la Cour.

4. La seule question est donc de savoir si la Colombie respecte, non pas votre arrêt de 2012 en tant que tel, mais les droits en résultant en ce qui concerne aussi bien leur extension spatiale que leur intégrité — intégrité : cela veut dire, les droits *souverains* appartenant au Nicaragua dans sa zone économique *exclusive*. Il est clair que la Partie colombienne ne s'y résigne pas — ni dans les faits, ni dans les discours de ses dirigeants, ni même dans les plaidoiries de ses représentants devant la Cour de céans. Toutes leurs contorsions verbales ne peuvent nier l'évidence : la Colombie entend, pour reprendre la formule de son ancien président, «continuer à exercer un plein contrôle et une pleine juridiction» dans sa «zone contiguë intégrale réunissant les zones contiguës de toutes les îles et cayes [qu'elle possède] dans la partie occidentale de la mer des Caraïbes»[3] ; ou bien, selon le titulaire actuel de cette haute fonction, «conserver tous les outils qui nous permettent d'assurer l'intégrité du territoire colombien»[4], et cela au détriment des zones maritimes relevant du Nicaragua.

5. Dans sa nouvelle présentation de l'affaire, la Colombie s'emploie essentiellement à minimiser ses activités dans la ZEE du Nicaragua. Elle se fait la représentante des intérêts de la communauté internationale dans son ensemble et la gardienne de la préservation de l'environnement sans égard pour les droits souverains du Nicaragua. Elle ne contrôle point ; elle ne contraint pas, elle «observe et informe» — l'expression constitue la clé de voûte de toute la plaidoirie de la professeure Boisson de Chazournes, dans laquelle elle n'apparaît pas moins de treize fois[5]. Cela n'est évidemment pas tenable, ne serait-ce que parce que ce n'est pas avec des navires de guerre que l'on procède à l'observation et à l'information relatives à la protection de l'environnement. Me Reichler

---

[3] Déclaration du président Juan Manuel Santos concernant la stratégie globale de la Colombie face à l'arrêt de la Cour internationale de Justice, 9 septembre 2013 (MN, annexe 4) ou https://www.radionacional.co/actualidad/colombia-va-defender-sus-intereses-sobre-litigio-con-nicaragua.

[4] «Presidente Duque ve con buenos ojos propuesta de Uribe sobre «consulta popular» para confirmar límite con Nicaragua», *Semana*, 23 septembre 2021, https://www.semana.com/nacion/articulo/presidente-duque-ve-con-buenos-ojos-propuesta-de-uribe-sobre-consulta-popular-para-confirmar-limite-con-nicaragua/202112/ (espagnol original : «seguir manteniendo vivas todas las herramientas que nos permitan tener la integralidad del territorio colombiano»).

[5] CR 2021/14, p. 36, par. 7 et 8, p. 37, par. 11, p. 41, par. 25, p. 43, par. 30, p. 45-46, par. 40-42, 46 et sect. I et II (Boisson de Chazournes). Voir aussi : p. 18, par. 43 (Cepeda Espinosa) ; p. 29, par. 22 et p. 33, par. 41 (Wood) ; CR 2021/15, p. 19, par. 50 (Bundy).

y reviendra plus longuement ; et le professeur Lowe, pour sa part, montrera que la conception qu'a l'Etat défendeur des droits lui revenant dans la zone contiguë «intégrale» qu'il prétend instaurer est totalement incompatible avec les règles coutumières applicables à la zone économique exclusive et à la zone contiguë.

6. En transformant leur défense des intérêts de la Colombie en une attaque, vaine, mal fondée, hors de cause, dirigée contre la politique nicaraguayenne de protection de l'environnement, nos contradicteurs confirment une nouvelle fois que l'Etat défendeur fait fi des décisions de votre haute juridiction.

7. Il se soucie comme d'une guigne de votre ordonnance du 15 novembre 2017 relative à ses demandes reconventionnelles. Il se comporte comme si vous n'aviez pas rejeté les deux premières exceptions se rapportant, l'une comme l'autre, selon le résumé que vous en avez fait, «aux prétendues violations, par le Nicaragua, de l'obligation qui lui incombe de protéger et de préserver l'environnement marin»[6]. Constatant «l'absence de connexité directe, tant en fait qu'en droit, entre [ces] demandes reconventionnelles de la Colombie et les demandes principales du Nicaragua»[7], vous avez jugé ces demandes «irrecevable[s] comme telle[s]» et, dès lors, comme *ne faisant «pas partie de l'instance en cours»*[8]. Elles n'en font pas partie, et la Colombie ne peut pas aujourd'hui réintroduire par la fenêtre, à l'occasion de ses plaidoiries sur le fond, ce que vous aviez exclu par la grande porte, à la majorité de 15 voix contre une. A cette occasion, la Colombie avait déjà fait valoir, selon le résumé qu'en a donné la Cour au paragraphe 29 de son ordonnance, que le Nicaragua aurait manqué aux obligations lui incombant «en matière de préservation et de protection de l'environnement marin et [dans] l'exercice de la diligence requise à cet égard...»[9]. La Colombie avait précisé que ces manquements se seraient produits dans «la zone couvrant certaines parties de la réserve de biosphère Seaflower et l'aire marine protégée du même nom, dont l'espace maritime entourant le banc de Luna Verde, … ainsi que la zone contiguë qu'elle a proclamée»[10]. Il est assez

---

[6] *Violations alléguées de droits souverains et d'espaces maritimes dans la mer des Caraïbes (Nicaragua c. Colombie), demandes reconventionnelles, ordonnance du 15 novembre 2017, C.I.J. Recueil 2017*, p. 300, par. 35.

[7] *Ibid.*, p. 302, par. 39.

[8] *Ibid.*, p. 314, par. 82.A(1) et (2) (les italiques sont de nous).

[9] *Ibid.*, p. 298, par. 29.

[10] *Ibid.*

plaisant (et en même temps choquant) de constater que toute la plaidoirie de Laurence Boisson de Chazournes a consisté en fait à reprendre et développer très exactement ces mêmes arguments.

8. Madame la présidente, nous ne suivrons pas cet exemple — ce mauvais exemple — et les conclusions que notre agent va lire tout à l'heure s'en tiendront strictement aux limites que la Cour a définies dans son arrêt sur les exceptions préliminaires. Je souhaite cependant ajouter une remarque : on peut avoir des doutes sur certaines conclusions demandant à la Cour d'ordonner à l'Etat défendeur d'offrir des garanties de non-répétition. Mais s'il y a un cas dans lequel cette forme de réparation s'impose, c'est assurément celui, très exceptionnel, dans lequel un Etat mauvais perdant se refuse à mettre en œuvre les droits résultant de l'un de vos arrêts. Nous maintenons donc cette conclusion visant à ce que la Colombie reconnaisse («acknowledge» en anglais), formellement et définitivement, la frontière maritime délimitée par la Cour dans son arrêt du 19 novembre 2012 et qu'il la respectera[11].

9. Mais nous croyons aussi que, compte tenu des circonstances particulières de cette affaire, au cours de laquelle la Colombie a montré le peu de cas qu'elle fait des décisions de l'organe judiciaire principal des Nations Unies, il serait approprié à tous points de vue que la Cour elle-même s'associe à cette garantie et déclare qu'elle restera saisie de l'affaire jusqu'à ce que la Colombie reconnaisse (toujours «acknowledge») et respecte les droits du Nicaragua que votre arrêt du 19 novembre 2012 lui a attribués dans la mer des Caraïbes.

10. Nous sommes bien conscients qu'il s'agit d'une demande inhabituelle ; elle est à la mesure du caractère exceptionnel de l'affaire. Et d'ailleurs, elle n'est pas sans précédent. Ainsi, dans les affaires des *Essais nucléaires*, la Cour a spontanément fait observer que : «si le fondement du présent arrêt [de 1974] était remis en cause, le requérant pourrait demander un examen de la situation conformément aux dispositions du Statut». Et vous avez ajouté que la dénonciation par la France du fondement «de la compétence de la Cour en l'espèce … ne saurait en soi faire obstacle à la présentation d'une telle demande»[12].

11. Vous avez dit ceci alors même que vous aviez précisé qu'il n'entre pas dans votre fonction d'envisager qu'«un Etat [qui] a pris un engagement quant à son comportement futur ... ne le respecte

---

[11] Voir MN, par. 4.66-4.73, conclusion 2 *d)*, et RN, conclusion 1 *g)*.

[12] *Essais nucléaires (Nouvelle-Zélande c. France), arrêt, C.I.J. Recueil 1974*, p. 477, par. 63.

pas»[13]. Dans notre affaire, l'inenvisageable s'est produit : l'Etat défendeur se refuse délibérément à respecter les droits découlant de votre arrêt ; c'est au moins aussi inacceptable et illicite que le non-respect d'un engagement unilatéral. La Cour a confirmé, dans son ordonnance du 22 septembre 1995, qu'une telle «procédure spéciale pouvait être envisagée lorsque les circonstances l'exigent»[14]. Nous espérons vivement qu'elles ne l'exigeront pas ; on ne peut toutefois pas totalement l'exclure au vu du comportement de la Colombie au cours des années écoulées.

II. L'étendue de la compétence de la Cour

12. Mesdames et Messieurs les juges, la plaidoirie de Me Bundy était censée établir que la Colombie n'a commis aucune violation des droits du Nicaragua dans la ZEE que lui a reconnue votre arrêt de 2012. Mon contradicteur, et néanmoins ami, n'en a pas moins consacré la plus grande partie de son intervention à tenter de neutraliser un très grand nombre des faits sur lesquels le Nicaragua s'appuie en invoquant la prétendue incompétence de la Cour pour en connaître. La raison en serait que «the Court lacks jurisdiction *ratione temporis* under the Pact of Bogotá to consider any events claimed to have occurred after 27 November 2013»[15], date à laquelle le pacte a cessé d'être en vigueur à l'égard de la Colombie, suite à sa dénonciation, survenue un an plus tôt.

13. Je ne discuterai pas la consistance et la portée de ces nombreux faits illicites, qui mettent la Colombie si mal à l'aise ; Paul Reichler s'en chargera avec son talent habituel. Il m'incombe seulement de rappeler[16] que, contrairement aux affirmations de Rodman Bundy, tous ces faits relèvent du différend que le Nicaragua a soumis à la Cour par sa requête du 26 novembre 2013.

14. Pour le montrer, je m'étais principalement appuyé lundi dernier sur l'interprétation généralement admise de l'article LVI du pacte de Bogotá. Elle semble l'être aussi par mon contradicteur puisque celui-ci ne nous reproche pas d'avoir mal interprété cette disposition. Mais il nous critique pour avoir négligé l'article XXXI. «Yet», he argued, «it is Article XXXI that not only contains the Contracting Parties' consent to the Court's jurisdiction, but equally importantly, the

---

[13] *Ibid.*

[14] *Demande d'examen de la situation au titre du paragraphe 63 de l'arrêt rendu par la Cour le 20 décembre 1974 dans l'affaire des* Essais nucléaires (Nouvelle-Zélande c. France) *(Nouvelle-Zélande c. France), ordonnance du 22 septembre 1995, C.I.J. Recueil 1995*, p. 303-304, par. 52-54.

[15] CR 2021/14, p. 48, par. 4 (Bundy).

[16] Voir CR 2021/13, p. 37-39 (Pellet).

limits of that consent, including consent to the Court's jurisdiction *ratione temporis* to decide disputes referred to in that Article»[17].

15. Avec votre permission, Madame la présidente, revoyons donc ce que dit l'article XXXI (dans sa partie utile pour nous aujourd'hui) — le texte complet se trouve à l'onglet AP-1 du dossier des juges :

> «Conformément au paragraphe 2 de l'article 36 du Statut de la Cour internationale de Justice, les Hautes Parties Contractantes en ce qui concerne tout autre Etat américain déclarent reconnaître comme obligatoire de plein droit, et sans convention spéciale tant que le présent Traité restera en vigueur, la juridiction de la Cour sur tous les différends d'ordre juridique surgissant entre elles».

16. L'expression «tant que le présent Traité restera en vigueur» serait la clé de la question puisque cette disposition contient, comme l'a dit Rodman Bundy, «a clear temporal limitation to Colombia's consent to the Court's jurisdiction over a dispute concerning the existence of any fact which, if established, could constitute the breach of an international obligation»[18]. Nous en sommes bien conscients ; mais cette «limitation temporelle» n'ajoute rien à ce que dit l'article LVI. Comme la Cour l'a constaté dans son arrêt de 2016, après une analyse soigneuse des relations entre les articles XXXI et LVI du pacte et l'article 36, paragraphe 2, du Statut : «L'extinction ultérieure du pacte entre le Nicaragua et la Colombie n'a pas d'incidence sur la compétence qui existait à la date à laquelle l'instance a été introduite.»[19] Aucune nouvelle instance ne peut être introduite mais la limitation temporelle contenue dans l'article XXXI ne concerne que *le différend* soumis à la Cour, étant entendu qu'il l'est *dans son ensemble*, sans pouvoir être divisé, saucissonné, entre plusieurs litiges. Celui qui vous a été soumis par le Nicaragua est né avant la dénonciation du pacte par la Colombie ; il concerne «des violations des droits souverains et des espaces maritimes du Nicaragua qui lui ont été reconnus par la Cour dans son arrêt du 19 novembre 2012»[20]. Ces violations, qui trouvent leur origine commune dans le refus continu de la Colombie de respecter les droits que le Nicaragua tient de votre arrêt, forment un tout.

---

[17] CR 2021/15, p. 15, par. 35 (Bundy).

[18] Voir CR 2021/15, p. 15, par. 37 (Bundy).

[19] *Violations alléguées de droits souverains et d'espaces maritimes dans la mer des Caraïbes (Nicaragua c. Colombie), exceptions préliminaires, arrêt, C.I.J. Recueil 2016 (I)*, p. 26, par. 48.

[20] Requête, par. 2.

17. En réalité, Me Bundy invente une limitation temporelle de la compétence de la Cour en vertu de l'article XXXI totalement incompatible avec le texte et le contexte de cette disposition. Je relève que la Colombie — qui a soulevé quatre exceptions préliminaires pour tenter de s'opposer, en tout ou en partie, à la compétence de la Cour dans notre affaire — n'avait pas élevé cette objection. On le comprend : elle brille davantage par son originalité que par sa solidité et consiste à transformer sans raison une exception de compétence *ratione materiae* en une exception *ratione temporis*.

18. Nous convenons, bien entendu, que la compétence de la Cour s'étend exclusivement aux différends de nature juridique survenus pendant que le pacte était en vigueur pour les deux Parties. La Cour a déjà décidé, dans son arrêt de 2016, qu'un tel différend, né avant la dénonciation du pacte par la Colombie, a effectivement surgi en l'espèce, et qu'elle a compétence pour en connaître. Mais M. Bundy va plus loin, et prétend trouver une limitation supplémentaire à la compétence *temporelle* de la Cour dans les alinéas *a)* à *d)* de l'article XXXI, en particulier l'alinéa *c)*[21]. Vous ne sauriez l'admettre : ces alinéas — qui reprennent le texte de ceux figurant à l'article 36, paragraphe 2, du Statut de la Cour — concernent sa compétence matérielle, *ratione materiae*, et non sa compétence temporelle, *ratione temporis*. Il n'est donc nécessaire, ni selon l'article XXXI, ni selon l'article 36, paragraphe 2, que *les faits* constituant des violations du droit international se produisent tous avant que la base de juridiction ait pris fin. Il suffit que *le différend* ait pris naissance alors que ces instruments de consentement étaient en vigueur et que les faits survenus ultérieurement fassent partie de ce même différend. En l'espèce, les faits dont se prévaut le Nicaragua font, indépendamment de leur date, partie intégrante du différend — objet de sa requête. Me Reichler y reviendra.

19. Dès lors, n'en déplaise à notre contradicteur, le problème se pose exactement dans les mêmes termes que cela était le cas dans les affaires qu'il s'efforce en vain de distinguer, relatives à la légalité de l'usage de la force ou à la *Compétence en matière de pêcheries* :

— dans le premier cas, selon les propres termes de Rodman Bundy, la question posée à la Cour était de savoir «si le *différend* — le mot «différend» *(dispute)* est souligné dans le compte rendu —

[21] CR 2021/15, p. 15-16, par. 36, 39 (Bundy).

était né avant ou après la déclaration facultative de la Yougoslavie» («whether the *dispute* arose before or after Yugoslavia's optional clause declaration»)[22], et,

— dans le second cas (dans l'affaire des *Pêcheries* entre l'Allemagne et l'Islande), il s'agissait de savoir — toujours selon notre contradicteur — si «one of Germany's submissions that was based on facts subsequent to the filing of the Application but arising directly out of the question which was the subject-matter of the Application»[23].

De la même manière, dans l'affaire qui nous occupe, qu'ils soient antérieurs à la requête ou postérieurs, *tous* les faits attribuables à la Colombie et invoqués par le Nicaragua établissent la réalité de la violation continue des droits du Nicaragua, qui est l'objet même (le subject matter) du différend.

20. La Colombie ne peut davantage se fonder sur l'affaire relative à *Certains biens*[24] : dans celle-ci, le différend portait exclusivement sur des faits pré-datant l'acceptation de la juridiction de la Cour par les deux parties et la question qui se posait était celle de la rétroactivité de l'exercice de la compétence.

21. Ce qui est fondamental dans l'affaire présente, c'est que le refus obstiné, persistant, continu, de la Colombie de reconnaître et respecter la juridiction et les droits souverains et exclusifs appartenant au Nicaragua dans sa ZEE ne résulte pas d'un fait isolé. Il s'agit d'un fait illicite composite au sens de l'article 15 des Articles de la CDI sur la responsabilité de l'Etat de 2001 — dont le texte avec les commentaires est reproduit à l'onglet AP-2 du dossier des juges. Il consiste en «une série d'actions … ou d'omissions, définie dans son ensemble comme illicite».

> «Dans un tel cas», comme le précise la Commission, «la violation s'étend sur toute la période débutant avec la première des actions ou omissions de la série et dure aussi longtemps que ces actions ou omissions se répètent et restent non conformes à ladite obligation internationale.»

22. Comme l'indique le commentaire de ce projet d'article : «le fait illicite est réputé s'étendre tout au long de la période commençant avec la commission de la première action ou omission»[25] ; au surplus, «cela n'exclut pas pour autant la possibilité que chacun des faits qui constituent la série soit

---

[22] *Ibid.*, p. 17, par. 41, se référant, sans citer à *Licéité de l'emploi de la force (Yougoslavie c. Belgique), mesures conservatoires, ordonnance du 2 juin 1999, C.I.J. Recueil 1999 (I)*, p. 134, par. 28.

[23] CR 2021/15, p. 17-18, par. 45 (Bundy) ; voir *Compétence en matière de pêcheries (République fédérale d'Allemagne c. Islande), fond, arrêt, C.I.J. Recueil 1974*, p. 203, par. 72.

[24] CR 2021/15, p. 16, par. 39 (Bundy).

[25] Draft articles on Responsibility of States for Internationally Wrongful Acts, with commentaries, *Yearbook of the International Law Commission*, 2001, vol. II, Part Two, p. 158, par. 10.

lui-même illicite…»[26]. Dans notre affaire, le fait déclencheur du fait composite illicite a été le refus de mettre en œuvre l'arrêt de 2012 dont est résultée une série d'actions, elles-mêmes illicites, violant la juridiction et les droits souverains du Nicaragua dans sa zone économique exclusive.

23. J'ajoute pour surplus de droit que même si, par impossible, la Cour estimait ne pas avoir compétence pour se prononcer sur l'illicéité, en tant que telle, de faits postérieurs à la dénonciation du pacte, il n'en résulterait nullement qu'elle devrait faire abstraction de ces faits pour apprécier celle des comportements de la Colombie antérieurs au 27 novembre 2013 — d'autant moins qu'ils sont dans la continuité des activités passées de la Colombie et confirment qu'elle n'a nullement l'intention de respecter les droits souverains et la juridiction du Nicaragua dans la ZEE que l'arrêt de 2012 lui a reconnus.

III. Le droit applicable

24. Mesdames et Messieurs de la Cour, je voudrais, pour terminer, relever certaines bizarreries persistantes dans l'argumentation colombienne en ce qui concerne maintenant le droit applicable.

25. La première, et non la moindre, concerne les explications embrouillées qu'a données le coagent de la Colombie au sujet des relations entre le droit interne de son pays et le droit international et, plus précisément, l'application de votre arrêt de 2012. Pour autant que je les ai comprises, il semble en résulter que cet arrêt serait applicable dans l'ordre international mais pas dans l'ordre interne, aussi longtemps en tout cas qu'un traité (international donc…) lui donnant effet n'aura pas été conclu[27]… Ceci résulterait de la sentence de la Cour constitutionnelle de 2014 (dont, curieusement, il n'a d'ailleurs plus du tout été question dans la suite des plaidoiries après la présentation du coagent). Selon cette décision, «the rulings of the International Court of Justice ha[ve] binding international effects and … Colombia ha[s] a "duty to comply [with it] in good faith", until a treaty [i]s concluded» — this is good news. And the Co-Agent added : «The Constitutional Court went on to say that Colombia "recognizes the binding character of the decisions adopted by an international court in the performance of treaties previously entered into, approved and ratified by Colombia".»[28]

---

[26] *Ibid.*, par. 9.

[27] Voir CR 2021/14, notamment p. 13, par. 19 (Cepeda Espinosa).

[28] *Ibid.*, p. 12, par. 14.

26. C'est que, nous a-t-on expliqué : «La Colombie est un pays dualiste pour ce qui est des frontières territoriales et maritimes.» («Colombia is a dualist country in matters of territorial and maritime boundaries»)[29]. Le dualisme a bon dos, Madame la présidente ! D'abord, il s'agit d'un dualisme «à la carte», car je peine à voir dans les articles 150 et 224 de la Constitution de la Colombie une adhésion de ce pays à la doctrine dualiste. (Les articles pertinents figurent à l'onglet AP-3 du dossier des juges.) De toute manière, il ne s'agit pas *d'incorporation* d'un éventuel traité dans le droit interne mais *de sa conclusion*, qui serait nécessaire pour donner effet à votre arrêt (sans considération pour l'article 94, paragraphe 1, de la Charte des Nations Unies ni pour l'article 60 de votre Statut). Je note également que l'article 101 de la Constitution, sur lequel s'appuie principalement la Cour constitutionnelle, dispose :

> «Les frontières de la Colombie sont celles établies dans les traités internationaux approuvés par le Congrès et dûment ratifiés par le président de la République, *et celles définies dans les sentences arbitrales auxquelles la nation est partie*.»

Il semble assez évident que ce qui vaut pour les sentences arbitrales vaut, au moins tout autant, pour les arrêts de la Cour mondiale.

27. Au demeurant, l'arrêt de la Cour de céans a été rendu en application de son Statut et du pacte de Bogotá, c'est-à-dire de traités dûment ratifiés par la Colombie. Malheureusement, ce ne sont apparemment pas de ces traités-là qu'il s'agit mais d'un futur traité, éventuel, à conclure avec le Nicaragua, qui aurait pour objet de donner effet à l'arrêt de 2012. Le Nicaragua, par la voix de son président[30], s'est d'ailleurs déclaré disposé à conclure un tel traité ; mais il n'en a plus été question par la suite et le coagent de la Colombie s'est bien gardé de prendre un engagement quelconque à cette fin pour l'avenir. Je constate d'ailleurs que, neuf ans après que la Cour a rendu son arrêt, aucune initiative n'a été prise par la Colombie en ce sens. Je comprends que ses conseils aient jugé plus prudent de laisser l'ambassadeur Cepeda Espinosa se débrouiller de cet imbroglio.

---

[29] *Ibid.*, par. 15.

[30] Voir «Daniel : 40 ans après le martyre d'Allende, la paix doit prévaloir», *El 19 Digital*, 11 septembre 2013, MN, annexe 39. Voir aussi «L'Assemblée nicaraguayenne favorable au dialogue avec la Colombie», *El Universal*, 12 septembre 2013 (MN, annexe 40) ; «Le Nicaragua propose à la Colombie de collaborer en vue de la mise en œuvre de l'arrêt de La Haye», *AFP*, 9 mai 2014, MN, annexe 46 (http://www.noticiasrcn.com/internacional-america/nicaragua-propone-coordinar-fallo-haya-colombia).

28. A défaut de respecter la Charte des Nations Unies et le Statut de la Cour, la Colombie s'appuie en revanche sur plusieurs traités qu'elle interprète à sa façon — qui n'est pas toujours orthodoxe, et est même souvent franchement imaginative.

29. En ce qui concerne le droit coutumier, Sir Michael Wood, qui en est spécialiste, a essayé de vous convaincre que la Colombie en avait identifié les règles avec grand soin. Mais en dehors d'une forte affirmation en ce sens au paragraphe 7 de sa plaidoirie de mercredi dernier[31], ni lui ni ses collègues n'ont tenté, comme il s'en targue, d'identifier sérieusement, sur la base de la pratique et de l'*opinio juris*, les règles coutumières qui s'éloigneraient de celles consacrées dans la convention de Vienne. Et, au fond, ils ont accepté, dans la quasi-totalité des cas, que les dispositions de la convention de Montego Bay les reflètent — surtout lorsqu'il s'agit de les opposer au Nicaragua[32].

30. En ce qui concerne la ZEE, Sir Michael a reconnu que l'essence même de son régime juridique est que «l'Etat côtier a «des droits souverains *aux fins d'exploration et d'exploitation, de conservation et de gestion des ressources naturelles*, biologiques ou non biologiques, des eaux surjacentes aux fonds marins, des fonds marins et de leur sous-sol»»[33] — ce faisant, il cite le texte de l'article 56, auquel il reconnaît donc une valeur coutumière. Il y ajoute, dans une note de bas de page[34], une mention de l'article 193 de la convention qui mérite que l'on s'y arrête un instant (il figure sous l'onglet AP-4 de vos dossiers) :

> «Les Etats ont le droit souverain d'exploiter *leurs* ressources naturelles selon *leur* politique en matière d'environnement et conformément à leur obligation de protéger et de préserver le milieu marin.»

— *leurs* ressources naturelles, selon *leur* politique en matière d'environnement…

31. Cette disposition suit l'article 192 aux termes duquel : «Les Etats ont l'obligation de protéger et de préserver le milieu marin.» Cette «obligation d'ordre général» (c'est le titre de l'article 192) est qualifiée par la règle spéciale énoncée à l'article suivant ; elle s'applique sous réserve du droit souverain qu'ont les Etats d'exploiter et de gérer les ressources naturelles des zones marines sur lesquelles ils ont juridiction, notamment dans leur zone économique *exclusive*. Dans

---

[31] CR 2021/14, p. 24, par. 7 (Wood).

[32] Voir notamment *ibid.*, p. 24-25, par. 8, p. 27, par. 17, p. 31, par. 31, p. 33, par. 40 (Wood) ; p. 44, par. 35 (Boisson de Chazournes).

[33] CR 2021/14, p. 24-25, par. 8, citant l'article 56.1 *a)* de la CNUDM (les italiques sont dans l'original).

[34] *Ibid.*, p. 25, note 25.

celle-ci, c'est l'article 56 qui s'applique (ou plutôt, dans notre espèce, son équivalent coutumier). Quoi qu'en ait dit Sir Michael, le Nicaragua ne demande rien de plus et il ne s'oppose nullement à l'exercice par d'autres Etats, y compris, bien sûr, la Colombie, des droits qui leur appartiennent dans les domaines non couverts par l'article 56 — domaines qui sont d'ailleurs énumérés à l'article 58 et ont également valeur coutumière (ce que Sir Michael semble reconnaître implicitement).

32. Au fond, qu'il s'agisse de l'affaire principale ou de ses demandes reconventionnelles, tout le raisonnement de la Colombie et de ses conseils consiste à nier l'existence même d'une zone économique *exclusive* caractérisée par les droits, limitativement énumérés certes, mais *souverains*, et la juridiction dont bénéficie l'Etat côtier.

33. Oui, Madame la présidente, tous les Etats ont des droits et des obligations en matière de préservation de l'environnement ou de lutte contre le trafic de drogues. Mais ils doivent les exercer dans le cadre des règles applicables propres aux différentes zones maritimes concernées.

34. Juste un exemple : bien sûr que la Colombie, comme le Nicaragua, doit respecter les dispositions de la convention de Carthagène, à laquelle ils sont tous deux parties et dont la professeure Boisson de Chazournes (qui a une petite tendance à plaider un peu trop par l'intermédiaire de notes de bas de page[35]) fait grand cas[36]. Mais il faut relever que l'article 3, paragraphe 2, de cette convention précise que : «La présente Convention et ses protocoles doivent s'interpréter *conformément au droit international applicable en la matière.*»[37]

35. L'article 3, paragraphe 1, du protocole de 1990 à la convention, dont la Colombie a souligné, dans son contre-mémoire, l'importance aux fins de la présente affaire[38], mais que ma contradictrice a opportunément omis de citer, explicite ce principe plus clairement encore :

> «Chaque Partie au présent Protocole, conformément [à] sa législation et réglementation et aux termes du Protocole, prend les mesures nécessaires pour protéger,

---

[35] Voir notamment les notes 87, 91, 102 reproduites dans le CR 2021/14.

[36] *Ibid.*, p. 35-36, par. 5-8, p. 38, par. 16, p. 41, par. 24-25, section III, et p. 46, par. 47-48.

[37] Convention pour la protection et la mise en valeur du milieu marin dans la région des Caraïbes, 24 mars 1983, CMC, annexe 17.

[38] CMC, p. 38-39, par. 2.38.

> préserver et gérer de manière durable, *dans les zones de la région des Caraïbes dans laquelle s'exerce sa souveraineté, ses droits souverains ou sa juridiction*».[39]

Le texte complet du protocole figure à l'onglet AP-5 de votre dossier ; il contient d'autres dispositions confirmant cette limitation spatiale dans lesquelles s'exercent les droits et obligations imposés aux Parties par la convention et ses protocoles — sur lesquels le professeur Lowe reviendra tout à l'heure. La Colombie n'exerce pas sa souveraineté et n'a ni droits souverains ni juridiction dans la ZEE du Nicaragua. Celui-ci en a ! C'est à lui, et à lui seul, qu'il revient de gérer les ressources naturelles de cette zone et d'y exercer sa juridiction (exclusive) en ce qui concerne «la protection et la préservation du milieu marin».

36. Décidément, Mesdames et Messieurs les juges, la Colombie se prévaut de droits totalement «imaginaires»[40]. Or, pour le dire comme le professeur Reisman : «la Cour ne se préoccupe pas de questions théoriques»[41]. Le Nicaragua ne doute pas que, conformément à votre mission et à votre jurisprudence constante, vous direz le droit existant et ne céderez pas à la tentation de légiférer[42] comme la Colombie vous y invite avec insistance.

37. Je vous remercie pour votre attention. Et je voudrais en profiter pour remercier aussi Tessa Barsac et Sébastien Le Drean pour leur assistance dans ces plaidoiries à distance. Je vous prie, Madame la présidente, de bien vouloir donner la parole à Me Reichler.

The PRESIDENT: I thank Professor Pellet. I now invite the next speaker, Mr. Reichler, to take the floor.

Mr. REICHLER: Madam President, Members of the Court, good afternoon.

---

[39] Protocole relatif aux zones et à la vie sauvage spécialement protégées à la Convention pour la protection et la mise en valeur du milieu marin de la région des Caraïbes, 18 janvier 1990, CMC, annexe 18 (les italiques sont de nous). Voir aussi l'article II 2) du protocole 3 (de 1999).

[40] Voir CR 2021/14, p. 46, par. 45 (Boisson de Chazournes).

[41] CR 2021/15, p. 25, par. 3 (Reisman).

[42] Voir *Licéité de la menace ou de l'emploi d'armes nucléaires, avis consultatif, C.I.J. Recueil 1996 (I)*, p. 237, par. 18. Voir aussi *Compétence en matière de pêcheries (Royaume-Uni c. Islande) (République fédérale d'Allemagne c. Islande), fond, arrêt, C.I.J. Recueil 1974*, p. 23-24, par. 53, et p. 192, par. 45 ; ou *Activités armées sur le territoire du Congo (République démocratique du Congo c. Ouganda), arrêt, C.I.J. Recueil 2005*, p. 190, par. 26.

The evidence of Colombia's violations of Nicaragua's rights under the Judgment of 19 November 2012

1. Last Wednesday, Colombia claimed to be "astonished" that Nicaragua, in its first round, set out the evidence of eleven incidents in which the Colombian Navy violated Nicaragua's sovereign rights under the Court's 2012 Judgment, all of which occurred after the "critical date" of 27 November 2013.

2. There were good reasons for this. First, as Professor Pellet has just demonstrated, the Court has jurisdiction over these post-critical-date violations, just as it has over the violations that preceded it, because all these violations are part of the same dispute, over which the Court found that it has jurisdiction in its Judgment of March 2016.

3. Second, as we said last Monday, we focused on these eleven violations because they are emblematic of those that Colombia has committed, on an ongoing basis since 2013, and because we have irrefutable proof that Colombia committed them, in the form of audio recordings, some of which we played for the Court, and others that we displayed in transcription.

4. What is most revealing about Colombia's response, and quite "astonishing" in its own right, is that it had absolutely nothing to say about nine of these violations — precisely the nine for which we played audio recordings or displayed transcriptions before the Court. Their silence about these nine incidents last week speaks loudly. It confirms that they have no credible defence for these blatant violations of Nicaragua's sovereign rights, as I will discuss further in the course of my presentation.

5. But first: what other compelling evidence of Colombia's violations of Nicaragua's sovereign rights, in its EEZ, as determined by the Court, did we present that Colombia kept absolutely quiet about?

6. How about the official statements by the President of Colombia that Colombia regards the 2012 Judgment as inapplicable?[43] Colombia made no attempt to explain or justify them, only accusing Nicaragua of quoting them "out of context"[44].

---

[43] See "Declaration of President Juan Manuel Santos on the judgment of the International Court of Justice, Bogotá, 19 November 2012", Spanish original available at https://www.cancilleria.gov.co/newsroom/news/alocucion-presidente-juan-manuel-santos-fallo-corte-internacional-justicia, MN, Ann. 1; "Colombia denounces the Pact of Bogotá after Judgement of the ICJ", *DW*, 28 Nov. 2012, Spanish original available at https://www.dw.com/es/colombia-denuncia-pacto-de-bogot%C3%A1-tras-fallo-de-la-cij/a-16414772, MN, Ann. 2; "Declaration of President Juan Manuel Santos on the integral strategy of Colombia on the Judgment of the International Court of Justice", 9 Sept. 2013, Spanish original available at https://www.cancilleria.gov.co/newsroom/news/colombia-presenta-su-estrategia-integral-frente-fallo-haya, MN, Ann. 4.

[44] CR 2021/14, p. 14, para. 25 (Cepeda Espinosa).

7. What about the official statements by the President of Colombia, including its current President, earlier this month[45], that the boundary with Nicaragua is the 82nd meridian, notwithstanding the Court's Judgment rejecting that claim[46]. On these statements, not a word was heard from Colombia last week.

8. Then there were the statements by commanders of the Colombian Navy, and other senior naval officers, that Colombia does not regard the Court's 2012 Judgment as applicable; that the boundary with Nicaragua is the 82nd meridian; and that the Navy exercises and protects Colombia's sovereignty all along that meridian and in all the maritime space lying east of it[47]. Not a peep from the other side about any of this, either.

9. Colombia also had nothing to say about the three maps published by the Colombian Navy showing the boundary with Nicaragua as the 82nd meridian and indicating, specifically, that the Navy's responsibility included exercising and protecting the sovereignty and sovereign rights that Colombia claims for itself, despite the Court's Judgment, in all areas east of that meridian[48]. Absolutely nothing from Colombia about these. Instead, its counsel chose to ignore them, and to spend his time on a map produced by the National Hydrocarbon Agency, making a grand show of the fact that, although it depicts petroleum blocks available for licence up to the 82nd meridian, in Nicaragua's EEZ, Colombia has not actually licensed any exploration there[49]. But we had already said that to the Court on Monday[50]. Our purpose in displaying that map was simply to show that the Navy is not the only Colombian State organ publishing official maps showing that the boundary with Nicaragua is the 82nd meridian, exactly as Colombia's presidents have been declaring from 2012 through 2021.

---

[45] "Presidente Duque ve con buenos ojos propuesta de Uribe sobre 'consulta popular' para confirmar límite con Nicaragua", *Semana*, 1 Sept. 2021.

[46] "Declaration of President Juan Manuel Santos on the integral strategy of Colombia on the Judgment of the International Court of Justice", 9 Sept. 20, MN, Ann. 4.

[47] See "Santos orders defense of the continental shelf with cloak and sword", *El Espectador*, 19 Sept. 2013, Spanish original available at https://www.elespectador.com/politica/santos-ordena-defender-plataforma-continental-a-capa-y-espada-article-447445/, MN, Ann. 41; "*There are no vetoed zones for the fishermen in San Andrés: National Navy*," *El País*, 3 Dec. 2015, RN, Ann. 26; "La Armada continúa patrullando el meridiano 82" *El Nuevo Siglo*, 7 Dec. 2019, Spanish original available at https://www.elnuevosiglo.com.co/articulos/12-2019-la-armada-continua-patrullando-el-meridiano-82.

[48] Admiral Hernando Wills Vélez, *Proyectando el Futuro, Poder Marítimo Colombiano*, pp. 5-7 ("Areas of Responsibility of the National Army").

[49] CR 2021/15, p. 21, para. 59 (Bundy).

[50] CR 2021/13, p. 48, para. 23 (Reichler).

10. Colombia attempts to portray all the post-November 2013 incidents as disconnected from the dispute that arose prior thereto, and thus, beyond the scope of the dispute over which the Court confirmed its jurisdiction, when it rejected Colombia's second preliminary objection in March 2016. This is an untenable argument, as Professor Pellet has explained.

11. Let me illustrate further the impeccable logic of Professor Pellet's analysis. As we showed you last Monday, in November 2012, President Santos declared that Colombia "emphatically rejects" the boundary established by the Court[51] and, in September 2013, he emphasized that "[t]he [J]udgment of the International Court of Justice is NOT APPLICABLE"[52]. On 17 November 2013, in an incident that occurred prior to the critical date, which I did not discuss last week, the Colombian naval frigate ARC *Almirante Padilla* ordered a Nicaraguan fishing vessel, the *Miss Sofia*, to leave what it said were Colombian waters — in the location now shown on your screens, which is plainly within Nicaragua's EEZ[53]. This is at tab PR-1 of our folder for today.

12. The *Miss Sofia* radioed a Nicaraguan coast guard vessel, the CG-205, calling for help[54]. The CG-205 advised the Colombian Navy by radio that it was in Nicaraguan waters, pursuant to the Judgment of the International Court of Justice[55]. The Colombian vessel responded, according to the official report sent by the CG-205 to Nicaragua's naval command, that "*ellos no reconocían la sentencia y que por lo tanto se mantendrían en el lugar*"[56]. In English, the message from Colombia was that "they did not recognize the Judgment and therefore would maintain their position"[57]. This was a clear reflection of President Santos' declaration, just a short while earlier, that, for Colombia, the Court's Judgment was "inapplicable". And it is the same message that Colombian naval vessels communicated to Nicaragua's Coast Guard repeatedly during the incidents after 27 November 2013, as you heard during our presentation last week.

---

51 "Declaration of President Juan Manuel Santos on the integral strategy of Colombia on the Judgment of the International Court of Justice", 9 Sept. 2013, MN, Ann. 4.

52 *Ibid.*

53 MN, 3 Oct. 2014, Ann. 23-A, p. 297.

54 MN, 3 Oct. 2014, Ann. 23-A, p. 297.

55 *Ibid.*

56 *Ibid.*, p. 281.

57 *Ibid.*, p. 297.

13. The same Colombian policy expressed in various declarations by President Santos in 2012 and 2013 — that the Court's 2012 Judgment is inapplicable, that Colombia does not recognize it, and that Colombia is therefore free to prevent Nicaragua from exercising sovereign rights in its own EEZ — is reflected in all the incidents that occurred after November 2013, in which Colombia's naval vessels repeatedly invoked the same policy, in virtually the same language reflected in the President of Colombia's earlier pronouncements.

14. To recall briefly, in the incident of 18 March 2015, Colombia's ARC *Independiente* radioed Nicaragua's CG-401 that "[t]he Colombian state has established that the ruling of The Hague is not applicable; therefore, the units of the Navy of the Republic of Colombia will continue to exercise sovereignty in these waters"[58]. Likewise, in the incident occurring on 23 March 2015, Colombia's Navy radioed to the Nicaraguan Coast Guard: "I inform you that the Colombian government has not abided by the ruling in The Hague."[59] On 26 March 2015, Colombia's *ARC 11 de Noviembre* insisted to Nicaragua's CG-401: "According to the Colombian government, the ruling of The Hague is inapplicable"[60].

15. In light of this evidence, it is simply untenable for Colombia to argue that the incidents after 27 November 2013 — all to the very same effect and purpose, and all repeating, almost word for word, the declarations of Colombia's President which gave rise to them — are not part of the same dispute, that is, the dispute over Nicaragua's allegations that Colombia has violated its sovereign rights under the Court's 2012 Judgment. All of these incidents are plainly part of the same, indivisible and ongoing dispute over Colombia's violations of Nicaragua's sovereign rights in its EEZ. Colombia cannot artificially divide them into separate disputes, in order to escape responsibility for its violations after November 2013.

16. The first documented incident in this series occurred in February 2013, well before the critical date. It also involved the ARC *Almirante Padilla*, which, at that time, prevented a Nicaraguan naval vessel from inspecting a Colombian-flagged fishing boat operating in the Luna Verde area, which is well within Nicaragua's EEZ. A Colombian media report directly quoted a Colombian naval

---

[58] RN, Ann. 32, audio transcription of 18.03.2015.

[59] *Ibid.*, audio transcription of 23.03.2015.

[60] RN, Ann. 32, audio transcription of 26.03.2015 *(a)*.

commander, Roberto Garcia Marquez, as confirming that this incident occurred[61]. Colombia disputes it on the ground that the *Almirante Padilla* was in its home port on the date the media report was published. But that media report was published several days after the incident[62]. Colombia has not accounted, in its written pleadings, for the whereabouts of the *Almirante Padilla* on the date of the incident or produced evidence that it was in another location on that date. Nor has it discredited the statement of its naval commander. My friend Mr. Bundy, reading from an older Nicaragua case, reminded the Court that it "takes the view that statements of this kind . . . are of particular probative value when they acknowledge facts or conduct unfavourable to the State represented by the person who made them"[63].

17. There was another incident on 18 September 2013, also before the critical date, and just prior to President Santos' issuance of Decree 1946 establishing Colombia's Integral Contiguous Zone[64]. On that date, the President, along with the Minister of Defence and the commanders of Colombia's armed forces, conducted what they themselves called a "sovereignty exercise" in the waters between San Andrés and the 82nd meridian[65]. During the exercise, inside Nicaragua's EEZ, President Santos said: "We find ourselves patrolling and exercising sovereignty over Colombian waters"[66]. Exercising sovereignty in Nicaragua's EEZ is plainly a violation of Nicaragua's sovereign rights under the 2012 Judgment. In its written pleadings, Colombia's first response was that this was nothing more than an exercise of Colombia's freedom of navigation[67], but that conflicted with President Santos' own description of it as a "sovereignty exercise". Then they gave another equally untenable explanation, that this was all about protection of Colombia's biosphere reserve[68]. But, of course, the biosphere reserve in Nicaragua's EEZ and continental shelf is Nicaraguan, not Colombian.

---

[61] "Colombia avoided boundary frictions with the Army of Nicaragua", *Caracol*, 19 Feb. 2013, MN, Ann. 34.

[62] See *ibid.*; RN, 15 May 2018, para. 4.53.

[63] CR 2021/15, p. 11, para. 22 (Bundy), citing to *Military and Paramilitary Activities in and against Nicaragua (Nicaragua* v. *United States of America), Merits, Judgment, I.C.J. Reports 1986*, p. 41, para. 64.

[64] "Declaration of President Juan Manuel Santos during the Sovereignty Exercises Performed in the Caribbean Sea", 18 Sept. 2013, MN, Ann. 5.

[65] *Ibid.*

[66] *Ibid.*

[67] CMC, Vol. 1, para. 4.24.

[68] *Ibid.* para. 4.25.

18. I have already mentioned the incident involving the *Almirante Padilla*, the *Miss Sofia* and Nicaraguan coast guard vessel CG-205 on 17 November 2013, also prior to the critical date. Colombia does not deny that the incident occurred, but claims that the *Almirante Padilla* performed a humanitarian service, rescuing two of the *Miss Sofia's* crew, who had fallen overboard during the incident[69]. But this is not inconsistent with the evidence submitted by Nicaragua. Nicaragua has not accused Colombia of acting inhumanely to its nationals, or violating human rights, but of violating its sovereign rights, including its right to control fishing activities in its own EEZ, as determined by the Court. Colombia's answer, in its written pleadings, does not refute Nicaragua's evidence.

19. All three of these incidents, which occurred prior to 27 November 2013, elicited from Colombia an attempt to brush them off, based on public statements by Nicaraguan officials during this period that there was no conflict with the Colombian Navy, and no incidents of which to complain. We have already accounted for Nicaragua's reluctance to speak out at that time. My good friend Mr. Bundy scoffed at our explanation and redoubled his emphasis on Nicaragua's statements. But what he failed to mention was that the last such statement was made in March 2014[70]. Thereafter, as Colombia's violations of Nicaragua's sovereign rights continued, Nicaragua not only began to protest them, it began to record the radio communications exchanged during these incidents. Nicaragua has submitted audio recordings and accompanying transcriptions of many of these exchanges, beginning in early 2014, as part of Annexes 23A and B of its Memorial and Annex 2 of its Reply.

20. Here is a transcription of one of those early recordings, from 8 May 2014, which is in today's folder at tab PR-2. The incident occurred in the location depicted on the map, well within Nicaragua's EEZ. What may be of particular interest to the Court is this part of the message from Colombia's ARC *20 de Julio* to Nicaragua's CG-201: "I remind you that this is a unit of the Coast Guard of the *Armada* [that is, the Navy] of the Republic of Colombia, which is protecting the historical fishing rights of the Colombian State . . . This communication is being recorded for legal purposes."

---

[69] *Ibid.*, paras. 4.40, 4.45.

[70] "Nicaragua denies intimidation of Colombia in San Andrés", *El Economista*, 18 Mar. 2014, POC, Ann. 26, p. 367.

21. Madam President, Nicaragua was not the only Party recording these exchanges. Colombia was, as well. Yet Colombia has submitted no recordings and no transcriptions of any of them to the Court. Surely, if their recordings contradicted what is on those submitted by Nicaragua, Colombia would have included them with its written pleadings. We can only presume, from Colombia's withholding of its own audio recordings, that they confirm, or at least do not contradict, what is on Nicaragua's.

22. I turn next to the nine incidents after 27 November 2013 for which we played recordings, or displayed transcriptions, last week. Colombia's silence in the face of this evidence may reflect more than the absence of a credible defence. It may also indicate a deliberate litigation strategy of saving their arguments for the second round and denying us an opportunity to respond to them. In consequence, we urge the Court to approach with caution anything that may be said for the first time on Wednesday. In the meantime, we will respond to what Colombia has already said about these incidents in its written pleadings, especially in Appendix 1 of its Rejoinder, which is where Mr. Bundy, in his only comment on these incidents, said Colombia's response could be found[71].

23. We begin with the incident that occurred on 18 March 2015, as depicted at tab 17 of our folder from last Monday. Colombia responds to Nicaragua's evidence as follows: "The authenticity of that audio cannot be confirmed by Colombia. Moreover, the circumstances of where and when the alleged interaction took place cannot be established from the said recording, since neither the date nor the position of the vessels are stated in the dialogue."[72] That is their entire defence, even at this late stage of the proceedings.

24. To which Nicaragua responds: first, Colombia only states that it cannot confirm the authenticity of the audio, which is not the same thing as claiming, let alone offering evidence, that the audio is inauthentic[73]. And Nicaragua has vouched for its authenticity, having been recorded contemporaneously at the time radio communications between the two vessels were exchanged, and having been furnished to the Nicaraguan naval command pursuant to standard procedures, and in turn to the Foreign Ministry, from which counsel for Nicaragua obtained it. Colombia did not argue

---

[71] CR 2021/15, p. 48, para. 7 (Bundy).

[72] RC, Vol. II, App. 1, p. 52, para. 2.

[73] *Ibid.*

that its naval officials did not make the statements that are reflected in the recording. Presumably, that is because its own recording is to the same effect.

25. In regard to the location of the incident, Colombia is correct that this is not stated in the radio communications. The source of that information is the official daily report by the Nicaraguan coast guard vessel, and the official log of such reports maintained by the naval command, which was submitted to the Court as part of Annex 2 to Nicaragua's Reply[74]. Notably, Colombia does not argue that the incident did not occur, or that it did not occur on the date or in the location shown in Nicaragua's evidence. This is significant because Colombia praises itself, repeatedly, about "the Colombian Navy's thoroughness in keeping record of its activities"[75]. Accordingly, if Colombia's records showed that the ARC *Independiente* was in another location on the date of the incident, Colombia would not have failed to mention that in its written pleadings.

26. I turn to the second of the nine incidents that we discussed last week, which occurred on 23 March 2015, as depicted at tab 18 of last week's folder. Here again, Colombia's defence is that it cannot confirm the authenticity of Nicaragua's audio recording, and that the date and location of the incident are not in it[76]. Nicaragua's response is the same as for the incident of 18 March 2015: the authenticity of the recording and the date and location of the incident are confirmed by Nicaragua's evidence, submitted with its Reply. Colombia also contends that the Honduran-flagged *Lucky Lady* was not authorized by Colombia to fish at Luna Verde, but only in Colombian waters[77]. But it does not dispute that the incident occurred in the location depicted on this map when Nicaragua's coast guard vessel encountered it, or that Colombia's ARC *Independiente* intervened to prevent Nicaragua from approaching that fishing vessel, claiming that it was in Colombian waters.

27. The third incident that we discussed last week occurred on 26 March 2015, as depicted at tab 19 of last week's folder. Again, Colombia's main defence is that it cannot confirm the authenticity of the audio recording[78]. Beyond this, Colombia claims that the ARC *11 de Noviembre*'s conduct

---

[74] RN, Ann. 2, p. 210.

[75] RC, Vol. II, App. 1, p. 62, para. 3.

[76] RC, Vol. II, App. 1, p. 53, para. 2.

[77] *Ibid.*, para. 3.

[78] *Ibid.*, p. 54, para. 2.

was "far from hostile"[79]. But that is beside the point. The indisputable fact is it was in Nicaragua's EEZ, as defined by the Court, where it was claiming to protect "the historic fishing rights of the Colombian State" in those waters. This, in itself, was a violation of Nicaragua's sovereign rights.

28. The fourth incident also occurred on 26 March 2015, depicted at tab 20 of our first-round folder. This is also evidenced by an audio recording, and by the official daily report of Nicaragua's BL-405 and the logs of the naval command[80]. Colombia argues that "no evidence of the *[Doña Emilia*'s*]* flag has been produced by Nicaragua"[81]. Yet, two paragraphs later in the Appendix to its Rejoinder, Colombia quotes one of its own naval officers as having radioed to the *Doña Emilia* that "your country has a restriction . . . which forbids snail and lobster fishing"[82]. Colombia thus admits that it knew that the *Doña Emilia* was flagged by Nicaragua. Colombia then accuses Nicaragua of having "manipulated" the recording, because "the only audible parts of the audio are the statements by the alleged Colombian officer; the responses by the crew of the *Doña Emilia* are not on record"[83]. Nicaragua emphatically rejects Colombia's unfounded accusation, and it denies any manipulation of the recording. Significantly, Colombia admits that the statements by its naval officer are indeed "audible", and does not deny that these were made, as transcribed by Nicaragua.

29. In regard to the fifth incident, on 5 April 2015, depicted at tab 21 of the first-round folder, Colombia's only defence is the now familiar refrain that it cannot confirm the authenticity of the recording, and that the recording itself does not identify the date or location of the incident[84]. As with previous incantations of these mantras, Nicaragua has furnished uncontradicted evidence of the authenticity of its recordings and the date and location of the incident, in Annex 2 of its Reply[85].

30. I turn next to the sixth incident, on 7 April 2015, depicted at tab 22 of last week's folder. Here, Colombia claims that the recording is "incomplete and inaudible in several parts"[86]. But the part that we displayed last Monday is complete and perfectly clear. Colombia further argues that

---

[79] *Ibid.*, para. 3.

[80] RN, Ann. 2, p. 213; RN, Ann. 32, audio transcription 26.03.2015 *(b)*.

[81] RC, Vol. II, App. 1, p. 56, para. 1.

[82] RN, Ann. 32, audio transcription 26.03.2015 *(b)*.

[83] RC, 15 Dec. 2018, Vol. II, App. 1, p. 56, para. 2.

[84] *Ibid.*, p. 59, para. 2.

[85] RN, Ann. 2, p. 215.

[86] RC, Vol. II, App. 1, p. 61, para. 2.

"[i]n the Maritime Travel Report of the A.R.C. 'San Andrés' there are no records of the said interactions as claimed by Nicaragua"[87]. Regardless, the audio recording plainly establishes that the ARC *San Andrés* was in radio communication with Nicaragua's BL-405, in close proximity to it[88]. And there is no doubt that this was the ARC *San Andrés*, whatever Colombia's maritime travel report fails to say, because the vessel identified itself as such. Maybe Colombia's maritime travel reports are not as thorough or as accurate as Colombia claims.

31. The seventh incident we discussed last week is the one that took place on 12 September 2015, depicted at tab 23 of the first-round folder, in which the Colombian naval vessel instructed Nicaragua's BL-405 to stay away from the Tanzanian-flagged fishing vessel, *Miss Dolores*, which, it said, was fishing "for the Colombian government". Here again, Colombia's only defence is that it cannot confirm the authenticity of the recording, and that the recording itself does not identify the date or location of the incident[89]. They have not denied, though, that the incident occurred as described by Nicaragua, at least not in their written pleadings.

32. We come next to the eighth incident, which occurred on 12 January 2016, as depicted at tab 25 of our earlier folder. Here, Colombia once again states that the "authenticity of the said audios cannot be confirmed"[90], but it does not contest that an incident occurred on 12 January 2016, nor does it contest the location, within Nicaragua's EEZ, as depicted by Nicaragua in this chart. Nor does it challenge Nicaragua's version of events, as evidenced by the recording, which we played aloud for you last week and showed you in transcription. Colombia's main argument is that Nicaragua's CG-403 claimed that it was "in Nicaraguan territorial waters", when, in fact, "according to the coordinates where it claims the interaction to have occurred, it was clearly in its EEZ, not territorial sea"[91]. Nicaragua will gladly stipulate to this: that is, that the incident took place in Nicaragua's EEZ, and not its territorial sea. As such, Colombia has plainly acknowledged violating Nicaragua's sovereign rights when it admitted to CG-403, on tape, that "the motorboat Observer is authorized to

---

[87] *Ibid.*, p. 62, para. 3.

[88] Audio transcription 7.04.2015 *(a)*: mins. 2:20-2:25; 3:26-3:35.

[89] RC, Vol. II, App. 1, p. 66, para. 2.

[90] *Ibid.*, p. 69, para. 2.

[91] *Ibid.*, p. 70, para. 5.

fish in this area by the Colombian maritime authority, according to the historic fishing rights of the State of Colombia"[92].

33. The ninth incident that we discussed last Monday occurred on 6 January 2017, as depicted at tab 26 of that folder. This is the incident in which the Colombian Navy instructed Nicaragua's CG-405 "to abort any attempt to board and any attempt to abort the fishing of the *Capitán Geovanie* motorboat", on the ground that the "*Capitán Geovanie* is authorized by the Colombian maritime authority, fishing in historically Colombian waters"[93]. Colombia's first defence is that its naval ship was "in the area watching over the safety of the vessels" and "exercising its freedom of navigation"[94]. But that explanation is directly contradicted by the message delivered by the Colombian naval vessel to CG-405. Colombia further argues that the *Capitán Geovanie* "was authorized to fish, not in Nicaragua's EEZ, but rather in the 'Northern Islands', i.e., in Colombian waters"[95]. But the audio recording contradicts that assertion, too. It shows that the Colombian naval vessel prevented Nicaragua's Coast Guard from enforcing Nicaragua's fisheries jurisdiction, in Nicaragua's EEZ, on the ground that the "*Capitán Geovanie* is authorized by the Colombian maritime authority, fishing in historically Colombian waters"[96].

34. In sum, the arguments and evidence that Colombia offered in its written pleadings, in respect of the nine incidents it studiously ignored at the oral hearings last week, come nowhere close to refuting Nicaragua's evidence, including its audio recordings, or justifying Colombia's interference with Nicaragua's exercise of its sovereign rights in relation to any of these incidents.

35. In contrast to its silence last week on these nine recorded incidents, Columbia did attempt to respond to our contentions regarding two other incidents.

36. The first of these was the incident of 10 December 2018, where Nicaragua's BL-405 *Tayacán* encountered, again, the Honduran-flagged *Observer*, in Nicaragua's EEZ, as depicted at tab 27 of last week's folder. Colombia argued last week that the *Observer* was in transit between

---

[92] RN, Ann. 32, audio transcription of 12.01.2016.

[93] *Ibid.*, audio transcription of 06.01.2017.

[94] RC, Vol. II, App. 1, p. 73, para. 3.

[95] RC, Vol. II, App. 1, p. 74, para. 4.1.

[96] RN, Ann. 32, audio transcription of 06.01.2017.

Quitasueño and Serrana[97]. Nicaragua does not dispute that. Wherever it might have been headed, it was plainly in Nicaragua's EEZ at the time it was intercepted by Nicaragua's coast guard vessel, boarded, and towed toward the Nicaraguan mainland.

37. The incident with Colombia occurred the following day. Colombia's ARC *Antioquía* approached and ordered Nicaragua's coast guard vessel to release the *Observer.* The Nicaraguan vessel refused, successfully manoeuvred to escape the Colombian vessel, and hauled the *Observer* to Nicaragua. Although Colombia failed in its attempt to prevent Nicaragua from doing so, the attempt itself is another example of Colombia's violation of Nicaragua's sovereign right to control and regulate fishing in its EEZ, and to exercise its law enforcement jurisdiction over unlicensed fishing in its waters.

38. On Monday, we said that the captain of the *Observer* admitted that it had been fishing in Nicaragua's EEZ without a Nicaraguan licence at the time of its arrest[98]. Counsel for Colombia insisted that this was not correct[99]. He was right. It was the owner of the *Observer*, not the captain, who admitted that his vessel was fishing illegally in Nicaragua's waters[100]. The real question is this: what right does Colombia have to challenge Nicaragua's enforcement of its fisheries jurisdiction, in its own EEZ, against a vessel flagged by a third State that is unlicensed by Nicaragua and that it believes to be fishing illegally in its waters? Colombia has given no answer to this question.

39. Instead, it argues that the manoeuvres by the BL-405 *Tayacán* threatened the safety of the *Observer*, which was bumped in the process[101]. This, of course, is irrelevant to these proceedings, which do not involve Nicaragua's compliance with international rules of navigation. Whether or not the Nicaraguan vessel's manoeuvres violated such rules, which is denied, they were undertaken to escape and avoid Colombia's naval vessel, which had no right to interfere with Nicaragua's exercise of its law enforcement rights in regard to fishing in its EEZ.

---

[97] CR 2021/15, p. 20, para. 53 (Bundy).

[98] CR 2021/13, p. 56, para. 43 (Reichler).

[99] CR 2021/15, p. 20, para. 53 (Bundy).

[100] Judgment of Nicaragua's Supreme Court of Justice No. 086, 26 October 2020, p. 10. Spanish original available at https://www.poderjudicial.gob.ni/pjupload/sconten2012/pdf/certificacion_caso_observer.pdf.

[101] CR 2021/15, p. 20, para. 53 (Bundy).

40. Colombia has challenged our assertion that it licensed and encouraged Colombian and foreign-flagged vessels, including industrial-commercial vessels, to fish in waters that the Court determined to fall within Nicaragua's EEZ, and it has disputed our reading of a Colombian-issued industrial commercial fishing permit that expressly refers to fishing in the areas known as Luna Verde and La Esquina, which are indisputably located in Nicaragua's EEZ[102].

41. We stand by our reading of that permit, which is at tab 29 of our folder from last week. But this case does not turn on Colombia's fishing licences. It turns on the actions by Colombia's Navy, in Nicaragua's EEZ, including the physical protection given by the Colombian Navy to Colombian and foreign-flag fishing vessels at Luna Verde and La Esquina, and, according to Mr. Valencia Ospina, various other locations in Nicaragua's EEZ[103]; and, it includes especially, the Colombian Navy's prevention of Nicaragua's enforcement of its own fishing laws and regulations in regard to these vessels, which have not been authorized by Nicaragua to fish in these areas. My friend Mr. Bundy appears to have conceded this. As he said last week, correctly: "in most of the exchanges, the Colombian vessels indicated that they were protecting Colombia's historical fishing rights"[104]. Protecting them from whom? From Nicaragua, of course. And that is exactly why their actions violated Nicaragua's sovereign rights over fishing in its own EEZ.

42. The only other incident, of the eleven that we discussed last Monday, with which Colombia chose to engage, is the one in which Colombia's *Almirante Padilla* intervened to prevent a Mexican scientific research vessel, licensed by Nicaragua, from carrying out its research activities in Nicaragua's EEZ[105]. What was Colombia's defence? There was none. Mr. Bundy cavalierly dismissed the incident as a "non-event", on the ground that Mexico did not complain to Colombia about it[106]. That is all they said on Wednesday. They did not dispute that the Mexican vessel was conducting marine scientific research under a Nicaraguan license, that it was in Nicaragua's EEZ, or that Colombia prevented it from carrying out its mission. In other words, they were unable to defend

---

[102] CR 2021/15, p. 20, para. 55 (Bundy).

[103] CR 2021/15, pp. 42-43, para. 21 (Valencia Ospina).

[104] CR 2021/15, p. 18, para. 48 (Bundy).

[105] Letter of the Agent of Nicaragua to the International Court of Justice, REF: HOL-EMB-098-2019, 23 Sept. 2019, p. 1, Anns. 1, 2 (p. 2), 7, 10.

[106] CR 2021/15, p. 21, para. 56 (Bundy).

Colombia's clear violation of Nicaragua's right to authorize marine scientific research in its own EEZ.

43. Madam President, as in most situations, context is relevant. All 11 of these incidents, plus the 3 incidents prior to 27 November 2013 that I discussed earlier, and the 37 others described in our written pleadings, occurred within a context that was framed by the repeated declarations of Colombia's presidents and senior naval commanders that the Judgment of the Court is inapplicable, that the boundary with Nicaragua is the 82nd meridian, that Colombia alone has sovereignty or exclusive sovereign rights in all the waters east of that meridian, and that the Colombian Navy would actively exercise Colombia's sovereignty or sovereign rights in those waters and, specifically, that it would protect what they called Colombia's historic fishing rights east of the meridian. The actions by Colombia's Navy that we have described in all of these incidents are entirely consistent with these presidential and naval declarations; indeed, they follow directly from them, and are linked to each other by them. They are the inevitable result of the policies expressed, and directions given, in the official statements by Colombia's presidents and naval commanders, commencing in November 2012 and continuing through to the present.

44. Most of these statements can be found on Colombian government websites[107]. Three of the naval commanders' statements were published by online news sources[108]. Consistent with the Court's treatment of media reports, Nicaragua has not relied on them as proof of the events that the reports themselves narrate. We have only relied on them as evidence of the public statements by Colombian naval authorities directly quoted therein. As Mr. Bundy helpfully reminded us, such statements, against the interests of the State these high officials represent, "are of particular probative value".

---

[107] "Declaration of President Juan Manuel Santos on the judgment of the International Court of Justice", Spanish original available at https://www.cancilleria.gov.co/newsroom/news/alocucion-presidente-juan-manuel-santos-fallo-corte-internacional-justicia 19 November 2012, MN, Ann. 1; "Colombia denounces the Pact of Bogota after Judgement of the ICJ", *DW*, 28 Nov. 2012, Spanish original available at https://www.dw.com/es/colombia-denuncia-pacto-de-bogot%C3%A1-tras-fallo-de-la-cij/a- 16414772, MN, Ann. 2; Declaration of President Juan Manuel Santos on the integral strategy of Colombia on the Judgment of the International Court of Justice", 9 Sept. 2013, Spanish original available at https://www.cancilleria.gov.co/newsroom/news/colombia-presenta-su-estrategia-integral-frente-fallo-haya, MN, Ann. 4.

[108] See "Santos orders defense of the continental shelf with cloak and sword", *El Espectador*, 19 Sept. 2013, Spanish original available at https://www.elespectador.com/politica/santos-ordena-defender-plataforma-continental-a-capa-y-espada-article-447445/, MN, Ann. 41; "*There are no vetoed zones for the fishermen in San Andrés: National Navy*," *El País*, 3 December 2015, RN, Ann. 26; "La Armada continúa patrullando el meridiano 82" *El Nuevo Siglo*, 7 Dec. 2019, Spanish original available at https://www.elnuevosiglo.com.co/articulos/12-2019-la-armada-continua-patrullando-el-meridiano-82.

45. As you have seen, Nicaragua has also relied on audio recordings made contemporaneously, and transcribed faithfully, as well as on official daily reports of its naval and coast guard vessels, routinely submitted in the regular course of operations to the naval command. To be sure, the reports concerning events after Nicaragua's Application was filed were prepared while this case was in progress. Mr. Bundy attempts to demean them as "prepared for purposes of litigation"[109]. But it is unavoidable that evidence of this nature would be produced during litigation in any case where the alleged violations are ongoing. In this case, the Nicaraguan naval and coast guard officers who recorded and reported on the incidents did so in the regular performance of their official duties. There is no reason to doubt the credibility of the recordings or the reports, especially after Colombia has had every opportunity to discredit them in its written pleadings, and it failed to do so, or to submit its own audio recordings of the incidents. Nicaragua trusts the Court will give this evidence its proper weight.

46. Colombia's primary response to all the evidence of its repeated and ongoing violations of Nicaragua's sovereign rights, as defined by the Court in its November 2012 Judgment, is to place its bet on a long-shot jurisdictional argument, pursuant to which, it hopes, the Court will ignore most of the violations, including those that are recorded. But, as Professor Pellet has explained, Colombia has got the law wrong, especially its strained and implausible interpretation of Article XXXI of the Pact of Bogotá. And the facts show, beyond reasonable argument, that Colombia's violations of Nicaragua's rights after the critical date are inextricably part of the same dispute that arose in November 2012, when Colombia first denounced, rejected and declared inapplicable the Judgment of the Court, and vowed that its Navy would disregard it.

47. In closing, Nicaragua reaffirms what it said last week: Colombia cannot escape international responsibility for violating Nicaragua's sovereign rights either on jurisdictional grounds, or on the merits.

48. Madam President, Members of the Court, it has been an honour for me to appear before you in these proceedings, and I thank you for your kind courtesy and patient attention, and ask that you call my colleague, Professor Lowe, to speak next.

---

[109] CR 2021/14, p. 51, para. 15 (Bundy).

The PRESIDENT: I thank Mr. Reichler. I will now give the floor to Professor Lowe. You have the floor, Sir.

Mr. LOWE:

COLOMBIA'S INTEGRAL CONTIGUOUS ZONE IS INCONSISTENT WITH INTERNATIONAL LAW

1. Madam President, Members of the Court: last Wednesday, Colombia addressed four arguments concerning the contiguous zone that it attributed to Nicaragua[110].

2. I shall respond to those arguments, but first let me address a preliminary point. Colombia said that we were referring to an "obsolete" version of Decree 1946. It is true that the Decree was amended by Decree 1119 of 17 June 2014; and this is apparently regarded as an exception to Colombia's principle that you should look at the position as at the date of the Application in this case, which was filed in 2013.

3. You have the amended Decree, Annex 7 from Colombia's Counter-Memorial, in your folders as tab VL-1. You will see in paragraph 2 of its preamble that it says that "the contiguous zone . . . [is] also *part of Colombia*".

4. In paragraph 7, it says that "the Government will proceed to indicate . . . the lines from which the various maritime spaces in which the Colombian nation exercises sovereignty are measured, including sovereign rights and jurisdiction in accordance with customary international law".

5. In paragraph 10, it says:

> "In accordance with customary international law, in the contiguous zone States exercise *sovereign rights and jurisdiction and control* in matters of *security*, control of the trafficking in drugs and illicit substances, the *protection of the environment*, fiscal and customs matters, immigration, health, *and other matters*."

6. In paragraph 11, it says that "[t]he extent of the contiguous zone of the island territories forming the Western Caribbean needs to be determined . . . *in order to secure the protection of the environment and resources, and the maintenance of comprehensive security and public order*".

---

[110] CR 2021/15, pp. 25-26. para. 7 (Reisman).

7. I pause to ask if this is the language of a measure intended to record that Colombia is doing no more than "observing" those in its contiguous zone and "informing" them of their legal position[111], rather like a schoolteacher gently "advising" her sometimes mischievous infant pupils on their behaviour.

8. The Decree itself, as amended, says in Article 1 that

> "Colombia exercises full sovereignty over its insular territories and territorial sea; *jurisdiction and sovereign rights over the rest of the maritime spaces* generated by its insular territories in the terms prescribed by international law, the Political Constitution, Law [No.] 10 of 1978, and by the present Decree, in what corresponds to each of them".

9. Article 2 reaffirms that "the contiguous zone . . . [is] *part of Colombia*".

10. And then comes Article 5. It is too long to read out in full, but it is central to this case. It establishes, in Section 2, "a continuous and uninterrupted Contiguous Zone, across the whole of the Department of the Archipelago of San Andrés, Providencia and Santa Catalina". That Department's website lists Serranilla, and also Bajo Nuevo, as part of the Department[112], though Bajo Nuevo is apparently left outside the Integral Contiguous Zone.

11. Article 5, Section 3 *(a)* says that in this contiguous zone

> "Colombia exercises the faculties of enforcement and control necessary to:
>
> *(a)* Prevent and control the infractions of the laws and regulations *related with the integral security of the State*, including piracy and trafficking of drugs and psychotropic substances, as well as *conduct contrary to the security in the sea* and *the national maritime interests*, the customs, fiscal, migration and sanitary matters which take place in its insular territories or in their territorial sea. In the same manner, violations against the laws and regulations related with *the preservation of the marine environment and the cultural heritage* will be prevented and controlled."

12. It is not clear how Colombia thinks the 2014 amendments to Decree 1946 affect Nicaragua's case. I have shown you the law. Last Wednesday, Colombia stated that "the map it produced in the record is its most accurate illustration of the contiguous zone", and that it "will publish official charts depicting its contiguous zone when ready"[113]. That map is now on the screen.

---

[111] CR 2021/14, p. 29, para. 22, p. 33, para. 41 (Wood); CR 2021/14, p. 36, paras. 7-8, p. 41, para. 25, p. 43, para. 30, p. 45, paras. 40-42, p. 46, para. 46 (Boisson de Chazournes); etc.

[112] Available at https://sanandres.gov.co/index.php/archipielago/informacion-general/geografia (accessed 24 Sept. 2021).

[113] CR 2021/15, p. 25. para. 4 (Reisman). The reference is to the map in RC, p. 212, Figure CR 4.3.

There is no key to the map, but you can see the "simplified" zone in the south and the zone around Serranilla, and the joint régime area in the north connected to it by the purple dotted line.

13. Having established that we are on the same page as our Colombian friends as far as the text of the Decree is concerned, let me turn to the four matters addressed by Colombia. Three of them can be dealt with briefly; and I begin with their second assertion, that Nicaragua "contends that a State may not resort to *any* reasonable geodetic lines to simplify the jagged and indented contours of its contiguous zone"[114].

14. That is not true. Colombia can draw a smooth contiguous zone boundary if it wishes. Nicaragua says only that it may not extend more than 24 nautical miles from the territorial sea baselines and may not extend beyond the Court's 2012 boundary; and that the suggestion of Colombia that its ICZ has jagged and indented contours comparable to the Norwegian coast is not credible.

15. Colombia made no attempt to establish that international law permits a contiguous zone in excess of 24 nautical miles — all of the red areas on the figure now on the screen — or that it permits the contiguous zone to be drawn from anything other than the baselines from which the breadth of territorial sea is measured. Its only point is that this is a "modest use of geodetic lines to smooth out and simplify the otherwise impractical outer limits of the contiguous zone . . . dictated by geography"[115]. I referred you to the State practice on the point[116], and it offers no support for Colombia's claim to exceed 24 nautical miles.

16. It is for you to decide whether, as Colombia claims, "without simplification, the contiguous zone of Colombia would be a tangle of interconnected arcs, representing difficulties in its practical implication" — a question of fact — and, if that were so, whether Colombia has any legal right to make the "simplification" that it claims — a question of law.

17. I add only that when Colombia says that "smoothing the [contiguous zone contours] has no adverse effects on the rights or interests of other States"[117], we disagree. Subjecting foreign

---

114 CR 2021/15, p. 25. para. 7 (Reisman).

115 CR 2021/15, p. 26. para. 8 (Reisman).

116 CR 2021/13, pp. 70-71, paras. 41-46 (Lowe).

117 CR 2021/15, pp. 30-31, para. 35 (Reisman).

shipping to Colombian control beyond the limits permitted by international law self-evidently has an adverse effect on the rights and interests of other States: that is what the whole history of debates over the freedom of the seas has been about.

18. Next, Colombia alleges that we say that customary international law confines contiguous zone powers to those enumerated in UNCLOS Article 33 — "customs, fiscal, immigration [and] sanitary" — and that they cannot evolve to adjust to new circumstances[118]. Colombia says that those terms have a "generic meaning"[119] and must be given an "evolutionary interpretation"[120].

19. Evolution is one thing: but Colombia's contiguous zone claim is more like a metamorphosis. Maybe "customs, fiscal, immigration [and] sanitary" can evolve to include some other matters, given the normal requirements of State practice and *opinio juris*. But where is the proof that it *has* done so?

20. I took you to the 2020 Roach study of 103 States claiming contiguous zones and said that the evidence of State practice was that most claims to jurisdiction over matters other than those listed had been related to security and to the underwater cultural heritage. Security claims have been protested by roughly as many States as have made them; and cultural heritage is covered by UNCLOS Article 303, which is binding on Nicaragua. So what does that prove about the content of customary international law?

21. What has Colombia produced? Annex B to its Counter-Memorial paraphrases extracts from the laws of under half that number of States — 40, taking account of the fact that one State appears in the list twice, as "Burma" and as "Myanmar".

22. Some do claim jurisdiction over "other matters" apart from the four accepted purposes. Jamaica and Palau, for example, assert jurisdiction over living resources: but they have that jurisdiction anyway because the contiguous zone is part of the EEZ, in which jurisdiction over living resources is uncontroversial.

---

[118] CR 2021/15, pp. 25-26. para. 7 (Reisman).

[119] CR 2021/15, p. 31, paras. 38. (Reisman).

[120] CR 2021/15, pp. 31-32, paras. 38-40 (Reisman).

23. Some entries are outdated. Cameroon is listed by Colombia as claiming a fifty-nautical-mile territorial sea: but 20 years ago it told the Court in the *Cameroon* v. *Nigeria* case that that provision was no longer in effect[121].

24. Only Albania appears to claim anything like the range of purposes within the Colombian contiguous zone claim; and its inclusion seems to be the result of a misapprehension. Neither DOALOS nor the Roach study list Albania as a contiguous zone claimant; and the Albanian law cited by Colombia appears to do no more than list the entire range of "tasks" that the Albanian coastguard may be called upon to discharge in Albania's maritime zones in general[122].

25. Where is the proof of a "general practice accepted as law" that establishes the rights that Colombia claims under customary international law?

26. I shall return to this point in a moment in order to focus on one of the most egregious of Colombia's claims — the claim to control environmental matters; but let me first address the last of the three brief points — Colombia's argument that the mere enactment of the Decree does not violate Nicaragua's rights: only its implementation could do so[123].

27. There are two common-sense answers. One: Colombia *has been implementing it*. That is what Mr. Reichler has been talking about. Two, in any event, telling Nicaraguan and other ships in Nicaragua's EEZ that they are subject to Colombian control is intended to affect their behaviour, and it cannot fail to do so. If a policeman, in uniform and on duty, acting under the authority of Decree 1946 tells you that he is "observing" your activities and "informing [you] of the consequences of [your] actions"[124] in Colombia's contiguous zone, that is very different from a cheerful wave from a passing fellow seafarer. Colombia asserts the right to *prevent and control infractions of Colombian laws and regulations* in Nicaragua's EEZ.

28. There is also a legal answer. The promulgation of a law that is manifestly incompatible with the international obligations assumed by a State can certainly constitute a violation of those

---

[121] *Land and Maritime Boundary between Cameroon and Nigeria (Cameroon* v. *Nigeria: Equatorial Guinea intervening)*, Reply of the Republic of Cameroon, 4 Apr. 2000, pp. 387-388, paras. 9.02–9.05.

[122] See Law No 8875, 4 Apr. 2002, Article 5, available at http://extwprlegs1.fao.org/docs/pdf/alb60863E.pdf.

[123] CR 2021/15, p. 25, para. 7. (Reisman).

[124] CR 2021/14, p. 29, para. 22 (Wood).

obligations[125]. That is why the ILC Articles restate the well-established rule of international law that the acts of the legislature are imputable to the State for the purposes of State responsibility[126].

29. Let me then turn to Colombia's first assertion: that Nicaragua "contends that, as a general rule, customary international law denies a State a protective contiguous zone if its territorial sea abuts another State's EEZ"[127].

30. What Nicaragua actually says is that a State's contiguous zone may not extend for more than 24 nautical miles from the baseline, and that in any event it must stop at the State's international maritime boundary.

31. Let me illustrate the point. One of Colombia's most egregious claims is the assertion of the right to exercise "the faculties of enforcement and control necessary to: . . . [p]revent and control . . . violations against the laws and regulations related with the preservation of the marine environment", in the words of Article 5 of Decree 1946.

32. Colombia asks which of Nicaragua's "enumerated environmental jurisdictions in [UNCLOS] Part XII the Colombian Decree violates"[128] — accepting that the UNCLOS provisions reflect customary international law for this purpose.

33. Our first point is that it is really for Colombia to establish what right it has to exercise those powers in the EEZ of another State. But let me respond directly to the question.

34. Nicaragua's case is based on UNCLOS Part V, which embodies the customary rules defining the rights and jurisdictions of the coastal State in the EEZ[129]. Article 56 asserts that "the coastal State has: . . . jurisdiction as provided for in the relevant provisions of this Convention with regard to: . . . the protection and preservation of the marine environment".

35. The relevant provisions are set out in UNCLOS Part XII. Articles 192-206 address general principles and international co-operation; Articles 207–212 address jurisdiction to prescribe rules to

---

[125] Inter-American Court of Human Rights, *International Responsibility for the Promulgation and Enforcement of Laws in Violation of the Convention, Advisory Opinion OC-14/94*, *International Law Reports*, 1994, Vol. 116, p. 320, paras. 31-50. Cf. *Applicability of the Obligation to Arbitrate under Section 21 of the United Nations Headquarters Agreement of 26 June 1947, Advisory Opinion, I.C.J. Reports 1988*, pp. 29-30, para. 42. Lord McNair, *The Law of Treaties* (1961), p. 550.

[126] *YILC*, 2001, Articles on State Responsibility, Art. 4.

[127] CR 2021/15, p. 25, para. 7. (Reisman).

[128] CR 2021/15, p. 33, para. 47 (Reisman).

[129] UNCLOS, Art. 55.

prevent, reduce and control pollution of the marine environment[130]; and Articles 213-222 address the enforcement of those rules.

36. For example, Article 210 concerns dumping at sea and provides in paragraph 5 that dumping within the territorial sea and EEZ "shall not be carried out without the express prior approval *of the coastal State*, which has *the right to permit, regulate and control such dumping* after due consideration of the matter with other States which . . . may be adversely affected thereby".

37. Colombia's Decree asserts the right to prevent and control violations of *Colombia's* environmental laws in Nicaragua's EEZ, in flat contradiction of Article 210.

38. You will note that despite Colombia's rather odd assertion that "none of the provisions in Part XII or anywhere else in the UNCLOS grant an EEZ State the jurisdiction to protect the environment of another State's territorial sea and land territory"[131], Article 210 establishes not only the right but the *duty* to take account of the interests of other States that may be affected — as, indeed, do other provisions in Part XII, such as Articles 194, 198 and 204[132]. The duty on coastal States under Part XII is to prevent, reduce and control pollution, not simply to prevent, reduce and control pollution of their own waters[133].

39. Article 211 goes on to address vessel source pollution and sets out coastal States' rights to adopt laws and regulations on that matter, and so on.

40. Then comes Section 6 of Part XII, on "enforcement". It refers to enforcement by flag States[134], port States[135] and coastal States[136]. No others. The only right of any other State acknowledged in Part XII is the right to intervene in the event of a maritime casualty which may reasonably be expected to result in major harmful consequences. That is the preservation in UNCLOS of the pre-existing right of intervention established after the *Torrey Canyon* incident in 1967 and set

[130] The *chapeau* of Part XII, Sec. 5.

[131] CR 2021/15, p. 33, para. 48 (Reisman).

[132] See UNCLOS, Arts. 193-195, 197-199, 204 (2) and 206.

[133] See e.g. Arts. 192 and 208 (1) and (2).

[134] UNCLOS, Art. 217.

[135] UNCLOS, Art. 218.

[136] UNCLOS, Art. 220.

out in the 1969 International Convention relating to Intervention on the High Seas in Cases of Oil Pollution Casualties[137], as amended[138].

41. That exceptional right to intervene in respect of major casualties has nothing to do with the routine "observing and informing" of ships or the "prevention and control" of Colombian laws, in the Nicaraguan EEZ; and it provides no support for Colombia's claimed contiguous zone powers. Nor does anything else in Part XII.

42. So if Colombia attempts to prevent dumping in the Nicaraguan EEZ authorized by Nicaragua, there is an obvious conflict of rights. So, too, if Colombia tries to enforce some other Colombian environmental laws and to prevent conduct lawful under Nicaraguan law.

43. We are not dealing with an exercise of high seas freedoms by Colombia. Colombia is establishing and implementing a zone in which it will prevent and control activities subject to Colombian law; and it is doing so in Nicaragua's EEZ, and in matters that directly overlap with Nicaragua's rights. And it is hard to believe that Colombia is not doing so precisely so as to make its point that the Court was wrong to draw the maritime boundary where it did. We cannot find *any* other example of a State unilaterally establishing a maritime zone in the waters of another State.

44. In passing, I should note that the one publication that Colombia cites as expressing the view that contiguous zone claims of neighbouring States may overlap is now included in your judges' folder as tab VL-6[139]. We leave it to the Court to decide how much weight to attach to it — a single, unsupported sentence on page 39 of a booklet on ocean management in the Pacific published almost forty years ago. It is what statisticians would call an "outlier".

45. Important as these — very obvious — points are, they must not obscure the larger picture. Colombia has made impassioned pleas concerning the environment of the western Caribbean, as if to give the impression that this is its main concern.

---

[137] United Nations, *Treaty Series (UNTS)*, Vol. 970, p. 211.

[138] Protocol relating to Intervention on the High Seas in Cases of Pollution by Substances other than Oil (Intervention Protocol 1973), *UNTS*, Vol. 1313, p. 4.

[139] Commonwealth Group of Experts, *Ocean Management: A Regional Perspective — The Prospects for Commonwealth Maritime Co-operation in Asia and the Pacific* (1984), Commonwealth Secretariat, p. 39, para. 2.35.

46. But both Nicaragua and Colombia are among the more than two dozen parties to the 1983 Cartagena Convention for the Protection and Development of the Marine Environment in the Wider Caribbean Region[140].

47. The Cartagena Convention provides a comprehensive framework for international action in the Caribbean to protect the environment. Article 4 of the Convention obliges States parties to "take all appropriate measures . . . to prevent, reduce and control pollution of the Convention area", and Article 11 obliges them to co-operate in taking necessary measures to respond to pollution emergencies.

48. Protocols such as the 1983 Protocol concerning Co-operation in Combatting Oil Spills amplify the provisions for the co-ordination of national efforts and mutual assistance[141].

49. But nowhere in that Convention is there any indication that one State has the right unilaterally to exercise powers of prevention and control in the waters of another. The whole Cartagena scheme is based on the principle that each State party will act in areas in which it exercises sovereignty, or sovereign rights, or jurisdiction, as Professor Pellet has shown you[142].

50. Perhaps the clearest example of this point is in Article 9 of the Cartagena Protocol concerning Specially Protected Areas, in today's folders as tab AP-5. This makes provision for "protected areas and buffer zones contiguous to international boundaries". Much as you might expect, it requires the two neighbouring States to "consult each other with a view to reaching agreement on the measures to be taken".

51. There is no suggestion that State A may declare an overlapping zone in which it can exercise powers to control activities in State B's EEZ. When States wish to take action regarding problems that straddle jurisdictional boundaries, they *have to agree* on how to do so. And for all Colombia's protests about its vital need to establish contiguous zone to safeguard the environment, the whole legal framework for safeguarding the Caribbean has been there — under the Cartagena Convention — for decades.

---

[140] Available at https://www.unep.org/cep/who-we-are/cartagena-convention.

[141] Available at https://www.unep.org/cep/who-we-are/cartagena-convention.

[142] See e.g. Arts. 3 (1), 5 (1), 6 (1), 7 (1) and 8 of the Protocol concerning Specially Protected Areas and Wildlife, available at https://www.unep.org/cep/who-we-are/cartagena-convention.

52. And if Colombia thinks that its partners in the Cartagena Convention are failing in their duties, then the dispute settlement procedures of Cartagena Article 23, including arbitration, are open to it, and it should use them.

53. When States wish to exercise their jurisdiction at sea beyond their national limits, they do so by agreement, not by denying the validity of those limits or by unilaterally establishing maritime zones in other States' waters. Colombia should do likewise.

54. Madam President, Members of the Court, that brings to an end my submissions on behalf of Nicaragua in this case. I thank you for your attention, and unless I can assist you further, I would ask you now to invite Nicaragua's Agent to the podium to present Nicaragua's final submissions.

The PRESIDENT: I thank Professor Lowe. I shall now give the floor to the Agent of Nicaragua, H.E. Mr. Carlos José Argüello Gómez. You have the floor, Your Excellency.

Mr. ARGÜELLO GÓMEZ:

1. Madam President, Members of the Court, good afternoon. Before proceeding to deliver Nicaragua's submissions on its case against Colombia, allow me to address very briefly a couple of issues that Colombia has directly or indirectly argued about the legal questions that are properly before the Court.

2. One of these questions is that of the environment. It should be recalled that Colombia filed four counter-claims. Two of these were related to questions of the environment and the Court did not admit them.

3. Madam President, in spite of Colombia's insistence on the topic, environmental issues are not part of the subject-matter of the present case, as has been clearly pointed out by Professor Pellet. Nevertheless, allow me a few additional remarks.

4. Since 2007, Nicaragua has increased its attention to the environment and has taken concrete steps that go well beyond its international commitments. For example, Nicaragua is one of the few countries in the world to have included in its Constitution, since 2014, a recognition of Mother Earth's rights[143].

---

[143] Nicaraguan Constitution, Article 60, available at https://www.asamblea.gob.ni/assets/constitucion.pdf (accessed 26 Sept. 2021).

5. In a country that has a continental territory of just over 130,000 sq km, it has declared 73 protected areas including 4 biosphere reserves adding up to 7,261,860 hectares of protected areas; that is, 72,000 sq km of protected areas[144].

6. The protection of the environment is an ongoing process for Nicaragua. Just this past January, Nicaragua established a biosphere reserve of 44,157 sq km in its Caribbean area that extends roughly from the Miskito archipelago out to the EEZ attributed by the Court to Nicaragua. Colombia promptly protested that it was located in its Seaflower Biosphere Reserve, which it is not[145]. The Nicaraguan biosphere is entirely in Nicaraguan territory and waters, and the law clearly and in so many words, spells out that it does not include or affect the Colombian keys of Quitasueño and Serrana or any of the areas attributed by the Court to Colombia. The text of the law with a map of the area and the co-ordinates were published in the *Official Gazette* on 2 February 2021, which is a readily available publication[146]. The Colombian protest note and Nicaragua's response are part of the record of this case, despite Colombia's opposition[147].

7. Madam President, it is ironic that Colombian counsel should state that Nicaragua treats the environment with disdain — "mépris"[148] — whilst Colombian authorities are trying to hinder Nicaragua's attempts to enhance this protection.

8. In conclusion, Colombia's attempt to portray Nicaragua as a country that does not care for the environment is no more than a bid to divert the attention of the public, and this Court, to matters that are not part of the case. In any event, it also fails on the merits.

9. Another point that has been the object of comments by the Co-Agent and by Colombian counsel is the right of Colombian vessels to fight crime they encounter in the Nicaraguan EEZ. Mr. Cepeda, the Co-Agent, notes that 38 States take part in joint operations (Operation Orion) against

---

144 Ministry of the Environment, available at http://www.marena.gob.ni/ (accessed 26 Sept. 2021).

145 Nicaragua's letter to the Court of 30 July 2021 (Ref.: HOL-EMB-384-2021); see also Registrar's letter to the Agent of Nicaragua, Ref.: 155258, 1 Sept. 2021.

146 La Gaceta, Diario Oficial, No. 22, 22 Feb. 2021 available at https://www.lagaceta.gob.ni/2021/02/022/ (accessed 26 Sept. 2021).

147 Nicaragua's letter to the Court of 30 July 2021 (Ref.: HOL-EMB-384-2021); see also Registrar's letter to the Agent of Nicaragua, Ref.: 155223, 16 Aug. 2021, and Ref.: 155258, 1 Sept. 2021.

148 CR 2021/14, p. 34, para. 2 (Boisson de Chazournes).

drug trafficking "including Nicaragua", and then states that "[i]t is unclear, to say the least, why Nicaragua maintains that all these countries can be present in the area, but Colombia cannot"[149].

10. For my part, it is unclear for me, to say the least, how Nicaragua can be participating in an operation of which Colombia is an important part and at the same time the distinguished Co-Agent should allege that Nicaragua opposes this. Nicaragua has never opposed in any way, openly or tacitly, Colombia's participation in multinational operations against the scourge of drug traffic.

11. Sir Michael Wood also continues with this strange argument that Nicaragua is opposed to Colombia combatting drug traffic in the Caribbean and in the same breath he states: "The Chief of the Nicaraguan Army applauded the 'high level of cooperation' with the Colombian Navy against drug trafficking, through participation in Operation Orion."[150]

12. Madam President, let me state it very clearly: Nicaragua does not object that Colombia should take measures for the control of the criminal activities that might occur in the Caribbean, particularly drug trafficking. After all, it is only logical that Colombia do so since most of this criminal activity has its origin in Colombia. But Colombian naval forces are also protecting illegal fishing in Nicaraguan waters, harrying Nicaraguan fishermen in Nicaraguan waters and, in general, carrying out activities in the Nicaraguan EEZ which are plain usurpations of Nicaragua's sovereign rights and jurisdiction there. If Colombia wishes to act beyond its jurisdictional limits as set by international law, it must do so by agreement, not by unilaterally asserting its control over the waters of neighbouring States.

13. Madam President, in compliance with Article 60 of the Rules of Court, I will now proceed to read into the record Nicaragua's final submissions. A copy of the written text of these submissions, duly signed, is being communicated to the Court and transmitted to the other Party.

FINAL SUBMISSIONS

1. In the case concerning *Alleged Violations of Sovereign Rights and Maritime Spaces in the Caribbean Sea (Nicaragua* v. *Colombia)*, for the reasons explained in the Written and Oral phase, Nicaragua respectfully requests the Court to adjudge and declare that:

---

[149] CR 2021/14, p. 16, para. 36 (Cepeda).

[150] CR 2021/14, p. 31, para. 30 (Wood).

(a) By its conduct, the Republic of Colombia has breached its international obligation to respect Nicaragua's maritime zones as delimited in paragraph 251 of the Court Judgment of 19 November 2012, as well as Nicaragua's sovereign rights and jurisdiction in these zones; and that, in consequence

(b) Colombia must immediately cease its internationally wrongful conduct in Nicaragua's maritime zones, as delimited by the Court in its Judgment of 19 November 2012, including its violations of Nicaragua's sovereign rights and jurisdiction in those maritime zones and take all necessary measures effectively to respect Nicaragua's sovereign rights and jurisdiction; these measures include but are not limited to revoking, by means of its choice:

(i) all laws and regulations, permits, licences, and other legal instruments which are incompatible with the Court's Judgment of 19 November 2012, including those related to marine protected areas;

(ii) the provisions of Decrees 1946 of 9 September 2013 and 1119 of 17 June 2014 in so far as they relate to maritime areas which have been recognized as under the jurisdiction or sovereign rights of Nicaragua; and

(iii) permits granted to fishing vessels to operate in Nicaragua's exclusive economic zone, as delimited in the Court's Judgment of 19 November 2012;

(c) Colombia must ensure that the decision of the Constitutional Court of Colombia of 2 May 2014 or of any other National Authority will not bar compliance with the 19 November 2012 Judgment of the Court;

(d) Colombia must compensate Nicaragua for all damage caused by its violations of its international legal obligations, including but not limited to damages caused by the exploitation of the living resources of the Nicaraguan exclusive economic zone by fishing vessels unlawfully "authorized" by Colombia to operate in that zone, and the loss of revenue caused by Colombia's refusal to allow, or by its deterrence of, fishing by Nicaraguan vessels or third State vessels authorized by Nicaragua and, generally, for the damages caused by its actions and declarations to the proper exploitation of the resources in Nicaragua's exclusive economic zone, with the amount of the compensation to be determined in a subsequent phase of the case; and

(e) Colombia must give appropriate guarantees of non-repetition of its internationally wrongful acts, including by formally acknowledging that the boundary as delimited by the Court in its Judgment of 19 November 2012 will be respected as the international maritime boundary between Colombia and Nicaragua.

(f) Nicaragua also requests that the Court adjudge and declare that it will remain seised of the case until Colombia recognizes and respects Nicaragua's rights in the Caribbean Sea as attributed by the Judgment of the Court of 19 November 2012.

This is the end of Nicaragua's submissions, Madam President, and with this I end the pleading of Nicaragua. I wish to thank you, Madam President, Members of the Court, for your kind attention.

The PRESIDENT: I thank the Agent of Nicaragua. The Court takes note of the final submissions which you have just read on behalf of Nicaragua in relation to its own claims.

Your statement brings to an end Nicaragua's second round of oral argument on its own claims. I recall that on Wednesday 29 September 2021, between 3 p.m. and 6 p.m., Colombia will present its second round of oral argument on the claims of Nicaragua and on its own counter-claims, and on Friday 1 October 2021, between 3 p.m. and 4 p.m., Nicaragua will present its second round of oral argument on the counter-claims of Colombia.

The sitting is adjourned.

The Court rose at 5 p.m.

Corrigé
Corrected

CR 2021/18

International Court of Justice

THE HAGUE

Cour internationale de Justice

LA HAYE

YEAR 2021

Public sitting

held on Wednesday 29 September 2021, at 3 p.m., at the Peace Palace,

President Donoghue presiding,

***in the case concerning* Alleged Violations of Sovereign Rights and Maritime Spaces in the Caribbean Sea (Nicaragua *v.* Colombia)**

VERBATIM RECORD

ANNÉE 2021

Audience publique

tenue le mercredi 29 septembre 2021, à 15 heures, au Palais de la Paix,

sous la présidence de Mme Donoghue, présidente,

***en l'affaire relative à des* Violations alléguées de droits souverains et d'espaces maritimes dans la mer des Caraïbes (Nicaragua c. Colombie)**

COMPTE RENDU

Present:	President	Donoghue
	Vice-President	Gevorgian
	Judges	Tomka
		Abraham
		Bennouna
		Yusuf
		Xue
		Sebutinde
		Bhandari
		Robinson
		Salam
		Iwasawa
		Nolte
	Judges *ad hoc*	Daudet
		McRae
	Registrar	Gautier

Présents :	Mme	Donoghue, présidente
	M.	Gevorgian, vice-président
	MM.	Tomka
		Abraham
		Bennouna
		Yusuf
	Mmes	Xue
		Sebutinde
	MM.	Bhandari
		Robinson
		Salam
		Iwasawa
		Nolte, juges
	MM.	Daudet
		McRae, juges *ad hoc*
	M.	Gautier, greffier

The Government of Nicaragua is represented by:

H.E. Mr. Carlos José Argüello Gómez, Ambassador of the Republic of Nicaragua to the Kingdom of the Netherlands,

as Agent and Counsel;

Mr. Alex Oude Elferink, Director, Netherlands Institute for the Law of the Sea, Professor of International Law of the Sea at Utrecht University,

Mr. Vaughan Lowe, QC, Emeritus Chichele Professor of Public International Law, University of Oxford, member of the Institut de droit international, member of the Bar of England and Wales,

Mr. Lawrence H. Martin, Attorney at Law, Foley Hoag LLP, member of the Bars of the United States Supreme Court, the District of Columbia and the Commonwealth of Massachusetts,

Mr. Alain Pellet, Emeritus Professor of the University Paris Nanterre, former Chairman of the International Law Commission, President of the Institut de droit international,

Mr. Paul Reichler, Attorney at Law, Foley Hoag LLP, member of the Bars of the United States Supreme Court and the District of Columbia,

as Counsel and Advocates;

Ms Claudia Loza Obregon, Legal Adviser, Ministry of Foreign Affairs of Nicaragua,

Ms Tessa Barsac, Consultant in International Law, Master (University Paris Nanterre), LLM (Leiden University),

as Assistant Counsel;

Mr. Robin Cleverly, MA, DPhil, CGeol, FGS, Law of the Sea Consultant, Marbdy Consulting Ltd,

as Scientific and Technical Adviser;

Ms Sherly Noguera de Argüello, MBA,

as Administrator.

The Government of Colombia is represented by:

H.E. Mr. Carlos Gustavo Arrieta Padilla, former Judge of the Council of State of Colombia, former Attorney General of Colombia and former Ambassador of Colombia to the Netherlands,

as Agent;

H.E. Mr. Manuel José Cepeda Espinosa, former President of the Constitutional Court of Colombia, former Permanent Delegate of Colombia to UNESCO and former Ambassador of Colombia to the Swiss Confederation,

as Co-Agent;

Le Gouvernement du Nicaragua est représenté par :

S. Exc. M. Carlos José Argüello Gómez, ambassadeur de la République du Nicaragua auprès du Royaume des Pays-Bas,

comme agent et conseil ;

M. Alex Oude Elferink, directeur de l'Institut néerlandais du droit de la mer, professeur de droit international de la mer à l'Université d'Utrecht,

M. Vaughan Lowe, QC, professeur émérite de droit international public à l'Université d'Oxford, titulaire de la chaire Chichele, membre de l'Institut de droit international, membre du barreau d'Angleterre et du pays de Galles,

M. Lawrence H. Martin, avocat au cabinet Foley Hoag LLP, membre des barreaux de la Cour suprême des Etats-Unis d'Amérique, du district de Colombia et du Commonwealth du Massachusetts,

M. Alain Pellet, professeur émérite de l'Université Paris Nanterre, ancien président de la Commission du droit international, président de l'Institut de droit international,

M. Paul Reichler, avocat au cabinet Foley Hoag LLP, membre des barreaux de la Cour suprême des Etats-Unis d'Amérique et du district de Colombia,

comme conseils et avocats ;

Mme Claudia Loza Obregon, conseillère juridique auprès du ministère des affaires étrangères du Nicaragua,

Mme Tessa Barsac, consultante en droit international, master (Université Paris Nanterre), LLM (Université de Leyde),

comme conseils adjoints ;

M. Robin Cleverly, MA, DPhil, CGeol, FGS, consultant en droit de la mer, Marbdy Consulting Ltd,

comme conseiller scientifique et technique ;

Mme Sherly Noguera de Argüello, MBA,

comme administrateur.

Le Gouvernement de la Colombie est représenté par :

S. Exc. M. Carlos Gustavo Arrieta Padilla, ancien juge au conseil d'Etat colombien, ancien *Procurador General de la Nación* et ancien ambassadeur de Colombie aux Pays-Bas,

comme agent ;

S. Exc. M. Manuel José Cepeda Espinosa, ancien président de la Cour constitutionnelle de Colombie, ancien représentant permanent de la Colombie auprès de l'UNESCO et ancien ambassadeur de Colombie auprès de la Confédération suisse,

comme coagent ;

H.E. Ms Marta Lucía Ramírez Blanco, Vice-President and Minister for Foreign Affairs of the Republic of Colombia,

H.E. Mr. Everth Hawkins Sjogreen, Governor of San Andrés, Providencia and Santa Catalina, Colombia,

as National Authorities;

Mr. W. Michael Reisman, McDougal Professor of International Law at Yale University, member of the Institut de droit international,

Mr. Rodman R. Bundy, former *avocat à la Cour d'appel de Paris*, member of the Bar of the State of New York, partner at Squire Patton Boggs LLP, Singapore,

Sir Michael Wood, KCMG, member of the International Law Commission, member of the Bar of England and Wales,

Mr. Eduardo Valencia-Ospina, former Registrar and Deputy-Registrar of the International Court of Justice, member and former Special Rapporteur and Chair of the International Law Commission, former Chair of the Latin American Society of International Law,

Mr. Jean-Marc Thouvenin, Professor at the University Paris Nanterre, Secretary-General of the Hague Academy of International Law, associate member of the Institut de droit international, member of the Paris Bar, Sygna Partners,

Ms Laurence Boisson de Chazournes, Professor of International Law and International Organization at the University of Geneva, member of the Institut de droit international,

H.E. Mr. Kent Francis James, former Ambassador of Colombia to Belize, former Ambassador of Colombia to Jamaica,

as Counsel and Advocates;

Mr. Andrés Villegas Jaramillo, LLM, Co-ordinator, Group of Affairs before the International Court of Justice at the Ministry of Foreign Affairs of Colombia, member of the Legal Sub-Commission of the Caribbean Sea Commission, Association of Caribbean States,

Mr. Makane Moïse Mbengue, Professor at the University of Geneva, Director of the Department of Public International Law and International Organization, associate member of the Institut de droit international,

Mr. Luke Vidal, member of the Paris Bar, Sygna Partners,

Mr. Eran Sthoeger, Esq., member of the Bar of the State of New York, Adjunct Professor of International Law at Brooklyn Law School and Seton Hall Law School,

Mr. Alvin Yap, Advocate and Solicitor of the Supreme Court of Singapore, Squire Patton Boggs LLP, Singapore,

Mr. Lorenzo Palestini, PhD, Lecturer at the Graduate Institute of International and Development Studies and at the University of Geneva,

as Counsel;

S. Exc. Mme Marta Lucía Ramírez Blanco, vice-présidente et ministre des affaires étrangères de la République de Colombie,

S. Exc. M. Everth Hawkins Sjogreen, gouverneur de San Andrés, Providencia et Santa Catalina, Colombie,

comme représentants de l'Etat ;

M. W. Michael Reisman, professeur de droit international à l'Université de Yale, titulaire de la chaire McDougal, membre de l'Institut de droit international,

M. Rodman R. Bundy, ancien avocat à la Cour d'appel de Paris, membre du barreau de l'Etat de New York, associé au cabinet Squire Patton Boggs LLP (Singapour),

Sir Michael Wood, KCMG, membre de la Commission du droit international, membre du barreau d'Angleterre et du pays de Galles,

M. Eduardo Valencia-Ospina, ancien greffier et greffier adjoint de la Cour internationale de Justice, membre et ancien rapporteur spécial et président de la Commission du droit international, ancien président de l'association latino-américaine de droit international,

M. Jean-Marc Thouvenin, professeur à l'Université Paris Nanterre, secrétaire général de l'Académie de droit international de La Haye, membre associé de l'Institut de droit international, membre du barreau de Paris, cabinet Sygna Partners,

Mme Laurence Boisson de Chazournes, professeure de droit international public et organisation internationale à l'Université de Genève, membre de l'Institut de droit international,

S. Exc. M. Kent Francis James, ancien ambassadeur de Colombie au Belize et ancien ambassadeur de Colombie en Jamaïque,

comme conseils et avocats ;

M. Andrés Villegas Jaramillo, LLM, coordonnateur du groupe chargé des affaires portées devant la Cour internationale de Justice au sein du ministère des affaires étrangères de la Colombie, membre de la sous-commission juridique relevant de la Commission de la mer des Caraïbes de l'Association des Etats de la Caraïbe,

M. Makane Moïse Mbengue, professeur à l'Université de Genève, directeur du département de droit international public et organisation internationale, membre associé de l'Institut de droit international,

M. Luke Vidal, membre du barreau de Paris, cabinet Sygna Partners,

M. Eran Sthoeger, membre du barreau de l'Etat de New York, professeur adjoint de droit international à la Brooklyn Law School et à la faculté de droit de l'université de Seton Hall,

M. Alvin Yap, avocat et *solicitor* à la Cour suprême de Singapour, cabinet Squire Patton Boggs LLP (Singapour),

M. Lorenzo Palestini, PhD, chargé d'enseignement à l'Institut de hautes études internationales et du développement et à l'Université de Genève,

comme conseils ;

H.E. Mr. Juan José Quintana Aranguren, Head of Multilateral Affairs, former Ambassador of Colombia to the Netherlands,

H.E. Mr. Fernando Antonio Grillo Rubiano, Ambassador of the Republic of Colombia to the Kingdom of the Netherlands and Permanent Representative of Colombia to the Organisation for the Prohibition of Chemical Weapons,

Ms Jenny Sharyne Bowie Wilches, Second Secretary, Embassy of Colombia in the Netherlands,

Ms Viviana Andrea Medina Cruz, Second Secretary, Embassy of Colombia in the Netherlands,

Mr. Sebastián Correa Cruz, Third Secretary,

Mr. Raúl Alfonso Simancas Gómez, Third Secretary, Group of Affairs before the International Court of Justice,

Ministry of Foreign Affairs of Colombia;

Rear Admiral Ernesto Segovia Forero, Chief of Naval Operations,

CN Hermann León, Delegate of Colombia to the International Maritime Organization,

CN William Pedroza, National Navy of Colombia, Director of Maritime and Fluvial Interests Office,

Navy of the Republic of Colombia;

Mr. Scott Edmonds, Cartographer, Director of International Mapping,

Ms Victoria Taylor, Cartographer, International Mapping,

as Technical Advisers;

Mr. Gershon Hasin, LLM, JSD, Yale Law School,

as Legal Assistant;

Mr. Mark Taylor Archbold, Consultant for the National Unit of Disaster Risk Management,

Mr. Joseph Richard Jessie Martinez, Consultant for the National Unit of Disaster Risk Management,

as Advisers.

S. Exc. M. Juan José Quintana Aranguren, chef des affaires multilatérales, ancien ambassadeur de Colombie aux Pays-Bas,

S. Exc. M. Fernando Antonio Grillo Rubiano, ambassadeur de la République de Colombie auprès du Royaume des Pays-Bas et représentant permanent de la Colombie auprès de l'Organisation pour l'interdiction des armes chimiques,

Mme Jenny Sharyne Bowie Wilches, deuxième secrétaire, ambassade de Colombie aux Pays-Bas,

Mme Viviana Andrea Medina Cruz, deuxième secrétaire, ambassade de Colombie aux Pays-Bas,

M. Sebastián Correa Cruz, troisième secrétaire,

M. Raúl Alfonso Simancas Gómez, troisième secrétaire, groupe chargé des affaires portées devant la Cour internationale de Justice,

ministère des affaires étrangères de la République de Colombie ;

Le contre-amiral Ernesto Segovia Forero, chef des opérations navales,

Le capitaine de vaisseau Hermann León, représentant de la Colombie auprès de l'Organisation maritime internationale,

Le capitaine de vaisseau William Pedroza, marine nationale de Colombie, chef de la direction chargée des intérêts maritimes et fluviaux,

marine de la République de Colombie ;

M. Scott Edmonds, cartographe, directeur de International Mapping,

Mme Victoria Taylor, cartographe, International Mapping,

comme conseillers techniques ;

M. Gershon Hasin, LLM, JSD, faculté de droit de l'Université de Yale,

comme assistant juridique ;

M. Mark Taylor Archbold, consultant auprès de l'unité nationale de gestion des risques de catastrophe,

M. Joseph Richard Jessie Martinez, consultant auprès de l'unité nationale de gestion des risques de catastrophe,

comme conseillers.

The PRESIDENT: Please be seated. The sitting is open. The Court meets this afternoon to hear Colombia's second round of oral argument on the claims of Nicaragua and on its own counter-claims.

I note the presence this afternoon of Her Excellency Ms Marta Lucía Ramírez Blanco, Vice-President as well as Minister for Foreign Affairs of Colombia, whom I am pleased to welcome.

I invite Sir Michael Wood to address the Court.

Sir Michael WOOD:

THE APPLICABLE LAW; REMEDIES

1. Madam President, Members of the Court. I shall respond to some applicable law points made by counsel for Nicaragua. And I shall refer briefly to the remedies sought by Nicaragua.

2. I shall be followed by Professor Boisson de Charzounes, Mr. Bundy and Professor Reisman, who will respond to Nicaragua's claims.

3. They will be followed by Mr. Valencia-Ospina and Professor Thouvenin, who will respond to what Nicaragua said about our counter-claims.

4. Finally, the Agent of the Republic of Colombia will make some general observations and read Colombia's submissions.

Subject-matter of the dispute

5. Before turning to the applicable law, I must say a few words about the subject-matter of the dispute. Nicaragua's case concerns alleged violations of its sovereign rights. Nothing else. Nicaragua is the Applicant and, like any applicant, must establish that its rights have been violated in some way. This case is not about determining the international responsibility of the State for political statements made by its officials or former officials. This is not a case about a PowerPoint presentation by former President Santos[1].

---

[1] E.g. CR 2021/13, p. 45, para. 15 (Reichler); CR 2021/17, p. 24, para. 9 (Reichler); CR 2021/17, p. 11, para. 5 (Pellet).

6. By arguing that "Colombia must establish that the rights that it claims in Nicaragua's EEZ are 'attributed' to it, and not to Nicaragua, by the regime of the EEZ"[2], Nicaragua presents a simplistic view of the EEZ régime, and seeks to reverse the burden of proof.

7. That burden is on the Applicant, who must show such violations and their repercussions. It would not be enough for Nicaragua to establish that Colombia has exceeded its rights in the EEZ. Rather, as the Applicant, Nicaragua has to establish that Colombia's actions violated Nicaragua's rights and to what effect.

8. On Monday, Professor Pellet said he would explain what the case was about and what it was not about[3]. I could agree when he says that the only question is whether Colombia respects Nicaragua's sovereign rights, not whether Colombia respects the 2012 Judgment[4]. They say that, but then they repeatedly accuse Colombia of rejecting the Judgment. Notwithstanding Professor Pellet's rhetoric, there is nothing "exceptional" about this case[5] — save, perhaps, Nicaragua's repeated references to political statements that, whatever their content, are legally speaking irrelevant. On that, the position is perfectly clear and was explained by Colombia's Co-Agent last week[6].

9. The law that is applicable is not an imaginary law regarding political statements and intentions. Even taken at face value, Nicaragua has, at best, cobbled together a handful of alleged events that cannot change the wider reality existing over the last decade: the reality that Nicaragua and its nationals have not been hindered from exercising their rights as part of an alleged continuous pattern of conduct. The Court then is left to deal with the various specific actions alleged by Nicaragua. Nicaragua must prove, for each separate "incident", that its sovereign rights have been violated.

10. The subject-matter of the dispute in the Application consisted of the 13 pre-critical date alleged incidents at sea and Decree 1946. The 13 non-events, as we say, are unconnected to the post-critical date alleged incidents. This much is obvious from the fact that Nicaragua, in its first round, did not even mention any of the pre-critical date alleged incidents. As for Nicaragua's second

---

[2] RN, para. 2.10.

[3] CR 2021/17, p. 10, para. 2 (Pellet).

[4] CR 2021/17, p. 11, para. 4 (Pellet).

[5] CR 2021/17, p. 13, para. 10 (Pellet).

[6] CR 2021/14, p. 12, para. 15 (Cepeda Espinosa).

round, Mr. Reichler strained to find a connection between the pre- and post-critical date non-events. This will be further elaborated by Mr. Bundy.

Applicable law

11. Madam President, on Monday Nicaragua once more distorted Colombia's position on the applicable law. I shall not reply to all they said; instead I respectfully refer the Court to the position set out in our written pleadings[7] as well as last week[8].

12. We differ on at least two basic matters: the extent of the rights and duties of all States in the EEZ; and the fact that the rules reflected in Part V are not self-contained, whether as a matter of customary or conventional law.

13. The essence of the applicable régime is that the coastal State has sovereign rights for the purposes of exploring and exploiting, conserving and managing natural resources, and limited jurisdiction concerning specific matters, while all other States enjoy the high seas freedoms of navigation and overflight, and other internationally lawful uses of the sea related to those freedoms. These freedoms are the same as anywhere on the high seas. They apply to all ships and aircraft. They go beyond mere "passage". They include the right to navigate and overfly for any purpose[9].

14. Professor Pellet misstates our position in order to criticize it. He said last week that for Colombia, everything that was not prohibited for third States was permitted, and that for the coastal State everything that was expressly permitted had to be interpreted restrictively[10]. That is not what we said. The simple point we are making is that Nicaragua has the burden of showing, as a matter of law, which of its rights under the specific legal régime Colombia, so it claims, has violated. That it has not done. For our part, we were not suggesting that the customary régime reflected in Part V attributes all rights and jurisdiction within the zone. We would not contest the passage from *M/V Saiga* (*No. 2*) cited by Professor Pellet[11]. In any event, in relation to the specific "incidents" of

---

[7] CMC, paras. 3.1-3.76; RC, Chap. 2.

[8] See, in particular, CR 2021/14, pp. 23-28, paras. 5-19 (Wood); CR 2021/14, pp. 43-46, paras. 33-44 (Boisson de Chazournes); CR 2021/15, pp. 26-27, 32-33, paras. 10-16, 44-45 (Reisman).

[9] CR 2021/14, pp. 26-28; paras. 13-18 (Wood).

[10] CR 2021/13, p. 32, para. 20 (Pellet).

[11] CR 2021/13, p. 32, para. 20 (Pellet).

which complaint is made in the present case, the specific legal régime does attribute to all States high seas freedoms in the zone[12] and it applies to the zone virtually all the rules concerning the high seas[13]. Under UNCLOS this is done "subject to the relevant provisions of this Convention" and "in so far as they are not incompatible with [Part V]". Under customary international law that could correspond to something like "subject to the relevant rules of the law of the sea" and "in so far as they are not incompatible with the specific legal regime applicable to the zone".

15. On Friday, Mr. Martin muddied the waters even further. He sought, at some length, to interpret the customary international law on the EEZ by reference to a close textual analysis of a whole series of provisions of UNCLOS and detailed reference to its *travaux préparatoires*[14]. He ignored the fact that the customary international law developed in parallel with the work at the Conference[15]. There was State practice well before the conclusion of UNCLOS in 1982 and its entry into force in 1994. It is not the case, as Nicaragua would have you believe, that customary law excluded all traditional fishing rights. Mr. Martin likewise sought to distinguish, in an obscure and inaccurate way, between the territorial sea and the EEZ by suggesting that the former had a "hybrid" legal régime, being "governed by both UNCLOS and general international law", whereas the EEZ was "a creation of UNCLOS and governed by the provisions of Part V of UNCLOS"[16]. For him, apparently, other rules of international law do not apply within the EEZ. That, with respect, is plainly wrong. Indeed, Part V itself contains many references to other rules, including those concerning the high seas and the protection of the environment.

16. Throughout these oral proceedings, Nicaragua has taken peculiar and contradictory approaches to the identification of customary international law. For one of its counsel, UNCLOS should just be presumed to reflect customary international law[17]. For another, customary international law is clearly not reflected in the Convention[18]. For a third, the existence of customary international

[12] Cf. UNCLOS, Art. 58.1.

[13] Cf. UNCLOS, Art. 58.2.

[14] CR 2021/16, pp. 20-22, paras. 12 and 20 (Martin).

[15] CR 2021/14, p. 68, paras. 29-30 (Lowe).

[16] CR 2021/16, pp. 22-23, paras. 23-24 (Martin).

[17] CR 2021/13, p. 32, para. 18 (Pellet).

[18] CR 2021/13, p. 66, paras. 19-20 (Lowe); CR 2021/17, p. 42, para. 25 (Lowe).

law must be reflected in State practice and *opinio juris* — but this basic methodology is no longer required if a rule is mentioned in UNCLOS[19].

17. Madam President, last week I described the limited "presence" of Colombia in the area, and the important objectives which it served. I also said that the Colombian activities included observing and informing: that is to say, Colombian vessels and aircraft navigate and overfly the area, among other things, in order to see what is happening. They do so for many reasons and Nicaragua itself has acknowledged the usefulness of this presence both in terms of search and rescue[20] as well as regards transnational criminal activity and anti-drug trafficking operations[21]. Colombia also observes and informs on environmental risk and damage. Its vessels and aircraft inform the vessels concerned, as well as their own headquarters, about illicit activities. Professor Pellet wonders why naval ships are necessary for observing and informing[22]. Navies and coastguards are precisely the people who are best placed routinely to carry out such activities in the high seas. Their actions are all well within the rights of all States where high seas freedoms apply. And they are important both for Colombia's interests as a coastal State in the south-western Caribbean and for the interests of the international community as a whole.

18. Nicaragua continues to treat the specific legal régime of the EEZ as if it were self-contained[23]. Of course, UNCLOS is not applicable between the Parties to this case, and you will decide on the basis of the customary international law of the sea. But that does not mean that other sources of international law can be ignored. Far from it! Account needs to be taken of other rules of customary international law, including those of particular (local) custom; of commitments undertaken in unilateral declarations, such as those of the most senior Nicaraguan officials; and of applicable treaties such as the Cartagena Convention and the Search and Rescue Convention. These particular rules, in turn, assist in a correct understanding of the customary international law of the

---

[19] CR 2021/16, p. 39, para. 11 (Oude Elferink).

[20] CR 2021/17, p. 28, para. 18 (Reichler).

[21] CR 2021/17, pp. 48-49, paras. 9-12 (Argüello Gómez).

[22] CR 2021/17, p. 11, para. 5 (Pellet).

[23] CR 2021/13, p. 31, para. 15 *et seq.* (Pellet).

sea, as it applies between the Parties. Nicaragua is quite wrong when it urges you to minimize the relevance or even disregard other sources of the law[24].

19. It's good to see that our friends opposite now accept the applicability of the Cartagena Convention[25]. However, Professor Pellet seemed to be suggesting that the Convention did not impose any obligations on the States parties[26]. But that cannot be right. Even if the Convention were to be described as a framework convention, that would not mean it was devoid of legal effect. Obligations under a framework convention are not without legal effect until "implemented" by more detailed provisions. A well-known example is Part XII of UNCLOS itself, often thought of as a framework convention, but which contains fundamental obligations on the protection of the environment, obligations that largely reflect customary international law.

20. Madam President, Professor Lowe too had some curious ways of identifying the applicable law. He said last week that "there is no evidence of States carving out or reserving their position in relation to contiguous zone rights when they delimit maritime boundaries — for example by establishing a contiguous zone straddling the delimited boundary"[27]. But what does that prove? The fact that most maritime boundary agreements delimit the territorial sea, the EEZ and the continental shelf, without mentioning the contiguous zone, tends to confirm that States see no need to delimit contiguous zones; they are not concerned by potential overlaps.

21. Professor Lowe's basic argument was that the contiguous zone and EEZ rights cannot coexist in the same area[28]. His argument here was broad-brush and unconvincing. "The jurisdictional clash is obvious"[29], he asserted. With respect, it is far from obvious. "As was apparent to the ITLOS in the *Saiga* and the *Virginia G* cases", he went on to say. Again, with respect, reading the passages listed in his footnote 212, one finds nothing to support this argument or convey any apparent tension between the contiguous zone and EEZ rights. Professor Lowe is also plain wrong when he asserts

---

[24] Churchill and Lowe, *The Law of the Sea* (3rd. ed., 1999), pp. 24-25.

[25] CR 2021/17, pp. 45-46, paras. 45-50 (Lowe).

[26] CR 2021/13, p. 35, para. 26 (Pellet).

[27] CR 2021/13, p. 67, para. 25 (Lowe).

[28] CR 2021/13, pp. 71-73, paras. 47-55 (Lowe).

[29] CR 2021/13, p. 72, para. 49 (Lowe).

that EEZ rights and contiguous zone rights "do not address entirely different matters"[30]. As the book by Churchill and Lowe puts it, with respect to the contiguous zone and the EEZ, "the distinction between the two kinds of zone was put beyond argument"[31].

22. As he did last week, in describing Colombia's Decree 1946, as amended, Professor Lowe overlooked the fact that the contiguous zone powers in the Decree are, in accordance with international law, expressly limited to powers to prevent and punish infringements of its laws and regulations within its territory and territorial sea. In addition, Article 5 of the Decree, as amended, expressly and unequivocally states, that "[t]he application of this article [Article 5] will be carried out in conformity with international law".

23. Worse still, Professor Lowe gave the impression that Colombia was exercising contiguous zone powers beyond the contiguous zone. At various points, he seemed deliberately to confuse the contiguous zone powers of the coastal State with the rights and freedoms of all States in the EEZ. Indeed, as soon as he turned to the central point about one State's contiguous zone overlapping another State's EEZ[32], he headed off on a long digression about the rights of the coastal State and others in the EEZ[33]. That had nothing to do with contiguous zone rights. He said indeed that the Decree "asserts the right to prevent and control violations of Colombia's environmental laws in Nicaragua's EEZ"[34].

24. Of course, the Decree does no such thing. It is limited, as I have just said, to violations in Colombia's territory and territorial sea. Earlier, Professor Lowe suggested that Colombia had been implementing the Decree in the EEZ: "That is what Mr. Reichler has been talking about"[35], he said. With respect, that was not what Mr. Reichler spoke about. None of the so-called alleged "incidents" Mr. Reichler discussed concern Nicaraguan vessels in Colombia's contiguous zone.

---

30 CR 2021/13, p. 72, para. 50 (Lowe).

31 Churchill and Lowe, *The Law of the Sea* (3rd. ed, 1999), p. 135.

32 CR 2021/17, p. 43, para. 29 (Lowe).

33 CR 2021/17, p. 43, para. 31 *et seq.* (Lowe).

34 CR 2021/17, p. 44, para. 37 (Lowe).

35 CR 2021/17, p. 42, para. 27 (Lowe).

25. Professor Lowe asserted on Wednesday that if any of the terms of the Decree were contrary to international law, its mere enactment would violate Nicaragua's EEZ rights[36]. Professor Reisman dealt with this last week[37] and we set out the position at some length in our Rejoinder[38]. Professor Lowe, for his part, merely asserted that "[t]he promulgation of a law . . . can certainly constitute a violation of [a State's international obligations]". Yes, it *can*, but that is the exception rather than the rule. Professor Lowe's reference to Article 4 of the ILC Articles on State does not assist his argument. Article 4 deals with the attribution of the conduct of State organs to a State, not with the content of the international obligation concerned. More relevant is the commentary to Article 12, which we cited in our Rejoinder[39]. Whether the mere enactment of a law violates international law turns on the content of the primary obligation concerned. This has mainly been discussed in the context of human rights obligations, where the jurisprudence is rather clear: it is only when the enactment has a continuous and direct effect on the individual applicant that its mere existence may involve a breach of his or her right to private life[40]. The exceptional circumstances which may give rise to a chilling effect in the human rights context are simply not present in the case of Decree 1946.

26. Professor Lowe cited two advisory opinions in a footnote (again pleading by footnote Professor Pellet — to use Professor Pellet's expression)[41]. One of the advisory opinions was by this Court; the other by the Inter-American Court of Human Rights. These opinions do not support Nicaragua. This Court's opinion concerned the existence of a dispute, not the merits of the case. The advisory opinion of the Inter-American Court concerned access to the Court by the Inter-American Commission, not the merits of a dispute.

---

[36] CR 2021/17, pp. 42-43, para. 28 (Lowe).

[37] CR 2021/15, pp. 35-36, paras. 56-60 (Reisman).

[38] CR, paras. 4.122-4.150.

[39] CR, para. 4.132.

[40] RC, paras. 4.135-4.139, citing *European Court of Human Rights, Case of Dudgeon* v. *The United Kingdom, 22 October 1981, Series A No. 45* and *European Court of Human Rights, Case of Modinos* v. *Cyprus, 22 April 1993, Series A No. 259.*

[41] CR 2021/17, p. 43, para. 28, fn. 125 (Lowe), citing Inter-American Court of Human Rights, *International Responsibility for the Promulgation and Enforcement of Laws in Violation of the Convention, Advisory Opinion OC-14/94, International Law Reports*, 1994, Vol. 116, p. 320, paras. 31-50. Cf. *Applicability of the Obligation to Arbitrate under Section 21 of the United Nations Headquarters Agreement of 26 June 1947, Advisory Opinion, I.C.J. Reports 1988*, pp. 29-30, para. 42.

27. Nor does Professor Lowe's footnote invocation of Lord McNair[42] avail him. The reference appears to be to a short passage from the *North Atlantic Coast Fisheries* case, which deals with good faith in the performance of treaty obligations.

Remedies

28. Madam President, Members of the Court, I now turn to the remedies sought by Nicaragua in connection with its claims[43].

29. Nicaragua has not made out any case for remedies. Even if there were a breach, Nicaragua has not begun to show any material or moral damage, indeed they have not even attempted to do so. So there could be no question of reparation for injury, or any justification for holding a separate procedural phase for that purpose[44]. I refer you to our written pleadings[45].

30. Nicaragua has also deemed it appropriate — if Colombia is found to have violated its rights — to ask the Court to order Colombia to take intrusive actions such as revoking laws, decrees, regulations, permits and licenses. This request is wholly inappropriate in proceedings such as the present one. It contradicts the jurisprudence of the Court, whereby the "choice of means" of compliance with a Judgment of the Court "must be left" to the relevant party[46].

31. On Monday, Professor Pellet invited the Court to insist that Colombia give guarantees of non-repetition. He further invited you to remain seised of the case[47]. Nicaragua's final submissions were changed, at the very last moment, to request "that the Court adjudge and declare that it will remain seised of the case until Colombia recognizes and respects Nicaragua's rights in the Caribbean Sea as attributed by the Judgment of the Court of 19 November 2012".

32. Madam President, Members of the Court, the Court's case law is clear: it will only consider assurances of non-repetition if special circumstances so warrant. In the present case, and despite Nicaragua's reliance yet again on statements by high Colombian officials, no such circumstances

---

[42] CR 2021/17, p. 43, para. 28, fn. 125 (Lowe), citing Lord McNair, *The Law of Treaties* (1961), p. 550.

[43] MN, Chap. 6.

[44] CR 2021/13, p. 74, para. 62 (Lowe).

[45] CMC, Chap. 6.

[46] *LaGrand (Germany* v. *United States of America), Judgment, I. C.J. Reports 2001*, p. 514, para. 125.

[47] CR 2021/17, pp. 13-14, paras. 8-11 (Pellet).

exist which would justify the Court in demanding cessation and non-repetition[48]. Professor Pellet himself admitted that these requests were very exceptional, and that the request that you remain seised was, in his words, *"une demande inhabituelle"*.

33. Professor Pellet argued there was a precedent in the *Nuclear Tests* case[49]. Madam President, Members of the Court, we are all of course aware of the wholly exceptional paragraph 63 of the Court's Judgment in *Nuclear Tests*, and of New Zealand's 1995 Application.

34. Professor Pellet knows the case well — all too well; he was counsel for France when it argued forcefully that the proceedings did not even amount to a case. The New Zealand Application was, of course, very unusual indeed. There is no comparison between that case, involving nuclear weapons testing, and the circumstances of the present case. In 1975 the Court had declined to exercise jurisdiction on the ground that the matter was moot, having regard to France's unilateral commitments to stop testing. And even in that extreme situation the procedure was highly controversial. We can see no basis whatsoever, in the present case, for the Court to remain seised of the matter. There is no provision for this in the Statute or the Rules, which provide only for the interpretation or revision of a judgment in strictly limited circumstances. No special circumstances exist in the present case to justify such an exceptional measure. By issuing its judgment, the Court will have exercised its jurisdiction to the full.

35. We would therefore strongly urge you, to reject this remarkable suggestion, which would be clearly contrary to the Statute and to the Charter of the United Nations, both of which provide other routes for post-judgment action. As you know well, Article 94 of the United Nations Charter specifically addresses a situation of alleged non-compliance with a judgment of the Court, which is the whole basis for Nicaragua's extraordinary submission.

36. Nicaragua cannot properly use your judgment in the present case to control indefinitely what it claims are violations of the 2012 Judgment. Over the years it has made no effort to use options that were open to it to this end, including Article L of the Pact of Bogotá[50]. As I said earlier, and as

---

[48] *Dispute regarding Navigational and Related Rights (Costa Rica* v. *Nicaragua), Judgment, I.C.J. Reports 2009*, p. 267, para. 150; see also *Pulp Mills on the River Uruguay (Argentina* v. *Uruguay), Judgment, I.C.J. Reports 2010 (I)*, p. 105, para. 278.

[49] CR 2021/17, p. 13, para. 9 (Pellet).

[50] POC, Vol. II, Ann. 33.

seems to be agreed between the Parties, the present case is not about compliance with the earlier Judgment.

37. Madam President, Members of the Court, that concludes my statement. I thank you for your attention, and I request that you invite Professor Boisson de Chazournes to the podium.

38. I thank you.

The PRESIDENT: I thank Sir Michael, and I now invite the next speaker, Prof. Laurence Boisson de Chazournes to take the floor. You have the floor, Madam.

Mme BOISSON DE CHAZOURNES :

LA DÉFORMATION PAR LE NICARAGUA DES ACTIVITÉS D'OBSERVATION ET D'INFORMATION DE LA COLOMBIE À DES FINS ENVIRONNEMENTALES

1. Madame la présidente, Mesdames et Messieurs les juges, c'est un honneur de me présenter à nouveau devant vous.

2. La Cour l'aura sûrement constaté : le Nicaragua s'est finalement résigné à évoquer l'environnement par la voix autorisée de ses conseils[51] et de son agent[52]. Malheureusement, ces références lui ont tout simplement servi de façade pour donner l'illusion à la Cour que le Nicaragua se préoccuperait également des écosystèmes fragiles de la mer des Caraïbes. Toutefois, de manière obstinée, le Nicaragua continue à nier que l'environnement fait partie intégrante du présent différend. Pour ce faire, le professeur Pellet a ressuscité un subterfuge auquel le Nicaragua n'a pas eu recours lors du premier tour des plaidoiries ; il a affirmé sans ambages que la Cour aurait exclu *ipso facto* et *ipso jure* l'environnement du présent différend en déclarant inadmissibles les demandes reconventionnelles de la Colombie y afférentes[53].

3. En plus d'être infondée, une telle affirmation contredit le soi-disant attachement du Nicaragua au respect des décisions de la Cour de céans. Mes contradicteurs sont trop fins juristes pour ignorer que les décisions de cette dernière, dans les procédures incidentes, ne préjugent pas du

---

[51] CR 2021/17, p. 11, par. 5, et p. 21, par. 33 (Pellet) ; CR 2021/17, p. 45, par. 45, et p. 46, par. 47 (Lowe).

[52] CR 2021/17, p. 47, par. 4, p. 48, par. 6 (Argüello Gómez).

[53] CR 2021/17, p. 12, par. 7 (Pellet).

fond[54]. La Cour n'a pas dit et n'aurait pu dire, avec l'autorité de la chose jugée, que l'environnement n'a aucune pertinence pour apprécier la licéité du comportement de la Colombie.

4. Alors pourquoi le Nicaragua s'entête-t-il donc à vouloir exclure l'environnement ? Mesdames et Messieurs les juges, la réponse est simple. La stratégie d'évitement du Nicaragua s'explique par le fait que l'environnement, *à lui seul*, révèle le caractère artificiel de la requête du Nicaragua. Il met à nu une évidence : aucune des violations alléguées par le Nicaragua n'est avérée.

5. Le Nicaragua sait que les écosystèmes fragiles de la mer des Caraïbes justifient la présence *licite* de la marine colombienne dans certains espaces du sud-ouest de cette mer. Le Nicaragua sait que les activités d'observation et d'information de la Colombie à des fins environnementales et la manière dont elles sont menées ne violent en aucun cas les droits souverains du Nicaragua. Le Nicaragua sait que la prise en compte des considérations environnementales est vitale pour la protection des habitats fragiles et cruciale pour l'exercice des droits traditionnels de pêche pour les Raizals. Cela explique, Mesdames et Messieurs les juges, pourquoi le Nicaragua s'obstine à présenter l'environnement comme un aspect étranger au différend dont vous avez à connaître. Il le fait en niant les liens intrinsèques entre environnement et santé[55] et la nécessité de protéger l'environnement dans tous les espaces maritimes.

6. Cette déformation stratégique par le Nicaragua de la pertinence de la protection de l'environnement ne vous lie bien évidemment pas. Dans son appréciation de l'objet d'un différend, la Cour se repose sur les arguments et positions des *deux* parties, ainsi que sur des éléments objectifs[56]. Or, il ne fait pas de doute que l'environnement est au cœur du présent différend[57].

7. En tenant dûment compte du droit applicable au présent différend, la Cour constatera que les activités d'observation et d'information de la Colombie à des fins environnementales respectent

---

[54] *Activités armées sur le territoire du Congo (République démocratique du Congo c. Ouganda), demandes reconventionnelles, ordonnance du 29 novembre 2001, C.I.J. Recueil 2001*, p. 681, par. 46 ; *Application de la convention pour la prévention et la répression du crime de génocide (Bosnie-Herzégovine c. Yougoslavie), demandes reconventionnelles, ordonnance du 17 décembre 1997, C.I.J. Recueil 1997*, p. 259, par. 38.

[55] *Projet Gabčíkovo-Nagymaros (Hongrie/Slovaquie), arrêt, C.I.J. Recueil 1997*, p. 41, par. 53 : «l'environnement n'est pas une abstraction, mais bien l'espace où vivent les êtres humains et dont dépendent la qualité de leur vie et leur santé, y compris pour les générations à venir».

[56] *Immunités et procédures pénales (Guinée équatoriale c. France), exceptions préliminaires, arrêt, C.I.J. Recueil 2018 (I)*, p. 308, par. 48.

[57] CR 2021/14, p. 16, par. 34 (Cepeda Espinosa) ; CR 2021/14, p. 35, par. 3-4, et p. 36-38, par. 9-14 (Boisson de Chazournes).

les droits souverains du Nicaragua (I) et que ces activités sont conformes aux obligations de prévention de la Colombie (II).

I. Les activités d'observation et d'information à des fins environnementales de la Colombie respectent les droits souverains du Nicaragua

8. Le régime de la zone économique exclusive, comme l'a souligné Sir Michael Wood[58], n'a jamais eu pour objectif d'exclure les droits d'Etats tiers en matière de protection de l'environnement. Il permet bel et bien l'exercice de tels droits. Contrairement à ce que prétend le Nicaragua, ce dernier ne jouit pas de juridiction «exclusive»[59] en matière de protection et de préservation du milieu marin en vertu de l'article 56 de la convention sur le droit de la mer. La juridiction de l'Etat côtier est explicitement liée aux autres «dispositions pertinentes de la convention», qui viennent apporter une «substance» à ladite juridiction[60].

9. Le régime de la zone économique exclusive ne peut, en effet, être lu en isolation clinique des règles pertinentes en matière de protection de l'environnement marin de la partie XII de la convention, laquelle lie le Nicaragua et reflète le droit coutumier. Ces règles, qui sont pleinement applicables à la zone économique exclusive, reconnaissent des obligations mais aussi des droits à tous les Etats — je dis bien à *tous* les Etats, n'en déplaise au professeur Lowe[61] — en matière de protection[62] et de préservation de l'environnement marin.

10. En outre, le Nicaragua, si prompt à citer ses «droits souverains», a insisté lourdement sur l'adjectif «souverain», comme pour suggérer une forme d'absolutisme. Il ne peut pourtant nier qu'il est obligé dans sa zone économique exclusive de «tenir dûment compte» des droits et intérêts des Etats tiers en vertu du droit international coutumier et de ses obligations conventionnelles tels que reflétés dans l'article 56 de la convention. Ces droits et intérêts ne sont pas des droits et intérêts à la carte comme l'insinue le Nicaragua. Ce dernier doit, là encore, «tenir *dûment* compte» de *tous* les droits et de *tous* les intérêts. Cette obligation de «tenir *dûment* compte» est inhérente au

---

[58] CR 2021/14, p. 25, par. 9 (Wood).

[59] CR 2021/13, p. 35-36, par. 29 (Pellet) ; CR 2021/17, p. 22, par. 35 (Pellet).

[60] Alexander Proelss, "The Law on the Exclusive Economic Zone in Perspective: Legal Status and Resolution of User Conflicts Revisited" (2012) 26 *Ocean Yearbook*, 87-112, p. 103.

[61] CR 2021/17, p. 43-44, par. 35-38 (Lowe).

[62] Article 56 1) *b)* iii) de la convention sur le droit de la mer.

«compromis»[63] que représente la zone économique exclusive dans le droit contemporain de la mer. Elle s'impose d'autant plus au regard de «l'importance» des droits et devoirs de l'Etat tiers concerné comme cela a été reconnu par le tribunal arbitral dans l'affaire de la *Chagos Marine Protected Area*[64].

11. La Colombie a expliqué à la Cour dans ses plaidoiries écrites et orales pourquoi les activités d'observation et d'information à des fins environnementales sont essentielles à la préservation des écosystèmes fragiles de la mer des Caraïbes, ainsi que pour les habitats et les droits des Raizals.

12. Ces activités ne violent pas les droits souverains du Nicaragua. L'observation et l'information ne constituent pas des actes inamicaux visant à empêcher le Nicaragua d'exercer ses droits souverains. Ce dernier peut exercer son droit d'observer et d'informer à des fins environnementales dans sa zone économique exclusive. De même, l'observation et l'information ne constituent pas par eux-mêmes des actes constitutifs de violations des droits souverains du Nicaragua. L'observation vise tout simplement à *évaluer* la situation écologique d'écosystèmes fragiles et nécessaires à la survie des Raizals. L'information, quant à elle, vise tout simplement à *alerter* sur les risques que certaines pratiques de pêche peuvent avoir sur la préservation des écosystèmes, ainsi que mon collègue Rodman Bundy le dira quand il montrera que les soi-disant incidents ne sont en rien étayés juridiquement.

13. Les droits de tout Etat côtier dans sa zone économique exclusive, y compris le Nicaragua, doivent être interprétés raisonnablement[65]. Or, il n'est pas raisonnable de la part du Nicaragua de chercher à empêcher la Colombie de mener des activités d'observation et d'information à des fins environnementales. Il est encore plus déraisonnable de voir dans ces activités des actes hostiles au Nicaragua et de nature à violer ses droits souverains. Qui plus est, ces activités d'observation et d'information bénéficient au Nicaragua, puisque les écosystèmes en cause sont interdépendants et partagés.

---

[63] C. Goodman, "Rights, Obligations, Prohibitions: A Practical Guide to Understanding Judicial Decisions on Coastal State Jurisdiction over Living Resources in the Exclusive Economic Zone" (2017) 33 *The International Journal of Marine and Coastal Law*, 1-27, p. 26.

[64] *Chagos Marine Protected Area (Maurice c. Royaume-Uni de Grande-Bretagne et d'Irlande du Nord)*, sentence, affaire CPA n° 2011-3, 18 mars 2015, par. 519.

[65] Affaire de l'*Arctic Sunrise (Royaume des Pays-Bas c. Fédération de Russie)*, sentence sur le fond, affaire CPA n° 2014-02, 14 août 2015, par. 327-328 ; *Affaire concernant le filetage à l'intérieur du golfe du Saint-Laurent*, sentence, 17 juin 1986, *Recueil des sentences arbitrales*, vol. XIX, p. 258-259.

14. L'observation et l'information à des fins environnementales, loin d'être illicites, permettent de garantir la coopération étroite et continue entre les nations dont le destin est de partager des écosystèmes interdépendants et fragiles. Elles permettent, en outre, à la Colombie de se conformer à ses obligations internationales en matière de protection de l'environnement.

II. Les activités d'observation et d'information de la Colombie à des fins environnementales visent à prévenir des dommages aux écosystèmes de la mer des Caraïbes

15. Le Nicaragua, fidèle à sa stratégie, a tenté de passer sous silence les obligations environnementales en cause dans le contexte du présent différend. Pourtant, ce sont ces obligations qui permettent de saisir toute la licéité des activités d'observation et d'information de la Colombie.

16. Parmi ces obligations[66], il y a bien entendu l'obligation de diligence requise en vertu du droit international coutumier de l'environnement. Votre Cour, à travers sa jurisprudence constante, a souligné l'importance de ces obligations[67]. La Cour a notamment insisté sur «la vigilance et la prévention» qui découlent de l'obligation de *due diligence* en raison du «caractère souvent irréversible des dommages causés à l'environnement»[68].

17. Les Etats, y compris le Nicaragua et la Colombie, sont tenus d'exercer vigilance et prévention en matière de protection de l'environnement marin et notamment pour des écosystèmes interdépendants. La vigilance et la prévention ne perdent certainement pas de leur importance lorsque les écosystèmes concernés se trouvent dans une ZEE. Des activités d'information et d'observation contribuent à la vigilance et à la prévention.

18. Le Nicaragua se présente devant vous et prétend et répète sans cesse qu'il a des droits souverains exclusifs en matière de protection de l'environnement dans sa ZEE, et cela en méconnaissant, comme je l'ai dit précédemment, les autres règles et principes applicables dans cet espace. Ce même Etat, qui est assez passif en matière de protection des écosystèmes fragiles, comme l'a reconnu la communauté scientifique et environnementale nicaraguayenne[69], reproche à un autre

---

[66] CR 2021/14, p. 43-46, par. 33-44 (Boisson de Chazournes).

[67] Voir, par exemple, *Certaines activités menées par le Nicaragua dans la région frontalière (Costa Rica c. Nicaragua)* et *Construction d'une route au Costa Rica le long du fleuve San Juan (Nicaragua c. Costa Rica), arrêt, C.I.J. Recueil 2015 (II)*, p. 706-707, par. 104.

[68] *Projet Gabčíkovo-Nagymaros (Hongrie/Slovaquie), arrêt, C.I.J. Recueil 1997*, p. 78, par. 140.

[69] Voir Commentaires de la Colombie sur les nouveaux documents produits par le Nicaragua, 9 septembre 2021, par. 20.

Etat, en l'occurrence la Colombie, de mener des activités licites d'observation et d'information à des fins environnementales. La logique du Nicaragua consiste, en fait, à favoriser le «*wait and see*» en matière environnementale. Cette logique consiste à demander aux Etats tiers, en vertu de son interprétation erronée du régime de la ZEE, de se soumettre à son bon vouloir unilatéral en matière de protection de l'environnement, et cela malgré les risques avérés qui pèsent sur les écosystèmes fragiles et les habitats des Raizals. Il ne fait guère de doute qu'une telle vision de la protection de l'environnement s'inscrit en porte-à-faux avec la vigilance et la prévention qui sont attendues des Etats en matière environnementale.

19. C'est aussi la vigilance et la prévention dans tous les espaces maritimes, y compris la ZEE, qui sont requises des Etats parties à la convention de Carthagène. Le Nicaragua a maintenant accepté que la convention de Carthagène s'applique et ne tente plus de réduire la portée de cet instrument conventionnel[70]. Il est difficile, en effet, en vertu des canons traditionnels de l'interprétation des traités, de faire abstraction du fait que cette convention contient des obligations positives pour les Etats parties[71]. Les canons du droit des traités rendent en outre sans effet le nouvel argument du Nicaragua selon lequel le protocole relatif aux zones et à la vie sauvage spécialement protégées[72] interdirait les activités d'observation et d'information de la Colombie. Ce protocole, que le Nicaragua a ratifié très récemment pour des raisons vraisemblablement opportunistes, n'est entré en vigueur pour le Nicaragua que le 3 juin 2021[73]. Il ne s'applique donc pas au présent différend. Par ailleurs, ledit protocole, qui a un objet spécifique, n'a pas et n'a jamais eu pour objet de se substituer à la convention de Carthagène. Il s'agit là donc d'une énième tentative douteuse du Nicaragua en vue de rendre illicite ce qui est licite dans le cadre de la convention de Carthagène.

---

[70] CR 2021/13, p. 35, par. 27 (Pellet).

[71] Convention de Carthagène, article 4 intitulé «Obligations générales».

[72] Protocole relatif aux zones et à la vie sauvage spécialement protégées, à la convention pour la protection et la mise en valeur du milieu marin dans la région des Caraïbes, 18 janvier 1990.

[73] Ministry of Foreign Affairs of Colombia, SPAW Protocol, list of signatures and ratifications, disponible à l'adresse suivante : https://www.cancilleria.gov.co/sites/default/files/FOTOS2020/protocolo_relativo_a_las_areas_y_flora_y_fauna_silvestres_especialmente_protegidas_del_convenio_para_la_proteccion_y_el_desarrollo_del_medio_marino_de_la_region_del_gran_caribe.pdf (consulté le 28 septembre 2021).

Conclusion

20. Madame la présidente, Mesdames et Messieurs les juges, vous l'aurez compris : la ZEE n'est pas une zone environnementale exclusive comme l'insinue le Nicaragua. Ce dernier, à travers ses écritures et ses deux tours de plaidoiries, vous a présenté une vision tronquée du régime de la ZEE. En outre, cette vision ne tient pas compte du caractère évolutif du droit international et de la nécessité d'interpréter le droit international à la lumière des préoccupations actuelles de la communauté internationale en matière de protection de l'environnement. De plus, elle s'éloigne fondamentalement de la notion de juridiction telle qu'interprétée par la Cour interaméricaine des droits de l'homme.

21. A l'heure où la communauté internationale dans son unanimité a accepté la nécessité de réaliser l'objectif du développement durable n° 14[74] dédié à la conservation des mers et ressources marines, la Cour se doit de déclarer les arguments du Nicaragua comme insoutenables, infondés et les rejeter purement et simplement. La Cour contribuera ainsi, comme elle l'a fait dans le passé, à la clarification de la portée du droit international relatif à la protection de l'environnement. Une telle contribution, qui n'implique pas pour la Cour de «légiférer», comme l'ont soutenu à tort les conseils du Nicaragua[75], serait significative et bienvenue à moins d'un an de la célébration du cinquantenaire de la conférence de Stockholm (Stockholm +50), laquelle a marqué le point de départ des normes et exigences environnementales auxquelles tous les Etats devraient se soumettre.

22. Mesdames et Messieurs les juges, je vous remercie de votre bienveillante attention. Madame la présidente, puis-je vous demander de donner la parole à M. Rodman Bundy ?

The PRESIDENT: I thank Professor Boisson de Chazournes. I now invite the next speaker, Mr. Rodman Bundy, to take the floor.

---

[74] ODD14 : «Conserver et exploiter de manière durable les océans, les mers et les ressources marines aux fins du développement durable», https://www.un.org/sustainabledevelopment/fr/oceans/ (consulté le 28 septembre 2021).

[75] CR 2021/17, p. 22, par. 36 (Pellet).

Mr. BUNDY:

COLOMBIA DID NOT VIOLATE NICARAGUA'S SOVEREIGN RIGHTS

Introduction

1. Thank you, Madam President, distinguished judges. In this presentation, I shall respond to Nicaragua's contentions concerning alleged violations of sovereign rights by Colombia's naval vessels and aircraft. This is the first strand of Nicaragua's claim. Professor Reisman will follow me with the second strand; the contiguous zone Decree. My presentation will be in four parts.

2. *First*, I will address Nicaragua's new "composite act" theory of liability that Professor Pellet advanced on Monday. *Second*, I will respond to what counsel had to say about pre-critical date events on Monday. These are the events that Nicaragua studiously avoided discussing in the first round. *Third*, I will turn to the jurisdictional issues in order to show that the arguments we heard two days ago from Professor Pellet do not change the fact that, under Article XXXI of the Pact, Colombia did not consent to the Court's jurisdiction over disputes concerning facts which, if established, would constitute breaches of international obligations after the Pact was no longer in force for Colombia. *Lastly*, I will take up the post-critical date alleged wrongful acts that counsel mentioned on Monday.

1. The alleged "pattern of conduct argument" and "composite act" argument

3. Nicaragua's case is based on a number of discrete alleged acts — 51 such acts over nine years, Mr. Reichler told us on Monday[76]. An average of less than six incidents per year. And even on Nicaragua's version of the facts each of these so-called "incidents" lasted no more than a few minutes. We have shown that the contemporary evidence, such as it is, does not support the proposition that any of these events rose to the level of a violation of Nicaragua's sovereign rights.

4. Recognizing the evidentiary fragility of its case, Nicaragua changed its tune in the Reply. There, Nicaragua claimed that, "[e]ven if Colombia might try to excuse some of these actions, it cannot avoid the conclusion that its behaviour, viewed as a whole, is internationally wrongful"[77].

---

[76] CR 2021/17, p. 36, para. 43 (Reichler).

[77] RN, para. 4.90.

5. This attempt to play down the actual facts in favour of a broad brush "pattern of conduct" approach is misplaced both factually and legally. Not only must Nicaragua demonstrate, based on proven facts and event-by-event, that Colombia violated its rights; it must also overcome the reality, attested to by the statements of its political and military leaders and the significant increase in its own fishing since the 2012 Judgment, that there was no pattern of wrongful conduct on the part of Colombia. Despite the efforts of Nicaragua's counsel, this Nicaragua has not done.

6. In the *Oil Platforms* case, the United States raised a similar argument. It advanced a generic claim to the effect that, as a result of an alleged cumulation of attacks on United States and other vessels in the Persian Gulf, Iran breached its obligation with respect to freedom of commerce and navigation that was the subject-matter of the dispute under Article X of the Treaty of Amity between those two countries. The Court rejected this approach in its 2003 Judgment. The Court stated the following:

> "The Court considers that, in the circumstances of this case, a generic claim of breach of Article X, paragraph 1, of the 1955 Treaty cannot be made out independently of the specific incidents whereby, it is alleged, the actions of Iran made the Persian Gulf unsafe for commerce and navigation, and specifically for commerce and navigation between the territories of the parties. However, [the Court continued] the examination in paragraph 120 above [— that was the paragraph where the Court had addressed each of the individual incidents — the examination in that paragraph] shows that none of them individually involved any interference with the commerce and navigation protected by the 1955 Treaty; accordingly the generic claim of the United States cannot be upheld"[78].

The same holds true in this case.

7. Two days ago, Professor Pellet seized yet another opportunity to change the nature of Nicaragua's case. He asserted that Colombia's acts can also be viewed as a breach consisting of a composite act under Article 15 of the Articles on State Responsibility. Now, this notion of a composite act was entirely new; it was not mentioned in Nicaragua's Application, nor in its Memorial nor in its Reply.

8. While Professor Pellet took you to the Commentary on Article 15, he neglected to mention that paragraph (2) of that Commentary notes that "Composite acts covered by article 15 are limited to breaches of obligations which concern some aggregate of conduct *and not individual acts as such*"

---

[78] *Oil Platforms (Islamic Republic of Iran* v. *United States of America), Judgment, I.C.J. Reports 2003*, pp. 217-218, para. 123.

(emphasis added). Here, we are dealing precisely with a number of individual acts — "incidents" to use Nicaragua's words — each of which Nicaragua advanced in its written pleadings as a violation of its sovereign rights. That is exactly the opposite of a composite act. Indeed, counsel was unable to say when the last act of this so-called "composite act" occurred although, on Nicaragua's theory of the case, it must have been well after the Pact of Bogotá ceased to be in force for Colombia. Moreover, my learned friend also passed over the Commentary's observation that examples of composite acts include genocide, apartheid, or crimes against humanity, systematic acts of racial discrimination and systematic acts of discrimination prohibited by a trade agreement[79]. Those examples are clearly legally different. They require a series of acts before a wrongful act is committed, and do not even remotely reflect what we are dealing with in the present case.

9. Thus, it is to the individual acts alleged by Nicaragua that we must turn. And Nicaragua's eleventh-hour tactic in advancing a "composite act" theory, which combines pre-critical date and post-critical date events, is no more than a rather transparent effort to overcome the temporal limits to the Court's jurisdiction contained in the Pact's compromissory clause — Article XXXI. As I shall show, this tactic is unavailing.

2. Pre-critical date events

10. I now turn to the pre-critical date events that Mr. Reichler belatedly discussed on Monday. In doing so, it is useful to recall that Nicaragua's Application made no reference, nor attached any annexes, dealing with any specific "incident" that involved interference by Colombia with the exercise by Nicaragua of its sovereign rights.

11. Instead, the documentation furnished by Nicaragua mostly concerned statements made by political or military officials — statements which, in themselves, do not constitute a violation of Nicaragua's sovereign rights. Moreover, we now have, as Sir Michael said, a new Nicaraguan submission in which it requests the Court to remain seised of the case until Colombia recognizes and respects Nicaragua's rights in the Caribbean Sea. But the Applicant forgets that, as the Court itself noted at paragraph 106 of its 2016 Judgment on the preliminary objections, "Nicaragua denies that

[79] Draft Articles on State Responsibility for Internationally Wrongful Acts, Art. 15, para. 2 of the Commentary.

its Application . . . represents an attempt to obtain post adjudication enforcement measures”[80]. That denial sits badly with Nicaragua’s new submission.

12. The first pre-critical date act that Mr. Reichler mentioned on Monday is claimed to have involved a Nicaraguan lobster boat, the *Miss Sofia*. Counsel asserted that the boat was chased away by a Colombian vessel, after which it radioed a Nicaraguan vessel for help, and that two men, whom the Colombian Navy subsequently rescued, had fallen over during this “incident”[81].

13. Now with respect, Madam President, this version of events is a product of Mr. Reichler’s rather fertile imagination. The only source counsel cited to support his account was the famous 26 August 2014 letter from Admiral Corrales to Nicaragua’s Foreign Ministry, prepared some 18 months after the event is alleged to have taken place, and *one day* before Admiral Corrales himself expressly affirmed that “we have not had any problems with the Colombian Navy”[82].

14. The 26 August 2014 letter contained no contemporaneous evidence to support the allegations. There is also no mention whatsoever that the two crew members on the lobster boat had fallen off during the incident. Regrettably, that again seems to be invention on counsel’s part. In contrast, Colombia produced as Annex 53 to its Counter-Memorial a naval report prepared just three days after the event — a contemporaneous report — recounting what had actually happened. The Colombian naval vessel had no contact with the *Miss Sofia*. Rather, it encountered two people set adrift in a canoe who said they were crew members of the *Miss Sofia* lobster boat and the Colombian Navy rescued them. The Colombian vessel then tried to contact the *Miss Sofia*, but the lobster boat failed to respond. So the Colombian vessel then contacted a Nicaraguan patrol boat that could also not reach the *Miss Sofia*, which had mysteriously disappeared abandoning two of its crewmen. Thereafter, the Nicaraguan patrol boat said that it would receive the two crewmen from Colombia, but later changed its mind and indicated that the crewmen could be received by yet a different vessel, which the Colombian Navy did after giving the crewmen food and medical attention. That is a violation of Nicaragua’s sovereign rights? I think not.

---

[80] *Alleged Violations of Sovereign Rights and Maritime Spaces in the Caribbean Sea (Nicaragua* v. *Colombia), Preliminary Objections, Judgment, I.C.J. Reports 2016 (I)*, p. 40, para. 106.

[81] CR 2021/17, p. 25, paras. 11-12 (Reichler).

[82] Preliminary Objections of Colombia, Ann. 43.

15. Mr. Reichler next mentioned an event dated 18 September 2013 reported on Colombian radio as to which he claimed that President Santos was conducting a "'sovereignty exercise' in the waters between San Andrés and the 82nd [degree] meridian"[83]. Regrettably, this too is a distortion. The media report nowhere mentions the 82nd meridian or any exercise of sovereignty up to it. The document in question simply reports President Santos saying: "We are patrolling and exercising sovereignty on Colombian waters."[84] No more, no less. How Mr. Reichler can assert right after quoting this passage that "[e]xercising sovereignty in Nicaragua's EEZ is plainly a violation of Nicaragua's sovereign rights"[85] is not only a *non sequitur*, it is also unsupported by the very report he relies on.

16. Mr. Reichler's last pre-critical date "incident" was described by Nicaragua as having taken place on 19 February 2013 when the Colombian vessel the *Almirante Padilla* was claimed to have prevented a Nicaraguan vessel from inspecting a Colombian fishing vessel in the Luna Verde area[86]. But Colombia produced the navigation logbook of the *Almirante Padilla* showing that, on the day in question, that is, 19 February 2013, the Colombian Naval vessel was berthed at the Cartagena Naval Base which is over 800 kilometres away![87] It could not have done what counsel asserts.

17. That is the sum total of the pre-critical date "incidents" that Mr. Reichler chose to discuss, presumably because he felt they represented Nicaragua's best examples. It is a pretty thin soup, Madam President. They amount to nothing, and are an undocumented, unsupported nothing at just that. As I noted last week, there were no Nicaraguan complaints at the time or for well over a year afterwards. To the contrary, the statements of Nicaragua's President, its Head of the Naval Forces and its Chief of the Army in 2013 fundamentally undermine any notion that Nicaragua considered that its sovereign rights had somehow been violated. So much for the pre-critical date events on which the Application was founded.

---

[83] CR 2021/17, p. 27, para. 17 (Reichler).

[84] MN, Ann. 5.

[85] CR 2021/17, p. 27, para. 17 (Reichler).

[86] MN, para. 2.39.

[87] CMC, Ann. 31.

3. Lack of jurisdiction over post-critical date events

18. I turn to the post-critical date events now starting with the question of jurisdiction.

19. Last week I noted that, in considering the scope of the Court's jurisdiction *ratione temporis*, Nicaragua's counsel had completely avoided even mentioning Article XXXI of the Pact in their first round. They preferred to rely exclusively on Article LVI. This was rather surprising given that Nicaragua expressly stated in paragraph 16 of its Application: "The jurisdiction of the Court in this case is based on Article XXXI of the American Treaty on Pacific Settlement (Pact of Bogotá) of 30 April 1948."

20. On Monday, Professor Pellet at last addressed Article XXXI, but only to say that it adds nothing to Article LVI[88], and that Article XXXI only concerns the Court's jurisdiction *ratione materiae*[89].

21. To borrow Professor Pellet's words, that is a "bizarre" thesis. First, the two Articles clearly deal with different matters: Article LVI with the denunciation of the Pact and its consequences; Article XXXI with the scope of the Contracting Parties' consent to the Court's jurisdiction. Contrary to my friend's contention, Article XXXI is scarcely limited to jurisdiction *ratione materiae*. It covers jurisdiction *ratione personae* — "the High Contracting Parties declare that they recognize . . . [the Court's jurisdiction]". It deals with jurisdiction *ratione temporis*, "without the necessity of any special agreement so long as the present Treaty is in force". And it deals with jurisdiction *ratione materiae* — sub-paragraphs *(a)* through *(d)* of Article XXXI.

22. Counsel's whole thesis is based on two propositions. The first is based on the second paragraph of Article LVI, that provides: "The denunciation shall have no effect with respect to pending procedures initiated prior to the transmission of the particular notification." The second proposition is that the Court can take into consideration facts that are alleged to have taken place after the filing of the application provided they are directly connected with the subject-matter of the Application. Neither of those propositions withstands scrutiny in the light of the actual wording of Article XXXI.

---

[88] CR 2021/17, p. 15, para. 16 (Pellet).

[89] CR 2021/17, p. 16, para. 18 (Pellet).

23. Colombia has no problem with Article LVI. Colombia accepts that the Court has jurisdiction over the claims that formed the basis for Nicaragua's Application — namely, alleged wrongful acts of Colombia that existed as of the date of the Application — pre-critical date events. However, the Court's 2016 Judgment on Colombia's preliminary objections —and contrary to counsel for Nicaragua's suggestion — while upholding the Court's jurisdiction over matters that were the subject of Nicaragua's Application, in no way prejudged the question of its jurisdiction over post-treaty facts.

24. On Monday, counsel questioned why Colombia had not advanced the jurisdictional position it takes with respect to post-treaty facts in its preliminary objections[90]. The answer is straightforward. This question depended on how Nicaragua was framing and was to frame its case and the materials it would introduce to support that case. We have seen that Nicaragua's case has consistently evolved from a claim based on a series of discrete acts, to a "continuing violation" theory, to a "pattern of conduct" argument, and finally, just on Monday, to a "composite act" thesis. Moreover, this evolution has been accompanied by the repeated introduction of new documents and new so-called "facts", and in these circumstances, the question of jurisdiction over post-treaty facts was closely connected to the merits of the case and did not have an exclusively preliminary character making it ripe for a preliminary objection.

25. Professor Pellet's Article LVI does not exist in a vacuum. It must be read in conjunction with Article XXXI, which after all is the provision actually providing for the Court's jurisdiction. This is where Nicaragua's case falls down.

26. Notwithstanding the text of Article XXXI, Nicaragua's counsel continued to argue that the Court's jurisprudence stands for the proposition that it has jurisdiction to consider facts and events introduced subsequent to the filing of the Application provided they are connected to facts and events already falling within the Court's jurisdiction and that they do not transform the nature of the dispute. But that is not the key question. Quite simply, none of the cases — *none of the cases* — cited by my opponents to support their argument deal with a compromissory clause drafted in the way that Article XXXI is, and they are not apposite to the situation we have here.

---

[90] CR 2021/17, p. 16, para. 17 (Pellet).

27. Take the *Certain Property* case. On that, on Monday, Professor Pellet was economical. He simply stated that that case concerned facts that predated the acceptance of jurisdiction by the two parties and thus the question posed concerned the retroactive exercise of jurisdiction[91]. But what my opponent failed to grapple with was the point I made last week: namely, if the Court had no jurisdiction over facts that were alleged to have occurred before there was a title of jurisdiction between the Parties, why would the situation be different with respect to jurisdiction over facts that are claimed to have transpired after the treaty was no longer in force between the Parties and there was thus no longer any applicable jurisdictional title? No answer from counsel on that point.

28. I will not come back at any length to Professor Pellet's treatment of the other cases I mentioned last week — the *Fisheries Jurisdiction* case and the *Legality of the Use of Force* case. Suffice it to note that my distinguished *contradicteur's* response was equally thin. Once again, he failed to address the critical point, which is that neither of the instruments which the Applicant relied on for jurisdictional purposes in those cases contained a temporal limitation to the Parties' consent to jurisdiction like that in Article XXXI. As the Court observed many years ago in the *Anglo-Iranian Oil Co.* case, and I think it still holds true today, "the jurisdiction of the Court to deal with and decide a case on the merits depends on the will of the Parties"[92]. Here, the will of the Parties with respect to jurisdiction *ratione temporis* was clearly expressed in Article XXXI. That consent only existed with respect to facts or claims that could constitute a breach of an international obligation as long as the Pact remained in force. But after 27 November 2013, the Pact was no longer in force for Colombia.

29. In its written pleadings, Nicaragua relied heavily on what it termed the "*Nottebohm* rule", which the Court recalled in its Order on the admissibility of Colombia's counter-claims in the following way: "Once the Court has established jurisdiction to entertain a case, it has jurisdiction to deal with all its phases; the subsequent lapse of the title cannot deprive the Court of its jurisdiction."[93] Again, Colombia has no problem with that, and while counsel did not return to this case on Monday, it is instructive for purposes of the jurisdictional issue before the Court to have a closer look at that case.

---

[91] CR 2021/17, p. 17, para. 20 (Pellet).

[92] *Anglo-Iranian Oil Co. (United Kingdom* v. *Iran), Preliminary Objection, Judgment, I.C.J. Reports 1952*, p. 103.

[93] *Alleged Violations of Sovereign Rights and Maritime Spaces in the Caribbean Sea (Nicaragua* v. *Colombia), Counter-Claims, Order of 15 November 2017, I.C.J. Reports 2017*, p. 310, para. 67.

30. Jurisdiction to deal with a dispute over the legal consequences of facts that are in existence during the period when a jurisdictional title exists is not the same thing as ruling on the legal consequences of facts that occur *after* a compromissory clause has lapsed. That is not tantamount to a "phase" of the case, such as a request for provisional measures, or the written or oral phases of the proceedings. Nicaragua is asking the Court to rule on the legality of events that are said to have occurred at a time when the Pact no longer applied as between Nicaragua and Colombia. In *Nottebohm*, the Court was not called upon to decide the legality of any events that transpired after Guatemala's optional clause declaration was no longer operative. Indeed, the Court noted in its Judgment that an Application filed after the expiration of Guatemala's declaration would not have had the effect of legally seising the Court[94].

31. Just as the Court would not have been legally seised if Nicaragua had filed a separate case relating to events occurring after 27 November 2013, so also Nicaragua cannot overcome the temporal limitation to Colombia's consent contained in Article XXXI by attempting to tack such events onto a pre-existing case. That is a stratagem by which Nicaragua is seeking to evade the basic principle of consent to jurisdiction.

32. Last week, I noted that Nicaragua's counsel had not pointed to a single case where the Court has exercised jurisdiction with respect to the legality of a State's conduct when that conduct occurred at a time when there was no applicable jurisdictional title in force between the parties to the case[95]. On Monday, Nicaragua's counsel were unable to counter that statement.

33. The key point is that, to the extent Nicaragua relies on facts or events that transpired after the Pact ceased to be in force for Colombia, the Court lacks jurisdiction *ratione temporis* to decide whether they constitute a breach of an international obligation.

4. There were no post-critical date breaches in any event

34. So let me last turn to the post-critical date events that Mr. Reichler came back to on Monday, notwithstanding the jurisdictional argument. A good part of Mr. Reichler's presentation consisted in rehashing nine "incidents" that he had discussed last week. But before turning to those

---

[94] *Nottebohm (Liechtenstein* v. *Guatemala), Preliminary Objection, Judgment, I.C.J. Reports 1953*, p. 121.

[95] CR 2021/15, p. 18, para. 46 (Bundy).

matters, it is important to recall what counsel was *not* able to show in order to keep Nicaragua's claims in context.

35. The point I would emphasize is that *none* of the events discussed by counsel showed any interference or hostile actions on the part of Colombia's Navy with respect to the activities of Nicaragua's fishermen, who were always able to carry out their activities. Nor did Colombia ever prevent Nicaragua from exercising its sovereign rights with respect to the exploration and exploitation of the resources in maritime areas where it has such rights. Despite the fact that counsel last week stated that he was addressing what he called the "more egregious of these actions of the Colombian Navy"[96], counsel's presentation of individual "incidents" — both last week and again on Monday — failed to demonstrate the contrary. Certainly, none of Mr. Reichler's nine "incidents", or any of the other events he discussed, show any such interference by Colombia on Nicaragua or its fishermen's ability to carry out their activities.

36. Instead — and this is quite striking — the incidents on which Mr. Reichler dwelled all had a common theme. If you flip though the tabs that counsel redirected you to on Monday, you will see that in most of them the Colombian Navy said it was there to protect the historic fishing rights of the Colombian State, provide security for all vessels and combat international crime. In certain others, the statements only refer to the protection of the historic rights of the fishermen.

37. Nicaragua takes no issue with the presence of Colombia's vessels for purposes of providing security to all vessels. There is no breach of any sovereign rights there. Nor does Nicaragua contest the right of Colombia's Navy to monitor the situation for international criminal activities, such as the transport of narcotics or arms. On Monday, Nicaragua's distinguished Agent confirmed what Nicaragua had in fact already said in its Reply, that "Nicaragua does not object that Colombia should take measures for the control of the criminal activities that might occur in the Caribbean, particularly drug trafficking"[97].

38. It follows that Nicaragua's case with respect to alleged violations of its rights boils down to only one thing: Colombia's presence in the area to protect the historical fishing rights of Colombia and its nationals, which Mr. Reichler asserted, in itself, constitutes a violation of Nicaragua's

---

96 CR 2021/13, p. 51, para. 29 (Reichler).

97 CR 2021/17, p. 49, para. 12 (Argüello Gómez).

sovereign rights[98]. But once again on this point, counsel failed to respond to what I had pointed out last week.

39. We have shown that Nicaragua's President, it's Head of State, was on record at the time as stating the following: "I told President Santos, and I have said publicly, that the [Raizales] can continue fishing. That Nicaragua will not affect them in their Rights"[99]. And he also stated that Nicaragua would authorize fishing in the area where Colombian traditionally fished, "both artisanal and industrial fisheries"[100].

40. Colombia was entitled to rely on the good faith of those statements that were directed at the highest level to Colombia's Head of State from none other than Nicaragua's Head of State. But the problem was that Nicaragua's naval forces did not respect the promises of its own president. They continued to approach Colombian fishermen and harassed them. And in these circumstances, it was entirely reasonable for the Colombian Navy to take President Ortega at his word and to offer protection to the fishermen as needed and when it could do so, without at the same time interfering at all with Nicaragua's own fishing or other activities. And that, in Colombia's submission, does not amount to a violation of Nicaragua's sovereign rights.

41. As for the other "incidents" that Mr. Reichler mentioned on Monday, they too have been presented unfortunately in a misleading manner.

42. For example, Nicaragua alleges that a Colombian vessel ordered a Nicaraguan-licensed fishing vessel, the *Doña Emilia*, to stop fishing. This was one of the events Mr. Reichler returned to on Monday[101]. This event was addressed by us in Appendix 1 to the Rejoinder (pp. 56-57), and the transcript of the audio recording shows that, even though the Nicaraguan fishing boat was carrying out clearly predatory fishing practices, Colombia did no more than to advise the crew to suspend those harmful practices[102]. There was no "order" and no interference with their fishing. In fact, Colombia's officers even informed the fishermen about the need to protect and preserve the species

---

[98] CR 2021/17, p. 31, para. 27 (Reichler).

[99] CR 2021/15, p. 19, para. 49 (Bundy).

[100] CR 2021/15, p. 19, para. 49 (Bundy).

[101] CR 2021/13, p. 53, para. 34 (Reichler) and CR 2021/17, p. 31, para. 28 (Reichler).

[102] RN, Ann. 32, p. 405.

for their children. Mere informatory statements like this do not amount to a violation of sovereign rights.

43. Counsel also referred to a matter involving a fishing vessel for Colombia, the *Miss Dolores*, with respect to which a Colombian naval vessel was claimed to have warned off a Nicaraguan patrol boat[103]. But counsel was unable to show that the *Miss Dolores* was even fishing in Nicaragua's waters because the date and the location of the event were unascertainable and have not been evidenced at all by anything Nicaragua has produced. It follows that Nicaragua has simply not sustained any burden of proof that its sovereign rights were infringed in this instance.

44. As for Nicaragua's reliance on the 10 December 2018 matter involving the *Observer*, I explained last week how our opponents' version of events is badly skewed[104]. Mr. Reichler agrees, finally, that, contrary to what he asserted last week, the captain of the *Observer* never admitted he was fishing in areas where Nicaragua has sovereign rights. Mr. Reichler now says it was the owner who admitted as much[105]. But the owner was not even on the *Observer* and he had absolutely no first-hand evidence of what happened. Moreover, to support his argument, counsel referred to a document mentioned in a footnote to his pleading — again pleading by footnote — a document that is not on the record[106], and that Nicaragua has not produced or shown is published or readily available, and for which there is no translation in one of the official languages of the Court. All of this is in complete non-compliance with Practice Direction 9*bis* of the Court, that renders any such reference inadmissible and unreliable, because even if it had been properly produced, Colombia should be given, under Practice Direction 9*bis*, the right to comment; none of that has happened.

45. Mr. Reichler also returned to an episode that is said to have involved a Colombian vessel interfering with a Mexican research ship[107]. But this, again, was a non-event. Colombia's 16 December 2019 letter to the Court, which was in response to new documents filed by Nicaragua and which was not referred to by counsel, explained that the official correspondence from the Mexican authority to which the research vessel was affiliated — an organization called

---

[103] CR 2021/17, p. 32, para. 31 (Reichler).

[104] CR 2021/15, pp. 19-20, paras. 52-53 (Bundy).

[105] CR 2021/17, p. 34, para. 37 (Reichler).

[106] CR 2021/13, p. 56, para. 43, and fn. 145 (Reichler).

[107] CR 2021/17, p. 35, para. 42 (Reichler).

INAPESCA — confirmed itself that the vessel carried out its scientific research work without interference. Hence, no Mexican protest.

46. And as for the matter of the claim that Colombia has violated Nicaragua's sovereign rights through the issuances of petroleum contracts, counsel now concedes that no such contracts have been issued[108]. So where is the violation of Nicaragua's sovereign rights?

47. And as for the assertion that Colombia issued a fishing licence for one of its registered boats to fish in the Luna Verde bank — and this my final point, Madam President — counsel had no response to my showing that the document Nicaragua relies on was not a fishing permit: it was only an authorization for the boat to be affiliated with a particular person's fishing fleet. But in any event, Mr. Reichler observed on Monday, "this case does not turn on Colombia's fishing licences"[109]. We agree. So even if the Court had jurisdiction over post-critical events, *quod non*, there were no breaches.

Madam President, distinguished judges, thank you for your attention. That concludes my presentation, and I would be grateful if the floor could be given to Professor Reisman. Thank you very much.

The PRESIDENT: I thank Mr. Bundy. I now invite the next speaker, Professor Michael Reisman, to take the floor.

Mr. REISMAN: Thank you, Madam President.

The contiguous zone of Colombia in the south-western Caribbean is lawful

1. Madam President, Members of the Court, it is an honour to appear before you on behalf of the Republic of Colombia. I will focus on Nicaragua's main arguments against the contiguous zone. In brief, contrary to Nicaragua's claims, the overlap is lawful, the simplification is lawful and the powers are lawful. In sum, Nicaragua has failed to prove that Decree 1946 violated any Colombian obligation towards it.

---

[108] CR 2021/17, p. 24, para. 9 (Reichler).

[109] CR 2021/17, p. 35, para. 41 (Reichler).

2. The powers exercised by a State in its contiguous zone attach, as of right, to the territorial sea and form part of that régime. These powers encompass *two* functions. Both concern the infringement of the State's protective laws within its territory and territorial sea. First, with respect to outbound activities, a State may punish perpetrators of such violations within its territory and territorial sea. Second, the inbound power concerns preventing perpetrators from executing violations within its territory or territorial sea. These powers do not "control" shipping or apply its laws in the contiguous zone as Nicaragua suggested[110], are entirely unrelated to other States' maritime resource rights and do not produce any adverse effects on any user. That is, of course, except for those who will or have violated Colombia's protective laws and regulations in its territory or territorial sea.

3. In its second pleading, Nicaragua quoted, very selectively, from the Decree's introduction, before — to use Nicaragua's words — turning to "[t]he Decree itself"[111]. Selectivity enables Nicaragua to focus on the vague reference to the contiguous zone as part of Colombia while ignoring the words "in accordance with international law". Even more egregiously, Nicaragua quotes two introductory paragraphs, excluding the bridging paragraph and distorting its meaning.

4. Consider the missing quotation and its effect.

5. Together both paragraphs not only condition the contiguous zone powers to "in accordance with customary international law", but also make clear that the place of those powers is within the territory and the territorial sea and not the zone itself. Nicaragua's repetition that the Decree enforces Colombia's laws in the contiguous zone is incorrect[112].

6. "The Decree itself" provides in Article 5: "Prevent and control infractions of the laws and regulations . . . which take place in its insular territories or in their territorial sea". Like any other contiguous zone, there is no "control" of "foreign shipping", or regulation of the EEZ's environment, as Nicaragua suggests[113].

7. Three points must be emphasized. First, contiguous zone powers are not exclusive and require neither delimitation, delineation nor even proclamation. Second, the simplification of the

[110] CR 2021/17, pp. 40-41, para. 17, p. 42, para. 27, and pp. 44-45, paras. 37 and 43 (Lowe).

[111] CR 2021/17, p. 39, para. 8 (Lowe).

[112] See e.g. CR 2021/17, pp. 44-45, paras. 37, 41, 42 and 43 (Lowe).

[113] CR 2021/17, pp. 40-41, para. 17 (Lowe).

contiguous zone is lawful and causes no injury to Nicaragua — by contrast with its straight baselines which Professor Thouvenin will deal with. Third, the powers in the Decree directed at preventing and punishing the infringement of the security, environment and cultural heritage within Colombia's territory or territorial sea are not "additions" to the terms in UNCLOS Article 33, but simply their elaboration.

8. Madam President, from the *Anglo-Norwegian Fisheries* case on, the Court has adjusted the Law of the Sea to maintain a balance between inclusive and exclusive uses. Both EEZ rights and contiguous zone rights are permissible uses. Contiguous zone powers are inclusive, as they may be exercised by various States in the same location, without interfering with the rights of the other users — whether exclusive or not. The EEZ does not "outrank" the contiguous zone. Both concern distinct and different rights having the *same normative force*. When occurring in the same space, they do not cancel each other out.

A. Inclusive contiguous zone powers may lawfully co-exist with exclusive EEZ rights

9. Nicaragua portrays the contiguous zone as a zone which trumps or excludes all the rights of other users because it has a spatial extent. Indeed, a contiguous zone does have a spatial extent, but it is inherently different from exclusive jurisdictions, such as the EEZ régime.

10. When a State's territorial sea abuts the EEZ of another State, its contiguous zone perforce extends into the EEZ of the latter. There is no conflict because the EEZ State's resource rights are substantially different from the contiguous zone State's "prevent and punish" powers. Keep in mind that the contiguous zone is a set of rights and not a conveyance of space. In its second round, Nicaragua artfully argued that "[w]hat Nicaragua actually says is that a State's contiguous zone may not extend for more than 24 nautical miles from the baseline, and that in any event it must stop at the State's international maritime boundary". Left unsaid is that the "boundary" for the purposes of contiguous zone powers is the outer limit of another State's territorial sea, as confirmed by the proclamation of the United States I quoted last week[114]. So Nicaragua, arguing circularly, in effect

[114] CR 2021/15, pp. 27-28, para. 17 (Reisman).

has no reasoned argument to support its denial of a contiguous zone for Colombia's islands' fronting Nicaragua's EEZ.

11. Nicaragua asserted that Colombia only offered a single authority to support the proposition of a permissible overlap between a contiguous zone and an EEZ[115]. Nicaragua errs. This passage, from a contemporary 1984 report by the Commonwealth Group of Experts, was offered as the explanation for the removal of the delimitation provision by the authoritative Virginia Commentary[116]. But Nicaragua misreads the Commentary, overlooking paragraph 33.8 *(c)*, which explains that: "There is nothing in article 33 corresponding to article 16, and there is no specific requirement for notice to be given of the establishment of a contiguous zone for the purposes indicated in article 33". No specific requirement for notice.

12. UNCLOS and the Commentary recognized that contiguous zone powers are not exclusive, do not affect the protected rights of others, and require no delimitation, delineation or even publication. For a coastal State's exclusive jurisdictions which affect the rights of others, UNCLOS requires publishing detailed charts depicting their spatial extent.

13. For example, Article 16 mandates that the coastal State publish charts or geographical coordinates for the territorial sea and baselines, "of a scale or scales adequate for ascertaining their position". They must be made public and deposited with the United Nations.

14. Articles 47, 75, and 84 on archipelagic baselines, the EEZ, the continental shelf and the outer continental shelf, which are in tab 6 of your folder, are to the same effects.

15. The reasons for such requirements are clear. These exclusive jurisdictions perforce affect the rights of other users, who must know their precise locations if they are to respect them. But there is no need for comparable notice for contiguous zone powers, which concern violations of laws *within* the territorial sea or territory of the contiguous zone State.

16. Given the nature of contiguous zone powers, the effects of their exercise on another State or user are minimal, if not non-existent. As I explained last week, the freedom of navigation does not include violating Colombia's protective laws in its territorial sea. As evident from Article 111 on

---

[115] CR 2021/17, p. 45, para. 44 (Lowe).

[116] Myron H. Nordquist, Satya N. Nandan and Shabtai Rosenne (eds.), *United Nations Convention on the Law of the Sea, 1982: A Commentary*, pp. 273-274, para. 33.8 (hereinafter Virginia Commentary).

hot pursuit, where a State defines the extent of its contiguous zone, it is primarily to direct the activities of its law enforcement officers when they are called on to prevent and punish such violations.

17. It is therefore clear that contiguous zone powers, which require no delineation, no publication and no delimitation, may lawfully co-exist with exclusive EEZ rights of an adjacent State. The focus of these powers is the State's own territory and territorial sea. In any event, the Court should approve the overlap in the unique circumstances of this case, given the location of the islands and their fragile marine environment.

B. The simplification of the contiguous zone is lawful

18. Nicaragua accepts that simplifications may be lawful, but objects to Colombia's simplification because it extends beyond 24 nautical miles[117].

19. Simplifications of the extent of these inclusive powers should be allowed when three conditions are met. First, when they promise efficient management by the contiguous zone State. Second, when they impose no deprivations on other users. And third, when they are modest and not excessive. The simplification provided by Colombia's Decree 1946, as amended, meets these conditions and should be allowed.

20. As Colombia explained, the simplification ensures that Colombian authorities may effectively prevent and punish violations of its protective laws in its territory or territorial sea. As a question of fact[118], the practical application problems generated by the tangle of interconnected arcs generated by these islands has been confirmed by this Court[119]. Second, the simplification of the contiguous zone, most of which falls in Colombia's EEZ, imposes no limits on the rights of others. Thus, Nicaraguan vessels may conduct their activities within the simplified contiguous zone and encounter no interference, indeed, be oblivious to the Decree.

---

[117] CR 2021/17, p. 40, para. 14 (Lowe).

[118] CR 2021/17, pp. 40-41, paras. 16-17 (Lowe).

[119] *Territorial and Maritime Dispute (Nicaragua* v. *Colombia), Judgment, I.C.J. Reports 2012 (II)*, p. 710, para. 235.

21. If contiguous zone powers impacted the rights of others, as Nicaragua asserts[120], there would have been a requirement to give notice or to publicize their spatial extent. Yet none exists[121]. This shows why the contiguous zone powers have a limited effect, if any, on the rights of other States. Given that the simplification of the Archipelago's contiguous zone portends no effect on others, or specifically, on Nicaragua, it should enjoy a wider margin of discretion than that of baselines, which is the question of law[122].

22. One last point on simplification. In its first and second pleading, as well as its written submissions, Nicaragua relied upon a sketch of Colombia's contiguous zone presented as an illustration in a televised press conference by former President Santos and on a purported map Nicaragua produced by itself[123]. But none is accurate since Colombia did not finalize the localization of its baselines. The only relevant map, for illustrative purposes, is the one produced by Colombia and is tab 7 of your folders. But as international law does not require the publication of a detailed map or even notice of a contiguous zone establishment, a televised map cannot be dispositive.

C. The powers in Decree 1946, as amended, are lawful

23. Nicaragua only disputes the Decree's powers of security and environment[124]. I will focus on them. But I must note that Colombia's contiguous zone obligation within Nicaragua's EEZ is to have "due regard" to the EEZ rights and jurisdictions when applying the Decree.

24. Nicaragua has failed to produce proof that the Decree has ever been applied against it, or that it has suffered any injury. Nicaragua's examples, whatever their value, do not, except one, even relate to events in the contiguous zone. Without regard to the absence of incidents, Nicaragua's claims that the mere promulgation of Decree 1946 *ipso facto* violated its rights because it may have a chilling effect on its claimed EEZ rights is wrong[125].

---

[120] CR 2021/17, p. 42, para. 27 (Lowe).

[121] UNCLOS, Art. 16; Virginia Commentary, p. 274.

[122] CR 2021/17, p. 40, para. 16 (Lowe).

[123] CR 2021/13, judges' folder, tab 7 (Reichler-5 and Reichler-6) (Reichler); CR 2021/13, judges' folder, tab 35 (VL1-4), tab 36 (VL1-5) and tab 39 (VL1-8) (Lowe); CR 2021/17, judges' folder, tab VL-2 (VL2-7) (Lowe).

[124] CR 2021/13, p. 71, para. 52 (Lowe).

[125] CR 2021/17, pp. 42, para. 27 (Lowe).

25. But just what is chilled? In the area in which it claims EEZ rights, Nicaragua enjoys no preferential freedoms of navigation beyond those availing other users. In the remote case of a conflict between activities implementing Decree 1946 and Nicaragua's EEZ rights, which are unrelated, those would be solved by the "due regard" obligation, as EEZ rights and contiguous zone rights are equal in normative force.

26. Nicaragua's proposition that there could be a theoretical chilling effect on its fishing activities due to the mere promulgation of contiguous zone powers may be quickly disposed of. First, Decree 1946, as amended, does not address fishing. Second, Nicaragua assumes the Decree would be misapplied by Colombia. Yet every State is entitled to the presumption that it will abide by its international obligations and apply the Decree in conformity with international law, as the Decree prescribes. Third, a theoretical chilling effect in a particular instance does not automatically justify denying Colombia the right to effectively protect its islands and territorial sea.

27. Nicaragua seems to accept that the terms in Article 33, dating back over seventy years to the ILC's 1956 draft, are generic and their interpretation may evolve[126]. But it muddles the rules for identifying custom and those for interpretation[127]. Evolutionary interpretation concerns the rules of interpretation as a recent ILC report made clear[128], not practice and *opinio juris*.

28. The terms mentioned in Article 33 were not defined in 1956, nor in 1958, nor the 1982 Convention. So determining their contemporary scope, one has to take account of the development of international law. Viewed in these terms, Decree 1946, as amended, does not add to the powers in UNCLOS Article 33, but simply provides an elaboration of these powers originating more than half a century ago.

29. In the Namibia Advisory Opinion, you explained that "the Court must take into consideration the changes which have occurred in the supervening half-century" and that

---

[126] CR 2021/17, p. 41, para. 19 (Lowe).

[127] CR 2021/17, p. 41, para. 19 (Lowe).

[128] ILC, *Draft conclusions on subsequent agreements and subsequent practice in relation to the interpretation of treaties, with commentaries*, 2018, UN doc. A/73/10, available at https://legal.un.org/ilc/texts/instruments/english/commentaries/1_11_2018.pdf.

"an international instrument has to be interpreted and applied within the framework of the entire legal system prevailing at the time of the interpretation"[129].

The PRESIDENT: Mr. Reisman, may I kindly interrupt you before you continue, as it appears that it would be a good time to adjourn for a coffee break of 10 minutes.

Mr. REISMAN: Thank you, Madam President, I will recess.

The PRESIDENT: The sitting is adjourned.

The Court adjourned from 4.35 p.m. to 4.50 p.m.

The PRESIDENT: Please be seated. I now give the floor back to Professor Reisman to continue his presentation.

Mr. REISMAN:

30. Thank you, Madam President. Recently, the International Law Commission adopted its draft conclusions on "subsequent agreements and subsequent practice in relation to the interpretation of treaties"[130]. Four of the ILC conclusions are on point.

31. First, in conclusion 5, the ILC states that, under the Vienna Convention, subsequent practice consists of "*any* conduct of a party in the application of a treaty, whether in the exercise of its executive, legislative, judicial or other functions". Second, in conclusion 7, the ILC observed that "[t]his may result in narrowing, widening, or otherwise determining the range of possible interpretations, including any scope for the exercise of discretion which the treaty accords to the parties". Third, this subsequent practice, as conclusion 8 explains, may "assist in determining whether or not the presumed intentions of the parties upon the conclusion of the treaty was to give a term used a meaning which is capable of evolving over time". And fourth, conclusion 10 of the ILC

---

[129] *Legal Consequences for States of the Continued Presence of South Africa in Namibia (South West Africa) notwithstanding Security Council Resolution 276 (1970), Advisory Opinion, I.C.J. Reports 1971*, p. 31, para. 53.

[130] ILC, *Subsequent agreements and subsequent practice in relation to interpretation of treaties*, available at https://legal.un.org/ilc/guide/1_11.shtml.

states that "[s]ilence on the part of one or more parties may constitute acceptance of the subsequent practice when the circumstances call for some reaction"[131].

32. Colombia submits that a contemporary interpretation of the generic terms in Article 33 now includes the powers specified in Decree 1946, as amended. Contiguous zone laws of other States provide some elaboration of the generic terms in Article 33. Jamaica, for example, includes "safety"[132], China and India "security"[133], Malta "pollution"[134], Saudi Arabia and Sierra Leone "environmental"[135]. But rather than "additions" to Article 33 or "violations", these are more in the way of elaborations on its generic terms, reflecting modern realities and understandings of the perils confronting coastal States[136] and the contemporary practice of other States.

33. Nicaragua's objection to the environmental power ignores the now widely appreciated link between environmental protection and the health of the population. Colombia submits that contiguous zone powers include powers to prevent or punish violations of a State's environmental protection laws *in its territory or territorial sea*. This is consistent with the practice of other States and is a contemporary interpretation of the term "sanitary". It is both inspired by and consistent with foundational instruments of contemporary international law.

34. Nicaragua suggested that UNCLOS Article 210 on dumping provides an example for a theoretical conflict between the power to protect the island's environment and its own EEZ right to regulate dumping. Colombia would assume of course that, as a State claiming to value environmental protection, Nicaragua would not authorize activities adversely affecting the Archipelago's fragile environment. But if it were to, the Decree can only be applied "in conformity with international

---

[131] ILC, *Draft conclusions on subsequent agreements and subsequent practice in relation to the interpretation of treaties*, 2018, UN doc. A/73/10, para. 51, available at https://legal.un.org/ilc/texts/instruments/english/draft_articles/1_11_2018.pdf.

[132] Maritime Areas Act of 1996, Art. 28, available at https://www.un.org/depts/los/LEGISLATIONANDTREATIES/PDFFILES/JAM_1996_Act.pdf.

[133] Law on the Territorial Sea and the Contiguous Zone of 25 February 1992, Art. 13, available at https://www.un.org/depts/los/LEGISLATIONANDTREATIES/PDFFILES/CHN_1992_Law.pdf; http://www.mod.gov.cn/big5/regulatory/2021-01/23/content_4877678.htm; The Territorial Waters, Continental Shelf, Exclusive Economic Zone and other Maritime Zones Act, 1976, Act No. 80, 28 May 1976, Art. 5, available at https://www.un.org/depts/los/LEGISLATIONANDTREATIES/PDFFILES/IND_1976_Act.pdf.

[134] Territorial Waters and Contiguous Zone, Art. 4, available at http://extwprlegs1.fao.org/docs/pdf/mlt1897.pdf.

[135] Translation of Royal Decree No. 6, dated 18/1/1433H, available at https://www.un.org/Depts/los/LEGISLATIONANDTREATIES/PDFFILES/SAU_2011_Decree.pdf; The Maritime Zones (Establishment) Decree, 1996, Art. 7, available at https://www.un.org/depts/los/LEGISLATIONANDTREATIES/PDFFILES/SLE_1996_Decree.pdf.

[136] See Alexander Proelβ, *The United Nations Convention on the Law of the Sea: A Commentary* (2017), p. 267.

law"[137]. So if such a theoretical conflict were to occur, in addition to the "due regard" obligation, the Colombian authorities would be required to respect Nicaragua's right to regulate dumping. This one, theoretical and remote, conflict cannot reasonably be used to deny Colombia the power to protect and punish infringements of its environmental laws in its territory or territorial sea.

35. Madam President, Colombia assumes that security risks, primarily those stemming from drug trafficking and piracy, pose a grave risk to the health and well-being of its population, not to speak of the fact that they violate its customs law. To support its proposition that such "security" powers in the contiguous zone are not reflective of an emerging custom or a modern interpretation of the treaty terms, Nicaragua claims that "[s]ecurity claims have been protested by roughly as many States as have made them"[138]. But, for the inclusion of security in contiguous zone powers, the 2021 study on which Nicaragua bases its claim relied on objections filed by one non-party State, and an uncorroborated note by a single author, as the Court can appreciate in tab 10 of the folder[139]. This study identifies 16 States that have proclaimed contiguous zone powers to prevent and punish violations of their security laws. Of these, 11 are UNCLOS States parties, among them: China, India, Sri Lanka and Saudi Arabia. Does Nicaragua assume that the practice of these *parties* to UNCLOS may not serve to interpret the generic terms in Article 33? Does it ignore the apparent silence of the other State parties?

36. If such practices, per the ILC conclusions, may "result in narrowing, widening, or otherwise determining the range of possible interpretations", such practice necessarily affects the interpretation of generic terms. Colombia thus submits that the power to punish or prevent security threats is an elaboration of the generic terms in Article 33, as reflected in customary international law and consistent with State practice, specifically that of UNCLOS parties.

37. I may note, Madam President, that in addition to the Roach study on which Nicaragua relies, two additional States include in their contiguous zone the punishment or prevention of acts violating the protective security laws in their territory or territorial sea. First, Colombia claims such a power in Decree 1946. Second, Nicaragua's unlimited claim to punish or prevent the violation of

---

[137] CMC, Ann. 7, Decree 1946, as amended, Art. 3.

[138] CR 2021/17, p. 41, para. 20 (Lowe); CR 2021/13, p. 69, para. 34 (Lowe).

[139] J. Ashley Roach, *Excessive Maritime Claims* (4th ed., 2021), pp. 146-149, fns. 14 and 16.

its entire portfolio of criminal laws necessarily includes such power. If Nicaragua criminalizes acts which undermine its security, environment, or even its political interests, such as its widely discussed law criminalizing activities on social media[140], then is it not claiming powers in the contiguous zone to prevent and punish such activities?

38. To conclude, Madam President, Colombia submits that the powers in Decree 1946 concerning its protective laws on security and the environment are lawful.

39. Madam President, Members of the Court, thank you for your attention. May I ask you to call on my colleague Eduardo Valencia-Ospina.

The PRESIDENT: I thank Professor Reisman, and I now give the floor to Mr. Eduardo Valencia-Ospina. You have the floor.

Mr. VALENCIA-OSPINA:

COUNTER-CLAIM: NICARAGUA'S INFRINGEMENT OF THE TRADITIONAL FISHING RIGHTS OF THE INHABITANTS OF THE SAN ANDRÉS ARCHIPELAGO

I. Introduction

1. Madam President, distinguished judges, Nicaragua's position on the traditional fishing rights counter-claim is based on three negative propositions: no recognition of the traditional fishing rights, no such rights in the EEZ, and no evidence of their existence and violation.

2. Colombia has advanced two *alternative* and *independently* decisive propositions.

3. The first Colombian proposition is that traditional rights run with the land *as well as with the sea*[141]. The creation and expansion of maritime areas, the transfer of territory and maritime delimitation have no bearing on their existence. There is no exception for the EEZ, and recognition of traditional rights is not a requirement for establishing their existence, though it would bear *decisive* value from the evidentiary standpoint. The second alternative Colombian proposition is that, assuming traditional rights were prohibited in the EEZ *(quod non)*, no one could deny that such

---

[140] Human Rights Watch, Nicaragua Events of 2021, available at https://www.hrw.org/world-report/2021/country-chapters/nicaragua#.

[141] CR 2021/15, pp. 44-45, para. 27 and fn. 81 (Valencia-Ospina); CMC, paras. 3.98-3.99, 3.106, and 9.12-9.13; RC, para. 5.12.

prohibition would fall under *jus dispositivum* and, thus, that States could set aside such notional ban, recognizing between themselves that certain practices amount to rights that survived the EEZ[142].

4. In this presentation I will first address the recognition of the traditional fishing rights while touching upon the evidence. I will then show that, should recognition not be established *(quod non)*, the traditional fishing rights would still be protected as a matter of principle, including in the EEZ. Finally, I will deal with the infringement of these vested rights.

II. The recognition and existence of the traditional fishing rights

5. Colombia must emphasize that we are not confronted with an expression of the will that is difficult to establish. Colombia does *not* rely on absence of reaction and does *not* infer recognition from a *tacit* expression of the will. Colombia simply gives meaning to the words of Nicaragua's President. Did he not speak of "historical rights"[143]? Did he not declare that the Raizales can "fish freely" and that "they already have a permanent permit"[144]? This leads me to a straightforward point. This case is about *express* recognition, but Nicaragua's first strategy is to portray a quasi-apocalyptic background[145], in the hope that the Court will forgive the words of its President.

6. Nicaragua does *not* deny that the Presidents of Nicaragua and Colombia can commit to internationally binding obligations, including through unilateral declarations[146], oral agreements[147] and approval that certain local practices are accepted as law[148]. Notwithstanding its depiction of the supposedly "critical diplomatic context"[149], Nicaragua does *not* argue that the will of its President was expressed in the absence of freedom, or that coercion rendered the act of recognition null and

[142] CR 2021/15, p. 49, para. 40 (Valencia-Ospina); RC, paras. 5.25-5.26.

[143] RC, Ann. 6.

[144] *Ibid.*

[145] CR 2021/16, p. 24, paras. 28-29 (Martin); RN, paras. 6.64-6.66; APN, paras. 2.29-2.30 and 2.36.

[146] See for example ILC, *Guiding Principles applicable to unilateral declarations of States capable of creating legal obligations*, 2006; *Nuclear Tests (Australia* v. *France), Judgment, I.C.J. Reports 1974*, pp. 267 *et seq.*, paras. 42 *et seq.*; *Nuclear Tests (New Zealand* v. *France), Judgment, I.C.J. Reports 1974*, pp. 472 *et seq.*, paras. 45 *et seq.*

[147] See for example Vienna Convention on the Law of Treaties, concluded at Vienna on 23 May 1969, *UNTS*, No. 18232, Vol. 1115, p. 331, Article 3 *(a)*.

[148] See for example ILC, *Conclusions on Identification of customary international law, Conclusion 16, annexed to General Assembly resolution 73/203 of 20 December 2018; Asylum (Colombian/Peruvian), Judgment, I.C.J. Reports 1950*, pp. 276-278; *Right of Passage over Indian Territory (Portugal* v. *India), Merits, Judgment, I.C.J. Reports 1960*, pp. 40-43; *Dispute regarding Navigational and Related Rights (Costa Rica* v. *Nicaragua), Judgment, I.C.J. Reports 2009*, pp. 265-266, para. 141; see also, CMC, paras. 3.87-3.92.

[149] RN, para. 6.67.

void. Nicaragua *only* suggests that, when evaluating its President's statements, account should be taken of the supposedly "furious" and "hostile" behaviour of Colombia[150]. For Nicaragua, context — together with a psychological inquiry into the real will of its President — reveal a different intention from the one expressed in his statements discussed last week. Unfortunately for Nicaragua, what matters is the *expressed* will, the *exteriorized* will of States. Context alone cannot change the fact that Nicaragua's President declared that the Raizales "can *continue* fishing", that "they are in *their* waters" and "in *their* natural habitat"[151].

7. Nicaragua thus overstated its contextual argument. More importantly, it is the context *as such* that Nicaragua overstated. When the Presidents of Nicaragua and Colombia spoke in Mexico, they disproved Nicaragua's depiction of a "particularly delicate context"[152]. Interestingly, Nicaragua's President stressed that "there is permanent communication between the different authorities"[153], adding that "this meeting . . . offer[ed] a message of peace and tranquillity to the brother country of Colombia and to the people of Nicaragua"[154]. This is the real context within which Nicaragua's President declared "[b]e sure that we will respect the historical rights that they (the Raizales) have had over those territories"[155].

8. This brings me to the second Nicaraguan strategy. As explained by Colombia, Nicaragua persists in its attempt to blur the *recognition* of the traditional rights with the creation of mechanisms aimed at *ensuring* these rights[156]. According to Nicaragua, "the artisanal fishing 'rights' do not exist independently of 'mechanisms' to be approved by Nicaragua"[157]. However, the conclusion of technical arrangements "should not be confused with *the existence* and *recognition of the existence* of the traditional fishing rights"[158]. If these rights do not exist as of today, how is it that

---

[150] RN, paras. 6.64-6.65; APN, para. 2.30; CR 2021/16, p. 24, para. 28 (Martin).

[151] RC, Ann. 6.

[152] RN, para. 6.64.

[153] CMC, Ann. 74.

[154] *Ibid.*

[155] *Ibid.*

[156] RC, paras. 5.2 and 5.30.

[157] RN, para. 6.70. Cf. also APN, paras. 2.33-2.41; CR 2021/16, p. 25, para. 32 (Martin).

[158] CR 2021/15, p. 38, para. 5 (Valencia-Ospina)

Nicaragua's President *consistently* speaks of "*historical rights*"?[159] If recognition is contingent on the creation of mechanisms, how is it that Nicaragua's President said that "they *already* have a permanent permit" and that they "can *continue* fishing"?[160]

9. Last week, Colombia went through the Nicaraguan presidential statements to show that recognition had *already* occurred, that it was subject to *no* condition, and that the aim of the foreseen "mechanisms"[161] would be *to ensure* the traditional fishing rights, not to establish their existence anew. But from what Nicaragua argued since then it would appear that, with regard to traditional fishing by the Raizales, *everything* has yet to be decided and *everything* will eventually depend on its "willingness"[162]. For the time being, though, Nicaragua shows *no* discomfort in declaring that it remains "ready to accommodate Colombia's concerns about the Raizales' artisanal fishing interests"[163]. Nicaragua's judicial strategy has left it no other choice since it cannot deny that its President paid a great deal of consideration to the "Raizal brethren"[164]. Nicaragua cannot disregard the fact that its President took pride in proclaiming Nicaragua's respect for the "Principle of the Native Peoples"[165]. What Nicaragua does, instead, is to build a narrative according to which these statements only stand for the proposition that fishing will have to be the subject of an agreement[166].

10. Nicaragua makes it look as though *everything* has yet to be defined, but in reality the *scope* of these vested rights has already been delineated. We know that traditional fishing rights relate to *artisanal* practices. For Nicaragua's President, revealingly, it is "industrial fishing", not artisanal fishing, that requires "permission from INPESCA"[167]. We likewise know that the artisanal practices at stake are those of individuals and of small companies. "If the Raizales have a company", says

[159] RC, Ann. 6.

[160] *Ibid.*

[161] CMC, Anns. 73-74.

[162] CR 2021/16, p. 25, para. 32 (Martin).

[163] APN, para. 2.41.

[164] MN, Ann. 27.

[165] *Ibid.*

[166] CR 2021/16, p. 25 para. 32 (Martin); RN, para. 6.73.

[167] RC, Ann. 6.

Nicaragua's President, "this company that belongs to the Raizales can fish *freely* as well, because these are their *original* areas as *original* people."[168]

11. The statements of Nicaragua's President are consistent with Colombia's evidence. Already in November 2012, he acknowledged that the Raizales are the "Native Peoples" that have "historically" fished and navigated the maritime areas discussed last week[169]. In perfect conformity with that evidence, he stressed the permanent connection between the Raizales and those he described as "their relatives in Bluefields [and] Pearl Lagoon"[170]. When later in February he explained that the artisanal companies can also "fish freely"[171], his words were once more consistent with the evidence that suggests that artisanal fishing is a *commercial* and *social* activity that implicates co-operatives and associations based in San Andrés and Providencia[172].

12. In spite of its distorted reading by Nicaragua, Colombia's evidence indeed shows that the artisanal fishermen and their ancestors have long navigated and fished in the shallow banks of Cape Bank and Luna Verde, as well as the deep-sea banks located east of La Esquina and in between the Northern Islands referred to in Colombia's first round tabs 41 to 43. These traditional banks are located no farther, and sometimes much closer, than some of the Northern Islands, which Nicaragua accepts are traditional grounds[173]. In this connection, I refer you to tab 11: San Andrés is located closer to Cape Bank and La Esquina compared to Roncador, Serrana and Quitasueño. As for Providencia, roughly the same distance separates it from Luna Verde, Roncador and Serrana. Providencia is in fact located significantly closer to La Esquina and the Northern banks situated between Providencia and Quitasueño. If the artisanal fishermen reach Serrana, Roncador and Quitasueño, they are per force able to reach Luna Verde and La Esquina.

13. Last week Nicaragua collected censuses and declared that the San Andrés Archipelago was not always as densely populated as today[174]. Yet traditional rights do not require high volume of

---

[168] RC, Ann. 6.

[169] MN, Ann. 27.

[170] *Ibid.*

[171] RC, Ann. 6

[172] Cf. in particular CMC, paras. 2.70-2.71, Anns. 62, 65, 68 and 71; RC, para. 5.8.

[173] Cf. for example, CR 2021/16, p. 29, para. 47 (Martin).

[174] CR 2021/16, pp. 11-12, paras. 11-12 and pp. 12-13, paras. 15-17 (Argüello).

fishing to come into being[175]. In addition, Nicaragua pointed out that, even though the artisanal fishermen often refer to the aforementioned banks, they do not always *expressly* say that they are traditional ones[176]. In a similar vein, Nicaragua stressed that common references to fishing do not suffice if these references are not *systematically* preceded by the term "traditional"[177]. These verbal tricks are certainly — to quote Nicaragua — "not the stuff of which serious international cases are made"[178]. The affidavits, some excerpts of which you will find in tab 12, are clear and compelling. The artisanal fishermen and their ancestors have for generations fished in these banks. This is a fact that is established in the affidavits, as well as in other documents adduced by Colombia[179]. This is a fact, which is fully *corroborated* by the statements of Nicaragua's President, all of which were made well before the affidavits now being looked at with suspicion by Nicaragua.

14. There is one last Nicaraguan strategy, addressed by Colombia in its Rejoinder[180], according to which a Section of the Colombian Ministry of Labour made a statement against interest in proceedings brought by Raizales before the ILO Committee of Experts[181]. What Colombia already showed when annexing all relevant documents is that that Section did not provide any evidence to maintain that the traditional banks had not been impacted by the 2012 Judgment[182]. This *unsupported* statement cannot undo the recognition by both the then President and Foreign Minister of Colombia[183]. This three-line assertion cannot be reconciled with the Colombian investments to support the artisanal fishermen in the aftermath of that Judgment[184]. What the proceedings before the Committee reveal is that the Raizales are consistent, regardless of whether their claims are supported

---

[175] *Award of the Arbitral Tribunal in the Second Stage of the Proceedings between Eritrea and Yemen (Maritime Delimitation), Decision of 17 December 1999, RIAA*, Vol. XXII, p. 358, para. 95.

[176] CR 2021/16, p. 31, para. 57 (Martin).

[177] *Ibid.*, p. 30, para. 51 (Martin).

[178] *Ibid.*, p. 34, para. 70 (Martin).

[179] Cf. CMC, Anns. 62-72, 85, 91 and 93.

[180] RC, paras. 5.55-5.61 and Anns. 24 and 67.

[181] CR 2021/16, pp. 27–28, paras. 40-43 (Martin).

[182] RC, para. 5.56 and Ann. 24.

[183] RC, para. 5.55; CMC Ann. 20; POC, Anns. 10 and 38.

[184] RC, paras. 5.57-5.60.

by Colombia or brought against Colombia[185]. This tells a lot about the integrity of the artisanal fishermen.

15. To conclude with recognition, Nicaragua need look no further than its own President if it wishes to discuss speeches against interest. Following the meeting in Mexico, the Nicaraguan President remarked: "I told President Santos, and I have said publicly, that the Raizal Community can continue fishing . . . Nicaragua will not affect them in their Rights as Original People"[186]. To quote *Libya/Chad*, his recognition entailed "first and foremost accepting", thus "respecting . . . and refraining from contesting . . . in the future"[187].

III. Traditional fishing rights are not qualified by the maritime areas or territories in which they took shape

16. I turn to the second part of my presentation. Although judicial economy militates against considering the EEZ argument of extinction, I will review it nonetheless since Nicaragua remains in denial with regard to recognition.

17. Let me begin by stressing the Colombian points that Nicaragua does not challenge.

— First, States may recognize traditional rights in the EEZ. Should recognition be established, the extinction theory would be of no avail.

— Secondly, traditional rights are compatible with the rights of States within their territories, territorial seas, archipelagic waters and internal waters. Revealingly, in all of these areas, *exclusive* sovereign rights are exercised over natural resources.

— Lastly, the *legal rationale* of traditional rights is the understanding that border communities may acquire vested rights after years of practice carried out in keeping with the tradition of their forebears. This *rationale* applies in an equally rational manner regardless of where the practices took place. Are traditional grazing rights of border communities that depend on their livestock[188] more important than traditional fishing rights of border communities that depend on their fishing

---

[185] RC, para. 5.61 and Anns. 67 and 68.

[186] RC, Ann. 6.

[187] *Territorial Dispute (Libyan Arab Jamahiriya/Chad), Judgment, I.C.J. Reports 1994*, p. 22, para. 42.

[188] *Award in the Arbitration regarding the delimitation of the Abyei Area between the Government of Sudan and the Sudan People's Liberation Movement/Army, Award of 22 July 2009, Reports of International Arbitral Awards (RIAA)*, Vol. XXX, p. 412, para. 766.

activities? Does the rationale suddenly become irrational if the fishing activities occur at 13 rather than 12 nautical miles from the nearest shore?

18. The whole strategy of Nicaragua is premised on *exceptionalism*, the proposition that traditional fishing rights must cease to exist in *one area and one alone*, the EEZ. This is precisely the area of interest to the Raizales, where you find the shallow and deep-sea banks already discussed[189]. Last week, we heard again the "legal monopoly" plea[190]. As Nicaragua puts it so peremptorily, the rights over the living resources of the *exclusive* economic zone cannot be but "*exclusive*", exactly as the name of this maritime area would suggest[191]. Yet, no matter the name, exclusivity of rights over natural resources is *not* specific to the EEZ. Traditional rights have been found to exist on land and at sea, in all areas where States possess *exclusive* rights over natural resources. It is, therefore, remarkable to hear from Nicaragua that exclusivity "is the *foundation* of [their] case"[192]. For if it is the foundation, it is a feeble one to say the least; one that would reveal that the entire jurisprudence on vested rights[193] is premised on a legal blunder, the failure to note that traditional rights are *always*, to quote Nicaragua, "inconsistent"[194] since they *always* relate to areas in which States possess exclusive rights over natural resources.

19. Nicaragua acknowledges that its extinction theory, premised on exceptionalism, finds no explicit support in UNCLOS, a treaty to which in any event, it bears repeating, Colombia is not a party. This is why Nicaragua came forth with the argument that what matters is that its Part V and customary international law contain no express carve-out preserving traditional rights in the EEZ[195].

---

189 CR 2021/15, pp. 41-44, paras. 16-24 (Valencia-Ospina).

190 CR 2021/16, pp. 18-19, paras. 7-8 (Martin); cf. also, APN, paras. 2.13, 2.22 and 2.26.

191 CR 2021/16, pp. 18-19, paras. 3 and 7; p. 20, para. 13; p. 21, para. 17; and p. 23, para. 24 (Martin). See also, RN, para. 6.9; APN, para. 2.5.

192 CR 2021/16, p. 20, para. 13 (Martin); emphasis added.

193 *Award in the Arbitration regarding the delimitation of the Abyei Area between the Government of Sudan and the Sudan People's Liberation Movement/Army, Award of 22 July 2009, RIAA*, Vol. XXX, p. 408, para. 753; *Award of the Arbitral Tribunal in the First Stage of the Proceedings between Eritrea and Yemen (Territorial Sovereignty and Scope of the Dispute), Decision of 9 October 1998, RIAA*, Vol. XXII, p. 244, para. 126; *Award of the Arbitral Tribunal in the Second Stage of the Proceedings between Eritrea and Yemen (Maritime Delimitation), Decision of 17 December 1999, RIAA*, Vol. XXII, p. 361, paras. 110-111; *Arbitration between Barbados and the Republic of Trinidad and Tobago, relating to the Delimitation of the Exclusive Economic Zone and the Continental Shelf between Them, RIAA*, Vol. XXVII, p. 227, para. 292; *Land, Island and Maritime Frontier Dispute (El Salvador/Honduras: Nicaragua intervening), Judgment, I.C.J. Reports 1992*, pp. 400-401, para. 66; *German Settlers in Poland, Advisory Opinion, 1923, P.C.I.J., Series B, No. 6*, p. 36.

194 CR 2021/16, pp. 18-19, para. 7 (Martin).

195 CR 2021/16, p. 21, para. 15 (Martin); cf. RN, para. 6.13. Cf. also, RC, para. 5.13.

The downside of the carve-out theory is that there is *no* such carve-out for the territory and territorial sea of States[196]. The jurisprudence goes precisely in the opposite direction. The principle applied in *El Salvador/Honduras*[197], *Abyei Area* and *Eritrea/Yemen*[198], is that vested rights are protected as a matter of principle, not as a matter of exception. The *Eritrea/Yemen* Tribunal, the only tribunal ever *formally* tasked with addressing traditional rights in the EEZ specifically, put it best: "traditional fishing . . . is not limited to . . . territorial waters" and "is not qualified by the maritime zones specified under . . . [UNCLOS]"[199]. The Tribunal did not rely on exceptionalism, but instead followed the usual presumption that, unless there is an "*explicit* prohibition to the contrary", traditional rights are not to be construed as being extinguished[200].

20. This is indeed the specificity of non-exclusive traditional rights compared to other *more intrusive* historic rights. Traditional rights vested in border communities, *unlike* historic rights that presuppose assertions of sovereignty or *exclusive* sovereign rights, do not entail at the outset violations of international law. Because traditional fishing first took place in conformity with the freedoms of the high seas, it is *free* from the original sin that characterizes *other* historic rights. This specificity of traditional rights clarifies why the jurisprudence *never* rests their existence upon consent or acquiescence. This specificity clarifies why Nicaragua's carve-out theory is unfounded.

21. This point was also developed by Sir Gerald Fitzmaurice[201] in the excerpt to be found in your folders at tab 13. Admittedly, Sir Gerald was not writing about the EEZ. But what mattered to the view he supported is that traditional fishing took shape *in the high seas*, not that the high seas later became part of broader territorial seas, or newly invented archipelagic waters or EEZ. Whether

---

[196] RC, para. 5.19.

[197] *Land, Island and Maritime Frontier Dispute (El Salvador/Honduras; Nicaragua intervening), Judgment, I.C.J. Reports 1992,* pp. 400-401, para. 66.

[198] *Award in the Arbitration regarding the delimitation of the Abyei Area between the Government of Sudan and the Sudan People's Liberation Movement/Army, Award of 22 July 2009, RIAA*, Vol. XXX, p. 408, para. 753; *Award of the Arbitral Tribunal in the Second Stage of the Proceedings between Eritrea and Yemen (Maritime Delimitation), Decision of 17 December 1999, RIAA*, Vol. XXII, p. 361, paras. 110-111.

[199] *Award of the Arbitral Tribunal in the Second Stage of the Proceedings between Eritrea and Yemen (Maritime Delimitation), Decision of 17 December 1999, RIAA*, Vol. XXII, p. 361, para. 109.

[200] *Award in the Arbitration regarding the delimitation of the Abyei Area between the Government of Sudan and the Sudan People's Liberation Movement/Army, Award of 22 July 2009, RIAA*, Vol. XXX, p. 408, para. 753.

[201] G. Fitzmaurice, "The Law and Procedure of ICJ, 1951-54: General Principles and Sources of Law", *British Yearbook of International Law*, 1953, Vol. 30, p. 31. See also RC, paras. 5.16-5.17. See also United Nations, Juridical régime of historic waters including historic bays — Study prepared by the Secretariat, UN doc. A/CN.4/143, pp. 7–11, paras. 42–61.

the coastal State is exercising *full-fledged exclusive sovereignty*, as is the case in the territorial sea, or *functional exclusive sovereign rights*, as is the case in the EEZ, has no bearing on the *rationale* supporting the jurisprudence on vested rights.

22. Nicaragua reads too much into *Gulf of Maine*[202], a case that Colombia addressed last week[203]. The short answer is that *Gulf of Maine* was *not* about traditional fishing rights. This case stands for the proposition, already discussed, according to which private practice has no impact on delimitation[204]. It says nothing, conversely, on the impact of delimitation on vested rights. To postulate a fundamental incompatibility between the EEZ and traditional rights on account of exclusivity alone is to fall again into contradiction, since the jurisprudence on vested rights always relates to areas in which there is monopoly over natural resources.

23. Colombia has explained that it is wrong to insinuate, as Nicaragua did[205], that the *Eritrea/Yemen* Tribunal applied other factors, such as Islamic law or a bilateral agreement[206] to depart from what would have otherwise been the black letter of international law[207]. On the contrary, the Tribunal said, in *unequivocal* terms that "traditional fishing . . . is not qualified by the maritime zones specified under . . . [UNCLOS]"[208].

24. Nicaragua's extinction theory rests on unconvincing *implications* to be apparently drawn from two UNCLOS provisions, the first pertaining to archipelagic waters, the second to the EEZ. Thus, as to the former, Nicaragua believes that Article 51, paragraph 1, with its reference to traditional fishing rights, supports the carve-out theory[209]. A more reasonable interpretation, which takes into account the *travaux* and *rationale* of acquired rights, indicates that this reference was made, not because of an *entrenched* belief that a carve-out was necessary, but because an example was

---

[202] CR 2021/16, pp. 19-20, paras. 8-11 (Martin).

[203] CR 2021/15, p. 49, para. 38 (Valencia-Ospina).

[204] CR 2021/15, pp. 44-45, para. 27 (Valencia-Ospina); see also CMC, paras. 3.98-3.111.

[205] RN, paras. 6.24-6.29.

[206] CR 2021/16, p. 23, para. 25 (Martin).

[207] RC, paras. 5.21-5.22.

[208] *Award of the Arbitral Tribunal in the Second Stage of the Proceedings between Eritrea and Yemen (Maritime Delimitation), Decision of 17 December 1999, RIAA*, Vol. XXII, p. 361, para. 109.

[209] CR 2021/16, p. 21, para. 15 (Martin); see also RN, para. 6.14; APN, fn. 38.

discussed and a few delegations felt reassured by its addition[210]. To suggest that, absent this reference, traditional rights would have been extinguished in archipelagic waters is speculation. There is indeed no similar provision in UNCLOS Part II, which concerns the territorial sea.

25. According to the second provision, Article 62, paragraph 3, when granting access to the surplus of the allowable catch, coastal States shall take into account "the need to minimize economic dislocation in States whose nationals have habitually fished in the zone"[211]. But *habitual* fishing is not the same as *traditional* fishing, the term of art used elsewhere in the Convention and the jurisprudence[212]. Unlike what happened with regard to archipelagic waters, and contrary to what Nicaragua would have you believe[213], the Conference did not consider the acquired rights of border communities and indigenous peoples in the EEZ. Instead, it considered habitual fishing, and what some *equivocally* labelled traditional fishing. These expressions were used by the major fishing powers with long-range fleets operating in many parts of the high seas[214]. In other words, unlike traditional fishing, habitual fishing need not be artisanal, need not occur in the adjacent waters of neighbouring States, and need not to have taken place for more than, say, a decade. The fact that these habitual fishing activities are deserving of consideration when granting access to surpluses neither suggests, nor hints, that traditional rights vested in border communities were extinguished by the EEZ. What this provision does is clarify that traditional rights, unlike habitual fishing activities, are not made dependent on the harvesting capacity and discretionary conduct of coastal States.

26. To sum up, the EEZ did not extinguish traditional fishing rights. Instead, these rank among those "other rules of international law"[215] which, according to general international law and UNCLOS, are compatible with the EEZ. Simply put, and as stated in the preamble of UNCLOS, these are "matters not regulated by this Convention" and which "continue to be governed by the rules and principles of general international law"[216]. Yet, I would be remiss if I were not to end this part

---

[210] Summary Records of Meetings of the Second Committee, 36th meeting, A/CONF.62/C.2/SR.36, paras. 1-8 (Indonesia); A/CONF.62/C.2/SR.37, paras. 26-29 (Singapore).

[211] UNCLOS, Article 62 (3).

[212] RC, para. 5.18.

[213] CR 2021/16, pp. 21-22, paras. 18-20 (Martin).

[214] See for example A/CONF.62/C.2/SR.27, para. 34 (Turkey); A/CONF.62/C.2/SR.22, para. 92 (Barbados).

[215] UNCLOS, Article 58 (3).

[216] UNCLOS, preamble.

of my presentation with the reminder that an *obiter dictum* from an arbitration which Nicaragua has not invoked, stressed that extinction, of course, would be no bar to "recognition", which, "would, in most instances, be commendable"[217].

IV. The infringement of the traditional fishing rights

27. Last week, Nicaragua contested the probative value of Colombia's evidence, bringing nothing new to the table. The Nicaraguan position is that *all* the evidence amounts to hearsay[218]. There are good reasons, not requiring much elaboration, that explain why Colombia cannot rely on first-hand accounts *only*. To these reasons, well reflected in the reports of international and non-governmental organizations, one may add that the associations and co-operatives, with whom the artisanal fishermen interact, neither have records, nor protocols in case of incidents at sea.

28. However, the affidavits, press-reports and observations of the ILO attest to the fact that the Nicaraguan Naval Force has inflicted fines and seized products, gears and vessels[219]. One might think that boarding a vessel to request food, cigarettes or coffee reveals just lack of professionalism. But if one were to put himself or herself in the shoes of the artisanal fishermen, it would become altogether clear that these encounters are far from benign. How to deal with them is one of the issues that Nicaragua and Colombia will have to resolve when discussing the means to ensure the traditional fishing rights.

29. Madam President, distinguished judges, this brings me to the end of my presentation. I thank you for your attention and request that you invite Professor Thouvenin to the podium.

The PRESIDENT: I thank Mr. Valencia-Ospina. I now invite the next speaker, Professor Jean-Marc Thouvenin, to take the floor.

---

[217] *The South China Sea Arbitration between the Republic of the Philippines and the People's Republic of China, Award of 12 July 2016, RIAA*, Vol. XXXIII, p. 469, para. 804 *(b)*.

[218] See for example CR 2021/16, pp. 33-34, paras. 65-70 (Martin); RN, para. 6.79; APN, para. 2.60.

[219] See in particular RC, paras. 5.62-5.73; CMC, Anns. 64, 65, 67, 69, 70, 71 and 72; MN, Ann. 12; RN, Ann. 20; ILO, Committee of Experts on the Application of Conventions and Recommendations, "Observations (CEACR) — adopted 2014, published 104rd ILC session (2015)", Indigenous and Tribal Peoples Convention, 1989, No. 169, Colombia, (Ratification: 1991); "San Andrés: entre la corrupción y el riesgo sanitario", press report by RCN, 16 Nov. 2019, available at https://www.noticiasrcn.com/nacional/san-andres-entre-la-corrupcion-y-el-riesgo-sanitario-349613 (accessed 22 Sept. 2021); "El fallo de la Haya se acató y se aplicó", press report by Caracol, 9 Oct. 2019, available at https://caracol.com.co/programa/2019/10/09/6am_hoy_por_hoy/1570633564_762159.html (accessed 22 Sept. 2021).

M. THOUVENIN : Merci beaucoup, Madame la présidente.

DEMANDE RECONVENTIONNELLE : ILLÉGALITÉ DU DÉCRET N° 33-2013

1. Madame la présidente, Mesdames et Messieurs les juges, je reviens aujourd'hui sur la deuxième demande reconventionnelle.

La Colombie maintient que le décret établissant les lignes de base droites du Nicaragua n'est pas conforme au droit international :

— Le sud de la côte nicaraguayenne n'est pas bardé de profondes échancrures[220]. Ses légères concavités ne sont même pas *bien marquées*[221] : si tel était le cas, le croquis que vous voyez ici, comme tous les autres disponibles, en attesterait. Aucun ne le fait ! Et même si tel était le cas, cela n'autoriserait pas à tirer une ligne droite entre un point de la côte (le point 9) et une île du large (le point 8).

— Il n'y a pas davantage de chapelet d'îles le long et à proximité immédiate de la côte[222]. Le Nicaragua n'essaie même pas de le démontrer par la géographie. Mon contradicteur préfère s'appuyer sur la longueur des lignes de base droites[223] que le Nicaragua s'estime en droit de tirer pour tenter de justifier que Ned Thomas Cay et Man of War Cay contribuent substantiellement, sur le plan géographique, à constituer un chapelet d'îles le long de la côte. Soixante-quinze milles marins séparent ces deux insignifiantes formations maritimes. C'est plus que la distance Rotterdam-Bruxelles. Puis de vous montrer l'archipel de la Recherche, en Australie, composé lui, indubitablement, d'un chapelet d'îles à l'effet masquant, abondamment réparties le long et à proximité très immédiate de la côte, et de suggérer que la géographie nicaraguayenne serait comparable[224], alors qu'elle ne l'est manifestement pas.

— Il est inutile, je pense, de marteler que les lignes de base contestées ne suivent en rien la direction générale de la côte : cela saute aux yeux[225]. Quant à la connexité des nouvelles eaux intérieures

[220] Voir notamment, CR 2021/15, p. 54-55, par. 17 (Thouvenin) ; voir également Colombie, dossier des juges du mercredi 22 septembre 2021, onglet n° 50.

[221] CR 2021/15, p. 55, par. 18 (Thouvenin).

[222] Voir notamment CR 2021/15, p. 57-60, par. 27-47 (Thouvenin).

[223] CR 2021/16, p. 40, par. 13 (Oude Elferink).

[224] CR 2021/16, p. 43, par. 22-23 (Oude Elferink)

[225] CR 2021/15, p. 61-62, par. 51-55 (Thouvenin) ; voir également Colombie, dossier des juges du mercredi 22 septembre 2021, onglet n° 56.

avec la côte, nous verrons tout à l'heure que le Nicaragua n'a jamais été capable de prouver l'existence même des formations maritimes qu'il prétend maintenant tellement «connectées» avec ses terres.

2. Ceci posé, quatre controverses nécessitent d'y consacrer quelques minutes. Elles concernent :

— l'objet du différend ;

— les effets du décret ;

— la question de la preuve de la multitude d'îles dont le Nicaragua se prévaut ; et, last but not least,

— la question des prétendues îles situées à Edinburgh Cay.

A. L'objet du différend relatif aux lignes de base droites

3. Madame la présidente, Mesdames et Messieurs les juges, quoi qu'en dise la Partie adverse, le différend n'a jamais porté, ne porte pas, et ne peut pas porter sur les lignes de bases *colombiennes*[226]. La seule question est de savoir si les lignes de base droites nicaraguayennes sont conformes au droit international.

4. Le différend ne porte pas non plus sur les nouvelles allégations nicaraguayennes relatives à de prétendues lignes de base normales soudainement apparues sur de prétendus hauts-fonds découvrants, à partir desquels serait mesurée la largeur de la ZEE et du plateau continental.

5. La question est réglée par l'article premier du décret n° 33-2013 qui énonce sans ambiguïté que les lignes de base droites sont celles : «à partir desquelles sera mesurée la largeur … *de sa zone économique exclusive et de son plateau continental dans la mer des Caraïbes*»[227].

6. J'ajoute que ce décret a été signé par le président Ortega le 19 août 2013, deux mois après que le Nicaragua a saisi la Commission des limites du plateau continental d'une demande dont le résumé public fait apparaître un croquis contenant deux mystérieux points surajoutés au feutre rouge[228]. Quelle qu'ait été l'intention de l'auteur de cet ajout, le décret précise de manière limpide à

---

[226] CR 2021/15, p. 51, par. 5.

[227] CMC, annexe 13, article premier (les italiques sont de nous).

[228] République du Nicaragua, «Submission to the Commission on the Limites of the Continental Shelf, Part I: Executive Summary», juin 2013, p. 4 (disponible à l'adresse suivante : www.un.org/depts/los/clcs_new/submissions_files/nic66_13/Executive%20Summary.pdf).

son article 5 que : «Toutes les dispositions légales et réglementaires qui contreviennent au présent décret sont abrogées.»[229]

7. En somme, le décret nº 33-2013 est l'objet précis, circonscrit, et unique de la demande reconventionnelle.

8. Au demeurant, le différend sur les lignes tracées par ce décret est le seul sur lequel la Cour peut exercer sa compétence. La Partie adverse reconnaît que : «Colombia's counter-claim indeed did not impugn the validity of Nicaragua's baseline along its low-water line.»[230] Evidemment, puisque c'est le décret qui fixe les lignes de base à partir desquelles se mesure la distance des zones, comme on vient de le voir. Mais mon contradicteur ajoute aussitôt : «But that is not the point.»[231] Mais si, that is *precisely* the point car, comme la Cour en a décidé, c'est à propos de la légalité de ce seul décret qu'un différend concernant les lignes de base droites nicaraguayennes est né avant la date d'effet de la dénonciation du pacte de Bogotá. L'extrait pertinent de votre ordonnance est reproduit à l'onglet nº 16 du dossier des juges[232].

B. Les effets du décret nº 33-2013

9. J'en viens à mon deuxième point, Madame la présidente, relatif aux effets du décret contesté.

10. Il ne fait à l'évidence aucun doute que les droits des Etats tiers, y compris de la Colombie, en sont affectés. Indubitablement, de larges portions de ZEE et de mer territoriale deviennent eaux intérieures, et de larges portions de ZEE deviennent mer territoriale. Mes contradicteurs suggèrent que tout ceci n'aurait pas grande importance puisque le droit de passage inoffensif serait maintenu dans les nouvelles eaux intérieures nicaraguayennes[233].

11. Mais, Madame la présidente, le Nicaragua ne conteste pas que de vastes espaces de ZEE tomberaient alors sous ce régime, là où devraient prévaloir non seulement la liberté de navigation — ce qui inclut, n'en déplaise au professeur Pellet[234], la liberté d'observer et d'informer sur les

---

[229] CMC, annexe 13, art. 5.

[230] CR 2021/16, p. 37, par. 8 (Oude Elferink)

[231] *Ibid.*

[232] *Violations alléguées de droits souverains et d'espaces maritimes dans la mer des Caraïbes (Nicaragua c. Colombie), demandes reconventionnelles, ordonnance du 15 novembre 2017, C.I.J. Recueil 2017*, p. 312, par. 73.

[233] CR 2021/16, p. 36, par. 4 (Oude Elferink), et p. 16, par. 29 (Argüello).

[234] CR 2021/17, p. 10, par. 1 (Pellet).

méfaits de certaines pratiques sur l'environnement[235] —, mais également les autres droits coutumiers reflétés dans le texte de l'article 58 de la convention de 1982[236].

12. Tout cela est inhérent au tracé des lignes de base droites, vous a-t-on dit vendredi[237]. Mais c'est précisément à cause de cet effet «inhérent», par définition dommageable aux autres Etats, que le droit international n'autorise à recourir à cette méthode que de manière exceptionnelle. Mais il est vrai que l'avocat de la Partie adverse ignore totalement la mise en garde de la Cour dans *Qatar c. Bahreïn* selon laquelle la méthode des lignes de base droites «doit être appliquée de façon restrictive»[238].

13. En outre, la Partie adverse s'est bien gardée de préciser que, dans ces mêmes espaces, le Nicaragua s'absout, par le seul jeu du décret contesté, des obligations applicables dans la ZEE au titre du régime international de conservation des ressources biologiques, notamment halieutiques, établi par la convention de 1982. Dans les eaux annexées par le décret, le Nicaragua n'a plus l'obligation de prendre «des mesures appropriées de conservation et de gestion pour éviter que le maintien des ressources biologiques de sa zone économique exclusive soit compromis par une surexploitation»[239]. Même chose s'agissant de ses obligations au titre des articles 62, 63, etc., de la convention à laquelle il est partie. Toutes obligations dont la portée *erga omnes* ne saurait faire de doute, car on ne protège pas l'environnement marin *inter partes* ; on le protège au bénéfice de tous.

14. Ces dernières remarques conduisent d'ailleurs à la parenthèse ouverte par l'agent du Nicaragua vendredi révélant que l'une des raisons de l'adoption des lignes de base droites : «is because it considered it appropriate in view of the rights of the population to fish and exploit those areas within 25 nautical miles of the adjacent islands and keys»[240].

15. Tout expert du droit de la mer saurait que les nouvelles lignes de base droites nicaraguayennes n'ont strictement aucun emport, du point de vue du droit international, sur les droits des populations nicaraguayennes de pêcher ou de conduire d'autres activités au large de la côte

---

[235] CPA, *The Arctic Sunrise Arbitration (Netherlands* v. *Russia)*, Award on the merits, 14 août 2015, par. 227.

[236] CNUDM, art. 58.

[237] CR 2021/16, p. 36, par. 4 (Oude Elferink).

[238] *Délimitation maritime et questions territoriales entre Qatar et Bahreïn (Qatar c. Bahreïn), fond, arrêt, C.I.J. Recueil 2001*, p. 103, par. 212.

[239] CNUDM, art. 61, par. 2.

[240] CR 2021/16, p. 14, par. 22 (Argüello).

nicaraguayenne. Ils le pouvaient avant, ils le peuvent après les lignes de base droites. La seule différence, mais elle est de taille, est que, désormais, leurs activités ne sont plus encadrées par le droit international qui protège contre la surexploitation.

16. Le Nicaragua fait d'ailleurs d'une pierre deux coups, puisqu'il s'absout aussi, dans ses immenses eaux intérieures conquises par décret, des obligations spécifiques de protection du milieu marin des Caraïbes auxquelles il s'est engagé en ratifiant la convention de Carthagène, dont le premier article précise qu'elle ne s'applique pas, sauf exception, aux eaux intérieures[241]. Grâce au décret, *exit*, l'obligation posée par cette convention de combattre la pollution et de gérer rationnellement l'environnement[242]. *Idem*, de l'obligation de protéger et préserver les écosystèmes rares ou fragiles ainsi que l'habitat des espèces en régression, menacées ou en voie d'extinction[243].

17. Le Nicaragua ne découvre évidemment pas aujourd'hui que son décret emporte l'effet majeur de le dégager, dans les eaux concernées, de ses obligations internationales les plus importantes de la période contemporaine, en particulier pour ses voisins caribéens.

18. Madame la présidente, Mesdames et Messieurs les juges, pas plus sur ce terrain que sur les autres, le Nicaragua ne peut sérieusement prétendre que le décret contesté n'a que peu d'effets sur les droits des tiers, y compris de la Colombie.

C. La question de la preuve de l'existence des îles

19. Je passerai dans un instant à Edinburgh Cay. Permettez-moi auparavant un mot sur la multitude d'îles dont le Nicaragua se prévaut. Dans ses diverses plaidoiries, le Nicaragua a balayé la question de leur preuve d'un revers de main en avançant deux arguments erronés.

20. Premièrement, il suffirait de regarder les cartes pour voir que les 95 îles listées en annexe 31 à la plaidoirie additionnelle sont bien là[244]. J'ai déjà mentionné quelques déficiences de cette liste. Il y en a d'autres : sur la carte qui vous a été montrée par le Nicaragua, la semaine dernière, comme preuve de l'existence d'îles sur Edinburgh Cay ou Edinburgh Reef, «The Witties», qui est dans la liste des prétendues îles, n'est qu'un haut-fond découvrant. Il en va de même pour

[241] CMC, annexe 17, article premier.

[242] Ibid., article 4 (1).

[243] Ibid., article 10.

[244] PAN, p. 56, par. 3.38 ; voir également, CR 2021/17, p. 40, par. 16 (Oude Elferink).

Ned Thomas Cay, sur lequel le Nicaragua pose un de ses points de base, mais aussi des trois prétendues îles de Lamarka Reef, et de Dennis Prong. Quant à Dry Rock et Sand Cay, je ne les ai pas trouvées.

21. Qu'en déduire ? Que les cartes de la zone, comme preuves de la géographie locale, ne sont pas fiables. Surtout quand on leur fait dire ce qu'elles ne disent pas. Ainsi du montage projeté par le professeur Oude Elferink, qui est à l'onglet n° 13 du dossier des juges de vendredi, surchargeant la carte extraite du site Internet de la convention Ramsar que j'avais montrée mercredi, dans sa version «bio» — c'est-à-dire sans aucune surcharge artificielle — et que voici à nouveau sur vos écrans. Cette carte dit simplement que les zones humides protégées au niveau de Miskito Cay et de la bande côtière ne sont pas connectées.

22. La Partie adverse a jugé bon de triturer cette même carte pour, apparemment, vous convaincre qu'un tapis d'îles connecterait la côte à Miskito Cay[245].

23. Ce que vous voyez à l'écran maintenant n'est rien d'autre que le montage du professeur Oude Elferink, mais en retirant tout ce qui n'est pas une île, en respectant fidèlement pour ce faire la légende de la carte qu'il a utilisée. La carte bio disait vrai. Il n'y a pas de connexion. Et on ne voit certainement ni un tapis ni un chapelet d'îles le long et à proximité de la côte.

24. Deuxièmement, pour prouver l'existence de ses îles, le Nicaragua croit avoir trouvé le Graal en renvoyant à la figure 9.2 annexée au contre-mémoire de la Colombie dans l'affaire clôturée en 2012[246].

25. Le Nicaragua se garde bien de rappeler que cette figure a été composée avec beaucoup de difficultés par la Colombie pour les seuls besoins du litige d'alors, sur la base, concernant la zone nicaraguayenne, d'informations cartographiques qui étaient à la fois imprécises et non vérifiées.

26. La Partie adverse veut en particulier oublier que, dans son contre-mémoire d'alors, la Colombie mettait en garde :

> «[L]a Colombie identifiera les points de base du Nicaragua en fonction des renseignements dont elle dispose. Comme la Colombie l'a noté, l'un des nombreux défauts du mémoire du Nicaragua tient au fait que ce pays n'a fourni aucun renseignement utile concernant les détails de sa géographie. En conséquence,

---

[245] CR 2021/16, p. 45, par. 28 (Oude Elferink).

[246] CR 2021/16, p. 40, par. 16 (Oude Elferink) ; voir également, Nicaragua, dossier des juges du vendredi 24 septembre 2021, onglet n° 14.

> l'identification des points de base du côté nicaraguayen de la ligne médiane a été basée sur les cartes disponibles de ces zones.»[247]

27. Et la Colombie de préciser on ne peut plus nettement que «les cartes … ont été établies à des échelles différentes et ne sont plus d'actualité à certains égards»[248].

28. Le Nicaragua n'entreprit rien de nature à clarifier la situation, se complaisant dans une connaissance très approximative des abords de sa côte. Pourquoi se donnerait-il du mal quand sa désinvolture paye ?

D. La question d'Edinburgh Cay

29. Cette désinvolture du Nicaragua à propos de sa propre géographie nous conduit au cas emblématique d'Edinburgh Cay.

30. La Cour a entendu parler pour la première fois de cette formation maritime dans *Nicaragua c. Honduras*[249].

31. S'interrogeant dans sa réplique sur le point de savoir si certaines formations — comme Edinburgh Cay et Edinburgh Reef — sont dotées d'une mer territoriale, le Honduras manifestait de sérieux doutes[250]. Le Nicaragua reconnaissait pour sa part, à propos des petites formations côtières dont il était avéré que certaines disparaissent au cours du temps : «the instability of these islets … indicates that they should in no case provide the basis for the delimitation of a maritime boundary»[251].

32. Le Nicaragua confirmait lors des plaidoiries qu'il

> «ignore le nombre d'îles et de formations qui sont en cause et leur emplacement étant donné que les principaux relevés se rapportant à cette zone remontent à la première moitié du XIXe siècle et qu'il s'agit d'une zone où ces formations ont nettement tendance à émerger et disparaître»[252].

---

[247] *Différend territorial et maritime (Nicaragua c. Colombie),* contre-mémoire de la Colombie, 11 novembre 2008, par. 9.20.

[248] *Ibid.*, par. 9.19.

[249] *Différend territorial et maritime entre le Nicaragua et le Honduras dans la mer des Caraïbes (Nicaragua c. Honduras).*

[250] *Différend territorial et maritime entre le Nicaragua et le Honduras dans la mer des Caraïbes (Nicaragua c. Honduras),* duplique du Honduras, p. 114, par. 6.27 et p. 115, par. 6.29.

[251] *Différend territorial et maritime entre le Nicaragua et le Honduras dans la mer des Caraïbes (Nicaragua c. Honduras)*, réplique du Nicaragua, p. 32, par. 3.17.

[252] *Différend territorial et maritime entre le Nicaragua et le Honduras dans la mer des Caraïbes (Nicaragua c. Honduras)*, CR 2007/11, p. 27, par. 70 (Argüello) *[traduction du Greffe]*.

33. Le Nicaragua évoquait ici ce qui se trouve à quelques milles au nord du 15e parallèle, mais sa remarque valait évidemment tout autant pour la zone d'Edinburgh Cay et d'Edinburgh Reef, qui se trouvent à quelques encablures au sud du 15e parallèle.

34. Le professeur Oude Elferink l'avait d'ailleurs confirmé dans sa plaidoirie du 19 mars 2007. Alors que le conseil du Honduras remarquait que «le Nicaragua n'a[vait] rien fait pour éclairer la Cour au sujet de ces formations, et le Honduras ne dispos[ait] d'aucun élément de preuve indépendant quant à leurs caractéristiques», et se plaignait du fait que le Honduras en était réduit à leur donner ce qu'il appelait «le bénéfice du doute»[253], le professeur Oude Elferink répondait :

> «*Que se passerait-il si l'on découvrait qu'Edinburgh Cay et les cayes situées sur Edinburgh Reef n'existaient pas ?* Cela ne serait en rien pertinent aux fins de déterminer la situation qui prévalait en 1821. Que peut-on prouver à propos des cayes à cette date ? La carte 2425 du service hydrographique du Royaume-Uni, initialement établie à partir de levés réalisés entre 1830 et 1843, montre six cayes sur Edinburgh Reef.»[254]

35. Bref, le Nicaragua reconnaissait qu'il était incapable de confirmer si les îles en question existaient encore. D'ailleurs, un rapport établi à sa demande dans cette affaire confirmait le peu de fiabilité actuelle des cartes marines de la zone : «The fact that features thought no longer to exist remain clearly marked on a current UKHO chart is not at all surprising.»[255]

36. C'est sur cette base qu'Edinburgh Cay a été prise en compte par la Cour dans sa décision. De guerre lasse, au bénéfice du doute.

37. En août 2013, date d'adoption du décret contesté devant vous, le Nicaragua n'avait toujours rien vérifié. Aujourd'hui encore, le doute demeure intact. Au bénéfice du Nicaragua qui n'a aucun intérêt à vérifier qu'Edinburgh Cay n'est plus aujourd'hui qu'une chimère insulaire. D'ailleurs, vous avez pu constater que, pour prouver l'existence d'Edinburgh Cay en tant qu'île, le professeur Oude Elferink s'est borné à vous renvoyer à la carte qu'il avait produite dans l'affaire *Nicaragua c. Honduras*[256].

---

[253] CR 2007/11, p. 57, par. 17 (Oude Elferink) *[traduction du Greffe]*.

[254] CR 2007/11, p. 57, par. 19 (Oude Elferink) (les italiques sont de nous) *[traduction du Greffe]*.

[255] *Ibid.*, réponse écrite de la République du Nicaragua à la question posée par M. le juge *ad hoc* Gaja lors de l'audience publique tenue le 16 mars 2007, 5 avril 2007.

[256] CR 2021/16, p. 41, par. 17 (Oude Elferink).

38. Je ne méconnais pas, bien sûr, que mon contradicteur a fait valoir non seulement qu'Edinburgh Cay est une île, mais encore qu'il y a d'autres îles, à Edinburgh Reef[257]. La carte que j'ai montrée la semaine dernière tend à attester qu'Edinburgh Cay n'est pas une île[258]. Il n'en existe pas davantage à Edinburgh Reef.

39. J'invite à cet égard la Cour à bien vouloir se référer aux instructions nautiques établies par les services hydrographiques des Etats-Unis. Ces instructions entendent décrire les formations marines rencontrées par les navigateurs, et ce, de manière précise en fonction des connaissances concrètes disponibles. Lorsque l'information n'est pas certaine, l'instruction le mentionne. Lorsque le doute n'est pas permis, l'information est sans réserve. Ainsi, alors qu'au début du XXe siècle, Edinburgh Reef était décrit comme «apparently awash»[259] — «apparemment submergée» en français —, les relevés ultérieurs ont permis à la National Geospatial-Intelligence Agency de lever ce doute, et d'affirmer, de manière constante depuis les années 1950, que : «Edinburgh Reef, about 4 miles long, *lies awash* about 8 ¼ miles northward of the northern limits of the Cayos Miskitos group»[260].

40. Ce témoignage récent, d'une partie tierce qui n'a aucun intérêt dans la présente espèce, est déterminant. La Cour sera également intéressée de savoir que, quelques années plus tard, le naturaliste Peter Matthiesen, que l'on ne saurait davantage soupçonner de partialité, faisait rapport sur sa propre visite de la zone de la manière suivante : «At Edinburgh Reef, no land was visible — only irregular patterns of white surf.»[261] Il notait aussi les similitudes entre Edinburgh Reef et «Cape Bank» — aujourd'hui Banco del Cabo Falso au Honduras : «Like Edinburgh, this reef is barely below the surface…»[262].

---

[257] CR 2021/16, p. 41, par. 17 (Oude Elferink).

[258] Colombie, dossier des juges du mercredi 22 septembre 2021, onglet n° 51.

[259] *Central America and Mexico Pilot*, H.O. No. 130, Government Printing Office, 2nd ed., 1920 (disponible à l'adresse suivante : books.google.nl/books?id=uEAPAQAAMAAJ).

[260] *Sailing Directions for the East Coasts of Central America and Mexico*, Pub. 20, Defense Mapping Agency, Hydrographic Center, 5e éd., 1952. (disponible à l'adresse suivante : books.google.nl/books?id=ibEnMMtvivAC — les italiques sont de nous) ; voir également, *Sailing Directions (enroute) for the Caribbean Sea*, Pub. 144, Defense Mapping Agency, Hydrographic/Topographic Center, 1re éd., 1976 (disponible à l'adresse suivante : books.google.nl/books?id=sOPgS6jBpsIC), *Sailing Directions (enroute) for the Caribbean Sea*, Numero 148, vol. 2, Defense Mapping Agency, Hydrographic/Topographic Center, 4e éd., 1993 (disponible à l'adresse suivante : books.google.nl/books?id=O_KrJAWvqw4C), *ibid.*, 6e éd., 1998 (disponible à l'adresse suivante : books.google.nl/books?id=TFaDH-1zPsoC) & *ibid.*, 17e éd., 2017 (disponible à l'adresse suivante : msi.nga.mil/Publications/SDEnroute).

[261] P. Matthiessen, «A Reporter at large to the Miskito Bank», *The New Yorker*, 28 octobre 1967, p. 154.

[262] *Ibid.*, p. 158.

41. Madame la présidente, Mesdames et Messieurs les Juges, j'en viens à ma conclusion. Premièrement, la géographie ne permet manifestement pas au Nicaragua de tracer des lignes de base droites au long de sa côte ; deuxièmement, même si tel était le cas, les lignes qu'il trace ne respectent en rien les règles s'appliquant à cette méthode ; enfin, et en tout état de cause, ces lignes s'appuient sur une géographie et de prétendus points de base qui ne pourraient exister qu'au bénéfice du doute.

Madame la présidente, ceci conclut ma plaidoirie. Mesdames et Messieurs les juges, je vous remercie de votre patiente attention. Madame la présidente, je vous prie de bien vouloir appeler à la barre M. l'agent de la Colombie.

The PRESIDENT: I thank Professor Thouvenin. I shall now give the floor to the Agent of Colombia, H.E. Mr. Carlos Gustavo Arrieta Padilla. You have the floor, Your Excellency.

Mr. ARRIETA PADILLA:

1. Madam President, distinguished judges, it is an honour to stand before you, once again, as the Agent of the Republic of Colombia.

2. Throughout these hearings, Nicaragua has tried to present a case that does not correspond to reality. It has tried to make this a case of non-compliance of the 2012 ruling, which it is not. The scope of this case was clearly defined by the Court in its 2016 decision on preliminary objections, which clearly stated that this is a case concerning alleged violations by Colombia of Nicaragua's sovereign rights, and nothing else.

3. Nicaragua's desire to change the scope of the case has led it to present a false narrative of Colombia's position and of the actual situation in the south-western Caribbean, based on misrepresented statements by Colombian presidents and a distorted presentation of some alleged events. Nicaragua has done this in order to be able to say that Colombia has had a systematic policy of disregarding the 2012 Judgment and Nicaragua's sovereign rights.

4. However, as a consequence of its desire to misrepresent the facts, Nicaragua has forgotten to pay attention to everything the presidential statements — on which they so heavily rely — did *not* say: Colombia never said that it will not respect its international obligations; Colombia never said that Nicaragua could not fish in its waters; and the Colombian Navy never received an order to stop Nicaraguan vessels. On the contrary, in line with our constitutional court's 2014 decision, as was

explained by the Co-Agent, our country has always tried to act in compliance with its international obligations.

5. Madam President, distinguished judges, Nicaragua is trying to make, as we say in Colombia, a storm in a teacup. It has intentionally forgotten to mention the reality in the area throughout the past nine years. That is, from the day after your ruling of 2012, Nicaraguan fishing boats have been able to fish freely east of the 82nd meridian, and Colombia has never opposed it. Based on a sporadic list of alleged incidents, Nicaragua has tried to ignore that overwhelming reality: since November 2012, vessels from that country have carried out no less than 10,000 fishing operations in these waters, and since November 2012 their fishing income has multiplied exponentially. All of this was demonstrated by Colombia in their pleadings.

6. If we look at this in terms of numbers, and even assuming that all the alleged incidents were true, which they are not of course, as Mr. Bundy explained, events have only occurred in 0.4 per cent of Nicaragua's fishing operations. This implies, *contrario senso*, that there have been no problems at all in at least 99.6 per cent of the fishing tasks carried out on Nicaraguan boats since 2012. That is, out of 10,000 fishing sorties made in the area by Nicaraguan fishing boats in 2012, 9,960 have had no problem at all. If we add the fact that in none of the cases alleged by Nicaragua our Navy has ever prevented Nicaraguan fishing vessels from continuing their fishing activities, it is easy to conclude that Colombia has never had a policy of systematic violations of Nicaragua's rights. On the contrary, these numbers show the opposite, that is that Colombia has always had a policy of respect for the sovereign rights of Nicaragua.

7. Even though this is a minor issue, Colombia wants to clarify a statement made by Nicaragua's counsel: we do not have a fleet in the area. The Colombian Navy has only one coast guard in the area, and occasionally two, which only coincide when one is replacing the other. In these conditions, that is, with just one coast guard in an area, as Nicaragua's Agent calls it, the size of the Adriatic Sea, one can hardly say that Colombia is trying to systematically impede Nicaragua from exercising their rights.

8. Colombia understands that lawyers sometimes get excited about their cases and exaggerate their positions. But in this case, they cannot hide the fact that during the past nine years more than 99.9 per cent of their fishing sorties have not had any problem at all, and that their fishing has increased monumentally.

9. Nicaragua has also tried to convey a false image of Colombia before the Court: it has said, not once but several times, that Colombia's actions and positions have intentionally disrespected the Court and its 2012 ruling, and has asked the Court to react by sanctioning my country. Madam President and distinguished judges, what Nicaragua has said is simply not true. Nicaragua seems to forget that this is a case of Nicaragua against Colombia, and not, as they try to portray it, a case of Colombia against the Court.

10. Colombia has been very clear from the beginning of the case. We have explained with total transparency our country's reaction after the 2012 Judgment; and throughout our written pleadings we have explained how our legal régime works, what our constitutional limitations are, and how we have tried to handle them. Colombia could not act otherwise: we are a country with a tradition of respect for judges, for national and international courts, and for their decisions. That has been one of the constants in the republican history of our country, which is the oldest in South America, that we will never change. I wish other countries could say the same.

11. Madam President, distinguished judges, Colombia has not had and will not have a policy of disregard of the Court or of Nicaragua's rights. What we have is a constitutional limitation. As the Co-Agent explained in his initial intervention, Colombia is a dualist country, whose political constitution provides that State boundaries can only be modified by a treaty. The second part of Article 101 of the Colombian Constitution has a very specific mandate, which Professor Pellet, by the way, chose to ignore in his presentation. It says that the existing boundaries, in 1991, "can only be modified by virtue of a treaty". Colombia cannot ignore that reality, nor the rule of law, nor the rule of the separation of powers.

12. Madam President, distinguished judges, the image of Colombia that Nicaragua wants to present is ill-intentioned, and completely removed from what Colombia is. We strongly reject that message, and also the fact that Nicaragua resorts to such attempts at manipulation to defend its indefensible positions.

13. It is worth repeating, as the Co-Agent said in his initial speech, that Colombia has been willing to open paths for dialogue with Nicaragua. It tried in 1977, in 1995, in 2001 and in 2015. Unfortunately, Nicaragua did not accept. In spite of this attitude, Colombia has left the door open since 2015.

14. Madam President, distinguished judges, Colombia has appeared in these proceedings to defend the rights conferred upon us by international law and to reject the unfounded accusations of Nicaragua. Colombia is convinced: (i) that it has the right to have a contiguous zone of the islands of the Archipelago of San Andrés, and to exercise in it the functions conferred by international law, as Professor Reisman explained; (ii) that it has the right to have a presence in the south-western Caribbean, to exercise its freedom of navigation and overflight, and to observe and report illegal activities that may occur, as allowed by international law, as my colleague explained; and (iii) that it has the duty to protect the natural habitat of the Raizal communities and to protect the maritime environment around the Archipelago from the predatory activities of Nicaragua and other countries that threaten the stability of the Archipelago and of the habitat of the Raizales, on which the survival of the islands depends.

15. I would finally refer – make a brief comment on Colombia's counter-claims:

16. First, the Raizal community of the islands of the San Andrés Archipelago has fished in the waters of south-western Caribbean for hundreds of years; members of that community settled the Mosquitia coast and were the origin of the Raizal groups in that area. The Raizales of San Andrés Archipelago discovered and named almost all the fishing grounds between the islands and the coast of Nicaragua. As Kent Francis James said last Wednesday, the sea is the Raizales' life and raison d'être. It is their gift from God. They have travelled and fished without impediment or limitation, but they did so until 2012, when Nicaragua impeded them to continue all this, in spite of their rights, and recognition made by Nicaragua's own President. Unfortunately, today, they face the possibility of not being able to continue fishing in their traditional banks, and they suffer the fear of moving freely between the islands of the Archipelago.

17. Far from what Nicaragua's Agent said, this would directly or indirectly affect not a small number of Raizales, but the entire community that inhabits the Colombian islands. This situation is inacceptable from any legal or social perspective, as it would affect a cultural and ethnical minority,

who just happen to be the original inhabitants of the islands. If they are so few fishermen, as Nicaragua contends, why does Nicaragua insist on denying them access to their traditional fishing grounds? Colombia considers that international law cannot support or be the cause of this situation. International law exists, among many other reasons, to correct such situations.

18. Madam President, distinguished judges, Colombia thanks the Court for having held these hearings and for having been heard. We thank you, Madam President, and your Colleagues. We also thank the Registrar and all his staff, who have made these hearings possible under extraordinary circumstances. And a special word of appreciation is due to the interpreters and the technicians who have made these hybrid proceedings possible.

19. Madam President, I know I will exceed a couple of minutes our allotted time, but please, I shall now read Colombia's concluding submissions, written copies of which will be made available in accordance with the Rules of the Court:

FINAL SUBMISSIONS

I. For the reasons stated in its written and oral pleadings, the Republic of Colombia respectfully requests the Court to reject each of the Submissions of the Republic of Nicaragua, and to adjudge and declare that

1. Colombia has not in any manner violated Nicaragua's sovereign rights or maritime spaces in the Southwestern Caribbean Sea.
2. Colombia's Decree No. 1946 of 9 September 2013 (as amended by Decree No. 1119 of 17 June 2014) has not given rise to any violation of Nicaragua's sovereign rights or maritime spaces.
   - *(a)* There is nothing in international law that precludes the contiguous zone of one State from overlapping with the exclusive economic zone of another State;
   - *(b)* The geodetic lines established in the Decree connecting the outermost points of Colombia's contiguous zones do not violate international law;
   - *(c)* The specific powers concerning the contiguous zone enumerated in the Decree do not violate international law;

(d) No Colombian action in the contiguous zone has given rise to any violation of Nicaragua's sovereign rights or maritime spaces.

II. Further, the Republic of Colombia respectfully requests the Court to adjudge and declare that

3. The inhabitants of the San Andrés Archipelago, in particular the Raizales, enjoy artisanal fishing rights in the traditional fishing grounds located beyond the territorial sea of the islands of the San Andrés Archipelago.
4. Nicaragua has violated the traditional fishing rights of the inhabitants of the San Andrés Archipelago.
5. Nicaragua's straight baselines established in Decree No. 33-2013 of 19 August 2013 are contrary to international law and violate Colombia's rights and maritime spaces.

III. The Court is further requested to order Nicaragua

6. With regard to submissions 3 and 4, to ensure that the inhabitants of the San Andrés Archipelago engaged in traditional fishing enjoy unfettered access to:
   (a) Their traditional fishing banks located in the maritime areas beyond the territorial sea of the islands of San Andrés Archipelago; and,
   (b) The banks located in Colombian maritime areas when access to them requires navigating outside the territorial sea of the islands of the San Andrés Archipelago.
7. To compensate Colombia for all damages caused, including loss of profits, resulting from Nicaragua's violation of its international obligations.
8. To give Colombia appropriate guarantees of non-repetition.

Madam President, distinguished judges, thank you very much for your attention. This concludes Colombia's presentation.

The PRESIDENT: I thank the Agent of Colombia. The Court takes note of the final submissions which you have now read on behalf of Colombia.

Your statement brings to an end Colombia's second round of oral arguments on the claims of Nicaragua and on Colombia's counter-claims. I recall that on Friday 1 October 2021, between 3 p.m.

and 4 p.m., Nicaragua will present its second round of oral argument on Colombia's counter-claims. The sitting is adjourned.

The Court rose at 6.10 p.m.

Non corrigé
Uncorrected

CR 2021/19

International Court of Justice

THE HAGUE

Cour internationale de Justice

LA HAYE

YEAR 2021

Public sitting

held on Friday 1 October 2021, at 3 p.m., at the Peace Palace,

President Donoghue presiding,

***in the case concerning* Alleged Violations of Sovereign Rights and Maritime Spaces in the Caribbean Sea (Nicaragua *v.* Colombia)**

VERBATIM RECORD

ANNÉE 2021

Audience publique

tenue le vendredi 1er octobre 2021, à 15 heures, au Palais de la Paix,

sous la présidence de Mme Donoghue, présidente,

***en l'affaire relative à des* Violations alléguées de droits souverains et d'espaces maritimes dans la mer des Caraïbes (Nicaragua c. Colombie)**

COMPTE RENDU

Present: President Donoghue
Vice-President Gevorgian
Judges Tomka
Abraham
Bennouna
Yusuf
Xue
Sebutinde
Robinson
Salam
Iwasawa
Nolte
Judges *ad hoc* Daudet
McRae

Registrar Gautier

Présents :	Mme	Donoghue, présidente
	M.	Gevorgian, vice-président
	MM.	Tomka
		Abraham
		Bennouna
		Yusuf
	Mmes	Xue
		Sebutinde
	MM.	Robinson
		Salam
		Iwasawa
		Nolte, juges
	MM.	Daudet
		McRae, juges *ad hoc*
	M.	Gautier, greffier

The Government of Nicaragua is represented by:

H.E. Mr. Carlos José Argüello Gómez, Ambassador of the Republic of Nicaragua to the Kingdom of the Netherlands,

as Agent and Counsel;

Mr. Alex Oude Elferink, Director, Netherlands Institute for the Law of the Sea, Professor of International Law of the Sea at Utrecht University,

Mr. Vaughan Lowe, QC, Emeritus Chichele Professor of Public International Law, University of Oxford, member of the Institut de droit international, member of the Bar of England and Wales,

Mr. Lawrence H. Martin, Attorney at Law, Foley Hoag LLP, member of the Bars of the United States Supreme Court, the District of Columbia and the Commonwealth of Massachusetts,

Mr. Alain Pellet, Emeritus Professor of the University Paris Nanterre, former Chairman of the International Law Commission, President of the Institut de droit international,

Mr. Paul Reichler, Attorney at Law, Foley Hoag LLP, member of the Bars of the United States Supreme Court and the District of Columbia,

as Counsel and Advocates;

Ms Claudia Loza Obregon, Legal Adviser, Ministry of Foreign Affairs of Nicaragua,

Ms Tessa Barsac, Consultant in International Law, Master (University Paris Nanterre), LLM (Leiden University),

as Assistant Counsel;

Mr. Robin Cleverly, MA, DPhil, CGeol, FGS, Law of the Sea Consultant, Marbdy Consulting Ltd,

as Scientific and Technical Adviser;

Ms Sherly Noguera de Argüello, MBA,

as Administrator.

The Government of Colombia is represented by:

H.E. Mr. Carlos Gustavo Arrieta Padilla, former Judge of the Council of State of Colombia, former Attorney General of Colombia and former Ambassador of Colombia to the Netherlands,

as Agent;

H.E. Mr. Manuel José Cepeda Espinosa, former President of the Constitutional Court of Colombia, former Permanent Delegate of Colombia to UNESCO and former Ambassador of Colombia to the Swiss Confederation,

as Co-Agent;

Le Gouvernement du Nicaragua est représenté par :

S. Exc. M. Carlos José Argüello Gómez, ambassadeur de la République du Nicaragua auprès du Royaume des Pays-Bas,

comme agent et conseil ;

M. Alex Oude Elferink, directeur de l'Institut néerlandais du droit de la mer, professeur de droit international de la mer à l'Université d'Utrecht,

M. Vaughan Lowe, QC, professeur émérite de droit international public à l'Université d'Oxford, titulaire de la chaire Chichele, membre de l'Institut de droit international, membre du barreau d'Angleterre et du pays de Galles,

M. Lawrence H. Martin, avocat au cabinet Foley Hoag LLP, membre des barreaux de la Cour suprême des Etats-Unis d'Amérique, du district de Colombia et du Commonwealth du Massachusetts,

M. Alain Pellet, professeur émérite de l'Université Paris Nanterre, ancien président de la Commission du droit international, président de l'Institut de droit international,

M. Paul Reichler, avocat au cabinet Foley Hoag LLP, membre des barreaux de la Cour suprême des Etats-Unis d'Amérique et du district de Colombia,

comme conseils et avocats ;

Mme Claudia Loza Obregon, conseillère juridique auprès du ministère des affaires étrangères du Nicaragua,

Mme Tessa Barsac, consultante en droit international, master (Université Paris Nanterre), LLM (Université de Leyde),

comme conseils adjoints ;

M. Robin Cleverly, MA, DPhil, CGeol, FGS, consultant en droit de la mer, Marbdy Consulting Ltd,

comme conseiller scientifique et technique ;

Mme Sherly Noguera de Argüello, MBA,

comme administrateur.

Le Gouvernement de la Colombie est représenté par :

S. Exc. M. Carlos Gustavo Arrieta Padilla, ancien juge au conseil d'Etat colombien, ancien *Procurador General de la Nación* et ancien ambassadeur de Colombie aux Pays-Bas,

comme agent ;

S. Exc. M. Manuel José Cepeda Espinosa, ancien président de la Cour constitutionnelle de Colombie, ancien représentant permanent de la Colombie auprès de l'UNESCO et ancien ambassadeur de Colombie auprès de la Confédération suisse,

comme coagent ;

H.E. Ms Marta Lucía Ramírez Blanco, Vice-President and Minister for Foreign Affairs of the Republic of Colombia,

H.E. Mr. Everth Hawkins Sjogreen, Governor of San Andrés, Providencia and Santa Catalina, Colombia,

as National Authorities;

Mr. W. Michael Reisman, McDougal Professor of International Law at Yale University, member of the Institut de droit international,

Mr. Rodman R. Bundy, former *avocat à la Cour d'appel de Paris*, member of the Bar of the State of New York, partner at Squire Patton Boggs LLP, Singapore,

Sir Michael Wood, KCMG, member of the International Law Commission, member of the Bar of England and Wales,

Mr. Eduardo Valencia-Ospina, former Registrar and Deputy-Registrar of the International Court of Justice, member and former Special Rapporteur and Chair of the International Law Commission, former Chair of the Latin American Society of International Law,

Mr. Jean-Marc Thouvenin, Professor at the University Paris Nanterre, Secretary-General of the Hague Academy of International Law, associate member of the Institut de droit international, member of the Paris Bar, Sygna Partners,

Ms Laurence Boisson de Chazournes, Professor of International Law and International Organization at the University of Geneva, member of the Institut de droit international,

H.E. Mr. Kent Francis James, former Ambassador of Colombia to Belize, former Ambassador of Colombia to Jamaica,

as Counsel and Advocates;

Mr. Andrés Villegas Jaramillo, LLM, Co-ordinator, Group of Affairs before the International Court of Justice at the Ministry of Foreign Affairs of Colombia, member of the Legal Sub-Commission of the Caribbean Sea Commission, Association of Caribbean States,

Mr. Makane Moïse Mbengue, Professor at the University of Geneva, Director of the Department of Public International Law and International Organization, associate member of the Institut de droit international,

Mr. Luke Vidal, member of the Paris Bar, Sygna Partners,

Eran Sthoeger, Esq., member of the Bar of the State of New York,

Mr. Alvin Yap, Advocate and Solicitor of the Supreme Court of Singapore, Squire Patton Boggs LLP, Singapore,

Mr. Lorenzo Palestini, PhD, Lecturer at the Graduate Institute of International and Development Studies and at the University of Geneva,

as Counsel;

S. Exc. Mme Marta Lucía Ramírez Blanco, vice-présidente et ministre des affaires étrangères de la République de Colombie,

S. Exc. M. Everth Hawkins Sjogreen, gouverneur de San Andrés, Providencia et Santa Catalina, Colombie,

comme représentants de l'Etat ;

M. W. Michael Reisman, professeur de droit international à l'Université de Yale, titulaire de la chaire McDougal, membre de l'Institut de droit international,

M. Rodman R. Bundy, ancien avocat à la Cour d'appel de Paris, membre du barreau de l'Etat de New York, associé au cabinet Squire Patton Boggs LLP (Singapour),

Sir Michael Wood, KCMG, membre de la Commission du droit international, membre du barreau d'Angleterre et du pays de Galles,

M. Eduardo Valencia-Ospina, ancien greffier et greffier adjoint de la Cour internationale de Justice, membre et ancien rapporteur spécial et président de la Commission du droit international, ancien président de l'association latino-américaine de droit international,

M. Jean-Marc Thouvenin, professeur à l'Université Paris Nanterre, secrétaire général de l'Académie de droit international de La Haye, membre associé de l'Institut de droit international, membre du barreau de Paris, cabinet Sygna Partners,

Mme Laurence Boisson de Chazournes, professeure de droit international public et organisation internationale à l'Université de Genève, membre de l'Institut de droit international,

S. Exc. M. Kent Francis James, ancien ambassadeur de Colombie au Belize et ancien ambassadeur de Colombie en Jamaïque,

comme conseils et avocats ;

M. Andrés Villegas Jaramillo, LLM, coordonnateur du groupe chargé des affaires portées devant la Cour internationale de Justice au sein du ministère des affaires étrangères de la Colombie, membre de la sous-commission juridique relevant de la Commission de la mer des Caraïbes de l'Association des Etats de la Caraïbe,

M. Makane Moïse Mbengue, professeur à l'Université de Genève, directeur du département de droit international public et organisation internationale, membre associé de l'Institut de droit international,

M. Luke Vidal, membre du barreau de Paris, cabinet Sygna Partners,

M. Eran Sthoeger, membre du barreau de l'Etat de New York,

M. Alvin Yap, avocat et *solicitor* à la Cour suprême de Singapour, cabinet Squire Patton Boggs LLP (Singapour),

M. Lorenzo Palestini, PhD, chargé d'enseignement à l'Institut de hautes études internationales et du développement et à l'Université de Genève,

comme conseils ;

H.E. Mr. Juan José Quintana Aranguren, Head of Multilateral Affairs, former Ambassador of Colombia to the Netherlands,

H.E. Mr. Fernando Antonio Grillo Rubiano, Ambassador of the Republic of Colombia to the Kingdom of the Netherlands and Permanent Representative of Colombia to the Organisation for the Prohibition of Chemical Weapons,

Ms Jenny Sharyne Bowie Wilches, Second Secretary, Embassy of Colombia in the Netherlands,

Ms Viviana Andrea Medina Cruz, Second Secretary, Embassy of Colombia in the Netherlands,

Mr. Sebastián Correa Cruz, Third Secretary,

Mr. Raúl Alfonso Simancas Gómez, Third Secretary, Group of Affairs before the International Court of Justice,

Ministry of Foreign Affairs of Colombia;

Rear Admiral Ernesto Segovia Forero, Chief of Naval Operations,

CN Hermann León, Delegate of Colombia to the International Maritime Organization,

CN William Pedroza, National Navy of Colombia, Director of Maritime and Fluvial Interests Office,

Navy of the Republic of Colombia;

Mr. Scott Edmonds, Cartographer, Director of International Mapping,

Ms Victoria Taylor, Cartographer, International Mapping,

as Technical Advisers;

Mr. Gershon Hasin, LLM, JSD, Yale Law School,

as Legal Assistant;

Mr. Mark Taylor Archbold, Consultant for the National Unit of Disaster Risk Management,

Mr. Joseph Richard Jessie Martinez, Consultant for the National Unit of Disaster Risk Management,

as Advisers.

S. Exc. M. Juan José Quintana Aranguren, chef des affaires multilatérales, ancien ambassadeur de Colombie aux Pays-Bas,

S. Exc. M. Fernando Antonio Grillo Rubiano, ambassadeur de la République de Colombie auprès du Royaume des Pays-Bas et représentant permanent de la Colombie auprès de l'Organisation pour l'interdiction des armes chimiques,

Mme Jenny Sharyne Bowie Wilches, deuxième secrétaire, ambassade de Colombie aux Pays-Bas,

Mme Viviana Andrea Medina Cruz, deuxième secrétaire, ambassade de Colombie aux Pays-Bas,

M. Sebastián Correa Cruz, troisième secrétaire,

M. Raúl Alfonso Simancas Gómez, troisième secrétaire, groupe chargé des affaires portées devant la Cour internationale de Justice,

ministère des affaires étrangères de la République de Colombie ;

Le contre-amiral Ernesto Segovia Forero, chef des opérations navales,

Le capitaine de vaisseau Hermann León, représentant de la Colombie auprès de l'Organisation maritime internationale,

Le capitaine de vaisseau William Pedroza, marine nationale de Colombie, chef de la direction chargée des intérêts maritimes et fluviaux,

marine de la République de Colombie ;

M. Scott Edmonds, cartographe, directeur de International Mapping,

Mme Victoria Taylor, cartographe, International Mapping,

comme conseillers techniques ;

M. Gershon Hasin, LLM, JSD, faculté de droit de l'Université de Yale,

comme assistant juridique ;

M. Mark Taylor Archbold, consultant auprès de l'unité nationale de gestion des risques de catastrophe,

M. Joseph Richard Jessie Martinez, consultant auprès de l'unité nationale de gestion des risques de catastrophe,

comme conseillers.

The PRESIDENT: Please be seated. The sitting is open. For reasons duly made known to me, Judge Bhandari is unable to join us for today's sitting. The Court meets this afternoon to hear Nicaragua's second round of oral argument on Colombia's counter-claims. I invite Mr. Lawrence Martin to address the Court.

Mr. MARTIN:

COLOMBIA'S COUNTER-CLAIM RELATING TO THE ALLEGED TRADITIONAL FISHING RIGHTS OF THE RAIZALES FAILS

1. Madam President, distinguished Members of the Court, good afternoon. My task today, as it was last Friday, is to respond to Colombia's arguments concerning the alleged traditional fishing rights of the Raizales. I am mindful of your admonition not to repeat points already made. I will therefore try to be as brief and to the point as possible. For the avoidance of doubt, however, we stand by our prior arguments in their entirety.

I. President Ortega's statements do not have the effects Colombia claims

2. You will have noticed from Mr. Valencia-Ospina's intervention on Wednesday that Colombia has gone all in on President Ortega's statements relating to the Raizales' alleged traditional fishing rights. Colombia now relies on those statements to support its *entire* case, both on the facts and the law. President Ortega's statements cannot, however, support the weight Colombia tries to place on them.

3. I explained many of those reasons last Friday. I do not intend to reiterate those points now. On Wednesday, Sir Michael and Mr. Valencia-Ospina helpfully hinted at a different way to think about the issue. They referred to President Ortega's statements as a form of "unilateral declaration"[1] capable of having legal effect. Looking at the question that way and examining President Ortega's statements through the lens of the law relating to unilateral undertakings only further underscores the fact that they do not have the effects that Colombia might wish.

---

[1] CR 2021/18, p. 14, para. 18 (Wood); CR 2021/18, p. 50, para. 6 (Valencia-Ospina).

4. In the *Nuclear Tests* cases, the Court stated:

> "It is well recognized that declarations made by way of unilateral acts, concerning legal or factual situations, may have the effect of creating legal obligations.
>
> . . . .
>
> Of course, not all unilateral acts imply obligation; but a State may choose to take up a certain position in relation to a particular matter with the intention of being bound — the intention is to be ascertained by interpretation of the act. *When States make statements by which their freedom of action is to be limited, a restrictive interpretation is called for*."[2]

5. Guiding Principle 7 of the International Law Commission's 2006 *Guiding Principles applicable to unilateral declarations of States capable of creating legal obligations* (hereinafter *"Guiding Principles"*) echoes the Court's language. According to Guiding Principle 7:

> "A unilateral declaration entails obligations for the formulating State only if it is stated *in clear and specific terms*. In the case of doubt as to the scope of the obligations resulting from such a declaration, such obligations *must be interpreted in a restrictive manner*."[3]

6. To the extent that President Ortega's statements were made "in clear and specific terms", they were clearly and specifically conditioned on appropriate "authorization"[4] being given in the future, or on "agreements"[5] or "mechanisms"[6] being worked out later. Colombia cannot casually seize on the alleged obligation assumed without also accepting the express conditions placed thereon.

7. Moreover, in the case concerning the *Frontier Dispute (Burkina Faso* v. *Republic of Mali)*, the Chamber of the Court was careful to point out that when it comes to determining the effect of an alleged unilateral undertaking "it all depends on the intention of the State in question"[7]. Guiding Principle 3 of the ILC's *Guiding Principles* is to similar effect. It states: "To determine the legal effects of such declarations, it is necessary to take account of their content, of *all the factual circumstances in which they were made*, and of the reactions to which they gave rise."[8]

---

[2] *Nuclear Tests (Australia* v. *France), Judgment, I.C.J. Reports 1974*, p. 267, paras. 43-44; *Nuclear Tests (New Zealand* v. *France), Judgment, I.C.J. Reports 1974*, pp. 472-473, paras. 46-47. Emphasis added.

[3] ILC, *Guiding Principles applicable to unilateral declarations of States capable of creating legal obligations*, 2006, Guiding Principle 7; emphasis added.

[4] CMC, para. 3.94 (citing MN, Ann. 27).

[5] CMC, para. 3.94 (citing CMC, Anns. 73 and 74).

[6] CMC, para. 3.94 (citing MN, Ann. 77).

[7] *Frontier Dispute (Burkina Faso v. Republic of Mali), Judgment, I.C.J. Reports 1986*, p. 573, para. 39.

[8] *Guiding Principles*, Guiding Principle 3; emphasis added.

8. Here, considering all the circumstances in which President Ortega's statements were made, it could not be more clear that they do not reflect an unqualified intent to be bound. As we explained — and Colombia does not seriously deny — they were made in the context of the highly fraught political situation created by Colombia's rejection of the Court's 2012 Judgment (a rejection that remains Colombia's policy to this day). President Ortega was simply, and very obviously, trying to entice Colombia back to the table by offering to take account of its expressed concerns as part of an agreement that would confirm Nicaragua's rights under the Court's 2012 Judgment.

9. This is not a question of conducting a "psychological inquiry into the real will of [Nicaragua's] President"[9], as Mr. Valencia-Ospina would have it. It is objective reality. The Court delivered its unanimous delimitation Judgment in November 2012 and Colombia rejected it. Nicaragua wanted to see it implemented but understood the only way that was possible, given Colombia's defiant reaction to it, was by seeking an agreement with Colombia that would allow it to save face and say that its concerns had been addressed. President Ortega was plainly seeking a solution that would be politically acceptable to both Parties.

10. Thus, accepting Colombia's invitation to view the issue through the prism of the law relating to unilateral undertakings and considering whether President Ortega's statements are sufficiently "clear and specific" to create the effects that Colombia says they do, the answer is clear: they do not.

11. Two final points on this issue, if I may. *First*, I would be remiss if I did not point out that Colombia itself has effectively admitted in its written pleadings that President Ortega's statements are insufficient to create any rights. Specifically, in its Counter-Memorial, in the context of setting out President Ortega's statements, Colombia itself rightly acknowledged that requiring mechanisms to be put in place "would have deprived the recognition of the Raizales' historic [fishing] rights of any meaning"[10]. Exactly right. A "right" subject to "authorization", conditioned on the adoption of "mechanisms" or subject to subsequent "agreement", is no right at all.

12. *Second*, Mr. Valencia-Ospina was not the only counsel for Colombia who tried to read more into President Ortega's statements than they actually say. Mr. Bundy went even further and

---

[9] CR 2021/18, p. 51, para. 6 (Valencia-Ospina).

[10] CMC, para. 3.94.

argued that President Ortega's statements not only granted fishing rights to Colombian fishermen, but also effectively invited the Colombian Navy into Nicaragua's EEZ to protect those rights[11]. As he did in the first round, Mr. Bundy admitted that Colombia's naval vessels were exercising police powers, in what was indisputably Nicaragua's waters under the Court's 2012 Judgment, to protect what they claimed were the Colombian State's historic fishing rights[12]. On Wednesday, his argument seemed to be that when Colombia's Navy intervened to stop Nicaragua's coast guard from approaching Colombian and foreign-flagged fishing boats, they did so pursuant to the authority conferred on them by President Ortega.

13. But that argument is directly contradicted by what the Colombian Navy said in its radio communications to the Nicaraguan coast guard, as the Court saw for itself during our presentation on 20 September. At no time did any Colombian naval vessel claim that it was acting pursuant to authority conveyed by President Ortega. To the contrary, in each incident, the Colombian naval vessel insisted that it was in Colombia's own waters, not Nicaragua's, because Colombia did not consider applicable, or abide by, the Court's ruling[13].

14. As that unchallenged evidence shows, the Colombian Navy did not act on anything President Ortega said. It was acting pursuant to what Colombia's own President said: that the boundary with Nicaragua was the 82nd meridian, and that all the waters east of it were Colombian.

II. The régime of the EEZ extinguished any traditional fishing rights

15. Not only are President Ortega's statements insufficient to vest the Raizales with the traditional fishing rights Colombia claims, those would-be rights are also inconsistent with the régime of the EEZ.

16. On Wednesday, Mr. Valencia-Ospina seemed irritated about once again hearing what he called "the 'legal monopoly' plea"[14]. I apologize for trying his patience, but the truth is that this is much more than just a "plea" from Nicaragua. It is a juridical fact established by a chamber of this Court — under customary international law, no less — in the *Gulf of Maine* case. As I pointed out

[11] CR 2021/18, p. 37, para. 40 (Bundy).

[12] CR 2021/15, p. 18, para. 48 (Bundy).

[13] CR 2021/17, pp. 25-26, paras. 11-12, 14 (Reichler).

[14] CR 2021/18, p. 56, para. 18 (Valencia-Ospina).

last time, the Chamber held that, with the advent of the EEZ, "[t]hird States *and their nationals found themselves deprived of any right of access to the sea areas within those zones*"[15]. I know Colombia finds this fact uncomfortable, but a fact it remains.

17. On Wednesday, for the very first time in the very long history of this case, we heard Colombia at least make an attempt to distinguish *Gulf of Maine*. Mr. Valencia-Ospina said first that that case "was not about traditional fishing rights"[16]. That may technically be true, but it is also irrelevant. The Court's language could not be any more clear. The coastal State has a "legal monopoly" that deprives "[t]hird States *and their nationals*" of any right of access. There is no room to read any ambiguity into that language.

18. Mr. Valencia-Ospina also said that the *Gulf of Maine* decision "says nothing . . . on the impact of delimitation on vested rights"[17]. But that assertion too cannot stand in the face of the Court's emphatic language. The effect of delimitation is precisely to determine the extent of the relevant States' EEZs and, with them, the extent of their "legal monopol[ies]" and the areas from which other States and their nationals are excluded.

19. At the end of the day, Colombia's case rests on two arguments, unpersuasive though they may be. *First*, it says, because traditional rights can exist on land and in the territorial sea, they can also exist in the EEZ. Mr. Valencia-Ospina came back to this argument at some length on Wednesday[18]. But I have already responded to it and I will not burden the Court by repeating those points now, all the more since Mr. Valencia-Ospina did not add anything new to the conversation on Wednesday.

20. Colombia's second argument is what might be termed the "but *Eritrea/Yemen*" argument. In Colombia's telling, the *Eritrea/Yemen* Tribunal was "the only tribunal ever *formally* tasked with addressing traditional rights in the EEZ" and decided that "traditional fishing . . . is not qualified by the maritime zones specified under . . . [UNCLOS]"[19]. The first part of this assertion is just wrong as

---

[15] *Delimitation of the Maritime Boundary in the Gulf of Maine Area (Canada* v. *United States), Judgment, I.C.J. Reports 1984*, pp. 341-342, para. 235; emphases added.

[16] CR 2021/18, p. 58, para. 22 (Valencia-Ospina).

[17] CR 2021/18, p. 58, para. 22 (Valencia-Ospina).

[18] CR 2021/18, pp. 49-50, para. 3; p. 56, para. 18 (Valencia-Ospina).

[19] CR 2021/18, p. 57, para. 19 (Valencia-Ospina).

a matter of fact. Indeed, a case Mr. Valencia-Ospina himself cites[20], the *South China Sea* arbitration, specifically addressed the question of whether traditional rights could exist in the EEZ and decisively concluded that they could not[21].

21. Moreover, the language from *Eritrea/Yemen* that Colombia is so fond of does not sweep as broadly as Colombia suggests. Here, greater precision is in order. The relevant passage from the tribunal's decision is on the screen now. The sentence to which Colombia devotes such attention reads: "By its very nature *it* is not qualified by the maritime zones specified under [UNCLOS]"[22]. But what is the "it" that is the subject of this sentence? The rest of the passage makes clear that this "it" is "the traditional fishing regime", which "has existed for the benefit of the fishermen of both countries throughout the region". In other words, the "it" is referring to the *specific* régime applicable between Eritrea and Yemen.

22. This is critical because, as I explained last Friday and Colombia dares not dispute, the traditional fishing régime between Eritrea and Yemen is characterized by an express agreement to allow traditional fishing in the EEZ[23]. This agreement was integral to the existing "traditional fishing regime" that was not qualified by the maritime zones under UNCLOS. This is a far cry from saying generally that, absent agreement, traditional fishing is compatible with the régime of the EEZ. Indeed, for all the reasons we have previously explained in our written and oral pleadings, traditional fishing is *not* compatible with the EEZ régime.

III. Colombia's evidence does not prove the existence of the rights it claims or their violation

23. I can be much briefer on the facts relating both to the alleged existence of the rights Colombia claims and Nicaragua's ostensible violation of them. The Court will recall that on Friday, I devoted roughly half my speech to a discussion of Colombia's evidence on these points and

---

[20] CR 2021/18, p. 60, para. 26, fn. 217 (Valencia-Ospina).

[21] *The South China Sea Arbitration between the Republic of the Philippines and the People's Republic of China, Award of 12 July 2016, RIAA*, Vol. XXXIII, p. 287, para. 261.

[22] *Award of the Arbitral Tribunal in the Second Stage of the Proceedings between Eritrea and Yemen (Maritime Delimitation), Decision of 17 December 1999, RIAA*, Vol. XXII, p. 361, para. 109.

[23] CR 2021/16, p. 23, para. 25 (Martin), citing the "Memorandum of Understanding between the State of Eritrea and the Republic of Yemen for Cooperation in the Areas of Maritime Fishing, Trade, Investment, and Transportation", 15 Nov. 1994, para. 1 (reproduced in Eritrea/Yemen, PCA Case No. 1996-04, Award of the Arbitral Tribunal in the Second Stage — Maritime Delimitation, 17 Dec. 1999, Ann. 3).

examined Colombia's 11 affidavits in some detail. On Wednesday, Mr. Valencia-Ospina was conspicuously more reserved.

24. On the first point — that is, the evidence ostensibly proving the existence of the alleged rights — Mr. Valencia-Ospina asserted only that "Colombia's evidence indeed shows that . . . artisanal fishermen and their ancestors have long navigated and fished in the shallow banks of Cape Bank and Luna Verde, as well as the deep-sea banks located east of La Esquina and in between the Northern Islands"[24]. This assertion, however, is entirely unsupported by any citation to the evidence. Not a single source is listed in footnote or elsewhere. And for good reason. As I explained last Friday, while some of Colombia's affidavits do *mention* Cape Bank and other features, none of them claim they were traditional fishing grounds fished by any of the affiants or their ancestors[25].

25. The only other point Colombia made on Wednesday was to return to the statement against interest made by an office of Colombia's Ministry of Labour. As it did in its written pleadings, Colombia dismissed this statement claiming that the relevant office "did not provide any evidence to maintain that the traditional banks had not been impacted by the 2012 Judgment"[26]. Of course, the same may be said about Colombia's claims before this Court. For the reasons we have explained, there is no evidence to maintain that the traditional fishing banks *were* impacted by the 2012 Judgment. Moreover, and in any event, the statement stands as Colombia's officially espoused view, stated on more than one occasion before an organ of the International Labour Organization.

26. Colombia was even more brief on the issue of Nicaragua's putative violations of the Raizales' alleged rights. In response to our observation that all of the allegations were hearsay, Mr. Valencia Ospina said: "There are good reasons, not requiring much elaboration, that explain why Colombia cannot rely on first-hand accounts *only*."[27] With respect, we actually think it would have been helpful to have those reasons elaborated. It is not at all clear to us why Colombia cannot rely on first-hand accounts. Moreover, it is not true that Colombia did not rely "only" on first-hand accounts; it did not rely on *any* first-hand accounts. Given that Colombia was able to collect

---

[24] CR 2021/18, p. 53, para. 12 (Valencia-Ospina).

[25] CR 2021/16, p. 31, para. 57 (Martin).

[26] CR 2021/18, p. 54, para. 14 (Valencia-Ospina).

[27] CR 2021/18, p. 60, para. 27 (Valencia-Ospina).

first-hand testimonies from a number of local fishermen, there is no reason whatsoever it could not have — and should not be expected to have — produced testimonies from directly affected fishermen, including those cited by name in Colombia's affidavits.

27. Colombia also tried to excuse the paucity of its evidence by asserting that "the associations and co-operatives, with whom the artisanal fishermen interact, neither have records, nor protocols in case of incidents at sea"[28]. Again, with respect, the record proves precisely the opposite. I explained last Friday that the co-ops have a detailed procedure pursuant to which fishermen report to the port captaincy after every trip[29]. And, indeed, one of Colombia's own affiants specifically refers to multiple incidents involving illegal fishermen from other countries that have been reported to local authorities[30]. There is therefore no excuse for Colombia's total reliance on hearsay to prove its case.

28. Madam President, for all these reasons, Nicaragua respectfully submits that the Court should reject Colombia's counter-claim relating to the alleged traditional fishing rights of the Raizales. The rights do not exist and they have not been violated.

29. Thank you for your ever patient attention. May I ask that you invite Professor Alex Oude Elferink to the podium once more?

The PRESIDENT: I thank Mr. Martin. I shall now give the floor to Professor Alex Oude Elferink. You have the floor, Sir.

Mr. OUDE ELFERINK: Madam President, Members of the Court, good afternoon.

NICARAGUA'S BASELINES

A. Introduction

1. Madam President, Professor Thouvenin this Wednesday pleaded with pathos and innuendo. However, taking a step back and looking at the content of his presentation, there was very little in terms of engaging with Nicaragua's arguments both on the law and on the facts. I would like to take this opportunity to discuss what Professor Thouvenin said, and perhaps even more importantly, what he did not say. To assist the Court, I will comment on all aspects of the applicable law as it relates to

[28] CR 2021/18, p. 60, para. 27 (Valencia-Ospina).

[29] CR 2021/16, p. 32, paras. 61-62 (Martin).

[30] CR 2021/16, p. 33, para. 63 (Martin).

straight baselines and also will briefly revisit the issue of Nicaragua's normal baselines seaward of its straight baselines.

B. Colombia's straight baseline practice

2. Madam President, this Wednesday counsel for Colombia again argued that Colombia's fourth counter-claim is concerned with Nicaragua's straight baselines, not Colombia's straight baselines[31]. It should be more than obvious by now that Nicaragua is not contesting that.

3. However, as Professor Thouvenin also submitted, the question is whether Nicaragua's straight baselines are in conformity with international law[32]. Now, that is a question that requires looking at the practice of States other than Nicaragua. For example, Colombia's fourth counter-claim also is not concerned with the legality of the straight baselines of Norway or Australia, but the practice of both States has been discussed in Colombia's pleadings[33].

4. Colombia's straight baselines practice is even more relevant in this connection. Colombia's straight baselines show how Colombia considers the law has to be interpreted and applied. That practice reveals that Colombia has adopted a different and self-serving standard specifically for the purposes of its fourth counter-claim[34]. It might be regrettable that the Court does not have the benefit of Colombia's explanation of how it has interpreted and applied the law in establishing its straight baselines. However, its tenacious silence really says it all.

C. Nicaragua's straight baselines

***(a)* The length of Nicaragua's straight baselines**

5. I now turn to a discussion of the various aspects of customary international law as they relate to Nicaragua's straight baselines. My first point concerns the length of Nicaragua's straight baselines. This Wednesday, counsel for Colombia submitted that I relied on the length of Nicaragua's baselines to justify that certain of Nicaragua's islands constituted part of the fringe of islands in the immediate

---

[31] CR2021/18, p. 62, para. 3 (Thouvenin).

[32] *Ibid.*

[33] See e.g. RC, para. 6.45; CR 2021/15, pp. 58-59, paras. 39-40 (Thouvenin); CR 2021/18, p. 61, para. 1 (Thouvenin).

[34] CR 2021/16, p. 40, para. 12 (Oude Elferink).

vicinity of Nicaragua's coast[35]. I did nothing of the kind. I observed that Nicaragua's straight baselines were unexceptional as regards their length in the light of State practice, including that of Colombia[36]. Professor Thouvenin had nothing to say on that point this Wednesday.

***(b)* The presence of a fringe of islands**

6. Madam President, one of the main planks of Colombia's argument on its fourth counter-claim has been that Nicaragua has not proven the existence of a fringe of islands along its coast[37]. This Wednesday Professor Thouvenin again played this same record.

7. He started by revisiting my argument on the Archipelago of the Recherche off the coast of Western Australia. He submitted that I had argued that Nicaragua's geography was comparable to that of the Archipelago of the Recherche[38]. That is not the point I was making. So, what was it? Let me illustrate that graphically. Last Friday, I argued that to the west of the town of Esperance, there is only a limited number of small islands, which are all included in the Australian system of straight baselines.

8. In its written pleadings, Colombia had argued that Nicaragua's islands had a very limited masking effect of the mainland, and as such were not fringing islands[39]. If you apply Colombia's methodology to determine this effect to the islands to the west of Esperance, there also is hardly any masking effect. Colombia's methodology, which was criticized in Nicaragua's Reply[40], consists of looking at the part of the mainland coast that is covered by the frontal projection of the islands in front of it. Not a very substantial part in this case. This figure is at tab AOE-1 of today's judges' folder. My point last Friday was that this example belies the high threshold Colombia is now seeking to impose on Nicaragua in relation to the criterion of fringing islands[41], not that the geography of Western Australia and Nicaragua is comparable.

---

[35] CR 2021/18, p. 61, para. 1 (Thouvenin).

[36] CR 2021/16, p. 40, para. 13 (Oude Elferink).

[37] APN, paras. 3.31 and following; CR 2021/15, para. 28 and following (Reisman).

[38] CR 2021/18, p. 61, para. 1 (Thouvenin).

[39] See RC, paras. 6.36 and following.

[40] RN, paras. 7.34-7.35.

[41] CR 2021/16, p. 43, para. 23 (Oude Elferink).

9. As a matter of fact, last Friday I discussed the coast of Trondheim to explain that straight baselines may also be used to connect separate groups of islands that are a distance apart[42]. Professor Thouvenin had nothing to say in reply this Wednesday. Now that this figure is on screen, allow me to also make another point. Colombia has sought to make much of the extent of the sea areas that are enclosed by Nicaragua's straight baselines. In 1952, when Norway established the straight baselines in the Trondheim area[43], it had a 4-nautical mile territorial sea. All of the area that is now coloured in red, avowedly Professor Thouvenin's favourite colour[44], were part of the high seas and the régime of freedom of navigation before Norway established its straight baselines. This figure is at tab AOE-2 of today's judges' folder.

10. I now turn to Professor Thouvenin's discussion of Nicaragua's islands. First, he sought to downplay the significance of the figures Colombia had previously used and which illustrated the presence and close proximity of Nicaragua's fringing islands to its mainland coast[45]. Now, what did he actually say? Nicaragua had allegedly overlooked Colombia's Counter-Memorial in this previous case. But as counsel for Colombia pointed out, the only thing the Counter-Memorial observes is that the charts Colombia had used were "on different scales, and . . . outdated in some respects"[46]. In some respects. No further information is provided. If the presence of islands had been in issue, it would have stood to reason that Colombia would have done one of two things. First, it could have acquired further data. Second, it could have given this matter the necessary attention in its pleadings, not the bland reference counsel for Colombia quoted this Wednesday. Colombia used base points on Nicaragua's islands to determine its boundary claim in relation to Nicaragua. A not unimportant matter. In this light, Nicaragua maintains that Colombia's earlier position squarely confirms the presence of the islands and that they fringe Nicaragua's mainland coast and are in close proximity of

---

[42] CR 2021/16, p. 42, para. 20 (Oude Elferink).

[43] Royal Decree of 18 July 1952 relating to the Baselines for the Norwegian Fishery Zone as regards that part of Norway which is situated to the south of 66° 28' 8 N Latitude, available at http://www.un.org/Depts/los/LEGISLATIONANDTREATIES/PDFFILES/NOR_1952_Decree.pdf (accessed 30 Sept. 2021). It should be noted that base points 49 and 50 in the Royal Decree are numbered as respectively base points 54 and 55.

[44] CR 2021/18, p. 62, para. 6 (Thouvenin).

[45] CR 2021/18, p. 66, para. 25 (Thouvenin).

[46] CR 2021/18, pp. 66-67, paras. 26-27 (Thouvenin).

that coast, as I also observed last Friday with reference to the baselines study of the United Nations Office for Ocean Affairs and the Law of the Sea[47].

11. Professor Thouvenin also revisited the map he showed of the Miskito biosphere reserve. It is welcome to see that he now admits that at least in this area there are many more islands than Miskito Cay. I will return to this point shortly. On the map he concluded: "La carte bio disait vrai. Il n'y a pas de connexion. Et on ne voit certainement ni un tapis ni un chapelet d'îles le long et à proximité de la côte."[48] That is not exactly true. The islands closest to the mainland are only some 9 nautical miles distant from it. As may be recalled, the baselines study of the United Nations Office for Ocean Affairs and the Law of the Sea observes that a distance of 24 nautical miles would satisfy the condition of "in the immediate vicinity"[49] for the islands that are closest to the coast. And Nicaragua has no doubt that this is a fringe of islands. Let me only add that, by omitting the areas of drying reefs in the Miskito Cays, which we have now added again to the figure, Professor Thouvenin's adjusted figure still did not do justice to the closely knit unit the Miskito Cays constitute. This figure is at tab AOE-3 of today's judges' folder.

12. But let me return to the larger picture. If Nicaragua's islands are such ephemeral features as Colombia claims them to be, one would have expected that Colombia should have been able to come up with some contemporary sources discussing this phenomenon. Nothing of the sort was done. To be truthful, counsel for Colombia did refer to one article that allegedly proved that Edinburgh Cay does not exist. An article from 1967[50]. That is all.

13. But more certainly has been published. Nicaragua in its Additional Pleading on Colombia's Counter-Claims already referred to a number of publications and the figures they include that describe and depict the islands fringing Nicaragua's Caribbean coast[51]. As these texts and figures also indicate, Nicaragua's mainland coast is also strewn with lagoons that cut deep into the mainland coast.

---

[47] CR 2021/16, pp. 40-41, para. 16 (Oude Elferink).

[48] CR 2021/18, p. 66, para. 23 (Thouvenin).

[49] See United Nations, Office for Ocean Affairs and the Law of the Sea, *The Law of the Sea. Baselines: An Examination of the Relevant Provisions of the United Nations Convention on the Law of the Sea*, 1989, New York, para. 46.

[50] CR 2021/18, p. 69, para. 40 (Thouvenin).

[51] APN, para. 3.38 and figs. 6 and 7.

14. It is not really difficult to find additional contemporary sources. A 2008 article on the coral reefs of the Miskito Cays, which is at tab AOE-4 of the judges' folder, describes them as consisting of "eighty mangrove and two sand and gravel cays, surrounded by seagrass beds, octocoral gardens, patch reefs, reef crests, extended algae platforms, short reef walls, and two marginal reefs around the sand cays"[52]. Again, evidence of the interconnectedness of the islands and the surrounding waters.

15. The figure that is now on screen is included in a 2011 article[53], which is at tab AOE-5 of today's judges' folder. It identifies 17 cays in the Pearl Cays by name. The 2014 Annual Report of the Hawksbill Conservation Project in the Pearl Cays observes that "[t]he Pearl Cays are located from 3-22 km east of the mainland, off the central Caribbean coast of Nicaragua . . . and encompass an area of approximately 700 km^2. The study area is comprised of 11 of the 22 Pearl Cays"[54]. The United States Navy Sailing Directions of 2017 describe Man O War Cays as "a cluster of islets, with the largest being 15 m high, [lying] 11 miles offshore"[55]. A 2003 article on coral reefs in Nicaragua indicates that Man O War, Tara and King's Cays are located in an area of coral reef measuring approximately 100 sq km[56]. These three publications I just quoted are reproduced in relevant part at tab AOE-5 of the judges' folder.

(c) A deeply indented and cut-into coast

16. Counsel for Colombia was very brief on the requirement of a deeply indented and cut-into coast. In that connection he had a figure on screen, which is at tab 14 of Colombia's judges' folder of this Wednesday. He submitted that this figure clearly illustrated that the southern coast of Nicaragua was not deeply indented and cut into[57]. That figure again is an example of Colombia's

---

[52] A. C. Fonseca, "Coral Reefs of Miskitus Cays, Nicaragua", *Gulf and Caribbean Research*, 2008, Vol. 20, p. 1, available at https://aquila.usm.edu/cgi/viewcontent.cgi?article=1431&context=gcr (accessed 30 Sept. 2021).

[53] C. Gonzalez and S. Jentoft, "MPA in Labor: Securing the Pearl Cays of Nicaragua", *Environmental Management*, 2011, Vol. 47, p. 620, available at https://link.springer.com/article/10.1007/s00267-010-9587-y (accessed 30 Sept. 2021).

[54] L. Irvine and P. J. Fletcher, WCS Hawksbill Conservation Project 2014 Annual Report — Pearl Cays, Nicaragua, Technical Report, May 2015 DOI: 10.13140/RG.2.1.4549.8322, available at https://www.researchgate.net/publication/283502960_WCS_Hawksbill_Conservation_Project_2014_Annual_Report_-_Pearl_Cays_Nicaragua (accessed 30 Sept. 2021).

[55] Sailings Directions (Enroute), Caribbean Sea Vol. II, 2017, 17th ed., available at https://msi.nga.mil>api>publications>download (accessed 30 Sept. 2021).

[56] J. Ryan and Y. Zapata, "Nicaragua's Coral Reefs, Status, Health and Management Strategies" in J. Cortés (ed.) *Latin American Coral Reefs* (2003), Elsevier, p. 212, available at https://www.elsevier.com/books/latin-american-coral-reefs/cortes/978-0-444-51388-5 (accessed 30 Sept. 2021).

[57] CR 2021/18, p. 61, para. 1 (Thouvenin).

cavalier use of graphics. It is at a scale at which Nicaragua's mainland coast is just over 2 cm. In reality it is over 530 km in length, measured along its general direction[58]. It would be an understatement to say that this is hardly a scale to assess a system of straight baselines. Neither does it allow for determining the location of any of the islands fringing Nicaragua's coast, nor the lagoons cutting into that coast. Counsel for Colombia also complained that Nicaragua, in any case, was not allowed to draw a straight baseline between an island and a point on the coast[59]. A somewhat bizarre proposition that was not supported by any legal authority. And since Colombia is not a party to the Convention, it would have to prove that this prohibition, which is not included in Article 7 of the Convention, meets the thresholds for the formation of a rule of customary international law.

***(d)* The general direction of the coast**

17. Counsel for Colombia also submitted that it was useless to hammer home ("inutile . . . de marteler") the point that Nicaragua's straight baselines do not follow the general direction of the coast. "[C]ela saute aux yeux", he said[60]. No attempt at all to reply to my detailed assessment of this point last Friday, which proves that Nicaragua's straight baselines comply with this condition[61].

***(e)* Close linkage of the enclosed waters with the land domain**

18. As regards the criterion of close linkage of the waters within straight baselines with the land domain, Professor Thouvenin again sang the worn-out refrain that Nicaragua has never proven the existence of the islands along its coast[62]. I beg to disagree. And not a word by counsel of Colombia on the fact that most of the waters inside Nicaragua's straight baselines overlap with traditional tenure areas of the indigenous population living on the coast, which also proves the close linkage[63].

---

[58] *Territorial and Maritime Dispute (Nicaragua* v. *Colombia), Judgment, I.C.J. Reports 2012 (II)*, p. 678, para. 145.

[59] CR 2021/18, p. 61, para. 1 (Thouvenin).

[60] *Ibid.*

[61] See CR 2021/16, pp. 44-46, paras. 26-32 (Oude Elferink).

[62] CR 2021/18, p. 61, para. 1 (Thouvenin). For Colombia's written pleadings on this point, see e.g. RC, paras. 6.28-6.29, 6.32, 6.34, 6.39, 6.43, 6.47.

[63] See CR 2021/16, pp. 46-47, para. 34 (Oude Elferink).

D. Edinburgh Cay

19. Professor Thouvenin did find it necessary to hammer home the point that Edinburgh Cay does not exist — *quod non*. Colombia's judges' folder contains no less than eight versions of the Sailing Directions of the United States Navy, published between 1920 and 2017[64]. Well, they all, every single one of them, attest to the existence of Edinburgh Cay. Professor Thouvenin even showed you this himself this Wednesday. We have added a highlight to the text on Edinburgh Cay. This figure is at tab AOE-6 of today's judges' folder.

20. And as a point of law, it is up to Nicaragua to determine its baselines and which nautical charts to use in that connection[65]. A point Professor Thouvenin conveniently overlooked. His misguided reference to the United States Navy Sailing Directions, and his ignoring that Edinburgh Cay was used as a base point in *Territorial and Maritime Dispute between Nicaragua and Honduras*[66] — a case in which the parties were in disagreement about the existence of several cays, but not Edinburgh Cay[67] — all indicate that Colombia has not even started making a case that Nicaragua has misapplied the law in using Edinburgh Cay as a base point[68].

21. As an aside, it may be noted, even if Colombia were right that Edinburgh Cay does not exist, *quod non*, it is a non-issue. A similar straight baseline segment as that connecting Cape Gracias a Dios to Edinburgh Cay may be drawn to several cays in the Miskito Cays.

E. Nicaragua's 2013 Decree on straight baselines and the low-water line seaward of it

22. Madam President, I now turn to the relationship between Nicaragua's straight baselines and its base points on the low-water line seaward of them. Professor Thouvenin seems to have abandoned the idea that different baselines may not be used at the same time. At least, he did not

---

[64] Colombia's judges' folder, second round, session of 29 September 2021, tab 24.

[65] See *Award in the arbitration regarding the delimitation of the maritime boundary between Guyana and Suriname, Award of 17 September 2007, RIAA*, Vol. XXX, paras. 395-396; *Award of the Arbitral Tribunal in the Second Stage of the Proceedings between Eritrea and Yemen (Maritime Delimitation)*, para. 135; *Arbitration between Barbados and the Republic of Trinidad and Tobago, relating to the Delimitation of the Exclusive Economic Zone and the Continental Shelf between Them, RIAA*, Vol. XXVII, para. 224

[66] See CR 2021/16, p. 41, para. 17 (Oude Elferink).

[67] See *Territorial and Maritime Dispute between Nicaragua and Honduras in the Caribbean Sea (Nicaragua* v. *Honduras), Judgment, I.C.J. Reports 2007 (II)*, p. 760.

[68] See also *Guyana/Suriname, Award of 17 September 2007, RIAA*, Vol. XXX, paras. 395-396.

respond to my invitation to point out the rule of customary law prohibiting such use[69]. He now made two different points. First, for some reason, he has difficulty with the features concerned, referring to Nee Reef and London Reef as "soudainement apparues" and "deux mystérieux points"[70]. Let me just remind the Court that Nicaragua in its written pleadings introduced a report on a survey confirming that Nee Reef and London Reef are low-tide elevations as defined in Article 13 of the Convention and customary law and may be used as part of the baseline for measuring the breadth of the territorial sea and also the exclusive economic zone[71]. Colombia has not said a word about the veracity of that survey and information.

23. Professor Thouvenin's second point was that Nicaragua's Decree No. 33-2013 is the only legislation that is relevant to determining Nicaragua's baselines and outer limits in the Caribbean Sea[72]. That is plainly an incorrect reading of the Decree.

24. After ratifying the United Nations Convention on the Law of the Sea on 3 May 2000, Nicaragua updated its legislation on maritime zones through Law No. 420 on Maritime Spaces of 15 March 2002. The law provides that the baselines from which the breadth of the territorial sea is measured are either straight baselines or the low-water line along the coast[73]. Law No. 420 thus provides for the option of combining the two methods. Nicaragua has done so along its Caribbean coast.

25. The Decree does not provide that this is the only legislation defining Nicaragua's baselines in the Caribbean Sea, as Professor Thouvenin claims. Instead, Article 1 only provides that the Decree establishes the straight baselines that are relevant in that connection. The Decree is not concerned with defining the normal baseline, which was already done through Law No. 420 itself.

26. Professor Thouvenin also rehashed his argument about the scope of Colombia's fourth counter-claim to argue that the Court should not consider base points on Nicaragua's low-water line.

---

[69] See CR 2021/16, p. 38, para. 9 (Oude Elferink).

[70] CR 2021/18, p. 62, paras. 4 and 6 (Thouvenin).

[71] See APN, paras. 3.25-3.26, and Ann. 5, Technical Report, Fieldwork Results in the Nee Reef and London Reef, Feb. 2019.

[72] CR 2021/18, pp. 62-63, paras. 4-8 (Thouvenin).

[73] See Law No. 420 on Maritime Spaces, Art. 3 (reproduced in APN, Ann. 1), Art. 7.

I already addressed that point last Friday[74], and I do not want to further test the patience of the Court by again engaging with the same argument.

F. Colombia's rights are not infringed by Nicaragua's baselines

27. Last Friday, I explained why Colombia's rights are not infringed by Nicaragua's baselines. I stand by that argument and I see no need to repeat it. There is, however, one comment I feel I have to make on Professor Thouvenin's argument on this point. This concerns his completely baseless argument that Nicaragua, by establishing its system of straight baselines, is seeking to free itself from environmental obligations it has under international law[75]. But, perhaps, we should simply see this as a measure of Colombia's misguided and desperate attempts to draw the Court's attention away from the mainline case.

28. Madam President, Members of the Court, that brings to an end my submissions on behalf of Nicaragua in this case. I ask that you now invite Nicaragua's Agent to the podium, to present Nicaragua's final submissions on Colombia's counter-claims. I thank you for your attention.

The PRESIDENT: I thank Professor Oude Elferink. I shall now give the floor to the Agent of Nicaragua, H.E. Mr. Carlos José Argüello Gómez. You have the floor, Your Excellency.

Mr. ARGÜELLO GÓMEZ:

1. Madam President, Members of the Court, good afternoon. Before reading Nicaragua's submissions on the counter-claims of Colombia, please allow me a few comments on the question of the Raizales and the use of straight baselines.

The straight baselines

2. The counter-claim on the question of the straight baselines used by Nicaragua has been amply analysed and set to rights by Professor Oude Elferink.

3. One important issue is that since Colombia is not a party to UNCLOS and there are no other treaties binding the Parties on matters of baselines or base points, the law applicable is customary

---

[74] CR 2021/16, p. 37, para. 8.

[75] CR 2021/18, p. 65, paras. 16-17.

international law. In the present case, what I would emphasize is that Colombia has established its own straight baseline system, but its counsel insists that they not be taken into consideration[76].

4. Colombia, for example, questions the length of Nicaragua's straight baselines and yet has even lengthier straight baselines of its own. Can Colombia claim that Nicaragua is violating a rule that it does not itself respect?

5. The Court cannot allow the application of a double standard. As this Court has stated, and the International Law Commission has reiterated, the rules of customary international law, "by their very nature, must have equal force for all members of the international community, and cannot therefore be the subject of any right of unilateral exclusion exercisable at will by any one of them in its own favour"[77].

6. On the question of baselines, the only rules that can be applied are those that have "equal force" for Nicaragua and for Colombia. Colombia does not have "any right of unilateral exclusion" of its own practice. Quite the contrary, this practice is conclusive.

The question of the alleged traditional fishing rights

7. Madam President, on the question of the Raizales, Colombia's submissions on 29 September request the Court to declare that "[t]he inhabitants of the San Andrés Archipelago, in particular the Raizales, enjoy artisanal fishing rights"[78]; and further ask that the Court declare that "Nicaragua has violated the traditional fishing rights of the inhabitants of the San Andrés Archipelago[79].

8. First, it should be emphasized that what Colombia is claiming is artisanal fishing rights and not, for example, industrial fishing rights, which they have nevertheless granted to Colombia and foreign-flagged vessels so that they could fish in Nicaragua's EEZ without Nicaragua's authorization.

9. With respect to artisanal fishing by the Raizales, Nicaragua has made it clear that it is willing, and even happy, to help the Raizal population, which has close relations with the Caribbean

---

[76] CR 2021/15, p. 51, para. 5 (Thouvenin).

[77] *North Sea Continental Shelf, Judgment, I.C.J. Reports 1969*, pp. 38-39, para. 63; see also *Report of the International Law Commission, Seventieth session*, 2018, UN doc. A/73/10, para. 66, Conclusion 15, Commentary 1.

[78] CR 2021/18, p. 75, para. II.3 (Arrieta).

[79] CR 2021/18, p. 75, para. II.4 (Arrieta).

population of Nicaragua. Obviously, as in other similar situations, fishing is not a free-for-all and artisanal fishermen need to identify themselves and fulfil certain requirements, including registering with Nicaragua. This is also a requirement for Nicaraguan artisanal fishermen. As indicated in my previous presentation: in 2018, all 8,907 Nicaraguan artisanal fishermen were registered[80]. All these procedures for the Colombian Raizales have to be worked out in an agreement between our two States.

10. Second, these potential rights in no way apply to the non-Raizal population of San Andrés. As I indicated before, these newcomers from the mainland arrived in the 1950s when San Andrés was converted into a freeport and a tourist destination[81]. In 1925, as I indicated before, the population of the Raizales in San Andrés was approximately 5,000 people and the non-Raizal population was only 30 — 30 people[82]. At present, as I explained in my earlier presentation, the majority of the population is non-Raizal and this population has not been part of any traditional artisanal fishing[83]. The newcomers simply took over from the Raizal the most lucrative businesses of the islands, which did not include artisanal fishing[84].

11. For this reason, it is necessary to emphasize that the offer made by Nicaragua to reach an agreement to facilitate the artisanal fishing of the Raizales refers to that population only. This, of course, does not close the door on the possibility of other fishing agreements, but that is not the point under discussion.

12. Third, Nicaragua has not violated any fishing rights of the inhabitants of San Andrés as claimed in the Colombian submissions. This claim is based on the affidavits of 11 persons and has been totally disproved by Mr. Martin in his first presentation[85], and again this afternoon.

13. In this regard, it should be emphasized that the Raizales could not and did not traditionally fish in Luna Verde, La Esquina and Cape Bank as Mr. Valencia stated[86]. This has already been

[80] CR 2021/16, p. 14, para. 23 (Argüello).

[81] CR 2021/16, p. 12, para. 12 (Argüello).

[82] CR 2021/16, p. 13, para. 17 (Argüello).

[83] CR 2021/16, pp. 12-13, paras. 15-17 (Argüello).

[84] CR 2021/16, p. 12, para. 12 (Argüello).

[85] CR 2021/16, pp. 28-31, paras. 46-58 (Martin).

[86] CR 2021/18, p. 53, para. 12 (Valencia-Ospina).

pointed out by Mr. Martin, who emphasized that this assertion is without any reference to proof. Permit me to add another consideration. It was simply impractical for the Raizales to have fished traditionally in artisan boats in areas located approximately 100 nautical miles from their home bases. This might occasionally have happened in the so-called northern keys of Serrana and Roncador, because in these places there was land and the fishermen could rest and preserve their catch from rotting. In Luna Verde, La Esquina and Cape Bank, there are no land areas so artisanal fishing is not practical from San Andrés or Providencia.

14. All this, does not mean that the Raizales could not travel longer distances. Of course they could, and they did. In fact, the original population of these islands arrived from the Miskito or Caribbean coast of Nicaragua[87]. But there is no evidence to support Colombia's claim that the Raizales who came to inhabit San Andrés and its sister islands fished with a degree of regularity, or over a prolonged period, sufficient to establish traditional rights at Luna Verde, La Esquina, Cape Bank or any other location in Nicaragua's EEZ, as delimited by the Court.

15. It should also be noted, in this regard, that all the incidents of illegal fishing in its waters that Nicaragua has brought to the Court's attention in these oral hearings — where the intervention of the Colombian Navy has been recorded, in some cases, played for the Court — involved industrial fishing, not artisanal fishing. And it should also be noted that most of these industrial fishing boats, were not even Colombian-flagged but Honduran[88] and even Tanzanian[89]. Not a single one was an artisanal Raizal fishing boat.

The statements of President Ortega

16. Madam President, Mr. Valencia and other speakers have expounded on the statements made by President Ortega with respect to the Raizales. Mr. Martin has amply covered this subject both in his first statement and his statement this afternoon. I will only add that President Ortega's statements in no way reflect an intention to make a unilateral cession of Nicaragua's sovereign rights over its EEZ, which took Nicaragua more than a dozen hard-fought years to secure in the Judgment

---

[87] A. Olmos-Pinzón, "Artisanal Fisheries in the San Andres Island: between cooperation and cooperativism", *Jangwa Pana:* Vol. 18 (2), p. 309, available at http://oaji.net/articles/2020/2336-1580499670.pdf (accessed 30 Sept. 2021).

[88] See for example CR 2021/13, p. 52, para. 32; p. 54, para. 39; p. 55, paras. 40-41 (Reichler).

[89] CR 2021/13, p. 53, para. 37 (Reichler).

of the Court of 19 November 2012. Precisely in order to enjoy those sovereign rights, in the face of Colombia's refusal to accept the Court's Judgment, President Ortega hoped that by offering to reach an agreement granting fishing rights to Colombia's Raizal population, Colombia could be coaxed into accepting and respecting Nicaragua's sovereign rights in its EEZ. The offer has never been withdrawn. But sadly, Colombia has shown no interest in reaching an agreement with Nicaragua, even if it would benefit its Raizal population.

17. Instead, Colombia hides behind its Constitution, claiming that it cannot accept the Court's Judgment or Nicaragua's rights without a treaty, while at the same time, refusing to enter into any discussions with Nicaragua that might lead to such a treaty.

18. Meanwhile, Colombia has not changed its attitude toward the Court's Judgment. It continues to reject and disregard it. This leaves us with a fundamental question: does the Court's Judgment matter? Nicaragua believes that it does. And that is why we are here before you.

19. Madam President, in compliance with Article 60 of the Rules of Court, I will now proceed to read into the record Nicaragua's final submissions on Colombia's counter-claims. A signed copy of the written text of these submissions is being duly communicated to the Court and transmitted to the other Party.

FINAL SUBMISSIONS

20. In the case concerning *Alleged Violations of Sovereign Rights and Maritime Spaces in the Caribbean Sea (Nicaragua* v. *Colombia)*, for the reasons explained in the Written and Oral phase, Nicaragua respectfully requests the Court to adjudge and declare that the counter-claims of the Republic of Colombia are rejected with all legal consequences.

21. Madam President, Members of the Court, this ends Nicaragua's oral pleadings on Colombia's counter-claims. On my behalf, and that of the Nicaraguan team, we wish to extend our thanks to the Members of the Court, the Registrar and his staff, the translators and interpreters, secretaries and assistants, as well as to the technicians who have made this hybrid oral hearing possible. Our thanks also to the Colombian delegation for their attention.

The PRESIDENT: I thank the Agent of Nicaragua. The Court takes note of the final submissions which you have just read on behalf of Nicaragua on the counter-claims of Colombia.

This brings us to the end of the hearings in the case concerning *Alleged Violations of Sovereign Rights and Maritime Spaces in the Caribbean Sea (Nicaragua* v. *Colombia)*. I thank the representatives of the Parties for the assistance they have given the Court by their presentations in the course of these hearings. In accordance with practice, I shall request the Agents of the Parties to remain at the Court's disposal to provide any additional information the Court may require.

The Court will now retire for deliberation. The Agents of the Parties will be advised in due course as to the date on which the Court will deliver its Judgment. Since the Court has no other business before it today, the sitting is now closed.

The Court rose at 3.55 p.m.

OTHER DOCUMENTS

AUTRES DOCUMENTS

SUMMARY — SOMMAIRE

QR CODE ACCESS TO OTHER DOCUMENTS